Fodor

Germany

"When it comes to information on regional history, what to see and do, and shopping, these guides are exhaustive."

—*USAir Magazine*

"Usable, sophisticated restaurant coverage, with an emphasis on good value."

—Andy Birsh, *Gourmet Magazine* columnist

"Valuable because of their comprehensiveness."

—*Minneapolis Star-Tribune*

"Fodor's always delivers high quality...thoughtfully presented...thorough."

—*Houston Post*

"An excellent choice for those who want everything under one cover."

—*Washington Post*

Fodor's Travel Publications, Inc.
New York • Toronto • London • Sydney • Auckland
http://www.fodors.com/

Fodor's Germany

Editor: David Low

Editorial Contributors: Robert Andrews, Robert Blake, Hannah Borgeson, David Brown, Audra Epstein, Janet Foley, Brent Gregston, Laura Kidder, Graham Lees, Heidi Sarna, Helayne Schiff, Mary Ellen Schultz, M. T. Schwartzman (Gold Guide editor), Jürgen Scheunemann, Dinah Spritzer, Robert Tilley

Creative Director: Fabrizio La Rocca

Cartographer: David Lindroth

Cover Photograph: Owen Franken

Text Design: Between the Covers

Copyright

Special Sales

PRINTED IN THE UNITED STATES OF AMERICA

10 9 8 7 6 5 4 3 2 1

CONTENTS

Maps

ON THE ROAD WITH FODOR'S

WE'RE ALWAYS THRILLED to get letters from readers, especially one like this:

It took us an hour to decide what book to buy and we now know we picked the best one. Your book was wonderful, easy to follow, very accurate, and good on pointing out eating places, informal as well as formal. When we saw other people using your book, we would look at each other and smile.

Our editors and writers are deeply committed to making every Fodor's guide "the best one"—not only accurate but always charming, brimming with sound recommendations and solid ideas, right on the mark in describing restaurants and hotels, and full of fascinating facts that make you view what you've traveled to see in a rich new light.

About Our Writers

Robert Tilley, who revised several chapters of this guide, landed in Germany more than 25 years ago (via Central Africa, South Africa, and England), intending to stay a year before settling somewhere *really* civilized. German women were responsible for his extended stay—he married one, and she's now a seasoned Fodor's researcher. Robert runs a media company in Munich and writes (mostly for English-language programs he produces for German TV) in a lakeside hideaway in the Bavarian Alps. His branch office is in a local brewery cellar.

Brent Gregston revised the chapters on the Black Forest, Heidelberg and the Neckar Valley, Frankfurt, the Rhineland Palatinate, and the Rhineland. After studying philosophy at the Albert-Ludwig University in Freiberg, he worked as a translator for the U.S. State Department and as an editor for Fodor's Worldview. Brent now unpacks his luggage in Amsterdam but often travels to the Black Forest and the Rhine as a journalist and travel writer.

Jürgen Scheunemann revised the chapters on Hamburg, Berlin, and the Baltic Coast. He is a native Hamburger but fell in love with Berlin eight years ago when he moved to the German capital to study North American history and German literature. Since then, Jürgen has worked as a professional journalist, editor, and book writer. Among other assignments, he was a contract writer for Berlin's leading daily *Der Tagesspiegel,* and wrote, published, and translated a number of picture books on Berlin and the United States. His latest works include contributions to the *BBC Television London.*

We'd also like to thank Helga Brenner-Khan, of the German National Tourist Office, and the German Wine Information Bureau.

New This Year

This year we've reformatted our guides to make them easier to use. Each chapter of *Germany '97* begins with brand-new recommended itineraries to help you decide what to see in the time you have. You may also notice our fresh graphics, new in 1996. More readable and more helpful than ever? We think so—and we hope you do, too.

On the Web

Also check out Fodor's Web site (http://www.fodors.com/), where you'll find travel information on major destinations around the world and an ever-changing array of travel-savvy interactive features.

How to Use This Book

Organization

Up front is the **Gold Guide.** Its first section, **Important Contacts A to Z,** gives addresses and telephone numbers of organizations and companies that offer destination-related services and detailed information and publications. **Smart Travel Tips A to Z,** the Gold Guide's second section, gives specific information on how to accomplish what you need to in Germany, as well as tips on savvy traveling. Both sections are in alphabetical order by topic.

Chapters in *Germany '97* are arranged geographically, going roughly from south to north. Each city chapter begins with an Exploring section, which is subdivided by neighborhood; each subsection recommends a walking or driving tour and lists sights in alphabetical order. Each regional chapter is divided by geographical area; within each area, towns are covered in logical geographical order, and attractive stretches of road and minor points of interest between them are indicated by the designation *En Route*. Throughout, Off the Beaten Path sights appear after the places from which they are most easily accessible. And within town sections, all restaurants and lodgings are grouped together.

To help you decide what to visit in the time you have, all chapters begin with recommended itineraries; you can mix and match those from several chapters to create a complete vacation. The A to Z section that ends all chapters covers getting there, getting around, and helpful contacts and resources.

At the end of the book you'll find Portraits, with an historical chronology and suggestions for pretrip reading, both fiction and nonfiction.

Icons and Symbols

★ Our special recommendations
✕ Restaurant
🏠 Lodging establishment
✕🏠 Lodging establishment with a restaurant that usually warrants a detour
🐤 Rubber duckie (good for kids)
☞ Sends you to another section of the guide for more info
✉ Address
☎ Telephone number
🕓 Opening and closing times
💰 Admission prices (those we give apply only to adults; substantially reduced fees are almost always available for children, students, and senior citizens)

Numbers in white and black circles—②
and ❷, for example—that appear on the maps, in the margins, and within the tours correspond to one another.

Dining and Lodging

The restaurants and lodgings we list are the cream of the crop in each price range. Price charts appear in the Pleasures and Pastimes section that follows each chapter introduction.

Hotel Facilities

We always list the facilities that are available—but we don't specify whether they cost extra: When pricing accommodations, always ask what's included.

Restaurant Reservations and Dress Codes

Reservations are always a good idea; we note only when they're essential or when they are not accepted. Book as far ahead as you can, and reconfirm when you get to town. Unless otherwise noted, the restaurants listed are open daily for lunch and dinner. We mention dress only when men are required to wear a jacket or a jacket and tie. Look for an overview of local habits under Dining in Smart Travel Tips A to Z and in the Pleasures and Pastimes section that follows each chapter introduction.

Credit Cards

The following abbreviations are used: **AE**, American Express; **DC**, Diners Club; **MC**, MasterCard; and **V**, Visa.

Please Write to Us

You can use this book in the confidence that all prices and opening times are based on information supplied to us at press time; Fodor's cannot accept responsibility for any errors. Time inevitably brings changes, so always confirm information when it matters—especially if you're making a detour to visit a specific place. In addition, when making reservations be sure to mention if you have a disability or are traveling with children, if you prefer a private bath or a certain type of bed, or if you have specific dietary needs or any other concerns.

Were the restaurants we recommended as described? Did our hotel picks exceed your expectations? Did you find a museum we recommended a waste of time? If you have complaints, we'll look into them and revise our entries when the facts warrant it. If you've discovered a special place that we haven't included, we'll pass the information along to our correspondents and have them check it out. So send your feedback, positive *and* negative, to the Germany Editor at 201 East 50th Street, New York, New York 10022—and have a wonderful trip!

Karen Cure

Karen Cure
Editorial Director

Germany

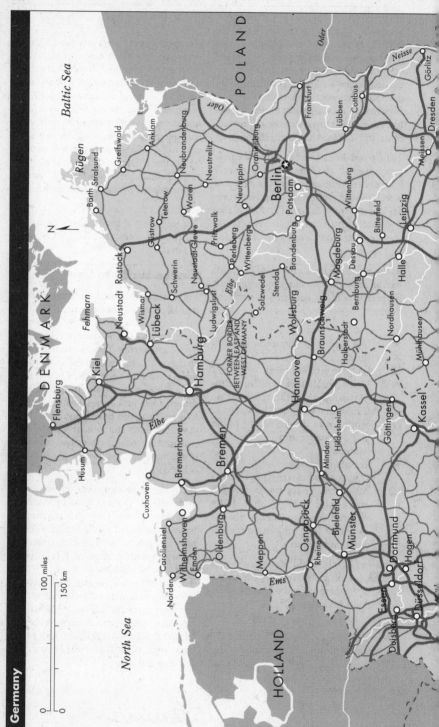

Baltic Sea

North Sea

POLAND

DENMARK

HOLLAND

Oder

Neisse

Görlitz

Dresden

Meißen

Cottbus

Lübben

Frankfurt

Leipzig

Halle

Bitterfeld

Wittenberg

Dessau

Berlin

Potsdam

Oranienburg

Brandenburg

Magdeburg

Bernburg

Nordhausen

Mühlhausen

Neuruppin

Neustrelitz

Neubrandenburg

Anklam

Greifswald

Rügen

Barth Stralsund

Pritzwalk

Perleberg

Wittenberge

Salzwedel

Stendal

Wolfsburg

Braunschweig

Halberstadt

Kassel

Göttingen

Hildesheim

Hannover

Minden

Bielefeld

Münster

Dortmund

Hagen

Essen

Düsseldorf

Duisburg

Osnabrück

Rheine

Meppen

Oldenburg

Bremen

Bremerhaven

Cuxhaven

Wilhelmshaven

Emden

Carolinensiel

Norden

Ems

Hamburg

Lüneburg

Ludwigslust

Neustadt-Gleeve

Schwerin

Wismar

Lübeck

Neustadt

Rostock

Güstrow

Teterow

Waren

Elbe

FORMER BORDER
BETWEEN EAST AND
WEST GERMANY

Kiel

Flensburg

Husum

Fehmarn

N

0 ——— 100 miles
0 ——— 150 km

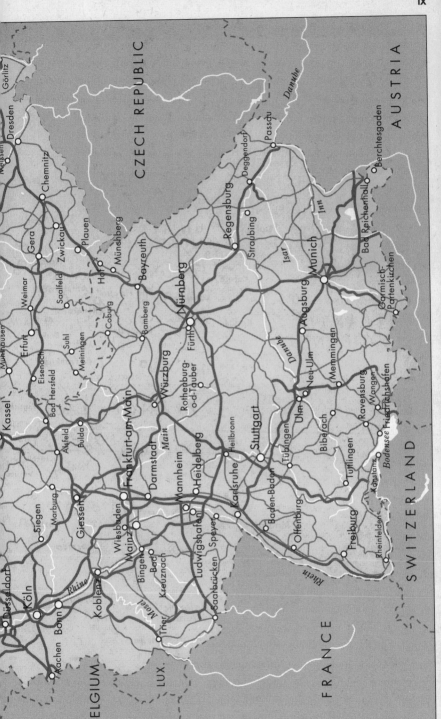

x

Reykjavik
ICELAND

NORWAY
Bergen

SCOTLAND
NORTHERN
IRELAND
Edinburgh
North
Sea
Skagerrak
Belfast
IRELAND
Irish
Sea
DENMARK
Dublin
UNITED
KINGDOM
WALES
Hamburg
Cardiff
ENGLAND
NETHERLANDS
London
The Hague
Amsterdam
Rotterdam
GERMA
English Channel
Brussels
BELGIUM
Bonn
ATLANTIC
OCEAN
Paris
LUXEMBOURG
Frankfurt

FRANCE
Zürich
Munich
Bern
SWITZERLAND
Lyon
LIECHTENSTEIN
Milan
Venice
Lj
Monte
Carlo
PORTUGAL
Madrid
ANDORRA
Marseille
Nice
MONACO
Florence
Lisbon
SPAIN
Barcelona
Corsica
Seville
Granada
Balearic
Islands
Sardinia
Gibraltar
Mediterranean Sea
Tyrrhenian S

MOROCCO
ALGERIA
0
400 miles
0
600 km
TUNISIA

FINLAND

Gulf of Bothnia

Oslo ✪

SWEDEN

Helsinki ✪

Gulf of Finland

St. Petersburg ○

Tallinn ✪

ESTONIA

Stockholm ✪

Göteborg ○

Riga ✪

LATVIA

Moscow ✪

Kattegat

Copenhagen ✪

Baltic Sea

LITHUANIA

Kaunas ○

RUSSIA

Vilnius ✪

Minsk ✪

Kaliningrad ○

Berlin ✪

POLAND

BELARUS

MANY

Warsaw ✪

Kraków ○

Kiev ✪

Prague ✪
CZECH
REPUBLIC

UKRAINE

SLOVAKIA

ich ○

Vienna ○

Bratislava ✪

MOLDOVA

Salzburg ✪

Budapest ✪

AUSTRIA

HUNGARY

Chişinău ✪

EIN

SLOVENIA

Ljubljana ✪

Zagreb ✪

ROMANIA

nice ○

CROATIA

Novi Sad ○

Bucharest ✪

BOSNIA AND
HERZEGOVINA

Belgrade ✪

Black Sea

Adriatic Sea

SERBIA

Sarajevo ✪

Rome ✪

MONTENEGRO

Priština ✪

BULGARIA

ITALY

Podgorica ○

Skopje ✪

Sofia ✪

Istanbul ○

F.Y.R. of
MACEDONIA

Tiranë ✪

Ankara ✪

Naples ○

ALBANIA

TURKEY

nian Sea

GREECE

Aegean
Sea

Sicily

Ionian
Sea

Athens ✪

CYPRUS

MALTA

Crete

Mediterranean Sea

World Time Zones

Numbers below vertical bands relate each zone to Greenwich Mean Time (0 hrs.).
Local times frequently differ from these general indications,
as indicated by light-face numbers on map.

Algiers, **29**

Anchorage, **3**

Athens, **41**

Auckland, **1**

Baghdad, **46**

Bangkok, **50**

Beijing, **54**

Berlin, **34**

Bogotá, **19**

Budapest, **37**

Buenos Aires, **24**

Caracas, **22**

Chicago, **9**

Copenhagen, **33**

Dallas, **10**

Delhi, **48**

Denver, **8**

Djakarta, **53**

Dublin, **26**

Edmonton, **7**

Hong Kong, **56**

Honolulu, **2**

Istanbul, **40**

Jerusalem, **42**

Johannesburg, **44**

Lima, **20**

Lisbon, **28**

London
(Greenwich), **27**

Los Angeles, **6**

Madrid, **38**

Manila, **57**

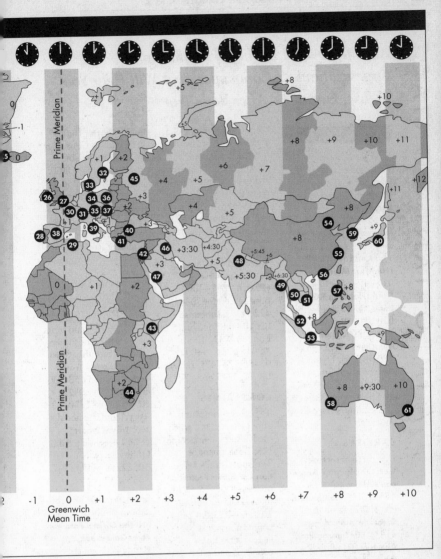

Mecca, **47**	Ottawa, **14**	San Francisco, **5**	Toronto, **13**
Mexico City, **12**	Paris, **30**	Santiago, **21**	Vancouver, **4**
Miami, **18**	Perth, **58**	Seoul, **59**	Vienna, **35**
Montréal, **15**	Reykjavík, **25**	Shanghai, **55**	Warsaw, **36**
Moscow, **45**	Rio de Janeiro, **23**	Singapore, **52**	Washington, D.C., **17**
Nairobi, **43**	Rome, **39**	Stockholm, **32**	Yangon, **49**
New Orleans, **11**	Saigon (Ho Chi Minh City), **51**	Sydney, **61**	Zürich, **31**
New York City, **16**		Tokyo, **60**	

IMPORTANT CONTACTS A TO Z

An Alphabetical Listing of Publications, Organizations & Companies That Will Help You Before, During & After Your Trip

A

AIR TRAVEL

The major gateways to Germany include Berlin (**Flughafen Tegel Tempelhof**, ☎ 011–49–30/69–510), Düsseldorf (**Flughafen Düsseldorf**, ☎ 011–49–211/421–1), Frankfurt (**Flughafen Frankfurt Main**, ☎ 011–49–69/690–1), Köln (**Fluhafen Köln/ Bonn**, ☎ 011–49–2203/40–0), and Munich (**Flughafen München**, ☎ 011–49–89/97–500). Flying time to Frankfurt is 7½ hours from New York, 10 hours from Chicago, and 12 hours from Los Angeles.

CARRIERS

U.S. carriers serving Germany include **American Airlines** (☎ 800/433–7300), **Continental** (☎ 800/231–0856), **Delta** (☎ 800/241–4141), **LTU International Airways** (☎ 800/888–0200), **Lufthansa** (☎ 800/645–3880), **Northwest Airlines** (☎ 800/447–4747), **TWA** (☎ 800/892–4141), **United** (☎ 800/241–6522), and **USAir** (☎ 800/622–1015).

Carriers flying into **Berlin** include American Airlines, Delta, Lufthansa, and Northwest. **Düsseldorf** arriving airlines include American, LTU International, and Lufthansa. Flying into **Frankfurt** are American, Continental, Delta, Lufthansa, Northwest, TWA, United, and USAir. The only carrier flying direct into **Köln** from the U.S. is Lufthansa. Arriving from the U.S. into **Munich** are Continental, Delta, LTU, and Lufthansa.

FROM THE U.K.➤ Contact **British Airways** (☎ 0181/897–4000; outside London, 0345/222–111), **Lufthansa** (✉ 10 Old Bond St., London W1X 4EN, ☎ 0181/750–3300 or 0345/737–747), and **Air UK** (☎ 0345/666–777).

COMPLAINTS

To register complaints about charter and scheduled airlines, contact the U.S. Department of Transportation's **Aviation Consumer Protection Division** (✉ C-75, Washington, DC 20590, ☎ 202/366–2220). Complaints about lost baggage or ticketing problems and safety concerns may also be logged with the **Federal Aviation Administration (FAA) Consumer Hotline** (☎ 800/322–7873).

CONSOLIDATORS

For services that will help you find the lowest airfares, *see* Discounts & Deals, *below.*

PUBLICATIONS

For general information about charter carriers, ask for the Department of Transportation's free brochure **"Plane Talk: Public Charter Flights"** (✉ Aviation Consumer Protection Division, C-75, Washington, DC 20590, ☎ 202/366–2220). The Department of Transportation also publishes a 58-page booklet, **"Fly Rights,"** available from the Consumer Information Center (✉ Supt. of Documents, Dept. 136C, Pueblo, CO 81009; $1.75).

For other tips and hints, consult the Consumers Union's monthly **"Consumer Reports Travel Letter"** (✉ Box 53629, Boulder, CO 80322, ☎ 800/234–1970; $39 1st yr) and the newsletter **"Travel Smart"** (✉ 40 Beechdale Rd., Dobbs Ferry, NY 10522, ☎ 800/327–3633; $37 per yr).

Some worthwhile publications on the subject are *The Official Frequent Flyer Guidebook,* by Randy Petersen (✉ Airpress, 4715-C Town Center Dr., Colorado Springs, CO 80916, ☎ 719/597–8899 or 800/487–8893; $14.99 plus $3 shipping); *Airfare Secrets Exposed,* by Sharon Tyler and Matthew Wunder (✉ Studio 4 Productions, Box 280400, Northridge, CA 91328, ☎ 818/700–2522 or 800/408–7369; $16.95 plus $2.50 shipping); *202 Tips Even the Best Business Travelers May Not Know,* by Christo-

pher McGinnis (⊠ Irwin
Professional Publishing,
1333 Burr Ridge Pkwy.,
Burr Ridge, IL 60521,
☎ 800/634–3966;
$11 plus $3.25 ship-
ping); and *Travel Rights,*
by Charles Leocha (⊠
World Leisure Corpora-
tion, 177 Paris St.,
Boston, MA 02128,
☎ 800/444–2524;
$7.95 plus $3.95
shipping).

For information on how
to avoid jet lag, there
are two publications: *Jet
Lag, A Pocket Guide to
Modern Treatment,* by
Peter Casano M.D.
(⊠ MedEd Publications,
Box 12415, Columbus,
OH 43212, ☎ 614/
488–9457; $5.95) and
How to Beat Jet Lag
(⊠ Henry Holt, 115 W.
18th St., New York, NY
10011, ☎ 800/288–
2131; $14.95).

Travelers who experi-
ence motion sickness or
ear problems in flight
should get the brochures
**"Ears, Altitude, and
Airplane Travel"** and
**"What You Can Do for
Dizziness & Motion
Sickness"** from the
American Academy of
Otolaryngology (⊠ 1
Prince St., Alexandria,
VA 22314, ☎ 703/836–
4444, FAX 703/683–
5100, TTY 703/
519–1585).

WITHIN GERMANY

Details of air travel
services are available
from travel agents;
otherwise, contact
Deutsche BA at its Munich headquarters at
Franz-Josef-Strauss
International Airport
(☎ 089/292121), **LTU** at
any of its city offices (in
Munich, ☎ 089/231–
1200), or **Lufthansa** at

any German airport or
downtown office

B

BETTER BUSINESS BUREAU

For local contacts in the
hometown of a tour
operator you may be
considering, consult the
**Council of Better Busi-
ness Bureaus** (⊠ 4200
Wilson Blvd., Suite 800,
Arlington, VA 22203,
☎ 703/276–0100, FAX
703/525–8277).

BUS TRAVEL

FROM THE U.K.

Eurolines (☎ 071/730–
3499) has up to three
departures a day from
London's Victoria
Coach Station. The
buses cross the Channel
on Sealink's Dover–
Zeebrugge ferry service
and then drive via the
Netherlands and Bel-
gium to Köln (14½
hours), Frankfurt (17½
hours), Mannheim (18¾
hours), Stuttgart/Nürn-
berg (20½ hours), and
Munich (22¾ hours).
Hoverspeed (☎ 01304/
240–241) runs two
buses in winter and one
in summer to Berlin
from Victoria Station.
Travel time is 23 hours,
including a three-hour
stopover in Brussels.

WITHIN GERMANY

The railways, in the
guise of **Deutsche Tour-
ing,** operate the Ger-
man sections of the
Europabus network.
Contact them at ⊠ Am
Römerhof 17, D-60426
Frankfurt/Main, ☎
069/79030, for regular
schedule details and
information about a
range of two- to seven-
day package tours.

C

CAR RENTAL

The major car-rental
companies represented
in Germany are **Alamo**
(☎ 800/327–9633; in
the U.K., 0800/272–
2000), **Avis** (☎ 800/
331–1084; in Canada,
800/879–2847), **Budget**
(☎ 800/527–0700; in
the U.K., 0800/181181),
Dollar (☎ 800/800–
4000; in the U.K., 0990/
565656, where it is
known as Eurodollar),
Hertz (☎ 800/654–
3001; in Canada, 800/
263–0600; in the U.K.,
0345/555888), and
National InterRent
(sometimes known as
Europcar InterRent
outside North America;
☎ 800/227–3876; in
the U.K., 01345/222–
525). Rates vary consid-
erably, depending upon
type of car and rental
location. In Munich or
Berlin, prices begin at
$52 a day and $101 a
week for an economy
car with unlimited
mileage. This does not
include tax on car
rentals, which is 15%.

RENTAL WHOLESALERS

Contact **Auto Europe**
(☎ 207/828–2525 or
800/223–5555), **Europe
by Car** (☎ 800/223–
1516; in CA, 800/252–
9401), or the **Kemwel
Group** (☎ 914/835–
5555 or 800/678–
0678).

THE CHANNEL TUNNEL

For information, con-
tact **Le Shuttle** (in the
U.S., ☎ 800/388–3876;
in the U.K., 0990/
353535), which trans-
ports cars, or **Eurostar**
(in the U.S., ☎ 800/

942–4866; in the U.K., 0345/881881), the high-speed train service between London (Waterloo) and Paris (Gare du Nord). Eurostar tickets are available in the United Kingdom through **InterCity Europe**, the international wing of BritRail (⊠ Victoria Station, London, ☎ 0171/834–2345 or 0171/828–0892 for credit-card bookings), and in the United States through **Rail Europe** (☎ 800/942–4866) and **BritRail Travel** (☎ 800/677–8585).

CHILDREN & TRAVEL

BABY-SITTING

The departure of the bulk of American forces from Germany has brought an end to the baby-sitting services once offered by U.S. Forces Women's Clubs, but local tourist offices are usually able to help out with names and addresses of reliable sitters. Many hotels also have their own contacts.

FLYING

Look into **"Flying with Baby"** (⊠ Third Street Press, Box 261250, Littleton, CO 80163, ☎ 303/595–5959; $4.95 includes shipping), cowritten by a flight attendant. **"Kids and Teens in Flight,"** free from the U.S. Department of Transportation's Aviation Consumer Protection Division (⊠ C-75, Washington, DC 20590, ☎ 202/366–2220), offers tips on children flying alone. Every two years the February issue of *Family Travel Times* (☞ Know-

How, *below*) details children's services on three dozen airlines. **"Flying Alone, Handy Advice for Kids Traveling Solo"** is available free from the American Automobile Association (AAA) (Send legal-size SASE: ⊠ Flying Alone, Mail Stop 800, 1000 AAA Dr., Heathrow, FL 32746).

KNOW-HOW

Family Travel Times, published quarterly by Travel with Your Children (TWYCH, ⊠ 40 5th Ave., New York, NY 10011, ☎ 212/477–5524; $40 per yr), covers destinations, types of vacations, and modes of travel.

LOCAL INFORMATION

"Young People's Guide to Munich" is a free pamphlet available from the German National Tourist Office.

TOUR OPERATORS

If you're outdoorsy, look into family-oriented programs run by the **American Museum of Natural History** (⊠ 79th St. and Central Park W, New York, NY 10024, ☎ 212/769–5700 or 800/462–8687).

CUSTOMS

IN THE U.S.

The **U.S. Customs Service** (⊠ Box 7407, Washington, DC 20044, ☎ 202/927–6724) can answer questions on duty-free limits and publishes a helpful brochure, "Know Before You Go." For information on registering foreign-made articles, call 202/927–0540.

COMPLAINTS⊳ Note the inspector's badge number and write to the commissioner's office (⊠ 1301 Constitution Ave. NW, Washington, DC 20229).

CANADIANS

Contact **Revenue Canada** (⊠ 2265 St. Laurent Blvd. S, Ottawa, Ontario K1G 4K3, ☎ 613/993–0534) for a copy of the free brochure **"I Declare/Je Déclare"** and for details on duty-free limits. For recorded information (within Canada only), call 800/461–9999.

U.K. CITIZENS

HM Customs and Excise (⊠ Dorset House, Stamford St., London SE1 9NG, ☎ 0171/202–4227) can answer questions about U.K. customs regulations and publishes a free pamphlet, **"A Guide for Travellers,"** detailing standard procedures and import rules.

D

DISABILITIES & ACCESSIBILITY

COMPLAINTS

To register complaints under the provisions of the Americans with Disabilities Act, contact the U.S. Department of Justice's **Disability Rights Section** (⊠ Box 66738, Washington, DC 20035, ☎ 202/514–0301 or 800/514–0301, FAX 202/307–1198, TTY 202/514–0383 or 800/514–0383). For airline-related problems, contact the U.S. Department of Transportation's **Aviation Consumer Protection Division** (☞ Air Travel, *above*). For complaints about surface transportation, contact the Department of Transportation's **Civil Rights Office** (☎ 202/366–4648).

ORGANIZATIONS

TRAVELERS WITH HEARING IMPAIRMENTS➤ The **American Academy of Otolaryngology** (✉ 1 Prince St., Alexandria, VA 22314, ☎ 703/836–4444, FAX 703/683–5100, TTY 703/519–1585) publishes a brochure, "Travel Tips for Hearing Impaired People."

TRAVELERS WITH MOBILITY PROBLEMS➤ Contact the **Information Center for Individuals with Disabilities** (✉ Box 256, Boston, MA 02117, ☎ 617/450–9888; in MA, 800/462–5015; TTY 617/424–6855); **Mobility International USA** (✉ Box 10767, Eugene, OR 97440, ☎ and TTY 541/343–1284, FAX 541/343–6812), the U.S. branch of a Belgium-based organization (☞ *below*) with affiliates in 30 countries; **MossRehab Hospital Travel Information Service** (☎ 215/456–9600, TTY 215/456–9602), a telephone information resource for travelers with physical disabilities; the **Society for the Advancement of Travel for the Handicapped** (✉ 347 5th Ave., Suite 610, New York, NY 10016, ☎ 212/447–7284, FAX 212/725–8253; membership $45); and **Travelin' Talk** (✉ Box 3534, Clarksville, TN 37043, ☎ 615/552–6670, FAX 615/552–1182), which provides local contacts worldwide for travelers with disabilities.

TRAVELERS WITH VISION IMPAIRMENTS➤ Contact the **American Council of the Blind** (✉ 1155 15th St. NW, Suite 720, Washington, DC 20005, ☎ 202/467–5081, FAX 202/467–5085) for a list of travelers' resources or the **American Foundation for the Blind** (✉ 11 Penn Plaza, Suite 300, New York, NY 10001, ☎ 212/502–7600 or 800/232–5463, TTY 212/502–7662), which provides general advice and publishes "Access to Art" ($19.95), a directory of museums that accommodate travelers with vision impairments.

IN THE U.K.

Contact the **Royal Association for Disability and Rehabilitation** (✉ RADAR, 12 City Forum, 250 City Rd., London EC1V 8AF, ☎ 0171/250–3222) or **Mobility International** (✉ Rue de Manchester 25, B-1080 Brussels, Belgium, ☎ 00–322–410–6297, FAX 00–322–410–6874), an international travel-information clearinghouse for people with disabilities.

PUBLICATIONS

Several publications for travelers with disabilities are available from the **Consumer Information Center** (✉ Box 100, Pueblo, CO 81009, ☎ 719/948–3334). Call or write for its free catalog of current titles. The Society for the Advancement of Travel for the Handicapped (☞ Organizations, *above*) publishes the quarterly magazine **"Access to Travel"** ($13 for 1-yr subscription).

The 500-page **Travelin' Talk Directory** (✉ Box 3534, Clarksville, TN 37043, ☎ 615/552–6670, FAX 615/552–1182; $35) lists people and organizations who help travelers with disabilities. For travel agents worldwide, consult the **Directory of Travel Agencies for the Disabled** (✉ Twin Peaks Press, Box 129, Vancouver, WA 98666, ☎ 360/694–2462 or 800/637–2256, FAX 360/696–3210; $19.95 plus $3 shipping).

TRAIN TRAVEL

The German Railways issues a booklet dealing with its services for travelers with disabilities, with an English-language section. It can be obtained from **Deutsche Bahn AG** (German Rail, ✉ Stephensonstr. 1, D–60326 Frankfurt am Main, ☎ 069/11111. Assistance can also be obtained from individual railroad stations by calling the local number 19419 (without the town or city prefix).

TRAVEL AGENCIES & TOUR OPERATORS

The Americans with Disabilities Act requires that all travel firms serve the needs of all travelers. That said, you should note that some agencies and operators specialize in making travel arrangements for individuals and groups with disabilities, among them **Access Adventures** (✉ 206 Chestnut Ridge Rd., Rochester, NY 14624, ☎ 716/889–9096), run by a former physical-rehab counselor.

THE GOLD GUIDE / IMPORTANT CONTACTS

TRAVELERS WITH MOBIL-
ITY PROBLEMS> Contact
Flying Wheels Travel
(✉ 143 W. Bridge St.,
Box 382, Owatonna,
MN 55060, ☎ 507/
451–5005 or 800/535–
6790), a travel agency
specializing in Euro-
pean cruises and tours;
Hinsdale Travel Service
(✉ 201 E. Ogden Ave.,
Suite 100, Hinsdale, IL
60521, ☎ 708/325–
1335), a travel agency
that benefits from the
advice of wheelchair
traveler Janice Perkins;
and **Wheelchair Jour-
neys** (✉ 16979 Red-
mond Way, Redmond,
WA 98052, ☎ 206/
885–2210 or 800/313–
4751), which can
handle arrangements
worldwide.

TRAVELERS WITH DEVEL-
OPMENTAL DISABILITIES>
Contact the nonprofit
New Directions (✉
5276 Hollister Ave.,
Suite 207, Santa Bar-
bara, CA 93111,
☎ 805/967–2841).

TRAVEL GEAR

The **Magellan's** catalog
(☎ 800/962–4943,
FAX 805/568–5406),
includes a range of
products designed
for travelers with
disabilities.

DISCOUNTS & DEALS

AIRFARES

For the lowest airfares
to Germany, call 800/
FLY–4–LESS.

CLUBS

Contact **Entertainment
Travel Editions** (✉ Box
1068, Trumbull, CT
06611, ☎ 800/445–
4137; $28–$53, de-
pending on destination),
Great American Traveler
(✉ Box 27965, Salt

Lake City, UT 84127,
☎ 800/548–2812;
$49.95 per yr), **Mo-
ment's Notice Discount
Travel Club** (✉ 7301
New Utrecht Ave.,
Brooklyn, NY 11204,
☎ 718/234–6295; $25
per yr, single or family),
Privilege Card (✉ 3391
Peachtree Rd. NE, Suite
110, Atlanta, GA
30326, ☎ 404/262–
0222 or 800/236–9732;
$74.95 per yr), **Travelers
Advantage** (✉ CUC
Travel Service, 49 Music
Sq. W, Nashville, TN
37203, ☎ 800/548–
1116 or 800/648–4037;
$49 per yr, single or
family), or **Worldwide
Discount Travel Club**
(✉ 1674 Meridian Ave.,
Miami Beach, FL
33139, ☎ 305/534–
2082; $50 per yr for
family, $40 single).

HOTEL ROOMS

For hotel room rates
guaranteed in U.S.
dollars, call **Steigen-
berger Reservation
Service** (☎ 800/223–
5652).

PASSES

☞ Train Travel, *below.*

STUDENTS

Members of Hostelling
International–American
Youth Hostels (☞
Students, *below*) are
eligible for discounts on
car rentals, admissions
to attractions, and other
selected travel expenses.

PUBLICATIONS

Consult **The Frugal
Globetrotter,** by Bruce
Northam (✉ Fulcrum
Publishing, 350 Indiana
St., Suite 350, Golden,
CO 80401, ☎ 800/
992–2908; $15.95).
For publications that
tell how to find the
lowest prices on plane

tickets, *see* Air Travel,
above.

Also see Fodor's **Affordable Europe** (available
in bookstores, or
☎ 800/533–6478;
$18.50).

DRIVING

There are three princi-
pal automobile clubs:
ADAC (Allgemeiner
Deutscher Automobil-
Club, ✉ Am Westpark
8, D–81373 Munich, ☎
089/76760), **AvD** (Auto-
mobilclub von Deutsch-
land, ✉ Lyonerstr. 16,
D–60528 Frankfurt,
☎ 069/66060), and **DTC**
(Deutscher Touring-
Automobil Club, ✉
Amalienburgstr. 23,
D–81247 Munich,
☎ 089/8911330).

FROM THE U.K.

The following compa-
nies operate car ferries
between the United
Kingdom and ports in
the Netherlands:
Sealink (☎ 01233/
646–801), **Eurolink
Ferries** (☎ 01795/581–
000), **P&O European
Ferries** (☎ 0181/575–
8555), **North Sea
Ferries** (☎ 01482/795–
141), and **Motorail**
(☎ 071/409–3518).

G

GAY & LESBIAN TRAVEL

ORGANIZATIONS

The **International Gay
Travel Association** (✉
Box 4974, Key West, FL
33041, ☎ 800/448–
8550, FAX 305/296–
6633), a consortium of
more than 1,000 travel
companies, can supply
names of gay-friendly
travel agents, tour
operators, and accom-
modations.

PUBLICATIONS

The premier international travel magazine for gays and lesbians is *Our World* (✉ 1104 N. Nova Rd., Suite 251, Daytona Beach, FL 32117, ☎ 904/441–5367, FAX 904/441–5604; $35 for 10 issues). The 16-page monthly *"Out & About"* (☎ 212/645–6922 or 800/929–2268, FAX 800/929–2215; $49 for 10 issues and quarterly calendar) covers gay-friendly resorts, hotels, cruise lines, and airlines.

TOUR OPERATORS

Toto Tours (✉ 1326 W. Albion Ave., Suite 3W, Chicago, IL 60626, ☎ 312/274–8686 or 800/565–1241, FAX 312/274–8695) offers group tours to worldwide destinations.

TRAVEL AGENCIES

The largest agencies serving gay travelers are **Advance Travel** (✉ 10700 Northwest Fwy., Suite 160, Houston, TX 77092, ☎ 713/682–2002 or 800/292–0500), **Islanders/ Kennedy Travel** (✉ 183 W. 10th St., New York, NY 10014, ☎ 212/242–3222 or 800/988–1181), **Now Voyager** (✉ 4406 18th St., San Francisco, CA 94114, ☎ 415/626–1169 or 800/255–6951), and **Yellowbrick Road** (✉ 1500 W. Balmoral Ave., Chicago, IL 60640, ☎ 312/561–1800 or 800/642–2488). **Skylink Women's Travel** (✉ 2460 W. 3rd St., Suite 215, Santa Rosa, CA 95401, ☎ 707/570–0105 or 800/225–5759) serves lesbian travelers.

H
HEALTH ISSUES

FINDING A DOCTOR

For its members, the **International Association for Medical Assistance to Travellers** (IAMAT, membership free; ✉ 417 Center St., Lewiston, NY 14092, ☎ 716/754–4883; ✉ 40 Regal Rd., Guelph, Ontario N1K 1B5, ☎ 519/836–0102; ✉ 1287 St. Clair Ave., Toronto, Ontario M6E 1B8, ☎ 416/652–0137; ✉ 57 Voirets, 1212 Grand-Lancy, Geneva, Switzerland, no phone) publishes a worldwide directory of English-speaking physicians meeting IAMAT standards.

MEDICAL ASSISTANCE COMPANIES

The following companies are concerned primarily with emergency medical assistance, although they may provide some insurance as part of their coverage. For a list of full-service travel insurance companies, *see* Insurance, *below.*

Contact **International SOS Assistance** (✉ Box 11568, Philadelphia, PA 19116, ☎ 215/244–1500 or 800/523–8930; ✉ Box 466, Pl. Bonaventure, Montréal, Québec H5A 1C1, ☎ 514/874–7674 or 800/363–0263; ✉ 7 Old Lodge Pl., St. Margarets, Twickenham TW1 1RQ, England, ☎ 0181/744–0033), **Medex Assistance Corporation** (✉ Box 5375, Timonium, MD 21094-5375, ☎ 410/453–6300 or 800/537–2029), **Traveler's Emergency Network** (✉ 3100 Tower Blvd., Suite 3100A, Durham, NC 27702, ☎ 919/490–6065 or 800/275–4836, FAX 919/493–8262), **TravMed** (✉ Box 5375, Timonium, MD 21094, ☎ 410/453–6380 or 800/732–5309), or **Worldwide Assistance Services** (✉ 1133 15th St. NW, Suite 400, Washington, DC 20005, ☎ 202/331–1609 or 800/821–2828, FAX 202/828–5896).

I
INSURANCE

IN CANADA

Contact **Mutual of Omaha** (✉ Travel Division, 500 University Ave., Toronto, Ontario M5G 1V8, ☎ 416/598–4083; in Canada, 800/465–0267).

IN THE U.S.

Travel insurance covering baggage, health, and trip cancellation or interruptions is available from **Access America** (✉ 6600 W. Broad St., Richmond, VA 23230, ☎ 804/285–3300 or 800/334–7525), **Carefree Travel Insurance** (✉ Box 9366, 100 Garden City Plaza, Garden City, NY 11530, ☎ 516/294–0220 or 800/323–3149), **Near Travel Services** (✉ Box 1339, Calumet City, IL 60409, ☎ 708/868–6700 or 800/654–6700), **Tele-Trip** (✉ Mutual of Omaha Plaza, Box 31716, Omaha, NE 68131, ☎ 800/228–9792), **Travel Guard International** (✉ 1145

Clark St., Stevens Point, WI 54481, ☎ 715/345–0505 or 800/826–1300), **Travel Insured International** (✉ Box 280568, East Hartford, CT 06128, ☎ 203/528–7663 or 800/243–3174), and **Wallach & Company** (✉ 107 W. Federal St., Box 480, Middleburg, VA 22117, ☎ 540/687–3166 or 800/237–6615).

IN THE U.K.

The **Association of British Insurers** (✉ 51 Gresham St., London EC2V 7HQ, ☎ 0171/600–3333) gives advice by phone and publishes the free pamphlet **"Holiday Insurance,"** which sets out typical policy provisions and costs.

L
LODGING

For information on hotel consolidators, *see* Discounts & Deals, *above.*

APARTMENT & VILLA RENTAL

Among the companies to contact are **EuropaLet** (✉ 92 N. Main St., Ashland, OR 97520, ☎ 541/482–5806 or 800/462–4486, FAX 541/482–0660), **Interhome** (✉ 124 Little Falls Rd., Fairfield, NJ 07004, ☎ 201/882–6864, FAX 201/808–1742), **Property Rentals International** (✉ 1008 Mansfield Crossing Rd., Richmond, VA 23236, ☎ 804/378–6054 or 800/220–3332, FAX 804/379–2073), **Rent-a-Home International** (✉ 7200 34th Ave. NW, Seattle, WA 98117, ☎ 206/789–9377 or 800/488–7368, FAX 206/

789–9379), and **Villas International** (✉ 605 Market St., Suite 510, San Francisco, CA 94105, ☎ 415/281–0910 or 800/221–2260, FAX 415/281–0919).

The German Automobile Association issues listings of family holiday apartments; write **ADAC Reisen** (✉ Am Westpark 8, D–81373 Munich).

CAMPING

For a listing of camping sites throughout Germany contact the **DCC,** or German Camping Club (✉ Mandlstr. 28, D–80802 Munich, ☎ 089/380–1420).

CASTLE HOTELS

For a brochure listing nearly 60 castle hotels, contact **Gast im Schloss** (✉ D 4, 9–10, Postfach 120620, D–68057 Mannheim, Germany, ☎ 0621/126–620). This organization and your travel agent can also advise on a number of packages available for castle hotels, including four- to six-night tours.

FARM VACATIONS

The **DLG** (German Agricultural Association) produces an illustrated brochure listing more than 1,500 inspected and graded farms, from the Alps to the North Sea, that offer accommodations. It costs DM 7.50 (send an international reply coupon if writing from the United States) and is available from **DLG Reisedienst, Agratour** (✉ Eschborner Landstr. 122, D–60489 Frankfurt/Main, ☎ 069/247–880) or the National Tourist Office.

HOME EXCHANGE

Some of the principal clearinghouses are **HomeLink International/Vacation Exchange Club** (✉ Box 650, Key West, FL 33041, ☎ 305/294–1448 or 800/638–3841, FAX 305/294–1148; $70 per yr), which sends members three annual directories, with a listing in one, plus updates; and **Intervac International** (✉ Box 590504, San Francisco, CA 94159, ☎ 415/435–3497, FAX 415/435–7440; $65 per yr), which publishes four annual directories.

HOTELS

An excellent nationwide hotel reservation service is also operated by **ADZ** (✉ Corneliusstr. 34, D–60325 Frankfurt/Main, ☎ 069/740–767, FAX 069/751–056), weekdays 9–5. The service is free of charge.

ROMANTIK HOTELS

A detailed brochure listing all Romantik Hotels and Restaurants, which costs $7.50 (including mailing), and a free miniguide are available from **Romantik Hotels Reservations** (✉ Box 1278, Woodinville, WA 98072, ☎ 206/486–9394; for reservations, ☎ 800/826–0015); information is also supplied by the National Tourist Office.

SPAS

A complete list of spas, giving full details of their springs and treatments, is available from the German National Tourist Office, or from **Deutsche Bäderverband,** the German Health Resort and Spa Association (✉ Postfach 190

147, D–53037 Bonn,
☎ 0228/262–010).

M
MONEY MATTERS

ATMS

For specific foreign
Cirrus locations, call
800/424–7787; for
foreign **Plus** locations,
consult the Plus direc-
tory at your local bank.

CURRENCY EXCHANGE

If your bank doesn't
exchange currency,
contact **Thomas Cook
Currency Services**
(☎ 800/287–7362
for locations). **Ruesch
International** (☎ 800/
424–2923 for loca-
tions) can also provide
you with foreign bank-
notes before you leave
home and publishes
a number of useful
brochures, including a
"Foreign Currency
Guide" and "Foreign
Exchange Tips."

WIRING FUNDS

Funds can be wired via
MoneyGram℠ (for
locations and informa-
tion in the U.S. and
Canada, ☎ 800/926–
9400) or **Western Union**
(for agent locations or
to send money using
MasterCard or Visa,
☎ 800/325–6000; in
Canada, 800/321–
2923; in the U.K.,
0800/833833; or visit
the Western Union
office at the nearest
major post office).

P
PACKING

For strategies on pack-
ing light, get a copy of
The Packing Book, by
Judith Gilford (✉ Ten
Speed Press, Box 7123,
Berkeley, CA 94707,
☎ 510/559–1600 or

800/841–2665, FAX 510/
524–4588; $7.95).

PASSPORTS & VISAS

IN THE U.S.

For fees, documentation
requirements, and other
information, call the
State Department's
**Office of Passport Ser-
vices** information line
(☎ 202/647–0518).

CANADIANS

For fees, documentation
requirements, and other
information, call the
Ministry of Foreign
Affairs and Interna-
tional Trade's **Passport
Office** (☎ 819/994–
3500 or 800/567–
6868).

U.K. CITIZENS

For fees, documentation
requirements, and to
request an emergency
passport, call the **Lon-
don Passport Office**
(☎ 0990/210410).

PHOTO HELP

The **Kodak Information
Center** (☎ 800/242–
2424) answers con-
sumer questions about
film and photography.
The **Kodak Guide to
Shooting Great Travel
Pictures** (available in
bookstores; or contact
Fodor's Travel Publica-
tions, ☎ 800/533–
6478; $16.50) explains
how to take expert
travel photographs.

S
SAFETY

"Trouble-Free Travel,"
from the AAA, is a
booklet of tips for
protecting yourself and
your belongings when
away from home. Send a
stamped, self-addressed,
legal-size envelope to
Flying Alone (✉ Mail

Stop 75, 1000 AAA Dr.,
Heathrow, FL 32746).

SENIOR CITIZENS

EDUCATIONAL TRAVEL

The nonprofit **Elderhos-
tel** (✉ 75 Federal St.,
3rd floor, Boston, MA
02110, ☎ 617/426–
7788), for people 60
and older, has offered
inexpensive study
programs since 1975.
Courses cover every-
thing from marine
science to Greek
mythology and cowboy
poetry. Costs for two-
to three-week interna-
tional trips—including
room, board, and
transportation from the
United States—range
from $1,800 to $4,500.

For people 50 and over
and their children and
grandchildren, **Interhos-
tel** (✉ University of
New Hampshire, 6
Garrison Ave., Durham,
NH 03824, ☎ 603/
862–1147 or 800/733–
9753) runs 10-day
summer programs that
feature lectures, field
trips, and sightseeing.
Most last two weeks
and cost $2,125–
$3,100, including
airfare.

ORGANIZATIONS

Contact the **American
Association of Retired
Persons** (AARP, ✉ 601
E St. NW, Washington,
DC 20049, ☎ 202/
434–2277; annual dues
$8 per person or cou-
ple). Its Purchase Privi-
lege Program secures
discounts for members
on lodging, car rentals,
and sightseeing.

Additional sources for
discounts on lodgings,
car rentals, and other
travel expenses, as well
as helpful magazines
and newsletters, are the

National Council of Senior Citizens (✉ 1331 F St. NW, Washington, DC 20004, ☎ 202/347–8800; annual membership $12) and Sears's **Mature Outlook** (✉ Box 10448, Des Moines, IA 50306, ☎ 800/336–6330; annual membership $9.95).

SPORTS

BICYCLING

Information on all aspects of cycling in Germany is available from the **Allgemeiner Deutscher Fahrrad-Club** (The German Cycle Club; ✉ Postfach 107747, D–28077 Bremen, ☎ 0421/346–290).

FISHING

Details on fishing in Germany are available from local tourist offices or from the **Verband Deutscher Sportfischer** (✉ Siemensstr. 11–13, D–63071 Offenbach, ☎ 069/855–006).

GOLF

For information, contact the **Deutscher Golf-Verband** (German Golf Association; ✉ Friedrichstr. 12, D–65185 Wiesbaden, ☎ 0611/990–200).

HIKING AND CLIMBING

The **Verband Deutscher Gebirgs und Wandervereine e.V.** (✉ Postfach 103213, D–66032 Saarbrücken, ☎ 0681/390–070) can provide information on routes, hiking paths, overnight accommodations, and mountain huts.

For Alpine walking, contact the **Deutsche Alpenverein** (✉ Von-Kahr-Str. 2–4, D–80997 Munich, ☎ 089/140–

030). It administers more than 50 mountain huts and about 15,000 kilometers (9,500 miles) of Alpine paths. In addition, it can provide courses in mountaineering and touring suggestions for routes in both winter and summer. Foreigners may become members.

Various mountaineering schools offer weeklong courses ranging from basic techniques for beginners to advanced mountaineering. Tourist offices in all Bavarian Alpine resorts have details.

SAILING

For details on sailing vacations and sailboat rental, contact **Deutscher Segler-Verband** (✉ Gründgensstr. 18, D–22309 Hamburg, ☎ 040/632–0090).

WINDSURFING

For windsurfing information contact the German National Tourist Office or local tourist office at Germany's many lake resorts.

STUDENTS

GROUPS

The major tour operators specializing in student travel are **Contiki Holidays** (✉ 300 Plaza Alicante, Suite 900, Garden Grove, CA 92640, ☎ 714/740–0808 or 800/266–8454) and **AESU Travel** (✉ 2 Hamill Rd., Suite 248, Baltimore, MD 21210-1807, ☎ 410/323–4416 or 800/638–7640).

HOSTELING

In the United States, contact **Hostelling International–American Youth**

Hostels (✉ 733 15th St. NW, Suite 840, Washington, DC 20005, ☎ 202/783–6161 or 800/444–6111 for reservations at selected hostels, FAX 202/783–6171); in Canada, **Hostelling International–Canada** (✉ 205 Catherine St., Suite 400, Ottawa, Ontario K2P 1C3, ☎ 613/237–7884); and in the United Kingdom, the **Youth Hostel Association of England and Wales** (✉ Trevelyan House, 8 St. Stephen's Hill, St. Albans, Hertfordshire AL1 2DY, ☎ 01727/855215 or 01727/845047). Membership (in the U.S., $25; in Canada, C$26.75; in the U.K., £9.30) gives you access to 5,000 hostels in 77 countries that charge $5–$30 per person per night.

For listings of German youth hostels, contact the **Deutsches Jugendherbergswerk Hauptverband** (✉ Bismarckstr. 8, D–32754 Detmold, ☎ 05231/74010).

ORGANIZATIONS

A major contact is the **Council on International Educational Exchange** (✉ Mail orders only: CIEE, 205 E. 42nd St., 16th floor, New York, NY 10017, ☎ 212/822–2600). The **Educational Travel Centre** (✉ 438 N. Frances St., Madison, WI 53703, ☎ 608/256–5551 or 800/747–5551, FAX 608/256–2042) offers rail passes and low-cost airline tickets, mostly for flights that depart from Chicago.

In Canada, also contact **Travel Cuts** (✉ 187 College St., Toronto, Ontario M5T 1P7,

☎ 416/979–2406 or 800/667–2887).

PUBLICATIONS

Check out the **Berkeley Guide to Germany and Austria** (available in bookstores; or contact Fodor's Travel Publications, ☎ 800/533–6478; $17.95).

T

TELEPHONE MATTERS

The country code for Germany is 49. For local access numbers abroad, contact **AT&T** USADirect (☎ 800/874–4000), **MCI** Call USA (☎ 800/444–4444), or **Sprint** Express (☎ 800/793–1153).

TOUR OPERATORS

Among the companies that sell tours and packages to Germany, the following are nationally known, have a proven reputation, and offer plenty of options.

GROUP TOURS

SUPER-DELUXE➤ **Abercrombie & Kent** (⊠ 1520 Kensington Rd., Oak Brook, IL 60521–2141, ☎ 708/954–2944 or 800/323–7308, FAX 708/954–3324) and **Travcoa** (⊠ Box 2630, 2350 S.E. Bristol St., Newport Beach, CA 92660, ☎ 714/476–2800 or 800/992–2003, FAX 714/476–2538).

DELUXE➤ **Globus** (⊠ 5301 S. Federal Circle, Littleton, CO 80123–2980, ☎ 303/797–2800 or 800/221–0090, FAX 303/795–0962), **Maupintour** (⊠ Box 807, 1515 St. Andrews Dr., Lawrence, KS 66047, ☎ 913/843–1211 or 800/255–4266, FAX 913/843–8351), and

Tauck Tours (⊠ Box 5027, 276 Post Rd. W, Westport, CT 06881, ☎ 203/226–6911 or 800/468–2825, FAX 203/221–6828).

FIRST CLASS➤ **Brendan Tours** (⊠ 15137 Califa St., Van Nuys, CA 91411, ☎ 818/785–9696 or 800/421–8446, FAX 818/902–9876), **Caravan Tours** (⊠ 401 N. Michigan Ave., Chicago, IL 60611, ☎ 312/321–9800 or 800/227–2826), **Collette Tours** (⊠ 162 Middle St., Pawtucket, RI 02860, ☎ 401/728–3805 or 800/832–4656, FAX 401/728–1380), **DER Tours** (⊠ 11933 Wilshire Blvd., Los Angeles, CA 90025, ☎ 310/479–4140 or 800/782–2424), **Gadabout Tours** (⊠ 700 E. Tahquitz Canyon Way, Palm Springs, CA 92262, ☎ 619/325–5556 or 800/952–5068), **Insight International Tours** (⊠ 745 Atlantic Ave., #720, Boston, MA 02111, ☎ 617/482–2000 or 800/582–8380, FAX 617/482–2884 or 800/622–5015), and **Trafalgar Tours** (⊠ 11 E. 26th St., New York, NY 10010, ☎ 212/689–8977 or 800/854–0103, FAX 800/457–6644).

BUDGET➤ **Cosmos** (☞ Globus, *above*) and **Trafalgar** (☞ *above*).

PACKAGES

DER Tours (☞ Group Tours, *above*) has the greatest variety of independent vacation packages. Among the U.S. airlines offering packages to Germany are **American Airlines Fly AAway Vacations** (☎ 800/321–2121), **Continental Vacations**

(☎ 800/634–5555), **Delta Dream Vacations** (☎ 800/872–7786), **United Vacations** (☎ 800/328–6877), and **USAir Vacations** (☎ 800/455–0123). Another leading packager is **4th Dimension Tours** (7101 S.W. 99th Ave., #105, Miami, FL 33173, ☎ 305/279–0014 or 800/877–1525, FAX 305/273–9777). **Funjet Vacations**, based in Milwaukee, Wisconsin, and **Gogo Tours**, based in Ramsey, New Jersey, sell packages only through travel agents.

FROM THE U.K.

DER Travel Services Ltd. (⊠ 18 Conduit St., London W1R 9TD, ☎ 0171/408–0111) arranges self-catering, guest-house, and hotel holidays, and the **German Travel Centre** (⊠ 403–409 Rayner's La., Pinner, Middlesex, HA5 5ER, ☎ 0181/429–2900) arranges tailor-made holidays.

THEME TRIPS

ADVENTURE➤ **Himalayan Travel** (⊠ 112 Prospect St., Stamford, CT 06901, ☎ 203/359–3711 or 800/225–2380, FAX 203/359–3669) operates a range of active adventure tours. **Value Holidays** (⊠ 10224 N. Port Washington Rd., Mequon, WI 53092, ☎ 414/241–6373 or 800/558–6850) customizes theme tours.

ART AND ARCHITECTURE➤ Contact **Smithsonian Study Tours and Seminars** (⊠ 1100 Jefferson Dr. SW, Room 3045, MRC 702, Washington, DC 20560, ☎ 202/357–4700,

FAX 202/633–9250) for programs on Germany's artistic achievements.

BARGE/RIVER CRUISES➤ Contact **Abercrombie & Kent** (☞ Group Tours, *above*), **Alden Yacht Charters** (✉ 1909 Alden Landing, Portsmouth, RI 02871, ☎ 401/683–1782 or 800/662–2628, FAX 401/683–3668), **Esplanade Tours** (✉ 581 Boylston St., Boston, MA 02116, ☎ 617/266–7465 or 800/426–5492, FAX 617/262–9829), or **KD River Cruises of Europe** (✉ 2500 Westchester Ave., Purchase, NY 10577, ☎ 914/696–3600 or 800/346–6525, FAX 914/696–0833) for itineraries throughout Germany. For a cruise on the Mosel River, contact **Etoile De Champagne** (✉ 88 Broad St., Boston, MA 02110, ☎ 800/280–1492, FAX 617/426–4689).

BEER➤ **MIR Corporation** (✉ 85 S. Washington St., #210, Seattle, WA 98104, ☎ 206/624–7289 or 800/424–7289, FAX 206/624–7360) leads you to Germany's famous breweries. Virtually all the general-interest operators listed above run Oktoberfest tours.

BICYCLING➤ For bike tours through Germany, contact **Backroads** (✉ 1516 5th St., Berkeley, CA 94710-1740, ☎ 510/527–1555 or 800/462–2848, FAX 510/527–1444), **Classic Adventures** (✉ Box 153, Hamlin, NY 14464-0153, ☎ 716/964–8488 or 800/777–8090, FAX 716/964–7297), **Euro-Bike Tours** (✉ Box 990, De Kalb, IL 60115, ☎ 800/321–

6060, FAX 815/758–8851), **Rocky Mountain Worldwide Cycle Tours** (✉ Box 1978, Canmore, Alberta, Canada TOL OMO, ☎ 403/678–6770 or 800/661–2453, FAX 403/678–4451), and **Uniquely Europe** (✉ 2819 1st Ave., #280, Seattle, WA 98121-1113, ☎ 206/441–8682 or 800/426–3615, FAX 206/441–8862).

CRUISES➤ For all types and sizes of ships, call **EuroCruises** (✉ 303 W. 13th St., New York, NY 10014, ☎ 212/691–2099 or 800/688–3876).

FOOD AND WINE➤ **The German Wine Academy** (✉ c/o German Wine Information Bureau, 79 Madison Ave., New York, NY 10016, ☎ 212/213–7028) has seminars in English designed to improve your knowledge and enjoyment of German wine.

HEALTH➤ Contact **Spa-Finders** (✉ 91 5th Ave., #301, New York, NY 10003-3039, ☎ 212/924–6800 or 800/255–7727).

HORSEBACK RIDING➤ **FITS Equestrian** (✉ 685 Lateen Rd., Solvang, CA 93463, ☎ 805/688–9494 or 800/666–3487, FAX 805/688–2943) leads eight-day rides through the Black Forest.

LEARNING➤ **Earthwatch** (✉ Box 403, 680 Mount Auburn St., Watertown, MA 02272, ☎ 617/926–8200 or 800/776–0188, FAX 617/926–8532) recruits volunteers to serve in its EarthCorps as short-term assistants to scien-

tists on research expeditions. **Smithsonian Study Tours and Seminars** (✉ 1100 Jefferson Dr. SW, Room 3045, MRC 702, Washington, DC 20560, ☎ 202/357–4700, FAX 202/633–9250) operates tours focused on art and culture.

MOTORCYCLE➤ **Beach's Motorcycle Adventures** (✉ 2763 W. River Pkwy., Grand Island, NY 14072-2053, ☎ 716/773–4960, FAX 716/773–5227) can take you on a guided alpine adventure through Germany.

MUSIC➤ **Dailey-Thorp Travel** (✉ 330 W. 58th St., #610, New York, NY 10019-1817, ☎ 212/307–1555 or 800/998–4677, FAX 212/974–1420) specializes in classical music and opera programs throughout Germany.

VILLA RENTALS➤ Contact **Villas International** (✉ 605 Market St., San Francisco, CA 94105, ☎ 415/281–0910 or 800/221–2260, FAX 415/281–0919).

WALKING➤ **Euro-Bike Tours** (☞ Bicycling, *above*) has a walking tour through Bavaria. Also try **Above the Clouds Trekking** (✉ Box 398, Worcester, MA 01602, ☎ 508/799–4499 or 800/233–4499, FAX 508/797–4779), and **Uniquely Europe** (☞ Bicycling, *above*).

YACHT CHARTERS➤ **Ocean Voyages** (✉ 1709 Bridgeway, Sausalito, CA 94965, ☎ 415/332–4681, FAX 415/332–7460).

ORGANIZATIONS

The **National Tour Association** (NTA, ✉

546 E. Main St., Lexington, KY 40508, ☎ 606/226–4444 or 800/755–8687) and the **United States Tour Operators Association** (USTOA, ✉ 211 E. 51st St., Suite 12B, New York, NY 10022, ☎ 212/750–7371) can provide lists of members and information on booking tours.

PUBLICATIONS

Contact the USTOA (☞ Organizations, *above*) for its **"Smart Traveler's Planning Kit."** Pamphlets in the kit include the "Worldwide Tour and Vacation Package Finder," "How to Select a Tour or Vacation Package," and information on the organization's consumer protection plan. Also get a copy of the Better Business Bureau's **"Tips on Travel Packages"** (✉ Publication 24-195, 4200 Wilson Blvd., Arlington, VA 22203; $2).

TRAIN TRAVEL

BAGGAGE SERVICE

From train stations throughout Germany, you can use the Deutsche Bahn *KurierGepäck* service to send your baggage to Frankfurt Airport; call 0180/332–0520 to have them pick up you baggage from your hotel. The service costs DM 28 per suitcase (with a valid ticket), and overnight delivery is guaranteed on weekdays.

DISCOUNT PASSES

The German Rail Pass, Eurail, and EuroPasses are available through travel agents and **Rail Europe** (✉ 226-230 Westchester Ave., White Plains, NY 10604,

☎ 914/682–5172 or 800/438–7245; ✉ 2087 Dundas E, Suite 105, Mississauga, Ontario L4X 1M2, ☎ 416/602–4195), **DER Tours** (✉ Box 1606, Des Plaines, IL 60017, ☎ 800/782–2424, FAX 800/282–7474), or **CIT Tours Corp.** (✉ 342 Madison Ave., Suite 207, New York, NY 10173, ☎ 212/697–2100 or 800/248–8687; in western U.S., 800/ 248–7245).

FROM THE UNITED KINGDOM BY TRAIN

For information on rail travel between London and Germany, *see* The Channel Tunnel, *above*. For timetables and information about German rail services and fares, contact the **German Rail Passenger Services** (✉ 23 Oakhill Grove, Surbiton, Surrey KT6 6DU, ☎ 0181/ 390–8833).

TRAVEL AGENCIES

For names of reputable agencies in your area, contact the **American Society of Travel Agents** (ASTA, ☎ 1101 King St., Suite 200, Alexandria, VA 22314, ☎ 703/739–2782), the **Association of Canadian Travel Agents** (✉ 1729 Bank St., Suite 201, Ottawa, Ontario K1V 7Z5, ☎ 613/521–0474, FAX 613/521–0805) or the **Association of British Travel Agents** (✉ 55-57 Newman St., London W1P 4AH, ☎ 0171/637–2444, FAX 0171/637–0713).

TRAVEL GEAR

For travel apparel, appliances, personal-care items, and other

travel necessities, get a free catalog from **Magellan's** (☎ 800/ 962–4943, FAX 805/ 568–5406), **Orvis Travel** (☎ 800/541–3541, FAX 703/343–7053), or **TravelSmith** (☎ 800/950–1600, FAX 415/455–0554).

ELECTRICAL CONVERTERS

Send a self-addressed, stamped envelope to the **Franzus Company** (✉ Customer Service, Dept. B50, Murtha Industrial Park, Box 142, Beacon Falls, CT 06403, ☎ 203/723–6664) for a copy of the free brochure "Foreign Electricity Is No Deep, Dark Secret."

U

U.S. GOVERNMENT TRAVEL BRIEFINGS

The U.S. Department of State's American Citizens Services office (✉ Room 4811, Washington, DC 20520; enclose SASE) issues **Consular Information Sheets** on all foreign countries. These cover issues such as crime, security, political climate, and health risks as well as listing embassy locations, entry requirements, currency regulations, and providing other useful information. For the latest information, stop in at any U.S. passport office, consulate, or embassy; call the interactive hot line (☎ 202/647–5225, FAX 202/647–3000); or, with your PC's modem, tap into the department's computer bulletin board (☎ 202/ 647–9225).

THE GOLD GUIDE / IMPORTANT CONTACTS

V

VISITOR INFORMATION

IN THE U.S.

German National Tourist Office (⊠ 122 E. 42nd St., New York, NY 10168, ☎ 212/661–7200, FAX 212/661–7174; ⊠ 11766 Wilshire Blvd., Suite 750, Los Angeles, CA 90025, ☎ 310/575-9799, FAX 310/575–1565).

IN CANADA

German National Tourist Office (⊠ 175 Bloor St. E, North Tower, Suite 604, Toronto, Ontario M4 W3R8, ☎ 416/968–1570).

IN THE U.K.

German National Tourist Office (⊠ Nightingale House, 65 Curzon St., London W1Y 7PE, ☎ 0891/600–100). Calls cost 49p per minute peak rate or 39p per minute cheap rate.

W

WEATHER

For current conditions and forecasts, plus the local time and helpful travel tips, call the **Weather Channel Connection** (☎ 900/932–8437; 95¢ per minute) from a Touch-Tone phone.

The *International Traveler's Weather Guide* (⊠ Weather Press, Box 660606, Sacramento, CA 95866, ☎ 916/974–0201 or 800/972–0201; $10.95 includes shipping), written by two meteorologists, provides month-by-month information on temperature, humidity, and precipitation in more than 175 cities worldwide.

SMART TRAVEL TIPS A TO Z

Basic Information on Traveling in Germany & Savvy Tips to Make Your Trip a Breeze

A

AIR TRAVEL

If time is an issue, **always look for nonstop flights,** which require no change of plane. If possible, **avoid connecting flights,** which stop at least once and can involve a change of plane, even though the flight number remains the same; if the first leg is late, the second waits.

For better service, **fly smaller or regional carriers,** which often have higher passenger satisfaction ratings. Sometimes they have such in-flight amenities as leather seats or greater legroom and they often have better food.

CUTTING COSTS

The Sunday travel section of most newspapers is a good place to look for deals.

MAJOR AIRLINES➤ The least-expensive airfares from the major airlines are priced for round-trip travel and are subject to restrictions. Usually, you must **book in advance and buy the ticket within 24 hours** to get cheaper fares, and you may have to **stay over a Saturday night.** The lowest fare is subject to availability, and only a small percentage of the plane's total seats is sold at that price. It's smart to **call a number of airlines, and when you are quoted a good price, book it on the spot**—the same fare may not be available on the same flight the next day. Airlines generally allow you to change your return date for a $25 to $50 fee. If you don't use your ticket, you can apply the cost toward the purchase of a new ticket, again for a small charge. However, most low-fare tickets are nonrefundable. To get the lowest airfare, **check different routings.** If your destination has more than one gateway, **compare prices to different airports.**

FROM THE U.K.➤ To save money on flights, **look into an APEX or Super-PEX ticket.** APEX tickets must be booked in advance and have certain restrictions. Super-PEX tickets can be purchased right at the airport.

ALOFT

AIRLINE FOOD➤ If you hate airline food, **ask for special meals when booking.** These can be vegetarian, low-cholesterol, or kosher, for example; commonly prepared to order in smaller quantities than standard fare, they can be tastier.

SMOKING➤ Smoking is not allowed on flights of six hours or less within the continental United States. Smoking is also prohibited on flights within Canada. For U.S. flights longer than six hours or international flights, **contact your carrier regarding their smoking policy.** Some carriers have prohibited smoking throughout their system; others allow smoking only on certain routes or even certain departures of that route.

WITHIN GERMANY

Germany's internal air network is excellent, with frequent flights linking all major cities. Services are operated by **Deutsche BA,** a British Airways subsidiary, **Lufthansa,** and **LTU.** In addition, small airlines operate services between a limited number of northern cities and the East and North Frisian islands, though many of these flights operate only in the summer.

Lufthansa also offers train service from Köln to the Frankfurt airport, acting as a supplement to existing air services. Only passengers holding air tickets may use the train. It is cheaper than normal rail travel, and luggage is automatically transferred to your plane on arrival at the airport. Service is first class. German Rail operates a similar service called "Rail and Fly" (☞ Train Travel, *below*), and most trains that stop at Frankfurt City also stop at Frankfurt airport.

B

BOAT TRIPS

EurailPasses and German Rail Passes are valid on all services of the KD German Rhine Line and on the Mosel between Trier and Koblenz. (If you use the fast hydrofoil, a supplementary fee is required.) Regular rail tickets are also accepted, meaning that you can **go one way by ship and return by train.** All you have to do is pay a small surcharge to KD Rhine Line and get the ticket endorsed at one of the landing-stage offices. But note that you have to buy the rail ticket first and *then* get it changed.

KD Rhine Line also offers a program of luxury cruises along the Rhine, Main, Mosel, Elbe, and Danube rivers. The cruises include four-day trips from Frankfurt to Trier (from DM 660), five-day journeys from Amsterdam to Basel in Switzerland, and seven-day holidays from Passau to Budapest (from DM 1,320). Prices include all meals. The cruises are supplemented by trips of one day or less on the Rhine and Mosel. During the summer there are good services between Bonn and Koblenz and between Koblenz and between Koblenz and Bingen; both trips take around five hours.

The cruises, especially for the newer Elbe routes, are in great demand, so reservations are necessary several months in advance.

BUS TRAVEL

Germany has good local bus services, but no proper nationwide network like Greyhound. A large portion of services are operated by the railways (Bahn-

bus) and are closely integrated with train services, while on less busy rail lines, services are run by buses in off-peak periods—normally midday and weekends. Rail tickets are valid on these services.

One of the best services is the Romantic Road bus between Würzburg (with connections to and from Frankfurt and Wiesbaden) and Füssen (with connections to and from Munich, Augsburg, and Garmisch-Parten-kirchen). This is an all-reserved-seats bus with a stewardess, offering one- or two-day tours in each direction in summer, leaving in the morning and arriving in the evening. Details and reservations are available from Deutsche Touring (☞ Bus Travel *in* Important Contacts A to Z, *above*) or big city tourist offices.

All towns of any size operate their own local buses. For the most part, those link up with local trams (streetcars), electric railway (S-bahn), and subway (U-bahn) services. Fares vary according to distance, but a ticket usually allows you to transfer freely between the various forms of transportation. Most cities issue 24-hour tickets at special rates.

BUSINESS HOURS

BANKS

Times vary from state to state and city to city, but banks are generally open weekdays from 8:30 or 9 to 2 or 3 (5 or 6 on Thursday), with a lunch break of about an hour. Branches at airports and main train

stations open as early as 6:30 AM and close as late as 10:30 PM.

MUSEUMS

Most museums are open from Tuesday to Sunday 9–6. Some close for an hour or more at lunch, and some are open on Monday. Many stay open late on Wednesday or Thursday.

SHOPS

Most shops are open 9 or 9:15–6:30 weekdays and until 2 PM on Saturday, except for the first Saturday in the month, when the bigger stores stay open until 6 in winter and 4 in summer. Many shops also remain open on Thursday evening until 8:30. The German government was reconsidering legislation in 1996 allowing shops to stay open until 8 PM throughout the week.

C
CAMERAS, CAMCORDERS, & COMPUTERS

IN TRANSIT

Always **keep your film, tape, or disks out of the sun**; never put these on the dashboard of a car. Carry an extra supply of batteries, and **be prepared to turn on your camera, camcorder, or laptop computer for security personnel** to prove that it's real.

X-RAYS

Always **ask for hand inspection at security.** Such requests are virtually always honored at U.S. airports, and are usually accommodated abroad. Photographic film becomes clouded after successive exposure to airport X-ray machines. Videotape and computer disks are not by X-rays, but **keep your tapes and disks away from metal detectors.**

CUSTOMS

Before departing, **register your foreign-made camera or laptop with U.S. Customs.** If your equipment is U.S.-made, call the consulate of the country you'll be visiting to find out whether it should be registered with local customs upon arrival.

CAR RENTAL

CUTTING COSTS

To get the best deal, **book through a travel agent who is willing to shop around.** Ask your agent to **look for fly-drive packages,** which also save you money, and **ask if local taxes are included** in the rental or fly-drive price. These can be as high as 20% in some destinations. Don't forget to find out about required deposits, cancellation penalties, drop-off charges, and the cost of any required insurance coverage.

Also **ask your travel agent about a company's customer-service record.** How has it responded to late plane arrivals and vehicle mishaps? Are there often lines at the rental counter, and—if you're traveling during a holiday period—does a confirmed reservation guarantee you a car?

Always **find out what equipment is standard** at your destination before specifying what you want; automatic transmission and air-conditioning are usually optional—and very expensive.

Be sure to **look into wholesalers**—companies that do not own their own fleets but rent in bulk from those that do and often offer better rates than traditional car-rental operations. Prices are best during off-peak periods; rentals booked through wholesalers must be paid for before you leave the United States.

INSURANCE

When driving a rented car, you are generally responsible for any damage to or loss of the rental vehicle. Before you rent, **see what coverage you already have** under the terms of your personal auto insurance policy and credit cards.

If you do not have auto insurance or an umbrella insurance policy that covers damage to third parties, purchasing CDW or LDW is highly recommended.

Collision policies that car-rental companies sell for European rentals typically do not cover stolen vehicles. Before you buy additional coverage for theft, find out if your credit card or personal auto insurance will cover the loss.

LICENSE REQUIREMENTS

In Germany your own driver's license is acceptable. An International Driver's Permit is a good idea; it's available from the American or Canadian auto-

mobile associations, or, in the United Kingdom, from the AA or RAC.

SURCHARGES

Before you pick up a car in one city and leave it in another, **ask about drop-off charges or one-way service fees,** which can be substantial. Note, too, that some rental agencies charge extra if you return the car before the time specified on your contract. To avoid a hefty refueling fee, **fill the tank just before you turn in the car**—but be aware that gas stations near the rental outlet may overcharge.

THE CHANNEL TUNNEL

The "Chunnel" is the fastest way to cross the English Channel short of flying—35 minutes from Folkestone to Calais, 60 minutes from motorway to motorway, or three hours from Waterloo, London, to Paris's Gare du Nord. It consists of two large 50-kilometer- (31-mile-) long train tunnels, and a smaller service tunnel running between them.

CHILDREN & TRAVEL

Almost every city in Germany has its own children's theater, and the country's puppet theaters rank among the best in the world. Many movie theaters also screen films for children, normally in the morning and afternoon. Playgrounds are around virtually every corner, and about a half dozen major theme parks around the country now entertain the younger ones.

When traveling with children, **plan ahead** and **involve your youngsters** as you outline your trip. When packing, **include a supply of things to keep them busy** en route (☞ Children & Travel *in* Important Contacts A to Z). On sightseeing days, try to **schedule activities of special interest to your children,** like a trip to a zoo or a playground. If you **plan your itinerary around seasonal festivals,** you'll never lack for things to do. In addition, **check local newspapers for special events** mounted by public libraries, museums, and parks.

BABY-SITTING

For recommended local sitters, **check with your hotel desk.** Updated lists of well-screened baby-sitters are also available from most local tourist offices. Rates are usually about DM 25 per hour.

Many large department stores in Germany provide baby-sitting facilities or areas where children can play while their parents go shopping.

DRIVING

If you are renting a car, don't forget to **arrange for a car seat when you reserve.** Sometimes they're free.

FLYING

Always **ask about discounted children's fares.** On international flights, infants under two not occupying a seat generally travel free or for 10% of the accompanying adult's fare; the fare for children ages 2–11 is usually half to two-thirds of the adult fare. On domestic flights, children under two not occupying a seat travel free, and older children are charged at the lowest applicable adult rate.

BAGGAGE➤ In general, the adult baggage allowance applies to children paying half or more of the adult fare. If you are traveling with an infant, **ask about carry-on allowances** before departure. In general, for infants charged 10% of the adult fare you are allowed one carry-on bag and a collapsible stroller; you may be limited to less if the flight is full.

SAFETY SEATS➤ According to the FAA, it's a good idea to **use safety seats aloft** for children weighing less than 40 pounds. Airline policies vary. U.S. carriers allow FAA-approved models but usually require that you buy a ticket, even if your child would otherwise ride free, since the seats must be strapped into regular seats. Foreign carriers may not allow infant seats, may charge a child rather than an infant fare for their use, or may require you to hold your baby during takeoff and landing—defeating the seat's purpose.

FACILITIES➤ When making your reservation, **request children's meals or freestanding bassinets** if you need them; the latter are available only to those seated at the bulkhead, where there's enough legroom. If you don't need a bassinet, **think twice before requesting bulkhead seats**—the only storage space for in-flight necessities is in inconveniently distant overhead bins.

GAMES

Milton Bradley and Parker Brothers have travel versions of some of their most popular games, including Yahtzee, Trouble, Sorry, and Monopoly. Prices run from $5 to $8. Look for them in the travel section of your local toy store.

LODGING

Most hotels allow children under a certain age to stay in their parents' room at no extra charge; others charge them as extra adults. Be sure to **ask about the cutoff age.**

CUSTOMS & DUTIES

To speed your clearance through customs, **keep receipts for all your purchases abroad.** If you feel that you've been incorrectly or unfairly charged a duty, you can **appeal assessments in dispute.** First ask to see a supervisor. If you are still unsatisfied, **write to the port director** your point of entry, sending your customs receipt and any other appropriate documentation. The address will be listed on your receipt. If you still don't get satisfaction, you can take your case to customs headquarters in Washington.

IN GERMANY

Since a single, unrestricted market took

effect within the European Union (EU) early in 1993, there are no longer restrictions for citizens of the 15 member countries traveling between EU countries. For citizens of non-EU countries and anyone entering Germany from outside the Union, the following limitations apply.

On goods obtained (duty- and tax-paid) within another EU country, you are allowed (1) 800 cigarettes or 400 cigarillos or 200 cigars or 1 kg. of tobacco; (2) plus 10 liters of spirits, 20 liters of fortified wine, 90 liters of wine, and 110 liters of beer; (5) other goods to the value of DM 780.

On goods obtained anywhere outside the EU or for goods purchased in a duty-free shop within an EU country, you are allowed (1) 200 cigarettes or 100 cigarillos or 50 cigars or 250 grams of tobacco (twice that if you live outside of Europe); (2) 2 liters of still table wine; (3) 1 liter of spirits over 22% volume or 2 liters of spirits under 22% volume (fortified and sparkling wines) or 2 more liters of table wine; (4) 60 milliliters of perfume and 250 milliliters of toilet water; (5) other goods to the value of DM 115.

Tobacco and alcohol allowances are for visitors age 17 and over. Other items intended for personal use can be imported and exported freely. There are no restrictions on the import and export of German currency.

IN THE U.S.

You may bring home $400 worth of foreign goods duty-free if you've been out of the country for at least 48 hours and haven't already used the $400 allowance, or any part of it, in the past 30 days.

Travelers 21 or older may bring back 1 liter of alcohol duty-free, provided the beverage laws of the state through which they reenter the United States allow it. In addition, regardless of their age, they are allowed 100 non-Cuban cigars and 200 cigarettes. Antiques and works of art more than 100 years old are duty-free.

Duty-free, travelers may mail packages valued at up to $200 to themselves and up to $100 to others, with a limit of one parcel per addressee per day (and no alcohol or tobacco products or perfume valued at more than $5); on the outside, the package should be labeled as being either for personal use or an unsolicited gift, and a list of its contents and their retail value should be attached. Mailed items do not affect your duty-free allowance on your return.

IN CANADA

If you've been out of Canada for at least seven days, you may bring in C$500 worth of goods duty-free. If you've been away for fewer than seven days but for more than 48 hours, the duty-free allowance drops to C$200; if your trip lasts between 24 and 48 hours, the allowance is C$50. You cannot pool allowances with family members. Goods claimed under the C$500 exemption may follow you by mail; those claimed under the lesser exemptions must accompany you.

Alcohol and tobacco products may be included in the seven-day and 48-hour exemptions but not in the 24-hour exemption. If you meet the age requirements of the province or territory through which you reenter Canada, you may bring in, duty-free, 1.14 liters (40 imperial ounces) of wine or liquor or 24 12-ounce cans or bottles of beer or ale. If you are 16 or older, you may bring in, duty-free, 200 cigarettes, 50 cigars or cigarillos, and 400 tobacco sticks or 400 grams of manufactured tobacco. Alcohol and tobacco must accompany you on your return.

An unlimited number of gifts with a value of up to C$60 each may be mailed to Canada duty-free. These do not affect your duty-free allowance on your return. Label the package "Unsolicited Gift—Value Under $60." Alcohol and tobacco are excluded.

IN THE U.K.

If your journey was wholly within European Union (EU) countries, you no longer need to pass through customs when you return to the United Kingdom. If you plan to bring back large quantities of alcohol or tobacco, check in advance on EU limits.

D

DINING

The choice of eating places in Germany is varied both in style and price. The most sophisticated spots—and the most expensive—are in cities. At the opposite end of the scale, almost every street of the western Germany has its *Gaststätte,* a sort of combination diner and pub, and every village its *Gasthof,* or inn, and such places are almost as easy to find in eastern Germany. The emphasis in the Gaststätte and Gasthof is on *gutbürgerliche Küche,* or good home cooking—simple food, wholesome rather than sophisticated, at reasonable prices. These are also places where people meet in the evening for a chat, a beer, and a game of cards. They normally serve hot meals from 11:30 AM to 9 or 10 PM; many places stop serving hot meals between 2 and 6 PM, although you can still order cold dishes. Lunch rather than dinner is the main meal in Germany, a fact reflected in the almost universal appearance of a *Tageskarte,* or suggested menu, every lunchtime. And at a cost of less than DM 20, in either a Gaststätte or Gasthof, for soup, a main course, and simple dessert (though this is not always offered), it's an excellent value. Coffee is generally available, although quality may vary, and it's perfectly acceptable to go into a Gaststätte or country pub and order just a pot of coffee outside busy lunch periods. Some, though not all, expensive restaurants also offer a table d'hôte (suggested or special) daily menu. Prices will be much higher than in a Gaststätte or Gasthof, but considerably cheaper than à la carte.

Regional specialties are given in the Dining sections of individual chapters. For names of German foods and dishes, *see* the Menu Guide at the end of this book.

BUDGET EATING TIPS

BUTCHER SHOPS➤ Known as *Metzgerei,* these often have a corner that serves warm snacks. The **Vinzenz-Murr** chain in Munich and Bavaria has particularly good-value food. Try *Warmer Leberkäs mit Kartoffelsalat,* a typical Bavarian specialty, which is a sort of baked meat loaf with sweet mustard and potato salad. In north Germany, try *Bouletten,* small hamburgers, or *Currywurst,* sausages in a piquant curry sauce.

DEPARTMENT STORES➤ For lunch, restaurants in local department stores (*Kaufhäuser*) are especially recommended for wholesome, appetizing, and inexpensive food. **Kaufhof, Karstadt, Horton,** and **Hertie** are names to note, as well as the enormous **KaDeWe** in Berlin.

FAST FOOD➤ A number of fast-food chains exist all over the country. The best are **Wiener-wald, McDonald's, Pizza Hut,** and **Burger King.** There are also **Nordsee** fish bars, serving hot and cold fish dishes.

FOREIGN RESTAURANTS➤ Germany has a vast selection of moderately priced Turkish, Italian, Greek, Chinese, and Balkan restaurants. All offer good value. Italian restaurants are about the most popular of all specialty restaurants in Germany—the pizza-to-go is as much a part of the average German's diet as *Bratwurst* or a hamburger. You'll find that Chinese restaurants in particular offer special lunch menus.

PICNICS➤ Buy some wine or beer and some cold cuts and rolls (*Brötchen*) from a department store, supermarket, or delicatessen and turn lunchtimes into picnics. You'll not only save money, but you'll also be able to enjoy Germany's beautiful scenery. Or leave out the beer and take your picnic to a beer garden, sit down at one of the long wood tables, and order a *Mass* (liter) of beer.

STAND-UP SNACK BARS➤ Often located in pedestrian zones, *Imbiss* (snack) stands can be found in almost every busy shopping street, in parking lots, train stations, and near markets. They serve *Würste* (sausages), grilled, roasted, or boiled, of every shape and size, and rolls filled with cheese, cold meat, or fish. Prices range from DM 3 to DM 6 per portion.

RATINGS

The restaurants in our listings are divided by

price into four categories: $$$$, $$$, $$, and $. *See* Dining *in* individual chapters for specific prices. Nearly all restaurants display their menus, with prices, outside; all prices shown will include tax and service charge. Prices for wine also include tax and service charge.

DISABILITIES & ACCESSIBILITY

Nearly 100 German cities and towns issue special guides for visitors with disabilities, which offer information, usually in German, about how to get around destinations and suggestions for places to visit.

All the major hotel chains (Hilton, Sheraton, Marriott, Holiday Inn, Steigenberger, and Kempinski) have special facilities for guests with disabilities, including specially equipped and furnished rooms. Some leading privately owned hotels also cater to travelers with disabilities; local tourist offices can provide lists of these hotels and additional information.

The Deutsche Bahn (German Rail) provides a complete range of services and facilities for travelers with disabilities. All InterCity Express (ICE) and InterRegio trains and most EuroCity and InterCity trains have special areas for wheelchair users. Seat and wheelchair-space reservations are free of charge for wheelchair users. The German Red Cross and a welfare service called the Bahn-

hofs-Mission (Railway Station Mission) have support facilities at all major and many smaller, regional stations. They organize assistance in boarding, leaving, and changing trains and also help with reservations.

When discussing accessibility with an operator or reservationist, **ask hard questions.** Are there any stairs, inside *or* out? Are there grab bars next to the toilet *and* in the shower/tub? How wide is the doorway to the room? To the bathroom? For the most extensive facilities, meeting the latest legal specifications, **opt for newer accommodations,** which more often have been designed with access in mind. Older properties or ships must usually be retrofitted and may offer more limited facilities as a result. Be sure to **discuss your needs before booking.**

DISCOUNTS & DEALS

You shouldn't have to pay for a discount. In fact, you may already be eligible for all kinds of savings. Here are some time-honored strategies for getting the best deal.

LOOK IN YOUR WALLET

When you **use your credit card to make travel purchases,** you may get free travel-accident insurance, collision damage insurance, medical or legal assistance, depending on the card and bank that issued it. Visa and MasterCard provide one or more of these ser-

vices, so **get a copy of your card's travel benefits.** If you are a member of the AAA or an oil-company-sponsored road-assistance plan, always **ask hotel or car-rental reservationists for auto-club discounts.** Some clubs offer additional discounts on tours, cruises, or admission to attractions. And don't forget that auto-club membership entitles you to free maps and trip-planning services.

SENIORS CITIZENS & STUDENTS

As a senior-citizen traveler, you may be eligible for special rates, but you should mention your senior-citizen status up front. If you're a students or under 26 can also get discounts, especially if you have an official ID card (☞ Senior-Citizen Discounts *and* Students on the Road, *below*).

DIAL FOR DOLLARS

To save money, **look into "1-800" discount reservations services,** which often have lower rates. These services use their buying power to get a better price on hotels, airline tickets, and sometimes even car rentals. When booking a room, always **call the hotel's local toll-free number** (if one is available) rather than the central reservations number—you'll often get a better price. Ask the reservationist about special packages or corporate rates, which are usually available even if you're not traveling on business.

JOIN A CLUB?

Discount clubs can be a legitimate source of

SMART TRAVEL TIPS / THE GOLD GUIDE

savings, but you must use the participating hotels and visit the participating attractions in order to realize any benefits. Remember, too, that you have to pay a fee to join, so **determine if you'll save enough to warrant your membership fee.** Before booking with a club, **make sure the hotel or other supplier isn't offering a better deal.**

GET A GUARANTEE

When shopping for the best deal on hotels and car rentals, **look for guaranteed exchange rates,** which protect you against a falling dollar. With your rate locked in, you won't pay more even if the price goes up in the local currency.

DRIVING

Entry formalities for motorists are few: All you need is proof of insurance, an international car-registration document, and a U.S. or Canadian driver's license (an international license is helpful, but not a must). If you or your car are from an EU country, Norway, or Switzerland, all you need is your domestic license and proof of insurance. *All* foreign cars must have a country sticker.

Roads in the western part of the country are generally excellent, but many surfaces in eastern Germany, where an urgent improvement program is under way, are in poor condition.

ADAC and AvD operate tow trucks on all autobahns; they also have emergency telephones every 3 kilometers (2 miles). On minor roads, go to the nearest call box and dial 19211. Ask, in English, for road service assistance, if you have to use the service. Help is free, but all materials must be paid for.

FROM THE U.K.

It is recommended that drivers **get a green card** from their insurance companies, which extends insurance coverage to driving in Europe. Extra breakdown insurance and vehicle and personal security coverage is also advisable.

FUEL AVAILABILITY AND COSTS

Gasoline (petrol) costs are between DM 1.10 and DM 1.60 per liter. As part of antipollution efforts, most German cars now run on lead-free fuel. Some models use diesel fuel, so if you are renting a car, find out which fuel the car takes. Some older vehicles cannot take unleaded fuel. German filling stations are highly competitive and bargains are often available if you shop around, but *not* at autobahn filling stations. Self-service, or *SB-Tanken,* stations are cheapest. Pumps marked *Bleifrei* contain unleaded gas.

SCENIC ROUTES

Germany boasts many specially designated tourist roads, all covering areas of particular scenic and/or historic interest. The longest is the Deutsche Ferienstrasse, the German Holiday Road, which runs from the Baltic to the Alps, a distance of around 1,720 kilometers (1,070 miles). The most famous, however, and also the oldest, is the Romantische Strasse, the Romantic Road (☞ Chapter 5), which runs from Würzburg in Franconia to Füssen in the Alps, covering around 355 kilometers (220 miles) and passing through some of the most historic cities and towns in Germany.

Among other notable touring routes—all with expressive and descriptive names—are the Grüne Küstenstrasse (Green Coast Road), running along the North Sea coast from Denmark to Emden; the Burgenstrasse (Castle Road), running from Mannheim to Nürnberg; the Deutsche Weinstrasse (German Wine Road), running through the heartland of the German wine country; and the Deutsche Alpenstrasse (German Alpine Road), running the length of the country's south border. In addition, there are many other equally delightful, if less well-known, routes, such as the Märchenstrasse (Fairy-tale Road), the Schwarzwälder Hochstrasse (Black Forest High Road), and the Deutsche Edelsteinstrasse (German Gem Road).

RULES OF THE ROAD

In Germany you drive on the right, and road signs give distances in kilometers. There is no speed limit on autobahns, although drivers are advised to keep below 130 kilometers

(80 miles) per hour. Speed limits on non-autobahn country roads vary from 80 to 100 kilometers (50 to 60 miles) per hour. Alcohol limits on drivers are equivalent to two small beers or a quarter of a liter of wine. Note that seat belts must be worn at all times by front- *and* back-seat passengers.

H

HEALTH CONCERNS

Sanitation and health standards in Germany are as high as those anywhere in the world, and there are no serious health risks associated with travel there. No inoculations are required.

HOLIDAYS

The following national holidays are observed in Germany: January 1; January 6 (Epiphany, Bavaria and Baden-Württemberg only); March 28 (Good Friday); March 31 (Easter Monday); May 1 (Workers' Day); May 8 (Ascension); May 19 (Pentecost Monday); May 29 (Corpus Christi, south Germany only); August 15 (Assumption Day, Bavaria and Saarland only); October 3 (German Unity Day); November 1 (All Saints' Day); December 24–26 (Christmas).

I

INSURANCE

Travel insurance can protect your monetary investment, replace your luggage and its contents, or provide for medical coverage

should you fall ill during your trip. Most tour operators, travel agents, and insurance agents sell specialized health-and-accident, flight, trip-cancellation, and luggage insurance as well as comprehensive policies with some or all of these coverages. Comprehensive policies may also reimburse you for delays due to weather—an important consideration if you're traveling during the winter months. Some health-insurance policies do not cover preexisting conditions, but waivers may be available in specific cases. Coverage is sold by the companies listed in Important Contacts A to Z, *above*; these companies act as the policy's administrators. The actual insurance is usually underwritten by a well-known name, such as The Travelers or Continental Insurance.

Before you make any purchase, **review your existing health and home-owner's policies** to find out whether they cover expenses incurred while traveling.

BAGGAGE

Airline liability for baggage is limited to $1,250 per person on domestic flights. On international flights, it amounts to $9.07 per pound or $20 per kilogram for checked baggage (roughly $640 per 70-pound bag) and $400 per passenger for unchecked baggage. Insurance for losses exceeding the terms of your airline ticket can be bought directly from the airline at check-in

for about $10 per $1,000 of coverage; note that it excludes a rather extensive list of items, shown on your airline ticket.

COMPREHENSIVE

Comprehensive insurance policies include all the coverages described above plus some that may not be available in more specific policies. If you have purchased an expensive vacation, especially one that involves travel abroad, comprehensive insurance is a must; **look for policies that include trip delay insurance,** which will protect you in the event that weather problems cause you to miss your flight, tour, or cruise. A few insurers will also sell you a waiver for preexisting medical conditions. Some of the companies that offer both these features are Access America, Carefree Travel, Travel Insured International, and TravelGuard (☞ Insurance *in* Important Contacts A to Z, *above*).

FLIGHT

You should **think twice before buying flight insurance.** Often purchased as a last-minute impulse at the airport, it pays a lump sum when a plane crashes, either to a beneficiary if the insured dies or sometimes to a surviving passenger who loses his or her eyesight or a limb. Supplementing the airlines' coverage described in the limits-of-liability paragraphs on your ticket, it's expensive and basically unnecessary. Charging an airline ticket to a major

THE GOLD GUIDE / SMART TRAVEL TIPS

credit card often automatically provides you with coverage that may also extend to travel by bus, train, and ship.

HEALTH

Medicare generally does not cover health care costs outside the United States; nor do many privately issued policies. If your own health insurance policy does not cover you outside the United States, **consider buying supplemental medical coverage.** It can reimburse you for $1,000–$150,000 worth of medical and/or dental expenses incurred as a result of an accident or illness during a trip. These policies also may include a personal-accident, or death-and-dismemberment, provision, which pays a lump sum ranging from $15,000 to $500,000 to your beneficiaries if you die or to you if you lose one or more limbs or your eyesight, and a medical-assistance provision, which may either reimburse you for the cost of referrals, evacuation, or repatriation and other services, or automatically enroll you as a member of a particular medical-assistance company. (☞ Health Issues *in* Important Contacts A to Z, *above.*)

U.K. TRAVELERS

You can buy an annual travel insurance policy valid for most vacations during the year in which it's purchased. If you are pregnant or have a preexisting medical condition make sure you're covered before buying such a policy.

TRIP

Without insurance, you will lose all or most of your money if you cancel your trip regardless of the reason. Especially if your airline ticket, cruise, or package tour is nonrefundable and cannot be changed, it's essential that you **buy trip-cancellation-and-interruption insurance.** When considering how much coverage you need, look for a policy that will cover the cost of your trip plus the nondiscounted price of a one-way airline ticket should you need to return home early. Read the fine print carefully, especially sections that define "family member" and "preexisting medical conditions." Also **consider default or bankruptcy insurance,** which protects you against a supplier's failure to deliver. Be aware, however, that if you buy such a policy from a travel agency, tour operator, airline, or cruise line, it may not cover default by the firm in question.

L

LANGUAGE

The Germans are great linguists and you'll find that English is spoken in virtually all hotels, restaurants, airports, stations, museums, and other places of interest. However, English is not always widely spoken in rural areas; this is especially true of the eastern part of Germany.

Unless you speak fluent German, you may find some of the regional dialects hard to follow, particularly in Bavaria. While most Germans can speak "High," or standard, German, some older country people are only able to speak in their dialect.

LODGING

The standard of German hotels—from sophisticated luxury spots (of which the country has more than its fair share) to the humblest country inn—is very high. Rates vary enormously, though not disproportionately, in comparison with other northern European countries. You can nearly always expect courteous and polite service and clean and comfortable rooms. Larger hotels often have no-smoking rooms or even no-smoking floors, so it's always worth asking for one when you check in.

In addition to hotels proper, the country has numerous *Gasthöfe* or *Gasthäuser,* which are country inns that serve food and also have rooms; pensions, or *Fremdenheime* (guest houses); and, at the lowest end of the scale, *Fremdenzimmer,* meaning simply "rooms," normally in private houses (look for the sign reading ZIMMER FREI or ZU VERMIETEN on a green background, meaning "to rent"; a red sign reading BESETZT means that there are no vacancies).

Lists of German hotels are available from the German National Tourist Office and all regional and local tourist offices. (Most hotels have restaurants, but those listed as

Garni will provide breakfast only.) Tourist offices will also make bookings for you at a nominal fee, but they may have difficulty doing so after 4 PM in high season and on weekends, so don't wait until too late in the day to begin looking for your accommodations. (If you do get stuck, ask someone who looks like a native—a mail carrier, police officer, or waiter, for example—for directions to a house renting a Fremdenzimmer or a Gasthof; in rural areas especially you'll find that people are genuinely helpful).

Many major American hotel chains—Hilton, Sheraton, Holiday Inn, Radisson, Marriott, Preferred—have hotels in the larger German cities. European chains are similarly well represented.

The hotels in our listings are divided by price into four categories: $$$$, $$$, $$, and $. *See* Lodging sections in individual chapters for specific prices. Note that there is no official grading system for hotels in Germany. Rates are by no means inflexible, and depend very much on supply and demand; you can save money by inquiring about reductions. Many resort hotels offer substantial ones in winter, except in the Alps, where rates often rise then. Likewise, many $$$$ and $$$ hotels in cities cut their prices on weekends and when business is quiet. Always be careful about trying to book late in the day at peak times. During

trade fairs (most commonly held in the spring and fall), rates in city hotels can rise appreciably. Breakfast is usually but not always included. Inexpensive rooms may have neither shower nor tub. **Ask about breakfast and bathing facilities** when booking. Usually you pay more for the tub. When you arrive, if you don't like the room you're offered, ask to see another.

APARTMENT & VILLA RENTAL

If you want a home base that's roomy enough for a family and comes with cooking facilities, **consider taking a furnished rental.** This can also save you money, but not always—some rentals are luxury properties (economical only when your party is large). Home-exchange directories list rentals—often second homes owned by prospective house swappers—and some services search for a house or apartment for you (even a castle if that's your fancy) and handle the paperwork. Some send an illustrated catalog; others send photographs only of specific properties, sometimes at a charge; up-front registration fees may apply.

CAMPING

Campsites—some 2,000 in all—are scattered across the length and breadth of Germany. The DCC, or German Camping Club (☞ Lodging *in* Important Contacts A to Z, *above*) produces an annual listing of 1,600 sites; it also details sites where

trailers and mobile homes can be rented. Similarly, the German Automobile Association ADAC (☞ Driving *in* Important Contacts A to Z, *above*) publishes a listing of all campsites located at autobahn exits. In addition, the German National Tourist Office publishes a comprehensive and graded listing of campsites.

Sites are generally open from May to September, though about 400 are open year-round for the very rugged. Most sites get crowded during high season, however. Prices range from around DM 10 to DM 25 for a car, trailer, and two adults; less for tents. If you want to camp elsewhere, you must get permission from the landowner beforehand; ask the police if you can't track him or her down. Drivers of mobile homes may park for one night only on roadsides and in autobahn parking-lot areas, but may not set up camping equipment there.

CASTLE HOTELS

Of comparable interest and value are Germany's castle, or *Schloss*, hotels, all privately owned and run and all long on atmosphere. A number of the simpler ones may lack some amenities, but the majority combine four-star luxury with valuable antique furnishings, four-poster beds, stone passageways, and a baronial atmosphere. Some offer full resort facilities (tennis, swimming pools, horseback riding, hunting, and fishing).

Nearly all are away from cities and towns.

FARM VACATIONS

The *Urlaub auf dem Bauernhof,* or vacation down on the farm, has increased dramatically in popularity throughout Germany over the past five years, and almost every regional tourist office now produces a brochure listing farms in its area that offer bed-and-breakfasts, apartments, and entire farmhouses to rent.

HOME EXCHANGE

If you would like to find a house, an apartment, or some other type of vacation property to exchange for your own while on holiday, **become a member of a home-exchange organization,** which will send you its updated listings of available exchanges for a year, and will include your own listing in at least one of them. Arrangements for the actual exchange are made by the two parties involved, not by the organization.

ROMANTIK HOTELS

Among the most delightful places to stay—and eat—in Germany are the aptly named Romantik Hotels and Restaurants. The Romantik group now has establishments throughout northern Europe (and even a few in the United States), with more than 60 in Germany. All are in atmospheric and historic buildings—a precondition of membership—and are personally run by the owners, with the emphasis on excellent food and service. Prices vary considerably, but in general represent good value, particularly the special-weekends and short-holiday rates. A three- or four-day stay, for example, with one main meal, is available at about DM 300 to DM 400 per person.

In addition, German Rail offers a special Romantik Hotel Rail program, which, in conjunction with a German Rail Tourist Ticket, gives nine days' unlimited travel. You don't need to plan your route in advance—only your first night's accommodation needs to be reserved before you leave. The remaining nights can be reserved as you go. The package also includes sightseeing trips, a Rhine/Mosel cruise, bicycle rentals, and the like.

SPAS

Taking the waters in Germany, whether for curing the body or merely beautifying it, has been popular since Roman times. There are more than 300 health resorts and mineral springs in the country—the word *Bad* before the name of a place usually means it's a spa—offering treatments, normally at fairly high prices. Although spas exist in eastern Germany, most are run down and not highly recommended.

There are four main groups of spas and health resorts: (1) the mineral and moorland spas, where treatments are based on natural warm-water springs; (2) those by the sea on the Baltic and North Sea coasts; (3) hydropathic spas, which use an invigorating process developed during the 19th century; and (4) climatic health resorts, which depend on their climates—usually mountainous—for their health-giving properties.

The average cost for three weeks of treatment is from DM 3,000 to DM 5,000; for four weeks, DM 3,500 to DM 6,000. This includes board and lodging, doctors' fees, treatments, and tax.

M

MAIL

Airmail letters to the United States and Canada cost DM 3; postcards cost DM 2. All letters to the United Kingdom cost DM 1; postcards cost 80 pfennigs.

RECEIVING MAIL

You can arrange to have mail sent to you in care of any German post office; have the envelope marked "Postlagernd." This service is free. Alternatively, have mail sent to any American Express office in Germany. There's no charge to cardholders, holders of American Express traveler's checks, or anyone who has booked a vacation with American Express.

MEDICAL ASSISTANCE

No one plans to get sick while traveling, but it happens, so **consider signing up with a medical assistance company.** These outfits provide referrals, emergency evacuation or repatriation, 24-hour telephone hot lines for medical consultation, cash for emergencies, and other personal and legal assistance. They also dispatch medical personnel and arrange for the relay of medical records.

MONEY & EXPENSES

The unit of currency in Germany is the Deutschmark (DM), and it's divided into 100 pfennigs (pf). There are bills of 5 (rare), 10, 20, 50, 100, 200, 500, 1000 marks and coins of 1, 2, 5, 10, and 50 pf and 1, 2, and 5 marks. At press time, the mark stood strong at DM 1.47 to the U.S. dollar, DM 1.06 to the Canadian dollar, and DM 2.26 to the pound sterling.

ATMS

CASH ADVANCES➤ Cirrus, Plus, and many other networks that connect automated teller machines operate internationally. Chances are that you can **use your bank card, MasterCard, or Visa at ATMs** to withdraw money from an account or get a cash advance. Before leaving home, **check on frequency limits** for withdrawals and cash advances. Also **ask whether your card's PIN must be reprogrammed** for use in Germany. Four-digit numbers are commonly used overseas. Note that Discover is accepted mostly in the United States.

COSTS

Western Germany has an admirably high standard of living, and eastern Germany's prices are rapidly rising, making the country expensive for visitors, particularly those who spend time in the cities. Lots of things—gas, food, hotels, and trains, to name but a few—are more expensive than in the United States.

A way to cut your budget is to **visit lessknown cities and towns and avoid Alpine summer and winter resorts during their high season.** All along the Main and Neckar rivers, for example, you will find small towns as charming as, but significantly less expensive than, the likes of Rothenburg and Heidelberg; similarly, Westphalia offers atmosphere but lower prices than the fabled towns and cities of the Rhine. Wine lovers should explore the Palatinate instead of the classical Rhine-Mosel tour. Ski enthusiasts would do well to investigate the advantages of the Harz and Eifel mountains, the Bavarian Oberpfalz, and the Bayerischer Wald in Lower (East) Bavaria.

The five new states (Saxony, Thuringia, Mecklenburg, Saxon-Anhalt, Brandenburg) of former East Germany still have a lower standard of living than does old West Germany. Outside large cities you will find such things as public transportation and dining in moderate restaurants cheaper than they are in, say, the Black Forest or the Rhineland. Prices in leading hotels and restaurants in such places as Dresden and Leipzig already match rates in Frankfurt and Munich. As the standard of living in the new states continues to rise, so will the cost of traveling in them.

EXCHANGING CURRENCY

For the most favorable rates, **change money at banks.** You won't do as well at exchange booths in airports or rail and bus stations, in hotels, in restaurants, or in stores, although you may find their hours more convenient. To avoid lines at airport exchange booths, **get a small amount of the local currency before you leave home.**

P

PACKING FOR GERMANY

What you pack depends more on the time of year than on any particular dress code. Winters can be bitterly cold; summers are warm but with days that suddenly turn cool and rainy. In summer take a warm jacket or heavy sweater for the Bavarian Alps, where the nights can be chilly even after hot days.

For cities, pack as you would for an American city: dressy outfits for formal restaurants and nightclubs, casual clothes elsewhere. Jeans are as popular in Germany as anywhere else and are perfectly acceptable for sightseeing and informal dining. In the evening, men will probably feel more comfortable wearing a jacket and tie in more expensive restaurants although it is almost never required. Many German women are extremely fashion-conscious and wear stylish outfits to restaurants and the theater, especially in the larger cities.

To discourage purse snatchers and pickpockets, carry a handbag with long straps that you can sling across your body, bandolier-style, and a zippered compartment for money and other valuables.

For stays in budget hotels, take your own soap. Many provide no soap at all or only one small bar. Bring an extra pair of eyeglasses or contact lenses in your carry-on luggage, and if you have a health problem, **pack enough medication** to last the trip or have your doctor write you a prescription using the drug's generic name, because brand names vary from country to country (you'll then need a duplicate prescription from a local doctor). It's important that you **don't put prescription drugs or valuables in luggage to be checked,** for it could go astray. To avoid problems with customs officials, carry medications in the original packaging. Also, don't forget the addresses of offices that handle refunds of lost traveler's checks.

ELECTRICITY

To use your U.S.-purchased electric-powered equipment, **bring a converter and an adapter.** The electrical current in Germany is 220 volts, 50 cycles alternating current (AC); wall outlets take Continental-type plugs, with two round prongs.

If your appliances are dual-voltage, you'll need only an adapter. Hotels sometimes have 110-volt outlets for low-wattage appliances near the sink, marked FOR SHAVERS ONLY; don't use them for high-wattage appliances like blow-dryers. If your laptop computer is older, carry a converter; new laptops operate equally well on 110 and 220 volts, so you need only an adapter.

LUGGAGE

Airline baggage allowances depend on the airline, the route, and the class of your ticket; ask in advance. In general, on domestic flights and on international flights between the United States and foreign destinations, you are entitled to check two bags. A third piece may be brought on board, but it must fit easily under the seat in front of you or in the overhead compartment. In the United States, the FAA gives airlines broad latitude regarding carry-on allowances, and they tend to tailor them to different aircraft and operational conditions. Charges for excess, oversize, or overweight pieces vary.

If you are flying between two foreign destinations, note that baggage allowances may be determined not by piece but by weight—generally 88 pounds (40 kilograms) in first class, 66 pounds (30 kilograms) in business class, and 44 pounds (20 kilograms) in economy. If your flight between two cities abroad con-

nects with your transatlantic or transpacific flight, the piece method still applies.

SAFEGUARDING YOUR LUGGAGE➤ Before leaving home, **itemize your bags' contents** and their worth, and label them with your name, address, and phone number. (If you use your home address, cover it so that potential thieves can't see it readily.) Inside each bag, **pack a copy of your itinerary.** At check-in, **make sure that each bag is correctly tagged** with the destination airport's three-letter code. If your bags arrive damaged—or fail to arrive at all—file a written report with the airline before leaving the airport.

PASSPORTS & VISAS

If you don't already have one, **get a passport.** It is advisable that you **leave one photocopy of your passport's data page** with someone at home and keep another with you, separated from your passport, while traveling. If you lose your passport, promptly call the nearest embassy or consulate and the local police; having the data page information can speed replacement.

U.S. CITIZENS

All U.S. citizens, even infants, need only a valid passport to enter Germany for stays of up to three months. Application forms for both first-time and renewal passports are available at any of the 13 U.S. Passport Agency offices and at some post offices and courthouses. Passports are usually mailed within four weeks; allow five weeks or more in spring and summer.

CANADIANS

You need only a valid passport to enter Germany for stays of up to three months. Passport application forms are available at 28 regional passport offices, as well as post offices and travel agencies. Whether for a first or a renewal passport, you must apply in person. Children under 16 may be included on a parent's passport but must have their own to travel alone. Passports are valid for five years and are usually mailed within two to three weeks of application.

U.K. CITIZENS

Citizens of the United Kingdom need only a valid passport to enter Germany for stays of up to three months. Applications for new and renewal passports are available from main post offices and at the passport offices in Belfast, Glasgow, Liverpool, London, Newport, and Peterborough. You may apply in person at all passport offices, or by mail to all except the London office. Children under 16 may travel on an accompanying parent's passport. All passports are valid for 10 years. Allow a month for processing.

S

SENIOR-CITIZEN DISCOUNTS

In Germany, the number of citizens over 60 is growing; this section of the population has also become more affluent and demanding and even has its own political party, the Gray Panthers. The strength of this special-interest age group has won them special privileges in Germany—such as price adjustments on the railways and reduced admission to museums—and elderly visitors from abroad can also take advantage of these discounts. Contact the German National Tourist Board (☞ Visitor Information *in* Important Contacts A to Z, *above*).

To qualify for age-related discounts, **mention your senior-citizen status up front** when booking hotel reservations, not when checking out, and before you're seated in restaurants, not when paying the bill. Note that discounts may be limited to certain menus, days, or hours. When renting a car, **ask about promotional car-rental discounts**—they can net even lower costs than your senior-citizen discount.

STUDENTS ON THE ROAD

To save money, **look into deals available through student-oriented travel agencies.** To qualify, you'll need to have a bona fide student ID card. Members of international student groups are also eligible (☞ Students *in* Important Contacts A to Z, *above*).

HOSTELING

Germany's youth hostels—*Jugendherbergen*—are probably the most efficient, up-to-date, and proportionally numerous of any country's in the world. There are more than 600 in all, many located in castles that add a touch of romance to otherwise utilitarian accommodations. Since unification, many eastern German youth hostels have closed down. An effort is being made, however, to keep as many open as possible, and renovations are currently under way to bring eastern hostels up to the standards of their western counterparts.

Apart from Bavaria, where there is an age limit of 27, there are no restrictions on age, though those under 20 take preference when space is limited. Accommodation is available only to members of the International Youth Hostel Federation (IYHF); guest membership for non-Germans costs DM 36 annually in Germany. Accommodation charges range from about DM 15 to DM 21 for youth under 27 and DM 22 to DM 38 for adults (breakfast included). Cards are available from the American Youth Hostels Association, the Canadian Hostelling Association, and the United Kingdom's Youth Hostels Association (☞ Students *in* Important Contacts A to Z, *above*).

T

TELEPHONES

Apart from the more remote rural corners of eastern Germany, telephone links between western and eastern areas of the country have now been completely upgraded.

LOCAL CALLS

Local public phones charge a minimum 30 pfennigs per call (for six minutes). All public phones take 10 pf, DM 1, and DM 5 coins. If you're anticipating making a lot of phone calls, purchase a phone card at any German post office (also available at many exchange places). They come in denominations of DM 12 and DM 50, the latter good for DM 60 worth of calls. Most phone booths have instructions in English as well as German.

LONG-DISTANCE

International calls can be made from public phones bearing the sign INLANDS UND AUSLANDS-GESPRÄCHE. Using DM 5 coins is best for long-distance dialing; a four-minute call to the United States costs DM 15. To avoid weighing yourself down with coins, however, **make international calls from post offices**; even those in small country towns will have a special booth for international calls. You pay the clerk at the end of your call. Never make international calls from your hotel room; rates will be at least double the regular charge.

The long-distance services of AT&T, MCI, and Sprint make calling home relatively convenient, but in many hotels you may find it impossible to dial the access number. The hotel operator may also refuse to make the

connection. Instead, the hotel will charge you a premium rate—as much as 400% more than a calling card—for calls placed from your hotel room. To avoid such price gouging, travel with more than one company's long-distance calling card—a hotel may block Sprint but not MCI. If the hotel operator claims that you cannot use any phone card, ask to be connected to an international operator, who will help you to access your phone card. You can also dial the international operator yourself. If none of this works, try calling your phone company collect in the United States. If collect calls are also blocked, call from a pay phone in the hotel lobby. Before you go, **find out the local access codes** for your destinations.

OPERATORS AND INFORMATION

The German telephone system is fully automatic, and it's unlikely that you'll have to employ the services of an operator. If you do, dial 010, or 0010 for international calls. If the operator doesn't speak English (also unlikely), you'll be passed to one who does.

TIPPING

HOTELS

The service charges on bills suffice for most tips in your hotel, though you should **tip bellhops and porters**; DM 2 per bag or service is ample. It's also customary to leave a small tip (a couple of marks per night) for the room cleaning staff. Whether you tip the desk clerk

depends on whether he or she has given you any special service.

RESTAURANTS

Service charges are included in all checks (listed as *Bedienung*), as is tax (listed as *MWST*). Nonetheless, it is customary to **round out the bill to the nearest mark or to leave about 5%** (give it to the waiter or waitress as you pay the bill; don't leave it on the table).

TAXIS

Round out the fare to the nearest full mark as a tip. Only give more if you have particularly cumbersome or heavy luggage (though you will be charged 50 pfennigs for each piece of luggage anyway).

TOUR OPERATORS

A package or tour to Germany can make your vacation less expensive and more hassle-free. Firms that sell tours and packages reserve airline seats, hotel rooms, and rental cars in bulk and pass some of the savings on to you. In addition, the best operators have local representatives available to help you at your destination.

A GOOD DEAL?

The more your package or tour includes, the better you can predict the ultimate cost of your vacation. Make sure you know exactly what is covered, and **beware of hidden costs.** Are taxes, tips, and service charges included? Transfers and baggage handling? Entertainment and excursions? These can add up.

Most packages and tours are rated deluxe, first-class superior, first class, tourist, or budget. The key difference is usually accommodations. If the package or tour you are considering is priced lower than in your wildest dreams, **be skeptical.** Also, **make sure your travel agent knows the accommodations** and other services. Ask about the hotel's location, room size, beds, and whether it has a pool, room service, or programs for children, if you care about these. Has your agent been there in person or sent others you can contact?

BUYER BEWARE

Each year a number of consumers are stranded or lose their money when operators—even very large ones with excellent reputations—go out of business. To avoid becoming one of them, take the time to **check out the operator**—find out how long the company has been in business and ask several agents about its reputation. Next, **don't book unless the firm has a consumer-protection program.** Members of the USTOA and the NTA are required to set aside funds for the sole purpose of covering your payments and travel arrangements in case of default. Non-member operators may instead carry insurance; look for the details in the operator's brochure—and for the name of an underwriter with a solid reputation. Note: When it comes to tour operators, **don't trust escrow accounts.** Although there are

laws governing those of charter-flight operators, no governmental body prevents tour operators from raiding the till.

Next, **contact your local Better Business Bureau and the attorney general's offices** in both your own state and the operator's; have any complaints been filed? Finally, **pay with a major credit card.** Then you can cancel payment, provided that you can document your complaint. Always **consider trip-cancellation insurance** (☞ Insurance, *above*).

BIG VS. SMALL➤ Operators that handle several hundred thousand travelers per year can use their purchasing power to give you a good price. Their high volume may also indicate financial stability. But some small companies provide more personalized service; because they tend to specialize, they may also be more knowledgeable about a given area.

USING AN AGENT

Travel agents are excellent resources. In fact, large operators accept bookings made only through travel agents. But it's good to **collect brochures from several agencies** because some agents' suggestions may be skewed by promotional relationships with tour and package firms that reward them for volume sales. If you have a special interest, **find an agent with expertise in that area;** ASTA can provide leads in the United States. (Don't rely solely on

your agent, though; agents may be unaware of small-niche operators, and some special-interest travel companies only sell direct.)

SINGLE TRAVELERS

Prices are usually quoted per person, based on two sharing a room. If traveling solo, you may be required to pay the full double-occupancy rate. Some operators eliminate this surcharge if you agree to be matched up with a roommate of the same sex, even if one is not found by departure time.

TRAIN TRAVEL

The German railway system is being privatized, so routes and timetables may still change in some areas. The two separate rail networks of East and West Germany merged in 1994 into Deutsche Bahn (DB, or German Rail), bringing Berlin and the cities of the old German Democratic Republic much closer to the main railheads of the west. The electrification and renovation of the ancient tracks in eastern Germany also made big strides forward, allowing the extension there of the high-speed InterCity Express (ICE) service. InterCity (IC) and EuroCity services have been improved and expanded, and the regional InterRegio network now extends nationwide. All overnight InterCity services and the slower D-class trains have sleepers, with a first-class service that includes breakfast in bed.

All InterCity and InterCity Express trains have restaurant cars, InterRegio services have bright bistro-cars, and the Hamburg–Berchtesgaden service has an onboard McDonald's as an experiment. A DM 6 surcharge is added to the ticket price on all InterCity and EuroCity journeys irrespective of distance (DM 12 return). The charge is DM 8 if paid on board the train. InterCity Express fares are about 20% more expensive than normal ones. Seat reservations on InterCity, EuroCity, and InterCity Express trains cost DM 3. Bikes cannot be transported on InterCity Express services, but InterCity, EuroCity, and some D-class trains have special storage facilities, and InterRegio trains even have compartments where cyclists can travel next to their bikes.

Changing trains couldn't be easier. You often only have to cross to the other side of the platform. Special train maps on platform notice boards give details of the layout of trains arriving on that track, showing where first- and second-class cars and the restaurant car are, as well as where they will stop along the length of the platform.

Rail passengers with a valid round-trip air ticket can buy a heavily discounted "Rail and Fly" ticket for DB trains connecting with 14 German airports: Berlin's Schönefeld and Tegel airports, Bremen, Dresden, Düsseldorf, Frankfurt/Main, Hamburg, Hannover, Köln-Bonn, Leipzig/Halle, Munich, Münster/Osnabrück, Nürnberg, and Stuttgart.

Note that in high season you will frequently encounter lines at ticket offices for seat reservations. Unless you are prepared to board the train without a reserved seat, taking the chance of a seat being available, the only way to avoid these lines is to **make an advance reservation by phone.** Call the ticket office (Fahrkarten-Schalter) of the rail station from which you plan to depart. Here again, you will probably have to make several attempts before you get through to the reservations section (Reservierungen/Platzkarten), but you will then be able to collect your seat ticket from a special counter **without having to wait in line.**

DISCOUNT PASSES

If Germany is your only destination in Europe, **consider purchasing a German Rail Pass,** which allows 5, 10, or 15 days of unlimited travel within a one-month period. You can also **use your rail pass aboard KR River Steamers** along certain sections of the Rhine, Main, and Moselle rivers. Prices begin at $178 for a single traveler in second class and $260 in first class. Twinpasses, which are designed two adults traveling together, begin at $267 in second class and $390 in first class. Additional days may be added to either pass. Other rail pass options include a youth passes.

Germany is one of 17 countries in which you can **use EurailPasses,** which provide unlimited first-class rail travel in all of the participating countries for the duration of the pass. If you plan to rack up the miles, get a standard pass. These are available for 15 days ($522), 21 days ($678), one month ($838), two months ($1,148), and three months ($1,468). If your plans call for only limited train travel, **look into a Europass,** which costs less money than a EurailPass. Unlike EurailPasses, however, you get a limited number of travel days, in a limited number of countries, during a specified time period. For example, a two-month pass ($316) allows between 5 and 15 days of rail travel, but costs $200 less than the least expensive EurailPass. Keep in mind, however, that the Europass is good only in France, Germany, Italy, Spain, and Switzerland, and the number of countries you can visit is further limited by the type of pass you buy. For example, the basic two-month pass allows you to visit only three of the five participating countries.

In addition to standard EurailPasses, **ask about special rail-pass plans.** Among these are the Eurail Youthpass (for those under age 26), the Eurail Saverpass (which gives a discount for two or more people traveling together), a Eurail Flexipass (which allows a certain number of travel days within a set period), the Euraildrive

Pass, and the Europass Drive (which combines travel by train and rental car).

Whichever pass you choose, remember that you must **purchase your pass before you leave** for Europe.

Many travelers assume that rail passes guarantee them seats on the trains they wish to ride. Not so. You need to **book seats ahead even if you are using a rail pass**; seat reservations are required on some European trains, particularly high-speed trains, and are a good idea on trains that may be crowded—particularly in summer on popular routes. You will also need a reservation if you purchase sleeping accommodations.

STUDENT AND YOUTH PASSES

In 1995 a more comprehensive version of the popular InterRail ticket for young people became available. The system divides Europe into seven zones, with different InterRail tariffs within each one. Germany belongs to Zone C, along with Switzerland, Austria, and Denmark. A one-month InterRail ticket for travel within this zone and an additional zone of your choice costs DM 500. Travel within just Zone C is limited to two weeks, but the pass costs less: DM 420. The age limit is 26. Young travelers intending to tour only Germany can get an even better deal by buying a Euro Domino ticket, allowing travel on all German trains for 3, 5, or 10 days within

one month, but it must be bought outside the country and in local currency. With a Euro Domino ticket bought, for instance, in Salzburg, just across the Austrian-Bavarian border, young people under 26 can tour neighboring Germany for up to 10 days for the equivalent of around $400. No age limit is linked to other special deals, such as the Sparpreis and ICE-Super Sparpreis, which offer big savings on return journeys made on off-peak days. One tip: There is very little difference between first- and second-class compartments in the newer InterCity trains and all InterCity Express trains, but there's a big difference in fares.

SENIOR-CITIZEN PASSES

Holders of British Rail Senior Citizens' Rail Cards can buy an "add-on" European Senior Citizens' Rail Card that permits half-price train travel in most European countries, including Germany.

FROM THE U.K.

There are several ways to reach Germany from London on British Rail. Travelers coming from the United Kingdom should **take the Channel Tunnel to save time, the ferry to save money.** Fastest and most expensive is the route via the Channel Tunnel on Eurostar trains (☞ The Channel Tunnel *in* Important Contacts A to Z, *above*). Departures leave hourly from Waterloo and require a change of trains in Brussels. Cheapest, and

slowest, are the 8–10 departures daily from Victoria using the Ramsgate-Ostend ferry, jetfoil, or SeaCat catamaran service.

Travelers under 26 who have not invested in a rail pass should inquire about discount travel fares under the Billet International Jeune (BIJ) scheme. The special one-trip tariff (also known as a twen-tickets fare) is offered by EuroTrain International, with offices in 22 European cities. You can purchase a Eurotrain ticket at one of these offices or at travel-agent networks, mainline rail stations, and specialist youth-travel operators.

TRAVEL GEAR

Travel catalogs specialize in useful items that can **save space when packing** and make life on the road more convenient. Compact alarm clocks, travel irons, travel wallets, and personal-care kits are among the most common items you'll find. They also carry dual-voltage appliances, currency converters, and foreign-language phrase books. Some catalogs even carry miniature coffeemakers and water purifiers.

U.S. GOVERNMENT

The U.S. government can be an excellent source of travel information. Some of this is free and some is available for a nominal charge. When planning your trip, **find out what government materials**

THE GOLD GUIDE / SMART TRAVEL TIPS

are available. For just a couple of dollars, you can get a variety of publications from the Consumer Information Center in Pueblo, Colorado. Free consumer information also is available from individual government agencies, such as the Department of Transportation or the U.S. Customs Service. For specific titles, *see* the appropriate publications entry *in* Important Contacts A to Z, *above.*

W
WHEN TO GO

The tourist season in Germany runs from May to late October, when the weather is at its best. In addition to many tourist events, this period has hundreds of folk festivals. The winter sports season in the Bavarian Alps runs from Christmas to mid-March. Prices everywhere are generally higher during the summer, so you may find considerable advantages to visiting out of season. Most resorts offer between-season (*Zwi-*

schensaison) and edge-of-season (*Nebensaison*) rates, and tourist offices can provide lists of hotels that offer special low-price inclusive weekly packages (*Pauschal-angebote*). Many winter ski resorts lower rates for the periods between mid-January (after local school holidays) and Easter. The other advantage of out-of-season travel is fewer crowds. The disadvantages of visiting out-of-season, especially in winter, are that the weather is often cold and gloomy and some tourist attractions, especially in rural areas, are closed or have shorter hours. Ski resorts are the exception.

The major cities, especially Berlin, Hamburg, and Munich, are active year-round. Avoid Leipzig the first few weeks in March and September, when the trade fair commandeers all accommodations and prices soar.

CLIMATE

Germany's climate is temperate, although cold snaps can plunge

the thermometer well below freezing, particularly in the Alps, the Harz region of Lower Saxony, the Black Forest, and the higher regions of northern Franconia. Summers are usually sunny and warm, though you should be prepared for a few cloudy and wet days. The south is normally always a few degrees warmer than the north. As you get nearer the Alps, however, the summers get shorter, often not beginning until the end of May. Fall is sometimes spectacular in the south—warm and soothing. The only real exception to the above is the strikingly variable weather in South Bavaria caused by the *Föhn,* an Alpine wind that gives rise to clear but very warm conditions. The Föhn can occur in all seasons. Sudden atmospheric pressure changes associated with the Föhn give some people headaches.

The following are the average daily maximum and minimum temperatures for Munich.

Climate in Germany

Jan.	35F	1C	May	64F	18C	Sept.	67F	20C
	23	− 5		45	7		48	9
Feb.	38F	3C	June	70F	21C	Oct.	56F	14C
	23	− 5		51	11		40	4
Mar.	48F	9C	July	74F	23C	Nov.	44F	7C
	30	− 1		55	13		33	0
Apr.	56F	14C	Aug.	73F	23C	Dec.	36F	2C
	38	3		54	12		26	− 4

1 Destination: Germany

WHAT IS GERMANY?

THE HONEYMOON IS OVER, and a unified but still disunited Germany has entered what its residents call the *grauer Alltag,* or "gray everyday." With the passing of the fifth anniversary of the fall of the Berlin Wall (1994) as well as the 50th anniversary of the end of World War II (1995), 1996 is the first year in recent German memory outside the shadow cast by a date of sober remembrance. That doesn't mean Germany is any the happier; from all sides this country hears it is the powerhouse of Europe, but it's not certain that it matches the image. Nor is the new Germany so self-effacing. In many areas—politics and economics most notably—Germany is flexing muscles that have been growing stronger, while other nations have been accumulating flab. The Germans of the late '90s are self-confident citizens of a country they are finally proud to call their own.

Yet if you ask a German to define his or her country, you might get an evasive answer. Seven years after unification the country still has deep divisions and unhealed wounds, its people constantly reminded of their condition by statistics still reflecting unequal conditions in two halves of a single country—one that Chancellor Helmut Kohl had hoped would be a happy whole by now. Inflation and unemployment are higher in the east than in the west, and wages are lower. In mid-1995 one adult in five was out of work in moribund industrial towns of Brandenburg and Saxony near the East European border.

The monetary cost of unification, as well as the sheer human sacrifice involved, have vastly exceeded all predictions. A special tax levy, meant to be a temporary source of funding for the former East Germany, was reimposed at the start of 1995, rekindling resentment among western Germans, who felt they had already paid enough. This was closely followed by an authoritative report in *Der Spiegel*—neither confirmed nor denied by the government—claiming that 65 billion marks raised from taxes, designated for investment in the east, had been totally wasted through inefficiency, sheer ignorance, or criminal misuse.

No, it wasn't a happy country that Kohl and his paper-thin coalition majority surveyed in late 1995—from a capital city tottering on uncertain foundations. By the beginning of the 21st century, Berlin is to take its place as the seat of German government from Rhineland Bonn, which assumed the role in the postwar years because it had few logistical or historical issues. As the cold war grew ever icier and the East–West divide widened, Bonn's provisional role took on a kind of permanence. When reunited Berlin restaked its claim, the parliamentary vote in favor of moving the capital was close, and the extra-parliamentary debate about the wisdom of the move continues. Berlin, too, is having problems adjusting to its new role: In 1995 half the construction projects connected with the move still awaited official approval.

The tax burden caused by unification and the impending move weighed heavily on the Bonn government in 1995, testing the alliance between Chancellor Kohl's Christian Democrats and the liberal Free Democrats to an extent not seen since the coalition first came to power. Despite waning popularity that threatened its very existence, the small but resilient Free Democratic Party challenged the Kohl cabinet's tax package and opened a split that could bring early elections.

An irony of history is that after celebrating the fall of the Iron Curtain and triumphantly dismantling the barbed-wire fences that separated East and West Europe for nearly four decades, Germany is putting up new border defenses at many weak frontier points to keep out unwanted "refugees." New legislation is making it much more difficult for emigrants from the Third World, Russia, and Eastern Europe to find refuge in Germany. Guard dogs may be brought back into service, too.

With such signs of political instability it was perhaps surprising that the unpleasant specter of ultra-right-wing neo-Nazi militancy lost some of its menacing form in 1995. Although the number of attacks on foreigners in Germany decreased, the number of anti-Semitic offenses nearly doubled from 1993 to 1994, and the trend was equally disturbing in 1995. Developments like these have a significance of their own in Germany, and many concerned Germans warn against underestimating the extent of the threat from the racist right.

Thinking twice about that trip to Germany? Don't worry—apart from beggars in Bonn subway passages, junkies in Frankfurt parks, and homeless people camping out in central Munich, a tourist could travel from the Danish border in the north to the Bavarian Alps in the south without witnessing much more than a smudge on the travel posters that trumpet Germany's attractions. It is an undeniably beautiful country, full of contrasts. But this diversity makes it difficult to find a common element that defines Germany and its people.

There has always been a perceptible north–south division, across which the Hamburger and the Bavarian view each other with a theatrical animosity that reduces the rivalry between the English and the Scots to schoolboy banter. But now the symbiosis has been disturbed by the arrival of the east German Saxon—to many west Germans a very backward species who chirps an incomprehensible language.

Like the English–Scottish rivalry, these unneighborly sentiments within Germany are rooted in a shared history scarred by internecine quarrels and further complicated by the long parallel rule of two great royal dynasties, the Hohenzollerns and the Wittelsbachs. Bavarians are proud that their line—the Wittelsbachs—is older and lasted longer than the Prussian Hohenzollerns. That two latter-day Bavarian rulers were insane is smilingly dismissed as a slight deviation. Indeed, the insanity of young King Ludwig II is welcomed as *Glück im Unglück* (a common German expression meaning "fortune in misfortune"), for the eccentric ruler built a collection of castles that, although they bankrupted the royal purse, now reap huge sums of money in tourist revenues. Similarly, Ludwig's munificent patronage of Wagner cost the Bavarians dearly in hard cash—but what an investment!

There are other, more visible differences that distinguish Bavarians from their neighbors to the north or, for that matter, the Berliner from the Rhinelander, and all of them from the Saarlander or the Saxon. You've only got to join them at the table and watch what they eat and particularly what and how they drink to sort out one from another.

The Berliner and Bavarian both enjoy a beer brewed from wheat—but the Bavarian watches with horror how the Berliner sweetens it with fruit juice. In the Rhineland, beer is served in small glasses that have been known to provoke threats of legal action from Bavarians believing they were getting short measure. Saarlanders claim to produce the best German beer and Bavarians the purest (brewed, despite European Union pressure to conform, according to a 16th-century purity law).

Germany produces great wines too, of course, but beer is the country's national beverage and its emblem; there are more breweries in Germany than in the rest of Europe put together. Unification gave German brewing a boost, and Germany regained its world title as number one in the per-capita consumption of beer. Germans down 144 liters (254 pints) a year, far surpassing Britain (197 pints) and the United States (165 pints). Bavarians drink a staggering 200 liters (352 pints) per person.

A great German institution is the beer garden, traditionally Bavarian but now being introduced throughout Germany. Beer gardens are the center of Bavarian life in the summer, which in a good year means the long, balmy span between Easter and the first cold snap of October. This is the time to visit Bavaria, and particularly Munich, when the velvety southern German nights draw families out to the lantern-hung chestnut tree bowers of throbbing beer gardens.

But the Bavarians by no means have a monopoly on outdoor delights such as these. In bustling Frankfurt, on off-duty summer nights, the city's businessmen can be found in the cider pubs of Sachsenhausen; in Berlin, the pavement cafés are an extension of the German living room; while along the Rhine, the arrival of the first new wine after the grape harvest signals party time.

In cities like Munich it's always party season, with even Lent producing an excuse for brewing an especially strong beer (locals say it kept monks going during their 40 days' fast). The weeks preceding Lent are Carnival time (known in southern Germany as Fasching), celebrated in Germany with an abandon found scarcely anywhere else in Europe.

Behind the uninhibited fun, though, is a precision-made mechanism that is peculiarly German, a kind of "Now you will enjoy yourself" compulsion. The Carnival season begins precisely at 11 AM on the 11th day of the 11th month and ends at the stroke of midnight on Shrove Tuesday—you can't organize your fun more efficiently. Since the Germans are so good at arranging their hedonism, we can be confident they will sort out their problems, too. And that's good news for us all.

— *Robert Tilley*

WHAT'S WHERE

Munich

Chic and cosmopolitan, carefree and kitschy—as Bavaria's capital and one of Germany's biggest cities, Munich has more than its share of great museums, architectural treasures, historic sites, and world-class shops, restaurants, and hotels. The same could be said of its abundance of lederhosen and oompah bands. But it's the overall feeling of *Gemütlichkeit* (conviviality) that makes the city so special—an open-air market here, a park there, and beer halls everywhere. Tourists flock to Munich year-round, but festival dates—especially Fasching, or Carnival, in the winter, and Oktoberfest in the fall—draw the most.

The Bavarian Alps

This region of fir-clad mountains stretches from Munich south to the Austrian border. Quaint towns full of half-timbered houses fronted by flowers in the summer, buried by snow in the winter, pop up among the peaks, as do the creations of "Mad" King Ludwig II. Shimmering Alpine lakes abound, and the whole area has sporting opportunities galore, centering on Garmisch-Partenkirchen. Long before sports were a part of the region's livelihood, however, wood carving was quite the industry; you'll still see it in many towns, notably Oberammergau and Berchtesgaden.

The Bavarian Forest

Low-key and understated, the Bavarian Forest is a welcome alternative to Germany's hyped-up, overcrowded tourist regions. Good-quality dining and lodging at budget prices make it even more attractive. Farming and forestry are mainstay industries, tourism is growing, and glass-blowing shouldn't be missed. Passau, a 2,000-year-old town at the confluence of three rivers, is visited for its beauty as much as its history.

The Romantic Road

One of Germany's so perfectly planned tourist routes, the Romantic Road is just that, albeit in the sense meaning wondrous and fanciful. *Minnesänger* Walther von der Vogelweide and medieval sculptor Tilman Riemenschneider are among the people whose legacies you'll discover as you travel the route. You'll also visit Würzburg, home to a glorious Baroque palace; the wonderfully preserved medieval town of Rothenburg-ob-der-Tauber; and Ludwig II's fantastic Neuschwanstein castle.

Franconia

A predominantly rural area, Franconia was most important politically in the days of the Holy Roman Empire. You'll want to see its beautiful and historic towns: Coburg, Bayreuth, Bamberg, Nürnberg, and Regensburg. Wagner fans especially shouldn't miss Bayreuth, where the great composer settled and built his theater. The annual festival that honors him brings other town functions to a halt every summer.

The Bodensee

If you're in the area, be sure to take at least one boat trip on the Bodensee, the largest lake in the German-speaking world. Some towns are built on islands near the shore, and their incredible beauty is best surveyed from the water. Other features of the area appreciated by tourists are its climate, which allows near-tropical growth in places, and its proximity to Switzerland and Liechtenstein. Konstanz, the largest city on the lake, is German but has parts in Switzerland.

The Black Forest

Cake and smoked ham aren't the only reasons to visit the Black Forest, but they are good ones. Spa and casino resorts, outdoor activities, and cuckoo clocks are other draws. The Romans were the first to take advantage of the area's healing waters, 19 centuries ago, and royalty and the cultural elite paraded about the region in the 1800s. Today watching vacationers here is a study in contrasts; some tourists flock to high-fashion, high-cost towns like Baden-Baden, while others feel more at home in down-home German country villages.

Heidelberg and the Neckar Valley

The Neckar Valley contains industrial cities and quaint university towns—Mannheim and Stuttgart among the former, Heidelberg and Tübingen among the latter—with castles, small villages, and the Neckar River throughout. Along the scenic Burgenstrasse (Castle Road), each medieval town is guarded by a castle, but arguably Heidelberg is most worth a stop (just ask—and beware of—its 2.5 million visitors annually). This town seems to work magic for all who give it a chance; look for signs of Johann Wolfgang von Goethe, Mark Twain, Carl Maria von Weber, and Robert Schumann, for example.

Frankfurt

Because it is the air gateway to Germany—and to Europe—you'll probably at least land in Frankfurt. Many German banks are headquartered here, and the Frankfurt Börse is Germany's leading stock exchange. All this has contributed to a high-rise-spiked skyline that would stun the 30 Holy Roman Emperors who were elected and crowned here. Their portraits line the banquet hall of the Römer, or city hall. Across the River Main from the heart of downtown is the residential, medieval-feeling Sachsenhausen Quarter, home to many of the city's best museums.

Rhineland Palatinate

This stretch of the Rhine has less dramatic scenery than along the riverbanks farther north, but it's also less crowded and less expensive. It's a region where few autobahns penetrate and where most other roads lead to truly off-the-beaten-track territory. One of these roads is Germany's first specially designated Weinstrasse (Wine Road), a winding, often narrow route guarded by ancient castles and lined with vineyards that beckon the traveler to sample current vintages. North and west of Weinstrasse are Speyer, Worms, and Mainz, all former imperial centers and each home to a Romanesque cathedral more spectacular than the last.

The Rhineland

Vater Rhein, or "Father Rhine," is Germany's historic lifeline, and the region from Mainz to Koblenz is its heart. Its banks are crowned by magnificent castle after castle and breathtaking, vine-terraced hills that provide the livelihood for many of the villages hugging the shores. Bigger cities, too, such as Bonn, Köln, and Koblenz, thrive along the great river. Koblenz lies at the meeting of the Rhine and its most famous tributary, the Mosel, on whose banks Germany's oldest city, Trier, was established. Other cities included in the chapter are Aachen and Düsseldorf.

The Fairy-Tale Road

If you're in search of Cinderella, Hansel and Gretel, the Pied Piper, and Rumpelstiltskin, the Fairy-Tale Road is the place to look. One of Germany's special tourist routes, it leads through parts of Germany where the brothers Grimm lived and worked. From its start in Hanau, just east of Frankfurt, to its end in Bremen, 600 kilometers (370 miles) north, it passes dozens of picturesque towns full of half-timbered houses and guarded by castles. Hannover is the site of a magnificent Baroque park.

Hamburg

The Free and Hanseatic City of Hamburg, the city's official title, is an apt description. Water—in the form of the Alster Lakes and the River Elbe—is its defining feature and the secret of its success. Even before the formation of the Hanseatic League, Hamburg shipped to and from all parts of the world; today the city's port is Germany's gateway to the world, making this city one of the most international ones in the country. The maritime heritage of Hamburg is also evident in many of the city's main attractions, including the Fischmarkt, its diverse restaurants, and the red-light district (the infamous Reeperbahn). A fire in the 1800s and wartime bombings destroyed much of Hamburg's early architecture but cleared room for fantastic new creations, among them beautiful art-nouveau and Nordic Renaissance structures.

Berlin

Reunited Berlin is a city born again, ready to assume its role as the capital of Germany and one of Europe's great metropolises. But it is still at odds with its newly found unity, after almost 30 years of artificial division. Today it is virtually the continent's largest construction site, with a skyline dominated by a forest of cranes. It is at the same time as lively, youthful, dramatic, international, and mercurial as ever. As central Europe's most important connection to the east, the city is a place where many international cultures mingle. Berlin has enough museums, notorious nightlife, shops, and restaurants to fill any itinerary, but sites related to its complex history make it worth an extended visit. Potsdam, site of Frederick the Great's magnificent Sanssouci Palace, is a popular excursion. Berlin isn't as old as many German cities, but it gets more than its share of space in the history books. It became capital of the newly unified German Empire under Bismarck in the late 1800s and hung on to that position until it was almost bombed out of existence by the Allies in the struggle against Hitler and Nazism. Following the war Berlin was artificially partitioned and later barricaded; reunification was like an impossible dream come true.

Saxony and Thuringia

This area is worth visiting for its traditional tourist sites and because it is in transition— for 45 years it was bound more closely with the Soviet Union than with West Germany. Dresden's Zwinger Palace complex is a cultural wonder; Leipzig, the largest eastern German city after Berlin, is an important commercial center (avoid the trade fair dates); and Weimar has many traces from its days as a cultural center in the 19th century.

The Baltic Coast

Between the medieval Hanseatic city of Lübeck and the Polish frontier, eastern Germany's vacation hot spot offers many beach towns that still seem trapped in the '30s. Miles of sandy coastline, peppered with chalk cliffs and charming little coves, have largely escaped the attention of developers. Evidence of the Hansa merchants and a wealth of architectural delights await inspection, from the well-preserved medieval town squares to the simple whitewashed seaside cottages with their roofs of reed thatch.

PLEASURES AND PASTIMES

Beer

The Germans don't just produce *a* beverage called beer; they brew more than 5,000 varieties in a range of tastes and colors. Germany has about 1,300 breweries, 40% of the world's total. The hallmark of the country's dedication to beer is the purity law, *das Reinheitsgebot,* unchanged since Duke Wilhelm IV introduced it in Bavaria in 1516. The law decrees that only malted barley, hops, yeast, and water may be used to make beer, except for specialty wheat beers.

Asking for a beer in most German hostelries is like going into a cheese shop and asking for cheese. Even the simplest country inn will likely have a choice of beers, and in many pubs there may be several different draft beers in addition to the standard selection of bottled beers. The type available varies from one part of the country to another, and in areas of southern Germany, the choice can also depend on the time of year.

In northern Germany the most popular standard beers are export lagers or the paler, more pungent Pilsners. The breweries of Rhine cities Köln and Düsseldorf produce "old-fashioned" beers similar to English ales.

Germany's biggest breweries are in the northern city of Dortmund, which feeds the industrial Ruhr region. But Bavaria is where the majority of the country's breweries—and beer traditions—are found. Indeed, while Germany as a whole is at the head of the international beer-drinking table, the Bavarians and the Saarlanders to the southwest consume more beer per person than does any other group in the country.

Ultimately, all beer routes lead to the world's beer-drinking capital: Munich. This is where you'll find the biggest beer halls, the largest beer gardens, the most famous breweries, the biggest and most indulgent beer festival, and the widest selection of brews; even the beer glasses are bigger. It's a measure of how seriously the Germans take their beer that they see no conflict in the fact that one of the most cosmopolitan cities in the country—a place with great art galleries and museums, an opulent opera house, and chic lifestyles—is internationally recognized as the most beer-drenched city on Earth. Postcards are framed with the message, "Munich, the Beer City."

Bavarians are sometimes regarded with disdain by their less-indulgent Prussian brothers to the north. But not even the widest-girthed southerners can be held wholly responsible for the staggering consumption of beer and food at the annual Oktoberfest, which starts in September. Typically, 5 million *liters* of beer, as well as 750,000 roasted chickens and 650,000 sausages, are put away by revelers. Clearly, visitors must be helping a little.

A BEER GLOSSARY➤ The alcohol content of German beers varies considerably. At the weaker end of the scale is the light Munich Helles (3.7% alcohol by volume); stronger brews are Pilsner (around 5%) and Doppelbock (more than 7%).

Alt: literally, "old," referring to beer made according to an old formula.

Bock: strong beer, which can be light or dark, sweet or dry.

Doppelbock: stronger than Bock, usually dark, and not to be trifled with.

Dunkles: dark beer, often slightly sweeter or maltier than pale (light) beers.

Export: usually a pale (light-colored) beer of medium strength.

Feierabend: called out when a drinking establishment is closing for the day.

Halbe: half a Mass, the standard beer measure in Bavaria (☞ *below*).

Hefe: yeast.

Helles: light beer.

Klar, Kristall: wheat beer with the yeast removed.

Kleines: a small glass of beer (in Bavaria).

Krug: an earthenware drinking vessel, often referred to as a stein.

Lager: In Germany the term, which means "store," refers to that stage of the brewing process during which beer matures in the brewery.

Leichtbier: beer with low alcohol and calorie content, usually pale in color.

Mass: a 1-liter (almost 2-pint) glass or earthenware mug.

Naturtrüb: a new term for unfiltered beer, implying the yeast has not been removed.

Obergärig: top-fermented.

O' zapftis!: "Barrel is tapped!"—the cry that announces the opening of the Munich Oktoberfest.

Pils, Pilsner: A golden-color, dry, bitter-flavor beer named after Pilsen, the Czech town where in the 19th century the style was first developed.

Polizei Stunde: literally, "police hour"—closing time. Midnight or 1 AM in some big cities, usually earlier in small towns and villages.

Prost: German for "cheers."

Radler: lemonade and beer mixed.

Rauchbier: smoked beer. Usually a dark brew with a smoky flavor that comes from infusing the malted barley with beech-wood smoke.

Untergärig: bottom-fermented.

Weissbier, Weizenbier: wheat beer. A highly carbonated, sharp, and sour brew, often with floating yeast particles.

Boat Trips

River and lake trips are among the greatest delights of a vacation in Germany, especially along the Rhine, Germany's longest river. The Rhine may be viewed in a variety of modes. For those in a hurry, there is a daily hydrofoil service from Düsseldorf right through to Mainz (book in advance). For gentler souls, there is a wide range of more leisurely cruises. German cruise ships also operate on the Upper Rhine as far as Basel, Switzerland; on the Main between Frankfurt and Mainz; on the Danube to Vienna and Budapest; on the Europe Canal joining the Main and the Danube; on the Elbe and Weser and their estuaries; on the Inn and Ilz; and on the Ammersee, Chiemsee, Königsee, Bodensee, and many other smaller German lakes.

History

Germany's past is glorious at times, horrifying at others. No matter what part of the country you visit, you'll be bombarded with it. In northern Germany the devastation of the Thirty Years' War is as visible as the riches brought by the Hanseatic

League. Throughout the country are remainders of leading figures—Charlemagne's throne in Aachen, Wittelsbach castles in Bavaria, Hitler's Alpine retreat. Many concentration camps, including Dachau, outside Munich, and Sachsenhausen, outside Berlin, have been reopened as education centers and memorials to their victims. In the former East Germany, many reminders of Communism—such as statues of Marx—were obliterated, but citizens fought to retain some, and won.

Theme tours can help you focus on an area of specific interest. You can organize a trip by visiting the Castles of Ludwig II, for example, or take a theme road, such as the tourist office's new Martin Luther route, to explore the country's past.

Scenery

Many of the tours in this book are designed to help you take in Germany's beauty. From the medieval brick buildings in the tiny towns on the Baltic Coast, to the spectacular castle- and vine-covered hills along the Rhine, to the densely wooded forests in the south, to the crystal-clear Alpine lakes, Germany's scenery is as diverse as it is breathtaking. Whether you're in the shadow of high-rises or driving past geranium-bedecked, half-timbered houses on a country road, be sure to appreciate what's around you.

Sports and Outdoor Activities

The Germans are nothing if not sports-crazy, and practically every sport, however arcane, can be arranged almost anywhere in the country. A good number of sports packages—for sailing, tennis, climbing, walking, horseback riding, to name only a few—are also available. Below, we give details of some of the more popular participant sports. Information about important sporting events is also published every month by regional and local tourist offices.

BICYCLING➤ There are no formalities governing the importation of bikes into Germany, and no duty is required. Bikes can also be carried on trains—though not on ICE trains—if you buy a Fahrradkarte, or bicycle ticket. These cost DM 8.60 per journey and can be bought at any train station. It is also possible to send your bike to your next destination for DM 21, where it will be held for you in storage until your arrival. Full details are given in German Rail's brochure Radler-Bahn.

Bicycles are also available for rental at more than 370 train stations throughout the country, most of them in southern Germany, from April to October. The cost is DM 11–DM 13 per day, DM 7–DM 9 if you have a valid rail ticket.

FISHING➤ Fishing is possible at many locations in Germany, but a permit, valid for one year at a cost of DM 10–DM 20, available from local tourist offices, is required, as is a local permit to fish in a particular spot. Get this from the owner of the stretch of water in which you plan to fish.

A number of hotels offer fishing for guests, but you will normally be expected to deliver your catch—if any—to the hotel.

GOLF➤ The popularity of golf in Germany is rapidly increasing, as is the number of courses. If they are not too busy, clubs will usually allow nonmembers to play; charges will be about DM 30 during the week and up to DM 60 on weekends and on public holidays.

HIKING AND CLIMBING➤ Germany's hill and mountain regions have thousands of miles of marked hiking and mountain-walking tracks. They are administered by regional hiking clubs and, where appropriate, mountaineering groups, all of which are affiliated with the Verband Deutscher Gebirgs- und Wandervereine e.V. (☞ Sports *in* Important Contacts A to Z.)

Local tourist offices and sports shops can usually supply details about mountain guides.

HORSEBACK RIDING➤ Riding schools and clubs can be found all over Germany. Rates are generally high, and most schools will insist on a minimum standard of competence before allowing novices to venture out. As an alternative, pony treks are available in many parts of the country.

SAILING➤ Sailing vacations and opportunities to rent sailboats are available throughout Germany. Most North Sea and Baltic resorts and harbors have either sailing schools or sailboats of varying types to rent. Lake sailing is equally popular, particularly on the Chiemsee in Bavaria and on the Bodensee.

SWIMMING➤ Almost all larger towns and resorts have open-air and indoor pools, the former frequently heated, the latter often with wave or whirlpool machines. In addition, practically all coastal resorts have indoor seawater pools, as well as good, if bracing, beaches. Similarly, all German spas have thermal or mineral-water indoor pools (☞ Lodging *in* Smart Travel Tips A to Z). Finally, Bavaria's Alpine lakes and a large number of artificial lakes elsewhere have marked-off swimming and sunbathing areas.

Note that swimming in rivers, especially the larger ones, is not recommended and in some cases is forbidden—look for the Baden signs—because of shipping, pollution, or both.

You'll probably notice that many Germans sunbathe nude. Some pools will have special days designated only for nude bathing, and nudity is also allowed on beaches with posted signs.

TENNIS➤ In the home country of champions Steffi Graf and Boris Becker, courts are available practically everywhere, summer and winter. Local tourist offices will supply details about where to play, charges, and how to book—the latter is essential in most areas. Charges vary from DM 20 to DM 30 for outdoor courts and DM 25 to DM 35 for indoor courts.

WINDSURFING➤ This has become so popular, particularly on the Bavarian lakes, that it has been restricted on some beaches as a result of collisions between surfers and swimmers. Nonetheless, there are still many places where you can rent and use Windsurfers. Lessons, at around DM 25 per hour, are also generally available.

WINTER SPORTS➤ South Bavaria is the big winter-sports region, and Garmisch-Partenkirchen is the best-known center. There are also winter-sports resorts in the Black Forest, the Harz region, the Bavarian Forest, the Rhön mountains, the Fichtelgebirge, the Sauerland, and the Swabian mountains. The season generally runs from the middle of December to the end of March, but at higher altitudes, such as the Zugspitze (near Garmisch), you can usually ski from as early as the end of November to as late as the middle of May. There's no need to bring skis with you—you can rent or buy them on the spot. Look for the special winter off-season rates (Weisse Wochen) offered by most winter-sports resorts for cross-country and downhill skiing vacations. Prices include seven days' bed-and-breakfast (or half board) plus ski lessons.

For cross-country (*Langlauf*) skiing, which is becoming increasingly popular, there are stretches of prepared tracks (*Loipen*) in the valleys and foothills of most winter-sports centers, as well as in the suburbs of larger towns in south Bavaria.

Skibobbing is on the increase. There are runs and schools at Bayrischzell, Berchtesgaden, Garmisch-Partenkirchen, Füssen, and Oberstdorf in the Alps, as well as at Altglashütten, Bernau, and Feldberg in the Black Forest. Ice rinks, many open all year, can be found everywhere.

Wine

More than 2,000 years ago, Romans saw the potential for grape growing in their newly conquered land, and vineyards have held their own in the beer-guzzling country ever since. Germany has nearly 240,000 acres of vineyards, about 87% of which are planted with white-wine grapes. Because it is so far north, the wines Germany produces are light and delicate; Riesling grapes and wines are the best known.

Wine grapes grow in 13 specified regions in the area around the Bodensee; along the Rhine and its tributaries, up to near Bonn; east of the French border, on the slopes of the Black Forest; and on the Elbe north of Dresden. As with beer, German law governs different aspects of wine production and labeling. A stipulation of the Treaty of Versailles states that Germany (and all other European countries) may not use the name "champagne"; Sekt is what German sparkling wines are called. The grape harvest takes place in October and November, but its products are celebrated by festivals year-round. The "Rivers of Wine" itinerary, below, and the Wine Road tour in Chapter 11 are good tours for connoisseurs.

FODOR'S CHOICE

Dining

★**Bado-La Poele d'Or, Köln,** with surprisingly simple and light classical cuisine in a hushed setting. $$$$

★**Bareiss, Baiersbronn, The Black Forest,** whose outstanding, award-winning cuisine even attracts diners from across the nearby French border. $$$$

★**Colombi, Freiburg,** has two sections: one rustic, the other elegant. Both serve excellent meat dishes. $$$$

★**Im Schiffchen, Düsseldorf,** one of Germany's two remaining exceptional restaurants and the pride of the whole Rhineland. $$$$

★**Landhaus Scherrer, Hamburg,** for sophisticated nouvelle specialties and down-to-earth local dishes. $$$$

★**Säumerhof, Grafenau,** an unexpectedly good restaurant in the middle of the Bavarian Forest. It serves original, nouvelle-inspired dishes made with ingredients found locally. $$$$

★**Wullenwewer, Lübeck,** a particularly attractive setting for sophisticated cuisine. $$$–$$$$

★**Schloss Bevern, Bevern,** a romantic and stylish restaurant where you'll dine on such traditional country dishes as roast pheasant or partridge. $$$

★**Weinhaus Brückenkeller, Frankfurt,** where you'll find time-honored yet light German specialties in an arched cellar. $$$

★**Alte Schwede, Wismar,** for traditional game and fish dishes. $$

★**Bad Dürkheimer Riesenfass, Bad Dürkheim,** which serves 420 people in the biggest wine barrel in the world. $$

★**Fischerhaus, Hamburg,** a busy restaurant that specializes in classic fish dishes. $

★**Weinhaus Moschner, Rottach-Egern,** a dark, old tavern with a menu that's heavy on sausage. The camaraderie and atmosphere are just as important as the food. $

★**Zum Stachel, Würzburg,** for satisfying Franconian fare served beneath a canopy of vine leaves. $

Lodging

★**Brenner's Park Hotel, Baden-Baden,** a stately mansion outfitted with luxury accommodations. $$$$

★**Dom-Hotel, Köln,** old-fashioned, formal, and gracious, with a stunning location right by the cathedral. It offers old-world elegance and discreetly efficient service. $$$$

★**Rafael, Munich,** a newer downtown hotel in an older building. Service and style are the hallmarks. $$$$

★**Romantik Hotel zum Ritter St. Georg, Heidelberg,** with Renaissance atmosphere by the barrel. $$$$

★**Schlosshotel Bühlerhöhe, Bühl,** a castle-hotel with spectacular views over the heights of the Black Forest. $$$$

★**Schlosshotel Vier Jahreszeiten, Berlin,** a new, and rather intimate Grand Hotel, with unique interior designs by Karl Lagerfeld. $$$$

★**Vier Jahreszeiten, Hamburg,** has antiques lining the public rooms and embellishing the stylish bedrooms; armloads of flowers standing in massive vases; and rare oil paintings hanging on the walls; of course, all rooms are individually decorated in superb taste. $$$$

★**Garden Hotels Pöseldorf, Hamburg,** has classy accommodations in three attractive city mansions. $$$

★**Pannonia Parkhotel, Meissen,** a *Jugendstil* (art deco) villa on the banks of the Elbe, with incredible suites under its eaves. $$$

★**Parkhotel Luisenbad, Bad Reichenhall,** the quintessential fin de siècle German spa hotel. Outside are pink porticoes and pillars, inside it's deep comfort and dark woods. $$$

★**Deidesheimer Hof, Deidesheim,** a traditional old Deidesheimer house, immaculate and comfortable. $$–$$$

★**Dornröschenschloss, Sababurg,** a small luxury hotel set in castle walls. $$–$$$

★**Wilder Mann, Passau,** with beds of carved oak beneath chandeliers and richly stuccoed ceilings in a tastefully modernized 11th-century house. $$–$$$

★**Hotel Ludwig der Bayer, Ettal,** a fine old hotel backed by mountains. $$

Castles and Palaces

★**The Altes Schloss,** in Meersburg, a private residence, it watches majestically over the town and lake and only some of its rooms are open to the public.

★**Burg Eltz,** in Mosel, is the real thing—an 800-year-old castle perched on the spine of an isolated rocky outcrop, bristling with towers and pinnacles.

★**Burg Trifels,** in Annweiler, first constructed during the mid-12th century by the emperor Barbarossa. Today's castle is a 1937 replica.

★**Heidelberg Schloss,** a mix of architectural styles. It has a particularly harmonious, graceful, and ornate Renaissance courtyard.

★**Neuschwanstein,** in Füssen. The most fanciful of Ludwig II's fantasy castles, it rises out of the mountainside like nothing you've ever seen.

★**Schloss Sanssouci,** in Potsdam, Frederick the Great's magnificent summer palace and grounds.

★**Wartburg Castle,** in Eisenach, begun in 1067 and added to throughout the centuries. It hosted the German minstrels Walter von der Vogelweide and Wolfram von Eschenbach, Martin Luther, Richard Wagner, and Goethe. It's captivating inside and out.

Museums

★**Deutsches Museum,** in Munich, a monumental building full of stimulating, innovative scientific exhibits, a planetarium, and an IMAX theater.

★**Domschatzkammer,** in Aachen, is one of the richest cathedral treasuries in Europe. Among its prizes are Charlemagne's bones, interred in a golden shrine, and his throne.

★**Kunsthalle,** in Hamburg, the city's principal gallery. It has one of the most important art collections in Germany, with paintings from the Middle Ages to the present.

★**Museum der Bildenden Künste,** in Leipzig, an art gallery of international standard.

★**Museum für Moderne Kunst,** in Frankfurt, a distinctive triangular building with a great collection of contemporary art.

★**Pergamonmuseum,** in Berlin, one of the world's greatest museums. It showcases the original Pergamon altar and other antique monuments.

★**Römisch-Germanisches Museum,** in Köln, built around a huge Dionysus mosaic, houses stone Roman coffins and a series of memorial tablets, among other Roman-related exhibits.

★**Wallraf-Richartz Museum and Museum Ludwig,** in Köln. The former contains pictures spanning the years 1300 to 1900, with Dutch and Flemish schools particularly well represented, and the latter is devoted to 20th-century works. Together they form the Rhineland's largest art collection.

Churches

★**The Kaiserdom,** in Aachen, built over the course of 1,000 years. It reflects architectural styles from the Middle Ages to the 19th century. Its commanding image is its magnificent octagonal royal chapel, rising in two arched stories to end in the cap of the dome.

★**Kaiserdom,** in Speyer, one of the finest Romanesque cathedrals in Europe. It conveys, more than any other building in Germany, the pomp and majesty of the early Holy Roman emperors.

★**Kölner Dom,** in Köln, an extraordinary Gothic cathedral. Its 515-foot towers soar heavenward, and its immense interior is illuminated by light filtering through acres of stained glass.

★**Mainzer Dom,** in Mainz, basically finished in the 12th century; alterations to its Romanesque purity include an 18th-century Baroque spire.

★**Münster,** in Freiburg. That the cathedral took more than 300 years to build is evidenced by different architectural styles. Its 370-foot spire is delicately perforated.

★**St. Margaretha,** in Osterhofen. Frescoist and painter Cosmas Damian Asam and sculptors Egid Quirin Asam and Johann Michael Fischer decorated here in a rare partnership between 1728 and 1741.

★**Trierer Dom,** in Trier, an architectural jumble of Romanesque, Gothic, and Baroque styles, has the air of a vast antiques shop.

★**Vierzehnheiligen,** in Franconia, built by Balthasar Neumann between 1743 and 1772. The entire building seems to be in motion—almost all the walls are curved and alive with delicate stucco.

★ **Wieskirche,** near Rottenbuch, has a simple exterior that gives little hint of the brilliantly colored stuccos, statues, and gilt and the luminous ceiling fresco inside.

★ **Wörmser Dom,** in Worms. A Romanesque masterpiece, though it was remodeled in keeping with new styles and attitudes.

Towns Where Time Stands Still

★ **Alsfeld.** Its medieval town center consists of beautifully preserved half-timbered houses that in places lean out to almost touch one another across narrow, winding cobbled streets. The Rathaus, with two pointy towers amid all the jumble, is particularly remarkable.

★ **Bad Wimpfen,** founded by the Romans, has remains of Barbarossa's imperial palace and a picture-postcard jumble of Gothic and Renaissance buildings.

★ **Bernkastel-Kues,** complete with Marktplatz, fountain, fortress, and vineyards.

★ **Hameln,** the town of Pied Piper fame, which has a street where no music is ever played.

★ **Rothenburg-ob-der-Tauber,** still enclosed by a wall, is a treasure of gingerbread architecture, fountains, and flowers against a backdrop of towers and turrets.

★ **St. Martin,** where grape vines have practically taken over; they encroach on the narrow streets and link the ancient houses with curling green garlands.

★ **Wasserburg,** an auto-free island town in the Bodensee, started as a fortress built on the site of a Roman watchtower.

Memorable Sights

★ **Baden-Baden's casino,** designed along the lines of the greatest French imperial palaces, with a series of richly decorated gaming rooms.

★ **The Brandenburger Tor and Berlin Wall remains** in Berlin give pause for reflection.

★ **The confluence of the Inn and Danube rivers at Passau** produces a special quality of light, a lovely complement to the fine old houses that line the waterfront.

★ **Munich's Oktoberfest,** a 16-day festival of beer (5 million liters of it), pretzels, rides,

and oompah bands, on Munich's Theresienwiese exhibition grounds.

★ **Opera night in Bayreuth,** with a Wagner masterpiece performed in the theater he designed—an incredible thrill for Wagner fans.

★ **The Rhine in Flames fireworks,** an orgy of rockets and flares. It lights up St. Goar and St. Goarshausen and their surrounding vineyards every September.

★ **The Semper Opera House,** in Dresden, built and named after a Dresden architect, and then rebuilt twice. Its lavish interior is sure to impress.

★ **The Street Dragon Festival,** in Furth im Wald in August. It sees townsfolk dressed in period costume taking part in the ritual slaying of a fire-breathing "dragon" that stalks the main street.

Unforgettable Excursions

★ **A boat ride on Bavaria's Königsee,** driven by a silent electric motor, allows you to glide serenely along the cliffs that plunge into the dark-green water.

★ **A cruise on the Rhine,** a great way to appreciate this legendary river.

★ **A Hamburg harbor cruise at night** introduces you to the city like nothing else can.

★ **A round-trip ride from Freiburg on the Black Forest railway,** which will take you through Hell and other spectacular scenery.

★ **A steam-train ride from Bad Doberan to the Baltic Sea** aboard the Molli, the perfect way to make this 10-mile journey.

★ **A trek to the summit of the Zugspitze,** Germany's highest mountain, just 10 minutes by cable car.

★ **The depths of the country's largest salt mine,** at Berchtesgaden, once open only to select guests. Today anyone can don miner's clothes and ride the miniature train that tours the Salzbergwerk.

★ **A torchlit sleigh ride through the Bavarian snow** or a nighttime toboggan ride down an Alpine slope gives you a different view of the mountains.

GREAT ITINERARIES

The Castles of Ludwig II

Munich tour operators offer day trips to the four famous castles of Bavaria's flamboyant King Ludwig II, but if you want to get to know them without distracting interruptions, there's no alternative but to strike out into the magnificent countryside on your own. If you're relying on public transportation, you'll have to return to Munich to visit the fourth castle, Herrenchiemsee, but arrange your itinerary so you can spend the night outside the city.

DURATION➤ 6 to 7 days

GETTING AROUND➤ **By Car:** From Munich this is a 340-kilometer (210-mile) drive round-trip drive.

By Public Transportation: Füssen and the Chiemsee Lake are reached by fast trains from Munich, with local buses making connections. A train service links Munich with Oberammergau, but allow two hours.

THE MAIN ROUTE➤ **Two Nights: Füssen.** You can walk to both Neuschwanstein and Hohenschwangau (Ludwig's childhood home) from Füssen or rent bikes at the station. Allow at least a full day at Neuschwanstein.

Two Nights: Ettal. Buses run from the picturesque mountain village of Ettal to Linderhof, which some consider the finest product of Ludwig's imagination. Find time to visit the Ettal monastery. Oberammergau is a 10-minute bus ride away.

Two Nights: Chiemsee. The unfinished Herrenchiemsee Palace stands on Herren Island in the Chiemsee. Passenger boats offer regular service to the island (and to the smaller, equally charming Fraueninsel) from the lakeside resorts of Prien and Gstadt. A main-line train service runs from Munich to Prien, and the Munich-Salzburg Autobahn runs alongside the south shore of the Chiemsee.

Information: ☞ Chapters 2, 3, and 5.

The Castle Road

Just outside the city of Heilbronn, amid rich vineyards, are the romantic ruins of the castle of the "Faithful Women." The explanation of its strange name is as romantic as the castle's setting. The German King Konrad III laid siege to the castle in 1140 and, in a moment of uncharacteristic weakness, allowed the women living within its walls to leave with as many of their possessions as they could carry. He is said to have lost his regal cool when the women trooped out carrying their menfolk on their backs. But he kept his word—and the men of the castle were spared. It's a marvelous yarn, typical of the stories you'll hear throughout this castle trail. There are about 50 castles along the 291-kilometer (180-mile) route between Mannheim and Nürnberg, a greater concentration than in any other part of Germany. Time and other circumstances—some are in private hands or serve some municipal function and can't be visited—will prevent you from viewing them all. On the other hand, some are now hotels where you'll be tempted to linger at least for a meal, perhaps to stay the night.

DURATION➤ 12 to 14 days

GETTING AROUND➤ **By Car:** It's 291 kilometers (180 miles) from Mannheim to Nürnberg. Follow the Neckar Valley road, B–27, from Mannheim to Heilbronn, then take the Burgenstrasse (the Castle Road itself) to Rothenburg-ob-der-Tauber. From Rothenburg, head for Colmberg and Hessbach, joining B–13 for the final stretch to Ansbach and Nürnberg.

By Public Transportation: Mannheim, Heidelberg, Heilbronn, and Nürnberg are all connected by regular express train services, but you'll have to rely on country bus services to reach many of the more remote castles.

THE MAIN ROUTE➤ **One Night: Mannheim.** Spend part of the day visiting Mannheim's magnificent 18th-century Elector's Palace, one of the largest Baroque buildings in Europe, and the rest at the Reiss-Insel Park and its walks alongside the Rhine.

Two Nights: Heidelberg. Spend a full day exploring Heidelberg itself, then make an excursion to the Heiligenberg, into the Odenwald Forest or to the castles of Schadeck, Hornberg, Hirschorn (all of them hotels with excellent restaurants), or to Zwingenberg and Minneburg.

Three Nights: Heilbronn. Plan excursions to the remains of the imperial palace of Bad Wimpfen and to the castles of Horneck, Guttenberg (with its aviary of birds of prey, including some fine eagles), Bad Rappenau, Ehrenberg, Weinsberg (the castle of "Faithful Women"), Neuenstein, and perhaps to the museum of bicycle and motorcycle technology at Neckarsulm.

Two Nights: Rothenburg-ob-der-Tauber. You'll want to spend at least a full day exploring Rothenburg, Europe's best-preserved medieval town. After that, make excursions along the Tauber River valley and to the castles of Langenburg, Bartenstein, and Colmberg.

Two Nights: Ansbach. Visit the margraves' palace and the 12th-century monastery church of Heilsbronn.

Two Nights: Nürnberg.

INFORMATION➤ ☞ Chapters 5, 6, and 9.

Rivers of Wine

The Rhine and Mosel need no introduction, but who knows the attractions of their tributaries—the rivers Saar and Nahe? Or the remote villages scattered across the Hunsrück range of hills, which is bordered by all four rivers? A tour of the four "rivers of wine" will take you from the crowds and crush of the Rhine of picture-postcard fame to the less dramatic but much more peaceful valley of the Saar. The Hunsrück high road leads you back at your own pace to the point where the well-trodden tourist trail picks up again on the Nahe River. In little more than a week you'll have skirted (and perhaps visited) Germany's most famous vineyards—and you should have tasted some of the country's finest wines.

DURATION➤ 10 to 12 days

GETTING AROUND➤ **By Car:** It's a 454-kilometer (280-mile) round-trip drive from Wiesbaden.

By Public Transportation: The rail journey along the Rhine between Bingen and Koblenz is Germany's most spectacular train ride. Riverboats also make the journey, and you can stop off at any point on the way. From Koblenz the rail line hugs the contours of the Mosel River to Trier; alternatively, you can again choose to travel the river by boat. A combination of train and bus will complete the itinerary along the Saar and across the Hunsrück to the Nahe River. Bus tours are offered by travel

agencies in Wiesbaden, Bingen, Koblenz, and Trier.

THE MAIN ROUTE➤ **Two Nights:** The **Rheingau** region, between Eltville and Rüdesheim. Visit the vineyards of the Rheingau (they produce Germany's finest wine) and Bingen, at the mouth of the Nahe River.

Four Nights: Along the **Rhine** between Rüdesheim and Koblenz. See the vineyards of Bacharach, Boppard, Brey, Kaub, Lorch, Oberwesel, Spay, and St. Goar, and the castles (or what remains of them) of Ehrenfels, Katz, Reichenstein, Rheinstein, Schönburg, and Sooneck.

Four Nights: Along the **Mosel** between Koblenz and Trier. Take excursions to the Deutsche Eck (where the Mosel and Rhine meet) and to the vineyards of Alken, Bernkastel-Kues, Bremm (Europe's steepest vineyard), Ediger, Kobern-Gondorf, Kröv, Nehren, Neumagen (Germany's oldest wine town, praised by the 4th-century Roman poet Ausonius in his work Mosella), Piesport, Traben-Trarbach, Winningen (its August wine festival is one of Germany's oldest), Zell, and to the castles of Cochem, Ehrenburg, Eltz (a medieval picture-book castle so treasured by the Germans that they've engraved its image on their DM 500 banknotes), and Thurant.

Two Nights: Trier. Explore Trier and follow the Saar River to Saarburg, Mettlach, and as far as the great "Saar Bend," a spectacular point where the river nearly doubles back on itself.

Two Nights: Idar-Oberstein. Venture into the Hunsrück hills and along the Nahe River to Bad Kreuznach. Take a day tour of the Edelsteinstrasse, or Gem Road, a well-marked 48-kilometer (30-mile) itinerary, starting and ending in Idar Oberstein, where precious stones are still mined and polished.

INFORMATION➤ ☞ Chapter 12.

Through the Black Forest

Many first-time visitors to the Black Forest literally can't see the forest for the trees. There are so many contrasting attractions that the basic, enduring beauty of the area passes them by. So in your tour of the forest, take time to stray from the tourist path and inhale the cool, mysterious air of its darker recesses. Walk or ride through its shadowy corridors or across its open upland; row a canoe and tackle the wild water of the Nagold and Wolf rivers. Then take time out to relax in any of the many spas, order a Baden wine enlivened by a dash of local mineral water, and seek out the nearest restaurant that confesses to its food being influenced by the cuisine of neighboring France. And, if you have money to spare at the end of your tour, return to Baden-Baden, try your luck on the gaming tables, and celebrate your good fortune or forget ill fate at the bar of the casino's nightclub, Griffen's.

DURATION> 12 to 14 days

GETTING AROUND> **By Car:** It's a 405-kilometer (250-mile) round-trip drive from Stuttgart.

By Public Transportation: Stuttgart, Baden-Baden, and Freiburg are all on InterCity train routes, and local trains and buses link them with most towns and spas of the Black Forest. Bus tours of the Black Forest are offered by travel agencies in Baden-Baden and Freiburg.

THE MAIN ROUTE> **Two Nights: Freudenstadt.** Take excursions to the Schwarzwald Museum at Lossburg, the Freilicht Museum Vogtsbauernhof near Wolfach, the Alpirsbach brewery, and the Glasswald Lake near Schapbach.

One Night: Triberg area. See the Triberg waterfall and the clock museums of Triberg and Furtwangen.

Two Nights: Hinterzarten or Titisee. Visit the Feldberg, the Black Forest's highest mountain, and the lakes of Titisee and Schluchsee.

Two Nights: Freiburg. Explore Freiburg, the Schauinsland Mountain, the Dr. Faustus town of Staufen, and the vineyards on the slopes of the Kaiserstuhl.

One Night: Offenburg. Visit the surrounding vineyards.

Two Nights: Baden-Baden. Enjoy the sights in and around Baden-Baden and travel to the summit of nearby Merkur Mountain, to Schloss Favorite, and to Windeck Castle.

One Night: Bad Liebenzell. Stop by one of the region's oldest spas.

INFORMATION> ☞ Chapter 8.

Toward East Bavaria

There's a corner of Germany that's on the doorstep of the country's most popular tourist area and yet can seem 1,000 miles from it. It stretches east from Munich to the Austrian border, its south edge marked by the Salzburg-bound autobahn, which propels most visitors and tourists to the greater attractions of the Bavarian Alps looming in the hazy distance. It's a gentle, pastoral region of rolling farmland, of forgotten villages asserting their presence with hilltop, onion-dome Baroque churches, of reed-fringed lakes and willow-bordered rivers. And what rivers! You'll meet the Inn as it meanders northward in search of the Danube, Salzburg's Salzach River, then the mighty Danube itself as it surges into Austria, and finally the Isar, ice-green and—just as the poet promised—still "rolling rapidly" from its mountain source.

DURATION> 7 to 8 days

GETTING AROUND> **By Car:** It's a 405-kilometer (250-mile) round-trip drive from Munich.

By Public Transportation: The route can be covered entirely by train, beginning with the main-line route from Munich to Wasserburg and then using local services between the remaining towns.

THE MAIN ROUTE> **One Night: Wasserburg.** Visit the medieval Amerang Castle (in summer, scene of chamber-music concerts) and the farmhouse museum at Amerang.

One Night: Laufen, on the Austrian border. Take excursions to the Waginger See, Germany's warmest lake, and across the Salzach River to the Austrian town of Oberndorf, where the Christmas carol "Silent Night" was composed.

One Night: Burghausen. In Altötting see the 14th-century "Black Madonna" in an 8th-century chapel chosen by the Wittelsbachs to be the repository of silver urns containing the hearts of the Bavarian rulers.

Two Nights: Passau. Venture north into the Bavarian Forest and perhaps across the border into the Czech Republic.

One Night: Straubing. Travel to the Danube towns Deggendorf and Bogen.

INFORMATION> ☞ Chapters 3, 4, and 7.

FESTIVALS AND SEASONAL EVENTS

Top seasonal events in Germany include Carnival festivities throughout the country in January and February, spring festivals (nationwide), Munich's Opera Festival in July, Bayreuth's Richard Wagner Festival in August, horse racing at Baden-Baden in August, wine festivals throughout the Rhineland in August, the Oktoberfest in Munich in late September and early October, the Frankfurt Book Fair in October, and December's Christmas markets (nationwide).

WINTER

DECEMBER➤ **Christmas Markets** are held in Augsburg, Munich, Heidelberg, Hamburg, Nürnberg, Lübeck, Freiburg, Berlin, Essen, and numerous other cities and smaller towns.

Grand Slam Cup, in Munich, is the world's richest tennis tournament.

JANUARY➤ **New Year International Ski Jumping,** among other winter-sports competitions, occurs at Garmisch-Partenkirchen.

Fasching season. The Rhineland is Germany's capital of Carnival events, including proclamations of Carnival princes, street fairs, parades, masked balls, and more. Some of the main Carnival cities are Koblenz, Köln, Mainz, Bonn, and Düsseldorf, although there's also plenty of activity in Munich and in smaller cities

and towns throughout southern Germany. Festivities always run through February, finishing on Fasching Dienstag (Shrove Tuesday or Mardi Gras).

International Green Week Agricultural Fair is held in Berlin.

Max Ophüls Film Festival, in Saarbrücken, is one of Germany's smallest but most provocative film festivals.

FEBRUARY➤ **Black Forest Ski Marathon** is a 60-kilometer (37-mile) ski race in Schonach-Hinterzarten.

Frankfurt International Fair is a major consumer-goods trade fair.

International Clock, Watch, Jewelry, Gems, and Silverware Trade Fair is held in Munich.

International Filmfestspiele is one of Europe's leading film festival, held in Berlin.

International Toy Fair, with models, hobbies, and handicrafts, takes place in Nürnberg.

Handel Music Festival comes to Karlsruhe.

SPRING

MARCH➤ **ITB,** one of Europe's largest international tourism fairs, takes place in Berlin.

International Easter Egg Fair takes place in Köln.

Leipzig Trade Fair attracts businesspeople from throughout Europe.

Munich Fashion Week is a popular trade fair of the latest fashions.

Spring Fairs. In such towns as Erfurt, Münster, Hamburg, Nürnberg, Stuttgart, and Augsburg, festivities ring in the spring season.

APRIL➤ **Frankfurt International Art Fair.**

Mannheim May Fair is a traditional spring fair with flower floats and parades.

Munich Ballet Days.

Schwetzinger Festspiele (orchestral concerts, opera, and ballet) at the Schwetzingen Schloss starts in April and continues until June.

Stuttgart Jazz Festival.

Walpurgis festivals. Towns in the Harz Mountains celebrate this, the night before May Day.

MAY➤ **Dresden Musikfestspiele** (orchestral concerts and opera), at the Semper Opera House and some of the city's palaces, starts in late May and runs into June.

Hamburg Summer is a whole season of festivals, concerts, plays, and exhibitions; events runs through October.

Folk, jazz, rock, and pop music are featured on weekends of entertainment in Köln's Rheinpark.

Four Castles Illumination presents fireworks on the heights of Neckarsteinach.

German Open Tennis Tournament takes place in Hamburg.

Hamburg Ballet Festival, with the Hamburg State Opera company.

International May Festival brings a month of opera, ballet, and theater performances to Wiesbaden.

International Mime Festival, in Stuttgart, attracts some of the best in the world.

International Jazz Festival takes place in Nürnberg.

Mozart's Heritage, in Dresden, celebrates the composer with opera, symphony, and chamber music concerts.

Red Wine Festival is held at Assmannshausen near Rüdesheim.

SUMMER

EARLY JUNE–AUGUST➣ **Castle Concerts** and musical events are held in Munich's Residenz and Nymphenburg Palace.

Castle Illuminations, with spectacular fireworks, are presented in Heidelberg.

Festival of the Arts, with theater and ballet performances, takes place in Weimar.

Franco-German Folk Festival is held in Berlin.

Frankfurt Craft Week.

Frankfurt Summertime Festival features outdoor activities throughout the city.

Händel Festival is celebrated in Halle.

International Theater Festival takes place in Freiburg.

Kiel Week is an international sailing regatta in Kiel.

Kuntsfest Weimar is a monthlong series of concerts held in Weimar.

Mosel Wine Week celebrations take place in Cochem.

Munich Film Festival.

Music Days highlight Leipzig's cultural calendar.

Nymphenburg Summer Festival, with concerts at Nymphenburg Palace, is held in Munich.

Weilburg Castle Concerts.

Würzburg Mozart Festival is held in several Würzburg locations.

JULY➣ **Bach Festival,** in Berlin, pays homage to one of Germany's greatest composers.

Folk Festivals. Outdoor festivities are held in Krov, Wald-Michelbach, Waldshut-Tiengen, Würzburg, Geisenheim, Speyer, Lübeck, Karlsruhe, Düsseldorf, Oestrich-Winkel, and Paderhorn.

German-American Folk Festival is Berlin's celebration of two cultures.

International Weissenhof Tennis Tournament for the Mercedes Cup is played in Stuttgart.

Kulmbach Beer Festival.

Old Town Festival includes castle illuminations in Neckarsteinach.

Opera Festival is Munich's major operatic affair.

Theater der Welt Festival takes place in Essen.

AUGUST➣ **Bad Hersfeld Festival** of opera is performed amid monastery ruins.

BMW Golf International takes place at the Eschenried course near Munich.

Castle Festival features open-air theater presentations at the castle in Heidelberg.

Grand Baden-Baden Week highlights international horse racing at Iffezheim in Baden-Baden.

Partenkirchen Festival Week is held in Garmisch-Partenkirchen.

Rhine in Flames is Germany's oldest and largest fireworks display.

Richard Wagner Festival is a major musical event in Bayreuth.

Stuttgart European Music Festival.

Wine festivals break out throughout the Rhineland.

AUTUMN

SEPTEMBER➣ **Berlin Festival Weeks** feature classical music concerts all month long.

Berlin International Marathon.

Bonn's International Beethoven Festival begins in mid-September and continues into October.

Eltville Summer Festival, at Schloss Reinhartshausen, offers fine wine and music.

Leipzig Trade Fair again draws commercial interests to that city.

Oktoberfest (late Sept.–early Oct.), in Munich, attracts millions of visitors from throughout Germany, Europe, and abroad.

OCTOBER➣ **Art and Antiques Fair** happens in Munich.

Bremen Freimarkt is a centuries-old folk festival and procession in Bremen; it's the largest in northern Germany.

Frankfurt Book Fair is a famous annual literary event.

NOVEMBER➤ **Antiques Fair** is held in Berlin.

Art Cologne, held in Köln, is a festival of modern art.

St. Martin's Festival, with children's lantern processions, is celebrated throughout the Rhineland and Bavaria.

Six-Day Cycle Race takes place in Munich.

Forum Vini is Munich's annual wine bash in a beer hall.

2 Munich

Chic and cosmopolitan, carefree and kitschy. As Bavaria's capital and one of Germany's biggest cities, Munich has more than its share of great museums, architectural treasures, historic sites, and world-class shops, restaurants, and hotels. The same could be said of its abundance of lederhosen and oompah bands. But it's the overall feeling of Gemütlichkeit *that makes the city so special—an open-air market here, a park there, and beer halls everywhere.*

MUNICH—München to the Germans—third-largest city in the Federal Republic and capital of the Free State of Bavaria, is the single most popular tourist destination for Germans. This one statistic attests to the enduring appeal of what by any standard is a supremely likable city. Munich is kitsch and class, vulgarity and elegance. It's a city of ravishing rococo and smoky beer cellars, of soaring Gothic and sparkling shops, of pale stucco buildings and space-age factories, of millionaires and lederhosen-clad farmers.

Germany's favorite city is a place with extraordinary ambience and a vibrant lifestyle all its own, in a splendid setting within view—on a clear day—of the towering Alps.

Munich belongs to the relaxed and sunny south. Call it Germany with a southern exposure—although it may be an exaggeration to claim, as some Bavarians do, that Munich is the only Italian city north of the Alps.

Still, there's no mistaking the carefree spirit that infuses the city, and its easygoing approach to life, liberty, and the pursuit of happiness, Bavarian style. The Bavarians refer to this positively un-Teutonic joie de vivre as *Gemütlichkeit,* loosely translated as conviviality.

It may be too easy to point to the abundance of beer that flows through the city and to its numerous beer restaurants, beer cellars, and beer gardens as the most obvious manifestations of this take-life-as-it-comes attitude. Certainly it's hard not to feel something approaching awe at the realization that Munich University has a beer faculty.

What makes Munich so special? How can its secret be explained? Is it that Munich, despite a population in excess of 1.3 million, retains something of a small-town, almost villagelike, atmosphere? Is it in the variety of buildings that dot its center, giving the city both a Baroque grandeur and the semblance of a toy town.

One explanation is the flair for the fanciful that is deeply rooted in Bavarian culture. And no historical figure better personifies this tradition than Ludwig II, one of the last of the Wittelsbachs, the royal dynasty that for almost 750 years ruled over Munich and southern Germany, until the monarchy was forced to abdicate in 1918.

While Bismarck was striving from his Berlin power base to create a modern unified Germany, "Mad" Ludwig—also nicknamed the "Dream King"—was almost bankrupting the state's treasury by building a succession of fairy-tale castles and remote summer retreats in the mountains and countryside.

Munich bills itself as *Die Weltstadt mit Herz* (the cosmopolitan city with heart), which it most assuredly is. A survey suggests that most Germans would prefer to live in Munich than where they currently reside, even though it is probably the most expensive place in reunited Germany.

This is not to suggest that all Germans subscribe to the "I Love Munich" concept. Certain buttoned-up types—in Hamburg or Düsseldorf, for example—might look down their imperious noses at Munich as just a mite crass and somewhat tacky, and Bavarians as only a few rungs up from the barbarians. So be it.

Munich is obviously Germany's good-time city, its image indelibly tied to a series of splashy celebrations that have spread the city's fame far and wide. Mention of Munich invariably triggers thoughts of the colorful carnival season known as *Fasching* and the equally gaudy spectacle of *Oktoberfest*, the 16-day beer festival. The city has become synonymous with beer, *Wurst* (sausage), and Gemütlichkeit. This triad comes close to the essence of the Munich experience.

Its stock image is the cavernous beer hall (such as the world-famous Hofbräuhaus) filled with the deafening echo of a brass oompah band and rows of swaying, burly Bavarians in lederhosen being served by frumpy Fraus in flaring dirndl dresses. Every day in different parts of the city, you'll find scenes like this. But there are also many Müncheners who never step inside a beer hall, who never go near Oktoberfest. They belong to the *other* Munich: a city of charm, refinement, and sophistication, represented by two of the world's most important art galleries and a noted opera house; a city of expensive elegance, where high-fashion shops seem in competition to put the highest price tags on their wares; a city of five-star nouvelle cuisine.

Endowed with vast, green tracts of parks, gardens, and forests; grand boulevards set with remarkable edifices; fountains and statuaries; and a river spanned by graceful bridges, Munich is easily Germany's most beautiful and interesting city. If the traveler could visit only one city in Germany, this should be it—no question.

If you factor in the city's dramatic change over the past decade, a traveler who has not visited for awhile might find a whole new Munich has evolved in the interim. For, quietly and without fanfare, Munich has taken its place as the high-tech capital of Germany, developing into the number one postindustrial-age center in the country and one of the most important cities in Europe. The concentration of electronics and computer firms—Siemens, IBM, Apple, and the like—in and around the city has turned it into the Silicon Valley of Germany.

Pleasures and Pastimes

Beer and Beer Gardens
Other German cities may maintain they brew better and stronger beer, but the Münchner just laughs and raises his liter mug in a generous toast to such risible rivalry. Munich doesn't just maintain its beer is best—it *knows* it is. One of the great pleasures of visiting Munich is this immersion in a beer tradition both serious and frivolous. Drink a couple of steins of Munich brew and you feel as if the city belongs to you.

Munich has more than 100 beer gardens, ranging from huge establishments that seat several hundred guests to small terraces tucked behind neighborhood pubs and taverns. Beer gardens are such an integral part of Munich life that a council proposal to cut down their hours provoked a storm of protest in 1995, culminating in one of the largest mass demonstrations in the city's history. They open whenever the thermometer creeps above 10°C (42°F) or so and when the sun filters through the chestnut trees that are a necessary part of the beer-garden scenery. Most—but not all—allow you to bring along your own food, and if you do, try not to bring something so foreign as pizza or a burger from McDonalds.

Dining
Judged from reviews in Germany's restaurant guides and magazines, Munich has the most first-rate restaurants in the country. It certainly has the widest range of eating establishments in Germany and more trattorias than many Italian cities.

Old Munich restaurants, called *Gaststätten*, feature *gutbürgerliche Küche*, loosely translated as good regional fare, and include brewery restaurants, beer halls, beer gardens, rustic cellar establishments, and *Weinstuben* (wine houses).

Munich is also a great place for snacks. The city's pre-McDonald's-type fast food is a centuries-old tradition. A tempting array of delectables is available almost anytime day or night; knowing the various Bavarian names will help.

The generic term for Munich snacks is *Schmankerl*. And Schmankerl are served at *Brotzeit,* literally translated as "bread time": a snack break, or what the English might call elevenses. According to a saying, *"Brotzeit ist die schönste Zeit"* (snack time is the best time).

In the morning in Munich, one eats *Weisswurst,* a tender minced-veal sausage—made fresh daily, steamed, and served with sweet mustard, a crisp roll or a pretzel, and *Weissbier* (wheat beer). This white sausage is not to everyone's taste, but it is certainly worth trying. As legend has it, this sausage was invented in 1857 by a butcher who had a hangover and mixed the wrong ingredients. A plaque on a wall in Marienplatz marks where the "mistake" was made. It is claimed the genuine article is available only in and around Munich and served only between midnight and noon.

Another favorite Bavarian specialty is *Leberkäs*—literally "liver cheese," although neither liver nor cheese is involved in its construction. It is a spicy meat loaf baked to a crusty turn each morning and served in succulent slabs throughout the day. A *Leberkäs Semmel*—a wedge of the meat loaf between two halves of a crispy bread roll smeared with a bittersweet mustard—is the favorite Munich on-the-hoof snack.

After that comes the repertoire of sausages indigenous to Bavaria, including types from Regensburg and Nürnberg.

More substantial repasts include *Tellerfleisch,* boiled beef with freshly grated horseradish and boiled potatoes on the side, served on wooden plates. (There is a similar dish called *Tafelspitz*.)

Among roasts, *Sauerbraten* (beef) and *Schweinsbraten* (pork) are accompanied by dumplings and red cabbage or sauerkraut.

Haxn ham hocks roasted until they're crisp on the outside, juicy on the inside. They are served with sauerkraut and potato puree.

You'll also find soups, salads, fish and fowl, cutlets, game in season, casseroles, hearty stews, desserts, and what may well be the greatest variety and the highest quality of baked goods in Europe, including pretzels. In particular, seek out a *Käsestange*—a crispy long bread roll coated in baked cheese. No one need ever go hungry or thirsty in Munich.

Music and Opera
Munich and music complement each other marvelously. The city has two world-renowned orchestras, the Bavarian State Opera Company, wonderful choral ensembles, two opera houses, a rococo jewel of a court theater, and a modern Philharmonic concert hall of superb proportions and acoustics—and that's just for starters.

Shopping
Munich has three of Germany's most exclusive shopping streets. At the other end of the scale, its flea market at the old Riem Airport is Europe's biggest. In between are department stores, where acute German-style competition assures reasonable prices and often produces outstanding bargains. The Christmas markets, which spring up all over the city as November slides into December, draw from backroom-studio artisans and artists with wares of outstanding beauty and orig-

inality. Collect their business cards—in the summer you're sure to want to order another of those little gold baubles that were on sale in December.

EXPLORING MUNICH

Munich is one of Europe's wealthiest cities—and it shows. Here everything is extremely upscale and up-to-date. At times the aura of affluence may be all but overpowering. But that's what Munich is all about these days and nights: a new city superimposed on the old; conspicuous consumption on a scale we can hardly imagine as a way of life; a fresh patina of glitter along with the traditional rustic charms. Such are the dynamics and duality of this fascinating metropolis that remains a joy to explore and get to know.

Numbers in the text correspond to numbers in the margin and on the Munich map.

Great Itineraries

IF YOU HAVE 2 OR 3 DAYS

Begin your stay with a visit to the tourist information office at the main railway station, the **Hauptbahnhof,** and make for one of the cafés of the nearby pedestrian shopping zone to get your bearings. Plan an eastward course across (or rather under) **Karlsplatz** and into Neuhauserstrasse and Kaufingerstrasse, plunging into the shopping crowds in this busy center of Munich commerce. You can escape the crowds whenever you want by seeking out any one of the three churches that punctuate the route: the **Bürgersaal,** the **Michaelskirche,** or the **Frauenkirche,** Munich's soaring Gothic cathedral. Try to arrive in the city's central square, **Marienplatz,** in time for the 11 AM performance of the Glockenspiel in the tower of the neo-Gothic City Hall. Proceed to the city market, the **Viktualienmarkt,** for lunch, and then head a few blocks north for an afternoon visit to the **Residenz** the rambling palace of the Wittelsbach rulers. End your first day with coffee at Munich's oldest café, the Cafe Annast, on Odeonsplatz, or an early evening cocktail at nearby Käfer's, also on Odeonsplatz, where you might just be tempted to spend the evening. Set aside days two and three for visits to Munich's leading museums, in the Maxvorstadt District: the **Alte Pinakothek** and the **Neue Pinakothek,** and the **Glyptothek** and **Antikensammlungen** on expansive **Königsplatz.** Also find time for a stroll east to the **Englischer Garten,** Munich's city park, for an outdoor lunch or an evening meal at one of its beer gardens or, in inclement weather, in the Seehaus on the northern shore of the Kleinhesselohersee Lake.

IF YOU HAVE 4 OR MORE DAYS

For the first two days follow the itinerary described above. On the third day venture out to suburban Nymphenburg for a visit to the **Schloss Nymphenburg,** which served as the summer residence of the Wittelsbach rulers. Allow up to a whole day to view the palace buildings, its museums, and to stroll through its lovely park, breaking for lunch at the restaurant of the Botanical Gardens. Allow one full day, too, to tour the **Olympiapark** and ride to the top of the Olympic Tower for the best view you'll get of Munich and the surrounding countryside as far as the Alps. And if there is still a day left in your Munich itinerary, choose between a walk along the surprisingly quiet city banks of the Isar River, its rapid waters a translucent green from their mountain sources, or a visit to two of Munich's most delightful art museums, the **Villa Stuck** and the **Städtische Galerie im Lenbachhaus.**

24

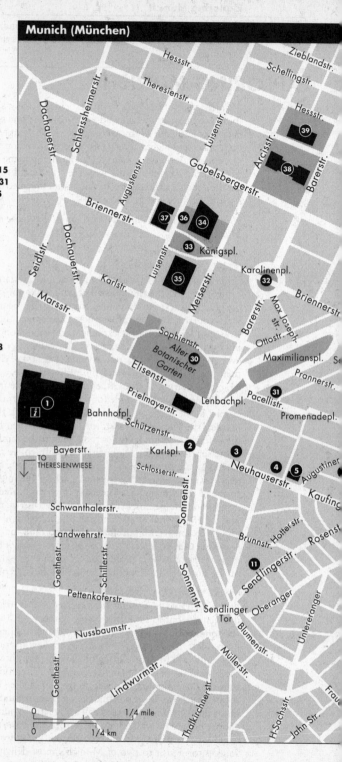

Munich (München)

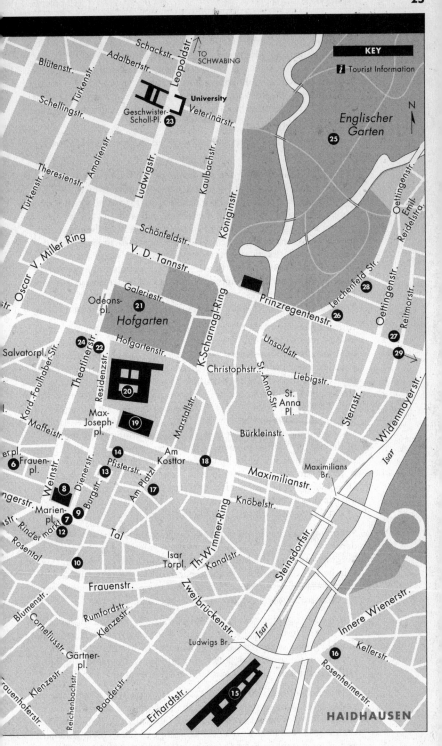

Schackstr.

Leopoldstr.

↑ TO
SCHWABING

Adalbertstr.

Blütenstr.

Türkenstr.

Schellingstr.

University

Geschwister-
Scholl-Pl. **23**

Veterinärstr.

Theresienstr.

Amalienstr.

Ludwigstr.

Kaulbachstr.

Türkenstr.

Schönfeldstr.

Königinstr.

KEY

ℹ Tourist Information

*Englischer
Garten*

25

Oettingenstr.

Emil-
Reidelstra.

Oscar V. Miller Ring

V. D. Tannstr.

Galeriestr.

Odeons-
pl. **21**

Hofgarten

Salvatorpl.-Str. **24** **22**

Kard.-Faulhaber-Str.

Theatinerstr.

Residenzstr.

Hofgartenstr.

K-Scharnagl-Ring

Prinzregentenstr.

Lerchenfeld Str.

28

26

Oettingenstr.

Reitmorstr.

27

29→

Unsoldstr.

Liebigstr.

Sternstr.

Widenmayerstr.

Christophstr.

St.-Anna-Str.

St.
Anna
Pl.

Maffeistr.

Max-
Joseph-
pl. **19**

20

Marstallstr.

Bürkleinstr.

Maximilianstr.

Maximilians
Br.

Isar

6 Frauen-
pl.

14

Dienerstr.

13

Pfisterstr.

Am platzl.

Am Kosttor

18

8

Weinstr.

Burgstr.

17

Knöbelstr.

7 Marien-
pl. **9**

12

Tal

Steinsdorfstr.

ngerstr.

Rindermarkt

Rosental

10

Isar
Torpl.

Th.-Wimmer-Ring

Kanalstr.

Frauenstr.

Zweibrückenstr.

Isar

Innere Wienerstr.

Blumenstr.

Rumfordstr.

Klenzestr.

Cornelliusstr.

Gärtner-
pl.

Ludwigs Br.

16

Kellerstr.

Klenzestr.

Reichenbachstr.

Baaderstr.

Erhardtstr.

15

Rosenheimerstr.

rauenhoferstr.

HAIDHAUSEN

The City Center

Munich is unique among German cities because it has no identifiable, homogeneous Old Town center. The historic heart of the city is a quiet courtyard unknown to most tourists, while clusters of centuries-old buildings that belong to Munich's origins are often separated by postwar developments of sometimes singular ugliness. The outer perimeter of this tour is defined more by a visitor's stamina than by ancient city walls.

A Good Walk

Numbers in the text correspond to numbers in the margin and on the Munich map.

Begin your walk through the city center at the **Hauptbahnhof** ①, the main train station and site of the city tourist office, which is on the corner of Bayerstrasse. Pick up a detailed city map here. Cross Bahnhofplatz, the square in front of the station, and walk toward Schützenstrasse, which marks the start of Munich's pedestrian shopping mall, the Fussgängerzone, 2 kilometers (1½ miles) of traffic-free streets. Running virtually the length of Schützenstrasse is Munich's largest department store, **Hertie.** At the end of the street you descend via the pedestrian underpass into another shopping empire, a vast underground complex of boutiques and cafés. Above you is the busy traffic intersection, **Karlsplatz** ②, known locally as Stachus, with a popular fountain area.

Ahead stands one of the city's oldest gates, the **Karlstor,** first mentioned in local records in 1302. Beyond it lies Munich's main shopping thoroughfare, **Neuhauserstrasse** and its extension, **Kaufingerstrasse.** On your left as you enter Neuhauserstrasse is another attractive Munich fountain: a jovial, late-19th-century figure of Bacchus. Neuhauserstrasse and Kaufingerstrasse are a jumble of ancient and modern buildings. This part of town was bombed almost to extinction during World War II and has been extensively rebuilt. Great efforts were made to ensure that the designs of these new buildings harmonized with the rest of the old city, although some of the newer structures are little more than functional. Still, even though this may not be an architectural high point of the city, there are at least some redeeming features. **Haus Oberpollinger,** on Neuhauestrasse, is one; it's a department store hiding behind an imposing 19th-century facade. Notice the weather vanes of old merchant ships on its high-gabled roof.

Shopping, however, is not the only attraction on these streets. Worldly department stores rub shoulders with two remarkable churches: the **Bürgersaal** ③ and the **Michaelskirche** ④. The 16th-century Michaelskirche was the first Renaissance church of this size in southern Germany. Its fanciful Renaissance facade contrasts finely with the surprisingly more severe Baroque exterior of the Bürgersaal.

The massive building next to Michaelskirche was once one of Munich's oldest churches, built during the late 13th century for Benedictine monks. It was secularized during the early 19th century, served as a warehouse for some years, and today houses the **Deutsches Jagd-und Fischereimuseum** (German Museum of Hunting and Fishing) ⑤.

Turn left here onto Augustinerstrasse and you will soon arrive in Frauenplatz, a quiet square with a shallow, sunken fountain. Towering over it is the **Frauenkirche** (Church of Our Lady) ⑥, Munich's cathedral, whose twin domes are at the same time the city's main landmark and its main symbol. From the cathedral follow any of the alleys heading east, and you'll reach the very heart of Munich, **Marienplatz** ⑦, which is surrounded by stores and dining spots. Marienplatz is dominated by the 19th-century **Neues Rathaus** (New Town Hall) ⑧, while the **Altes**

Rathaus (Old Town Hall) ⑨, a medieval building of assured charm, sits modestly, as if forgotten, in a corner of the square. Its great hall—destroyed in 1944 but now fully restored—was the work of architect Jörg von Halspach.

Hungry? Thirsty? Help is only a few steps away. From the Altes Rathaus cross the street, passing the **Heiliggeistkirche**, an early Munich church with a rococo interior added between 1724 and 1730. Heiliggeiststrasse brings you to the jumble of market stalls known as the **Viktualienmarkt** ⑩, the city's open-air food market.

From the market follow Rosental into **Sendlingerstrasse,** one of the city's most interesting shopping streets, and head left toward **Sendlinger Tor,** a finely restored medieval brick gate. On your right as you head down Sendlingerstrasse is the remarkable 18th-century Church of St. Johann Nepomuk, known as the **Asamkirche** ⑪ because of the two Asam brothers, Cosmas Damian and Egid Quirin, who built it. The exterior fits so snugly into the street's housefronts (the Asam brothers lived next door) that you might easily overlook the church as you pass; yet the raw rock foundation of the facade, with its gigantic pilasters, announces the presence of something unusual.

From the Asamkirche return down Sendlingerstrasse toward the city center and turn right into the Rindermarkt (the former cattle market), and you'll be beneath the soaring tower of **Peterskirche** ⑫, or Alter Peter (Old Peter), the city's oldest and best-loved parish church. From Peterskirche reenter Marienplatz and pass in front of the Altes Rathaus once again to step into Burgstrasse. You'll soon find yourself in the quiet, airy **Alter Hof** ⑬, the inner courtyard of the original palace of the Wittelsbach rulers of Bavaria.

A short distance beyond the northern archway of the Alter Hof, on the right-hand side of Pfisterstrasse, stands the former royal mint, the **Münze** ⑭.

If you'd like to visit some museums, extend your walk by a further 10 minutes, returning down Burgstrasse to broad Tal, once an important trading route that entered Munich at the Isartor, now beautifully restored to its original medieval appearance. Continue across Isartorplatz, into Zweibrückenstrasse, and you'll come to the Isar River. There on a river island is the massive bulk of the **Deutsches Museum** (German Museum of Science and Technology) ⑮, with a gigantic thermometer and barometer on its tower showing the way to the main entrance. Budding scientists and young dreamers alike will be delighted by its extensive collections and its many activities that provide buttons to push and cranks to turn.

On a rainy day you can pack your swimwear and splash around in the setting of the **Müllersches Volksbad,** a restored Jugendstil indoor swimming pool at Ludwigsbrücke, opposite the Deutsches Museum. On a sunny day join the locals for ice cream and a stroll along the Isar River, where the more daring sunbathe nude on pebble islands. Or walk up the hill from the Volksbad and see what art exhibition or avant-garde film (often in English) is showing at the modern, redbrick **Gasteig Culture Center** ⑯.

TIMING

Set aside at least a whole morning for this walk, arranging to be in Marienplatz when the Glockenspiel plays at 11 or noon. The churches along the route will each demand at least a half hour of your time. You'll also be tempted to look into one or more of the department stores in the pedestrian shopping zone, so if it's noon by the time you get to

Marienplatz, step into the nearby Viktualienmarkt for a stand-up lunch at any of the many stalls. Prepare for big crowds in Marienplatz when the Glockenspiel (chiming clock) plays, and try to avoid shopping between noon and 2, when German workers grab a lunch break and make for the department stores. If hunting, shooting, and fishing are your thing, you'll spend at least two hours in the Deutsches Jagd- und Fischereimuseum.

Sights to See

Numbers in the margin correspond to points of interest on the Munich map.

⑬ Alter Hof. This palace was the original residence of the Wittelsbach rulers of Bavaria, who held court starting in 1253. The palace now serves as local government offices. Something of the medieval flavor of those times has survived in the Alter Hof's quiet courtyard in the otherwise busy downtown area. Don't pass through without turning to admire the medieval oriel (bay window) that hides modestly on the south wall, just around the corner as you enter the courtyard.

⑨ Altes Rathaus. This was Munich's first city hall, built in 1474 and restored after wartime bomb damage. Its fine assembly hall is used for official receptions. The tower provides a satisfyingly atmospheric setting for a little toy museum, accessible via a winding staircase. It includes several exhibits from the United States. ⊠ *Marienpl.* ▣ *DM 4.* ☉ *Daily 10–5:30.*

★ ⑪ Asamkirche. Munich's most unusual church has a suitably extraordinary entrance, framed by raw rock foundations. The insignificant church door, crammed between its craggy shoulders, gives little idea of the splendor within. Before you enter, have a look above the doorway at the statue of St. Nepomuk, a 14th-century Bohemian monk who drowned in the Danube; you'll see that angels are conducting him to heaven from a rocky riverbank. Inside you'll discover a prime example of true southern German, late-Baroque architecture. Red stucco and rosy marble cover the walls; there is an explosion of frescoes, statuaries, and gilding. The little church overwhelms with its opulence and lavish detailing—take a look at the gilt skeletons in the little atrium—and creates a powerfully mystical atmosphere. This is a vision of paradise on earth that those more accustomed to the gaunt Gothic cathedrals of northern Europe may find disconcerting. It is a fine example, though, of the Bavarian taste for ornament and, possibly, overkill. Is it vulgar or a great work of architecture? You be the judge. ⊠ *Sendlingerstr.*

OFF THE
BEATEN PATH

FRANZISKANERKLOSTERKIRCHE ST. ANNA – This striking example of the two Asam brothers' work may be found in the city district of Lehel. Though less opulently decorated than the Asamkirche, this small Franciscan monastery church, consecrated in 1737, impresses with its sense of movement and its heroic scale. It was largely rebuilt after wartime bomb damage. The ceiling fresco by Cosmas Damian Asam was removed before the World War II and, after restoration, now glows in all its original vivid joyfulness. The ornate altar was also designed by the Asam brothers. ⊠ *St.-Anna-Str.,* ☎ *089/212–1820. You can get to Lehel on Tram 20 or U-bahn 5 or 6, from the city center.*

❸ Bürgersaal. Beneath the modest roof of this unassuming church are two contrasting levels. The Oberkiche upper level—the church proper—consists of a richly decorated Baroque oratory. Its elaborate stucco foliage and paintings of Bavarian places of pilgrimage project a distinctly different ambience from that of the Unterkirche lower level, reached by descending a double staircase. This gloomy, cryptlike chamber contains the tomb of Rupert Mayer, a famous Jesuit priest renowned for his energetic and outspoken opposition to the Nazis. ✉ *Neuhauserstr., 14,* ☎ *089/223–884.* ☉ *Oberkirche Mon.–Sat. 11 AM–1 PM, Sun. 9 AM–12:30 PM; Unterkirche Mon.–Sat. 6:30 AM–7 PM, Sun. 7–7.*

❺ Deutsches Jagd-und Fischereimuseum (German Museum of Hunting and Fishing). Lovers of the thrill of the chase will be fascinated by this museum. It contains the world's largest collection of fishhooks, some 500 stuffed animals (including a 6½-foot-tall North American grizzly bear), a 12,000-year-old skeleton of an Irish deer, and valuable collection of hunting weapons. ✉ *Neuhauserstr. 2,* ☎ *089/220522.* ▧ *DM 5.* ☉ *Tues., Wed., Fri.–Sun. 9:30–5; Mon. and Thurs. 9:30–9.*

★ ✋ ⓯ Deutsches Museum (German Museum of Science and Technology). Founded in 1903 and housed in its present monumental building since 1925, this is one of the most stimulating and innovative science museums in Europe. Nineteen kilometers (12 miles) of corridors, six floors of exhibits, and 30 departments make up the immense collections. Set aside a full day if you plan to do justice to the entire museum. The technically most advanced planetarium in Europe was recently opened within this huge museum complex. The planetarium has up to six shows daily, including a Laser Magic display. The old Deutsches Museum concert hall now houses an IMAX theater—a wraparound screen six stories high showing documentary films in which spectators feel as if they're part of the action. There are up to 14 performances daily. ✉ *Museumsinsel 1,* ☎ *089/21791, 089/2112–5180 to reserve tickets at both the planetarium and the IMAX cinema.* ▧ *Museum DM 8, planetarium DM 10.90–DM 24.90; IMAX DM 10.90.* ☉ *Daily 9–5.*

★ ❻ Frauenkirche (Church of Our Lady). Munich's cathedral or Dom is a distinctive late-Gothic brick structure with two enormous towers, which are Munich's main landmark and city symbol. Each is more than 300 feet high, and both are capped by very un-Gothic onion-shape domes. The towers have become the symbol of Munich's skyline—some say because they look like overflowing beer mugs.

The main body of the cathedral was completed in 20 years—a record time in those days. The towers were added, almost as an afterthought, between 1524 and 1525. Jörg von Polling, the Frauenkirche's original architect, is buried within the walls of the cathedral. The building suffered severe damage during the Allied bombing of Munich and was lovingly restored from 1947 to 1957. Inside, the church combines most of von Polling's original features with a stark, clean modernity and simplicity of line, emphasized by slender, white octagonal pillars that sweep up through the nave to the yellow-traced ceiling far above. As you enter the church, look on the stone floor for the dark imprint of a large footstep—the *Teufelstritt* (Devil's footprint). According to local lore, the Devil challenged von Polling to build a nave without windows. Von Polling wagered his soul and accepted the challenge, building a cathedral that is flooded with light from 66-foot-high windows that are invisible to anyone standing at the point marked by the Teufelstritt. The cathedral houses an elaborate, 15th-century black-marble memorial to Emperor Ludwig the Bavarian, guarded by four 16th-century armored knights.

A splendid view of the city is yours from an observation platform high in one of the towers. But beware—you must climb 86 steps to reach the tower elevator! ✉ *Frauenpl.,* ☎ *089/290–0820.* ▧ *Tower DM 4. Tower elevator operates Apr.–Oct., Mon.–Sat. 10–5.*

⑯ **Gasteig Culture Center.** This striking post-modern brick cultural complex for music, theater, and film has an open-plan interior and a maze of interior courtyards and plazas, sitting high above the Isar River. The center has two theaters, where plays in English are occasionally performed. ⌧ *Rosenheimerstr. 5,* ☎ *089/5481–8181.*

❶ **Hauptbahnhof** (Main Railway Station). Tourists often start their exploration here because it contains the city tourist office, with maps and helpful information on events around town. ⌧ *Bayerstr.*

OFF THE
BEATEN PATH

STREETCAR 19 – For the cheapest sight-seeing tour on wheels of the city center, board this streetcar outside the main train station on Bahnhofplatz and make the 15-minute journey to Max Weber Platz. Explore the streets around the square, part of the old bohemian residential area of Haidhausen (with some of the city's best bars and restaurants), and then return by a different route on Streetcar 18 to Karlsplatz.

THERESIENWIESE – The site of Munich's annual beer festival—the infamous Oktoberfest—is only a 10-minute walk from the main train station; or by subway it is one stop on the U–4 or U–5. The Theresienwiese is an enormous exhibition ground, named after a young woman whose engagement party gave rise to the Oktoberfest. In 1810 the party celebrated the betrothal of Princess Therese von Sachsen-Hildburghausen to the Bavarian crown prince Ludwig, later Ludwig I. It was such a success, attended by nearly the entire population of Munich, that it became an annual affair. Beer was served then as now, but what began as a night out for the locals has become a 16-day international bonanza at the end of September and the beginning of October, attracting more than 6 million people each year (it qualifies as the *Oktoberfest* by ending the first Sunday in October). In enormous wooden pavilions that heave and pulsate to the combined racket of brass bands, drinking songs, and thousands of dry throats demanding more, the hordes knock back around 5 million liters of beer.

Overlooking the Theresienwiese is a 19th-century hall of fame—one of the last works of Ludwig I—and a monumental bronze statue of the maiden **Bavaria**, more than 100 feet high. The statue is hollow, and 130 steps take you up into the braided head for a view of Munich through Bavaria's eyes.

❷ **Karlsplatz.** Known locally as Stachus, this busy intersection has one of Munich's most popular fountains, a circle of water jets that act as a magnet on hot summer days for city shoppers and office workers seeking a cool corner. The semicircle of yellow-front buildings that back the fountain, with their high windows and delicate cast-iron balconies, gives the area a southern, almost Mediterranean, air.

★ ❼ **Marienplatz.** Surrounded by shops, restaurants, and cafés, this square is named after the gilded statue of the Virgin Mary that has been watching over it for more than three centuries. It was erected in 1638 at the behest of Elector Maximilian I as an act of thanksgiving for the survival of the city during the Thirty Years' War, the cataclysmic religious struggle that devastated vast regions of Germany. When the statue, which stands on a marble column, was taken down to be cleaned for a eucharistic world congress in 1960, workmen found a small casket in the base containing a splinter of wood said to be from the cross of Christ. ⌧ *Bordered by Kaufingerstr., Rosenstr., Weinstr., and Dienerstr.*

❹ **Michaelskirche.** A curious story explains why this sturdy Renaissance church has no tower. Seven years after the start of construction the principal tower collapsed. Its patron, pious Duke Wilhelm V, regarded the disaster as a heavenly sign that the church wasn't big enough, so he ordered a change in the plans—this time without a tower. Completed seven years later, the Michaelskirche was the first Renaissance church of this size in southern Germany. The duke is buried in the crypt, along with 40 members of Bavaria's famous Wittelsbach family (the ruling dynasty for seven centuries), including the eccentric king Ludwig II. A severe neoclassical monument in the north transept contains the tomb of Napoléon's stepson, Eugene de Beauharnais, who married one of the daughters of Bavaria's King Maximilian I and died in Munich in 1824. You'll find the plain white stucco interior of the church and its slightly barnlike atmosphere soothingly simple after the lavish decoration of the nearby Bürgarsaal. ✉ *Neuhauserstr. 6,* ☎ *089/551–99257.* 🎫 *DM 5.* ⊗ *Guided tours of church Wed. at 2.*

NEED A BREAK?   Across the road from the Michaelskirche beckons the *Jugendstil* (art nouveau) facade of the **Augustiner Gaststätte** (✉ Neuhauserstr. 27, ☎ 089/551–99257). Within its late-19th-century interior, beer from Munich's oldest brewery is served. Even if you don't want a drink, look inside for more stunning examples of Bavarian Jugendstil.

---

⑭ **Münze.** Originally the royal stables, the Münze (mint) was created by court architect Wilhelm Egkl between 1563 and 1567 and now serves as an office building. A stern neoclassical facade emblazoned with gold was added in 1809; the interior courtyard retains has Renaissance-style arches. ✉ *Pfisterstr. 4. Courtyard* 🎫 *Free.* ⊗ *Mon.–Thurs., 8–4, Fri. 8–2.*

❽ **Neues Rathaus.** Munich's present city hall was built between 1867 and 1908 in the fussy, turreted, neo-Gothic style so beloved by King Ludwig II. Architectural historians are divided over its merits, though its dramatic scale and lavish detailing are impressive. Perhaps the most serious criticism is that the Dutch and Flemish style of the building seems out of place amid the Baroque and rococo of so much of the rest of the city. In 1904 a glockenspiel (a chiming clock with mechanical figures) was added to the tower; it plays daily at 11 AM and noon, with additional performances at 5 PM and 9 PM June–October. As chimes peal out over the square, doors flip open, and brightly colored dancers and jousting knights go through their paces. They act out two events from Munich's past: a tournament held in Marienplatz in 1568 and the *Schäfflertanz* (Dance of the Coopers), which commemorated the end of the plague of 1517. When Munich was in ruins after the war, an American soldier contributed some paint to restore the battered figures, and he was rewarded with a ride on one of the jousters' horses, high above the cheering crowds. You, too, can travel up there, by elevator, to an observation point near the top of one of the towers. On a clear day the view is spectacular. ✉ *Marienpl.,* ☎ *089/2331.* 🎫 *Tower DM 2.* ⊗ *Tower elevator operates Apr.–Oct., Mon.–Sat. 10–5.*

⑫ **Peterskirche.** Munich's oldest and smallest parish church traces its origins to the 11th century and over the years has been restored in a variety of architectural styles. Today you'll find a rich Baroque interior, with a magnificent late-Gothic high altar and aisle pillars decorated with exquisite 18th-century figures of the apostles. From the top of its 300-foot tower there's a fine view of the city. In clear weather it's well worth the climb—the view includes glimpses of the Alps to the south. Peterskirche has a Scottish priest who is glad to show English-speaking visitors around the church. ✉ *Rindermarkt.,* ☎ *089/260–4070.* 🎫 *Tower DM 2.50.* ⊗ *Weekdays 9–6, Sat. 8:30–6, Sun. 10–6.*

★ ⑩ **Viktualienmarkt.** The city's open-air food market (*Viktualien* is an old German word for food) has a wide range of produce, German and international food, Bavarian beer, and French wines, which make the area a feast for the eyes as well as the stomach. It is also the realm of the garrulous, sturdy market women, dressed in traditional country costumes, who run the stalls with dictatorial authority; one was roundly reprimanded by Munich's leading newspaper for rudely warning an American tourist not to touch the fruit!

On *Fasching Dienstag* (Shrove Tuesday), the last day of the carnival period and the day before Lent, the market women soften a little as they lead dancing and singing in the market square. There's more dancing on May Day (May 1), this time round the blue-and-white maypole. Figures adorning the pole represent the traditional crafts of the city. The characters atop several small fountains scattered about the market square represent legendary Bavarian music-hall stars, singers, and comedians.

In summer relax at a table in one of the lively beer gardens set up beneath great chestnut trees and enjoy an alfresco lunch of Bavarian sausages and sauerkraut.

Metzgereien (butcher shops) in and around the market dispense a variety of sausages and will make sandwiches either to go or to be eaten on the premises. For *Thüringer Rostbratwurstl*—a slightly spicy, long, thin sausage—or *Nürnberger Bratwurstl,* head for the Schlemmermeyer Brotzeit Standl stalls.

The market even has a champagne bar where high-tone tidbits complement the bubbly served by the glass. ⊠ *South of Marienpl.*

Royal Munich

From the relatively modest palace of the Alter Hof (☞ *above*), Munich's royal rulers expanded their quarters northward, where more space was to be found than in the jumble of narrow streets of the old quarter. The Wittelsbachs built a palace more suitable for their regal pretensions and laid out a fine garden, which was off limits at first to all but the nobility. Three avenues of regal dimension radiated outward from this new center of royal rule, and fine homes arose along them. One of them—Prinzregentstrasse—marks the southern end of Munich's huge public park, the Englischer Garten, which was also the creation of a Wittelsbach ruler.

A Good Walk
Numbers in the text correspond to numbers in the margin and on the Munich map.

A good way to start this virtually endless walk is to stoke up first with a Bavarian breakfast of white sausage, pretzels, and beer at the suitably named **Hofbräuhaus** (Royal Brewery) ⑰, perhaps Munich's best-known beer hall, on Am Platzl. Turn right from the Hofbräuhaus for the short walk along Orlandostrasse to **Maximilianstrasse** ⑱, Munich's most elegant shopping street, named after King Maximilian II, whose statue you'll see far down on the right. This wide boulevard has many grand buildings, which contain government offices and the city's ethnological museum, the **Staatliches Museum für Völkerkunde.** The **Maximilianeum,** on a rise beyond the Isar River, is an impressive mid-19th-century palace where the Bavarian state government now meets.

Across Maximilianstrasse as you enter from the Hofbräuhaus stands a handsome city palace: the **Hotel Vier Jahreszeiten,** a historic watering hole for princes, millionaires, and the expense-account jet set.

Turn left down Maximilianstrasse, away from the Maximilianeum, and you'll enter the square called Max-Joseph-Platz, dominated by the pillared portico of the 19th-century **Nationaltheater** ⑲, home of the Bavarian State Opera Company. The statue in the square's center is of Bavaria's first king, Max Joseph. Along the north side of this untidily arranged square (marred by the entrance to an underground parking lot) is the lofty and austere south wall of the **Residenz** ⑳, the royal palace of Wittelsbach rulers for more than six centuries.

Directly north of the Residenz, on Hofgartenstrasse, lies the former royal garden, the **Hofgarten** ㉑. You can be forgiven for any confusion about your whereabouts ("Can this really be Germany?") when you step from the Hofgarten onto Odeonsplatz. To your left is the 19th-century **Feldherrnhalle** ㉒, a local hall of fame modeled after a Florentine loggia.

Looking north up Ludwigstrasse, the arrow-straight avenue that ends at the Feldherrnhalle, you'll see the **Siegestor** ㉓, or victory arch, which marks the beginning of Leopoldstrasse. Completing this impressively Italianate panorama is the great yellow bulk of the former royal church of St. Kajetan, the **Theatinerkirche** ㉔, an imposing Baroque building. Its lofty towers frame a restrained facade capped by a massive dome.

Now head north up Ludwigstrasse. The first stretch of the street was designed by court architect Leo von Klenze. In much the same way that Baron Haussmann would later demolish many of the old streets and buildings in Paris, replacing them with stately boulevards, so von Klenze swept aside the small dwellings and alleys that stood here to build his great avenue. His high-windowed and formal buildings have never quite been accepted by Müncheners, and indeed there's still a sense that Ludwigstrasse is an intruder. Most visitors either love it or hate it. Von Klenze's buildings end just before Ludwigstrasse becomes Leopoldstrasse, and it is easy to see where he handed construction over to another leading architect, Friedrich von Gärtner. The severe neoclassical buildings that line southern Ludwigstrasse—including the **Bayerische Staatsbibliothek** (Bavarian State Library), the **Universität** (University) and the peculiarly Byzantine **Ludwigskirche**—fragment into the lighter styles of Leopoldstrasse. The more delicate structures are echoed by the busy street life you'll find here in summer. Once the hub of the legendary artists' district of **Schwabing,** Leopoldstrasse still throbs with life from spring to fall, exuding the atmosphere of a Mediterranean boulevard, with cafés, wine terraces, and artists' stalls. In comparison, Ludwigstrasse is inhabited by ghosts of the past.

At the south end of Leopoldstrasse, beyond the Siegestor, lies the great open quadrangle of the university, **Geschwister-Scholl-Platz,** named after brother and sister Hans and Sophie Scholl, who were executed in 1943 for leading the short-lived anti-Nazi resistance movement known as the Weisse Rose (White Rose). At its north end Leopoldstrasse leads into Schwabing itself, once Munich's Bohemian quarter but now distinctly upscale. Explore the streets of old Schwabing around Wedekindplatz to get the feel of the place. (Those in search of the Bohemian mood that once animated Schwabing should head to **Haidhausen,** on the other side of the Isar.)

Bordering the east side of Schwabing is the **Englischer Garten** (English Garden) ㉕. Five kilometers (3 miles) long and 1½ kilometers (about 1 mile) wide, it's Germany's largest city park, stretching from the Prinzregentenstrasse, the broad avenue laid out by Prince Regent Luitpold at the end of the 19th century, to the city's northern boundary, where the lush parkland is taken over by the rough embrace of open countryside. Dominating the park's southern border is one of the few examples of Hitler-era architecture still standing in Munich: the colonnaded Haus der Kunst (House of Art), home of the **Staatsgalerie Moderner Kunst**—and also of Munich's most fashionable disco, the PI.

A few 100 yards farther along Prinzregentenstrasse are two other leading museums, the **Bayerisches Nationalmuseum** (Bavarian National Museum) ㉖ and the **Schack-Galerie** ㉗, while around the first left-hand corner, on Lerchenfeldstrasse, is a museum of prehistory that brings the ancient past to life in fascinating form, the **Prähistorische Staatssammlung** ㉘.

The column you see standing triumphant on a hill at the eastern end of Prinzregentstrasse, just across the Isar River from the Schackgalerie, is Munich's well-loved **Friedensengel** (Angel of Peace). This striking gilded angel crowns a marble column in a small park overlooking the Isar River. It marks one end of Prinzregentenstrasse, the broad, arrow-straight boulevard laid out by Prince Regent Luitpold at the end of the 19th century. Just across the river, beyond the Friedensengel, is another historic home, which became a major Munich art gallery—the **Villa Stuck** ㉙, a jewel of art-nouveau fantasy.

There are innumerable walks here along the banks of the Isar River and in the nearby Englischer Garten, where you have the choice of ending your stroll with a stop at one of its three beer gardens (the Chinese Tower is the largest and most popular) or with a visit to the Seehaus, on the banks of the park's lake, the Kleinhesseloher See. Here you'll have another choice to make: a smart restaurant or a cozy bierstube.

TIMING
You'll need a day (and good walking shoes) for this stroll, which ends in the virtually endless Englischer Garten. Set aside at least two hours for a tour of the Residenz. If the weather is fine, try to return to the southern end of the Englischer Garten at dusk, when you'll be treated to an unforgettable silhouette of the Munich skyline, black against the retreating light.

Sights to See

Numbers in the margin correspond to points of interest on the Munich map.

㉖ **Bayerisches Nationalmuseum.** The Bavarian National Museum contains an extensive collection of Bavarian and other German art and artifacts. The highlight for some will be the medieval and Renaissance wood carvings, with many works by the great Renaissance sculptor Tilman Riemenschneider. Fine tapestries, arms and armor, a unique collection of Christmas crèches (the Krippenschau), Bavarian arts and crafts, and folk artifacts compete for your attention. Although the Bayerisches Nationalmuseum places emphasis on Bavarian cultural history, it has exhibits of outstanding international importance and stages regular exhibitions that attract worldwide attention. ⊠ *Prinzregentenstr. 3,* ☎ *089/211241.* 🖃 *DM 5, free Sun. and holidays.* ☉ *Tues.–Sun. 9:30–5.*

★ ㉕ **Englischer Garten.** This virtually endless park, which is embraced by open countryside at Munich's northern city limits, was designed for the Bavarian prince Karl Theodor by a refugee from the American War of Independence, Count Rumford. Although Rumford was of English descent, it was the open, informal nature of the park—reminiscent of the rolling parklands with which English aristocrats of the 18th century liked to surround their country homes—that determined its name. It has an appealing boating lake, four beer gardens, and a series of curious decorative and monumental constructions, including the Monopteros, a Greek temple designed by von Klenze for King Ludwig I and built on an artificial hill in the southern section of the park. In the center of one of the park's most popular beer gardens is a Chinese pagoda erected in 1789, destroyed during the war, and then reconstructed. The Chinese Tower beer garden is world famous, but the park has prettier places for downing a beer: the Aumeister, for example, along the northern perimeter. The Aumeister's restaurant is in an early 19th-century hunting lodge.

The Englischer Garten is a paradise for joggers, cyclists, and, in winter, cross-country skiers. The Munich Cricket Club grounds are in the southern section—proof, perhaps, that even that most British of games is not invulnerable to the single-minded Germans—and spectators are welcome. The park also has specially designated areas for nude sunbathing—the Germans have a positively pagan attitude toward the sun—so don't be surprised to see naked bodies bordering the flower beds and paths.

㉒ Feldherrnhalle. This local hall of fame was modeled on the 14th-century Loggia dei Lanzi in Florence. In the '30s and '40s it was the site of a key Nazi shrine, marking the marking the site of Hitler's abortive rising, or putsch, took place in 1923. All who passed it had to give the Nazi salute. ⊠ *South end of Odeonspl.*

⑰ Hofbräuhaus. Duke Wilhelm V founded Munich's most famous brewery in 1589, and although it still boasts royal patronage in its title, it's now state-owned. If the downstairs hall is too noisy for you, try the quiet restaurant upstairs. Beer is what you're expected to order here. Hofbräu means "royal brew," a term that aptly describes the golden beer served here in king-size liter mugs. ⊠ *Am Platzl 9,* ☎ *089/221676.*

㉑ Hofgarten. Two sides of the pretty, formal garden that was once part of the royal palace grounds are bordered by arcades designed during the 19th century by the royal architect Leo von Klenze. On the east side of the garden stands the new state chancellery, built around the ruins of the 19th-century Army Museum and incorporating the remains of a Renaissance arcade. Its most prominent feature is a large copper dome. Bombed during World War II air raids, the museum stood untouched for almost 40 years as a grim reminder of the war.

In front of the chancellery stands one of Europe's most unusual—some say most effective—war memorials. Instead of looking up at the monument, you are led down to it—it is a sunken crypt covered by a massive granite block. In the crypt lies a German soldier from World War I. ⊠ *Hofgartenstr., north of the Residenz.*

Ludwigskirche. Planted halfway along the severe, neoclassical Ludwigstrasse is this curious neo-Byzantine/early Renaissance–style church. It was built at the behest of Ludwig I to provide his newly completed suburb with a parish church. Though most visitors will find the building a curiosity at best, it can be worth a stop to see the fresco of the *Last Judgment* in the choir. At 60 feet by 37 feet, it is one of the world's largest. ⊠ *Ludwigstr. 22,* ☎ *089/288–334.* ☉ *Daily 7–7.*

⑱ Maximilianstrasse. Munich's sophisticated shopping street was named after King Maximilian II, who wanted to break away from the Greek-influenced classical style of city architecture favored by his father, Ludwig I, so he ingenuously asked his cabinet whether he could be allowed to create something original. Maximilianstrasse was the result. This broad boulevard, its central stretch lined with majestic buildings (now government offices and the city's ethnological museum, the ☞ **Staatliches Museum für Völkerkunde,** culminates on a rise beyond the Isar River in the stately outlines of the **Maximilianeum,** a lavish 19th-century arcaded palace built for Maximilian II as part of an ambitious city-planning scheme and now the home of the Bavarian state parliament. Today only the terrace can be visited.

⑲ Nationaltheater. Built in the late 19th century as a royal opera house in the classical style, with a pillared portico, this large theater was bombed during the war but is now restored to its original splendor. It has some of the world's most advanced stage technology.

㉘ Prähistorische Staatssammlung (State Prehistoric Collection). This is Bavaria's principal record of its prehistoric, Roman, and Celtic past. The perfectly preserved body of a young girl who was ritually sacrificed, recovered from a Bavarian peat moor, is among its more spine-chilling exhibits. Head down to the basement to see the fine Roman mosaic floor. ⊠ *Lerchenfeldstr. 2,* ☏ *089/293911.* ⊡ *DM 4, free Sun. and holidays.* ☉ *Tues., Wed., and Fri.–Sun. 9–4, Thurs. 9–8.*

★ ⑳ Residenz. Munich's royal palace began as a small castle, to which the Wittelsbach dukes moved during the 14th century, when the Alter Hof became surrounded by the teeming tenements of an expanding Munich. In succeeding centuries the royal residence developed parallel to the importance, requirements, and interests of its occupants. As the complex expanded, it came to include the Königsbau (on Max-Josef-Platz) and then (clockwise) the Alte Residenz; the Festsaal (Banquet Hall); the Altes Residenztheater (Cuvilliés Theater); Allerheiligenhofkirche (All Soul's Church, now ruined); the Residenz theater; and the Nationaltheater.

Building began in 1385 with the **Neuveste** (New Fortress), which comprised the northeast section; it burned to the ground in 1750, but one of its finest rooms survived: the 16th-century **Antiquarium,** which was built for Duke Albrecht V's collection of antique statues (today it's used chiefly for state receptions). The throne room of King Ludwig I, the **Neuer Herkulessaal,** is now a concert hall. The accumulated treasures of the Wittelsbachs can be seen in the **Schatzkammer,** or treasury (one rich centerpiece is a small Renaissance statue of St. George, studded with 2,291 diamonds, 209 pearls, and 406 rubies), and a representative collection of paintings and tapestries is housed in the **Residenzmuseum.** Antique coins and Egyptian works of art are in the two other museums of this vast palace. In the center of the complex, entered through an inner courtyard where chamber-music concerts are given in summer, is a small rococo theater, built by François Cuvilliés from 1751 to 1755. The French-born Cuvilliés was a dwarf who was admitted to the Bavarian court as a decorative "bauble." Prince Max Emanuel recognized his latent artistic ability and had him trained as an architect. The prince's eye for talent gave Germany some of its richest rococo treasures. ⊠ *Max-Joseph-Pl. 3,* ☏ *089/290671. Treasury and Residenzmuseum:* ⊡ *DM 4;* ☉ *Tues.–Sun. 10–4:30. Staatliche Münzsammlung (coin collection), accessible at Residenzstr. 1:* ⊡ *DM 3.50, free Sun. and holidays;* ☉ *Tues.–Sun. 10–4:30. Staatliche Sammlung Ägyptischer Kunst (Egyptian art), accessible at the Hofgarten entrance to the Residenz:* ⊡ *DM 4.50, free Sun. and holidays;* ☉ *Tues. 9–9, Wed.–Fri. 9–4, weekends 10–5. Cuvilliés Theater:* ⊡ *DM 2.50;* ☉ *Mon.–Sat. 2–5, Sun. 10–5.*

㉗ Schack-Galerie. Those with a taste for florid and romantic 19th-century German paintings will appreciate the collections of the Schack-Galerie, originally the private collection of one Count Schack. Others may find the gallery dull, filled with plodding and repetitive works by painters who now repose in well-deserved obscurity. ⊠ *Prinzregentenstr. 9,* ☏ *089/23805224.* ⊡ *DM 3, free Sun. and holidays.* ☉ *Wed.–Mon. 10–5.*

㉓ Siegestor (Victory Arch). Marking the beginning of Leopoldstrasse, the Siegestor has Italian origins—it was modeled on the Arch of Constantine in Rome—and was built to honor the achievements of the Bavarian army during the Wars of Liberation (1813–15).

Staatliches Museum für Völkerkunde (State Museum of Ethnology). Arts and crafts from around the world are displayed in this extensive museum. There are also regular ethnological exhibits. ⊠ *Maximilianstr. 42,* ☎ *089/2285506.* ☞ *DM 3.50, free Sun. and holidays.* ⊙ *Tues.–Sun. 9:30–4:30.*

Staatsgalerie Moderner Kunst (State Gallery of Modern Art). The gallery is in the west wing of the Hitler-era Haus der Kunst, a monumental pillared building at the south end of the Englischer Garten (☞ *above*) (the east wing has regularly changing exhibits). It features one of the finest collections of 20th-century paintings and sculptures in the world. ⊠ *Prinzregentenstr. 1,* ☎ *089/21127137.* ☞ *DM 5, free Sun. and holidays.* ⊙ *Tues., Wed., and Fri.–Sun. 10–5, Thurs. 10–8.*

㉔ Theatinerkirche. This mighty Baroque church owes its Italian appearance to its founder, Princess Henriette Adelaide, who commissioned it as an act of thanksgiving for the birth of her son and heir, Max Emanuel, in 1663. A native of Turin, the princess distrusted Bavarian architects and builders and thus summoned a master builder from Bologna, Agostino Barelli, to construct her church. He took as his model the Roman mother church of the newly formed Theatine Order. Barelli worked on the building for 11 years but was dismissed before the project was completed. It was another 100 years before the Theatinerkirche was finished. Step inside to admire its austere stucco interior. ⊠ *Odeonspl,* ☎ *089/221650.* ⊙ *Daily 7–7.*

NEED A
BREAK?

Munich's oldest café, the **Annast** (⊠ Odeonpspl., ☎ 089/290–7530) is across from the Theatinerkirche on the busy square, Odeonsplatz. In summer you have the choice of watching the hustle and bustle from a pavement table or retreating through a gate in the Hofgarten's western wall to the café's quiet, tree-shaded beer garden.

㉙ Villa Stuck. This museum is the former home of one of Munich's leading turn-of-the-century artists, Franz von Stuck. His work covers the walls of the haunting rooms of the neoclassical villa, which is also used for regular art exhibits organized by the museum's newly appointed Australian director. ⊠ *Prinzregentenstr. 60,* ☎ *089/23805224.* ☞ *DM 6 and upward, according to exhibit.* ⊙ *Tues., Wed., and Fri.–Sun. 10–5, Thurs. 10–9.*

The Maxvorstadt and Schwabing

Here is the artistic center of Munich: Schwabing, the old artists' quarter, and the neighboring Maxvorstadt, where most of the city's leading art galleries and museums are congregated. Schwabing is no longer the Bohemian area where such diverse residents as Lenin and Kandinsky were once neighbors, but at least the solid cultural foundations of the Maxvorsadt are immutable. Where the two areas meet (in the streets behind the university) life hums with a creative vibrancy that is difficult to detect elsewhere in Munich.

A Good Walk

Numbers in the text correspond to numbers in the margin and on the Munich map.

Begin with a stroll through the city's old botanical garden, the **Alter Botanischer Garten** ㉚. The grand-looking building opposite the entrance to the botanical garden is the **Palace of Justice,** law courts built in 1897 in suitable awe-inspiring dimensions. Across the square, at one corner of busy Lenbachplatz, you can't fail to notice one of Munich's most impressive fountains: the monumental late-19th-century **Wittelsbacher Brunnen.** Just beyond the fountain, in Pacellistrasse, is the Baroque **Dreifaltigkeitskirche**(Church of the Holy Trinity) ③.

Leave the Alter Botanischer Garten at its northern end and walk up Meiserstrasse, passing on the right-hand side two solemn neoclassical buildings, one of which houses a fascinating collection of drawings and prints from the late-Gothic period to the present day. The neighboring building is the **Music Academy,** the site of the prewar pact carving up Czechoslovakia, signed by Hitler, Mussolini, Britain's Chamberlain, and France's Deladier.

At the junction of Meiserstrasse and Briennerstrasse look right to see Munich's Egyptian obelisk dominating the circular **Karolinenplatz** ㉜. On your left, at the crossroads of Meiserstrasse and Briennerstrasse, is an expansive square, **Königsplatz** ㉝, lined on three sides with the monumental Grecian-style buildings that house two museums, the **Glyptothek** ㉞ and the **Antikensammlungen** (Antiquities Collection) ㉟. Beyond the great triumphal gate that marks the western boundary of the square is a third museum leading into the past, the **Paläontoligisches Museum** ㊱. Young dinosaur fans will love the reconstructed monsters on display here.

Turn right into Luisenstrasse after leaving Königsplatz, and you'll arrive at one of Munich's most delightful art galleries, the **Städtische Galerie im Lenbachhaus** ㊲, a Florentine-style villa containing an outstanding collection of works from the Gothic period to the present. Continue down Luisenstrasse, turning right on Theresienstrasse to reach Munich's two leading art galleries, the **Alte Pinakothek** ㊳ and the **Neue Pinakothek** ㊴, opposite it. They are as complementary as their buildings are contrasting: the Alte Pinakothek severe and serious in style, the Neue Pinakothek almost frivolously Florentine.

After a few hours immersed in culture, end your walk with a leisurely stroll through the neighboring streets of **Schwabing,** lined with boutiques, bars, and restaurants. If it's a fine day, head for the **Elisabethmarkt,** Schwabing's permanent market.

TIMING

This walk may take an entire day, depending on how long you're tempted to linger at the several major museums en route. Avoid the museum crowds by timing your visits as early in the day as possible. All Munich seems to discover an interest in art on admission-free Sundays, particularly during foul weather, so you might find it worth spending that bit extra on admission to guarantee relatively undisturbed viewing. Many Schwabing bars have happy hours between 6 and 8—a tip for those who want to time the end of their walk with a watering-hole stop.

Sights to See

Numbers in the margin correspond to points of interest on the Munich map.

㊳ **Alte Pinakothek.** The towering, brick Alte Pinakothek (Old Picture Gallery) was constructed by von Klenze between 1826 and 1836 to exhibit the collection of Old Masters begun by Duke Wilhelm IV during the 16th century. It's now judged one of the world's great picture galleries. Closed in 1994 for renovations, at press time it was scheduled to reopen in early 1997. The gallery's most famous include Dürers, Rembrandts, Rubenses, and two celebrated Murillos; if the museum has not yet reopened when you're visiting Munich, you can find its paintings on display at the Neue Pinakothek. ⊠ *Barerstr. 27,* ☎ *089/23805215. Hrs and admission charges not available at press time.*

③⓪ Alter Botanischer Garten. Munich's first botanical garden began as the site of a huge glass palace, built here in 1853 for Germany's first industrial exhibition. In 1931 the immense structure burned down; six years later the garden was redesigned as a public park. Two features from the '30s remain: a small, square **exhibition hall,** still used for art shows; and the 1933 **Neptune Fountain,** an enormous work in the heavy, monumental style of the prewar years. At the international electricity exhibition of 1882, the world's first high-tension electricity cable was run from the park to a Bavarian village 48 kilometers (30 miles) away. ⊠ *Entrance at Lenbachpl.*

NEED A BREAK? Tucked away on the north edge of the Alter Botanischer Garten is one of the city's central beer gardens. It's part of the **Park Café** (⊠ Sophienstr. 7, ☎ 089/598–313), which at night becomes a fashionable disco serving magnums of champagne for DM 1,500 apiece. Prices in the beer garden are more realistic.

③⑤ Antikensammlungen (Antiquities Collection). This museum at Königsplatz has a fine group of smaller sculptures, Etruscan art, Greek vases, gold, and glass. ⊠ *Königspl. 1,* ☎ *089/598359.* ▣ *DM 5, free Sun. and holidays. Combined ticket to the Antikensammlungen and the* ☞ *Gyptothek costs DM 8.* ◷ *Tues. and Thurs.–Sun. 10–4:30, Wed. noon–8:30. Free guided tour of museum Wed. at 6.*

③① Dreifaltigkeitskirche. This striking Baroque edifice is the Church of the Holy Trinity, built between 1711 and 1718 after a local woman prophesied doom for the city unless a new church was erected. It has heroic frescoes by Cosmas Damian Asam. ⊠ *Pacellistr. 10,* ☎ *089/290-0820.* ◷ *Daily 7–7.*

Elisabethmarkt. Schwabing's permanent market is smaller than the popular Viktualienmarkt but hardly less colorful. It has a pocket-size beer garden, where a jazz band performs every Saturday from spring to autumn. *Corner of Arcistr. and Elisabethstr.*

③④ Glyptothek. This museum at Königsplatz features a permanent exhibition of Greek and Roman sculptures. ⊠ *Königspl. 3,* ☎ *089/286100.* ▣ *DM 5, free Sun. and holidays. Combined ticket to the Gyptothek and the* ☞ *Antikensammlungen costs DM 8.* ◷ *Tues., Wed., and Fri.–Sun. 10–4:30, Thurs. noon–8:30. Free guided tour of museum Thurs. at 6.*

③② Karolinenplatz. At the junction of Meiserstrasse and Briennerstrasse, this circular area is dominated by an Egyptian obelisk, actually a memorial, unveiled in 1812, to Bavarians killed fighting Napoléon. **Amerikahaus** (America House) faces Karolinenplatz. It has an extensive library and a year-round program of cultural events. ⊠ *Karolinenpl. 3,* ☎ *089/552–5370.*

③③ Königsplatz. This expansive square is lined on three sides with the monumental Grecian-style buildings by Leo von Klenze that gave Munich the nickname "Athens on the Isar." The two templelike buildings he had constructed there are now the ☞ **Glyptothek** and the ☞ **Antikensammlungen** museums. In the '30s the great parklike square was laid with granite slabs, which resounded with the thud of jackboots as the Nazis commandeered the area for their rallies. Only recently were the slabs removed; since then the square has taken on something of the green and peaceful appearance originally intended by Ludwig I.

③⑨ **Neue Pinakothek.** The Neue Pinakothek (New Picture Gallery) was opened in 1981 to house the royal collection of modern art left homeless when its former building was destroyed in the war. It's a low, brick building that combines high-tech and Italianate influences in equal measure. From outside the museum does not seem to measure up to the standards set by so many of Munich's other great public buildings. Yet the interior offers a magnificent environment for picture gazing, at least partly due to the superb natural light flooding in from the skylights. The highlights of the collection are probably the Impressionist and other French 19th-century works—Monet, Degas, and Manet are all well represented. But there's also a substantial collection of 19th-century German and Scandinavian paintings—misty landscapes predominate—that are only now coming to be recognized as admirable and worthy products of their time. ⊠ *Barerstr. 29,* ☎ *089/3805195.* ☞ *DM 6, free Sun. and holidays.* ⊙ *Tues. and Thurs. 10–8, Wed. and Fri. 10–5, weekends 10–5.*

NEED A   The Neue Pinakothek has an airy basement restaurant and café, the
BREAK?   **Pina,** with an outdoor courtyard area, where in summer you can relax to
            the splashing of a fountain that rivals some of the artwork within.

③⑥ **Paläontologisches Museum.** The 10-million-year-old skeleton of a mammoth is the centerpiece of this paleontological and geological collection. ⊠ *Richard-Wagner-Str. 10,* ☎ *089/5203361.* ☞ *Free.* ⊙ *Mon.–Thurs. 8–4, Fri. 8–2.*

③⑦ **Städtische Galerie im Lenbachhaus.** You'll find an internationally renowned picture collection inside a delightful late-19th-century Florentine-style villa, former home and studio of the artist Franz von Lenbach. It contains a rich collection of works from the Gothic period to the present, including an exciting assemblage of art from the early 20th-century *Blaue Reiter* (Blue Rider) group: Kandinsky, Klee, Jawlensky, Macke, Marc, and Münter. ⊠ *Luisenstr. 33,* ☎ *089/23332000.* ☞ *DM 6, free Sun. and holidays.* ⊙ *Tues.–Sun. 10–6.*

Outside the Center

BMW Museum. On the eastern edge of the Olympiapark, you can't miss this museum, a circular tower building that looks as if it served as a set for *Star Wars.* Munich is the home of the famous car firm, and the museum contains a dazzling collection of BMWs old and new; it adjoins the BMW factory. ⊠ *Petuelring 130 (U-bahn 2 or 3 to Olympiazentrum station).* ☞ *DM 4.50.* ⊙ *Daily 9–5 (last entry 4 PM).*

Botanischer Garten (Botanical Garden). A collection of 14,000 plants, including orchids, cacti, cyads, Alpine flowers, and rhododendrons, makes up one of the most extensive botanical gardens in Europe. The garden lies on the eastern edge of ☞ Schloss Nymphenburg Park. Take Tram 12 or Bus 41 from the city center to the garden. ⊠ *Menzingerstr. 65.* ☞ *DM 3.* ⊙ *Daily 9–4:30; hothouses daily 9–noon and 1–4.*

Geiselgasteig Movie Studios. Munich is Germany's leading moviemaking center, and in the summer the studios at Geiselgasteig, on the southern outskirts of the city, open their doors to visitors. A "Filmexpress" transports you on a 1½-hour tour of the sets of *Das Boot (The Boat), Enemy Mine, The Neverending Story,* and other productions. Children should enjoy the stunt shows (mid-Apr.–Oct., weekends and public holidays, 11:30 AM, 1 PM, and 2:30 PM) or the newly opened

"Showscan" super-wide-screen cinema. Take the U-bahn 1 or 2 from the city center to Silberhornstrasse and then change to Tram 25 to Bavari-afilmplatz. ☎ *DM 14, stunt shows DM 9, combined ticket for tour of studios, stunt show, and Showscan cinema DM 28.* ⊙ *Mar.–Oct., daily 9–5. Last tour begins at 4 daily.*

Hellabrun Zoo. On the southern edge of the city this is one of the most attractive zoos in Germany. There's a minimum of cages and many park-like enclosures. Animals are arranged according to their geographical origin. The zoo's 170 acres include restaurants and children's areas. Take Bus 52 from Marienplatz or the U-bahn 3. ✉ *Tierparkstr. 30,* ☎ *089/625–080.* ☎ *DM 7.* ⊙ *Apr.–Sept., daily 8–6; Oct.–Mar., daily 9–5.*

Olympiapark. The undulating circus-tent-like roofs that cover the stadia built for the 1972 Olympic Games are unobtrusively tucked away in what is now known as Olympiapark on the northern edge of Schwabing. The roofs are made of translucent tiles that glisten in the midday sun and act as amplifiers for such visiting rock bands as the Rolling Stones. Tours of the park on a Disneyland-style train run throughout the day from March through November. Take the elevator up the 960-foot Olympia Tower for a view of the city and the Alps; there's also a revolving restaurant near the top. Take the U-bahn 3 to the park. ☎ *089/3067–2414. Main stadium:* ☎ *DM 1;* ⊙ *Daily 9–4:30. Tower:* ☎ *Elevator ride DM 5;* ⊙ *Daily 9 AM–midnight. Combined ticket for park tour and ride up the tower is DM 7. Restaurant:* ☎ *089/3067–2818 for reservations;* ⊙ *Daily 11–5:30 and 6:30 PM–midnight.*

Schloss Blutenburg. Beyond Nymphenburg, on the northwest edge of Munich, lies this medieval palace, now the home of an international collection of 500,000 children's books in more than 100 languages. Alongside this library are collections of original manuscripts, illustrations, and posters. The castle chapel, built in 1488 by Duke Sigismund, has some fine 15th-century stained glass. Take any S-bahn train to Pasing station, then Bus 73 or 76 to the castle gate. ✉ *Blutenberg 35,* ☎ *089/811–3132.* ☎ *Free.* ⊙ *Weekdays 10–5.*

★ **Schloss Nymphenburg.** The major attraction away from downtown Munich is this glorious Baroque and rococo palace in the northwest suburb that was a summer home to five generations of Bavarian royalty. Nymphenburg is the largest palace of its kind in Germany, stretching more than a half mile from one wing to the other. The palace grew in size and scope over a period of more than 200 years, beginning as a summer residence built on land given by Prince Ferdinand Maria to his beloved wife, Henriette Adelaide, on the occasion of the birth of their son and heir, Max Emanuel, in 1663. She had the Theatinerkirche built as a personal expression of thanks for the birth. The Italian architect Agostino Barelli, was brought from Bologna to build the palace. It was completed in 1675 by his successor, Enrico Zuccalli. Within that original building, now the central axis of the palace complex, is a magnificent hall, the Steinerner Saal, extending over two floors and richly decorated with stucco and swirling frescoes. In the summer chamber-music concerts are given here. The decoration of the Steinerner Saal spills over into the surrounding royal chambers, one of which houses the famous **Schönheitsgalerie** (Gallery of Beauties). The walls are hung from floor to ceiling with portraits of women who caught the roving eye of Ludwig I, among them a butcher's daughter and an English duchess. The most famous portrait is of Lola Montez, a sultry beauty and high-class courtesan who, after a time as the mistress of Franz Liszt and later Alexandre Dumas, captivated Ludwig I to such an extent that he gave up his throne for her.

The palace is set in a fine park, laid out in formal French style, with low hedges and gravel walks extending into woodland. Tucked away among the ancient trees are three fascinating structures built as Nymphenburg expanded and changed occupants. Don't miss the **Amalienburg** hunting lodge, a rococo gem built by François Cuvilliés, architect of the Residenztheater. The silver-and-blue stucco of the little Amalienburg creates an atmosphere of courtly high life, making clear that the pleasures of the chase here did not always take place outdoors. In the lavishly appointed kennels you'll see that even the dogs lived in luxury. For royal tea parties another building, the **Pagodenburg**, was constructed. It has an elegant French exterior that disguises a suitably Asian interior in which exotic teas from India and China were served. Swimming parties were held in the **Badenburg**, Europe's first post-Roman heated pool.

Nymphenburg contains so much of interest that a day hardly provides enough time. Don't leave without visiting the former royal stables, the **Marstallmuseum,** or Museum of Royal Carriages. It houses a fleet of vehicles, including an elaborately decorated sleigh in which King Ludwig II once glided through the Bavarian twilight, postilion torches lighting the way. On the floor above are fine examples of Nymphenburg porcelain, produced here between 1747 and the 1920s.

A newly opened museum in the north wing of the palace has nothing to do with the Wittelsbachs but nevertheless has become one of Nymphenburg's major attractions. The **Museum Mensch und Natur** (Museum of Man and Nature) concentrates on three areas of interest: the history of man, the variety of life on Earth, and man's place in the environment. Main exhibits include a huge representation of the human brain and a chunk of Alpine crystal weighing half a ton.

To reach Schloss Nymphenburg, take the U-bahn 1 from the Hauptbahnhof to Rotkreuzplatz, then pick up Tram 12, heading for Amalienburg. ☎ 089/179–080. ✉ *Admission to entire Schloss Nymphenburg complex, DM 6 (ask for a Gesamtkarte, or combined ticket). A ticket for just the palace, Schönheitsgalerie, and Marstallmuseum DM 2.50.* ☉ *Apr.–Sept., daily 9–12:30 and 1:30–5; Oct.–Mar., daily 10–12:30 and 1:30–4. Museum Mensch und Natur:* ✉ *DM 3; free on Sun. and public holidays;* ☉ *Tues.–Sun. 9–5. All except Amalienburg and gardens closed Mon. (Munich's botanical garden with its interesting tree collection and tropical greenhouses is adjacent to the palace grounds.)*

Schloss Schleissheim. In 1597 Duke Wilhelm V decided to look for a peaceful retreat outside Munich and found what he wanted at this palace, then far beyond the city walls but now only short ride on a train and a bus. A later ruler, Prince Max Emanuel, extended the palace and added a second, smaller one, the Lustheim. Separated from the main palace by a formal garden and a decorative canal, the Lustheim houses Germany's largest collection of Meissen porcelain. To reach the palace, take the suburban S-bahn 1 line (to Oberschleissheim station) and then Bus 292 (which doesn't run on weekends). ✉ *Oberschleissheim,* ☎ *089/315–8720.* ✉ *Combined ticket for the palaces and the porcelain collection DM 4.* ☉ *Tues.–Sun. 10–12:30 and 1:30–5.*

Südfriedhof. At this museum-piece cemetery, you'll find many famous names but few tourists. Four hundred years ago it was a graveyard beyond the city walls for plague victims and paupers. During the 19th century it was refashioned into an upscale last resting place by the city architect Friedrich von Gärtner. Royal architect Leo von Klenze designed some of the headstones, and both he and von Gärtner are among the famous names you'll find there. The last burial here took place more than 40 years ago. The Südfriedhof is a short 10-minute walk south from the U-bahn station at Sendlinger-Tor-Platz. ⊠ *Thalkirchnerstr.*

DINING

Munich rates as Germany's gourmet capital, and it has an inordinate number of high-class French restaurants, some with chef-owners who honed their skills under such Gallic masters as Paul Bocuse. For connoisseurs, wining and dining at Tantris or the Königshof could well turn into the equivalent of a religious experience; culinary creations are accorded the status of works of art on a par with a Bach fugue or Dürer painting, with tabs worthy of a king's ransom. Epicureans are convinced that one can dine as well in Munich as in any other city on the Continent, including Paris, Brussels, and Rome, and perhaps it's true. It certainly is in a number of the top-rated restaurants listed below.

However, for many the true glory of Munich's kitchen artistry is to be experienced in those rustically decorated traditional eating places that serve down-home Bavarian specialties in ample portions. The city's renowned beer and wine restaurants offer superb atmosphere, low prices, and as much wholesome German food as you'll ever want. They're open at just about any hour of the day or night—you can order your roast pork at 11 AM or 11 PM.

What to Wear

Many Munich restaurants serve sophisticated cuisine, and they require their patrons to dress for the occasion. Other, usually less-expensive, restaurants will serve you regardless of what you wear.

CATEGORY	COST*
$$$$	over DM 95
$$$	DM 65–DM 95
$$	DM 45–DM 65
$	DM 30–DM 45

per person for a three-course meal, excluding drinks

$$$$ ✕ **Königshof.** The view here is great inside and out—ask for a panoramic window table overlooking Karlsplatz—in what is probably Munich's most exquisitely decorated restaurant. The service is of equally high standard. French nouvelle cuisine dominates. ⊠ *Karlspl. 25,* ☎ *089/551–360. Reservations essential. Jacket and tie. AE, DC, MC, V.*

$$$$ ✕ **Tantris.** Chef Hans Haas has kept this restaurant with a modernist
★ look among the top five dining establishments in Munich, and in 1994 Germany's premier food critics voted him the country's top chef. You, too, will be impressed by the exotic nouvelle cuisine on the menu, including such specialties as shellfish and creamed potato soup and roasted wood pigeon with scented rice. But you may wish to ignore the bare concrete surroundings and the garish orange-and-yellow decor. ⊠ *Johann-Fichter-Str. 7,* ☎ *0889/362–061. Reservations essential. Jacket and tie. AE, DC, MC, V. Closed Sun., Dec. 25, and Whitsun.*

$$$ ✕ **Bistro Terrine.** Tucked away self-effacingly in a corner of a Schwabing shopping arcade, the misnamed bistro is one of this lively area's most charming upmarket restaurants. Crisp blue-and-white linen, caneback chairs, and art-nouveau lamps give it a French atmosphere matched by the excellent Gallic-influenced menu. A cozy aperitif bar completes the harmonious picture. ⊠ *Amalienstr. 89,* ☎ *089/281780. AE, DC, MC, V. Closed Sun. No lunch Mon.*

$$$ ✕ **Käfers am Odeonsplatz.** This smart restaurant and even smarter piano
★ bar is Michael Käfer's latest addition to his impressive collection of nightspots; it meets the exacting standards he sets for himself and his

44

Altes Hackerhaus, **5**
Augustiner Keller, **33**
Austernkeller, **18**
Bamberger Haus, **29**
Bistro Terrine, **27**
Brauhaus zum
Brez'n, **30**
Dürnbräu, **20**
Erstes Münchner
Kartoffelhaus, **17**
Franziskaner, **9**
Friesenstube, **21**
Glockenbach, **1**
Grüne Gans, **8**
Halali, **23**
Haxnbauer, **15**
Hofbräuhaus, **16**
Hundskugel, **4**
James Cafe, **19**
Jeeta's, **22**
Käfers am
Odeonsplatz, **13**
Käferschänke, **24**
Königshof, **2**
Max—Emanuel-
Brauerei, **28**
Pfälzer
Weinprobierstube, **12**
Preysing Keller, **25**
Ratskeller, **7**
Santa Fe, **26**
Spatenhaus, **10**
Spöckmeier, **6**
Tantris, **31**
Weichandhof, **32**
Weinhaus Neuner, **3**
Welser Küche, **11**
Wirtshaus im
Weinstadl, **14**

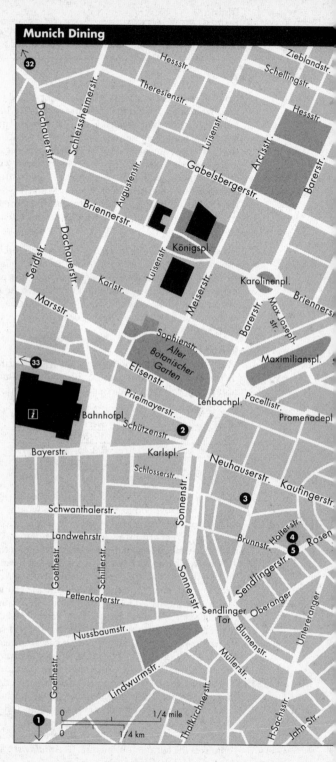

Munich Dining

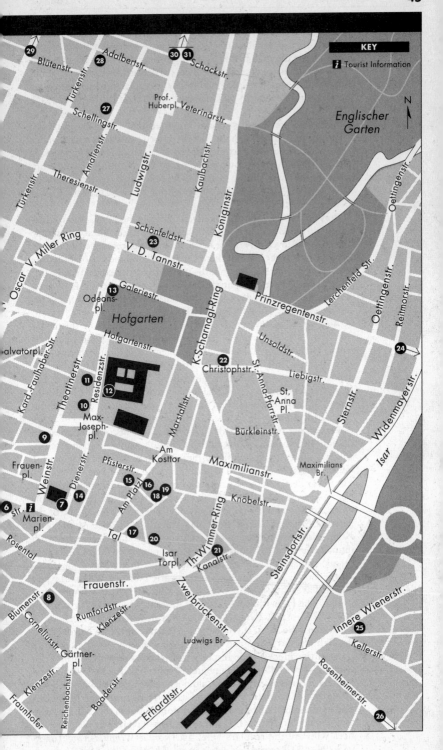

N

Englischer Garten

Blütenstr.

Adalbertstr.

Türkenstr.

Schellingstr.

Amalienstr.

Theresienstr.

Türkenstr.

Schackstr.

Prof.-Huberpl. Veterinärstr.

Kaulbachstr.

Königinstr.

Ludwigstr.

Schönfeldstr.

V. D. Tannstr.

Oscar V. Miller Ring

Prinzregentenstr.

Lerchenfeld Str.

Oettingenstr.

Reitmorstr.

Galeriestr.

Odeons-pl.

Hofgarten

Hofgartenstr.

K.-Scharnagl-Ring

Unsoldstr.

Liebigstr.

Widenmayerstr.

alvatorpl.

Kard.-Faulhaber-Str.

Theatinerstr.

Residenzstr.

Christophstr.

St.-Anna-Pfarrstr.

St. Anna Pl.

Sternstr.

Isar

Max-Joseph-pl.

Marstallstr.

Bürkleinstr.

Frauen-pl.

Weinstr.

Dienerstr.

Pfisterstr.

Am Kosttor

Maximilianstr.

Maximilians Br.

Str.

i

Marien-pl.

Am Platzl

Knöbelstr.

Rosental

Tal

Th.-Wimmer-Ring

Steinsdorfstr.

Isar Torpl.

Kanalstr.

Frauenstr.

Zweibrückenstr.

Innere Wienerstr.

Blumenstr.

Cornelliusstr.

Rumfordstr.

Klenzestr.

Kellerstr.

Gärtner-pl.

Klenzestr.

Baaderstr.

Ludwigs Br.

Rosenheimerstr.

Reichenbachstr.

Fraunhofer

Erhardtstr.

team. Spotless white linen and the finest crystal set the tone of a restaurant that looks out onto elegant Odeonsplatz. The accent is on fish, with fine Scottish salmon sharing menu space with imaginative creations like house-made ravioli stuffed with lobster. Before or after the meal a stop at the busy bar is recommended, particularly if the concert-grand piano is in use (and especially if one of the regular American guest pianists is at the keyboard). ⊠ *Odeonspl. 3,* ☎ *089/290–7530. AE, DC, MC, V.*

$$$ ✕ **Käferschänke.** Fresh seafood, imported daily from the south of France, is the attraction here. Try the grilled prawns in a sweet-and-sour sauce. The rustic decor, complemented by some fine antiques, is sure to delight no matter what you order. The restaurant is in the upscale Bogenhausen suburb, a 10-minute taxi ride from downtown. ⊠ *Schumannstr. 1,* ☎ *089/41681. Jacket and tie. AE, DC, MC. Closed Sun. and holidays.*

$$$ ✕ **Preysing Keller.** Devotees of all that's best in modern German cooking—food that's light and sophisticated but with recognizably Teutonic touches—will love the Preysing Keller. It's in a 16th-century cellar, though it has been so overrestored there's practically no indication of its age or original character. Never mind—it's the food, the extensive wine list, and the perfect service that make this restaurant special. ⊠ *Innere-Wiener-Str. 6,* ☎ *089/481–015. Reservations essential. Jacket and tie. No credit cards. Closed Sun. and Dec. 23–Jan. 10.*

$$ ✕ **Austernkeller.** Oysters (*Austern*) are the specialty of this cellar restaurant, although many other varieties of seafood—all flown in daily from France—help fill its imaginative menu. The lobster thermidor is expensive (DM 46) but surpasses that served elsewhere in Munich, while a richly stocked fish soup can be ordered for less than DM 10. The fussy, fishnet-hung decor is a shade too maritime, especially for downtown Munich, but the starched white linen and glittering glassware and cutlery add a note of elegance. ⊠ *Stollbergstr. 11,* ☎ *298–787. MC.*

$$ ✕ **Bamberger Haus.** The faded elegance of this historic old house on the edge of Schwabing's Luitpold Park disguises an up-to-date kitchen, which conjures up inexpensive dishes of modern flair and imagination. Vegetarians are well catered to with cheap and filling vegetable gratins. The cellar beer tavern was reopened in 1996 after extensive renovations and serves one of the best ales in town. In summer reserve a table on the terrace and eat under shady chestnut trees with a view of the park. ⊠ *Brunnerstr. 2,* ☎ *089/3088966. MC. No lunch Mon.*

$$ ✕ **Franziskaner.** Vaulted archways, cavernous rooms interspersed with intimate dining areas, bold blue frescoes, long wood tables, and a sort of spic-and-span medieval atmosphere—the look without the dirt—set the mood. This is the place for an early morning *Weisswurst* and a beer; Bavarians swear it will banish all trace of that morning-after feeling. The Franziskaner is right by the State Opera. ⊠ *Perusastr. 5,* ☎ *089/231–8120. Reservations not accepted. No credit cards.*

$$ ✕ **Friesenstube.** Even if you won't be journeying to the North Sea or the Baltic resorts, you can taste authentic cuisine from Germany's coast at this modest little restaurant. Delicious Busumer shrimp is a welcome staple; *Labskaus,* Hamburg's favorite stew, has its day on Thursday. The menu is mostly seafood, although some Westphalian meat dishes do intrude. The place is small and easily recognizable by its timber-clad exterior, reminiscent of a harbor pub. But alas, this is in Munich, and it's late-working officials from nearby Bavarian government offices who are the regulars here. ⊠ *Thomas-Wimmer-Ring 16,* ☎ *089/294–600. Reservations not accepted. AE, MC. Closed Sat. No lunch.*

$$ ✕ **Glockenbach.** This small, highly popular restaurant with dark-wood paneling inside serves mostly fish entrées, prepared by the acclaimed chef and owner, Karl Ederer. Book ahead to enjoy such specialties as freshwater fish ragout from the Starnberger Lake or marinated wild hare fillets with perfumed horseradish. ⌧ *Kapuzinerstr. 29,* ☎ *089/534–043. Reservations essential. MC, V. Closed Sun., Mon., Dec. 25, Jan. 1, and 2 wks in July.*

$$ ✕ **Halali.** The Halali is an old-style Munich restaurant—polished wood paneling and antlers on the walls—that offers new-style regional specialties, such as venison in juniper-berry sauce and marinated beef on a bean salad. Save room for the homemade vanilla ice cream. ⌧ *Schönfeldstr. 22,* ☎ *089/285–909. Jacket and tie. MC. Closed Sun. and holidays.*

$$ ✕ **James Cafe.** James is an immigrant from Kenya, but there aren't any African specialties on his restaurant's small but very fine menu. James cooks Italian—so well that his cozy café is considered by local aficionados to be one of *the* Italian eating places in town. One of Munich's leading restaurant critics said most of the city's Italian cooks should turn "green, white, and red with shame." The menu changes daily; if pheasant is on it, that's the dish to order. ⌧ *Hochbrückenstr. 14,* ☎ *089/298–940. No credit cards. No lunch Sun.*

$$ ✕ **Jeeta's.** The restaurant that is arguably Munich's best for Indian food is just a tiny neighborhood eatery, tucked away in a side street of upmarket Lehel. The food is pungently Punjabi, although concessions are also made to other regional influences. Don't miss the bean-curd soup. The few tables are packed close together, so this isn't the place for a quiet tête-à-tête or a large party. ⌧ *Seitzstr. 13 (corner of Christophstr.),* ☎ *089/223931. Reservations essential. AE, MC.*

$$ ✕ **Ratskeller.** Munich's Ratskeller is one of the few city-hall cellar restaurants to offer vegetarian dishes alongside the normal array of hearty and filling traditional fare. If turnip in cheese sauce is on the menu, you won't need to be a vegetarian to appreciate it. The decor is much as you would expect, with vaulted stone ceilings and flickering candles. ⌧ *Marienpl. 8,* ☎ *089/220–313. AE, MC, V.*

$$ ✕ **Spatenhaus.** A view of the opera house and the royal palace com-
★ plements the Bavarian mood of the wood-paneled and beamed Spatenhaus. The menu is international, however, with more or less everything from artichokes to *Zuppa Romana* (alcohol-soaked, fruity Italian cake-pudding). But since you're in Bavaria, why not do as the Bavarians do? Try the Bavarian Plate, an enormous mixture of local meats and sausages. ⌧ *Residenzstr. 12,* ☎ *089/227–841. DC, MC, V.*

$$ ✕ **Spöckmeier.** This rambling, solidly Bavarian beer restaurant spread over three floors, including a snug *Keller* (cellar), is famous for its homemade Weisswurst. If you've just stopped in for a snack and don't fancy the fat breakfast sausage, order coffee and pretzels or, in the afternoons, a wedge of cheesecake. The daily changing menu also offers more than two dozen hearty main-course dishes and a choice of four draft beers. The house *Eintopf* (a rich broth of noodles and pork) is a meal in itself. The Spöckmeier is only 50 yards from Marienplatz; on sunny summer days tables are set outside in the auto-free street. ⌧ *Rosenstr. 9,* ☎ *089/268–088. AE, DC, MC, V.*

$$ ✕ **Weichandhof.** This rambling old farmhouse-style restaurant is on the northwestern outskirts of town, in the leafy residential suburb of Obermenzing and near the start of the Stuttgart Autobahn. If you're heading that way, a stop here is strongly recommended, but even a special trip from the city center is worthwhile. The food is excellent, with a menu based on traditional Bavarian and regional German and Austrian fare; roast suckling pig, pork knuckle, and Vienna-style boiled beef are basic staples. In summer or on warm spring and autumn evenings the vine-clad terrace beckons. In winter tiled stoves give a warm glow to the wood-paneled dining rooms. ⌧ *Betzenweg 81,* ☎ *089/111–621. MC. Closed weekends.*

$$ ✕ **Welser Kuche.** It's less a question of what you eat at this medieval-style cellar restaurant than how you eat it—with your fingers and a hunting knife, in the manner of 16th-century baronial banquets. You're welcomed by pretty "serving wenches" who tie a protective bib around your neck, proffer a hunting horn of mead, and show you to one of the oak trestle tables that complete the authentic-looking surroundings. It's best to go in a group, but room will always be found for couples or those dining alone. The full menu runs to 10 dishes, although you can settle for less and choose à la carte. ⊠ *Residenzstr. 2,* ☎ *089/296–565. MC. No lunch.*

$$ ✕ **Wirtshaus im Weinstadl.** Tucked away at the end of a small alley off a busy shopping street and overlooked by most passersby, the historic Weinstadl is well worth hunting out. In summer the courtyard beer garden is a cool delight, with a humorous fountain depicting a Munich burgher quaffing a glass of wine; the fountain splashes away beneath original Renaissance galleries. In winter the brass-studded oaken door opens onto a vaulted dining room where traditional Bavarian fare is served at bench-lined tables. A lunchtime menu and a glass of excellent beer leave change from DM 20. The equally atmospheric cellar, reached via a winding staircase, features live music on Friday and Saturday evenings. ⊠ *Burgstr. 5,* ☎ *089/290–4044. AE, DC, MC.*

$ ✕ **Altes Hackerhaus.** Since 1570 beer has been brewed or served here, the birthplace of Hacher-Pschorr, a still-active Munich brewery. Today the site is a cozy, upscale restaurant with three floors of wood-paneled rooms. In summer you can order a cheese plate and beer in the cool, flower-decorated inner courtyard; in winter you can snuggle in a corner of the Ratsstube and warm up on thick homemade potato broth, followed by schnitzel and *Bratkartoffein* (pan-fried potatoes). ⊠ *Sendlinger-Str. 75,* ☎ *089/260–5026. No credit cards.*

$ ✕ **Augustiner Keller.** This 19th-century establishment is the flagship beer restaurant of one of Munich's oldest breweries, Augustiner. The decor emphasizes wood—from the refurbished parquet floors to the wood barrels from which the beer is drawn. The menu changes daily and offers a full range of Bavarian specialties, but try to order *Tellerfleisch*—cold roast beef with lashings of horseradish, served on a big wood board. Follow that with *Dampfnudeln* (suet pudding served with custard), and you won't feel hungry again for 24 hours. The communal atmosphere of the two baronial hall–like rooms makes this a better place for meeting locals than for attempting a quiet meal for two. ⊠ *Arnulfstr. 52,* ☎ *089/594–393. No credit cards.*

$ ✕ **Brauhaus zum Brez'n.** This hostelry is bedecked in the blue-and-white-check colors of the Bavarian flag. The eating and drinking are spread over three floors and cater to a broad clientele—from local business lunchers to hungry night owls emerging from Schwabing's bars and looking for a bite at 2 AM. Brez'n offers a big all-day menu of traditional roasts, to be washed down with a choice of three draft beers. ⊠ *Leopoldstr. 72,* ☎ *089/390–092. No credit cards.*

$ ✕ **Dürnbräu.** A fountain plays outside this picturesque old Bavarian inn. Inside, the mood is crowded and noisy. Expect to share a table; your fellow diners will range from businesspeople to students. The food is resolutely traditional. Try the cream of spinach soup and the boiled beef. ⊠ *Dürnbräugasse 2,* ☎ *089/222–195. AE, DC, MC, V.*

$ ✕ **Erstes Münchner Kartoffelhaus.** When potatoes were first introduced to Germany, they were dismissed as fodder fit only for animals or the very lowest layers of society. Frederick the Great was largely responsible for putting them on the dining tables of even the nobility, and now the lowly potato is an indispensable part of the German diet. In "Munich's first potato house" they come in all forms, from the simplest baked potato with sour cream to gratin creations with shrimps and salmon. This newly opened restaurant is great fun and a great value, too. ☒ *Hochbrückenstr. 3,* ☏ *089/296331. AE, DC, MC, V.*

$ ✗ Grüne Gans. This small, chummy restaurant near Viktualienmarkt is popular with local entertainers, whose photographs clutter the walls. International fare with regional German influences dominates the menu, although there are a few Chinese dishes. Try the chervil cream soup, followed by calves' kidneys in tarragon sauce. ☒ *Am Einlass 5,* ☏ *089/266–228. Reservations essential. MC. Closed Sat. No lunch.*

$ ✗ Haxnbauer. This is one of Munich's more sophisticated beer restaurants. There's the usual series of interlinking rooms—some large, some small—and the usual sturdy yet pretty Bavarian decoration. But there is a much greater emphasis on the food here than in similar places. Try the *Schweineshaxn* (pork shanks) cooked over a charcoal fire. ☒ *Munzstr. 2,* ☏ *089/221–922. MC, V.*

$ ✗ Hofbräuhaus. The sound of the constantly playing oompah band draws passersby into this father of all beer halls, in which trumpet, drum, and accordion music blends with singing and shouting drinkers to produce an earsplitting din. This is no place for the fainthearted, although a trip to Munich would be incomplete without a visit to the Hofbräuhaus. Upstairs is a more peaceful restaurant. In March, May, and September ask for one of the special, extra-strong seasonal beers (Starkbier, Maibock, Märzen), which complement the heavy, traditional Bavarian fare. ☒ *Am Platzl,* ☏ *089/221–676. Reservations not accepted. No credit cards.*

$ ✗ Hundskugel. This is Munich's oldest tavern, dating from 1440; his-
★ tory positively drips from its crooked walls. The food is surprisingly good. If *Spanferkel*—roast suckling pig—is on the menu, make a point of ordering it. This is simple Bavarian fare at its best. ☒ *Hotterstr. 18,* ☏ *089/264–272. No credit cards.*

$ ✗ Max-Emanuel-Brauerei. Visit this historic old brewery tavern and restaurant on a Monday or a Tuesday and you're expected to bargain over the bill. "Pay what you feel the meal is worth" is the management's unique offer, and (surprise, surprise) the system was working well—at least at the start of 1996. Even if the practice has been abandoned by 1997 (and, of course, on other days of the week) the Max-Emanuel is great value, with hearty Bavarian dishes rarely costing more than DM 20. The main dining room has a stage, so the bill often includes a cabaret or jazz concert. In summer take a table outside in the secluded little beer garden. ☒ *Adalbertstr. 33,* ☏ *089/2715158. No credit cards.*

$ ✗ Pfälzer Weinprobierstube. A warren of stone-vaulted rooms of various sizes, wood tables, flickering candles, dirndl-clad waitresses, and a vast range of wines add up to an experience as close to everyone's image of timeless Germany as you're likely to get. The food is reliable rather than spectacular. Local specialties predominate. ☒ *Residenzstr. 1,* ☏ *089/225–628. Reservations not accepted. No credit cards.*

$ ✗ Santa Fe. Munich's surprisingly large Native American population holds regular powwows in this authentic southwestern American bar and restaurant, which is run by a German and a New Mexico native. A real totem pole sits solemnly in a place of honor, and Native American handicrafts and paintings adorn the rough-plastered adobe-esque walls. The food is convincingly New Mexican (turkey with pumpkin and maize-bread stuffing, for instance) and the portions are American-size (large). On Sunday American breakfasts are served all day long, with cowboy-style coffee cans on the rough wood tables. You'll find the Santa Fe in the center of Munich's lively Haidhausen District, behind the Gasteig, a cultural center. ☒ *Balanstr. 16,* ☏ *089/484736. Reservations not accepted. AE, MC.*

$ ✕ **Weinhaus Neuner.** Munich's oldest wine tavern serves good food as well as superior wines in its three varied nooks and crannies: the wood-paneled restaurant, the wine tavern (*Weinstübl*), and the small bistro. The choice of food is remarkable, from nouvelle German to old-fashioned country. Specialties include home-smoked beef and salmon. ✉ *Herzogspitalstr. 8,* ☎ *089/260–3954. AE, DC, MC. Closed Sun. and holidays. No lunch Sat.*

LODGING

Make reservations well in advance, and be prepared for higher-than-average rates. Though Munich has a vast number of hotels in all price ranges, many of the most popular are fully booked year-round; this is a major trade and convention city as well as a prime tourist destination. If you plan to visit during *Mode Wochen* (Fashion Weeks) in March and September or during the Oktoberfest at the end of September, make reservations at least four months in advance.

Some of the large, very expensive ($$$$) hotels that cater to expense-account business travelers have very attractive weekend discount rates—sometimes as much as 50% below normal prices. Conversely, regular rates can go up during big trade fairs. Check well in advance, either through your travel agent or directly with the hotel.

The tourist office at Rindermarkt 1, D–80331 Munich 1, has a reservations department, but it will not accept telephone reservations. There's also a reservations office at the airport. The best bet for finding a room if you arrive without a reservation is the tourist office in the main train station, on the south side abutting Bayerstrasse, which is open daily 8 AM–10 PM (no telephone bookings).

CATEGORY	COST*
$$$$	over DM 300
$$$	DM 200–DM 300
$$	DM 140–DM 200
$	under DM 140

All prices are for two people in a double room, including tax and service charge.

$$$$ 🏨 **Bayerischer Hof.** This is one of Munich's most traditional luxury hotels. It's on a ritzy shopping street, and there's a series of exclusive shops right outside the imposing marble entrance. Public rooms are decorated with antiques, fine paintings, marble, and painted wood. Old-fashioned comfort and class abound in the older rooms; some of the newer rooms are more functional. ✉ *Promenadenpl. 2–6, D–80333,* ☎ *089/21200,* FAX *089/212–0906. 440 rooms with bath. 3 restaurants, pool, beauty salon, massage, sauna, nightclub, parking. AE, DC, MC, V.*

$$$$ 🏨 **Grand Continental.** Part of the Royal Classic chain, this hotel combines supermodern luxury with old-fashioned style. Bedrooms are individually furnished with antiques, and the ornately designed public rooms feature marble and sculptures. ✉ *Max-Joseph-Str. 5, D–80333,* ☎ *089/551–570,* FAX *089/5199–5420. 149 rooms with bath. 2 restaurants, bar, beauty salon, parking. AE, DC, MC, V.*

$$$$ 🏨 **Park Hilton.** The hotel is big on the outside but intimate on the inside, with as cheerful and accommodating a staff as you're likely to encounter in any European hotel, the glitziness of the lobby and reception area notwithstanding. The hotel is beside the vast Englischer Garten, away from the city center, but a downtown-bound tram stops nearby—or you can take the hotel's own courtesy minibus, which runs a return service for guests. A fast-flowing stream with a beer garden beside it runs throughout the grounds. ✉ *Am Tucherpark 7,*

On the road with **Fodors**

Costumes at Karnival (Fasching) in the Black Forest, Germany
Photo © 1992 Owen Franken

Fodor's is a registered trademark of Fodor's Travel Publications, Inc.

D–80538, ☎ *089/38450,* FAX *089/3845–1845. 477 rooms with bath. 3 restaurants, pool, massage, sauna, health club. AE, DC, MC, V.*

$$$$ 🏠 **Platzl.** This hotel stands in the historic heart of Munich, near the famous Hofbräuhaus beer hall and a couple of minutes' walk from Marienplatz and many other landmarks. The Aying brewery owners have done the soundproof rooms in rustic Bavarian style. Adjoining the hotel is Platzl Bühne, a famous Bavarian folk theater, where you may not understand the thigh-slapping humor, but you're sure to have fun. ⊠ *Sparkassenstr. 10, D–80331,* ☎ *089/237-030; toll-free booking in the U.S.,* ☎ *800/4488355;* FAX *089/2370–3800. 167 rooms with bath. Restaurant, bar, sauna, steam room, exercise room, parking. AE, DC, MC, V.*

$$$$ 🏠 **Rafael.** This elegant downtown hotel opened in 1989 in a beauti-
★ fully renovated neo-Renaissance building that was a high-society ballroom during the late 19th century. Today it tries to recapture some of that bygone era with 24-hour service, including such personalized amenities as in-house butlers. Rooms are individually furnished and extravagantly decorated, in addition to offering many extras, including fax machines. The hotel staged a coup in 1995 by attracting the patronage of Britain's Prince Charles, who broke with royal tradition by electing to stay here during a visit to Germany. ⊠ *Neuturmstr. 1, D–80331,* ☎ *089/290–980,* FAX *089/222–539. 54 rooms and 19 suites (up to DM 1,150 per night) with bath. Restaurant, 2 bars, pool, sauna. AE, DC, MC, V.*

$$$$ 🏠 **Vier Jahreszeiten Kempinski.** The Vier Jahreszeiten (Four Seasons)
★ has been playing host to the world's wealthy and titled for more than a century. It has an unbeatable location on Maximilianstrasse, Munich's premier shopping street, only a few minutes' walk from the heart of the city. Elegance and luxury set the tone throughout; many rooms have handsome antique pieces. The main floor's restaurant is Bistro Eck, and the Theater bar/restaurant is in the cellar. ⊠ *Maximilianstr. 17, D–80539,* ☎ *089/21250; reservations in the U.S. from Kempinski Reservation Service,* ☎ *516/794–2670;* FAX *089/21252000. 268 rooms with bath, 30 suites, presidential suite, 17 apartments. 2 restaurants, piano bar, pool, massage, sauna, exercise room, car rental, parking. AE, DC, MC, V.*

$$$–$$$$ 🏠 **Eden Hotel Wolff.** Chandeliers and dark-wood paneling in the public rooms underline the old-fashioned elegance of this downtown favorite. It's directly across the street from the train station and near the Theresienwiese fairgrounds. The rooms are comfortable, and most are spacious. You can dine on excellent Bavarian specialties in the intimate Zirbelstube restaurant. ⊠ *Arnulfstr. 4, D–80335,* ☎ *089/551–150,* FAX *089/5511–5555. 209 rooms, 2 suites with bath. Restaurant, bar, café, parking (fee). AE, DC, MC, V.*

$$$–$$$$ 🏠 **Torbräu.** You'll sleep under the shadow of one of Munich's ancient city gates—the 14th-century Isartor—if you stay here. This snug hotel offers comfortable rooms decorated in plush and ornate Italian style and an excellent location midway between the Marienplatz and the Deutsches Museum (and around the corner from the Hofbräuhaus). The Torbräu has a moderately priced Italian restaurant, the Firenze, and a good café tucked away in a corner of the arcaded facade. ⊠ *Tal 41, D–80331,* ☎ *089/225–016,* FAX *089/225–019. 97 rooms and 3 suites with bath. Restaurant, café, bowling. AE, MC, V.*

$$$ 🏠 **Admiral.** Although it's in the heart of the city, close to the Isar River
★ and Deutsches Museum, the small, privately owned Admiral enjoys a quiet side-street location and its own garden. Many of the cozily furnished and warmly decorated bedrooms have a balcony overlooking the garden. Bowls of fresh fruit are part of the friendly welcome awaiting guests. The breakfast buffet is a dream, complete with homemade

52

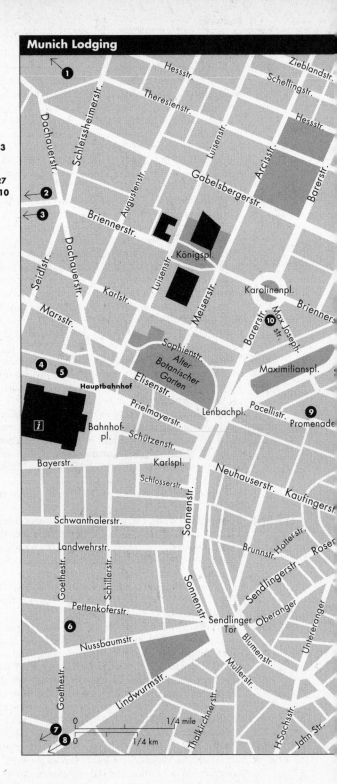

Munich Lodging

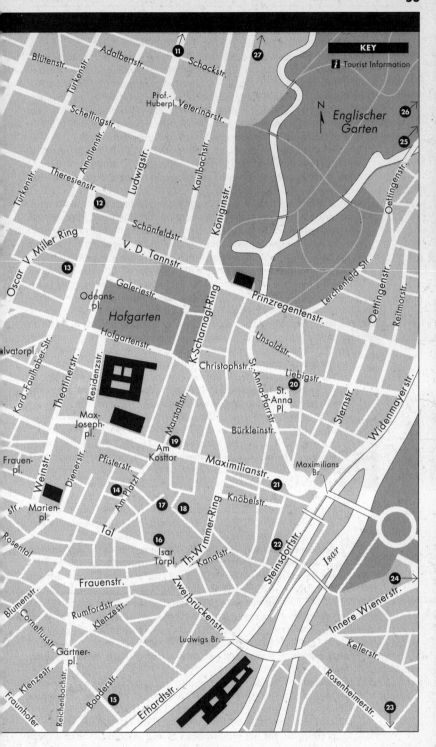

KEY

i Tourist Information

Blütenstr.

Adalbertstr.

Schackstr.

Türkenstr.

Prof.-Huberpl.

Veterinärstr.

Schellingstr.

Amalienstr.

Ludwigstr.

Kaulbachstr.

Englischer Garten

N

Theresienstr.

Türkenstr.

Königinstr.

Oettingenstr.

Schönfeldstr.

Oscar V. Miller Ring

V. D. Tannstr.

Prinzregentenstr.

Lerchenfeld Str.

Oettingenstr.

Rettmorstr.

Galeriestr.

Odeons-pl.

Hofgarten

Hofgartenstr.

Unsoldstr.

Ivatorpl.

Kard.-Faulhaber-Str.

Theatinerstr.

Residenzstr.

K.-Scharnagl-Ring

Christophstr.

St.-Anna-Pfarstr.

Liebigstr.

St. Anna Pl.

Sternstr.

Widenmayerstr.

Max-Joseph-pl.

Marstallstr.

Bürkleinstr.

Maximilianstr.

Maximilians Br.

Frauen-pl.

Weinstr.

Dienerstr.

Pfisterstr.

Am Kosttor

Am Platzl

Knöbelstr.

str.

Marien-pl.

Tal

Isar Torpl.

Th.-Wimmer-Ring

Kanalstr.

Steinsdorfstr.

Isar

Rosental

Frauenstr.

Zweibrückenstr.

Innere Wienerstr.

Blumenstr.

Cornellusstr.

Rumfordstr.

Klenzestr.

Ludwigs Br.

Kellerstr.

Klenzestr.

Gärtner-pl.

Rosenheimerstr.

Reichenbachstr.

Baaderstr.

Erhardtstr.

Fraunhofer

11 27 26 25 12 13 20 19 14 17 18 21 16 22 24 15 23

jams, in-season strawberries, and Italian and French delicacies. ⊠ *Kohlstr. 9, D–80469,* ☎ *089/226–6414,* FAX *089/293–674. 33 rooms with bath. Bar, garage. AE, DC, MC, V.*

$$$ ▣ **Arabella Airport.** This first-class lodging is only five minutes from the new Franz Josef Strauss Airport, and the hotel operates a courtesy shuttle bus. Built primarily to cater to businesspeople (there are numerous conference rooms), the Arabella has plenty of leisure facilities and is ideal for any traveler who has an early-morning departure or a late-evening arrival flight. The three-story, Bavarian rustic-style building is surrounded by greenery. Rooms are furnished in light pinewood, with Laura Ashley fabrics. ⊠ *Freisingerstr. 80, D–85445 Schwaig,* ☎ *08122/8480,* FAX *08122/848–800. 170 rooms, 7 suites with bath. 2 restaurants, bar, indoor pool, sauna, steam room, exercise room. AE, DC, MC, V.*

$$$ ▣ **Erzgiesserei Europe.** Its location on a dull little street in an uninteresting section of the city is this hotel's only drawback, but even that is easily overcome—the nearby subway whisks you in five minutes to central Karlsplatz, convenient to the pedestrian shopping area and the main railway station. Rooms in this attractive hotel are particularly bright, decorated in soft pastels with good reproductions on the walls. The cobblestone garden café is a haven of peace. ⊠ *Erzgiessereistr. 15, D–80335,* ☎ *089/126–820,* FAX *089/123–6198. 106 rooms with bath. Restaurant, bar, café, parking. AE, DC, MC, V.*

$$$ ▣ **Hotel Concorde.** The centrally located Concorde wants to do its bit toward relieving traffic congestion, so guests who arrive from the airport on the S-bahn can exchange their ticket at the reception desk for a welcome champagne or cocktail. With the nearest S-bahn station (Isartor) only a two-minute walk, why not take the hotel up on its offer? Rooms were completely refurnished in 1994 and decorated in pastel tones and light woods, with modern prints on the walls. The hotel has no restaurant, but a large breakfast buffet is served in its stylish, mirrored Salon Margarita. ⊠ *Herrnstr. 38, D–80539,* ☎ *089/224515,* FAX *089/2283282. 67 rooms and 4 suites with bath. Lounge. AE, DC, MC, V.*

$$$ ▣ **Pannonia Hotel Königin Elisabeth.** A bright, modern interior, with emphasis on the color pink, lies behind the protected neoclassical facade of this Pannonia-group hotel, opened in 1990 and a 15-minute tram ride northwest of the city center. Children under 12 stay free in their parents' room. ⊠ *Leonrodstr. 79, D–80636,* ☎ *089/126–860,* FAX *089/1268–6459. 79 rooms. Restaurant, bar, beer garden, hot tub, sauna, steam room, exercise room. AE, DC, MC, V.*

$$$ ▣ **Schloss-Hotel Grünwald.** On the southern edge of the city this rustic, newly renovated lodging offers quiet, eclectically designed rooms (from Bavarian farmhouse motifs to Laura Ashley), with cliff-top views of the Isar River valley stretching toward the Alps. Its restaurant has an international menu of high standard and an extensive wine list. Next door is a castle with a local-history museum. Nearby is the terminus of Tram 25, which will take you into the city. ⊠ *Zeillerstr. 1, D–81547,* ☎ *089/641–9300,* FAX *089/6419–3036. 13 rooms and 3 suites with bath. Restaurant, beer garden, wine bar. AE, DC, MC. Closed Jan. 1–14.*

$$$ ▣ **Splendid.** Chandelier-hung public rooms, complete with antiques
★ and Oriental rugs, give this small hotel something of the atmosphere of a spaciously grand 19th-century inn. The service is attentive and polished. Have breakfast in the small courtyard in summer. There's no restaurant, but the bar serves snacks as well as drinks. The chic shops of the Maximilianstrasse are a five-minute stroll in one direction; an equally brief walk in the other takes you to the Isar River. ⊠ *Maximilianstr. 54, D–80538,* ☎ *089/296–606,* FAX *089/291–3176. 40 rooms, 1 suite, and 5 apartments with bath. Bar. AE, DC MC, V.*

\$\$–\$\$\$ ☷ **Carlton.** This is a favorite of many diplomats: a small, elegant, discreet hotel on a quiet side street in the best area of downtown Munich. The American and British consulates are a short walk away, and so are some of the liveliest Schwabing bars and restaurants. Art galleries, museums, and cinemas are also in the immediate area. Rooms are on the small side, but there are four apartments with cooking facilities. ☒ *Fürstenstr. 12, D–80333,* ☎ *089/282–061,* ☒ *089/284–391. 49 rooms, 4 apartments with bath. AE, DC, MC, V.*

\$\$ ☷ **Adria.** This modern, comfortable hotel is ideally located in the upmarket area of Lehel, in the middle of Munich's museum quarter. Rooms are large and tastefully decorated, with old prints on the pale-pink walls, Oriental rugs on the floors, and flowers beside the double beds. A spectacular breakfast buffet (including a glass of sparkling wine) is included in the room rate. There's no hotel restaurant, but the area is rich in good restaurants, bistros, and bars. ☒ *Liebigstr. 8a, D–80538,* ☎ *089/293–081,* ☒ *089/227–015. 46 rooms, 43 with bath. AE, MC, V.*

\$\$ ☷ **Amba.** Families get an especially good deal at the Amba, member of a hotel group that prides itself on being child-friendly. A modern, brightly furnished double room goes for as little as DM 140, and additional beds cost DM 35. The hotel is right across the street from the main railway station and has its own porter service. A hotel bus collects guests from the airport. ☒ *Arnulfstr. 20, D–80335,* ☎ *089/545–140,* ☒ *089/5451–4555. 86 rooms, 73 with bath. Restaurant, coffee bar, parking. AE, DC, MC, V.*

\$\$ ☷ **Bauer.** Head here for a good-value Bavarian-rustic inn that provides country comforts (painted wardrobes, raw light pine, lots of blue-and-white-check patterns) yet is within easy reach of the city. The family-run Bauer, 10 kilometers (6 miles) from the city center, is best for those traveling by car, although the S-bahn train line S-3 is nearby. ☒ *Münchnerstr. 6, D–85622 Feldkirchen,* ☎ *089/90980,* ☒ *089/909–8414. 103 rooms with bath. Restaurant, café, indoor pool, sauna. AE, DC, MC, V.*

\$\$ ☷ **Brack.** This modest but comfortable hotel is on a tree-lined thoroughfare just south of the center, near the Oktoberfest grounds and opposite the Poccistrasse subway station. The Brack has no restaurant, but the buffet breakfast will set you up for the day. ☒ *Lindwurmstr. 153, D–80337,* ☎ *089/771–052,* ☒ *089/725–0615. 50 rooms with bath. AE, DC, MC, V.*

\$\$ ☷ **Gästehaus am Englischen Garten.** Reserve well in advance for a room
★ at this popular converted water mill, over 200 years old, adjoining the Englischer Garten. The hotel, complete with ivy-clad walls and shutter-framed windows, is only a five-minute walk from the bars and shops of Schwabing. There's no restaurant, but who needs one with Schwabing's numerous eating possibilities so close? Be sure to ask for a room in the main building; the modern annex down the road is cheaper but lacks charm. In summer breakfast is served on the terrace. ☒ *Liebergesellstr. 8, D–80802,* ☎ *089/392–034,* ☒ *089/391–233. 27 rooms, 22 with bath or shower. No credit cards.*

\$\$ ☷ **Mayer.** If you are willing to sacrifice a convenient location for good value, head for this family-run hotel 25 minutes by suburban train from the Hauptbahnhof. The Mayer's first-class comforts and facilities cost less than half what you'd pay at similar lodgings in town. Built in the 1970s, it is furnished in Bavarian country-rustic style—lots of pine and solid green, red, and check fabrics. Chef (and hotel owner) Rainer Radach was a student of two of Germany's most respected master chefs. The Mayer is a 10-minute walk or a short taxi ride from Germering station on the S-5 suburban line, eight stops west of the Hauptbahnhof.

     ⊠ *Augsburgerstr. 45, D–82110 Germering,* ☎ *089/840–1515,* FAX *089/844–094. 56 rooms with bath. Restaurant, indoor pool. AE, MC.*

$$ ⛫ **Tele-Hotel.** This modern, well-appointed hotel on the outskirts of
★   Munich is handy to the television studios at Unterföhring (hence the
name) and is also conveniently located on the airport S-bahn Line 8,
a 15-minute ride from downtown. Television people escape their drab
canteen fare by popping into the hotel's Bavarian Hackerbräu restau-
rant, where a lunchtime menu for less than DM 30 is a hot favorite.
Rooms are stylishly furnished in cherry wood. ⊠ *Bahnhofstr. 15,
D–85774 Unterföhring,* ☎ *089/950–146,* FAX *089/950–6652. 60
rooms with bath, 1 apartment. Restaurant, bar, bowling, parking. AE,
DC, MC, V.*

$–$$ ⛫ **Kriemhild.** If you're traveling with children, you'll appreciate this
welcoming, family-run pension in the western suburb of Nymphenburg.
It's a 10-minute walk from the palace itself and around the corner from
the Hirschgarten Park, site of one of the city's best beer gardens. The
tram ride (No. 12) from downtown is 30 minutes. There's no restaurant. ⊠ *Guntherstr. 16, D–80639,* ☎ *089/170–077,* FAX *089/177–478.
18 rooms, 14 with bath. Bar. MC, V.*

$ ⛫ **Fürst.** On a quiet street just off Odeonsplatz, on the edge of the uni-
★   versity quarter, this very basic, clean guest house is constantly busy with
families and students traveling on a budget. Book early. ⊠ *Kardinal-
Döpfnerstr. 8, D–80333,* ☎ *089/281–043,* FAX *089/280860. 19 rooms,
12 with bath. No credit cards.*

$ ⛫ **Hotel-Pension Beck.** American and British guests receive a particu-
★   larly warm welcome from the Anglophile owner of the rambling,
friendly Beck. Rooms were recently refurnished in pinewood. The
pension has a prime location in the heart of fashionable Lehel (handy
for museums and the Englischer Garten). ⊠ *Thierschstr. 36, D–80538,*
☎ *089/220–708 or 089/225–75768,* FAX *089/220–925. 44 rooms, 5
with shower. No credit cards.*

$ ⛫ **Mariandl.** Large families are catered to at this rambling, friendly pen-
sion with huge rooms furnished in a variety of styles. Only four rooms
have their own showers, so be specific when booking. The ground floor
is taken up by a Viennese-style restaurant, with Biedermeier furnishings and a menu featuring every variety of Wiener schnitzel. The large
grand piano isn't there just for decoration; soirees in the style of the
Viennese evenings once enjoyed by Schubert (portraits of the composer
adorn the walls) and his friends are given here every weeknight. ⊠
Goethestr. 51, ☎ *089/534–108 or 089/535–158. 30 rooms, 4 with
shower. Restaurant. AE, DC, MC, V.*

NIGHTLIFE AND THE ARTS

Nightlife

Munich's nighttime attractions vary with the seasons. The year starts
with the abandon of *Fasching,* the Bavarian carnival time, which begins quietly in mid-November with the crowning of the King and
Queen of Fools, expands with fancy-dress balls, and ends with a great
street party on *Fasching Dienstag* (Shrove Tuesday). No sooner has Lent
brought the sackcloth curtain down on Fasching than the local weather
office is asked to predict when the spring sunshine will be warm
enough to allow the city's 100 beer gardens to open. From then until
late fall the beer garden dictates the style and pace of Munich's nightlife.
When it rains, the indoor beer halls and taverns absorb the thirsty like
blotting paper.

The beer gardens and most beer halls close at midnight, but there's no need to go home to bed then: Some bars and nightclubs are open until 6 AM. A word of caution about some of those bars: Most are run honestly, and prices are only slightly higher than normal, but a few may be unscrupulous. The seedier are near the main train station. Stick to beer or wine if you can, and pay as you go. And if you feel you're being duped, call the cops—the customer is usually, if not always, right.

Clubs

Munich's club scene has fallen victim to changing tastes. Gone are the '60s-generation nightclubs combining a good restaurant, a dance combo, and high-class exotic dancers. In their place are tiny cabaret stages and even smaller strip bars. The cabarets, mostly in Schwabing, usually perform political satire in dialects that are incomprehensible to non-Germans.

The Bayericher Hof's **Night Club** (⌧ Promenadenpl. 2–6, ☎ 089/21200) has dancing to live music and a very lively bar. American visitors will also do well at the **Park Hilton Hotel** (⌧ Am Tucherpark 7, ☎ 089/38450), which has an intimate piano bar with dance floor, or in the **Vier Jahreszeiten Kempinski** (⌧ Maximilianstr. 17, ☎ 089/21250), where there's piano music until 9 and then dancing.

Discos

Schwabing is disco land. There are more than a dozen in the immediate area around Schwabing's central square, the Münchner-Freiheit. One, the **Skyline** (☎ 089/348–470), is at the top of the Hertie department store that towers above the busy square. Other old-time favorites in a constantly changing scene include **Peaches** (☎ 089/348–470), on nearby Feilitzstrasse, and **Albatros** (☎ 089/344–972), just up the street on Occamstrasse (which is lined with lively clubs and pubs). Schwabing's central boulevard, Leopoldstrasse, also has its share of discos: **Ba-Ba-Lu** (☎ 089/343–535) has survived here for 30 years, updating its tape collection with every swing in musical taste. Across town, **PI** (⌧ Prinzregentenstr., on the west side of the Haus der Kunst, ☎ 089294–252), **Maximilian's Nightclub** (⌧ Maximilianpl. 16, ☎ 089/223–252), and the **Park-Café** (⌧ Sophienstr. 7, ☎ 089/598–313) are the most fashionable discos in town, but you'll have to talk yourself past the doorman to join the chic crowds inside. Munich's former airport and its new Franz-Josef-Strauss Airport both have cavernous discos; those at the former Riem Airport double as concert venues. The real ravers ride the S-bahn to Franz-Josef-Strauss, alighting at the Besucherpark station and bop till dawn at the **Night Flight** (☎ 089/9759–7999), where it's becoming fashionable for package-tour travelers to start their holidays with a pre-check-in, early-morning turn round the dance floor and a bar breakfast. **Nachtwerk** (⌧ Landsbergerstr. 185, ☎ 089/570—7390), in a converted factory, blasts out a range of sounds from punk to avant-garde nightly between 8 PM and 4 AM. Live bands also perform there regularly.

Bars and Singles

Every Munich bar is singles territory. Try **Schumann's** (⌧ Maximilianstr. 36, ☎ 089/229–268) anytime after the curtain comes down at the nearby opera house (and watch the barmen shake those cocktails; closed Sat.). Wait till after midnight before venturing into the **Alter Simpl** (⌧ Türkenstr. 57, ☎ 089/272–3083) for a sparkling crowd despite the gloomy surroundings. Back on fashionable Maximilianstrasse, **O'Reilly's Irish Cellar Pub** (☎ 089/292–311) offers escape from the German bar scene, and it serves genuine Irish Guinness. Great Caribbean cocktails and a powerful Irish-German Black and Tan (Guinness and strong German beer) are served at the English nautical-

style **Pusser's** bar (⊠ Falkenturmstr. 9, ☎ 089/220–500); it replaced
Munich's own Harry's Bar. Stiff competition is nearby at **Havana** (⊠
Herrnstr. 3, ☎ 089/291–884), which does its darnedest to look like
a rundown Cuban dive, although the chic clientele spoils those pretensions. Making contact at the **Wunderbar** (⊠ Hochbrückenstr. 3,
☎ 089/295–118) is easier on Tuesday nights, when telephones are
installed on the tables and at the bar and the place hums like a sty-
gian switchboard. The lively (at any time) basement bar is run by an
innovative young New Yorker. Munich's gay scene is found between
Sendlingertorplatz and Isartorplatz. Its most popular bars are **Nil** (⊠
Hans-Sachs-Str. 2, ☎ 089/265–545), **Ochsengarten** (Müllerstr. 47,
☎ 089/266–446), and **Pimpernel** (⊠ Müllerstr. 56, ☎ 089/267–176).

Jazz

Munich likes to think it's Germany's jazz capital, and to reinforce the
claim, some beer gardens have taken to replacing their brass bands with
funky combos. Purists don't like it, but jazz enthusiasts are happy. The
combination certainly works at **Waldwirtschaft Grosshesselohe** (⊠
Georg Kalb-Str. 3, ☎ 089/795–088), in the southern suburb of Grosshesselohe. Sundays are set aside for jazz, and if it's a nice day, the excursion is much recommended. Some city pubs also set aside Sunday
midday for jazz; try **Doktor Flotte** (⊠ Occamstr. 8). The best of the jazz
clubs are the **Scala Music Bar** (⊠ Brienner Str. 20, ☎ 089/285–858),
Nachtcafé (⊠ Maximilianpl. 5, ☎ 089/595–900), **Schwabinger Podium**
(⊠ Wagnerstr. 1, ☎ 089/399–482), and **Unterfahrt** (⊠ Kirchenstr. 96,
☎ 089/448–279). The **CD** (⊠ Ungererstr. 75) has a good jazz program
featuring regular performances by vivacious English actress and singer
Jenny Evans, who has a terrific voice and a warm welcome for visitors from the United States and Britain.

The Arts

Details of concerts and theater performances are listed in "Vorschau"
and "Monatsprogramm," booklets available at most hotel reception
desks, newsstands, and tourist offices. Some hotels will make ticket reservations; otherwise use a ticket agency in the city center, such as either
of the two kiosks in the underground concourse at Marienplatz; the
Abdendzeitung Schalterhalle (⊠ Sendlingerstr. 10, ☎ 089/267–024);
Residenz Bücherstube (concert tickets only; ⊠ Residenzstr. 1, ☎
089/220–868); or the **Max Hieber Konzertkasse** (⊠ Liebfrauenstr. 1,
☎ 089/290–080). There's also a special ticket agency for visitors with
disabilities: **abr-Theaterkasse** (⊠ Neuhauser Str. 9, ☎ 089/12040).

Concerts

Munich and music go together. Paradoxically, however, it's only since
1984 that the city has had a world-class concert hall: the Gasteig, a
lavish brick complex standing high above the Isar River, east of downtown. It's the permanent home of the Munich Philharmonic Orchestra, which regularly performs in its Philharmonic Hall. The city has
three other orchestras: the Bavarian State Orchestra, based at the National Theater; the Bavarian Radio Orchestra, which gives regular
Sunday concerts at the Gasteig; and the Kurt Graunke Symphony Orchestra, which performs at the Gärtnerplatz Theater. The leading
choral ensembles are the Munich Bach Choir, the Munich Motetten-
chor, and Musica Viva—the latter specializing in contemporary music.

Bayerischer Rundfunk (⊠ Rundfunkpl. 1, ☎ 089/558–080). The box
office is open weekdays 9–noon and 1–5.

Herkulessaal in der Residenz (⊠ Hofgarten, ☎ 089/2906–7263). The
box office opens one hour before performances.

Hochschule für Musik (✉ Arcisstr. 12, ☎ 089/559–101). Concerts featuring music students are given free of charge.

Olympiahalle (☎ 089/306–13577). The box office is open Monday–Saturday 11–6. Pop concerts are presented here. The box office is open Monday–Saturday 11–6.

Opera, Ballet, Operetta, and Musicals

Munich's Bavarian State Opera Company and its ballet ensemble perform at the **Nationaltheater** (also called the Bayerisches Staatsoper). The ticket office is at Maximilianstrasse 11 (☎ 0889/2185–1920). The evening ticket office, at the Maximilianstrasse entrance to the theater, opens one hour before curtain time. At the romantic Jugendstil **Staatstheater am Gärtnerplatz** (✉ Gärtnerpl. 3, ☎ 089/201-6767), a less ambitious but nevertheless high-quality program of opera, ballet, operetta, and musicals is presented. The ticket office is also at Maximilianstrasse 11. An evening ticket office opens at the theater one hour before performances.

Theater

Munich has scores of theaters and variety-show haunts, although most productions will be largely impenetrable if your German is shaky. A very active American company, the American Drama Group Europe, presents regular productions at the **Theater an der Leopoldstrasse** (✉ Leopoldstr. 17, ☎ 089/343–803 for program details), while a British theater group, the Munich English Theater (MET) is at home in the **Theater im Karlshof** (✉ Kalstr. 43, ☎ 089/596–611), a backyard theater with a friendly bar . Listed here are all the better-known theaters, as well as some of the smaller and more progressive spots. A visit to one or more will underline just why the Bavarian capital has such an enviable reputation as an artistic hot spot. Note that most theaters are closed during July and August.

Bayerisches Staatsschauspiel/Neues Residenztheater (Bavarian State Theater/New Residence Theater) (✉ Max-Joseph-Pl., box office is at Maximilianstr. 11, ☎ 089/2185–1920). Open weekdays 10–1 and 2–6, Saturday 10–1, and one hour before the performance.

Cuvilliés-Theater/Altes Residenztheater (Old Residence Theater) (✉ Max-Joseph-Pl.; entrance on Residenzstr.). The box office, at Maximilianstrasse 11 (☎ 089/221–1316), is open weekdays 10–1 and 2–6, Saturday 10–1, and one hour before the performance.

Deutsches Theater (✉ Schwanthalerstr. 13, ☎ 089/5523–4360). The box office is open weekdays noon–6, Saturday 10–1:30.

Gasteig (✉ Rosenheimerstr. 5, ☎ 089/5481–8181). This modern cultural complex includes two theaters—the Carl-Orff Saal and the Black Box—where plays in English are occasionally performed. The box office is open weekdays 10:30–2 and 3–6, Saturday 10:30–2.

Kleine Komödie, two theaters sharing a program of light comedy and farce (✉ Bayerischer Hof Hotel, Promenadepl., ☎ 089/292–810; ✉ Max-II-Denkmal, Maximilianstr. 27, ☎ 089/221–859). The box office at Bayerischer Hof is open Monday–Saturday 11–8, Sunday and holidays 3–8. The box office at Max-II-Denkmal is open Tuesday–Saturday 11–8, Monday 11–7, Sunday and holidays 3–8.

Marionettentheater (✉ Blumenstr. 29A, ☎ 089/265–712). The box office is open Tuesday–Sunday 10–noon.

Münchner Kammerspiele-Schauspielhaus (✉ Maximilianstr. 26, ☎ 089/237–21328). The box office is open weekdays 10–6, Saturday 10–1, closed Sundays and holidays.

Platzl Bühne (⌧ Am Platzl 1, ☎ 089/237–030) has a daily show (except Sunday and Monday) with typical Bavarian humor, yodeling, and *Schuhplattler* (the slapping of Bavarian leather shorts in time to the oompah music).

Prinzregententheater (⌧ Prinzregentenpl. 12, ☎ 089/470–6270). The box office, at Maximilian Strasse 11, is open weekdays 10–1 and 2–6, Saturday 10–1, and one hour before the performance.

Theater an der Leopoldstrasse (⌧ Leopoldstr. 17, ☎ 089/343–803) features the American Drama Group Europe, which gives English-language performances. No box office.

Munich also has several **theaters for children.** With pantomime such a strong part of the repertoire, the language problem disappears. The best of them is the **Münchner Theater für Kinder** (⌧ Dachauerstr. 46, ☎ 089/595–454 or 089/593–858). Two puppet theaters offer regular performances for children: the **Münchner Marionettentheater** (⌧ Blumenstr. 29a, ☎ 089/265–712) and **Otto Bille's Marionettenbühne** (⌧ Breiterangerstr. 15, ☎ 089/150–2168 or 089/310–1278). Munich is the winter quarters of the **Circus Krone** (⌧ Marsstr. 43, ☎ 089/558–166), which has its own permanent building. The circus performs there from Christmas until the end of March.

OUTDOOR ACTIVITIES AND SPORTS

The **Olympiapark,** built for the 1972 Olympics, is one of the largest sports and recreation centers in Europe. For general information about clubs, organizations, and events, contact the **Haus des Sports** (⌧ Briennerstr. 50, ☎ 089/520–151) or the **Städtisches Sportamt** (⌧ Neuhauserstr. 26, ☎ 089/233–6224).

Beaches and Water Sports
There is sailing and windsurfing on Ammersee and Starnbergersee. Windsurfers should pay attention to restricted areas at bathing beaches. Information on sailing is available from **Bayrischer Segler-Verband** (⌧ Georg-Brauchle-Ring 93, ☎ 089/157–02366). Information on windsurfing is available from **Verband der Deutschen Windsurfing Schulen** (⌧ Weilheim, ☎ 0881/5267).

Golf
Munich Golf Club has two courses that admit visitors on weekdays. Visitors must be members of a club at home. Its 18-hole course is at Strasslach in the suburb of Grünwald, south of the city (☎ 08170/450). Its nine-hole course is more centrally located, at Thalkirchen, on the Isar River (☎ 089/723–1304). The greens fee is DM 75 for both courses.

Hiking and Climbing
Information is available from **Deutscher Alpeinverein** (⌧ Praterinsel, ☎ 089/235–0900) and from the sporting-goods stores **Sport Scheck** (☎ 089/21660) and **Sport Schuster** (☎ 089/237–070).

Hotel Fitness Centers
Bayerischer Hof (⌧ Promenadepl. 2–6, ☎ 089/21200) has a rooftop pool, a sun terrace, a sauna, and nearby tennis.

München Sheraton (⌧ Arabellstr. 6, ☎ 089/92640) has a large indoor pool that opens onto a garden. In the pool room are weights and some exercise equipment.

Park Hilton International München (⌧ Am Tucherpark 7, ☎ 089/38450), facing the Englischer Garten, has marked running trails, an indoor pool, a sauna, and massage and spa facilities.

Vier Jahreszeiten Kempinski (⊠ Maximilianstr. 17, ☎ 089/230–390) is proud of its rooftop swimming pool; it also has a gym with weights and exercise equipment, sauna, massage room and solarium, and jogging maps in each room.

Ice-Skating

There is an indoor ice rink at the **Eissportstadion** in Olympiapark (⊠ Spiridon-Louis-Ring 3) and outdoor rinks at **Prinzregenten Stadium** (⊠ Prinzregentenstr. 80) and **Eisbahn-West** (⊠ Agnes-Bernauer Str. 241). There is outdoor skating in winter on the lake in the **Englischer Garten** and on the **Nymphenburger Canal,** where you can also go curling (*Eisstockschiessen*) by renting equipment from little wooden huts, which also sell hot drinks. Players rent sections of machine-smoothed ice on the canal. Watch out for the *Gefahr* (danger) signs warning of thin ice. Additional information is available from **Bayerischer Eissportverband** (⊠ Betzenweg 34, ☎ 089/81820).

Jogging

The best place to jog is the **Englischer Garten** (U-bahn: München-Freiheit or Universität), which is 11 kilometers (7 miles) around and has lakes and dirt and asphalt paths. You can also jog through **Olympiapark** (U-bahn: Olympiazentrum). A pleasant morning or evening jog can be had along the **Isar River,** or you can go for a jog in the 500-acre park of **Schloss Nymphenburg.** For a longer jog along the Isar River, take the S-bahn to Unterföhring and pace yourself back to Münchner-Freiheit—a distance of 6½ kilometers (4 miles).

Rowing

Rowboats can be rented on the southern bank of the **Olympiasee** in Olympiapark and at the **Kleinhesseloher See** in the Englischer Garten.

Swimming

You can try swimming outdoors in the Isar River at Maria-Einsiedel, but be warned that because the river flows from the Alps the water is frigid even in summer. Warmer swimming can be found off the beaches of the lakes near Munich—for example, the **Ammersee** and **Starnbergersee.** There are pools at **Cosima Bad** (⊠ Corner of Englschalkingerstr. and Cosimastr., in Bogenhausen), with man-made waves; **Dantebad** (⊠ Dantestr. 6); **Nordbad** (⊠ Schleissheimerstr. 142, in the Schwabing District); **Michaelibad** (⊠ Heinrich-Wieland-Str. 24); **Olympia-Schwimmhalle** (⊠ Olympiapark); and **Volksbad** (⊠ Rosenheimerstr. 1).

Tennis

There are indoor and outdoor courts at **Münchnerstrasse 15,** in München-Unterfohring; at the corner of **Drygalski-Allee** and **Kistlerhofstrasse,** in München-Fürstenried; and at **Rothof Sportanlage** (⊠ Denningerstr.), behind the Arabella and Sheraton hotels. In addition, there are about 200 outdoor courts all over Munich. Many can be booked via **Sport Scheck** (☎ 089/21660), which has installations around town. Prices vary from DM 18 to DM 25 an hour, depending on the time of day. Full details on tennis in Munich are available from the **Bayerischer Tennis Verband** (⊠ Georg-Brauchle-Ring 93, ☎ 089/157–02640).

SHOPPING

Shopping Districts

Munich has an immense **central shopping area,** 2 kilometers (1½ miles) of pedestrian streets stretching from the train station to Marienplatz and north to Odeonsplatz. The two main streets here are Neuhauserstrasse and Kaufingerstrasse, the sites of most major department stores

(☞ Department Stores, *below*). For upscale shopping, Maximilianstrasse, Residenzstrasse, and Theatinerstrasse are unbeatable and contain a fine array of classy and tempting stores that are the equal of any in Europe. **Schwabing,** north of the university, has several of the city's most intriguing and offbeat shopping streets—Schellingstrasse and Hohenzollernstrasse are two to try.

Antiques

Bavarian antiques can be found in the many small shops around the Viktualienmarkt; Westenriederstrasse is lined with antiques shops. Also try the area north of the university; Türkenstrasse, Theresienstrasse, and Barerstrasse are all filled with stores that sell antiques. **Seidl Antiquitäten** (⊠ Sieges-Str. 21, near Münchner Freiheit, ☎ 089/349–568) is so full of antique goods you might literally stumble over what you've always wanted to put on that corner of the mantelpiece. **Carl Jagemann's** (⊠ Residenzstr. 3, ☎ 089/225–493) has been in the antiques business for more than a century despite the shop's high prices. Perhaps friendly and knowledgeable service are the secret of its success. **Robert Müller's** antiques shop (⊠ Westenriederstr. 4, ☎ 089/221–726) is where you'll find German military memorabilia (spiked helmets from the First World War sell for upwards of DM 600).

Horst Fuchs (⊠ Westenriederstr. 17, ☎ 089/223–791) has one of Munich's best selections of antique beer mugs. His crowded shelves also hide sentimental embroidered pictures, kitschy souvenirs, and other amusing and inexpensive German knickknacks.

In **Antike Uhren Eder** (⊠ Prannerstr. 4, in the Hotel Bayerischer Hof building, ☎ 089/220–305), the silence is broken only by the ticking of dozens of highly valuable German antique clocks and by discreet bargaining over the high prices. The nearby **Antike Uhren H. Schley** (⊠ Kardinal-Faulhaber-Str. 14a, ☎ 089/226–188) specializes in antique clocks.

Interesting and/or cheap antiques and assorted junk from all over eastern Europe are laid out on the tarmac of the old airport at Riem (take the S-6 S-bahn). The flea market there on Fridays and Saturdays is one of Europe's largest.

Department Stores

Hertie (☎ 089/55120) occupying an entire city block between the train station and Karlsplatz, is the largest and, some claim, the best department store in the city. The basement has a high-class delicatessen with champagne bar and a stand-up bistro offering a daily changing menu that puts many high-price Munich restaurants to shame. Hertie's Schwabing branch (at the square known as Münchner-Freiheit) was recently given a top-to-bottom face-lift, which left it loaded with high-gloss steel and glass. **Kaufhof** has two central Munich stores (⊠ Karlspl. 2, opposite Hertie, ☎ 089/51250; ⊠ Corner of Marienpl., ☎ 089/231–851). Both offer a wide range of goods in the middle price range. If you catch an end-of-season sale, you're sure of a bargain.

Karstadt (☎ 089/290–230), in the 100-year-old Haus Oberpollinger, at the start of the Kaufingerstrasse shopping mall, is another high-class department store, with a very wide range of Bavarian arts and crafts. **Ludwig Beck** (⊠ Marienpl. 11, ☎ 089/236–910) is one of the smaller department stores, but it's packed from top to bottom with highly original wares—from fine feather boas to roughly finished Bavarian pottery. It comes into its own as Christmas approaches, when a series of booths, each delicately and lovingly decorated, are occupied by craftsmen turning out traditional German toys and decorations. **Hirmer** (⊠ Kaufingertr. 22, ☎ 089/236–830) has Munich's most comprehensive collection of German-made men's clothes, with a markedly friendly and knowledgeable staff. **K & L Ruppert** (⊠ Kaufingerstr. 15, ☎ 089/231–1470) has a good, fashionable range of German-made clothes in the lower price brackets.

Folk Costumes

Those who feel the need to deck themselves out in lederhosen or a dirndl, or to sport a green loden coat and little pointed hat with feathers, have a wide choice in the Bavarian capital. **Loden-Frey** (⊠ Maffeistr. 7–9, ☎ 089/236–930) is the top address for traditional Bavarian wear, although its rich brass-and-mahogany shelves also have other fine-quality German-made clothes. **Wallach** (⊠ Residenzstr. 3, ☎ 089/220–871) is small and exclusive and sets its clothes off against amusing shop-window displays (a Bavarian forest, for instance, with real trees). The aptly named **Lederhosen Wagner** (⊠ Tal 77, ☎ 089/225–697) has been in business since 1825, and the one-story shop hasn't changed much over the years—nor have the traditionally styled lederhosen.

Food Markets

Munich's **Viktualienmarkt** is *the* place to shop. Just south of Marienplatz, it's home to an array of colorful stands that sell everything from cheese to sausages, from flowers to wine. A visit here is more than just an excuse to buy picnic makings; it's central to an understanding of the easy-come–easy-go nature of Müncheners. If you are staying in the Schwabing area, the daily market at **Elisabethplatz** is worth a visit—it's much, much smaller than the Viktualienmarkt, but the range and quality of produce are comparable.

Dallmayr (⊠ Dienerstr. 14-15, ☎ 089/21350) is an elegant gourmet food store, with delights ranging from the most exotic fruits to English jams, served by efficient Munich matrons in smart blue-and-white linen costumes. The store's famous specialty is coffee, with more than 50 varieties to blend as you wish. There's also an enormous range of breads and a temperature-controlled cigar room.

The **Zerwick Gewölbe** (⊠ Ledererstr. 3, ☎ 089/226–824) is Munich's oldest venison shop, with a mouthwatering selection of smoked meats, including wild boar.

Gift Ideas

Munich is a city of beer, and items related to its consumption are obvious choices for souvenirs and gifts. **Ludwig Mory** (⊠ Marienpl. 8, ☎ 089/224–542) is the most centrally located beer-mug and coaster specialty shop, tucked away inconspicuously in the arcades of the City Hall on Marienplatz. **Sebastian Wesely** (⊠ Peterspl., ☎ 089/264–519) has shelves of glistening pewter mugs and plates and ceiling-high piles of Baroque-style, colorfully decorated candles, another Bavarian specialty.

Munich is also the home of the famous **Nymphenburg Porcelain** factory. The **Nymphenburg** store (⊠ corner of Odeonspl. and Briennerstr., ☎ 089/282–428) resembles a drawing room of the famous Munich palace, with dove-gray soft furnishings and the delicate, expensive porcelain safely locked away in bowfront cabinets.

You can also buy direct from the factory, on the grounds of Schloss Nymphenburg (⊠ Nördliches Schlossrondell 8). For Dresden and Meissen ware, go to **Kunstring Meissen** (⊠ Briennerstr. 4, ☎ 089/281–532).

Otto Kellnberger's Holzhandlung (⊠ Heiliggeiststr. 7–8, ☎ 089/226–479) specializes in another Bavarian craft—woodwork. **Geschenk Alm** (⊠ Heiliggeiststr. 7–8, ☎ 089/225–147) has nooks and crannies where brushes of every kind are stowed. Looking for that pig's-

64

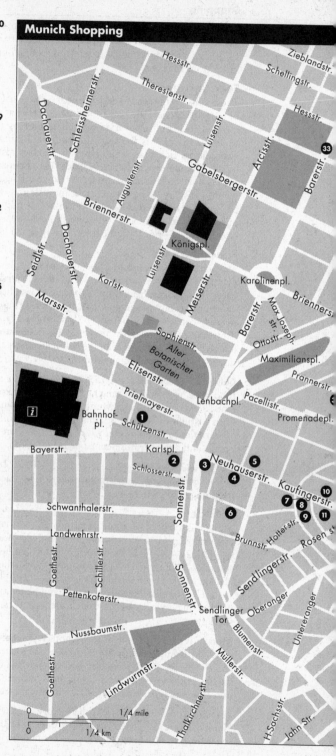

Munich Shopping

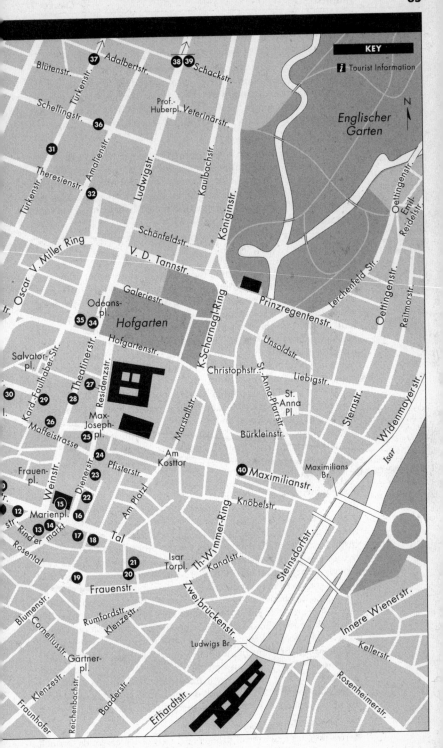

Blütenstr.

Adalbertstr.

37

38 39 Schackstr.

Türkenstr.

Schellingstr.

Prof.-
Huberpl. Veterinärstr.

36

31

Ludwigstr.

Amalienstr.

Theresienstr.

Kaulbachstr.

Königinstr.

32

Schönfeldstr.

Englischer
Garten

N

V. D. Tannstr.

Oettingenstr.

Emil-
Reidelstr.

K-Scharnagl-Ring

Prinzregentenstr.

Lerchenfeld Str.

Oettingenstr.

Oscar V. Miller Ring

Galeriestr.

Odeons-
pl.

Hofgarten

Reitmorstr.

35 34

Hofgartenstr.

Unsoldstr.

Liebigstr.

Theatinerstr.

Salvator-
pl.

Christophstr.

St. Anna-Pfarrstr.

St.
Anna
Pl.

Sternstr.

Karl-Faulhaber-Str.

Residenzstr.

27

Marstallstr.

Bürkleinstr.

Widenmayerstr.

30

29

28

Isar

26

Max-
Joseph-
pl.

25

Am
Kosttor

Maffeistrasse

24

Pfisterstr.

23

40 Maximilianstr.

Maximilians
Br.

Frauen-
pl.

Weinstr.

Dienerstr.

22

Am Platzl

Knöbelstr.

12

15

16

Marienpl.

Steinsdorfstr.

13 14

Rind er markt

17 18

Tal

Rosental

21

Isar
Torpl. Th-Wimmer-Ring

Kanalstr.

19

20

Innere Wienerstr.

Frauenstr.

Blumenstr.

Rumfordstr.

Klenzestr.

Zweibrückenstr.

Kellerstr.

Corneliusstr.

Gärtner-
pl.

Ludwigs Br.

Rosenheimerstr.

Klenzestr.

Reichenbachstr.

Baaderstr.

Fraunhofer

Erhardtstr.

bristle brush to get to the bottom of tall champagne glasses? This is the place to find it.

Obletter's (⊠ Karlspl. 8, ☎ 089/231–8601; ⊠ Marienpl., ☎ 089/264–062) has a total of five floors packed with toys, many of them hand-made German playthings of great charm and indestructible quality. An exceptionally friendly staff will help you make the right choice—to the point of engaging you in the latest computer game. This is also the place to find that great German market leader, the miniature train set.

Malls

Two new shopping malls have opened in recent years in the main pedestrian area, near Kaufingerstrasse and Neuhauserstrasse. **Kaufinger Tor** (⊠ Kaufingerstr. 117) has several floors of boutiques and cafés packed neatly together under a high glass roof. The aptly named **Arcade** (⊠ Neuhauserstr. 5) is where the young Munich crowd finds the best designer jeans and chunky jewelry.

SIDE TRIPS

Munich's excellent suburban railway network, the S-bahn, brings several outlying towns and attractive rural areas within easy reach for a day's excursion. The two nearest lakes, the Ammersee and Starnbergersee, are highly recommended in summer and winter alike, particularly for visitors who want to escape the bustle of Munich for a day. Dachau attracts overseas visitors, mostly because of its concentration-camp memorial site, but it's an attractive and historic town in its own right. Landshut, north of Munich, is way off the tourist track, but if it were the same distance south of Munich, this jewel of a Bavarian market town would have difficulty accommodating the crush. Wasserburg am Inn is another charming Bavarian town, held in the narrow embrace of the Inn River, and it's easily incorporated into an excursion to the nearby Chiemsee Lake. All these destinations have a wide choice of dining possibilities and hotels.

Ammersee

The Ammersee is the country cousin of the better-known, more cosmopolitan Starnbergersee, and many Bavarians (and tourists, too) like it all the more as a result. Fashionable Munich cosmopolites of centuries past thought it too distant for an excursion, not to mention too rustic for their sophisticated tastes. So the shores remained relatively free of the villas and parks that ring the Starnbergersee, and even though the upscale holiday homes of Munich's moneyed classes today claim some stretches of the eastern shore, the Ammersee still offers more open areas for bathing and boating than the bigger lake to the west. Bicyclists can circle the 19-kilometer-long (12-mile-long) lake (it's nearly 6 kilometers across at its widest point) on a path that rarely loses sight of the water. Hikers can spread out the tour for two or three days, staying overnight in any of the comfortable inns along the way. Dinghy sailors and Windsurfers can zip across in minutes with the help of the Alpine winds that swoop down from the mountains. A ferry boat cruises the lake at regular intervals during summer, dropping and picking up passengers at several pier stops. Join it at Herrsching.

Exploring Ammersee

Herrsching has a delightful promenade, part of which winds through the resort's park. The 100-year-old villa that sits so comfortably in the park, overlooking the lake and the Alps beyond, seems as if it were built by Ludwig II, such is the romantic and fanciful mixture of medieval turrets and Renaissance-style facades. It was actually built for the artist Ludwig Scheuermann in the late 19th century and became a favorite meeting place for Munich and Bavarian artists. It is now a municipal cultural center and the scene of chamber-music concerts on some summer weekends.

The Benedictine monastery of **Andechs,** one of southern Bavaria's most famous places of pilgrimage, lies 5 kilometers (3 miles) south of Herrsching. You can reach it on Bus 951 (connecting Ammersee and Starnbergersee). The crowds of pilgrims are drawn not only by the beauty of the hilltop monastery—its 15th-century pilgrimage church decked out with glorious rococo decoration in the mid-18th century and a repository of religious relics said to have been brought from the Holy Land 1,000 years ago—but also by the beer brewed there. The monastery makes its own cheese as well, and it's an excellent accompaniment to the rich, almost black, beer. You can enjoy both at large wood tables in the monastery tavern or on the terrace outside. The son of the last Austro-Hungarian emperor, Archduke Otto von Hapsburg, lives besides the lake. He celebrated his 80th birthday in the church in 1992, with a family party following in the tavern. ⊙ *Daily 7–7.*

The little town of **Diessen,** with its magnificent Baroque abbey-church, is situated at the southwest corner of the lake. Step inside the abbey to admire its opulent stucco decoration and sumptuous gilt-and-marble altar. Visit the church in late afternoon, when the light falls sharply on its crisp gray, white, and gold facade, etching the pencil-like tower and spire against the darkening sky over the lake. Don't go without at least peeping into neighboring St. Stephen's courtyard, its cloisters smothered in wild roses.

Dining

DIESSEN
The **Gasthaus Unterbräu** (⊠ Carl-Orff-Pl., ☎ 08807/8437; $) has a rustic exterior you'll admire; venture inside for an indelible culinary experience (or in summer find a table outside in the leafy beer garden). The **Hotel-Gasthof-Seefelder Hof** (⊠ Alexander-Koester-Weg 6, ☎ 08807/1022; $) has a delightful beer garden.

HERRSCHING
Gasthof zur Post (⊠ Andechsertr. 1, ☎ 08152/1210; $) is everything a Bavarian tavern should be. The weekday lunch menu is an unbeatable value, and the locally brewed dark beer is unbeatable, period. The **Hotel Promenade** (⊠ Summerstr. 6, ☎ 08152/1350; $) is one of the best of the several idyllic terrace restaurants you'll find along the lakeside promenade. The **Restaurante de Mario** (⊠ Am Mühlfeld 2, ☎ 08152/1486; $), at the end of the promenade, has the tastiest *tiramisù* outside Italy.

Ammersee A to Z

ARRIVING AND DEPARTING
By Car. Take Autobahn 96—follow the signs to Lindau—and 20 kilometers (12 miles) west of Munich take the exit for Herrsching, the lake's principal town. Herrsching is 40 kilometers (25 miles) from Munich.

By Train. Herrsching, on the east bank of the lake, is the end of the S-bahn 5 suburban line, a half-hour ride from Munich's central Marienplatz. From Herrsching station, Bus 952 runs north along the lake, and Bus 956 runs south.

VISITOR INFORMATION
Verkehrsamt, ⊠ Bahnhofspl. 2, ☎ 08152/5227.

Dachau

The first Nazi concentration camp was built just outside this town. Dachau preserves the memory of the camp and the horrors perpetrated there with deep contrition while trying, with commendable discretion, to signal that it also has other things to offer visitors. It's older than nearby Munich, for example, with local records going back to the time of Charlemagne in the 9th century. And it's a handsome town, too, built on a hilltop with fine views of Munich and the Alps.

Exploring Dachau

The site of the infamous camp, now the **Dachau Concentration Camp Memorial,** is just outside the town. Photographs, contemporary documents, the few remaining cell blocks, and the grim crematorium create a somber and moving picture of the camp, where many tens of thousands lost their lives. To reach the memorial by car, leave the center of the town along Schleissheimerstrasse and turn left into Alte Römerstrasse; the site is on the left. By public transport, take Bus 722 from the Dachau S-bahn train station to Robert-Boschstrasse and walk along Alte Römerstrasse for 100 yards, or board Bus 720 and get off at Ratiborer Strasse. ⊠ *Alte Römerstr. 75,* ☎ *08121/1741.* ☎ *Free.* ☉ *Tues.–Sun. 9–5. A guided tour of the site in English is given weekends at 12:30. A documentary film (in English) is shown daily at 11:30 and 3:30.*

Schloss Dachau, the hilltop castle, dominates the town. What you'll see is the one remaining wing of a palace built by the Munich architect Josef Effner for the Wittelsbach ruler Max Emanuel in 1715, a replacement for the original castle built during the 15th century. During the Napoleonic Wars at the beginning of the 19th century the palace served as a field hospital, treating French and Russian casualties from the Battle of Austerlitz (1805). The wars made a casualty, too, of the palace, and three of the four wings were demolished by order of King Max Joseph I. What's left is a handsome cream-and-white building, with an elegant pillared and lantern-hung café on the ground floor and the former ballroom above. Concerts are regularly held here, beneath a richly decorated and carved ceiling, with painted panels representing characters from ancient mythology. The east-facing terrace affords panoramic views of Munich and, on fine days, the distant Alps, while in summer the café opens out onto a very attractive south-facing terrace overlooking pretty, orchardlike gardens. There's also a 250-year-old *Schlossbrauerei* (castle brewery), which hosts the town's own beer and music festival each year during the first half of August. ⊠ *Schlosspl.,* ☎ *08131/87923.* ☎ *DM 2.* ☉ *May–Sept., weekends 2–5. A visit to the Schloss is included in a guided tour of the town, May–mid-Oct., Sat. at 10:30;* ☎ *DM 5.*

St. Jacob, Dachau's parish church, was built in the early 16th century in late-Renaissance style on the foundations of 14th-century Gothic building. Baroque features and a characteristic onion dome were added in the late 17th century. On the south wall you can admire a very fine 17th-century sundial clock. ⊠ *Konrad-Adenauer-Str. 7,* ☉ *Daily 7–7.*

Dachau served as a lively artists' colony during the 19th century, and the tradition lives on. The picturesque houses designed for the colony line Hermann-Stockmann-Strasse and part of Münchner Strasse, and many of them are still the homes of successful artists. The **Gemälde-galerie** displays the works of many of the town's 19th-century artists. ⊠ *Konrad-Adenauer-Str. 3,* ☎ *08131/567516.* ☎ *DM 3.* ☉ *Wed.–Fri. 11–5, weekends and public holidays 1–5.*

Dining and Lodging

The **Bräustüberl** (⌖ Schlossstr. 8, ☎ 08131/72553; $), 100 yards from the castle, has a shady beer garden for summer lunches and a cozy tavern for year-round Bavarian-style eating and drinking. The solid, historic **Zieglerbräu** (⌖ Konrad–Adenauer–Str. 8, ☎ 08131/4074; $–$$), once a 17th-century brewer's home, is now a wood-paneled restaurant; it's next to the ivy-covered Town Hall. The **Hörhammerbräu** (⌖ Konrad–Adenauer–Str. 12, ☎ 08131/4711; $–$$) serves its own beer, as well as hearty Bavarian dishes costing less than DM 20. The Hörhammerbräu also has 21 reasonably priced guest rooms.

Dachau A to Z

ARRIVING AND DEPARTING

By Car. Dachau is 20 kilometers (12 miles) northwest of Munich. Take the B–12 country road, or the Stuttgart Autobahn to the Dachau exit.

By Train. Dachau is on the S-bahn No 2 suburban line, a 20-minute ride from Munich's Marienplatz.

VISITOR INFORMATION

Verkehrsverein Dachau, ⌖ Konrad-Adenauer-Str. 3, ☎ 08131/84566.

Landshut

If fortune had placed Landshut 64 kilometers (40 miles) south of Munich, in the protective folds of the Alpine foothills, instead of the same distance north, in the dull flatlands of Lower Bavaria, this delightful, historic town would have been overrun by visitors long ago. All the same, Landshut's geographical misfortune is the discerning visitor's good luck, for the town is never overcrowded, with the possible exception of the three summer weeks every four years when the *Landshuter Hochzeit* is celebrated. The next celebration is in 1997, and then a visit to Landshut is really a must on any tour of this part of Germany. The festival commemorates the marriage in 1475 of Prince George of Bayern-Landshut, son of the expressively named Ludwig the Rich, to Princess Hedwig, daughter of the king of Poland. The entire town is swept away in a colorful reconstruction of the event, which increased its already regal importance and helped give it the majestic air you'll still find within its ancient walls.

Exploring Landshut

Landshut has two magnificent, cobbled market streets. The one in **Altstadt** (Old Town) is considered by many to be the most beautiful city street in Germany; the one in **Neustadt** (New Town) projects its own special appeal. The two streets run parallel to each other, tracing a course between the Isar River and the heights overlooking the town. A steep path from Altstadt takes you up to **Burg Trausnitz**, sitting commandingly on the heights. This castle was begun in 1204 and accommodated the Wittelsbach dukes of Bayern-Landshut until 1503. ☎ 0871/22638. ◨ *DM 4, including guided tour.* ☉ *Apr.–Sept., daily 9–noon and 1–5; Oct.–Mar., daily 10–noon and 1–4.*

The **Stadtresidenz** in Altstadt was the first Italian Renaissance building of its kind north of the Alps. During the 16th century the Wittelsbachs moved to the Altstadt and into this palace. The Renaissance facade of the palace forms an almost modest part of the architectural splendor and integrity of Altstadt, where even the ubiquitous McDonald's has to serve its hamburgers behind a Baroque exterior. ☎ 0871/22638. ◨ *DM 3.* ☉ *Apr.–Sept., daily 9–noon and 1–5; Oct.–Mar., daily 10–noon and 1–4.*

St. Martin's Church, with the tallest brick church tower in the world, soars above the other buildings with its 436-foot tower and bristling spire. The church contains some magnificent Gothic treasures and a 16th-century carved Madonna. Moreover, it is surely the only church in the world to contain an image of Hitler, albeit in devilish pose. The Führer and other Nazi leaders are portrayed as executioners in a 1946 stained-glass window showing the martyrdom of St. Kastulus. In the nave of the church is a clear and helpful description of its history and its treasures, an aid to English-speaking visitors that could profitably be copied by other churches and historical sites in Germany.

Dining and Lodging

DINING

There are several attractive Bavarian-style restaurants in Altstadt and Neustadt, most of them with charming beer gardens. The best are **Brauereigasthof Ainmiller** (⊠ Altstadt 195, ☎ 0871/21163; $), **Gasthaus Schwabl** (⊠ Neustadt 500, ☎ 0871/23930; $), **Zum Hofreiter** (⊠ Neustadt 505, ☎ 0871/24402; $), and the **Hotel Goldene Sonne** (⊠ Neustadt 520, ☎ 0871/92530; $).

The **Klausenberg Panorama-Restaurant** (⊠ Klausenberg 17; $) has a terrace with a fine view of the town and the surrounding countryside. For a reasonable three-course lunch, try the **Buddha** (⊠ Apotheker-gasse), which serves a good, fixed-price Chinese meal for around DM 15 per person. If you're looking for an authentic Bavarian dining experience, make your way to the old Episcopal town of Freising, halfway between Landshut and Munich. Here you'll find the **Bayerische Staatsbrauerei Weihenstephan** (☎ 08161/13004; $), the world's oldest brewery (dating from AD 1040), where you can select from 11 different brews. Freising is the final stop on the S-1 suburban railway line from Munich and one stop from Landshut by express train.

LODGING

Landshut has several hotels and a handful of reasonably priced, comfortable inns. The **Hotel Kaiserhof** (⊠ Papiererstr. 2, ☎ 0871/6870, FAX 0871/687–403; $$$) is housed in an attractive 18th-century-style riverside building. At the **Romantik Hotel Fürstenhof** (⊠ Stethaimerstr. 3, ☎ 0871/92550, FAX 0871/925544; $$$), you'll rest your head in a tastefully modernized villa. **Hotel Goldene Sonne** (⊠ Neustadt 520, ☎ 0871/92530, FAX 0871/9253350; $$) is a historic inn in the Old Town.

In 1996 the **Hotel Schloss Schönbrunn** (⊠ Schsnbrunn 1, ☎ 0871/95220, FAX 0871/952211; $$$) opened in the Schloss Schönbrunn palace, on the edge of Landshut. Rooms are suitably palatial and look out over the superb palace grounds.

Landshut A to Z

ARRIVING AND DEPARTING

By Car. Landshut is a 45-minute drive northwest from Munich on either Autobahn A–92—follow the signs to Deggendorf—or the B–11 highway.

By Train. Landshut is on the Plattling–Regensburg–Passau line, a 40-minute ride by express train from Munich.

VISITOR INFORMATION

Verkehrsverein, ⊠ *Altstadt 315,* ☎ *0871/922050.*

Starnbergersee

The Starnbergersee was one of Europe's first pleasure grounds. Royal coaches trundled out from Munich to its wooded banks in the Baroque years of the 17th century; in 1663 Elector Ferdinand Maria threw a huge shipboard party at which 500 guests wined and dined as 100 oarsmen propelled them around the lake. Today pleasure steamers perform the same task for visitors of less-than-noble rank. The lake is still lined with the Baroque palaces of Bavaria's aristocracy, but their owners must now share the lakeside with public parks, beaches, and boatyards. The Starnbergersee is one of Bavaria's largest lakes—19 kilometers (12 miles) long and 5 kilometers (3 miles) across at its widest point—so there's plenty of room for swimmers, sailors, and Windsurfers. On its west shore is one of Germany's finest golf courses, but it's about as difficult for the casual visitor to play a game there as it was for a Munich commoner to win an invitation to one of Prince Ferdinand's boating parties. Those on the trail of Ludwig II should note that Starnbergersee (beside the village of Berg) was where the doomed monarch met his watery death under circumstances that remain a mystery.

Exploring Starnbergersee

At Berg you'll find the **King Ludwig II Memorial Chapel,** on the eastern shore of the lake. A well-marked path leads through thick woods to the chapel, built near the point in the lake where the king's body was found on June 13, 1886. He had been confined in nearby Berg Castle after the Bavarian government took action against his withdrawal from reality and into expensive castle-building fantasyland. Look for the cross in the lake, which marks the point where his body was recovered.

The castle of **Possenhofen,** home of Ludwig's favorite cousin, Sissi, stands on the western shore of Starnbergersee, practically opposite Berg. Local lore says they used to send affectionate messages across the lake to each other. Sissi married the Austrian emperor Franz Joseph I but frequently returned to the Starnbergersee; she spent more than 20 consecutive summers in the lakeside castle, now converted into luxury apartments.

Just offshore is the tiny **Roseninsel** (Rose Island), where King Maximilian II built a summer villa. You can swim to its tree-fringed shores or sail across in a dinghy or on a Windsurfer (Possenhofen's boatyard is one of the lake's many rental points).

Dining and Lodging

The fine old **Bayerischer Hof** (⊠ Bahnhofstr. 12, ☎ 08151/918–888; $$) has an elegant café, with a sunny terrace, a Bavarian tavern named Fisher Stübe, and reasonably priced guest rooms. If you feel like a splurge, book the beamed König-Ludwig suite, with a terrace commanding a breathtaking view of the lake and the mountains beyond. The **Gasthof Zur Sonne** (⊠ Hanfelder Str. 7, ☎ 08151/14571; $$) has no lake views, but lake fish land every day on the menu of its beamed and wood-paneled restaurant. The **Seerestaurant Undosa** (⊠ Seepromenade 1, ☎ 08151/8021; $$), where the atmosphere is always boisterous, has uninterrupted lake views for your enjoyment. Farther down the lake, on the outskirts of Possenhofen, is the **Forsthaus am See** (⊠ Am See 1, Pocking-Possenhofen, ☎ 08157/93010; $$), where you dine beneath a carved panel ceiling imported from Austria's South Tyrol. The restaurant has a lakeside beer garden and its own pier for guests who arrive by boat. From Tutzing, at the end of the S-6 suburban line, a short walk up into the hills leads to the **Forsthaus Ilka-Höhe** (☎ 08158/8242; $$), a rustic lodge with a fine view of the lake and excellent Bavarian food. It's closed Tuesday, October–March. On the side of the lake near the Berg Castle grounds and the King Ludwig II Memorial Chapel, try the **Dorint Seehotel Leoni** (⊠ Assenbucherstr. 44, Berg-Leoni; $), where you can also rent bicycles (☎ 08151/5060). The **Park-und Strandhotel Schloss Berg** (⊠ Ölschlag 9; $) has a lakeside dining terrace.

Starnbergersee A to Z

By Car. The north end of the lake, where the resort of Starnberg sits in stately beauty, is a 30-minute drive from Munich on Autobahn A–95. Follow the signs to Garmisch and take the Starnberg exit. Country roads then skirt the west and east banks of the lake.

By Train. The S-bahn 6 suburban line runs from Munich's central Marienplatz to Starnberg and three other towns on the lake's west bank: Possenhofen, Feldafing, and Tutzing. The journey from Marienplatz to Starnberg takes 35 minutes. The east bank of the lake can be reached by bus from the town of Wolfratshausen, the end of the S-bahn 7 suburban line.

Fremdenverkehrsverband, ⊠ Wittelsbacher Str. 9 (Am Kirchpl.), ☎ 08151/13008.

Wasserburg am Inn

Wasserburg floats like a faded ship of state in a benevolent, lazy loop of the Inn River, which comes within a few yards of cutting the ancient town off from the wooded slopes of the encroaching countryside. The river caresses the southern limits of the ancient town center, embraces its eastern boundary with rocky banks 200 feet high, returns westward as if looking for a way out of this geographical puzzle, and then heads north in search of its final destination, the Danube. Wasserburg sleeps on in its watery cradle, a perfectly preserved, beautifully set medieval town, once a vitally important trading post but later thankfully ignored by the industrialization that gripped Germany in the 19th century.

Exploring Wasserburg

You're never more than 100 yards or so from the river in Wasserburg's Old Town center, which huddles within the walls of the castle that originally gave Wasserburg (Water Castle) its name. The town has a southern, almost Italian look, typical of many Inn River towns. There are two large parking lots on the north and east banks, and you're advised to use one of them; the town council is expanding the traffic-free zone. It's only a few minutes' walk from the lots to central Marienplatz. There you'll find Wasserburg's late-Gothic brick **Town Hall.** ⊠ Marienpl. ☎ DM 1.50. ☉ Guided tours Tues.–Fri. at 10, 11, 2, 3, and 4; weekends at 10 and 11.

The 14th-century **Frauenkirche** on Marienplatz is the town's oldest church. It incorporates an ancient watchtower. The Baroque altar frames a beautiful Madonna by an unknown 14th-century artist.

Wasserburg's imposing 15th-century parish church, **St. Jakob,** has a finely crafted intricate Baroque pulpit, carved in 1640.

The **Erstes Imaginäres Museum,** at the town end of Wasserburg's only bridge, next to the 14th-century town gate, is one of Germany's most unusual museums. The museum has a collection of more than 400 world-famous paintings, without an original among them; every single one is a precise copy. ☎ DM 3. ☉ May–Sept., Tues.–Sun. 11–5; Oct.–Apr., Tues.–Sun. 1–5.

Wasserburg is a convenient base for enticing walks along the banks of the Inn River and into the surrounding countryside. A pretty path west leads to the village of **Attel.** Another half hour into the Attel River valley and one reaches the enchanting castle-restaurant of **Schloss Hart** (☎ 08039/1774).

Dining and Lodging

DINING

The **Herrenhaus** (⌧ Herrengasse 17, ☎ 08071/2800; $$) has the most compelling atmosphere for dining in Wasserburg—there's a centuries-old vaulted wine cellar. For simple and traditional Bavarian fare, try the **Gasthaus Zum Löwen** (⌧ Marienpl. 10, ☎ 08071/7400; $$), a wood-paneled restaurant whose tables spill out onto the sidewalk in summer.

LODGING

Try the **Hotel Fletzinger** (⌧ Fletzingergasse 1, ☎ 08071/8010, FAX 08071/40810; $$) for solid comfort, along with antiques in some rooms, good, hearty food, and a beer garden. On Marienplatz, the ancient **Paulanerstuben** (⌧ Marienpl. 9, ☎ 08071/3903; $), with its delightful rococo facade, offers simple yet reassuring comforts.

Wasserburg A to Z

ARRIVING AND DEPARTING

By Car. Take the B–304 highway from Munich, which leads directly to Wasserburg. It's a 45-minute drive.

By Train. Take either the S-bahn 4 suburban line to Ebersberg and change to a local train to Wasserburg, or the Salzburg express, changing at Grafing Bahnhof to the local line. Both trips take 90 minutes.

VISITOR INFORMATION

Verkehrsamt, ⌧ Rathaus, Rathauspl. 1, ☎ 08071/1050.

MUNICH A TO Z

Arriving and Departing

By Bus

Long-distance buses arrive at and depart from the north side of the main train station. A taxi stand is right next to it.

By Car

From the north (Nürnberg and Frankfurt) leave the autobahn at the Schwabing exit. From Stuttgart and the west the autobahn ends at Obermenzing. The autobahns from Salzburg and the east, Garmisch and the south, and Lindau and the southwest all join the Mittlerer Ring (city beltway). When leaving any autobahn, follow the Stadtmitte signs for downtown Munich.

By Plane

Munich's **Franz Josef Strauss (FJS) Airport**—named after the late Bavarian state premier—opened in 1992. It is 28 kilometers (18 miles) northeast of the city center, between the small towns of Freising and Erding. One of the biggest and most modern airports in Europe, FJS took 10 years to build. It is capable of handling 14 million passengers a year and replaces the old Riem Airport, which is now a collection of discos and concert halls.

BETWEEN FJS AIRPORT AND DOWNTOWN

A fast train service links **FJS Airport** with Munich's Hauptbahnhof (the main train station). The S-8 line operates from a terminal directly beneath the airport's arrival and departure halls. Trains leave every 20 minutes, and the journey takes 38 minutes. Several intermediate stops are made, including Ostbahnhof (convenient for lodgings east of the Isar River) and such city-center stations as Marienplatz. A one-way ticket costs DM 13.20, DM 10.40 if you purchase a multiple-use "strip" ticket (☞ Getting Around, *below*). A family of up to five (two adults and three children) can make the trip for DM 24 by buying a *Tageskarte* ticket. A bus service was reintroduced in 1994, but it's slower and more expensive (DM 15) than the S-bahn link (☞ Getting Around by Public Transportation, *below*), and only to be recommended if you are traveling with a lot of luggage. The taxi fare from the airport costs between DM 90 and DM 100. During rush hour (7 AM–10 AM and 4 PM–7 PM), you need to allow up to one hour of traveling time. If you're driving from the airport to the city, take route A–9 and follow the signs for München Stadtmitte. If you're driving to FJS from the city center, head north through Schwabing, join the A–9 Autobahn at the Frankfurter Ring intersection, and follow the signs for the airport (FLUGHAFEN).

By Train

All long-distance rail services arrive at and depart from the main train station; trains to and from some destinations in Bavaria use the adjoining Starnbergerbahnhof, which is under the same roof as the Hauptbahnhof. The high-speed InterCity Express trains connect Munich, Frankfurt, and Hamburg on one line; Munich, Würzburg, and Hamburg on another. For information on train schedules, call 089/19419; most railroad information staff speak English. For tickets and travel information, go to the station information office or try the ABR travel agency, right by the station, on Bahnhofplatz.

Getting Around

By Bicycle

Munich and its environs are easily navigated on two wheels. The city is threaded with a network of specially designated bike paths. A free map showing all bike trails is available at all city tourist offices.

You can rent bicycles at the **Englischer Garten** (✉ Corner of Königstr. and Veterinärstr., ☎ 089/397–016) for DM 5 per hour or DM 15 for the day from May–October, weekends in good weather; **Aktiv-Rad** (✉ Hans-Sachs Str. 7, ☎ 089/266–506) and **A–Z Fahrräder** (✉ Zweibrückenstr. 8, ☎ 089/223–272) hire them out for DM 70 to DM 90 per week. Bikes can also be rented at the Hauptbahnhof (Radius Touristik, opposite platform 31), and at some S-bahn and mainline stations around Munich. A list of stations that offer the service is available from the Deutsche Bahn. The cost is DM 6–DM 8 a day if you've used public transportation to reach the station; otherwise it's DM 10–DM 12, depending on the type of bike.

On Foot

Downtown Munich is only a mile square and is easily explored on foot. Almost all the major sights in the city center are on the interlinking web of pedestrian streets that run from Karlsplatz by the main train station to Marienplatz and the Viktualienmarkt and extend north around the Frauenkirche and up to Odeonsplatz. The central tourist office issues a free map with suggested walking tours.

By Public Transportation

Munich has an efficient and well-integrated public transportation system, consisting of the **U-bahn** (subway), the **S-bahn** (suburban railway), the **Strassenbahn** (streetcars), and buses. Marienplatz forms the heart of the U-bahn and S-bahn network, which operates from around 5 AM to 1 AM. An all-night tram and bus service was introduced on main city routes in 1994. For a clear explanation in English of how the system works, pick up a copy of *Rendezvous mit München*, available free of charge at all tourist offices.

Fares are uniform for the entire system. As long as you are traveling in the same direction, you can transfer from one mode of transporta-

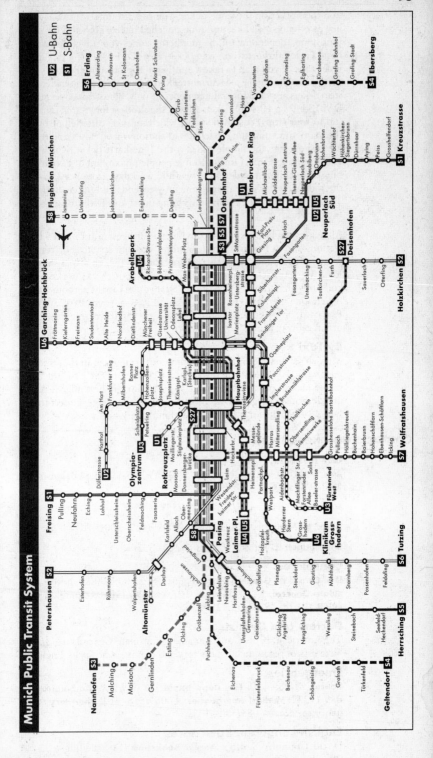

Munich Public Transit System

U2 U-Bahn
S1 S-Bahn

tion to another on the same ticket. You can also interrupt your journey as often as you like, and time-punched tickets are valid for up to four hours, depending on the number of zones you travel through. A basic **Einzelfahrkarte** (one-way ticket) costs DM 3.40 for a ride in the inner zone; if you plan to take a number of trips around the city, you'll save money by buying a **Mehrfahrtenkarte,** or multiple strip ticket. Red strip tickets are valid for children under 15 only. Blue strips cover adults. DM 13 buys a 10-strip ticket. All but the shortest inner-area journeys (up to four stops) cost two strips, which must be canceled at one of the many time-punching machines at stations or on buses and trams. For a short stay the simplest idea is the **Tageskarte** ticket, which provides unlimited travel for up to five people (maximum of two adults, plus three children under 15). It is valid weekdays from 9 AM to 4 AM the following day and at any time on weekends and public holidays. The costs are DM 12 for an inner-zone ticket and DM 24 for the entire network.

All tickets can be purchased from the blue dispensers at U- and S-bahn stations and at bus and streetcar stops. Bus and streetcar drivers, all tourist offices, and Mehrfahrtenkarten booths (which display a white *K* on a green background) also sell tickets. Spot checks are common and carry an automatic fine of DM 60 if you're caught without a valid ticket. One final tip: Holders of a Eurail Pass, a Youth Pass, an Inter-Rail card, or a Deutsche Bahn Tourist Card can travel free on all suburban railway trains.

By Taxi
Munich's cream-color taxis are numerous. Hail them in the street; or telephone 089/21610 (there's an extra charge of DM 2 for the drive to the pickup point). Rates start at DM 4 for the first mile. There is an additional charge of DM 1 for each piece of luggage. Expect to pay DM 12–DM 13 for a short trip within the city.

Contacts and Resources

Car Rentals
Avis: ✉ Nymphenburgerstr. 61, ☎ 089/1260–0020; ✉ Balanstr. 74, ☎ 089/403–091.

Europcar: ✉ Hirtenstr. 14, ☎ 089/557–145.

Hertz: ✉ Nymphenburgerstr. 81, ☎ 089/129–5001.

Sixt-Budget: ✉ Seitzstr. 9, ☎ 089/223–333.

Consulates
U.S. Consulate General, ✉ Königinstr. 5, ☎ 089/28880. **British Consulate General,** ✉ Bürkleinstr. 10, ☎ 089/211090. **Canadian Consulate,** ✉ Tal 29, ☎ 089/290650.

Doctors and Dentists
The American, British, and Canadian Consulate-Generals (☞ *above*) have lists of recommended doctors and dentists who speak English.

Emergencies
Police: ☎ 089/110. **Fire department:** ☎ 089/112. **Ambulance:** ☎ 089/19222. **Medical emergencies:** ☎ 089/558–661. **Pharmacy emergency service:** ☎ 089/594–475.

English-Language Bookstores
David Connolly Smith's **Anglia Bookshop** (✉ Schellingstr. 3, ☎ 089/283–642) has been in business for a quarter of a century and can claim to be the leading English-language bookstore in Munich. You may have trouble finding what you're looking for, however, because

of the shop's incredible disorder. **Wordsworth** (✉ Schellingstr. 21a, ☎ 089/280–9141) is a well-kept shop with books in English. The **Internationale Presse** store is at the main train station. The **Hugendubel** bookshop (✉ 2nd floor, at Marienpl., and at Karlspl.) has a good selection.

Guided Tours

EXCURSIONS

Bus excursions to the Alps, to Austria, to the royal palaces and castles of Bavaria, or along the Romantic Road can be booked through **ABR** (✉ Hauptbahnhof, ☎ 089/591–315 or 089/59041). **PanoramaTours** (✉ Arnulfstr. 8, next to the Hauptbahnhof, ☎ 089/120–4248) operates numerous trips, including the Royal Castles Tour (Schlösserfahrt) of "Mad" King Ludwig's dream palaces; the cost is DM 75, excluding entrance fees to the palaces. Bookings can also be made through all major hotels in the city. The tours depart from in front of the Hauptbahnhof outside the Hertie department store.

The Upper Bavarian Regional Tourist Office (☞ Visitor Information, *below*) provides information and brochures for excursions and accommodations outside Munich.

The **S-bahn** can quickly take you to some of the most beautiful places in the countryside around Munich. Line S-6, for example, will whisk you lakeside to Starnberger See in a half hour; Line S-4 runs to the depths of the Ebersberger Forest. You can take a bicycle on S-bahn trains.

ORIENTATION TOURS

A variety of city bus tours is offered by **Panorama Tours** (✉ Arnulfstr. 8, ☎ 089/120–4248). The blue buses operate year-round, departing from in front of the Hertie department store on Bahnhofplatz (across from the main entrance to the train station). The Kleine Rundfahrt, a one-hour city tour, leaves daily at 10 AM and 2:30 PM, as well as 11:30 AM in midsummer. The cost is DM 15. The "Olympiatour," which lasts about 2½ hours, explores the Olympia Tower and grounds; it departs daily at 10 AM and 2:30 PM, and the cost is DM 27. The Grosse Rundfahrt, or extended city tour, comes in two varieties; each lasts around 2½ hours and costs DM 27. The morning tour includes visits to the Frauenkirche and Alte Pinakothek; the afternoon tour visits Schloss Nymphenburg. They run Tuesday–Sunday, leaving at 10 and 2:30, respectively. The München bei Nacht tour provides five hours of Munich by night and includes dinner and visits to three nightspots. It departs May–October, Friday and Saturday at 7:30 PM; the cost is DM 100.

WALKING AND BICYCLING TOURS

The **Munich tourist office** (☞ Visitor Information, *below*) organizes guided walking tours for groups or individuals; no advance booking is necessary. The meeting place is the Fischbrunnen (Fish Fountain) on Marienplatz on Monday, Tuesday, and Thursday at 10 AM; the cost is DM 6 per person. **Münchner Stadtrundgänge** has a daily tour, starting at 9:30 AM at the Mariensäule in the middle of Marienplatz. The tour costs DM 10. Call Siegfried Sturm (☎ 089/181273) to book. **City Hopper Touren** (☎ 089/272–1131) offers daily escorted bike tours March–October. Bookings must be made in advance, and starting times are negotiable. A newcomer to the bike-tour scene is a 27-year-old American who hires German students to take visitors on a two- to three-hour spin through Munich. The tours start daily at the Old Town Hall, the Altes Rathaus, at 11:20 and 3:50. They cost DM 25, including bike rental. For more information call Mike at 089/6514275.

Pharmacies

Internationale Ludwigs-Apotheke (✉ Neuhauserstr. 11, ☎ 089/260–3021), open weekdays 8–6 and Saturday 8–1, and **Europa-Apotheke**

(✉ Schützenstr. 12, near the Hauptbahnhof, ☎ 089/595–423), open weekdays 8–6 and Saturday 8–1, stock a large variety of over-the-counter medications and personal-hygiene products. Munich pharmacies stay open late on a rotating basis, and every pharmacy has a sign in its window with the address of the nearest drug store that's open late.

Travel Agencies

American Express, ✉ Promenadepl. 6, ☎ 089/21990. **ABR,** the official Bavarian travel agency, has outlets all over Munich; call 089/12040 for information.

Visitor Information

The **Fremdenverkehrsamt** (central tourist office) is in the heart of the city (✉ Rindermarkt 10, just up the street from central Marienplatz, ☎ 089/23911). It is open Monday–Thursday 8:30–4 and Friday 8:30–2). Longer hours are kept by the city tourist office at the **Hauptbahnhof** train station (✉ At the entrance on Bayerstr., ☎ 089/239–1256), open Monday–Saturday 8 AM–10 PM and Sunday and holidays 11–7. There is also a tourist office at Munich's airport that is open Monday–Saturday 8:30 AM–10 PM and Sunday and holidays 1–9.

For information on the Bavarian mountain region south of Munich, contact the **Fremdenverkehrsverband München-Oberbayern** (Upper Bavarian Regional Tourist Office, ✉ Sonnenstr. 10, ☎ 089/597–347).

Munich Found, an English-language monthly, has articles and information about the city as well as a complete calendar of events. It's sold (DM 4) in kiosks downtown. An official monthly listing of upcoming events, the *Monatsprogramm,* is available at most hotels and newsstands and all tourist offices for DM 2.50. Information in English about museums and galleries can be obtained round-the-clock by dialing 089/239–162, and about castles and city sights by dialing 089/239–172.

3 The Bavarian Alps

This region of fir-clad mountains stretches from Munich south to the Austrian border. Quaint towns full of half-timbered houses fronted by flowers in the summer, buried by snow in the winter, pop up among the peaks, as do the creations of "Mad" King Ludwig II. Shimmering Alpine lakes abound, and the whole area has sporting opportunities galore.

OBERBAYERN, OR UPPER BAVARIA, is Germany's favorite year-round vacationland for visitors and Germans alike. This part of Bavaria, fanning south from Munich to the Austrian border, comes closest to what most of us think when we see or hear the name "Germany." Stock images from tourist-office posters—the fairy-tale castles you've seen in countless ads, those picture-book villages of too-good-to-be-true wood homes with brightly frescoed facades, with window boxes abloom in summer's warmth or sloping roofs heavy with winter's snow—are brought to life here. To complete the picture, onion-dome church spires rise out of the mist against the backdrop of the mighty Alps.

Coming south from Munich, you will soon find yourself on a gently rolling plain leading to a lovely land of lakes fed by Alpine rivers and streams and surrounded by ancient forests. In time the plain merges into foothills, which suddenly give way to a jagged line of Alpine peaks. In places such as Königsee, near Berchtesgaden, snowcapped mountains seem to rise straight up from the gemlike lakes.

If you continue south, you will encounter cheerful villages with richly frescoed houses, some of the finest Baroque churches in Germany, and any number of minor spas where you can stay to "take the waters" and tune up your system.

Sports possibilities are legion: downhill and cross-country skiing and ice-skating in winter; tennis, swimming, sailing, golf, and, above all (sometimes literally), hiking in summer. Marked hiking trails lead from the glorious countryside, along rivers and lakes, through woods, and high into the Alps.

Driving the Deutsche Alpenstrasse (German Alpine Road) is a spectacular journey. The entire route between Lindau, on the Bodensee, and Berchtesgaden adds up to about 485 kilometers (300 miles). The dramatic stretch between Garmisch-Partenkirchen and Berchtesgaden runs about 300 kilometers (185 miles) and affords wonderful views.

Pleasures and Pastimes

Castles

Popping up among the peaks are numerous curious castles that were created at the behest of a certain crazy king. For a proper appreciation of Linderhof and the other royal castles associated with Ludwig, it helps to understand the troubled man for whom they were created.

"Mad" King Ludwig II, the haunting presence indelibly associated with Alpine Bavaria, was one of a long line of dukes, electors, and kings of the Wittelsbach dynasty, which ruled Bavaria from 1180 to 1918. The Wittelsbachs are credited with fashioning the grandiose look of Munich. This art-loving family started the city's great art collections, promoted the fine arts and music (Ludwig II was a patron of Richard Wagner), and set up a building program that ran for centuries. Ludwig II concentrated on building monumental edifices for himself rather than for the people and devoted a good part of his time and energies (along with an inordinate percentage of the royal purse) to this endeavor.

The grandest of his extravagant projects is Neuschwanstein, the monumental structure to the king's monumental ego, which came close to breaking the Wittelsbach bank. It was built over a 17-year period starting in 1869, and today is one of Germany's top tourist attractions (☞ Toward the Alps *in* Chapter 5). Towering Neuschwanstein offered

The Bavarian Alps

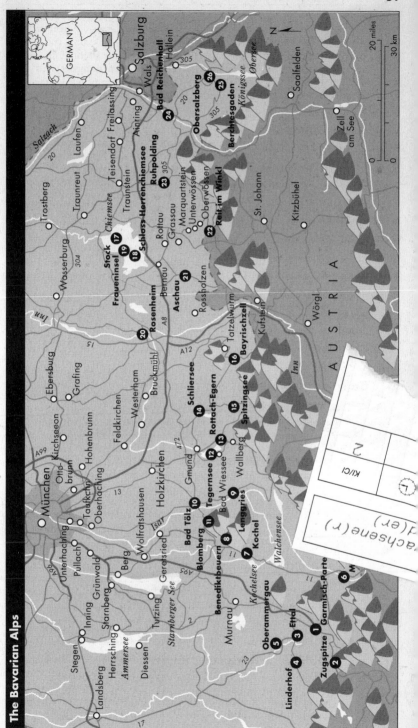

highly visible proof that the eccentric king had taken leave of his senses and was bleeding the treasury dry. In 1886 the government officially relieved Ludwig of his royal duties for reasons of insanity and had him confined in the small castle Schloss Berg on the shore of his beloved Starnbergersee (☞ Chapter 2), where he had spent summers in his youth. Schloss Linderhof and Schloss Herrencheimsee are included in this chapter's tours. Schloss Linderhof and Schloss Herrencheimsee, also constructed for Ludwig, are included in this chapter's tours.

Dining

The food in Bavaria's mountainous areas is understandably hearty and filling, designed to pack in the calories after a day's walking or skiing. Portions are usually huge, whether its great wedges of roast pork, dumplings big enough to fire from a cannon, or homemade *Apfelstrudel* that's a meal in itself. In lakeside inns and restaurants the day's catch will land directly on the menu—plump whitefish (*Renke*) or even trout in one form or another (*Forelle, Lachsforelle,* or *Bachsaibling*). Many inns have pools where the trout grow even fatter, although they lack the mountain water tang. Most districts in the Alps distill their own brand of schnapps from mountain herbs, while arguably the region's best beer is to be quaffed on the banks of the Tegernsee.

CATEGORY	COST*
$$$$	over DM 90
$$$	DM 55–DM 90
$$	DM 35–DM 55
$	under DM 35

*per person for a three-course meal, including service but not drinks.

Lodging

With few exceptions, all hotels and *Gasthäuser* in the Bavarian Alps and lower Alpine regions are traditionally styled, featuring geranium-covered balconies—the Bavarian summer standard—pine woodwork, and steep roofs. Quality is high even in simpler lodgings. Sophisticated Alpine resort areas are where you'll find luxury; cozy and much less expensive inns are in the villages. Garmisch-Partenkirchen and Berchtesgaden are bountifully supplied with accommodations in all price ranges. Check out the special seven-day packages. Private homes all through the region offer Germany's own version of bed-and-breakfasts, indicated by signs of ZIMMER FREI (rooms available). These rates may be under DM 25 per person. As a general rule, the farther from the popular Alpine resorts you stay, the lower the rates.

CATEGORY	COST*
$$$$	over DM 200
$$$	DM 160–DM 200
$$	DM 120–DM 160
$	under DM 120

*All prices are for two people in a double room, including tax and service charge.

Outdoor Activities and Sports

BIKING
With its lakeside and mountain trails this is a mountain biker's paradise. Sports shops in most mountain and lake resorts rent mountain bikes for around DM 20–DM 30 a day.

HIKING AND WALKING
The Bavarian Alpine range is great hiking country, with lower slopes that offer a suitably scaled-down challenge for walkers who just want an afternoon stroll in the champagne air. Serious hikers make for the mountain trails of the Zugspitze or the heights above Oberammergau,

Berchtesgaden, Bad Reichenhall or the lovely Walchensee. After three hours of steady uphill walking, you'll deserve a beer at a mountain-top inn on any of the well-marked trails around the Schliersee or Tegernsee lakes.

SAILING

All the Bavarian Alpine lakes have sailing schools that rent sailboards as well as boats of various rigs. The Starnbergersee lake alone has six; the largest is Captain Glas's picturesque boatyard at Possenhofen.

SKIING

Garmisch-Partenkirchen was the site of the 1936 winter Olympics and remains Germany's premier winter-sports resort. The upper slopes of the Zugspitze and surrounding mountains challenge the best ski buffs, while there are also plenty of runs for intermediate skiers and for families. The mountain slopes above Reit im Winkl (particularly the Winklmoosalm) are less crowded, but the skiing is comparable. All hotels in the region offer special skiing packages, often including ski rental and lift tickets.

Exploring the Bavarian Alps

Great Itineraries

The region is too extensive to cover fully in even a month's vacation, but it does have the advantage that one resort with its ring of mountains is as attractive as the next. So consider basing yourself in one resort (such as Garmisch-Partenkirchen, Berchtesgaden, or a point halfway between, such as the Chiemsee or Tegernsee lakes) and exploring the immediate area—you'll still be experiencing just about everything the Bavarian Alps has to offer. In winter snowfalls can make traveling a nightmare, but for visitors who want to cram in as much as possible, come fair weather or foul, the German Tourist Board has drawn up a recommended route, the "German Alpine Road." Allow a week to cover it.

Numbers in the text refer to numbers in the margin and on the Bavarian Alps map.

IF YOU HAVE 3 DAYS

Make a clear choice between the Garmisch-Partenkirchen area and the southeastern corner of Bavaria centered on Berchtesgaden. If ☷ **Garmisch** ① (as the resort is known for short) is your choice, make the busy little Alpine city your base and devote a couple of days to exploring the magnificent surrounding countryside. Wait or hope for good weather to take the cable-car or cog-railway trip to the summit of Germany's highest mountain, the **Zugspitze** ②. If it's summer or autumn (deep snow still clings to the upper slopes in spring) follow one of the well-marked paths to a point where you can pick up the railway to the bottom of the mountain again. A comfortable day trip takes in **Oberammergau** ⑤, the monastery at nearby **Ettal** ③, and one of King Ludwig's loveliest palaces, **Schloss Linderhof** ④. Allow a third day to visit **Mittenwald** ⑥ and its violin museum, taking in the little village of Klais (Germany's highest railroad station) on the way. If you choose instead to devote your three days to ☷ **Berchtesgaden** ㉕, allow one of them for the trip to the **Obersalzberg** ㉖, site of Hitler's "Eagle's Nest," and a second for a boat outing on **Königsee** deep into the mountains that embrace the beautiful little stretch of water. A third day gives you the Hobson's choice between a trip down Berchtesgaden's salt mine, the Salzbergwerk, or a cross-border run into the neighboring Austrian city of Salzburg.

IF YOU HAVE 5 DAYS
Consider spending a day or two in 🔲 **Garmisch** ①, then head for Berchtesgaden by way of the **Chiemsee** lake, overnighting in one of the several villages on its western shore (Prien has a main-line railway station and a boat harbor) and taking boat trips to **Schloss Herrenchiemsee** ⑱ island (to view the most magnificent of King Ludwig's castles) and to the smaller, quieter, and utterly enchanting **Fraueninsel** ⑲. Round off the journey with two days in 🔲 **Berchtesgaden** ㉕ and the surrounding countryside.

IF YOU HAVE 7 DAYS
Plan a tour of the Bavarian Alps, beginning with a day or two in 🔲 **Garmisch** ① to take in excursions to **Oberammergau** ⑤ and **Schloss Linderhof** ④ and then striking out along the well-signposted route of the German Alpine Road, which connects Garmisch in the west with Berchtesgaden in the east. Leave the route after 20 kilometers (12 miles), at Wallgau, to relax for an hour or two on the southern shore of picturesque **Walchensee**, doubling back later to compare its dark waters with the fresh mountain green of dammed-up Sylvenstein Stausee, then dodging in and out of Austria on a highland road that snakes through the tree-lined Aachen pass to 🔲 **Tegernsee** ⑫ lake. Book two or three nights at one of the moderately priced *Gasthöfe* in and around Tegernsee or spoil yourself at one of the luxurious hotels in upscale 🔲 **Rottach-Egern** ⑬. With a hiker's map of the region from Tegernsee's tourist office in hand, take off into the hills that dip from all sides into the lake. A day's walk (or a 20-minute drive) takes you to Tegernsee's neighboring lake, the shimmering **Schliersee** ⑭. From there the road becomes a switchback, climbing from narrow valleys to mountain ski resorts and finally plunging down to the Inn River valley. Consider leaving the Alpine route here for a stay on the shores of Bavaria's largest lake, **Chiemsee,** where the most sumptuous of King Ludwig's castles, **Schloss Herrenchiemsee** ⑱ stands on one of the three islands (reached by a regular boat service). Back on the Alpine route, the road heads inevitably back into the mountains, dropping down again into elegant 🔲 **Bad Reichenhall** ㉔, another recommended overnight stop. From there it's only 30 kilometers (18 miles) to Berchtesgaden, where a final two days should be spent viewing the town, its castle museum, Hitler's mountain-top retreat (the "Eagle's Nest"), and beautiful **Königsee.**

When to Tour the Bavarian Alps

This mountainous region is a year-round holiday destination, a snowy wonderland in winter and full of inviting lakes and alpine meadows in summer. Snow is promised by most resorts from December through March, while there's year-round skiing on the glacier slopes at the top of the Zugspitze. Spring and autumn are ideal times for mountain walking. November is a between-seasons time, when many hotels and restaurants close down for a welcome break or just to attend to renovations.

Garmisch-Partenkirchen

❶ *95 km (60 mi) southeast of Munich.*

Garmisch, as it's more commonly known, is the undisputed Alpine capital of Bavaria, a bustling, year-round resort and spa. Once two separate communities, Garmisch and Partenkirchen fused in 1936 to accommodate the winter Olympics. Today, with a population of 27,000, the area is large enough to offer every facility expected from a major Alpine resort but small enough not to overwhelm.

Although it looks modern—few of its buildings predate World War I—Garmisch-Partenkirchen has a long history. Partenkirchen, the older half, was founded by the Romans. The road the Romans built between Partenkirchen and neighboring Mittenwald, a section of the principal road between Rome and Germany that was a major route well into the 17th century, can still be followed. Much of the astounding wealth of the Fugger family in Augsburg (☞ the Northern Romantic Road *in* Chapter 5) resulted from trade between southern Germany and Venice, connected by the Roman route.

Partenkirchen was spared physical destruction but devastated economically by the Thirty Years' War. By the early 18th century it was rejuvenated by the discovery of iron ore. Today, of course, tourism keeps Garmisch-Partenkirchen thriving.

Winter sports rank high on the agenda here. There are more than 62 miles of downhill ski runs, 40 ski lifts and cable cars, and 115 miles of cross-country ski trails (called *Loipen*). One of the principal stops on the international winter-sports circuit, the area hosts a week of international races every January. You can usually count on good skiing from December through April, into May on the Zugspitze.

Garmisch-Partenkirchen isn't all sporty, however. In addition to two Olympic stadiums in the Partenkirchen side of the city, there are some other attractions worth seeing. In Garmisch, the 18th-century parish church of **St. Martin,** off the Marienplatz, contains some significant stuccowork by the Wessobrunn artists Schmuzer, Schmidt, and Bader. Across the Loisach River on Pfarrerhausweg stands a **St. Martin's** dating from 1280, whose Gothic wall paintings include a larger-than-life-size figure of St. Christopher. On Frühlingstrasse are some beautiful examples of **Upper Bavarian houses.** At the end of Zöppritzstrasse lies the villa of composer **Richard Strauss,** who lived there until his death in 1949.

2 The number one attraction in Garmisch is the **Zugspitze,** the highest mountain (9,731 feet) in Germany. The hotel that stood for so long at the summit has closed—a restaurant and sunny terrace are now in its place—so don't miss the last lift down to the valley. There are two ways up the mountain: a leisurely 75-minute ride on a cog railway from the train station in the center of town or a 10-minute hoist by cable car, which begins its giddy ascent from the Eibsee, just outside town on the road to Austria. Either way, a separate cable car carries you the final 1,037 feet to just below the peak. A round-trip combination ticket allows you to mix your mode of travel up and down the mountain. Prices are lower in winter than in summer, even though they include use of all the ski lifts on the mountain. A round-trip ticket costs DM 56; one-way fare is DM 37 for train or cable car.

You can take a cable car to the top of the one of the **lesser peaks.** The round-trip fare to **Alpspitze,** some 2,000 feet lower than the Zugspitze, is DM 34. To the top of the **Wank** and back costs DM 33 (you ride in four-seat cable cars). In winter months, fares include the use of all ski lifts on the respective mountains. Both mountains can be tackled on foot, provided you're properly shod and physically fit.

Dining and Lodging

$$$ ✕ **Posthotel Partenkirchen.** A 500-year-old vaulted cellar with a hand-painted ceiling is the setting for an elegant restaurant whose menu combines traditional Bavarian dishes with French and vegetarian specialties. ⊠ *Ludwigstr. 49,* ☎ *08821/51067. AE, DC, MC, V.*

$$$ ✕ **Reindl's.** Named after the proprietor, this pine-paneled restaurant at the Partenkirchner Hof Hotel serves high quality regional dishes, such as pork fillets in sour cream sauce. The chef's apple cake in vanilla sauce is recommended. ✉ *Bahnhofstr. 15,* ☎ *08821/58025. Jacket and tie. AE, DC, MC, V.*

$ ✕ **Riessersee.** Situated on the shores of a tranquil, small, green lake a 3-kilometer (2-mile) walk from town, this café-restaurant is an ideal spot for lunch or afternoon tea (on weekends there's live zither music 3–5 PM). House specialties are fresh trout and local game. The Riessersee also has five comfortable rooms. ✉ *Riess 6,* ☎ *08821/95440,* FAX *08821/72589. No credit cards.*

$$$$ ✕⬜ **Grand Hotel Sonnenbichl.** This elegant, established lodging on the outskirts of Garmish offers panoramic views of the Wetterstein Mountains and the Zugspitze, but only from its front rooms—the rear rooms face a wall of rock. ✉ *Burgstr. 97, D–82467,* ☎ *08821/7020,* FAX *08821/702–131. 90 rooms, 3 suites with bath. 3 restaurants, bar, indoor pool, beauty salon, hot tub, sauna, exercise room. AE, DC, MC, V.*

$$$ ✕⬜ **Wittelsbach.** Dramatic mountain vistas from bedroom balconies
★ and a spacious garden terrace make this hotel especially attractive. Public rooms are rustic, and the bedrooms are spacious with corner lounge areas. Ask for a room facing south for Zugspitze views. ✉ *Von-Brugstr. 24, D–82467,* ☎ *08821/53096,* FAX *08821/57312. 60 rooms with bath or shower, 2 family suites. Restaurant, piano bar, indoor pool, sauna. AE, DC, MC, V.*

$$–$$$ ✕⬜ **Vier Jahreszeiten.** This turn-of-the-century, four-story hotel, with red roof tiles and an attractive, yellow stonework exterior, is in the center of town, only two minutes from the special Zugspitze train departure point. Its rooms offer a curious mix of Bavarian pinewood and Scandinavian modern furnishings; some have mountain views. ✉ *Bahnhofstr. 23, D–82467,* ☎ *08821/58084,* FAX *08821/4486. 50 rooms, 45 with bath. Restaurant, beer garden. AE, DC, MC, V.*

$$ ✕⬜ **Gasthof Fraundorfer.** "Bavarian evenings"—lots of yodeling and
★ folk dancing—are held six nights a week in the bustling restaurant of this friendly Alpine Gasthof. The Bavarian influence extends throughout the house, from the pinewood-clad public rooms to the farmhouse furnishings of the cozy bedrooms, some of which have romantic four-poster beds. ✉ *Ludwigstr. 24, D–82467,* ☎ *08821/71071,* FAX *08821/ 71073. 29 rooms with shower. Restaurant, sauna, steam room. AE, MC, V.*

$$ ✕⬜ **Hotel-Gasthof Drei Mohren.** All the simple, homey comforts you'd expect of a 150-year-old Bavarian inn can be found here, in the historic Partenkirchen village. The rooms are painted in pastel colors, and most of them have pinewood furniture. The tavern and restaurant are spruced up with polished pine. ✉ *Ludwigstr. 65, D–82467,* ☎ *08821/ 9130,* FAX *08821/18974. 23 rooms, 1 apartment all with bath. Restaurant, bar. No credit cards.*

$–$$ ✕⬜ **Hotel Bergland.** Comfortable, reasonably priced, and well located—what more could you ask of this small, traditional guest house? Great views of Zugspitze? Well, from some rooms. This hotel, extensively renovated in 1995, is in the village of Grainau, on the lower slopes of the Zugspitze, 2 kilometers (1 mile) outside Garmisch. Rooms are furnished in traditional Bavarian style, right down to the painted cupboards and headboards. The cozy lounge, with its open fireplace, is just the place to relax after a day in the mountains. ✉ *Alpspitzstr. 14, D–82467,* ☎ *08821/8509,* FAX *08821/82368. 9 rooms, 1 apartment, all with bath. Restaurant, bar, café. AE, DC, M, V.*

$$ 🏨 **Edelweiss.** Not unlike its namesake, the Alpine flower, this small, downtown hotel oozes mountain charm. Inlaid with warm pinewood, it has Bavarian furnishings and a color scheme to match. In summer you'll find that other favorite Bavarian bloom—the geranium. There is no restaurant here, but there's a buffet breakfast. ✉ *Martinswinkelstr. 17, D–82467,* ☎ *08821/2458,* 📠 *0962? '24122. 13 rooms with bath. No credit cards.*

Hiking and Walking

There are innumerable spectacular walks on 300 kilometers (186 miles) of marked trails through the pine woods and upland meadows that cover the lower slopes of the mountains. If you have the time and stout walking shoes, try one of the two that lead to striking gorges. The **Höllentalklamm** route starts at the Zugspitze Mountain railway terminal in town and ends at the top of the mountain (you'll want to turn back before reaching the summit unless you have mountaineering experience). The **Partnachklamm** route is quite challenging; to do all of it, you'll have to stay overnight in one of the mountain huts along the way. It starts at the Olympic ice stadium in town and takes you through a spectacular, tunneled water gorge, past a pretty little mountain lake, and far up the Zugspitze. An easier way to tackle this route is to ride part of the way up in the **Eckbauer cable car** that sets out from the Olympic ice stadium. There's a handy inn at the top where you can gather strength for the hour-long walk back down to the cable-car station. **Horse-drawn carriages** also cover the first section of the route in summer; in winter you can skim along it in a **sleigh** (call the local coaching society, the Lohnkutschevereinigung, ☎ 08821/53167 for information). For details on mountain hikes and on staying in mountain huts, contact Deutscher Alpenverein (✉ German Alpine Association, Praterinsel 5, D–80538 Munich, ☎ 089/235–0900).

Nightlife and the Arts

Garmisch-Partenkirchen is a busy ski resort—and that means the **après-ski** scene is a busy one, too. Many hotels have dance floors and some have basement discos that pound away until the early hours. **Bavarian folk dancing** is a regular feature of Garmisch nightlife, and during the summer there's a weekly program of folk music and dancing every Saturday evening at the Bayernhalle (✉ Brauhausstr. 19). **Concerts** of classical and popular music are presented Saturday through Thursday, mid-May through September, in the resort park bandstand in Garmisch, and on Fridays in the Partenkirchen resort park. Garmisch-Partenkirchen also has a **folklore theater** company, although your German will have to be pretty good to make anything of the thigh-slapping farces that are the staple fare of this Bavarian-style entertainment. The sophisticated option is the Garmisch-Partenkirchen **casino** (☎ 08821/53099), open daily 3 PM to 3 AM.

Ettal

★ ❸ *16 km (10 mi) north of Garmisch-Partenkirchen.*

A charming village in its own right, Ettal is totally dominated by the massive bulk of **Kloster Ettal,** the great monastery founded in 1330 by Holy Roman Emperor Ludwig der Bayer (Ludwig the Bavarian) for a group of knights and a community of Benedictine monks. The abbey was replaced with new buildings during the 18th century and now serves as a school. Open to visitors, the original 10-sided church was brilliantly redecorated in 1744–53, becoming one of the foremost examples of Bavarian rococo. The church's chief treasure is its enormous dome fresco (83 feet wide), painted by Jacob Zeiller, circa 1751–52. The mass of swirling clouds and the pink-and-blue vision of heaven are typical of the rococo fondness for elaborate and glowing illusion-istic ceiling painting.

A liqueur with legendary health-giving properties, made from a cen-turies-old recipe, is still distilled at the monastery by the monks. It's made with more than 70 mountain herbs. You can't get the recipe, but you can buy bottles of the libation (about DM 20) from the small stall outside the monastery.

NEED A
BREAK?

Across the road from the monastery you'll find one of the area's best and coziest restaurants, within the traditional, old **Hotel Zur Post** (⊠ Kaiser-Ludwig-Pl. 18, ☎ 08822/3596). If it's a cold day, try for a spot near the ancient tile stove and order a steaming pot of the best coffee in town; if it's lunchtime, get a Bavarian garlic soup or venison stew.

Dining and Lodging

$$$ ✕🛏 **Hotel-Gasthof Zur Post.** This traditional Gasthof is in the center of town, but it has its own gardens. Its child-friendliness is also a plus: The restaurant has a children's menu, and there's a playground. ⊠ *Kaiser-Ludwig-Pl. 18, D–82488,* ☎ *08822/3596,* FAX *08822/6971. 18 rooms and 4 apartments, most with bath or shower. Restaurant, playground. AE, DC, MC, V. Closed Oct. 26–Dec. 18.*

$$ ✕🛏 **Benediktenhof.** The open beams and colorfully painted walls are part of this former farmstead's 250-year history. Bedrooms are furnished in Bavarian Baroque or peasant style, with brightly decorated cupboards and bedsteads. ⊠ *Zieglerstr. 1, D–82488,* ☎ *08822/4637,* FAX *08822/ 7288. 16 rooms and 1 apartment with bath or shower. Restaurant. No credit cards. Closed Nov.–Dec. 22.*

$$ ✕🛏 **Hotel Ludwig der Bayer.** Backed by mountains, this fine old Ettal hotel is run by the Benedictine order from across the road. But there's nothing monastic about it, except for the exquisite religious carvings and motifs that adorn the walls. Most of them come from the monastery's own carpentry shop, which also made much of the sturdy furniture in the comfortable bedrooms. The hotel also has its own Bavarian-style apartment houses equipped with individual kitchens, but its eateries would tempt even the most dedicated cook. Two atmospheric restau-rants and a vaulted tavern serve sturdy Bavarian fare (the pork knuckle and dumplings fuel even the most energetic mountain hiker for the day) and beer brewed at the monastery. Even the schnapps is distilled by the monks. ⊠ *Kaiser-Ludwig-Pl. 10–12, D–82488,* ☎ *08822/6601,* FAX *08822/74480. 70 rooms with bath, 32 apartments with kitchen. 2 restaurants, 2 bars, indoor pool, sauna, tennis court, bowling, exer-cise room, paddle tennis, bicycles. MC, V.*

Schloss Linderhof

❹ *10 km (6 mi) west of Ettal on B–23.*

Built on the grounds of his father's hunting lodge between 1874 and 1878, **Schloss Linderhof** was the only one of Ludwig II's royal residences to have been completed during the monarch's short life, and the only one in which he spent much time. According to stories, while staying at Linderhof the eccentric king would dress up as Lohengrin to be rowed in a swan boat on the grotto pond; in winter he took off on midnight sleigh rides behind six plumed horses and a platoon of outriders hold-ing flaring torches. On day two of the king's stay at the Schloss after his dethronement in 1886, however, he drowned under mysterious cir-cumstances. A cross in the lake in front of the castle marks the place where his body was recovered from the water.

Linderhof was the smallest of this ill-starred king's castles, and yet it was his favorite country retreat. Set in grandiose sylvan seclusion, between a reflecting pool and the green slopes of a gentle mountain, the charming, French-style, rococo confection is said to have been inspired by the Petit Trianon at Versailles. From an architectural standpoint it could well be considered a disaster—a mishmash of conflicting styles, lavish on the outside, vulgarly overdecorated on the inside. Ludwig's bedroom is filled with brilliantly colored and gilded ornaments, the Hall of Mirrors is a shimmering dreamworld, and the dining room boasts a fine piece of 19th-century engineering—a table that rises from and descends to the kitchens below. The formal gardens contain further touches of Ludwig's love of fantasy. There's a Moorish pavilion—bought wholesale from the 1867 Paris Universal Exposition—and a grotto, said to have been modeled on Capri's Blue Grotto, with a rock that slides back at the touch of a button. The gilded Neptune fountain in the palace lake shoots a jet of water 105 feet into the air, higher than the roof. *DM 8. ☉ Apr.–Sept., daily 9–12:15 and 12:45–5:30; Oct.–Mar., daily 10–12:15 and 12:45–4. Only the Schloss and grounds can be visited in winter months, for a reduced admission charge of DM 6.*

Oberammergau

❺ *20 km (12 mi) northwest of Garmisch-Partenkirchen, 4 km (2½ mi) northwest of Ettal.*

An amateur—and, some critics say, amateurish—theatrical production has given this small Bavarian town a fame quite out of proportion to its size. Its location alone, though, in an Alpine valley beneath a sentinel-like peak, would qualify it as a major tourist attraction. Its main streets are lined with beautifully frescoed houses, such as the 1784 Pilatushaus on Ludwig-Thoma-Strasse, and in summer the village explodes with color as geraniums pour from every window box. Many of these lovely houses are occupied by families whose men are highly skilled wood-carvers, a craft that has flourished here since the depredations of the Thirty Years' War.

Oberammergau, however, is best known for its **Passion Play,** begun in 1634 as an offering of thanks that the Black Death stopped just short of the village. In faithful accordance with a solemn vow, it has been presented every 10 years since 1680 (except 1940, and with an additional 350th-anniversary performance in 1984), so the next play year is 2000. Its 16 acts, which take 5½ hours, depict the final days of Christ, from the Last Supper through the Crucifixion and Resurrection. It is presented daily on a partly open-air stage against a mountain backdrop from late May to late September each Passion Play year.

A visit to Oberammergau when the play is on may be considered something of a mixed blessing, in view of the crowds (half a million or more visitors) and the difficulty of obtaining tickets (most are available only through package tours). The entire village is swept up by the production, with some 1,500 residents directly involved in its preparation and presentation. Men grow beards in hopes of capturing key roles; young women have been known to put off their weddings—the role of Mary went only to unmarried girls until the 1990 performances. In that year tradition was broken amid much local controversy when a 31-year-old mother of two was given the part.

Play year or no, you will find many **wood-carvers** at work here, and Oberammergau's shop windows will be crammed with their creations. From June through October, a workshop is open free to the public at the Pilatushaus (Verlegergasse); working potters and traditional painters can also be seen. You can even sign up for a weeklong course in wood carving (classes are in German), at a cost of between DM 460 and DM 650, bed and breakfast included.

If you travel to Oberammergau in a nonplay year you can still visit the theater, the **Oberammergau Passionsspielhaus,** and explore backstage. Tours of the huge building, with its 5,200-seat auditorium and vast stage open to the mountain air, are given by guides who will demonstrate the remarkable acoustics by reciting Shakespearean soliloquies. ⊠ *Passionstheater, Passionswiese.* ☒ *DM 4 (with guided tour).* ☉ *May–Oct., daily 9:30–noon and 1–4; Nov.–Apr., Tues.–Sun. 10–noon and 1:30–4; closed Jan. 5–31.* ☒ *DM 5.50 for combined ticket for admission to both the Passion Play theater and the Heimatmuseum.*

The **Heimatmuseum** has historic examples of the wood craftsman's art and one of Germany's finest collections of Christmas crèches, dating from the mid-18th century. ⊠ *Dorfstr. 8.* ☒ *DM 3; DM 5.50 for a combined ticket for admission to both the Passion Play theater and Heimatmuseum.* ☉ *Mid-Apr.–mid-Oct., Tues.–Sun. 2–6; mid–Oct.–mid-Apr., Sat. 2–6.*

Oberammergau's 18th-century **St. Peter and St. Paul Church** is regarded as the finest work of rococo architect Josef Schmuzer and has striking frescoes by Matthäus Günther. ☎ *08824/553.*

Dining and Lodging

$$ ✗ **Ammergauer Stubn.** A homey beer tavern in the Wittelsbach Hotel, the Stubn offers a comprehensive menu that combines Bavarian specialties with international dishes. ⊠ *Dorfstr. 21,* ☎ *08822/1011. AE, DC, MC. Closed Tues. and Nov. 7–Dec. 10.*

$ ✗ **Alte Post.** You can enjoy carefully prepared local cuisine on the original pine tables in this 350-year-old inn. There's a special children's menu, and in summer meals are also served in the beer garden. ⊠ *Dorfstr. 19,* ☎ *08822/1091. AE, MC, V.*

$$$ ✗🖭 **Hotel Turmwirt.** Rich wood paneling reaches from floor to ceiling
★   in this transformed 18th-century inn, in the shadow of Oberammergau's mountain, the Kofel. The hotel's own band presents regular Bavarian folk evenings. Rooms have corner lounge areas, and most come with balconies and sweeping mountain views. ⊠ *Ettalerstr. 2, D–82487,* ☎ *08822/3091, FAX 08822/1437. 22 rooms with bath. Restaurant, recreation room. AE, DC, MC, V. Closed most of Jan. and Nov.–mid-Dec.*

$$$ ✗🖭 **Parkhotel Sonnenhof.** Away from the sometimes crowded town center, the modern Sonnenhof provides a balcony with every guest room, where you can sun yourself and soak up the Alpine view. There's also a children's playroom. ⊠ *König-Ludwigstr. 12, D–82487,* ☎ *08822/ 1071, FAX 08822/3047. 70 rooms with bath. Restaurant, bar, indoor pool, sauna, bowling. AE, DC, MC, V.*

$$–$$$ ✗🖭 **Hotel Wolf.** Americans in particular value this attractive old hotel—about 30% of its guests are from the United States. Blue shutters punctuate its white walls; the steeply gabled upper stories bloom with flowers. The hotel's Hafner Stube is a popular local haunt. ⊠ *Dorfstr. 1, D–82487,* ☎ *08822/3071, FAX 08822/1096. 32 rooms with bath. Restaurant, 2 bars, café, pool, sauna. AE, DC, MC, V.*

$$–$$$ ✗🖭 **Landhaus Feldmeier.** This quiet, country-style hotel, built in 1990, has mostly spacious rooms decorated with modern pinewood furniture. It's only a five-minute walk from the town center. ⊠ *Ettalerstr. 29, D–82487,* ☎ *08822/3011, FAX 08822/6631. 22 rooms with bath. Restaurant, hot tub, sauna, steam room. AE, V.*

$$ ✕⊡ **Hotel Böld.** A boldly painted facade and geranium-hung balconies make the Böld one of the handsomest buildings in central Oberammergau. It's a rambling, friendly house, owned by the Ring group, but still family-run—and so keeps its old-fashioned Bavarian character. The restaurant prides itself on a menu that combines traditional fare with international cuisine. All rooms here are designed to accommodate people in wheelchairs. ✉ *König-Ludwig-Str. 10, D–82487,* ☎ *08822/3021,* FAX *08822/7102. 57 rooms with bath. Restaurant, beer garden, hot tub, sauna, steam room, exercise room, paddle tennis, bicycles.*

Mittenwald

❻ *20 km (12 mi) southeast of Garmisch.*

Many regard Mittenwald as the most beautiful town in the Bavarian Alps. Mittenwald itself takes the compliment so seriously it spent several years on a face-lift, giving the town a facade to match the magnificence of its mountain backdrop. The expensive program was completed in 1996 with the inauguration of a pedestrian zone to rival Germany's best. The town also restored an important historical feature by re-creating the stream that used to flow through the market square.

Mittenwald was an important medieval center, the staging point for goods shipped from Verona by way of the Brenner Pass and Innsbruck. From there, goods were transferred to rafts, which carried them down the Isar to Munich. As might be expected, Mittenwald grew rich on this traffic; its early prosperity is reflected in the splendidly decorated houses with ornately carved gables and brilliantly painted facades that line its main street. In the mid-17th century, however, the international trade route was moved to a different pass, and the fortunes of Mittenwald declined.

Prosperity returned in 1684, when farmer's-son-turned-master-violin-maker Matthias Klotz returned from a 20-year stay in Cremona. There he had studied with Nicolo Amati, who gave the violin its present form. Klotz brought his master's pioneering ideas back to Mittenwald and taught the art of violin making to his brothers and friends; before long, half the men in the village were creating the instruments. With woods from neighboring forests, the trade flourished. Mittenwald became known as "The Village of a Thousand Violins," and stringed instruments made in Mittenwald—violins, violas, and cellos—were shipped around the world. Klotz's craft is still carried on in Mittenwald.

The **Geigenbau und Heimatmuseum** describes in fascinating detail the history of violin making in Mittenwald. Ask the curator of the museum to direct you to the nearest of the several violin makers who are still active—they'll be happy to demonstrate the skills handed down to them by the successors of Klotz. ✉ *Ballenhausgasse 3,* ☎ *08823/2511.* ⊡ *DM 2.50.* ☉ *Weekdays 10–noon and 2–5, weekends and holidays 10–noon.*

On the back of the altar in the 18th-century **St. Peter and St. Paul Church,** you'll find Matthias Klotz's name, carved there by the violin maker himself. In front of the church is a monument to him. The church, with its elaborate and joyful stuccowork coiling and curling its way around the interior, is one of the most important rococo structures in Bavaria. Note its Gothic choir loft, incorporated into the church in the 18th century. The bold frescoes on its exterior are characteristic of *Lüftlmalerei,* an art form that reached its height in Mittenwald. You can see other fine examples on the facades of three famous houses: the

Goethehaus, the Pilgerhaus, and the Pichlerhaus. ⊠ *Next to Geigen-bau und Heimatsmuseum.*

NEED A
BREAK? Just down the street from the museum and the church is the 17th-century **Hotel Post** (⊠ Obermarkt 9). Ask for *Apfelkuchen* (apple cake) and coffee.

Dining and Lodging

$$–$$$ ✕ **Arnspitze.** Get a table at the large picture window and soak in the view of the towering Karwendel Mountain range as you ponder the choices on a menu that combines the best Bavarian traditional ingredients with international flair. The fish pot-au-feu is Mediterranean in flavor and appearance, while the jugged hare in red wine is truly Bavarian. ⊠ *Innsbrucker Str. 68,* ☎ *08823/2425. AE. Closed Tues. and Nov. No lunch Wed.*

$$$ ✕🏨 **Hotel Rieger.** A rustic Bavarian hotel of great charm, the Rieger boasts modern health-cure facilities and deep-pile comfort. ⊠ *Dekan-Karl-Pl. 28, D–82481,* ☎ *08823/5071,* FAX *08823/5662. 46 rooms with bath. Restaurant, indoor pool, hot tub, sauna, recreation room. AE, DC, MC, V. Closed mid-Oct.–Dec. 19.*

$$–$$$ ✕🏨 **Post.** Stagecoaches carrying travelers and mail across the Alps stopped here as far back as the 17th century. The hotel has changed a lot since then, but it still retains much of its historic charm. If you're planning dinner, pause by the open fire in the cozy lounge-bar while you choose between the wine tavern or the low-beamed Poststüberl. The food in each is excellent, with the emphasis on hearty Bavarian fare. ⊠ *Obermarkt 9, D–82481,* ☎ *08823/1094,* FAX *08823/1096. 80 rooms with bath, 7 apartments. 2 restaurants, bar, indoor pool, sauna, bowling. No credit cards.*

$$ ✕🏨 **Alpenrose.** Once part of a monastery and later given a beautiful baroque facade, the Alpenrose is one of handsomest hotels in the area. Bedrooms and public rooms are decorated in typical Bavarian style, with lots of wood paneling, farmhouse cupboards, and finely woven fabrics. The restaurant devotes the entire month of October to venison dishes, for which it has become renowned. ⊠ *Obermarkt 1, D–82481,* ☎ *08823/5055,* FAX *08823/3720. 18 rooms, 16 with bath. Restaurant, bar, indoor pool, sauna. AE, DC, MC, V.*

Shopping

It's not the kind of gift every visitor wants to take home, but just in case you'd like a violin, cello, or even a double bass from a town that has been making these instruments for centuries, the Alpine resort of Mittenwald can oblige. There are at least a dozen craftsmen whose work is coveted by musicians throughout the world. If you're buying or even just curious, call on **Benedict Lang** (⊠ Dammkarstr. 22, ☎ 08651/8544). A good place for the town's famous stringed instruments is **Geigenbau Leonhardt** (⊠ Mühlenweg 53a, ☎ 08651/8010). For traditional Bavarian costumes—dirndls, embroidered shirts and blouses, and lederhosen—try the **Trachtenstub'n** (⊠ Obermarkt 35, Mittenwald, ☎ 08651/3785). **Trachten Werner-Leichtl** has your basic Bavarian wear (⊠ Dekan Karl Pl. 1, Mittenwald, ☎ 08651/8282).

Kochel

❼ *North of Mittenwald, on the B–11.*

The hero of the attractive little lakeside town of Kochel is the Schmied von Kochel, or Blacksmith of Kochel. His fame stems from his role—and eventual death—in the 1705 peasants' uprising at Sendling, just outside Munich. You can see his statue in the town center. His town is on the shore of the **Kochelsee** and just north of the **Walchensee,** two popular Bavarian Alpine lakes. They are longtime favorites for summer getaways and offer good swimming, water sports, and mountain walks. The 5,300-foot-high **Herzogstand,** above the Walchensee, is suitable for the less adventurous—the summit can be reached by chairlift (DM 12 round-trip). The 5,400-foot-high **Benediktenwand,** east of Kochel, is a challenge for mountaineers.

The lido **Trimini,** on the shores of the Kochelsee, is one of the largest and most spectacular in Bavaria, with a collection of indoor and outdoor pools, water slides, and enough other games to keep a family amused the whole day. ⊠ *Trimini, Kochel,* ☎ *08851/5300.* ⊠ *3-hr ticket DM 8, all-day family ticket DM 33.* ☉ *Daily 9–8:30; closed 1st 3 wks of Dec.*

OFF THE BEATEN PATH — History is relived at the Freilichtmuseum an der Glentleiten (⊠ ☎ 08851/ 1850), an **open-air museum** that looks and functions just as a Bavarian village did centuries ago, complete with cobbler, blacksmith, and other craftsmen who kept the community self-sufficient. ⊠ *Grossweil, near the Kochelsee (just off the Munich-Garmisch Autobahn).* ⊠ *DM 7.* ☉ *Apr.–Oct., Tues.–Sun. 9–6.*

Benediktbeuren

❽ *45 km (27 mi) north of Mittenwald.*

The great mid-8th-century monastery in the village of Benediktbeuren is thought to be the oldest Benedictine institution north of the Alps. It was a flourishing cultural center in the Middle Ages; paradoxically, it also gave birth to one of the most profane musical works of those times, the *carmina burana* (also known as the Goliardic songs). The 1937 orchestration of the work by the Bavarian composer Carl Orff is regularly performed in the monastery courtyard, where the original piece was first heard during the 12th century. The frescoes of the monastery's 17th-century church were painted by the father of the Asam brothers, whose church building and artistic decoration made them famous far beyond the borders of 18th-century Bavaria. Cosmas Damian Asam, the eldest son, was born at Benediktbeuren. ☉ *Monastery church daily 8–6. Guided tours of monastery are given July–Sept., daily at 2:30; Oct.–mid-May, weekends 2:30; mid-May–June, Sat. and Wed. 2:30, Sun. 10:30 and 2:30.*

Dining and Lodging

$$–$$$ ✕🏨 **Alpenhotel Schmied von Kochel.** The Schmied von Kochel (Blacksmith of Kochel) was a local folk hero, and the use of his name is one of several traditional touches that distinguish this 100-year-old Alpine-style hotel, in the village of Kochel, south of Benediktbeuren. A zither player can be heard most summer evenings in the restaurant. ⊠ *Schlehdorferstr. 6, D–82431,* ☎ *08851/9010,* 𝔽𝔸𝕏 *08851/7331. 30 rooms with bath or shower. Restaurant, bar, café, hot tub, sauna. MC, V.*

$$ ✕🏨 **Post Hotel.** Traditional local fare becomes memorable when sampled in this old coach inn on the banks of the Walchensee. On warm days you can dine outside and watch the Windsurfers glide by. Specialties include Bavarian lake perch pike. Moderately priced rooms are available, as are lakeside apartments in a modern annex. ⊠ *Urfeld 8111, D–82431,* ☎ *08851/249,* 𝔽𝔸𝕏 *08851/5067. Restaurant. No credit cards.*

$ ✕🏨 **Grauer Bär.** The friendly atmosphere at this hotel, on the shores of the Kochelsee Lake, has much to do with the family that has owned and managed it since 1905. Ask for one of the spacious, newly renovated rooms overlooking the lake, where the hotel also has its own stretch of private beach. ⊠ *Mittenwalderstr. 82–86, D–82431,* ☎ *08851/861,* ℻ *08851/1607. 26 rooms, 4 apartments with bath. Restaurant, café. AE, DC, MC, V.*

En Route   Even though it's a section of the German Alpine Road, the route through the mountains south of Benediktbeuren is really off-the-beaten track territory, partly because the first 15 kilometers (10 miles) from Wallgau (the junction of the road north to Benediktbeuren) to Vorderiss is a toll road (DM 4 per vehicle). This should not deter you, however, for the road is one of the most beautiful stretches of the German Alpine Road, following the course of the still infant, fast-flowing Isar River and lined by fir-clad slopes and rocky peaks. Vorderiss is at the western end of the Sylvenstein dam-lake, a mysterious sliver of water whose dark surface covers a submerged village. Ghosts linger in the cool air. Halfway along the lake the road divides, east to the Achen Pass and on to Tegernsee and north to the Alpine resort of Lenggries and Bad Tölz.

Lenggries

❾   *40 km (24 mi) north of Wallgau, 12 km (8 mi) north of Sylvenstein Lake.*

Lenggries is a small but popular ski resort, wedged into a narrow valley between the towering Benediktenwand Mountain and the peaks of the Tegernsee Alps. There are fine walks into the mountains and along the Isar, and the skiing is the best in the region.

Dining and Lodging

$$$ ✕☵ **Arabella Brauneck Hotel.** Arabella is a German chain known for its refinements, and its leading Bavarian Alpine hotel does not disappoint. Many of the rooms have views of the area's skiing region, the Brauneck, and lifts are a short walk from the hotel. The Isargrotte sauna-whirlpool "grotto" offers great après-ski relaxation. ⊠ *Münchner Str. 25, D–83661,* ☎ *08042/5020,* ℻ *08042/4224. 98 rooms, 7 apartments with bath. Restaurant, bar, hot tub, sauna, steam room. AE, DC, MC, V.*

$ ✕☵ **Altwirt.** The history of this former coaching inn stretches back to the 15th century. Its restaurant serves such regional specialties as venison with cranberry sauce and egg noodles; its rooms are neat and plain. ⊠ *Marktstr. 13, D–83661,* ☎ *08042/8085,* ℻ *08042/5357. 22 rooms with bath. Restaurant, sauna. No credit cards.*

Bad Tölz

❿   *16 km (10 mi) northeast of Benediktbeuren, 45 km (27 mi) south of Munich.*

If you can, visit Bad Tölz on a Wednesday morning—market day—when the main street is lined with stalls that stretch to the Isar River, the dividing line between the Old and New towns. The latter, dating from the mid-19th century, sprang up with the discovery of iodine-laden springs, which allowed the locals to call their town *Bad* (bath or spa) Tölz. You can take the waters, either by drinking a cupful from the local springs or going the whole way with a full course of health treatment at a specially equipped hotel.

Bad Tölz clings to its ancient customs and traditions more tightly than does any other Bavarian community. Folk costumes, for example, are worn regularly. The town is also famous for its painted furniture, particularly farmhouse cupboards and chests. Several local shops specialize in this *Bauernmöbel* (farmhouse furniture) and will usually handle export formalities.

If you're in Bad Tölz on November 6, you'll witness one of the most colorful traditions of the Bavarian Alpine area: the *Leonhardifahrt* equestrian procession, which marks the feast day of St. Leonhard, the patron saint of horses. The procession ends north of the town at an 18th-century chapel on the Kalvarienberg, above the Isar River.

The **Alpamare,** Bad Tölz's very attractive lido, pumps spa water into its pools, one of which is disguised as a South Sea beach, complete with surf. Its four waterslides include a 330-meter-long (1,082-foot-long) adventure run, Germany's longest. Another—the "Alpa-Canyon"—has 90° drops, and only the hardiest swimmers are advised to try it. ⊠ *Ludwigstr. 13,* ☎ *08041/509–334.* 🎫 *4-hr ticket DM 29 (weekends DM 35). Until 9 AM and after 6 PM the ticket price drops by up to DM 11.* ⊙ *Sun.–Thurs. 8 AM–9 PM, Fri.–Sat. 8 AM–10 PM.*

The **Heimatmuseum,** housed in the Altes Rathaus (Old Town Hall), has many fine examples of Bauernmöbel, as well as a fascinating exhibition on the history of the town and surrounding area. ⊠ *Marktstr. 48,* ☎ *08041/504–688.* 🎫 *DM 3.* ⊙ *Tues.–Wed. and Fri.–Sat. 10–noon and 2–4, Thurs. 10–noon and 2–6, Sun. 10–1.*

⑪ Bad Tölz's local mountain, the **Blomberg,** 3 kilometers (2 miles) west of town, has moderately difficult ski runs, but the height can also be tackled on a toboggan in winter and in summer. The winter run of 5 kilometers (3 miles) is the longest in Bavaria, while the artificial, concrete channel used in summer is Germany's longest dry toboggan run, snaking 1,200 meters (3,938 feet) down the mountain. It's great fun for children, but it can be expensive unless you ration the number of runs. A ski-lift ride to the start of the run and toboggan rental are included in the price. 🎫 *DM 10 a ride.* ⊙ *Dec.–Nov., daily 9–5; Nov.–Dec., depending on weather conditions.*

Dining and Lodging

$$$$ ✕🏨 **Hotel Jodquellenhof-Alpamare.** *Jodquellen* are the iodine springs
★ that have made Bad Tölz wealthy. You can take advantage of these revitalizing waters at this luxurious spa hotel, where the emphasis is on fitness. The imposing 19th-century building, with private access to the Alpamare Lido, contains comfortable and stylish rooms, many of which were enlarged in 1994. ⊠ *Ludwigstr. 13–15, D–83646,* ☎ *08041/ 5090,* 🆑 *08041/509–441. 81 rooms with bath. Restaurant, pool, indoor thermal baths, sauna. AE, DC, MC, V.*

$$ ✕🏨 **Hotel Gasthof Pension Am Wald.** This modern but traditionally designed lodging is set in its own spacious grounds in the "new" half of town, a 10-minute stroll from Bad Tölz's ancient quarter. Rooms are decorated and furnished country style. ⊠ *Austr. 39, D–83646,* ☎ *08041/9014,* 🆑 *08041/72643. 32 rooms with bath, 2 apartments. Restaurant, indoor pool, sauna, exercise room. AE, DC, MC, V. Closed Nov. 7–Dec. 20.*

Nightlife and the Arts

Although Bad Tölz is a spa town, with a fair number of clinics and sanatoriums, it is by no means short on entertainment for younger visitors. It has four discos—the best is said to be **Arena** (⊠ Demmeljochstr. 42). The town is world renowned on the concert circuit for its outstanding **boys choir.** When it's not on tour, the choir gives regular concerts in the Kurhaus (program details available from the Städtische Kurverwaltung, ☎ 08041/70071).

Tegernsee

★ ⑫ *16 km (10 mi) east of Bad Tölz, 50 km (30 mi) south of Munich.*

The beautiful shores of the Tegernsee Lake are among the most expensive properties in all Germany, and so many wealthy Germans have their homes here that the locals dubbed it the *Lago di Bonzo* ("Bonze" means "big shot," while the Italian word "Lago" refers to expensive lakes where Mafia bosses lurk). Although many of the houses qualify as small palaces, most of the hotels have sensible rates, and a stay at Tegernsee need be no more expensive than anywhere else in Alpine Bavaria. Its wooded shores, rising gently to scaleable mountain peaks of no more than 2,000 meters (6,300 feet), invite hikers and walkers, while in summer the lake draws swimmers, yachting types, and picnicking families. In fall its russet-clad trees provide a colorful contrast to the dark, snowcapped mountains.

The former **Benedictine monastery,** which sits majestically on the eastern shore of the lake, in the town of Tegernsee, provides further proof that medieval monastic orders were very choosy about where they settled. Founded in the 8th century, this was one of the most productive cultural centers in southern Germany; the musician and poet Minnesänger Walther von der Vogelweide (1170–1230) was a welcome guest. Not so welcome were Hungarian invaders, who laid waste to the monastery in the 10th century. Fire caused further damage in following centuries, and secularization sealed the monastery's fate at the beginning of the 19th, when Bavarian king Maximilian I bought the surviving buildings for use as a summer retreat. Maximilian showed off this corner of his kingdom to Emperors Alexander of Russia and Franz-Josef of Austria during their journey to the Congress of Verona in October 1822, and you can follow their steps through the woods to one of the loveliest lookout points in Bavaria, the **Grosses Paraplui.** A plaque marks the spot where they admired the open expanse of the Tegernsee and the mountains beyond.

In addition to a church, the property houses a beer tavern, a brewery, a restaurant, and a high school. Students here, in what was the monastery, write their exams beneath inspiring Baroque frescoes. The late-Gothic **church** was refurbished in Italian Baroque style in the 18th century. Opinions remain divided as to the success of the remodeling, which was the work of a little-known Italian architect named Antonio Riva. Whatever you think of his designs, you'll admire the frescoes by Hans Georg Asam, whose work you saw at Benediktbeuern. The parish church of **Gmund,** at the north end of the lake, also has Baroque influences.

NEED A BREAK? You can follow King Max's footsteps, too, into the vaulted rooms of the neighboring **Bräustüberl** (✉ Schlosspl., ☎ 08022/4141), in which busy waitresses bustle where Benedictine monks once meditated. The dark beer is very strong; the food is basic Bavarian.

Dining and Lodging

$$$ ✕ **Der Leeberghof.** This gentrified country restaurant offers panoramic views and Bavarian cooking with flair. Try chef Michael Hamburger's jellied duck with plums or vegetable-stuffed pork with fried potato cakes. An alternative to dessert might be goat cheese and coriander bread. On warm evenings take an aperitif or an after-dinner Bavarian schnapps on the bar-terrace above the lake—the view will root you to the spot. If you really have problems leaving, the Leeberghof has six luxurious guest rooms. ✉ *Ellingerstr. 10,* ☎ *08022/3966. MC.*

$$–$$$ ✕ **Freihaus Brenner.** Proprietor Josef Brenner has brought a taste of nouvelle cuisine to the Tegernsee, where his attractive restaurant commands fine views from high above Bad Wiessee. Try any of his suggested dishes—ranging from wild rabbit in elderberry sauce to fresh lake fish. German chancellor Kohl and French president Mitterrand ate well here during one of their regular summits. ⊠ *Freihaushöhe 4,* ☎ *08022/82004. MC.*

$ ✕ **Herzogliches Bräustuberl.** Once part of Tegernsee's Benedictine monastery, then a royal retreat, the Bräustuberl is now a beer hall and brewery immensely popular with the locals, who pack it solid every night. Only basic Bavarian snacks (sausages, pretzels, a deliciously marshmallow-like baked Camembert) are served in this crowded place, but hearty Bavarian meals can be ordered in the adjoining Keller. In summer quaff it beneath the huge chestnuts and admire the lake and mountains over the rim of your glass. ⊠ *Schlosspl. 1,* ☎ *08022/4516. Reservations not accepted. No credit cards. Closed Nov.*

$$$$ ✕▥ **Hotel Bayern.** The elegant, turreted Bayern is a showpiece of the Silence group, whose hotels must guarantee a peaceful setting. The Bayern certainly meets that qualification, sitting high above the Tegernsee Lake, backed by the wooded slopes of the Neureuth Mountain. Rooms overlooking the lake are in big demand despite their relatively high cost, so book early. All guests, whatever their room, can enjoy panoramic views of the lake and the mountains from the extensive terrace fronting the castle-like building. ⊠ *Neureuthstr. 23, D–83684,* ☎ *08022/1820,* FAX *08022/3775. 92 rooms, 2 suites, all with bath. Restaurant, indoor pool. AE, DC, MC.*

$$$ ✕▥ **Seegarten.** This lakeside hotel in Bad Wiessee, with pinewood wall paneling and matching furniture, has cheerful rooms decorated in the bright primary colors typical of the Bavarian country-farmhouse style. Ask for a room with a balcony overlooking Tegernsee Lake. The Seegarten's kitchen is famous for its cakes. ⊠ *Adrian-Stoopstr. 4, D–83684,* ☎ *08022/81155,* FAX *08022/85087. 33 rooms with bath. Restaurant. AE, V.*

$$ ✕▥ **Seehotel Zur Post.** The fine lake views from most rooms in this hotel in Tegernsee are somewhat disturbed by the main road, which runs outside, but its central location and a fine winter garden and terrace are pluses. The restaurant serves fresh lake fish, but there are also special venison weeks, worthy of a long detour. ⊠ *Seestr. 3, D–83684,* ☎ *08022/3951. Restaurant. DC, MC, V. Closed Jan.–Feb. 15.*

$$ ▥ **Margaritenhaus.** This handsome Bavarian-style mansion has 25 individually designed and furnished apartments, all with their own kitchen facilities and either balconies or garden terraces, most with lake views. One (Apartment Mathilde) even has a modern, glassed-in fireplace for winter evenings. The lake and mountain slopes are just a short walk away. Also nearby are a number of Bavarian restaurants and taverns, and several hotels that have regular evenings of Bavarian zither music and dancing. ⊠ *Adrian-Stoopstr. 32, D–83684,* ☎ *08022/860340. 25 apartments. Laundry. No credit cards.*

Nightlife and the Arts

Bad Wiessee has a lakeside **casino** (☎ 08022/82028) that's open daily 3 PM–3 AM and sets the tone for a surprisingly lively after-dark scene around the Tegernsee lake. The **Leeberghof,** on the edge of Tegernsee town (⊠ Ellingerstr. 10), has a sensational terrace bar with prices to match, inclusive of one of Bavaria's finest views. Every resort has its **spa orchestra**—in the summer they play daily in the music-box-style bandstands that dot the lakeside promenades.

A strong Tegernsee tradition is the summer-long program of **festivals,** often deep in the forest. Tegernsee's lake festival in August, when sailing clubs deck their boats with garlands and lanterns, is an unforgettable experience.

Shopping

Trachten Brendl (✉ Hauptstr. 8, Tegernsee) has a colorful selection of Bavarian traditional costumes and other handmade fabrics. If at the end of your Upper Bavarian tour you're still looking for *something,* stop at the busy market town of Miesbach (between Tegernsee and Schliersee) and climb the stairs to **Cilly's Gschirrladn** (Cilly's china shop, ✉ Stadpl. 10, ☏ 08025/1705). A warren of rooms is packed ceiling high with every variety of item for the home, from embroidered tablecloths to fine German porcelain.

Rottach-Egern

⑬ *On the south shore of Tegnersee.*

Rottach-Egern is a fashionable and upscale resort. Its classy shops, chic restaurants, and expensive boutiques are as well stocked and interesting as many in Munich; its leading hotels, world-class. Its church, **St. Laurentius,** has Baroque influences. For a stylish visit to town, **Bachmair's** (✉ Seestr. 47, ☏ 08022/2720), on the water's edge, is the place to stay: It has a nightclub featuring international acts.

Dining and Lodging

$ ✕ **Weinhaus Moschner.** You're pretty much expected to drink wine in this dark, old tavern on the edge of fashionable, ritzy Rottach Egern. Beer, from the monastery brewery across the lake in Tegernsee, is also served, and the waitresses probably won't protest if you order it. The menu sticks to local Bavarian fare (heavy on the sausage), but nobody comes here just to eat. Join the locals at a rough wood table in the log-walled tavern tap room, order a plate of smoked pork and a glass of ale or Franconian wine, and leave the fine dining until tomorrow—it's the camaraderie and atmosphere here that counts. Under-thirties will love the first-floor disco, although the rough charm of the lederhosen-clad locals may distract you. ✉ *Kisslinger Str. 2,* ☏ *08022/5522. No credit cards. Closed Mon.–Tues., Dec. 25, Jan. 1.*

OFF THE   The mountain slopes above Bad Wiessee offer fine views, but for the
BEATEN PATH best vista of all climb the 5,700-foot **Wallberg,** at the south end of the Tegernsee. It's a hard, four-hour hike, though anyone in good shape should be able to make it since it involves no rock climbing. A cable car makes the ascent in just 15 minutes and costs DM 13 one-way, DM 22 round-trip. At the summit there's a restaurant and sun terrace and several trailheads; in winter the skiing is excellent.

Schliersee

⑭ *20 km (12 mi) east of Tegernsee, 55 km (32 mi) southeast of Munich.*

Schliersee is smaller, quieter, and less fashionable than Tegernsee, but scarcely less beautiful. The difference between the two lakes is made clear in the names local people have long given them: The Tegernsee is called the *Herrensee* (or Master's Lake), while the Schliersee is known as the *Bauernsee* (or Peasant's Lake). There are fine walking and ski trails on the mountain slopes that ring its placid waters. The lake is shallow and often freezes over in winter, when the tiny island in its center is a favorite hiking destination.

Like its neighbor, the Schliersee was the site of a monastery, built in the 8th century by a group of noblemen. It subsequently became a choral academy, which eventually moved to Munich. Today only the restored 17th-century **abbey church** recalls this piece of the Schliersee's history. The church has some fine frescoes and stuccowork by Johann Baptist Zimmermann.

Dining and Lodging

$$–$$$ ✕▥ **Schlieseer Hof am See.** You can eat and sleep well in this modern, traditional-style, lakeside hostelry with many facilities. The restaurant concentrates on local fish (ask for *Renke*, a delicate white fish from the lake) and game (if it's offered, try the braised venison in the rich house sauce). Rooms are fashioned with pinewood and bright check fabrics. ⊠ *Seestr. 21, D–83727,* ☎ *08026/4071,* ℻ *08206/4953. 43 rooms, 3 apartments. Restaurant, weinstube, pool, sauna, boating. AE, DC, MC, V.*

Spitzingsee

⑮   *10 km (6 mi) south of Schliersee.*

Arguably the most beautiful of this group of Bavarian lakes, Spitzingsee is cradled 3,500 feet up between the Taubenstein, Rosskopf, and Stumpfling peaks, and the ride there is spectacular. The lake is particularly beautiful in winter, usually frozen over and almost buried in the surrounding snow. Walking in this area is breathtaking during every season and in every sense. The skiing is very good, too.

Dining and Lodging

$$$$ ✕▥ **Arabella Alpenhotel.** For an out-of-the-way break in the mountains, head for this modern motel on the banks of the small and quiet Spitzingsee Lake. Rooms are decorated with modern Scandinavian furnishings. If you can't stay overnight, come for a leisurely lunch of lake fish or a vegetarian meal. In winter the frozen lake is used for ice sports. ⊠ *Seeweg 7, D–83727,* ☎ *08026/7980,* ℻ *08026/798–879. 122 rooms with bath. Restaurant, indoor pool, sauna, steam room, tennis courts, bowling, exercise room, boating, library. AE, DC, MC, V.*

Bayrischzell

⑯   *10 km (6 mi) east of Schliersee.*

Bayrischzell is in an attractive family-resort area, where many a Bavarian first learned to ski. The wide-open slopes of the Sudelfeld Mountain are ideal for those who enjoy undemanding skiing; in summer and fall they offer innumerable upland walking trails.

The town sits at the end of a wide valley overlooked by one of the highest mountains in the area, the 6,000-foot **Wendelstein,** which attracts expert skiers. At its summit is a tiny stone-and-slate-roof chapel that's much in demand as an unusual place for wedding ceremonies. The cross above the entrance was carried up the mountain by Max Kleiber, who designed the 19th-century church. Today there are two easier ways up: by cable car (which sets out from beside the train station at Osterhofen and costs DM 27 round-trip) and by historic cog railway (catch it at Brannenburg, on the north side of the mountain; round-trip DM 36).

Dining and Lodging

$$ ✕▥ **Hotel Alpenrose.** This friendly, family-run hotel, in Alpine style, is handy for the ski slopes and the town center. Rooms are cozy and mostly furnished in traditional Bavarian style, with lots of wood. ⊠ *Schlierseestr. 6, D–83735,* ☎ *08023/620,* ℻ *08023/1049. 37 rooms, 3 suites, 3 apartments, with bath or shower. Restaurant. No credit cards.*

En Route   A mile or two east of Bayrischzell on the Sudelfeld Road is the **Tatzel-wurm** gorge and waterfall, named for a winged dragon who suppos-edly inhabits these parts. Dragon or no, this can be an eerie place to drive through at dusk. From the gorge, the road drops sharply to the valley of the Inn River, leading to the busy ski resort of Oberaudorf.

The Inn River valley, an ancient trade route, carries the most impor-tant road link between Germany and Italy. The wide, green Inn gushes here, and in the parish church of St. Bartholomew at **Rossholzen** (16 kilometers [10 miles] north of Oberaudorf), you can see memorials to the local people who have lost their lives in its chilly waters. The church has a fine late-Gothic altar.

Stock

⑰   *30 km (18 mi) northeast of Rossholzen, 20 km (12 mi) east of Rosen-heim, 80 km (50 mi) east of Munich.*

Chiemsee is north of the German Alpine Road, but it demands a de-tour, if only to visit King Ludwig's huge palace on one of its idyllic is-lands. It's the largest Bavarian lake and although surrounded by reedy flatlands the nearby mountains provide a majestic backdrop. Stock is one of its main towns.

⑱   Despite its distance from Munich, the expansive beauty of the Chiem-see Lake drew Bavarian royalty to its shores. Its dreamlike, melancholy air caught the imagination of King Ludwig II, and it was on one of the lake's three islands that he built the sumptuous **Schloss Herrenchiem-see,** based on Louis XIV's great palace at Versailles. But this was the result of more than simple admiration of Versailles: Ludwig, whose name was the German equivalent of Louis, was keen to establish that he, too, possessed the absolute authority of his namesake, the Sun King. As with most of Ludwig's projects, the building was never completed, and Ludwig the "mad" king never stayed in its state rooms. Nonetheless, what remains is impressive—and ostentatious. Regular ferries out to the island depart from Stock, on the shore. If you want to make the journey in style, take the 100-year-old steam train—which glories in the name *Feuriger Elias,* or *Fiery Elias*—from the neighboring town of Prien to Stock. A horse-drawn carriage takes you to the palace it-self. Most spectacular in the palace is the Hall of Mirrors, a dazzling gallery (modeled on that at Versailles) where candlelit concerts are held in the summer. Also of interest are the ornate bedrooms Ludwig planned and the stately formal gardens. The south wing houses a mu-seum containing Ludwig's christening robe and death mask, as well as other artifacts of his life. ✉ *Palace and museum DM 7.50.* ☉ *Apr.–Sept., daily 9–5; Oct.–Mar., daily 10–4. Guided tours offered May–Sept.*

⑲   The smaller **Fraueninsel** (Ladies' Island), also reached by boat from Stock, is a charming retreat. The Benedictine convent, founded 1,200 years ago, now serves as a school. One of its earliest abbesses, Irmengard, daughter of King Ludwig der Deutscher, died here in the 9th century. Her grave was discovered in 1961, the same year that early frescoes in the convent chapel were brought to light.

OFF THE   The world's largest small-gauge model railway competes for attention
BEATEN PATH   with more than 200 old automobiles in the **German Automobile History Museum** (Museum für Deutsche Automobilgeschichte) at Ammerang, near the Chiemsee Lake. The two collections share 6,000 square meters (about 65,000 square feet) of exhibition space. ✉ *Wasserburger Str. 38.* ✉ *DM 10.* ☉ *Tues.–Sat. 10–6.*

Dining and Lodging

$$ ✕🏨 **Seehotel Wassermann.** The Wassermann stands in the village of Seebruck by the mouth of the River Alz, which flows into the Chiemsee. The hotel was built in the 1980s, in the traditional style of Bavarian pine. Ask for a balconied room with a four-poster bed. ⊠ *Ludwig-Thomastr. 1, D–83358, ☎ 08667/8710,* ꜰᴀꞟ *08667/871–498. 40 rooms, 2 apartments with bath. Restaurant, indoor pool, hot tub, sauna, steam room, boating, bicycles. AE, MC, V.*

$ ✕🏨 **Hotel Post.** This historic family-run coaching inn offers reasonably priced lodging in the center of Seebruck. Rooms are simply furnished in pinewood. In summer guests can dine in the tree-shaded beer garden. The hotel sponsors Bavarian music evenings. ⊠ *Ludwig-Thomastr. 8, D–83358, ☎ 08667/8870,* ꜰᴀꞟ *08667/1343. 35 rooms with bath, 31 with shower. Beer garden. AE, MC, V.*

$ ✕🏨 **Unterwirt zu Chieming.** You can catch the boat to the islands of the Chiemsee right outside this small pension. Rooms are cozily furnished in traditional Bavarian style. The cheerful little restaurant serves hearty portions of such local fare as pork knuckle and potato dumplings. ⊠ *Hauptstr. 32, D–83358, ☎ 08664/551,* ꜰᴀꞟ *08664/1649. 11 rooms with shower. Restaurant. No credit cards. Restaurant closed Mon.–Tues.; pension and restaurant are closed Nov.*

Rosenheim

㉚ *20 km (12 mi) west of Chiemsee, 55 km (33 mi) east of Munich.*

Bustling Rosenheim is an attractive medieval market town that has kept much of its character despite the onslaught of industrial development. The arcaded streets of low-eaved houses are characteristic of Inn Valley towns. It's an ideal center from which to explore nearby Chiemsee and has a handful of pretty rural lakes of its own on its doorstep (Simssee, Hofstättersee, and Rinssee).

Dining and Lodging

$$$$ ✕🏨 **Residenz Heinz Winkler.** In 1991 award-winning chef Heinz Winkler moved his kitchen from Munich to the red-roof village of Aschau, 6 kilometers (4 miles) south of Chiemsee, where he converted a 300-year-old coaching inn into one of the country's most sought-after restaurants. Gourmets, undismayed by Winkler's recent loss of one of his three Michelin stars, flock here to sample his expensive nouvelle-cuisine creations in elegant surroundings. Specialties include truffle soup, crab legs with basil, and carpaccio of beef fillet in cream sauce. The Residenz also offers individually designed guest rooms, many of them furnished with expensive antiques. ⊠ *Kirchpl. 1, D–83229, ☎ 08052/17990,* ꜰᴀꞟ *08052/179–966. 32 rooms with bath. Restaurant, bar, café, sauna. AE, DC, MC, V.*

Aschau

㉛ *10 km (6 mi) south of Chiemsee.*

Aschau is an enchanting village nestling in a fold of the Chiemgauer Alps and site of **Schloss Hohenaschau.** One of few medieval castles in southern Germany to have been restored in the 17th-century in Baroque style, the renovation gave its stately rooms a new elegance. Chamber-music concerts are presented regularly in the Rittersaal (Knights Hall) during the summer. ☎ *08052/392.* 🎟 *DM 3.* ◷ *Apr.–Oct., Tues.–Fri. 9–5.*

Dining and Lodging

$$$ ✕🏨 **Goldener Hirsch.** Rooms maintain a high standard of comfort in this central and established hotel in the heart of Rosenheim. It's an ideal place from which to explore the Alpine region, and in the car-free streets around the hotel you'll find a wealth of restaurants and taverns. The hotel's restaurant has a large menu that combines local dishes (roast pork and dumplings, Bavarian sausage) with international specialties. ✉ *Münchnerstr. 40, D–83022,* ☎ *08031/21290,* Ⅻ *08031/212–949. 33 rooms with bath. Restaurant. AE, DC, MC, V.*

En Route At Aschau you'll join the most scenic section of the Alpine Road, as it passes through a string of villages—Bernau, Rottau, Grassau, Marquartstein, and Oberwössen—pretty enough to make you want to linger. In summer the farmhouses of **Rottau** virtually disappear behind facades of flowers, which have won the village several awards. The houses of **Grassau** shrink beside the bulk of the 15th-century Church of the Ascension, worth visiting for its rich 17th-century stuccowork.

Reit im Winkl

㉒ *16 km (10 mi) south of Chiemsee.*

Reit im Winkl has produced at least two German ski champions, who trained on the demanding runs high above the village. The **Winklmoosalm Mountain,** towering above Reit im Winkl, can be reached by bus or chairlift and is a popular ski area in winter, a great place for bracing upland walks in summer and fall. In summer the town attracts artists because of the clarity of its light.

Dining and Lodging

$$ ✗ **Kupferkanne.** Outside, a garden surrounds the building; inside, you could be in an Alpine farmstead. The food is good country fare enhanced by some interesting Austrian specialties. Try the *Salzburger Brez'n,* a thick, creamy, bread-based soup. ✉ *Weitseestr. 18,* ☎ *08640/ 1450. No credit cards. Closed Sat. and Nov.*

$$ ✗🏠 **Landgasthof Rosi Mittermaier.** Rosi Mittermaier, skiing star of the 1976 Innsbruck Olympics, runs this charming Bavarian Gasthof with her husband, Christian Neureuther, a champion skier himself. If you're here to hit the slopes, you're in good hands—Rosi was skiing the runs here practically before she could walk. In summer she and Christian are also free with advice about the trails to the surrounding mountains. The Gasthof has only eight large apartments, so it's essential to book in advance. But even if you're not staying, a visit to its rustic Cafe Olympia or cozy, pine-paneled tavern-restaurant is recommended. The duck dishes are a specialty of the house, and the *Käsekuchen* is legendary. ✉ *Chiemseestr. 2a, D–83242,* ☎ *08640/1011,* Ⅻ *08640/1013. 8 apartments. 2 restaurants, café, sauna. AE, DC, MC, V.*

Ruhpolding

㉓ *24 km (14 mi) east of Reit im Winkl.*

The Bavarian tourist boom began in this picturesque resort back in the '30s. In those days tourists were greeted at the train station by a brass band. The welcome isn't quite so extravagant any more, but it's still warm. In the 16th century the Bavarian rulers journeyed to Ruhpolding to hunt, and the Renaissance-style hunting lodge of Prince Wilhelm V still stands (now used as the offices of the local forestry service). The hillside 18th-century **Pfarrkirche St. Georg** (Parish Church of St. George) is one of the finest Baroque and rococo churches in the Bavarian Alps. In one of its side altars stands a rare 13th-century carved Madonna, the Ruhpoldinger Madonna. Note also the atmospheric crypt chapel in the quiet churchyard.

In the village of Hasslberg near Ruhpolding you can visit a 300-year-old **bell foundry**, now a fascinating museum of the ancient craft of the foundry-man and blacksmith. ☜ DM 4.50. ☺ Mon.–Sat. 10–noon and 2–4.

Dining and Lodging

$$ ✕🏠 **Zur Post.** Look for the Zur Post sign in any Bavarian town or village, and you can be confident of good local fare. In business for more than 650 years, Ruhpolding's has been in the hands of the same family for 150. You can also obtain lodging here; call beforehand for room reservations. ✉ *Hauptstr. 35, D-83324,* ☎ *08663/1035,* 𝖥𝖠𝖷 *08663/1483. Reservations not accepted. MC. Closed Mon.*

Bad Reichenhall

㉔ *30 km (18 mi) east of Ruhpolding, 20 km (12 mi) west of Salzburg.*

Bad Reichenhall shares a remote corner of Bavaria, almost surrounded by the Austrian border, with another prominent resort, Berchtesgaden. Although the latter is more famous, Bad Reichenhall is older, with saline springs that made the town rich. Salt is so much a part of the town that you can practically taste it in the air. There's even a 19th-century "saline" chapel, part of the spa's facilities and built in exotic Byzantine style at the behest of Ludwig I. Many hotels base special spa treatments on the health-giving properties of the saline springs and the black mud from the surrounding waterlogged moors. The waters can also be taken in the attractive spa gardens throughout the year. It's open April–October, daily 7 AM–10 PM; November–March, daily 7–6. Bad Reichenhall's symphony orchestra performs five days a week during the summer season and four days a week in winter. Like most resorts in the area, this one also has a casino (☞ Nightlife and the Arts, *below*).

Europe's largest saline source was first tapped in pre-Christian times; salt mined during the Middle Ages supported the economies of cities as far away as Munich and Passau. In the early 19th century King Ludwig I built an elaborate saltworks and spa house in Bad Reichenhall—the **Alte Saline and Quellenhaus**—in vaulted, pseudomedieval style. Their pump installations are astonishing examples of 19th-century engineering. A fascinating **museum** in the same building looks at the history of the salt trade, which helped build Bad Reichenhall's wealthy foundations. *Quellenhaus and Salzmuseum,* ☎ *08651/700251.* ☜ *DM 4. ☺ Apr.–Oct., daily 10–11:30 and 2–4; Nov.–Mar., Tues. and Thurs. 2–4. The Alte Saline also houses a typical Upper Bavarian glass foundry and a showroom with articles for sale.* ☜ *Free. ☺ Weekdays 9–6, Sat. 9–1.*

Bad Reichenhall's ancient church of **Saint Zeno** is dedicated to the patron saint of those imperiled by floods and the dangers of the deep, an ironic note in a town that flourishes on the riches of its underground springs. Much of this 12th-century basilica was remodeled in the 16th and 17th centuries, but some of the original cloisters remain. ✉ *Kirchpl. 1,* ☎ *08651/4889.*

Dining and Lodging

$$$$ ✕🏠 **Parkhotel Luisenbad.** If you fancy spoiling yourself in a typical German fin de siècle spa hotel, this is *the* place—a fine porticoed and pillared building whose imposing pastel-pink facade holds the promise of spacious luxury. Inside, the promise is fulfilled. Rooms are large, furnished in deep-cushioned, dark-wood comfort, most of them with flower-smothered balconies or loggias. The elegant restaurant serves international and traditional Bavarian cuisines, while a pine-paneled

tavern, Die Holzstubn'n, is the place for a glass or two of the excellent local brew. ⊠ *Ludwigstr. 33, D–83435,* ☎ *08651/6040,* FAX *08651/62928. 80 rooms and 8 apartments with bath. Restaurant, bar, beer garden, indoor pool, hot tub, sauna, exercise room, bicycles, recreation room. DC, MC, V.*

$$$$ ✕⊡ **Steigenberger-Hotel Axelmannstein.** Ludwig would have enjoyed the palatial air that pervades this hotel—and he would have been able to afford the price, which rivals that of top hotels in Germany's most expensive cities. If you stay here, you'll reside in luxurious comfort, in rooms ranging in style from Bavarian rustic to Laura Ashley demure. Outside is a manicured park and the town center. ⊠ *Salzburgerstr. 2, D–83435,* ☎ *08651/7770,* FAX *08651/5932. 143 rooms with bath and 8 apartments. 2 restaurants, bar, indoor pool, beauty salon, sauna, spa, tennis court, exercise room, baby-sitting. AE, DC, MC, V.*

$ ✕⊡ **Pension Hubertus.** This delightfully traditional family-run lodg-
★   ing stands on the banks of the tiny Thumsee Lake, 5 kilometers (3 miles) from the town center. The Hubertus's private grounds lead down to the lake, where guests can swim or boat. Rooms are Bavarian rustic in style. Ask for one with a balcony overlooking the lake. Special, full-board discounts are offered October–May. ⊠ *Thumsee 5, D–83435,* ☎ *08651/2252,* FAX *08651/63845. 18 rooms with shower. Restaurant, exercise room, boating. AE.*

Nightlife and the Arts

Bad Reichenhall has an elegant **casino,** open 3 PM–3 AM (☎ 08651/4091). The resort is proud of its long musical tradition and of its **orchestra,** founded more than a century ago. It performs throughout the year in the chandelier-hung Kurgastzentrum theater or, when weather permits, in the open-air pavilion. Call the Kurgastzentrum, ☎ 08651/3003 for program details.

Shopping

The **Josef Mack Company** (⊠ Ludwigstr. 36, Bad Reichenhall, ☎ 08651/78280) has been in the business of making up medicinal herbal preparations since 1856, using flowers and herbs grown in the Bavarian Alps. **Dricoolo KG** (⊠ Ludwigstr. 27, Bad Reichenhall, ☎ 08651/78331) is another established herb vendor.

Berchtesgaden

㉕ *18 km (11 mi) south of Bad Reichenhall, 20 km (12 mi) south of Salzburg.*

Berchtesgaden's reputation is unjustly rooted in its brief association with Adolf Hitler, who dreamed besottedly of his 1,000-year "Reich" from the mountaintop where millions of tourists before and after him drank in only the superb beauty of the Alpine panorama. Below those giddy heights is a historic old market town and mountain resort of great charm. While as a high-altitude ski station it may not have quite the cachet of Garmisch-Partenkirchen, in summer it serves as one of the region's most popular (and crowded) resorts, with top-rated attractions in a heavenly setting. Members of the ruling Wittelsbach dynasty started coming here in 1810. Their ornate palace stands today and is one of the town's major attractions, along with a working salt mine and, of course, the mountaintop retreat used by Hitler.

Salt—or "white gold," as it was known in medieval times—was the basis of Berchtesgaden's wealth. In the 12th century Emperor Barbarossa gave mining rights to a Benedictine abbey that had been founded here a century earlier. The abbey was secularized early in the 19th century, when it was taken over by the Wittelsbach rulers. The last royal resident of the Berchtesgaden abbey, Crown Prince Rupprecht, who died here in 1955, furnished it with rare family treasures that now form the basis of a permanent collection—the **Königliches Schloss Berchtesgaden Museum.** Fine Renaissance rooms provide the principal exhibition spaces for the prince's collection of sacred art, which is particularly rich in wood sculptures by such great late-Gothic artists as Tilman Riemenschneider and Veit Stoss. You can also visit the abbey's original, cavernous 13th-century dormitory and cool cloisters, which still convey something of the quiet and orderly life led by medieval monks. ☎ 08652/2085. ⌑ DM 7. ☉ *Easter–Sept., Sun.–Fri. 10–1 and 2–5; Oct.–Easter, weekdays 10–1 and 2–5. No admission after 4, when last tour starts.*

Wood carving in Berchtesgaden dates back to long before Oberammergau established itself as the premier wood-carving center of the Alps. Examples of Berchtesgaden wood carvings and other local crafts are on display at one of the most interesting museums of its kind in the Alps, the **Heimatmuseum,** in the Schloss Adelsheim. ⌑ *Schroffenbergallee 6,* ☎ 08652/4410. ⌑ DM 3. ☉ *Entry allowed only as part of the guided tours given weekdays at 10 and 3.*

Berchtesgaden has its own salt mine, the **Salzbergwerk,** one of the chief tourist attractions of the entire region. In the days when the mine was owned by Berchtesgaden's princely rulers, only select guests were allowed to see how the source of the city's wealth was extracted from the earth. Today 90-minute tours of the mines are available. Dressed in traditional miner's clothing, visitors sit astride a miniature train that transports them nearly half a mile into the mountain to an enormous chamber where the salt is mined. Rides down the wooden chutes, used by the miners to get from one level to another, and a boat ride on an underground saline lake the size of a football field are included in the 1½-hour tour. ⌑ *1 mi from Berchtesgaden on the B–305 Salzburg Rd.,* ☎ 08652/60020. ⌑ DM 17. ☉ *May–mid-Oct., daily 8:30–5; mid-Oct.–Apr., Mon.–Sat. 12:30–3:30.*

㉖ The **Obersalzburg,** site of Hitler's luxurious mountain retreat, sits high above Berchtesgaden, on the north slope of the Hoher Goll. Most of the Nazi complex was destroyed in 1945, as was Hitler's chalet; only a few basement walls remain. Farther along, the hairpin bends of Germany's highest road come to the base of the 6,000-foot peak on which sat the so-called *Adlerhorst* (Eagle's Nest), the **Kehlsteinhaus** (☎ 08652/2969). Hitler had the road built in 1937–39. It climbs more than 2,000 feet in less than 6 kilometers (4 miles) and ends at a lot that clings to the mountain about 500 feet below the Kehlsteinhaus. A tunnel in the mountain brings you to an elevator that whisks you up to what appears to be the top of the world. There are refreshment rooms and a restaurant, where you can fill up before the giddy descent to Berchtesgaden. The round-trip by bus and lift (Berchtesgaden post office to Eagle's Nest and back) costs DM 25.50 per person. By car you can travel only as far as the Obersalzberg bus station. From there, the return fare is DM 19. The full round-trip takes one hour. ☉ *Mid-May–mid-Oct.*

Dining and Lodging

$$ ✕ **Alpenhotel Denninglehen.** Nonsmokers will appreciate the special dining room set aside just for them in this mountain hotel's restaurant. The restaurant is 3,000 feet up in the resort area of Oberau, just outside Berchtesgaden, and its terrace offers magnificent views. ⌑ *Am Priesterstein 7, Berchtesgaden-Oberau,* ☎ 08652/5085. *No credit cards. Closed Sat. and late Nov.–Dec. 25.*

$$ ✕ **Hotel Post.** This is a centrally located and solidly reliable hostelry with a well-presented international menu. If fish from the nearby Königsee is offered, order it. In summer you can eat in the beer garden. ✉ *Maximilianstr. 2,* ☎ *08652/5067. AE, DC, MC, V. Closed Tues.*

$ ✕ **Fischer.** You can pop into this farmhouse-style eatery for Apfelstrudel and coffee or for something more substantial from a frequently changing international and local menu. It's a short walk across the bridge from the railway station. ✉ *Königsseerstr. 51,* ☎ *08652/9550. MC. Closed Nov.–Dec. 18.*

$$$$ ✕🖫 **Geiger.** With steeply eaved, Bavarian green roofs that rival the dramatic mountain-peak backdrop, this hotel matches almost anyone's idea of how a German Alpine retreat should look. Since 1866 it has stood alone on a mountain slope overlooking the town, with forest firs creeping up to the rooms' flower-wreathed balconies. Antiques, thick Oriental rugs, hunting trophies, and old engravings complete the picture. You have a wide choice of dining rooms—from the paneled, Bavarian-style restaurant to the aptly named, cozy Biedermeier Salon or "farmer's tavern." ✉ *Alpenkette, Stanggass, D-83471,* ☎ *08652/9653,* FAX *08652/965–400. 41 rooms, 4 suites, 4 apartments, all with shower or bath. 2 restaurants, bar, indoor and outdoor pools, massage, sauna, exercise room, recreation room. V. Closed mid-Nov.–mid-Dec.*

$$–$$$ ✕🖫 **Stolls Hotel Alpina.** Set above the Königsee in the delightful little village of Schönau, the Alpina offers rural solitude and easy access to Berchtesgaden. Families are catered to with special family-size apartments, a resident doctor, and a playroom. ✉ *Ulmenweg 14, D-83471,* ☎ *08652/65090,* FAX *08652/61608. 44 rooms, 6 apartments with bath. Restaurant, indoor and outdoor pools, sauna, beauty salon. AE, DC, MC, V. Closed Nov. 4–Dec. 17.*

$$ ✕🖫 **Hotel Grünberger.** The cozy rooms at this older-style residence have farmhouse-style furnishings and some original antiques. Only a few strides from the train station, in the town center, the Grünberger overlooks the River Ache, beside which you can relax on a private sun terrace. ✉ *Hansererweg 1, D-83471,* ☎ *08652/4560,* FAX *08652/62254. 65 rooms with bath. Restaurant, beer garden, indoor pool, sauna. No credit cards. Closed Nov.–mid-Dec.*

$$ ✕🖫 **Hotel Wittelsbach.** Bearing the name of Bavaria's former royal rulers, this is one of the oldest (built in 1892) and most traditional lodgings in the area. The cozy rooms have dark pinewood furnishings and deep-red-and-green drapes and carpets. Ask for one with a balcony. ✉ *Maximilianstr. 16, D-83471,* ☎ *08652/96380,* FAX *08652/66304. 20 rooms, 3 apartments with bath. Restaurant. AE, DC, MC, V.*

$ ✕🖫 **Hotel Watzmann.** The USAF director of operations in Berchtesgaden awarded the Hotel Watzmann a special certificate of appreciation for its hospitality to American servicemen. Today's American visitors, in turn, appreciate its cozy Bavarian style and good restaurant. Rooms were recently refurbished with Bavarian antique furniture and offer remarkable value for money (a double comes as cheaply as DM 66). ✉ *Franziskanerpl., D-83471,* ☎ *08652/2055,* FAX *08652/ 5174. 35 rooms, 16 with shower. Restaurant. AE, MC, V. Closed early Nov.–mid-Dec.*

$ ✕🖫 **Seehotel Gamsbock.** Situated in the village of Ramsau, 7 kilometers (4 miles) west of Berchtesgaden, the Gamsbock stands directly on the banks of Hintersee Lake. It's ideal for anglers; the crystal-clear lake contains trout and saibling. Book one of the olde Worlde balconied rooms overlooking the lake; each is furnished in the Bavarian rustic style, with ornately hand-painted wardrobes, pinewood beds, and dried flowers. ✉ *Am See 75, Ramsau, D-83486,* ☎ *08657/279 or*

08657/439, ⟨FAX⟩ *08657/748. 25 rooms, 20 with bath. Restaurant. No credit cards.*

$–$$ ⟨⟩ **Hotel-Garni zum Türken.** The view alone justifies making the 10-minute journey from Berchtesgaden to this hotel. Confiscated during World War II by the Nazis, it's at the foot of the road to Hitler's mountaintop retreat. Remains of Nazi wartime bunkers adjoin the hotel. There's no restaurant, although evening meals can be ordered in advance. ⟨⟩ *Obersalzberg-Berchtesgaden, D–83471,* ☎ *08652/2428,* ⟨FAX⟩ *08652/4710. 17 rooms, 13 with bath or shower. AE, DC, MC, V. Closed Nov.–Dec. 20.*

<table>
<tr><td>OFF THE
BEATEN PATH</td><td>Schellenberg Caves – Germany's largest ice caves lie 10 kilometers (6 miles) north of Berchtesgaden. By car, take the B–305 to the village of Marktschellenberg, or take the bus from the Berchtesgaden post office to Marktschellenberg (fare DM 6.70). Once you arrive in Marktschellenberg, you can reach the caves on foot only by walking along a clearly marked route. The walk takes more than an hour, so you'll need to be in reasonably good physical shape. A guided tour of the caves takes one hour. ▨ DM 8. ☉ Mid-June–mid-Oct., daily 10–4 (guided tour included).</td></tr>
</table>

Berchtesgaden National Park

5 km (3 mi) south of Berchtesgaden.

The deep, mysterious, and fable-clad Königsee is the most photographed panorama in Germany, adorning millions of calendars. Together with its much smaller sister, the Obersee, it is nestled within the Berchtesgaden National Park, 210 square kilometers (82 square miles) of wild mountain country where flora and fauna have been left to develop as nature intended. No roads penetrate the area, and even the mountain paths are difficult to follow. The park administration organizes guided tours of the area from June until September (contact the Nationale Parkverwaltung, ⟨⟩ Doktorberg 6, D–83471 Berchtesgaden, ☎ 08652/61068).

One less strenuous way into the Berchtesgaden National Park is by **boat.**
★ A fleet of 21 excursion boats, electrically driven so that no noise disturbs the peace, operates on the **Königssee.** Only the skipper of the boat is allowed to shatter the silence with a trumpet fanfare to demonstrate the lake's remarkable echo. The notes from the trumpet bounce back and forth from the almost vertical cliffs that plunge into the dark, green water. A cross on a rocky promontory marks the spot where a boatload of pilgrims hit the cliffs and sank more than 100 years ago. The voyagers, most of whom drowned, were on their way to the tiny, twin-towered Baroque chapel of St. Bartholomä, built in the 17th century on a peninsula where an early Gothic church once stood. The princely rulers of Berchtesgaden built a hunting lodge at the side of the chapel; a tavern and a restaurant now occupy its rooms.

The much smaller but equally beautiful **Obersee** can be reached by a 15-minute walk from the second stop on the boat tour. The lake's backdrop of jagged mountains and precipitous cliffs is broken by a waterfall, the Rothbachfall, that plunges more than 1,000 feet to the valley floor. ⟨⟩ *Boat service on the Königsee runs year-round (except when lake freezes). Round-trips can be interrupted at St. Bartholomä and Salet, the landing stage for the Obersee. Boat trips stop only at St. Bartholomä Oct.–Apr. Round-trip to the Königsee and the Obersee* *lasts almost 2 hrs, without stops, and costs DM 19. The shorter trip to St. Bartholomä and back costs DM 15.50.*

THE BAVARIAN ALPS A TO Z

Arriving and Departing

By Bus

The Alpine region is not well served by long-distance buses. The southern section of the Europabus route, along the Romantische Strasse (Romantic Road), connects Frankfurt, Wiesbaden, Würzburg, Munich, and Augsburg with the resorts of Schongau and Füssen (☞ Chapter 5).

By Car

Three autobahns reach deep into the Bavarian Alps: A–7 coming in from the northwest (Frankfurt, Stuttgart, Ulm) to Füssen; A–95 from Munich to Garmisch; and A–8 from Munich to Salzburg, for Berchtesgaden. All provide speedy access to the Alpine foothills, where they connect with a comprehensive network of well-paved country roads that penetrate high into the mountains. (Germany's highest road runs through Berchtesgaden at more than 5,000 feet.)

By Plane

Munich, 95 kilometers (60 miles) northwest of Garmisch-Partenkirchen, is the main airport for the Bavarian Alps. There is easy access from Munich to the autobahns that lead to the Alps (☞ By Car, *above*). If you're staying in Berchtesgaden at the east end of the Alps, the airport at Salzburg in Austria is closer but has fewer international flights.

By Train

Garmisch-Partenkirchen and Mittenwald are on the InterCity network, which has regular direct service to all regions of the country. (Klais, just outside Garmisch, is Germany's highest InterCity train station.) Bad Reichenhall and Berchtesgaden are linked directly to north German cities by the FD (Fern-Express) "long-distance express" service.

Getting Around

By Boat

Passenger boats operate on all the major Bavarian lakes. They're mostly excursion boats and many run only in summer. However, there's an important year-round service on the Chiemsee that links the mainland with the islands of Herreninsel and Fraueninsel. Four boats on the Starnbergersee and four on the Ammersee (including a fine old paddle steamer) make round-trips of the lake several times a day (Apr.–Oct.), leaving from Starnberg and Stegen/Inning. Eight boats operate year-round on the Tegernsee, connecting the towns of Tegernsee, Rottach-Egern, Bad Wiessee, and Gmund, from which a regular train service runs to Munich. A fleet of 21 silent, electrically driven boats glides through the waters of the Königsee near Berchtesgaden to the most remote of Bavaria's lakes, the Obersee.

By Bus

Villages not served by train are connected by post bus. This is a fun and inexpensive way to get around, but service is slow and irregular. Larger resorts operate buses to outlying areas.

By Car

The Deutsche Alpenstrasse, not a continuous highway but a series of roads, runs from Lindau in the west to the Austrian border beyond Berchtesgaden in the east, skirting the northern edge of the Alps for most of the way before heading deep into the mountains on the final stretch between Inzell and Berchtesgaden. Another way, the Blaue Route (Blue Route), follows the valleys of the Inn and Salzach rivers along the German-Austrian border above Salzburg. This off-the-beaten-track territory includes three quiet lakes: the Tachingersee, the Wagingersee, and the Abstdorfersee. They are the warmest bodies of water in Upper Bavaria, ideal for family vacations. At Wasserburg, on the Inn River, southeast of Munich, you can join the final section of the Deutsche Ferienstrasse (German Holiday Road), another combination of roads that run on to Traunstein, east of Chiemsee, and then into the Alps. The Chiemsee and four other popular lakes—Tegernsee, Schliersee, Starnbergersee and Ammersee—are within easy reach of Munich by autobahn.

By Train

Most Alpine resorts are connected with Munich by regular express and slower services. Munich's S-bahn (suburban train) extends as far as two lakes, the Starnbergersee and the Ammersee, where the Alpine foothills really begin.

Contacts and Resources

Buses

Seat reservations, which are obligatory, can be made through **Deutsche Touring GmbH** (✉ Am Römerhof 17, D–60486 Frankfurt/Main 90, ☎ 069/790–3240). Many travel agents—ABR in Bavaria, for instance—can also make reservations.

Car Rentals

Avis: ✉ Nymphenburgerstr. 61, ☎ 089/126–0020, **Munich.**

Europcar: ✉ St. Martin-Str. 6, ☎ 08821/50168, **Garmisch-Partenkirchen**; ✉ Hirtenstr. 14, ☎ 089/557–145, **Munich.**

Hertz: ✉ Zugspitzstr. 81, ☎ 08821/18787, **Garmisch-Partenkirchen**; ✉ Nymphenburger-Str. 81, ☎ 089/129–5001, **Munich.**

Sixt-Budget: ✉ Wittelsbacher Str. 17, ☎ 08651/64450, **Bad Reichenhall**; ✉ Seitzstr. 9, ☎ 089/223–333, **Munich.**

Emergencies

Police: ☎ 110. **Fire, medical emergencies:** ☎ 112.

Guided Tours

Bus tours to King Ludwig II's castles at Neuschwanstein and Linderhof and to the Ettal monastery near Oberammergau are offered by the **ABR** travel agencies in Garmisch-Partenkirchen (☎ 08821/55125) and in Oberammergau (☎ 08822/1021 or 08822/4771). Tours to Neuschwanstein, Linderhof, Ettal, and into the neighboring Austrian Tyrol are also offered by a number of other Garmisch travel agencies: **Hans Biersack** (☎ 08821/4920), **Heinz Karrasch** (☎ 08821/2111), **Dominikus Kümmerle** (☎ 08821/4955), **Hilmar Röser** (☎ 08821/2926), and **Weiss-Blau-Reisen** (☎ 08821/3766). The Garmisch mountain railway company, the **Bayerische Zugspitzbahn** (☎ 08821/58058), offers special excursions to the top of the Zugspitze, Germany's highest mountain, by cog rail and/or cable car (☞ Garmisch-Partenkirchen, *above*). **Deutsche Bahn** (German Railways; ☎ 089/598–484 or 0821/19419) offers special excursion fares from Munich and Augsburg to the top of the Zugspitze. In Berchtesgaden the **Schwaiger** bus company (☎ 08652/2525) offers tours of the area and across the Austrian border as far as Salzburg.

Visitor Information

The Bavarian regional tourist office in Munich, **FVV München Oberbayern** (✉ Sonnenstr. 10, D–80331 Munich, ☎ 089/597–347), provides general information about Upper Bavaria and the Bavarian Alps. There are local tourist information offices in the following towns:

Bad Reichenhall: ✉ Kur-und-Verkehrsverein, im Kurgastzentrum, Wittelsbacherstr. 15, D–83424, ☎ 08651/3003.

Bad Tölz: ✉ Kurverwaltung, Ludwigstr. 11, D–83646, ☎ 08041/70071.

Bad Wiessee: ✉ Kuramt, Adrian-Stoop-Str., D–83684, ☎ 08022/86030.

Bayerischzell: ✉ Kuramt, Kirchpl. 2, D–83735, ☎ 08023/648.

Berchtesgaden: ✉ Kurdirektion, Königseerstr. 2, D–83463, ☎ 08652/9670. — ☎ 08652

Garmisch-Partenkirchen: ✉ Verkehrsamt der Kurverwaltung, Richard-Strauss-Pl. 2, D–82467, ☎ 08821/1806.

Mittenwald: ✉ Kurverwaltung, Dammkarstr. 3, D–82481, ☎ 08823/33981.

Oberammergau: ✉ Verkehrsamt, Eugen-Papst-Str. 9a, D–82487, ☎ 08822/1021.

Prien am Chiemsee: ✉ Kurverwaltung, Alter Rathausstr. 11, D–83209, ☎ 08051/69050.

Reit im Winkl: ✉ Verkehrsamt, Rathauspl. 1, D–83242, ☎ 08640/80020.

Rottach-Egern/Tegernsee: ✉ Kuramt, Hauptstr. 2, D–83684, ☎ 08022/180–140.

Germany | Tourist Office München — 089/2330300
Tourist Office (Regional) — 089/8292180

Austria | Tourist Office Salzburg — 0043-662 889870
Tourist Office Kaprun — 0043-65 4786430
Tourist Office Zell am See — 0043-65 42770

4 The Bavarian Forest

Low-key and understated, the Bavarian Forest is a welcome alternative to Germany's hyped-up, overcrowded tourist regions. Good-quality, budget-priced dining and lodging make it even more attractive. Farming and forestry are mainstay industries, tourism is growing, and glassblowing shouldn't be missed. Passau, a 2,000-year-old town at the confluence of three rivers, is visited for its beauty as much as its history.

FOR YEARS THIS PICTURESQUE, WOODED REGION of southeast Germany was an isolated part of western Europe, with its eastern boundary flanked by the Iron Curtain, and its flavor is still vastly different from the stock concept of Bavaria (that world supposedly populated by men in lederhosen and funny, feathered, green hats and buxom women in flowing dirndls, who spend their time singing along with oompah bands and knocking back great mugs of beer). Instead, people here are reserved; even their accent is gentler than that of their southern countrymen. Farming and forestry are the chief industries, and the centuries-old craft of glassmaking still survives. Ancient villages of jumbled red roofs and onion-dome churches still pepper the vast forest—a result of both its isolation and the protection of a tract of the Bayerischer Wald (Bavarian Forest) from further development.

The collapse of Communism in Czechoslovakia and the formation of the Czech Republic made possible the renewal of old contacts between Germans and Bohemian Czechs. The centuries-old trading route between Deggendorf and Prague—the Böhmweg—has been revived for walkers. No visit to the Bavarian Forest would be complete without at least a day trip across the border; bus trips into Bohemia are organized by every local tourist office.

The Bavarian Forest has long been a secret with Germans in search of relaxing, affordable holidays at mountainside lodges or country inns, and tourism is growing as the region opens up. All those in search of peace and quiet—hikers, nature lovers, anglers, horseback riders, skiers looking for uncrowded slopes, and golfers distressed by steep greens fees at more fashionable courses—will do well here.

Pleasures and Pastimes

Dining

Food in the Bavarian Forest tends toward the wholesome and the hearty; large portions are very much the norm. Specialties include *Regensburger* (short, thick, spicy sausages, rather like the *Bratwurst* of Nürnberg) and *Bauernseufzer* (farmer's sigh) sausage. Dumplings, made out of anything and everything, appear on practically every menu. Try *Deggendorfer Knödel* if you fancy something really local. The Danube provides a number of excellent types of fish, particularly *Donauwaller* (Danube catfish), from Passau, served *blau* (boiled) or *gebacken* (breaded and fried). The town of Tirschenreuth, in the north, is the home of the equally delicious *Karpfen* (carp). Radishes are a specialty, especially *Weichser Rettiche,* and are a good accompaniment to the many local beers. Passau alone has four breweries—at the Hacklberg, one of the most photogenic in all Germany, you can sample excellent beer at the brewery's tavern.

CATEGORY	COST*
$$$$	over DM 90
$$$	DM 55–DM 90
$$	DM 35–DM 55
$	under DM 35

per person for a three-course meal, including tax and tip but not drinks.

Lodging

Prices here are among the lowest in Germany. Many hotels offer special 14-day packages for the price of a 10-day stay, and 10 days for the price of seven. There are also numerous sports packages, with accommodations at low rates. All local tourist offices can supply lists of accommodations; most can help with reservations.

CATEGORY	COST*
$$$$	over DM 200
$$$	DM 160–DM 200
$$	DM 120–160
$	under DM 120

All prices are for a standard double room for two, including tax and service charge.

Outdoor Activities and Sports

GOLF

The rolling, wooded hills of the Bavarian Forest are golfing country, and apart from some of Germany's most attractive courses, golfers can enjoy at least two important local advantages: lower greens fees (sometimes a fraction of what's charged in Upper Bavaria) and clubs that welcome visitors. Guests at some hotels (the Gasthof Deutscher Rhein in Zwiesel, for example) enjoy reduced green fees at clubs in the region.

HIKING

The Bavarian Forest is prime hiking country, crisscrossed with trails of varied challenge. The longest, the **Pandurensteig**, runs nearly 167 kilometers (100 miles), from Waldmünchen in the northwest to Passau in the southeast across the heights of the Bavarian Forest National Park. The trail can be covered in stages with the aid of a special tourist program that transfers hikers' luggage from one overnight stop to the next. Get details from Fremdenverkehrsverband Ostbayern (✉ Landshuterstr. 13, D–93047 Regensburg, ☎ 0941/57186). Resorts between Deggendorf and Bayerisch Eisenstein on the Czech border have remapped the centuries-old **Böhmweg** trading route, and it can be comfortably covered in three or four days, with accommodations at village taverns en route (maps and information from the Bavarian Forest National Park authority, the **Natur Park Bayerischer Wald Informationshaus,** ✉ D–8372 Zwiesel, ☎ 09922/5555). Three Bavarian Forest resorts—Kellberg, Hauzenberg, and Buchelberg—have joined in a hiking-holiday scheme called **Wandern mit Tapetenwechsel** (Hiking with Change of Scene). The package consists of 14 days' hiking, bed-and-breakfast accommodations, tour assistance, and luggage transportation, all for around DM 450. For details, contact the **Verkehrsamt Kellberg** (✉ D–94136 Thyrnau, ☎ 08501/320) or the **Lichtenauer Pension** (☎ 08501/426).

SKIING

Advanced **downhill skiers** make for the World Cup slopes of the **Grosser Arber.** The summit is reached by chairlifts from Bayerisch-Eisenstein and from just outside Bodenmais. Other ski areas in the Bavarian Forest are not as demanding, and many resorts are ideal for **family skiing** vacations. St. Englmar, Frauenau, Furth im Wald, Waldmünchen, and the villages around the Brotjackelriegel, near Deggendorf, are the best.

Cross-country skiing trails are everywhere in the Bavarian Forest; a map of 22 of the finest can be obtained free of charge from the Fremdenverkehrsverband Ostbayern (☞ Hiking, *above*). The pretty resort of **Thurmansbang** has a trail that stops at all the best bargain inns of the area. For around DM 250 Thurmansbang offers a week's bed-and-breakfast accommodations, cross-country ski instructions, and equipment rentals. Contact the **Verkehrsamt Thurmansbang** (☎ 08504/1642).

Exploring the Bavarian Forest

The Bavarian Forest is a well-defined area sandwiched between the Danube River and the borders of Austria and the Czech Republic, and planning tours is easy. The region has only two major towns, Deggendorf and Passau, both good bases for day trips into the forest or for longer outings. If the bright lights aren't an important consideration, many of the larger country hotels are ideal for a family vacation, as they usually offer a very wide range of leisure and sports facilities. You could spend a week or two at such a resort and enjoy everything the Bavarian Forest has to offer without venturing beyond the village boundaries.

Numbers in the text refer to numbers in the margin and on the Bavarian Forest map.

IF YOU HAVE 3 DAYS

Base yourself in either Deggendorf or Passau and make day trips into the surrounding countryside. From ⊞ **Deggendorf** ⑦ it's only 7 kilometers (4 miles) along the Danube to the spectacular Benedictine abbey of **Metten**, founded in the 9th century by Charlemagne. It's a full day's trip north of Deggendorf to the **Grosser Arber** mountain, the highest in both the Bavarian Forest and the Bohemian Forest on the other side of the nearby Czech frontier. There's a great view of this darkly mysterious central European stretch of woodland from the Arber's summit.

From ⊞ **Passau** ⑪–㉑ take a boat trip down the Danube into neighboring Austria and spend another day exploring the **Bavarian Forest National Park** ⑨, 50 kilometers (30 miles) north of the city. If you're driving, take the B–85 along the valley of the pretty river Ilz.

IF YOU HAVE 5 DAYS

Make ⊞ **Deggendorf** ⑦ your starting point, and after a day or two touring the town and the nearby **Metten** abbey, head north to the **Grosser Arber** mountain, overnighting in ⊞ **Bodenmais** ③, ⊞ **Zwiesel** ⑥, or ⊞ **Viechtach** ②, all famous for the fine glass still made in traditional foundries. From Zwiesel follow the course of the Regen River as far as Frauenau and head into the **Bavarian Forest National Park** ⑨, staying farther on in ⊞ **Grafenau** (and dining in one of southern Germany's finest restaurants, the Säumerhof). From Grafenau follow the Ilz River down to ⊞ **Passau** ⑪–㉑, where it spills into the Danube at that river's confluence with the Inn. Passau takes at least two days to explore, but leave time for a boat trip down the Danube and into neighboring Austria.

IF YOU HAVE 7 DAYS

Enter the Bavarian Forest at its northwest corner, the little town of **Cham** ①, stopping to admire the remains of its medieval walls and its 15th-century Town Hall. Head past Deggendorf, watching for the ruins of a medieval castle on the summit of the 2,500-foot-high **Haidstein** peak. Around the year 1200 it was home to poet Wolfram von Eschenbach. Farther on, between Prackenbach and Viechtach villages, you'll view an extraordinary geological phenomenon, the **Pfahl,** a ridge of glistening white quartz. Overnight in ⊞ **Viechtach** ②, and don't miss a visit to the Gläserne Scheune, a glassmaker's studio where even the roof is a work of glazier's art. At the next village, Patersdorf, turn left into the depths of the forest and make for **Bodenmais** ③, a pretty resort overlooked by the region's highest mountain, the 4,800-foot-high **Grosser Arber.** The Czech border cuts through the forest on the mountain's northern slopes, and in the border town of **Bayerischer Eisenstein** ④

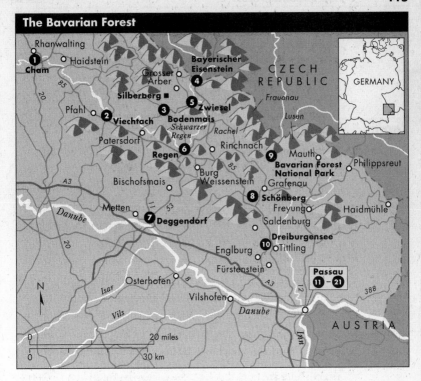

The Bavarian Forest

Rhanwalting
Haidstein
Cham ①
**Bayerischer
Eisenstein** ④
Grosser
Arber
Silberberg ■
Viechtach ②
③
⑤ **Zwiesel**
Bodenmais
*Schwarzer
Regen*
Pfahl
Patersdorf
Regen ⑥
Frauenau
Lusen
Rachel
Rinchnach
⑨ Mauth
Philippsreut
**Bavarian Forest
National Park**
Grafenau
⑧ **Schönberg**
Freyung
Saldenburg
Haidmühle
Deggendorf ⑦
Metten
Burg
Weissenstein
Bischofsmais
Danube
Dreiburgensee
⑩ Tittling
Englburg
Fürstenstein
Passau
⑪ – ㉑
Osterhofen
Isar
Vilshofen
Vils
Danube
Inn
N
C Z E C H
R E P U B L I C
GERMANY
AUSTRIA

0   20 miles

0   30 km

the curious can peer into the country. The center of the Bavarian Forest's glass industry, ☎ **Zwiesel** ⑤, is 15 kilometers (10 miles) south of Bayerisch Eisenstein. It also produces good beers and a notorious schnapps, so an overnight is recommended here. The road continues south to **Regen** ⑥, a busy market town that's a good lunch stop, and then snakes through wooded uplands before dropping into Deggendorf, in the wide valley of the Danube. Allow two days for ☎ **Deggendorf** ⑦, including several hours for its still-expanding "culture quarter." Make a side trip to the ancient Benedictine abbey of **Metten,** cross the Danube for a visit to the beautiful Baroque church of St. Margaretha in **Osterhofen,** follow the south bank of the river to Vilshofen, and then cross the Danube bridge there to head north again into the forest. Base yourself at Grafenau and explore the **Bavarian Forest National Park** ⑨, where wolves and lynx are being resettled in their natural habitat. On the road south to ☎ **Passau** ⑪ you'll pass through the Dreiburgenland, so named because of three famous castles that mark the route. Plan a stop at the ☎ **Dreiburgensee** ⑩ Lake in Tittling to see the open-air museum of 50 reconstructed Bavarian Forest houses. From there it's an easy 20-kilometer (12-mile) trip south back to Passau.

When to Tour the Bavarian Forest

Summer is really the time to visit the Bavarian Forest. Although local tourist offices do their best to publicize events spread throughout the calendar year, only winter-sports fans and hardy types dare venture deep into the forest in the months between late fall and early spring. November is so unpleasant—shrouding the whole region in cold, damp fog for days on end—that many hotels put up the shutters until the December vacation season begins.

THE WESTERN BAVARIAN FOREST

Although the Bavarian Forest has no recognized boundaries, it can be said to end in the west where the upland, wooded slopes drop to the Franconian flatlands north of Regensburg.

Numbers in the margin correspond to points of interest on the Bavarian Forest map.

Cham

❶ *58 km (35 mi) northeast of Regensburg, 58 km (35 mi) northwest of Deggendorf, 140 km (75 mi) north of Munich.*

Beautifully located on the scenic Regen River, Cham regards itself as the gateway to the forest and is further distinguished by its intact sections of original 14th-century town walls, including the massive Straubinger Turm (tower). It also possesses a 15th-century Town Hall and an even older town-wall gate, the Biertor.

Dining and Lodging

$$ ✕ **Bürgerstuben.** The Stuben is in Cham's central Stadthalle (City Hall). Tasty local dishes and an appealingly simple atmosphere add up to an authentic Bavarian experience. ✉ *Fürtherstr. 11,* ☎ *09971/1707. No credit cards. Closed Mon.*

$$ ✕🏠 **Randsbergerhof.** A German knight lived here before this house became a hotel. It's a rambling, old building with beamed ceilings and ornate, hand-painted walls. An indoor pool and a Finnish sauna were recently added to its facilities. ✉ *Randsbergerhofstr. 15–17, D–93413,* ☎ *09971/126–669,* 🆑 *09971/20299. 71 rooms with bath or shower, 4 apartments. 2 restaurants, indoor pool, sauna, bowling, squash. AE, DC, MC, V.*

$$ 🏠 **Hotel am Stadtpark.** Upgraded recently to a hotel, this popular lodging offers unbeatable value, with comfortable double rooms costing just DM 78—including a view of the forest and a large breakfast. The house stands on the edge of Cham's resort park. ✉ *Tilsiterstr. 3, D–93413,* ☎ *09971/2253,* 🆑 *09971/79253. 11 rooms, 9 with shower. AE.*

Golf

Furth im Wald (north of Cham) has a nine-hole course (☎ 09973/2089).

Nightlife and the Arts

At Furth im Wald (north of Cham), August brings Germany's oldest street **folk festival,** dating from medieval times. Dressed in period costume, townsfolk take part in the ritual slaying of a fire-breathing "dragon" that stalks the main street. Call ☎ 09973/3813 for exact dates and seat reservations.

OFF THE BEATEN PATH

CHURPFALZ PARK – In Loifling, near Cham, this park offers hours of fun—from a puppet theater to miniature trains and a water carousel—while parents can wander around the extensive gardens. 🎫 *DM 9.50.* ☉ *Apr.–mid-Oct., daily 9–6.*

En Route As you head southeast of Cham on B–85, watch on the left for the ruins of a medieval castle perched on the 2,500-foot-high **Haidstein** peak. Around the year 1200 it was home to the German poet Wolfram von Eschenbach. On the mountain slopes is a 1,000-year-old linden tree known as Wolframslinde (Wolfram's linden tree). With a circumference of more than 50 feet, its hollow trunk could easily shelter 50 people. Continuing on B–85 you'll pass sunny villages with trim streets and gardens and see two sinuous lakes created by the dammed Regen River. From here the Weisser (white) Regen soon becomes the Schwarzer (black) Regen.

Between the village of Prackenbach and the little town of Viechtach you'll see a dramatic section of the **Pfahl,** one of Europe's most extraordinary geological phenomena. The ridge of glistening white quartz juts dramatically out of the ground in an arrow-straight spur that extends more than 100 kilometers (60 miles) through the Bavarian Forest. Here the quartz rises in folds to heights of 100 feet or more.

Viechtach

❷ *30 km (18 mi) southeast of Cham, 29 km north of Deggendorf.*

This little market town nestled in the folds of the Bavarian Forest won a major government prize for its environmental-protection programs, and the award includes a special seal of approval (a fir tree) designating hotels and guest houses deemed "ecologically friendly." The little fir is now proudly displayed on most Viechtach houses. The town is also a center of Bavarian Forest glassmaking.

The spectacularly decorated rococo church of St. Augustin dominates Viechtach's central **market square,** its severe white-and-yellow west front contrasting colorfully with the high-gabled Renaissance and Baroque buildings that make up the other three sides.

In the **Gläserne Scheune,** glass artist Rudolf Schmid produces his highly original sculptures of glass and wood under a studio roof made from a mosaic of painted glass fragments. ✉ *Raubühl 3,* ☎ *09942/8147.* 🎫 *DM 4.* ⏲ *Apr.–Sept., daily 10–5; Oct., daily 10–4.*

Four centuries of glassmaking are documented in Viechtach's **Kristallmuseum,** which also has a vivid exhibition on the Pfahl, together with samples of 600 crystals and minerals. ✉ *Linprunstr. 4,* ☎ *09942/5497.* 🎫 *DM 4.* ⏲ *Mon.–Sat. 9–6; Sun. and public holidays 10–4.*

Dining and Lodging

$$–$$$ ✕🏨 **Kur- und Ferienhotel Viechtach.** Among the beauty treatments offered by this newly opened spa hotel complex is a "Cleopatra bath," although management hasn't disclosed what distinguishes that from other water-based treatments guaranteed to put new life into old or overtaxed limbs. Other treatments include Dr. Kneipp's cold-water "cure." The hotel does have its hedonist side, though, with a friendly bar, a good restaurant, and a Sunday brunch with live music. ✉ *Waldschmidtstr. 2, D–94234,* ☎ *09942/953–408,* FAX *09942/953–400. 72 rooms with bath. 2 restaurants, indoor pool, barbershop, beauty salon, sauna. AE, DC, MC, V.*

$$ ✕🏨 **Hotel Schmaus.** Run by the same family for generations, this place is for the energetic. The kitchen turns out meals on the assumption that every guest has just finished a 25-mile hike through the forest, although the all-weather sports facilities could make you equally hungry. In summer dine in the grill garden. Ask to stay in the older section—some of the modern rooms are somewhat plain. ✉ *Stadtpl. 5, D–94234,* ☎ *09942/1627,* FAX *09942/6042. 42 rooms with bath. Restaurant, weinstube, pool, sauna, tennis. AE, DC, MC, V. Closed last 3 wks of Jan.*

Nightlife and the Arts

A **theater festival** with its roots in the Middle Ages is held every summer in the Neunussberg Castle, just outside Viechtach. Call the Viechtach tourist office, ☎ 09942/1661, for details.

Shopping

For **glass objects** and other Bavarian Forest **arts and crafts**, try the **Viechtacher Kunststube**, in Alten Rathaus, (⌧ Stadtpl. 1). **Glas Rötzer** sells forest **handicrafts** (⌧ Hafnerhöhe).

Bodenmais

❸ *24 km (15 mi) east of Viechtach, 34 km (20 mi) north of Deggendorf.*

This health resort is tucked into a valley below the Bavarian Forest's highest mountain, the 4,800-foot-high Grosser Arber. A nearby silver mine helped Bodenmais prosper before tourism reached this isolated part of the country.

Bodenmais's long tradition of **glassmaking** includes Bavaria's largest glassworks, the **Joska Waldglashütte**, which welcomes visitors at both of its foundries, at Scharebenstrasse and in the Am Moosbach industrial zone. Both are open to visitors weekdays 9–11:45 and 1–3:45, Saturdays 9–1:45; showrooms are open weekdays 9–6 and Saturdays 9–2. The **Austen Glashütte** foundry can also be visited weekdays 9:30–5:30 and Saturdays 9:30–2:30.

OFF THE
BEATEN PATH

SILVERBERG (SILVER MOUNTAIN) – The 700-year-old silver mine was closed in 1962, but you can still view its workings near the summit of the 3,000-foot-high Silberberg. Take the chairlift from the Arber Road, about 3 kilometers (2 miles) north of Bodenmais, or enjoy the easy, 25-minute walk from the road to the entrance of the mine. ☎ 09924/304 for details on guided tours. ⌧ DM 9. ☼ Apr.–June, daily 10–4; July–Sept., daily 9–5; Oct., daily 10–4; Jan.–Mar., daily 1–3.

Dining and Lodging

$$ ✕🏠 **Bodenmaiser Hof.** The geranium-bedecked Hof's quality and reputation bring German visitors back year after year. Guest rooms paneled in pale pine are a cut above the average, with ample facilities. The Hof even has its own bakery and butcher shop, which ensures the freshness and quality of the food prepared for guests. ⌧ *Risslochweg 4, D–94249,* ☎ *09924/1841,* ℻ *09924/7457. 30 rooms with bath. Restaurant, café, sauna, exercise room. No credit cards.*

$$ ✕🏠 **Böhmhof.** The Böhmhof estate, beautifully located on the edge of the forest, has been owned by the Geiger family for more than three centuries. Their long tradition can be felt throughout, from the friendly reception to the comfortable, spacious rooms, several of which were recently converted to "country-house suites" with separate living areas. One estate building now provides farmhouse-style accommodations, ideal for children. The outdoor and indoor pools allow for year-round swimming; walking and cross-country ski trails start at the front door. ⌧ *Böhmhof 1, D–94249,* ☎ *09924/222,* ℻ *09924/1718. 26 rooms with bath. Restaurant, café, indoor and outdoor pools, sauna, hot tub, recreation room. No credit cards. Closed mid-Nov.–mid Dec.*

OFF THE
BEATEN PATH

GROSSER ARBER – The highest mountain of both the Bavarian Forest and the Bohemian Forest on the other side of the border is 13 kilometers (8 miles) north of Bodenmais. A bus service runs from Bodenmais to the base of the mountain, where a chairlift makes the 10-minute trip to the summit. A short walk from the bottom of the lift leads to the **Arbersee** Lake, surrounded by thick forest.

Beside the Arbersee Lake children can wander through the **Märchen-wald** (Fairytale Wood), which features a collection of colorful model scenes from famous stories. *Entrance opposite Hotel Arberseehaus.* ☉ *Easter–mid-Oct., daily 9–5.*

NEED A BREAK?	You can quench your thirst or fortify yourself for a hike up the Arber at the friendly **Gasthof Schareben** on the shores of the lake.

Bayerischer Eisenstein

❹ *17 km (10 mi) north of Bodenmais, 7 km (4 mi) east of the Frosser Arber.*

Travelers who can't resist quirky sights may wish to make the detour north to this little town that sits on the Czech Republic border. The frontier actually cuts the local train station in half.

Dining and Lodging

$–$$ ✕🏨 **Ferienhotel Waldspitze.** The former Hotel Waldwinkel has changed hands and name, which now identifies it as a "holiday hotel." Its forest location and range of facilities certainly make it an ideal vacation base. Rooms have been enlarged and extensively renovated, with new bathrooms and heavy, Bavarian-style furniture. ⊠ *Hauptstr. 4, D–94252,* ☎ *09925/308,* 🆑 *09925/1287. 55 rooms with bath. Restaurant, café, indoor pool, sauna, steam room, exercise room, table tennis, billiards. No credit cards.*

Zwiesel

❺ *14 km (8 mi) south of Bayerisch Eisenstein, 40 km (24 mi) northeast of Deggendorf.*

As the region's **glassmaking** center, Zwiesel has 18 firms and more than 2,000 townspeople involved in shaping, engraving, or painting glass. Most open their foundries to visitors. At **Kunstglasbläserei Seemann** (⊠ Stormbergerstr. 36, ☎ 09922/1091) in the village of Rabenstein, you can try your own skill at blowing glass (Thursday only, 10–11), taking the result of your efforts home with you (for a fee).

The **Waldmuseum Zwiesel** offers displays dedicated to the customs and heritage of the entire forest region during the past few centuries. ⊠ *Stadtpl. 29,* ☎ *09922/60888.* 🎟 *DM 3.* ☉ *Mid-May–mid-Oct., weekdays 9–5, weekends 10–noon and 2–4; mid-Oct.–mid-May, weekdays 10–noon and 2–5, weekends 10–noon; closed Nov.*

The Bavarian Forest has a long toy-making tradition, and Zwiesel has one of the region's largest collection of playthings, ancient and modern—the **Zwiesel Spielzeugmuseum.** ⊠ *Stadtpl. 35,* ☎ *09922/5526.* ☉ *June–Sept., daily 9–5; Oct.–May, daily 10–5; closed Nov.–Dec. 26.*

Zwiesel produces a variety of beers and a notorious schnapps, Bärwurz. You can sample the house-brewed bitter Janka Pils or a malty, dark wheat brew at the **Gasthof Deutscher Rhein,** a 300-year-old inn (☞ Dining and Lodging, *below*). The **Bärwurz distillery** (Bayerwald Bärwurzerei, Heinrich Hieke, ⊠ Frauenauer Str. 80–82, ☎ 09922/1515) has added a liqueur to its products that at 20% alcohol volume rivals the schnapps for pure head-spinning effect. The distillery welcomes visitors during regular shop hours on Sunday in summer.

OFF THE BEATEN PATH	**THE GLASMUSEUM (ZUM SCHLÖSSL) –** In the village of Theresienthal, 2 kilometers (1 mile) north of Zwiesel, this museum is one of the biggest of its kind in the Bavarian Forest. Here you'll see how glassblowing de-

veloped through the centuries. ✉ *Glaspark Theresienthal,* ☎ *09922/
1030.* ⊙ *Weekdays 10–2.*

Dining and Lodging

$$ ✕⊞ **Gasthof Deutscher Rhein.** Although this lodging is in the Bavarian
Forest, it exudes a Bohemian atmosphere—from the crenulated facade
of the 300-year-old building bearing the founder's Czech name to the
specialties from the kitchen and the house brewery. You can sample tra-
ditional game dishes and enjoy Pilsner, which tastes as if it really comes
from Pilsen, the famous Czech brewing town across the border. The mod-
ern rooms were recently refurbished to make this the Bavarian Forest
showpiece of the Ring hotel group. The wood-paneled Wirtsstube tav-
ern provides visitors with a warm, country-style welcome. ✉ *Am
Stadtpl. 42, D-94227,* ☎ *09922/84100,* FAX *09922/1652. 20 rooms with
bath. Restaurant. AE, DC, MC, V. Closed 1st 3 wks of Dec.*

$$ ✕⊞ **Hotel zur Waldbahn.** The great-grandfather of the current owner,
assisted by 13 children, built the Hotel zur Waldbahn more than 100
years ago to accommodate train passengers traveling between
Czechoslovakia and points south. Today the emphasis is still on making the traveler feel at home within the hotel's wood-paneled walls.
✉ *Bahnhofpl. 2, D-94227,* ☎ FAX *09922/3001. 28 rooms with bath
or shower. Restaurant, hot tub, sauna, exercise room. No credit cards.
Closed Nov.*

$$ ✕⊞ **Kurhotel Sonnenberg.** High above Zwiesel, the Sonnenberg of-
fers fine views of the forest and quick access to mountain walks and
ski runs. It's a sporty hotel, with numerous fitness facilities and large,
plushly furnished rooms, most with balcony. ✉ *Augustinerstr. 9,
D-94227,* ☎ *09922/2031,* FAX *09922/2913. 20 rooms, 1 apartment,
all with bath or shower. Restaurant, indoor pool, beauty salon, sauna,
exercise room. No credit cards.*

Golf

An 18-hole course recently opened at **Oberzwieselau,** near Zwiesel
(☎ 09922/2367).

Regen

❻ *10 km (6 mi) southwest of Zwiesel, 28 km (15 mi) northeast of
Deggendorf.*

Regen, a busy market town with fine 16th-century houses around its
large central square, is famous because of the annual event celebrated
the last weekend in July: a great party commemorating the 17th-cen-
tury creation of *Pichelsteiner Eintopf* (pork-and-vegetable stew), a fill-
ing dish that has become a staple throughout Germany. The stylish
celebrations include sports events on the Regen River; so pack a swim-
suit if you fancy joining in. Regen's other claim to fame is an ex-
traordinary display of Christmas crèches.

Frau Maria-Elisabeth Pscheidl, a Regen resident who has been mak-
ing the items for more than 30 years, has amassed an inordinate num-
ber of **Christmas crèches.** Her collection is claimed to be the largest,
and the best (according to the local tourist office), in the world—it even
has the Vatican seal of approval. Many of her creations are displayed
in the **Pscheidl Bayerwald-Krippe Museum,** run by the town council
in Frau Pscheidl's home. ✉ *Ludwigsbrücke 3,* ☎ *09921/2893.* ⌦ *DM
2.* ⊙ *Weekdays 8–11:30 and 2–4.*

OFF THE   **WEISSENSTEIN CASTLE** – The world's largest snuffbox collection is on the
BEATEN PATH   third floor of Weissenstein Castle, near Regen. The 1,300 snuffboxes on
                 display were collected over a period of 46 years by Regen's former

mayor, Alois Reitbauer. His reward was an entry in the *Guinness Book of Records.* ⊙ *Late May–mid-Sept., daily 10–noon and 1–5.*

Dining and Lodging

$ ✕🏨 **Burggasthof Weissenstein.** The ruins of the neighboring medieval Weissenstein Castle loom above you as you breakfast on the sunny terrace overlooking the Old Town. Ask for a room with a view of either. The recently opened cellar tavern has dancing on weekends. ⊠ *Weissenstein 32, D–94209,* ☎ *09921/2259,* 🅵🅰🅇 *09921/8759. 15 rooms with bath. Restaurant. No credit cards. Closed Nov.*

$ ✕🏨 **Pension Panorama.** This modern, friendly hotel on the outskirts of Regen chose this name because most of its rooms enjoy fine south-facing views of the Bavarian Forest. In summer a spacious sun terrace and garden are open for relaxation. In winter a log fire blazes in the open hearth of the beamed lounge. Rooms are furnished in light veneers with bright prints on the walls. ⊠ *Johannesfeldstr. 27, D–94209,* ☎ *09921/2356. 17 rooms with bath. Restaurant, bar, indoor pool, paddle tennis. MC.*

OFF THE   **RINCHNACH** – This village, 8 kilometers (5 miles) east of Regen, has an
BEATEN PATH   impressive monastery that began as an 11th-century monk's lonely retreat. Built in the 15th century, the church had extensive Baroque renovations done by Johann Michael Fischer in the 1720s. Visit its expansive and lordly interior to see his masterful wrought-iron work and some typically heroic frescoes. Two early 18th-century altar paintings by Cosmas Damian Asam are also on view.

THE EASTERN BAVARIAN FOREST

East of Deggendorf the countryside falls in hilly folds to the Danube and the beautiful border city of Passau. North of Passau the forest climbs again to the remote Dreiländereck, the corner of Germany bordering Austria and Czechoslovakia.

Deggendorf

❼ *28 km (15 mi) southwest of Regen, 140 km (84 mi) northeast of Munich.*

Nestled between the Danube and the forested hills that rise in tiers to the Czech border, Deggendorf justifiably regards itself as the Bavarian Forest's southern gateway. The town was once on the banks of the Danube, but repeated flooding forced its inhabitants to higher ground in the 13th century. You can still see a 30-yard stretch of the protective wall built around the medieval town.

Deggendorf is unique in Lower Bavaria for its specially developed "cultural quarter," created from a section of Old Town. Lining the leafy, traffic-free square are the city museum; a public library; a new handicrafts museum, the only one of its kind in the Bavarian Forest; and the Kapuzinerstadl, a warehouse converted into a concert hall and a large foyer that is frequently used as a theater venue.

The 16th-century **Rathaus** (Town Hall), in the center of the wide main street, the Marktstrasse, has a central tower with a tiny apartment that traditionally housed the town watchman and lookout. From its windows you can enjoy a fine view. The rooms haven't changed over the centuries. ☎ *0991/296–0169.* 🎫 *DM 5.* ⊙ *Tower can be visited as part of guided tour of the town, June–Sept.*

★ The **Heilig Grabkirche** was originally built as a Gothic basilica in the 14th century. Its lofty tower—regarded as the finest Baroque church tower in southern Germany—was added 400 years later by the Munich master builder Johann Michael Fischer. ⊠ *Marktstr.* 🎟 *Free.* ☉ *Daily 9– sunset.*

Exhibits at the **Handwerksmuseum** (Museum of Trades and Crafts) study typical regional handicrafts. 🎟 *DM 2.* ☉ *Tues.–Sun. 10–4, Thurs. 10–6.*

The **Stadtmuseum** (City Museum) traces the history of the Danube people. 🎟 *DM 2.* ☉ *Tues.–Sun. 10–4, Thurs. 10–6.*

Dining and Lodging

$$ ✕ **Ratskeller.** If you eat here, beneath the vaulted ceilings of the Rathaus, you could easily find yourself sharing a table with a town councillor, perhaps even the mayor. The menu is strictly Bavarian; the beer flows freely. ⊠ *Oberer Stadtpl. 1,* 🕿 *0991/6737. Reservations not accepted. No credit cards.*

$$ ✕ **Zum Grafenwirt.** In winter ask the host for a table near the fine old tile stove that sits in the dining room. Try such filling dishes as roast pork and Bavarian dumplings. In summer watch for Danube fish on the menu. ⊠ *Bahnhofstr. 7,* 🕿 *0991/8729. AE, DC, MC, V. Closed Tues. and 1st 2 wks in June.*

$$$$ ✕🏠 **Schlosshotel Egg.** The "Egg" isn't for something you might eat in this castle-hotel's excellent restaurant; it's derived from Ekke, the name of the 12th-century owner. Today the hotel, 13 kilometers (9 miles) northwest of Deggendorf, is an atmospheric and memorable place in which to lay your head. Try for a room in the castle rather than in the adjoining guest house. ⊠ *94505 Schloss Egg-Bernried, D–94505,* 🕿 *09905/289 or 09905/8316,* FAX *09905/691. 19 rooms with bath. Restaurant. AE, DC, MC, V.*

$$$ ✕🏠 **Flamberg Parkhotel.** This luxury hotel opened in 1991 and has rapidly established itself as one of the region's best. A monumental mural by Elvira Bach welcomes you in the reception area, and the artistic touch is continued in the large and airy guest rooms, all with original paintings on the walls. The Tassilo restaurant and adjoining winter garden have an international menu with an Italian flair. In summer a shady beer garden beckons; in winter a log fire burns invitingly in the lounge. The Danube promenade and the Old Town center are both a few minutes' walk away. ⊠ *Edlmairstr. 4, D–94469,* 🕿 *0991/6013,* FAX *0991/31551. 125 rooms and 13 suites, all with bath. Restaurant, bar, beer garden, hot tub, sauna, exercise room, bicycles. AE, DC, MC, V.*

$$ ✕🏠 **Donauhof.** This lovely 19th-century stone warehouse, painted
★ cream and white, was converted into a hotel in 1988. The spotless rooms have modern Scandinavian furniture. The Wintergarden Café is a local favorite for its homemade cakes and coffee. ⊠ *Hafenstr. 1, D–94469,* 🕿 *0991/38990,* FAX *0991/389–966. 42 rooms with bath, 3 apartments. Restaurant, weinstube, sauna. AE, MC, DC, V.*

Golf

There's a challenging course (🕿 0991/8911) at **Schaufling,** high above Deggendorf, that offers fine views of the Bavarian Forest and the Danube plain.

OFF THE   **METTEN** – To see two outstanding examples of Baroque art, you can take
BEATEN PATH   the 7-kilometer (4-mile) trip along the Danube, heading northwest from Deggendorf, to the ancient Benedictine abbey of Metten, founded in the 9th century by Charlemagne. Within its white walls and quiet cloisters is an outstanding 18th-century library, with a collection of 160,000 books

whose gilded leather spines are complemented by the heroic splendor of their surroundings—Herculean figures support the frescoed, vaulted ceiling, and allegorical paintings and fine stuccowork identify different categories of books. In the **monastery church** is Cosmas Damian Asam's altar painting of *Lucifer Destroyed by St. Michael*, created about 1720, its vivid coloring and swirling composition typical of the time. ☎ 0991/ 91080. 🎟 *Free (donations welcome).* ⊙ *Guided tours Mon.–Sat. at 10 and 3, Sun. at 3 only; closed Easter.*

En Route If you are driving, cross the Danube just outside Deggendorf or take the ferry at Winzer and then the Passau road (B–15) to the village of **Osterhofen** and the **church of St. Margaretha.** This structure contains important work by Baroque artists, including a series of large, ornate frescoes and altar paintings by Cosmas Damian Asam, as well as elaborate sculptures of angels and cherubs, entwined on the church pillars, by Egid Quirin Asam and Johann Michael Fischer. The three worked here in a rare partnership between 1728 and 1741. Look for Cosmas Damian's self-portrait amid the extravagant decor. ⊙ *Daily 9–7, except during Sun. services. Free guided tours on Tues. and Thurs. at 3. (Assemble at main church door.)*

Schönberg

❽ *40 km (24 mi) northeast of Deggendorf.*

In little Schönberg's **Marktplatz** (market square), arcaded shops and houses present an almost Italian air. As you head farther south down the Inn Valley, this Italian influence—the so-called Inn Valley style—becomes more pronounced.

Dining and Lodging

$$ ✕🏨 **Hotel Antonios Hof.** This chalet-style lodging, on the edge of the Bavarian Forest National Park, has an exterior distinguished by ornately carved Victorian balconies. Inside, the pinewood trimmings—from the low beams of the snug tavern to the restaurant's carved pillars—help to create a warm, homey atmosphere. The rooms are equally welcoming, decorated in the Bavarian country style with pinewood furnishings. Try the fish if you eat here; it comes directly from the hotel's pond. ⊠ *Unterer Marktpl. 12, D–94139,* ☎ *08554/9700,* ℻ *08554/970–100. 40 rooms with bath. Restaurant, indoor pool, sauna, bowling. AE, DC, MC, V.*

Bavarian Forest National Park

★ ❾ *15 km (9 mi) northeast of Schönberg, main entrance at Neuschönau.*

The Bavarian Forest National Park is a 32,000-acre stretch of protected dense forest. Bears, wolves, and lynx roamed wild in these parts until well into the 19th century. Substantial efforts have been made to reintroduce these and other animals to the park, though today the animals are restricted to large enclosures. Well-marked paths lead to points where the animals can best be seen. Bracing walks also take you through the thickly wooded terrain to the two highest peaks of the park, the 4,350-foot **Rachel** and the 4,116-foot **Lusen.** Specially marked educational trails trace the geological and botanical history of the area, and picnic spots and playgrounds abound. In winter park wardens will lead you through the snow to where wild deer from the mountains feed. A visitor center—**The National Park-Haus**—is at the main entrance to the park. Slide shows and English-language brochures provide introductions to the area.

Dining and Lodging

$$ ✕ **Adalbert Stifter.** Named for a popular 19th-century Bavarian Forest poet, this friendly country hotel–restaurant at the foot of the Dreisessel Mountain is at its best turning out the sort of time-honored dishes Stifter knew. Try one of the Bohemian-style roasts, served with fresh dumplings. ✉ *Frauenberg 32,* ☎ *08556/355. MC. Closed Nov.–Dec. 20.*

$$$$ ✕⌂ **Säumerhof.** The Bavarian Forest isn't known for haute cuisine,
★   but here in Grafenau, one of its prettiest resorts, is a restaurant that bears comparison with Germany's best. It's part of a small country hotel (with 10 moderately priced and homey rooms), run by the Endl family. Gebhard Endl's territory is the kitchen, where he produces original, nouvelle-inspired dishes, using ingredients obtainable locally. Try the pheasant on champagne cabbage or the roast rabbit in herb-cream sauce. ✉ *Steinberg 32, D–94481 Grafenau,* ☎ *08552/2401. 10 rooms with bath. AE, DC, MC, V.*

$$$$ ✕⌂ **Steigenberger-Avance Sonnenhof.** If you are traveling with children, this is the hotel for you: The staff includes a *Spieltante* (playtime auntie) who keeps youngsters amused. The ultramodern hotel is set on extensive grounds, and there's lots to do—even horse-drawn sleigh rides in winter. ✉ *Sonnenstr. 12, D–94481,* ☎ *08552/4480,* FAX *08552/4680. 194 rooms with bath. 2 restaurants, bar, indoor pool, beauty salon, saunas, spa, indoor and outdoor tennis courts, miniature golf, bowling, exercise room, nightclub. AE, DC, MC, V.*

$$$–$$$$ ✕⌂ **Bierhütte.** The name means "beer hut," and it was once a royal brewery. Now a member of the select Romantik hotel group, the elegant 18th-century building has its own quiet grounds beside a lake, near the village of Hohenau. It has all the trappings of a regal residence, with ornate furnishings and tapestries in public rooms and bedrooms. ✉ *Bierhutte 10, Hohenau, D–94545 Hohenau,* ☎ *08558/315,* FAX *08558/2387. 37 rooms with bath, 6 suites. Restaurant, sauna, exercise room, recreation room, library. AE, DC, MC, V.*

$$ ✕⌂ **Barnriegel.** This family-run restaurant on the edge of the Bavarian Forest National Park caters to those made hungry by a day's walking. Sauerbraten is one of the best dishes on the menu; local lake fish is also a specialty. The weary can stay here, too, in one of 13 inexpensive rooms. ✉ *Hauptstr. 2, D–94151 Finsterau,* ☎ *08557/96020. 13 rooms, 6 with bath. No credit cards. Closed Mon. and Apr.–June.*

Dreiburgenland

On the Ostmarkstrasse (B–85) south of Schönberg.

Dreiburgenland, or the Land of the Three Castles, is named for **Fürstenstein, Englburg,** and **Saldenburg.** The little village of Fürstenstein likes to call itself the "Pearl of the Dreiburgenland." From the walls of its castle you can get a fine view of the Danube plain to the south and the mountains of the Bavarian Forest to the north.

❿   On the shores of the **Dreiburgensee** in Tittling, you'll find the **Freilichtmuseum** (Open-Air Museum), which boasts 50 reconstructed Bavarian Forest houses. You can sit on the benches of a 17th-century schoolhouse, drink schnapps in an 18th-century tavern, or see how grain was ground in a 15th-century mill. ✉ *Museumsdorf Bayerischer Wald, by Hotel Dreiburgensee, Tittling,* ☎ *08504/8482.* 🎫 *DM 3.* ☉ *Daily 8–5.*

NEED A   After your tour of the village you'll probably be hungry and thirsty; the
BREAK?   **Gasthaus Mühhiasl** waits at the end of the main street, with a menu of hearty and inexpensive Bavarian fare and locally brewed beer. In summer the shady beer garden is the place to be.

Dining and Lodging

$–$$ ✕🏨 **Ferienhotel Dreiburgensee.** This is primarily for longer vacations, but it's also convenient for an overnight stop if you're touring the Bavarian Forest or visiting the nearby Dreiburgensee open-air museum. All of the hotel's rooms have balconies with views of the Dreiburgensee Lake or the surrounding forest. Some have Bavarian-style four-poster beds with painted headboards and large, fluffy goose-down covers. Children love the sturdy bunk beds in the spacious family rooms. ✉ *Am Dreiburgensee, D–94104,* ☎ *08504/2092,* ℻ *08504/1094. 100 rooms with bath or shower. Restaurant, café, indoor pool, sauna, exercise room, miniature golf, boating, bicycles, playground. No credit cards. Closed Nov.–Jan.*

Passau

❶❶ *66 km (40 mi) southeast of Deggendorf, 160 km (96 mi) northeast of Munich.*

The city perches on a narrow point of land where the Inn and the Danube meet, with wooded heights rising on the far sides of both rivers; the much smaller River Ilz also joins the Danube nearby. Most of its finest and oldest homes face the busy waterfront, where freighters and barges load and unload during journeys to and from the Black Sea and the Rhine. Narrow streets of varying levels rise to a hill in the center of the old city. These harmonious proportions are complemented by the typical Inn Valley houses that line the streets, joined to one another by picturesque archways. While Passau is no "Venice of the North" (as it's sometimes described), it does have a Mediterranean air, due in part to the many Italian architects who worked here and to a special quality of light that painters through the centuries have been attracted to and tried to capture in their work.

Passau is a remote yet important embarkation point for the traffic that has plied its way along the Danube for centuries, traveling between Germany, central Europe, and the Black Sea. Settled more than 2,000 years ago by the Celts, then by the Romans, Passau later passed into the possession of prince-bishops whose power stretched into present-day Hungary. The influence they wielded over nearly six centuries has left its traces in the town's Residenz (bishop's palace), the Veste Oberhaus (the bishop's summer castle), and the magnificent Dom (cathedral).

For 45 years Passau was a backwater in a "lost" corner of West Germany, but recent political changes have placed the old city back in the limelight, and you will find it elegant and dignified; its grande-dame atmosphere has far more in common with the stately demeanor of Vienna or Prague than some of the brasher cities of the Federal Republic.

Numbers in the margin correspond to points of interest on the Passau map.

★ ❶❷ The city panorama of Passau is dominated by its mighty **Dom,** the cathedral, which stands majestically on the highest point of the earliest-settled part of the city, between the Danube and Inn. A baptismal church stood here in the 6th century. Two hundred years later, when Passau became the seat of a bishop, the first basilica was built. It was dedicated to St. Stephan and became the original mother church of St. Stephan's Cathedral in Vienna. Little was left of the medieval basilica after a fire reduced it to smoking ruins in the 17th century. What you see today is an impressive Baroque building, complete with dome and flanking towers. Little in its marble- and stucco-encrusted interior reminds you of Germany, and much proclaims the exuberance of Rome. Beneath the octagonal dome is the largest church **organ** in the world. Built between 1924 and 1928, and enlarged from 1979 to 1980, it claims

Passau

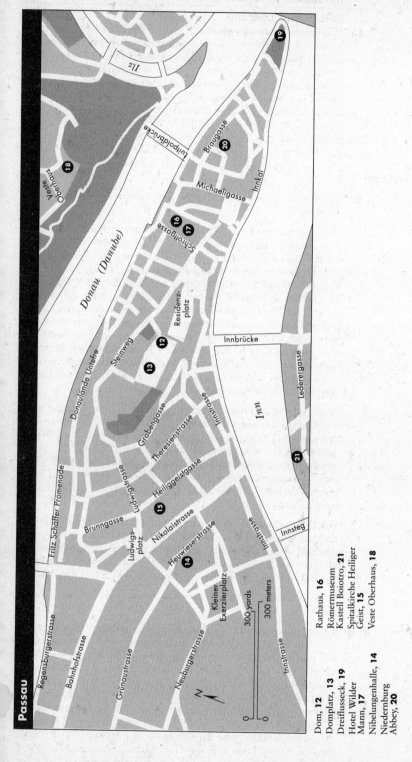

Il-

Luitpoldbrücke

Braugasse

20

Veste Oberhaus

18

Michaeligasse

Innkai

16

Schrollgasse

17

Donau (Danube)

Residenz-platz

Steinweg

12

Donaulände Untere

13

Innbrücke

Grabengasse

Ledergasse

Theresienstrasse

Innstrasse

Inn

Fritz Schäffer Promenade

Ludwigsgasse

Heiliggeistgasse

21

15

Brunngasse

Nikolaistrasse

Innstrasse

Regensburgerstrasse

Ludwigs-platz

Heuwiesenstrasse

Innsteg

Bahnhofstrasse

14

Kleiner Exerzierplatz

Grünaustrasse

Neuburgerstrasse

300 yards

N

300 meters

Innstrasse

0

Dom, **12**
Domplatz, **13**
Dreiflusseck, **19**
Hotel Wilder
Mann, **17**
Nibelungenhalle, **14**
Niedernburg
Abbey, **20**

Rathaus, **16**
Römermuseum
Kastell Boiotro, **21**
Spitalkirche Heiliger
Geist, **15**
Veste Oberhaus **18**

no fewer than 17,388 pipes and 231 stops. Concerts (🔊 DM 4) are given on the enormous instrument from May through October, weekdays at noon and Thursday at 7:30 PM (🔊 DM 6–DM 10 depending on the program). The Dom is open May–October, 8–11 and 12:30–6; October–May, 8–dusk.

The **Domschatz-und Diözesanmuseum** (cathedral treasury and museum) houses one of Bavaria's largest collections of religious treasures, the legacy of Passau's episcopal history. The museum is part of the **Neue Residenz,** which has a stately Baroque entrance opening onto a magnificent staircase—a scintillating study in marble, fresco, and stucco. ⊠ *Dom Pl.* 🔊 *DM 2.* 🕓 *May–Oct. and mid-Dec.–mid-Jan., Mon.–Sat. 10–4.*

🔞 **Domplatz,** the large square in front of the cathedral (with a fine statue of Bavarian king Maximilian Joseph I in its center), is bordered by a number of sturdy 17th- and 18th-century buildings, including the **Alte Residenz,** the former bishop's palace. Today it's a courthouse.

Young visitors to Passau love the city's fascinating toy museum, the **Spielzeugmuseum,** which includes many exhibits from the United States. There is a good collection of dolls, as well as many ancient model steam engines. ⊠ *Residenzpl.* 🔊 *DM 3.* 🕓 *Apr.–Oct., daily 9:30–5:30; Nov.–Mar., weekends only.*

🔞 Passau's great **Kleiner Exerzierplatz** was once a Benedictine monastery garden but is now a parking lot and the site of the ugly **Nibelungenhalle,** a Nazi-era hall, which seats 8,000. The name is taken from the *Nibelungenlied,* an epic poem about German mythology, written in Passau during the 12th century. Richard Wagner chose it as the theme for his immense 19th-century operatic cycle, *The Ring of the Nibelung.* Later Hitler recast the legend in an attempt to legitimize the Nazi creed. His obsession with Wagner—almost surpassing that of Ludwig II—was an example of how he saw himself as an extension of an established Germanic tradition. The hall is still used for political rallies and was also the reception center for the first refugees who fled East Germany in late summer 1989, presaging the collapse of the Berlin Wall. From late November until just before Christmas it takes on a very apolitical appearance, housing Passau's glittering Christmas market, the Christkindlmarkt. There's a tourist office adjoining the hall. ⊠ *Kleiner Exerzierpl.*

🔞 The 15th-century **Spitalkirche Heiliger Geist** (Infirmary Church of the Holy Ghost) has fine 16th-century stained glass and an exquisite 15th-century marble relief depicting the Way of the Cross. Evidence of the influence of Passau's religious establishments and of their central European, as opposed to purely Germanic interests, is shown by the vineyards in neighboring Austria still owned by the church. ⊠ *Heiliggeiststr., a short walk from the Nibelungenhalle.*

🔞 Passau's 13th-century **Rathaus** (Town Hall) sits like a Venetian merchant's house on a small square fronting the Danube. It was the home of a wealthy German merchant before being declared the seat of city government after a 1298 uprising. Two assembly rooms contain wall paintings depicting scenes from local history and lore, including the (fictional) arrival in the city of Siegfried's fair Kriemhild. The Rathaus can be visited only on guided tours arranged by the tourist office.

🔞 The **Hotel Wilder Mann,** fronting the Rathaus square, has a museum tracing the history of central Europe's glassmaking with an exquisite display of 20,000 items. *Glasmuseum.* ⊠ *Hotel Wilder Mann, Am Rathauspl.* 🔊 *DM 3.* 🕓 *Mar.–Sept., daily 10–5; Oct.–Feb., daily 2–4.*

18 The **Veste Oberhaus,** the powerful fortress and summer castle commissioned by Bishop Ulrich II in 1219, looks down on downtown Passau from an impregnable site on the other side of the river, opposite the Rathaus. Today the Veste Oberhaus is Passau's most important museum, containing exhibits that illustrate the 2,000-year history of the city. It also commands a magnificent **view** of Passau and the three rivers that converge on it. ⌨ *Museum DM 4.* ☽ *Mar.–Jan., Tues.–Sun. 10–5. Bus takes visitors from Rathauspl. to museum Apr.–Oct. every ½ hr 11:30–5.*

From the terrace of the Veste Oberhaus there's a bird's-eye view of the **19** **Dreiflusseck** (Corner of the Three Rivers), where the Inn's green water, typical of a mountain river, slowly gives way to the darker hues of the Danube, and the brownish Ilz adds its small contribution to this colorful natural phenomenon. It's the end of the journey for the Inn—which flows here from the mountains of Switzerland and through Austria—and the much shorter Ilz, which rises in the Bavarian Forest; from here their waters are carried by the Danube to the Black Sea.

20 **Niedernburg Abbey** (⌨ Bräugasse) was founded in the 8th century as a convent. It was destroyed by fire and rebuilt in the last century in a clumsy Romanesque style. Today it's a girls' school. In its church you can see the 11th-century tomb of a queen who was once abbess here—Gisela, sister of the emperor Heinrich II and widow of Hungary's first and subsequently sainted king, Stephan, who became the patron of the Passau Cathedral.

The **Mariahilfberg,** site of a 17th-century monastery pilgrimage church, is on the southern side of the Inn, in the so-called Innstadt, or Inn City. In 1974 archaeologists here uncovered the site of the Roman citadel of Boiotro, a stout fortress with five defense towers and walls more than 12 feet thick. A Roman well was also found, its water still plentiful and fresh. The pottery, lead figures, and other archaeological dis-**21** coveries from the site are housed at the nearby **Römermuseum Kastell Boiotro.** ⌨ *Lederergasse 43.* ⌨ *DM 2.* ☽ *Mar.–Nov., Tues.–Sun. 10–noon and 2–4; June–Aug. 1–4.*

Dining and Lodging

$$ ✕ **Heilig-Geist-Stiftsschänke.** For atmospheric dining, this 14th-century monastery turned wine cellar is a must. In summer you eat beneath chestnut trees; in winter seek out the warmth of the vaulted dining rooms. The wines—made in Austria from the Spitalkirche Heiliger Geist vineyards—are excellent and suit all seasons. ⌨ *Heiliggeistgasse 4,* ☎ *0851/2607. AE, DC, MC, V. Closed Wed. and Jan. 10–Feb. 10.*

$ ✕ **Gasthof Andorfer.** A good wheat beer is brewed and served here, and you can drink it on a lime-tree-shaded terrace overlooking the grain fields. The brewery tavern is in Passau-Ries, a couple miles north of the city center, near the Veste Oberhaus fortress. The menu is basic, but the beer and the surroundings are what count. There are a few rooms if you fancy spending the night. ⌨ *Rennweg 2,* ☎ *0851/51372. Reservations not accepted. No credit cards. Closed Sat.*

$ ✕ **Peschl Terrasse.** The beer you sip on the high sunny terrace overlooking the Danube is brought fresh from the Old Town brewery below, which, along with this traditional Bavarian restaurant, has been in the same family since 1855. ⌨ *Rosstränke 4,* ☎ *0851/2489. Reservations not accepted. AE, DC, MC, V. Closed Mon.*

$ ✕ **Zum Hirschen.** This is a traditional Bavarian hostelry, with blue-and-white-checked tablecloths and a menu of solid fare, ranging from roast pork and dumplings to vanilla steamed pudding. The 400-year-old building stands beside the Niedernburg Abbey. ⌨ *Im Ort 6,* ☎ *0851/36238. Reservations not accepted. No credit cards. Closed Mon.*

$$$ ✕⊞ **Hotel Weisser Hase.** The White Rabbit was accommodating travelers at the beginning of the 16th century. Rooms are decorated in sleek Ring-group style, with cherry wood and mahogany veneers and soft matching colors. It stands sturdily in the town center, at the start of the pedestrian shopping zone, a short walk from all the major sights. All rooms have satellite TV. ⊠ *Ludwigstr. 23, D–94302,* ☎ *0851/92110,* FAX *0851/921–1100. 108 rooms with bath. Restaurant, in-room modem lines. AE, DC, MC, V.*

$$$ ✕⊞ **Passauer Wolf.** Try for a room with a view of the Danube at this leading riverside hotel, where elegance and comfort are matched by outstanding cuisine. The restaurant attracts diners from neighboring Austria, who come for its light French touch. The accent is on fish—if freshly caught Danube pike perch is on the menu, you're in for a treat. ⊠ *Rindermarkt 6, D–94032,* ☎ *0851/34046,* FAX *0851/36757. 40 rooms with bath. Restaurant, bar. AE, DC, MC, V.*

$$–$$$ ✕⊞ **Wilder Mann.** Passau's most historic hotel shares prominence
★ with the ancient city hall on the waterfront market square. You sleep beneath chandeliers and richly stuccoed ceilings in beds of carved oak in a house that dates from the 11th century (renovated in the 19th and 20th centuries and subsequently kept up to contemporary standards of comfort). Guests have ranged from the consort of the Austrian emperor Franz-Josef to the American astronaut Neil Armstrong. The swimming pool is in the 11th-century vaulted cellars. ⊠ *Am Rathauspl. 1, D–94302,* ☎ *0851/35071,* FAX *0851/31712. 48 rooms with bath, 5 apartments. Restaurant, bar, café, indoor pool. AE, DC, MC, V.*

$$$ ⊞ **Hotel König.** Though built only in 1984, the König blends successfully with the graceful Italian-style buildings alongside its elegant waterfront setting on the Danube. Rooms are large and airy; most have a fine view of the river. ⊠ *Untere Donaulände 1, D–94302,* ☎ *0851/3850,* FAX *0851/385–460. 41 rooms with bath. Bar, sauna, steam room. AE, DC, MC, V.*

$ ⊞ **Rotel Inn.** "Rotels" are usually hotels on wheels, an idea developed by a local entrepreneur to accommodate tour groups in North Africa and Asia. Now he has built the first permanent Rotel Inn, on the banks of the Danube in central Passau. Its rooms are small and cabin-like, but they're clean, decorated in a lively pop-art style, and amazingly cheap (DM 60 for a double). The whole building breaks with traditional styles, and its design—red, white, and blue facade and flowing roof lines—has actually been patented. It's a definite for young travelers—but also fun for families. ⊠ *Am Hauptbahnhof/Donauufer, D–94032,* ☎ *0851/95160,* FAX *0851/951–6100. 93 rooms. No credit cards. Closed Nov.–Mar.*

Golf

There is an 18-hole course at **Thyrnau** (☎ 08501/1313).

Nightlife and the Arts

Passau is the cultural center of Lower Bavaria. The **Stiftung Wörlen Museum Moderner Kunst** (⊠ Bräugasse 17, ☎ 0851/34091), a modern-art gallery, opened in Passau in 1990. The **Europäische Wochen** (European Weeks) Festival—featuring everything from opera to pantomime—is now a major event on the European music calendar. The festival runs from June to early August. For program details and reservations, write the Kartenzentrale der Europäischen Wochen Passau (⊠ Dr. Hans Kapfinger Str. 22, Passau, ☎ 0851/7966).

Passau's thriving theater company, the **Stadttheater,** has its home in the beautiful little Baroque opera house of Passau's prince-bishops. Get program details and reservations from Stadttheater Passau (✉ Gottfried-Schäffer-Str., ☎ 0851/929–1913).

Jazz fans head to nearby Vilshofen every June for the annual international jazz festival, staged in a special tent on the banks of the Danube. For program details and reservations, call ☎ 08541/2080. Live jazz programs are regularly presented at Passau's **Theater im Scharfrichter-Haus** (✉ Milchgasse 2, ☎ 0851/35900), home of the city's nationally famous cabaret company. The company hosts a German **cabaret** festival every fall between October and December.

Passau's **Christmas fair**—the Christkindlmarkt—is the biggest and most spectacular of the Bavarian Forest. It's held in and around the Nibelungenhalle from late November until just before Christmas.

OFF THE
BEATEN PATH
MT. DREISESSEL – You can't get much more off the beaten track than in the remote corner of the country north of Passau, where the German frontier winds in and out of the Czech Republic and Austria. Where the border cuts across the summit of Mt. Dreisessel, west of Altreichenau, it's possible to walk in and out of a virtually forgotten corner of the Czech Republic—a feat that was possible even when the border was guarded everywhere else by heavily armed soldiers. *Dreisessel* means "three armchairs," an apt description of the summit and its boulders, which are shaped like the furniture of a giant's castle. If you're driving to the Dreisessel, take B–12 to Philippsreut, just before the frontier, then follow the well-marked country road. The mountain is about 67 kilometers (40 miles) from Passau. Several bus operators in Passau and surrounding villages offer tours.

BAVARIAN FOREST A TO Z

Arriving and Departing

By Car
The principal road links with the Bavarian Forest are the A–3 Autobahn from Nürnberg and the A–92 Autobahn from Munich. Nürnberg is 104 kilometers (65 miles) from Regensburg and 229 kilometers (140 miles) from Passau. Munich is 120 kilometers (75 miles) from Regensburg and 179 kilometers (110 miles) from Passau. Traffic on both roads is always relatively light.

By Plane
The nearest airports are at Munich and Nürnberg. Each is about 160 kilometers (100 miles) from the western edge of the Bavarian Forest.

Getting Around

By Boat
Ludwig Wurm (✉ Donaustr. 71, D–93464 Irlbach, ☎ 09424/1341) concentrates on a range of small cruise-ship services upriver between Passau and Regensburg, taking in Deggendorf, Metten, Straubing, and Walhalla, while its bigger sister company, **Wurm & Köck** (✉ Höllgasse 26, D–94032 Passau, ☎ 0851/929–292), and its rival, **Erste Donau-Dampfschiffahrts-Gesellschaft**, or DDSG-Donaureisen (✉ Im Ort 14a, D–94032 Passau, ☎ 0851/33035), operate bigger ships and cruises from Passau into Austria as far as Vienna. In 1993 Wurm & Köck added to its fleet the *Regina Danubia*, a 225-foot luxury day-cruise vessel that travels between Passau and Austria, usually as far as Linz.

By Bus
Villages not on the railway line are well served by post bus. Passau has a municipal bus service that reaches into the hinterland.

By Car

The small country highways and side roads within this region are less traveled, making the entire area something of a paradise for those who have experienced only the high-speed mayhem of most other German roads. B–85 runs the length of the Bavarian Forest from Passau to Cham, and its designation as a route of special scenic interest (the Ostmark-strasse) extends northward to Bayreuth.

By Train

Two main rail lines cross the region: One runs west–east via Nürnberg, Regensburg, Passau, and Vienna; the other runs south–north via Munich, Landshut, and Straubing. This latter route slices right through the heart of the Bavarian Forest on its way to the Czech Republic (if you fancy overnighting in Prague, this is the train to take). Plattling, just south of Deggendorf, and Cham are the main rail junctions for the area. Passau is the principal rail gateway on the border between southeast Germany and Austria.

Contacts and Resources

Car Rentals

Budget: ✉ Stelzlhof 7 (on the Franz Josef Strauss bridge), ☎ 0851/603–839, **Passau.**

Europcar: ✉ Graflingerstr. 125, ☎ 0991/28181, **Deggendorf;** ✉ Bahnhofstr. 29 (west wing of main railway station), ☎ 0851/54235, **Passau.**

Hertz: ✉ Industriestr. 12, ☎ 0851/801211, **Passau.**

Emergencies

Police: ☎ 110. **Fire and emergency medical attention:** ☎ 112.

Guided Tours

The tourist offices at Freyung, Grafenau, and Tittling organize bus tours of the region and excursions into **Czechoslovakia.** The Freyung tourist office (☎ 08551/58850) has weekly half-day trips to the **Bavarian National Park** and to the **Dreisessel Mountain** for DM 8. The **Wolff Ost-Reisen** bus company in Furth im Wald (☎ 09973/5080) offers one- and two-day excursions to **Prague,** twice a week between May and October, as well trips to the former royal spa town of **Karlsbad** (now Karlovy Vary) in Bohemia, as do the tourist offices of Grafenau (☎ 08552/42743) and Tittling (☎ 08504/40114). In Tittling the **Hötl** bus company (☎ 08504/4040) has daily excursions into the **Bavarian Forest** in summer. The **Furth im Wald** tourist office (☎ 09973/3813) publishes a sight-seeing guide to border areas of the Czech Republic, including the historic town of Domazlice.

Guided tours of **Passau** are organized from April through October by the city tourist office (☎ 0851/39190). There are two tours (at 10:30 and 2:30) on weekdays and one (at 2:30) on weekends. Tours start at King Max Joseph monument in the Domplatz (the cathedral square) and last one hour. The cost is DM 3.50. Tours of the **Dom** take place Monday through Saturday from May through October at 12:30 (assemble at the front right-hand aisle of the cathedral), and from November through April at noon (assemble under the cathedral organ). The tour costs DM 2.

Cruises on Passau's three rivers begin and end at the Danube jetties on Fritz-Schäffer Promenade. Forty-five-minute trips on the Danube, Inn, and Ilz are run from March through October by **Wurm & Köck** (☎ 0851/929292). The cost is DM 10. The Three Rivers trip can be combined with a cruise as far as **Linz,** Austria (including an overnight stay in Passau or Linz), for DM 135. Another cruise overnights in four-star hotels in **Linz and Vienna** and ends with a rail journey back to Passau (✉ DM 379–DM 399). Every Friday and Saturday from May through October a Wurm & Köck ship becomes a floating dance floor, with live bands performing on deck during evening cruises on the Danube (for DM 25). From mid-May through September the **Hungarian cruise** ship *Rakoczi* invites revelers aboard every Thursday and Saturday for an evening of Hungarian music, food, and wine. The DDSG company (☎ 0851/33035) offers two-day cruises to **Vienna,** with passengers sleeping in two-bed cabins, for around DM 250 per person one-way. DDSG also offers Danube cruise connections via Budapest all the way to the **Black Sea.**

On the Inn River an Austrian shipping operator, **M. Schaurecker** (✉ A.-Stifterstr. 581, A–4780 Schärding, ☎ 0043/771–23231), runs a daily service Tuesday through Sunday, mid-March through October, between Passau and the enchanting Austrian river town of **Schärding.** The round-trip fare is DM 12.

Visitor Information

Bayerisch-Eisenstein: ✉ Verkehrsamt Bayerisch-Eisenstein, Schulbergstr., D–94252 Bayerisch-Eisenstein, ☎ 09925/327.

Bodenmais: ✉ Kur-Verkehrsamt, Bahnhofstr. 56, D–94249 Bodenmais, ☎ 09924/77835.

Cham: ✉ Verkehrsverein Cham, Propsteistr. 46, D–93413 Cham, ☎ 09971/78233.

Deggendorf: ✉ Verkehrsverein Deggendorf, Oberer Stadtpl. 4, D–94469 Deggendorf, ☎ 0991/296–0169.

Freyung: ✉ Verkehrsamt Freyung, Rathausweg 1, D–94078 Freyung, ☎ 08551/58850.

Furth im Wald: ✉ Verkehrsverein Furth im Wald, Schlosspl. 1, D–93437 Furth im Wald, ☎ 09973/3813.

Grafenau: ✉ Verkehrsamt Grafenau, Rathausgasse 1, D–94481 Grafenau, ☎ 08552/96230.

Passau: ✉ Fremdenverkehrsverein Passau, Rathauspl. 3, D–94032 Passau, ☎ 0851/39190.

Regen: ✉ Verkehrsamt Haus des Gastes, Stadtpl., D–94209 Regen, ☎ 09921/2929.

St. Englmar: ✉ Verkehrsamt St. Englmar, Rathausstr. 6, D–94379 St. Englmar, ☎ 09965/221.

Straubing: ✉ Städtisches Verkehrsamt Straubing, Rathaus, Theresienpl., D–94315 Straubing, ☎ 09421/944–307.

Tittling: ✉ Verkehrsamt Tittling, Marktpl. 10, D–94104 Tittling, ☎ 08504/40114.

Viechtach: ✉ Städtisches Kur- und Verkehrsamt, Rathaus, D–94234 Viechtach, ☎ 09942/1661.

Waldkirchen: ✉ Fremdenverkehrsamt Waldkirchen, Ringmauerstr. 14, D–94065 Waldkirchen, ☎ 08581/20250.

Zwiesel: ✉ Kurverwaltung, Stadtpl. 27, D–94227 Zwiesel, ☎ 09922/840–523.

5 The Romantic Road

One of Germany's so perfectly planned tourist routes, the Romantic Road is just that, albeit in the sense meaning wondrous and fanciful. Minnesänger Walther von der Vogelweide and medieval sculptor Tilman Riemenschneider are among the people whose legacies you'll discover as you travel the route. You'll also visit Würzburg, home to a glorious Baroque palace; the wonderfully preserved medieval town of Rothenburg-ob-der-Tauber; and Ludwig II's fantastic Neuschwanstein castle.

OF ALL THE SPECIALLY DESIGNATED TOURIST ROUTES that crisscross Germany, none rivals the aptly named Romantische Strasse, or Romantic Road. The scenery along the road (with a few exceptions) is more domestic and rural than spectacular, but the Romantic Road is memorable because of the medieval towns, villages, castles, and churches that stud its 420-kilometer (260-mile) length. Many of these are tucked away beyond low hills, their spires and towers poking up through the greenery.

Within the massive gates of formerly fortified settlements, half-timbered houses lean against one another along narrow cobbled lanes. Ancient squares are adorned with fountains and flowers, and formidable walls are punctuated by watchtowers built to keep a lookout for marauding enemies. The sights add up to a pageant of marvels of history, art, and architecture, providing an essence of Germany at its most picturesque and romantic.

The road runs south from Würzburg in the north of Bavaria to Füssen on the border with Austria. You can, of course, follow it in the opposite direction, as a number of bus tours do. Either way, among the major sights you'll see are one of Europe's most scintillating Rococo palaces, in Würzburg, and Rothenburg-ob-der-Tauber, perhaps the best-preserved medieval town on the Continent. Ulm, a short trip off the Romantic Road, is included here because of its magnificent cathedral. Then there's the handsome Renaissance city of Augsburg. Finally, for most visitors, the highlight will be Ludwig II's captivating fantasy castle of Neuschwanstein.

The concept of the Romantic Road developed as West Germany was trying to rebuild its tourist industry in the wake of World War II. An enterprising public-relations type dreamed up the catchy title for a historic passage through several regions of southern Germany so they could be advertised as a unit. And in 1950 the Romantic Road was born, soon to evolve into one of Europe's most heavily traveled tourist trails.

The name itself refers not so much to the kind of romance of lovers as to a variation of the word meaning wonderful, fabulous, imaginative. And, of course, the Romantic Road started as a road on which the Romans traveled.

On its way the road crosses former battlefields where armies fought for control of the region. It was the most cataclysmic of these conflicts, the Thirty Years' War, that destroyed the region's economic base in the 17th century, thereby assuring the survival of the historic Romantic Road towns.

As you travel the Romantic Road, two names crop up again and again: Walther von der Vogelweide and Tilman Riemenschneider. It might be helpful to know a little about these masters of the Middle Ages.

Walther von der Vogelweide, who died in Würzburg in 1230, was the most famous of the German *Minnesänger,* poet-musicians who wrote and sang of courtly love in the age of chivalry. Knights and other nobles would hire them for their artistic services to help win the favors of fair ladies. Von der Vogelweide broke with this tradition by writing love songs to maidens of less-than-noble rank. He also accepted commissions of a political nature, producing what amounted to medieval political manifestos. His work was romantic, lyrical, witty, and filled with a sighing wistfulness and philosophical questioning.

Tilman Riemenschneider, Germany's master of late-Gothic sculpture, lived an extraordinary life. His skill with wood and stone was recognized at an early age. His success became so great that he soon presided over a major Würzburg workshop, with a team of assistants. Riemenschneider worked alone, however, on the life-size figures that dominate his sculptures. His characteristic grace and harmony of line can be identified in such features as the folds of a robe.

At the height of his career Riemenschneider was appointed city councillor; later he became mayor of Würzburg. In 1523, however, he made the fateful error of siding with the revolutionaries in the Peasants' Revolt. He was arrested and held for eight weeks in the dungeons of the Marienburg fortress above Würzburg, where he was frequently tortured. Most of his wealth was confiscated, and he returned home a broken man with little will to continue his work. He died in 1531.

For nearly three centuries he and his sculptures were all but forgotten. Only in 1822, when ditchdiggers uncovered the site of his grave, did Riemenschneider once again come to be included among Germany's greatest artists. Today Riemenschneider is recognized as the giant of German sculpture. The richest collection of his works is in Würzburg, although other masterpieces are on view in churches and museums in other cities along the Romantic Road as well as in other parts of Germany; for example, the renowned Windsheim Altar of the Twelve Apostles is found in the Palatine Museum in Heidelberg. Two major Riemenschneider works were discovered in 1994–95 and are now on display in Würzburg.

Pleasures and Pastimes

Dining

The best Franconian and Swabian food combines hearty regional specialties with nouvelle elements. Various forms of pasta are common. Try *Pfannkuchen* (pancakes) and *Spätzle* (small tagliatelle-like ribbons of rolled dough), the latter often served with roast beef, or *Rinderbraten,* the traditional Sunday lunchtime dish. One of the best regional dishes is *Maultaschen,* a Swabian version of ravioli, usually served floating in broth strewn with chives. Würzburg is one of the leading wine-producing areas of Germany, and beer lovers will want to try the many Franconian beers, whose brands and flavors change from one town to another.

CATEGORY	COST*
$$$$	over DM 90
$$$	DM 55–DM 90
$$	DM 35–DM 55
$	DM 20–DM 35

*per person for a three-course meal, including tax and excluding drinks

Golf

The rolling countryside along the Romantic Road route is ideal territory for golf, and there are several golf courses along its length; you can tee off in Augsburg, in Aschaffenburg, at Würzburg, at Schloss Colberg (east of Rothenburg), and at Schloss Igling, just outside Landsberg.

Lodging

With a few exceptions the Romantic Road hotels are quiet and rustic rather than slick, modern city lodgings. You'll find high standards of comfort and cleanliness throughout the region. Make reservations as far in advance as possible if you plan to visit in the summer. Hotels in Würzburg, Rothenburg, and Füssen in particular are often full year-round. Augsburg hotels are in great demand during trade fairs in nearby Munich because of accommodation shortages in the Bavarian capital. Tourist information offices can sometimes help with accommodations, even in high season, especially if you arrive early in the day.

CATEGORY	COST*
$$$$	over DM 200
$$$	DM 160–DM 200
$$	DM 120–DM 160
$	under DM 120

*All prices are for two people in a double room, excluding service charges.

Water Sports

The Lech River, which follows the southern stretch of the Romantic Road for much of its way, offers excellent canoeing. There's good sport, too, on the Tauber and Wörnitz rivers. The lakes around Füssen are excellent for sailing and windsurfing.

Exploring the Romantic Road

Geographically, the Romantic Road runs from the vineyard-hung slopes of the Main River valley at Würzburg to the snow-covered mountains overlooking Füssen in the Allgäuer Alps. For much of its route it follows two enchanting rivers, the Tauber and the Lech, and at one point crosses the great Danube. The city of Augsburg, because of its proximity to Munich and the Bavarian capital's pivotal place in German road and rail communications, marks the natural halfway point of the Romantic Road. South of Augsburg, the road climbs gradually into the Alpine foothills and the landscape changes from the lush green of Franconian river valleys to mountain-ringed meadows and forests.

Great Itineraries

Although a long-distance bus covers the Romantic Road route daily during summer in less than 12 hours, the same number of days would be needed to get to know the route thoroughly. Each town that marks the route tugs insistently at the visitor, and it's difficult to resist an overnight stay when one is sent to bed with the help of a night watchman's bell (as in Rothenburg or Dinkelsbühl). Two or three days are too short a time to devote to Würzburg or Augsburg, while such attractions as the minster of Ulm are time-consuming but rewarding diversions from the recognized Romantic Road route.

Numbers in the text correspond to numbers in the margin and on the maps.

IF YOU HAVE 3 DAYS

Join the Romantic Road at ⛰ **Augsburg** ㉖–㊴, and spend your first day and night immersing yourself in its fascinating Fugger family history. On the second day, head north, making stops at **Donauwörth** ㉔ (lingering for a lunchtime view of the Danube), **Nördlingen** ㉓, **Dinkelsbühl** ㉒, and **Feuchtwangen** ㉑; stay overnight within the ancient walls of ⛰ **Rothenburg ob-der-Tauber** ⑫–⑳. On the third day, continue on to **Creglingen** ⑩ to admire the Tilman Riemenschneider altar in the **Herrgottskirche** ⑪, just outside the village, and then travel through the lovely Tauber River valley, visiting the historic towns of **Weikersheim** ⑨, **Bad Mergentheim** ⑧, and **Tauberbischofsheim** ⑤, until you reach your final destination, ⛰ **Würzburg** ⑦.

IF YOU HAVE 5 DAYS

Tackle the entire length of the Romantic Road, starting at ⛰ **Würzburg** ⑦ (via Frankfurt). From Würzburg, follow the three-day itinerary described above in reverse order, with overnight stays in ⛰ **Rothenburg** ⑫ and either **Dinkelsbühl** ㉒ or **Nördlingen** ㉓. Stop at the southern part of

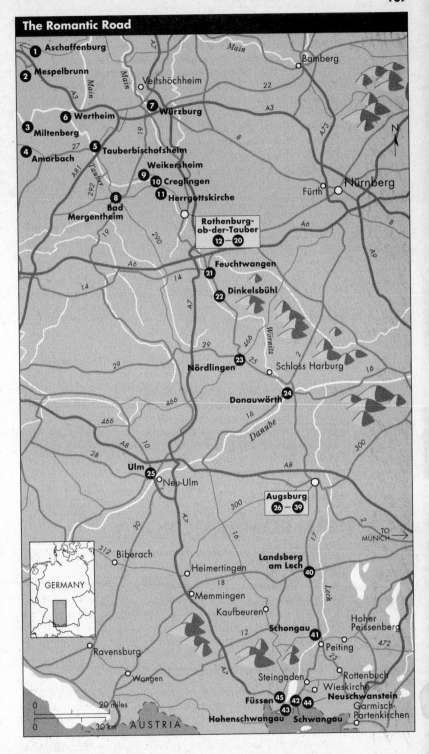

The Romantic Road

1 Aschaffenburg
2 Mespelbrunn
Veitshöchheim
Bamberg
22
7 Würzburg
6 Wertheim
3 Miltenberg
A3
5 Tauberbischofsheim
27
4 Amorbach
9 Weikersheim
10 Creglingen
11 Herrgottskirche
Fürth
Nürnberg
8 Bad Mergentheim
Rothenburg-ob-der-Tauber
12 — 20
A6
21 Feuchtwangen
22 Dinkelsbühl
Wörnitz
23 Nördlingen
25
Schloss Harburg
24 Donauwörth
Danube
Ulm 25
Neu-Ulm
A8
Augsburg
26 — 39
TO MÜNCHEN
GERMANY
Biberach
312
Heimertingen
Landsberg am Lech
40
Memmingen
18
Kaufbeuren
Hoher Peissenberg
Schongau
41
Peiting
472
12
Ravensburg
Steingaden
Rottenbuch
Wieskirche
Wangen
45
42 44 Neuschwanstein
Füssen
43 Schwangau
Garmisch-Partenkirchen
Hohenschwangau
AUSTRIA

0 _____ 20 miles
0 _____ 30 km

the Romantic Road at 🏰 **Augsburg** ㉖, where a side trip to Munich obviously beckons. South of Augsburg, join the Lech River valley at **Landsberg** ㊵ (where Hitler wrote *Mein Kampf* while in the town prison). Continue on to **Schongau** ㊶, where you'll see the Alps rising up ahead of you; they're the signal to watch for one of the most glorious sights of the Romantic Road, the rococo **Wieskirche,** which stands (as its name promises) in a heavenly Alpine meadow. As it heads into the Alps, the Romantic Road has even more spectacular sights, particularly the most eccentric of "mad" King Ludwig's castles, **Neuschwanstein** ㊹. Finally, spend the day in the frontier town of 🏰 **Füssen** ㊺ (the natural end of the Romantic Road).

IF YOU HAVE 7 DAYS

Begin your Romantic Road tour at **Aschaffenburg** ①, 50 kilometers (30 miles) east of Frankfurt, with its magnificent Renaissance castle, the Schloss Johannisburg. Next head toward Würzburg, stopping on the way to visit a smaller but no less impressive castle, **Mespelbrunn** ② in the Spessart uplands. Then continue through the Main Valley and take some time to explore the lovely old medieval towns of **Miltenberg** ③ and **Wertheim** ⑥. Devote two days to 🏰 **Würzburg** ⑦ before heading south along the entire Romantic Road to **Füssen** ㊺. Take day five to investigate 🏰 **Rothenburg-ob-der-Tauber** ⑫ (overnighting within its medieval walls), and spend the sixth day of your tour visiting two other exquisitely preserved medieval towns, **Dinkelsbühl** ㉒ and **Nördlingen** ㉓. On the seventh day, complete your trip in 🏰 **Füssen.** If your schedule allows, make a side trip to **Ulm** ㉕, and possibly Munich. Füssen provides a good base for day trips to **Neuschwanstein** ㊹, and the lovely **Wieskirche** church.

When to Tour the Romantic Road

Late summer and early autumn are the best time to travel the Romantic Road, when the grapes ripen on the vines around Würzburg and the geraniums run riot on the medieval walls of towns like Rothenburg and Dinkelsbühl. You'll also miss the high-season summer crush of tourists. Otherwise, consider visiting the region in the depths of December, when Christmas markets pack the ancient squares of the Romantic Road towns and snow gives turreted Schloss Neuschwanstein its final magic touch.

NORTHERN ROMANTIC ROAD

Numbers in the margin correspond to points of interest on the Romantic Road map.

The northern section of the Romantic Road skirts the wild open countryside of the Spessart uplands, following the sinuous course of the Main River eastwards as far as Würzburg, before heading south through the plains of

Aschaffenburg

❶ *50 km (30 mi) east from Frankfurt.*

Strictly speaking, Aschaffenburg isn't on the Romantic Road; it's one of the highlights of another German holiday route, the Strasse der Residenzen. The town has been included in this chapter because of its imposing Renaissance castle, the **Schloss Johannisburg,** residence of the prince-electors of Mainz, hereditary rulers of Aschaffenburg in the 17th and 18th centuries. The exterior of the doughty sandstone castle harks back to the Middle Ages. Four massive corner towers guard the inner courtyard. The interior contains the **Schloss Museum** (Castle Museum), which charts the history of the town and contains a representative collection of German glass, and the **Staatsgalerie** (City Art Gallery). A small section of the latter is devoted to Lucas Cranach the Elder (1472–1553), a leading painter of the German Renaissance, including his typical enigmatic nudes and haunting landscapes. The palace grounds contain a striking copy of the temple of Castor and Pollux in Pompeii, constructed for Ludwig I of Bavaria in 1840. If you've admired the lavish neoclassical buildings Ludwig put up in Munich, this powerful structure will also impress you. ☏ 06021/22417. 🎟 *Castle and museums DM 4.* ⊙ *Apr.–Sept., Tues.–Sun. 9–noon and 1–5; Oct.–Mar., Tues.–Sun. 11–4.*

NEED A BREAK? For an ideal introduction to Franconian wines and regional specialties, stop at the **Schlossweinstuben** (☏ 06021/12440), a wine cellar/restaurant in the castle. From the terrace there's a fine view over the Main Valley.

The **Stiftskirche** (Collegiate Church) of Sts. Peter and Alexander has a gaunt and haunting painting by Matthias Grünewald (circa 1475–1528), *The Lamentation of Christ.* It was part of a much larger and now lost altarpiece. See how, in spite of the lessons of Italian Renaissance painting, naturalism and perspective still produce an essentially Gothic image, attenuated and otherworldly. Little remains of the original Romanesque building here, save the cloisters; most of what you see dates from the 16th and 17th centuries. Pause before you go in to admire the tapering green spire and the imposing, slightly out-of-kilter facade. ✉ *Lanlingstr.* ⊙ *9–dusk.*

The **Automuseum Rosso Bianco** claims to have the largest collection of historic sports cars in the world. ✉ *Obernauer Str. 125,* ☏ *06021/21358.* 🎟 *DM 10.* ⊙ *Apr.–Oct., Tues.–Sun. 10–6; Nov.–Mar., Sun. 10–6.*

Ballooning

Englishman James Seyfert-Joiner (☏ 06106/79641) has a fleet of hot-air balloons based near Aschaffenburg and takes visitors on flights over the Romantic Road region and, from his Chiemgau base, over the Bavarian Alps.

Dining and Lodging

$$$ ✕🏨 **Romantik Hotel Post.** This is the number one choice in town for
★ both dining and lodging. Despite extensive wartime damage, the restored Post exudes class and that inimitable German coziness. All rooms are individually furnished. Eating here can be an experience, not just for the excellent local specialties but because there's an original 19th-century mail coach in the rustic-looking restaurant. ✉ *Goldbacherstr. 19–21, D–63739,* ☏ *06021/3340,* FAX *06021/13483. 71 rooms with bath or shower. Restaurant, bar, indoor pool, sauna. DC, MC, V.*

$$ ✕🏨 **Zum Goldenen Ochsen.** Just around the corner from Schloss Johannisburg, this cozy old hotel-tavern serves hearty Franconian fare at very reasonable prices. Rooms offer a high standard of comfort, with mostly traditional Bavarian furnishings. ✉ *Karlstr. 16, D–63739,* ☏ *06021/23132,* FAX *06021/25785. 39 rooms. Restaurant, café. AE, DC, MC, V. Closed 3 wks in Aug., 1 wk in Jan.*

Mespelbrunn

❷ *14 km (9 mi) southeast of Aschaffenburg.*

The main attraction of Mespelbrunn is a **castle,** surrounded by a moat and dominated by a massive round tower dating from the mid-16th century. The **Rittersaal** (Knight's Room) on the first floor displays Teutonic suits of armor, assorted weapons, and massive, dark furniture. A more delicate note is struck by the 18th-century **Chinesische Salon** (Chinese Room) upstairs. From the castle, hiking paths lead into the forested surroundings. ☎ 06092/269. ▨ *DM 5 (includes guided tour).* ◔ *Mid-Mar.–mid-Nov., Mon.–Sat. 9–noon and 1–5, Sun. 9–5.*

En Route   The road south now cuts through the still sparsely populated forest area of the **Spessart,** a walker's paradise that used to be the hunting grounds of the archbishops of Mainz and the haunt of Robin Hood–type outlaws, who have claimed a place in German lore. At the village of **Grossheubach,** the road meets up with the river Main and then follows it on a picturesque, serpentine route to Würzburg.

Miltenberg

❸ *30 km (18 mi) south of Mespelbrunn, 70 km (40 mi) west of Würzburg.*

If you've seen Rothenburg-ob-der-Tauber and loved it but hated the crowds, Miltenberg—a sleepy riverside town on the southern slopes of the forested Spessart—will provide the ideal antidote. For most, the Marktplatz, the steeply sloping town square, is the standout attraction. A 16th-century fountain, bordered by geraniums, splashes in its center; tall half-timbered houses—some six stories high, with crooked windows bright with yet more flowers—stand guard all around. To see more of these appealing buildings, stroll down Hauptstrasse, site of the **Rathaus** (Town Hall) and the 15th-century **Haus zum Riesen** (House of the Giant). The town takes its name from its castle, whose entrance is on the Marktplatz. You can peek into the courtyard (open in summer only) to see the standing stone in it. Though the stone's origins and meaning are obscure, most scholars agree it's probably Roman and is connected with a fertility rite, as there's no denying its phallic qualities.

Dining

$ ✕ **Haus zum Riesen,** Built in 1590, the "giant's house" is one of the oldest inns in Germany—so old that the origins of its strange name are lost in antiquity. Hearty Franconian dishes (great roasts and fat sausages) are served with excellent local beer and wines. ▨ *Hauptstr. 99. No credit cards.*

En Route   From Miltenberg you can take one of two routes to Würzburg. Both have lovely scenery along the way. One road, B–426, follows the meanderings of the Main River, while the other, A–8, cuts south, leading you to historic towns such as Tauberbischofsheim and Amorbach.

Amorbach

❹ *12 km (7 mi) south of Miltenberg.*

The little town of Amorbach, in the beautiful Odenwald forest, has the impressive onetime Benedictine abbey church of **St. Maria.** The building is interesting chiefly as an example of the continuity of German architectural traditions, the superimposition of one style on another. You'll see examples of works here from the 8th through the 18th century. The facade of the church seems a run-of-the-mill example of Baroque work, with twin domed towers flanking a lively and well-proportioned central section; in fact, it is a rare example of the Baroque grafted directly onto a Romanesque building. Look closely and you'll notice the characteristic round arches of the Romanesque marching up the muscular towers. It's the onion-shape domes at their summits and the colored stucco applied in the 18th century that make them seem Baroque. There are no such stylistic confusions in the interior, however; all is Baroque power and ornamentation. The mighty Baroque organ, built by the revered Stumm family, is recognized as one of the finest in Europe. ⊠ *Kirchpl.* ⊠ *DM 4 (includes guided tour of church and former monastery buildings).* ☺ *Apr. and Oct., Mon.–Sat. 9:20–noon and 1:20–5:20, Sun. 11:20–5:20; Mar., Mon.–Sat. 9:40–11:40 and 1:40–5, Sun. 1–6; May–Sept., Mon.–Sat. 9:20–noon and 1:20–6, Sun. 11:20–6; Nov.–Feb., by prior appointment only. Call* ☎ *09373/971545. Brief recitals on the organ are given in conjunction with tours of church, May–Oct., Tues.–Fri. 3, Sat. 11 and 3.* ⊠ *DM 5.*

Amorbach has several rustic half-timbered houses; one of the oldest in Germany is found here: the **Templerhaus,** built in 1291 by a local nobleman. ⊠ *Free.* ☺ *May–Oct., Wed. 4:30–5:30, Sat. 11–noon.*

Sammlung Berger (Teapot Museum) may have Europe's largest collection of teapots—17,000 of them, mostly from Britain and the United States. An unusual exhibit traces the story of Pepsi-Cola. A local firm produces a wide range of teapots, which are on sale at the museum. ⊠ *Wolkmannstr. 2,* ☎ *09373/618.* ⊠ *Free.* ☺ *Apr.–Oct., Tues.–Sun. 1:30–5.*

OFF THE BEATEN PATH   **WILDENBERG CASTLE** – Part of Germany's Parzival legend is thought to have been written within the walls of this 1,000-year-old structure, whose ruins are 5 kilometers (3 miles) southeast of Amorbach. The castle keep is still standing, and it affords a fine view of the Odenwald Forest. ⊠ *DM 2.50.* ☺ *Sun. and public holidays only.*

The Arts
Regular recitals are held on the great organ of the former abbey church. Call 09373/971545 for program details.

Dining
$ ✕ **Cafe Schlossmühle.** This charming café-restaurant is in the former mill of the abbey, and on warm days you can eat outside beside the mill stream. The simple menu has reasonably priced dishes, and the pastries are scrumptious. ⊠ *Schlosspl. 4,* ☎ *09373/1254. No credit cards.*

Tauberbischofsheim
❺ *40 km (24 mi) east of Amorbach, 36 km (22 mi) southwest of Würzburg.*

The bustling little Tauber River town of Tauberbischofsheim has a parish church with a side altar richly carved by a follower of Tilman Riemenschneider. ☺ *9–dusk.*

Wertheim
❻ *30 km (18 mi) east of Miltenberg, 40 km (24 mi) west of Würzburg.*

Wertheim is the chief town on the northern Main Valley road to Würzburg; it has a beautifully location at the confluence of the Main and Tauber rivers. The town was founded in 1306 and proclaims its medieval origins through a jumble of half-timbered houses with jutting gables. Those in the central Marktplatz are the most attractive.

The romantic ruins of **Kurmainzisches Schloss,** an 11th-century castle built for the counts of Wertheim, has a memorable view of the Main Valley.

Würzburg

❼ *40 km (24 mi) east of Wertheim, 172 km (103 mi) east of Frankfurt.*

The basically Baroque city of Würzburg, the pearl of the Romantic Road, is a heady example of what happens when great genius teams up with great wealth. Beginning in the 10th century, Würzburg was ruled by the powerful (and rich) prince-bishops, who created the city with all the glittering attributes you see today.

Situated at the junction of two age-old trade routes, this glorious old city is on the banks of the Main River as it passes through a calm valley backed by vineyard-covered hills. Festung Marienberg, a fortified castle on high ground across the river, overlooks the town. Constructed between 1200 and 1600, the fortress was the residence of the prince-bishops for 450 years.

Present-day Würzburg is by no means 100% original. On March 16, 1945, seven weeks before Germany capitulated, Würzburg was all but obliterated by Allied saturation bombing. Although the bombing raid lasted no more than 20 minutes, 87% of Würzburg was wiped off the map, with some 4,000 buildings destroyed and at least that many people killed. Reconstruction, in many cases using original stones from the bombed-out structures, has returned most of the city's famous sights to their former splendor. Those who knew prewar Würzburg insist the heart of the city is now every bit as impressive as it was prior to 1945. Except for a new pedestrian zone, it remains a largely authentic restoration.

The ★**Residenz,** Würburg's major attraction, is the glorious Baroque palace where the line of prince-bishops lived after coming down from Festung Marienberg, their hilltop fortress. Construction started in 1719 under the brilliant direction of Balthasar Neumann, the German architectural genius of his age. Most of the interior decoration was entrusted to the Italian stuccoist Antonio Bossi and the Venetian painter Giovanni Battista Tiepolo. But the man whose spirit infuses the Residenz is pleasure-loving Prince-Bishop Johann Phillip Franz von Schönborn, who financed the venture but did not live to see the completion of what is now considered the most beautiful palace of Germany's Baroque era and one of Europe's most sumptuous buildings, frequently referred to as the "Palace of Palaces." This dazzling structure is a 10-minute walk from the railway station, along pedestrian-only Kaiserstrasse and then Theaterstrasse.

From the moment you enter the building, the splendor of the Residenz is evident, as the largest Baroque staircase in the country, the **Treppenhaus,** stretches away from you into the heights. Halfway to the second floor, the stairway splits and peels away at 180 degrees to the left and right.

Dominating the upper reaches of this vast space is Tiepolo's giant fresco *The Four Continents,* a gorgeous exercise in blue and pink, with allegorical figures at the corners representing the four continents known at the time. Tiepolo immortalized himself and Balthasar Neumann as two of the figures. See if you can find them; they're not too difficult to spot. Sadly, although the fresco survived the devastating wartime bombing raid on the town, it is showing signs of crumbling and needs urgent restoration work. Nineteen ninety-seven might be the last year to view the painting before its restoration, a job that could take four years or more.

Next, make your way to the **Weissersaal** (White Room) and then beyond to the grandest of the state rooms, the **Kaisersaal** (Throne Room). The Baroque/rococo ideal of *Gesamtkunstwerk*—the fusion of the arts—is perfectly illustrated here. Architecture melts into stucco; stucco invades the frescoes; the frescoes extend the real space of the room into their fantasy world. Nothing is quite what it seems, and no expense was spared to make it so. Tiepolo's frescoes show the 12th-century visit of the emperor Frederick Barbarossa to Würzburg to claim his bride. The fact that the characters all wear 16th-century Venetian dress hardly seems to matter. Few interiors anywhere use such startling opulence to similar effect. You'll find more of this expansive spirit in the **Hofkirche**, the chapel, which offers proof that the prince-bishops experienced little or no conflict between their love of ostentation and their service to God. Among the lavish marbles, rich gilding, and delicate stuccowork, note the Tiepolo altarpieces, ethereal visions of *The Fall of the Angels* and *The Assumption of the Virgin*. Finally, tour the palace garden, the **Hofgarten**; the entrance is next to the chapel. This 18th-century formal garden, with its stately gushing fountains and trim, ankle-high shrubs outlining geometric flower beds and gravel walks, is the equal of any in the country. ☎ *0931/3551712.* ▨ *DM 7, including guided tour.* ☯ *Apr.–Oct., Tues.–Sun. 9–5; Nov.–Mar., Tues.–Sun. 10–4.*

NEED A BREAK?

Sample your first Würzburg wine either in the extensive cellars of the Residenz, where you'll find a cozy tavern, or by making for one of two famous institutions in the immediate area. The nearest is the **Bürgerspital.** To get there from the square fronting the Residenz, take the first street on the right, Theaterstrasse; the Bürgerspital is about halfway down the street on the right. Originally this was a medieval hospice established by wealthy burghers for Würzburg's poor and old. Ask for a tour of the wine cellar—its barrels are the size of a Volkswagen. Just down the road, on Juliuspromenade, is another of these charitable institutions, the **Juliusspital** (Julius Hospice), established in 1576 by a Würzburg bishop.

The distinctive Baroque **Augustinerkirche** (Church of St. Augustine) stands significantly on Schönbornstrasse, the street named after Bishop Schönborn, who commissioned Balthasar Neumann to build the Residenz. The church, another fine example of Neumann's work, was a 13th-century Dominican chapel; Neumann's additions date from the early 18th century. Würzburg's Romanesque cathedral, the **Dom,** begun in 1045, stands at the end of Schönbornstrasse. Step inside and you'll find yourself, somewhat disconcertingly, in a shimmering Rococo treasure house. This is only fitting: Prince-bishop von Schönborn is buried here, and it's hard to imagine him slumbering amid the dour weightiness of a Romanesque edifice. ☯ *9–dusk.*

The **Neumünster,** alongside the Dom, was built above the grave of the early Irish martyr St. Kilian, who brought Christianity to Würzburg and, with two companions, was put to death here in 689. Their missionary zeal bore fruit, however—17 years after their death a church was consecrated in their memory. By 742 Würzburg had become a diocese, and over the following centuries 39 churches flourished throughout the city. The Neumünster's former cloistered churchyard contains the grave of Walther von der Vogelweide, the most famous minstrel in German history. ☯ *9–dusk.*

The 14th- to 15th-century **Marienkapelle** (St. Mary's Chapel), tucked modestly away at one end of Würzburg's market square, is almost lost amid the historic old facades that frame the busy heart of this city. Balthasar Neumann lies buried in this lovely church. Pause beneath the finely carved portal of the building and inspect the striking figures of Adam and Eve; you shouldn't have great difficulty recognizing the style of Tilman Riemenschneider. The original statues are in Würzburg's museum, the Mainfränkisches Museum (☞ *below*); the ones in the portal are copies. ✉ *Marktpl.* ⊙ *9–dusk.*

Exquisite **house Madonnas** may be seen on your explorations along the edge of the pedestrian zone and market square; these small statues of the Virgin are set in corner niches on the second level of many old homes. So many of these representations of the city's protective patron can be found that Würzburg is frequently referred to as "the town of Madonnas."

Old Main Bridge, which crosses the Main River, was already standing when Columbus sighted America. Twin rows of infinitely graceful statues of saints line the bridge. Note particularly the *Patronna Franconiae* (commonly known as the Weeping Madonna). There's also a beautiful view of the Marienburg fortress from the bridge—statues in the foreground, Marienburg and its surrounding vineyards as the focal point—which makes a perfect photograph to treasure as a souvenir of this historic city.

The **Marienburg** was the original home of the prince-bishops, beginning in the 13th century. The oldest buildings—note especially the **Marienkirche,** the core of the complex—date from around 700. In addition to the rough-hewn medieval fortifications, there are a number of fine Renaissance and Baroque apartments. To reach the Marienburg, you can make the fairly stiff climb on foot top the top of a hill, or take the bus from the Old Main Bridge. It runs every half hour starting at 9:45 AM.

The highlight of a visit to the Marienburg is the **Mainfränkisches Museum** (the Main-Franconian Museum). The rich and varied history of Würzburg is brought alive by this remarkable collection of art treasures. The standout is the gallery devoted to Würzburg-born sculptor Riemenschneider, including the originals of the great Adam and Eve statues, copies of which adorn the portal of the Marienkapelle. Two previously unknown works by Riemenschneider—a Madonna and child and a crucifixion—were discovered in 1994–95 in what German art critics hailed as a "sensational find." Both had been in private collections, where they had remained for decades without anyone suspecting they were by Riemenschneider. They were added to the Mainfränkisches Museum collection, together with two other works recently discovered in private possession and thought to be by pupils of Riemenschneider. You'll also be exposed to fine paintings by Tiepolo and Cranach the Elder and to exhibits of porcelain, firearms, antique toys, and ancient Greek and Roman art. Wine lovers won't want to miss the old winepresses, some of which are enormous. Other exhibits chart the history of Franconian wine. ☎ *0931/43016.* ✉ *Marienburg Fortress is free.* ⊙ *Apr.–Sept., Tues.–Sun. 9–noon and 1–5; Oct.–Mar., Tues.–Sun. 10–noon and 1–5.* ✉ *Mainfränkisches Museum DM 3.50.* ⊙ *Apr.–Oct., Tues.–Sun. 10–5; Nov.–Mar., Tues.–Sun. 10–4.*

The Marienburg collections are so vast that they spill over into another outstanding museum that is part of the fortress, the **Fürstenbaumuseum;** it traces the 1,200 years of Würzburg's history. There are some breathtaking exhibits of local goldsmiths' art. ☎ *0931/43838.* ✉ *DM 4. Com-*

bined ticket for both Mainfränkisches and Fürstenbaum museums DM
6. ☉ *Apr.–Sept., Tues.–Sun. 9–12:30 and 1–5; Oct.–Mar., Tues.–Sun.*
10–12:30 and 1–4.

Schloss Veitshöchheim, the original summer palace of the prince-
bishops, is situated 8 kilometers (5 miles) north of Würzburg, at Veitshöchheim. Though it has little of the glamorous appeal of the Residenz, the sturdy Baroque building provides further evidence of the great
wealth of the worldly rulers of Würzburg. ☎ *0931/91582.* 🎟 *DM 3*
(including guided tour). ☉ *Apr.–Sept., Tues.–Sun. 9–noon and 1–5.*

Dining and Lodging

$$ ✕ **Juliusspital Weinstuen.** The wine you drink here is from the tavern's
own vineyard; the food—predominantly hearty Franconian specialties—
takes second billing. ⊠ *Juliuspromenade 19,* ☎ *0931/54080. No credit*
cards. Closed Wed.

$$ ✕ **Ratskeller.** The vaulted cellars of Würzburg's Rathaus shelter one
★ of the city's most popular restaurants. Beer is served, but Franconian
wine is what the regulars drink. The food is staunch Franconian fare.
⊠ *Beim Grafeneckart, Langgasse 1,* ☎ *0931/13021. Reservations not*
accepted. AE, DC, MC, V.

$ ✕ **Backofele.** More than 400 years of tradition are sustained by this
historic old tavern. You can dine well and inexpensively on such dishes
as oxtail in Burgundy sauce and homemade *Rissoles* (filled pastries)
in wild-mushroom sauce. ⊠ *Ursulinergasse 2,* ☎ *0931/59059. AE,*
MC, V.

$ ✕ **Zum Stachel.** On a warm spring or summer day, take a bench in the
★ ancient Mediterranean-like courtyard of the Stachel, which is shaded by
a canopy of vine leaves and girded by high walls of mellow, creeper-hung
stone. The food is satisfying Franconian fare, from lightly baked onion
cake to hearty roast pork, but the reason for stopping here is to sample
the wine, made from grapes grown in the tavern's own vineyard. ⊠ *Gres-*
sengasse 1, ☎ *0931/52770. MC. Closed Sun. and holidays.*

$$$$ ✕🛏 **Hotel Rebstock.** Centuries of hospitality are contained behind
★ this hotel's rococo facade. The spacious lobby, with its open fireplace
and beckoning bar, sets the tone. All rooms are individually decorated.
⊠ *Neubaustr. 7, D–97070,* ☎ *0931/30930,* 🖷 *0931/309–3100. 52*
rooms, 27 suites with bath. Restaurant, bar, weinstube, no-smoking
rooms. AE, DC, MC, V.

$$$$ ✕🛏 **Hotel Walfisch.** You'll breakfast on the banks of the Main in a dining room that commands views of the river valley and the vineyard-
covered Marienberg above Würzburg. For lunch and dinner try the
hotel's cozy Walfischstube restaurant. Guest rooms are furnished in solid
Franconian style with farmhouse cupboards, floral fabrics, and heavy
drapes. ⊠ *Am Pleidenturm 5, D–97070,* ☎ *0931/50055,* 🖷
0931/51690. 41 rooms with bath. Restaurant. AE, DC, MC, V.

$$$–$$$$ ✕🛏 **Ringhotel Wittelsbacher Höh.** From most of the cozy, newly re-
furbished rooms under the steep eaves of this historic redbrick man-
sion, you'll have a fine view of Würzburg and the surrounding vineyards.
The restaurant's wine list embraces most of the leading local vintages,
and Franconian and international dishes pack the menu. In summer
take a table on the terrace and soak in the view. ⊠ *Hexenbruchweg*
10, D–97082, ☎ *0931/42085,* 🖷 *0931/415–458. 75 rooms with*
bath. Restaurant, sauna. AE, DC, MC, V.

$$$ ✕🛏 **Fränkischer Hotelgasthof zur Stadt Mainz.** This traditional Fran-
conian inn dates from the 15th century, and recipes from its 19th-
century cookbook form the basis of the restaurant's imaginative, fish-
dominated menu. Eel from the Main River, prepared in a dill sauce,
and locally caught carp and pike are specialties of the house. Home-

made apple strudel is served with afternoon coffee and also finds its way onto the dinner dessert menu. The breakfast buffet is enormous. Rooms are comfortably furnished with old-fashioned touches such as gilt mirrors and heavy drapes. ⊠ *Semmelstr. 39, D–97070,* ☎ *0931/53155,* FAX *0931/58510. 15 rooms with bath or shower. Restaurant. AE, MC, V. Closed Dec. 20–Jan. 20.*

$$–$$$ ✕▥ **Hotel Greifenstein.** The Greifenstein, recently modernized with care and taste, offers comfortable, individually furnished rooms in a quiet corner of the city, just off the market square. The cheaper doubles are small but lack no comforts or facilities. The hotel restaurant, the Fränkische Stuben, has very good cuisine—mostly Franconian specialties. ⊠ *Häfnergasse 1, D–97070,* ☎ *0931/35170,* FAX *0931/57057. 37 rooms with bath. Restaurant. AE, DC, MC, V.*

$$ ✕▥ **Strauss.** Close to the river and the pedestrian-only center, this lodging has been run by the same family for more than 100 years. The emphasis is on clean, simple comforts. The restaurant specializes in Franconian cuisine. ⊠ *Juliuspromenade 5,* ☎ *0931/30570,* FAX *0931/305–7555. 77 rooms and 2 suites with bath or shower. Restaurant. AE, DC, MC, V. Closed Dec. 20–mid-Jan.*

Nightlife and the Arts

Würzburg is the major cultural center of this region of Franconia. The cultural year starts with a Classical Music Days festival in January and ends with a Johann Sebastian Bach festival in November. Its annual Mozart Festival in June attracts visitors from all over the world. Most of the concerts are held in the magnificent setting of the Residenz. Jazz fans also claim their part of the arts program with an annual jazz festival in November. The town hosts a series of wine festivals, climaxing in the Vintners' Festival in September.

Shopping

Würzburg is the true wine center of the Romantic Road. Visit any of the vineyards that rise from the Main River and choose a *Bocksbeutel,* the distinctive green, flagon-shape wine bottles of Franconia. It's claimed that the shape came about because wine-guzzling monks found it the easiest to hide under their robes. In Würzburg itself, you'll want to linger on traffic-free **Schönbornstrasse** and the adjacent marketplace. Wine and the familiar goblets in which it is served in this part of the world are sold in many of the shops here.

Bürgerspital (⊠ Theaterstr. 19, ☎ 0931/13861) is an ancient city institution selling wine. The **Juliusspital** (⊠ Juliuspromenade 19, ☎ 0931/30840), also old, sells wine from its own vineyards, as well as the glasses from which to drink it. The **Haus des Frankenwein** (House of Franconian Wine) (⊠ Kranenkai 1, ☎ 0931/57066) has wine tastings for individual visitors. Some 600 Franconian wines and a wide range of wine accessories can be purchased.

En Route   From Würzburg follow the Romantic Road through Bavarian Franconia and Swabia and into the mountains of Upper Bavaria. For the first stretch, to Bad Mergentheim, take either the B–27 to Tauberbischofsheim and then the B–290, or the more direct B–19. Both routes take you through the open countryside of the Hohenloher Plain.

Bad Mergentheim

❽ *44 km (26 mi) south of Würzburg.*

Between 1525 and 1809 Bad Mergentheim was the home of the Teutonic Knights, one of the most successful medieval orders of chivalry. Their greatest glories came during the 15th century, when they had established themselves as one of the dominant powers of the Baltic, ruling large areas of present-day eastern Germany, Poland, and Lithuania. The following centuries saw a steady decline in the order's commercial success. In 1809 Napoléon expelled the Teutonic Knights from Bad Mergentheim. The French emperor had little time for what he considered the medieval superstition of orders such as this and felt no compunction for disbanding them as he marched east through Germany in the opening stages of his ultimately disastrous Russian campaign. The expulsion of the order seemed to sound the death knell of the little town. But in 1826 a shepherd discovered mineral springs on the north bank of the river. They proved to be the strongest sodium sulfate and bitter-salt waters in Europe, with health-giving properties that ensured the little town's future prosperity. Excavations subsequently showed the springs had been known in the Iron and Bronze ages, before becoming choked with silt.

The **Deutschordensschloss,** the Teutonic Knights' former castle at the eastern end of the town, has a museum that traces the history of the order. ⌧ *Deutschordensmuseum, Schloss 16,* ☎ *07931/52212.* ⌧ *DM 3.* ☉ *Tues.–Sat. 2:30–5:30, Sun. 10–noon and 2:30–5:30. Guided tours, costing DM 4, are given Sun. and Thurs. at 3.*

OFF THE
BEATEN PATH

STUPPACH – This village, 11 kilometers (7 miles) southeast of Bad Mergentheim, has a chapel guarding one of the great Renaissance German paintings, the so-called *Stuppacher Madonna* by Matthias Grünewald (circa 1475–1528). The painting is believed to have been produced for a church in nearby Aschaffenburg; no one seems clear on how it found its way here in 1812. It was only in 1908 that experts finally recognized it as the work of Grünewald; repainting in the 17th century had turned it into a flat and unexceptional work. Grünewald was one of the leading painters of the early Renaissance in Germany. Though he was familiar with the developments in perspective and natural lighting of Italian Renaissance painting, his work remained resolutely anti-Renaissance in spirit: tortured, emotional, dark. You'll want to compare it with that of Dürer, his contemporary, if you know his work. Whereas Dürer used the lessons of Italian painting to reproduce its clarity and rationalism, Grünewald used them for expressionistic purposes to heighten his essentially Gothic imagery. *Chapel:* ☉ *9–dusk.*

Dining and Lodging

$ ✗ **Kettler's Altfränkische Weinstube.** You'll want to come here to try the *Nürnberger Bratwürste*—finger-size spicy sausages—and to enjoy the atmosphere of a snug 180-year-old Franconian tavern. The wine list is enormous. ⌧ *Krumme Gasse 12,* ☎ *07931/7308. No credit cards. Closed Wed.*

$$$$ ✗⌧ **Victoria.** This is one of the area's finest spa hotels, combining cosmopolitan flair with rural peace and quiet. Rooms are large, luxurious, and furnished in the style of a country mansion, with king-size beds, well-cushioned armchairs, subdued lighting, and fine prints on the textile-hung walls. The lounge is scarcely less opulent, with an open fireplace and a library. The excellent restaurant, with a magnificent tile oven taking pride of place, draws a clientele from far afield. ⌧ *Post-str. 2–4, D–96980,* ☎ *07931/5930,* FAX *07931/593–500. 80 rooms with bath. Restaurant, bar, pub, beauty salon, sauna. AE, DC, MC, V.*

Weikersheim

❾ *10 km (6 mi) east of Bad Mergentheim.*

The Tauber River town of Weikersheim is dominated by the castle of the counts of Hohenlohe. The great hall of the castle is the scene each summer of an international youth music festival, and the Rittersaal (Knight's Hall) contains life-size stucco wall sculptures of animals, reflecting the counts' love of hunting. In the cellars you can drink a glass of cool wine drawn from the huge casks that seem to prop up the building. Outside again, stroll through the enchanting gardens and enjoy the view of the Tauber and its leafy valley.

Dining and Lodging

$$ ✕⊡ **Flair Hotel Laurentius.** This traditional old hotel on Weikersheim's market square is an ideal stopover on a tour of the Romantic Road. You can avoid the crowds and the relatively high prices of nearby Rothenburg and still be within an hour's car ride of most sights on the northern part of the route. Owners Heinrich and Lony Koch, who ran the hotel for many years, recently handed it over to their son Jürgen, who continues the family tradition with winning charm. Rooms are very comfortable and individually furnished, some with fine German antiques. The vaulted ground floor has a cozy wine tavern, a very good restaurant named, like the hotel, after the patron saint of cooks (and, slyly, after the family Koch—German for cook), and a newly opened brasserie. The very capable Jürgen Koch, who recently won one of Germany's top gastronomic awards, runs the kitchen. ✉ *Marktpl. 5, D–97990,* ☎ *07934/7007,* ᴀᴄ *07934/7077. 13 rooms with bath. Restaurant, brasserie, café, weinstube. DC, MC, V.*

Creglingen

❿ *20 km (12 mi) east of Weikersheim.*

The village of Creglingen has been an important place of pilgrimage since the 14th century, when a farmer had a vision of a heavenly host
⓫ plowing his field. The **Herrgottskirche** (Chapel of Our Lord) is situated in a side valley, the Herrgottstal (Valley of the Lord), 3 kilometers (2 miles) south of Creglingen; the way there is well signposted. The chapel was built by the counts of Hohenlohe, and during the early 16th century Tilman Riemenschneider was commissioned to carve an altarpiece for it. This enormous work, 33 feet high, depicts in minute detail the life and ascension of the Virgin Mary. Riemenschneider entrusted much of the background detail to the craftsmen of his Würzburg workshop, but he allowed no one but himself to attempt the life-size figures of this masterpiece. Its intricate detail and attenuated figures are a high point of late-Gothic sculpture. ☾ *9–dusk.*

The **Fingerhutmuseum,** one of Germany's most unusual museums, can be found opposite the Herrgottskirche. *Fingerhut* is German for "thimble," and the museum has thousands of them, some dating from Roman times. ⊡ *Free.* ☾ *Apr.–Oct., daily 9–6; Nov.–Mar., daily 1–4.*

The fascinating **Fire-Brigade Museum,** with an impressive collection of old fire engines, lies 8 kilometers (5 miles) outside Creglingen, within the stout castle walls of Schloss Waldmannshofen. ⊡ *Free.* ☾ *Easter–Oct., daily 10–noon and 2–4.*

Lodging

$ ⊡ **Bauernhof Hans Stahl.** For an off-the-beaten-track experience that also provides an overnight accommodation, book a space in the hayloft of the Stahl family's farm at Creglingen. The Stahls have opened what they describe as southern Germany's first "hay hotel," where visitors bed down in freshly turned hay in the farmhouse granary. If the hay is too prickly, bed linen and blankets can be borrowed. The overnight rate of DM 28 includes a cold supper and breakfast. ⊠ *Weidenhof 1, D–97993,* ☎ *07933/378. No credit cards.*

Rothenburg-ob-der-Tauber

★ ⑫ *20 km (12 mi) southeast of Creglingen.*

Rothenburg-ob-der-Tauber (literally, "the red castle on the Tauber") is the kind of medieval town that even Walt Disney might have thought too good to be true, with gingerbread architecture galore and a wealth of fountains and flowers against a backdrop of towers and turrets. The reason for its survival is simple. Rothenburg was a small but thriving 17th-century town that had grown up around the ruins of two 12th-century churches destroyed by an earthquake. Then it was laid low economically by the havoc of the Thirty Years' War, the cataclysmic religious struggle that all but destroyed Germany in the 17th century. The town's economic base was devastated, and it slumbered until modern tourism rediscovered it. And here it is, milking its "best-preserved-medieval-town-in-Europe" image to the fullest, undoubtedly something of a tourist trap, but genuine enough for all the hype. There really is no place quite like it. Whether Rothenburg is at its most appealing in summer, when the balconies of its ancient houses are festooned with flowers, or in winter, when snow lies on its steep gables and narrow streets, is a matter of taste. Few people are likely to find this extraordinary little survivor from another age anything short of remarkable.

Numbers in the margin correspond to points of interest on the Rothenburg-ob-der-Tauber map.

⑬ Rothenburg's **city walls** are more than a mile long and provide an excellent way of introduction to the town. Stairs every 200 or 300 yards provide ready access. There are superb views of the tangle of pointed and tiled red roofs, and of the rolling country beyond.

⑭ The **Rathaus** (City Hall) on Rathausplatz is a logical place to begin your exploration of Rothenburg. Half the building is Gothic, begun in 1240; the other half is classical, started in 1572. A fire in 1501 destroyed the part of the structure that is now the newer, Renaissance section, which faces the main square. Go inside to the vaults below the building to see the **Historiengewölbe**, a museum that charts Rothenburg's role in the Thirty Years' War. Great prominence is given to an account of the Meistertrunk (Master Drink), an event that will follow you around Rothenburg. It came about when the Protestant town was captured by Catholic forces. During the victory celebrations, so the story goes, the conquering general was embarrassed to find himself unable to drink a great tankard of wine in one go, as his manhood demanded. He volunteered to spare the town further destruction if any of the city councillors could drain the mighty draught. The mayor, a man by the name of Nusch, took up the challenge and succeeded, and Rothenburg was preserved. The tankard itself is on display at the Reichsstadtmuseum (☞ *below*). As it holds 6 pints, the wonder is not so much that the conquering general was unable to knock it back but that he should have tried it in the first place. On the north side of the main square is a fine clock, placed there 50 years after Nusch's feat. Today he's surmounted by a mechanical figure that acts out the epic Master Drink daily on the hour from 11 to 3 and at 8, 9, and 10 PM. The town also holds an annual pageant celebrating the feat, with townsfolk parading through the streets dressed in 17th-century garb. The festival be-

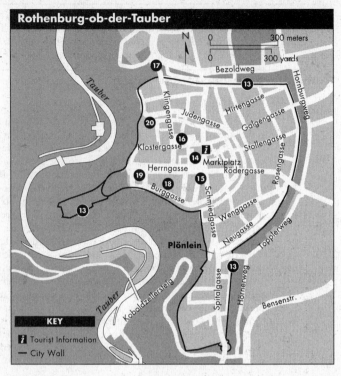

Rothenburg-ob-der-Tauber

KEY

ℹ️ Tourist Information
— City Wall

gins in the courtroom of the Town Hall, where the event is said to have occurred. ✉️ *Rathauspl. Rathaus tower,* ☎ *09861/40492.* 🎫 *DM 1.* ⏱ *Weekdays 9:30–12:30 and 1–5, weekends and holidays noon–3. Historiengewölbe museum (and dungeons):* 🎫 *DM 2.50.* ⏱ *Mid-Mar.–Apr., daily 10–5; May–Oct., daily 9–6; Nov.–Dec., Fri. and weekends 10–5.*

⑮ The **Herterlichbrunnen,** an ornate Renaissance fountain, may be found at Rothenburg's central Marktplatz (Market Square). To celebrate some momentous event—the end of a war, say, or the passing of an epidemic—the *Schäfertanz* (Shepherds' Dance) was performed around the fountain. The dance is still done, though for the benefit of tourists rather than to commemorate the end of a threat to Rothenburg. It takes place in front of the Rathaus several times a year, chiefly at Easter, in late May, and throughout June and July.

⑯ The **Stadtpfarrkirche St. Jakob** (Parish Church of St. James) serves as the repository of additional Riemenschneider works, including the famous Heiliges Blut (Holy Blood) altar. Above the altar a crystal capsule is said to contain drops of Christ's blood. The church has other items of interest, including three 14th- and 15th-century stained-glass windows in the choir and the famous Herlin-Altar, with its 15th-century painted panels. ☎ *09861/40492.* ⏱ *Easter–Oct., daily 9–5; Nov.–Easter, daily 10–noon and 2–4.*

⑰ **St. Wolfgang's** is a church built into the defenses of the town. From within the town it looks like a peaceful parish church; from outside it blends into the forbidding city wall. Through an underground passage you can reach the sentry walk above and follow the wall for almost its entire length. ⏱ *9–dusk.*

⓲ The town has two museums you won't want to miss. The **Mittelalter-liches Kriminalmuseum** (Medieval Criminal Museum) sets out to document the history of German legal processes in the Middle Ages and contains an impressive array of instruments of torture. ⊠ *Burggasse 3,* ☎ *09861/5359.* 🎟 *DM 5.* ☉ *Apr.–Oct., daily 9:30–6; Nov.–Mar., daily 2–4.*

👆 ⓳ The **Puppen und Spielzeugmuseum** (Doll and Toy Museum) is housed in a 15th-century building near the Rathaus. There are 300 dolls, the oldest dating from 1780, the newest from 1940. ⊠ *Hofronnengasse 13.* 🎟 *DM 5.* ☉ *Mar.–Dec., daily 9:30–6; Jan.–Feb., daily 11–5.*

⓴ The **Reichsstadtmuseum** (Imperial City Museum) turns out to be two attractions in one. It's the city museum, and it contains artifacts that illustrate Rothenburg and its history. Among them is the great tankard, or *Pokal,* of the Meistertrunk. The setting of the museum is the other attraction; it's a former convent, the oldest parts of which date from the 13th century. Tour the building to see the cloister, the kitchens, and the dormitory; then see the collections. ⊠ *Hofronnengasse 13,* ☎ *09861/40458.* 🎟 *DM 4.* ☉ *Apr.–Oct., daily 10–5; Nov.–Mar., daily 1–4.*

Dining and Lodging

$$$ ✕ **Die Blaue Terrasse.** The view of the Tauber Valley from the windows
★ of the Hotel Goldener Hirsch's restaurant almost rivals its nouvelle cuisine, prepared with regional touches. Snails and asparagus (in season) are perennial favorites. ⊠ *Untere Schmiedgasse 16/25,* ☎ *09861/7080. Jacket and tie. AE, DC, MC, V. Closed mid-Dec.–Jan.*

$$ ✕ **Baumeisterhaus.** In summer you can dine in one of Rothenburg's
★ loveliest courtyards, a half-timbered oasis of peace that's part of a magnificent Renaissance house. If the weather's cooler, move inside to the paneled dining room. The menu, changed daily, features Bavarian and Franconian specialties. ⊠ *Obere Schmiedgasse 3,* ☎ *09861/94700. AE, DC, MC, V.*

$$$$ ✕🏨 **Hotel Eisenhut.** It's appropriate that the prettiest small town in Ger-
★ many should have one of the prettiest small hotels in the country. It stands in the center of town and is in what were originally four separate town houses, the oldest dating from the 12th century, the newest from the 16th. Inside there are enough oil paintings, antiques, and heavy beams to make any Teutonic knight feel at home. ⊠ *Herrngasse 3, D–91541,* ☎ *09861/7050,* 🖷 *09861/70545. 79 rooms, with bath. Restaurant, café, piano bar. AE, DC, MC, V.*

$$$–$$$$ ✕🏨 **Romantik Hotel Markusturm.** This hotel belongs to the Roman-
★ tik group, and romantic it certainly is: a 13th-century (but fully modernized) sharp-eaved house that is practically embraced by the ancient Markus tower and gate. If you stay at the height of the season, you'll hear the night watchman making his rounds. ⊠ *Rödergasse 1, D–91541,* ☎ *09861/2098,* 🖷 *09861/2692. 21 rooms, 5 suites with bath. Restaurant, no-smoking rooms, sauna. DC, MC, V.*

$$–$$$$ ✕🏨 **Hotel-Gasthof Zum Rappen.** Close to the Würzburger Tor (a town gate) and first mentioned in town records in 1603, this tavern offers a surprisingly high standard of comfort behind its stout, yellow-stucco, geranium-smothered facade. Guest rooms have a colorful, airy touch, with light woods and pastel-shaded and floral furnishings. Those in the modern annex have balconies overlooking a quiet courtyard. If you ask for traditional German furnishings, the Rappen will oblige. Friday and Saturday nights are dance nights in the atmospheric "Rappenschmiede" weinstube. ⊠ *Würzburger Tor 6 and 10, D–91541,* ☎ *09861/6071,* 🖷 *09861/6076. 60 rooms, 11 apartments with bath or*

shower. Restaurant, bar, beer garden weinstube. AE, DC, MC, V. Closed Jan.

$$–$$$ ✕🖭 **Flair Hotel Reichs-Küchenmeister.** Master chefs in the service of the Holy Roman Empire were the inspiration for the name of this historic hotel-restaurant, one of the oldest trader's houses in Rothenburg. The present proprietors, Barbara and Wolfgang Niedner, carry on the tradition with energy and flair. The excellent fish come from their own tanks; the venison, from hunters they know. Rooms are furnished in a stylish mixture of old and new, light veneer pieces sharing space with heavy oak bedsteads and painted cupboards. A delightful attic room, tucked up under the steep eaves, has exposed beams and timbering and is furnished with select cane pieces. ✉ *Kirchpl. 8, D–91541,* ☎ *09861/2046,* 🖷 *09861/86965. 44 rooms and 6 apartments with bath. Restaurant, pub, hot tub, sauna. AE, DC, MC, V.*

$ ✕🖭 **Gasthof Klingentor.** This sturdy old staging post is outside the city walls but still within a 10-minute walk of Rothenburg's Old Town center. Rooms have recently been redecorated and furnished to a high standard of comfort. A well-marked cycle and hiking path starts outside the front door. ✉ *Mergentheimer Str. 14, D–91541,* ☎ *09861/3468. 22 rooms, most with bath. Restaurant. MC, V.*

$ ✕🖭 **Hotel Zapf "An der Wörnitzquelle."** You can escape the crowds and high prices of Rothenburg accommodations at this enchanting and remarkably good-value country hotel in the village of Schillingfurst, 20 kilometers (12 miles) from Rothenburg and just 5 kilometers (3 miles) from the Romantic Road. The river Wörnitz rises practically in its back garden, hence the hotel's name, which means "source of the Wörnitz." Although this inn has a striking stepped-gable Renaissance facade, most rooms are in the less lovely modern extension; they are nevertheless comfortable and well-furnished, with balconies offering views of the fortified town of Schillingfurst and the surrounding countryside. ✉ *Dombühlerstr. 9, D–91583,* ☎ *09868/5029,* 🖷 *09868/5464. 20 rooms with bath/shower, 1 apartment. Restaurant, beer garden, café, sauna, paddle tennis, bicycles. AE, DC, MC, V.*

$$$–$$$$ 🖭 **Hotel Goldener Hirsch.** This lantern-hung, green-shuttered 15th-century patrician house is an inextricable part of Rothenburg's history. It was here that the Meistertrunk play was first performed. Baroque antiques are everywhere, from the lobby to the uppermost, bay-windowed bedroom. ✉ *Untere Schmiedgasse 16–25, D–91541,* ☎ *09861/7080,* 🖷 *09861/708100. 72 rooms with bath or shower. AE, DC, MC, V. Closed mid-Dec.–Jan.*

Nightlife and the Arts

The highlight of Rothenburg's annual calendar is the "Meistertrunk" festival in early June, celebrating a famous wager that saved the town from destruction in the Thirty Years' War.

Shopping

Unger's (✉ Herrngasse 10, ☎ 09861/8904) and the **Kunstwerke Friese** (✉ Grüner Markt, near the Rathaus, ☎ 09861/1425) stock a selection of Hummel figures and beautifully crafted porcelain birds made by the Hummel manufacturer, the Goebel Porzellanfabrik; they also carry porcelain and glassware by other German manufacturers.

Burggasse, the centuries-old onetime home of Georg Nusch—the Rothenburg councillor who saved the town by accepting General Tilly's wine-drinking challenge—is a shop stacked high with local glassware and other handicrafts.

Käthe Wohlfahrt's shop (✉ Herrngasse 1, ☎ 09861/4090) carries children's toys. **Weihnachtsdorf** (Christmas Village) is a wonderland of locally made toys and decorations; even in summer there are Christmas trees hung with brightly painted wood baubles.

Numbers in the margin correspond to points of interest on the Romantic Road map.

Feuchtwangen

㉑ *30 km (18 mi) south of Rothenburg-ob-der-Tauber.*

Feuchtwangen has a central market square, with a splashing fountain and an ideal setting of half-timbered houses, that rivals even the attractions of Rothenburg and Dinkelsbühl. Summer is the time to visit, when open-air theater productions are staged in the low, graceful cloisters next to the **Stiftskirche**, the collegiate church, from mid-June to the beginning of August. Inside the church is a 15th-century altar carved by Albrecht Dürer's teacher, Michael Wohlgemut.

The **Heimatmuseum** (Local History Museum) has an excellent collection of folk arts and crafts. ⊠ *Museumstr. 19,* ☎ *09852/575.* ⊒ *DM 4.* ☉ *Mar.–Dec., daily 10–noon and 2–5.*

NEED A BREAK?	Stop for a coffee at the half-timbered house opposite the Heimatmuseum, the **Cafe am Kreuzgang,** which makes its own chocolates as well as delicious pastries.

Dining and Lodging

$$$$ ✕▥ **Romantik Hotel Greifen Post.** The solid, market-square exterior
★ of this historic house (formerly a staging post on the medieval route between Paris and Prague) gives little hint of the luxuries within. Ask for the room with the four-poster. If that's taken, settle for the Louis XVI romantic room, the Biedermeier room, or the Laura Ashley English country-house-style room. In the indoor pool you'll splash around within the original Renaissance walls of this ancient part of the house. In the hotel's fine restaurant you'll dine within walls decorated with frescoes of Feuchtwangen's past; the pictures illustrate that past guests here included a German emperor and the notorious dancer who cost a king his throne, Lola Montez. ⊠ *Marktpl. 8, D–91555,* ☎ *09852/6800,* ⅎⱯ *09852/68068. 38 rooms with bath. Restaurant, bar, indoor pool, sauna, bicycles. AE, DC, MC, V.*

Dinkelsbühl

★ **㉒** *12 km (8 mi) south of Feuchtwangen.*

Within the mellow walls of Dinkelsbühl, a beautifully preserved medieval town, the rush of traffic seems an eternity away. There's less to see here than in Rothenburg, but the mood is much less tourist-oriented. It's thought that the town originated during the 6th century as the court of a Franconian king. Like Rothenburg, Dinkelsbühl was caught up in the Thirty Years' War, and, again like Rothenburg, it preserves a fanciful episode from those bloody times. Local lore says that when Dinkelsbühl was under siege by Swedish forces and in imminent danger of destruction, a young girl led the children of the town to the enemy commander and implored him in their name for mercy. The commander of the Swedish army, Colonel Klaus Dietrich von Sperreuth, is said to have been moved almost to tears, and he spared the town. Whether or not it's true, the story is a charming one, and it is retold every year during the Kinderzech Festival, a pageant by the children of Dinkelsbühl during a 10-day festival in July.

Touring Dinkelsbühl is not so much a matter of taking in specific sights—museums, palaces, parks, and churches, say—as of simply wandering around the historic area, pausing to admire a facade, a shop window, or the juxtaposition of architectural styles—from Gothic through Baroque—that makes this little town memorable.

The **Stadtpfarrkirche St. Georg** on the Marktplatz is the one standout sight for many. Large enough, at 235 feet in length, to be a cathedral, St. Georg's is among the best examples in Bavaria of the late-Gothic style. Note especially the complex fan vaulting that spreads sinuously across the ceiling. If you can face the climb, head up the 200-foot tower for amazing views over the jumble of Dinkelsbühl's rooftops. ✉ *Marktpl.*

The **Museum 3 Dimension** is the world's first museum of three-dimensional technology. Exhibitions describe how three-dimensional effects are achieved in photography, the cinema, and other art forms. Children enjoy the 3-D film run at various times during the day, as well as the 3-D art on display. ✉ *Nördlinger Tor.* ☉ *Apr.–Oct., daily 10–6; Nov.–Mar., weekends 11–4.*

Dining and Lodging

$$$–$$$$ ✕⊡ **Hotel Goldene Kanne.** Within its historic walls this centrally located hotel (now a member of the budget-conscious Minotel group) offers a high standard of comfort. Rooms were recently renovated and furnished with solid German oak; many of them have sitting-room corners with desks. The rooms even have fax connections—a rarity in this part of Germany. It's particularly recommended for families (seven of the rooms have children's beds), although lovers are also catered to with a special honeymoon suite. The cozy restaurant offers both local and international cuisine and has regular offbeat specialty weeks, featuring exotic pancake preparations and potato recipes. ✉ *Segringerstr. 8, D–91550,* ☎ *09851/6011,* FAX *09851/2281. 23 rooms and 2 suites, all with bath/shower. Restaurant, café. AE, MC, V.*

$$–$$$ ✕⊡ **Deutsches Haus.** This picture-postcard medieval inn, with a facade of half-timbered gables and flower boxes, has many rooms fitted with antique furniture. One of them has a romantic four-poster bed. ✉ *Weinmarkt 3, D–91550,* ☎ *09851/6058,* FAX *09851/7911. 7 rooms and 2 suites with bath. Restaurant, sauna, exercise room. AE, DC, MC, V. Closed Dec. 24–Jan. 6.*

$$ ⊡ **Blauer Hecht.** A brewery-tavern in the 18th century (they still brew in the backyard), this Ring hotel has been renovated and furnished with the sleek, dark-veneer and pastel-shaded contrasts favored by the group's interior designers. It's central but quiet. ✉ *Schweinemarkt 1, D–91550,* ☎ *09851/811,* FAX *09851/814. 44 rooms with bath. Indoor pool, sauna, steam room. AE, DC, MC, V. Closed Jan.*

Nightlife and the Arts

An annual open-air theater festival from late June until mid-August has the ancient walls of Dinkelsbühl as its backdrop.

Shopping

At **Weschke and Ries** (✉ Segringerstr. 20, ☎ 09851/9439), Hummel porcelain figures share window space with other German porcelain and glassware.

Jürgen Pleilkles (✉ Segringerstr. 53, ☎ 09851/7596) is energetically trying to restore his town's former reputation for fine earthenware; he also offers courses at the potter's wheel. **Reichstadt** gallery (✉ Segringerstr. 33, ☎ 09851/3123) displays a large selection of local artists' work.

Nördlingen

❷❸ *32 km (19 mi) southeast of Dinkelsbühl.*

In Nördlingen the cry of *So G'sell so*—"All's well"—still rings out every night across its ancient walls and turrets. The town employs sentries to sound out the traditional message from the 300-foot-high tower of the central parish church of St. Georg at half-hour intervals between 10 PM and midnight. The tradition goes back to an incident during the Thirty Years' War, when an enemy attempt to slip into the town was detected by an alert townswoman. From the church tower—known locally as the Daniel—you'll get an unsurpassed view of the town and the surrounding countryside, including, on clear days, 99 villages. However, the climb is only for the fit: The tower has 365 steps, one for each day of the year. The tower is open daily 9 AM to dusk. The ground plan of the town is two concentric circles. The inner circle of streets, whose central point is St. Georg's, marks the earliest boundary of the medieval town. A few hundred yards beyond it is the outer boundary, a wall built to accommodate the expanding town. Fortified with 11 towers and punctuated by five massive gates, it's one of the best-preserved town walls in Germany. You can stroll along 1.2 kilometers (2 miles) of its length.

For an even more spectacular view of Nördlingen, contact the local flying club, the **Rieser Flugsportverein** (☎ 09081/4099), and take to the sky in a light aircraft. The sight of Nördlingen nestling in the trim, green Swabian (southwestern Germany) landscape is well worth the cost. The basinlike formation of the **Ries**, a 24-kilometer-wide (15-mile-wide) crater, is best seen from above. Until the beginning of this century it was believed that the crater was the remains of an extinct volcano. In 1960 it was proven by two Americans that the Ries was caused by a meteorite at least 1 kilometer (½ mile) in diameter that hit the ground at more than 100,000 miles per hour. The impact had the destructive energy of 250,000 atomic bombs of the size that obliterated Hiroshima. It also turned the surface rock and subsoil upside down, hurling debris as far as what is now Slovakia and wiping out virtually all plant and animal life within a radius of more than 100 miles. The compressed rock, or *Suevit*, formed by the explosive impact of the meteorite was used to construct many of the town's buildings, including St. Georg's tower.

The **Rieskrater Museum,** housed in a converted 15th-century barn, tells the story of the Ries crater. ⊠ *Hintere Gerbergasse 3,* ☎ *09081/84143.* ☎ *DM 5.* ☉ *Tues.–Sun. 10–noon and 1:30–4:30.*

Dining and Lodging

$$$$ ✕ **Meyer's-Keller.** An unassuming exterior belies the cozy, rustic interior of this restaurant, a short walk from Nördlingen's Altstadt. The menu is anything but simple Bavarian; try any of the fish dishes, all prepared with flair. ⊠ *Marienhöhe 8,* ☎ *09081/4493. AE, MC, V. Closed Mon. No lunch Tues.*

$$$–$$$$ ✕🏨 **Kaiserhof-Hotel-Sonne.** The great German poet Goethe stayed here and was only one in a long line of distinguished guests, headed by Emperor Friedrich III in 1487. The vaulted cellar wine tavern is a reminder of those days. The three honeymoon suites are furnished in 18th-century style, with hand-painted four-poster beds. ⊠ *Marktpl. 3, D–86720,* ☎ *09081/5068,* 🆋 *09081/23999. 40 rooms, all with bath or shower. Restaurant, weinstube. AE, MC, V. Closed Dec. 26–mid-Jan.*

$$$ ✕🏨 **Flamberg Hotel Klösterle.** Where monks of the Barfuss order once went about their frugal daily routine, you can dine in a restaurant that

incorporates the ancient stonework of the original monastery. Guest rooms are anything but monastic—modern and comfortably furnished in pastel tones with bright prints on the walls. The hotel's striking white-and-yellow facade, with its Renaissance-look windows and steeply stepped gables, fits snugly into the old-town center, whose jumble of roofs you can admire while relaxing in the fitness center and sauna–steam bath on the hotel's top floor. ⊠ *Beim Klösterle 1, D–86720,* ☎ *09081/88054,* FAX *09081/22740. 98 rooms, 11 suites with bath. Restaurant, weinstube, sauna, exercise room, bicycles. AE, DC, MC, V.*

$$–$$$ ✕⌂ **Hotel Schützenhof.** This small, comfortable hotel in the traditional style, on the outskirts of town, is known for its excellent restaurant, which specializes in fresh fish from the surrounding lakes and rivers. ⊠ *Kaiserwiese 2, D–86720,* ☎ *09081/3940 or 09081/3948,* FAX *09081/88815. 15 rooms with shower. Restaurant, beer garden, bowling. AE, DC, MC, V. Closed 1st 2 wks in Aug. and 2 wks in Jan.*

Nightlife and the Arts

An annual open-air theater festival has the ancient walls of Nördlingen's "Alter Bastei" (Old Bastion) as a backdrop. It's held from the end of June through July. A traditional horse race with medieval origins is held annually in mid-July. It's the central focus of a show-jumping festival of international stature.

Shopping

Otto Wolf (⊠ Marktpl., ☎ 09081/841–161) stocks a wide selection of Hummel figures at competitive prices. Nördlingen has a twice-weekly market in the pedestrian shopping zone on Wednesday and Saturday.

En Route At the point where the little Wörnitz River breaks through the Franconian Jura Mountains, 20 kilometers (12 miles) southeast of Nördlingen, you'll find one of southern Germany's best-preserved medieval castles. **Schloss Harburg** was already old when it passed into the possession of the counts of Oettingen in 1295; before that time it belonged to the Hohenstaufen emperors. The ancient and noble house of Oettingen still owns the castle, and inside you can view treasures collected by the family through the centuries. The collection includes some works by Tilman Riemenschneider, along with illuminated manuscripts dating as far back as the 8th century and an exquisite 12th-century ivory crucifix. ⊡ *DM 5 (including guided tour).* ⊙ *Mid-Mar.–Sept., Tues.–Sun. 9–5; Oct., Tues.–Sun. 9:30–4:30.*

Donauwörth

㉔ *11 km (7 mi) south of Harburg.*

At the old walled town of Donauwörth, the Wörnitz River meets the Danube. If you're driving, pull off into the clearly marked lot on B–25, just north of town. Below you sprawls a striking natural relief map of Donauwörth and its two rivers. The oldest part of town is on an island in the river, connected to the rest of town by a wood bridge and greeted on the north bank by the single surviving town gate, the Riederstor. North of the gate is one of the finest avenues of the Romantic Road: Reichsstrasse (Empire Street), so named because it was once a vital link in the Road of the Holy Roman Empire between Nürnberg and Augsburg. The broad street—known by the locals as the Gute Stube (front room) of their town—is lined by solid, centuries-old houses and shops that tell their own tales of Donauwörth's prosperous past. The Fuggers, a famous family of traders and bankers from Augsburg, acquired a palatial home here in the 16th century; its fine Renaissance-style facade under a steeply gabled roof stands proudly at the upper end of Reichsstrasse.

Dining and Lodging

$$–$$$ ✕🏨 **Posthotel Traube.** Mozart and Goethe are among the notable guests who have stayed at the Traube in the course of its 300-year history. It's one of the oldest coaching inns in the area. Part of the Ring group now, the hotel offers a high degree of comfort within its sturdy old walls. The restaurant is one of Donauwörth's best, with a wide-ranging menu featuring local and international cuisines. ⊠ *Kapellstr. 14–16, D–86609,* ☎ *0906/6096,* 🅵🅰🆇 *0906/23390. 41 rooms, 2 suites with bath. Restaurant, weinstube, sauna. AE, DC, MC, V.*

$$$ 🏨 **Parkhotel.** A recently established group brings together hotels that
★ have one feature in common: an idyllic location. This one qualifies because of its fine site high above Donauwörth. Rooms were renovated in 1994, and most have balconies with panoramic views. ⊠ *Stern-schanzenstr. 1, D–86609,* ☎ *0906/6037,* 🅵🅰🆇 *0906/23283. 45 rooms with bath or shower. Weinstube, indoor pool, bowling. AE, DC, MC, V.*

Shopping

Donauwörth is the home of the famous and well-loved Käthe-Kruse dolls. At the **Heimatmuseum,** you can see these toys being made. ⊠ *Im Ried.* ⊙ *May–Sept., Tues.–Sun. 2–5.*

Ulm

㉕ *70 km (40 mi) southwest of Donauwörth, 65 km (39 km) west of Augsburg.*

Ulm isn't strictly on the Romantic Road, but it's definitely worth visiting, if only for one reason: its mighty minster, with the world's tallest church tower (528 feet). It has two other claims to fame: the birthplace of Albert Einstein in 1879 and the site of the most spectacular attempt to fly since Icarus, made by a local tailor (☞ *Rathaus, below.*). To get to Ulm from Donauwörth, take the B–16 highway west, connecting with the B–28. For a prettier ride, head back to Nördlingen and take the Schwäische Albstrasse (Swabian Alp Road, the B–466 highway) south to Ulm. From Nördlingen, it's about 60 kilometers (36 miles).

Ulm grew as a medieval trading city thanks to its location on the Danube and, like so many towns in the area, declined as a result of the Thirty Years' War. It was transferred between neighboring states of Baden-Württemberg and Bavaria, becoming part of the latter in 1810. In response, Bavaria built Neu-Ulm in its territory, on the southern shore of the Danube. World War II bombing caused extensive damage, but there's been considerable restoration work. Today Ulm's Old Town presses against the river; its cobblestone alleys and stone-and-wood bridges over the Blau (a small Danube tributary) in its Fisherman's and Tanner's quarters are especially picturesque.

Ulm's **Münster,** the largest church in southern Germany, was unscathed by bombing. It stands over the huddled medieval gables of old Ulm, visible long before you hit the ugly suburbs encroaching on the Swabian countryside. Its single, filigreed tower challenges stout-hearted tourists to plod 143 meters (472 feet) up 768 steps through the giddily twisting, spiral stone staircase to a spectacular observation point below the spire. The climb may be rewarded by views of the Swiss and Bavarian Alps, 160 kilometers (100 miles) to the south. The Münster was begun in the late-Gothic age (1377) and took five centuries to build, with completion in the neo-Gothic years of the late 19th century. It contains some notable treasures, including fine late-Gothic choir stalls and a Renaissance altar. ⊠ *Münsterpl.* 🔲 *Tower DM 3.50.* ☉ *Daily 9–5. Organ recitals weekdays at 11.*

Ulm's central **Marktplatz** is bordered by handsome medieval houses with stepped gables. A colorful market is held here on Wednesday and Saturday mornings.

The **Rathaus** on Marktplatz has a reproduction of Ludwig Berblinger's flying machine hanging from the ceiling of the central hall. In 1811 Berblinger, a tailor and local eccentric, cobbled together a pair of wings and made a big splash by trying to fly across the river. He didn't make it, but he grabbed a place in German history books. ⊠ *Marktpl. 1.*

The **Ulmer Museum,** on the southern side of Marktplatz, is an excellent natural history and art museum. Exhibits illustrate centuries of development in this part of the Danube Valley, and a modern art section has works by Kandinsky, Klee, Léger, and Roy Lichtenstein. ⊠ *Marktplatz 9.* ☎ *0731/1614330.* 🔲 *DM 5.* ☉ *Tues., Wed., and Fri.–Sun. 11–5, Thurs. 10–8; guided tour on Thurs. at 6.*

Einstein's home was a casualty of an Allied raid and never rebuilt. The **Einstein Monument,** erected in 1979, marks the site. ⊠ *Eastern side of Friedrich-Ebert Str., opposite main railway station.*

German bread is world renowned, so it's not surprising that a national museum is devoted to bread making. The **Deutsches Brotmuseum** is housed in a former salt warehouse, just north of the Münster. It's by no means as crusty or dry as some might fear, with some often-amusing tableaux illustrating how bread has been baked over the centuries. ⊠ *Salzstadelgasse 10,* ☎ *0731/69955.* 🔲 *DM 5.* ☉ *Tues and Thurs.–Sun. 10–5, Wed. 10–8:30.*

A ticket covering entry to Ulm's two museums and other attractions costs DM 8.

NEED A BREAK?	Head back toward Münsterplatz, turning left onto the street called Lautenberg. Here you'll find the **Barfüsser** (⊠ *Lautenberg 1,* ☎ *0731/602–1110*), a brewery-tavern that prepares its own delicious, Swabian variety of pretzels and brews its own beer in a shining copper *Kessel* that forms part of the brick-walled restaurant's decor.

Complete your visit to Ulm with a walk down to the banks of the Danube, where you'll find long sections of the old city wall and fortifications intact. Every four years the river is the scene of one of Germany's strangest festivals, the Ulmer Fischerstechen, in which teams of young men, dressed in historical costume and balancing on narrow canoe-like craft, try to knock each other into the river with long poles—rather like jousting, but from boats. The next festival is scheduled for July 1997.

Dining and Lodging

$$ ✕ **Zunfthaus.** The sturdy, half-timbered Zunfthaus has stood here for more than 500 years, first as a fishermen's pub and now a tavern-restaurant of great charm. Ulm fishermen used the building as their guild headquarters, and when the nearby Danube flooded, the fish swam right up to the door. Today they land on the menu. "Foreign" intruders on the menu include Bavarian white sausage, the *Weisswurst,* which even in Ulm should be eaten by midday. The local beer is an excellent accompaniment. ⊠ *Fischergasse 31,* ☎ *0731/64411. No credit cards.*

\$\$–\$\$\$ ✗🏨 **Hotel-Landgasthof Hirsch.** A barn was converted 100 years ago into this country tavern, which expanded in recent times into a comfortable hotel. In winter a fire burns in the large fireplace of the rustic lounge, while the excellent restaurant is a draw throughout the year. The hotel is 3 kilometers (2 miles) from Ulm, in the Finnigen District, but bus stops are nearby. ✉ *Dorfstr. 4, D-89233 Finningen,* ☎ *0731/70171,* FAX *0731/724–131. 22 rooms with shower. Restaurant, lounge, bowling. AE, DC, MC, V.*

\$\$\$ 🏨 **Inter-City Hotel.** This is one of the newest and smartest of the German Inter-City hotels you'll find at many main railway stations. Although Ulm is a busy rail junction, you won't hear a thing within your soundproof room, and the hotel has the advantage of being located directly in the city center. Rooms have special work corners (with small desks and fax-modem outlets) for visitors who are traveling on business. ✉ *Bahnhofpl. 1,* ☎ *0731/96550, D-89073,* FAX *0731/965–5999. 135 rooms with shower. Restaurant, bar. AE, DC, MC, V.*

Nightlife and the Arts

Ulm has quite a lively after-hours scene. **Crazy Horse** (✉ Lessingstr. 2, Neu-Ulm, ☎ 0731/723875) is one of the best nightclubs this side of Munich, with high-class striptease and cabaret.

The mighty organ of the **Münster** can be heard in special recitals every Sunday at 11:15 from Easter until November.

Numbers in the margin correspond to points of interest on the Romantic Road map.

Augsburg

26 *65 km (39 mi) east of Ulm, 41 km south of Donauwörth, 60 km (36 mi) west of Munich.*

Augsburg is Bavaria's third-largest city, after Munich and Nürnberg. It dates to 15 years before the birth of Christ, when one Drusus, son of the Roman emperor Augustus, set up a military camp here on the banks of the Lech River. The settlement that grew up around it was known as Augusta, a name Italian visitors to the city still call it. It was granted city rights in 1156, and 200 years later the first mention of it can be found in municipal records of the Fugger family, who were to Augsburg what the de' Medicis were to Florence. On your tour of the city you will encounter traces of that extraordinary family at almost every turn.

Touring Augsburg is easy for the visitor because signs on almost every street corner point the way to the city's chief sights. The signs are integrated into three color-charted tours plotted by the tourist office, the Verkehrsverein. The office is on Bahnhofstrasse, the street running into the city center from the main railway station, or Hauptbahnhof.

Numbers in the margin correspond to points of interest on the Augsburg map.

27 The true center of the city is **Maximilianstrasse,** once a medieval wine market and today Augsburg's main shopping street, where the high-gabled, pastel-color facades of the 16th-century merchant houses assert themselves against encroaching post–World War II shops. Most of the city's chief sights are on this thoroughfare or a short walk away. Two monumental and elaborate fountains punctuate the long street. At the north end the Mercury Fountain, designed in 1599 by the Dutch master Adrian de Vries (after a Florentine sculpture by Giovanni da Bologna), shows winged Mercury in his classic pose. Farther up Maximilianstrasse is another de Vries fountain: a bronze Hercules struggling to defeat the many-headed Hydra.

The former home and business quarters of the Fuggers is on the right of Maximilianstrasse as you walk up the slight incline of the street. The 16th-century building now houses a restaurant in its cellar and offices on the upper floors. In the ground-floor entrance are busts of two of Augsburg's most industrious Fuggers, Raymund and Anton. They are tributes from a grateful city to the wealth these merchants brought to the community. Beyond a modern glass door is a quiet courtyard with colonnades, originally reserved for the Fugger women.

28 The **Von Schaezler Stadtpalais** was originally built by a wealthy family, the von Liebenhofens. The 18th-century palace bears the name of a baron who married into the banking family. The von Liebenhofens wanted to outdo the Fugger merchant family—but not at any price. Thus, to save money in an age when property was taxed according to the size of the street frontage, they constructed a long, narrow building running far back from Maximilianstrasse. The palace is composed of a series of interconnecting rooms that lead into a green-and-white rococo ballroom: an extravagant, two-story hall heavily decorated with mirrors, chandeliers, and wall sconces. Marie Antoinette, on her way from Vienna to Paris to marry Louis XVI, was guest of honor at the inauguration ball in 1770.

Descendants of the von Liebenhofens bequeathed the palace to the city of Augsburg after the war; today its rooms contain the **Deutsche Barockgalerie** (German Baroque Gallery), a major art collection that features works of the 17th and 18th centuries. The palace adjoins the former church of a Dominican monastery. A steel door behind the banquet hall of the palace leads into another world of high-vaulted ceilings, where the Bavarian State Collection highlights an exhibition of early Swabian Old Master paintings. Among them is a Dürer portrait of one of the Fuggers. ⊠ *Maximilianstr. 46.* ▢ *DM 4.* ⊙ *May–Sept., Tues.–Fri. 10–1 and 2–5, weekends 11–1 and 2–5; Oct.–Apr., Tues.–Fri. 10–1, weekends 11–1 and 2–4.*

29 The former monastery churches of **Sts. Ulrich and Afra** stand at the highest point of the city. These two churches were built on the site of a Roman cemetery, where St. Afra was martyred in AD 304. The original, Catholic building was begun as a late-Gothic construction in 1467; a Baroque-style preaching hall was added in 1710 as the Protestant church of St. Ulrich. St. Afra is buried in the crypt, near the tomb of St. Ulrich, a 10th-century bishop credited with helping to stop a Hungarian army at the doors of Augsburg in the Battle of the Lech River. The remains of a third patron of the church, St. Simpert, are preserved in one of the church's most elaborate side chapels. From the steps of the magnificent altar, look back along the high nave to the finely carved Baroque wrought-iron and wood railing that borders the entrance. As you leave, pause to look into the separate but adjacent Protestant church of St. Ulrich, the former monastery assembly hall that was taken over and reconstructed by the Lutherans after the Reformation. ⊠ *Ulrichspl. at top of Maximilianstr.* ⊙ *9–dusk.*

30 Many of the city's ancient fortifications are still intact. The **Rotes Tor** (Red Gate), Ausburg's most important medieval entrance gate, once straddled the main trading road to Italy. From here you can follow the traces of the early city fortifications northward and back to the city center, passing the Gothic **Vogeltor** (Bird Gate) astride Oberer Graben.

If you have time and energy, you can continue your tour with a walk along the remains of the city's ancient north and east defenses. At the

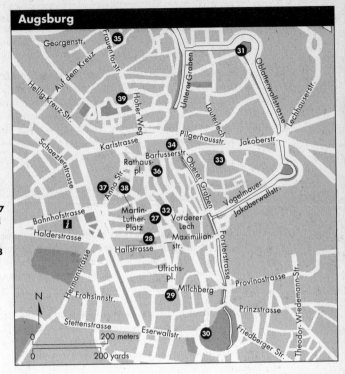

Augsburg

31 Oblatter Wall you can rent a boat and row between the green, leafy banks.

32 Otherwise, retrace your steps to the city center. On the street called Vorderer Lech is **Holbein Haus,** the rebuilt 16th-century home of Hans Holbein the Elder, one of Augsburg's most famous sons (the homes of two others, Leopold Mozart and Bertolt Brecht, are also on our tour). The Holbein Haus is now a city art gallery, with a regularly changing program of exhibitions. ⊠ *Vorderer Lech 20.* ⊙ *May–Oct., Tues., Wed., and Fri.–Sun. 10–5, Thurs. 10–8; Nov.–Apr., Tues., Wed., and Fri.–Sun. 10–4, Thurs. 10–8.*

33 The famous **Fuggerei** is the world's oldest social housing project, established by the Fugger family to accommodate the city's deserving poor. The 147 homes still serve the same purpose; the annual rent of "one Rheinish Guilder" (DM 1.72) hasn't changed, either. Understandably, there's quite a demand to take up residence in this peaceful, leafy estate. There are four requirements: Residents must be Augsburg citizens, Catholic, destitute through no fault of their own, and they must pray daily for their original benefactors, the Fugger family.

NEED A BREAK? If you make a sharp left as you leave the Fuggerei, into Jakobenstrasse, you'll find a welcoming tavern and restaurant, the **Fuggerei Stube** (⊠ Jakoberstr. 26) built into the outside walls of the ancient enclave.

34 Augsburg honors two of its famous sons with museums devoted to their lives and work. The **Brecht Haus** is a modest artisan's house, where the renowned playwright Bertolt Brecht, author of *The Threepenny Opera,* was born. He lived here until he moved to Munich and then, during Hitler's reign, to Scandinavia and later the United States. After the war he settled in East Berlin to direct the Berliner Ensemble. Today the house serves as a memorial center dedicated to Brecht's life and work. ⊠ *Auf dem Rain 7.* ▦ *DM 2.50.* ☉ *May–Sept., Tues.–Fri. 10–1 and 2–5, weekends 11–1 and 2–5; Oct.–Apr., Tues.–Fri. 10–1, weekends 11–1 and 2–4.*

35 The **Mozarthaus** is the birthplace of Leopold Mozart, the father of Wolfgang Amadeus Mozart and an accomplished composer and musician in his own right. A comfortable 17th-century home, it now serves as a Mozart memorial and museum, with some fascinating contemporary documents on the Mozart family. The last Augsburg family connection died just a few years ago. ⊠ *Frauentorstr. 30.* ▦ *DM 2.50.* ☉ *May–Sept., weekdays 10–1 and 2–5, weekends 11–1; Oct.–Apr., weekdays 10–1, weekends 11–1.*

Rathausplatz is the central square of Augsburg, with several attractions, including the 258-foot-high **Perlachturm** (Tower). ☉ *Apr.–Sept., daily 10–6.*

36 The massive, square **Rathaus** (City Hall) on the main square was Germany's largest city hall when it was built during the early 17th century. It remains one of the finest Renaissance structures north of the Alps. ⊠ *Rathauspl.* ▦ *Free.* ☉ *10–6 on days when no official functions are taking place.*

NEED A BREAK? Directly opposite the Rathaus, on the western side of the great square, you'll find the **Cafe Bertele,** a convenient stop for coffee or a meal. Its downstairs café makes delicious pastries and chocolates, while the smart first-floor restaurant serves an excellent lunch.

37 Martin Luther is another name closely associated with Augsburg. In 1518 the recalcitrant monk stayed in **St. Annakirche** (St. Anna's Church), a former Carmelite monastery, during his meetings with Cardinal Cajetanus, the papal legate sent from Rome to persuade the reformist to renounce his heretical views. Luther refused, and the place where he publicly declared his rejection of papal pressure is marked with a plaque on Augsburg's main street, the Maximilianstrasse. Visitors can wander through the quiet cloisters of the former monastery, dating from the 14th century, and view the chapel used by the Fugger family until the Reformation. ⊠ *Annastr., west of Rathauspl.* ☉ *9–dusk.*

38 The **Maximilian-Museum,** across the Rathaus square in front of St. Anna's Church, is the city's chief museum. Its permanent exhibition of Augsburg arts and crafts is housed in a 16th-century merchant's mansion. ⊠ *Phillipine-Welser-Str. 24.* ▦ *DM 4.* ☉ *May–Sept., Tues.–Fri. 10–1 and 2–5, weekends 11–1 and 2–5; Oct.–Apr., Tues.–Fri. 10–1, weekends 11–1 and 2–4.*

★ **39** Augsburg's cathedral, the **Dom St. Maria** (Cathedral of the Virgin Mary), is distinctive in the city's panorama because of its square Gothic towers; it dates from the 9th century, when an Episcopal church stood here. A 10th-century Romanesque crypt, built in the time of Bishop Ulrich, remains from those early years. The heavy bronze doors on the south portal reflect 11th-century craftsmanship; 11th-century windows on the south side of the nave, depicting the prophets Jonah, Daniel, Hosea, Moses, and David, form the oldest cycle of stained glass in central Europe. Five important paintings by Hans Holbein the Elder adorn the altar. The cathedral's treasures are displayed in the Maximilian-Museum, pending the opening of an Episcopal museum in the complex of ancient buildings on Domplatz. ☉ *9–dusk.*

A short walk from the cathedral will take you to the quiet courtyards and small raised garden of the former Episcopal residence, a series of fine 18th-century buildings in Baroque and rococo styles that now serve as the offices of the Swabian regional government. Although less than 64 kilometers (40 miles) from the capital of Bavaria, we're now firmly in Swabia, once such a powerful dukedom under the Hohenstaufens that its territory covered virtually all of present-day Switzerland. Today Swabia has become an administrative district of Bavaria, and Augsburg has yielded the position it once held to the younger city of Munich.

Despite the heavy accent on its history and culture, Augsburg has much to offer young visitors. Children enjoy the fascinating **nature museum and planetarium.** ⊠ *Ludwigstr. 2.* ⊙ *Tues., Wed., and Fri.–Sun. 9–5, Thurs. 9–8.*

At Königsbrunn, just outside Augsburg, is a **lido** with five heated pools, complete with water cannons, chutes, and geysers. ⊒ *2 hrs: DM 14.* ⊙ *Daily 10:30–7:30.*

Dining and Lodging

$$$ ✕ **Zum alten Fischertor.** This is one of the culinary high points along the Romantic Road, offering a mix of regional specialties and French haute cuisine. Try the Swabian dumplings with cuttlefish filling. The Augsburg-style herb soup is also delicious. ⊠ *Pfärrle 14,* ☎ *0821/518–662. Jacket and tie. AE, DC, MC, V. Closed Mon., Aug. 1–19, and Dec. 24–30. No dinner Sun.*

$$ ✕ **Die Ecke.** *Ecke* means "corner," and that describes the location of this attractive and popular restaurant, tucked away behind Augsburg's very fine city hall. Die Ecke is valued for the imaginative variety of its cuisine and the scope of its wine list. In season the venison dishes are among Bavaria's best. Fish—in particular, locally caught trout (the *truit meunière* is magnificent)—is another house specialty. ⊠ *Elias-Holl-Pl. 2,* ☎ *0821/510–600. Reservations essential. AE, DC, MC, V.*

$$ ✕ **Fuggerkeller.** The vaulted cellars of the former Fugger home on Augsburg's historic Maximilianstrasse are now a bright and comfortable restaurant, owned and run by the luxurious Drei Mohren Hotel above it. The midday specials are a particularly good value; try the Swabian-style stuffed cabbage rolls in a spiced meat sauce. Prices for dinner are higher. ⊠ *Maximilianstr. 38,* ☎ *0821/516–260. AE, DC, MC, V. Closed 1st 3 wks in Aug. No dinner Sun.*

$$ ✕ **Welser Kuche.** You can practically hear the great oak tables groan
★ under the eight-course menus of Swabian specialties offered here. You'll need to give a day's notice if you want the eight-course menu, however. Be sure to try spaetzle. ⊠ *Maximilianstr. 83,* ☎ *0821/96110. No lunch.*

$$$$ ✕🛏 **Steigenberger Drei Mohren Hotel.** Kings, princes, even Napoléon slept here; so did the duke of Wellington, who defeated him at Waterloo. The historic hotel, however, takes its name from three very early guests of less renown: Abyssinian bishops who sought shelter in this worldly German city. ⊠ *Maximilianstr. 40, D–86150,* ☎ *0821/50360,* FAX *0821/157864. 100 rooms and 5 suites with bath. Restaurant, bar, beauty salon. AE, DC, MC, V.*

$$–$$$ ✕🛏 **Romantikhotel Augsburger Hof.** A preservation order protects the beautiful Renaissance facade of this charming old Augsburg mansion, the interior of which was completely reconstructed to create a comfortable and up-to-date hotel. The cathedral is around the corner; the town center is a five-minute stroll away. ⊠ *Auf dem Kreuz 2, D–86152,* ☎ *0821/314–083,* FAX *0821/38322. 36 rooms with bath. Restaurant, sauna. AE, DC, MC, V.*

$–$$ ✕⊞ **Gaststätte-Hotel-Pension Jakoberhof.** This sturdy, turreted city mansion has been in the Schoderer family's possession for more than 75 years. One son reigns in the kitchen, while his parents attend to the everyday hotel tasks. The lodging is centrally located and only a few minutes' walk from the famous Fuggerei. Rooms are simply but cheerfully furnished. ⊠ *Jakoberstr. 39–41, D–86150,* ☎ *0821/510–030,* FAX *0821/150–844. 36 rooms, most with bath or shower. Restaurant, bar, beer garden. No credit cards.*

$$$ ⊞ **Hotel am Rathaus.** This hotel derives its name from its unrivaled position, tucked neatly away down a quiet side street, literally within the shadow of Augsburg's superb city hall. The attractive lobby, furnished with deep-seated armchairs, Tiffany lamps, and Oriental rugs, sets the style for the subdued, dark-wood decor of the comfortable rooms, all of which underwent extensive renovation in 1996. ⊠ *Am Hinteren Perlachberg 1, D–86150,* ☎ *0821/509–000,* FAX *0821/517–746. 32 rooms and 1 apartment with bath. AE, DC, MC, V.*

$$–$$$ ⊞ **Dom Hotel.** Just across the street from Augsburg's cathedral, this is a snug, comfortable establishment with a personal touch. Ask for one of the attic rooms, where you'll sleep under beam ceilings and wake to a rooftop view of the city. Recent additions to the hotel include a garden terrace bordering the old city walls and an indoor pool with sauna and solarium. ⊠ *Frauentorstr. 8, D–86152,* ☎ *0821/153–031,* FAX *0821/510–126. 43 rooms with bath or shower. Indoor pool, sauna. AE, DC, MC, V.*

Nightlife and the Arts

Augsburg has chamber and symphony orchestras, as well as a ballet and opera companies. The **Kongresshalle** (⊠ Göggingerstr. 10, ☎ 0821/324–2348) presents music and dance performances from September through July. For information about programs, call 0931/58686. The city stages a Mozart Festival of international stature in September.

Augsburg also has an annual open-air drama season, with the old city walls as a backdrop, in June and July; plays move to the romantic setting of the inner courtyard of the Fugger Palace for part of July and August (for details, ☎ 0821/36604).

☾ Children love the city's excellent **puppet theater** (⊠ Spitalgasse 15, next to the Rotes Tor).

Shopping

Viktoria Passage, an arcade of diverse shops and boutiques opposite the main railway station, has some of Augsburg's best shopping. **Maximilianstrasse,** the city's broad, main street, was once the city's wine market and is now a good shopping area.

TOWARD THE ALPS

South of Augsburg, the Romantic Road climbs gradually into the foothills of the Bavarian Alps, which burst into view between Landsberg and Schongau. The route ends dramatically at the northern wall of the Alps at Füssen, on the Austrian border.

Numbers in the margin correspond to points of interest on the Romantic Road map.

En Route   Leaving Augsburg southward on B–17—the southern stretch of the Romantic Road—you'll drive across the Lech battlefield, where the Hungarian invaders were stopped in 955. Rich Bavarian pastures extend as far as the Lech River, which the Romantic Road meets at the historic town of Landsberg.

Numbers in the margin correspond to points of interest on the Romantic Road map.

Landsberg am Lech

40 *35 km (21 mi) south of Augsburg, 58 km (35 mi) west of Munich.*

Although Landsberg has a colorful history, it is most famous today because of one notorious guest—Adolf Hitler, who wrote much of *Mein Kampf* while in prison there. The town was founded by the Bavarian ruler Heinrich der Löwe (Henry the Lion) during the 12th century and grew wealthy from the salt trade. You'll see impressive evidence of Landsberg's early wealth among the solid old houses packed within its turreted walls; the early 18th-century **Altes Rathaus** (Old Town Hall) is one of the finest in the region.

The German artist Sir Hubert von Herkomer was born in a small village just outside Landsberg. Within the town walls is an unusual monument—not to Sir Hubert (he was knighted in England in 1907) but to his mother, Josefine. It's a romantic, medieval-style tower, bristling with turrets and galleries, built by Sir Hubert. He called it his Mutterturm, or "mother tower." The young Hubert was taken by his parents to the United States and later, when they couldn't settle happily in America, to England. He died in Devon in 1914. A permanent exhibition on the life and work of this remarkable man can be seen within its rough-stone walls. ☎ *Free.* ⏰ *Tues.–Sun. 2–5.*

Schongau

41 *28 km (17 mi) south of Landsberg.*

Schongau, founded in the 11th century at about the same time as Landsberg, has virtually intact wall fortifications, together with towers and gates. In medieval and Renaissance times, the town was an important trading post on the route from Italy to Augsburg. The steeply gabled, 16th-century Ballenhaus was a warehouse before it was elevated to the rank of **Rathaus** (Town Hall).

☼ One of the popular **Märchenwälder** (fairy-tale forests) that dot the German landscape lies 1½ kilometers (1 mile) outside Schongau, suitably set in a wood. It comes complete with mechanical models of fairy-tale scenes, deer enclosures, and an old-time miniature railway. ⊠ *Diessenerstr. 6.* ☎ *DM 4.* ⏰ *Easter–Oct., daily 9–7.*

Dining and Lodging

$$ ☒ **Hotel Holl.** The Holl is a 10-minute stroll from the town center, but it's on wooded slopes, with great views from most rooms—ideal for travelers seeking peace and quiet. The restaurant under the steep eaves of the Alpine-style hotel draws on local rivers and lakes to stock the menu with fresh, imaginative fish dishes. ⊠ *Altenstädter Str. 39, D–86956,* ☎ *08861/4051,* FAX *08861/9843. 22 rooms with bath. Restaurant, recreation room. AE, DC, MC, V.*

$$ ☒ **Hotel Rössle.** Although it was built in 1987, the Rössle has a traditional atmosphere, with old copper lamps lighting up its arched entrance and setting the general tone of this comfortable, friendly hotel. The location, in the Old Town and right next to the Old Town Hall, couldn't be better. ⊠ *Christophstr. 49, D–86956,* ☎ *08861/2305,* FAX *08861/2648. 17 rooms with bath. Restaurant. AE, DC, MC, V.*

Outdoor Activities and Sports

☼ If you're in Schongau during the winter, take a **sleigh ride** (☎ 08362/8581) into the mountains to feed the wild deer. Josef Kotz sets off daily from the Karbrücke Bridge at 2:30.

OFF THE
BEATEN PATH

HOHER PEISSENBERG – The mountains of the Bavarian Alps rise up above the lush meadowland to the south and signal the approaching end of the Romantic Road. Some 15 kilometers (9 miles) east of Schongau (on the B–472) is the first real peak of the Alpine chain, the 3,000-foot-high Hoher Pessenberg. A pilgrimage chapel was consecrated on the mountain in the 16th century; a century later a larger church was added, with a fine ceiling fresco and delicate carvings by local Bavarian masters.

ROTTENBUCH – The small country road B–23 (watch for the turning just before the village of Peissenberg) leads to this town, 13 kilometers (8 miles) south of Schongau. Here the Augustinian order built an impressive monastery on the Ammer River during the 11th century. The Gothic basilica was redecorated in rococo style during the 18th century. The lavish interior of cream, gold, and rose stuccowork and statuary is stunning.

WIESKIRCHE – This church—a glorious example of German rococo architecture—stands in an Alpine meadow just off the Romantic Road near the village of Steingaden, which is 9 kilometers (5 miles) east of Rottenbuch, on the Steingaden road, and is well signposted. The church is open again after four years of extensive restoration work (alarming cracks in the stucco had been caused by low-flying military aircraft). Its yellow-and-white walls and steep red roof are set off by the dark backdrop of the Trauchgauer Mountains. The architect Dominicus Zimmermann, former mayor of Landsberg and creator of much of that town's Rococo architecture, was commissioned in 1745 to build the church on this spot, where six years earlier a local woman claimed to have seen tears running down the face of a picture of Christ. Although the church was dedicated as the Pilgrimage Church of the Scourged Christ, it is now known as the Wieskirche (Church of the Meadow). Visit it on a bright day if you can, when Alpine light streaming through its high windows displays the full glory of the glittering interior. Together with the pilgrimage church of Vierzehnheiligen in north Bavaria, the Wieskirche represents the culmination of German rococo ecclesiastical architecture. As at Vierzehnheiligen, the simple exterior gives little hint of the ravishing interior. A complex oval plan is animated by a series of brilliantly colored stuccos, statues, and gilt. A luminous ceiling fresco completes the decoration. Note the beautifully detailed choir and organ loft. Concerts are presented in the church in the summer. Contact the tourist office (☎ 08861/7216) in Schongau for details. Zimmermann, the architect of the church, is buried in the 12th-century former abbey church of Steingaden. Although his work was the antithesis of Romanesque architecture, he was laid to rest in a dour, late-Romanesque side chapel. 🖼 Free. ☉ 9–dusk.

Schwangau

 18 km (11 mi) south of Steingaden.

The lakeside resort town of Schwangau is an ideal center from which to explore the surrounding mountains. Here you'll encounter the heritage of Bavaria's famous 19th-century king, Ludwig II. Ludwig spent much of his youth at Schloss Hohenschwangau; it is said that its neo-Gothic atmosphere provided the primary influences that shaped the construction of the wildly romantic Schloss Neuschwanstein, the fairy-tale castle Ludwig built across the valley after he became king.

The two castles are a half mile from each other and about 1 mile from the center of Schwangau. Cars and buses are barred from the approach roads, but the 1-mile journey to Neuschwanstein can be made by horse-drawn carriages, which stop in the village of Hohenschwangau. A bus from the village takes a back route to the Aussichtspunkt Jugend; from there it's only a 10-minute walk to the castle. The Schloss Hohenschwangau is a 15-minute walk from the village.

❸ Schloss Hohenschwangau was built by the knights of Schwangau during the 12th century. Later it was remodeled by Ludwig's father, the Bavarian crown prince (and later king) Maximilian, between 1832 and 1836. It was here that the young Ludwig met the composer Richard Wagner. Their friendship shaped and deepened the future king's interest in theater, music, and German mythology—the mythology upon which Wagner drew for his "Ring" cycle of operas. Wagner saw the impressionable Ludwig principally as a potential source of financing for his extravagant operas, rather than as a kindred spirit. For all his lofty idealism, the composer was hardly a man to let scruples interfere with his self-aggrandizement. *DM 8 (including guided tour).* *Apr.–Sept., daily 8:30–5:30; Oct.–Mar., daily 10–4.*

★ **❹ Schloss Neuschwanstein** was conceived by a set designer instead of an architect, thanks to Ludwig's deep love of the theater. The castle soars from its mountainside like a stage creation—it should hardly come as a surprise that Walt Disney took it as the model for his castle in the movie *Sleeping Beauty* and later for the Disneyland castle itself.

The life of the proprietor of this spectacular castle reads like one of the great Gothic mysteries of the 19th century. Here was a king, a member of the Wittelsbach dynasty that had ruled Bavaria since 1180, who devoted his time and energies to creating architectural flights of fancy that came close to bankrupting the Bavarian government. Finally, in 1886, before Neuschwanstein was finished, members of the government became convinced that Ludwig had taken leave of his senses. A medical commission set out to prove that the king was insane and forced him to give up his throne. Ludwig was incarcerated in the much more modest lakeside castle of Berg on the Starnbergersee. Then, on the evening of June 13, 1886, the king and the doctor attending him disappeared. Late that night their bodies were pulled from the lake. The circumstances of their deaths remain a mystery.

The interior of Ludwig's fantasy castle is a fitting setting for this grim tale. His bedroom is tomblike, dominated by a great Gothic-style bed. The throne room is without a throne; Ludwig died before one could be installed. Corridors are outfitted as a ghostly grotto, reminiscent of Wagner's *Tannhäuser*. During the 17 years from the start of construction until his death, the king spent only 102 days in this country residence. Chamber concerts are held at the beginning of September in the gaily decorated minstrels' hall, one room, at least, that was completed as Ludwig conceived it. (Program details are available from the Verkehrsamt, Schwangau, ☎ 08362/81980.) There are some spectacular walks around the castle. Be sure to visit the **Marienbrücke** (Mary's Bridge), spun like a medieval maiden's hair across a deep, narrow gorge. From this vantage point there are giddy views of the castle and the great Upper Bavarian Plain beyond. *Schloss Neuschwanstein (including guided tour) DM 8.* *Apr.–Sept., daily 8:30–5:30; Oct.–Mar., daily 10–4.*

If you plan to visit Hohenschwangau or Neuschwanstein, bear in mind that more than 1 million people pass through the two castles every year. Authorities estimate that on some summer weekends the number of people who tour Neuschwanstein is matched by the number who give up at the prospect of standing in line for up to two hours. If you visit in the summer, get there early. The best time to see either castle without waiting in a long line is a weekday in January, February, or early March. The prettiest time, however, is in the fall.

Dining and Lodging

$$$–$$$$ ✕☎ **Hotel Müller.** Built in 1910, this sturdy family-run hotel retains many of its art-nouveau features, despite extensive renovations over the years. It's ideally located between the Neuschwanstein and Hohenschwangau castles—some rooms have views of both. The rustic-style restaurant has a creative menu, with Bavarian roast meats a good bet. ✉ *Alpseestr. 16, D–87643, Hohenschwangau,* ☎ *08362/81990,* FAX *08362/819–913. 42 rooms and 3 suites, with bath or shower. Restaurant, café. AE, DC, MC, V.*

$$$–$$$$ ✕☎ **König Ludwig.** This handsome Alpine hotel-restaurant, smothered in flowers in summer and in snow in deep winter, is named for the king who felt so at home in these surroundings. The wood-paneled restaurant serves Bavarian fare with an international touch, and venison is a specialty when it's in season. Rooms are cozily furnished in rustic Bavarian style. Room rates include a substantial breakfast buffet. ✉ *Kreuzweg 11–15, D–87645 Schwangau,* ☎ *08362/8890,* FAX *08362/81779. 102 rooms and 36 apartments with bath. Restaurant, pub, indoor and outdoor pools, tennis court, beauty salon, massage, sauna, steam room, bowling, bicycles. No credit cards.*

Nightlife and the Arts

The throne chamber of **Schloss Neuschwanstein** is the magnificent setting for chamber concerts held at regular intervals throughout the year. Call 08362/81980 for program details.

Füssen

45 *5 km (3 mi) southwest of Schwangau.*

Füssen has a beautiful location at the foot of the mountains that separate Bavaria from the Austrian Tyrol—and a notable castle. **Hohes Schloss** is one of the best-preserved late-Gothic castles in Germany. It was built on the site of the Roman fortress that once guarded this Alpine section of the Via Claudia, the trade route from Rome to the Danube. The castle was the seat of Bavarian rulers before Emperor Heinrich VII mortgaged it and the rest of the town to the bishop of Augsburg for 400 pieces of silver. The mortgage was never redeemed, and Füssen remained the property of the Augsburg episcopate until secularization during the early 19th century. The castle was put to good use by the bishops of Augsburg as their summer Alpine residence. It has a spectacular 16th-century Rittersaal (Knights Hall) with a fine carved ceiling and a princes' chamber with a Gothic tiled heating oven. ✉ *Magnuspl. 10.* 🎫 *DM 10.* 🕐 *Daily 10–4.*

The presence, at least in summer, of the bishops of Augsburg ensured that Füssen received an impressive number of Baroque and rococo churches. Füssen's **Rathaus** (Town Hall) was once a Benedictine abbey, built during the 9th century at the site of the grave of St. Magnus, who spent most of his life ministering in Füssen and the surrounding countryside. A Romanesque crypt beneath the Baroque abbey church has a partially preserved 10th-century fresco, the oldest in Bavaria.

In summer, chamber concerts are held in the high-ceiling, Baroque splendor of the abbey's **Fürstensaal** (Princes Hall). Program details are available from the Füssen tourist office (✉ Augsburger Torpl. 1, ☎ 08362/7077).

Füssen's main shopping street was once part of the Roman Via Claudia like Augsburg's Maximilianstrasse. This cobblestone pedestrian walkway is lined with high-gabled medieval houses and backed by the bulwarks of the castle and the easternmost buttresses of the Allgäu Alps.

The Lech River, which has accompanied you for much of the final section of the Romantic Road, rises in those mountains and embraces the town as it rushes northward. One of several lakes in the area, the **Forggensee,** is formed from a broadening of the river. Pleasure boats cruise the lake June–September. *Fares for cruises vary (according to length) from DM 9 to DM 14.*

Dining and Lodging

$ ✕ **Gasthaus zum Schwanen.** This modest, cozy establishment offers good regional cooking with no frills, at low prices. The excellent Swabian *Maultaschen* are made on the premises. ⊠ *Brotmarkt 4,* ☎ *08362/6174. No credit cards. Closed Mon. and Nov. No dinner Sun.*

$$–$$$ ✕🏨 **Alpen-Schlössle.** A *Schlössle* is a small castle. Although this comfortable, rustic hotel and restaurant isn't one, it is on a mountain site, just outside Füssen, that King Ludwig might well have chosen for one of his homes. If wild duck is on the restaurant's menu, don't leave without tasting it. The restaurant is closed Tuesday. There are 11 cozy rooms, richly furnished with Russian pine, larch, and cherry wood. ⊠ *Alatseestr. 28, D–87629,* ☎ *08362/4017,* 🆁🅰🅇 *08362/39847. 11 rooms. Restaurant. No credit cards.*

$$–$$$ ✕🏨 **Hotel Sonne.** The arcaded street level of this sturdy old hotel is part of Füssen's pedestrian shopping zone, and all the town's attractions are just a short walk away. *Sonne* means "sun," and sunny certainly describes the hotel's friendly service and warm atmosphere. Rooms are furnished in a mixture of modern and traditional Bavarian styles. ⊠ *Reichenstr. 37, D–87629,* ☎ *08362/9080,* 🆁🅰🅇 *08362/908100. 32 rooms with bath or shower. Restaurant, café, nightclub. AE, DC, MC, V.*

$–$$ ✕🏨 **Hotel-Schlossgasthof Zum Hechten.** Geraniums flower for most of the year in the balcony boxes in front of the bedroom windows at this comfortable guest house, one of the town's oldest. It has been in the possession of the Pfeiffer family for several generations and is noted for its personalized service. The family's butcher shop provides the meat for the restaurant, where you'll eat at sturdy, round tables within colorfully frescoed walls. ⊠ *Ritterstr. 6, D–87629,* ☎ *08362/7906,* 🆁🅰🅇 *08362/39841. 29 rooms, 24 with bath or shower, 6 apartments. Restaurant, bowling, exercise room, paddle tennis. AE, DC, MC, V.*

THE ROMANTIC ROAD A TO Z

Arriving and Departing

By Bus

From April until the end of October, daily bus service covers the northern stretch of the Romantic Road, leaving Frankfurt at 8 AM and arriving in Munich at 8 PM. A second bus covers the section of the route between Dinkelsbühl and Füssen. Buses leave Dinkelsbühl daily at 4:15 PM and arrive in Füssen at 9 PM. In the other direction, also from April until the end of October, buses leave Füssen daily at 8 AM, arriving in Dinkelsbühl at 1:05 PM. Buses leave Munich daily at 9 AM and arrive in Frankfurt at 8:30 PM. All buses stop at the major sights along the road. Reservations are essential; contact **Deutsche Touring GmbH** (⊠ Am Römerhof 17, D–60486 Frankfurt/Main, ☎ 069/790–3256). Local buses cover much of the route but are infrequent and slow.

By Car

The northernmost city of the Romantic Road—and the natural starting point for a tour—is Würzburg on the Frankfurt–Nürnberg Autobahn. It's 115 kilometers (72 miles) from Frankfurt and 280 kilometers (175 miles) from Munich. Augsburg, the largest city on the Romantic Road, is 70 kilometers (44 miles) from Munich and 365 kilometers (228 miles) from Frankfurt. Full information on the Romantic Road is available from **Tourist Information Land an der Romantischen Strasse** (✉ Kreisverkehrsamt, Crailsheimerstr. 1, D–91522 Ansbach, ☎ 0981/4680) or from **Arbeitsgemeinschaft Romantische Strasse** (✉ Marktpl., D–91550 Dinkelsbühl, ☎ 09851/90271).

By Plane

The major international airports serving the Romantic Road are Frankfurt, at its north end, and Munich, at its south end. Regional airports include Nürnberg, Stuttgart, and Augsburg, home base of the private airline Interot.

By Train

Both Würzburg and Augsburg are on the InterCity and high-speed InterCity Express routes and have fast, frequent service to and from Frankfurt, Munich, Stuttgart, and Hamburg. Less frequent trains link most of the other major towns of the Romantic Road.

Getting Around

By Boat

Three shipping companies offer excursions on the Main River from Würzburg. The **Fränkische Personenschiffahrt** (✉ Kranenkai 1, ☎ 0931/51722) and the **Würzburger Personenschiffahrt Kurth and Schiebe** (✉ Am Alten Kranen, ☎ 0931/58573) operate excursions to the vineyards in and around Würzburg; wine tasting is included in the price. Fränkische Personenschiffahrt (FPS for short) also offers cruises of up to two weeks on the Main, Neckar, and Danube rivers, and on the Main–Danube Canal. **Kurth and Schiebe** and **Veitschöchheimer Personenschiffahrt** (✉ Am Alten Kranen, ☎ 0931/55633) offer daily service to Veitschöchheim, site of the palace that was once the summer residence of the bishops of Augsburg. Passenger service on the most romantic section of the Main, between Lohr and Miltenberg, is operated by a Wertheim line, the Wertheimer (✉ Personenschiffahrt, ☎ 09342/1414).

By Car

The Romantic Road is most easily traveled by car, starting from Frankfurt or Würzburg as outlined above and following the B–27 country highway south to meet roads B–290, B–19, B–292, and along the Wörnitz River on B–25.

Contacts and Resources

Car Rentals

Avis: ✉ Klinkerberg 31, ☎ 0821/38241, **Augsburg**; ✉ Nürnbergerstr. 107, ☎ 0931/200–3939, **Würzburg.**

Europcar: ✉ Pilgerhausstr. 24, ☎ 0821/312–033, **Augsburg**; ✉ Am Hauptbahnhof (at the main railway station), ☎ 0931/12060 **Würzburg.**

Hertz: ✉ Steinerne Furt 76, ☎ 0821/700–8101, **Augsburg**; ✉ Höchbergerstr. 10, ☎ 0931/415–221, **Würzburg.**

Sixt-Budget: ✉ Meierweg 3, ☎ 0821/412003, **Augsburg**; ✉ Rottendorferstr. 46, ☎ 0931/72093, **Würzburg.**

Emergencies

Police: ☎ 110.

Fire and urgent medical aid: ☎ 112.

Guided Tours

BUS TOURS

From April through October, the **Deutsche Touring** company (☞ Arriving and Departing by Bus, *above*) operates four tours of one to three days' duration to Rothenburg and sections of the Romantic Road. Prices vary from DM 435 (for a tour including one night in Rothenburg) to DM 1,085 (with overnights in Rothenburg and Heidelberg).

CITY TOURS

All the cities and towns on the Romantic Road offer guided tours, either on foot or by bus. Details are available from the local tourist information offices. Following is a sample of the more typical tours.

In **Würzburg,** guided tours on foot and by bus (in German) start at the tourist office at 10:30 AM Monday through Saturday, early April through October. Tours in English are given Tuesday to Saturday at 11 AM from early April through October. The German-language tour costs DM 8 and the English-language tour is DM 12. The latter tour includes a visit to the Residenz.

Augsburg has self-guided walking tours, with routes of varying lengths posted on color-coded signs throughout the downtown area. A daily bus tour starts out from the Rathaus at 10:30 from May through October. The cost is DM 12. Tours on foot set out from the Rathaus daily at 2 PM, May–October.

Rothenburg-ob-der-Tauber's night watchman, dressed in traditional garb, conducts visitors on a nightly tour of the town, leading the way with a lantern. Tours in English begin at 8 PM from April through December and cost DM 4. There is also a daytime tour at 1:30 (April–October), also costing DM 4. The night watchman in **Dinkelsbühl** does a nightly round at 9 PM from April through October, and though he doesn't give official tours, he is always happy to answer questions from inquisitive visitors (but don't expect a reply in fluent English). Daily guided tours of Dinkelsbühl in horse-drawn carriages (April–October) are a fun way to see the little town; the cost is DM 8.

Ulm has a 90-minute guided tour offered by the tourist office, including a visit to the Münster, the Old Town Hall, the Fischerviertel, and the Danube riverbank. From May through October there are tours at 10 and 2:30 Monday–Saturday, 11 and 2:30 Sunday and public holidays; from November to April, tours are at 10 on Saturday and 11 on Sunday. The departure point is the tourist information office at Münsterplatz; the cost is DM 7.

TRAIN TOURS

The **Deutsche Bahn** (German Railways) offers special weekend excursion rates covering travel from most German railroad stations to Würzburg and hotel accommodations for up to four nights. Details are available at any train station.

Outdoor Activities and Sports

GOLF

Augsburg Golf Club (☎ 08234/5621) welcomes visiting members of overseas golf clubs. For scenery and a mild challenge, try the nine-hole course at **Schloss Colberg** (☎ 09803/615). It's 20 kilometers (12 miles) east of Rothenburg. There are also attractive nine-hole courses at Aschaffenburg (✉ Am Heigenberg, Hösbach-Feldkahl, ☎ 06024/4666),

Würzburg (⊠ Rottendorfer Str. 16, ☎ 0931/71092), and just outside Landsberg, at Schloss Igling (☎ 08248/1003).

Contact **Kanu-Laden in Donauwörth** (⊠ Alte Augsburger Str., ☎ 0906/8086) in Krezschmer about water sports opportunities in the area.

If you're visiting the lakes around Füssen, **Selbach Bootsvermietung** has several boathouses, two of which, Hopfensee and Weissensee (☎ 08362/7164), rent dinghies and Windsurfers. For boats and Windsurfers on the larger Forggensee, try the **Yachtschule Gruber und Jürgensen** (☎ 08367/471).

Visitor Information

A central tourist office based in Dinkelsbühl covers the entire Romantic Road: the **Touristik-Arbeitsgemeinschaft Romantische Strasse** (⊠ Marktpl., D–91550 Dinkelsbühl, ☎ 09851/90271, ℻ 09851/90279). The office produces a color brochure describing all the main towns and attractions along the Romantic Road.

Amorbach: Verkehrsamt, ⊠ Altes Rathaus, D–63916, ☎ 09373/20940.

Aschaffenburg: ⊠ Dalbergstr. 6, D–63739, ☎ 06021/395800.

Augsburg: Verkehrsverein, ⊠ Bahnhofstr. 7, D–86150, ☎ 0821/ 502–070.

Dinkelsbühl: Tourist-Information, ⊠ Marktpl., D–91550, ☎ 09851/90240.

Donauwörth: Städtisches Verkehrsamt, ⊠ Rathausgasse 1, D–86607, ☎ 0906/789–145.

Feuchtwangen: Fremdenverkehrsamt, ⊠ Marktpl. 1, D–91555, ☎ 09852/90444.

Füssen: Kurverwaltung, ⊠ Kaiser-Maximilian-Pl. 1, D–87629, ☎ 08362/7077.

Harburg: Fremdenverkehrsverein, ⊠ Schlossstr. 1, D–86655, ☎ 09003/96990.

Landsberg am Lech: Fremdenverkehrsamt, ⊠ Hauptpl. 1, D–89896, ☎ 08191/128–246.

Mespelbrunn: ⊠ Hauptstr. 173, D–63875, ☎ 06092/319.

Nördlingen: Städtisches Verkehrsamt, ⊠ Marktpl. 2, D–86720, ☎ 09081/84116.

Rothenburg-ob-der-Tauber: Tourist-Information, Rathaus, ⊠ Marktpl. 2, D–91541, ☎ 09861/40492.

Schongau: Verkehrsverein, ⊠ Münzstr. 5, D–86956, ☎ 08861/7216.

Schwangau: Kurverwaltung, Rathaus, ⊠ Münchenerstr. 2, D–87645, ☎ 08362/81980.

Ulm: Tourist-Information, ⊠ Münsterpl. (Stadthaus), D–89073 Ulm/Donau, ☎ 0731/161–2830.

Wertheim: ⊠ Am Spitzen Turm, D–97877, ☎ 09342/1066.

Würzburg: Fremdenverkehrsamt, ⊠ Am Congress-Centrum, D–97070, ☎ 0931/37335.

6 Franconia

A predominantly rural area, Franconia was most important politically in the days of the Holy Roman Empire. You'll want to see its beautiful and historic towns: Coburg, Bayreuth, Bamberg, Nürnberg, and Regensburg. Wagner fans especially shouldn't miss Bayreuth, where the great composer settled and built his theater. The annual festival that honors him brings other town functions to a halt every summer.

THE ANCIENT KINGDOM OF THE FRANKS is known today as Franconia or, in German, Franken. Although it's mainly rural, the castles and architecturally rich towns provide a solid reminder of the region's past importance in the Holy Roman Empire. It was only in the early 19th century, following Napoléon's conquest of what is now southern Germany, that the area was incorporated into northern Bavaria. Modern Franconia stretches from the Bohemian Forest on the Czech border in the east to the outskirts of Frankfurt in the west. But its heart—and the focal point of this tour—is an area known as the Fränkisches Schweiz (the Franconian Switzerland), bounded by Nürnberg (Nuremberg) on the south, Bamberg on the west, and the cultural center of Bayreuth on the east.

Despite its beauty and history, Franconia is not a mainstream tourist destination; many Germans simply drive straight through on their way south. But the region rates high with epicures in search of authentic German regional cuisine. It is also noted for its liquid refreshments, from both the grape and the grain. Franconian white wine, usually sold in distinctive stubby bottles called *Bocksbeutel,* is renowned as one of the driest in Germany. And the region has the largest concentration of village breweries in the world, producing a wide range of brews, the most distinctive of which is the dark and heady smoked *Rauchbier.*

Pleasures and Pastimes

Dining

Franconia offers a wide range of dining possibilities, though *Gasthäuser*—inns where the food is simple but filling and cheap—are definitely preponderant. Virtually all of them have inexpensive lunchtime menus. Traditional dishes worth trying include sauerbraten, *Schweinshaxe* (pork knuckle), and the omnipresent *Knödeln* (dumplings). The region has the largest concentration of small breweries in all Germany (Bamberg alone has 10, Bayreuth 7), so you should be able to get the local brew wherever you're staying. The banks of the river Main produce one of Germany's top wines, the Franken white, which comes in the familiar bulbous green bottles.

CATEGORY	COST*
$$$$	over DM 90
$$$	DM 55–DM 90
$$	DM 35–DM 55
$	under DM 35

per person for a three-course meal, including sales tax and excluding drinks and service charge

Hiking

The wild stretches of forest and numerous nature parks in northern Franconia make this ideal hiking country. There are more than 25,000 miles of hiking trails, with the greatest concentration in the Altmühltal Nature Park, Germany's largest, and in the Frankenwald.

Lodging

Make reservations well in advance for hotels in all the larger towns and cities if you plan to visit anytime between June and September. If you're visiting Bayreuth during the annual Wagner Festival in July and August, consider making reservations up to a year in advance. And remember, too, that during the festival prices can be double the normal rates. Standards of comfort and cleanliness are high throughout the

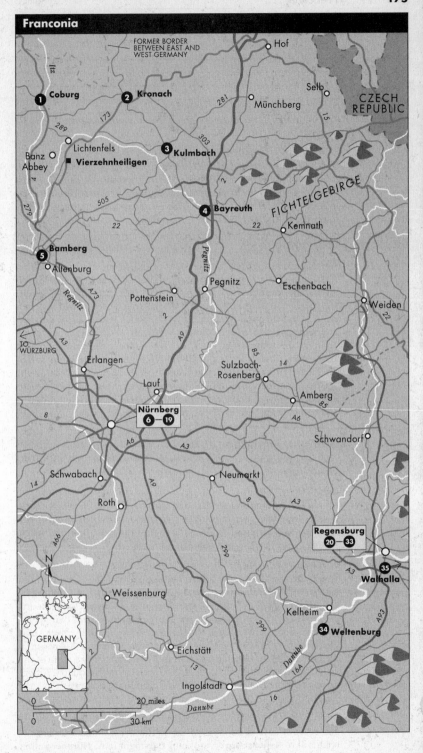

Franconia

FORMER BORDER
BETWEEN EAST AND
WEST GERMANY

Hof

① Coburg

② Kronach

Selb

Münchberg

CZECH
REPUBLIC

Lichtenfels

Banz
Abbey

Vierzehnheiligen

③ Kulmbach

FICHTELGEBIRGE

④ Bayreuth

Kemnath

⑤ Bamberg

Altenburg

Pegnitz

Pegnitz

Eschenbach

Weiden

Pottenstein

TO
WÜRZBURG

Erlangen

Sulzbach-
Rosenberg

Lauf

Amberg

Nürnberg

⑥—⑲

Schwandorf

Schwabach

Neumarkt

Roth

Regensburg

⑳—㉝

N

㉟
Walhalla

Weissenburg

GERMANY

Kelheim

㉞ Weltenburg

Eichstätt

Ingolstadt

Danube

0   20 miles

0   30 km

region, whether you stay in a simple pension or in a modern, international chain hotel.

CATEGORY	COST*
$$$$	over DM 200
$$$	DM 160–DM 200
$$	DM 120–DM 160
$	under DM 120

All prices are for two people in a double room, excluding service charges.

Skiing

The highest peaks of Franconia's upland region, the Fichtelgebirge and Frankenwald, rarely top 1,000 meters (3,300 feet), but their exposed location in central Germany assures them good snow conditions most winters. Cross-country skiers also make for this region because of its lack of mass tourism. Whether Alpine-style or cross-country, the skiing is cheap and ideally suited for families.

Exploring Franconia

Although many proud Franconians would dispute it, this historic homeland of the Franks, one of the oldest Germanic peoples, is unmistakably part of Bavaria. Its southern border areas end at the Danube and merge into Lower Bavaria and the Bavarian Forest, while its northern border is marked by the river Main, which is seen as the dividing line between northern and southern Germany. Despite its extensive geographic spread, however, Franconia is a homogenous region of rolling agricultural landscapes and thick forests climbing to the mountains of the Fichtelgebirge. You'll most likely pass through Franconia on the way to somewhere else, although a well-planned tour can be the highlight of any German holiday. Franconian towns like Bayreuth, Coburg, and Bamberg are practically places of cultural pilgrimage, while rebuilt Nürnberg is the epitome of German medieval beauty.

Great Itineraries

Numbers in the text correspond to numbers in the margin and on the Franconia map.

IF YOU HAVE 3 DAYS

Make 🏙 **Nürnberg** ⑥ your base and take day trips on each of the three days to **Bayreuth** ④ (an imperative visit whether or not it's Wagner Festival season); **Bamberg** ⑤, once the seat of the most powerful ruling families in the country; and **Coburg** ①, home of the royal Saxe-Coburgs.

IF YOU HAVE 5 DAYS

Spend the first three days following the itinerary above, making day trips from 🏙 **Nürnberg** ⑥ to **Bayreuth** ④, **Bamberg** ⑤, and **Coburg** ①. On the third and fourth days, stop overnight at 🏙 **Coburg.** On the fourth day take side trips to **Banz Abbey** and **Vierzehnheiligen,** two mighty churches that stand facing each other across a valley of the river Main. On the fifth day follow the Main upstream from Coburg to **Kulmbach** ③, the beer capital of Germany, a charming town that brews more of this alcoholic beverage per capita than anywhere else in the country. Among its several brands is reputedly the world's strongest brew.

IF YOU HAVE 7 DAYS

Begin by following the five-day itinerary above. Plan to spend your sixth and seventh days continuing to the southwest from 🏙 **Kulmbach** to medieval 🏙 **Regensburg** ⑳, stopping overnight in 🏙 **Nürnberg** along the way. At Regensburg, you'll meet the already broad Danube at the 12th-century **Steinerne Brücke** (Stone Bridge). From Regensburg, you may embark on boat tours between towering limestone cliffs to the great abbey church of **Weltenburg** ㉞ and to Germany's 19th-century hall of fame, the Doric temple at **Walhalla** ㉟.

When to Visit Franconia

Summer is the best time to explore Franconia, though spring and fall can also be good seasons to visit if the weather cooperates. In spring the leaves of the deciduous trees in the extensive forests take on several shades of emerald to contrast with the deep greens of the various all-weather firs. In the fall travelers enjoy the russet hues of the regional foliage. Avoid the cold and wet month of November, and January and February, unless you wish to come here to ski. If you're around in Nürnberg in December, you may shop at one of Germany's largest and loveliest Christmas markets.

NORTHERN FRANCONIA

Three major German cultural centers lie within this region of Franconia: Coburg, a town that can claim a blood link with royal dynasties throughout Europe; Bamberg, a lovely old city with its own claim to German regal history; and Bayreuth, the town where composer Richard Wagner finally settled and a place of musical pilgrimage for Wagner fans from all over the world.

Numbers in the margin correspond to points of interest on the Franconia map.

Coburg

❶ *105 km (63 mi) north of Nürnberg.*

Coburg is a treasure—and a surprisingly little-known one—whether it's glittering under the summer sky or frosted white with the snows of winter. It was founded in the 11th century and remained in the possession of the dukes of Saxe-Coburg-Gotha until 1918; the present duke still lives there. In fact, it's as the home of the remarkable Saxe-Coburgs, as they are generally known, that the town is most famous. Superficially just one among dozens of German ruling families, they established themselves as something of a royal stud farm, providing a seemingly inexhaustible supply of blue-blood marriage partners to ruling houses the length and breadth of Europe. The most famous of these royal mates was Prince Albert. He married Queen Victoria, after which she gained special renown in Coburg: Legend has it that on a visit to her new husband's hometown, she had the first flush toilet in Germany installed. Whether apocryphal or not, Albert and Victoria were a prolific pair. Their numerous children, married off among more of Europe's kings, queens, and emperors, helped to spread the tried-and-tested Saxe-Coburg stock even farther afield.

Coburg's **Marktplatz,** the main square, has a statue of Prince Albert, the high-minded consort, proudly standing surrounded by gracious Renaissance and Baroque buildings. The **Rathaus** (Town Hall), begun in 1500, is the most imposing structure on Marktplatz. A forest of ornate gables and spires projects from its well-proportioned facade. Look at the statue of the **Bratwurstmännla** on the building; the staff he carries is claimed to be the official length against which the town's famous bratwurst sausages are measured. If this sounds to you like guidebook babble, convince yourself otherwise by trying a bratwurst from one of the stands in the square, which sell them Monday–Saturday.

Schloss Ehrenburg, the ducal palace, is situated on Coburg's second main square, Schlossplatz. Built in the mid-16th century, it has been greatly altered over the years, principally following a fire in the early

19th century. The then-duke took the opportunity to rebuild the palace in a heavy Gothic style. It was in this dark and imposing heap that Prince Albert spent much of his childhood. The throne room; the Hall of Giants, named for the larger-than-life statues that support the stuccoed ceiling; and the Baroque-style chapel can all be visited. ⊠ *Schlosspl.,* ☎ *09561/80880.* ☎ *DM 4.* ☉ *Tours Apr.–Sept., Tues.–Sun. at 10, 11, 1:30, 2:30, 3:30, and 4:30; Oct.–Mar., Tues.–Sun. same hrs, except no 4:30 tour.*

🖑 **Coburger Puppenmuseum,** Coburg's doll museum, is a favorite with children. ⊠ *Rückertstr. 2, next to Schloss Ehrenburg,* ☎ *09561/74047.* ☎ *DM 4.* ☉ *Daily 10–5.*

The **Veste Coburg** fortress, one of the largest and most impressive in the country, is Coburg's main attraction. The brooding bulk of the castle lies on a small hill above the town. The first buildings were constructed around 1055, but with progressive rebuilding and remodeling through the centuries, today's predominantly late-Gothic/early Renaissance edifice bears little resemblance to the original rude fortress. It contains a number of museums. See the **Fürstenbau,** or Palace of the Princes, where Martin Luther was sheltered for six months in 1530. Among the main treasures are paintings by Cranach, Dürer, Rembrandt, and Cranach (again) are all represented at the **Kunstsammlungen,** the art museum in the fortress, as are many examples of German silver, porcelain, arms and armor, and furniture. Finally, there's the **Herzoginbau,** the duchess's building, a sort of 18th-century transportation museum, with carriages and ornate sleighs for speeding in style through the winter snows. ☎ *09561/8790. Castle:* ☉ *Apr.–Oct., Tues.–Sun. 9:30–5; Nov.–Mar., Tues.–Sun. 2–5. Kunstsammlungen and Herzoginbau:* ☎ *DM 4;* ☉ *Apr.–Oct., Tues.–Sun. 9:30–1 and 2–5; Nov.–Mar., Tues.–Sun. 2–5. Fürstenbau:* ☎ *DM 4.* ☉ *Apr.–Oct., Tues.–Sun. 9:30–noon and 2–4; Nov.–Mar., Tues.–Sun. 2–3:30; tours conducted every ½ hr.*

The **Naturkunde-museum** (Natural History Museum) is now found in the former palace gardens, the Hofgarten. This is the country's leading museum of its kind, with more than 8,000 exhibits of flora and fauna, as well as geological, ethnological, and mineralogical specimens. ⊠ *Veste Coburg,* ☎ *09561/75068.* ☎ *DM 2.* ☉ *Daily 9–noon and 1–5.*

NEED A BREAK?	In the **Burgschänke** (☎ 09561/75153), Veste Coburg's own tavern, you can soak up the history of centuries while sampling a Coburg beer and one of the traditional dishes from the basic but appetizing menu. The tavern is closed Mondays and January–mid-February.

OFF THE BEATEN PATH	**NEUSTADT –** This town north of Coburg is a center of toy and doll making. Its **Museum der Deutschen Spielzeugindustrie** (Museum of the German Toy Industry) shows how toys were made throughout the centuries, providing a fascinating diversion for a rainy afternoon. ⊠ *Hindenburgpl. 1,* ☎ *09568/5600.* ☎ *DM 5.* ☉ *Mon.–Sun. 10–5.*
	SCHLOSS ROSENAU – Halfway between Coburg and Neustadt is this 550-year-old castle in which Prince Albert was born in 1819. In an English-style park beside the Itz River near the village of Rödental, 9 kilometers (6 miles) north of Coburg, the castle was restored in 1990 and opened to the public. A mix of architectural styles ranging from Renaissance to neo-Gothic, the castle features furniture made especially for the Saxe-Coburg family by noted Viennese craftsmen and other pieces from the period of Albert's youth. One room houses exhibits devoted to Victoria and Albert.

Dining and Lodging

$$$$ ✕ **Coburger-Tor Restaurant Schaller.** This hotel-restaurant provides surprisingly upscale dining in softly lit and distinctly well-upholstered quarters just south of the city center. The food is sophisticated nouvelle, with such offerings as wild-duck breasts in sherry sauce and stuffed dates with nougat sauce. ✉ *Ketschendorfer Str. 22,* ☎ *09561/25074. Reservations essential. Jacket and tie. No credit cards. Closed Sun.*

$$ ✕ **Ratskeller.** An entirely different experience is offered in the stone vaults of this establishment, the sort of emphatically Teutonic place where local specialties always taste better. Try the sauerbraten, along with a glass of crisp Franken white wine. ✉ *Markt 1,* ☎ *09561/92400. No credit cards.*

$ ✕ **Goldenes Kreuz.** In business since 1477, this restaurant has all the
★ rustic decor you'll ever want to accompany large portions of equally authentic Franconian food. Goose with dumplings provides a hearty experience. Nouvelle cuisine it is not. ✉ *Herrngasse 1,* ☎ *09561/90473. No credit cards.*

$$$ ✕⌂ **Blankenburg Parkhotel.** North of the town center, this modern
★ hotel, an excellent value, encourages families with the offer of free lodging for children up to age 15 sharing their parents' room. A leafy park is the hotel's peaceful setting, and in summer breakfast is served on a sunny terrace. The stylish Kräutergarten restaurant has become noted for its gourmet fare. Admission to an adjoining indoor swimming and wave pool is free to guests. ✉ *Rosenauerstr. 30, D–96450,* ☎ *09561/75005,* FAX *09561/75674. 44 rooms and 2 suites with bath. Restaurant. AE, DC, MC, V.*

$$$ ✕⌂ **Romantic Hotel Goldene Traube.** Book a room overlooking the square, and on summer evenings you can fall asleep to the splash of the fountain named after Queen Victoria. The hotel feels such a strong link with Britain's former queen and empress that it even named its bar after her. The rooms are comfortable and all have cable TV. A recent addition is a sauna complex with solarium. ✉ *Am Viktoriabrunnen 2, D–96450,* ☎ *09561/8760,* FAX *09561/876–222. 77 rooms with bath or shower. Restaurant, bar, sauna, steam room, exercise room, miniature golf, bicycles. AE, MC, V.*

Nightlife and the Arts

Coburg's **Landestheater** has an opera season, from October through mid-July. Call 09561/92742 (from 9 to 1) for tickets.

Shopping

Coburg is a culinary delight, famous for its *Schmätzen* (gingerbread) and *Elizenkuchen* (almond cake). You'll find home-baked versions in any of the many excellent patisseries or at a Grossman store (there are three in Coburg).

En Route From Coburg avoid the main highway east to Bayreuth and take the smaller road (Number 289) to Lichtenfels, just across the Main River (a little town worth visiting because of its basket-weaving tradition). On the opposite heights, across the Main, are probably the two most remarkable churches in Franconia. **Banz Abbey** stands high above the Main on what some call the "holy mountain of Bavaria." There had been a monastery here since 1069, but the present buildings—now a political-seminar center and think tank—date from the end of the 17th century. The highlight of the complex is the **Klosterkirche** (Abbey Church), the work of architect and stuccoist Johann Dientzenhofer. Its two massive onion-dome towers soar above the restrained yellow sandstone facade. Note the animated statues of saints set in niches, a typical Baroque device. Inside, the church shimmers and glows with lustrous rococo decoration. ☉ *Apr.–Sept., daily 8:30–11:30 and 1–5:30; Oct.–Mar., Mon.–Sat. 8:30–11:30 and 1–4:30.*

★ From the terrace of Banz Abbey there's a striking view over the Main to **Vierzehnheiligen.** What you see is probably the single most ornate Rococo church in Europe, although you might not know it just from the exterior. There are those same onion-dome towers and the same lively curving facade, but little to suggest the almost explosive array of paintings, stucco, gilt, statuary, and rich rosy marble inside. The church was built by Balthasar Neumann (architect of the Residenz at Würzburg; ☞ Chapter 5) between 1743 and 1772 to commemorate a vision of Christ and 14 saints—*Vierzehnheiligen* means "14 saints"—that appeared to a shepherd in 1445. Your first impression will be of the richness of the decoration and the brilliance of the coloring, the whole more like some fantastic pleasure palace than a place of worship. Notice the way the entire building seems to be in motion—almost all the walls are curved—and how the walls and ceiling are alive with delicate stucco. In much the same way that builders of Gothic cathedrals aimed to overwhelm through scale and verticality, Neumann wanted to startle worshipers through light, color, and movement. Anyone who has seen the gaunt Romanesque cathedrals of Protestant northern Germany will have little difficulty understanding why the Reformation was never able to gain more than a toehold in Catholic southern Germany. Few buildings in Europe are more uplifting.

Kronach

❷ *13 km (8 mi) from Lichtenfels.g*

Kronach is a delightful small medieval town (take the signposted junction just outside the village of Hochstadt). It was here that Renaissance master painter Lucas Cranach the Elder was born at the end of the 15th century; you can visit his house at Marktplatz 1. A cluster of half-timbered buildings and a fine Renaissance Town Hall complete the appeal of this flower-strewn square. Outside the town, visit the **Rosenberg fortress.** ▨ *DM 2.* ☉ *Guided tours Tues.–Sun. at 11 and 2.*

Kulmbach

❸ *32 km (20 mi) from Lichtenfels.*

Kulmbach, a pretty market town on the Main, has a claim to fame that belies its size. In a country in which the brewing and drinking of beer breaks all records, this town produces more per capita than anywhere else in Germany: 9,000 pints per man, woman, and child. A quarter of the workforce in Kulmbach earns a living directly or indirectly from beer. As if to show the town didn't have *enough* breweries, a new one began production in 1994.

Kulmbach celebrates its beer every year in a nine-day festival that starts on the last Saturday in July. The main festival site, a mammoth tent, is called the Festspulhaus—literally "festival-house"—a none-too-subtle dig at nearby Bayreuth and its Festspielhaus, where Wagner's operas are performed.

The **Erste Kulmbacher Union brewery,** one of Kulmbach's six breweries, produces the strongest beer in the world—the *Doppelbock* Kulminator 28—which takes nine months to brew and has an alcohol content of more than 11%. The cost of a tour here is more than offset: At the end of the tour you're served a beer and a snack, *and* you walk away with a gift pack of six beers, two EKU glasses, and a handsome bottle opener! ⊠ *EKU-Str. 1,* ☎ *09221/882–283.* 🎦 *Tours DM 10.* 🕭 *Mon.–Thurs., on a reservation-only basis.*

The **Mönchshof-Bräu Brewery** has a museum. The cost of its tour is returned as a voucher to spend in the Kulmbacher Reichelbräu brewery's tavern (⊠ Lichtenfelser Str., ☎ 09221/705–225). ⊠ *Hofer Str. 20,* ☎ *09221/4264.* 🎦 *Tour DM 10.*

Another special local brew is *Eisbock,* which is frozen as part of the brewing process to make it stronger. The locals claim it's the sparkling clear spring water from the nearby Fichtelgebirge hills that makes their beer so special.

NEED A | The **Kupferpfanne** (⊠ Klostergasse 7) tavern-restaurant serves some of
BREAK? | Kulmbach's less potent brews on draft, plus a good selection of local dishes. Buy a bottle of Kulminator 28 as a souvenir.

Kulmbach, however, is much more than beer, beer, and more beer. The Old Town, for example, contains a warren of narrow streets that merit exploration. The **Plassenburg,** the town's castle and symbol, is the most important Renaissance castle in the country. It's on a rise overlooking Kulmbach, a 20-minute hike from the Old Town. The first building here, begun in the mid-12th century, was torched by marauding Bavarians who were anxious to put a stop to the ambitions of Duke Albrecht Alcibiades—a man who apparently had few scruples when it came to self-advancement, and who spent several years murdering, plundering, and pillaging his way through Franconia. His successors built today's castle, starting in about 1560. Externally, there's little to suggest the graceful Renaissance interior, but as you enter the main courtyard, the scene changes abruptly. The tiered space of the courtyard is covered with precisely carved figures, medallions, and other intricate ornaments, the whole comprising one of the most remarkable and delicate architectural ensembles in Europe. Inside, you may want to see the **Deutsches Zinnfigurenmuseum** (Tin Figures Museum), with more than 300,000 ministatuettes, the largest collection of its kind in the world. ☎ *069221/ 5550.* 🎦 *DM 3.* 🕭 *Apr.–Sept., Tues.–Sun. 10–5; Oct.–Mar., Tues.–Sun. 10–3.*

OFF THE | **NEUENMARKT –** Young railway fans are fascinated by Germany's "rail-
BEATEN PATH | way village," near Kulmbach. More than 20 beautifully preserved, gleaming old locomotives huff and puff here in a living railroad museum. A functioning 60-year-old restaurant car will take care of your appetite.

Dining and Lodging

$$$–$$$$ ✕🏨 **Romantik Posthotel.** This traditional country hotel, owned and run by the same family since 1870, is an excellent base from which to explore the area as well as an ideal getaway. It has a discreetly friendly and cozy atmosphere, whether you're relaxing in the gardens, at the putting green, in the library, at the rustic restaurant—or at the whirlpool. The newly enlarged spa gets tired muscles into action after a day in the country. The hotel is in the quiet village of Wirsberg, 5 kilometers (3 miles) east of Kulmbach. ⊠ *Markt 11, D–95339,* ☎ *09227/2080,* FAX *09227/5860. 35 rooms, 12 suites, and apartments with bath. Bar, café, hot tub, massage, sauna, steam room, exercise room, bicycles, library. AE, DC, MC, V.*

Shopping

The **Wanderer und Ramming** store (⊠ Obere Stadt 34) has an army of more than 1,000 toy soldiers in all shapes, sizes, and uniforms.

Bayreuth

❹ *75 km (45 mi) east of Coburg.*

Bayreuth is pronounced Bi-*roit*, though it might as well be called Wagner. This small Franconian town was where 19th-century composer and man of myth Richard Wagner finally settled after a lifetime of rootless shifting through Europe, and here he built his great theater, the Festspielhaus, as a suitable setting for his grandiose and heroic operas. The annual Wagner Festival, first held in 1876, regularly brings the town to a halt as hordes of Wagner lovers descend on Bayreuth, pushing prices sky-high, filling hotels to bursting, and earning themselves much-sought-after social kudos in the process (to some, it's one of *the* places to be seen). The festival is held from late July until late August, so unless you plan to visit the town specifically for it, this is the time to stay away. Likewise, those whose tastes do not include opera and the theater will find little here to divert them. Bayreuth has no picture-postcard setting, and there is little here that is not connected in some way with music, specifically Wagner's.

Built by Wagner, **Wahnfried** was the only house he ever owned. It's a simple, austere neoclassical building, constructed in 1874, just south of the town center. Today it's a museum celebrating the life of this maddening and compelling man, although, after wartime bomb damage, all that remains of the original construction is the facade. Here Wagner and his wife, Cosima, daughter of composer Franz Liszt, lived; and here they are buried. King Ludwig II of Bavaria, the young and impressionable "dream king," who provided much of the financial backing for Wagner's vaultingly ambitious works, is remembered, too; there's a bust of him in front of the entrance to the house. Though the house is something of a shrine to Wagner, even those who have little interest in the composer will find it intriguing and educational. Standout exhibits include the original scores for a number of his operas, including *Parsifal, Tristan und Isolde, Lohengrin, Der fliegende Holländer,* and *Die Götterdämmerung.* You can also see designs, many of them the originals, for productions of his operas, as well as his piano and huge library. At 10, noon, and 2, excerpts from his operas are played in the living room, and a video film on his life is shown at 11 and 3. ✉ *Richard-Wagner-Str. 48,* ☎ *0921/7572816.* 🎫 *DM 4.* ⏱ *Daily 9–5.*

The **Festspielhaus,** the famous theater where the annual Wagner Festival is held, is no beautiful building. In fact this high temple of the Wagner cult is disappointingly plain, almost intimidating, even though the composer himself conceived, planned, and financed it, specifically as a setting for his monumental operas. Today it is very much the focus of the annual Wagner Festival, still masterminded by descendants of the composer. The spartan look is explained partly by Wagner's near-permanent financial crises and partly by his desire to achieve perfect acoustics. For this reason the wood seats have no upholstering, and the walls are bare of all ornament. The stage is enormous, capable of holding the huge casts required for Wagner's largest operas. ✉ *Auf dem Grünen Hügel,* ☎ *0921/78780.* 🎫 *DM 2.50.* ⏱ *Tours are given Tues.–Sun. at 10, 10:45, 2:15, and 3; closed afternoons during festival and Nov.*

The **Neues Schloss** (New Palace) is close to Wahnfried. Though Wagner is the man most closely associated with Bayreuth, it's well to remember that he would never have come here in the first place had it not been for the woman who built this glamorous 18th-century palace. She was the Margravine Wilhelmina, sister of Frederick the Great of Prussia and a woman of enormous energy and decided tastes. She devoured books, wrote plays and operas (which she directed and, of course, acted in), and had buildings constructed, transforming much of the town and bringing it near bankruptcy. Her distinctive touch is much in evidence at the palace, built when a mysterious fire conveniently destroyed parts of the original palace. Anyone with a taste for the wilder flights of rococo decoration will love it. The **Staatsgalerie** (State Art Gallery), containing a representative collection of mainly 19th-century Bavarian paintings, is also housed in the palace, and rooms have also recently been given over to one of Europe's finest collections of faience ware. ✉ *Ludwigstr. 21,* ☎ *0921/759690.* ✎ *DM 4.* ⊙ *Apr.–Sept., Tues.–Sun. 10–noon and 1:30–4:30; Oct.–Mar., Tues.–Sun. 10–noon and 1:30–3. English-language tours of Schloss. Times vary; call ahead for details.*

★ The **Markgräfliches Opernhaus** (Margrave Opera House) is Wilhelmina's other great architectural legacy. Built between 1745 and 1748, it is a Rococo jewel, sumptuously decorated in red, gold, and blue. Apollo and the nine Muses cavort across the frescoed ceiling. It was this delicate 500-seat theater that originally drew Wagner to Bayreuth, since he felt that it might prove a suitable setting for his own operas. In fact, while it may be a perfect place to hear Mozart, it's hard to imagine a less suitable setting for Wagner's epic works. Catch a performance here if you can; otherwise, take a tour of the ravishing interior. ☎ *0921/759690.* ✎ *DM 3.* ⊙ *Apr.–Sept., Tues.–Sun. 9–11:30 and 1:30–4:30; Oct.–Mar., Tues.–Sun. 10–11:30 and 1:30–3.*

The **Altes Schloss Eremitage** (Old Palace and Hermitage), 5 kilometers (3 miles) north of Bayreuth, makes an appealing departure from the sonorous and austere Wagnerian mood of much of the town. It's an early 18th-century palace, built as a summer palace and remodeled in 1740 by the margravine Wilhelmina. While her taste is not much in evidence in the drab exterior, the interior, alive with light and color, displays her guiding hand in every elegant line. The standout is the extraordinary **Japanese Room,** filled with Asian treasures and chinoiserie furniture. The park and gardens, partly formal, partly natural, are enjoyable for idle strolling in summer. ☎ *0921/92561.* ✎ *Schloss (includes a guided tour given every 30 mins) DM 4.* ⊙ *Apr.–Sept., Tues.–Sun. 9–11:30 and 1–4:30; Oct.–Mar., Tues.–Sun. 10–11:30 and 1–2:30.*

NEED A BREAK? Seek out Bayreuth's oldest inn, the **Braunbierhaus** (✉ Kanzleistr. 15, off Maximilianstr.), for local atmosphere, Franconian dishes, and locally brewed beer.

☾ The **toy museum** in the Boltz auction rooms keeps kids at Wagner Festival busy. ✉ *Brandenburger Str. 36,* ☎ *0921/20616.* ⊙ *During Wagner festival only, and visitors are asked to make an appointment.*

Dining and Lodging

$$$$ ✗ **Schloss Hotel Thiergarten.** Just 6½ kilometers (4 miles) from Bayreuth in the Thiergarten suburb, this small, onetime hunting lodge, now beautifully converted into a hotel (☞ *below*) and two stunning restaurants, provides one of the most elegant dining experiences in Franconia. The intimate Kaminhalle (the name means fireplace, a reference to the lavishly ornate one here) and the Venezianischer Salon, dominated by a glittering 300-year-old Venetian chandelier, both offer regional and nouvelle specialties. ✉ *Oberthiergärtener Str. 36,* ☎ *09209/9840. Reservations essential. Jacket and tie. DC, MC, V. Closed Mon. and Feb. 15–Mar. 15. No dinner Sun.*

$$$ ✗ **Cuvee.** Within a couple of years owner Wolfgang Hauenstein elevated the status of this restaurant from elegant to the don't-miss category, with his mixture of nouvelle cuisine and traditional regional

specialties prepared with a modern twist. The cellar includes 14 varieties of champagne. ⊠ *Markgrafenallee 15,* ☎ *0921/23422. Jacket and tie. AE, MC. Closed Sun. and last 2 wks in Sept.*

$$ ✕ **Weihenstephan.** Long wood tables, fulsome regional specialties, and beer straight from the barrel (from the oldest brewery in Germany) make this a perennial favorite with tourists and locals alike. In summer the crowded, flower-strewn terrace is the place to be. ⊠ *Bahnhofstr. 5,* ☎ *0921/82288. No credit cards. Closed Fri.*

$ ✕ **Brauereischänke am Markt.** They make their own bratwurst (spicy grilled sausage) at this boisterous Old Town inn. Another local specialty is *Bierrippchen,* pork ribs braised in a dark beer sauce. The inn's yeasty Zwickel beer is the ideal accompaniment to a meal. On sunny summer days you'll enjoy the beer garden on the pedestrian street. ⊠ *Maximilianstr. 56,* ☎ *0921/64919. AE, MC.*

$$$$ ✕🏨 **Schloss Hotel Thiergarten.** If you plan to stay in this near-regal little hotel, be sure to make reservations well in advance. Rooms are furnished either in elegant white Venetian style or heavy German baroque, and all have a plush, lived-in character. A stay here is what you imagine staying with your favorite elderly millionaire aunt would be like. (☞ *above* for details of the two restaurants.) ⊠ *Oberthiergärtner Str. 36, D–95406,* ☎ *09209/9840,* 🅵🅰🅷 *09209/98429. 8 rooms with bath. 2 restaurants, bar, sauna. DC, MC, V. Closed Feb. 15–Mar. 15.*

$$$ ✕🏨 **Goldener Anker.** No question about it—if you're booking far
★   enough in advance, this is *the* place to stay while you're in Bayreuth. The hotel is right by the Markgräfliche's Opernhaus and has been entertaining composers, singers, conductors, and players for more than 100 years, as the signed photographs in the lobby and the signatures in the guest book make clear. Rooms are small but individually decorated; many have antique pieces. The restaurant is justly popular. ⊠ *Opernstr. 6, D–95445,* ☎ *0921/65051,* 🅵🅰🅷 *0921/65500. 38 rooms, 1 suite, 4 apartments with bath. Restaurant. MC, V. Closed Dec. 20–Jan. 10.*

$$ ✕🏨 **Goldener Löwe.** A trusty yet stylish old inn close to the town center, the Löwe (Lion) provides a traditional Franconian welcome, especially to overseas visitors. Rooms are furnished in Franconian farmhouse style, with pinewood, floral prints, and bright red-and-white–checked linen. The kitchen is known for its selection of *Klössen* (regional-style dumplings). At the tavern bar you may meet some friendly folks and find yourself invited to join in a game of cards. ⊠ *Kulmbacherstr. 30, D–95445,* ☎ *0921/41046,* 🅵🅰🅷 *0921/47777. 12 rooms with bath. Restaurant (closed Sun.), beer garden. AE, DC, MC, V.*

Nightlife and the Arts

Opera lovers cheerfully admit that there are few more intense operatic experiences than that offered by the annual **Wagner Festival** in Bayreuth, held in July–August. If you want tickets, write to the **Festspielhaus** (⊠ Festspielhügel 2, ☎ 0921/20221) or call 0921/78780, but be warned: The waiting list is years long! You have only a slim chance of obtaining tickets unless you plan your visit a couple of years in advance. Rooms can be nearly impossible to find during the festival, too. If you don't get tickets, you can console yourself with visits to the exquisite 18th-century **Markgräfliches Opernhaus** (☎ 0921/759690); performances are given most nights in July and August. Check with the tourist office for details.

Shopping

The **Hofgarten Passage,** off Richard-Wagner-Strasse, is one of the fanciest shopping arcades of the whole region; it's crammed with smart boutiques selling anything from high German fashion to simple local artifacts.

En Route The B–22 highway west, to Bamberg, is part of the officially designated **Strasse der Residenzen** (Road of Residences), so named because of the many episcopal and princely palaces along its way—including Bamberg's stunning Neue Residenz. The road cuts through the Fränkische Schweiz— or Franconian Switzerland—which got its name from its fir-clad upland landscape. Just north of Hollfeld, 23 kilometers (14 miles) west of Bayreuth, the jura rock of the region breaks through the surface in a bizarre, craggy formation known as the Felsgarten (Rock Garden).

Bamberg

⑤ *65 km (39 mi) west of Bayreuth, 80 km (50 mi) north of Nürnberg.*

Bamberg is one of the great historic cities of Germany, filled with buildings and monuments that recall its glorious days as the seat of one of the most powerful ruling families in the country. Though founded as early as the 2nd century, Bamberg rose to prominence only in the 11th century, under the irresistible impetus provided by its most famous son, Holy Roman Emperor Heinrich II. His imperial cathedral still dominates the historic area.

The city lies on the Regnitz River, and its historic center is a small island in the river; to the west is the so-called Bishops Town; to the east, the so-called Burghers Town. Connecting them is a bridge on which stands the **Altes Rathaus** (Old Town Hall), a highly colorful, rickety Gothic building dressed extravagantly in Rococo. It's best seen from the adjacent bridge upstream, where it appears to be practically in danger of being swept off by the river. The preeminent pleasure of a visit is to stroll through the narrow, sinuous streets of old Bamberg, past half-timbered and gabled houses and formal 18th-century mansions. Peek into cobbled, flower-filled courtyards or take time out in a waterside café, watching the little steamers as they chug past the colorful row of fishermen's houses that make up Klein Venedig (Little Venice).

The **Neue Residenz,** Bamberg's claim to a place of honor on the German Road of Residences, is an immense Baroque palace which was once the home of the prince-electors. Their wealth and prestige can easily be imagined as you tour the glittering interior. Most memorable is the **Kaisersaal** (Throne Room), complete with impressive ceiling frescoes and elaborate stuccowork. The palace also houses the **Staatsbibliothek** (State Library). Among the thousands of books and illuminated manuscripts are the original prayer books belonging to Heinrich and his wife, a 5th-century manuscript by the Roman historian Livy, and handwritten manuscripts by the 16th-century painters Dürer and Cranach. You'll also be able to visit the rose garden in back of the building. ⊠ *Dompl. 8.* 🎫 *DM 4.* ☉ *Apr.–Sept., daily 9–noon and 1:30– 5; Oct.–Mar., daily 9–noon and 1:30–4. Staatsbibliothek:* 🎫 *Free;* ☉ *Weekdays 9–5, Sat. 9–noon; closed afternoons in Aug.*

The great **Dom** is one of the most important of Germany's cathedrals, a building that tells not only Bamberg's story but that of much of Germany as well. The first building here was begun by Heinrich II in 1003, and it was in this partially completed cathedral that he was crowned Holy Roman Emperor in 1012. In 1237 it was mostly destroyed by fire, and the present late-Romanesque/early Gothic building was begun. From the outside, the dominant features are the massive towers at each corner. Heading into the dark interior, you'll find one of the most striking collections of monuments and art treasures of any European church.

★ The most famous is the ***Bamberger Reiter*** (*Bamberg Rider*), an equestrian statue, carved—no one knows by whom—around 1230 and thought to be an allegory of knightly virtue. The larger-than-life figure is an extraordinarily realistic work for the period, more like a Renaissance statue than a Gothic piece. Compare it with the mass of carved figures huddled in the tympana, the semicircular spaces above the doorways of the church; while these are stylized and obviously Gothic, the *Bamberg Rider* is poised and calm. In the center of the nave you'll find another great sculptural work, the massive tomb of Heinrich and his wife, Kunigunde. It's the work of Tilman Riemenschneider, Germany's greatest Renaissance sculptor. Pope Clement II is also buried in the cathedral in an imposing tomb under the high altar; he is the only pope to be buried north of the Alps. The cathedral stands suitably in the heart of so-called Bishops Town on Domplatz.

The **Diözesanmuseum** (Cathedral Museum), directly next to the cathedral, contains a splinter of wood and the *heilige Nagel,* or "holy nail," both reputedly from the cross of Jesus. A more macabre exhibit among the rich collection of ecclesiastical exhibits is Heinrich's and Kunigunde's skulls, mounted in elaborate metal supports. The building itself was designed by Balthasar Neumann, the architect of Vierzehnheiligen Church, and constructed between 1730 and 1733. ⊠ *Dompl. 5.* 🎫 *DM 3.* ⊙ *Tues.–Sun. 10–5. Free guided tours in English at 11 and 3.*

The **Alte Hofhaltung** is the former imperial and episcopal palace. It's a sturdy and weather-worn half-timbered Gothic building with a graceful Renaissance courtyard. Today it contains the **Historisches Museum,** with a collection of documents and maps charting Bamberg's history that will appeal most to avid history buffs and/or those who read German well. ⊠ *Dompl. 7.* 🎫 *DM 3.* ⊙ *May–Oct., Tues.–Sun. 9–5.*

Hoffmann Haus is the former home of Ernst Theodor Hoffmann, the Romantic writer, composer, and illustrator who lived and worked in Bamberg. Hoffmann is probably best remembered not for one of his own works but for *The Tales of Hoffmann,* an opera written *about* him and his stories, by composer Jacques Offenbach. The little house has been preserved much as it was when Hoffmann lived here—complete with the hole in the floor of his upstairs study through which he talked to his wife below. ⊠ *Schillerpl. 26.* 🎫 *DM 2.* ⊙ *May–Oct., Tues.–Fri. 4–6, weekends and public holidays 10–noon.*

NEED A BREAK?

The **Brauereiausschank Schlenkerla** (⊠ Dominikanerstr. 6, ☎ 0951/56060) is a centuries-old monastery turned beer tavern. The black furniture, wall paneling, and dresses worn by the waitresses match the beer—Rauchbier—a strong malty brew with a smoky aftertaste. The unusual flavor comes from a beech wood–smoke brewing process. There are also excellent Franconian specialties at reasonable prices. Try the *Rauchschinken* (smoked ham) or the *Bierbrauervesper*—composed of smoked meat, sour-milk cheese, and black bread and butter, all served on a wood platter. *Prost!*

Nightlife and the Arts

The **Sinfonie an der Regnitz** (⊠ Mussstr. 20, ☎ 0951/964–7200), a fine riverside concert hall, is home to Bamberg's world-class resident symphony orchestra; if it's performing during your visit, it's an experience not to be missed. The **Hoffmann Theater** (⊠ Schillerpl. 5, ☎ 0951/871–431), has opera and operetta, September through July. In June and July open-air performances are also given at the **Alte Hofhaltung** (☎ 0951/25256 for tickets). The city has a first-class choir concentrating on ancient music, the Capella Antiqua Bambergensis, while throughout the summer organ concerts are given in the Kaiserdom. For program details and tickets to all cultural events call 0951/871161.

En Route   From Bamberg you can either take the fast autobahn (A–73) south to Nürnberg or a parallel country road that follows the Rhine-Main-Danube Canal. This mighty feat of engineering, first dreamed up by Charlemagne, connects the North Sea and the Black Sea by linking the Rhine and the Danube via the Main and a man-made canal. The canal was one of the major environmental issues in Germany in the '80s, with ecologists protesting it would irreparably damage the natural beauty and wildlife of the area. Judge for yourself whether they were right.

SOUTHERN FRANCONIA

There's no tangible division between northern and southern Franconia. You do, however, leave the thickly wooded heights of the Fichtelgebirge and the Fränkische Schweiz behind, and the countryside opens up as if to announce the imminent arrival of a more populated region, where Nürnberg and Regensburg share a historically rooted hegemony.

Nürnberg

6   *63 km (38 mi) south of Bamberg, 162 km (100 mi) north of Munich.*

Nürnberg is the principal city of Franconia and second in size and significance in Bavaria only to Munich. With a recorded history stretching back to 1040, it's among the most historic and visitable of Germany's cities; the core of the Old Town, through which the Pegnitz River flows, is still surrounded by its original medieval walls. Nürnberg has always taken a leading role in German affairs. It was here, for example, that the first diet, or meeting of rulers, of every Holy Roman Emperor was held. And it was here, too, that Hitler staged the most grandiose Nazi rallies; later, this was the site of the Allies' war trials, where top-ranking Nazis were charged with—and almost without exception convicted of—"crimes against humanity." Wartime bombing destroyed much of medieval and Renaissance Nürnberg, though faithful reconstruction has largely re-created the city's prewar atmosphere.

The city grew because of its location at the meeting point of a number of medieval trade routes. With prosperity came a great flowering of the arts and sciences. Albrecht Dürer, the first indisputable genius of the Renaissance in Germany, was born here in 1471, and he returned in 1509 to live out the rest of his life. (His house is one of the most popular tourist shrines in the city.) Other leading Nürnberg artists of the Renaissance include wood carver Michael Wolgemut and sculptors Adam Kraft and Peter Vischer. Earlier the *Minnesingers*—medieval poets and musicians, chief among them Tannhäuser—had made the city a focal point in the development of German music. In the 15th and 16th centuries their traditions were continued by the *Meistersingers*. Both groups were celebrated much later by Wagner. Among a great host of inventions associated with Nürnberg, the most significant were the pocket watch, gun casting, the clarinet, and the geographical globe (the first of which was made before Columbus discovered the Americas).

Nürnberg is rich in special events and celebrations. By far the most famous is the Christkindlmarkt, an enormous pre-Christmas market that runs from November 27 to Christmas Eve. The highlight is the December 10 candle procession, in which thousands of children march through the city streets. There are few sights in Europe to compare with the flickering of their tiny lights in the cold night air, the entire scene played out against the backdrop of centuries-old buildings.

Numbers in the margin correspond to points of interest on the Nürnberg map.

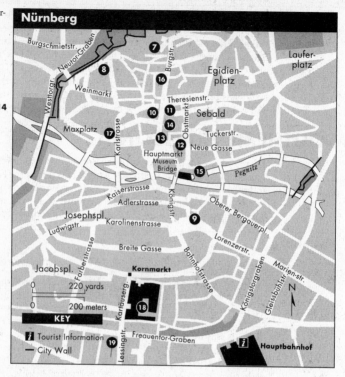

The historic heart of Nürnberg is compact; all principal sights are within easy walking distance. To get a sense of the city begin your tour by walking around all or part of the **city walls.** Finished in 1452, they come complete with moats, sturdy gateways, and watchtowers. Year-round floodlighting adds to their brooding romance.

7 **Die Kaiserburg** (the Imperial Castle), Nürnberg's main attraction, is an immense cluster of buildings, standing just inside the city walls; it was formerly the residence of the Holy Roman Emperors. Impressive rather than beautiful, the complex comprises three separate groups of buildings. The oldest, dating from around 1050, is the **Burggrafenburg,** the Burgrave's Castle, with a craggy, ruined seven-side tower and bailiff's house. It stands in the center of the complex. To the east is the **Kaiser-stallung** (Imperial Stables). These were built during the 15th century as a granary, then converted into a youth hostel after the war. (If you're backpacking, stay here—if only for the view of old Nürnberg from the bedrooms and dormitories.) The real interest of this vast complex of ancient buildings, however, centers on the Imperial Castle itself, the west-ernmost part of the fortress. The standout feature here is the Renais-sance **Doppelkappelle** (Double Chapel). The upper part—richer, larger, and more ornate than the lower chapel—was where the emperor and his family worshiped. Also visit the **Rittersaal** (Knight's Hall) and the **Kaisersaal** (Throne Room). Their heavy oak beams, painted ceilings, and sparse interiors have changed little since they were built in the 15th century. ⊠ *Burgstr.,* ☎ *0911/225726.* ⊡ *DM 5.* ⊙ *Apr.–Sept., daily 9–noon and 1–5; Oct.–Mar., daily 9:30–noon and 1–4.*

★ **8** The **Albrecht-Dürer-Haus,** opposite the Tiergärtner Gate, was the great painter's home from 1509 until his death in 1528. It is also just about the best-preserved late-medieval house in the city, typical of the prosperous merchants' homes that once filled Nürnberg. Before stepping inside, admire the half-timbering of the upper stories and the tapering gable. Dürer was the German Leonardo da Vinci, the Renaissance man incarnate, bursting with curiosity. His talent for painting was equaled by his printmaking ability; he raised the woodcut, a notoriously difficult medium, to new heights of technical sophistication, combining great skill with a haunting, immensely detailed drawing style and complex, allegorical subject matter. A number of original prints adorn the walls. The house also gives a realistic sense of what life was like in early 16th-century Germany. ✉ *Albrecht-Dürer-Str. 39,* ☎ *0911/2312568.* ☞ *DM 4.* ☉ *Mar.–Oct. and Christkindlmarkt, Tues. and Thurs.–Sun. 10–5, Wed. 1–9; Nov.–Feb., Tues., Thurs., and Fri. 1–5, Wed. 1–9, weekends 10–5.*

❾ **St. Lorenz Kirche** (St. Laurence's Church) is considered by many the most beautiful in Nürnberg, a city with several beautiful historical churches. St. Lorenz was begun around 1220 and completed in about 1475. It's a sizable church; two towers flank the main entrance, which is covered with a forest of carvings. In the lofty interior note the works by sculptors Adam Kraft and Veit Stoss: Kraft's great stone tabernacle to the left of the altar and Stoss's *Annunciation* at the east end of the nave are considered their finest works. There are many other carvings throughout the building, a fitting testimonial to the artistic richness of late-medieval Nürnberg. ✉ *Lorenzerstr.,* ☎ *0911/209–287.* ☉ *Daily 7–7.*

❿ The 13th-century **St. Sebaldus Kirche** lacks the number of art treasures boasted by rival St. Lorenz, but its lofty nave and choir are among the purest examples of Gothic ecclesiastical architecture in Germany: elegant, tall, and airy. Veit Stoss carved the crucifixion group at the east end of the nave, while the elaborate bronze shrine, containing the remains of St. Sebaldus himself, was cast by Peter Vischer and his five sons around 1520. ✉ *Sebaldkirchepl.,* ☎ *0911/225–613.* ☉ *Daily 7–7.*

⓫ The **Altes Rathaus** (Old Town Hall) abuts the rear of the St. Sebaldus Kirche; it was built in 1332, destroyed in World War II, and subsequently restored. It has intact medieval dungeons and a torture chamber that may cause young ones to break out in a cold sweat. ☎ *0911/23360.* ☞ *DM 3.* ☉ *Apr.–Sept., weekdays 10–4, weekends and public holidays 10–1.*

Like Munich's Viktualienmarkt, Nürnberg's market, the **Hauptmarkt,** is more than just a place to do the shopping. Its colorful stands, piled high with produce and shaded by striped awnings, are a central part of the city. The red-armed market women—whose acid wit and earthy, homespun philosophy you'll have to take on trust unless your command of German extends to an in-depth familiarity with the Nürnberg dialect—are a formidable-looking bunch, dispensing flowers, fruit, and abuse in equal measure. It's here that the Christkindlmarkt is held. The area has three principal sights.

⓬ The **Frauenkirche** (Church of Our Lady), on the central square, was built, with the approval of Holy Roman Emperor Charles IV, in 1350 on the site of a synagogue that was burned down during a pogrom in 1349. (The area covered by the Hauptmarkt was once the Jewish Quarter of the city.) These days most visitors are drawn not so much by the church itself as by the **Männleinlaufen,** a clock dating from 1500 that's set in its facade. It's one of those colorful mechanical marvels at which the Germans have long excelled—a perfect match of love of punctuality and ingenuity. Every day at noon the electors of the Holy Roman Empire glide out of the clock to bow to Emperor Charles IV before sliding back under cover. It's worth scheduling your morning to catch the display. ⊠ *Hauptmarkt.*

⓭ The **Schöner Brunnen** (Beautiful Fountain) is an elegant 60-foot-high Gothic fountain carved around the year 1400, looking for all the world as though it should be on the summit of some lofty Gothic cathedral. Thirty figures arranged in tiers stand sentinel on it. They include prophets, saints, local noblemen, sundry electors of the Holy Roman Empire, and one or two strays, such as Julius Caesar and Alexander the Great. A gold ring is set into the railing surrounding the fountain, reportedly placed there by an apprentice carver. Stroking it is said to bring good luck. Cynics will enjoy the sight of Germans and tourists alike examining the railing for the ring and then surreptitiously rubbing it.

⓮ Facing the Altes Rathaus is the bronze **Gänsemännchenbrunnen** (Gooseman's Fountain). It's an elegant work of great technical sophistication, cast in 1550.

⓯ The **Heilig-Geist-Spital** (Holy Ghost Hospital), south of Hauptmarkt, is set on graceful arcades over the Pegnitz River. Begun in 1381, it has a charming courtyard with elegant wood balconies and spacious arcades and now houses a restaurant. ⊠ *Spitalgasse 16*, ☎ *0911/221–761.*

⓰ Nürnberg has several interesting and unusual museums. The **Stadtmuseum** (City Museum) is housed in the Fembohaus, a dignified, patrician dwelling completed in 1598 and one of the finest Renaissance mansions in Nürnberg. Here you can learn in depth about the city's rich history. ⊠ *Burgstr. 15.*, ☎ *0911/2312595.* ⌨ *DM 4.* ☉ *Mar.–Oct., Tues–Sun. 10–5; Nov.–Feb., Tues.–Sun. 1–5, weekends 10–5.*

NEED A BREAK? In a medieval courtyard off Burgstrasse 19, under the shadow of the castle, the **Hausbrauerei Altstadthof** (☎ 0911/362–327) offers food, drink, and the chance to see a working cottage industry brewing beer. Reactivating brewing rights granted the tavern in the 16th century, the new owners use 19th-century equipment ordinarily confined to a museum.

⓱ The **Spielzeugmuseum** (Toy Museum) upholds Nürnberg's cherished title of "toy capital of the world." This captivating museum (and not only for children) has a few exhibits dating from the Renaissance; most, however, are from the 19th century. Simple dolls vie with mechanical toys of extraordinary complexity. There's even a little Ferris wheel. ⊠ *Karlstr. 13–15*, ☎ *0911/2313164.* ⌨ *DM 5.* ☉ *Tues. and Thurs.–Sun. 10–5, Wed. 10–9.*

⓲ The **Germanisches Nationalmuseum** (Germanic National Museum) showcases Germany's cultural achievements. You could spend an entire day visiting this vast and fascinating museum. It is the largest of its kind in Germany and about the best arranged. The setting gets everything off to a flying start; the museum is in what was once a Carthusian monastery, complete with cloisters and monastic outbuildings. There are few aspects of German culture, from the Stone Age to the 19th century, not covered here, and quantity and quality are evenly matched. For some visitors the highlight may be the superb collection of Renaissance German painting (with Dürer, Cranach, and Altdorfer well represented). Others may prefer the exquisite medieval ecclesiastical exhibits—manuscripts, altarpieces, statuary, stained glass, jewel-encrusted reliquaries—or the collections of arms and armor, or the scientific instruments, or the toys. Few will be disappointed. ⊠ *Kartäusergasse 1.*, ☎ *0911/13310.* ⌨ *DM 5, free Sun.* ☉ *Tues. and Thurs.–Sun. 10–5, Wed. 10–9.*

NEED A
BREAK?

The **Bratwurstglöcklein** (⊠ Am Königstor, ☎ 227–625), in the nearby Handwerkerhof medieval shopping mall, offers some of the best bratwurst in Nürnberg. Sauerkraut and potato salad are the traditional accompaniments. Wash it all down with a glass of beer.

⑲ The **Verkehrsmuseum** (Transportation Museum) is a favorite with children. December 7, 1835, saw the first-ever train trip in Germany, from Nürnberg to nearby Fürth. A model of the epochal train is here at the museum, along with a series of original 19th- and early 20th-century trains and stagecoaches. Philatelists will want to check out some of the 40,000-odd stamps in the extensive exhibits on the German postage system. There's also a fascinating exhibition on a mammoth, broad-gauge rail system planned by Hitler to link the Atlantic to the Urals but overtaken by the war. ⊠ *Lessingstr. 6.*, ☎ *0911/2192428.* ☞ *DM 5.* ⊙ *Daily 9:30–5.*

The enormous parade grounds where Hitler addressed his largest Nazi rallies lies on the eastern edge of the city. The vast site, the **Zeppelinfeld**, is big enough to accommodate four soccer fields and still leave room for a game of hockey. Nowadays it sometimes shakes to the amplified beat of pop concerts, but otherwise it is a depressing, empty stretch of wasteland, where dusty grass and weeds claw an existence from stone slabs that once resounded to the martial click and clack of Nazi jackboots. It's open to the public and reachable on the S–2 line (Frankenfeld station).

Nürnberg has a major, well-stocked **zoo**; children love its dolphinarium, which is worth the extra admission fee. ⊠ *Am Tiergarten 30,* ☎ *0911/543–0348.* ☞ *DM 8. (The dolphinarium costs an extra DM 6. Displays daily at 11, 2, and 4.)* ⊙ *Zoo and dolphinarium Apr.–Sept., daily 8–7:30; Oct. and Mar., daily 8–5:30; Nov.–Feb., daily 9–5.*

Dining and Lodging

$$$$ ✕ **Entenstub'n.** "Duck Tavern" seems an inappropriate name for such a regal restaurant, which looks like an 18th-century drawing room and was once a shooting lodge for Bavarian King Ludwig III. The menu, a mix of regional and nouvelle cooking styles, matches the elegant setting, with such specialties as parfait of creamed pigeon and white fish in chives galantine. ⊠ *Günthersbühlerstr. 145,* ☎ *0911/598–0413. AE, MC. Closed Sun.–Mon.*

$$$$ ✕ **Goldenes Posthorn.** The authentic heart of old Nürnberg still beats
★   in this ancient restaurant beside the cathedral, notwithstanding that it was built after the war. In their day both Dürer and the poet and *Meistersinger* Hans Sachs ate here. The food is nouvelle Franconian; try the venison in red wine with plums or the quail stuffed with walnuts and goose liver. The wine list is extensive. ⊠ *An der Sebalduskirche,* ☎ *0911/225–153. Reservations essential. AE, DC, MC, V. Closed Sun.*

$$$ ✕ **Essigbrätlein.** Some rank this the top restaurant in the city and even
★   among the best in Germany. As the oldest restaurant in Nürnberg, built in 1550 and originally used as a meeting place for wine merchants, it is unquestionably one of the most atmospheric. Today its elegant period interior is *the* place to eat *Essigbrätlein* (roast loin of beef). Other dishes blend Franconian and nouvelle recipes. ⊠ *Weinmarkt 3,* ☎ *0911/ 225–131. Reservations essential. AE, DC, MC, V. Closed Sun.–Mon., 1st 10 days in Jan.*

$$ ✕ **Nassauer Keller.** The exposed-beam-and-plaster decor complements the resolutely traditional cooking. Try the duck and the apple strudel. The restaurant has a memorable location in the cellar of a 13th-century tower beside the church of St. Lorenz. ⊠ *Karolinenstr. 2–4,* ☎ *0911/225–967. AE, DC, MC.*

\$ ✕ **Bratwurst Haüsle.** There are few better places to try Nürnberg's famous grilled sausages—roasted over an open fire and served on heavy pewter plates with horseradish and sauerkraut—than this dark, old, wood-paneled inn. The mood is noisy and cheerful. ⊠ *Rathauspl. 1,* ☎ *0911/227–695. No credit cards. Closed Sun.*

\$ ✕ **Heilig-Geist-Spital.** Heavy wood furnishings and a choice of more
★   than 100 wines make this 650-year-old wine tavern a popular spot for visitors. The traditional cuisine includes grilled pork chops, pan-fried potatoes, and German cheeses. ⊠ *Spitalgasse 16,* ☎ *0911/221–761. AE, DC, MC, V.*

\$\$\$\$ ✕⌂ **Carlton.** This stylish old hotel, sturdy in a grande-dame way, is quietly efficient and offers thick-carpeted, old-fashioned luxury. The restaurant is plushly expensive and a pleasure in summer, when you can sit on the shaded terrace. It's on a quiet side street close to the train station. Although room rates are in the higher price bracket, they are almost halved during off-peak periods (most of April and October) and on weekends. ⊠ *Eilgutstr. 13–15, D-90443,* ☎ *0911/20030,* fax *0911/ 200–3532. 126 rooms, 3 suites, and 1 apartment with bath. Restaurant, bar, weinstube, sauna, exercise room. AE, DC, MC, V.*

\$\$\$\$ ✕⌂ **Maritim.** If you value modern convenience over Old World charm, consider staying in this luxuriously modern hotel, opened in 1986. You won't find so much as a hint of the medieval glories of old Nürnberg here, but the service is impeccable, the spacious rooms are tastefully furnished, mostly with gleaming dark veneers and fabrics in pastel shades, and the public areas are elegantly well-heeled. The Maritim, part of a French chain, is just south of the historic area. Its French connection ensures fine cuisine in the Gourmet, its restaurant. Breakfast costs an extra DM 22, but the range and excellence of the buffet fully warrant the expense. ⊠ *Frauentorgraben 11, D-90443,* ☎ *0911/23630,* fax *0911/236– 3836. 306 rooms, 10 suites with bath. 2 restaurants, bar, indoor pool, massage, sauna, steam bath, exercise room. AE, DC, MC, V.*

\$\$\$ ✕⌂ **Hotel-Weinhaus Steichele.** This skillfully converted former 19th-century wine merchant's warehouse is now part of the Flair hotel group but is still managed by the family that has been running it for three generations. It's handily situated close to the main train station, yet on a quiet street of the old walled town. The rooms, decorated in Bavarian rustic decor, are cozy rather than luxurious. Two traditionally furnished taverns serve Franconian and Baden-Württemberg fare. ⊠ *Knorrstr. 2–8, D-90402,* ☎ *0911/204–377,* fax *0911/221–914. 49 rooms, 45 with shower. Restaurant, weinstube. AE, DC, MC, V.*

\$\$–\$\$\$ ⌂ **Burg-Hotel Grosses Haus, Burg-Hotel Kleines Haus.** These two hotels, with one name, both stand under the castle's gaze in the Old Town, a few blocks from each other. Both provide private-home comforts and facilities, such as indoor pools and saunas. Their chief difference is price: The larger hotel, Grosses Haus, offers smarter rooms, bedecked with Laura Ashley fabrics, and better views (it's next to Dürer's house), and therefore it's costlier than its smaller sister. It also has more facilities, including an indoor pool and solarium. Neither has a restaurant. ⊠ *Grosses Haus: Lammsgasse 3, D-90403,* ☎ *0911/204–414,* fax *0911/223–882. 41 rooms and 5 suites with bath. Indoor pool, sauna. AE, DC, MC, V.* ⊠ *Kleines Haus: Schildgasse 16, D-90403,* ☎ *0911/203–040,* fax *0911/ 226–503. 23 rooms with bath. AE, DC, MC, V.*

Nightlife and the Arts

Nürnberg has an annual summer festival, "Sommer ein Nürnberg," from May through September, with a program of more than 200 cultural highlights. From May through August classical music concerts are given in the Rittersaal of the Kaiserburg, while regular pop and rock shows are staged in the dry moat of the castle. In June and July open-air concerts are given in the castle's Serenadenhof.

Shopping

Step into the **Handwerkerhof,** near the main railway station, and you'll think you're back in the Middle Ages. Craftspeople are busy at work in a "medieval mall," turning out the kind of handiwork that has been produced in Nürnberg for centuries: pewter, glassware, basketwork, wood carvings, and, of course, toys. The mall is open mid-March–December 24, weekdays 10–6:30, Saturdays 10–2:30 (first Saturday of every month until 4). In December the mall is also open on Sundays, 10–6:30.

Numbers in the margin correspond to points of interest on the Franconia map.

Regensburg

❷⓿ *90 km (54 mi) southeast of Nürnberg, 120 km (72 mi) northwest of Munich.*

Regensburg is one of the best-preserved cities in Germany. Everything here is the original, because the city suffered no major damage in World War II. It is also one of Germany's most historic cities. The mystery then is why Regensburg is not better known. Few visitors to Bavaria (or even Franconia) venture this far off the well-trod tourist trails. Even Germans are astonished that such a remarkable city should exist in comparative obscurity.

The key to Regensburg is the Danube. The city marks the northernmost navigable point of the great river, and this simple geographic fact allowed Regensburg to control trade along the Danube between Germany and central Europe. The great river was a highway for more than commerce, however; it was a conduit of ideas as well. It was from Regensburg that Christianity was spread across much of central Europe during the 7th and 8th centuries. By the Middle Ages Regensburg had become a political, economic, and intellectual center of European significance. For many centuries it was the most important city in southeastern Germany, eclipsed by Munich only when Napoléon ordered the dismemberment of the Holy Roman Empire during the early years of the 19th century. That he presided over its decline from Regensburg, a Free Imperial City since the 13th century and meeting place of the Imperial Diet (parliament) since the 17th, was an irony he appreciated.

Regensburg's story begins with the Celts around 500 BC. They called their little settlement Radasbona. In AD 179, as an original marble inscription in the Museum der Stadt Regensburg proclaims, it became a Roman military post called Castra Regina. Little remains of the Roman occupation save a fortified gate, the Porta Praetoria, in the Old Town. When Bavarian tribes migrated to the area during the 6th century, they occupied what remained of the Roman town and, apparently on the basis of its Latin name, called it Regensburg. Irish missionaries led by St. Boniface in 739 made the town a bishopric before heading down the Danube to convert the heathen in lands even more far-flung. Charlemagne, first of the Holy Roman Emperors, arrived at the end of the 8th century, incorporating Regensburg into his burgeoning lands. And so, in one form or another, prospering all the while and growing into a glorious medieval and, later, Renaissance city, Regensburg remained until Napoléon turned up.

Any serious tour of Regensburg involves visiting an unusually large number of places of worship—not for nothing is it known as "the city of

Alte Kapelle, **24**
Altes Rathaus, **29**
Brückturm, **31**
Dom St. Peter, **21**
Karmelitenkirche, **25**
Museum der Stadt Regensburg, **28**
Neupfarrkirche, **22**
Niedermünster, **26**
Porta Praetoria, **27**
St. Emmeramus, **33**
St. Kassian, **23**
Schloss Emmeram complex, **32**
Steinerne Brücke, **30**

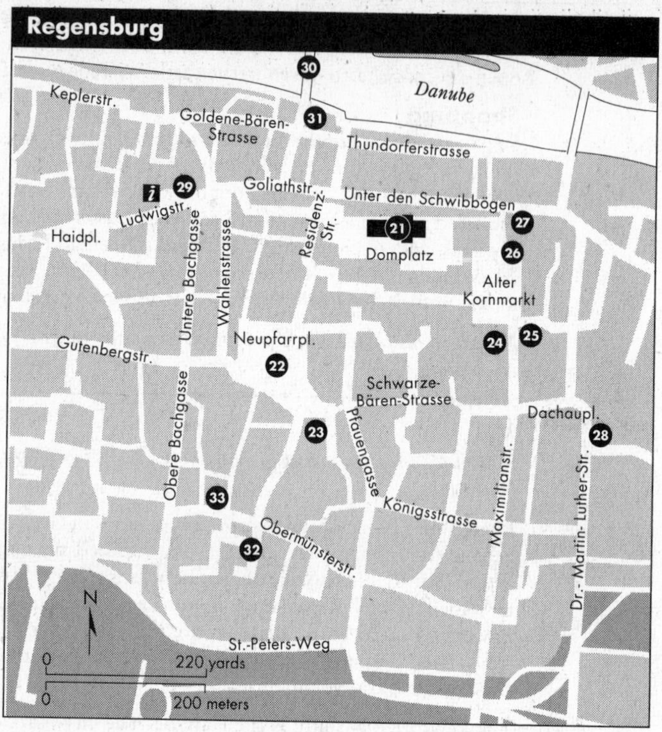

churches." If your spirits wilt at the thought of inspecting them all, you should at least see the Dom (cathedral), famous for its boys choir, and the Domspatzen (Cathedral Sparrows), before moving on to the secular attractions.

Numbers in the margin correspond to points of interest on the Regensburg map.

★ 21 **Dom St. Peter,** the soaring cathedral modeled on the airy, vertical lines of French Gothic architecture, is something of a rarity this far south in Germany—it wouldn't look out of place in Köln or Bonn. Begun during the 13th century, it stands on the site of a much earlier Carolingian church. Construction dragged on for almost 600 years, and it was finally finished when Ludwig I of Bavaria, then the ruler of Regensburg, had the towers built. These had to be replaced during the mid-1950s after their original soft limestone was found to be badly eroded.

Before heading into the Dom, admire its intricate and frothy facade, embellished with delicate and skillful carving. A remarkable feature of the cathedral is its capacity of 7,000 people, three times the population of Regensburg when construction began. Standouts of the austere interior are the glowing 14th-century stained glass in the choir and the exquisitely detailed statues of the archangel Gabriel and the Virgin in the crossing (the meeting point of nave and choir). ✉ *Dompl.,* ☎ *0941/56990.* 🎫 *Tours DM 3.* ⏲ *Cathedral tours May–Oct., weekdays at 10, 11, and 2, Sun. and public holidays at noon and 2; Nov.–Apr., weekdays at 11, Sun. and public holidays at noon.*

Complete your tour of the cathedral with a visit to the **cloisters,** reached via the garden. There you'll find a small octagonal chapel, the **Aller-**

heiligenkapelle (All Saints Chapel), a typically solid Romanesque building that is all sturdy grace and massive walls. You can barely make out the faded remains of stylized 11th-century frescoes on its ancient walls. The equally ancient shell of St. Stephan's Church, the **Alter Dom** (Old Cathedral), can also be visited. ✉ *DM 3. ☉ The cloisters, chapel, and Alter Dom can be seen only on guided tours: mid-May–Oct., daily at 10, 11, and 2; Nov.–Mar., weekdays at 11, Sun. at noon; Apr.–mid-May, daily at 11 and 2. Tours last about 1 hr.*

The **Domschatzmuseum** (Cathedral Museum) contains more valuable treasures. The entrance is in the nave of Dom St. Peter. ✉ *Dompl.,* ☎ *0941/51068.* ✉ *DM 3. ☉ Apr.–Nov., Tues.–Sat 10–5, Sun. noon–5; Dec.–Mar., Fri. and Sat. 10–4, Sun. noon–4.*

To the south of the cathedral are the Neupfarrkirche and the Church of St. Kassian. To the east lie the Niedermünster Church, the Karmelitenkirche, and the Alte Kapelle.

㉒ The **Neupfarrkirche,** built between 1519 and 1540, is the only Protestant church in Regensburg, indeed one of a very few in Franconia. It's an imposing building, substantially less ornate than any other in the city. Some may find its restraint welcome after the exuberance of so many of the other places of worship. ✉ *Neupfarrpl.*

㉓ **St. Kassian** is the oldest church in the city, founded during the 8th century. Don't be fooled by its dour exterior; inside, the church has been endowed with delicate rococo decoration.

㉔ The **Alte Kapelle** (Old Chapel) is another Carolingian structure, erected during the 9th century. As is the case at St. Kassian, the dowdy exterior gives little hint of the joyous rococo treasures within—extravagant concoctions of sinuous gilt stucco, rich marble, and giddy frescoes, the whole illuminated by light pouring in from the upper windows.

㉕ The **Karmelitenkirche,** adjoining the Alte Kapelle, is Baroque from crypt to cupola.

㉖ Formerly the parish church, the **Niedermünster** (construction started in 1150) has a Baroque interior. In 1982 workmen discovered a Roman altar, dating from AD 180–190, dedicated to the emperor Commodus. ✉ *Alter Kornmarkt 5,* ☎ *0941/57796.* ✉ *Advance booking only.*

㉗ The rough-hewn **Porta Praetoria,** an original city gate, is one of the most interesting relics of Roman times to be found in Regensburg. Look through the grille on its east side to see a section of the original Roman street, about 10 feet below today's street.

㉘ The **Museum der Stadt Regensburg** relates vividly the cultural history of Regensburg. For many the museum is one of the highlights of a visit to the city, both for its unusual and beautiful setting—a former Gothic monastery—and for its wide-ranging collections, from Roman artifacts to Renaissance tapestries, all helping to tell the story of Regensburg. The most significant exhibits are the paintings by Albrecht Altdorfer (1480–1538), a native of Regensburg and, along with Cranach, Grünewald, and Dürer, one of the leading painters of the German Renaissance. His work has the same sense of slight distortion—of heightened reality—found in that of his contemporaries, in which the lessons of Italian painting are used to produce an emotional rather than a rational effect. The real significance of Altdorfer's work is his interest in landscape not merely as the background of a painting but as its subject. In many of his works figures are incidental. Altdorfer's obviously emotional response to landscape is even more intriguing; his paintings would not have seemed out of place among those of 19th-century Romantics. Far from seeing the world around him as essentially hostile, or at least alien, he saw it as something intrinsically beautiful, to be admired for its own sake, whether wild or domesticated. ⌂ *Dachaupl. 2–4,* ☎ *0941/507–20448.* ⌂ *DM 4.* ☉ *Tues.–Sat. 10–4, Sun. and holidays 10–1.*

㉙ The **Altes Rathaus,** a picture-book complex of medieval buildings with half-timbering, windows large and small, and flowers in tubs, is among best preserved such building in the country, as well as one of the most historically important. It was here, in the imposing Gothic **Reichssaal** (Imperial Hall), that the "everlasting Imperial Diet" met from 1663 to 1805. This could be considered a forerunner of the German parliament, where representatives from every part of the Holy Roman Empire—plus the emperor and the prince-electors—assembled to discuss and determine the affairs of the far-reaching German lands. The hall is sumptuously appointed with tapestries, flags, and heraldic designs. Note especially the wood ceiling, built in 1408. If you have children in tow, they'll want to see the adjoining torture chamber, the **Fragstatt,** and execution room, the **Armesünderstübchen.** Any prisoner who withstood three days of "questioning" here without confessing was released—which tells you something about medieval notions of justice. ⌂ *Rathauspl,* ☎ *0941/5074411.* ⌂ *DM 5.* ☉ *Daily 9–4. Tours in English May–Sept., Mon.–Sat. 3:15.*

NEED A BREAK? The **Prinzessin Cafe** (⌂ Rathauspl. 2, ☎ 0941/57671), Germany's oldest coffeehouse, first opened its doors to the general public in 1686; it's across the square from the Altes Rathaus. Coffee is served on the first floor and tea one floor above in a lounge furnished like the living room of a Biedermeier mansion, with soft sofas and elaborate little side tables.

★ **㉚** The **Steinerne Brücke** (Stone Bridge), which spans the Danube, is Regensburg's most celebrated sight. The bridge is a central part of Regensburg history. Built in 1141, it was rightfully considered a miraculous piece of engineering at the time. As the only crossing point over the Danube for miles, it effectively cemented Regensburg's control of trade in the region. At the southern end of the Steinerne Brücke stands the **㉛** picturesque **Brückturm** (Bridge Tower): all tiny windows, weathered tiles, and pink plaster. (The brooding building with a massive roof to the left of the tower is an old salt warehouse that now serves as a restaurant where you can try your first Regensburger sausages.).

Regensburg is rarely out of the headlines in the German and even international press because of the flamboyant and often unpredictable lifestyle of one of its resident, Gloria of Thurn-und-Taxis. The young, widowed princess achieved wide fame because of the glamorous parties she threw at the family estate, the Schloss Emmeram (☞ *below*). Michael Jackson and Mick Jagger have been among her guests. In recent years the princess has fallen on hard times and was forced to sell much of the family treasure to pay the taxes that fell due when her husband, Prince Johannes, died. In 1996 the Bavarian authorities allowed her to keep what remains, on the condition that it be put on public display at the palace. So visitors in 1997 are due for a rare treat.

㉜ The vast **Schloss Emmeram complex,** formerly a Benedictine monastery, is bigger than Buckingham Palace. Its more than 500 rooms are a testimony to the fabulous wealth that the Thurn-und-Taxis family accumulated from running the German postal system, a monopoly they enjoyed until 1867. The former abbey cloisters are probably the palace's only architectural treasure, with their elegant and attenuated late-Gothic carving. As for the rest of the building, much of which was extensively rebuilt at the end of the 19th century, opinions remain divided. Some consider it the most vulgar and ponderously overdecorated specimen of its kind in Germany. Others admire its Victorian bombast and confidence. You can also visit the **Marstallmuseum** (Transport Museum) in the palace if you have a weakness for 18th- and 19th-century carriages and sleighs. ⊠ *Emmeramspl. 3,* ☎ *0941/50480.* ➤ *Palace and cloisters DM 12, Marstallmuseum DM 6, combined ticket DM 40.* ☉ *Palace and cloisters (guided tours only) Apr.–Oct., weekdays 11, 2, 3, and 4; weekends 10, 11, 2, 3, and 4. Nov.–Mar., weekends and holidays only, 10, 11, 2, and 3. Marstallmuseum (guided tours only) weekdays 2, 2:40, and 3:15, Sun. 10, 10:40, and 11:15.*

㉝ St. Emmeramus stands across from Schloss Emmerman. It's the work of the Asam brothers and is decorated in their customary and full-blown late-Baroque manner. ⊠ *Emmeramspl. 3,* ☎ *0941/51030.*

Dining and Lodging

$$$ ✕ **Historisches Eck.** A wealthy tradesman's family once owned this historic old house. Today paying customers sit at antique tables beneath the cross-vaulted ceiling that dates from the 13th century; leaded windows complete the medieval look. There's a less atmospheric dining room upstairs, so specify where you want to sit when you reserve a table. In both rooms the cuisine is identical and uniformly excellent, combining traditional fare with a light French-tinted flair—maize-fed roast chicken, for instance, with a delicate salad of *mange-tout* (snap beans). ⊠ *Watmarkt. 6,* ☎ *0941/58920. Reservations essential. AE, MC.*

$$ ✕ **Alter Simpl.** Sit in one of the cozy nooks and crannies of this old inn and try one of chef Harry Flashar's fresh beef steaks, a specialty of the house. ⊠ *Fischgässe 4,* ☎ *0941/999–395. No credit cards. Closed Sun.*

$ ✕ **Historische Wurstküche.** Succulent Regensburger sausages—the best in town—are prepared right before your eyes here on an open beechwood charcoal grill in the tiny kitchen, and if you eat them inside in the tiny dining room, you'll have to squeeze past the cook. In summer they are served at trestle tables set outside on the banks of the Danube. Inside are plaques recording the levels the river reached in the various floods that have doused the restaurant's kitchen in the past 100 years. ⊠ *Thundorferstr. 3,* ☎ *0941/59098. No credit cards.*

$$$$ ✕🏨 **Hotel-Restaurant Bischofshof am Dom.** This is one of Germany's most historic hostelries, a former bishop's palace where guests can sleep in an apartment that includes part of a Roman gateway. Other chambers are only slightly less historic, and some have seen emperors and princes as guests. Recent renovations have put well-equipped bathrooms into all rooms; they're still large and comfortably furnished. In summer the central, cobbled courtyard is a delight. If your room overlooks it, you'll awaken to a neighboring church's carillon playing a German hymn, and you'll retire to the strains of the Bavarian national anthem. The hotel's restaurant is a gourmet mecca in these reaches of Bavaria, yet the prices are sensible. The beer comes from a brewery founded in 1649. ⊠ *Krauterermarkt 3, D–93407,* ☎ *0941/59086,* 🆕 *0941/53508. 54 rooms with bath. Restaurant, bar, beer garden. AE, DC, MC, V.*

$$$$ ✕🏨 **Parkhotel Maximilian.** A handsome 18th-century building in the Old Town, this is the most elegant and sophisticated hotel in Regensburg. Its fine facade was restored in 1992, and public rooms are memorably exotic. Bedrooms are less opulent, but all are intelligently and comfortably decorated and come with cable TV. An extensive refurbishing program was under way at press time. If you're feeling homesick, you should eat at the American-style steak house. ⊠ *Maximilianstr. 28, D–93047,* ☎ *0941/568–5300,* 🆕 *0941/52942 (bookings can also be made in the U.S.:* ☎ *800/447–7462 or 800/223–0888). 46 rooms,*

6 *suites with bath. 2 restaurants, bar, café, beauty salon, recreation room. AE, DC, MC, V.*

$$$-$$$$ ✕🏨 **Altstadthotel Arch.** A beautifully renovated 18th-century house with foundations laid in the 12th century, this small family hotel in the center of the old city is convenient for visiting all the main attractions. Rooms are decorated in great style, mostly in warm blues, and shades of red and dark wood. Try for an attic room—you'll sleep beneath the original beams. The restaurant is in a Gothic-style stone-vaulted cellar. It offers an international menu, but it's dominated by Franconian dishes such as sauerbraten; the *Knödeln* are homemade. ⊠ *Haidpl. 4, D–93407,* ☎ *0941/502–060,* 🅵🅰🆇 *0941/5020–6168. 62 rooms, 6 apartments with bath or shower. Restaurant, bar. AE, DC, MC, V.*

$$ ✕🏨 **Kaiserhof am Dom.** Stay here for the great view of the cathedral. The building itself oozes 18th-century charm, with exposed beams, stone walls, and rough plaster. Rooms are more modern, with pastel-color walls, cherry-wood furnishings, and new carpeting. Try to get one with a view. ⊠ *Kramgasse 10, D–93407,* ☎ *0941/585–350,* 🅵🅰🆇 *0941/585–3595. 32 rooms with bath. Restaurant, café. AE, MC. Closed Dec. 23–Jan. 6.*

The Arts

Regensburg offers a range of musical experiences, though none so moving as a performance by the famous boys choir **Domspatzen** (Cathedral Sparrows) at Dom St. Peter. The best-sung mass is held on Sunday at 9 AM. It can be a remarkable experience, and it's worth scheduling your visit to the city to hear the choir.

Numbers in the margin correspond to points of interest on the Franconia map.

Weltenburg

★ ㉞ *25 km (15 mi) southwest of Regensberg.*

In Weltenburg you'll find the great abbey church of St. George and St. Martin, by the banks of the Danube. The most dramatic approach to the abbey is by boat from Kelheim, 10 kilometers (6 miles) downstream (☞ Contacts and Resources *in* Franconia A to Z, *below*). On the stunning ride, the boat winds between towering limestone cliffs that rise straight up from the tree-lined riverbanks. The abbey church, constructed between 1716 and 1718, is commonly regarded as the masterpiece of the brothers Cosmas Damian and Egid Quirin Asam, two leading Baroque architects and decorators of Bavaria (Cosmas Damian was the architect, Egid Quirin was the painter, sculptor, and stucco worker). If you've seen their little church of St. John Nepomuk in Munich, you'll know what pyrotechnics to expect here, albeit on a substantially larger scale. To some, this kind of frothy confection, with painted figures whirling on the ceiling, lavish and brilliantly polished marble, highly wrought statuary, and stucco dancing in rhythmic arabesques across the curving walls, is more high kitsch than high art. To others, the exuberance, drama, and sheer technical sophistication of this concentrated style may be appear to be a stone version of Mozart's music. Whichever view you take, it's hard not to be impressed by the bronze equestrian statue of St. George above the high altar, reaching down imperiously with his flamelike, twisted gilt sword to dispatch the winged dragon at his feet. ☉ *9–dusk.*

NEED A BREAK?   The abbey monks brew their own delicious dark beer, which you can sample on draft while sitting under ancient chestnut trees in the courtyard. Meals are also served. ☉ *Daily until 6.*

Walhalla

★ ⑤ *11 km (7 mi) east of Regensburg.*

Walhalla is an excursion from Regensburg you won't want to miss, especially if you have an interest in the wilder expressions of 19th-century German nationalism. The town has an incongruous Greek-style Doric temple that may be approached by a Danube riverboat (☞ Contacts and Resources *in* Franconia A to Z *below*). To get to the temple from the river you'll have to climb 358 marble steps; this is not a tour to take if you're not in good shape. There is, however, a parking lot near the top. To drive to it, take the Danube River valley country road (unnumbered) east from Regensburg 8 kilometers (5 miles) to Donaustauf. The Walhalla temple is 1 kilometer (about ½ mile) outside the village and well signposted.) Walhalla—a name resonant with Nordic mythology—was where the god Odin received the souls of dead heroes. This monumental temple, on a commanding site high above the Danube, was erected in 1840 for Ludwig I to honor German heroes through the ages. In the prevailing neoclassical style of the 19th century, it's actually a copy of the Parthenon in Athens. Even if you consider the building more a monument to kitsch than a tribute to the great men of Germany, you will at least be able to muse about its supremely well-built structure, its great, smooth-fitting stones, and its expanses of costly marble—evidence of both the financial resources and the craftsmanship that were Ludwig's to command.

FRANCONIA A TO Z

Arriving and Departing

By Car

Franconia is served by five main autobahns: A–7 from Hamburg; A–3 from Köln and Frankfurt; A–81 from Stuttgart; A–6 from Heilbronn; and A–9 from Munich. Nürnberg is 167 kilometers (104 miles) from Munich and 222 kilometers (139 miles) from Frankfurt. Regensburg is 120 kilometers (75 miles) from Munich and 332 kilometers (207 miles) from Frankfurt.

By Plane

The major international airports near Franconia are at Frankfurt and Munich; both have regular flights to and from the United States. The most important regional airports are at Nürnberg and Bayreuth. There are frequent flights between Frankfurt and Nürnberg.

By Train

Regular InterCity services connect Nürnberg and Regensburg with Frankfurt and other major German cities. Trains run hourly from Frankfurt to Munich, with stops at Würzburg and Nürnberg. The trip takes about three hours. There are also hourly trains from Munich direct to Regensburg and to Nürnberg.

Getting Around

By Bicycle

Renting bicycles is popular in Franconia, and the tourist authorities have made great efforts to attract cyclists. The scenic wooded terrain of the Altmühltal Valley is particularly suitable for biking. The tourist board for the Altmühltal (the Fremdenverkehrsamt Naturpark Altmühltal, ⊠ Notre Dame 1, D–85072 Eichstätt, ☎ 08421/6733) issues leaflets with suggested cycling tours and lists of outlets where you can rent bikes. Bicycles can also be rented from most major train stations (the cost is DM 12 per day, DM 6 if you have a rail ticket). Other tourist offices can supply details of special cycling routes in their regions.

By Boat

A total of 15 different lines operate cruises through the region from April through October. Contact the **Fremdenverkehrsverband Franken** (⊠ Am Plärrer 14, Nürnberg, ☎ 0911/264–202) and ask for details of their "Weisse Flotte" cruises. Or contact a travel agent in advance.

By Bus

The bus service between major centers in Franconia is poor; it's better to drive or ride the train. Other than the buses along the Romantic Road, the only major service is from Rothenburg-ob-der-Tauber to Nürnberg. Local buses run from most train stations to smaller towns and villages, though the service isn't frequent. Buses for the Fichtelgebirge in northern Franconia leave from Bayreuth's post office, near the train station.

By Car

The most famous scenic route in Franconia is the Romantic Road (☞ Chapter 5), but almost as interesting are the east section of the Burgenstrasse (Castle Road), which runs west to east from Heidelberg to Nürnberg; and the Bocksbeutel Strasse (Franconian Wine Road), which follows the course of the Main River from Zeil am Main along the wine-growing slopes of the valley to Aschaffenburg.

By Train

If you start in Frankfurt and plan to visit the wine towns along the Main River, you can take good local trains to Aschaffenburg, Miltenberg, and other small river towns (☞ Chapter 5). Some InterCity trains stop in Bamberg, which is most speedily reached from Munich. Locals trains from Nürnberg connect with Bayreuth and areas of southern Franconia.

Contacts and Resources

Car Rentals

Avis: ⊠ Markgrafenallee 6, ☎ 0921/789–550, **Bayreuth**; ⊠ Schmidt-str. 39, ☎ 069/730–111, **Frankfurt**; ⊠ Allersbergerstr. 139, ☎ 0911/49696, **Nürnberg.**

Europcar: ⊠ Schlossstr. 32, ☎ 069/775–033, **Frankfurt**; ⊠ Nürnberg Airport, ☎ 0911/528–484, **Nürnberg**; ⊠ Straubingerstr. 8, ☎ 0941/793–011, **Regensburg**; ⊠ Friendenstr. 15, ☎ 0931/881–150, **Würzburg.**

Hertz: ⊠ Gutleutstr. 87, ☎ 069/242–526627, **Frankfurt**; ⊠ Nürnberg Airport, ☎ 0911/527–719, **Nürnberg**; ⊠ Bahnhofstr. 22, ☎ 0941/51515, **Regensburg.**

Sixt-Budget: ⊠ Frankfurt Airport, ☎ 069/697–0070, **Frankfurt**; ⊠ In-golstädter Str. 21, ☎ 0911/438–710, **Nürnberg**; ⊠ Im Gewerbepark A7, ☎ 0941/401–035, **Regensburg.**

Emergencies

Police: ☎ 110. **Fire:** ☎ 112. **Emergency medical attention:** ☎ 19222.

Guided Tours

The most popular excursions are **boat trips** on the Danube from Regensburg to Ludwig I's imposing Greek-style Doric temple of Walhalla or to the monastery at Weltenburg. There are daily sailings to Walhalla from Easter through October. The round-trip costs DM 12 and takes three hours. Changing boats at Kelheim will allow you to reach Weltenburg from Regensburg, or you can pick up a shorter cruise from Kelheim. The Regensburg–Kelheim boat ride takes 2½ hours. The journey from Kelheim to Weltenburg takes only 30 minutes (the fare is DM 9). Daylong upstream cruises from Regensburg, which take in Weltenburg via the Altmühltal (a scenic wooded gorge), are also possible. Regensburg boats depart from the Steinerne Brücke; for information, call 0941/55359. For information on Kelheim departures, call 09441/3402 or 09441/8290.

There are also regular trips in the summer along scenic routes following the Main River from Aschaffenburg to Würzburg and from Würzburg to Bamberg. These are worth considering if you plan to spend a lot of time in the region. For information, contact **Fränkische Personen-Schiffahrt** (⊠ Kranenkai 1, Würzburg, ☎ 0931/55356 and 0931/51722) or the Würzburg tourist office (⊠ Marktpl., D–97070 Würzburg, ☎ 0931/37398).

For boat tours around Bamberg, contact **Fritz Kropf,** (⊠ Kapuzinerstr. 5, ☎ 0951/26679). Tours leave daily at 2:30 and 4; the cost is DM 5.50.

In Nürnberg tours of the Old Town center start daily at 2:30 at the tourist information office, Hauptmarkt. The two-hour tour, which is in German, costs DM 8 Two-and-a-half-hour tours in English start at 9:30 daily, May–October, in front of the Mauthalle, Hallplatz. The cost is DM 20.

Hiking

For maps of hiking trails in Franconia and further information, contact the Fremdenverkehrsverband Franken (⊠ Am Plärrer 14, D–90443 Nürnberg, ☎ 0911/264–202).

Skiing

For information on resorts and snow conditions, call the Tourist Information Fichtelgebirge (☎ 09272/6255).

Travel Agencies

American Express (⊠ Adlerstr. 2, Nürnberg, ☎ 0911/232–397) makes travel arrangements.

Visitor Information

The principal regional tourist office for Franconia is **Fremdenverkehrsverband Franken** (⊠ Am Plärrer 14, D–90443 Nürnberg, ☎ 0911/264–202). There are local tourist information offices in the following towns:

Ansbach: ⊠ Johann-Sebastian-Bach-Pl. 1, D–91522, ☎ 0981/51243.
Bamberg: Fremdenverkehrsamt, ⊠ Geyerswörthstr. 3, D–96047, ☎ 0951/871–161.
Bayreuth: Fremdenverkehrsverein, ⊠ Luitpoldpl. 7–9, D–95444, ☎ 0921/88588.
Coburg: Fremdenverkehrs-und Kongressbetrieb, ⊠ Herrngasse 4, D–96450, ☎ 09561/74180.
Ingolstadt: ⊠ Hallstr. 5, D–85049, ☎ 0841/305–417.
Kloster Banz and **Vierzehnheiligen:** ⊠ Alte Darre am Stadtturm, D–96231 Staffelstein, ☎ 09573/4192.
Kronach: ⊠ Marktpl., D–96317, ☎ 09261/97236.
Kulmbach: Fremdenverkehrsbüro, ⊠ Stadthalle, Sutte 2, D–95311, ☎ 09221/95880.
Lichtenfels: ⊠ Am Marktpl. 1, D–96215, ☎ 09571/795–221.
Nürnberg: Congress-und Tourismus-Zentrale, ⊠ Frauentorgraben 3, D–90443 Nürnberg 70, ☎ 0911/23360.
Regensburg: ⊠ Altes Rathaus, D–93047, ☎ 0941/507–4410.
Weissenburg: ⊠ Martin-Luther-Pl. 3, D–91781, ☎ 09141/907–124.

7 The Bodensee

Be sure to take at least one boat trip on the Bodensee if you're in the area. Some towns are built on islands near the shore, and their incredible beauty is best surveyed from the water. Other features of the area appreciated by tourists are its climate, which allows near-tropical growth in places, and its proximity to Switzerland and Liechtenstein. Konstanz, the largest city on the lake, is German, but parts of it are in Switzerland.

THE BODENSEE (Lake Constance) is the largest lake in the German-speaking world—424 kilometers square, 339 kilometers around (163 miles square, 210 miles around)—and is bordered by Germany, Switzerland, and Austria. Though called a lake, it's actually a vast swelling of the Rhine, gouged out by a massive glacier in the Ice Age and flooded by the river as the ice receded. The Rhine flows into its southeast corner, where Switzerland and Austria meet, and flows out at its west end.

Visitors should be grateful: These immense natural forces have created a ravishing corner of Germany—a natural summer playground, ringed with little towns and busy resorts. Gentle, vineyard-clad hills slope down to the lakeshore. To the south, the Alps are a jagged and dramatic backdrop. It's one of the warmest areas of the country, too, the result not just of its location—it's almost the southernmost region of Germany—but of the warming influence of the water, which gathers heat in the summer and releases it in the winter like a massive radiator. There are near-tropical corners of the Bodensee, where lemons, bougainvillea, and hibiscus flourish, and vines grow in abundance. The lake itself practically never freezes (it has done so only once this century and twice during the last).

R&R may be the major reason for visiting the Bodensee, but it's by no means the only one. The lake's natural attractions, not least its abundance of fresh fish and its fertile soil, were as compelling several thousand years ago as they are today, making this one of the oldest continually inhabited areas of Germany. Highlights include the medieval island town of Lindau; Friedrichshafen, birthplace of the zeppelin; the rococo abbey church of Birnau; and the town of Konstanz on the Swiss-German border. It would be a shame, too, not to take advantage of the area's proximity to Austria and Switzerland (and to little Liechtenstein). A day trip to one or more is easy to make, and formalities are few.

Pleasures and Pastimes

Dining
Fish specialties predominate around the Bodensee. There are 35 different types of fish in the lake, with *Renke* and *Felchen* (both meaty white fish) the most highly prized. Felchen belongs to the salmon family and is best eaten *blau* (poached) in rosemary sauce or *müllerin* (baked in almonds). Wash it down with a top-quality Meersburg white wine. If you venture north to Upper Swabia, *Pfannkuchen* and *Spaetzle,* both flour-and-egg dishes, are the most common specialties. Pfannkuchen (pancakes) are generally filled with meat, cheese, jam, or sultanas, or chopped into fine strips and scattered in a clear consommé known as *Flädlesuppe.* Spaetzle are roughly chopped, golden-color fried egg noodles that are the usual accompaniment to the Swabian Sunday roast-beef lunch of *Rinderbraten.* One of the best-known Swabian dishes is *Maultaschen,* a kind of ravioli, usually served floating in a broth strewn with chives.

CATEGORY	COST*
$$$$	over DM 90
$$$	DM 55–DM 90
$$	DM 35–DM 55
$	under DM 35

per person for a three-course meal, including tax and tip but not wine

Lodging

The towns and resorts around the lake have a wide range of hotels, from venerable, wedding-cake-style, fin de siècle palaces to more modest *Gasthöfe* (inns). If you're visiting in July and August, make reservations well in advance and expect higher-than-average prices. For lower rates and a more rural atmosphere, consider staying away from the lake in Upper Swabia or the Allgäu.

CATEGORY	COST*
$$$$	over DM 200
$$$	DM 160–DM 200
$$	DM 120–DM 160
$	under DM 120

All prices are for a standard double room for two, including tax and service charge.

Nightlife and the Arts

Most Bodensee towns and resorts have regular **entertainment evenings** for visitors, ranging from traditional folk music and dancing to jazz and pop concerts. Local tourist offices have schedules. Many resort hotels also organize regular *Heimatabende* (folk-music evenings) or *Gästeabende* (guests' evenings); in some, Saturday night really is dance night. The **Bodensee Festival,** a rich mixture of orchestral and chamber music concerts, opera and dance, is held from early May to early June in various towns around the lake.

Outdoor Activities and Sports

BICYCLING

Bikes can be rented at many train stations and from some sports shops (inquire at tourist offices). Bikes are allowed on all lake ferries.

Radeltours, set up by bike fan Dieter Siever, organizes bike tours of the Bodensee, including accommodations en route. Dieter's tours can be booked with Radeltours (⊠ J. A. Feuchtmayer-Str. 5, Konstanz, ☎ 07531/34793) or directly in the United States (⊠ Radeltours USA, 455 Elm St., Dartmouth, MA 02748, ☎ FAX 508/993–4122). Konstanz-based **Velotours** arranges bike tours with accommodations around the Bodensee (⊠ Mainaustr. 34, ☎ 07531/52083), and also rents out bikes at DM 20 per day, or DM 50 for three days.

BOATING

There are more than 30 boatyards and sailing schools where you can rent boats; most will ask to see written proof (a proficiency certificate from a sailing school, for example) that you can handle a sail vessel. Motorboats and rowboats can be rented in every resort without such formalities. Windsurfers will also have no trouble renting boards from any of 35 rental points around the lake. Water-skiers are catered to on the lake, although the fun isn't cheap. The Bodensee is fine cruising water, too, and many yards charter yachts.

Shopping

The Bodensee is artists' territory, and shopping means combing the many small **galleries** and artists' shops in lakeside towns and resorts for watercolors, engravings, and prints. Local potters practice their craft and sell their **pottery** in many places around the lake.

Exploring the Bodensee

You can travel the entire length of the German shore of the Bodensee easily in a day—by car, train, and even by boat—but the temptation to linger in one of the enchanting towns along the way will be strong. Lindau is a pretty and unusual resort, and it's close to Austria,

Liechtenstein, and the mountains of the German Allgäu. Friedrichshafen is busier but sits at the head of a road inland to Ravensburg, Weingarten, and the extraordinary churches of the "Baroque Road." Meersburg, built on a slope that slides down to the lakeside, is arguably the loveliest Bodensee town and is just a short ferry ride to the area's largest city, Konstanz, the local gateway to the Swiss Alps. The Bodensee region is compact enough to cover easily in five days.

Great Itineraries

Numbers in the text refer to numbers in the margin and on the Bodensee map.

IF YOU HAVE 3 DAYS

Prowl around **Lindau** ①, then make for the next "town in the lake," **Wasserburg** ②, perched above the water at the end of a narrow causeway. Next stop is **Friedrichshafen** ④, where you should reserve a couple of hours for the Zeppelin Museum, which celebrates the airships once built there. Overnight in lovely ⌐ **Meersburg** ⑤, rising early to catch the sunrise over the lake and the ferry to ⌐ **Konstanz** ⑪, on the opposite shore. From here there's a difficult choice—a day trip either to the Swiss Alps or to two Bodensee islands, **Mainau** ⑫ and **Reichenau** ⑬. After an overnight stay in Konstanz, return to Meersburg or make for the "German Nice," as the local tourist office calls **Überlingen** ⑦.

IF YOU HAVE 5 DAYS

Start your itinerary at **Lindau** ①, continuing to **Wasserburg** ②, **Langenargen** ③ (for a panoramic view of the lake from Montfort Castle), and **Friedrichshafen** ④, then heading inland via the B–30 to medieval ⌐ **Ravensburg** ⑧, where you can find food and accommodation in a number of historic hostelries. Although the great pilgrimage church of **Weingarten** ⑨ is only 5 kilometers (3 miles) north of Ravensburg, allow a morning or an afternoon to do the magnificent structure justice. Return south to the lake and an overnight stay in lovely ⌐ **Meersburg** ⑤. Catch the ferry to ⌐ **Konstanz** ⑪, on the opposite shore, and allow a full day to get to know this fascinating city. With five days on your hands, an excursion to Switzerland should be irresistible—but return to overnight in Konstanz or any of its German neighbors to avoid paying room rates in strong Swiss francs. Devote the next day to the islands of **Mainau** ⑫ and supper in one of the ancient taverns of **Reichenau** ⑬, and then head for **Radolfszell** ⑭, at the end of the peninsula that juts into the western end of the Bodensee. From there it's a short drive around the head of the lake to ⌐ **Überlingen** ⑦, where one or two days' relaxation in its balmy clime isn't really enough. A visit to the nearby pilgrimage church of **Birnau** ⑥—a rococo masterpiece—is a marvelous finale to any Bodensee tour.

When to Tour the Bodensee

The Bodensee's temperate climate means comfortable weather any time of year, with the possible exception of November when it may be cold and damp. In spring orchard blossoms explode everywhere, and on Minau, the "island of flowers," more than a million tulips, hyacinths, and narcissi burst into bloom. Holiday crowds come in summer, while autumn can be long and mellow. Early birds are rewarded with spectacular sunrises over the lake, although evenings also have splendor.

The Bodensee (Lake Constance)

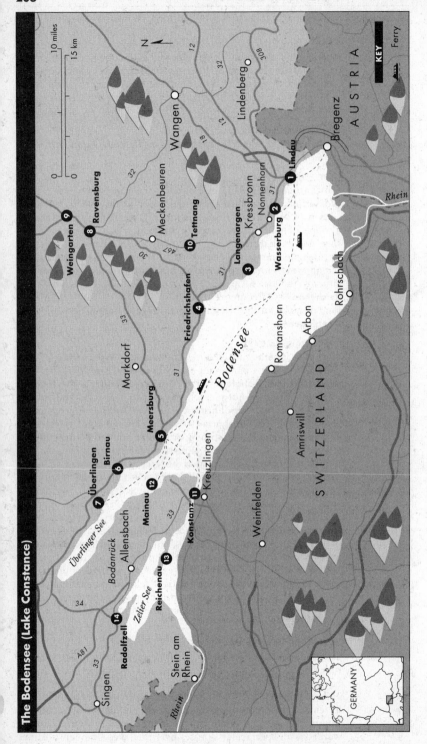

GERMANY

THE NORTHERN SHORE

Lindau, Wasserburg, Langenargen, Friedrichshafen, Meersburg, Birnau, and Überlingen

The Bodensee's northern shore marks this part of Germany's land boundary, and from the water's edge you can see snowcapped mountains in Switzerland and Liechtenstein rising majestically above the opposite bank. A clear day will bring the peaks of the Austrian Vorarlberg, to the east, into view. There's a feeling here, in the midst of a peaceful Alpine landscape, that you're a part of Germany and yet separated from it—often literally in towns like Lindau and Wasserburg, which sit in the lake tethered to land by narrow causeways. At the far western end of this northern shore, Überlingen, a fading beauty of a resort beached on a small finger of water, works to maintain its reputation as the "German Nice."

Numbers in the margin correspond to points of interest on the Bodensee map.

Lindau

❶ *180 km (108 mi) southwest of Munich.*

This ancient town, which once sheltered Roman ships of war and trade, is the Bodensee's very essence, so much so that it is surrounded by the lake. It's best to arrive by train, and even that seems boatlike as it teeters along the narrow causeway linking Lindau with the mainland. Stand at the water's edge in Lindau's newer, mainland section, the Gartenstadt (Garden Town, so named because of its abundance of flowers and shrubs) on a hazy summer's day, and the walls and roofs of old Lindau seem to float on the shimmering water, an illusion intensified by the miragelike backdrop of the Swiss and Liechtenstein Alps.

Lindau was originally three islands, on one of which the Romans built a military base. Under Roman rule the town developed as a fishing settlement and then as a trading center along the route between the rich lands of Swabia and Italy for hundreds of years. (The *Lindauer Bote,* an important stagecoach service between Germany and Italy in the 18th and 19th centuries, was based here; Goethe traveled on it on his first visit to Italy in 1786.) In 1275 little Lindau was made a Free Imperial City within the Holy Roman Empire. As the empire crumbled toward the end of the 18th century, battered by Napoléon's revolutionary armies, Lindau fell victim to competing political groups. It was ruled by the Austrian Empire before passing into Bavarian control in 1805.

The proud symbol of Bavaria, a **seated lion,** is one of Lindau's striking landmarks. The lion in question, 20 feet high and carved from Bavarian marble, stares out across the lake from a massive plinth at the end of one of the harbor walls. You can share the lion's view by climbing up to the viewing platform of the harbor lighthouse, the **Neuer Leuchtturm.** On a clear day you'll see the Three Sisters, three peaks in Liechtenstein. 🎟 *DM 1.* ☯ *Apr.–Oct., daily 9:30–6.*

The **Alter Leuchtturm,** or old lighthouse, stands at the edge of the inner harbor on the weathered remains of the original 13th-century city walls. A maze of ancient streets leading from the harbor make up the **Altstadt** (Old Town). The main street, pedestrians-only **Maximilianstrasse,** is lined by old half-timbered and gabled houses. Eventually all the Altstadt streets lead to the **Altes Rathaus** (Old Town Hall), the finest of Lindau's handsome historical buildings. It was constructed between 1422 and 1436 in the midst of a vineyard (now a busy thoroughfare) and given a Renaissance face-lift 150 years later, though the original stepped gables remain. Emperor Maximilian I held an imperial council here in 1496; a fresco on the south facade depicts a scene from this high point of local history. A part of the building that served as the town prison is identified by an ancient inscription enjoining the townsfolk "to turn aside from evil and learn to do good."

The **Barfüsserkirche,** (Church of the Barefoot Pilgrims), built from 1241 to 1270, is now Lindau's principal theater. The Gothic choir is a memorable location for concerts, especially church music. The tourist office on Bahnhofplatz can provide details of performances. Ludwigstrasse and Fischergasse lead to a watchtower, once part of the original city walls. Pause in the little park behind it, the **Stadtgarten.** If it's early evening, you'll see the first gamblers of the night making for the neighboring casino. **Peterskirche** (St. Peter's Church) on Schrannenplatz is an impressively solid Romanesque building, constructed in the 10th century and reputedly the oldest church in the Bodensee region. Step inside to see the frescoes by Hans Holbein the Elder (1465–1524), some of which depict scenes from the life of St. Peter, the patron saint of fishermen.

NEED A BREAK?   The **Weinstube Frey** is a 16th-century wine tavern. Try fresh lake fish and a crisp white Bodensee wine for an excellent lunch. Smoked ham from the Black Forest is also a specialty. ⊠ *Maximilianstr. 15.*

Lindau's market square, **Marktplatz,** is lined by a series of sturdily attractive old buildings, among them the 18th-century **Haus zum Cavazzen,** richly decorated with stucco and frescoes. Today it's the municipal art gallery and local history museum. Its permanent display includes a fascinating collection of mechanical musical instruments. ⊠ *Am Marktpl.* 🏛 *DM 3. Guided tour of musical instrument collection an extra DM 5.* ☉ *Apr.–Oct., Tues.–Sun. 10–noon and 2–5.*

The simple, sparely decorated Gothic **Stephanskirche** and the more elaborate Baroque **Marienkirche** stand on Marktplatz. Both have charm—the Stephanskirche for its simplicity, the Marienkirche for its exuberance.

OFF THE BEATEN PATH   **PEACE MUSEUM –** The achievements of the crusade for world peace are documented in Europe's first Peace Museum, in Bad Schachen. ⊠ *Lindenhofweg 25, just outside Lindau.* 🏛 *Free.* ☉ *Mid-Apr.–mid-Oct., Tues.–Sat. 10–noon and 2:30–5, Sun. 10–noon.*

Dining and Lodging

$$$$ ✕ **Restaurant Hoyerberg Schlössle.** A commanding view across the lake
★ to Bregenz and the Alps combined with elegant nouvelle cuisine make this just about the best dining experience in Lindau. The specialties are fish and game, which change seasonally, and there are fixed-price menus of six and eight courses; one offers lobster, noodles with white truffles and goose liver, and roast breast of squab. The decor features brick-trimmed arched windows, fresh flowers, and elegant high-back chairs. Dine on the terrace for the terrific view. ⊠ *Hoyerbergstr. 64,* ☎ *08382/25295. Reservations essential. Jacket and tie. AE, DC, MC, V. Closed Mon. and mid-Jan.–Feb.*

$ ✕ **Gasthaus zum Sünfzen.** In the heart of the Old Town, the Gasthaus zum Sünfzen is an appealing old inn with small leaded windows and a simple, wood-paneled interior. Entrées include venison shot on forest hunts led by landlord Hans Grättinger, as well as fish caught locally and sausage from the restaurant's own butcher shop. Try either the spinach spaetzle or the Felchen fillet. The menu changes daily and seasonally. ✉ *Maximilianstr. 1,* ☎ *08382/5865. AE, DC, MC, V. Closed Feb.*

$$$$ ✕🛏 **Hotel Bayerischer Hof.** This is *the* address in town, a stately hotel directly on the edge of the lake, bordered by gardens lush with semitropical, long-flowering plants, trees, and shrubs. Most of the luxuriously appointed rooms have views of the lake and the Swiss mountains beyond. Freshly caught lake pike perch is a highlight of the extensive menu in the stylish restaurant. If the hotel is full or can't provide the room you want, try one of the two neighboring, less expensive establishments under the same management (the Reutemann and the Seegarten). ✉ *Seepromenade, D–88131,* ☎ *08382/9150,* 🅵🅰🅇 *08382/915–591. 104 rooms with bath. Restaurant, bar, café, pool, massage, boating, bicycles, recreation room. DC, MC, V.*

$$ ✕🛏 **Schachen-Schlössle.** Though this turreted 15th-century manor house is not on Lindau Island, it is set amid peaceful gardens very close to the waterfront (in the Bad Schachen District of the mainland town) and is a remarkably good value. Rooms are decorated in authentic rustic style. The 16 apartments are ideal for families, spacious and with cooking facilities—book well in advance. The restaurant serves traditional German dishes with a light French accent, and lake fish is always on the menu. ✉ *Enzisweilerstr. 1–7, D–88131,* ☎ *08382/5069,* 🅵🅰🅇 *08382/3956. 16 rooms, 16 apartments with bath. Restaurant, bar, beer garden, indoor pool, sauna. AE, DC, MC, V. Closed Nov.–Feb.*

$ ✕🛏 **Gasthof Engel.** Claiming to be the oldest inn in Lindau, the Engel traces its pedigree back to 1390. Tucked into one of the Old Town's ancient, narrow streets, the family-run property creaks with history. Twisted oak beams are exposed inside and outside the terraced house. The bedrooms are simply furnished but comfortable. Frau Zech's changing menu features lake fish and local white wines. ✉ *Schafgasse 4, D–88131,* ☎ *08382/5240. 9 rooms, most with bath. Restaurant. No credit cards. Closed Nov.*

Nightlife and the Arts

Lindau has a **casino,** open 3 PM–3 AM daily (☎ 08382/5051). The Las Vegas of the Bodensee is **Bregenz,** in neighboring Austria, but it's only 8 kilometers (5 miles) away. Michael Zeller, who has two reputable shops in Lindau, organizes the celebrated, twice-yearly **Internationale Bodensee-Kunstauktion** (art auction); it's held in the spring and fall.

Outdoor Activities and Sports

BICYCLING

Bikes can be rented at the Lindau train station for DM 12 a day (DM 6 with a valid train ticket).

BOATING

The **Bodensee Yachtschule** in Lindau charters yachts (✉ Christoph Eychmüller Schiffswerfte 2, ☎ 08382/5140).

Shopping

Michael Zeller, who organizes the Bodensee art auction, has two reputable shops selling watercolors, engravings, and prints (✉ Bindergasse 7 and Hintere Metzgergasse 2, ☎ 08382/93020 for both). You can find fine pottery at **Angelika Ochsenreiter's** shop (✉ Ludwigstr. 29, ☎ 08382/23867).

Wasserburg

❷ *6 km (4 mi) west of Lindau.*

Wasserburg means "water castle," describing exactly what this enchanting town once was—a fortress built on the site of a Roman watchtower. The original owners, the counts of Montfort zu Tettnang, sold it to the Fugger family of Augsburg to pay off mounting debts. When the Fuggers fell on hard times in the 18th century, the castle passed into the hands of the Hapsburgs. In 1805 it was taken over by the Bavarian government.

The Fuggers, when they bought Wasserburg, were among the richest families in Europe. During the final days of their ownership, they were so impoverished they couldn't even afford to maintain the drawbridge that connected the castle with the shore. Instead they built a causeway. Cars aren't allowed into Wasserburg these days, and one of the pleasures here is to wander undisturbed through the tangle of ancient streets. The castle is now the Hotel Schloss.

Dining and Lodging

$$$ ×⊞ **Hotel Schloss Wasserburg.** You live like a lord in this lovely castle hotel, and at an astonishingly reasonable price. Rooms are nobly furnished, with Oriental rugs and carved bedsteads. Most have uninterrupted views of the lake. The beamed restaurant has an excellent menu featuring freshly caught lake fish, while in warm weather you can dine on an airy terrace above the water. ⊠ *Auf der Halbinsel, Hauptstr. 5, D–88142,* ☎ *08382/887–588,* ℻ *08382/8141. Restaurant, beach. AE, DC, MC, V.*

Langenargen

❸ *8 km (5 mi) west of Wasserburg.*

Langenargen is worth visiting because on its waterfront is the region's most unusual castle. The Baroque parish church and the town museum, both on the Marktplatz, are also interesting.

Montfort Castle—named for the original owners, the counts of Montfort-Werdenberg—was a conventional enough medieval fortification until the 19th century, when it was rebuilt in pseudo-Moorish style by its new owner, King Wilhelm I of Württemberg. If you can, see it from a steamer on the lake; the castle is especially memorable in the early morning or late afternoon, when the softened, watery light gives additional mystery to its outline. These days, very unromantically, the castle houses local government offices and is *not* open to the public. Its **tower**, however, can be climbed. ⊠ *Waterfront.* 🎫 *DM 1.50.* ⊙ *Easter–Oct., daily 9–5.*

The **Langenargen Stadtmuseum** (City Museum), which may appeal only to those with an advanced taste for lesser-known 20th-century works, contains a series of paintings by German Hans Purrmann (1880–1966), an admirer of Henri Matisse and cofounder of the Académie Matisse in Paris in 1908. The academy faltered soon after it was founded, and between 1915 and 1935 (at which point Purrmann's work was outlawed by the Nazis), Purrmann lived in Langenargen. ⊠ *Marktpl. 20,* ☎ *07543/3410.* 🎫 *DM 3.* ⊙ *Apr.–Oct., Tues.–Sun. 10–noon and 2:30–5.*

Friedrichshafen

❹ *10 km (6 mi) west of Langenargen.*

Named for its founder, King Friedrich I of Württemberg, Friedrichshafen is a young town (dating only to 1811) that was almost wiped off the map by wartime air raids on its munitions factories. Curious though it may seem in an area otherwise given over to resort towns and agriculture, Friedrichshafen played a central role in Germany's aeronautic tradition, which saw the development of the zeppelin airship before

World War I and the Dornier flying boat in the '20s and '30s. In both cases it was the broad, smooth waters of the lake that made Friedrichshafen attractive to the pioneer aeronauts: The zeppelins were built in enormous floating hangars on the lake; the Dorniers were tested on its calm surface.

★ The fascinating story of the zeppelin is told in the **Zeppelin–Museum Technik und Kunst,** with the aid of models (one 26 feet long), plans, photographs, and documents (☞ Dornier Museum in Meersburg, *below*). The museum is housed in a specially constructed wing of the Hafenbahnhof (harbor railway station). ☎ *07541/203–441.* ▣ *DM 8.* ☉ *Tues.–Sun. 10–5, Thurs. 10–8.*

Schloss Hofen, a short walk from town along the lakeside promenade, is a small palace that served as the summer residence of Württemberg kings until 1918. The palace was formerly a priory—its foundations date from the 11th century—and the adjoining priory **church** is a splendid example of local Baroque architecture. The swirling white stucco of the interior was executed by the Wessobrun Schmuzer family, whose master craftsman, Franz, was responsible for much of the finest work in the basilica of Weingarten. Franz Schmuzer also created the priory church's magnificent marble altar.

OFF THE
BEATEN PATH

SCHOOL MUSEUM – You can make a nostalgic return to the classroom with a visit to the School Museum. There are convincing reconstructions of schoolrooms from 1850, 1900, and 1930—and not a pocket calculator in sight. ⊠ *Friedrichstr. 14, in the Schnetzenhausen suburb,* ☎ *07541/32622.* ▣ *Free, but donations appreciated.* ☉ *Mid-Mar.–mid-Nov., daily 10–5; mid-Nov.–mid-Mar., Tues.–Sun. 2–5.*

Bicycling

Friedrichshafen's train station rents bikes for DM 12 a day (DM 6 with a valid train ticket). Twenty-five hotels and pensions in and around Friedrichshafen offer discounts of up to 20% on room rates for guests arriving by bike; the tourist office (☎ 07541/30010) has details.

Dining and Lodging

$$$–$$$$ ✕▥ **Hotel Restaurant Krone.** Not to be confused with the City-Krone, this hotel decorated in a Bavarian theme is in the Schnetzhausen District's quiet, semirural surroundings, ideal for a sporting holiday. All rooms have balconies. The restaurant specializes in game dishes and fish from the nearby Bodensee. ⊠ *Untere Mühlbachstr. 1, D–88046,* ☎ *07541/4080,* ℻ *07541/43601. 115 rooms with bath or shower. Restaurant, bar, indoor and outdoor pools, hot tub, sauna, indoor and outdoor tennis courts, bowling, exercise room, bicycles. AE, DC, MC, V. Closed Dec. 10–25.*

$$$–$$$$ ✕▥ **Ringhotel Buchhorner Hof.** This traditional lakeside hotel, now part of the Ring group, has been run by the same family since it opened in 1870. Hunting trophies on the walls, leather armchairs, and Turkish rugs decorate the public areas; bedrooms are large and comfortable, and all were totally renovated in the past two years. The restaurant is plush and subdued, with delicately carved chairs and mahogany-paneled walls. It offers a choice of menus that feature such dishes as pork medallions, perch fillet, and lamb chops. ⊠ *Friedrichstr. 33, D–88045,* ☎ *07541/2050,* ℻ *07541/32663. 64 rooms with bath, 1 suite, 1 apartment. Restaurant, bar, massage, sauna, miniature golf, exercise room, bicycles. AE, DC, MC, V. Closed mid-Dec.–mid-Jan.*

Nightlife and the Arts

From early May to early June Friedrichhafen's Graf-Zeppelin-Haus is the venue for the **Bodensee Festival** (☎ 07541/30010). The annual **Kul-**

turfer, an open-air festival of theater and musical, is in the first week of September.

Meersburg

⑤ *18 km (11 mi) west of Friedrichshafen.*

The most romantic way to approach Meersburg is from the lake. Seen from the water on a summer afternoon with the sun slanting low across the water, the steeply terraced town can seem floodlit, like an elaborate stage setting. (Meersburg is well aware of its too-good-to-be-true charm—some may find the gusto with which it has embraced tourism crass, and the town can get unpleasantly crowded.) Assuming your visit is by ferry boat, you'll step ashore in the Unterstadt, the lower town, which clings to the lakeshore about 150 feet below the Oberstadt, or upper town. The climb between the two halves is not arduous, but there's a bus if you can't face the hike.

Meersburg is said to have been founded in 628 by Dagobert, king of the Franks, who supposedly laid the first stone of the Altes Schloss, which watches majestically over the town and the lake far below. It's Germany's oldest inhabited castle and one of the most impressive. The market square, ringed by historic half-timbered houses including the medieval Rathaus, is unusually pretty and also bustling. In 1995 a hot spring was discovered on the outskirts of Meersburg, so you can expect that sometime the town will add "Bad" to its name. Meanwhile, the hot water is being fully exploited—in the municipal swimming pool, for example.

★   The massive central tower of the **Altes Schloss** (Old Castle) was named for King Dagobert and has walls 10 feet thick. In 1526 the Catholic bishop of Konstanz set himself up in the castle after he was thrown out by the newly Protestant Konstanz. Bishops remained in the castle until the middle of the 18th century, when they had built, as they saw it, a more suitable residence—the Baroque Neues Schloss. Plans to tear down the Altes Schloss in the early 19th century were shelved when it was taken over by one Baron Joseph von Lassberg, a man much taken by the castle's medieval romance. He turned it into a home for like-minded poets and artists, among them his sister-in-law, Annette von Droste-Hülshoff (1797–1848), generally considered one of Germany's finest poets. The Altes Schloss is still private property, but much of it can be visited, including the richly furnished rooms where von Droste-Hülshoff lived and the chamber where she died, as well as the imposing knights' hall, the minstrels' gallery, and the sinister dungeons. The **Altes Schloss Museum** contains a fascinating collection of weapons and armor, including a unique set of medieval jousting equipment. ☎ *07532/6441.* ✉ *DM 8.* ☼ *Daily 10–6.*

The spacious and elegant **Neues Schloss** (New Castle) is directly across from the Altes Schloss. It was built partly by Balthasar Neumann, the leading German architect of the 18th century, and partly by an Italian, Franz Anton Bagnato. Neumann's work is most obvious in the stately sweep of the grand double staircase, with its intricate grillwork and heroic statues. The interior's other standout is the glittering Speigelsaal, the Hall of Mirrors, now the site of an international music festival held in the summer (☞ Nightlife and the Arts, *below*). In an unlikely combination of 18th-century grace and 20th-century technology, the top floor of the palace houses the **Dornier Museum,** which traces the history of the German aircraft and aerospace industries. ☎ *07532/440–265.* ✉ *DM 4.*

🕙 *Apr.–Oct., daily 10–1 and 2–6. Guided tours in English can be arranged in advance* (☎ 07532/440–265).

Sunbathed, south-facing Meersburg has been a center of the Bodensee wine trade for centuries. You can pay your respects to the noble trade in the **Weinbau Museum,** one of the most comprehensive wine museums in Germany. A barrel capable of holding 50,000 liters and an immense wine press dating from 1607 are highlights of the collection. The museum has another claim to fame: It's in the house where Dr. Frank Anton Mesmer (1734–1815), pioneer of hypnotism—"mesmerism"—lived in the early 19th century. ⊠ *Vorburggasse 11,* ☎ *07532/431–110.* 🎫 *DM 1.* 🕙 *Apr.–Sept., Tues., Fri., and Sun. 2–5. Admission at other times during tourist-office tours of the town.*

NEED A BREAK?	The front door of **Weinkeller in Truben** (⊠ Steigstr.) is one end of a huge wine barrel. Inside, wine racks stretch from the floor to the whitewashed, vaulted ceiling. Order a bottle of local wine and try one of the cheese-based dishes.

An idyllic retreat almost hidden among the vineyards, the **Fürstenhäusle** was built in 1640 by a local vintner and later used as a holiday home by poet Annette von Droste-Hülshoff. It's now a museum containing many of her personal items and giving a vivid sense of Meersburg in her time. ⊠ *Stettenerstr. 9 (east of the Obertor, the town's north gate),* ☎ *07532/6088.* 🎫 *DM 4.* 🕙 *Easter.–mid-Oct., Mon.–Sat. 10–noon and 2–6, Sun. and holidays 2–6.*

Dining and Lodging

$$$-$$$$ ✕🏨 **Strandhotel Wilder Mann.** This 18th-century nobleman's home has its own 750-foot stretch of shoreline. Modern, deep-pile comforts are to be found in the antiques-filled guest rooms, with dark-pine furniture and tapestries predominating. The restaurant's pastries are first-rate, as is the wine cellar. ⊠ *Bismarckpl. 2, D–88709,* ☎ *07532/9011,* ℻ *07532/9014. 29 rooms, 2 apartments with bath. Restaurant, beach. AE. Closed Jan.–Feb.*

$$-$$$ ✕🏨 **Hotel-Cafe Off.** Although this small and friendly hotel fronts the lake, don't worry if you can't get a room overlooking the water—those on the side look out over vineyards. There's a bright, cheerful feel to the hotel, accentuated by the light woods and matching pastel tones of the furnishings. Rooms have broad beds and many homey touches. There's a playroom and sandpit for youngsters. ⊠ *Uferpromenade 51, D–88709,* ☎ *07532/333,* ℻ *07532/5805. 21 rooms with bath, 2 suites. Restaurant, café, bicycles. DC, MC, V.*

$$-$$$ ✕🏨 **Löwen.** This centuries-old, ivy-clad tavern on Meersburg's market square is a local landmark. Its cozy restaurant serves such regional specialties as spaetzle and Maultaschen, and in season venison and asparagus find their way onto the menu. Guest rooms are cozily furnished and have their own sitting corners, and some have genuine Biedermeier antique furniture. ⊠ *Marktpl. 2, D–88709,* ☎ *07532/43040,* ℻ *07532/430–410. 21 rooms with bath or shower. Restaurant, weinstube, no-smoking rooms, bicycles. AE, DC, MC, V.*

$$ ✕🏨 **Zum Bären.** Built in 1605 and incorporating 13th-century Gothic foundations, the Zum Bären was an important staging point for Germany's first postal service, and its fine tradition for hospitality lives on. The ivy-smothered facade, with its characteristic, steepled oriel, hasn't changed much over the centuries, but interior comforts certainly have. Some of the rooms are furnished with Bodensee antiques and brightly painted rustic wardrobes. ⊠ *Marktpl. 11, D–88709,*

☎ 07532/43220, 𝔽𝔸𝕏 07532/432–244. *17 rooms with shower. Restaurant. No credit cards. Closed Mon. and Dec.–Feb.*

Nightlife and the Arts

The glittering Spiegelsaal (Hall of Mirrors) of the Neues Schloss is the magnificent setting of an annual **international chamber music festival,** with concerts every Saturday from June through September. Call ☎ 07532/43112 for schedule information.

Birnau

❻ *10 km (6 mi) west of Meersberg.*

The **Wallfahrtskirche** (pilgrimage church) of Birnau was built by the masterful architect Peter Thumb between 1746 and 1750. Its simple exterior consists of plain gray-and-white plaster and a tapering clock tower spire above the main entrance; the interior, by contrast, is overwhelmingly rich, full of movement, light, and color. It's hard to single out highlights from such a profusion of ornament, but seek out the *Honigschlecker* (the Honey Sucker), a gold-and-white cherub beside the altar, dedicated to St. Bernard of Clairvaux, "whose words are sweet as honey" (it's the last altar on the right as you face the high altar). The cherub is sucking honey from his finger, which he's just pulled out of a beehive. If this sort of dainty punning strikes you as misplaced in a house of worship, you'll probably find equally tasteless the small squares of glass set into the pink screen that rises high above the main altar; the gilt dripping from the walls; the swaying, swooning statues; and the swooping figures on the ceiling. If, like many, you are entranced by the plump cherub, odds are the rest of the building will be very much to your liking. ☉ *Daily 7–7.*

En Route   Just south of Birnau, near the village of Uhldingen, you'll find a settlement stuck out in the lake—a reconstructed collection of early dwellings built on stilts. This is how the original lake dwellers lived, surviving off the fish who swam outside their humble huts. The settlement is open to visitors throughout the year.

Überlingen

❼ *3 km (2 mi) west of Birnau, 24 km (15 mi) west of Friedrichshafen.*

Überlingen's tourist office describes its town as the German Nice, and although that's a cheeky exaggeration, this Bodensee resort at least has an almost Mediterranean flair and an attractive waterside site. It's midway along the north shore of the Überlingersee, a narrow branch of the Bodensee that projects northwest out of the lake's main body. Überlingen is ancient, a Free Imperial City since the 13th century, with no fewer than seven of its original city gates and towers left as well as substantial portions of the old city walls. What was once the moat is now a delightfully grassy place in which to walk, with the walls of the Old Town towering over you on one side and the Stadtpark (city park) stretching away on the other. The heart of the city is the Münsterplatz.

★   The **Nikolausmünster** (Church of St. Nicholas) is a huge church for such a small town. It was built between 1512 and 1563 on the site of at least two previous churches. The interior is all Gothic solemnity and massiveness, with a lofty stone-vaulted ceiling and high, pointed arches lining the nave. The single most remarkable feature is not Gothic at all but opulently Renaissance—the massive high altar, carved from white-painted wood that looks almost like ivory. Statues, curlicues, and columns jostle for space on it. ✉ *Münsterpl.*

Inside the late-gothic **Altes Rathaus** (Old Town Hall) is a high point of Gothic decoration, the **Ratsaal**, or council chamber. Its most striking feature amid the riot of carving is the series of figures representing the states of the Holy Roman Empire. There's a naïveté to the figures—their beautifully carved heads are all just a little too large, their legs a little too spindly—that makes them easy to love. ⊠ *Münsterpl.* ⊞ *Free.* ⊘ *Apr.–mid-Oct., weekdays 9–noon and 2:30–5, Sat. 9–noon.*

The **Heimatmuseum** houses a vast collection of dollhouses and has exhibits tracing Bodensee history. ⊠ ☏ *07531/991–122.* ⊞ *DM 2.* ⊘ *Apr.–Oct., Tues.–Sat. 9–12:30 and 2–5, Sun. 10–3; Nov.–Mar., Tues.–Sat. 10:30–noon.*

Bicycling
Bikes at the train station rent for DM 12 a day (DM 6 with a valid train ticket).

Dining and Lodging

$$$$ ✕⊞ **Parkhotel St. Leonard.** About a mile from the lake on a vineyard-
★ covered hillside, the modern St. Leonard offers elegance and style. All rooms have balconies, but try for one with a view of the lake. Facilities include indoor and outdoor tennis courts as well as a tennis school. There are two restaurants, one sleekly contemporary and the other traditional, both in the hands of a French chef. Lake fish are a specialty, but also check to see if local lamb in spinach or the homemade Maultaschen are on the menu. In summer you'll dine on a canopied terrace. ⊠ *Obere St. Leonardstr. 71, D–88648,* ☏ *07551/808–100,* ℻ *07551/808–531. 140 rooms, 5 apartments with bath. 2 restaurants, bar, indoor pool, beauty salon, sauna, tennis courts, exercise room, bicycles, billiards. AE, MC, V.*

$$ ✕⊞ **Seehof.** This popular family hotel has direct access to a beach and boat pier, and most rooms have balconies looking out over the water. Fitness fanatics can book a cold-water cure within the hotel's health facility. The restaurant regularly serves fish caught in the lake—the pike perch is particularly tasty. ⊠ *Strandweg 6, D–88648,* ☏ *07551/63020,* ℻ *07551/68166. 35 rooms with bath. Restaurant, sauna, boating, bicycles. No credit cards. Closed Nov.–Mar.*

Nightlife and the Arts
An **international music festival** is held in Überlingen from May through September, with concerts every Tuesday in the newly renovated lakeside Kursaal (☏ 07551/991–122 for details).

NORTH TO THE UPPER SWABIAN BAROQUE ROAD, RAVENSBURG, AND WEINGARTEN

From Friedrichshafen a picturesque road (the B–30) leads north along the valley of the little river Schussen and links up with one of Germany's least-known but most attractive holiday routes, the Oberschwäbische Barockstrasse (Upper Swabian Baroque Road), so named because of the rich series of Baroque churches and abbeys that mark the route like milestones. They include the largest Baroque church in Germany, Weingarten, which is just 4 kilometers (2 miles) north of the ancient city of Ravensburg.

Ravensburg

❽ *20 km (12 mi) northeast of Friedrichshafen, 32 km (19 mi) north of Lindau.*

In what eventually proved an uneven contest, Ravensburg once competed with Augsburg and Nürnberg for economic supremacy in southern Germany. The Thirty Years' War finally put an end to Ravensburg's remaining hopes of economic leadership; after the war the city was reduced to little more than a medieval backwater. The city's loss proved fortuitous only in that many of its original features have remained much as they were when built. Fourteen of the town gates and towers survive, for example, and the Altstadt (Old Town) is among the best preserved in Germany. A wise municipal decision to ban cars from the Old Town has helped retain its character.

That ecclesiastical and commercial life were never entirely separate in medieval towns such as Ravensburg is demonstrated by the former **Karmelitenklosterkirche,** once part of a 14th-century monastery and now a Protestant church. The stairs on the west side of the church's chancel, for example, lead to the former meeting room of the Ravensburger Gesellschaft (the Ravensburg Society), an organization of linen merchants established in 1400 to direct trade of the product that was largely responsible for the town's rapid economic growth.

The central **Marienplatz Square** has many old buildings that recall Ravensburg's wealthy years: the late-Gothic Rathaus, with a picturesque Renaissance bay window; the 14th-century **Kornhaus,** once the corn exchange for all of Upper Swabia; the 15th-century **Waaghaus,** the town's weighing station and central warehouse, incorporating a tower where the watchman had his lookout; and the colorfully frescoed **Lederhaus,** once the headquarters of the leather workers.

NEED A BREAK?	Traffic-free Marienplatz is lined with historic facades. They front a variety of inns whose signs announce a welcome to thirsty visitors, with **Am Kornhaus** (✉ Marienpl. 8) among the friendliest. Step into its traditional interior for a taste of true Bodensee cooking. Ask for wine from any of the Bodensee vineyards or for the Ravensburg-brewed beer.

One of Ravensburg's **defensive towers** is visible from Marienplatz, the **Grüner Turm** (Green Tower), so called because of its green tiles; many are the 14th-century originals. Another stout defense tower is the massive **Obertor,** the oldest gate in the city walls. From it you can see one of the most curious of the city's towers, the **Mehlsack,** or Flour Sack Tower (because of its bulk and the original whitewash exterior), 170 feet high and standing on the highest point of the city. If you can stand the 240-step climb, head up to the summit for the view. 🎫 *Free.* 🕐 *Mid-Mar.–mid-Oct., 3rd Sun. of month only, 10–noon.*

Ravensburg's true parish church, the **Liebfrauenkirche** (Church of Our Lady), is a 14th-century structure, elegantly simple on the outside but almost entirely rebuilt inside. Some of the original stained glass remains, however, as does the heavily gilded altar. Seek out the *Ravensburger Schutzmantelmadonna,* a copy of the 15th-century original, which is now in Berlin's Dahlem Museum. ✉ *Kirchstr. 18,* ☎ *0751/23063.* 🕐 *Daily 7–7.*

Ravensburg is a familiar name to all jigsaw-puzzle fans, for its eponymous Ravensburg publishing house produces the world's largest selection of puzzles, in addition to many other popular games. In 1995 it opened a **puzzle museum,** in which the history of the jigsaw puzzle plays a central role. ⊠ *Robert Busch-str. 1,* ☎ *0751/860.* 🎟 *Free.* ⊙ *Thurs. 2–6.*

Dining and Lodging

$ ✕ **Gaststätte zur Brotlaube.** Franconian specialties and wine are featured on the menu of this traditional old inn, so expect hearty dishes with plenty of roast meat, sausages, and dumplings. The soups are freshly made and delicious. The daily lunch-time menu costs less than DM 20, an excellent value. ⊠ *Gespinstmarkt 25,* ☎ *0751/33734. No credit cards.*

$$$$ ✕🛏 **Romantikhotel Waldhorn.** This traditional old house has been welcoming travelers on Ravensburg's central Marienplatz since 1860. It's now a member of the Romantik group, and the accent certainly is on the "romantic." For a combination of romance and comfort, book a room or apartment in the annex. Those in the main house are more basic, though they do have new furnishings and modern facilities. The highly recommended restaurant is done in a Biedermeier style; you dine beneath sturdy beams at tables covered with crisp blue linen. ⊠ *Marienpl. 15, D–88212,* ☎ *0751/36120,* 𝐅𝐀𝐗 *0751/361–2100. 17 rooms with bath, 3 apartments. Restaurant, bar. AE, DC, MC, V.*

Weingarten

❾ *5 km (3 mi) north of Ravensburg.*

Weingarten is famous Germany-wide because of its huge and hugely impressive pilgrimage church, whose great bulk completely dominates the small town. It achieved additional recognition in the 1950s, when archaeologists discovered hundreds of Alamann graves from the 6th, 7th, and 8th centuries just outside town.

At 220 feet high and more than 300 feet long, **Weingarten Basilica** is the largest Baroque church in Germany, the basilica of one of the oldest and most venerable convents in the country, founded in 1056 by the wife of Guelph II. The Guelph dynasty ruled large areas of Upper Swabia, and generations of family members lie buried in the basilica. The majestic basilica was because of the little vial it possesses, said to contain drops of Christ's blood. First mentioned by Charlemagne, the vial passed to the convent in 1094, entrusted to its safekeeping by the Guelph queen Juditha, sister-in-law of William the Conqueror. At a stroke Weingarten became one of Germany's foremost places of pilgrimage. On the Friday after Ascension, the anniversary of the day the relic was entrusted to the convent, a huge procession of pilgrims, headed by 2,000 horsemen (many local farmers breed horses just for this procession) wends its way to the basilica. It was decorated by leading early-18th-century German and Austrian artists: stucco by Franz Schmuzer, ceiling frescoes by Cosmas Damian Asam, and a Donato Frisoni altar—one of the most breathtakingly ornate in Europe, with nearly 80-feet-high towers on either side. The organ, installed between 1737 and 1750, is among the largest in the country. ☎ *0751/43071.* ⊙ *Daily 8–6.*

If you want to learn about early Germans—residents from the 6th, 7th, and 8th centuries whose graves are just outside town—visit the **Alamannenmuseum** in the Kornhaus, at one time a granary. ⊠ *Karl-str. 28,* ☎ *0751/405125.* 🎟 *Free.* ⊙ *Wed. and weekends 3–5; closed Feb. and Nov.*

Bad Schussenried

32 km (19 mi) north of Weingarten on the B–30.

This small town lies on Germany's "Baroque Road," a vacation route north of the Bodensee studded with jewels of Baroque architecture. They include the extraordinary church of Steinhausen, claimed to be the world's most beautiful parish church and so out of the ordinary that it completely dominates the tiny community. Follow a visit to the Weingarten pilgrimage basilica with a detour to Steinhausen; you'll find the contrast breathtaking and well worth the drive.

The Bodensee region produces good wines *and* some fine beers. One local brewery in Bad Schussenried recently opened Germany's first **beer-mug museum,** with more than 1,000 exhibits of mugs spanning five centuries. *Schussenried Bierkrugmuseum,* ⊠ *Wilhelm-Schussen-Str. 12.* ☜ *DM 4.50.*

Tettnang

⑩ *13 km (8 mi) south of Ravensburg on the B–467.*

Former ancestral home of the counts of Montfort zu Tettnang, Tettnang is a Bodensee curiosity—by 1780 the Montfort zu Tettnang dynasty had fallen on such hard times that it ceded the town to the Hapsburgs for hard cash. Twenty-five years later it passed to the Bavarian Wittelsbachs. You'll want to visit principally to see what remains of its palace, the Neues Schloss.

The **Neues Schloss** is an extravagant Baroque palace that was built in the early 18th century, burned down in 1753, and then partially rebuilt before the Montfort finances ran dry. Enough remains, however, to give some idea of the rulers' former wealth and ostentatious lifestyle. ☎ *0751/403–418.* ☜ *DM 1.* ☉ *Apr.–Oct., daily 10–5.*

NEED A BREAK?   The last of the Montfort line, Count Anton IV, spent his declining years in a modest house in Tettnang, now the **Gasthof Krone,** which has its own brewery. If you visit in late spring, order an asparagus dish; Tettnang is one of Germany's leading asparagus-growing centers. ⊠ *Bärenpl.*

ACROSS THE LAKE, TO KONSTANZ, MAINAU, AND REICHENAU

Both Konstanz and Mainau, the "island of flowers," are reachable by ferry from Lindau or Meersburg. That's by far the most romantic way to cross the lake, although a main road (the B–31, then the B–34, and finally the B–33) skirts the eastern end of the Bodensee and ends its German journey at Konstanz.

Konstanz

⑪ *A ½-hr ferry ride from Meersburg.*

Konstanz is not really a German city—at least, not totally. Parts of it are actually in Switzerland; the border runs across the southern half of Konstanz. Crossing it is easy, with formalities reduced to a minimum. Because of its location, Konstanz (or Kreuzlingen, as the Swiss call their part) suffered no wartime bombing—the Allies were unwilling to risk inadvertent bombing of neutral Switzerland—and so Konstanz is among the best-preserved major medieval towns in Germany.

It's claimed that Konstanz was founded during the 3rd century by the emperor Constantine Chlorus, father of Constantine the Great. The story is probably untrue, though it's certain that there was a Roman garrison here. By the 6th century, Konstanz had become a bishopric; in 1192 it was made a Free Imperial City. But what really put Konstanz on the map was the Council of Konstanz, held between 1414 and 1417 and probably one of the medieval world's most remarkable gatherings. Upwards of 100,000 people are said to have descended on the city during the great assembly, and some of its profound consequences are still felt today. The council was not a political gathering so much as a religious one, though the point where politics stopped and the religion began was not always easy to identify: To enjoy either religious supremacy or political power in medieval Europe was, to a large extent, to enjoy both.

What was the council? It was convened to settle the Great Schism, the 14th-century rift in the church caused by the papacy's move from Rome to Avignon in the south of France. With the move a rival pope declared himself in Rome. Whatever else it may not have done, the council did at least resolve the problem of the pope: In 1417 it elected Martin V as the true, and only, pope. What it failed to do was solve the underlying problems about the nature of the church that, in part at least, had caused the schism in the first place. At stake was the primacy of the German Holy Roman Emperor in electing the pope (thus extending imperial power) and the primacy of the pope in determining church affairs (and thus extending the power of the Holy Roman Emperor still further).

Leading the rebel camp was Jan Hus (1372–1415), a theologian from Prague opposed both to the political power of the Holy Roman Emperor and to the religious primacy of the pope. He was, in effect, a church reformer 100 years before his time, a man calling for a fundamental reinterpretation of Christian dogma and for the cleansing of the church's corrupt practices. Hus attended the council, having been promised safe conduct by the emperor Sigismund on condition that he would not say mass or preach. The emperor, however, needed a deal with the church that would restore his role in electing the pope. The church agreed, on condition that Hus be done away with. (Sigismund, too, had much to gain from Hus's death; with Hus out of the way, he hoped to restore his control of Bohemia.) So, safe conduct notwithstanding, Hus was accused of breaking his side of the agreement—the emperor was seen to blush as the charges were read—and condemned to be burned at the stake, as indeed he duly was, in July 1415.

Neither the emperor nor the papacy gained much in the long run. Hus's death sparked violent uprisings in Bohemia, which took until 1436 to suppress. Likewise, his reforming doctrines gave direct inspiration, a century later, to Martin Luther, a man whose actions caused a far greater schism—the Reformation itself and the permanent division of the church between Catholics and Protestants. Konstanz itself became a Protestant city in the Reformation, a revenge of sorts for the brutal treatment of Hus.

Hus remains a key figure in Konstanz: There's a Hussenstrasse (Hus Street); the site of his execution is marked by a stone slab (the Hussenstein) and, appropriately, the square it's in is now the Lutherplatz; and a statue of Hus is outside the magnificent Konzilgebäude (Council Hall)—so called because it's claimed the council of cardinals met here to choose the new pope in 1415 (they actually met in the cathedral). The

Dominican monastery where Hus was held before his execution is still here, too, doing duty as a luxurious hotel, the Steigenberger Insel-Hotel (☞ Dining and Lodging, *below*).

For all its vivid history, most visitors find Konstanz a town to be enjoyed for its more world pleasures—its elegant Altstadt (Old Town), trips on the lake, walks along the promenade, the classy shops, the restaurants, the views. The heart of the city is the **Gondelhafen** (harbor), with the simple bulk of the Konzilgebäude looming behind it. Erected in 1388 as a warehouse, the building is now a concert hall. Alongside the Hus statue is one of Graf Zeppelin, born in Konstanz in 1837.

The **Hus Museum,** dedicated to the life of Hus and his movement, has been opened in a 16th-century house on the street named for him. The museum contains illustrations and documents tracing his life and his campaigns against Rome. To see where Hus was killed (**Lutherplatz**), continue past the Town Hall, walking along Paradiesstrasse. ⊠ *Hus-str. 64.* 🖾 *Free.* 🕑 *June–Sept., Tues.–Sun. 10–5; Oct.–May, Tues.–Sat. 10–noon and 2–4, Sun. 10–noon.*

Konstanz's Old Town Hall, the **Altes Rathaus,** was built during the Renaissance and painted with boldly vivid frescoes—swags of flowers and fruits, shields, architectural details, and sturdy knights wielding immense swords. Walk into the courtyard to admire its Renaissance restraint.

St. Stephanskirche, an austere, late-Gothic church with a very un-Gothic rococo chancel, stands in a little square surrounded by fine half-timbered houses. Look at the **Haus zur Katz**—on the right as you walk into the square. It was the headquarters of one of the city's trade guilds in the Middle Ages; now it houses the city archives.

Konstanz's cathedral, the **Münster,** was built on the site of the original Roman fortress. Construction on the cathedral continued from the 10th through the 19th century, resulting in today's oddly contrasting structure. The twin-towered facade is sturdily Romanesque, blunt and heavy-looking. However, the elegant and airy chapels along the aisles are full-blown 15th-century Gothic, the complex nave vaulting is Renaissance, and the choir is severely neoclassical. Make a point of seeing the Holy Sepulchre tomb in the Mauritius Chapel at the far end of the church, behind the altar. It's a richly worked, 13th-century Gothic structure, 12 feet high, with some of its original, vivid coloring and gilding, and it's studded with statues of the Apostles and figures from the childhood of Jesus.

The **Niederburg,** the oldest part of Konstanz, is a tangle of old, twisting streets leading to the Rhine. At the river take a look at the two city towers here: the **Rheintor,** the one nearer the lake, and the aptly named **Pulverturm** (Powder Tower), the former city arsenal.

Dining and Lodging

$ ✕ **Zum Guten Hirten.** At this late-15th-century wine tavern, whose name means good shepherd, owner Diana Zoeller maintains a traditional atmosphere. In the particularly authentic Bauernstübe (Country Corner), such Swiss specialties as *Rösti*—pan-fried potatoes and onions mixed with chopped, smoked ham—are served. Try the dish with a crisp white wine from the Bodensee vineyards. ⊠ *Zollernstr. 8,* ☎ *07531/27344. No credit cards. Closed Sun. and holidays.*

$$$$ ✕🖾 **Seehotel Siber.** The major attraction in this small hotel, in a turn-★   of-the-century villa, is its adjoining restaurant—the most elegant dining in the region (reservations essential; jacket and tie). Prepared by

Bertold Siber, one of Germany's leading chefs, the food is classical with regional touches. Try his lobster salad or bouillabaisse with local lake fish, followed by punch sorbet with ginger-flavor doughnuts. The restaurant is divided into three rooms: One resembles a library, with massive bookcases; the center room is airy and spacious, with a white ceiling and bold modern paintings; the third has mint-color walls and a deep-green carpet. In summer you can eat on a terrace overlooking the lake. Bedrooms 3 and 7 have balconies affording similar views. ⊠ *Seestr. 25, D–78464,* ☎ *07531/63044,* FAX *07531/64813. 11 rooms with bath, 1 suite. Restaurant, café, dance club. DC, MC, V. Hotel and restaurant closed in Feb.*

$$$$ ✕🖬 **Steigenberger Insel-Hotel.** If the Seehotel offers the best dining in
★   town, then this Steinberger group hotel must be the best lodging, or at least the most luxurious. It's a former 13th-century monastery, with its original cloisters, as well as the site where Jan Hus was held before his execution and where, much later, Graf Zeppelin was born. Bedrooms are spacious and stylish, more like those of a private home than a hotel, and many have lake views. The restaurant is very imposing, with some fine arches and superb views across the lake. The Dominikaner Stube has regional specialties, and there's the clubby, relaxed Zeppelin Bar. Gardens bright with flowers surround the hotel, keeping the bustle of Konstanz at bay. ⊠ *Auf der Insel 1, D–78464,* ☎ *07531/1250,* FAX *07531/26402. 100 rooms, 3 suites with bath. 2 restaurants, bar, beach, recreation room, baby-sitting. AE, DC, MC, V.*

$ ✕🖬 **Graf Zeppelin.** A small, family-run place in the historic heart of Konstanz, the Zeppelin has an eye-catching painted facade depicting town scenes from the Middle Ages. Rooms are modest but neat and clean, and there are special family accommodations, including an enormous tower room. Fresh fish from Lake Constance land daily on the restaurant's menu. ⊠ *St. Stephans-Pl. 15, D–78464,* ☎ *07531/23780,* FAX *07531/17226. 30 rooms, 22 with shower. Restaurant, café. AE, DC, MC, V.*

Nightlife and the Arts

The Bodensee **disco scene** is concentrated in Konstanz. Babalu (⊠ Kreuzlingerstr. 15) is a good disco, as is Excalibur (⊠ Hussenstr. 6). Konstanz's **casino** (⊠ Seestr. 2, ☎ 07531/54081) is open 3 PM–3 AM.

The Bodensee region's **Bodensee Symphony Orchestra,** founded in 1932, is based in Konstanz, with a season running from October through April. Schedule information and tickets are available from the Konstanz tourist office (☎ 07531/284–376). Konstanz's **summer music festival** runs from mid-June to mid-July, with a program of international events, including celebrated organ concerts in the cathedral. Performances are held in the picturesque Renaissancehof (courtyard) of the Town Hall. For program details and bookings, contact the Konstanz tourist office. Konstanz and Friedrichshafen (☞ *above*) stage the annual **Bodensee Festival,** which includes orchestral concerts and theater productions from early May to early June.

The **Stadttheater,** Germany's oldest active theater (⊠ Konzilstr.; or the festival office, ☎ 07531/52016), has staged plays since 1609 and has its own repertory company. The local season runs from September through June. During July through August the company moves to its summer theater in Meersburg. For program details, contact the Stadttheater Konstanz (⊠ Konzilstr. 11, D–78462 Konstanz, ☎ 07531/20070). For the Meersburg program, call ☎ 07532/82383.

Outdoor Activities and Sports

BICYCLING

Rent bikes at the train station for DM 12 a day (DM 6 with a valid train ticket).

BOATING

Canoes can be rented from the Huber sports shop (⊠ Gottlieberstr. 32). **Yachts** can be chartered from the **Segelschule Müller KN–Wallhausen** (⊠ Wittmoosstr. 10, ☎ 07531/4780).

OFF THE
BEATEN PATH

WOLLMATINGER RIED – Just north of Konstanz on the Bodanrück Peninsula is the 1,000-acre Wollmatinger Ried, moorland that's now a bird sanctuary. There are three-hour guided tours of the moor on Wednesday and Saturday, April through mid-October, at 4 PM, and two-hour tours June through mid-September on Tuesday, Thursday, and Friday at 9 AM. Most of the birds you'll see are water birds, naturally; there are also remains of prehistoric stilt houses. Bring sturdy, comfortable shoes and mosquito repellent (if you can). Binoculars can be rented. Contact DBV Naturschutzzentrum Wollmatinger Ried (⊠ Fritz Arnold-Str. 2e, Konstanz, ☎ 07531/78870).

Mainau

⑫ *7 km (4 mi) north of Konstanz (by road and ferry), 1 hour by ferry from Konstanz.*

One of the most unusual sites in Europe, Mainau is a tiny island given over to the cultivation of **rare plants.** Not many people visit Germany expecting to find banana plantations, let alone such exotic flora as bougainvillea and hibiscus. But these and hundreds of more commonplace species flourish, nurtured by the freakishly warm and moist climate. Visit in the spring and you'll find more than a million tulips, hyacinths, and narcissi in bloom; rhododendrons and roses flower in May and June; dahlias dominate the late-summer display. The island was originally the property of the Teutonic Knights, who settled here during the 13th century. During the 19th century Mainau passed to Grand Duke Friedrich I of Baden, a man with a passion for botany. He laid out most of the gardens and introduced many of the island's more exotic specimens. His daughter Victoria, later queen of Sweden, gave the island to her son, Prince Wilhelm, and it has remained Swedish ever since. Today it's owned by Prince Wilhelm's son, Count Lennart Bernadotte (who lives in the castle, which is closed to the public). The **children's zoo** helps keep younger visitors amused; its wandering groups of tiny potbelly pigs are a hit with all visitors. ◻ *DM 12.* ☉ *Mid-Mar.–mid-Oct., daily 7–7.*

Reichenau

⑬ *10 km (6 mi) northwest of Konstanz, 50 minutes by ferry from Konstanz.*

Reichenau has something in common with Mainau, the town on the other side of the small peninsula—plant life. Although in this case it's vegetables, not flowers, that dominate. In fact, Reichenau is the most important vegetable-growing area in Germany, with fully 15% of its area covered by greenhouses and vegetables of one kind or another growing on almost the entire island outside town.

Though it seems unlikely, amid the cabbages and the cauliflowers and the lettuces and the carrots and the potatoes, there are three of Europe's most important and, some say, most beautiful **Romanesque churches** on the island. Little Reichenau, 3 miles long and 1 mile wide, connected to the Bodanrück Peninsula by just a narrow causeway, was a great monastic center of the early Middle Ages. Secure from marauding tribesmen on its fertile island, the monastic community blossomed from the 8th to the 12th centuries, in the process developing into a major center of learning and the arts. Each of the island's villages—**Oberzell, Mittelzell,** and **Unterzell**—is the site of one church, with Mittelzell the site of the monastery itself.

The **Stiftskirche St. Georg** (Collegiate Church of St. George), in Oberzell, was built around 900; now cabbages grow in serried ranks up to its rough plaster walls. Small round-head windows, a simple tower, and russet-color tiles provide the only exterior decoration. Inside, look for the wall paintings along the nave; they date from around 1000 and show the miracles of Christ. Their simple colors and unsteady outlines have an innocent, almost childlike charm. The striped backgrounds are typical of Romanesque frescoes.

Begun in 816, the **Münster of St. Maria and St. Markus,** the monastery's church, is the largest and most important of the area's trio of Romanesque churches. The monastery was founded in 725 by St. Pirmin; under the abbots Waldo (786–806) and Hatto I (806–23), it became one of the most important cultural centers of the Carolingian Empire. It reached its zenith around 1000 under the rule of Abbot Hermanus Contractus, "the miracle of the century," when 700 monks lived here. It was then probably the most important center of book illumination in Germany. Though it's larger than St. George, this church has much the same simplicity. It's by no means crude (though it can't be called technically sophisticated), just marvelously simple, a building that's utterly at one with the fertile soil on which it stands. Visit the **Schatzkammer** to see some of its more important treasures. They include a 5th-century ivory goblet with two carefully incised scenes of Christ's miracles and some priceless stained glass that is almost 1,000 years old. 🏷 *DM 1. ⊙ May–Sept., daily 11–noon and 3–4. Guided tours (☎ 07534/276) possible at other times.*

The **Stiftskirche St. Peter and St. Paul,** at Niederzell, contains some Romanesque frescoes in the apse, uncovered in 1990 during restoration work.

A **local-history museum** in the Old Town Hall of Mittelzell offers interesting insights into life on the island over the centuries. 🏷 *DM 2. ⊙ May–Sept., Tues.–Sun. 3–5.*

Dining and Lodging

$$$–$$$$ ✕🏠 **Strandhotel Löchnerhaus.** The Strand (beach) hotel stands commandingly on the water's edge, a stone's throw from the lake and 50 meters from its own boat pier. Freshly caught lake fish figure prominently on the menu of the excellent restaurant. Most rooms have lake views; those that don't look out over a quiet, shady garden. ⊠ *An der Schiffslände 12, D–78479, ☎ 07534/8030, ℻ 07534/582. 44 rooms with bath or shower. Restaurant, beach, boating. MC, V.*

Radolfzell

❶❹ *22 km (14 mi) northwest of Konstanz.*

Radolfzell is an old lakeside town that wears its history with style, aside from the ugly high-rises surrounding it. It was an Austrian outpost for much of its existence—from 1267 to 1415 and again from 1455 to the early 19th century. There are the same half-timbered buildings and sinewy old streets that you'll find in other historic Bodensee towns, the same elegant lakeside promenade, and the same chic shops. But the tourist hype is less obtrusive; you don't feel as if Radolfzell exists only for its visitors. While it has no outstanding sights, it's an appealing stop for a night or two. And if you must have some culture, visit the 14th-century **Liebfrauenmünster,** a sturdy Gothic church right on the lakeshore.

Boating
Bodensee Yachtschule charters yachts (✉ Zeppelinstr. 23, ☎ 07732/
54390).

THE BODENSEE A TO Z

Arriving and Departing

By Car

The A–96 autobahn runs virtually all the way from Munich to Lindau, but for a less hurried, more scenic route take the B–12 via Landsberg and Kempten. If you want to take a more scenic but slower route
from Frankfurt, take the B–311 at Ulm and follow the Oberschwäbische
Barockstrasse (the Upper Swabian Baroque Road) to Friedrichshafen.
An alternative, no less scenic route to Lindau, at the east end of the
lake, is on the Deutsche Alpenstrasse (the German Alpine Road). It runs
east–west from Salzburg to Lindau, passing Garmisch-Partenkirchen
and Füssen along the way.

By Plane

The closest international airport to the Bodensee is Zurich, Switzerland, 60 kilometers (40 miles) from Konstanz. Munich Airport is 240
kilometers (150 miles) from Konstanz; Frankfurt Airport is 375 kilometers (230 miles) from Konstanz. The little airport at Friedrichshafen,
on the north shore of the lake, has flights from all three airports.

By Train

There are InterCity trains to Lindau from Frankfurt (via Stuttgart and
Ulm) and from Munich. There are also frequent and fast trains from
Zurich and Basel in Switzerland.

Getting Around

By Boat

The Weisse Flotte (White Fleet) line of boats links most of the larger
towns and resorts; numerous excursions are also available (☞ Guided
Tours *in* Contacts and Resources, *below*). If you plan to use the ferries extensively, buy a Bodensee Pass. It is valid for 15 days and allows
half-price travel on all ferries, as well as many Bodensee trains, buses,
and mountain cable cars (in Germany, Switzerland, and Austria). The
pass costs DM 48. Contact Bodensee-Schiffsbetriebe (✉ Hafenstr. 6,
D–78462 Konstanz, ☎ 07531/281–398). There are also offices in
Friedrichshafen (☎ 07541/201–389) and Lindau (☎ 08382/6099).

By Bus

Railway and post buses serve most smaller communities that have no
train links. Service is less than frequent, however; use local buses only
if time is no object.

By Car

Lakeside roads in the Bodensee area are good, if crowded, in summer;
all offer scenic diversions to compensate for the occasional slow going
in heavier traffic. You may want to drive around the entire lake, crossing into Switzerland and Austria; formalities at border crossing points
are few. However, in addition to your passport, you'll need insurance
and registration papers for your car. If you're taking a rental car, check
with the rental company to make verify it imposes no restrictions on
crossing these frontiers. Car ferries link Romanshorn, in Switzerland
on the south side of the lake, with Friedrichshafen, on the north side
next to Lindau, as well as connecting Konstanz with Meersburg. Taking either saves substantial mileage while driving around the lake.

By Train
Local trains encircle the Bodensee, stopping at most towns and villages.

Contacts and Resources

Car Rentals
Avis: ✉ Eberhardstr. 31, ☎ 07541/23030, **Friedrichshafen**; ✉ Reichenaustr. 45, ☎ 07531/66630, **Konstanz**.

Europcar: ✉ Eugenstr. 47, ☎ 07541/23053, **Friedrichshafen**; von-Emmerich-Str. 3, ☎ 07531/52833; **Konstanz**.

Hertz: ✉ **Friedrichshafen** Airport, ☎ 07541/930−700; ✉ Bregenzerstr. 25, ☎ 08382/940−000; **Lindau**.

Sixt-Budget: ✉ Zeppelinstr. 66, ☎ 07541/33066, **Friedrichshafen**; ✉ Karl-Benz-Str. 14, ☎ 07531/690044, **Konstanz**.

Emergencies
Police: ☎ 110. ✉ **Fire and medical emergencies:** ☎ 112.

Guided Tours

BOAT TOURS

The **Weisse Flotte** organizes numerous excursions around the lake, lasting from one hour to a full day. Many cross to Austria and Switzerland; some head west along the Rhine to the Schaffhausen Falls, the largest waterfall in Europe. (☞ Getting Around by Boat, *above*, for addresses.) Information on excursions on the lake is also available from all local tourist offices and travel agencies.

CITY TOURS

Most of the larger tourist centers have regular tours with English-speaking guides. In **Friedrichshafen** there are tours from May through September on Tuesday at 9:30, leaving from the tourist office (✉ Friedrichstr. 18). The tours are free of charge and include visits to the Zeppelin Museum and Schlosskirche. Tours of **Konstanz** leave from the tourist office (✉ Bahnhofpl. 13) from April through October on Monday (9:30 AM), Wednesday (4:30 PM), and Friday and Saturday (10:30 AM). **Lindau** offers tours, also starting from the tourist office (✉ Am Hauptbahnhof), from April through October on Tuesday and Friday at 10. The **Meersburg** tourist office (✉ Kirchstr. 4) offers guided tours that include a visit to the wine museum; tours are held from April through October on Wednesday at 10. The **Radolfzell** tourist office (✉ Marktpl. 2) arranges tours from May through September on Saturday at 10 for groups of 10 or more.

EXCURSIONS

Bus trips to destinations in and around the Bodensee can be booked from tour operators in all the larger towns. Typical tours include visits to cheese makers in the Allgäu, the rolling Alpine foothills east of the Bodensee; tours around the Black Forest; tours to Baroque churches and castles around the lake; and tours to the ancient town of St. Gallen across the border in Switzerland. Operators include **Reisebüro Rominger** (✉ Marktstätte 17, ☎ 07531/26031; ✉ Zähringerpl. 34, ☎ 07531/5503, Konstanz), **Reisebüro Lemke** (✉ Schmiedgasse 13, Lindau, ☎ 08382/25025), **Bregenzer Autoreisen** (✉ Rengoldhauserstr. 11, Überlingen, ☎ 07551/4044), and **Reisebüro Kast** (✉ Münsterstr. 31−33, Überlingen, ☎ 07551/63628).

SPECIAL-INTEREST TOURS

Flights around the Bodensee are offered by **Konair** (✉ Flugpl., Konstanz, ☎ 07531/61110). A 20-minute flight over Konstanz and part of the Bodensee costs DM 95 per person. A 45-minute flight over the entire lake costs DM 150. For DM 190, you can have the plane for an hour, easily time enough to fly south over parts of the Alps. Sight-seeing flights also operate from the Lindau-Wildberg airstrip (☎ 08389/271).

Wine-tasting tours are available in Überlingen, in the atmospheric Spitalweingut zum Heiligen Geist, (✉ Mühlbachstr. 115), on Thursday at 7 PM; contact the tourist office or call ☎ 07551/65855. In Konstanz, wine tasting is by appointment only at the Spitalkellerei (✉ Brückengasse 12, ☎ 07531/288–342). In Meersburg, tastings are held Tuesday and Friday at 6 PM; contact the tourist office (☎ 07532/431–110).

Visitor Information

Information on the entire Bodensee region is available from the **Internationaler Bodensee-Verkehrsverein** (✉ Schützenstr. 8, D–78462 Konstanz, ☎ 07531/22232). There are local tourist information offices in the following towns:

Friedrichshafen: ✉ Tourist-Information, Friedrichstr. 18, D–88045, ☎ 07541/30010.

Konstanz: ✉ Tourist-Information Konstanz, Bahnhofpl. 13, D–78462, ☎ 07531/900–377.

Langenargen: ✉ Langenargen Verkehrsamt, Obere Seestr. 2, D–88085, ☎ 07543/30292.

Lindau: ✉ Verkehrsverein Lindau, Ludwigstr. 68, D–8990, ☎ 08382/26000.

Meersburg: ✉ Kur- und Verkehrsverwaltung, Kirchstr. 4, D–88709, ☎ 07532/431–110.

Radolfzell: ✉ Städtisches Verkehrsamt, Rathaus, Marktpl. 2, D–78315, ☎ 07732/3800.

Ravensburg: ✉ Städtisches Verkehrsamt, Kirchstr. 16 Weingartner Hof, D–88212, ☎ 0751/82324.

Reichenau: ✉ Verkehrsbüro, Ergat 5, D–78479, ☎ 07534/276.

Tettnang: ✉ Verkehrsverein, Montfortpl. 1, D–88069, ☎ 07542/510–213.

Tuttlingen: ✉ Städtisches Verkehrsamt, Rathaus, D–78532, ☎ 07461/99203.

Überlingen: ✉ Städtische Kurverwaltung, Überlingen, Landungspl. 14, D–88648, ☎ 07551/991–122.

Weingarten: ✉ Kultur-und Verkehrsamt, Münsterpl. 1, D–88250, ☎ 0751/405125.

8 The Black Forest

Cake and smoked ham aren't the only reasons to visit the Black Forest, but they are good ones. Spa and casino resorts, outdoor activities, and cuckoo clocks are other draws. The Romans were the first to take advantage of the area's healing waters, 19 centuries ago, and royalty and the cultural elite paraded about the region in the 1800s. Today watching vacationers here is a study in contrasts; some tourists flock to high-fashion, high-cost towns like Baden-Baden, while others feel more at home in down-home German country villages.

THE NAME BLACK FOREST—Schwarzwald in German—
conjures up images of a wild, isolated place where time
passes so slowly it can be measured by the number
of rings on the trunks of felled trees. And this southwest corner of Germany is indeed a rural region where dense woodland stretches away
to the horizon, but it is neither an inaccessible nor a backwater area.
The first recorded tourists checked in here 19 centuries ago, when the
Roman emperor Caracalla and his army rested and soothed their battle wounds in the natural-spring waters of what later became Baden-
Baden.

Celebrated names have long been associated with the Black Forest. In
1770 the empress Maria Theresa's 15-year-old daughter—the future
queen Marie Antoinette—traveling between Vienna and Paris with an
entourage of 250 officials and servants in some 50 horse-drawn carriages, made her way along the coach road through the Höllental (Hell
Valley).

In the 19th century just about everyone who mattered in Europe grav-
itated to Baden-Baden: kings, queens, emperors, princes, princesses, members of Napoléon's family, and the Russian nobility, along with actors,
actresses, writers, and composers. Turgenev, Dostoyevsky, and Tolstoy
were among the Russian contingent. Victor Hugo was a frequent visitor. Brahms composed lilting melodies in this calm setting. Queen Victoria spent her vacations here. Today it's a favorite vacation setting for
millionaires, movie stars, and the new corporate royalty.

Mark Twain could be said to have put the Black Forest on the tourist
map for Americans. In his 1880 book *A Tramp Abroad* he waxed poetic on the beauties of this forest.

Today you can come here for rest and relaxation and to "take the waters," as the Romans first did, at thermal resorts large or small. The
Black Forest offers a wide range of sporting activities, catering particularly
to the German enthusiasm for hiking, with its virtually limitless trails
wending their way in and out of the woods. In winter these same trails
serve as tracks for cross-country skiing on some of Europe's most ideally suited terrain for this popular sport.

The Black Forest's enviable sporting scene is blessed by dependable
snow in winter and warming sun in summer. Freudenstadt, at the center of the Black Forest, claims the greatest number of annual hours
of sunshine of any town in Germany. You can play tennis, swim, or
bike at most resorts, and some have golf courses of international
standards.

The Black Forest is near Germany's southernmost wine region and is
home to some of the country's finest traditional food. Black Forest
smoked ham and Black Forest cake are both world famous—and that's
only the beginning.

The Black Forest also happens to be the home of the cuckoo clock, despite Orson Welles's claim in *The Third Man* that all Switzerland managed to create in 500 years of peace and prosperity was this trivial
timepiece. Cuckoo clocks are still made (and sold) here, as they have
been more or less since time immemorial, along with hand-carved
wood artifacts and exquisite examples of glassblowing.

Despite its fame and the wealth of some of its visitors, the Black Forest doesn't have to be an expensive place to visit. It's possible to stay
at a modest, family-run country inn or farmhouse where the enormous

breakfast will keep you going for the better part of the day—all for not much more than the price of a meal in a German city restaurant.

Pleasures and Pastimes

Bicycling

Bicycles can be rented at nearly all the train stations in the Black Forest and in many villages. Several regional tourist offices sponsor tours on which the biker's luggage is transported separately from one overnight stop to the next. Six- to 10-day tours are available for reasonable rates, including bed-and-breakfast and bike rental.

Dining

Restaurants in the Black Forest range from the well-upholstered luxury of Baden-Baden's chic eating spots to simple country inns. Old *Kachelöfen* (attractive yet functional large, traditional tiled heating stoves) are still in use in many area restaurants; try to sit by one if it's cold outside. Some specialties here betray the influence of neighboring France, but if you really want to go native, try *z'Nuni*, the local farmers' second breakfast, generally eaten around 9 AM. It consists of smoked bacon, called *Schwarzwaldgeräuchertes*—the most authentic is smoked over fir cones—a hunk of bread, and a glass of chilled white wine. No visitor to the Black Forest will want to pass up the chance to try *Schwarzwälder Kirschtorte* (Black Forest cherry cake). *Kirschwasser,* locally called *Chriesewässerle* (from the French *cerise,* meaning cherry), is cherry brandy, the most famous of the region's excellent schnapps.

CATEGORY	COST*
$$$$	over DM 90
$$$	DM 55–DM 90
$$	DM 35–DM 55
$	DM 25–DM 35

*per person for a three-course meal, excluding drinks, service charge, and tax

Fishing

The Black Forest, with its innumerable mountain rivers and streams, is a fisherman's paradise. Native trout are abundant in many rivers, including the Nagold, Elz, Alb, and Wildgutach, and in mountain lakes such as the Schluchsee and Titisee. Licenses are available from most local tourist offices, which usually also provide maps and rental equipment.

Hiking and Walking

The Black Forest is ideal country for walkers. The three principal trails are well marked and cross the region from north to south, the longest stretching from Pforzheim to the Swiss city of Basel, 280 kilometers (174 miles) away. Walks vary in length from a few hours to a week; here, as in many other German regions, the tourist office has gotten together with local inns to create "Hike Without Luggage" tours (*Wandern ohne Gepäck*) along the old clock-carriers route. Your bags are transported ahead by car to meet you each evening at that day's destination.

Horseback Riding

Farms throughout the Black Forest offer riding vacations; addresses are available from local tourist offices and the **Fremdenverkehrsverband Schwarzwald**, the regional tourist office, in Freiburg. Many of the larger towns have riding clubs and stables where visitors can rent horses.

Lodging

Accommodations in the Black Forest are varied and numerous, from simple rooms in farmhouses to five-star luxury. Some properties have been passed down through the generations of the same family for what seems an impossible amount of time. *Gasthofs* (inns) abound, all offering low prices and as much local color as you'll ever want.

CATEGORY	COST*
$$$$	over DM 230
$$$	DM 170–DM 230
$$	DM 120–DM 170
$	under DM 120

All prices are for two people in a double room, excluding service charge.

Spas and Health Resorts

The Black Forest region offers an amazing variety of places to "take the waters," from expensive spa towns to rustic places deep in the woods. Baden-Baden is stately and elegant. Bad Dürrheim has Europe's highest brine spa. For a garden setting, head for Bad Herrenalb. Bad Liebenzell has an Olympic size pool, while the spa towns of Feldberg and Hinterzarten also provide opportunities to hike.

Swimming

Most of the larger resorts and towns in the Black Forest have pools, either indoor or outdoor. You can also swim in any of the region's lakes, if you can stand the cold.

Winter Sports

Despite Swiss claims to the contrary, the Black Forest is the true home of downhill skiing. In 1891, a French diplomat was sighted sliding down the slopes of the **Feldberg,** the Black Forest's highest mountain, on what are thought to be the world's first downhill skis. The idea caught on among the locals, and a few months later, Germany's first ski club was formed. The world's first ski lift opened at Schollach in 1907. There are now more than 200 ski lifts in the Black Forest, but the slopes of the Feldberg are still the top ski area.

Exploring the Black Forest

Geographically, the Black Forest can be divided into three areas: northern, central, and southern. The northern area is known for its broad ridges and thickly forested slopes; it contains the largest number of spas. The central region is especially popular with tourists because of its associations with folklore, cuckoo clocks, and the Black Forest Railway; Triberg and its waterfalls attract a large number of visitors annually. The southern portion of the Black Forest has the most dramatic scenery and the most frequented recreation areas. Two main attractions are Titisee and Schluchsee, two beautiful lakes created by glaciers.

Great Itineraries

Many first-time visitors to the Black Forest literally can't see the forest for the trees. There are so many contrasting attractions that the basic, enduring beauty of the area passes them by. So, in touring the forest, take time to stray from the tourist path and inhale the cool, mysterious air of its darker recesses. Walk or ride through its shadowy corridors or across its open upland; row a canoe and tackle the wild water of the Nagold and Wolf rivers. Then take time out to relax in a spa, order a Baden wine enlivened by a dash of local mineral water, and seek out the nearest restaurant that devotes itself to local specialties. If you have money to spare at the end of your trip, return to Baden-

Baden, try your luck at the gaming tables, and blow your winnings—
or forget your losses at the bar of Griffen's, the casino's nightclub.

*Numbers in the text correspond to numbers in the margin and on the
Black Forest map.*

IF YOU HAVE 3 DAYS

Start your first day in **Pforzheim** ①, located at the confluence of
three rivers and visit the famous Schmuckmuseum, with its glittering jewelry collection, and then go on to nearby Maulbronn, with
its 12th-century Cistercian abbey, the most beautiful of all surviving
monasteries in Germany. Spend a night in the picturesque town of
⌂ **Bad Liebenzell** ② and on the second day, soak in one of the Black
Forest's oldest spas. After a visit to the ruined abbey in **Hirsau,** near
Calw ③, head south to **Freudenstadt** ⑤, which has one of the largest
market squares in Germany. Next, continue farther south to ⌂
Triberg ⑬, site of Germany's highest waterfall and the Schwarzwaldmuseum, with exhibits relating to regional folklore. On the last day,
go north to look at the farmhouses at the Freilicht Museum Vogtsbauernhof near **Wolfach,** before driving along the Schwarzwaldhochstrasse, the "Black Forest Highway" (with a stop at the legendary
lake, from **Mummelsee**) to **Baden-Baden** ⑥, saving plenty of time for
a walk around the fashionable spa.

IF YOU HAVE 5 DAYS

Begin your trip by following the first two days of the three-day itinerary
described above, starting at **Pforzheim** ①, and then stopping at
Maulbronn, **Bad Liebenzell** ②, **Calw** ③, **Freudenstadt** ⑤, and ⌂
Triberg ⑬. On the third day, continue directly south to **Furtwangen** ⑭
to survey Germany's largest clock museum. ⌂ **Titisee** ⑮, the jewel of
the Black Forest lakes, is a good place to spend the third night. On the
fourth day, after taking some time to enjoy the visual splendor of Titisee and the mountain-enclosed lake **Schluchsee** ⑰, you're ready to brave
the winding road northwest through **Höllental** (Hell Valley). End your
day at **Freiburg** ⑱, which lies at the foot of the Black Forest; its Münster, or cathedral, has the most perfect spire of any German Gothic
church. Drive north from Freiberg on Highway 3 through the vineyards
of the Rhine Valley to elegant ⌂ **Baden-Baden** ⑥, where you can relax
on the fifth day.

IF YOU HAVE 10 DAYS

Commence your trip by following the first two days of the three-day
itinerary described above, making your first stop at **Pforzheim** ①. Spend
the first two nights in ⌂ **Bad Liebenzell** ②. ⌂ **Freudenstadt** ⑤ is a
good base for the next two days; from here, make excursions to the
Schwarzwaldmuseum at **Lossburg,** the Schwarzwälder Freilichtmuseum Vogtsbauernhof (Black Forest Open Air Museum) near **Gutach,**
the **Alpirsbach** brewery, and the Glasswald Lake near Schapbach.
On the fifth day, continue on to ⌂ **Triberg** ⑬, with its waterfall; also
visit the cuckoo clock museums in Triberg and **Furtwangen** ⑭. Spend
the fifth and sixth nights near the lovely lake ⌂ **Titisee** ⑮. From the
lake, visit Feldberg, the Black Forest's highest mountain, and the ⌂
Schluchsee ⑰. Spend the following two days and nights in ⌂
Freiburg ⑱, allowing time for Schauinsland mountain; the town of
Staufen ⑲, where the legendary Dr. Faustus made a pact with the Devil;
and the vineyards on the slopes of the Kaiserstuhl. Finally, drive
north through the Rhine Valley for two nights in ⌂ **Baden-Baden** ⑥
to enjoy the sights in and around the city, including trips to the summit of nearby Merkur Mountain, to Schloss Favorite, and to Windeck
Castle.

The Black Forest

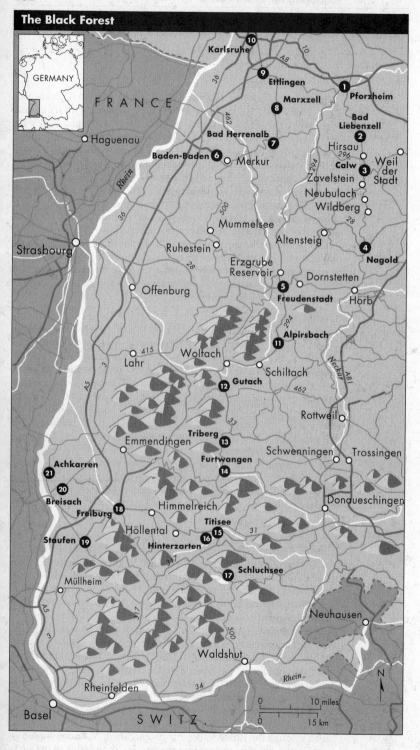

GERMANY

F R A N C E

Karlsruhe ❿
A8
10
Ettlingen ❾
Marxzell ❽
Pforzheim ❶
Bad Liebenzell ❷
Hirsau
Calw ❸
Weil der Stadt
Zavelstein
Neubulach
Wildberg
28
Bad Herrenalb ❼
Baden-Baden ❻ Merkur
Haguenau
462
296
294
Mummelsee
Altensteig
Nagold ❹
Ruhestein
Erzgrube Reservoir
Dornstetten
500
Offenburg
Freudenstadt ❺
Horb
28
294
Alpirsbach ⓫
Strasbourg
Rhein
36
Lahr
415
Woltach
Schiltach
Gutach ⓬
462
Neckar
A81
Rottweil
3
Emmendingen
Triberg ⓭
33
Furtwangen ⓮
Schwenningen
Trossingen
Achkarren ㉑
Breisach ⓴
Himmelreich
Donaueschingen
Freiburg ⓲
Höllental
Titisee
Titisee ⓯
31
Staufen ⓳
Hinterzarten
⓰
Müllheim
Schluchsee
⓱
317
Neuhausen
A5
3
500
Waldshut
Rheinfelden
34
Rhein
N
Basel
S W I T Z .
0   10 miles
0   15 km

When to Tour the Black Forest

The Black Forest is one of the most heavily visited mountain regions in Europe so reservations should be made well in advance for the better known spas and hotels. In summer, the areas around Schluchsee and Titisee are particularly crowded. Some spa hotels close for the winter. In early fall and late spring, the Black Forest scenery is less crowded but just as beautiful (with the exception of the Easter holidays).

THE NORTHERN BLACK FOREST

This region is crossed by broad ridges that are densely wooded, with little lakes such as Mummelsee and Wildsee. The Black Forest Spa Route (270 kilometers, 168 miles) links many of the spas in the region, from Baden-Baden (the best known town in the area) to Wildbad. Other regional treasures are the lovely Nagold River, ancient towns such as Bad Herrenalb and Hirsau, and the magnificent abbey at Maulbronn, near Pforzheim.

Numbers in the margin correspond to points of interest on the Black Forest map.

Pforzheim

❶ *35 km (22 mi) from Karlsruhe, just off the A–8 Autobahn, the main Munich–Karlsruhe route.*

The Romans founded Pforzheim at the meeting place of three rivers, the Nagold, the Enz, and the Würm. Almost totally destroyed in World War II, it has since been rebuilt in a blocky postwar style and continues to prosper. For a sense of its past, visit the restored church of **St. Michael** in the center of the city. The original mixture of 13th- and 15th-century styles has been faithfully reproduced; compare the airy Gothic choir with the church's sturdy Romanesque entrance.

Pforzheim owes its prosperity to Europe's jewelry trade, of which it is a center. To get a sense of "Gold City," explore the jewelry shops on streets around Leopoldplatz and the pedestrian area. The Reuchlinhaus, the city cultural center, has a jewelry museum, the **Schmuckmuseum.**
★ Its glittering collection of 3rd-century BC to 20th-century pieces is one of the finest in the world. ⊠ *Jahnstr. 42,* ☎ *07231/392–126.* 🎫 *DM 5.* 🕐 *Tues.–Sun. 10–5.*

Pforzheim has long been known as a center of the German clock-making industry. In the **Technisches Museum,** one of the country's leading museums devoted to the craft, you can see watch- and clock-makers at work; there's also a reconstructed 18th-century clock factory. ⊠ *Bleichstr. 81.* 🎫 *Free.* 🕐 *Wed. 9–noon and 3–6, and every 2nd and 4th Sun. of month 10–noon and 2–5.*

★ **Maulbronn Monastery,** located in the little town of Maulbronn, 18 kilometers (11 miles) northeast of Pforzheim, is probably the best-preserved medieval monastery north of the Alps, an entire complex of 30 buildings. The main buildings were constructed between the 12th and 14th centuries. The monastery's church was built in a time of architectural transition from Romanesque to Gothic style and had a significant influence on the spread of Gothic architecture through northern and central Europe. Next to the church is the cloister, with a fountain-house and refectories for the monks and lay brothers. The monastery's fortified walls still stand and its medieval water management system, with its elaborate network of drains, irrigation canals, and reservoirs, remains intact. ☎ 07043/7454. ☜ *DM 8.* ☼ *Mar.–Oct., daily 9–5:30; Nov.–Feb., Tues.–Sun. 9:30–5. Guided tours at 11:15 and 3.*

Dining and Lodging

$$$ ✕ **L'Escale.** Long Pforzheim's leading restaurant, L'Escale reopened under
★   new management in 1994 and has managed to retain its place high on
      the city's list of places to dine. The new menu features an expanded
      repertoire but still combines international cuisine (with a nouvelle
      twist) and regional specialties. ☒ *Parkstr. 16,* ☎ *07231/32075. No credit
      cards. Closed Sun., 3 wks in Aug.*

$$$ ✕ **Silberburg.** Serving nouvelle cuisine with a Swiss touch, emphasiz-
      ing poultry, fish, and fresh vegetables, is the policy of this cozy restau-
      rant. Try the duck in one of chef Gilbert Noesser's exquisite sauces.
      ☒ *Dietlingerstr. 27,* ☎ *07231/41159. AE, DC, MC, V. Closed Mon.,
      Tues. afternoon, and mid-July–mid-Aug.*

$$ ⊡ **Hotel Ruf.** When it opened at the beginning of the century, this hotel
      was described by a visiting English journalist as "a house that is aware
      of its importance for the numerous German and foreign visitors . . . to
      Pforzheim." Whether or not it is still of such importance, it aims to
      offer the same degree of reliable comfort—the hotel is nothing fancy,
      but it is dependably efficient and welcoming. The excellent restaurant
      is decorated with wrought iron and stained glass. ☒ *Bahnhofpl. 5,
      D–75175 Pforzheim,* ☎ *07231/106–011,* FAX *07231/33139. 90 rooms
      with bath. Restaurant. AE, DC, MC, V.*

Nightlife and the Arts

Pforzheim's recently built **Stadttheater** (☎ 07231/392–440) has a program that emphasizes operettas and musicals, but it also presents opera and theater.

En Route   The road south of Pforzheim, B–463, follows the twists and turns of the pretty little Nagold River. Gardening enthusiasts should follow the signs to the **Alpine Garden** (on the left as you leave the city limits). The garden, on the banks of the Würm River, stocks more than 100,000 varieties of plants, including the rarest Alpine flowers. ☼ *Mid-Apr.–Oct., daily 8–7.*

Bad Liebenzell

❷ *31 km (19 mi) south of Pforzheim on highway 463.*

The picturesque town of Bad Liebenzell has one of the Black Forest's oldest spas. Bathhouses were built here as early as 1403. Nearly six centuries later, the same hot springs feed the more modern installations that have taken the place of the medieval originals. Apart from medicinal baths (highly recommended for the treatment of circulatory problems), the town has the Paracelsusbad lido complex with outdoor and indoor hot-water pools. There's also mixed nude bathing at the Sauna Pinea, which some consider the most beautiful in the Black Forest, with its panoramic views of the surrounding wooded slopes. German swimming champions trained in the Paracelsusbad for the 1992 Barcelona Olympics. ☎ 07052/408–250. ☜ *DM 12 for 3 hrs.* ☼ *Apr.–Oct., Tues., Wed., Fri.–Sun. 7:30 AM–9 PM and Mon., Thurs. 7:30 AM–5 PM; Nov.–Mar., Tues., Wed., Fri.–Sun. 8:30 AM–8 PM, Mon., Thurs. 8:30 AM–5 PM.*

A principal pastime in and around Bad Liebenzell is walking along the Nagold River valley. Winding through the thick woods around the little town is a path that leads to the partially restored 13th-century castle of **Liebenzell,** today an international youth center and youth hostel.

NEED A
BREAK?
For morning coffee or afternoon tea, the **Cafe Schweigert** (⊠ Kurhaus-damm 11, ☎ 07052/4404) is ideally situated in the town center, over-looking the river.

Dining and Lodging

$$$ ✕⊞ **Kronen Hotel.** Most of the rooms at this relaxing hotel are situ-ated in a large modern wing; they have natural wood decor and large glass windows. The kitchen, which provides the food for the hotel's three different restaurants, prides itself on serving "vital cuisine" with lots of fresh vegetables and herbs, whole-grain products, and fruit. ⊠ *Badweg 7, D–75378,* ☎ *07052/4090,* FAX *07052/409–420. 3 restau-rants, café. AE, DC, V.*

$$–$$$ ✕⊞ **Waldhotel Post.** This hotel and spa has a fine view of the town of Bad Liebenzell and the surrounding Black Forest. The spacious rooms range from comfortable to luxurious; some have sunny, south-facing balconies. The Black Forest landscape creeps to the very edge of the garden. The Restaurant Krieg is one of the best in the region. Its en-ergetic chef produces creative regional cuisine such as Swabian-style lobster ravioli and mousse of Black Forest currents with cassis sauce. ⊠ *Hölderlinstr. 1, D–75378,* ☎ *07052/4070,* FAX *07052/40790. Restau-rant. café, indoor pool, beauty salon, massage, sauna, spa. AE, V.*

En Route **Weil der Stadt,** the former imperial city, is situated in the hills behind Bad Liebenzell. This small, sleepy town has only its well-preserved city walls and fortifications to remind the visitor of its onetime importance. The astronomer Johannes Kepler, born here in 1571, was the first man to track and accurately explain the orbits of the planets; the **Kepler Museum** in the town center is devoted to his discoveries. ⊠ *Kepler-gasse 2.* ▨ *DM 1.* ☉ *Tues.–Fri. 10–noon and 2–4, Sat. 11–noon and 2–4, Sun. and holidays 11–noon and 2–5; open only 1st and 3rd Sun. of month Oct.–May.*

Hirsau, 5 kilometers (3 miles) southwest of Bad Liebenzell on B–463, is the site of the ruins of a 9th-century monastery, now the setting for open-air theater performances in the summer.

Calw

❸ *3 km (2 mi) south of Hirsau on B–463.*

Calw, one of the Black Forest's prettiest towns, was the birthplace of novelist Hermann Hesse (1877–1962). Pause on the town's 15th-cen-tury bridge over the Nagold River; you might see a local tanner spread-ing hides on the river wall to dry, as his ancestors did for centuries. The town's market square, with its two sparkling fountains surrounded by 18th-century half-timbered houses whose sharp gables stab at the sky, is an ideal spot for relaxing, picnicking, or people-watching.

Dining and Lodging

$$ ✕⊞ **Klosterschenke–Kloster Hirsau.** Diners can choose between two
★ dining rooms and two cuisines in the Hotel Kloster Hirsau: haute cui-sine and regional cooking. Both are outstanding. The hotel itself, a model of comfort and gracious hospitality, is built near the ruins of a monastery. ⊠ *Wildbader Str. 2, D–75365,* ☎ *07051/5621,* FAX *07051/51795. 42 rooms with bath. Restaurant, indoor golf, bowling. DC, V.*

$$ ✕⊞ **Ratsstube.** Most of the original features, including 16th-century beams and brickwork, are still intact at this historic house in the cen-ter of Calw. Rooms aren't spacious, but they are brightly decorated with pastel colors and floral patterns. The restaurant offers sturdy, tra-ditional German fare, such as marinated beef and noodles, thick soups,

and Black Forest sausage. ⊠ *Marktpl. 12, D–75365,* ☎ *07051/1864,* 𝖥𝖠𝖷 *07051/70826. 13 rooms with bath. Restaurant. No credit cards.*

OFF THE
BEATEN PATH

ZAVELSTEIN – On the road south, watch for a sign to this tiny town 5 kilometers (3 miles) out of Calw. The short detour up a side valley to this spot is well worth taking, particularly in spring, when surrounding meadows are carpeted with wild crocuses.

En Route   Back on the main road going south, you'll come next to a turnoff marked **Talmühle/Seitzental.** From here, a winding road leads to **Neubulach,** a town that was home to one of the oldest and, until it closed in 1924, most productive silver mines of the Black Forest. Since then a new use has been found for the mine's extensive workings: Doctors discovered that the dust-free interior of the mine helped in the treatment of asthma patients. Today, rather incongruously, a therapy center is located in the mine. The ancient shafts can also be visited. ☜ *Guided tour of mine DM 4.* ☉ *Apr.–Nov., daily 10–4:15.*

Arrive in **Wildberg,** 8 kilometers (5 miles) farther south, on the third Sunday of July in an even-numbered year and you'll witness one of Germany's most picturesque contests, the **Schäferlauf,** in which Black Forest shepherds demonstrate their skill and speed in managing their flocks. Those unable to time their arrival quite so precisely will find the appealing little fortified town nonetheless has much to command attention, including a 15th-century wooden Town Hall and the remains of a medieval castle.

Nagold

❹   *40 km (25 mi) north of Freudenstadt, 10 km (7 mi) south of Wildberg.*

Nagold is worth a stop to drop in at the half-timbered **Alte Post** inn on the main street. Kings and queens have taken refreshment here on journeys through the Black Forest. Order a glass of the local beer and a plate of Black Forest smoked ham, or a pot of strong coffee and a slice of the famous Black Forest cake.

Dining and Lodging

$$$ ✕ **Romantik Restaurant Alte Post.** This 17th-century half-timbered
★   inn has the kind of ambience lesser establishments believe can be built in with false beams. The menu ranges from traditional Swabian dishes to classic French offerings. For the best value try the local food; the veal in mushroom sauce and venison (in season) are reliable favorites. ⊠ *Bahnhofstr. 2,* ☎ *07452/4221. Jacket and tie. AE, DC, MC, V. Closed Dec. 20–Jan. 8.*

$$–$$$ ⌂ **Hotel Post Gästehaus.** Run by the former proprietors of the neighboring Alte Post restaurant, this hotel is part of a historic and charming old coach inn. Parts of the ivy-clad building are modern, but the same standards of comfort are offered throughout. ⊠ *Bahnhofstr. 3, D–72202,* ☎ *07452/4048,* 𝖥𝖠𝖷 *07452/4040. 24 rooms with bath. AE, DC, MC, V.*

En Route   Leaving Nagold, head west toward Freudenstadt on local highway B–28. The road skirts another jewel of the Black Forest, the ancient town of **Altensteig,** which is on a sunny terracelike slope above the Nagold River. A steep, marked route up the hill through the narrow, medieval streets brings you (huffing and puffing) into a marvelous, unspoiled Old Town with half-timbered houses and a city museum in the old castle.

In summer, pause at the manmade reservoir by **Erzgrube,** 12 kilometers (8 miles) away (follow signs to Erzgrube), for a swim, a picnic, or a hike through one of the thickest parts of the Black Forest, where 200-year-old trees tower to heights of 150 feet or more.

B–28 continues, passing the oldest town of the northern Black Forest, **Dornstetten.** If you fancy another dip into the past, stop to see the 17th-century Town Hall, flanked by equally venerable old buildings, the low eaves of their red roofs framing magnificent half-timbered facades. The fountain dates from the 16th century.

Freudenstadt

⑤ *91 km (57 mi) north of Freiburg, 22 km (14 mi) southwest of Altensteig.*

Freudenstadt, a war-torn city rebuilt with painstaking care, is young by German standards, founded in 1599 to house workers from the nearby silver mines and refugees from religious persecution in what is now the Austrian province of Carinthia (*Freudenstadt* means "City of Joy"). You'll find the streets still laid out in the checkerboard formation decreed by the original planners, the vast central square still waiting for the palace that was intended to stand there. It was to have been built for the city's founder, Prince Frederick I of Württemberg; he, unfortunately, died before work could begin. Don't miss Freudenstadt's Protestant parish church, just off the square. Its lofty nave is L-shaped, a rare architectural liberty in the early 17th century, when this imposing church was built. Freudenstadt claims to have more annual hours of sunshine than any other German resort, so you should be able to sit in the sunbathed Renaissance arcades of the fine main square and bask in the warmth of the rays.

OFF THE BEATEN PATH

SCHAPBACH – From this town 22 kilometers (14 miles) southwest of Freudenstadt, in the enchanting Wolfach River valley, head up into the hills to **Glaswald Lake**; you should have this tree-fringed stretch of water all to yourself. Parts of the neighboring Poppel Valley are so wild that carnivorous flowers number among the rare plants carpeting the countryside. Visit the valley's **Hohloh Lake** nature reserve, near Enzklösterle, in July and August and you'll find the bug-eating *Sonnentau* in full bloom. Farther north, just off B–500, near **Hornisgrinde Mountain,** a path to the remote and romantic **Wildsee** lake passes through an experimental area of forest where the trees are left untended.

Bicycling

The **Kongresse–Touristik–Kur** (☎ 07441/8640, ☏ 07441/85176) organizes bike tours of the surrounding countryside.

Dining and Lodging

$$ ✕ **Ratskeller.** Ask for a table near the Kachelofen, a central feature of this atmospheric haunt on picturesque Marktplatz. Swabian dishes and venison are featured prominently on the menu, but try the homemade trout roulade with crab sauce if it's available. The fixed-price menu, starting at DM 15, is the best value. ✉ *Marktpl. 8,* ☎ *07441/2693. MC, V. Closed Mon.*

$$$ ✕▨ **Schwarzwaldhotel Birkenhof.** If you need to recharge tired batteries (figuratively speaking), there are few better places to do so than this superbly equipped hotel. Old-fashioned comfort and a woodland setting complement a wide range of sports facilities. The two restaurants offer a choice between classic French cuisine and sturdy Black Forest fare. ✉ *Wildbaderstr. 95, D–72250,* ☎ *07441/8920,* ☏ *07441/4763. 57* *rooms with bath. Restaurant, bar, café, indoor pool, sauna, bowling, squash. AE, DC, MC, V.*

$$ ✕⊡ **Bären.** The sturdy old Gasthof Bären has been owned by the same family since 1878, and they strive to maintain tradition and service with a personal touch. Rooms are modern but contain such homey touches as farmhouse-style bedsteads and cupboards. The beamed restaurant is a favorite with the locals and has a menu that combines heavy German dishes (roasts and hearty sauces) and lighter international fare. The trout is caught locally. ✉ *Lange Str. 33, D–72250,* ☎ *07441/2729,* ℻ *07441/2887. 23 rooms with bath. Restaurant, parking. DC, MC, V. Closed Mon.*

$$ ✕⊡ **Luz Posthotel.** This is an old coaching inn in the heart of the town that has also been managed by the same family for a long time—since 1809. However, there's nothing old-fashioned about the rooms, which are both modern and cozy. The restaurant offers Swabian delicacies. During the summer there's a coffee terrace. ✉ *Stuttgarterstr. 5, D–72250,* ☎ *07441/8970,* ℻ *07441/84533. 40 rooms, 4 apartments with bath, some with balcony. Wine bar, library. AE, DC, MC, V. Closed Nov.*

$$ ✕⊡ **Warteck.** This Biedermeier-style restaurant is a feast for all the
★ senses—with flowers everywhere, even in the nooks and crannies between the lead-paned windows. The menu strikes a delicious balance between local and extraregional cuisine. Choices include succulent lamb in meadow herbs, venison with Swabian noodles, and veal in mushroom sauce. In season, the asparagus is dressed in an aromatic hazelnut vinaigrette. The Biedermeier style extends to the cozy furnishings of the guest rooms. ✉ *Stuttgarter Str. 14, D–72250,* ☎ *07441/7418,* ℻ *07441/2957. 13 rooms with bath. Restaurant. DC, V. Restaurant closed Tues.; hotel and restaurant closed Nov., 1st 3 wks after Easter.*

Shopping

Black Forest smoked ham (*Schwarzwälder Schinken*) is an aromatic souvenir that's prized all over Germany. You can buy one at any butcher shop in the region, but it's more fun to visit a *Schinkenräucherei* (smokehouse), where the ham is actually cured. Hermann Wein's **Schinkenräucherei** (☎ 07443/2450), in the village of Musbach, near Freudenstadt, is one of the leading smokehouses in the area. If you have a group of people, call ahead to find out if the staff can show you around. The Schinkenräucherei's shop is open weekdays 9–6 and Saturday 9–noon.

Baiersbronn

7 km (4 mi) northwest of Freudenstadt.

The mountain resort of Baiersbronn, in the midst of the northern Black Forest, is blessed with two of Germany's leading hotel-restaurants—both famous for hospitality, cuisine, and service. Skiing, golf, and riding are among the area's most popular activities.

Dining and Lodging

$$$$ ✕⊡ **Bareiss.** The luxury hotel of the same name has dark-wood furniture and tapestry-papered walls are warmly lit by candles and traditional lamps. Guests, some from across the border in Alsace, are lured by the light, classic cuisine and carefully selected wines (30 brands of champagne alone). The hotel itself is among the most luxurious and best-equipped in the Black Forest. Suites (DM 710 and up; DM 840 in season) have their own sauna, solarium, and whirlpool baths. ✉ *Gärtenbühlweg 14, D–07442 Mitteltal/Baiersbronn,* ☎ *07442/470,* ℻ *07442/47320. 51 rooms with bath, 42 apartments, 7 suites. 2 restaurants, bar, 3 swimming pools, beauty salon, sauna, tennis courts, bowling, exercise room, bicycles, billiards. AE, DC, MC, V.*

$$$$ ✕⊞ **Traube Tonbach.** Baiersbronn's second award-winning restaurant,
★ the Schwarzwaldstube is also part of a luxurious mountain hotel. The
Traube Tonbach has two outstanding restaurants, and if the fabulous
Schwarzwaldstube is full or too expensive for your pocketbook (menus
range from DM 150 to DM 200), then the Köhlerstube is an acceptable alternative. In both, you dine beneath beamed ceilings at tables
bright with fine silver and glassware. The hotel is a harmonious blend
of old and new, each room enjoying sweeping views of the Black Forest. Guests are nearly outnumbered by a small army of extremely helpful and friendly staff. ⊠ *Tonbachstr. 237, D–72270,* ☎ *07442/4920,*
𝔽𝔸𝕏 *07442/492–692. 134 rooms with bath, 38 apartments, 8 suites. 2
restaurants, bars, cafeteria, 3 pools, beauty salon, sauna, tennis, bowling, exercise room. AE, DC, MC, V.*

$$–$$$ ✕⊞ **Hotel Lamm.** The half-timbered exterior of this 200-year-old build-
ing presents a clear picture of the traditional Black Forest hotel within.
Rooms are furnished with heavy oak fittings and some fine antiques. In
winter, logs flicker in the lounge's fireplace, a welcome sight for guests
returning from the slopes (the ski lift is nearby). In its beamed restaurant you can order fish fresh from the hotel's trout pools. ⊠ *Ellbacher-
str. 4, D–07442 Mitteltal/Baiersbronn,* ☎ *07442/4980,* 𝔽𝔸𝕏 *07442/49878.
Restaurant, indoor pool, sauna, billiards. AE, DC, MC, V.*

En Route Return to the Black Forest High Road now, the Schwarzwald
Hochstrasse, winding through the land of myth and fable. At the little village of **Ruhestein,** the side road on the left leads to the **Allerheiligen**
ruins. This 12th-century monastery was secularized in 1803, when plans
were drawn to turn it into a prison. Two days later lightning started
a fire that burned the monastery to the ground. To this day the locals
claim it was divine intervention.

Five kilometers (3 miles) north of Ruhestein is the source of a local myth.
This is the **Mummelsee,** a small, almost circular lake that has fascinated
local people and visitors alike for centuries. Because of the lake's high
mineral content, there are no fish in it. According to legend, however,
sprites and other spirits of the deep find it to their liking. The Romantic lyric poet Mörike (1804–75) immortalized the lake in his ballad "The
Spirits of the Mummelsee." The lake is a popular destination in the summer; if you can, visit during the mist-laden days of spring and allow
yourself to fall victim to its full mysterious appeal.

Bühlerhöhe

*On B–500, 3 km (2 mi) after the turnoff to town of Bühl, which is 17
km (11 mi) north of Ruhestein, 16 km (10 mi) south of Baden-Baden.*

Several of the finest hotels and restaurants in the Black Forest are in
Bühlerhöhe, the thickly wooded heights above the town of Bühl, making it an ideal place to stop for the night. In Bühl Valley and the surrounding area are spas, ruins, quaint villages, and a legendary local
wine called *Affenthaler.*

Dining and Lodging

$$$ ✕ **Wehlauer's.** This outstanding restaurant in the small Badischer Hof
★ Hotel mixes classic French cuisine and delicate variations on re-
gional dishes. Try the pigeon salad or halibut in horseradish sauce if
they're on the menu. In summer take a table in the shady garden at
the edge of the Bühlot River. ⊠ *Hauptstr. 36,* ☎ *07223/23063.
Reservations essential. Jacket and tie. AE, DC, MC, V. Closed Wed.,
Thurs., 3 wks in Jan.*

$$$$ ✕🏨 **Schlosshotel Bühlerhöhe.** One of the leading luxury hotels of the
★   entire Black Forest, this "castle hotel" stands majestically on its own
      extensive grounds high above Baden-Baden, with spectacular views over
      the heights of the Black Forest and walking trails starting virtually at
      the hotel door. The more expensive of its two restaurants, Imperial,
      features such delicacies as lamb and artichoke roulades. Both restau-
      rants are closed Wednesday, Thursday, and January–mid-February. ✉
      Schwarzwaldhochstr. 1, D–77815 Bühl/Baden-Baden, ☎ *07226/550,*
      FAX *07226/55777. 90 rooms, including 13 suites with bath. 2 restau-
      rants, bar, indoor pool, sauna, tennis, health club. AE, DC, MC, V.*

$$$ ✕🏨 **Plättig.** You can enjoy views across the Rhine into France at this
★   excellent traditional hotel. Under the same management as the neigh-
      boring Schlosshotel, but more affordable, it has such pleasantries as a
      summer terrace, where you can feast on homemade Black Forest cake.
      ✉ *Schwarzwaldhochstr. 1, D–77815 Bühl/Baden-Baden,* ☎ *07226/55300,*
      FAX *07226/55444. 38 rooms, 10 apartments with bath. Restaurant, wine
      bar, indoor pool, sauna, exercise room. AE, DC, MC, V.*

$$ ✕🏨 **Cafe-Pension Jägersteig.** Magnificent views of the wide Rhine Val-
      ley as far as the French Vosges Mountains are included in the reason-
      able room rate at this spectacularly located mountain pension, high
      above the town of Bühl and its surrounding vineyards. ✉ *Kappel-
      windeckstr. 95a, D–77815 Bühl/Baden-Baden,* ☎ *07223/24125,* FAX
      *07223/985–998. 14 rooms with bath or shower. Restaurant. No credit
      cards. Closed Thurs., mid-Jan.–mid-Feb.*

Baden-Baden

★ ❻   *24 km (15 mi) north of Mummelsee, 36 km (22 mi) south of Karlsruhe.*

Baden-Baden, the famous and fashionable spa, is downhill all the way
north on B–500 from the Mummelsee. The town sits in a wooded valley of the northern Black Forest and is atop the extensive underground
hot springs that gave the city its name. The Roman legions of the emperor Caracalla discovered the springs when they settled here in the
1st century and named the area Aquae. The leisure classes of the 19th
century rediscovered the bubbling waters, establishing Baden-Baden
as the unofficial summer residence of many European royal families,
who left their imprint on the city in the palatial homes and stately villas that still grace its tree-lined avenues.

This small, neat city, so harmoniously set within the surrounding forest, has a flair and style all its own. As Germany's ultimate high-fashion resort, it basks unabashedly in leisure and pleasure. Here the
splendor of the Belle Epoch lives on to a remarkable extent. Some claim
that one out of five residents is a millionaire. In the evening, Baden-
Baden is a soft-music-and-champagne-in-a-silver-bucket kind of place,
and in the daytime it follows the horseback-riding-along-the-bridle-paths
tradition. It has a crowded season of ballet performances, theater, concerts, and recitals, along with exciting horse racing and high-stakes action at its renowned casino.

Baden-Baden claims the casino, Germany's first, is the most beautiful
in the world, a boast that not even the French can challenge; it was a
Parisian, Jacques Bénazet, who persuaded the sleepy little Black Forest spa to build gambling rooms to enliven its evenings. In 1853 his
son Edouard Bénazet commissioned Charles Séchan, a stage designer
associated with the Paris opera house, to create a design along the lines
of the greatest French imperial palaces. The result was a series of richly
decorated gaming rooms in which even an emperor could feel at
home—and did. Kaiser Wilhelm I was a regular visitor, as was his chan-

cellor, Bismarck. Visitors as disparate as the Russian novelist Dostoyevsky, the Aga Khan, and Marlene Dietrich were all patrons.

Few people visit Baden-Baden to go sightseeing (though those who feel the urge might want to see the **Neues Schloss,** or New Castle, a 19th-century fortress that was rebuilt in the Renaissance style for the grand dukes of Baden; today it's a museum of local history). If you come here to take the waters, still be sure to have a flutter in the casino and perhaps take a swim in the positively palatial **Caracalla Baths,** a vast complex with no fewer than seven pools, opened in 1985. Above all, you'll want to stroll around this supremely elegant resort and sample the gracious atmosphere of a place that, more than almost anywhere else in Europe, retains the feeling of a more unhurried, leisured age.

Baden-Baden's **Spielzeugmuseum** (toy museum) features dollhouses, some of which are 200 years old. ⊠ *Gernsbacherstr. 48,* ☎ *07221/32511.* ⊠ *DM 3.50.* ⊙ *Tues.–Fri. and Sun. 3–6.*

NEED A BREAK?

At the start of the pedestrian shopping street, Lichtentalerstrasse, stands a Baden-Baden institution, the **Cafe König**; step inside to soak up its warmly inviting elegance. Order a pot of coffee and a wedge of Black Forest cake and listen to the hum of money and leisure from the spa crowd, who have made this quiet corner their haunt.

Dining and Lodging

$$$ ✗ **Zum Alde Gott.** The draw here is the classy combination of upscale rustic appeal with distinctive nouvelle German cooking. With only 12 tables, the mood is intimate and sophisticated. The restaurant has a spectacular location amid rolling vineyards in the suburb of Neuweier. In summer you can take a table on the broad terrace and enjoy the view as well as the local wine. Figs in beer pastry make for a memorable dessert anytime of the year. ⊠ *Weinstr. 10, Neuweier,* ☎ *07223/5513. AE, DC, MC, V. Closed Thurs., Fri., and Jan.*

$–$$ ✗ **Klosterschänke.** This rustic restaurant is a 10-minute drive from the center of Baden-Baden, and the food is well worth the trip, particularly on a summer evening, when you can dine outside on a tree-covered terrace. You'll probably share a rough oak table with locals; the Baden wine and locally brewed beer ensure conviviality. The menu is surprisingly imaginative, with Black Forest trout prepared in a local meunière variation. This is the best place for venison when it's in season. ⊠ *Landstr. 84,* ☎ *07221/25854. No credit cards. Closed Mon., 1 wk in summer. No lunch Tues.*

$ ✗ **Gasthaus Münchner Löwenbräu.** Munich's famous Löwenbräu is the only beer served at this Bavarian-style restaurant and in its tree-shaded beer garden—along with a wide selection of Baden wines. The food is simple and filling, with regional specialties predominating. ⊠ *Gernsbacherstr. 9,* ☎ *07221/22311. MC, V.*

$ ✗ **Weinstube Zum Engel.** The Frölich family has been in charge of "The Angel Wine Cellar" for four generations. Eduard Frölich is responsible for the wine; Gerti Frölich, for the kitchen. It is an ideal place for traditional German food such as sauerbraten or Wiener schnitzel. The selection of wines, served by the glass, does supreme justice to the fine local vintages. ⊠ *Mauerbergstr. 62,* ☎ *07223/57243. No credit cards. Closed Mon.–Tues. and 3 wks in Mar.*

$$$$ ✗▥ **Brenner's Park Hotel.** This hotel claims, with some justification, ★ to be one of the best in the world. It's a stately mansion off Baden-Baden's leafy Lichtentaler Allee, set on spacious private grounds. Luxury abounds, and all the rooms and suites (the latter costing up to DM 2,200 a day) are sumptuously furnished and appointed. ⊠ *Schillerstr.*

6, D–76530, ☎ 07221/9000, FAX 07221/38772. *68 rooms and 32 suites with bath. 2 restaurants, bar, indoor pool, beauty salon, sauna, spa, fitness room. AE, DC, MC, V.*

$$$$ ✕⊞ **Quisisana.** You could lock yourself away from the outside world for days in this elegant turn-of-the-century hotel, set in its own spacious park. Most of the guest rooms, decorated in the style of an English country house, have balconies, and the hotel's spa facilities are extensive. ⊠ *Bismarck-str. 21, D–76530,* ☎ *07221/369–100,* FAX *07221/38195. 46 rooms and 9 suites with bath. 2 restaurants, bar, indoor pool, beauty salon, massage, sauna, spa. MC, V.*

$$$$ ✕⊞ **Romantik Hotel Der Kleine Prinz.** This is the showpiece of the whole
★ Romantik organization. Owner Norbert Rademacher, a veteran of the New York Hilton and Waldorf Astoria, and his interior-designer wife have skillfully combined two elegant city mansions into a lodging of unique appeal. Each room is decorated in a different style, from Oriental ("Star of the East") to contemporary Manhattan. A penthouse suite, with open fireplace, covers the entire floor of half of the hotel. Two other rooms have fireplaces, and many come with double bathtubs with Jacuzzi. In winter take an armchair in front of a blazing log fire and wait to be called to your table in the hotel's romantic little restaurant. Chef Berthold Krieg has been in charge of the kitchen for more than a decade. By combining nouvelle-cuisine flair with unmistakable German thoroughness, he has elevated the restaurant to a leading position in demanding Baden-Baden. ⊠ *Lichtentalerstr. 36, D–76530,* ☎ *07221/3464,* FAX *07221/38264. 24 rooms, 15 junior suites, penthouse suite, all with bath. Restaurant, bar, laundry service, parking. AE, DC, MC, V.*

$$–$$$ ✕⊞ **Pospisil's Merkurius.** A log fire on cool days adds to the warm atmosphere of this country-style restaurant and small, friendly hotel in the district of Varnhalt on the southern fringe of Baden-Baden. The dining room's menu offers classic and regional dishes with a light touch: goose-liver soufflé and imaginative preparations of wild hare and pheasant, for example. The extensive wine list features a selection of fine vintages. The restaurant borders on the expensive (menus range up to DM 125), but the seven comfortable hotel rooms are very reasonably priced (DM 110–DM 130). ⊠ *Klosterbergstr. 2, D–76534 Varnhalt/Baden-Baden,* ☎ *07223/5474,* FAX *07223/60996. 7 rooms with bath. Restaurant. No credit cards.*

$$ ✕⊞ **Laterne.** Dating from the late 17th century, this is one of Baden-Baden's oldest hotels as well as one of its smallest. The public rooms, the restaurant, and some of the bedrooms have original beams and woodwork and antique Black Forest furnishings. It's centrally located in a pedestrian zone. ⊠ *Gernsbacherstr. 10–12, D–76530,* ☎ *07221/29999,* FAX *07221/38308. 16 rooms, 3 apartments, all with bath or shower. Restaurant, café. AE, DC, MC, V.*

$ ✕⊞ **Am Markt.** The Bogner family has run the place for more than three decades—a relatively short amount of time in the history of this 250-plus-year-old building. It's in the quiet, traffic-free zone and close to such major attractions as the Roman baths. They've just completed a partial renovation. ⊠ *Marktpl. 17–18, D–76530,* ☎ *07221/22747,* FAX *07221/391–887. 27 rooms, 14 with bath. Restaurant. AE, DC, MC, V.*

$$ ⊞ **Deutscher Kaiser.** This centrally located, old, established hotel offers homey and individually styled rooms at comfortable prices in an otherwise expensive town. All the double rooms have balconies on a quiet street off one of the main thoroughfares. The hotel is just a few minutes' stroll from the Kurhaus. ⊠ *Merkurstr. 9, D–76530,* ☎ *07221/2700,* FAX *07221/270–270. 28 rooms and 1 apartment, all with bath. AE, DC, MC, V.*

In case you want to be welcomed there.

We're here to see that you're always welcomed at establishments everywhere. That's why millions of people carry the American Express® Card – for peace of mind, confidence, and security, around the world or just around the corner.

do more

Cards

In case you're running low.

We're here to help with more than 118,000 Express Cash locations around the world. In order to enroll, just call American Express before you start your vacation.

do more

Express Cash

And just in case.

We're here with American Express® Travelers Cheques
and Cheques *for Two.*® They're the safest way to carry
money on your vacation and the surest way to get a
refund, practically anywhere, anytime.
Another way we help you...

do more ®

**Travelers
Cheques**

$$ ⌘ **Hotel Etol.** This centrally located old hotel has homey, individually decorated rooms at reasonable prices in an otherwise expensive town. All the double rooms have balconies facing a quiet street off one of the main thoroughfares. The hotel is just a few minutes' stroll from the Kurhaus. ⊠ *Merkurstr. 7, D–76530,* ☎ *07221/2700,* FAX *07221/270–270. 28 rooms and 1 apartment, all with bath. AE, DC, MC, V.*

Nightlife and the Arts

Nightlife means Baden-Baden's elegant **casino,** first and foremost. There's a DM 5 admission charge; bring your passport as ID. You'll have to sign a form guaranteeing that you can meet any debts you run up (minimum stake is DM 5; maximum DM 20,000). If your tastes run to the less formal, try the city's leading disco, **Griffon's** (closed Mon. and Tues.), in the same building. For a more subdued evening, stop by at the **Oleander Bar** in Baden-Baden's top hotel, Brenner's Park Hotel (⊠ Schillerstr.), or **Le Piano** piano bar (⊠ Sophienstr. 15).

Baden-Baden has one of Germany's most beautiful performance halls, the **Theater am Goetheplatz** (☎ 07221/275–268 for program details and tickets), a late-Baroque jewel built in 1860–62 in the style of the Paris Opera. It opened with the world premiere of Berlioz's opera *Beatrice et Benedict.* Today the theater presents a regular series of dramas, operas, and ballets.

Each summer Baden-Baden holds a two-week **Musikalischer Sommer Festival** (⊠ Postfach 540, Augustapl. 8, D–7570 Baden-Baden, ☎ 07221/275–228). Venues include the Kurhaus, Kurgarten, St. Jacob's, New Castle Courtyard, and the Brenner's Park Hotel. The **Kurhaus** (⊠ Werderstr., ☎ 07221/932–700) hosts concerts year-round.

Outdoor Activities and Sports

GOLF

The 18-hole Baden-Baden course is considered one of Europe's finest. Contact the **Golf Club** (⊠ Fremersbergstr. 127, Baden-Baden, ☎ 07221/23579).

HORSEBACK RIDING

Facilities in **Baden-Baden** include an equestrian hall, a special area for riding instructions, and a 1-kilometer-long sand track (⊠ Gunzenbachstr. 4a, ☎ 07221/31876).

SWIMMING

The **Caracalla** complex in Baden-Baden is the most lavish swimming pool in the Black Forest region. Enlarged and completely modernized, it has five indoor and two outdoor pools, a sauna, a solarium, and Jacuzzis, as well as courses of thermal water-therapy treatment. ⊠ *Römerpl. 11,* ☎ *07221/275–940.* ☞ *DM 18 for 2 hrs, DM 24 for 3 hrs.* ☉ *Daily 8* AM–10 PM.

The **Friedrichsbad** swimming pool in Baden-Baden offers mixed nude bathing. ⊠ *Römerpl. 1,* ☎ *07221/275–920.* ☞ *DM 48 (includes massage) for 3 hrs; children under 18 not admitted.* ☉ *Mon.–Sat. 9* AM–10 PM, Sun. 2–10.

Shopping

Gaisser (⊠ Lange Str. 22, ☎ 07221/24393), located in Baden-Baden's attractive pedestrian shopping zone, stocks glass, porcelain, and handicrafts from all over Germany, with many specialties from the Black Forest.

The region's wines, especially the dry Baden whites and delicate reds, are highly prized in Germany. Buy them directly from any vintner on the Wine Road. At Yburg, outside Baden-Baden, visit the 400-year-old

Nägelsförster Hof wine tavern and shop (☎ 07221/35550), where you can also enjoy panoramic views of the town. It has daily wine tastings (weekdays 8–6).

En Route   The road to **Gernsbach,** a couple of miles to the east of Baden-Baden, skirts the 2,000-foot-high mountain peak **Merkur,** named after a Roman monument to the god Mercury, which still stands just below the mountain summit. You can take the cable car to the summit, but it's not a trip for the fainthearted—with an incline of more than 50%, this is one of Europe's steepest mountain lifts. ▨ *DM 6 round-trip.* ⊙ *Mid-Feb.–mid-Dec., daily 10–6.*

Bad Herrenalb

❼ *21 km (13 mi) south of Baden-Baden, 8 km (5 mi) south of Marxzell.*

Bad Herrenalb is a popular Black Forest spa, set amid the wooded folds of the Alb River valley. Railway enthusiasts will admire the train station here; it's Baden-Baden's original station, built in the 19th century. It was saved from destruction during the modernization of the Baden-Baden station when it was transported and erected here.

Dining and Lodging

$$–$$$ ✕▨ **Mönchs Posthotel.** Beautiful gardens surround this half-timbered
  ★   building with an ornate turret. Two restaurants (Locanda, with Mediterranean fare, and Kloster Schänke, which serves local fare) and comfortable quarters await inside. Each room is elegantly furnished, and no two are the same. ✉ *Doblerstr. 2, D–76328,* ☎ *07083/7440,* FAX *07083/74422. 35 rooms with bath. 2 restaurants, pool, beauty salon, massage. AE, DC, MC.*

Marxzell

❽ *8 km (5 mi) north of Bad Herrenalb on the road to Karlsruhe.*

In the village of Marxzell a group of ancient locomotives and other old machines at the side of the road announces the presence of the
🄲 **Fahrzeugmuseum,** a wonderland for the technically minded. Every kind of early engine is represented in this museum dedicated to the German automobile pioneer Karl Benz (1844–1929). Germans claim it was he who built the first practical automobile, in 1888, a claim hotly disputed by the French. ✉ *Albtalstr. 2,* ☎ *07248/6262.* ▨ *DM 5.* ⊙ *Daily 2–5.*

Ettlingen

❾ *10 km (6 mi) south of Karlsruhe, 12 km (7 mi) north of Marxzell.*

Ettlingen is a 1,200-year-old town that's now practically a suburb of its newer and much larger neighbor, Karlsruhe. Bordered by the Alb River, Ettlingen's ancient center is a maze of auto-free cobbled streets. Come in the summer for the annual Schlossberg theater and music festival in the beautiful **Baroque Schloss** (palace). The palace was built in the mid-18th century, and its striking domed chapel—today a concert hall—was designed by Cosmas Damian Asam, a leading figure of south German Baroque. Its ornate, swirling ceiling fresco is typical of the heroic, large-scale, illusionistic decoration of the period. ☎ *07243/101.* ⊙ *Tues.–Sun.*

Dining and Lodging

$$ ✕ **Ratsstuben.** Originally used to store salt, this 16th-century cellar by the fast-flowing Als River is now a good place to eat. The food is heartily Teutonic. ✉ *Am Markt/Kirchgasse 1–3,* ☎ *07243/14754. DC, MC, V.*

$$$ ✕🏨 **Hotel-Restaurant Erbprinz.** This is one of the most historic hotels
★ in Ettlingen, and it even has its own trolley-car stop. For many the real
reason for staying here is the top-rated restaurant, which offers mag-
nificent nouvelle German specialties. In summer dine in the charming
garden, hidden away behind the hotel's green-and-gilt fencing. ✉ *Rhe-
instr. 1, D-76275,* ☎ *07243/3220,* 𝖥𝖠𝖷 *07243/16471. 41 rooms with
bath or shower, 6 apartments. Restaurant. AE, DC, V.*

Karlsruhe

★ ⑩ *127 km (79 mi) north of Freiburg.*

Karlsruhe, founded at the beginning of the 18th century, is a young
upstart compared with ancient Ettlingen. But what it lacks in years, it
makes up for in industrial and administrative importance, sitting, as
it does astride a vital autobahn and railroad crossroads. It holds little
major attraction for the visitor, apart from the former palace of the
margrave Karl Wilhelm, today the **Badisches Landesmuseum,** the mu-
seum of local history. ☎ *0721/926–6514.* ☉ *Tues. and Thurs.–Sun.
10–5, Wed. 10–8.*

The town quite literally grew up around the palace, which was begun
in 1715; 32 avenues radiate out from it, 23 leading into the extensive
grounds, and the remaining nine forming the grid of the Old Town.
It's said that the margrave fell asleep under a great oak while search-
ing for a fan lost by his wife and dreamed that his new city should be
laid out in the shape of a fan. True or false, the fact is that the city is
built in a fan pattern, and all but one of the principal streets lead di-
rectly to the palace. The exception is the Kaiserstrasse, constructed in
1800, which runs parallel to the palace.

Despite wartime bomb damage, much of the Old Town retains its orig-
inal and elegant 18th-century appearance thanks to faithful restora-
tion. Walk to the **Marktplatz,** the central square, to see the austere stone
pyramid that marks the margrave's tomb and the severe neoclassical
Stephanskirche (the church of St. Stephen), modeled on the Pantheon
in Rome and built around 1810. The interior, rebuilt after the war, is
incongruously modern.

Nightlife and the Arts

The **Badisches Staatstheater** (✉ Baumeisterstr. 11, ☎ 0721/60202)
in Karlsruhe is by far the best opera house in the Black Forest region.
Street theater is featured in Karlsruhe's annual **Schlossberg** festival in
August, a popular and informal carnival-like event centering on the
palace.

THE CENTRAL BLACK FOREST

The Central Black Forest takes in the Simonswald, Elz, and Glotter val-
leys as well as Triberg and Furtwangen, with their cuckoo clock mu-
seums. The area around the Triberg falls—the highest falls in
Germany—is also renowned for pom-pom hats, straw-covered farm-
houses, and mountain railways. The Black Forest Railway (Offen-
burg-Villingen line), which passes through Triberg, is one of the most
scenic in all of Europe.

Alpirsbach

⑪ *16 km (10 mi) south of Freudenstadt.*

Beer has been brewed in Alpirsbach since the Middle Ages. The un-
usually soft water gives the village-brewed beer a flavor that is widely

acclaimed. The brewery was once part of a monastic settlement, and visitors are welcome to look around. Take a break for a glass of beer at any of the small taverns. In summer concerts are held regularly in Alpirsbach's fine 11th-century parish church. If you have a group, call ahead (☎ 07444/670).

En Route South of Alpirsbach, stop at **Schiltach,** 10 kilometers (6 miles) along B–294, to admire the frescoes on the 16th-century Town Hall. They tell the town's history more vividly than any local chronicle could. Look for the figure of the Devil, who was blamed for burning down the town on more than one occasion.

Leaving Schiltach, follow the B–294 highway 14 kilometers (9 miles) to **Wolfach.** It's the site of the **Dorotheenhütte,** one of the only remaining Black Forest factories where glass is blown using the centuries-old techniques that were once common throughout the region. ▨ *Guided tours DM 4.* ⊙ *Mar.–Oct., weekdays 9–4:30, Sat. 9–2.*

Gutach

⑫ *8 km (5 mi) south of Wolfach, 17 km (11 mi) north of Triberg.*

Gutach lies in **Gutachtal,** a valley famous for the traditional costume, complete with pom-pom hats, worn by the women on feast days and holidays. The pom-poms' color has significance: Married women wear black pom-poms; those unmarried wear red. The village is one of the few places in the Black Forest where you can still see traditional thatched roofs. However, escalating costs caused by a decline in thatching skills, in addition to the ever-present risk of fire, mean that there are substantially fewer thatched roofs in Gutach than there were 20 years ago.

Near Gutach is one of the most diverting museums in the Black Forest, the Schwarzwälder Freilichtmuseum Vogtsbauernhof (Black Forest Open Air Museum). Farmhouses and other rural buildings from all parts of the region have been transported here from their original locations and reassembled, complete with traditional furniture, to create a living museum of Black Forest building types through the centuries. ☎ *07831/230.* ▨ *DM 6.* ⊙ *Apr.–Oct., daily 8:30–6.*

Dining and Lodging

$$$$ ✕▨ **Romantik Hotel Stollen.** The flower-strewn balconies and low
★   roofs of this hotel disguise a distinctive and luxurious interior. Run by the same family for 140 years, it combines understated comfort—some rooms have four-poster beds—with attentive service: You are treated as if you were staying in a family home rather than a hotel. The restaurant—complete with a roaring log fire—serves regional food with nouvelle touches. ⊠ *D–79261 Gutach im Elztal,* ☎ *07685/207,* ☎ *07685/1550. 12 rooms with bath. Restaurant. AE, MC, V. Closed 2 wks in Jan.; restaurant closed Tues.*

Triberg

★ **⑬** *49 km (30 mi) north of Freiburg, 25 km (16 mi) east of Villingen.*

At the head of the Gutach Valley lies the town of Triberg, the site of Germany's highest waterfall, where the Gutach River plunges nearly 500 feet over seven huge granite steps. The pleasant 30-minute walk from the center of Triberg to the top of the spectacular falls is well signposted. ▨ *To view waterfall: DM 2.50 (this may be waived in winter).*

The famous **Schwarzwaldmuseum** in Triberg has exhibits related to Black Forest culture. This is cuckoo-clock country, and the museum has an impressive collection of clocks. The oldest dates from 1640; its simple wooden mechanism is said to have been carved with a bread knife. ⊠ *Wallfahrtstr. 4.* ☎ *DM 5.* ⊘ *May–Oct., daily 9–6; Nov. 1–15 and mid-Dec.–Apr., daily 10–5; Nov.–mid-Dec., weekends only 10–5.*

For anyone who wants to own a cuckoo clock, the place to look is **House of 1000 Clocks.** The shop lives up to its name: Its town branches are two picturesque old houses overflowing with all manner of clocks; the main branch just out of town is distinguished by a huge cuckoo clock on the roof and a special section devoted exclusively to grandfather clocks (*Standuhren*). The staff is multilingual and very friendly, and shipping goods abroad and arranging tax refunds is a matter of course. ⊠ *Branches on Triberg's main street just down from entrance to waterfall and off B–33 toward Offenburg,* ☎ *07722/1085.* ⊘ *Mon.–Sat. 9–5.*

Dining and Lodging

$$–$$$ ✕🏨 **Parkhotel Wehrle.** This imposing mansion has been in the Wehrle family's possession since 1707; its steep-eaved, wisteria-covered facade dominates the town center between the marketplace and the municipal park. Guests should find the service impeccable. The comfortable rooms are individually furnished in a variety of woods with such pleasant touches as fresh flowers. The restaurant serves trout a dozen different ways, all delicious. Try it grilled over coals with fennel. ⊠ *Am Marktpl. 1, D–78098 Triberg im Schwarzwald,* ☎ *07722/86020,* FAX *07722/860–290. 54 rooms, all with bath, and 3 suites. Restaurant, outdoor and indoor pools, sauna, exercise room, parking. AE, DC, MC, V.*

$–$$ ✕🏨 **Römischer Kaiser.** The Roman Emperor has been owned by the same family for more than 150 years, and Black Forest tradition practically oozes from its walls. Rooms are comfortably furnished in solid Black Forest style, with heavy wooden bedsteads and painted furniture. The restaurant serves German and international dishes, with a bit of a French flair. Fresh mountain trout is on the menu almost daily. ⊠ *Sommeraustr. 35, Nussbach,* ☎ *07722/4418,* FAX *07722/4401. 26 rooms with bath. Restaurant, parking. AE, DC, MC, V. Restaurant closed Mon.; no dinner Sun.*

Furtwangen

⑭ *16 km (10 mi) south of Triberg, 37 km (23 mi) north of Titisee.*

Furtwangen is on a tourist route dubbed "The Cuckoo-Clock Road"; clock enthusiasts come to visit its **Uhren (Clock) Museum,** the largest such museum in Germany. It charts the development of Black Forest clocks, the cuckoo clock taking pride of place. Its massive centerpiece is a 25-hundredweight astronomical clock built by a local master. ⊠ *Gerwigstr. 11,* ☎ *07723/920–117.* ☎ *DM 4.* ⊘ *Apr.–Oct., daily 9–5. Nov.–Mar., daily 10–5.*

Across from the Clock Museum, the **Uhrenkabinett Wehrle** (⊠ Lindenstr. 2, ☎ 07223/53240) has an extensive selection of antique and modern clocks in all shapes and sizes—including, of course, plenty of cuckoo clocks.

THE SOUTHERN BLACK FOREST

In the south you'll find the most spectacular mountain scenery in the area, culminating in Feldberg—at 1493 meters (4899 feet), the highest mountain in the Black Forest. The region also has two large lakes created by glaciers: the Titisee and Schluchsee. The best Alpine skiing in the Black Forest occurs on the slopes of Feldberg and around Belchen and Herzogenhorn. Freiberg is a romantic university city whose boundaries contain vineyards, a Gothic cathedral, and Schauinsland mountain.

Titisee

⑮ *37 km (23 mi) south of Furtwangen, 7 km (4 mi) east of Hinterzarten.*

The Titisee, a rare jewel among lakes and the star attraction of the Black Forest's lakeland region, is set in a mighty forest. The 1½-mile-long lake is invariably crowded in summer with boats and Windsurfers. Boats and boards can be rented at several points along the shore.

Dining and Lodging

$$-$$$ ✕▥ **Romantik Hotel Adler Post.** Located in the Neustadt district of Titisee, about 5 kilometers (3 miles) from the lake, this solid old building has been owned and run by the Ketterer family for 140 years. All the rooms are comfortably and traditionally furnished. The restaurant, the Rotisserie zum Postillon, offers excellent local specialties. ✉ *Hauptstr. 16, D-79822 Titisee-Neustadt,* ☎ *07651/5066,* ℻ *07651/3729. 24 rooms, with bath, 4 apartments. Restaurant, indoor pool, beauty salon, massage, sauna. AE, DC, MC, V. Closed mid-Mar.–early Apr.*

Hinterzarten

⑯ *5 km (3 mi) from Titisee, 32 km (20 mi) east of Freiburg.*

The lovely 800-year-old town of Hinterzarten is the most important resort in the southern Black Forest. Some buildings date from the 12th century, among them **St. Oswald's** church, built in 1146. Hinterzarten's oldest inn, **Weisses Rossle,** has been in business since 1347. The **Park Hotel Adler** (☞ *below*), established in 1446, has been under the same family management for 14 generations, although the original building was burned down during the Thirty Years' War, and its successor has been altered considerably since Marie Antoinette and her retinue stayed there in 1770.

Dining and Lodging

$$$ ✕▥ **Park Hotel Adler.** The Riesterer family has owned this historic property since 1446. It's one of Germany's finest hotels, standing on nearly 2 acres of grounds that are ringed by the Black Forest. Marie Antoinette once ate here, and the highest standards are maintained in the French restaurant and a paneled 17th-century dining room. An orchestra accompanies dinner and later moves to the bar to play for dancing. All rooms are sumptuously appointed. ✉ *Adlerpl. 3, D-79854,* ☎ *07652/1270,* ℻ *07652/127–717. 42 rooms and 32 suites with bath. 2 restaurants, bar, indoor pool, sauna, driving range, tennis courts, paddle tennis. AE, DC, MC, V.*

$$-$$$ ▥ **Sassenhof.** Traditional Black Forest styles reign supreme here, from
★ the steep-eaved wood exterior to the comfortable rooms, furnished with rustic pieces that are brightly painted, many of them decoratively carved. There's no restaurant, but guests are welcome to use the kitchen. ✉ *Adlerweg 17, D-79854,* ☎ *07652/1515,* ℻ *07652/484. 16 rooms and 6 suites with bath. Indoor pool, beauty salon, massage, sauna, bicycles. No credit cards. Closed mid-Nov.–mid-Dec.*

Hiking and Skiing

Hinterzarten is situated at the highest point along the Freiburg–Donaueschingen road, and from it a network of far-ranging hiking trails fan out into the surrounding forest. In winter Hinterzarten is one of Germany's most popular centers for *langlauf* (cross-country skiing).

Schluchsee

⑰ *25 km (16 mi) from Hinterzarten (take highway B–317 then pick up B–500).*

The largest of the Black Forest lakes, mountain-enclosed Schluchsee, is near the 4,500-foot Feldberg, the Black Forest's highest mountain. Schluchsee is a diverse resort, where sports enthusiasts may revel in swimming, windsurfing, fishing, and, in winter, skiing. For details, contact the local tourist office (☎ 07656/7732).

Dining and Lodging

$$ ✕🏨 **Kur–und Sporthotel Feldberger Hof.** This is the biggest and best-appointed hotel in the area. Set amid woods and meadows on the slopes above Feldberg and a pleasant walk from the Schluchsee Lake, it has everything for sports-loving guests—from a large pool to ski lifts, which are right outside the hotel. ✉ *Am Seebuck, D–79859,* ☎ *07676/180,* 🖷 *07676/1220. 140 rooms with bath. 3 restaurants, bars, café, pool, beauty salon, health club, theater. AE, DC, MC, V.*

$ ✕🏨 **Hotel Waldeck.** In summer and autumn, geraniums smother the sun-drenched balconies of the Waldeck, while in winter snow piles up on the slopes outside and beckons skiers. Walking trails also begin practically at the front door, and the local forest creeps up to the hotel terrace. Some rooms have traditional furnishings, and others are generic, modern-hotel style. ✉ *Feldberg Altglasshütten, D–79859,* ☎ *07655/364 or 07655/374,* 🖷 *07655/231. 19 rooms with bath. Restaurant, bar, parking. DC, MC, V.*

En Route To get to Freiburg, the largest city in the southern Black Forest, you have to brave the curves of the winding road through **Höllental** (Hell Valley). The first stop at the end of the valley is a little village called, appropriately enough, **Himmelreich,** or Kingdom of Heaven. The village is said to have been given its name in the 19th century by railroad engineers who were grateful they had finally laid a line through Hell Valley. At the entrance to Höllental is a deep gorge, the **Ravennaschlucht.** It's worth scrambling through to reach the tiny 12th-century chapel of **St. Oswald,** the oldest parish church in the Black Forest. Watch for a bronze statue of a deer, situated high on a roadside cliff, 5 kilometers (3 miles) farther on. It commemorates the local legend of a deer that amazed hunters by leaping the deep gorge at this point. Another 16 kilometers (10 miles) will bring you to Freiburg.

Freiburg

⑱ *Via B–31, 23 km (14 mi) from turn-off (317) to Schluchsee.*

Freiburg, or Freiburg im Breisgau (as it's called to distinguish it from another Freiburg in eastern Germany), was founded in the 12th century. After extensive wartime bomb damage, skillful restoration has helped re-create the original and compelling medieval atmosphere of one of the loveliest historic towns in Germany. Freiburg has had its share of misadventures through the years. In 1632 and 1638 Protestant Swedish troops in the Thirty Years' War captured the city; in 1644 it was taken by Catholic Bavarian troops; and in 1677, 1713, and 1744 French troops captured it. Perhaps more interesting to Americans, the 16th-century geographer Martin Waldseemüller, who first put the name America on a map in 1507, was born here. Between April 15 and October 31, the tourist office sponsors English walking tours on

Monday and Friday at 2:30, Wednesday–Thursday and Saturday–Sunday at 10:30. The two-hour tours cost DM 8.

★ The **Münster** cathedral, Freiburg's most famous landmark, towers over the rebuilt medieval streets of the town. The pioneering 19th-century Swiss art historian Jacob Burckhardt described its delicately perforated 380-foot spire as the finest in Europe. The cathedral took three centuries to build, from around 1200 to 1515. You can easily trace the progress of generations of builders through the changing architectural styles, from the fat columns and solid, rounded arches of the Romanesque period to the lofty Gothic windows and airy interior of the choir, the last parts of the building to be completed. Of particular interest are the luminous 13th-century stained-glass windows; a 16th-century triptych (three-panel painting) by Hans Baldung Grien; and paintings by Holbein the Younger and Lucas Cranach the Elder. If you can summon the energy, climb the tower; the reward is a magnificent view of the city and the Black Forest beyond. ☎ 0761/31099; *tours 0761/36890–90.* ▣ *DM 2.50.* ☉ *Mon.–Sat. 10–6, Sun. 1–6.*

The Münsterplatz, the square around Freiburg's cathedral, hosts a daily market, where you can buy everything from strings of garlic to scented oils before the facade of the 16th-century market house, the **Kaufhaus.** The square is also lined with traditional taverns serving such local specialties as Black Forest ham and Swabian spaetzle (small, chewy noodles).

A visit to the Freiburg's cathedral is not really complete without also exploring the **Augustinermuseum,** located at the former **Augustine cloister.** Original sculpture from the cathedral is on display as well as other gold and silver reliquaries. The collection of stained-glass windows, ranging from the Middle Ages to today, is one of the most important in Germany. ✉ *Am Augustinerpl. (Salzstr. 32),* ☎ *0761/201–2531.* ▣ *DM 4.* ☉ *Tues.–Fri. 9:30–5, weekends 10:30–5.*

Located in the **Rathaus Platz,** Freiburg's famous **Rathaus** (Town Hall) is constructed from two 16th-century patrician houses joined together. Among its attractive Renaissance features is an oriel, or bay window, clinging to a corner and bearing a bas-relief of the romantic medieval legend of the Maiden and the Unicorn. ✉ *Rathauspl. 1.*

For a more intimate view of Freiburg, wander through the streets around the Münster or follow the main shopping artery of Josephstrasse. After you pass a reconstructed city gate (this one is **Martinstor;** the other is called **Schwabentor**), follow **Fischerau** off to the left. River fishermen used to live on this little alley. You'll come to quaint shops along the bank of one of the city's larger canals, which continues past the former **Augustine cloister** (☞ Augustinermuseum, *above*) to the equally picturesque area around the **Insel** (island). This canal is a larger version of the brooklets running through many streets in Freiburg's Old Town; tradition has it that anyone who steps into one of these *Bächle* is sure to return to Freiburg.

NEED A BREAK? The little weinstube on Fischerau, **Zur Trotte,** provides an atmospheric taste of Old Freiburg. This establishment serves simple, local specialties (both lunch and dinner) and a variety of local wines in a traditional, rustic interior featuring a big tile oven (*Kachelofen*).

Dining and Lodging

$$$ ✕ **Alte Weinstube zur Traube.** The fruit of the vine is not the only item on the menu at this cozy, old wine tavern, which offers a rich and varied selection of classic French and Swabian dishes. *Zander* (pike)

roulade with crab sauce and braised pork with lentils are especially recommended. ✉ *Schusterstr. 17,* ☎ *0761/32190. AE, MC, V. Closed Sun. and 2–3 wks July–Aug. No lunch Mon.*

$$–$$$ ✕ **Oberkirchs Weinstuben.** Located across from the Gothic cathedral and next to the Renaissance Kaufhaus, this wine cellar is a bastion of tradition and local *gemütlichkeit* (conviviality). Approximately 20 Baden wines are served by the glass, from white Gutedel to red Spätburgunder. The proprietor personally bags some of the game that ends up in the kitchen. Fresh trout is another specialty. In summer the dark-oak dining tables spill onto a garden terrace. ✉ *Münsterpl. 22,* ☎ *0761/31011. V. Closed Sun., public holidays, and Jan. 10–Feb. 2.*

$$ ✕ **Kleiner Meyerhof.** Here you'll find weinstube atmosphere with more places to sit. It's a good place to try regional specialties at comfortable prices. In the fall and winter they serve goose and wild game. ✉ *Rathausgasse 27,* ☎ *0761/26941. MC. Closed Sun. between June and Aug.*

$$ ✕ **Kühler Krug.** Venison dominates the proceedings at this restaurant, which has even given its name to a distinctive saddle-of-venison dish. Those who prefer fish shouldn't despair: There's an imaginative range of freshwater varieties available. ✉ *Torpl. 1,* ☎ *0761/29103. MC. Closed Wed., Thurs., and 3 wks in June.*

$ ✕ **Freiburger Salatstuben.** Come here for healthy, vegetarian food prepared in creative ways—try the homemade whole-wheat noodles with cauliflower in a pepper cream sauce—and served cafeteria style. And all that nutrition and fiber costs no more than a meal at the McDonald's around the corner. It's crowded at peak hours with students from the university up the street. ✉ *Am Martinstor-Löwenstr. 1,* ☎ *0761/35155. No credit cards. Closed Sun., public holidays. No dinner Sat.*

$$$$ ✕▣ **Colombi.** ★ Freiburg's most luxurious hotel also has the city's finest and most original restaurant in two reconstructed 18th-century Austrian farmhouse guest rooms, now luxuriously furnished and decorated with selected Black Forest antiques (including a handsome cuckoo clock, of course). In the rustic part of the restaurant, which is named after the Black Forest artist Hans Thoma, you can order such hearty local dishes as lentil soup and venison, while in its more elegant section the menu goes decidedly upmarket, combining traditional meat and fish dishes with innovative sauces. Restaurant reservations are essential. The hotel, centrally located but very quiet, received an addition in 1995. ✉ *Am Colombi Park/Rotteckring 16, D–79098 Freiburg im Breisgau,* ☎ *0761/21060,* 𝖥𝖠𝖷 *0761/31410. 86 rooms, 42 suites with bath. Restaurant. AE, DC, MC, V.*

$$$$ ✕▣ **Zum Roten Bären.** Now a showpiece of the Ring Group, this inn, which dates from 1311, has retained its individual character, with very comfortable lodging and excellent dining in a cozy warren of four restaurants and taverns. If it's a chilly evening, order a table next to the large *Kachelofen* (glazed-tile stove), which dominates the main, beamed restaurant. A tour of the two basement floors of cellars, dating from the original 12th-century foundation of Freiburg and now well stocked with fine wines, is also recommended. ✉ *Oberlinden 12, D–79098 Freiburg im Breisgau,* ☎ *0761/36913,* 𝖥𝖠𝖷 *0761/36916. 19 rooms with bath, 3 apartments. Restaurant, wine bar, sauna, parking. AE, DC, MC, V.*

$$–$$$ ✕▣ **Schwär's Hotel Löwen.** Heinrich Schwär's "Lion Hotel" stands imposingly on the edge of town, with its back on Freiburg's golf course. Ask for a room with a south-facing balcony and soak up the sun in summer and the Black Forest view in winter. Most of the rooms are furnished in rustic Black Forest style; all are spacious. The hotel operates a minibus service that takes guests into town. ✉ *Kapplerstr. 120, D–79117*

Freiburg–Littenweiler, ☎ *0761/63041,* ⅋ *0761/60690. 62 rooms, 42 with bath or shower. Restaurant, bar, parking. AE, DC, MC, V.*

$$ ✕🖭 **Rappen.** In the heart of the pedestrian-only Old Town, this hotel's brightly painted, farmhouse-style rooms overlook the marketplace and cathedral (and overhear the latter's bells). The rustic theme extends to the restaurant, where wine lovers will appreciate the wide choice—more than 200—of regional vintages. ✉ *Münsterpl. 13, D–79098 Freiburg im Breisgau,* ☎ *0761/31353,* ⅋ *0761/382–252. 25 rooms, 13 with bath. Restaurant. AE, DC, MC, V.*

$$$$ 🖭 **Park Hotel Post.** Located near the train station, the Post has been a hotel since the turn of the century, with good, old-fashioned service to prove it. The Jugendstil facade with stone balconies and central copper-dome tower has earned the building protected status. A large breakfast buffet is included in the room price. ✉ *Eisenbahnstr. 35, D–79098 Freiburg im Breisgau,* ☎ *0761/385–480,* ⅋ *0761/31680. 41 rooms with bath. AE, DC, MC, V.*

Nightlife and the Arts

Nightlife in Freiburg revolves around the city's *Kneipen* (pubs), wine bars, and wine cellars. On Münsterplatz, **Oberkirchs Weinstuben** (✉ Münsterpl. 22, ☎ 0761/31011) is typically atmospheric; you can also look for night spots on any of the streets around the cathedral. For student pubs, wander around Stühlinger, the neighborhood immediately south of the train station. Leading discos in Freiburg's constantly changing scene are **Agar** (✉ Löwenstr. 8, ☎ 0761/380–650) and **Arena** (✉ Schwarzwaldstr. 2, ☎ 0761/73924). Freiburg's **Jazz Haus** (✉ Schnewlinstr. 1, ☎ 0761/34973) has live music nightly and draws big acts and serious up-and-coming artists to its brick cellar.

Freiburg has opened a new multistage complex, the **Konzerthaus,** near the train station. Summer is when the music scene really comes alive. The annual **Zeltmusik** (tent music) festival is a musical jamboree held in June and July, so named because many of the musical events are held in huge tents. The emphasis is on jazz, but most types of music, including classical, can be heard. There are summer chamber music concerts in the courtyard of the ancient Kaufhaus, opposite the Münster, and the Münster itself hosts an annual summer program of organ recitals. For program details and tickets for the above, contact **Freiburg Verkehrsamt** (✉ Rotteckring 14, ☎ 0761/368–9090). Performances in Freiburg's annual summer-theater festival are centered in the city's theater complex, spilling out into the streets and squares.

Staufen

🔞 *20 km (12 mi) south of Freiburg via B–31.*

Once you've braved Hell Valley to get to Freiburg, a visit to the nearby town of Staufen, where Dr. Faustus is reputed to have made his pact with the Devil, should hold no horrors. The legend of Faustus is remembered today chiefly because of Goethe's 1808 drama *Faust,* the leading single work of German literature. Goethe's Faust, fed up with life and the futility of academic studies, is driven to make a pact with the Devil, selling his soul in return for youth, action, and other satanic favors. In fact, the original Faustus was an alchemist and a scientist in the 16th century. His pact was not with the Devil but with a local baron who was convinced that Faustus could make his fortune by discovering the secret of how to make gold from base metals. In his attempts Dr. Faustus died in an explosion that produced such noise and sulfurous stink the townspeople were convinced the Devil had carried him off. You can visit the ancient inn called the **Gasthaus zum Löwen** in the center of Staufen (⊠ Hauptstr. 47), where Faustus lived and died. The frescoes on its walls tell his story in vivid detail.

Breisach

20 *20 km (12 mi) northwest of Freiburg on B–31.*

The town of Breisach stands by the Rhine River; everything you see to the west on the opposite bank is in France. Towering high above the town and the surrounding vineyards is the **Stephansmünster,** the cathedral of St. Stephen, built between 1200 and 1500 (and almost entirely rebuilt after World War II). As at Freiburg, the transition from sturdy Romanesque styles to airy and vertical Gothic styles is easy to see. North of Breisach rises the **Kaiserstuhl,** or Emperor's Chair, a volcanic outcrop clothed in vineyards that produce some of Baden's best wines—reds from the Spätburgunder grape and whites that have an uncanny depth.

Achkarren

21 *5 km (3 mi) north of Breisach.*

Sample high-quality wines—the Weissherbst in particular—in one of the taverns of Achkarren or visit the fine little **wine museum** in the village. ⊠ *Museum DM 2.* ☺ *Apr.–Oct., weekdays 2–5, weekends 11–4 by arrangement.*

THE BLACK FOREST A TO Z

Arriving and Departing

By Car
The Rhine Valley Autobahn, A–5, runs the length of the Black Forest, connecting with the rest of the autobahn system at Karlsruhe, north of the Black Forest.

Freiburg, the region's major city, is 410 kilometers (255 miles) from Munich and 275 kilometers (168 miles) from Frankfurt.

By Plane
The closest international airports are at Stuttgart, Strasbourg in neighboring French Alsace, and the Swiss border city of Basel, the latter just 70 kilometers (40 miles) from Freiburg, the largest city in the Black Forest.

By Train
The main rail route through the Black Forest runs north–south, following the Rhine Valley from Karlsruhe to Basel. There are fast and frequent trains to Freiburg and Baden-Baden from most major German cities (you generally have to change at Karlsruhe).

Getting Around

By Bus
There is an extensive system of local buses in the region, particularly in the northern and central Black Forest. Details are available from the Regionalbusverkehr Südwest (Regional Bus Lines): Karlsruhe, ☎ 0721/1816–6568; Offenburg, ☎ 0781/935–420; Freudenstadt, ☎ 07441/1555.

By Car
Good two-lane highways crisscross the entire region. The main highways that connect the towns of the Black Forest are the A–5 (Frankfurt–Karlsruhe–Basel) running through the Rhine Valley; the A–81

(Stuttgart–Bodensee) in the east; and the A–8 (Karlsruhe–Stuttgart) in the north. Traffic jams on weekends and holidays are not uncommon. Taking the side roads might not save time but they are a lot more interesting. The Schwarzwaldhochstrasse (Black Forest Highway) is one of the area's most scenic routes. The region's tourist office (☞ Contacts and Resources, *below*) has established a series of specially designated tourist driving routes: the High Road, the Low Road, the Spa Road, the Wine Road, and the Clock Road. Though the routes are intended primarily for drivers, most points along them can also be reached by train or bus.

By Train

Local lines connect most of the smaller towns. Two east–west routes—the Black Forest Railway and the Höllental Railway—are among the most spectacular in the country. Details are available from **Deutsche Bahn** (German Railways) in Freiburg (☎ 0761/19419).

Contacts and Resources

Car Rentals

Avis: in **Baden-Baden,** ⊠ Maximilianstr. 54–56, ☎ 07221/71088; in **Freiburg,** ⊠ St-Georgenerstr. 7, ☎ 0761/19719; in **Pforzheim,** ⊠ Westliche Karl-Friedrich-Str. 141, ☎ 07231/40828.

Europcar: in **Baden-Baden,** ⊠ Rheinstr. 29, ☎ 07221/64031; in **Freiburg,** ⊠ Wilhelmstrasse 1A, ☎ 0761/515–100.

Hertz: in **Baden-Baden,** ⊠ Langestr. 101, ☎ 07221/60004; in **Freiburg,** ⊠ Lörracherstr. 49, ☎ 0761/475–051.

Consulates

British Consulate, ⊠ Buchenstr. 4, Gundelfingen, ☎ 583–117. **Canadian Consulate** (nearest one), ⊠ Friedrich-Wilhelm Str. 18, Bonn, ☎ 0228/231–061. **U.S. Consulate** (nearest one), ⊠ Urbahnstr. 7, D–70173 Stuttgart, ☎ 0711/210–080.

Guided Tours

BICYCLE TOURS

Bicycles can be rented at nearly all the train stations in the Black Forest from April 1 to October 1. The cost is DM 11–DM 13 a day (DM 7–DM 9 if you have a valid railway ticket). Several regional tourist offices offer tours on which the biker's luggage is transported separately from one overnight stop to the next. Six- to 10-day tours are available for as little as DM 174 per person, including bed-and-breakfast and bike rental. For the superfit, Titisee-Neustadt organizes a tour through 12 of the Black Forest's mountain passes. Contact the **Kurverwaltung** (⊠ D–79822 Titisee-Neustadt, ☎ 07651/20668) for details.

BUS TOURS

Bus tours of the Black Forest are available from **Freiburg.** The Freiburg tourist information office (☞ Visitor Information, *below*) offers a number of one-day tours, in English, of the Black Forest and parts of neighboring France and Switzerland. Tours start at DM 32.

Outdoor Activities and Sports

FISHING

Fishing without a license is forbidden, and fines are automatically levied on anyone caught doing so. Licenses cost DM 8–DM 12 a day and are available from most local tourist offices, which can also usually provide maps and rental equipment. Contact the **Fremdenverkehrsverband Schwarzwald** (⊠ Bertoldstr. 45, D–79098 Freiburg, ☎ 0761/31317) for details.

The regional tourist office has gotten together with local inns to create "Hike Without Luggage" tours (*Wandern ohne Gepäck*) along the old clock-carriers route. Your bags are transported ahead by car to meet you each evening at that day's destination. Prices are reasonable: Three nights with hotel and breakfast start at DM 305. For reservations and information, contact the Uhrenträgergemeinschaft in Triberg (⊠ Postfach 1423, 78094 Triberg, ☎ 07722/860236, FAX 860290).

The resort of **Wehr** (☎ 07762/80888) offers a 14-day stay in a bed-and-breakfast and 10 hours of riding; similar vacation packages are offered throughout the region.

Cross-country ski instruction is given in every resort, and tours of two days and more are offered by many tourist offices. Call the **Verkehrsamt,** Hinterzarten, ☎ 07652/120–642, for details.

Visitor Information

Information for the entire Black Forest is available from **Fremden-verkehrsverband,** ⊠ Bertoldstr. 45, D–79098 Freiburg, ☎ 0761/31317, FAX 0761/36021. There are local tourist information offices in the following towns:

Baden-Baden: Baden-Baden Marketing Gmbh, ⊠ Augustapl. 8, D–76530, ☎ 07221/275–200, FAX 07221/275–202

Badenweiler: Kurverwaltung, ⊠ Ernst-Eisenlohr-Str. 4, D–79410, ☎ 07632/72110.

Bad Herrenalb: Kurverwaltung, ⊠ D–76332, ☎ 07083/7933.

Bad Liebenzell: Kurverwaltung, ⊠ Kurhausdamm 4, D–75378, ☎ 07052/4080.

Feldberg: Kurverwaltung im Ortsteil Altglashütten, ⊠ Kirchgasse, 1, D–79868, ☎ 07655/8019.

Freiburg: Verkehrsamt, ⊠ Rotteckring 14, D–79098, ☎ 0761/368–9090.

Freudenstadt: Kongresse–Touristik–Kur, ⊠ Promenadenpl. 1, D–72250, ☎ 07441/8640.

Pforzheim: Stadtinformation, ⊠ Rathaus, Marktpl. 1, D–75175, ☎ 07231/39900.

Schluchsee: Kurverwaltung, ⊠ Fischbacherstr. 7, D–79859, ☎ 07656/7732.

Titisee-Neustadt: Kurverwaltung, ⊠ Kurhaus, D–79822, ☎ 07651/980–421.

Triberg: Kurverwaltung im Kurhaus, ⊠ Luisenstr. 10, D–78098, ☎ 07722/953–230.

9 Heidelberg and the Neckar Valley

This area bounces between industrial cities and quaint university towns— Mannheim and Stuttgart among the former, Heidelberg and Tübingen among the latter—with castles, small villages, and the Neckar River throughout. Along the scenic Burgenstrasse (Castle Road), each medieval town is guarded by a castle.

LIKE THE RHINE, THE NECKAR RIVER possesses beauty and historic resonance, but on a more intimate scale; the attractions along its banks make for a memorable vacation. Much of the following route is on the Burgenstrasse, the Castle Road, which charms every bit as much as the Romantic Road without all the tourist hype. This section of the Neckar has proportionately more castles than any comparable stretch of the Rhine. Along the way there are opportunities aplenty to escape into quiet side valleys and visit little towns that slumber in leafy peace. Scarcely one of these towns is without its guardian castle, standing in stern splendor above medieval streets. This is a region that can delight—and sometimes surprise—even the most hardened traveler.

Pleasures and Pastimes

Dining

Heidelberg, Mannheim, and Stuttgart offer the most elegant dining in the region, although in Heidelberg you'll be dining with tradition at your table—there are few restaurants in the city that don't have decor to match the stage-set atmosphere of the town. Atmospheric restaurants in the castle hotels along the Neckar serve excellent food more often than not. In smaller towns along the valley, simple inns, dark and timbered, are the norm. Outside Heidelberg, Mannheim, and Stuttgart, prices can be low. Specialties in the Neckar Valley are much the same as those along the Wine Road, with sausages and local wines figuring prominently. Many restaurants in Heilbronn, Stuttgart and Tübingen feature one of Germany's truly great authentic regional cuisines, based on age-old Swabian recipes.

CATEGORY	COST*
$$$$	over DM 90
$$$	DM 55–DM 90
$$	DM 35–DM 55
$	under DM 35

*per person for a three-course meal including tax but not drinks

Lodging

Staying in a castle hotel can be fun. This area is second only to the Rhine for baronial-style castle hotels studding the hilltops. Most have terrific views as well as a stone-passageway-and-four-poster-bed atmosphere. Stuttgart's hotels cater, on the one hand, to the expense-account business traveler, along with jet-setters from around the world who come to pick up their new Mercedes or Porsche at the source, and, on the other, to German families on vacation. Thus Stuttgart has several luxury hotels as well as a wide range of family-style hotels at a relatively modest cost.

CATEGORY	COST*
$$$$	over DM 250
$$$	DM 180–DM 250
$$	DM 120–DM 180
$	under DM 120

*Prices are for two people in a double room.

Exploring Heidelberg and the Neckar Valley

In addition to the ancient university town of Heidelberg, the geographic area covered in this chapter includes Mannheim, where the Neckar empties into the Rhine, 80 kilometers (55 miles) south of

Frankfurt. From Heidelberg the route runs mostly southeast, with the exception of a detour south to Schwetzingen and one north to Weinheim. The Neckar snakes its scenic way east and then south, between the river and the wooded slopes of the Odenwald Forest, before hitting the rolling, vine-covered countryside around Heilbronn. From there it's a 50-kilometer (31-mile) drive, partly along the Neckar, to Stuttgart; about 40 kilometers (25 miles) farther, you rejoin the banks of the Neckar at the picturesque university town of Tübingen.

Great Itineraries

For most tourists, Heidelberg is a destination unto itself, but it can also be seen as the major stop on the Castle Road, which makes its way through the narrower parts of the Neckar Valley. Beyond that, you reach the cities of Heilbronn, Stuttgart, and Tübingen, which reflect the region's industry and history.

Numbers in the text correspond to numbers in the margin and on the Heidelberg and the Neckar Valley maps.

IF YOU HAVE 3 DAYS

Spend a full day and night exploring ⊞ **Heidelberg** ①, with its university pleasures. On the second day take a trip up the Neckar to the castles of ⊞ **Neckarsteinach**, ⊞ **Hirschhorn** ㉓, and ⊞ **Hornberg** ㉕ (all of them have hotels for an overnight stay, with excellent restaurants). On the third day visit the **Staatsgalerie** (State Gallery) in **Stuttgart** ㉙.

IF YOU HAVE 5 DAYS

Begin your first day exploring **Mannheim** ⑲, with the 18th-century Elector's Palace, one of the largest Baroque buildings in Europe, and the Reiss-Insel Park alongside the Rhine. Proceed to ⊞ **Heidelberg** ① for two overnight stays and spend the second day taking in its quaint university atmosphere. On the third day, continue up the Neckar to stop at the Burg Guttenberg (with its aviary of birds of prey) and the castles of **Neckarsteinach, Hirschhorn** ㉓, and ⊞ **Hornberg** ㉕. Stay overnight at Hornberg's hotel. Plan to spend your fourth day investigating the remains of the imperial palace and other sights in **Bad Wimpfen** ㉖ and end the trip in the medieval atmosphere of ⊞ **Tübingen** ㉛, which you can explore on the fifth day, if time allows.

IF YOU HAVE 7 DAYS

After a half day in Mannheim, explore ⊞ **Heidelberg** ①, spending two nights there. On the third day, head up the Neckar to **Burg Guttenberg** and the castles of **Neckarsteinach** and ⊞ **Hirschhorn** ㉓, staying at Hirschhorn for two nights. Continue on to explore **Mosbach** ㉔, the castle at **Hornberg** ㉕, the rebuilt medieval castle of **Horneck,** and the spa town of **Bad Rappenau.** Spend the sixth day and night in ⊞ **Bad Wimpfen** ㉖, with a possible side trip to the museum of bicycle and motorcycle technology at **Neckarsulm** ㉗. On the seventh day, visit the Staatgalerie in **Stuttgart** ㉙ en route to ⊞ **Tübingen** ㉛ for the last night of the journey.

When to Tour Heidelberg and the Neckar Valley

If you plan to visit Heidelberg in summer, make reservations well in advance and expect to pay top rates. To get away from the crowds, consider staying out of town—at Neckargemünd, say—and driving or taking the bus into the city. Hotels and restaurants are much cheaper just a little upriver. A visit in late fall, when the vines turn a faded gold, or early spring, with the first green shoots of the year, can be captivating. In the depths of winter river mists creep through the narrow streets of the Old Town and awaken the ghosts of a romantic past.

HEIDELBERG AND THE NECKAR-RHINE TRIANGLE

The natural beauty of Heidelberg is created by the embrace of mountains, forests, vineyards, and the Neckar River, crowned by its ruined castle. The Neckar and the Rhine meet at nearby Mannheim, a major industrial center and the second-largest river port in Europe. Inside its industrial sprawl lurks an elegant Old Town that was carefully rebuilt after wartime bomb damage. Schwetzingen, known as known as Germany's asparagus capital, lies in the triangle's center.

Heidelberg

❶ *57 km (35 mi) northeast of Karlsruhe*

If any city in Germany encapsulates the spirit of the country, it is Heidelberg. Scores of poets and composers—virtually the entire 19th-century German Romantic movement—have sung its praises. Goethe and Mark Twain both fell in love here: the German writer with a beautiful young woman, the American author with the city itself. Sigmund Romberg set his operetta *The Student Prince* in the city; Carl Maria von Weber wrote his lushly Romantic opera *Der Freischütz* (The Marksman) here. Composer Robert Schumann was a student at the university. It was the university, the oldest in the country, that gave impetus to the artistic movement that claimed Heidelberg as its own. The campaign these artists waged on behalf of the town has been astoundingly successful. Heidelberg's fame is out of all proportion to its size; more than 2.5 million visitors crowd its streets every year.

Heidelberg was the political center of the Rhineland Palatinate. At the end of the Thirty Years' War (1618–48), the elector Carl Ludwig married his daughter to the brother of Louis XIV in hopes of bringing peace to the Rhineland. But when the elector's son died without an heir, Louis XIV used the marriage alliance as an excuse to claim Heidelberg, and in 1689 the town was sacked and laid waste. Four years later he sacked the town again. From its ashes arose what you see today: a Baroque town built on Gothic foundations, with narrow, twisting streets and alleyways. The new Heidelberg changed under the influence of U.S. army barracks and industrial development stretching into the suburbs, but the old heart of the city remains intact, exuding the spirit of romantic Germany.

Extending west to east through the Old Town is **Hauptstrasse,** an elegant pedestrian mall that runs straight as an arrow for 1½ miles through the city. The main square, **Marktplatz,** is surrounded by narrow side streets that should be explored before going on to the castle. **❷** You reach the first part of the **university** (there are four separate university complexes in the town) by walking down Hauptstrasse west of Marktplatz.

On Hauptstrasse, pause in front of the **Haus zum Riesen** (the Giant's House), so-called because the local worthy who built it in 1707 (using stone from the destroyed castle) put up the larger-than-life statue of himself above the front door. Not far from Haus zum Riezen, on Hauptstrasse on your right, is the Protestant **Providence Church,** built by the elector Carl Ludwig in the mid-17th century. The richly ornate doorway of the **Wormser Hof** is a reminder that Heidelberg was the seat of the bishops of Worms. Look at its lead-paned Renaissance oriel (bay window) on the second floor—it's one of the finest in the city.

The Neckar Valley

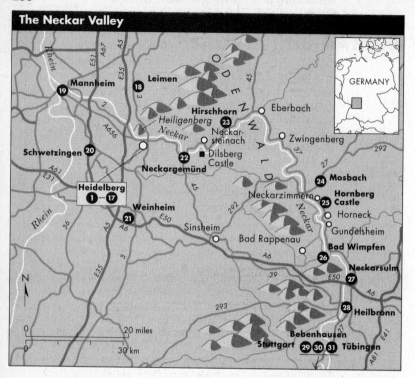

❹ The **Kurpfälzisches Museum** (Electoral Palatinate Museum), Heidelberg's leading museum, is housed in a Baroque palace opposite Wormser Hof. Its collections chart the history of Heidelberg. Among the exhibits are two contrasting standouts. One is a replica of the jaw of Heidelberg Man, a key link in the evolutionary chain thought to date from a half-million years ago; the original was unearthed near the city in 1907. You'll need rare powers of imagination to get much of a sense of this early ancestor from just his (or her) jaw, however. The other attraction presents no such problems. It's the **Twelve Apostles Altarpiece**, one of the largest and finest works of early Renaissance sculptor Tilman Riemenschneider. Its exquisite detailing and technical sophistication are matched by the simple faith that radiates from the faces of the apostles. On the top floor of the museum there's a rich range of 19th-century German paintings and drawings, many depicting Heidelberg. ✉ *Hauptstr. 97,* ☎ *06221/583–402.* ✉ *DM 5, free Sun. and public holidays.* ☉ *Tues.–Sun. 10–5, Wed. 10–9.*

❺ Two blocks from the Kurpfälzisches Museum lies the **Old University**, founded in 1386 and rebuilt during the early 18th century for the elector Johann Wilhelm. Behind the Old University, in Augustinerstrasse,

❻ is the **Studentenkarzer,** the former students prison where, from 1784 to 1914, unruly students were incarcerated (tradition dictated that students couldn't be thrown into the town jail). The students could be held for up to 14 days; they were left to subsist on bread and water for the first three days but thereafter were allowed to attend lectures, receive guests, and have food brought in from the outside. A stay in the jail became as coveted as a scar inflicted in the university's fencing clubs. There's bravado, even poetic flair, to be deciphered from two centuries of graffiti that cover the walls and ceiling of the narrow cells. ✉ *Augustingasse,* ☎ *06221/542–334.* ✉ *DM 1.50.* ☉ *Tues.–Fri. 10–noon and 2–5, Sat. 10–1; closed public holidays.*

Alte Brücke, **17**

Castle, **11**

Heiliggeist-
kirche, **15**

Hotel zum
Ritter, **16**

Königstuhl, **13**

Königstuhl
funicular, **10**

Kurpfälzisches
Museum, **4**

Molkenkur, **12**

New
University, **7**

Old
University, **5**

Rathaus, **14**

St. Peter's
Church, **9**

Studenten-
karzer, **6**

Universitäts-
bibliothek, **8**

University, **2**

Wormser
Hof, **3**

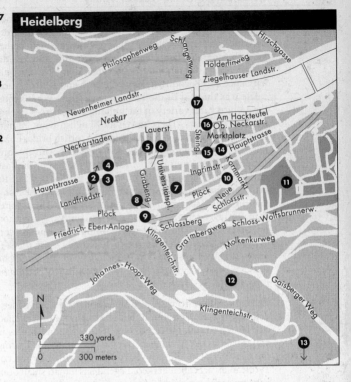

Heidelberg

7 The **New University,** across Universitätsplatz (University Square), was
built between 1930 and 1932 with funds raised in the United States
by a former American student at the university who became U.S. am-
bassador to Germany, J. G. Schurman. An ancient section incorporated
into the new building is all that remains of the old city walls. It's the
Hexenturm (Witches Tower), where witches were locked up in the Middle Ages. ⊠ *Grabengasse.*

8 The **Universitätsbibliothek,** the university library, stands opposite the
New University on the street called Plöck. Its 2.5 million volumes in-
clude the 14th-century *Manesse Codex,* a collection of medieval songs
and poetry once performed in the courts of Germany by the Minnesänger.
⊠ *Plöck 107–109.* ☏ *06221/542–380.* ⬚ *Free.* ☾ *Mon.–Sat. 10–7
(Easter–Nov. 1, Mon.–Sat. 10–7), Sun. and holidays 11–4.*

9 Across from the university library is the Gothic **St. Peter's Church,** the
city's oldest parish church. In its graveyard are the final resting places,
some more than 500 years old, of many leading Heidelberg citizens.
The Baroque building immediately east of St. Peter's Church was originally a Jesuit seminary; it later became a lunatic asylum and is now a
student dormitory.

10 East of St. Peter's Church on Plöck is the **Königstuhl funicular,** which
hoists visitors to the Königstuhl heights, 1700 feet (568 meters) above
Heidelberg. On the way the funicular stops at the ruined castle. The
round-trip fare to the castle is DM 4.50; the 17-minute journey to the
Königstuhl heights and back costs DM 7. The funicular leaves every
10 minutes in the summer and every 20 minutes in the winter. A winding road provides a slower way to the castle; if you take it, you'll be
following in the footsteps of generations of earlier visitors. If you don't
fancy the hike up but want to pretend to be Mark Twain, you can walk
down from the castle.

⑪ The **castle** was already in ruins when Germany's 19th-century Romantics fell under its spell, drawn by the mystery of its Gothic turrets and Renaissance walls etched against the verdant background of the thick woodland above Heidelberg. The oldest parts still standing date from the 15th century, though most of the great complex was built in the Renaissance and Baroque styles of the 16th and 17th centuries, when the castle was the seat of the Palatinate electors. What's most striking is the architectural variety of the building, vivid proof of changing tastes through the years. There's even an "English wing," built in 1612 by the elector Friedrich V for his teenage Scottish bride, Elizabeth Stuart; its plain, square-windowed facade appears positively foreign in comparison with the more opulent styles of the rest of the castle. (The enamored Friedrich also had a charming garden laid out for his young bride; its imposing arched entryway, the Elisabethentor, was put up overnight as a surprise for her 19th birthday.) The architectural highlight, however, remains the Renaissance courtyard—harmonious, graceful, and ornate. Allow at least two hours to tour the complex—and expect long lines in summer (up to 30 minutes is usual). ☎ 06221/538–414. 🖭 DM 2 (castle); DM 4 (includes tour of castle courtyard and Fass; ☞ below). ☉ Daily 9–5; guided tours 9–4:30 and by special arrangement.

Even if you have to wait, you should make a point of seeing the **Heidelberger Fass,** an enormous wine barrel in the cellars, made from 130 oak trees and capable of holding 49,000 gallons. It was used to hold wines paid as tax by winegrowers in the Palatinate. During the rule of the elector Carl Philip, the barrel was guarded by the court jester, a Tyrolean dwarf called Perkeo. Legend has it that, small or not, he could consume frighteningly large quantities of wine—he was said to have been the most prodigious drinker in Germany—and that he died when he drank a glass of water by mistake. A statue of Perkeo stands opposite the massive barrel.

★ The fascinating **Apothekenmuseum** is a delight, filled with ancient carboys and other flagons and receptacles (each with a carefully painted enamel label), beautifully made scales, little drawers, shelves, a marvelous reconstruction of an 18th-century apothecary shop, dried beetles and toads, and a mummy with a full head of hair. 🖭 DM 3 (Apothekenmuseum). ☉ Mid–Mar.–Oct., daily 10–5; Nov.–Mar., weekends only 11–5.

The castle is floodlit in June, July, and September, and fireworks are shot from the terraces at night. In August the castle is the setting for an open-air theater festival. Performances of *The Student Prince* figure prominently.

There are fine views of the Old Town from the castle terraces, but for an even better view ride the funicular up to either of the next two stops:

⑫ ★ ⑬ **Molkenkur** and, at the summit, **Königstuhl.** If the weather's clear, you can see south as far as the Black Forest and west to the Vosges Mountains of France.

NEED A BREAK?   Both the Molkenkur and Königstuhl stops have comfortable restaurants with terraces commanding sweeping views. If you don't want a full-fledged lunch, stop in for a cup of coffee and a pastry.

Back in town, walk toward the river from the funicular station to **Kornmarkt,** one of the oldest squares in Heidelberg, graced with a fine Baroque statue of the Virgin Mary. The impressive building on the corner of Mittelgasse was once Heidelberg's foremost hostelry, the Prinz Karl, where Mark Twain stayed in 1878. A few years earlier it was used as a barracks by Bismarck's triumphant Prussian army as it swept through the Rhineland, forcibly uniting Germany. The young Prince Wilhelm von Preussen, later Kaiser Wilhelm I, was among the soldiers stationed there; prudently, he brought along his own camp bed.

⑭ The **Rathaus** (Town Hall), a stately Baroque building dating from 1701, fronts Heidelberg's market square, the Marktplatz. Be here at 7 PM to hear melodious chimes ring out from the building. Criminals were tortured and decapitated and witches were burned in the tower-
⑮ ing shadow of the 14th-century **Heiliggeistkirche** (Church of the Holy Ghost) on Markplatz. The church itself fell victim to the plundering General Tilly, leader of the Catholic League during the Thirty Years' War. Tilly loaded the church's greatest treasure—the *Biblioteka Palatina*, at the time the largest library in Germany—onto 500 carts and trundled it off to Rome, where he presented it to the pope. Few volumes found their way back to Heidelberg. At the end of the 17th century French troops plundered the church again, destroying the family tombs of the Palatinate electors; only the 15th-century tomb of Elector Ruprecht III and his wife, Elisabeth von Hohenzollern, remain today.

★ ⑯ **Hotel zum Ritter,** with its elaborate Renaissance facade of curclicues, columns, and gables, stands opposite Heiliggeistkirche, on Haupstrasse. The hotel takes its name from the statue of a Roman knight ("Ritter") atop one of the many gables. Its French builder, Charles Bélier, had the Latin inscription *Persta Invicta Venus* added to the facade in gold letters—"Venus, Remain Unconquerable." It appears this injunction was effective, as this was the city's only Renaissance building to be spared the attentions of the invading French in 1689 and 1693. Between 1695 and 1705 it was used as Heidelberg's Town Hall; later it became an inn. Today it's the most atmospheric hotel in town (☞ Dining and Lodging *below*). ⊠ *Hauptstr. 178,* ☎ *06221/24272.*

Skirt the cathedral, cross the former fish market, the Fischmarkt, and turn down picturesque Steingasse. Within a few steps you'll have reached
⑰ the Neckar. The romantically turreted **Alte Brücke** (Old Bridge) spans the river. It's the ninth bridge to be built here since medieval times, its predecessors suffering various unhappy fates, included several destroyed by ice floes. The elector Carl Theodor, who built it in 1786–88, must have been confident this one would last: He had a statue of himself put on it, the plinth decorated with river gods and goddesses (symbolic of the Rhine, Danube, Neckar, and Mosel rivers). Just to be safe, he also put up a statue of the saint appointed to guard over it, St. John Nepomuk. You can walk onto the bridge from the Old Town under a portcullis spanned by two *Spitzhelm* towers (so called for their resemblance to old-time German helmets). In the left (west) tower are three dank dungeons that once held common criminals. Between the towers, above the gate, were more salubrious lockups, with views of the river and the castle; these were reserved for debtors. Above the portcullis you'll see a memorial plaque that pays warm tribute to the Austrian forces who helped Heidelberg beat back a French attempt to capture the bridge in 1799. From the bridge, or from the road leading along the other bank of the river, you'll have some of the finest views of the Old Town and the castle above. For the best view of Heidelberg, climb up
★ the steep, winding **Schlangenweg** (Snake Path) to **Philosophenweg**, a path through the woods above the river. Be here as the sun sets, turning the castle to gold, for a vision to cherish for a lifetime.

Dining and Lodging

$$$ ✕ **Zur Herrenmühle.** Delicately prepared French-inspired cuisine is
★ served on pewter plates adorning rough-hewn tables at this 17th-century tavern in the Old Town. Fish is the specialty here, and the desserts

are noteworthy. In summer diners can eat in a peaceful inner court-yard. ⊠ *Hauptstr. 237–239,* ☎ *06221/12909. AE, DC, MC, V. Closed Sun. No lunch.*

$$ ✕ **Hackteufel.** Once a popular student pub, the Hackteufel now has a
★ broader clientele; a friendly atmosphere and the host's good cooking are the draws. Low-slung lamps hung from dark beams cast a warm glow over the rough wood tables. If it's winter, choose a place by the handsome tile oven. ⊠ *Steingasse 7,* ☎ *06221/27162, AE, DC, MC, V. Closed Dec. 23–Jan. 2.*

$ ✕ **Cafe Journal.** Here is an Old World paradise for coffee, pastries, and people-watching. The pedestrians strutting on the Hauptstrasse pro-vide local theater as do the people chatting, conspiring, and flirting in-doors. Yes, Heidelbergers love the place, although it gets more than its share of tourists. Newspapers from around the world, hung on hooks, line the walls. ⊠ *Hauptstr. 162,* ☎ *06221/161712. No credit cards.*

$ ✕ **Perkeo.** Ask for a table in the atmospheric Schlosstube Room and request suckling pig if it's on the menu. You'll then be dining in the style for which this historic restaurant has been known for nearly three cen-turies. ⊠ *Hauptstr. 75,* ☎ *06221/160–613. AE, DC, MC, V.*

$ ✕ **Schnookeloch.** This picturesque and lively old tavern dates from 1407 and is inextricably linked with Heidelberg's history and its uni-versity. Look for men both old and young, with scars on their cheeks. There is still handful of students who duel with swords, crazy as it might sound. Every evening a piano player chimes in. ⊠ *Haspelgasse 8,* ☎ *06221/14460,* FAX *06221/22733. AE, DC, MC, V.*

$ ✕ **Vetters Alt–Heidelberger Brauhaus.** This brewery-tavern also has a butcher shop in the back. It sells sausage by the centimeter, little pots of lard, and roast pig in "quarters, halves, and wholes." The closest thing to a vegetable is cheese. Elbow your way in by all means. The brewed-on-the-premises beer is excellent. ⊠ *Steingasse 9,* ☎ *06221/165–850. No credit cards.*

$ ✕ **Zum Roten Ochsen.** Many of the oak tables here have initials carved
★ into them, a legacy of the thousands upon thousands who have visited Heidelberg's most famous and time-honored old tavern. Over many, many decades Bismarck, Mark Twain, and John Foster Dulles, may have left their mark—they all ate here. It's been run by the Spengel fam-ily for more than a century, and they jealously guard the rough-hewn, half-timbered atmosphere. ⊠ *Hauptstr. 217,* ☎ *06221/20977. Reser-vations essential. No credit cards. Closed Sun., holidays, and mid-Dec.–mid-Jan.*

$$$$ ✕🏠 **Europäischer Hof–Hotel Europa.** This is the classiest and most
★ luxurious of Heidelberg's hotels, close to just about everything in town and offering a wide range of facilities. Public rooms are sumptuously furnished, and bedrooms are spacious and tasteful. If you fancy a splurge, ask for one of the suites; the best have whirlpools. ⊠ *Friedrich-Ebert-Anlage 1, D–69117,* ☎ *06221/5150,* FAX *06221/515–555 or 06221/515–556. 122 rooms, 13 suites, all with bath. Restaurant, bar, coffee shop, beauty salon. AE, DC, MC, V.*

$$$$ ✕🏠 **Romantik Hotel zum Ritter St. Georg.** If this is your first visit to
★ Germany, try to stay here. It's the only Renaissance building in Hei-delberg, and it dishes atmosphere by the barrel load. The Red Baron would feel right at home with the exposed beams and the suit of armor in the dining room, feasting on *Wild* (game) specialties such as *Hirsch* (venison) from nearby Odenwald Forest. Bedrooms are clean and com-fortable—some traditional, some more modern. ⊠ *Hauptstr. 178, D–69117,* ☎ *06221/24272,* FAX *06221/12683. 39 rooms, 36 with bath. Restaurant. AE, DC, MC, V.*

$$$ ✕⊞ **Gutschänke Grenzhof.** The Grenzhof estate existed as a simple homestead long before Heidelberg was founded. Today it's a very comfortable hotel, recently enlarged and completely renovated in German country-house style. Four more expensive maisonette suites have been added; they are done in the style of a city apartment, yet they have views of rural parkland. There's also a gourmet restaurant. ⊠ *Heidelberg-Grenzhof 9, D–69117,* ☎ *06202/9430,* ⒻⒶⓍ *06202/943–100. 22 rooms, 4 maisonettes, 1 junior suite, all with bath. Restaurant, bar, beer garden, café. AE, DC, MC, V.*

$$$ ✕⊞ **Hotel Hirschgasse.** Across the river on the edge of town, yet only
★   a 10-minute walk from the city center, the Hirschgasse began as a farmhouse. Its 500-year history, which places it among the oldest buildings in the area, also includes a stint as a tavern, where university students indulged their fencing duels, and a mention in Mark Twain's *A Tramp Abroad.* Only suites, all decorated Laura Ashley–style, are available. The restaurant is exceptional. ⊠ *Hirschgasse 3, D–69120,* ☎ *06221/4540,* ⒻⒶⓍ *06221/454–111. 22 suites with bath. Restaurant. AE, DC, MC, V. Closed Dec. 23–Jan. 7.*

$$ ✕⊞ **Gasthaus Backmulde.** This traditional tavern in the heart of Heidelberg has a surprising range of items on its restaurant menu, from delicately marinated fresh vegetables that accompany the excellent meat dishes to imaginative soups that add modern flair to ancient recipes (a Franconian potato broth, for instance, rich with garden herbs). Guest rooms are small but comfortable. ⊠ *Schiffgasse 11, D–69117,* ☎ *06221/53660. 13 rooms with bath. Restaurant. No credit cards.*

$$$ ⊞ **Holländer Hof.** The pink-and-white painted facade of this ornate 19th-century building, across from the Old Bridge, stands out on the old-town waterfront of the Neckar River. Many of its rooms overlook the busy waterway and the forested hillside above the opposite shore. In 1996 the second floor was renovated and the rooms newly furnished. ⊠ *Neckarstaden 66, D–69117,* ☎ *6221/12091,* ⒻⒶⓍ *06221/22085. 40 rooms and 1 suite with bath. Baby-sitting. AE, DC, MC, V.*

Nightlife and the Arts

Information on all upcoming events in **Heidelberg** is listed in the monthly *Konzerte im Heidelberger Stern* and *Heidelberg Aktuell,* both free and available from the tourist office. Tickets for theaters in Heidelberg are available from **Theaterkasse** (⊠ Theaterstr. 4, ☎ 06221/583–520).

BARS AND CLUBS

Heidelberg's nightlife is concentrated in the area around the Heiliggeistkirche (Church of the Holy Ghost), in the Old Town. For a fun night out try the **Hard Rock Cafe** (⊠ Hauptstr. 142); it's not exactly *Student Prince* territory, but it's a good place for videos and burgers. For blues, jazz, and funk try **Eckstein** (⊠ Fischmarkt 3); admission is free. Germany's oldest jazz cellar is **Cave 54** (⊠ Krämergasse 2). The mood is smoky and loud at the **Goldener Reichsapfel** (⊠ Unterestr. 35), always crowded after 10 PM. **Club 1900** (⊠ Hauptstr. 117) is a well-established disco. The fanciest bars, along with many trendy cafés, are along the main pedestrian street, Haupstrasse. For most, however, nightlife in Heidelberg means a visit to one of the student taverns to drink wine and beer, lock arms, and sing. There are no better places to try than **Zum Roten Ochsen** and **Schnookeloch,** both of which have been in business for several centuries (☞ Dining, *above*).

THEATER AND MUSIC

Heidelberg has a thriving theater scene. The **Theater der Stadt** (⊠ Friedrichstr. 5, ☎ 06221/583–502) is the best-known theater in town. The **Zimmer Theater** (⊠ Hauptstr. 118, ☎ 06221/21069) is known for avant-garde productions. For information on performances at the castle during the annual Schloss-Spiele festival, call 06221/58976.

The **Zwingenberg,** above the Neckar River, holds annual Schloss-Spiele festivals throughout the summer within its ancient walls. For program information and tickets, contact Rathaus Zwingenberg (✉ D–69439 Zwingenberg, ☎ 06251/70030).

Outdoor Activities and Sports

GOLF

There are two golf clubs in the vicinity of Heidelberg. The **Golfclub Heidelberg** (☎ 06226/40490), in the neighboring village of Lobbach-Lobenfeld, welcomes visitors on weekdays only. You must be accompanied by a member to play at the **Hohenhardter Hof Club** (✉ Wiesloch, 20 min south of Heidelberg, ☎ 06222/72081) on weekends.

HORSEBACK RIDING

In Heidelberg there are stables near the **city zoo** (✉ Tiergartenstr. 1b, ☎ 06221/412–728). One can also go riding at **Pleikartsforstenhof 5** (✉ Pleikartsförsterhof 3, ☎ 06221/700–476).

SWIMMING

You'll find indoor and outdoor swimming pools in all towns and most villages along your way. Heidelberg has a pool fed by thermal water at Vangerowstrasse 4, and pools at the extensive **Tiergartenschwimm-bad,** next to the zoo.

TENNIS

Most towns and villages along the Neckar have tennis clubs that accept visitors. In Heidelberg you can play at the **Tennis-Inn** (✉ Harbig-weg 1, ☎ 06221/12106).

Shopping

Heidelberg's **Hauptstrasse,** or main street, is a pedestrian zone lined with shops, sights, and restaurants that stretches more than half a mile through the heart of town. Look here for the glass and crystal for which the Neckar Valley region is renowned. You can find a selection of crystal at **Edm. König** (✉ Hauptstr. 124, am Uni-Pl., ☎ 06221/20929), along with a selection of porcelain, ceramics, and handicrafts. **Unholtz** (✉ Hauptstr. 160, ☎ 06221/20964) carries cutlery and tableware by Solingen, a famous German manufacturer of some of the best knives in Europe.

The city can also be a good place to find reasonably priced German antiques. Look in at **Spiess & Walther** (✉ Friedrich-Ebert-Anlage 23a, ☎ 06221/22233) for an interesting selection. Antique hounds can also check out **B & B Antiques** (✉ Sofienstr. 27, ☎ 06221/23003).

Heidelberg has many tempting **markets.** On Wednesday and Sunday mornings go to the central market square, Marktplatz; on Tuesday and Friday mornings make for Friedrich-Ebert-Platz. The weekday offerings include produce and other edibles; on Sunday there's a flea market. A flea market is also held every other Saturday on the Güteramtsstrasse (near the customs office).

Leimen

⑱ *7 km (4 mi) south of Heidelberg.*

Leimen is best known as tennis star Boris Becker's hometown; otherwise, it's just a pleasant wine village—and therefore has more modestly priced alternatives to the usually expensive accommodations in the larger cities of the Neckar Valley.

Lodging

$$ 🏨 **Hotel Seipel.** The Seipel is a clean, modern hotel on the edge of a sports park and woodland. The rooms are furnished in dark redwood, with dove-gray drapes and upholstery. ⊠ *Am Sportpark,* ☎ *06224/71089,* 𝔽𝔸𝕏 *06224/71080. 30 rooms with bath. Sauna, steam room, exercise room. AE, DC, MC, V. Closed 1st wk of Jan.*

Mannheim

🅳 *10 km (6 mi) northwest of Heidelberg.*

Mannheim, is not as "old" as other Rhine cities. It was not founded until 1606, and is even more unusual for having been laid out on a grid pattern. The forward-looking Palatinate elector Friedrich IV, who built the city, imposed the rigid street plan that forms the heart of the
★ Old Town, or **Quadratestadt** (literally, "squared town"). Streets running northeast–southwest—from one river to the other—are labeled A through U; those running northwest–southeast are numbered 1 through 7. The central Marktplatz is G–1 on your map; the best restaurant in town—Da Gianni—is R–7. Rationalism rules. The only exceptions to this system are the two main streets of the pedestrian shopping zone—Heidelbergerstrasse, which runs a parallel course to the two rivers, and Kurpfalzstrasse, which cuts through the heart of the town, leading southwest.

Though it was the elector Friedrich IV who built Mannheim, his court was at Heidelberg. In 1720, the elector Carl Philip went one stage further, moving the court to Mannheim rather than rebuilding what remained of his castle at Heidelberg after it had been sacked by Louis XIV's French troops in 1689 and again in 1693. (What, ironically, helped prompt his decision was the desire to build a palace modeled on the absolutist, classical lines of Louis XIV's great palace at Versailles; like many 18th-century German rulers, Carl Philip eagerly seized the example provided by Louis XIV to reinforce his own absolute right to rule.)

The **Residenzschloss** (palace) was 40 years in the building, completed only in 1768. Five separate architects were employed, their combined efforts producing one of the largest buildings in Europe: a vast, relentlessly symmetrical edifice containing more than 400 rooms and 2,000 windows, with a frontage more than a quarter-mile long. The palace was reduced to a smoking ruin in World War II, rebuilt in the '50s, and today belongs to Mannheim University. The great hall and some of the state rooms can be visited; they're impressive but strangely lifeless now. ⊠ *Kurfürstlichtes Residenzschloss,* ☎ *0621/292–2890.* 🎫 *DM 3.* ⊙ *Apr.–Oct., Tues.–Sun. 10–noon and 3–5; Nov.–Mar., weekends 10–1 and 2–5. Tours daily Apr.–Oct.*

From the palace you can either head off to the right to visit the Städtische Kunsthalle (City Art Museum) or make a left to see the **Jesuitenkirche** (Jesuit Church) three blocks away at A–4. The Jesuitenkirche is the largest and most important Baroque church in this part of Germany, its immense, rigorously classical facade flanked by graceful dome spires and topped by a massive dome. It was begun in 1733, commissioned by the elector Carl Philip to commemorate his family's return to Catholicism. The church, too, was severely bombed during the war, and most of the internal decorations were lost, including what were probably the most lavish ceiling and dome paintings in the country. Although plainer now, the airy grandeur of the interior suggests something of its former magnificence. Pause as you go in to look at the ornate wrought-iron gates at the entrance.

The **Städtische Kunsthalle** (City Art Museum) is on Friedrichsplatz, at the eastern fringe of the Quadratstadt, a 10-minute walk from the Jesuit Church. The building itself is a prime example of *Jugendstil* (art nouveau) architecture, constructed in 1907. Provocative and large-scale modern sculptures stand outside. Inside you'll find one of the largest and best collections of modern art in Germany. All the big names are here, from Manet (including his famous painting *The Execution of the Emperor Maximilian*) to Warhol. Regular exhibitions of major importance are also presented, giving Mannheim a reputation as one of Germany's leading fine-arts centers. ⊠ *Friedrichspl. 4,* ☎ *0621/293–6413.* 🎫 *DM 4.* ☉ *Tues.–Wed., Fri.–Sun. 10–5, Thurs. noon–5.*

Ⓒ Mannheim has two attractions children will enjoy. The **planetarium** has a special show for children on Sundays and holidays. The regular program, which changes every few months and is geared to stargazers of all ages. ⊠ *Wilhelm-Varnholt-Allee 1,* ☎ *0621/415–692.* 🎫 *DM 8.* ☉ *Show times Tues. 10, 3; Wed. and Fri. 3, 8; weekends 5.*

Ⓒ **Mannheim's Museumsschiff** (Museum Ship) is a restored paddle-wheel steamboat filled with information on boats and machines through the ages. ⊠ *Am Museumsufer, by the Kurpfalz Bridge.* 🎫 *Free.* ☉ *Tues., Thurs.–Sun. 10–5, Wed. 10–8.*

Dining and Lodging

$$$$ ✕ **Da Gianni.** Sophisticated Italian dishes with a distinctly nouvelle ac-
★   cent are served in this classy haunt in the Quadratstadt. Chef Wolfgang Staudenmaier's sauces give the menu a Gallic-Italian flair; St. Peter fish, for instance, is served in a combination of tomatoes, potatoes, and olives. ⊠ *R–7 34,* ☎ *0621/20326. Reservations essential. Jacket and tie. AE, DC, MC, V. Closed Mon. and 3 wks starting late July.*

$$$ ✕ **L'Epi d'Or.** French nouvelle cuisine and sophisticated local special-
★   ties are the hallmarks of Norbert Dobler's city-center restaurant. The warm lobster salad is a classic; the saddle of lamb is a good alternative. ⊠ *H–7 3,* ☎ *0621/14397. Reservations essential. Jacket and tie. AE, MC, V. Closed Sun. and 2 wks in summer (time varies) and around Christmas. No lunch Sat. and Mon.*

$$ ✕ **Alte Munz.** For old German atmosphere, local specialties, and a wide range of beers, the Alte Munz is hard to beat. Try the suckling pig if it's available. ⊠ *P–7 1,* ☎ *0621/28262,* 🅵🅰🆇 *0621/26555. AE, MC, V.*

$$$$ ✕🛏 **Maritim Parkhotel.** The turn-of-the-century Parkhotel is the num-
★   ber one choice in town, grandly offering opulent comforts. The pillared, chandelier-hung lobby sets the mood; rooms are spacious and elegant. ⊠ *Friedrichspl. 2, D–68165,* ☎ *0621/45071,* 🅵🅰🆇 *0621/152–424. 184 rooms and 3 suites, all with bath. Restaurant, bar, indoor pool, beauty salon, sauna, steam room, exercise room. AE, DC, MC, V.*

$$–$$$ ✕🛏 **Gasthof zum Ochsen.** Mannheim's oldest inn is about 8 kilometers (5 miles) from the city center, in the Feudenheim district, but it's well worth the journey, particularly on clear summer days when you can eat and drink on the chestnut-tree–shaded terrace. The menu here is a mixture of French and Baden cuisines. Twelve comfortable bedrooms, furnished in fine cherry wood, are tucked away under the steep eaves. ⊠ *Hauptstr. 70, D–68259 Feudenheim/Mannheim,* ☎ *0621/799–550,* 🅵🅰🆇 *0621/799–5533. AE, DC, MC, V.*

$$–$$$ ✕🛏 **Hotel Löwen-Seckenheim.** Light-wood furnishings and contemporary fabrics create a cheerful atmosphere in the rooms at this friendly, efficiently run hotel. Frequent trams run between Seckenheim, on the edge of the city, and the city center. A large breakfast buffet is included in the room rate. ⊠ *Seckenheimer Hauptstr. 159–163,* ☎ *0621/48080,*

FAX *0621/481–4154. 60 rooms with bath or shower. Restaurant, free parking. AE, MC; V.*

The Arts

Mannheim has a respectable opera company, and its theater has recently been renovated (National theater box office ☎ 0621/24844).

Shopping

Stores in Mannheim carry some of the best in German fashions. Clothes by Jil Sander, a famous German women's designer, are stocked at the **CC-Boutique** (✉ 17 Q–7 St., ☎ 0621/25148). Browse through **Kurfürsten Passage,** the city's stylish shopping mall, on P–7 Street.

Schwetzingen

⓴ *8 km (5 mi) south of Mannheim on A–6, 12 km (7 mi) west of Heidelberg.*

Schwetzingen is famous for its palace, a formal 18th-century building constructed as a summer residence by the Palatinate electors. It's a noble, rose-color building, imposing and harmonious; a highlight is the charming rococo theater in one wing. The extensive park is worth visiting. It blends formal French and informal English styles, with neatly bordered gravel walks trailing off into the dark woodland. The 18th-century planners of this delightful oasis had fun adding such touches as an exotic mosque, complete with minarets and a shimmering pool (although they got a little confused and gave the building a very German Baroque portal), and the "Classical ruin," virtually de rigueur for landscape gardeners of this period. ☎ *06202/81482. Palace* ☉ *Apr.–Oct., Tues.–Sun. Gardens open daily.*

Another rare pleasure awaits you if you're in Schwetzingen in April, May, or June: The town is Germany's asparagus center, and fresh-asparagus dishes dominate the menu of every local restaurant.

Dining and Lodging

$$$–$$$$ ✕🏨 **Romantik Hotel Löwe.** The "Lion" has been a favorite staging post for travelers for two centuries. The attractive old house, with its steeply eaved, dormer-window red roof, was originally a butcher shop and wine tavern. Now it's a very welcoming hotel and an excellent restaurant, although the wine tavern is still in place, basically unchanged. The restaurant serves imaginatively prepared Palatinate specialties—the marinated beef is a must—and the famous Schwetzingen asparagus dominates the menu throughout the summer. There are comfortable rooms, some with exposed beams, all individually furnished. ✉ *Schlossstr. 4–6, D–68165,* ☎ *06202/26066,* FAX *06202/10726. 22 rooms with bath. Restaurant. AE, DC, MC, V.*

The Arts

The leading arts event in this region is the annual **Schwetzingen Festival** in May and June, which features operas and concerts by international artists in the lovely rococo theater of Schwetzingen Palace (for information, call the local tourist office ☎ 06202/4933).

Weinheim

㉑ *17 km (10 mi) north of Heidelberg, 17 km (10 mi) east of Mannheim.*

Weinheim lies on the lovely Bergstrasse (Mountain Route), about the same distance from Mannheim and Heidelberg—ideal for visitors who want to avoid the summer crush of both cities. Part of the medieval walls of Weinheim still defend it, and the historic Old Town has many half-timbered houses from the 15th and 16th centuries. Schloss Berckheim, which overlooks it, has a beautiful park, and, higher up, the melancholy ruins of Burg Windeck provide fine views of the area.

Dining and Lodging

$$$ ✕🏨 **Hotel Ottheinrich.** The virtues of this privately run hotel include high standards, individuality, and charm. The rooms have stylish Italian furniture as well as TVs. ⊠ *Hauptstr. 126, D–69469,* ☎ *06201/18070,* 🖷 *06201/180–788. 15 rooms and 9 suites with bath. Restaurant, bar. AE, DC, MC, V.*

ALONG THE BURGENSTRASSE (CASTLE ROAD)

Upstream from Heidelberg, the Neckar Valley narrows. Along the banks of the Neckar River is a landscape of orchards, vineyards, and wooded hills, crowned with castles rising above the soft-flowing water. It is one of the most impressive stretches of the Burgenstrasse, a tourist route that goes all the way to Prague. All the small valleys along the Neckar Valley road (B–27)—the locals call them "Klingen"—that cut north into the Odenwald are off-the-beaten-track territory. One of the most atmospheric is the **Wolfsschlucht,** which starts below the castle at Zwingenberg. The dank, shadowy little gorge features in Carl Maria von Weber's opera *Der Freischütz.* If you see a vulture circling overhead, don't be alarmed. It's likely to be from Claus Fentzloff's unusual **aviary** at Guttenberg Castle (☞ Burg Guttenberg, *below*).

Neckargemünd

㉒ *12 km (8 mi) upstream from Heidelberg.*

The first town on the Burgenstrasse is Neckargemünd, once a bustling river town. Today it's a sleepy sort of place, although it can make a good base from which to see Heidelberg if you want to avoid the summertime crowds there.

Dining and Lodging

$$ ✕ **Landgasthof Die Rainbach.** This long-popular country inn just outside Neckargemünd, in the Rainbach district, changed hands recently, but the quality of its cuisine remains just as good, with the accent still on hearty traditional fare. If the weather's good, take a table on the terrace, which commands a fine view of the river. In winter warm up in the paneled restaurant with a dish of venison stew or any of the freshly prepared soups. ⊠ *Rainbach 9,* ☎ *06223/2455. MC. Closed Mon. and Jan.*

$$ ✕🏨 **Zum Röss'l.** The Röss'l has been catering to Neckar Valley travelers for nearly 350 years. You'll dine in a wood-paneled restaurant or on the delightful garden terrace in summer. Be sure to try the excellent brandy that is produced in the Röss'l's own distillery. Above the restaurant are 14 small but comfortably furnished rooms, 12 with bath. ⊠ *Heidelberger Str. 15, D–69151,* ☎ *06223/2665,* 🖷 *06223/6859. 14 rooms. No credit cards.*

$$–$$$ 🏨 **Hotel zum Ritter.** Built during the 16th century, the half-timbered zum Ritter has appropriately aged exposed beams and satisfyingly creaky passages. The hotel overlooks the Neckar, as do some of its rooms. ⊠ *Neckarstr. 40,* ☎ *06223/7035,* 🖷 *06223/73–339. 40 rooms with bath. AE, MC, V.*

En Route   Eight kilometers (5 miles) farther along the Neckar Valley road, perched impregnably on a hill, is **Dilsberg Castle,** one of the few castles hereabouts to have withstood General Tilly's otherwise all-conquering forces in the Thirty Years' War. Until the student jail in Heidelberg was built, its dungeons were used to accommodate the university's more unruly dissidents. The view from its battlements, over the valley and the green expanse of the Odenwald Forest beyond, is worth the climb.

Opposite Dilsberg is **Neckarsteinach,** known as the **Vierburgenstadt** (Town of the Four Castles), for the fairly obvious reason that there are four castles here. They form one large complex—the **Schadeck**—most of which dates from the 12th century. What remains is largely ruins. But the sections that are still intact comprise the baronial residence of an aristocratic German family.

Hirschhorn

❷❸ *10 km (6 mi) east of Neckarsteinach, 22 km (14 mi) east of Heidelberg.*

The pretty little town of Hirschhorn has a castle, which is one of a number of ancient structures standing on the Neckar that have been converted into hotel-restaurants. The view is superb. If you don't plan to stay here, a stop for lunch would certainly be worthwhile.

Dining and Lodging

$$$ ✕🏨 **Schlosshotel auf Burg Hirschhorn.** Not so much a castle hotel as a pleasant if undistinguished modern hotel in a castle, the Hirschhorn is perched on a hilltop overlooking the medieval village and the Neckar River. Hallways have that rough-plaster medieval look, less you forget where you are; rooms are furnished in approved *Student Prince* style. The views are terrific, and the is restaurant much better than average. ✉ *D–69434 Hirschhorn/Neckar,* ☎ *06272/1373,* 📠 *06272/3267. 23 rooms and 2 suites with bath. Restaurant, café. AE, MC, V. Closed Dec.–Jan.*

En Route If you prefer a less formal lunchtime layover than the Schlosshotel in Hirschhorn, carry on to the next village—**Eberbach**—just a few miles up the valley, and visit the **Krabbenstein.** It's a 17th-century inn, one of the oldest along the river. The walls are decorated with frescoes that illustrate the trades carried on in the village since the Middle Ages.

Eight kilometers (5 miles) beyond Eberbach, there's another castle. This one stands above the village of **Zwingenberg,** its medieval towers thrusting through the dark woodland. Some say it's the most romantic of all the castles along the Neckar (the one at Heidelberg excepted). It's owned by the margraves of Baden and is open on a limited basis only, but if you happen along at the right time, stop in to admire the frescoed 15th-century chapel and the collection of hunting trophies. 🎟 *DM 3.* ☉ *May–Sept., Tues., Fri., and Sun. 2–4.*

Mosbach

❷❹ *16 km (10 mi) up the valley (southeast) from Hirschhorn.*

The little town of Mosbach is one of the most charming towns on the Neckar, and its ancient market square, Marktplatz, contains one of Germany's most exquisite half-timbered buildings. It's the early 17th-century **Palmsches Haus,** its upper stories smothered with intricate timbering. The **Rathaus,** built 50 years earlier, is a modest affair by comparison.

Dining and Lodging

$$ ✕🏨 **Zum Lamm.** The half-timbered Lamm (Lamb) Inn on Mosbach's main street is one of the town's prettiest houses. Its cozy rooms are individually furnished, with flowers filling the window boxes. The restaurant, complete with requisite exposed beams, serves local and international dishes, incorporating meat from the hotel's own butcher shop. ✉ *Hauptstr. 59, D–74821,* ☎ *06261/89020,* 𝔽𝔸𝕏 *06261/890– 291. 53 rooms with bath. Restaurant. AE, DC, MC, V.*

Outdoor Activities and Sports

BALLOONING

Hot-air-balloon tours of the Neckar Valley and surrounding country-side are offered by **Balloon Tours** (☎ 06261/18477) in Mosbach.

Neckarzimmern

5 km (3 mi) south of Mosbach.

㉕ The massive circular bulk of **Hornberg Castle** rises above the woods that drop to the riverbank and the town of Neckarzimmern. The road to the castle leads through vineyards that have been providing excellent dry white wines for centuries. Today the castle is part hotel and restaurant and part museum. During the 16th century it was home to the larger-than-life knight Götz von Berlichingen (1480–1562). Von Berlichingen was a remarkable fellow. When he lost his right arm fighting in a petty dynastic squabble—the Landshut War of Succession in 1504—he had a blacksmith fashion an iron replacement for him. The original designs for this fearsome artificial limb are on view in the castle, as is a suit of armor that belonged to him. Scenes from his life are also represented. For most Germans, the rambunctious knight is best remembered for a remark he delivered to the Palatinate elector that was faithfully reproduced by Goethe in his play (called, simply, *Götz von Berlichingen*). Responding to a reprimand from the elector, von Berlichingen told the elector, more or less, to "kiss my ass" (the original German is substantially more earthy). To this day the polite version of this insult is known as a "Götz von Berlichingen"; practice it on the autobahn when a BMW screeches on its brakes, headlights flashing, inches from your rear bumper. 🎫 *DM 2.50.* ☺ *Apr.–Nov., daily 9–5.*

Dining and Lodging

$$$ ✕⌂ **Burg Hornberg.** Your host is the present baron of the castle. The
★   hotel's rooms are comfortable, and some have magnificent views over the hotel's own vineyards to the river. The restaurant features venison (in season) and fresh fish. ✉ *D–74865 Neckarzimmern,* ☎ *06261/92460,* 𝔽𝔸𝕏 *06261/18864. 23 rooms with bath. Restaurant, bar, miniature golf. MC, V. Closed mid-Dec.–Feb.*

Shopping

In Neckarzimmern you can get a closer look at why the Neckar Valley is famous for its glassware. The factory **Franz Kaspar,** known for its fine crystal, gives tours that demonstrate the manufacturing process; it also has an exhibition space and an outlet with a wide selection and some special offers. ✉ *Hauptstr. 11,* ☎ *06261/923–014.* ☺ *Weekdays 8–6:30, Sat. 8–2. Tours: weekdays 8–3, Sat. 8–noon.*

For sheer historical worth you can't beat a bottle from the **Hornberg Castle** estate, which once stocked the table of the knight Götz von Berlichingen. The vineyards here belong to the castle hotel; you can buy wine by the bottle or the case (☎ 06261/5001).

En Route   The fine medieval castle of **Horneck,** 5 kilometers (3 miles) upriver, south of Hornburg, was destroyed during the Peasants' War (1525) by Götz von Berlichingen and his troops. It was subsequently rebuilt and stands in all its medieval glory. Once it was owned by the Teutonic Order of Knights; today it has a more mundane role as the retirement home of a German charity.

A few bends of the river south of Horneck bring you to one of the best preserved of the Neckar castles, the 15th-century **Burg Guttenberg.**

Within its stout stone walls is a restaurant with fine views of the river valley. The castle is also home to Europe's leading center for the study and protection of birds of prey, and some are released on demonstration flights from the castle walls, from March through November, daily at 11 and 3. The spa of **Bad Rappenau** awaits the tired traveler. Bad Rappenau's brine baths are said to ease not just aching limbs but asthma, rheumatism, and circulatory problems. It's an attractive little town, with a picturesque Rathaus that was once a moated castle.

Bad Wimpfen

26 *10 km (6 mi) south of Mosbach.*

Bad Wimpfen is of both historic and aesthetic interest. The Romans founded it, building a fortress here and a bridge across the Neckar, in the 1st century AD. By the early Middle Ages, Bad Wimpfen had become an imperial center; the 12th-century emperor Barbarossa built his largest palace here. Much of what remains can be visited, including the imperial living quarters with their stately pillared windows, from which the royal inhabitants enjoyed fine views of the river below. ⊠ *Kaiserpl.* ☎ *07063/53151.* ☉ *Guided tours are given daily but must be booked in advance.*

★ After you've seen the fortress, you'll want to explore the small, winding streets of the historic center, a picture-postcard jumble of Gothic and Renaissance buildings. **Klostergasse,** a stage set of a street, is the standout. If you want to see the town in more detail, follow the marked walking tour; it begins at the Rathaus and is marked by signs bearing the town arms—an eagle with a key in its beak. Highlights of the tour are two churches: the early **Gothic Ritterstiftskirche (Knights' Church) of Sts. Peter and Paul**; and the **parish church** on the market square, Marktplatz. Sts. Peter and Paul stands on a charming square, shaded by gnarled chestnut trees. The rough-hewn Romanesque facade is the oldest part of the church, left standing when the town ran out of money after rebuilding the remainder of the church in Gothic style during the 13th century. The outline of the original walls are clearly visible on the floor inside. The cloisters are delightful, an example of German Gothic at its purest and most uncluttered. In the parish church be sure to see the 13th-century stained glass; it's among the oldest in the country.

Dining and Lodging

$–$$ ✕⊡ **Hotel Blauer Turm.** Germany's oldest sentry watchtower, Bad Wimpfen's spectacular turreted Blue Tower, stands sentinel outside your bedroom window at this handsome, old half-timbered hotel in the town center. A fine view of the Neckar River can also be enjoyed from most of the double rooms. In summer claim a table within the leafy bower of the pergola-terrace and watch the Neckar meander by. Both on the terrace and in the smart restaurant you'll be offered a comprehensive menu that features Swabian specialties, such as spaetzle, and fresh fish from the river. ⊠ *Burgviertel 5, D–74206,* ☎ *07063/7884,* FAX *07063/6701. 22 rooms, most with bath. Restaurant. No credit cards. Restaurant closed Mon.*

Neckarsulm

27 *10 km (6 mi) south of Bad Wimpfen.*

Motorbike fans won't want to miss the town of Neckarsulm. It's a busy little industrial center, home of the German automobile manufacturer Audi and site of the **Deutsches Zweirad Museum** (German Motorcycle Museum). It's close to the factory, where motorbikes were first manufactured in Germany. Among its 180 exhibits are the world's first mass-produced machine (the Hildebrand and Wolfmüller), a number of famous racing machines, and a rare Daimler machine, the first made by that legendary name. The museum also has an exhibit of early bicycles, dating from 1817, as well as early automobiles. All are arranged over four floors in a handsome 400-year-old building that belonged to the Teutonic Order of Knights until 1806. ⊠ *Urbanstr. 11.* 🎫 *DM 7.* ⊘ *Weekdays 9–noon and 1:30–5, weekends and holidays 9–5.*

Dining and Lodging

$$$ ✕🏨 **Astron Hotel.** Ask for a mansard room at the modern Astron—the rooms under the steep eaves are very cozy, decorated in harmonious pastel tones. Fresh flowers are a welcome touch. ⊠ *Sulmstr. 2, D-74172,* ☎ *07132/3880,* 𝖥𝖠𝖷 *07132/388–113. 82 rooms, 2 suites with bath. Restaurant, bar, beauty salon, sauna. AE, DC, MC, V.*

Outdoor Activities and Sports

Neckarsulm boasts an "adventure bathing" complex—complete with palm trees and white-water river—called **AQUAtoll** (☎ 07132/2052).

SWABIAN CITIES: HEILBRONN, STUTTGART, TÜBINGEN

Heilbronn, Stuttgart, and Tübingen are all part of the ancient province of Swabia, a region strongly influenced by Protestantism and Calvinism. The inhabitants speak the Swabian dialect of German. Visitors to the area will want to make a point of eating Swabian food, one of the best regional cuisines in Germany. At the top of the list are *Maultaschen,* somewhat similar to Italian ravioli, served in a delicate broth; and spaetzle, the tiny noodlelike dumplings that take the place of potatoes in this part of Germany.

Heilbronn lies on both sides of the Neckar. Stuttgart, the capital of the Land (State) of Baden-Würtemberg and one of Germany's leading industrial cities, is surrounded by hills on three sides, with the fourth side opening up toward its river harbor. The medieval town of Tübingen is found on the steep slopes and hilltops above the Neckar, with views of the surrounding countryside.

Heilbronn

28   *6 km (4 mi) south of Neckarsulm, 50 km (31 mi) north of Stuttgart.*

The city of Heilbronn owes its name to Heiligen Brunne (holy well), a little fountain that bubbles from the ground by the church of St. Kilian; it owes its fame to the German Romantic classic *Das Käthchen von Heilbronn,* by early 19th-century writer Heinrich von Kleist. The virtuous, put-upon Käthchen was modeled by von Kleist on the daughter of Heilbronn's lord mayor, and the family home still stands on the west side of the central square, Marktplatz. Its ornate oriel, decorated with figures of four of the prophets, makes it easy to spot.

★   Most of the leading sights in Heilbronn are grouped in and around Marktplatz, dominated by the sturdy **Rathaus,** built in the Gothic style in 1417 and remodeled during the Renaissance. Set into the clean-lined Renaissance facade of Heilbronn's Rathaus, beneath the steeply eaved red roof, is a magnificently ornate 16th-century **clock.** It's divided into four distinct parts. The lowest is an astronomical clock, showing the day of the week, the month, and the year. Above it is the main clock—note how its hour hand is larger than the minute hand, a convention common in the 16th century. Above this there's a smaller dial that shows the phases of the sun and the moon. The final clock is a bell at the top-

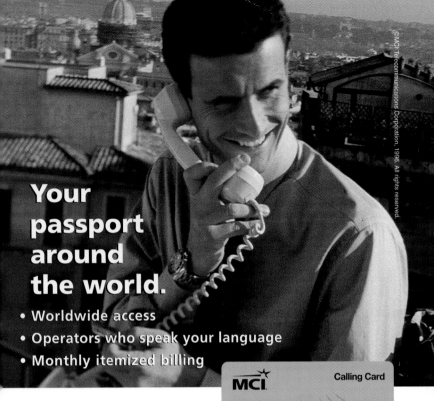

Your passport around the world.

- Worldwide access
- Operators who speak your language
- Monthly itemized billing

MCI   Calling Card

415 555 1234 2244
J.D. SMITH

Use your MCI Card® and these access numbers for an easy way to call when traveling worldwide.

Austria (CC)♦†	022-903-012
Belarus	
From Gomel and Mogilev regions	8-10-800-103
From all other localities	8-800-103
Belgium (CC)♦†	0800-10012
Bulgaria	00800-0001
Croatia (CC)★	99-385-0112
Czech Republic (CC)♦	00-42-000112
Denmark (CC)♦†	8001-0022
Finland (CC)♦†	9800-102-80
France (CC)♦†	0800-99-0019
Germany (CC)†	0130-0012
Greece (CC)♦†	00-800-1211
Hungary (CC)♦	00▼800-01411
Iceland (CC)♦†	800-9002
Ireland (CC)†	1-800-55-1001
Italy (CC)♦†	172-1022
Kazakhstan (CC)	1-800-131-4321
Liechtenstein (CC)♦	155-0222
Luxembourg†	0800-0112
Monaco (CC)♦	800-90-19

Netherlands (CC)♦†	06-022-91-22
Norway (CC)♦†	800-19912
Poland (CC)✜†	00-800-111-21-22
Portugal (CC)✜†	05-017-1234
Romania (CC)✜	01-800-1800
Russia (CC)✜♦	747-3322
For a Russian-speaking operator	747-3320
San Marino (CC)♦	172-1022
Slovak Republic (CC)	00-42-000112
Slovenia	080-8808
Spain (CC)†	900-99-0014
Sweden (CC)♦†	020-795-922
Switzerland (CC)♦†	155-0222
Turkey (CC)♦†	00-8001-1177
Ukraine (CC)✜	8▼10-013
United Kingdom (CC)†	
To call to the U.S. using BT ■	0800-89-0222
To call to the U.S. using Mercury ■	0500-89-0222
Vatican City (CC)†	172-1022

To sign up for the MCI Card, dial the access number of the country you are in and ask to speak with a customer service representative.

http://www.mci.com

(CC) Country-to-country calling available. May not be available to/from all international locations. (Canada, Puerto Rico, and U.S. Virgin Islands are considered Domestic Access locations.) ♦ Public phones may require deposit of coin or phone card for dial tone. † Automation available from most locations. ★ Not available from public pay phones. ▼ Wait for second dial tone. ✜ Limited availability. ■ International communications carrier.

It helps to be pushy in airports.

Introducing the revolutionary new TransPorter™ from American Tourister. It's the first suitcase you can push around without a fight. TransPorter's™ exclusive four-wheel design lets you push it in front of you with almost no effort–the wheels take the weight. Or pull it on two wheels if you choose. You can even stack on other bags and use it like a luggage cart.

Stable 4-wheel design.

TransPorter™ is designed like a dresser, with built-in shelves to organize your belongings. Or collapse the shelves and pack it like a traditional suitcase. Inside, there's a suiter feature to help keep suits and dresses from wrinkling. When push comes to shove, you can't beat a TransPorter™. For more information on how you can be this pushy, call 1-800-542-1300.

Shelves collapse on command.

Making travel less primitive.

©1996 American Tourister

most level. Suspended from a delicate stone surround, it's struck alternately by the two angels on either side. Be here at noon, when the entire elaborate mechanism swings into action. As the hour strikes, an angel at the base of the clock sounds a trumpet; another turns an hour glass and counts the hours with a scepter. Simultaneously, the twin golden rams between them charge each other and lock horns while a cockerel spreads its wings and crows.

Behind the market square is the **Kilianskirche** (Church of St. Kilian), Heilbronn's most famous church, dedicated to the Irish monk who brought Christianity to the Rhineland in the Dark Ages, and who lies buried in Würzburg. Its lofty Gothic tower was capped in the early 16th century with a fussy, lanternlike structure that ranks as the first major Renaissance work north of the Alps. At its summit there's a soldier carrying a banner decorated with the city arms. Walk around the church to the south side (the side opposite the main entrance) to see the well that gave the city its name.

OFF THE
BEATEN PATH

FREIZEITPARK TRIPSDRILL – Twenty kilometers (12 miles) south of Heilbronn, on B–27, this is one of southern Germany's best amusement parks in Cleebronn/Tripsdill. ☎ *07135/4081.* ▦ *DM 22.* ☉ *Apr.–Oct., daily 9–6.*

EBERSTÄDTER HÖHLEN – These intriguing caves lie north of Heilbronn on the B–27. ☎ *06292/578.* ☉ *Daily 10–4.*

Dining and Lodging

$$ ✕ **Ratskeller.** For sturdy and dependable regional specialties—try
★ Swabian *Maultaschen,* a kind of local ravioli—and as much Teutonic atmosphere as you'll ever want, you won't go wrong in this basement restaurant of the Town Hall. ⊠ *Marktpl. 7,* ☎ *07131/84628. No credit cards. Closed holidays. No dinner Sun.*

$$ ✕ **Restaurant-Café Harmonie.** Eat on the terrace in summer to enjoy
★ the view of the city park. Inside, the decor is traditional with a modern twist, as is the menu. For best value, try one of the fixed-price menus. ⊠ *Am Stadtgarten, Allee 28,* ☎ *07131/87954. Reservations essential. Jacket and tie. Closed Tues. and most of Aug. AE, DC, MC, V.*

$$$$ ✕▦ **Insel-Hotel.** Is it possible to sleep in the middle of the Neckar River
★ and yet be within walking distance of Heilbronn's Old Town center? You bet. *Insel* means "island," and that's where the luxurious Insel-Hotel is—on a river island tethered to the city by the busy Friedrich-Ebert Bridge. A family-run establishment, the Insel combines a personal touch and the sleek service and facilities expected of a large chain. ⊠ *Friedrich-Ebert-Brücke, D–74072,* ☎ *07131/6300,* ☎ *07131/626–060. 120 rooms with bath and 5 suites. Restaurant, bar, café, weinstube, no-smoking rooms, indoor pool, sauna, free parking. AE, DC, MC, V.*

$$$$ ✕▦ **Schlosshotel Liebenstein.** Nestled in the hills above the Neckar-westheim village, south of Heilbronn, is one of the area's most beautiful castles, Schloss Liebenstein, a Renaissance jewel whose restaurant draws diners from as far away as Stuttgart. Guest rooms have views of the surrounding forests and vineyards. Within the 3-foot-thick castle walls the peaceful hush of centuries reigns over a setting of comfort and noble elegance. ⊠ *Schloss Liebenstein, D–74382, Neckarwestheim,* ☎ *07133/6041,* ☎ *07133/6045. 24 rooms with bath or shower. Restaurant. AE, DC, MC, V.*

$–$$ ▦ **Hotel Zur Post.** The Mangler family, who runs this sturdy hotel, offers their guests comfort and friendly service at a very reasonable price. Personal touches include bright prints on the pastel walls and fresh flowers. The Zur Post doesn't have a restaurant, but there's no shortage of places to eat in the neighborhood. The Manglers also run the nearby Hotel Allee-Post; ask for rooms there if the Zur Post is full. ⊠ *Bismarckstr. 5,* ☎ *07131/627–040, D-74072,* FAX *07131/82193. 20 rooms with shower. (Hotel Allee-Post,* ⊠ *Titotstr. 12,* ☎ *07131/81656.) MC, V.*

Nightlife and the Arts

The **Heilbronn** tourist office publishes a monthly listings magazine, *Heilbronn Today & Tomorrow,* available free of charge. You can buy tickets from the Heilbronn tourist office (☎ 07131/562–270 or dial the hot line, ☎ 07131/19433).

Heilbronn has one of the biggest and liveliest wine festivals in the Neckar Valley—the **Weindorf,** held in mid-September in the streets and squares around the City Hall. But it's not all tradition in Heilbronn. The city has a colorful nightlife—for discos, try the **BOSS-Club** (⊠ Mosbacherstr. 8) or **Apfelbaum** (⊠ Neckargartacher Str. 111).

THEATER AND MUSIC

Heilbronn's **Stadttheater** (⊠ Berliner Pl. 1, ☎ 07131/563–001) is the leading venue in the city.

Outdoor Activities and Sports

GOLF

You can play at the **Golfclub Heilbronn-Hohenlohe,** in the village of Friedrichsruhe (☎ 07941/7886). Neckarwestheim, south of Heilbronn, has an excellent course, the **Golf and Country Club Liebenstein** (☎ 07133/16019).

HORSEBACK RIDING

Heilbronn has a riding club where you can rent horses and also take lessons, the **Reiterverein Heilbronn** (⊠ Im Sternberg 5, ☎ 07131/178–469).

SWIMMING

Heilbronn's favorite lido, the **Freibad Neckarhalde** (☎ 07131/255–100), has a view of the river. Also try **Freibad Gesundbrunnen** (☎ 07131/46700), a public swimming pool. Swimming in the Neckar River is not advisable.

TENNIS

Heilbronn's tennis schools at Böckingerstrasse 170 (☎ 07131/46166) and Viehweide 91 (☎ 07131/34343) can arrange lessons and partners.

Shopping

Wine is the chief product of the Neckar region, and Heilbronn is the place to buy it. The city's internationally renowned wine festival (the Weindorf), during the second week of September, showcases more than 200 wines from the Heilbronn region alone. Outside festival time, you'll find numerous shops stocking wine along Heilbronn's central pedestrian shopping zone, and you can also buy directly from vineyards. A good, no-frills wine outlet is the **Amalienhof** (⊠ Lukas-Cranach-Weg 5, ☎ 07131/251–735). Only the vineyard's own wines are for sale—80 of them, to be precise.

Stuttgart

 50 km (31 mi) south on B–27 from Heilbronn; the road follows the Neckar only for a short distance.

Stuttgart is a place of fairly extreme contradictions. It has been called, among other things, "Germany's biggest small town" and "the city where work is a pleasure." For centuries Stuttgart, whose name derives from *Stutengarten,* or "stud farm," remained a pastoral backwater along the Neckar. Then the Industrial Revolution propelled the city into the machine age, after which it was leveled in World War II. Since then Stuttgart has regained its position as one of Germany's top industrial centers.

Here, *schaffen*—"to do, make, produce"—is all. This is Germany's can-do city, whose native sons have turned out Mercedes-Benz and Porsche cars, Bosch electrical equipment, and a host of other products exported worldwide. It is only fitting that one end of the main street, Königstrasse, should be emblazoned with a neon sign proclaiming BOSCH on a high-rise, and the other end should shine with the Mercedes star.

Yet Stuttgart is also a city of culture and the arts, with world-class museums and a famous ballet company. Moreover, it's the domain of fine local wines; the vineyards actually approach the city center in a rim of green hills. Forests, vineyards, meadows, fields, and orchards comprise more than half the city, which is enclosed on three sides by seemingly endless woods.

An ideal introduction to the contrasts of Stuttgart is a guided city bus tour (☞ Guided Tours *in* Heidelberg and the Neckar Valley A to Z, *below*). Included is a visit to the needle-nose TV tower, high on a mountaintop above the city, affording stupendous views. Built in 1956, it was the first of its kind in the world. On your own the best place to begin your exploration of Stuttgart is at the Hauptbahnhof (main train station) end of Königstrasse, a pedestrian shopping street, continuing on to the Schlossplatz.

Schlossplatz (Castle or Royal Square) is a huge area enclosed by reconstructed royal palaces, with elegant arcades branching off to other stately plazas. The magnificent Baroque **Neues Schloss** (New Castle), now occupied by the Baden-Württemberg state government offices, dominates the square.

Across the street from Neues Schloss stands **Altes Schloss** (Old Castle), the former residence of the counts and dukes of Württemberg. Built as a moated castle around 1320, with wings added during the mid-15th century to turn this into a Renaissance palace, the Altes Schloss was considerably rebuilt between 1948 and 1970 to repair wartime damage. The palace now houses the **Württemberggisches Landesmuseum** (Württemberg State Museum), with imaginative exhibits tracing the development of the area from the Stone Age to modern times. The displays of medieval life are especially noteworthy. ⌂ *Schillerpl. 6,* ☎ *0711/279–3400.* ☞ *Free.* ⊙ *Tues., Thurs.–Sun. 10–5, Wed. 10–7.*

The **Stiftskirche** (Collegiate Church) is a late-Gothic church built in 1433–1531. ⌂ *Schillerpl.*

Schlossgarten borders the Schlossplatz. If you continue in this park across Schillerstrasse, you'll come to the **Park Wilhelma,** home to botanical gardens and the city's renowned zoo. Here you can walk along the banks of the Neckar River.

★ The **Staatsgalerie** (State Gallery) is sure to please lovers of modern art and architecture. You can reach the museum from the Oberer Schlossgarten by crossing Konrad-Adenauer-Strasse. The old part of the complex, dating from 1843, contains paintings from the Middle Ages through the 19th century, including works by Cranach, Holbein, Hals, Memling, Rubens, Rembrandt, Cézanne, Courbet, and Manet. Connected to the original building is the New State Gallery, designed by British architect James Stirling in 1984 as a melding of classical and modern, sometimes jarring, elements (such as chartreuse window mullions!). Considered one of the most successful postmodern buildings, it houses works by such 20th-century artists as Braque, Chagall, de Chirico, Dali, Kandinsky, Klee, Mondrian, and Picasso. Look for Otto

Dix's *Grosstadt (Big City)* triptych, which distills the essence of 1920s Germany on canvas. ☒ *Konrad-Adenauer-Str. 30–32,* ☎ *0711/212–4050.* ☜ *DM 5.* ☉ *Wed., Fri.–Sun. 10–5, Tues. and Thurs. 10–8.*

OFF THE
BEATEN PATH

GOTTLIEB DAIMLER MEMORIAL WORKSHOP – The first successful internal combustion engine was perfected here in 1883, and you can see the tools, blueprints, and models of early cars that helped pave the way for the Mercedes line. ☒ *Taubenheimstr. 13, Stuttgart-Bad Cannstatt,* ☎ *0711/1756-9399.* ☜ *Free.* ☉ *Tues.–Sun. 10–4.*

MERCEDES-BENZ MUSEUM – Auto enthusiasts will want to venture somewhat out of town to visit this museum, the oldest car factory in the world, to view the collection of historic racing and luxury cars, as well as pioneering engines for ships and planes. ☒ *Mercedesstr. 136, Stuttgart-Untertürkheim,* ☎ *0711/172-2578.* ☜ *Free.* ☉ *Tues.–Sun. 9–5; closed holidays.*

PORSCHE MUSEUM – Perhaps only true auto aficionados will venture as far as this Porsche factory in the northern suburb of Zuffenhausen, to view a small but significant collection of legendary Porsche racing cars. Still, serious auto buffs will find the trip worthwhile. ☒ *Porschestr. 42, Stuttgart-Zuffenhausen,* ☎ *071/827-5685.* ☜ *Free.* ☉ *Weekdays 9–4, weekends and holidays 9–5.*

WEISSENHOFSIEDLUNG (WEISSENHOF COLONY) – Architecture buffs should seek out this minicity created for a 1927 exhibition of the "New Home." Using a zoning plan designed by Mies van der Rohe, 16 leading architects from five countries—among them van der Rohe, Le Corbusier, and Walter Gropius—were invited to create residences that offered optimal living conditions at affordable prices. The still-functioning colony, which had a significant influence on the development of 20th-century housing, is on a hillside overlooking Friedrich-Ebert-Strasse. To get there from the city center, take Tram 10 toward Killesberg to the Kunstakadamie stop. The Stuttgart tourist office issues a brochure indicating which architects designed the various homes.

Dining and Lodging

$$$$ ✕ **Wielandshöhe.** Stuttgart's leading restaurant fits neatly into the city's
  ★   sleek, businesslike image. It consists of a bright space devoid of all decoration, except for bowls of flamboyant flowers that stand out against the white and gray decor. The menu is full of surprises, including breast of pigeon nestled in a tangle of tagliolini, tender duck with farmhouse red cabbage, and swordfish served with a vinaigrette sauce. The wine list is exemplary. ☒ *Alte Weinsteige 71, Degerloch,* ☎ *0711/640–8848. Reservations essential. Jacket and tie. AE, DC, MC, V. Closed Sun.–Mon.*

$$–$$$ ✕ **Zeppelin-Stüble.** Hearty down-home Swabian dishes are the specialties at this friendly restaurant in the otherwise buttoned-up Steigenberger-Hotel Graf Zeppelin. ☒ *Arnulf-Klett-Pl. 7,* ☎ *0711/20480. AE, DC, MC, V.*

$$ ✕ **Der Zauberlehrling.** "The Sorcerer's Apprentice" is aptly named. The
  ★   enchantment on the menu includes imaginative salads, beautifully presented rack of venison, and heart-shaped waffles with cherries and cinnamon ice cream. You'll find excellent choices on the wine list. ☒ *Rosenstr. 38,* ☎ *0711/237–7770,* ⅢⅪ *0711/237–7775. No credit cards.*

$$$$ ✕▣ **Am Schlossgarten.** This pricey, modern eight-story glass-and-concrete hotel is set in spacious gardens in the heart of the city, a stone's throw from the Staatstheater, the state parliament, and several other landmarks. The hotel's Schlossgarten restaurant offers a mixture of international and regional dishes. Try the consommé of fresh forest

mushrooms and the turbot with leeks and lobster cream sauce. ⊠ *Schillerstr. 23, D–70173,* ☎ *0711–20260,* FAX *0711/202–6888. 125 beds with bath. 2 restaurants, bar, café. AE, DC, MC, V.*

$$$ ✗▥ **Alter Fritz.** Katrin Fritsche describes her small country mansion as a "hotel for individualists." With only 10 rooms, she is able to cater to guests' most exacting requirements with a friendly and personal touch rare in a city the size of Stuttgart. The picturesque house with its steep eaves and shuttered windows, high up on the wooded Killesberg Hill, is ideally located for visitors to the nearby trade fairground and a 15-minute bus ride from the main railway station. ⊠ *Feuerbach Weg 101, D–70192,* ☎ *0711/135–650,* FAX *0711/135–6565. 10 rooms with bath or shower. Restaurant, free parking. No credit cards.*

$$$ ✗▥ **Hotel Mercure Fasanenhof.** This recent addition to the Mercure chain offers the latest in comfort and service. The design is light and airy, with large windows throughout the spacious lobby, restaurant, public rooms, and the comfortable bedrooms; everything is decorated in tasteful, pastel colors. ⊠ *Eichwiesenring 1–1, D–70567,* ☎ *0711/72660,* FAX *0711/726–6444. 148 rooms with bath. Restaurant, bar, sauna, free parking. AE, DC, MC, V.*

Nightlife and the Arts

The **Stuttgart** tourist office issues the English-language *Stuttgart's Theatres-Museums* booklet, with detailed information on the city's theaters and museums, and the monthly *Monatsspiegel* (DM 2 a copy), which lists cultural, artistic, and sporting events.

Stuttgart's most vibrant nightlife is likely to be encountered in the numerous popular wine taverns, where just about everyone orders a *Viertelesglas,* local wine served in the typically Swabian quarter-liter glass mug. Throughout the region, between November and February, join the crowds in the *Besenwirtschaften* (broom inns), private inns serving the owner's new wine of the season; these are usually in nondescript houses, but you can recognize them by the broom hanging over the door. Night owls congregate at the **Schwabenzentrum** on Eberhardstrasse, where the pubs are open until 5 AM.

THEATER AND MUSIC

The **Staatstheater** (⊠ Oberer Schlossgarten 6, ☎ 0711/221–795) presents performances by Stuttgart's internationally renowned ballet company. The ballet alternates with opera performances by the respected State Opera; the season runs from September through June. For program details contact the Stuttgart tourist office (☞ Contacts and Resources *in* Heidelberg and the Neckar Valley A to Z, *below*). The box office is open weekdays 9–1 and 2–5. The **Stuttgart Musical Hall** showcases remarkable musicals, usually from Great Britain. This is the center of an entire entertainment complex (hotels, bars, restaurants, shows) built to house the touring blockbuster musical *Miss Saigon* (rumored to be sold to capacity through 1998 or so). Call 0711/222–8246 for information and tickets.

Outdoor Activities and Sports

HIKING

Stuttgart has a 53-kilometer (33-mile) network of marked hiking trails in the surrounding hills; follow the signs with the city's emblem: a horse set in a yellow ring.

HORSEBACK RIDING

You can hire horses at the **Schwarzbach** riding school (⊠ Handwerkstr. 39, ☎ 0711/780–2122).

TENNIS

Stuttgart is the true tennis center of the region, and the city has several clubs that welcome visitors. The largest is **Jens Weinberger's tennis and sports school** (⊠ Emerholzweg 73, ☎ 0711/808–018).

Shopping

Two of Germany's top men's fashion designers—Hugo Boss and Ulli Knecht—base themselves in Stuttgart. **Holy's** (⊠ Königstr. 54, ☎ 0711/221–872) is an exclusive men's boutique, which carries clothes by all the most sought-after designers.

Günter Krauss's glittering shop (⊠ Kronprinzstr. 21, ☎ 0711/297–395) specializes in designer jewelry. The design of the shop itself—walls of white Italian marble with gilded fixtures and mirrors—has won many awards.

Calwer Strasse, one of the city's leading shopping streets, is home to the glitzy arcade **Calwer Passage,** full of elegant chrome and glass. Here you'll find numerous shopping opportunities, from local women's fashion (Beate Mössinger), to furniture, to a shop devoted to pipes and accessories.

Breuninger (⊠ Marktstr. 1–3, ☎ 0711/2110), a leading regional department-store chain, has glass elevators that rise and fall under the dome of the several-stories-high central arcade. They're carrying customers to floors that contain everything from fashion to housewares.

Stuttgart's central market hall (entrances on Spörerstr. and on Dorotheenstr.) is an excellent place to buy local wines and other edible regional specialties.

Bebenhausen

③⓪ *5 km (3 mi) north of Tübingen, right at the side of the road.*

The little settlement of Bebenhausen is the first sign that you're approaching the lovely town of Tübingen. If you blink, you'll miss the turnoff, and that would be a shame because it is really worth a visit. The **Zisterzienkloster** (Cistercian Monastery) is a rare example of an almost perfectly preserved medieval monastery, dating from the late 12th century. Due to the secularization of 1806, the abbot's abode was rebuilt as a hunting castle for King Frederick of Württemberg. Expansion and restoration went on as the castle and monastery continued to be a royal residence into this century. Even after the monarchy was dissolved in 1918, the last Württembergs were given lifetime rights here; this came to an end in 1946 with the death of Charlotte, wife of Wilhelm II. For a few years after the war the state senate convened in the castle; today both castle and monastery are open to the public, although the castle is open for guided tours only. ⊠ *Zisterzienkloster DM 2, castle DM 2.50, combined admission for monastery and castle DM 4.* ☉ *Tues.–Fri. 9–noon and 2–5, weekends and holidays 10–noon and 2–5. Guided tours Tues.–Fri. hourly 9–4, weekends and holidays hourly 10–4.*

Dining

$$$ ✕ **Waldhorn.** This establishment shows how wonderful Swabian restaurants can be. It's been in the same family for generations, but the present owners are the ones who turned it into the area's best address for this type of cuisine. Everything is made by hand, down to the chocolates that come with the bill, but for all its elegant furnishings and fanciness, the restaurant hasn't lost its local flavor—from the warmth of the proprietors to the lunchtime menu that showcases traditional local specialties. ⊠ *Schönbuchstr. 49 (on the B-27),* ☎ *07071/61270,* 𝖥𝖠𝖷 *07071/610–581. Reservations essential. No credit cards. Closed Mon., Tues., and 2 wks in summer.*

Tübingen

③ *40 km (25 mi) south of Stuttgart on B–27 on the Neckar River.*

With its half-timbered houses, winding alleyways, hilltop location, and views overlooking the Neckar, Tübingen is popular with both German and foreign travelers. Dating to the 11th century, the town flourished as a trade center; in fact, Tübingen weights and measures, along with its currency, were the standard through much of the area. The town declined in importance after the 14th century, when it was taken over by the counts of Württemberg. Between the 14th and the 19th centuries, its size hardly changed as it became a university and residential town, its castle the only symbol of ruling power. Too bad, perhaps, for the merchants, but marvelous for visitors: Untouched by wartime bombings or even, it sometimes seems, the passage of time, the little town still has an authentic medieval flavor, providing the quintessential German experience.

Yet Tübingen hasn't been sheltered from the world. It resonates with a youthful air. Even more than Heidelberg, Tübingen is virtually synonymous with its university, a leading center of learning since it was founded in 1477. Illustrious students of yesteryear include the astronomer Johannes Kepler and the philosopher G. W. F. The latter studied at the Protestant theological seminary, still a cornerstone of the university's international reputation in academic circles. One of Hegel's roommates was Friedrich Hölderlin, a great poet of the German Romantic movement—who went mad and died young. Tübingen's population is around 80,000, of which nearly 26,000 are students. During term time, it can be hard to find a seat in pubs and cafés; during vacations, the town sometimes seems deserted. The best way to see and appreciate Tübingen is simply to stroll around, soaking up its age-old atmosphere of quiet erudition.

★ The **Marktplatz,** a sloping, uneven, cobblestone parallelogram, dominates the heart of Tübingen's Old City (Altstadt). As is common in medieval squares, the marketplace contains a fountain—the **Neptune Fountain,** graced with a statue of the sea god. The ornate facade of the
★ Renaissance **Rathaus** is bright with colorful wall paintings and a marvelous astronomical clock (dating from 1511). Built around 1435, the Rathaus was altered and expanded for another 150 years or so. The halls and reception rooms are adorned with half-timbering and paintings from the late 19th century.

The **Stiftskirche** (Collegiate Church) is just a short stroll from the Marktplatz. This late-Gothic building is one of Tübingen's finest architectural monuments. Because of the city's peaceful history, many of its original features have lasted through the ages, including the stained-glass windows, the choir stalls, the ornate baptismal font, and the elaborate stone pulpit. It's here that the dukes of Württemberg from the 15th to the 17th century are interred. ⊠ *Holzmarkt.* ⊙ *Feb.–Oct., daily 9–5; Nov.–Jan., daily 9–4.*

On and near the Stiftskirche and Holzmarkt you'll also find evidence of Tübingen's role as a center of publishing; the first books were published here in 1498. Around the corner, on Münzgasse, is the former headquarters of Cotta, a leading publishing house. And just across from the church is the Heckenhauer Bookstore, in a building where the writer Herman Hesse lived for a few years.

From Hechenhauer Bookstore, follow Neckargasse or Bursagasse south to the scenic bank of the Neckar; during the season you'll find pun-ters to rival Oxford's (☞ Guided Tours *in* Heidelberg and the Neckar Valley A to Z, *below*).

The **Hölderlinturm,** a residential house, stands at the end of a walk by the Neckar River. The "mad poet" Friedrich Hölderlin resided here with the Zimmer family for 36 years, until his death in 1843. Today the building is a museum commemorating the poet's life and work. If you don't speak German, you may want to arrange for an English tour to get the most out of the exhibits. You can also acquaint yourself with a couple of Hölderlin poems in translation to get a sense of the writer's Romantic imagery and notably "modern" style. ☒ Bursagasse 6, ☎ 07071/22040. 🎫 DM 3. *Tours weekends and holidays at 5 PM; English-language tours available by arrangement.* ☉ *Tues.–Fri. 10–12 and 3–5, weekends and holidays 2–5.*

Near the Hölderlinturm is the 15th-century **Bursa,** a former student dormitory. Farther on along is the **Evangelisches Stift** (Protestant Seminary), richer in history than in immediate visual interest. From the outside you can't tell that this site has served for centuries as a center of European intellectual thought. It was founded in 1534, partly as a political move during the Reformation; the Protestant duke of Württemberg, Ulrich, wanted facilities to train Protestant clerics so that Protestantism could retain its foothold in the region. (He would have been disappointed to know a major Catholic seminary arrived here in 1817.) Since that time philosophical rather than political considerations have prevailed within these walls. Hegel, Hölderlin, and the philosopher Schelling all shared a room during their studies—even in a university town this seems an unusually high concentration of brain power.

The narrow steps and cobblestones of **Burgsteige** pave one of the oldest thoroughfares in the town, and it's lined with equally aged houses. The street's name translates as "Castle Climb," which is at least honest advertising—you'll be more than a little breathless when you finally arrive at the top.

The almost 400-year-old castle **Hohentübingen,** at the summit of Burgsteige, is a replacement for 11th-century fortifications. Its portal is fitted as a Roman-style triumphal arch in true Renaissance spirit. Like so many sites in southern Germany, it was a bone of contention during the Thirty Years' War, and the French blew up one of its towers in 1647. Now it serves an altogether more peaceable function: housing classical archaeology and several other university departments. A main attraction is the magnificent view over river and town.

As the university has grown, so has Tübingen expanded, spreading modern buildings and housing developments across the hillsides. North of the Neckar, above the city, are the parks and greenhouses of its **Botanische Garten** (Botanical Garden) one of Tübingen's favorite modern attractions. ☒ *Hartmeyerstr. 123.*

The **Kunsthalle** has become a venue for some of the leading exhibitions in Germany. Like the Botanische Garten, it is situated north of the Neckar. The Kunsthalle generates a special kind of "art tourism," making it nearly impossible to find lodging if a popular show (such as the Renoir exhibition in 1996) is on. ☒ *Philosophenweg 76,* ☎ 07071/96910. 🎫 *Varies depending on the show: for Renoir, it was DM 12.* ☉ *Tues.–Sun. 10–8.*

The **Auto- und Spielzeug-Museum "Boxstop"** is devoted to cars and toys—there's something for everyone. ☒ *Brunnenstr. 18,* ☎ 07071/929–020. 🎫 *DM 4.* ☉ *Apr.–Oct., Wed. and Fri.–Sun. 10–noon and 2–5; Nov.–Mar., Sun. and holidays or by arrangement.*

Dining and Lodging

$ ✕ **Café/Bistro Neckartor.** The café has light and airy modern decor and a beautiful view up and down the Neckar. Hölderlin's Tower is just a few houses down river. The short menu has only freshly prepared entrees. The eclectic menu includes such dishes as cassoulet, lasagna, and *Maultaschen* (German-style ravioli). Don't even try to resist the pastries. ✉ *Neckargasse 22,* ☎ FAX *07071/22122. No credit cards.*

$$ ✕🖳 **Hotel Hospiz.** This little hotel has a central Altstadt location and was renovated in 1995. Although it's modern and not especially beautiful, it provides plenty in the way of comfort, good food, convenience, and friendly service. ✉ *Neckarhalde 2, D–72070,* ☎ *07071/9240,* FAX *07071/924–200. 50 rooms, most with bath or shower. Restaurant, bar, meeting room, free parking. AE, DC, MC, V.*

$ ✕🖳 **Hotel Am Schloss.** The climb is steep from the Altstadt to this hotel, next to the castle that towers over the town, but the reward is lovely views from the geranium-bedecked windows of the comfortable rooms. The hotel's restaurant is known for local specialties; proprietor Herbert Rösch has written a number of books about regional cuisine. In warm weather you can partake of meals on the small terrace overlooking the city. ✉ *Burgsteige 18, D–72070,* ☎ *07071/92940,* FAX *07071/929–410. 28 rooms with shower. Restaurant, free parking. AE, DC, MC, V.*

$$ 🖳 **Krone.** Between the train station and the Neckar River, not far from the university, the Krone is over 100 years old and attracts more than its share of distinguished guests behind its Renaissance-style facade. Rooms here are very basic but comfortable, and many of them have city views. There is no restaurant, but a substantial breakfast is provided. ✉ *Uhlandstr. 1, D–72072,* ☎ *07071/31036,* FAX *07071/38718. 48 rooms, most with bath or shower. AE, DC, MC, V.*

Nightlife and the Arts

Patty (✉ Schlachthausstr. 9, ☎ 07071/51612) is a very popular club in a former factory right on the Neckar. The very high student-to-resident ratio in Tübingen explains the dynamic scene inside. Salsa, reggae, and blues all get a piece of the action.

As a student town, Tübingen has an active small-theater scene. Check with the tourist office for a listing of what is going on—the more eclectic offerings are likely to be the better ones.

Outdoor Activities and Sports

HIKING

The Tübingen tourist office has maps with routes around the town, including historic and geologic "*Lehrpfad*," or educational walks. A classic Tübingen walk goes from the castle down to the little chapel called the **Wurmlinger Kapelle,** taking about two hours. On the way it's customary to stop off at the restaurant Schwärzlocher Hof to sample the good food and great views. The tourist office can give you a map detailing the way.

HEIDELBERG AND THE NECKAR VALLEY A TO Z

Arriving and Departing

By Plane

The airports nearest to the Neckar Valley are at Frankfurt and Stuttgart. From both there's fast and easy access, by car and train, to all major centers along the Neckar.

Getting Around

By Bus

Europabus 189 runs the length of the Burgenstrasse daily from May through September. There are stops at towns and villages all along the Neckar. For information, timetables, and reservations, contact **Deutsche Touring GmBH** (✉ AmRömerhof 17, D–60486 Frankfurt/Main 90, ☎ 069/79030). Local buses run from Mannheim, Heidelberg, Heilbronn, and Stuttgart to most places along the river; post buses connect the rest.

By Car

Mannheim is a major junction of the autobahn system, easily reached from all parts of the country. Heidelberg and Heilbronn are also served by the autobahn. A 15-minute drive on A–656 speeds you from Mannheim to Heidelberg; Heilbronn stands beside the east–west A–6 and the north–south A–81. The route followed in this chapter, the Burgenstrasse—also unromantically designated A–37—follows the north bank of the Neckar from Heidelberg to Mosbach, from which it runs down to Heilbronn as A–27. It's a busy road—and a fast one. If you need a change of pace, cross the river at Mosbach to Obrigheim and continue south on the slower B–39.

By Train

Mannheim is western Germany's most important rail junction, with hourly InterCity trains from all major German cities. Nearby Heidelberg is equally easy to get to. Mannheim is also a major stop for the super-high-speed InterCity Express service, which reaches 250 kilometers (155 miles) per hour on the Mannheim–Stuttgart stretch. There are express trains to Heilbronn from Heidelberg and Stuttgart and direct trains from Stuttgart to Tübingen. Local services link many of the smaller towns along the Neckar.

Contacts and Resources

Car Rentals

Avis: ✉ Karlsruherstr. 43, ☎ 06221/22215, **Heidelberg**; ✉ Salzstr. 112, ☎ 07131/172–077, **Heilbronn**; ✉ Augartenstr. 112–114, ☎ 0621/442–091, **Mannheim**; ✉ Katharinenstr. 18, ☎ 0711/239–320, **Stuttgart.**

Europcar: ✉ Bergheimerstr. 159, ☎ 06221/20845, **Heidelberg**; ✉ Neckarauerstr. 50–52, ☎ 0621/852–055, **Mannheim**; ✉ Alexanderstr. 42, ☎ 0711/236–4863, **Stuttgart**; ✉ Eisenbahnstr. 17, ☎ 07071/36303, **Tübingen.**

Hertz: ✉ Kurfürstenanlage 1 (in the Holiday Inn), ☎ 06221/23434, **Heidelberg**; ✉ Friedrichsring 36, ☎ 0621/22997, **Mannheim**; ✉ Leitzstr. 51, ☎ 0711/817–233, **Stuttgart.**

Guided Tours

BOAT TOURS

From Easter through October there are regular trips on the Neckar from Stuttgart and Heilbronn. Contact the **Neckar-Personen-Schiffahrt** (☎ 0711/541–073), **Personenschiffahrt Stumpf** (☎ 07131/85430), or the tourist offices for details. The **Tübingen** tourist office organizes punting on the Neckar (Apr.–Oct.); trips leave Saturday at 4 PM from the quay by the Neckar Bridge (✉ DM 6).

CITY TOURS

There are guided bus tours of **Heidelberg** at 2 Thursday, 10 and 2 Friday–Saturday, and 10 on Sunday and holidays from April to October (Sat. only at 2, Nov.–Mar.) leaving from the train station and Bismarckplatz. Call 06221/21341 or 06221/513–2000 for details. The tours cost DM 20. The **Heidelberg Card** (✉ DM 25) is a one-day ticket that includes admission to all of Heidelberg's tourist attractions as well as unlimited use of all public transportation and other extras. It can be purchased at the Tourist Information Office at the main train station, in local hotels, restaurants and cultural institutions.

In **Heilbronn** the tourist office offers a **"Viertel nach Sechs"** tour, meaning "quarter after six," which is just when the tour begins (that's 6:15 PM). The tours are given every Thursday from early May through September; the cost is DM 7, and all tours end with a free glass of wine. On the first Wednesday in June, July, August, and September, you can take a tour in a 1927 Paris city bus. The cost of DM 21 includes a welcome-aboard drink. Contact the tourist office for details (☎ 07131/562–270). Two or three times a month, except July and August, a "Heilbronn by Night" bus tour is offered. The DM 72 cost includes a visit to seven wine taverns/restaurants and to a strip club, with drinks and snacks in each; the tour ends at a discotheque. There are bus tours of **Mannheim** May–October, Monday–Saturday at 10:30. Tours leave from the Wasserturm and cost DM 18.

The tourist office in **Stuttgart,** open November to March, Saturday to Monday, offers daily 2½-hour sight-seeing tours of the city (✉ DM 32) as well as evening-long "Stuttgart by Night" tours every Saturday night that go to shows and nightclubs (✉ DM 105). For details, go to the tourist board *"i-Punkt"* (☎ 0711/222–8240) in the underground Klett-Passage at the main train station.

From April to October the **Tübingen** tourist office runs guided city tours Wednesday at 10 AM, weekends and holidays at 2:30 PM; the cost is DM 5.

Visitor Information

For information on the entire Burgenstrasse, contact **Arbeitsgemeinschaft Burgenstrasse** (✉ Rathaus, Marktpl., D–74072 Heilbronn, ☎ 07131/562–271). There are local tourist information offices in the following towns and cities:

Bad Wimpfen: Verkehrsamt, ✉ Hauptstr. 45, D–74206, ☎ 07063/53151.

Heidelberg: Verkehrsverein Heidelberg, ✉ Friedrich-Ebert-Anlage 2, D–69117; ✉ Am Hauptbahnhof, D–69115, ☎ 06221/21341.

Heilbronn: Verkehrsverein Heilbronn, Rathaus, Marktpl., D–74072, ☎ 07131/562–270.

Mannheim: Tourist-Information, ✉ Kaiserring 10/16, D–68161, ☎ 0621/101–011.

Mosbach: Städtisches Verkehrsamt, ✉ Rathaus, D–74821, ☎ 06261/82236.

Stuttgart: Stuttgart Marketing, Gmhb, ✉ Königstr. 1a, D–70173, ☎ 0711/222–8240.

Tübingen: Verkehrsverein Tübingen, ✉ An der Neckarbrücke, D–72016, ☎ 07071/91360.

10 Frankfurt

*Because it is the air gateway to
Germany—and to Europe—you'll
probably at least land in Frankfurt.
Many German banks are
headquartered here, and the Frankfurt
Börse is Germany's leading stock
exchange. All this has contributed to a
high-rise-spiked skyline that would
stun the 30 Holy Roman emperors
who were elected and crowned here.
Their portraits line the banquet hall of
the Römer, or City Hall. Across the
River Main from the heart of
downtown is the residential, medieval-
feeling Sachsenhausen quarter, home to
many of the city's best museums.*

HOME OF THE BIGGEST AIRPORT ON THE CONTI-NENT, Frankfurt is the gateway to Germany for most air travelers. Although it ranks fifth in size among German cities (population: 650,000), it became the country's financial capital after World War II, and although larger cities such as Munich have reclaimed the physical character of their past, Frankfurt deliberately developed a New York–style skyline. You may hear the city referred to as Mainhattan, a reference to the River Main, by which it stands. The temperament of Frankfurters has also been compared with that of Americans—aggressive and competitive yet open and hospitable.

So why come to Frankfurt? Partly because of its history, which spans more than 1,200 years. It was: one of the joint capitals of Charlemagne's empire; the city where no fewer than 30 emperors of the Holy Roman Empire were elected and crowned; the site of Gutenberg's print shop; the birthplace of Goethe, for many Germany's greatest poet; and the city where the first German parliament met.

Frankfurt's commercial clout has its historic side as well. The city was a major trading center as early as the 12th century. Its first international Autumn Fair was held in 1240; in 1330 its Spring Fair was inaugurated. Both are still going strong today. The stock exchange, one of the half dozen most important in the world, was established in 1595. The Rothschilds opened their first bank here in 1798.

And though Frankfurt may be a city of balance sheets and share prices, it still possesses something of the glitzy panache and high living that are such conspicuous features of today's German cities. It's more than just a question of expense-account restaurants and sleek cars. There's the feeling that you are in the heart of a powerful, sophisticated, and cosmopolitan nation. There may not be much here to remind you of the Old World, but there's a great deal that explains Germany's success story.

Pleasures and Pastimes

Dining

The range and quality of the city's restaurants are excellent. You can find everything from the most sophisticated French haute cuisine to neighborhood *Gasthofs* (beer restaurants) serving earthy local dishes. But dining in Frankfurt—the expense-account city par excellence—can be expensive. You'll need to make reservations well in advance, too, if you plan to eat in any of the fancier restaurants.

CATEGORY	COST*
$$$$	over DM 95
$$$	DM 65–DM 95
$$	DM 45–DM 65
$	under DM 45

per person for a three-course meal, excluding drinks

Jazz

Frankfurt's nightlife has at least one trump card—*jazz*. Many German cities like to call themselves the jazz capital of the country, but Frankfurt probably has a better claim to the title than most. Fittingly, it's here, in the fall, that the German Jazz Festival is held. There are hundreds of jazz venues, from smoky back-street cafés all the way to the Old Opera House. But Der Jazzkeller has been the most noted venue for German jazz fans for decades (☞ Nightlife and the Arts, *below*).

Lodging

Businesspeople descend on Frankfurt year-round, so most hotels are expensive. The majority of the larger hotels are situated around the main train station. Lower prices and—for some, anyway—more atmosphere are found at smaller hotels and pensions in the suburbs; the efficient public transportation network makes them easy to reach.

CATEGORY	COST*
$$$$	over DM 275
$$$	DM 180–DM 275
$$	DM 120–DM 180
$	under DM 120

All prices are for two people in a double room, including tax and service.

Museums

Frankfurt is a city full of museums, and during the 1980s, 13 of them were newly built or renovated. Interesting for their architecture as well as for their content, the exhibition halls have increased the city's popularity. Sachsenhausen, which is now largely residential, is home to no fewer than eight of these museums. They line the side of the Main, on Schaumainkai, known locally as the Museumsufer (Museum Riverbank).

EXPLORING FRANKFURT

The neighborhood around the Hauptbahnhof (main train station) is mostly devoted to business and banking, where many of the major hotels are. There is also a red-light district that has been downsized and cleaned up. The department stores of the Hauptwache and Zeil are only a few blocks away. But visitors who want a sense of the past, or to let the good times roll, head to the Old Town with its restored medieval quarter and to Sachsenhausen across the river, where the pubs and museums greatly outnumber the banks.

Numbers in the text correspond to numbers in the margin and on the Frankfurt map.

Great Itineraries

IF YOU HAVE 1 DAY

Begin your visit to Frankfurt in **Römerberg Square,** the heart of the city, and take a look at the **Römer,** or Town Hall, and its **Kaisersaal** (Imperial Hall), before exploring the **Goethehaus und Goethemuseum** (Goethe's House and Museum), the home of Germany's greatest poet. Then go to the **Museum für Moderne Kunst** (Museum of Modern Art), one of Frankfurt's modern architectural monuments. Walk a few blocks and several centuries back in time to **St. Bartholomäus** (Church of St. Bartholomew) and admire the original magnificent Gothic carvings. After lunch cross over the **Eiserner Steg** (Iron Bridge) to the Museumufer (Museum Riverbank) to reach the **Städelsches Kunstinstitut und Städtische Galerie** (Städel Art Institute and Municipal Gallery), with its important collection of Old Masters and Impressionists, and the **Städtische Galerie Liebieghaus** (Liebieg Municipal Museum of Sculpture), a former mansion containing sculpture from the third millennium BC up to the modern age. In the evening stroll around **Sachsenhausen** and eat in one of the neighborhood apple-cider taverns.

IF YOU HAVE 2 DAYS

First visit **Römerberg Square** and the **Römer.** Then take a look at the **Nikolaikirche** (Church of St. Nicholas), where the carillon chimes at 9 AM, noon, and 5 PM; the **Historisches Museum** (Historical Museum) to see maps of medieval Frankfurt and a model of the city as it looked just after the war; and the **Paulskirche** (Church of St. Paul's)—now a monument to Germany's failed democratic revolution in the 19th century. Then continue on to the **Goethehaus und Goethemuseum** (Goethe's House and Museum), the **Museum für Moderne Kunst** (Museum of Modern Art), and **St. Bartholomäus** (Church of St. Bartholomew). Take a midday break in the **Steinernes Haus** (Stone House; ☞ Dining, *below*) before visiting Germany's shop-till-you-drop district on the **Zeil** and the **Zoologischer Garten** (Zoological Garden), one of Europe's best zoos. End the first evening in **Der Frankfurter Jazzkeller** (☞ Nightlife and the Arts, *below*). The entire second day can be devoted to the **Museumufer** (Museum Riverbank), starting with the **Städelsches Kunstinstitut und Städtische Galerie** (Städel Art Institute and Municipal Gallery) and the **Städtische Galerie Liebieghaus** (Liebieg Municipal Museum of Sculpture). A patrician house serves as the setting for the extremely popular **Deutsches Architekturmuseum** (German Architectural Museum). The **Deutsches Filmmuseum** (German Film Museum) allows you to play with early cameras and projectors; Europe's largest collection of contemporary art from the Third World complements collections of earlier non-Western art and religious artifacts at **Museum für Völkerkunde** (Ethnological Museum). The white house along the Main River, designed by New York architect Richard Meier, is home to the **Museum für Kunsthandwerk** (Museum of Applied Arts). Finally, explore **Sachsenhausen**'s nightlife.

IF YOU HAVE 3 DAYS

Few tourists spend three full days in Frankfurt, but an extended visit is more than justified. Spend your first two days following the itinerary outlined above. On the morning of the third day, see the **Naturkundemuseum Senckenberg** (Natural History Museum), one of Europe's best; it has a famous collection of dinosaurs and giant whales from early geological eras. Afterward visit the nearby **Palmengarten und Botanischer Garten** (Tropical Garden and Botanical Garden), which has climatic zones from tropical to sub-Antarctic and a dazzling range of orchids. Taking the U-bahn to the Opernplatz, emerge above ground before the 19th-century splendor of the **Alte Oper** (Old Opera House); lunch is not far away in the appropriately named **Fressgasse** (Pig-Out Alley). In the afternoon, go to the visitors gallery of the **Börse** (Stock Exchange) to feel the pulse of Europe's banking capital. Then continue on to the less worldly **Karmeliterkirche** (Carmelite Church and Monastery). Secularized in 1803, the church and buildings were renovated in the 1980s and now house the **Museum für Vor- und Frügeschichte** (Museum of Prehistory and Early History). Just around the corner on the shore of the Main, in the former Rothschild Palace, the **Jüdisches Museum** (Jewish Museum) tells the thousand-year story of Frankfurt's Jewish quarter and its end in the Holocaust.

The Old Town

Frankfurt was rebuilt after the World War II with little attention paid to the past. Nevertheless, important architectural monuments from its long history are still standing, and the city also has its share of modern architectural masterpieces. Despite the city's incredible prosperity and growth, it remains a good city for walking, with parks, gardens, pedestrian arcades, and outdoor cafés. Across the Main River, Sachsenhausen still has cobblestone streets, half-timbered houses, beer gardens, and atmospheric cider taverns.

A Good Walk

Numbers in the text correspond to numbers in the margin and on the Frankfurt map.

Frankfurt

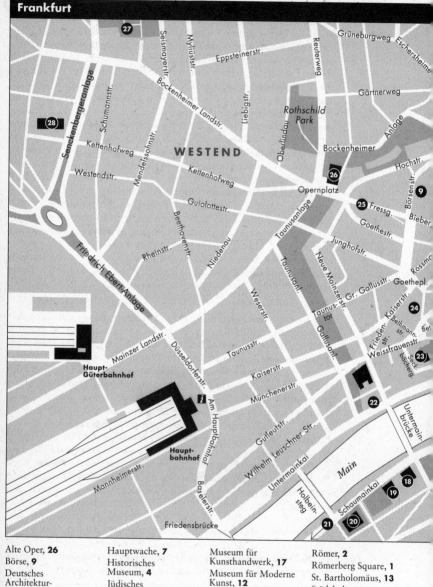

Alte Oper, **26**

Börse, **9**

Deutsches
Architektur-
museum, **19**

Deutsches
Filmmuseum, **18**

Eiserner Steg, **14**

Fressgasse, **25**

Goethehaus und
Goethemuseum, **24**

Hauptwache, **7**

Historisches
Museum, **4**

Jüdisches
Museum, **22**

Karmeliterkirche, **23**

Katharinenkirche, **8**

Kuhhirtenturm, **16**

Leonhardskirche, **15**

Liebfrauenkirche, **6**

Museum für
Kunsthandwerk, **17**

Museum für Moderne
Kunst, **12**

Naturkundemuseum
Senckenberg, **28**

Nikolaikirche, **3**

Palmengarten und
Botanischer
Garten, **27**

Paulskirche, **5**

Römer, **2**

Römerberg Square, **1**

St. Bartholomäus, **13**

Städelsches
Kunstinstitut und
Städtische Galerie, **20**

Städtische Galerie
Liebieghaus, **21**

Staufenmauer, **11**

Zoologischer
Garten, **10**

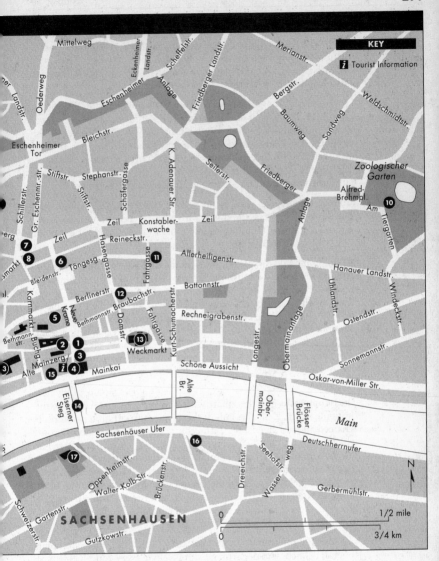

KEY

i Tourist Information

Mittelweg

Eckenheimer Landstr.

Scheffelstr.

Merianstr.

Eschenheimer Anlage

Friedberger Landstr.

Bergstr.

Weldschmidtstr.

Oederweg

Eschenheimer Landstr.

Baumweg

Sandweg

Bleichstr.

Eschenheimer Tor

Stiftstr.

Stephanstr.

Schäfergasse

K. Adenauer Str.

Seiterstr.

Friedberger

Zoologischer Garten

Schillerstr.

Gr. Eschenmr.-str.

Stiftstr.

Alfred-Brehmpl.

Am Tiergarten

10

Zeil

Konstabler-wache

Zeil

Anlage

7

Zeil

Reineckstr.

Hasengasse

Fahrgasse

Allerheiligenstr.

Hanauer Landstr.

Windeckstr.

8

6

Töngesg.

11

Battonnstr.

Uhlandstr.

Ostendstr.

Bleidenstr.

Berlinerstr.

12

Braubachstr.

Rechneigrabenstr.

Obermainanlage

Sonnemannstr.

Kornmarkt

Bethmann-str.

5

Neue Krame

Bethmannstr.

Domstr.

Fahrgasse

Kurt-Schumacherstr.

Langestr.

2

1

13

Bethmann-str.

Bachg.

Weckmarkt

Schöne Aussicht

Oskar-von-Miller Str.

3

Alte

Mainzerg.

3

i

4

Mainkai

Alte Br.

Ober-mainbr.

Flösser Brücke

Main

15

14

Eiserner Steg

Sachsenhäuser Ufer

Deutschherrnufer

16

17

Oppenheimstr.

Walter-Kolb-Str.

Brückenstr.

Dreieichstr.

Seehofstr.

Wasserweg

Gerbermühlstr.

Schweizerstr.

Gartenstr.

SACHSENHAUSEN

Gutzkowstr.

N

0

1/2 mile

0

3/4 km

Römerberg Square ① has been the center of civic life for centuries; it is still the historic—albeit reconstructed—heart of Frankfurt. Taking up most of the west side of the square is the City Hall, called the **Römer** ②. It's a modest-looking building compared with many of Germany's city halls, though it has undeniable charm. In the center of the square stands the fine 16th-century Fountain of Justitia (Justice).

On the south side of the Römerberg is the **Nikolaikirche** (St. Nicholas's Church) ③. It was built during the late 13th century as the court chapel for the emperors of the Holy Roman Empire. Beside the Nikolaikirche stands the **Historisches Museum** (Historical Museum) ④, where you can see a perfect scale model of historic Frankfurt. On the east side of Römerberg Square is a row of painstakingly restored half-timbered houses called the **Ostzeile,** dating from the 15th and 16th centuries.

From the Römerberg, walk up the pedestrian street called Neue Krame. On your left you'll pass the Gothic turrets and crenellations of the **Steinernes Haus** (Stone House), originally built in 1464 and rebuilt from 1957 to 1960. Today it houses an art gallery.

Next, looming up on the left is the circular bulk of the **Paulskirche** (St. Paul's Church) ⑤, a handsome, mostly 18th-century church building, more interesting for its political than its religious significance. It was here that the short-lived German parliament met for the first time in May 1848. Today the building remains a focus for the democratic aspirations of the German people. From Paulskirche, keep heading along the Neue Krame, which becomes Liebfrauenstrasse. Here, in more peaceful surroundings, you will come to the **Liebfrauenkirche** (Church of Our Lady) ⑥, a late-Gothic church dating from the end of the 14th century.

The **Hauptwache** ⑦ is the square where Liebfrauenstrasse runs into the shopping street, Zeil. The hub of the city's transportation network, it is named after the handsome 18th-century building with a sloping roof, which is still on the square. Now a café, this structure once served as the city's guardhouse and prison. A vast shopping mall extends below the square. To the south of Hauptwache Square is the **Katharinenkirche** (St. Katherine's Church) ⑧, the most important Protestant church in the city. North of the Hauptwache, Schillerstrasse leads to the on Börsenplatz and Frankfurt's **Börse** (Stock Exchange) ⑨, the leading stock exchange and financial powerhouse of Germany.

The **Zeil** is Frankfurt's largest pedestrian zone and main shopping street. It is lined with department stores selling every conceivable type of consumer goods and can get very crowded. A 15- to 20-minute walk all the way to the end of the Zeil brings you to Alfred-Brehm Platz and the entrance to the **Zoologischer Garten** (Zoological Garden) ⑩. This is one of Frankfurt's chief attractions, ranking among the best zoos in Europe. If you don't want to go all the way down the Zeil, turn right at the square Konstabler Wache onto Fahrgasse. Follow the signs reading "An der Staufenmauer" to the **Staufenmauer** ⑪, which is one of the few surviving stretches of the old city wall.

Continue down Fahrgasses, then go left at Battonstrasse. From the corner of Berlinerstrasse and Domstrasse you'll see the striking wedge-shape outline of Frankfurt's **Museum für Moderne Kunst** (Museum of Modern Art) ⑫, opened in 1991. Cross Berlinerstrasse at a convenient point, bear left along Braubachstrasse for a few yards, and then turn left onto Domstrasse. You are now at the grand Gothic church of **St. Bartholomäus** (St. Bartholomew's Church) ⑬ or Kaiserdom (Imperial Cathedral), as it is more popularly known. "Cathedral" is a courtesy title; Frankfurt was never the seat of a bishopric. From this archaeological site dating from 1290, walk through the pedestrian zone alongside the modern edifice of the **Schirn Kunsthalle,** a major venue for art exhibitions.

Continuing on will take you back to the Römerberg. From here, turn left and walk to Mainkai, the busy street that runs parallel to the tree-lined river. On your left you will see the **Rententurm,** one of the city's medieval gates, with its pinnacled towers at the base of the main spire extending out over the walls. To your right and in front is the **Eiserner Steg** ⑭, an iron footbridge that was the first suspension bridge in Europe, connecting central Frankfurt with the old district of Sachsenhausen. River trips, boat excursions, and the old steam train leave from here. (☞ Guided Tours *in* Frankfurt A to Z, *below.*)

Past the Eiserner Steg is **Leonhardskirche** (St. Leonard's Church) ⑮. Started in the Romanesque style and continued in the late-Gothic style, it still contains two 13th-century Romanesque arches, as well as one of the few 15th-century stained-glass windows to have survived World War II.

Return to the Eiserner Steg and cross the river to **Sachsenhausen.** Formerly a village separate from Frankfurt, Sachsenhausen is said to have been established by Charlemagne, who arrived here with a group of Saxon families during the 8th century and formed a settlement on the banks of the Main. It was an important bridgehead for the crusader Knights of the Teutonic Order and in 1318 officially became part of Frankfurt. Down the bank to your left you'll catch a glimpse of the 15th-century **Kuhhirtenturm** (Shepherd's Tower) ⑯, the only remaining part of Sachsenhausen's original fortifications.

Turn right and follow the Main River on Schaumainkai, to reach a row of museums. The spacious **Museum für Kunsthandwerk** (Museum of Decorative Arts) ⑰, houses a stunning collection of European and Asian applied art. Germany's first museum devoted exclusively to the cinema, the **Deutsches Filmmuseum** (German Film Museum) ⑱, imaginatively presents its collection of film artifacts. Just next door, the popular **Deutsches Architekturmuseum** (German Architectural Museum) ⑲ lies within a 19th-century villa, although the interior is entirely modern.

If you have time and energy, step away from the waterfront to explore more of the up-and-coming district of Sachsenhausen. The area has a distinctly medieval air, with narrow back alleys, quaint little inns, and quiet squares that escaped the modern developer, yet it's also full of new shops, boutiques, cafés, and bars thronging with people and activity. Follow Schweizer Strasse (the street where the Film Museum is) to **Schweizer Platz** to see the heart of Sachsenhausen.

From the Architectural Museum, continue along the riverbank past the Deutsches Post Museum to the **Städelsches Kunstinstitut und Städtische Galerie** (Städel Art Institute and Municipal Gallery) ⑳, which houses one of the most significant art collections in Germany, with fine examples of Flemish, Dutch, German, and Italian Old Masters, plus a sprinkling of French Impressionists. Next, go past the pedestrian Holbeinsteg Bridge in front of the Städel to the next building on the riverbank, the **Städtische Galerie Liebieghaus** (Liebieg Municipal Museum of Sculpture) ㉑, with an internationally famous collection of classical, medieval, and Renaissance sculpture on display in a charming 17th-century villa.

From here you can backtrack along the Schaumainkai to the Holbeinsteg Bridge, cross over to the other side of the river, and turn left into Untermainkai. The **Jüdisches Museum** (Jewish Museum) ㉒ is No. 14–15 in the former Rothschild Palais and focuses on Frankfurt's centuries-old Jewish community, the second largest in Germany after Berlin.

As you head back toward the Römer, Untermainkai becomes Mainkai. Continue a short way, then turn left into the narrow Seckbächer Gasse, which will take you to the **Karmeliterkirche** (Carmelite Church and Monastery) ㉓. Secularized in 1803 the church and buildings were renovated in the 1980s and now house the **Museum für Vor- und Frügeschichte** (Museum of Prehistory and Early History). At the other side of the building, the main cloister contains the largest religious fresco north of the Alps.

Coming out of the Karmeliterkirche into Münzgasse, turn left and go to the junction of Bethmannstrasse and Berliner Strasse. Use the pedestrian walkway and cross over to the north side of Berliner Strasse, then turn left again onto Grosser Hirschgraben. Outside No. 23 there will probably be a small crowd of visitors entering and leaving the **Goethehaus und Goethemuseum** (Goethe's House and Museum) ㉔. This is where the renowned author Johann Wolfgang von Goethe was born in 1749. What Shakespeare is to English literature, Goethe is to German.

On leaving the Goethehaus turn left, and at the end of Grosser Hirschgraben bear left again and retrace your steps up Rossmarkt. Cross over to the Gutenberg Memorial and continue along the pedestrian zone to Rathenau-Platz. At the end of the square, turn left onto Grosse Bockenheimer Strasse, known locally as **Fressgasse** (Pig-Out Alley) ㉕ because of its many delicatessens, bakeries, and cafés.

Fressgasse ends at Opernplatz and Frankfurt's reconstructed opera house, the **Alte Oper** ㉖. Destroyed by incendiary bombs in 1944, it was finally reopened in 1981 and is now a prime venue for classical concerts as well as conferences and, every now and then, an opera. The steps of the opera house, or the Rothschild Park opposite, are a good spot from which to take in the impressive sight of Frankfurt's modern architecture. In this part of the new town you are close to the financial center (the West End), and if you look down Taunusanlage and Mainzer Landstrasse, the view both right and left is dominated by gleaming skyscrapers that house the headquarters of West Germany's biggest and richest banks. More than 422 banks (275 of which are foreign) have offices here, confirming Frankfurt's position as the country's financial capital. Nearest to you on the right is the 155-meter- (508-foot-) tall skyscraper housing the headquarters of the Deutsche Bank, the largest in Germany.

Next, you can wander from the Alte Oper up Bockenheimer Landstrasse until you come to Siesmayerstrasse on your right; this street leads to the delightful **Palmengarten und Botanischer Garten** (Tropical Garden and Botanical Garden) ㉗. From here, by walking southwest, you can easily reach the **Naturkundemuseum Senckenberg** (Natural History Museum) ㉘, with fascinating hands-on exhibits that please both children and adults.

TIMING

Count on spending at least three hours just to look at the buildings and major sights. It is impossible to see all the museums on one trip. You should block out 45 minutes for the **Goethehaus und Goethemuseum,** an hour and 15 minutes for the **Städelsches Kunstinstitut und Städtische Galerie,** and an hour for the **Städtische Galerie Liebieghaus.** For the remaining museums, it is a question of your individual taste, how much you can absorb, and how much time you have left. Take your pick from the following and allow at least 45 minutes for each: the **Historisches Museum,** the **Deutsches Filmmuseum,** the **Museum für Kunsthandwerk,** the **Deutsches Architekturmuseum,** and the **Jüdisches Museum.** If you intend to visit the **Zoologischer Garten** (Zoo), expect to spend an hour and a half there.

Numbers in the margin correspond to points of interest on the Frankfurt map.

Sights to See

㉖ **Alte Oper** (Old Opera House). Built between 1873 and 1880 and destroyed during World War II, Frankfurt's Old Opera House has been beautifully reconstructed in the style of the original. Kaiser Wilhelm II traveled all the way from Berlin for the gala opening in 1880. After World War II the opera house remained in ruins for many years while controversy raged over its reconstruction. The new building is faithful to the classical proportions and style of the original. ⊠ *Opernpl.,* ☎ *069/134–0405.*

Alter Jüdischer Friedhof (Old Jewish Cemetery) The old Jewish quarter is within Frankfurt, near Börneplatz. The Old Jewish Cemetery lies on the east side of the square and was in use between the 13th and 19th centuries. Partly vandalized in the Nazi era, it is nearly all that remains of prewar Jewish life in Frankfurt. The cemetery can be visited by prior arrangement only. ⊠ *Corner of Kurt-Schumacher-Str. and Battonstr.,* ☎ *069/561–826.*

Anlagenring. When the fortification wall surrounding Frankfurt was demolished during the 19th century, the open space on both sides of the structure was turned into a park. A 3-mile ring of green now encircles the city center, north of the Main River.

⑨ **Börse** (Stock Exchange). The Börse was founded by Frankfurt merchants in 1558 to establish some order in their often chaotic dealings, but the present building dates from the 1870s. This is the center of Germany's stock and money market. In the past the trading on the dealers' floor was hectic. These days computerized networks and international telephone systems have removed some of the drama, but it is still an exciting scene to watch. There is a visitors gallery. ⊠ *Börsepl.,* ☎ *069/21010.* ▱ *Free.* ⊙ *Weekdays 9:30–1:30.*

⑲ **Deutsches Architekturmuseum** (German Architecture Museum). Created by German architect Oswald Mathias Ungers, this 19th-century villa setting contains an entirely modern interior. There are five floors of drawings, models, and audiovisual displays that chart the progress of German architecture through the ages, as well as many special exhibits. ⊠ *Schaumainkai 43,* ☎ *069/2123–8844.* ▱ *DM 6; free Wed.* ⊙ *Tues., Thurs., and weekends 11–6; Wed. and Fri. noon–8.*

⑱ **Deutsches Filmmuseum** (German Film Museum). Germany's first museum of cinematography houses an exciting collection of film artifacts. ⊠ *Schaumainkai 41,* ☎ *069/2123–8830.* ▱ *DM 5; free Wed.* ⊙ *Tues., Thurs., Fri., and Sun. 10–5; Wed. 10–8; Sat. 2–8.*

Deutsches Postmuseum (Postal Museum). On display are the various means of transporting mail through the ages—from the mail coach to the airplane. There's also an exhibition of stamps and stamp-printing machines, as well as a reconstructed 19th-century post office. ⊠ *Schaumainkai 53,* ☎ *069/60600.* ▱ *Free.* ⊙ *Tues. and Thurs.–Sun. 10–5, Wed. 10–8.*

Deutschordenshaus (House of the Teutonic Order). A Baroque building, it once belonged to the Knights of the Teutonic Order. It was built in 1709 above a Gothic cellar. Next door is a church that dates from 1309. ⊠ *Brueckenstr. 3–7,* ☎ *069/609–10860.* ⊙ *Church can be visited by prior arrangement only.*

⑭ **Eiserner Steg** (Iron Bridge). A pedestrian walkway, the bridge connects the center of Frankfurt with Sachsenhausen.

Eschenheimer Turm (Eschenheimer Tower). Built during the early 15th century, this tower remains the finest example of the city's original 42 towers. ⊠ *Eschenheimer Tor.*

㉕ Fressgasse (Pig-Out Alley). One of the city's liveliest thoroughfares, the street's proper name is Grosse Bockenheimer Strasse, but Frankfurters have given it this sobriquet because of the amazing choice of delicatessens, wine merchants, cafés, and restaurants to be found here. Food shops offer fresh or smoked fish, cheeses, and a wide range of local specialties, including frankfurters. In the summer you can sit at tables on the sidewalk and dine alfresco. *Prost!*

★ ㉔ Goethehaus und Goethemuseum (Goethe's House and Museum). The birthplace of Germany's most famous poet is furnished with many original pieces that belonged to his family. Although the original house was destroyed by Allied bombing, it has been carefully rebuilt and restored in every detail as the young Goethe would have known it. In Goethe senior's study look for the little window that was installed so he could keep an eye on the street outside and, in particular, on young Johann, who was well known to wander afield. Although he studied law and became a member of the bar in Frankfurt, Goethe preferred the life of a writer and published his first best-seller at the age of 20 (*Götz von Berlichingen*). He sealed his fame a few years later with the tragic love story *The Sorrows of Young Werther.* Goethe also wrote the first version of his masterpiece, *Faust,* in Frankfurt. The adjoining museum is closed for renovations until 1998. ⊠ *Grosser Hirschgraben 23–25,* ☎ *069/282–824.* ☜ *DM 4.* ☉ *Apr.–Sept., Mon.–Sat. 9–5:30, Sun. 10–1; Oct.–Mar, Mon.–Sat. 9–4, Sun. 10–1.*

Goetheturm (Goethe's Tower). At the edge of the Stadtwald on the Sachsenhauser Berg, this is Germany's highest wood tower.

❼ Hauptwache. This square is situated where Liebfrauenstrasse runs into the ☞ Zeil, a main shopping street. It is named after the attractive Baroque building on the square. This edifice with a steeply sloping roof was originally constructed as a municipal guardhouse in 1729. Today it houses a café and a tourist information office. A vast underground shopping mall stretches below the square.

❹ Historisches Museum (History Museum). This fascinating museum encompasses all aspects of the city's history over the past eight centuries. It contains a scale model of historic Frankfurt, complete with every street, house, and church. There is also an astonishing display of silver, exhibits covering all aspects of the city's life from the 16th to the 20th century, and a children's museum. ⊠ *Saalgasse 19,* ☎ *069/2123–5599.* ☜ *DM 5; free Wed.* ☉ *Tues.–Sun. 10–5, Wed. 10–8. Children's museum 1–5.*

☾ International Airport. Frankfurt's airport is the busiest in mainland Europe, but it is also one of Germany's leading tourist attractions. There's a display of old aircraft and a viewing platform above departure level A, and admission includes a ride on the "Sightseeing Train." Terminal 2, opened in 1994, also has a huge observation deck. The airport is just a few miles outside the city and probably the most accessible major airport in Europe (average travel time from and to Frankfurt central station is 11 minutes). The S-bahn to the airport departs every 15 minutes from track 3 at the central station. ☎ *069/30511.* ☜ *DM 7.* ☉ *9:30 AM–8 PM.*

㉒ Jüdisches Museum (Jewish Museum). Housed in the former Rothschild Palace, this museum tells the story of Frankfurt's Jewish quarter. Prior to the Holocaust it was the second largest in Germany. The museum contains extensive archives of Jewish history and culture, including a library of 5,000 books, a large photographic collection, and a documentation center. ⊠ *Untermainkai 14–15,* ☎ *069/2123–5000.* ▥ *DM 5; free Wed.* ☽ *Tues.–Sun. 10–5, Wed. 10–8.*

㉓ Karmeliterkirche (Carmelite Church and Monastery). Secularized in 1803, the church and buildings were renovated in the 1980s and now contain the **Museum für Vor- und Frügeschichte** (Museum of Prehistory and Early History). The main cloister of this former monastery houses the largest religious fresco north of the Alps, a 16th-century representation of Christ's birth and death by Jörg Ratgeb. The cloister's *Galerie im Karmeliterkloster* displays rotating exhibitions of modern art and the largest religious fresco north of the Alps. *Galerie im Karmeliterkloster:* ⊠ *Münzgasse 9.* ▥ *DM 3.* ☽ *Tues.–Sun. 11–6. Museum für Vor-und Frühgeschichte:* ⊠ *Karmelitergasse 1,* ☎ *069/2123–5896.* ▥ *DM 5; free Wed.* ☽ *Tues. and Thurs.–Sun. 10–5, Wed. 10–8.*

❽ Katharinenkirche (St. Katherine's Church). This church was originally built between 1678 and 1681, the first independent Protestant church in the Gothic style. It was in the original church here that the first Protestant sermon was preached in Frankfurt, in 1522. Goethe was confirmed here. Step inside to see the simple, postwar stained glass. ⊠ *Corner of An der Hauptwache and Katherinenpfad.* ☽ *Daily 10–5.*

⓰ Kuhhirtenturm (Shepherd's Tower). This is the last of nine towers, built in the 15th century, that formed part of Sachsenhausen's fortifications. The composer Paul Hindemith lived in the tower from 1923 to 1927 while working at the Frankfurt Opera.

⓯ Leonhardskirche (St. Leonard's Church). This beautifully preserved 13th-century building with five naves has some fine old stained glass. The hanging "pending vaulting" (a hanging, ornately carved piece of the ceiling vault) was already a major Frankfurt tourist attraction during the 17th century. ⊠ *Corner of Leonhardstr. and Untermainkai.* ☽ *Wed., Fri., and Sat. 10–noon and 3–6; Tues. and Thurs. 10–noon and 3–6:30; Sun. 9–1 and 3–6.*

❻ Liebfrauenkirche (Church of Our Lady). Dating from the 14th century, this late-Gothic church still has a fine tympanum relief over the south door and ornate rococo wood carvings inside. Outside there is also a delightful rococo fountain. ⊠ *Corner of Liebfrauenstr. and Bleidenstr.*

Messe (Exhibition Halls). This huge complex of buildings hosts some of the most important trade fairs in the world. In addition to the two major fairs in spring and fall, among the more important smaller ones are the Automobile Show in March, the Fur Fair at Easter, and the International Book Fair in early fall. ⊠ *Ludwig-Erhard-Anlage 1,* ☎ *069/75750.*

⓱ Museum für Kunsthandwerk (Museum of Decorative Arts). The American architect Richard Meier designed this museum, which opened in 1985. Here more than 30,000 objects, representing European and Asian handicrafts, are exhibited in displays with changing themes, including furniture, glassware, and porcelain. ⊠ *Schaumainkai 17,* ☎ *069/2123–5896.* ▥ *DM 8; free Wed.* ☽ *Tues. and Thurs.–Sun. 10–5, Wed. 10–8.*

⓬ Museum für Moderne Kunst (Museum of Modern Art). Housed in a distinctive triangular building designed by Austrian architect Hans Hollein, this collection features American pop art and works by such German artists as Gerhard Richter and Joseph Beuys. The distinctive triangular building was designed by Austrian architect Hans Holbein. ⊠ *Domstr. 10,* ☎ *069/2123–5896.* ▥ *DM 7.* ☽ *Tues. and Thurs.–Sun. 10–5, Wed. 10–8.*

Museum für Völkerkunde (Ethnological Museum). The exhibits depict the lifestyles and customs of aboriginal societies from different parts of the world. The collection includes masks, ritual objects, and jewelry. ⊠ *Schaumainkai 29,* ☎ *069/2123–5391.* ▣ *DM 4.* ⊙ *Tues. and Thurs.–Sun. 10–5, Wed. 10–8.*

🐣 **28** **Naturkundemuseum Senckenberg** (Natural History Museum). Fossils, animals, plants, and geological exhibits are all displayed in an exciting, hands-on environment. The most important single exhibit is the diplodocus dinosaur, imported from New York, the only complete specimen of its kind in Europe. Many of the exhibitions on prehistoric animals have been designed partly with children in mind. ⊠ *Senckenberganlage 25,* ☎ *069/75420.* ▣ *DM 5.* ⊙ *Mon., Tues., Thurs., and Fri. 9–5; Wed. 9–8; weekends 9–6.*

3 **Nikolaikirche** (St. Nicholas's Church). This small red sandstone church dates from the late 13th century. Try to time your visit to coincide with the chimes of the glockenspiel carillon, which ring out three times a day. It's a wonderful sound. ⊠ *South side of Römerberg. Carillon chimes daily at 9, noon, and 5.* ⊙ *Mon.–Sat. 10–5.*

Ostzeile. This row of carefully restored half-timbered houses dates from the 15th and 16th centuries. They are an excellent example of how the people of Frankfurt have begun, albeit belatedly, to take seriously the reconstruction of their historic buildings. ⊠ *East side of Römerberg.*

🐣 **27** **Palmengarten und Botanischer Garten** (Tropical Garden and Botanical Gardens). A splendid cluster of tropical and semitropical greenhouses contains a wide variety of flora, including cacti, orchids, and palms. The surrounding park has many recreational facilities. There is a little lake where you can rent rowboats, a play area for children, and a wading pool. Situated between the Palmengarten and the adjoining Grüneburgpark, the botanical gardens contain a wide assortment of wild, ornamental, and rare plants from around the world. They also feature a number of special collections, including a 2½-acre rock garden as well as rose and rhododendron gardens. During most of the year there are flower shows and exhibitions; in summer, concerts are held in an outdoor music pavilion. ⊠ *Siesmayerstr. 63,* ☎ *069/2123–7856.* ▣ *DM 5.* ⊙ *Mar.–Sept., daily 9–6; Oct. and Feb., daily 9–5; Nov.–Jan., daily 9–4.*

5 **Paulskirche** (St. Paul's Church). This church was the site of the first all-German parliament meeting in 1848. The parliament lasted only a year, having achieved little more than offering the Prussian king the crown of Germany. Today the church is used mainly for formal ceremonial occasions. The building you see today, modeled loosely on the original, was rebuilt after the war in the expectation that it would become the home of the new German parliament. The German Book Dealers' annual Peace Prize is awarded in the hall, as is the Goethe Prize. ⊠ *Paulspl.* ⊙ *Daily 11–3.*

2 **Römer** (City Hall). Its gabled Gothic facade with ornate balcony is widely known as the city's official emblem. Three individual patrician buildings make up the Römer. From left to right, they are the Alt-Limpurg, the Zum Römer (from which the entire structure takes its name), and the Löwenstein. The mercantile-minded Frankfurt burghers used the complex not only for political and ceremonial purposes but also for trade fairs and other commercial ventures.

The most important events to take place in the Römer were the banquets held to celebrate the coronations of the Holy Roman emperors. These were mounted starting in 1562 in the glittering and aptly named

Kaisersaal (Imperial Hall), last used in 1792 to celebrate the election of the emperor Francis II, who would later be forced by Napoléon to abdicate. It is said that a 16-year-old Goethe posing as a waiter smuggled himself into the banquet celebrating the coronation of Emperor Joseph II to get a firsthand impression of the festivities. The most vivid description of the ceremony is contained in his book, *Dichtung und Wahrheit* (*Poetry and Truth*). When no official business is being conducted, visitors are permitted to see the impressive full-length 19th-century portraits of the 52 emperors of the Holy Roman Empire, which line the walls of the reconstructed banquet hall. ⊠ *West side of Römerberg,* ☎ *069/2123–4814.* ▦ *DM 3.* ⊙ *Tues.–Sun. 11–3; closed during official functions.*

❶ Römerberg Square. This square north of the Main River, lovingly restored after wartime bomb damage, is the historical focal point of the city. The ☞ **Römer,** the ☞ **Nikolaikirche,** the ☞ **Historiches Museum,** and the ☞ **Ostzeile** are all found here. The fine 16th-century Fountain of Justitia (Justice) stands in the center of Römerberg. At the coronation of Emperor Matthias in 1612, wine instead of water flowed from the fountain. This practice has recently been revived by the city fathers, but only for special festive occasions.

Saalhofkapelle (Saalhof Chapel). Near the Eiserner Steg (Iron Bridge) and behind the Rententurm, this small 12th-century chapel is one of the oldest buildings in the city. ⊠ *Saalgasse 31.*

★ Sachsenhausen. The old quarter of Sachsenhausen, on the south bank of the Main River, has been sensitively preserved and continues to be very popular with residents and tourists alike. The neighborhood is the home of the famous *Ebbelwei* (apple-wine or cider) taverns. A green pine wreath above the entrance tells passersby that a freshly pressed—and alcoholic—apple juice is on tap. You can eat well in these small inns, too, though the menu might need some explanation. For example, *Handkas mit Musik* does not promise music at your table. The Musik means that the cheese, or *Kas* (from Käse), will be served with raw onions, oil, vinegar, and bread and butter. Most traditional apple-wine taverns serve this specialty without a fork, and those who ask for one give themselves away as strangers.

NEED A BREAK?   Sachsenhausen has about 15 apple-wine taverns; two of the best known are **Zum Gemalten Haus** (⊠ Schweizerstr. 67) and **Lorsbacher Tal** (⊠ Grosse Rittergasse 49).

⓭ St. Bartholomäus. (Church of St. Bartholomew). Also known as the Kaiserdom (Imperial Cathedral), this impressive structure isn't really a cathedral. It was built largely between the 13th and 15th centuries and survived the bombs of World War II with most of its original treasures intact. It was built to replace an earlier church established by Charlemagne's son, Ludwig the Pious, on the present site of the Römerberg. The cathedral still contains many of its original magnificent Gothic carvings, including a life-size crucifixion group and a fine 15th-century altar. Its most impressive exterior feature is the tall, red sandstone tower (almost 300 feet high), which was added between 1415 and 1514. Excavations in front of the main entrance in 1953 revealed the remains of a Roman settlement and the foundations of a Carolingian imperial palace. ⊠ *Domstr.* ▦ *Free.* ⊙ *Apr.–Oct., Mon. 9–12:30 and 3–6, Tues.–Sun. 8–6; Nov.–Feb., daily 9–noon and 3–5.*

Schirn Kunsthalle (Schirn Art Gallery). One of Frankfurt's most modern museums houses a good collection of 20th-century art. It's located opposite St. Bartholomäus Church. ⊠ *Am Römerberg 6a,* ☎ *069/299–*

8820. ⊠ DM 6–DM 9, *depending on current exhibition.* ⊙ *Tues. and Fri.–Sun. 10–7, Wed.–Thurs. 10–10.*

NEED A
BREAK?

A designer watering hole adjoining the Schirn Art Gallery, **Schirn Café** (⊠ 6a am Roemerberg, ☎ 069/291–732) has a 120-foot-long bar that makes a perfect outpost for a drink and people-watching. The tapas-style bar food is good, and a counter in one corner sells delicious chocolates.

❷⓿ **Städelsches Kunstinstitut and Städtische Galerie** (Städel Art Institute and Municipal Gallery). Here you may find one of west Germany's most important art collections, with paintings by Dürer, Vermeer, Rembrandt, Rubens, Monet, Renoir, and other great masters. ⊠ *Schaumainkai 63,* ☎ *069/605–0980.* ⊠ *DM 8; free Wed.* ⊙ *Tues. and Thurs.–Sun. 10–5, Wed. 10–8.*

★ ❷① **Städtische Galerie Liebieghaus** (Liebieg Municipal Museum of Sculpture). The sculpture collection from different civilizations and epochs here is considered one of the most important in Europe. Some pieces are exhibited in the lovely gardens surrounding the house. ⊠ *Schaumainkai 71,* ☎ *069/2123–8617.* ⊠ *DM 5.* ⊙ *Tues. and Thurs.–Sun. 10–5, Wed. 10–8.*

⓫ **Staufenmauer.** The Staufenmauer and the Saalhofkapelle (Chapel) (near the Eiserner Steg bridge) are the two oldest parts of the medieval city in evidence today. The Staufenmauer, one of the few remaining sections of the old city's fortifications, dates from the 12th century. ⊠ *Free.* ⊙ *Saalhofkapelle Tues. and Thurs.–Sat. 10–5, Wed. 10–8, Sun. 10–5.*

Steinernes Haus (Stone House). Originally built in 1464, destroyed in World War II, and rebuilt from 1957 to 1960 with an altered interior, this Gothic-style patrician house has also served as a trading post. The Frankfurt Kunstverein (Arts Association) regularly mounts special exhibits (☎ 069/285–339 for details). ⊠ *Markt 44.* ⊠ *DM 8.* ⊙ *Tues.–Sat. noon–7.*

☙ **Struwwelpeter-Museum.** This museum contains a collection of letters, sketches, and manuscripts by Dr. Heinrich Hoffmann, physician and creator of the children's-book hero Struwwelpeter, or "Slovenly Peter," the character you see as a puppet or doll in Frankfurt's shops. ⊠ *Bendergasse 1 (Römerberg),* ☎ *069/281–333.* ⊠ *Free.* ⊙ *Tues. and Thurs.–Sun. 11–5, Wed. 11–8.*

Zeil. The heart of Frankfurt's shopping district is this ritzy pedestrian street, running east from Hauptwache Square. City officials claim it's the country's busiest shopping street, with an unrivaled annual turnover of more than 1 billion deutsche marks. The Zeil is also known as "the golden mile." (☞ Shopping, *below.*)

☙ ⓾ **Zoologischer Garten** (Zoo). Founded in 1858, this is one of the most important and attractive zoos in Europe, with many of the animals and birds living in a natural environment. Its remarkable collection includes some 5,000 animals of 600 different species, a bears' castle, an exotarium (aquarium plus reptiles), and an aviary, reputedly the largest in Europe. Many of the birds can be seen in a natural setting. In the nocturnal section you can see nighttime creatures moving about. The zoo is an ideal place for a family outing, as it also has a restaurant and a café, along with afternoon concerts in summer. ⊠ *Alfred-Brehm Pl. 16,* ☎ *069/2123–3727.* ⊠ *DM 11.* ⊙ *Mar. 31–Oct. 26, weekdays 9–7, weekends 8–7; Oct. 27–Dec. and Jan.–Mar. 30, daily 9–5.*

OFF THE
BEATEN PATH

EUROPATURM (Telecommunications Tower) – At 332 meters (1,090 feet), this is the highest tower in Western Europe and the fourth highest in the world. For the best view of Frankfurt take the lift to the viewing platform of the television tower. At the 730-foot level there's a spectacular son-et-lumière show; one floor below that is a classy restaurant named Windows. Europaturn is northwest of the Old Town; take the U-bahn 1, 2, or 3 to Dornbush station, then tram 34 going west. ⊠ *Wilhelm-Epstein-Str. 20, Ginnheim.*

SECKBACH – In this district north of the city, Frankfurters like to visit the 590-foot Lohrberg Hill, as the climb yields a fabulous view of the town and the Taunus, Spessart, and Odenwald hills. Along the way you'll also see the last remaining vineyard within Frankfurt, the Seckbach Vineyard. *Take the U–4 subway to Seckbacher Landstr., then Bus 43 or 38.*

STADTWALD (City Forest) – With its innumerable paths and trails, bird sanctuaries, and sports facilities, the Stadtwald is used by citizens and visitors alike for recreation and relaxation. The forest is threaded with lovely paths and trails and contains one of Germany's most impressive sports stadiums. Of particular interest is the Waldehrpfad—a trail leading past a series of rare trees, each identified by a small sign. The Stadtwald was the first place in Europe where trees were planted from seed (they were oaks, sown in 1398), and there are still many extremely old trees in evidence. In addition to bird sanctuaries and wild-animal enclosures, the forest also has a number of good restaurants and is a pleasant place in which to eat and linger. *Take Bus 36 from Konstablerwache to Hainer Weg.*

DINING

For any of the fancier restaurants in Frankfurt, you're advised to make reservations well in advance.

$$$$ ★ ✗ **Avocado.** Huge arrangements of fresh flowers make this classy restaurant as ideal for a romantic dinner as for a business lunch. The fine bistro food with truly excellent service doesn't hurt either. Recent offerings included guinea fowl baked in a potato coating and served in a sherry sauce. ⊠ *Hochstr. 27,* ☎ *069/292–867. AE, MC, V. Closed Sun.*

$$$$ ✗ **Erno's Bistro.** Erno's is something of a Frankfurt institution. It's small and chic—*very* popular with visiting power brokers—and offers classy French cuisine. Fish dishes predominate—all the fish is flown in daily, most of it from France—with specialties varying according to what's available in the markets that day. This is one of those rare restaurants where you can sit back and let the staff—all the waiters speak English—choose your meal for you. ⊠ *Liebigstr. 15,* ☎ *069/721–997. Reservations essential. Jacket and tie. AE, DC, MC, V. Closed weekends, 1 wk at Easter, and mid-June–mid-July.*

$$$$ ✗ **Papillon.** Although it's part of the airport Sheraton, the Papillon has won over the country's most respected food critics—who agree that this is Germany's best airport restaurant. No whisper of a jet engine can be heard, and there's no rush or bustle in the velvety, luxurious dining room. Kitchen manager Klaus Bohler concentrates on a small but vividly imaginative daily changing menu, on which you'll find such delicacies as rolled pike perch coated in wild rice or lamb fillet served with eggplant baked in a sour-cream dough. ⊠ *Sheraton Hotel, Frankfurt Airport (Terminal Mitte),* ☎ *069/6977–1238. Jacket and tie. AE, DC, MC, V. Closed Sun. No lunch Sat.*

302

Altes Zollhaus, **12**
Avocado, **4**
Bistro 77, **19**
Börsenkeller, **5**
Brückenkeller, **14**
Cafe GegenwART, **13**
Cafe Karin, **8**
Charlot, **3**
Erno's Bistro, **2**
Germania, **18**
Gilde Stuben, **11**
Jaspers, **16**
Melange, **1**
Papillon, **20**
Restaurant Français, **6**
Steinernes Haus, **10**
Tequila, **9**
Wolkenbruch, **17**
Zum Gemalten
Haus, **15**
Zur Müllerin, **7**

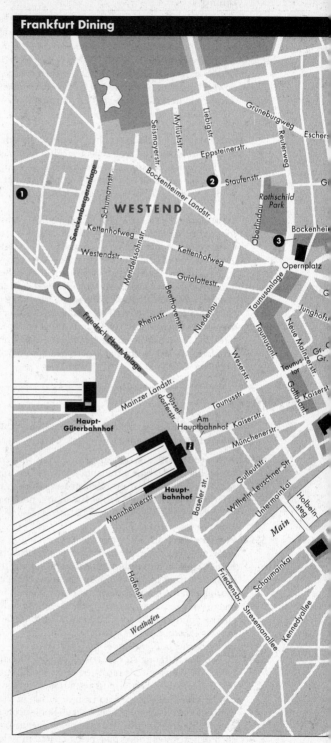

Frankfurt Dining

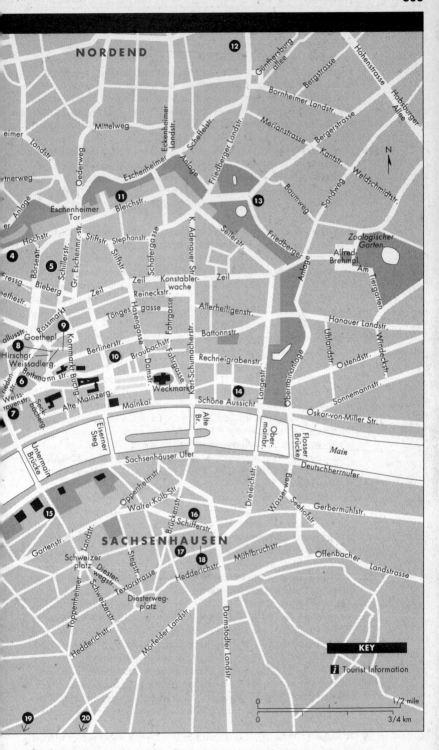

$$$$ ✕ **Restaurant Français.** The crystal chandeliers, tapestries on the walls,
★   and green-and-gold surroundings of this restaurant of the incomparably luxurious Steigenberger Hotel Frankfurter Hof provide an appropriately sumptuous setting for some of the finest food in Frankfurt. The food is French (of course), traditional rather than nouvelle, and served with the sort of panache you might expect in one of the best restaurants in Paris. For a memorable gastronomic treat, try the stuffed quail in truffle butter sauce. ✉ *Am Kaiserpl.,* ☎ *069/215–865. Reservations essential. Jacket and tie. AE, DC, MC, V. Closed Sun., Mon., and 4 wks in July or Aug. No lunch Sat.*

$$$ ✕ **Altes Zollhaus.** Within this beautiful, 200-year-old half-timbered house you can enjoy very good traditional German specialties. Try one of the game dishes, or the sliced pork with mushrooms in apple-wine sauce. In summer you can eat outside while chefs grill in the huge garden. ✉ *Friedberger Landstr. 531,* ☎ *069/472–707. AE, DC, MC, V. Closed Mon. No lunch.*

$$$ ✕ **Bistrot 77.** Proprietor-chef Dominique, who learned his trade in the French Alsace, serves outstanding food in this spare bistro with plain walls and a tile floor. The accent is on fresh vegetables and fine cuts of meat, such as rosettes of lamb with young runner beans. Various special dinners are offered during the week—bouillabaisse on Tuesdays, a three-course regional meal on Thursdays—and there's always one three-course lunch for DM 48. ✉ *Ziegelhüttenweg 1–3,* ☎ *069/614–040. AE, MC, V. Closed Sun.*

$$$ ✕ **Brückenkeller.** Sophisticated dining in Frankfurt isn't just a matter
★   of refined French food in expense-account restaurants. This establishment offers magnificent German specialties in the sort of time-honored arched cellar that would have brought a lump to Bismarck's throat. What's more, though the food may be unmistakably Teutonic, it's light and delicate—for example, cream of cucumber soup, or veal in tomato vinaigrette. In addition to the terrific antiques-strewn surroundings and the classy food, there's a phenomenal range of wines to choose from: The cellars—don't be shy about asking to see them—hold around 85,000 bottles. ✉ *Schützenstr. 6,* ☎ *069/284–238. Jacket and tie. AE, DC, MC, V. Closed Sun. No lunch.*

$$ ✕ **Börsenkeller.** The dark (some would say masculine) atmosphere of this restaurant reflects its favored status among workers from the nearby stock exchange. Soft lighting, heavy arches, and high-back booths establish the mood. The food is traditional and substantial, though always prepared with some style. See if venison stew is on the day's menu. ✉ *Schillerstr. 11,* ☎ *069/281–115. AE, DC, MC, V. Closed Sun. No dinner Sat.*

$$ ✕ **Charlot.** The French cuisine of this very popular restaurant has acquired an Italian touch since the arrival of Chef Mario, but it has survived the transition well. The Alte Oper is just across the street, so after the curtain falls you'll be fighting with the music buffs for a place in the French bistro–style dining rooms, spread over two floors. But you might also be sharing a table with Luciano Pavarotti. ✉ *Opernpl. 10,* ☎ *069/287–007. AE, DC, MC, V. No lunch Sun.*

$$ ✕ **Gilde Stuben.** This is a lusty Bohemian beer tavern with a spacious beer garden overlooking a park. Sample such Czech dishes as *Svickova* (smoked beef and cranberry sauce with juicy dumplings). Wash your choice down with genuine Pilsener Urquell and Budvar beers. ✉ *Bleichstr. 38,* ☎ *069/283–228. AE, DC, MC, V.*

$$ ✕ **Jaspers.** Although this is technically a French restaurant, the food
★   is very Germanic because it serves Alsatian specialties. The service and cooking set a standard that puts many better known and more expensive restaurants to shame. The simple dining room has white-painted, unadorned walls and wooden tables, and there's a small courtyard for

summer evenings. Try the fish soup with croutons, mushroom crepes, snails in calvados sauce over spinach, Wiener schnitzel with roast potatoes and salad, and Muenster cheese. The good wine list is definitely affordable. ⊠ *Schifferstr. 8 (just off Affentorpl.), Sachsenhausen,* ☎ *069/614–117. AE, MC, V. Closed Sun.*

$$ ✕ **Wolkenbruch.** The name of the restaurant means "Cloud Burst," a rather dramatic description for a place that serves whole-grain pizza, tofu burgers, vegetable frittata, and organic wine. The Scandinavian-style furniture is certainly comfy, and you'll appreciate the courteous service. It's one of Frankfurt's best vegetarian restaurants. ⊠ *Textorstr. 26,* ☎ *069/622–612. Reservations essential. No credit cards. No lunch weekdays.*

$$ ✕ **Zur Müllerin.** The *Müllerin* (miller's wife) is Lieselotte Müller, who has been running this restaurant since the 1950s. Her regulars are artists and actors from the nearby theaters; expressions of appreciation for their beloved Müllerin's cooking skills decorate the restaurant walls. ⊠ *Weissfrauenstr. 18,* ☎ *069/285–182. AE, DC, MC, V. No lunch weekends.*

$ ✕ **Cafe GegenwART.** *Gegenwart* means "the present," and the emphasis on the second syllable means regularly changing exhibitions by local artists on the walls of this friendly, noisy café-restaurant. It's frequented by a young crowd, and in the summer diners spill out onto the pavement, where Riviera-style tables brighten up the scene. There's a French accent on the menu, too—the tomato fondue is a dream. ⊠ *Berger Str. 6,* ☎ *069/497–0544. No credit cards.*

$ ✕ **Cafe Karin.** This understated café has flair and attracts an interesting slice of Frankfurt life. This is great place to breakfast (for only a few marks); also come here to recover from a shopping spree or to eat something healthy in preparation for a night out. Sample the goat cheese salad or whole-grain ratatouille crepes. Cakes and baked goods come from the whole-grain bakery next door. There is a no-smoking section. ⊠ *28 Grosser Hirschgraben,* ☎ *069/295–217. No credit cards.*

$ ✕ **Germania.** In a city not known for sentimentality, customers feel
★ affectionate toward Germania, one of Sachsenhausen's most authentic apple-cider taverns, in a courtyard off Textorstrasse. All the guests sit at long wooden tables in an open room. Waves of conviviality in a confined space, accompanied by a lot of elbow rubbing and raised glasses, create a flow of feeling known in German as *Gemuetlichkeit*. It's noisy, smoky, claustrophobic, and a lot of fun, with good traditional food such as *Rippchen mit Kraut* (herbed pork ribs) and *Handkäse mit Musik* (cheese and onions). There's great cider but absolutely no beer! ⊠ *Textorstr. 16, Sachsenhausen,* ☎ *069/613–336. Reservations not accepted. No credit cards. Closed Mon.*

$ ✕ **Melange.** Inexpensive but imaginative dishes from a daily changing menu are served up on pink-lined decked tables to students and professors from the nearby university. This is one place where vegetarians are not in the minority—there is an unusually good selection of vegetarian food and meatless Italian appetizers. In summer a boulevard terrace opens for business. ⊠ *Jordanstr. 19,* ☎ *069/701–287. No credit cards.*

$ ✕ **Steinernes Haus.** Here's a piece of Frankfurt's history and the perfect place to take your German grandmother if you have one. The diners sit like schoolchildren at long wooden tables beneath prints of old Frankfurt and traditional clothing mounted on the walls. The house specialty is a rump steak brought to the table uncooked with a heated rock tablet on which it is prepared. The beef broth is the perfect antidote to cold weather. The menu has other old German standards along with daily specials. If you don't specify a *Kleines,* or small glass of beer, you'll automatically get a liter mug. Traditional fare popular with locals includes *Frankfurter Rippchen* (smoked pork) and *Zigeuner-hackbraten* (spicy meat loaf). ⊠ *Braubachstr. 35,* ☎ *069/283–491. Reservations not accepted. No credit cards.*

$ ✕ **Tequila.** Beef and vegetarian burritos, a choice of 46 kinds of tequila, and *Apfel* (apple) strudel with vanilla ice cream: What more could you want at midnight in the center of Frankfurt? All you have to do is get the attention of one of the four pretty and busy young waitresses. It helps to wear a sombrero. ⊠ *Weissadlergasse 5,* ☎ *069/287–142. No credit cards.*

$ ✕ **Zum Gemalten Haus.** This is the real thing—a traditional apple-wine
★   tavern in the heart of Sachsenhausen. Its name means "At the Painted House," a reference to the frescoes that cover the walls inside and out. In summer the courtyard is the place to be; in winter you sit in the noisy tavern proper at long tables with benches. It's often crowded, so if there isn't room when you arrive, order a glass of apple cider and hang around until someone leaves. Traditional cider-tavern dishes include *Rippchen* (smoked pork), but come here for *Rinderselcher* (smoked beef). ⊠ *Schweizerstr. 67,* ☎ *069/614–559. Reservations not accepted. No credit cards. Closed Mon.–Tues.*

LODGING

Businesspeople descend on Frankfurt year-round, so most hotels in the city are expensive (though many also offer significant reductions on weekends, an option worth checking out) and are frequently booked up well in advance. The majority of the larger hotels are around the main train station, close to the business district and the trade-fair center and a 15- to 20-minute walk from the Old Town. Many hotels add as much as a 50% surcharge during trade fairs (*Messen*), of which there are generally about 30 a year. Some dates to avoid (unless you intend to visit one of the fairs in question) are: January 8–11 (Home Textiles); January 25–29 (Premiere); February 15–19 (Ambiente); June 8–14 (Achema); August 23–27 (Autumn International Fair); September 11–21 (IAA); and the Frankfurt Book Fair October 15–20. These dates may change, so it's best to confirm them with the German-American Chamber of Commerce (☎ 212/974–8830; in London, 0171/734–0543) or the local tourist office.

$$$$ 🏢 **An der Messe.** This little place, whose name means "at the fair-
★   grounds," is a pleasing change from the giant hotels of the city. It's stylish, with a distinctive pink marble lobby and chicly appointed bedrooms. The staff is courteously efficient. The only drawback is the absence of a restaurant. ⊠ *Westendstr. 104, D–60325 Frankfurt am Main,* ☎ *069/747–979,* 🖷 *069/748–349. 46 rooms with bath. Parking. AE, DC, MC, V.*

$$$$ 🏢 **Arabella Grand Hotel.** The emphasis at this recent addition to Frankfurt's list of luxury hotels is on the "grand." Everything is large-scale, from the palatial public rooms to the vast double bedrooms. The center-city location means many rooms have views of backyards and parking lots, but pull the heavy drapes and it's a world of understated luxury. ⊠ *Konrad-Adenauer-Str. 7, D–60313 Frankfurt am Main,* ☎ *069/29810,* 🖷 *069/298–1810. 378 rooms with bath, 11 suites. 2 restaurants, bar, pool, beauty parlor, sauna, fitness center, parking. AE, DC, MC, V.*

$$$$ 🏢 **Dorint Hotel.** The Frankfurt member of the Dorint chain is a mod-ern, well-appointed hotel with all the comfort and facilities expected from this well-run group—including a palm-fringed indoor pool. The hotel is south of the river in the Niederrad district, but there are good bus and subway connections with the city center and Sachsenhausen.

✉ *Hahnstr. 9, D–60492 Frankfurt am Main,* ☎ *069/663–060,* FAX *069/6630–6600. 183 rooms (29 reserved for nonsmokers), 8 suites. Restaurant, 2 bars, indoor pool, sauna, parking. AE, DC, MC, V.*

$$$$ 🏨 **Hessischer Hof.** This is the choice of many businesspeople, not just
★ because of its location opposite the trade-fair building but for the air of class and style that pervades its handsome and imposing interior (the exterior is nondescript). The public rooms are subdued and traditional; bedrooms are elegantly chic, and many of them are furnished with antiques. The restaurant features excellent nouvelle cuisine; it also has a fine display of Sevres porcelain arranged around the walls. ✉ *Friedrich-Ebert-Anlage 40, D–60325 Frankfurt am Main,* ☎ *069/75400,* FAX *069/754–0924. 106 rooms and 11 suites with bath. Restaurant, 2 bars, parking. AE, DC, MC, V.*

$$$$ 🏨 **Hotel Gravenbruch Kempinski.** The atmosphere of the 16th-century
★ manor house, which this elegant, sophisticated hotel was built around, still remains at this parkland sight, a 15-minute drive south of the downtown area. It's a combination of substantial modern luxury with Old World charm that works. All the rooms are spacious and classy and have views of the lake or the park. Six of Germany's finest golf courses are nearby. ✉ *D–63263 Neu Isenberg,* ☎ *06102/5050,* FAX *06102/505– 445. 288 rooms and 29 suites with bath. 2 restaurants, bar, indoor and outdoor pools, beauty salon, massage, sauna, tennis, convention center. AE, DC, MC, V.*

$$$$ 🏨 **Palmenhof.** Named for its proximity to the botanical garden, Palmengarten, this luxuriously modernized hotel occupies a renovated Art Deco *Jugendstil* (German Art Nouveau) building in Frankfurt's West End. The high-ceiling rooms have up-to-date comfort but retain the elegance of the old building. In the basement is a cozy restaurant, the Bastei, with an expensive nouvelle menu. ✉ *Bockenheimer Landstr. 89–91, D–60325 Frankfurt am Main,* ☎ *069/753–0060,* FAX *069/7530– 0666. 47 rooms with bath, 40 apartments. Restaurant, parking. AE, DC, MC, V.*

$$$$ 🏨 **Parkhotel.** A member of the Forte chain, this is a businessperson's favorite, conveniently located just across from the train station. The structure successfully fuses the original 19th-century red-stone building and a postwar addition. It was renovated between 1989 and 1995. ✉ *Wiesenhüttenpl. 28–38, D–60329 Frankfurt am Main,* ☎ *069/26970,* FAX *069/2697884. 300 rooms with bath. 2 restaurants, bar, weinstube, sauna, fitness room. AE, DC, MC, V.*

$$$$ 🏨 **Steigenberger Frankfurter Hof.** The combination of an Old Town
★ location, an imposing 19th-century Renaissance-style building, and full-bodied luxury makes this the leading choice for many visitors. The atmosphere throughout is one of old-fashioned, formal elegance, with burnished woods, fresh flowers, and a thick-carpeted hush. The Restaurant Français is among the gourmet high spots of Germany; the bar is a classy late-night rendezvous. ✉ *Am Kaiserpl., D–60311 Frankfurt am Main,* ☎ *069/21502,* FAX *069/215–900. 347 rooms and 10 suites with bath. 4 restaurants, 2 bars. AE, DC, MC, V.*

$$$ 🏨 **Liebig.** A comfortable, family-run hotel, this establishment has spacious, high-ceiling rooms and a friendly feel. Ask for a room at the back— it's much quieter. ✉ *Liebigstr. 45, D–60323 Frankfurt am Main,* ☎ *069/727–551,* FAX *069/727–555. 20 rooms with bath. Restaurant. AE, MC, DC, V.*

$$$ 🏨 **Schwille.** Frankfurt's famous *Fressgasse* is right outside the door, although you don't have to venture too far in search of culinary attractions; the Schwille itself has an excellent café-restaurant that's so popular among the locals that it opens at six in the morning to cater to early risers. Despite the hotel's central location, its rooms are quiet. They are dark wood–toned, decorated with pleasing floral prints, but

308

Frankfurt Lodging

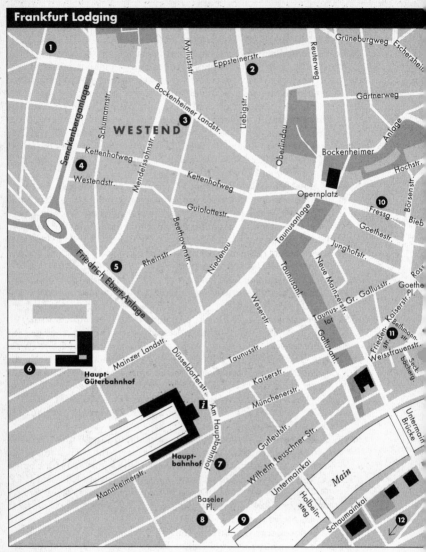

An der Messe, **4**
Arabella Grand
Hotel, **13**
Attache, **6**
Dorint Hotel, **12**
Hessischer Hof, **5**
Hotel Gravenbruch
Kempinski, **15**
Hotel Ibis Frankfurt
Friedensbrüke, **8**
Hotel-Pension
West, **1**

Hotelschiff *Peter
Schlott*, **9**
Liebig, **2**
Maingau, **14**
Palmenhof, **3**
Parkhotel, **7**
Schwille, **10**
Steigenberger
Frankfurter Hof, **11**
Waldhotel Hensels
Felsenkeller, **16**

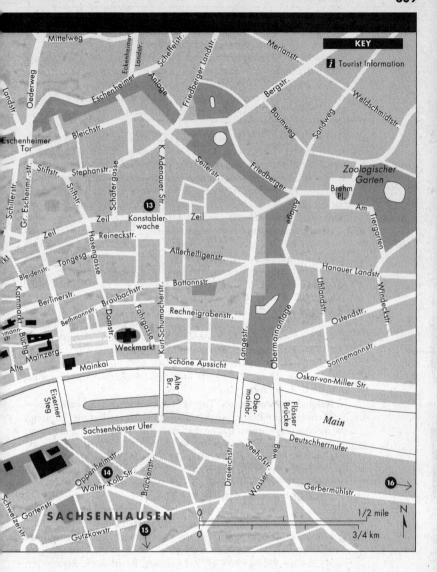

Mittelweg

Oederweg

Landstr.

Eschenheimer Landstr.

Scheffelstr.

Eschenheimer Anlage

Merianstr.

Bergstr.

Baumweg

Sandweg

Weldschmidtstr.

Eschenheimer Tor

Bleichstr.

Friedberger Landstr.

Stiftstr.

Stephanstr.

Schäfergasse

K. Adenauer Str.

Seilerstr.

Friedberger Anlage

Zoologischer Garten

Brehm Pl.

Am Tiergarten

Schillerstr.

Gr. Eschenmr.-str.

Stiftstr.

13

Zeil

Konstabler-wache

Zeil

Zeil

Reineckstr.

Hasengasse

Tongesg.

Allerheiligenstr.

Hanauer Landstr.

Uhlandstr.

Ostendstr.

Windeckstr.

Bleidenstr.

Berlinerstr.

Braubachstr.

Bethmannstr.

Domstr.

Battonnstr.

Rechneigrabenstr.

Obermainanlage

Sonnemannstr.

Kormarkt

Buchg.

mann-str.

Weckmarkt

Kurt-Schumacherstr.

Fahrgasse

Langestr.

Alte Mainzerg.

Mainkai

Schöne Aussicht

Oskar-von-Miller Str.

Alte Br.

Eiserner Steg

Ober-mainbr.

Flösser Brücke

Main

Sachsenhäuser Ufer

Deutschherrnufer

Oppenheimstr.

14

Walter-Kolb-Str.

Brückenstr.

Dreieichstr.

Seehofstr.

Wasser

Dem.

Gerbermühlstr.

16 →

SACHSENHAUSEN

Schweizerstr.

Gartenstr.

0 | 1/2 mile

0 | 3/4 km

N ↑

Gutzkowstr.

15
↓

on the small side. ⊠ *Grosse Bockenheimerstr. 50, D–60313 Frankfurt am Main,* ☎ *069/920–100,* 𝕱𝕬𝕏 *069/9201–0999. 51 rooms with shower or bath. Restaurant, parking. AE, DC, MC, V.*

$$ 🏨 **Attache.** This simple but comfortable downtown hotel has no restaurant, but a buffet breakfast provides a hearty start to the day. Rooms are comfortably if unspectacularly furnished and have such amenities as color TV. ⊠ *Kölnerstr. 10, D–60327 Frankfurt am Main,* ☎ *069/730282,* 𝕱𝕬𝕏 *069/7392194. 46 rooms with shower or bath. Bar. AE, MC, V.*

$$ 🏨 **Hotel Ibis Frankfurt Friedensbrüke.** This modern hotel was recently acquired by the Ibis chain, known for providing modern comfort at affordable prices. Ask for a room overlooking the River Main and you'll have a good view and a convenient location: near the main railway station and downtown Frankfurt. ⊠ *Speicherstr. 3–5, D–60327 Frankfurt am Main,* ☎ *069/273–030,* 𝕱𝕬𝕏 *069/237–024. 233 rooms with bath. Restaurant, bar, parking. AE, DC, MC, V.*

$$ 🏨 **Hotel-Pension West.** For home comforts, a handy location (close to
★ the university), and good value, try this family-run pension. It's in an older building and scores high for old-fashioned appeal. The rooms are hardly luxurious, but they're more than adequate for a night or two. ⊠ *Gräfstr. 81, D–60486 Frankfurt am Main,* ☎ *069/247–9020,* 𝕱𝕬𝕏 *069/707–5309. 20 rooms with shower. AE, DC, MC, V.*

$$ 🏨 **Maingau.** This excellent-value hotel is within easy reach of the downtown area, close to the lively Sachsenhausen quarter and its cheery apple-wine taverns. Rooms are basic but clean and comfortable, and all have TVs. Families with children are welcome. The room rate includes a substantial breakfast buffet. ⊠ *Schifferstr. 38–40, D–60594 Frankfurt am Main,* ☎ *069/617–001,* 𝕱𝕬𝕏 *069/620–790. 100 rooms with bath. Restaurant, parking. AE, MC.*

$ 🏨 **Hotelschiff Peter Schlott.** This is Frankfurt's most unusual hotel— a riverboat moored near Höchst. Few comforts are lacking, although the rooms are unsurprisingly on the small side. Still, they offer fine views of the Main River, which laps outside the portholes. Caution is advised when guests return home after a night out in Frankfurt. ⊠ *Mainberg, D–65929 Frankfurt am Main,* ☎ *069/315–480,* 𝕱𝕬𝕏 *069/307–671. 19 rooms, half with shower. Restaurant, parking. AE, MC.*

$ 🏨 **Waldhotel Hensels Felsenkeller.** Helmut Braun's traditional old hotel backs onto the woods that ring Frankfurt, yet the city center is just a 15-minute train ride away (the nearest stop is a three-minute walk). Rooms are quite basic, but there are plans to modernize them and add more amenities. ⊠ *Buchrainstr. 95, D–60599 Frankfurt am Main,* ☎ *069/652–086,* 𝕱𝕬𝕏 *069/658–379. 15 rooms, 7 with bath. Restaurant, parking. MC.*

NIGHTLIFE AND THE ARTS

Nightlife

Frankfurt, for all its unabashed internationalism and sophisticated expense-account living, is unlikely to win many votes as Germany's premier after-hours town. Most of the larger hotels have bars, discos, and nightclubs. There's little to distinguish them from thousands of similar haunts the world over, but they're tried and tested. True, Frankfurt also has a red-light district, centered on the tawdry streets around the train station, though it's hardly in the same league as Hamburg's Reeperbahn.

For more genuinely local nightlife, head across the river to **Sachsenhausen,** Frankfurt's "Left Bank." It's hardly the quaint old bohemian quarter it likes to bill itself as, but for bars, discos, clubs, and beer and wine restaurants, this is about the best place to try. If you're in search of a rowdy night out, check out the **Apfelwein** (cider) taverns—some of them are touristy, but they're still fun. A green wreath above the door identifies them. If Sachsenhausen doesn't agree with you, try the ever-more-fashionable district of **Bornheim,** northeast of downtown. It has an almost equal number of bars, clubs, and the like, but the atmosphere is less forced, more authentic.

Bars and Nightclubs

Cooky's (⊠ Am Salzhaus 4, ☎ 069/287–662) is one of the most popular local haunts for listening to rock music; live bands perform on Monday night. You can also dance and have a meal. It's open nightly until 4 AM. If you're seeking something soothing, try the **Casablanca Bar** (⊠ Parkhotel, Wiesenhüttenpl. 28, ☎ 069/26970) for piano music and a little crooning. It's open Monday–Saturday 8 PM–2 AM. **Jimmy's Bar** (⊠ Friedrich-Ebert-Anlage 40, ☎ 069/614–559), in the Hessischer Hof Hotel, is classy—and expensive. It's a favorite with high-flying executives and other big spenders but attracts local color as well. Irish pub **An Sibin** (⊠ Wallstr. 9, ☎ 069/603–2159) is in a cellar decorated with wagons and pushcarts, presumably to remind you of the Emerald Island's folksy character. There is live music most nights along with Guinness right out of the keg and some good pub grub. Serious elbow lifting and heartfelt conversations take place in English, Gaelic, Hessian dialect, and German. It's closed Sunday. **Al Andalus** (⊠ Affentorpl. 1, ☎ 069/617–032) is known far and wide for flamenco. The Andalusian owner, Catalina Romero, prides herself on presenting the "real thing"—serious Spanish musicians and dancers from the land of Lorca, bullfights, and Gypsies. Admission is charged for the better-known acts. Good tapas are served. It's closed Sunday and Monday.

Discos

Dorian Gray (☎ 069/690–2212) may be the best disco in the city. Bizarre as it may seem, it's at the airport. It's easily reached by S-bahn, and is in Section C, Level O. It attracts a surprisingly upscale crowd and has loud music and soft lights. Dance temple **Funkadelic** (⊠ Broennerstr. 11, ☎ 069/283–808) is one of the hottest crossroads of funk and reggae in Frankfurt's nightlife. Try to come before midnight on weekends; it gets very crowded. **Fantasy Garden** (⊠ Seilerstr. 34, ☎ 069/285–055) is a bistro–café–dance club–bar with Asian-Egyptian-California atmosphere. Drinks have names like "Sex on the Beach" and "Orgasmus" and mescal is served with a worm. California-style food leans toward salads and vegetables (served until midnight). There is a terrace for cooling off. **Nachtleben** (Night Life: ⊠ Kurt Schumacher Str. 45, ☎ 069/20650) has a disco in the basement and café-bar upstairs. If you are over 20, you should probably skip the disco. But upstairs is a good place to end up at the very end of the night; the service is still awake, and the café attracts a diverse contingent of Frankfurters and foreigners who refuse to let the night die young. Both the disco and the café are closed Monday.

Jazz

Der Frankfurter Jazzkeller (⊠ Kleine Bockenheimer Str. 18a, (☎ 069/288–537) is the oldest jazz cellar in Germany, founded by legendary trumpeter Carlo Bohländer. It offers hot, modern jazz, often free (but the cover charge for some performances is around DM 25). **Schlachthof** (⊠ Deutschherrnufer 36, ☎ 069/623–201) is the place for Dixieland jazz, although it's scheduled to move in the near future. **Sinkkasten** (⊠ Brönnerstr. 5–9, ☎ 069/280–385) celebrated its 25th birthday in 1996. The club is still a class act and a great place for jazz, rock, pop, and African music; it's sometimes hard to get in but worth the effort for serious fans. It's closed Monday. **Jazz-Life Podium** (⊠ Kleine Rittergasse 22–26, ☎ 069/626–346) has been around for a few years and has kept its personality and following intact. There is live music by national and international groups daily. The program is often jazz, but, depending on the evening, you may also hear rock, beat, romantic-punk, or pop music. Although admission is usually free, an *Aufschlag* (extra charge) is added to the price of each drink. It's closed Sunday. **Dreikoenigskeller** (⊠ Faerberstr. 71, ☎ 069/629–273) fills up with jazz and jazz enthusiasts as well as smoke. Anything can happen, and you might hear '40s or '50s jazz, blues, funk, rock-wave, or indie-punk. It's patronized mostly by students, as well as by plenty of older, mature-but-hip people. It's closed Monday.

The Arts

Frankfurt has the largest budget for cultural expenditure of any city in the country. Unfortunately, economic recession hit the city hard, and in 1994 it also had the highest debt of any German city. This meant introducing or raising admission fees for city museums and reducing the number of opera performances. Still, what you *can* see is likely to be first-rate. The **Städtische Bühnen**—municipal theaters, including the city's opera company—are the leading venues. Frankfurt also has what is probably the most lavish theater in the country, the **Alte Oper** (Old Opera House), a magnificently ornate heap that was rebuilt and reopened in 1981 after near-total destruction in the war. However, the building is used mainly for classical concerts rather than opera performances.

Theater tickets can be purchased from the tourist office at Römerberg 27 and from all theaters. Alternatively, try the **Kartenvorverkauf am Liebfrauenberg** (⊠ Liebfrauenberg 52–54, ☎ 069/293–131), the ticket office in the **Hertie** department store (⊠ Zeil 90, ☎ 069/294–848), or **Kartenkiosk Sandrock** (⊠ Hauptwache Passage, ☎ 069/20115/6). Call for information about concerts (☎ 069/11517). Pick up a copy of the twice-monthly listings magazine *Frankfurter Wochenschau* from any tourist office.

Concerts and Opera

The most glamorous venue for classical-music concerts is the **Alte Oper** (Old Opera) (⊠ Opernpl. ☎ 069/134–0405 or 069/134–0406). Even if you don't go to a performance, it's worth having a look at the ponderous and ornate lobby, an example of 19th-century classicism at its most self-confident. Under conductor Sylvain Cambreling, the **Frankfurt Opera** is making a new name for itself as a company for dramatic artistry, while the **Frankfurt Ballet**, directed by William Forsythe, is world renowned. Both perform at the **Städtische Bühnen** (⊠ Willy-Brandt-Pl.).

The **Festhalle** (☎ 069/75750) at the trade-fair building is the scene of many rock concerts and other large-scale spectaculars.

Theater

If you speak German, you can understand the highbrow drama at the **Kammerspiele** (⊠ Hofstr. 2, ☎ 069/2123–7444) or the municipally owned **Schauspiel,** or Playhouse (⊠ Willy-Brandt-Pl., ☎ 069/2123–7444), and lighter fare at **Die Komödie** (⊠ Neue Mainzer Str. 18, ☎ 069/284–580). For a zany theatrical experience, try **Die Schmiere** (⊠ Seckbächer Gasse 2, ☎ 069/281–066), which offers trenchant satire and also disarmingly calls itself "the worst theater in the world." Renowned for international experimental productions, including dance theater and other forms of nonverbal drama, is **Theater am Turm** (TAT) (☎ 069/154–5100) in the Bockenheimer Depot. The **Künstlerhaus Mouson Turm** (⊠ Waldschmidtstr. 4, ☎ 069/4058–9520) is a cultural center that hosts a regular series of concerts of all kinds, as well as plays and exhibits. If you're looking for English-language productions, try the **Frankfurt Entertainment** (⊠ Hansaallee 150, ☎ 069/320–5835) or the **English Theater** (⊠ Kaiserstr. 52, ☎ 069/242–3160). The **Tiger Palast** (⊠ Heiligkreuzgasse 16–20, ☎ 069/289–691) is the best place in Frankfurt to see variety shows, as well as circus performances, dance, and much more. Shows often sell out, so you are advised to book tickets as far in advance as possible. Open nightly 5:30 PM–3 AM.

OUTDOOR ACTIVITIES AND SPORTS

For information on sport clubs and organizations in Frankfurt, as well as public pools, call the city sports office (☎ 069/212–33887).

Bicycling

Opportunities in the city are limited, but get away from the downtown area and Frankfurt's parks and forests offer terrific places for recreational biking. In summer you can rent bikes at the **Goetheturm** (☎ 069/49111) on the northern edge of the Stadtwald.

Fitness Centers

Fitness Company (⊠ Zeil 109, ☎ 069/280–565) is centrally located near the Hauptwache and offers everything anyone needs to work out. There are more than 60 aerobic and gym classes and 150 different fitness machines, from Nautilus to StairMaster. English is spoken. A day's training costs DM 25; the price includes a sauna.

Intercontinental (⊠ Wilhelm-Leuschner-Str. 43, ☎ 069/26050) overlooks the Main River, along whose banks you can jog. The hotel has an indoor pool, health club, gym, and sauna.

Hotel Gravenbruch Kempinski (⊠ Neu-Isenburg 2, ☎ 06102/5050) is about 15 minutes by car outside Frankfurt. It's in a 37-acre park, with tennis courts, two Olympic-size pools, and jogging paths through the woods.

Jogging

One good place to jog in Frankfurt is along the banks of the Main River. To avoid retracing your steps, you can always cross a bridge and return down the opposite side. In the center city, **Grüneberg Park** is 1 mile around, with a Trimm Dich (get fit) exercise facility in the northeast corner. The **Anlagenring,** a park following the line of the old city walls around the city, is also popular with local joggers. For a vigorous forest run, take the streetcar to **Hohemark** (a 30-minute ride); a streetcar will also bring you to the **Stadtwald,** a 4,000-acre forest park south of the city, where you can jog, swim, or play tennis.

Skating

Eissporthalle has two rinks—one outdoor, the other indoor. ⊠ *Am Bornheimer Hang 4, Ratsweg,* ☎ *069/2123–0825.* ☜ *DM 10; skate rental DM 6 for 3 hrs.* ☉ *Nov.–Feb., daily 9 AM–10:30 PM.*

Swimming

The **Rebstockbad** leisure center has an indoor pool, a pool with a wave machine and a palm-fringed beach, and an outdoor pool with giant water chutes. ⊠ *August-Euler-Str. 7,* ☎ *069/708–078.* ☜ *DM 13 for 3 hrs.* ☉ *Mon. 2–10, Tues. and Thurs. 9–6, Wed. and Fri.–Sun. 9 AM–10 PM.*

The **Titus Therme** pool complex has everything from "adventure pools" to squash courts. ⊠ *Walter-Möller-Pl. 2,* ☎ *069/958–050.* ☜ *DM 10 for 4 hrs.* ☉ *Mon. 1–10, Tues.–Wed. 6:30 AM–10 PM, Thurs.–Fri. 6:30 AM–11 PM, weekends 7 AM–10 PM.*

The **Stadionbad** has an outdoor pool, a giant water chute, a solarium, and exercise lawns. ✉ *Morfelder Landstr. 362,* ☎ *069/678–040.* ☉ *Mid-May–Sept.*

A number of city pools are open in the summer, such as the **Brentanobad,** an outdoor pool surrounded by lawns and old trees. It is often crowded during the summer. ✉ *Rödelheimer Parkweg,* ☎ *069/2123–9020.* ✉ *DM 5.*

Tennis

Courts are available at the **Nidda Park** sports center. Next to the **Stadionbad** (☞ *above*) you'll find 20 courts (cost is about DM 20 per hour, depending on the time and day of the week). Call (☎ *069/678–040*) for reservations.

SHOPPING

Gift Ideas

Gifts and souvenirs are not the first things that spring to mind when one thinks of the financial capital of Germany. Like all other cities, however, Frankfurt has its shopping treasures. It is, for example, the home of the largest selection of Meissen porcelain outside Meissen itself, found, improbably, in the Japanese department store **Mitsukoshi** (✉ Kaiserstr. 13, ☎ 069/293–085 or 069/293–086).

Porcelain direct from the manufacturer is available in the suburb of Höchst at the **Höchster Porzellan Manufaktur** outlet in the center of town (✉ Berlinerstr. 60, at the Kornmarkt, ☎ 069/295–299). Here you'll find everything from figurines to dinner services, as well as a selection of glassware and silver.

La Galleria (✉ Berlinerstr. 66, ☎ 069/281–461) has a good selection of jewelry designed and made by local craftsmen (*Goldschmeide*). Don't make the mistake of thinking local means rustic: Jewelry-making in Germany is a highly developed and sophisticated art, as is reflected in the prices.

Frankfurt may not have an abundance of fashion centers, but you'll certainly find plenty of pricey apparel here. One of the best-known designers is **Jil Sander,** whose Frankfurt outlet is on the Goethestrasse, the "fashion street" (✉ Goethestr. 29, ☎ 069/283–469). A former fashion model, Sander still models her own creations in photo ads from time to time. The more affordable **Escada** sells collections made up of infinitely combinable separates and accessories (✉ Goethestr. 31, ☎ 069/287–799).

For children, you can pick up a *Struwwelpeter* (Slovenly Peter) puppet or doll, named after the character in the famous children's book by Frankfurt resident Heinrich Hoffmann. The **Struwwelpeter Museum** (✉ Schirm am Römerberg, ☎ 069/281–333) has a few such dolls, as well as a range of Struwwelpeter children's books.

One typical Frankfurt specialty is Apfelwein, the famous Ebbelwei, or "apple wine," sold in most supermarkets and in the taverns in Sachsenhausen, south of the river.

If you want to stock up on "regular" local wine, stop in at the Weinverkauf des Städtische **Weingutes** in the Römer; this outlet sells wine produced in the city's own vineyards of the Rheingau. ✉ *Limpurger Gasse 2,* ☎ *069/2123–3680.* ☉ *Mon.–Thurs. 7:30–12:30 and 1–4, Fri. 7:30–1.*

For typical Frankfurter baked specialties, go to the pastry shop **Konditorei Lochner** on the Fressgasse (Karl-Becher-Str. 10, ☎ 069/920–7320).

Here you can find local delicacies such as *Bethmännchen und Brenten* (marzipan cookies) or *Frankfurter Kranz* (a kind of creamy cake). All types of sweets are found at the café **Laumer** (⊠ Bockenheimer Landstr. 64, ☎ 069/727–912); Laumer goodies are also found at the café in the Hauptwache.

Shopping Districts
The heart of Frankfurt's shopping district is the pedestrian street called **Zeil**, running east from Hauptwache Square. City officials claim it's the country's busiest shopping street, with an unrivaled annual turnover of more than DM 1 billion. The seven-story, metal-and-glass mall of the **Zeil Galerie** is at the beginning of the street, near the Hauptwache (⊠ Zeil 112-114, ☎ 069/9207–3414). This complex includes 56 shops and boutiques, generally ranging from low- to mid-price, as well as several types of eateries, including cafés and Japanese fare. The streets running off Zeil and the Hauptwache are home to a series of upscale fashion shops. **Goethestrasse** is the best known of Frankfurt's luxury-shopping "quarter," with boutiques, art galleries, jewelry stores, and antiques shops.

A more upscale mall is the new **Schillerstrasse** (Schiller Passage), around the corner from the Börse. This small, elegant shopping arcade is gradually filling with everything from shoe stores to lingerie boutiques. It centers, in the most literal sense, around the **Cafe Cult**, a restaurant, meeting point, music bar, and late-night spot for the young and beautiful. There's also a ritzy mall in the BFG building on the corner of Willy-Brandt-Platz and Neue-Mainzer-Strasse.

Extending west from the Hauptwache is **Grosse Bockenheimer Strasse** (known as Fressgasse, or food street, to the locals). Cafés, restaurants, and, above all, food shops are the draw here. This is the place for fish—fresh or smoked—cheeses, and a wide range of local specialties, including frankfurters. Arcades such as the **Galerie Fressgasse** provide additional dining and shopping possibilities.

The multitude of stores and antiques shops across the river in **Sachsenhausen** is ever more chic. The **Metzgerei Willi Meyer** (⊠ Schweizer Str. 42, ☎ 069/615–010) is worth a look for its decor alone. Stark green-and-black Italian tiles and subtle spotlighting make this probably the classiest butcher shop in Germany; it looks more like a jewelry store than a place that sells sausages.

Flea Markets
Frankfurt has two weekend flea markets: on Saturday from 9 to 2 on Schaumainkai below the Eiserner Steg, and on Sunday from 8 to 2 at the Schlachthof (slaughterhouse) on Seehoferstrasse in Sachsenhausen. Whichever you choose, get there early for the bargains. There's a wide range of goods on display, a lot of them pretty junky, but sometimes better-quality items reward the diligent browser. Shopping success or no, both markets are fun to explore and show a different shade of Frankfurt's local color.

SIDE TRIPS

Frankfurt is so centrally located in Germany that the list of possible excursions—day trips and longer treks—is nearly endless. It is a gateway to the Rhineland in the west, the Neckar Valley in the south, and Franconia in the southeast, and it's the ideal starting point for journeys into all of these regions. Thus the list of excursions here is merely a selection of destinations that are not covered in other chapters.

Bad Homburg

Just a few miles north of Frankfurt, Bad Homburg lies at the foot of the **Taunus Hills.** The Taunus, with its rich forests, medieval castles, and photogenic towns, are regarded by many Frankfurters as their territory. On weekends you can see them enjoying "their" playground: hiking through the hills; climbing the **Grosse Feldberg**; taking the waters at a health-giving mineral spring; or just lazing in the sun. The Bad Homburg spa was first known to the Romans but was rediscovered and made famous during the 19th century. Illustrious visitors included the Prince of Wales, the son of Queen Victoria, and Czar Nicholas II. And one of the world's first casinos was founded here in 1841. Today Bad Homburg has a lovely Altstadt (Old Town).

One of the town's greatest attractions over the centuries has been the Kurpark in the heart of the Old Town, with its more than 31 fountains. In the park you'll find not only the popular, highly saline Elisabethenbrunnen spring but also a Siamese temple and a Russian chapel, mementos left by two distinguished guests—King Chulalongkorn of Siam and Czar Nicholas II. The Kurpark is a good place to begin a walking tour of the town; Bad Homburg's tourist office is located here (☞ *Visitor Information below*). ⊠ *Between Paul-Ehrlich-Weg and Kaiser-Fredrich-Promenade.*

The most historically noteworthy sight in Bad Homburg is the 17th-century **Schloss.** The 172-foot **Weisser Turm** (White Tower) is all that remains of the medieval castle that once stood here. The Schloss that stands today was built between 1680 and 1685 by Friedrich II of Hesse-Homburg, and a few alterations were made during the 19th century. The state apartments are exquisitely furnished, and the Spiegelkabinett (Hall of Mirrors) is especially worthy of a visit. In the surrounding park, look for two venerable trees from Lebanon, both now almost 150 years old. ⊠ *Schlosspl,* ☎ *06172/121–310.* ☑ *DM 4.* ☯ *Mar.–Oct., Tues.–Sun. 10–5; Nov.–Feb., Tues.–Sun. 10–4.*

Only 6½ kilometers (4 miles) from Bad Homburg, and accessible by direct bus service, is the **Saalburg Limes** fort, the best-preserved Roman fort in Germany. Built in AD 120, the fort could accommodate a cohort (500 men) and was part of the fortifications along the 550-meter-long (342-mile-long) Limes Wall. The fort has been rebuilt as the Romans originally left it—with wells, armories, parade grounds, and catapults, as well as shops, houses, baths, and temples. ☑ *DM 3.* ☯ *Fort and museums daily 8–5.*

About a 30-minute walk from the Saalburg Limes fort is a fine open-air museum at **Hessenpark,** near Neu Anspach. The museum consists of 135 acres of rebuilt villages with houses, schools, and farms typical of the 18th and 19th centuries. A visit here yields a clear, concrete picture of the world in which the 18th- and 19th-century Hessians lived. The park is 15 kilometers (10 miles) outside of Bad Homburg in the direction of Usingen. ☎ *06081/58854.* ☑ *DM 7.* ☯ *Mar.–Oct., Tues.–Sun. 9–6.*

Just a short, convenient bus ride from Bad Homburg is the highest mountain in the Taunus, the 2,850-foot, eminently hikeable **Feldberg.** From here there are easy bus connections to the towns of Königstein and Kronberg. **Königstein** is a health-resort town that contains the ruins of a 13th-century castle and a noteworthy **Rathaus** (Town Hall). Many painters have chosen a town in the Taunus, **Kronberg,** as their setting. This picturesque Old Town, with its half-timbered houses and winding streets, was the home of the Kronberger School, an important contributor to 19th-century German art. Visit the 15th-century **Johaniskirche** with its late-Gothic murals.

Dining and Lodging

Most of the well-known spas in Bad Homburg have restaurants, but they tend to be very expensive. For an inexpensive and enjoyable meal, try one of the numerous Italian or Greek restaurants throughout the city.

$$$ ✕ **Sänger's Restaurant.** You get a quintessential spa experience here: fine dining at high prices. But service is friendly, and the truffle risotto may make you forget the bill. ✉ *Kaiser-Friedrich-Promenade 85,* ☎ *06172/24425. AE, MC. Closed Sun. No lunch Mon. and Sat.*

$$ ✕ **Zum Wasserweibchen.** Chef Inge Kuper is a local, culinary legend. Although prices are high for some items on the menu, the portions are large. Despite a clientele that sometimes includes celebrities, the service remains friendly and unpretentious. You can't go wrong with the potato cakes with salmon mousse, sour cream, and herbs; the brisket of beef with green sauce; or any of the desserts. ✉ *Am Mühlberg 57,* ☎ *06172/29878. AE, MC. Closed Sat.*

$ ✕ **Kartoffelküche.** The name means "potato kitchen." It's a simple restaurant serving traditional dishes accompanied by potatoes cooked every way imaginable. The potato and broccoli gratin and the potato pizza are excellent, and for dessert try potato strudel with vanilla sauce. ✉ *Audenstr. 4,* ☎ *06172/21500. No credit cards. No lunch weekends.*

$$$ ✕🏨 **Maritim Kurhaus Hotel.** Standing on the edge of a spa park, the hotel offers large, richly furnished rooms with king-size beds and deep armchairs, most covered in pastel fabrics. You have the choice here between dining in style in the hotel's elegant Park restaurant (pink table linen, fine silverware, and candlelight) with nouvelle cuisine, or more cheaply (but evenings only) in the cozy Burgerstube with traditional fare dominated by local meat dishes; the latter is worth a visit just for the collection of dolls that forms part of the rustic decor. Despite the difference in prices, both restaurants draw on the same excellently managed kitchen. ✉ *Ludwigstr., D–61348 Bad Homburg,* ☎ *06172/6600,* FAX *06172/660–100. 148 rooms with bath. Restaurant, 2 bars, 2 cafés. AE, DC, MC, V.*

$$$$ 🏨 **Steigenberger Bad Homburg.** This prestigious hotel chain is well represented in Bad Homburg. Across from the Kurpark, the hotel has luxurious rooms furnished in art deco style. One of its restaurants, Charly's Le Bistro, serves traditional bistro-style cuisine while the other, Charly's Parkside Restaurant, is devoted to American cooking. ✉ *Kaiser-Friedrich-Promenade 69–75, D–61348 Bad Homburg v. d. Höhe,* ☎ *06172/1810,* FAX *06172/181–630. 169 rooms with bath. 2 restaurants, bar, café. AE, DC, MC, V.*

$$$ 🏨 **Hartdwald Hotel.** The flowers that spill from the window boxes covering the white facade of the Hartdwald have won this distinctive woodland hotel numerous local awards. These blooms are one of the many touches that make the property special. Its location couldn't be better—in the woods yet near the town center and spa park. ✉ *Philosophenweg 31, D–61350 Bad Homburg v. d. Höhe,* ☎ *06172/81026 or 06172/9880,* FAX *06172/82512. 42 rooms. Restaurant, café, laundry service, parking. AE, DC, MC, V.*

$–$$ 🏨 **Haus Fischer Garni.** This family-operated pension is simple and clean. It is near a park and is convenient to the Old Town. ✉ *Landgrafenstr. 12, D–61348 Bad Homburg,* ☎ *06172/85927. 10 rooms with bath. No credit cards.*

Bad Homburg A to Z

By Car. About 30–45 minutes of driving on the A–5 Autobahn (Frankfurt–Dortmund) will take you to Bad Homburg.

By Train and Bus. Bad Homburg has its own station. Take the S-bahn
from Frankfurt at Konstabler Wache (S-5 line). Buses and streetcars
can also get you there.

The first stop you'll want to make in Bad Homburg is at the **tourist
bureau** downtown. There you'll find local maps, advice, and assistance
in booking accommodations, if necessary. You can also get information about and tickets to various local events. ⊠ *Verkehrsamt. Louisen-
str. 58*, ☎ *06172/675–110.* ⊙ *Weekdays 8:30–6, Sat. 9–1.*

Höchst

Frankfurt's most western suburb is best known today as the headquarters
of the chemical concern Hoechst AG. On the Main River, during the
Middle Ages it was a town in its own right, governed by Mainz until
it was engulfed by the spread of Frankfurt. Unlike Frankfurt, however,
Höchst was not devastated by wartime bombing and still possesses many
of its original historic buildings.

It's worth taking the time to explore the picturesque Altstadt (Old Town),
with its attractive market and half-timbered houses. Of special interest in the town is the factory of **Höchster Porzellan Manufaktur.** Höchst
was once a porcelain-manufacturing town to rival Dresden and Vienna.
Production ceased during the late 18th century but was revived by an
enterprising businessman in 1965. ⊠ *Bolongaro Str. 186*, ☎ *069/300–
9020 or 06023/30581 to arrange guided tour of the works.*

On Bolongaro Strasse you can also see a fine exhibit of porcelain at
the **Bolongaropalast** (Bolongaro Palace), a magnificent residence facing the river. It was built during the late 18th century by an Italian snuff
manufacturer. Its facade—almost the size of a football field—is nothing
to sneeze at. Not far from the palace is the **Höchster Schloss.** Built in
1360, this castle was originally the seat and customshouse of the archbishop of Mainz. Destroyed and rebuilt several times, it now houses
the **Höchst City Museum** and the **Hoechst AG company Museum.** ☎
069/303–249. ▣ *Free.* ⊙ *Daily 10–4.*

Hochst's most interesting attraction is the **Justiniuskirche,** Frankfurt's
oldest building. Dating from the 7th century, the church is part early
Romanesque and part 15th-century Gothic. The view from the top of
the hill is well worth the walk. ⊠ *Corner of Justiniuspl. and Bolongaro Str.*

Getting There

Höchst can be reached via the S-1 and S-2 suburban trains from Frankfurt's main train station, or Konstablerwache station.

Limburg

The imposing seven-spired cathedral at Limburg that greets you upon
arrival seems to grow out of the cliff that holds it. Modern Limburg
grew around its Old Town—a city that developed because it was at
the crossroads of the Köln–Frankfurt and Hessen–Koblenz highways
in the 9th century. The Old Town still has a number of beautiful patrician and merchant houses, evidence of the city's importance in the
Middle Ages.

The first sight to take in is the **Dom St. Georg und Nikolaus,** the cathedral that you'll see towering above the Lahn River. Construction of the cathedral began in 1220, and evident in the building is the transition from Romanesque to Gothic style; each side presents a new perspective. Extensive restoration recently uncovered the original medieval coloring and bright frescoes from the 13th century.

Treasures from the cathedral are on display in the Diözesanmuseum in the Lyenschen Haus, near the cathedral. It houses ecclesiastical art treasures from the bishopric of Limburg. Be sure to see the Byzantine cross reliquary that was stolen from the palace church in Constantinople in 1204 and the *Patri-Stab* (Peter's Staff), set with precious stones and adorned with gold. *Domschatz und Diözesanmusem:* ⊠ *Domstr. 12,* ☎ *06431/295–233 for appointment.* ⌑ *DM 2.* ⊙ *Mid-Mar.–mid-Nov., Tues.–Sat. 10–1 and 2–5, Sun. and holidays 11–5; late Nov.–early Mar.*

The Schloss adjacent to the Dom St. Georg und Nikolaus dates from the 7th or 8th century, although the castle's current building only goes back to the 13th century. The group of residences, the chapel, and other buildings added in the 14th to 16th centuries serve as an architectural counterbalance to the cathedral. The castle is closed to visitors; it is used as a facility for conferences. ⊠ *Am Dompl.*

Only 6 kilometers (4 miles) from Limburg is the small town of **Runkel,** with an impressive 12th-century fortress. The fortress tower provides a panoramic view over the Taunus and the Westerwald.

About 20 kilometers (12 miles) south of Limburg is the state-recognized spa resort of **Bad Camberg,** a historic town in the western foothills of the **Hochtaunus** (Taunus highlands). This city offers numerous half-timbered houses, remains of the city's gate and fortifications, and an attractive ensemble of buildings in the center of town, including the **Hohenfeldsche Kapelle** (chapel) of 1650. They stand in striking contrast to the modern **Kurhaus** (Spa) across the street.

Limburg is on one of the new driving routes called the **Deutsche Fachwerkstrassen,** or "Half-Timbered Roads," an initiative designed to make people aware of the beauty of some lesser-known villages and to furnish an impetus to restore some decaying half-timbered houses. The "West and Central Hessia" route runs from the Frankfurt suburb of Höchst north through Limburg to Marburg and is highly recommended to anyone interested in seeing an untouristed, truly beautiful side of the country. For information, contact the Limburg tourist office.

Dining and Lodging

$$ ✕ **St. Georgs-Stuben.** In the Stadthalle, only a few minutes' walk from the center of Limburg, this pleasant restaurant serves local and international dishes. Try the house specialty, the St. Georgsteller, a filling pork-steak meal. ⊠ *Hospitalstr. 4,* ☎ *06431/26027. No credit cards.*

$$–$$$ 🏨 **Dom Hotel.** Centrally located and ideal for a brief visit to see the Old Town, this old established hotel offers standard comforts backed by friendly service. ⊠ *Grabenstr. 57,* ☎ *06431/24077,* 🖷 *06431/6856. 48 rooms with bath or shower. Restaurant. AE, DC, MC, V. Closed late Dec.*

$$–$$$ 🏨 **Romantik Hotel Zimmermann.** The privately owned Zimmermann is one of the showpieces of the Romantik group. A beautifully renovated town house in the center of Lahn, it is on a small, quiet side street. Rooms are individually and stylishly decorated, and those in a neighboring annex are furnished in English country-house style. The service is attentive; the breakfasts hearty. ⊠ *Blumenröderstr. 1,* ☎ *06431/4611,*

FAX *06431/41314. 30 rooms with bath or shower. Restaurant, parking.*
AE, DC, MC, V. Closed late Dec.

Limburg A to Z

GETTING THERE

By Car. The Frankfurt–Köln Autobahn (A–3) has two Limburg exits.
Take either of them. The drive should take you less than an hour from
Frankfurt.

By Train and Bus. Limburg has its own railway station as well as regular bus service from Frankfurt, Koblenz, Wiesbaden, and Frankfurt
Airport.

VISITOR INFORMATION

Upon arriving in the center of Limburg, visit the **Verkehrsamt** (tourist
office) to receive city maps, help with accommodations, if necessary,
and general information. ⊠ *Hospitalstr. 2,* ☎ *06431/203–222.* ⊙
Apr.–Oct., weekdays 8–12:30 and 1:30–6, Sat. 10–noon; Nov.–Mar.,
Mon.–Thurs. 8–12:30 and 1:30–5, Fri. 8–12:30.

FRANKFURT A TO Z

Arriving and Departing

By Bus

More than 200 European cities—including all major former West German cities—have bus links with Frankfurt. Buses arrive and depart from
the south side of the Hauptbahnhof. For information and tickets, contact **Deutsche Touring,** ⊠ *Am Römerhof 17,* ☎ *069/79030.*

By Car

Frankfurt is the meeting point of a number of major Autobahns, of
which the most important are: A–3, running south from Köln and then
on to Würzburg, Nürnberg, and Munich; and A–5, running south
from Giessen and then on to Mannheim, Heidelberg, Karlsruhe, and
the Swiss-German border at Basel. A complex series of beltways surround the city. If you're driving to Frankfurt on A–5 from either north
or south, exit at Nordwestkreuz and follow A–66 to the Nordend District, just north of downtown. Driving south on A–3, exit onto A–66
and follow the signs to Frankfurt-Höchst and then the Nordend District. Driving north on A–3, exit at Offenbach onto A–661 and follow
the signs for Frankfurt-Stadtmitte.

By Plane

Frankfurt Airport is the biggest on the Continent, second in Europe
only to London's Heathrow. There are direct flights to Frankfurt from
many U.S. cities and from all major European cities. It's 10 kilometers (6 miles) southwest of the downtown area, by the Köln–Munich
Autobahn.

BETWEEN THE AIRPORT AND DOWNTOWN

Getting into Frankfurt from the airport is easy. The line S-8 is the S-
Bahn (suburban train) that runs from the airport to downtown Frankfurt. It goes to the Hauptbahnhof (main train station) and then to
Hauptwache Square in the heart of Frankfurt. Trains run every 15 minutes and the trip takes about 15 minutes. The one-way fare is DM 5.50.
InterCity and InterCity Express (ICE) trains to and from most major
West German cities also stop at the airport. There are hourly services
to Köln, Hamburg, and Munich, for example. City Bus 61 also serves
the airport, running between it and the Südbahnhof train station in Sachsenhausen, south of the downtown area. The trip takes about 30 minutes; the fare is DM 5.50. A taxi from the airport into the city center

normally takes around 20 minutes; allow double that during rush hours. The fare is around DM 40. If you're picking up a rental car at the airport, getting into Frankfurt is easy: Take the main road out of the airport and follow the signs for Stadtmitte (downtown).

By Train

EuroCity and InterCity trains connect Frankfurt with all German cities and many major European cities. The new InterCity Express line links Frankfurt with Hamburg, Munich, and a number of other major German cities. All long-distance trains arrive at and depart from the Hauptbahnhof. For information, call **Deutsche Bahn** (German Railways, ☎ 069/19419) or ask at the information office in the station.

Getting Around

By Bicycle

Theo Intra's shop (✉ Westerbachstr. 273, ☎ 069/342–780) has a large selection of bikes, from tandems to racing models.

In summer you can rent bikes at the **Goetheturm** (Goethe Tower) at the edge of the Frankfurt Stadtwald (☎ 069/49111).

By Boat

Frankfurt is the starting point for many boat excursions, ranging from day trips on the River Main to cruises along the Rhine and Mosel as far as Trier, lasting up to three days. The **Köln-Dusseldorfer** line offers the most trips; they run from March to October and leave from the Frankfurt Mainkai am Eisernen Steg, just south of the Römer complex. For tickets and information call the Köln-Dusseldorfer agent, Malachi Faughnan (✉ Am Eisernen Steg, ☎ 069/285–728), which is open daily 11–6. The **Fahrgastshiff Wikinger** company (☎ 069/282–886) has boat trips along the Main and excursions to the Rhine. **Deutsche Touring** (☎ 069/79030) combines boat trips with wine tasting. At Easter and from May to October, pleasure boats of the **Primus Line** cruise the Main and Rhine rivers from Frankfurt, sailing as far as the Lorelei and back in a day. For details and reservations, contact Frankfurter Personenschiffahrt (✉ Mainkai 36, ☎ 069/281–884).

By Car

CAR RENTALS

Avis, ✉ Schmidtstr. 39, ☎ 069/730–111.

Europcar, ✉ Schlosstr. 32, ☎ 069/775–033.

Hertz, ✉ Hanauer Landstr. 106–108, ☎ 069/449–090.

On Foot

Downtown Frankfurt is compact and easily explored on foot. There are fewer pedestrian-only streets in the downtown area than in some other major German cities; the most important radiate from Hauptwache Square. The Römer complex, south of Hauptwache, is also a pedestrian zone. From here you can easily cross the river on the Eisener Steg (Iron Bridge) to Sachsenhausen, where the tangle of small streets is best explored on foot.

By Public Transportation

Frankfurt's smooth-running, well-integrated public transportation system consists of the U-bahn (subway), S-bahn (suburban railway), and Strassenbahn (streetcars). Fares for the entire system are uniform, though they are based on a complex zone system that can be hard to figure out. A basic one-way ticket for a ride in the inner zone costs DM 2.70 (DM 3.20 during rush hours). For rides of just a stop or two, buy a *Kurzstrecke* ticket for DM 1.80 (DM 2.50 during rush hours). A day ticket for unlimited travel in the inner zone costs DM 8.50. The Frankfurt Tourist Office offers a two-day ticket called the Frankfurt Card. The card costs DM 13 and allows unlimited travel in the inner zone and a 50% reduction on admission to 14 museums in Frankfurt. If you're caught on the subway without a ticket, there's a fine of DM 60. Call for information and assistance (☎ 069/269–462).

By Taxi

Fares start at DM 2.50 and increase by DM 2.15–DM 2.53 per kilometer, depending on the time of day. There is an extra charge if the driver is asked to carry baggage. You can hail taxis in the street or call them (☎ 069/250–001, 069/230–033, or 069/545–011). There's an extra charge to have the driver come to the pickup point.

Contacts and Resources

Consulates

U.S. Consulate General, ✉ Siesmayerst. 21, ☎ 069/75350.

British Consulate General, ✉ Bockenheimer Landstr. 42, ☎ 069/170–0020.

The nearest **Canadian Consulate** is ✉ Prinz-Georg-Str. 126, D–40479 Düsseldorf, ☎ 0211/172–170.

Emergencies

Police: ☎ 110. **Fire:** ☎ 112. **Medical Emergencies:** ☎ 069/7950–2200 or 069/19292. **Pharmacies:** ☎ 069/11500. **Dental Emergencies:** ☎ 069/660–7271.

English-Language Bookstores

American Book Center (ABC), ✉ Jahnstr. 36, ☎ 069/552–816.

Amerika Haus (library, newspapers, cultural events), ✉ Staufenstr. 1, ☎ 069/971–4480.

British Bookshop, ✉ Börsenstr. 17, ☎ 069/280–492.

Guided Tours

ORIENTATION TOURS

Two-and-a-half-hour bus tours with English-speaking guides, which take in all the main sights, are offered throughout the year. From March through October, tours leave from outside the main tourist information office at Römerberg 27 daily at 10 AM and 2 PM; all of these buses leave from the train station tourist office (opposite Track 23) 15 minutes later. The tour includes a visit to the Goethe Haus. In winter (November–February), tours leave on weekends and holidays at 1 PM from the Römer office, stopping at 1:15 at the train station tourist office. The cost is DM 39. Gray Line (☎ 069/230–492) offers two-hour city tours four times a day; the price (DM 50) includes a typical Frankfurt snack.

SPECIAL-INTEREST TOURS

The city transit authority (☎ 069/2132–2425) runs a brightly painted old-time streetcar—the **Ebbelwei Express** (Cider Express)—weekends and holidays every 40 minutes between 1:32 and 5:32. Departures are from the Bornheim-Mitte U- and S-Bahn station and the fare—which includes a free glass of cider (or apple juice) and a pretzel—is DM 4. All the major attractions in the city are covered as the streetcar trundles along. The ride lasts just over 30 minutes. The **Historische Eisenbahn Frankfurt** (☎ 069/436–093) runs a vintage steam train along the banks of the Main River one weekend each month. The train runs from the Eisener Steg west to Frankfurt–Griesham and east to Frankfurt–Mainkur. The fare is DM 6. There are special tours offered by the tourist office by prior arrangement: The first covers Frankfurt's architecture (from its historic remains to its skyscrapers), the second traces the city's Jewish history, and the third follows Goethe's footsteps. The tours aren't cheap—for an English-speaking guide, the cost is DM 90–DM 100 per hour, plus tax. For further information, call Mr. Wolf (☎ 069/2123–8953).

The Frankfurt tourist office arranges walking tours on demand (☎ 069/2123–8849). Tours are tailored to suit individual requirements, and costs vary accordingly. For those who want to tour Frankfurt on foot on their own, the tourist office lends Walkman tape players equipped with a taped guided tour. The tapes cost DM 12, and a DM 50 deposit is charged for the loan of the Walkman.

EXCURSIONS

Noblesse Limousine Service (✉ Bad Vilbel, ☎ 06101/12055), **Deutsche Touring** (✉ Am Römerhof 17, ☎ 069/790–3268) and **Gray Line** (✉ Wiesenhüttenpl. 39, ☎ 069/230–492) offer a variety of tours in the areas immediately around Frankfurt as well as farther afield. Destinations include the Rhine Valley, with steamship cruises and wine tasting, as well as day trips to the historic towns of Heidelberg and Rothenburg-ob-der-Tauber. Additional information is available from all three organizations. A **Casino Bus** runs daily to the casino at Bad Homburg in the Taunus. It leaves every hour between 2 PM and 11 PM (the last bus back to Frankfurt leaves Bad Homburg at 3 AM) from the Frankfurt Hauptbahnhof (south side). The DM 9.50 fare includes entry to the casino.

Travel Agencies

American Express International, ✉ Kaiserstr. 8, ☎ 069/210–548.

Thomas Cook, ✉ Kaiserstr. 11, ☎ 069/134–733.

D.E.R. Deutsches Reisebüro, ✉ Emil-von-Behring Str. 6, ☎ 069/9588–3650.

Hapag-Lloyd Reisebüro, ✉ Kaiserstr. 14, ☎ 069/216–2286.

Visitor Information

For advance information, write to the **Verkehrsamt Frankfurt/Main** (✉ Kaiserstr. 52, 60329 Frankfurt, ☎ 069/2123–8800). The main tourist office is at Römerberg 27 (☎ 069/2123–8708) in the heart of the Old Town. It's open daily 9 AM–6 PM. A secondary information office is at the main train station (Hauptbahnhof) opposite Track 23 (☎ 069/2123–8849). This branch is open weekdays 8 AM–9 PM, weekends 9 AM–6 PM. Both offices can help you find accommodations.

Two information offices at the airport can also help with accommodations. The **FAG Flughafen-Information,** on the first floor of arrivals hall B, is open daily 6:45 AM–10:15 PM. The **DER Deutsches Reisebüro,** in arrivals hall B-6, is open daily 8 AM–9 PM.

11 Rhineland Palatinate

This stretch of the Rhine has less dramatic scenery than along the riverbanks farther north, but it's also less crowded and less expensive. Few autobahns penetrate this region, and most other roads lead to truly off-the-beaten-track territory. One of these roads is the specially designated Weinstrasse (Wine Road). A winding, often narrow route, it is guarded by ancient castles and lined with vineyards that beckon the traveler to sample the current vintage. North and west of it are Speyer, Worms, and Mainz, all former imperial centers that are home to Romanesque cathedrals, each more spectacular than the last.

FOR MOST TRAVELERS—EVEN SEASONED ONES—the Rhineland means the spectacular stretch between Bingen (where the river leaves the Rheingau region and swings north) and the ancient city of Koblenz (at the mouth of the Mosel). But there's another part of the Rhineland, where vineyards climb slopes crowned by ancient castles. This is the Rhineland Palatinate (Rheinland-Pfalz in German). It lacks the spectacular grandeur of the river above Bingen, the elegance of the resorts of Boppard and Koblenz, and the cachet of the wines of the Rheingau. But for that reason the crowds are smaller, the prices lower, and the pace slower. And there are attractions here, including an area with the warmest climate in Germany, that you won't find in the more popular stretch of the river farther north. The south-facing folds of the Palatinate Hills shelter communities where lemons, figs, and sweet chestnuts grow alongside vines.

Few autobahns penetrate this region, and most other roads lead to truly off-the-beaten-track territory. One of these roads is Germany's first specially designated Weinstrasse (Wine Road), a winding, often narrow route guarded by ancient castles and lined with vineyards that beckon the traveler to sample the current vintage.

Pleasures and Pastimes

Bicycling

The vineyard-lined country roads on either side of the Wine Road are a cyclist's dream. You can rent bikes at any of the main train stations for DM 12 a day (DM 6 if you have a valid train ticket). The tourist offices have arranged a number of bike trips where a flat fee includes meals and accommodations in some lovely hotels and restaurants (contact the Pfalz Tourist Office; ☞ Contacts and Resources *in* the Rhineland Palatinate A to Z, *below*). Many of the towns and villages along the Wine Road also have shops where you can rent a bike.

Dining

Local specialties, served in local inns, are what you'll eat in the towns and villages here. The bigger cities, such as Mainz and Worms, have more elegant establishments. Sausages are more popular in the Rhineland Palatinate than in almost any other area of the country, with the herb-flavored *Pfälzer* a favorite. *Hase im Topf*, a highly flavored rabbit pâté made with port, Madeira, brandy, and red wine, is another specialty to look for. The Rhineland Palatinate produces more wine than any other region in Germany, and all restaurants will offer a range of wine.

CATEGORY	COST*
$$$$	over DM 90
$$$	DM 55–DM 90
$$	DM 35–DM 55
$	under DM 35

per person for a three-course meal, excluding drinks

Hiking

You can cover the entire Wine Road on foot along a clearly marked trail that winds its way among the vineyards covering the slopes of the Palatinate Forest. Contact the Wine Road tourist offices (☞ Contacts and Resources *in* the Rhineland Palatinate A to Z, *below*) for maps and information. Local tourist offices and hotels also have a wide variety of other walking tours lasting anywhere from two days to a week, where a fixed price pays for accommodation, meals, and the transportation of your baggage from one hotel to the next. There are all kinds of perks on the various tours, down to a walking stick and a bottle of locally made schnapps to help you cover the distance; on the "gourmet walking tours," the meals are especially good. The Palatinate Forest is Germany's largest single tract of woodland—and offers fine walking, notably in one edge of the Wasgau Nature Park. Contact the Pfalz Tourist Office in Neustadt (☞ Contacts and Resources *in* the Rhineland Palatinate A to Z, *below*) or local tourist offices for a complete list of walking routes.

Lodging

Accommodations are plentiful, with those along the Wine Road mostly simple and inexpensive inns. The region has many bed-and-breakfasts; keep an eye open for signs reading ZIMMER FREI, meaning "rooms available." If you plan to visit during any of the wine festivals in the late summer and fall, make reservations well in advance—and expect higher prices.

CATEGORY	COST*
$$$$	over DM 200
$$$	DM 150–DM 200
$$	DM 100–DM 150
$	under DM 100

All prices are for two people in a double room.

Shopping

Shopping in the Rhineland Palatinate means *wine*. Entire streets in many towns and villages are dominated by shops devoted to the product of the grape. Likewise, vineyards along the roadside invite you in to pass judgment on the year's vintage. Bad Dürkheim is one particularly inviting center.

Wine Festivals

The wine festivals of the towns and villages of the Wine Road are numerous enough to take up several vacations. From late May through October the entire area seems caught up in one long celebration. The most important festivals are the **Dürkheimer Wurstmarkt** (Germany's biggest wine festival), in mid-September; the **Weinlesefest**, in Neustadt-an-der-Weinstrasse (with the coronation of the local Wine Queen), in the first half of October; Schweigen-Rechtenbach's **Rebenblütenfest**, in the first week of July; Bad Bergzabern's **Böhammerfest**, in early July; Landau's **Herbstmarkt**, in mid-September; Edenkoben's **Südliches Weinstrasse Grosses Weinfest**, in late September; and the **Mainzer Weinmarkt** in Mainz's Volkspark, the last weekend of August and the first weekend of September.

Exploring the Rhineland Palatinate

The southern end of the Deutsche Weinstrasse (German Wine Road) begins near the border of France in Schweigen. It crosses the largest uninterrupted wine-growing region in Germany, along the east side of the Pfälzerwald (Palatinate Forest) through vineyards, orchards, and idyllic wine towns. It is still guarded by numerous old castles. The ancient city of Speyer is a convenient excursion from the Wine Road at Neustadt-an-der-Weinstrasse. At the northern end of the Wine Road, two other cities are within easy reach: Worms, and Mainz. All three were among the Rhineland's great imperial centers, where emperors and princes met and where the three greatest Romanesque cathedrals in Europe stand. From the most northerly, Mainz, you are poised to explore the remainder of the Rhineland. (For full details, ☞ Chapter 12.)

Great Itineraries

Mainz is the only major city in the region with regular InterCity services; there are hourly connections to and from major German cities. For the Wine Road it is best to rent a car. Most roads in the region are narrow and winding, a far cry from the highways of much of the rest of Germany. It is a good idea to take along a nondrinker as codriver, or split the driving between you. And take your time.

Numbers in the text correspond to numbers in the margin and on the Rhineland Palatinate map.

IF YOU HAVE 3 DAYS

Start your first day at the French border in **Schweigen-Rechtenbach** ① and then visit the enchanted village of **Dörrenbach** and the legendary **Burg Trifels** ⑤, said to have been the site of the Holy Grail. Stay overnight in the picturesque village of ⌘ **St. Martin** ⑧. The next day get back on the Wine Road and travel through **Neustadt-an-der-Weinstrasse** ⑨ before making the detour to **Speyer** ⑩ to see its **Kaiserdom,** the most important Romanesque cathedral in the Rhineland. Continue on to **Deidesheim** ⑪ and ⌘ **Bad Dürkheim** ⑫, home of the biggest sausage fair in Europe and the world's biggest wine cask. Begin your third day with a visit to the old Limburg Monastery above Bad Dürkheim, a masterpiece of Romanesque architecture, and stop in **Freinsheim,** where medieval walls surround high-gabled, half-timbered buildings and a stately Baroque Rathaus (Town Hall). End your journey in **Bockenheim.**

IF YOU HAVE 5 DAYS

On your first day begin at **Schweigen-Rechtenbach** ① and explore the first part of the Wine Road from Dörrenbach to Neustadt-on-der-Weinstrasse ②–⑨, staying two nights in ⌘ **St. Martin** ⑧. On your third day take a detour to **Speyer** ⑩ to see the **Kaiserdom** and then return to the Wine Road and stop in **Deidesheim** ⑪ on the way to ⌘ **Bad Dürkheim** ⑫, where you can spend the night. Visit Limburg Monastery and the Pfälzerwald Nature Park, then continue north by way of **Freinsheim** and **Neuleiningen** ⑬ to ⌘ **Worms** ⑭ for a look at the **Worms Cathedral,** a magnificent amalgam of Gothic and Romanesque architecture, and the **Judenfriedhof,** the oldest and largest Jewish cemetery in Europe.

IF YOU HAVE 7 DAYS

From **Schweigen-Rechtenbach** ①, explore the first part of the Wine Road from Dörrenbach to Neustadt-an-der-Weinstrasse ②–⑨, staying two nights in ⌘ **St. Martin** ⑧. After a detour to **Speyer** ⑩ to see the **Kaiserdom,** return to the Wine Road and make a stop in **Deidesheim** ⑪ before arriving in ⌘ **Bad Dürkheim** ⑫ for two nights. Go cycling or horseback riding in the Palatinate Forest Nature Park and visit Limburg Monastery, Frankenstein Castle, and local wine villages such as Forst and Wachenheim. Continue north by way of **Freinsheim** and **Neuleiningen** ⑬ to ⌘ **Worms** ⑭ for a visit to the **Worms Cathedral,** the **Judenfriedhof,** and the Liebfrauen vineyard. Plan to spend the last night in ⌘ **Oppenheim** ㉒, an ancient wine village on the Rhine, with an excursion to nearby Nierstein ㉓. Spend the seventh day in **Mainz** ㉔, home to another impressive cathedral, the **Dom,** and the **Gutenberg Museum,** which tells the history of printing beginning with Europe's first printed book, the Gutenberg Bible.

When to Tour the Rhineland Palatinate

Late spring and early summer are a fine time to visit because the vines and hillside meadows are in flower. The area is less crowded and less expensive than the Rhineland in high summer but fills up for the wine

Rhineland Palatinate

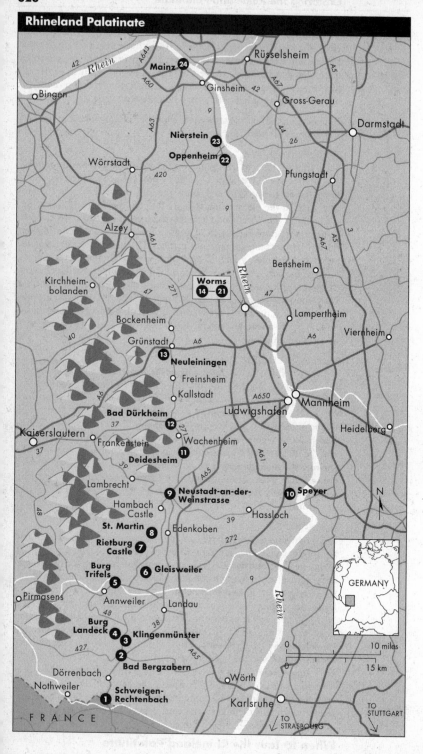

Rhein

42

A643

Mainz 24

A60

Rüsselsheim

A5

A67

Bingen

Ginsheim

42

9

Gross-Gerau

44

Darmstadt

26

A63

Wörrstadt

420

Nierstein 23

Oppenheim 22

Pfungstadt

A5

A67

Bensheim

Rhein

9

3

Alzey

A61

47

Worms 14 — 21

47

Lampertheim

Kirchheim-
bolanden

271

Viernheim

40

Bockenheim

A6

Grünstadt

A6

13

Neuleiningen

Freinsheim

Kallstadt

A650

Mannheim

Ludwigshafen

Bad Dürkheim

37

12

271

Wachenheim

9

Heidelberg

Kaiserslautern

Frankenstein

11

A61

37

39

Deidesheim

A65

Lambrecht

9

Neustadt-an-der-
Weinstrasse

Hambach
Castle

St. Martin 8

39

10 Speyer

Hassloch

Rietburg
Castle 7

Edenkoben

272

Burg
Trifels

6 Gleisweiler

9

5

Pirmasens

Annweiler

48

Landau

Rhein

N

Burg
Landeck

4 3 Klingenmünster

38

A65

427

2

Bad Bergzabern

Dörrenbach

Wörth

0   10 miles

Nothweiler

1 Schweigen-
Rechtenbach

0   15 km

Karlsruhe

F R A N C E

TO
STRASBOURG

TO
STUTTGART

GERMANY

festivals, most of which are in late summer and early fall. Winter has its pleasures, too, including wild game served in restaurants and a hearty welcome wherever you go.

THE WINE ROAD

Although the north end of the Wine Road is a favored starting point for many visitors because of its proximity to Mainz and Frankfurt, it is just as logical to begin a tour at its southern point—at the town in which the Wine Road itself began.

Schweigen-Rechtenbach

❶ *10 km (6 mi) south of Bad Bergzabern on B–38.*

The little wine village of Schweigen-Rechtenbach lies on the French border. It was here in July 1935 that a group of vintners hit on the idea of establishing a tourist route through the vineyards of the region. To get the road off to a suitable start, they put up a massive stone arch, the **Deutsches Weintor** (German Wine Gate). There's an open gallery halfway up the arch that offers a fine view of the vineyards that crowd the countryside between the Vosges Mountains over the French border and the Rhine away to the east. Some of Schweigen's best wine comes from the vineyards on the French side of the border; you can walk across the frontier—it's only 200 yards from the arch—with no formalities and compare vintages. For further investigation of the region's wines, follow the **Weinlehrpfad,** the "wine inspection path." It begins in Schweigen and ambles for about a mile through the vineyards of the nearby Sonnenberg. It is the first of scores of such walking routes that you'll find in wine-producing areas throughout Germany. The path is well marked and easy to follow.

En Route   Drive north on B–38 toward Bad Bergzabern. A mile before you reach the town turn left to see the village of **Dörrenbach.** It's an enchanting place, tucked snugly in a protective fold of the Palatinate Hills. The Renaissance **Rathaus** has a flower-hung facade crisscrossed with so many half-timbers that there's hardly room for the tiny-paned windows.

Bad Bergzabern

❷ *10 km (6 mi) north on B–38.*

The little spa town of Bad Bergzabern rivals any in Germany for its wealth of old half-timbered houses. Notable among these—in age and appearance—is the distinctive Renaissance stone building of the tavern Zum Engel. Its exterior is marked by unusual bay windows at the corners of the facade; inside, there's food and wine aplenty. ⊠ *Königstr. 45,* ☎ *06343/4933. Closed Tues.*

Klingenmünster

❸ *8 km (5 mi) north of Bad Bergzaben on B–38.*

The village of Klingenmünster has the ruins of a 7th-century Benedictine monastery, with a still-intact Baroque chapel. If castles are your
❹ thing, you should walk from the monastery to the ruins of **Burg Landeck.** The walk, through silent woods of chestnut trees, takes about half an hour. Your reward will be a magnificent view from the castle over the Rhine Valley and south as far as the Black Forest.

Annweiler

★ *8 km (5 mi) north of Klingenmünster on B–38.*

⑤ The most famous castle in the Rhineland Palatinate region is outside the village of Annweiler. This is **Burg Trifels,** one of the most romantic buildings in the country, its drama only slightly spoiled by the rather free reconstruction of the original Romanesque castle, rebuilt in 1937 (a period when a lot of Germans were keen on reestablishing what they saw as the glories of their "race"). The original castle was constructed during the mid-12th century by the emperor Barbarossa, who once wrote: "Whoever has Trifels possesses the empire." From 1126 to 1273 Burg Trifels housed the imperial crown jewels. This inspired the legend that Burg Trifels was the site of the Holy Grail, the bowl used by Christ at the Last Supper. In the Middle Ages the Holy Grail was the object of numerous knightly quests, not so much to find the Grail as to prove one's steadfastness and Christian virtue by embarking on an impossible task. Replicas of the imperial crown jewels are on display in the castle museum. ⌖ *DM 5.* ☾ *Jan.–Nov., daily 9–5.*

If you visit Burg Trifels, you'll pass the ruins of two neighboring castles as you head up the hill. These are the castles of **Scharfenberg** and **Anebos.** Their craggy, overgrown silhouettes add greatly to the romance of visiting their neighbor.

Dining and Lodging

$$ ✕ **Burg-Restaurant Trifels.** Eat in the shadows of Burg Trifels, where Richard the Lion-Hearted once stayed in less happy circumstances. In summer try for a table on the terrace; the view is terrific. Palatinate specialties—including delicious dumplings—are featured on the menu. ⌖ *Auf den Schlossackern,* ☎ *06346/8479. MC, V. Closed Mon.*

$ ✕▥ **Zum Goldenen Lamm.** At this half-timbered country inn at Ramberg, 7 kilometers (4½ miles) north of Annweiler, the Lergenmüller family carries on an old rural tradition of supplying beer, wine, and meat to the neighborhood—there's a butcher shop in the inn. ⌖ *D–76857 Ramberg,* ☎ *06345/8286,* ℻ *06345/3354. 35 rooms with bath. Restaurant. No credit cards. Restaurant closed Tues.*

Outdoor Activities and Sports

BICYCLING

You can rent bicycles at the **Fahrradgeschäft Seel** (⌖ Gerbergasse 27).

CLIMBING

The sandstone cliffs of the Palatinate Forest (Pfälzerwald) are fun and relatively safe to tackle. The tourist office in **Annweiler am Trifels** (☎ 06346/2200) will tell you the best places to climb.

HORSEBACK RIDING

There is ample opportunity in this fine riding country. Recommended stables include the **Gut Hohenberg** (☎ 06346/2592). The **Ferien und Reiterhof Münz** (☎ 06346/5272) is near Annweiler am Trifels.

Shopping

Located on the edge of the Palatinate Forest, the Pfälzerwald, Pirmasens is Germany's shoe center; it can be worth a detour from the Wine Road to stock up on a pair or two from factory outlets. **Buchholz** (⌖ Horebstr. 38, ☎ 06331/24790) stocks men's shoes. The place for children's shoes is **Hummel** (⌖ Charlottenstr. 8, ☎ 06331/76085). Women, however, will have to content themselves with the selection in regular (nonoutlet) shoe stores, of which the town has plenty.

Gleisweiler

❻ *12 km (8 mi) north of Anweiler on B-38 (follow signs toward Edenkoben).*

The little town of Gleisweiler is reputedly the warmest spot in Germany. A flourishing subtropical park supports the claim. Further proof is supplied by the fig trees that grow in abundance on many south-facing walls. This is also just about the only area in Germany in which lemons are grown.

The sun-drenched charms of the region attracted Bavaria's King Ludwig I in the middle of the 19th century. He called it "a garden of God" and compared its light to that of Italy. In the 1850s he built himself a summerhouse in the hills above the town. The nearby community of Edenkoben responded by putting up a statue of its royal guest in the main square.

You can pay your respects to the Bavarian monarch by visiting his handsome neoclassical residence, **Villa Ludwighöhe.** Today it displays paintings by the German Impressionist Max Slevogt (1868–1932). The paintings have a certain dreamy charm, but many visitors will find the grandiose setting more diverting. ☎ 06323/3148. ☐ DM 5 *(includes guided tour in German).* ☉ *Apr.–Sept., Tues.–Sun. 9–1 and 2–6; Oct.–Mar., Tues.–Sun. 9–1 and 2–5.*

❼ The ruins of **Rietburg Castle** lie on the opposite (north) side of the valley, facing the Villa Ludwigshöhe. The only chairlift in the Rhineland Palatinate will whisk you up to them, if you feel like checking out the terrific view.

NEED A BREAK? The other reason for visiting Rietburg Castle is to have lunch on the terrace of the **café** here. Drink in the view as you eat.

St. Martin

★ **❽** *5 km (3 mi) north of Gleisweiler.*

Back on the Wine Road, a mile or two will bring you to the village of St. Martin. It's known as one of the most beautiful in the area, a reputation it nurtures by encouraging the surrounding vineyards to encroach on its narrow streets. You'll find vines clinging everywhere, with curling green garlands linking the ancient houses. Visit the little 15th-century church to see the imposing Renaissance tomb of the Dalberg family. Their castle, now romantically ruined, stands guard over the village.

Dining and Lodging

$$–$$$ ✗🏨 **St. Martiner Castell.** An ancient vintner's house, once virtually a ruin, was transformed into a fine hotel and restaurant in the late 1980s. Many of the building's original features were retained and restored—the restaurant's gnarled beams and old wine press, for example. Guest rooms are adorned with antique furnishings and decorative pieces; most rooms have balconies that afford views of the surrounding vineyards. ⊠ *Maikammer Str. 2,* ☎ 06323/9510, ⚠ 06323/2098. *18 rooms with bath. Restaurant, weinstube, sauna. No credit cards. Closed Feb.–mid-Mar.*

En Route There's another castle hereabouts that you can visit, especially if your blood is stirred by tales of German nationalism and the overthrow of tyranny. It's **Hambach Castle,** standing about a half mile outside the village of Hambach, itself about 8 kilometers (5 miles) north of St. Martin. It's not the castle, built in the 11th century and largely ruined in the 17th, that's the attraction. Rather you'll visit to honor an event that happened here in May 1832. Fired by the revolutionary turmoil that was sweeping across Europe and groaning under the repressive yoke of a distant and aristocratic government, 30,000 stalwart Germans assembled at the castle demanding democracy, the overthrow of the Bavarian ruling house of Wittelsbach, and a united Germany. The symbol of their heroic demands was a flag—striped red, black, and yellow—that they flew from the castle. The old order proved rather more robust than these protodemocrats had reckoned on; the crowd was rapidly dispersed with some loss of life. The new flag was banned. It was not until 1919 that the monarchy was ousted and a united Germany became fully democratic. Fittingly, the flag flown from Hambach nearly 90 years earlier was adopted as that of the new German nation. (It was a short-lived triumph. Hitler did away with both democracy and the flag, when he came to power in 1932, and it was not until 1949, with the creation of the Federal Republic of Germany, that both were restored.) The castle remains a focus of the democratic aspirations of the Germans. Exhibits chart the progress of democracy in Germany. ☎ 06321/30881. ⌨ DM 5. ⊙ Mar.–Nov., daily 9–6:30.

Neustadt-an-der-Weinstrasse

❾ 5 km (3 mi) north of Hambach.

High-rises announce the presence of Neustadt-an-der-Weinstrasse, the biggest town on the Wine Road and the most important wine-producing center in the region. It's a bustling town, the narrow streets of its old center still following the medieval street plan. It's wine that makes Neustadt tick, and practically every shop seems linked with the wine trade. A remarkable 5,000 acres of vineyards lie within the official town limits. The **Stiftskirche** (Collegiate Church) in the central Marktplatz is an austere Gothic building, constructed during the 14th century for the elector of the Rhineland Palatinate. Inside, a wall divides the church in two, a striking reminder of former religious strife. The church, indeed the entire region, became Protestant in the Reformation during the 16th century. At the beginning of the 18th century the Catholic population of the town petitioned successfully to be allowed a share of the church. The choir (the area around the altar) was accordingly designated the Catholic half of the church; the nave, the main body of the church, was reserved for the Protestants. To keep the squabbling communities apart, the wall was built inside the church. Is it an instance of religious tolerance or intolerance? And who got the better deal? As you wander around the church—be sure to look at the intricate 15th-century choir stalls and the little figures, monkeys, and vine leaves carved into the capitals of the nave columns—you can ponder these matters.

....

NEED A BREAK?   Duck into the ancient confines of the **Herberge aus der Zunftzeit** (✉ Mittelgasse 3, ☎ 06321/7688), a 14th-century tavern offering excellent local wines and specialties. Try a slice of Zwiebelkuchen (onion tart) and a glass of Kirchberg wine.

....

℃   Neustadt has a **railway museum** that's packed with old-timers from the age of steam. From May to October you can take the historic steam train along the 11-kilometer (7-mile) stretch from Neustadt to Elmstein (☎ 06325/8626 for information). ✉ Neustadt railway station, Schillerstr. entrance, ☎ 06321/30390. ⌨ DM 4. ⊙ Weekends and holidays 10–4.

Dining

$$ ✕ **Gerberhaus.** Two floors of a half-timbered 17th-century tanner's house, next to the medieval gate leading to the Old Town, are occupied by this fine old Pfalz restaurant. The menu ranges from stout local fare (Pfälzer sausage and cuts of marinated pork) to more sophisticated international dishes (lamb medallions with young beans in bacon). The local wines are excellent. ⊠ *Hintergasse 6,* ☎ *06321/88700. MC. Closed Wed.*

$$ ✕ **Ratsherrenstuben.** Local vintners often meet in this half-timbered building; if you come here, you're likely to overhear them discussing business, and perhaps you'll pick up advice on which wine to order from the long list available. The comprehensive menu specializes in Palatinate dishes, such as the Pfälzer butcher's plate, piled high with various meats. ⊠ *Marktpl. 10–12,* ☎ *06321/2070. MC, V. Closed Mon.*

$ ✕ **Weinstube Eselsburg.** A consummate artist is in charge here. The tavern's jovial landlord finds time between serving creative Palatinate dishes to sketch and paint. He sings, too—the evenings can lengthen into quite a party. The tavern is in the Mussbach area of Neustadt, a 10-minute drive from the town center. ⊠ *Kurpfalzstr. 62, Neustadt-Mussbach,* ☎ *06321/66984. No credit cards. Closed Sun.–Tues.*

Nightlife

If you tire of the wine taverns of the Wine Road, try the exotic **Bahama Club** (⊠ Landauerstr. 65) in Neustadt-an-der-Weinstrasse. Neustadt has a surprisingly upbeat nightlife; **Madison** (⊠ am Kartoffelmarkt 2) is the "in" place.

Outdoor Activities and Sports

BICYCLING

In Neustadt one can rent bicycles at **Fahrradladen Pirad** (⊠ Ludwigstrasse 31, ☎ 06321/33790).

GOLF

The Palatinate has its own golf club, the **Golf Club Pfalz e.V.** (☎ 06327/97420), with an 18-hole course at Geinsheim, near Neustadt-an-der-Weinstrasse.

En Route On the Wine Road you'll find what is claimed to be one of Europe's biggest leisure parks, the **Hassloch Holidaypark.** It's at Hassloch, on B–39 between Neustadt and Speyer. A circus, a dolphinarium, a replica of the Lilliputians' town from the book *Gulliver's Travels,* an adventure playground, and an elaborate medieval mock-up, the "Robber Knights of Falkenstein Mountain," number among the attractions. ⊠ *D-67454 Hassloch-Pfalz,* ☎ *06324/599–3900.* ☞ *DM 27.50.* ☉ *Apr.–Oct., daily 9–6.*

Speyer

🔟 *29 km (18 mi) east of Neustadt, 22 km (14 mi) north of Mannheim.*

Speyer was one of the great cities of the Holy Roman Empire, probably founded in Celtic times, taken over by the Romans, and expanded during the 11th century by the Salian Holy Roman emperors. Between 1294 and 1570 no fewer than 50 full diets (meetings of the rulers of the Holy Roman Empire) were convened here.

★ The focus of a visit to Speyer is the imperial cathedral, the **Kaiserdom,** one of the largest medieval churches in Europe. It is certainly one of the finest Romanesque cathedrals, and more than any other building in Germany conveys the pomp and majesty of the early Holy Roman emperors. It was built in only 30 years, between 1030 and 1060, by the emperors Konrad II, Heinrich III, and Heinrich IV. A four-year restoration program in the 1950s returned the building to almost exactly its original condition. If you have any interest in the achievements of the early Middle Ages, don't miss this building. It embodies all that is best in Romanesque architecture.

There's an understandable tendency to dismiss most Romanesque architecture as little more than a cruder version of Gothic, the style that followed it and that many consider to be the supreme architectural achievement of the Middle Ages. Where the Gothic is seen as delicate, soaring, and noble, the Romanesque by contrast seems lumpy and earthbound, more fortresslike than divine. It's true that even the most successful Romanesque buildings are ponderously massive, but they possess a severe confidence and potency that can be overwhelming. What's more, look carefully at the decorative details and you'll see vivid and often delicate craftsmanship.

See as much of the building from the outside as you can before you venture inside. You can walk most of the way around it, and there's a fine view of the east end from the park by the Rhine. If you've seen Köln Cathedral, the finest Gothic cathedral in Germany, you'll be struck at once by how much more massive Speyer Cathedral is. The few windows are small, as if crushed by the surrounding masonry. Notice, too, their round tops, a key characteristic of the style. The position of the space-rocket–like towers, four in all (two at either end), and the immense, smoothly sloping dome at the east end give the building a distinctive, animated profile; it has a barely suppressed energy and dynamism. Notice, too, how much of a piece it is; having been built all in one go, the church remains faithful to a single vision. Inside, the cathedral is dimly mysterious, stretching to the high altar in the distance. In contrast to Gothic cathedrals, whose walls are supported externally by flying buttresses, allowing the interior the minimum of masonry and the maximum of light, at Speyer the columns supporting the roof are massive. Their bulk naturally disguises the side aisles, drawing your eye to the altar. Look up at the roof; it's a shallow stone vault, the earliest such vaulted roof in Europe. Look, too, at the richly carved capitals of the columns, filled with naturalistic details—foliage, dogs, birds, faces.

No fewer than eight Holy Roman emperors, many kings, and four queens are buried in the cathedral, including, fittingly enough, the three who built it. They lie in the crypt, which also should be visited to see its simple beauty, uninterrupted by anything save the barest minimum of decorative detail. The entrance is in the south aisle. ⊠ *Dompl. Kaiserdom. For information about guided tours,* ☎ *06232/102–267.* ⊘ *Weekdays 9–5, Sat. 9–6, Sun. 1:30–5.*

Treasures from the cathedral and the imperial tombs of Speyer are kept in the city's excellent museum, the **Historisches Museum der Pfalz,** opposite the cathedral. ⊠ *Dompl.* ⊠ *DM 8.* ⊘ *Tues.–Sun. 10–6.*

☾ A turn-of-the-century factory hall in Speyer houses the **Technology Museum,** a huge collection of locomotives, aircraft, old automobiles, and fire engines. A major attraction here is the 420-ton U-boat on display outside. The museum also has added an IMAX cinema (one of only two in Germany). ⊠ *Geibstr. 2,* ☎ *06232/78844.* ⊠ *DM 12, IMAX cinema DM 10.* ⊘ *Daily 9–6.*

Dining and Lodging

$$ ✕ **Wirtschaft zum Alten Engel.** Regional dishes from the Palatinate and
★ the French Alsace region dominate the menu in this historic cellar tavern in the heart of the city. Try the mushroom gratinée. ⊠ *Mühlturmstr. 1,* ☎ *06232/70914. AE, DC, MC, V. Closed Sun. and Aug. No lunch.*

$$ ✕⊡ **Hotel Morgenstern.** Flowers in window boxes adorn the immaculate white facade of this stately modern mansion in Speyer's Römerberg district. It was built in a combination of attractive styles, with high French windows under an imposing mansard roof. The interior lives up to the exterior—bright and airy rooms are furnished in a combination of modern and traditional styles. ⊠ *Römerberg 1 at Berghausen, D–67354,* ☎ *06232/8001,* ⅎⅨ *06232/8028. 21 rooms with bath. Restaurant, bar. AE, MC.*

$$–$$$ ⊡ **Goldener Engel.** The "Golden Angel" has been in business since 1701 and offers a simple, traditional atmosphere with appealing modern comfort. The rooms have modern furniture, wall-to-wall carpeting, and painted oak beams. There's no restaurant, but it adjoins the Wirtschaft zum Alten Engel (☞ *above*). ⊠ *Mühlturmstr. 1a, D–67346,* ☎ *06232/13260,* ⅎⅨ *06232/132–695. 45 rooms and 2 apartments with bath. AE, DC, MC, V. Closed Dec. 23–Jan. 10.*

The Arts

In Speyer the city's theater is the **Stadthalle** (⊠ Obere Langgasse, ☎ 06232/14392); contact the local tourist office, the Verkehrsamt (⊠ Maximilianstr. 11, ☎ 06232/14392), for program details and tickets.

Outdoor Activities and Sports

SWIMMING

Speyer's **lido** (⊠ Geibstr. 4) has a spectacular water slide.

TENNIS

Speyer has a tennis club that accepts visitors: the **Tennisclub Weiss-Rot Speyer** (⊠ Holzstr., ☎ 06232/76423).

Deidesheim

⑪ *6 km (4 mi) north of Neustadt.*

Back on the Wine Road, the wine town of Deidesheim is the next stop north. It was here that the bishops of Speyer, among the most powerful clerics in Germany during the Middle Ages, had their administrative headquarters. Their former palace is now mostly a ruin, its moat a green and shady park. Make sure you see the town square, **Marktplatz.** It's bordered on three sides by flower-smothered, half-timbered houses, the whole forming one of the most picturesque ensembles in the Rhineland Palatinate. Climb the impressive stairway to the **Rathaus;** the entrance is through a curious porch crowned by a helmetlike roof and spire. Ask to view the fine wood-paneled assembly hall, where councillors and envoys of successive bishops of Speyer haggled over church finances. Don't leave Deidesheim without strolling down the street called Feigengasse. It's named after the *Feigen* (fig trees) that grow in front of practically every house.

NEED A
BREAK?
Look for the golden lion sign of the **Deidesheimer Hof** (⊠ Marktpl., ☎ 06326/1811) on the right side of the three-cornered market square. Within this ancient inn is one of the best restaurants in the region. There's also the more affordable St. Urban wine tavern, where you can eat and drink in quiet comfort. Look, too, for the names Gerümpel and Goldbächel on the wine list—they are the very best the area has to offer.

Dining and Lodging

$$$–$$$$ ✕⊡ **Deidesheimer Hof.** This is the showpiece hotel of the Deidesheim-
★ based Hahnhof group, a countrywide chain of wine restaurants. It's a traditional old Deidesheimer house, immaculately clean, comfortable,

and run with slick but friendly efficiency. German chancellor Kohl likes to entertain official guests in the hotel's Schwarzer Hahn restaurant. It's one of the best establishments in the region, with traditional oak and pine furnishings and broad vaulted ceilings. The menu includes German-style nouvelle cuisine and hearty Palatinate dishes. Margaret Thatcher and Mikhail Gorbachev have been among the restaurant's distinguished guests. ⊠ *Am Marktpl., D–67146,* ☎ *06326/1811,* ⅢX *06326/7685. 18 rooms, 2 suites with bath. Restaurant, weinstube. AE, DC, MC, V. Closed Jan. and Aug.*

$$–$$$ ✕⛨ **Haardt Hotel Zum Geissbock.** The pillared front facade of this lodging stands directly on the Wine Road, in the center of Deidesheim. Front-facing rooms can be noisy, so ask for one at the back. Under the steeply pitched roof is a well-designed pool and sauna/solarium area, where you can swim and enjoy views of the neighboring countryside. The renowned Reichsrat von Buhl vineyard supplies the excellent wines served in the hotel's restaurant and basement wine-tasting tavern. ⊠ *Weinstr. 11, D–67146,* ☎ *06326/7070,* ⅢX *06326/707–112. 80 rooms with bath. Restaurant, bar, pool, sauna, bowling, paddle tennis. DC, MC, V.*

$$ ✕⛨ **Hotel St. Urban.** The oriel windows under the steep eaves afford a complete view of Deidesheim—ask for a room with one. Even if your request isn't granted, the village center is just a few minutes' walk. The hotel is well-modernized and elegantly appointed; a soothing dove gray is the predominant color, from the walls of the restaurant to the carpeting of the comfortable rooms. ⊠ *Im oberen Grain 1, D–67146,* ☎ *06326/6024,* ⅢX *06326/79485. 18 rooms with bath. Restaurant, café, weinstube, sauna. AE, MC, V.*

En Route   At the foot of the castle ruins of Wachtenburg, between Deidesheim and Bad Dürkheim, the regional **Winzergenossenschaft** (Vintner's Association) in Wachenheim is a great place to taste a wide variety of the local vintages—and, if you like, to purchase some. ⊠ *Weinstr. 2,* ☎ *06322/8101.* ☉ *Weekdays 8–noon and 1–5, Sat. 8–noon.*

Bad Dürkheim

⑫ *8 km (5 mi) and two charming wine villages (Forst and Wachenheim) north of Deidesheim.*

The bustling little Wine Road town of Bad Dürkheim has a distinction that's hard to beat: a wine cask so big it contains a restaurant with seating for 420 (the Bad Dürkheimer Riesenfass, ⊠ Am Wurstmarktgelände) and a live brass band on weekends. In mid-September it's the focal point of what the locals claim is the world's biggest wine festival, a week of revelry and partying during which the wine flows freely.

The click and whir of roulette balls may not suggest an off-the-beaten-track activity, but Bad Dürkheim's little **casino** is definitely a change from the high rollers of Baden-Baden and Mainz. If you fancy a quiet flutter, try your luck here. 🎴 *DM 5. Jacket and tie.* ☉ *Daily 2 PM–2 AM.*

The remains of the old **Limburg Monastery** above town are an impressive reminder of Bad Dürkheim's past. It is counted as one of the most important Romanesque buildings in Germany.

The **Pfälzerwald** nature park begins just beyond Bad Dürkheim's town limits. It's Germany's largest uninterrupted area of forest and a favorite stretch for hiking. If you don't fancy a full-fledged walking tour, at least give yourself an hour or two to experience its lonely, rugged grandeur.

Stroll through the groves of **sweet chestnut trees** in the hills above Bad Dürkheim. The descendants of saplings planted by the Romans

2,000 years ago, the trees are among the few of their kind remaining in Germany.

OFF THE
BEATEN PATH

FRANKENSTEIN – Climb through the woods above this town (west of Bad Dürkheim on A–37 on the way to Kaiserslautern) to the ruins of the medieval castle that watches over the ugly, brooding town. Whether it's the castle that helped inspire Mary Shelley, author of Frankenstein, no one knows, but it's easy to imagine how a romantic soul might be stirred by the ruins.

NOTHWEILER – In this town near Bad Dürkheim, you'll find an ancient iron mine, the **St. Anna Ironworks,** said to date from Celtic times, before the birth of Christ. ☒ DM 4. ☉ Apr.–Oct., Tues.–Fri. 2–6, Sat. 1–6, Sun. 11–6.

Dining and Lodging

$$ ★ ✕ **Bad Dürkheimer Riesenfass.** This must be Germany's most unusual restaurant, in the biggest wine barrel in the world, with room for 420 people inside and an additional 230 on the terrace. The food, like the wine, is robustly local. It's touristy but fun. ☒ Am Wurstmarktgelände, ☎ 06322/2143. No credit cards.

$$ ✕ **Restaurant-Weinstube Käsbüro.** Despite the name—it means "cheese office"—this historic old tavern specializes in fish and game dishes. It's about a mile from the center of Bad Dürkheim, in Seebach, and is well worth hunting down. ☒ Dorfpl., Seebach, ☎ 06322/8694. MC, V. Closed Wed.

$$$–$$$$ ✕▥ **Kurparkhotel.** Ask for a room overlooking the little spa park; on summer evenings you'll be serenaded by the orchestra that plays on its bandstand. Rooms are large and airy, and some have views of the vineyards above the town. Temptation lurks in the lobby—the hotel has direct access to the spa's casino. ☒ Schlosspl. 1–4, ☎ 06322/7970, D–67098, ℻ 06322/797–158. 110 rooms, 3 suites with bath. Restaurant, bar, indoor pool, beauty salon, sauna, spa. AE, DC, MC, V.

$$$ ▥ **Garten-Hotel Heusser.** This hotel describes itself as an "oasis of peace"—and that's not much of an exaggeration. There are vineyards all around, and most rooms have fine views of the rolling Palatinate countryside. One disadvantage: This vineyard oasis is a thirsty 20-minute walk from the town center. ☒ Seebacherstr. 50–52, ☎ 06322/9300, ℻ 06322/930–499. 80 rooms with bath. Restaurant, indoor pool, outdoor pool, sauna. AE, DC, MC, V.

$$$ ▥ **Hotel-Restaurant Fronmühle.** Located on the edge of Bad Dürkheim's spa park, this whitewashed farmhouse-style hotel has won first prize several times in a district-wide competition for hotel management. If your tastes are similar to those of the judges, you'll praise the Fronmühle's high-quality accommodations and services and the efficient management of the Kraus family. Bathrooms are a bit small for a hotel of this price category—there are no bathtubs—but large, airy rooms make up for that; they're individually decorated with dark-wood furnishings and brightly colored prints. ☒ Salinenstr. 15, D–67098, ☎ 06322/94090. 22 rooms with shower. Restaurant, pool, sauna. AE, DC, MC, V.

$ ▥ **Weingut und Gästehaus Ernst Karst and Sohn.** You'll stay in the midst of vineyards, and proprietor Ernst Karst will gladly and proudly show you around his own cellars, inviting you to try his vintages. Rooms are light and airy, furnished mostly in pine; all of them have splendid views of the surrounding countryside—which you are invited to explore on the bikes that Herr Karst loans out. The hotel's lovely restaurant is 1 kilometer (½ mile) from the hotel itself. ☒ In den Almen 15, D–67098,

☎ 06322/2862, FAX 06322/65965. *4 rooms with shower, 1 apartment with bath. Restaurant, bicycles. No credit cards. Closed Nov.–Jan.*

Outdoor Activities and Sports

BICYCLING
In Bad Dürkheim you can rent bicycles at **Robl Sport** (✉ Bruchstr. 51).

SWIMMING
At the **thermal baths** (☎ 06322/66727) you can splash around in warm pools overlooking the sun-drenched vineyards that clothe the hills surrounding the town.

TENNIS
Tennis courts in the **Kurpark** (☎ 06322/67979) are so beautifully located that concentrating on the game becomes difficult.

Shopping
Bad Dürkheim is a particularly inviting wine center. Most wine outlets are family-run affairs; don't expect to be able to use credit cards. **Heinrich Bühler** (✉ Hinterbergstr. 12, ☎ 06322/2102) offers wine tastings accompanied by explanations in English. You can taste and learn with vintner **Roland Bauer** (✉ Seebacher Str. 12, ☎ 06322/2487). Local winegrower **Hermann Frey** has a reasonably priced package deal on eight different kinds of wine and a plate of homemade sausages (✉ Michelsbergstr. 5, ☎ 06322/4151).

En Route   Four kilometers (2½ miles) north from of Dürkheim and a couple of miles after Kallstadt is **Freinsheim.** The little town is one of the best preserved in the region, a winning combination of winding medieval streets and high-gabled, half-timbered buildings. At regular intervals conical-roofed towers punctuate the original medieval walls that still encircle the Old Town. A counterpoint to this toy-town charm is provided by the stately Baroque Rathaus, an elegantly classical building with an unusual covered staircase leading up to the imposing main entrance.

Neuleiningen

🔞 *10 km (6 mi) north of Kallstadt.*

Too-good-to-be-true charm is provided by the town of Neuleiningen. Until quite recently this was among the most backward and impoverished areas of the country. The people were called *Geesbocke,* or "billy goats," a mocking reference to the only animals the townspeople could afford to keep. The name lives on today in the village's most historic inn, Zum Gäsbock. Stop in to sample a glass or two of local wine or for a tasty bite and to admire the Renaissance interior. The Wine Road ends at **Bockenheim,** 10 kilometers (6 miles) north of Neuleiningen.

Dining and Lodging
$$$ ✕▥ **Pfalzhotel Asselheim.** This fine old country hotel stands on the outskirts of Grünstadt, a town near Neuleiningen, at the north end of the Wine Road. Surrounded by vineyards, the Pfalzhotel is situated near the edge of the Pfälzerwald nature park. Low beams, fine wood paneling, rustic antiques, and huge tile ovens combine harmoniously in the restaurant and public areas—even the indoor swimming pool has half-timbered walls. The bedrooms aren't quite so atmospheric, but they are modern and comfortable. ✉ *Holzweg 6, D–67269 Grünstadt-Asselheim,* ☎ *06359/80030,* FAX *06359/800–399. 33 rooms with bath or shower, 2 apartments. Restaurant, weinstube, indoor pool, sauna, bowling, paddle tennis, bicycles. AE, DC, MC, V.*

WORMS TO MAINZ

Like Speyer, the Rhine cities of Worms and Mainz were once among the Rhineland's great imperial centers. Mainz and Worms both possess cathedrals to rival Speyer's. From Mainz you may continue on to explore the rest of the Rhineland. (☞ Chapter 12.)

Worms

⑭ *13 km (8 mi) east of Bockenheim, 44 km (27 mi) south of Mainz.*

Numbers in the margin correspond to points of interest on the Worms map.

There are several reasons to visit the ancient imperial city of Worms (pronounced *Vawrms*). First you should see the great, gaunt Romanesque cathedral; it presents a less-perfect expression of the Romanesque spirit than does Speyer Cathedral but exudes much of the same craggy magnificence. Second, Worms, though devastated in World War II, is among the most ancient cities in Germany: founded as early as 6,000 years ago, settled by the Romans, and later one of the major centers of the Holy Roman Empire. More than 100 diets of the empire were held here, including the 1521 meeting where Martin Luther came to plead his "heretical" case. Its standing as one of the most important German wine centers is the third reason to travel to Worms. Anyone who has fallen under the spell of the Rhineland Palatinate's golden wines will want to sample more here. There's some industry on the outskirts of the city, but the rebuilt Old Town is compact and easy to explore.

It was the Romans who made Worms important, but it was a Burgundian tribe, established in Worms in the 5th century, that gave the city its most compelling legend—the *Nibelungenlied*. The story, probably written during the 12th century and considerably elaborated throughout the years, is complex and sprawling, telling of love, betrayal, greed, war, and death. It ends when Attila the Hun defeats the Nibelungen (the Burgundians) who find their court destroyed, their treasure lost, and their heroes dead. (One of the most famous incidents tells how Hagen, treacherous and scheming, hurls the court riches into the Rhine; by the Nibelungen bridge there's a bronze statue of him caught in the act.) The *Nibelungenlied* may be legend, but the story is based on fact. For instance, a Queen Brunhilda is supposed to have lived here. It's known, furthermore, that a Burgundian tribe was defeated in 437 by Attila the Hun in what is present-day Hungary.

Not until Charlemagne resettled Worms almost 400 years later, making it one of the major cities of his empire, did the city prosper again. Worms wasn't just an administrative and commercial center but a great ecclesiastic city as well. The first expression of this religious importance was the original cathedral, consecrated in 1018. In 1171 construction began on another cathedral; this is the one that brings visitors to Worms.

★ **⑮** If you've seen Speyer Cathedral, you'll quickly realize that **Worms Cathedral,** by contrast, contains many Gothic elements. In part this is simply a matter of chronology. Speyer Cathedral was completed more than 100 years before the one at Worms was even begun, long before the lighter, more vertical lines of the Gothic style were developed. But there's another reason. Once built, Speyer Cathedral was left largely untouched in later periods; the Worms Cathedral was remodeled frequently as new architectural styles and new values developed. Nonetheless, you'll find that same muscular confidence, that same blocky

340

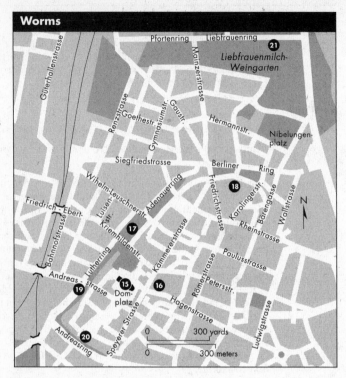

Worms

massiveness, characteristic of Speyer. The ground plan of the church is similar, too, framed with two towers on each side, a prominent apse at the east end, and short transepts (the "arms" of the church). The Gothic influence is most obvious inside, especially in the great rose window at the west end (over the main entrance). It could almost be in a French church and presents a striking contrast to the tiny, round-headed windows high up in the nave. Notice, too, how a number of the main arches in the nave are pointed, a key characteristic of the Gothic style. It wasn't only in the Gothic period that the cathedral was altered, however. As you near the main altar you'll see the lavish Baroque screen of columns supporting a gold crown that towers above the marvelous altar by the great Balthasar Neumann:—an example of Baroque at its most opulent. The choir stalls, installed in 1760, are equally opposed in spirit to the body of the church. Intricately carved and gilded, they proclaim the courtly and sophisticated glamour of the rococo. ☉ *Apr.–Oct., daily 8–6; Nov.–Mar., daily 9–5.*

Outside the Worms Cathedral cross the square to see the simple **Dreifaltigkeit Church** (Church of the Holy Trinity). Remodeling of the church during the 19th and 20th centuries produced today's austere building, although the facade and tower are still joyfully Baroque. It's a Lutheran church and therefore a reminder of the beginnings of Protestantism, which started as Martin Luther's "protest" against the excesses and corruption of the Catholic church in that period. Luther called for reform (hence the term Reformation) and defended his supposedly heretical beliefs here in 1521 before the Holy Roman Emperor and the massed ranks of Catholic theologians. After his passionate defense, he was duly excommunicated. ⊙ *Daily 9–5, tours of tower 2nd Sun. of month at 2 and 4.*

⑰ The **Lutherdenkmal (Luther monument)** commemorates the speech Luther made before the Holy Roman Emperor. Luther ended his speech with: "Here I stand, I can do no different. God help me. Amen!" The monument is a 19th-century group of statues of Luther and other figures from the Reformation, set in a small park on the street appropriately named Lutherring.

Worms was also one of the most important Jewish cities in Germany, a role that came to a brutal end with the rise of the Nazis. The rebuilt ★ **⑱** **synagogue,** one of the oldest in the country, was founded during the 11th century; it was entirely destroyed in 1938 during the Kristallnacht assaults. In 1961 the synagogue was rebuilt, using as much of the original masonry as had survived. ⊙ *May–Oct., daily 10–noon and 2–5; Nov.–Apr., daily 10–noon and 2–4.*

Next to the synagogue of Worms in a former Jewish family home is the **Judaica Museum,** which documents the history of the Jewish community in Worms. The exhibits include artifacts from as far back as the 11th century. ⊠ *Raschi-Haus, Judengasse.* ▨ *DM 3.* ⊙ *Tues.–Sun. 10–noon and 2–5.*

⑲ Worms's **Judenfriedhof** is the oldest Jewish cemetery in Europe, with graves dating back to 1076. ⊠ *West of Dompl. off the Lutherring.* ▨ *Free.* ⊙ *Daily 10–noon and 2–4.*

⑳ To bone up on the history of Worms, visit the **Städtisches Museum** (Municipal Museum). It's housed in the cloisters of a former Romanesque church; the exhibits shed considerable light on Worms's Roman past. ⊠ *Weckerlingpl.* ▨ *DM 3.* ⊙ *Tues.–Sun. 10–noon and 2–5.*

If you visit Worms in late August or early September, you'll find it embroiled in its carnival, the improbably named *Backfischfest,* or Baked Fish Festival. The highlight is the **Fischerstechen,** a kind of waterborne jousting in which contestants spar with long poles while balancing on the wobbly decks of flat-bottom boats. The winner is crowned King of the River; the losers get a dunking. Baked fish is the culinary highlight of the festival, of course. The wine is never in short supply.

Don't leave Worms without visiting the Gothic pilgrimage church of **㉑** the **Liebfrauen** convent, the **Liebfrauenkirche,** an easy 20-minute walk north from the Old Town. The church is surrounded by the vineyard that gave birth to Germany's most famous export wine, Liebfraumilch (Our Lady's Milk). Buy a bottle or two from the shop at the vineyard. *Church and vineyard* ⊙ *Apr.–Oct., daily 9–6; Nov.–Mar., daily 9–5.*

Dining and Lodging

$$$ ✕ **Bei Bacchus.** The name is apt: Here you'll drink some of the best ★ wine in the region. This restaurant is perhaps a bit stuffy, but the food is quite good, with local specialties predominating. ⊠ *Obermarkt 10,* ☎ *06241/6913. Jacket and tie. AE, DC, MC, V. Closed Sun.*

$$$ ✕ **Rotisserie Dubs.** Make the trek to Wolfgang Dubs's sleekly appointed restaurant to eat his excellent steak in snail sauce, a substantially more appetizing dish than it sounds. The restaurant is in the suburb of Rheindürkheim, a 10-minute ride from downtown. ⊠ *Kirchstr. 6,* ☎ *06242/2023. Reservations essential. Jacket and tie. MC. Closed Tues. and 2 wks in July. No lunch Sat.*

$$$ ✕▣ **Dom Hotel.** Although this modern and centrally located hotel is the best in Worms, all it really provides is functional comfort. The restaurant, Bei Bacchus (☞ *above*), compensates, however. ⊠ *Obermarkt*

10, D–67547, ☎ 06241/6913, FAX 06241/23515. *60 rooms with bath, 2 apartments. Restaurant. AE, DC, MC, V.*

$$–$$$ ✕🏨 **Hotel and Restaurant Römischer Kaiser.** Despite what you'd expect from a hotel with this name in this region, the ground floor is a high-class Asian restaurant that serves Chinese, Japanese, and Korean dishes. Rooms at the hotel are sturdy and affordable, with sleek dark-wood furnishings and such individual touches as oil paintings on the walls and fresh flowers on the dressing tables. ✉ *Römerstr. 72, D–67547,* ☎ *06241/6936,* FAX *06241/229–953. 11 rooms with bath. AE, DC, MC, V.*

$$–$$$ ✕🏨 **Kriemhilde.** Reliable comfort and a central location next to the cathedral are the advantages of this rustic-style hotel. Its restaurant's menu offers a wide range of German specialties, including seasonal dishes: asparagus in May, wild boar in December, and goose for St. Martin's Day, November 11. The wine list is also gratifying—to anyone, at least, who wants to sample the local vintages. ✉ *Hofgasse 2–4, D–67547,* ☎ *06241/ 6278,* FAX *06241/6277. 20 rooms with bath. AE, DC, MC, V.*

$–$$ ✕🏨 **Lortze–Eck.** Just renovated, this hotel has Spanish-style decor outside and comfortable furnishings inside. It is one of the better deals in town; there are daily specials in the restaurant for DM 10 and good local wines by the glass. The management is friendly and keeps everything running smoothly. Although centrally located, the surrounding buildings (it is behind the Kaufhof) are of postwar concrete. ✉ *Schlossergasse 10–14, D–67547 Worms,* ☎ *06241/26349. 15 rooms with bath. AE, DC, MC, V.*

$ 🏨 **Gästehaus Bech.** The Bechtel family expanded its vineyard farmhouse to create this guest house. Rooms are comfortable and have TVs and telephones. The guest house lies on the outskirts of Worms, in the village of Heppenheim, with fine views of the surrounding vineyards. ✉ *Pfälzerwaldstr. 98,* ☎ *06241/36536,* FAX *06241/34745. 12 rooms with bath or shower. No credit cards.*

Nightlife and the Arts

Worms has a square-dance club, the **Crackers,** which welcomes guests. Call 06241/23400 if you'd like to join in. The discotheques and bars of **Worms** are concentrated around Judengasse.

THEATER

Worms has a city theater, the **Städtisches Spiel und Festhaus,** where concerts and drama productions are staged. For program details and tickets, contact the box office on Rathenaustrasse (☎ 06241/22525.)

Shopping

Even if you're not buying wine, you can still pick up such related souvenirs as wineglasses, bottle openers (some of them elaborately carved from local wood), or wine coolers at Worms's **tourist office** (✉ Verkehrsverein, Neumarkt 14, ☎ 06241/25045); they sell a most original wine cooler: a terra-cotta replica of a Roman model unearthed in the region by archaeologists.

Oppenheim

🔢 *26 km (16 mi) north of Worms on B–9.*

One of Germany's most famous wine towns, Oppenheim lies between Worms and Mainz. The town is said to have been the center of Charlemagne's wine estates. Take a look at the fine market square, fussily bordered on all sides by time-honored half-timbered buildings. Then climb the steep stepped streets to the Gothic church of St. Catherine, the **Katharinenkirche.**

Dining and Lodging

$$$ ✕🏨 **Rondo.** "Rondo" (in the round) is exactly what this hotel is. Every room has a view, and many of them look out over the nearby Rhine. The best view of all is from the hotel's roof-terrace café. Because of its circular construction, the hotel's interior is light and airy; this is complemented in guest rooms by light-wood furnishings and bright fabrics. ✉ *Sant-Ambrogio-Ring,* ☎ *06133/70001,* ᴲᴬˣ *06133/2034. 35 rooms with bath. Restaurant, café, sauna, recreation room. AE, DC, MC, V.*

Outdoor Activities and Sports

HORSEBACK RIDING

In a nature-preserve area midway between Worms and Oppenheim is the **Gut Liebfrauenthal** in Eich, a stable (with a hotel and restaurant) offering a range of riding classes (☎ 06246/7578). Local tourist offices can give you more information.

Nierstein

㉓ *29 km (18 mi) north of Worms on B–9.*

Nierstein is a town that lives for wine; entire streets contain shops that sell nothing but the precious liquid. Many have ornate wood or wrought-iron signs, brilliantly painted and gilded, advertising their wares.

Mainz

㉔ *44 km (27 mi) north of Worms on B–9, 40 km (25 mi) west of Frankfurt.*

The city of Mainz is a bustling, businesslike, but friendly Rhine-side city. With its half-timbered buildings housing shops, restaurants, and wine taverns, it's a fine example of sensitive postwar reconstruction, following near-total destruction by bombings. The well-planned central pedestrian zone makes touring on foot a pleasure. All streets lead to the spacious market square, filled with stalls selling produce and other articles.

★ Watching over Mainz is the sturdy, turreted **Dom,** the third of the Rhine's great Romanesque cathedrals. Inside you'll find that the mantle of 1,000 years of history accompanies you through the aisles and chapels. The first cathedral here—dedicated to Saints Martin and Stephan—was built at the end of the 10th century. In 1002 Heinrich I, the last Saxon emperor of the Holy Roman Empire, was crowned in the still-far-from-complete building. In 1009, on the very day of its consecration, the cathedral burned to the ground. Rebuilding began almost immediately. The cathedral you see today, though substantially rebuilt at the end of World War II, was largely finished at the end of the 11th century. During the Gothic period, however, rebuilding and remodeling diluted the Romanesque purity of the original; and an imposing Baroque spire was added in the 18th century. Despite these additions and modifications, the building remains essentially Romanesque. At the very least its ground plan demonstrates a clear link to the cathedrals at Speyer and Mainz. Notice the towers at each end and the spires that rise between them; one may be Baroque, but its positioning and something of its bold impact produce an effect that is nothing if not Romanesque. Inside, though pointed arches proliferate, the walls have the same grim, fortresslike massiveness of Speyer. True, there's more stained glass, but the weight of masonry is full-fledged Romanesque. 🎫 *DM 8.* ☉ *English-language tours of cathedral and old city are given July–Aug., daily at 2.*

The **Dom und Diözesan Museum** (Cathedral Treasury and Museum) displays the Mainz cathedral's treasures. These include some marvelous Romanesque stone carvings including a figure of Atlas groaning and holding his lower back from the strain of supporting a heavy stone arch; and a group of damned souls, not at all pleased about having to go to hell. ☎ *Free.* ⊘ *Mon.–Wed. and Fri. 10–4, Thurs. 10–5, Sat. 10–2; closed holidays.*

★ Opposite the east end of the cathedral is the **Gutenberg Museum,** one of the most popular attractions in the Rhineland, devoted to the life and times of Mainz's most famous and influential son, Johannes Gutenberg (1390–1468). It was in Mainz, in 1456, that Gutenberg built the first machine that could print from movable type. The significance of his invention was immense, leading to an explosion in the availability of information. This wasn't actually the building in which Gutenberg worked—that's long since disappeared—but you can see fine reconstructions of his printing machine and get a sense of his original workshop. Exhibits explain the history of printing through the ages, with machines displayed below and manuscripts above. Among the latter the unquestioned highlight is one of only 47 existing copies of the Gutenberg Bible, not only one of the most historically significant books in the world but one of the most beautiful. Gutenberg is so important to Mainz that he has his own festival, *Johannisnacht,* in mid-June. ⊠ *Liebfrauenpl. 5,* ☎ *06131/122–640.* ☎ *DM 5.* ⊘ *Tues.–Sat. 10–6, Sun. 10–1.*

From the Gutenberg Museum, if you walk north along the Rhine, you'll find a confrontation of historic styles in the face-off between the **Eisenturm,** a reconstruction of one of the original city gates, on your left; and the unabashedly modern, 20th-century **Rathaus,** on your right. ⊠ *Rathauspl.,* ☎ *06131/122382.*

Continuing along the Rhine you'll come to the **Kurfürstliches Schloss** (Electoral Palace), a building oddly asymmetrical for its day (it appears to be missing a wing but was, in fact, built that way). This houses testimony to Mainz's even more ancient past: the **Römisch-Germanisches Museum.** Exhibited are artifacts, from statues to armor to jewelry, of the Roman settlement that once flourished here. ⊘ *Tues.–Sun. 10–6.*

☪ The animals in Mainz's **Natural History Museum** may all be stuffed and mounted, but these lifelike groups can demonstrate the relationships among various families of fauna better than any zoo. ⊠ *Reichklarastr. 1,* ☎ *06131/122–646.* ☎ *DM 5.* ⊘ *Tues. and Thurs. 10–8; Wed., Fri., and Sat. 10–5.*

The church of **St. Stephan** allows a hilltop view of the city. It's worth making the climb up, and not only for the view. The church itself is one of the oldest single-nave Gothic buildings in this part of the Rhineland. Its main highlight, however, is far newer: Around the choir, behind the altar, are six stained-glass windows depicting scenes from the Bible, designed in the 1970s by Russian-born painter Marc Chagall. The windows' vivid blue is a beautiful complement to the austere Gothic design of the rest of the church. ⊠ *Kleine Weissgasse 12,* ☎ *06131/231640.* ⊘ *Weekdays 10–noon and 2–5 (Dec.–Jan. 2–4:30).*

Not far from the church of St. Stephan is the **Kupferberg Sektkellerei,** the local producer of *Sekt* (sparkling wine), a little more upscale than the local wine. The oldest cellars here date to the days of the Romans; newer additions include the spectacular Art Deco (*Jugendstil*) Traubensaal, or "Grape Hall." The two-hour tour of the facility includes, of course, a sampling of its product. ⊠ *Am Kupferbergterrasse,* ☎ *06131/ 5550.* ☎ *DM 15.*

Mainz claims to host the wildest pre-Lent carnival in Germany. Be here in early February if you want to put that claim to the test. The city erupts in a Rhineland riot of revelry, the high point of which is the procession through the Old Town.

Dining and Lodging

$$ ✕ **Fischrestaurant Jackob.** Fresh fish (the fish shop next door belongs to the restaurant) is served at affordable prices in an atmosphere of old foghorns and ship photographs. A plate of *matjes* (herring) is DM 12. ⊠ *Fischtor 7,* ☎ *06131/229–299. No credit cards. Closed Sun. No dinner Sat.*

$$ ✕ **Kartäuser Hof.** If the weather is warm, try for a table in the walled courtyard, a pretty sunlit area smothered in flowers in the summer. There's a warm welcome at any time of year, however, in this pleasant restaurant that often features locally caught fish. There's also an impressive wine list, dominated by local vineyards. ⊠ *Kartäuser Str. 14,* ☎ *06131/222–956. AE, DC, MC, V.*

$$ ✕ **Rats und Zunftstuben Heilig Geist.** The most atmospheric dining in
★ Mainz is offered here. Parts of the building date from Roman times, but most of it is Gothic, with vaulted ceilings and stone floors. The menu features Bavarian specialties with nouvelle touches. ⊠ *Rentengasse 2,* ☎ *06131/225–757. AE, DC, MC, V. Closed Mon. No dinner Sun.*

$ ✕ **HDW.** The abbreviated name stands for "House of German Wine." This German bistro has a modern approach to traditional food. The Mainz *Spuntekäse* is excellent as are the salad with fish and venison ragout with spaetzle (homemade noodles). It's near the Gutenberg Museum. ⊠ *Gutenbergpl. 3,* ☎ *06131/228–676. No credit cards.*

$ ✕ **Weinhaus Schreiner.** Mainz's oldest wine tavern has been in the hands of the Schreiner family since the mid-18th century and has won many awards from the local Vintners Association. The menu is shorter than the wine list, but it's full of robust Palatinate fare. It's your lucky day if marinated beef Rhineland style is available when you visit. ⊠ *Rheinstr. 38,* ☎ *06131/225–720. No credit cards. Closed Sun.*

$$$$ ✕▦ **Hilton International.** A terrific location right by the Rhine, allied
★ with the reliable standards of comfort and service expected of the chain, makes the Hilton the number one choice in Mainz. Don't come looking for too much in the way of old German atmosphere, however. The hotel has a casino and two restaurants; one serves an international menu with nouvelle cuisine, and the other has plainer, more traditional fare. ⊠ *Rheinstr. 68, D–55116,* ☎ *06131/2450,* ☒ *06131/245–589. 419 rooms and 14 suites, all with bath. 2 restaurants, beauty salon, sauna, exercise room. AE, DC, MC, V.*

$$$ ✕▦ **Hotel-Restaurant Am Lerchenberg.** The location isn't ideal—some 6½ kilometers (4 miles) from the city center—but this family-run hotel is friendly, comfortable, and peaceful—and there's a bus stop right outside the door. This could be a very good choice, though, if you're interested in biking and hiking—open countryside is only a few steps away. ⊠ *Hindemithstr. 5,* ☎ *06131/934–300,* ☒ *06131/934–3099. 53 rooms with shower. Restaurant, sauna, exercise room. AE, DC, MC, V.*

$$–$$$ ✕▦ **Hotel Ibis.** If you're visiting Mainz on the weekend, you can stay here for a discount of up to 50%—a very good deal. The hotel offers the sleek, though somewhat spartan, comfort and facilities that have enabled the Ibis group to keep its prices down. This one (unlike some of its German siblings) is also centrally located, with a restaurant that can be recommended. ⊠ *Holzhofstr. 2, D–55116,* ☎ *06131/ 2470,* ☒ *06131/234–126. 144 rooms with bath. Restaurant, bar. AE, DC, MC, V.*

$ ✕▦ **Hotel Stadt Coblenz.** In the heart of town, you get what you pay for at this hotel: budget rooms (bath in the hall) at budget prices. Ask for a room facing the back to avoid the noise of street traffic, and spend the money you saved on dinner in the rustic restaurant, which serves local and German specialties. ⊠ *Rheinstr. 49, D–55116,* ☎ *06131/ 227602. Restaurant. No credit cards.*

Nightlife and the Arts

Night owls congregate in the Altstadt, the Old Town, which is full of historic old wine and beer taverns (**Schinderhannes** is recommended). The central Marktplatz is the scene of a nightly program of open-air pop music, jazz, and street cabaret from May through September. Disco fans dance at **M Discothek** (⊠ Rheinallee 175) and the **Lindenbaum** (⊠ Holzstr. 32).

Mainz's recently acquired cultural center, the **Frankfurter Hof** (⊠ Augustinerstr. 55, ☎ 06131/220–438), offers a constantly changing music program of classical, pop, folk, and jazz. The **Kurfürstliches Schloss** presents classical concerts. You can get complete information on concerts in Mainz, as well as tickets, from the ticket office Kartenhaus (⊠ Schillerstr. 11, ☎ 06131/228–729).

Mainz has an annual **cathedral-music festival** that lasts through the summer. Organ recitals are given in the cathedral every Saturday at noon from mid-August to mid-September.

THEATER

The theater life of the Rhine-Palatinate region is concentrated in Mainz. The city's resident company, the **Theater der Landeshauptstadt Mainz,** performs regularly in the Staatstheater, Gutenbergerplatz, and at two other smaller venues. Opera and ballet productions are also staged at the Staatstheater. Call 06131/285–1222 for program details and tickets.

Shopping

Mainz boasts the area's oldest merchant district, **Am Brand,** a pedestrian zone that runs parallel to the marketplace toward the river. Locals did their shopping here as long ago as the late 13th century; today the merchant tradition is still carried on with a modern area of shops, boutiques, and supermarkets. Mainz's largest clothing store is **Sinn** (⊠ Am Brand 41, ☎ 06131/2730), with a selection of both men's and women's clothing. Centrally located in Mainz is a leading store, **Leininger** (⊠ Ludwigstr. 11, ☎ 06131/288820), which stocks articles for women and children only.

Such souvenirs of Mainz as distinctive local wineglasses emblazoned with the city's coat of arms are available from the **tourist office** (⊠ Bahnhofstr. 15, ☎ 06131/286–210). One of the local products is *Sekt* (champagne by any other name) from the local **Kupfenberg Sektkellerei.** You can buy it from the facility itself (⊠ Am Kupfenbergterrasse, ☎ 06131/5550) or at most local shops.

Mainz's famous **flea market,** the Krempelmarkt, is held along the banks of the Rhine every third Saturday of the month (except Apr. and Oct.).

RHINELAND PALATINATE A TO Z

Arriving and Departing

By Plane

Frankfurt, which has regular flights from the United States, is the closest major international airport for the entire Rhineland. Autobahn access to Mainz, the northernmost point of the itinerary, is fast and easy. Stuttgart Airport serves the southern half of the region. Take Autobahn

8 to Karlsruhe and then drive the 36 kilometers (22 miles) to the southern point of the wine route.

Getting Around

By Bus

Buses crisscross the Rhineland-Palatinate region, with most running to and from Mainz. Post buses connect smaller towns and villages. For information, timetables, and reservations, contact **Deutsche Touring GmbH** (✉ Am Römerhof 17, D–60486 Frankfurt/Main, ☎ 069/79030).

By Car

Most roads in the region are narrow and winding, a far cry from the highways of much of the rest of Germany. Autobahn 6 runs northeast–southwest across much of the southern part of the region, from Saarbrücken on the French border to the Rhine, reaching the river just above Mannheim. Halfway along take 61 to 63 north to Mainz. Driving conditions are good everywhere, with all roads well surfaced.

CAR RENTALS

Avis: ✉ Schmidtstr. 39, ☎ 069/730–111, **Frankfurt**; ✉ Wormser Landstr. 22, ☎ 06232/32068, **Speyer**; ✉ Alzeyer Str. 44, ☎ 06241/591–081, **Worms.**

Europcar: ✉ Schlossstr. 32, ☎ 069/775–033, **Frankfurt**; ✉ Rheinallee 107, ☎ 06131/677–073, **Mainz.**

Hertz: ✉ Hanauer Landstr. 106–108, ☎ 069/449–090, **Frankfurt**; ✉ Bensheimerstr. 1, ☎ 06241/43790, **Worms.**

By Train

Mainz is the only major city in the region with regular InterCity services; there are hourly connections to and from major German cities. To reach the southern part of the region, travel through Karlsruhe and Landau. Railroad buses serve those towns not on the rail network.

Contacts and Resources

Guided Tours

A number of the smaller towns and villages offer sightseeing tours in the summer, some including visits to neighboring vineyards. At Annweiler, for example, tours of the town are given on Wednesdays from May to October, beginning with a glass of wine at the Rathaus at 10 AM. Details of this and all other tours in the region are available from local tourist information offices.

There are city tours of Speyer and Worms. Mainz has a walking tour of its Old Town on Saturdays, starting from the tourist office at 10 AM (✉ DM 6); in July and August, there are English-language tours of the cathedral, Gutenberg Museum, and old city daily at 2 PM. The shipping company **Köln-Düsseldorfer Deutsche Rheinsschiffarht** has daily tours from Mainz to Köln between Good Friday and October (☎ 06131/286–2126). For details of Rhine River tours in the United States, contact **JFO CruiseService Corp.** (✉ 2500 Westchester Ave., Purchase, NY 10577, ☎ 914/696–3600, 800/346–6525); and **KD River Cruises of Europe** (✉ 323 Geary St., Suite 603, San Francisco, CA 94102, ☎ 415/392–8817 or 800/858–8587).

Visitor Information

The central tourist office for the Palatinate is the **Pfalz Tourist Office** (✉ Martin-Luther-Str. 69, 67433 Neustadt-an-der-Weinstrasse, ☎ 06321/39160). Information on the Wine Road can be obtained from the **Weinstrasse Zentrale für Tourismus** (✉ Postfach 2124, D–76829 Landau);

Fremdenverkehrsverband (✉ Bezirksstelle Pfalz, Hindenburgstr. 12, D–67433 Neustadt-an-der-Weinstrasse); and **Mittelhaardt-Deutsche Weinstrasse** (✉ Weinstr. 32, D–67146 Deidesheim-an-der-Weinstrasse). There are local tourist-information offices in the following towns:

Bad Dürkheim: Verkehrsamt, ✉ Mannheimer Str. 24, D–67098, ☎ 06322/935–156.

Deidesheim: Verkehrsamt Stadthalle, ✉ Bahnhofstr. 11, D–67146, ☎ 06326/5021.

Landau: Büro für Tourismus, ✉ Marktstr. 50, D–76825, ☎ 06341/13181.

Mainz: Verkehrsverein Mainz, ✉ Bahnhofstr 15, D–55116, ☎ 06131/286–210.

Neustadt-an-der-Weinstrasse: Verkehrsamt, ✉ Exterstr. 2, D–67433, ☎ 06321/926–892.

Speyer: Verkehrsamt der Stadt Speyer, ✉ Maximilianstr. 11, D–67346, ☎ 06232/14392.

Worms: Verkehrsverein der Stadt Worms, ✉ Neumarkt 14, D–67547, ☎ 06241/25045.

12 The Rhineland

Vater Rhein, or "Father Rhine," is Germany's historic lifeline, and the region from Mainz to Koblenz is its heart. Its banks are crowned by magnificent castle after castle and by breathtaking, vine-terraced hills that provide the livelihood for many of the villages hugging the shores. Bigger cities, such as Bonn, Köln, and Koblenz, also thrive along the great river. Koblenz lies at the meeting of the Rhine and its most famous tributary, the Mosel, on whose banks Germany's oldest city, Trier, was established. Other cities included in the chapter are Aachen and Düsseldorf.

THE IMPORTANCE OF THE RHINE can hardly be over-estimated. Throughout recorded history the Rhine has served as Europe's leading waterway. While not the longest river in Europe (the Danube is more than twice its length), it has been the main river-trade artery between the heart of the Continent and the North Sea.

The Rhine runs 1,355 kilometers (840 miles), from Lake Constance to Basel in Switzerland, then north through Germany, and finally west through the Netherlands to Rotterdam. For part of its length, it forms a natural frontier between Germany and France and was Europe's major highway between Basel and the Atlantic before the advent of overland transportation.

The Rhine is also a river of legend and myth. The Lorelei, a steep, jutting mountain of rock, was once believed the home of a beautiful and bewitching maiden who lured boatmen to a watery end in the swift currents. It was the home, too, of the Nibelungen, a Burgundian race said to have lived on its riverbanks, who serve as subjects for Wagner's epic opera cycle *Der Ring des Nibelungen*.

The Rhine became Germany's top tourist site 200 years ago. Around 1790 a spearhead of adventurous travelers from throughout Europe arrived by horse-drawn carriages to explore the sector of the river between Bingen and Koblenz, now known as the Middle Rhine Valley. They were all but overwhelmed by the dramatic and romantic scenery. It didn't take long for the word to spread. Other travelers followed in their coach tracks, and soon the first sightseeing cruises went into operation.

Poets, painters, and other artists were attracted by this magnet: Goethe, Germany's greatest poet, was enthralled; Heinrich Heine wrote a poem about the Lorelei legend that was eventually set to music and made the unofficial theme of the landmark; and William Turner captured misty Rhine sunsets on canvas. In 1834 the first-ever Baedeker guidebook described the attractions of this stretch of the river in meticulous detail. At about the same time the railroad opened the region to an early form of mass tourism. By the mid-19th century the Rhine Valley was known throughout Europe; in 1878 Mark Twain's *A Tramp Abroad* spread the word to potential travelers in the United States.

The most famous tributary of the Rhine is the Mosel, which flows into the river at Koblenz. It snakes its passage through another great wine-producing area with scenery almost as striking as that found along the Rhine. At its west end, almost on the French border, is Trier, once the third-greatest city in the Roman Empire, after Rome and Constantinople.

Today the passage through the Rhine and Mosel valleys still provides one of Europe's most memorable journeys.

Pleasures and Pastimes

Dining

The local specialties in the Rhineland tend to be more hearty than sophisticated: *Himmel und Erde,* a mixture of blood sausage, potatoes, onions, and apples; *Hämmchen* (pork knuckle); *Hunsrücker Festessen* (sauerkraut with potatoes, horseradish, and ham). There are many small inns and restaurants serving these and other regional dishes. At the other end of the scale, Düsseldorf, Köln, and Wiesbaden boast some of the most sophisticated restaurants in Europe, many offering delectable nouvelle cuisine.

CATEGORY	COST*
$$$$	over DM 90
$$$	DM 55–DM 90
$$	DM 35–DM 55
$	under DM 35

per person for a three-course meal, including tax but not alcohol

Lodging

The most romantic places to lay your head are the old riverside inns and hotels and the castle-hotels, some of which are enormously luxurious. The most expensive hotels in the cities of the Rhineland are among the finest in Europe. Modern high rises are common, as are more interesting, affordable quarters. A great many hotels close for the winter; most are also booked well in advance, especially for the wine festivals in the fall and during important trade fairs, as in Köln and Düsseldorf. Whenever possible, make reservations long before you visit.

CATEGORY	COST*
$$$$	over DM 250
$$$	DM 175–DM 250
$$	DM 125–DM 175
$	under DM 125

Prices are for two people in a double room, excluding service charges.

Music

Few regions in Europe rival the quality of classical performances and venues on the Rhine. Beethoven was born in Bonn, and the city will be hosting a Beethoven festival in 1997. Düsseldorf, once home to Mendelssohn, Schumann, and Brahms, boasts the finest concert hall in Germany after Berlin's Philharmonie: the Tonhalle, in a former planetarium. Cologne also has one of Germany's best concert halls, and its opera company is known for exciting classical and contemporary productions. The cathedrals of Aachen, Köln, and Trier are magnificent settings for concerts and organ recitals.

Wine

The Rheingau and the Mosel valleys are the two finest wine-producing regions in Germany, but other areas in the Rhineland also produce good wine. Overall, it is one of the best regions in Europe for wine tourism because most young German wines are delicious. In the vineyards a visitor will normally be served wine that is at its best at that very moment, not in five or 10 years. Almost every restaurant and café in the region has a good selection; many proudly serve wines from neighboring vineyards.

Exploring the Rhineland

The Mittel Rhein (Middle Rhine) could be considered an obligatory day trip out of Frankfurt—it's quite possibly Germany's number one, not-to-be-missed excursion. The Mosel is the Rhine's most important tributary, with scenery almost as striking. Just north of Bonn, the Rhine wends its way a little farther and the landscape flattens out. The Cologne Lowlands, the German part of the Lower Rhine, has two principal cities: Köln (Cologne), the greatest of the Rhine cities, and its rival, Düsseldorf. Not far from the Rhine, on the Belgian and Dutch borders, is the city of Aachen, site of the most important Carolingian (pre-Romanesque) cathedral in Europe.

The Rhineland

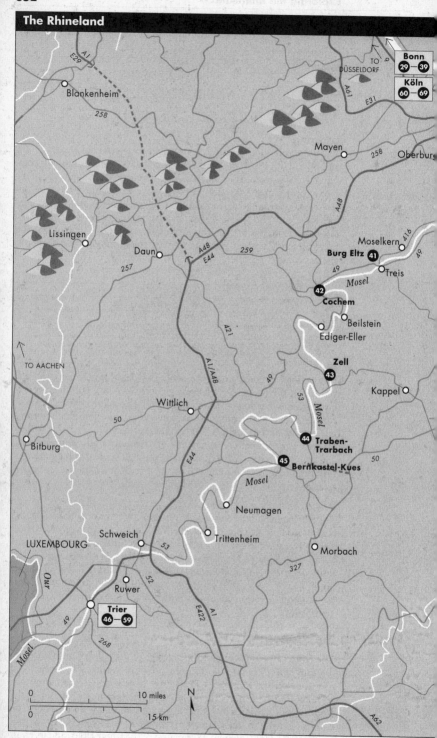

Blankenheim

Mayen

Oberbur

TO DÜSSELDORF

Bonn 29 — 39

Köln 60 — 69

Lissingen

Daun

Moselkern

Burg Eltz 41

Treis

Mosel

42 **Cochem**

Beilstein

Ediger-Eller

Zell 43

Kappel

Wittlich

Mosel

53

44 **Traben-Trarbach**

45 **Bernkastel-Kues**

Bitburg

Mosel

Neumagen

LUXEMBOURG

Schweich

Trittenheim

Morbach

Our

Ruwer

Trier 46 — 59

Mosel

TO AACHEN

0   10 miles
0   15 km

N

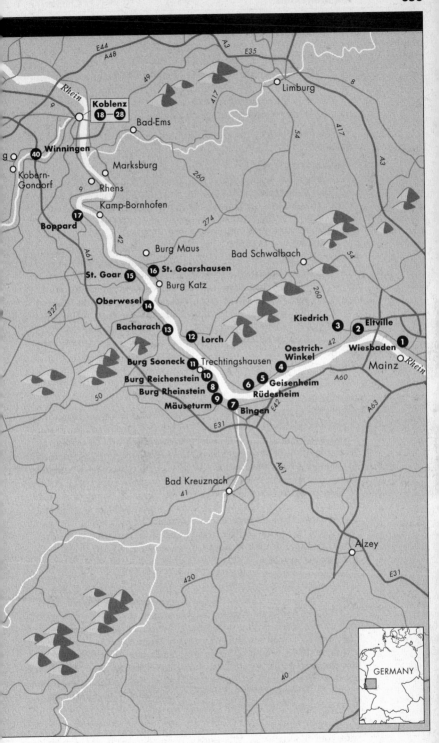

Koblenz
18—**28**

Bad-Ems

Limbburg

40 **Winningen**

g○

Kobern-
Gondorf

Marksburg

Rhein

9

Rhens

Kamp-Bornhofen

17

Boppard

Burg Maus

Bad Schwalbach

16 **St. Goarshausen**

St. Goar **15**

Burg Katz

Oberwesel **14**

Kiedrich

3

2 **Elfville**

Bacharach **13**

12 **Lorch**

1

Wiesbaden

**Oestrich-
Winkel**

4

Burg Sooneck **11** Trechtingshausen

Mainz

Rhein

Burg Reichenstein **10**

Burg Rheinstein **8**

5

6

Geisenheim

Mäuseturm **9**

7 **Rüdesheim**

Bingen

Bad Kreuznach

Alzey

GERMANY

Great Itineraries

Driving is the ideal way to travel—up one side of the Rhine and down
the other—with time out for a cruise. But even the train route between
Wiesbaden and Koblenz offers thrilling views—the landmarks may flash
by at top speed, a little like an out-of-control home movie, but you
still gain exposure to the essential aspects of the Rhine's beauty: hilltop castles silhouetted against the sky, ravishing river sights, and
glimpses of pretty-as-a-picture wine villages.

*Numbers in the text correspond to numbers in the margin and on
the maps.*

IF YOU HAVE 3 DAYS

Focus on the Rheingau region. Start your first day by traveling down
the Rhine from **Eltville** ②. Visit the local vineyards, which produce Germany's finest wine, at **Oestrich-Winkel** ④ (the largest in the area),
Geisenheim ⑤ (arguably the best in the region), **Rüdesheim** ⑥, and 🚋
Bingen ⑦, at the mouth of the Nahe River, where you can spend your
first night. On the second day, begin a tour of the famous Rhine castles (or their remains) with the fanciful and romantic **Burg Rheinstein** ⑧,
near Bingen and **Burg Reichenstein** ⑩ (now a fancy hotel), and also make
stops at **Lorch** ⑫, a small town with ancient walls, **Bacharach** ⑬, a thriving wine center in the Middle Ages, **Oberwesel** ⑭, and 🚋 **St. Goar** ⑮.
On the third day, continue on to **Burg Katz** and **Burg Maus**, whose 14th-
century owners feuded continuously. Also stop at **Boppard** ⑰, with
first-rate hotels, restaurants, and spas, and the unconquered **Marksburg**,
the final castle on this fortress-studded stretch. End your trip in
Koblenz ⑱–㉘, the region's cultural and business center, where the
Mosel and Rhine rivers meet.

IF YOU HAVE 7 DAYS

Begin your first day in **Eltville**. Plan to spend your first three days tour-
ing the Middle Rhine vineyards and lovely historic medieval towns from
Eltville to **Bingen** ②–⑦, and **Lorch** ⑫, **Bacharach** ⑬, and **Oberwesel** ⑭.
Also stop at the towering castles (or their remains) in the region, from
the romantic **Burg Rheinstein** to **Burg Sooneck** ⑧–⑪ and from **Burg
Katz** to the impregnable **Marksburg**. Plan to spend your first night in
🚋 **Bingen** and your second and third evenings in 🚋 **Boppard** ⑰, with
its first-rate lodgings. On your fourth day, explore **Koblenz** ⑱–㉘, making sure to visit the **Festung Ehrenbreitstein**, Europe's largest fortress;
then travel up the Mosel River for the rest of the trip. During the fifth
day, take time out at the vineyards of **Winningen** ㊵ and spend an
afternoon at **Burg Eltz** ㊶, a medieval picture-book castle that was never
destroyed and has scarcely been touched in 500 years. Move on to
🚋 **Cochem** ㊷ for an overnight stay. On the sixth day, stop at **Zell** ㊸,
Traben-Trarbach ㊹ (with one of Germany's oldest wine festivals, held
each August), **Bernkastel-Kues** ㊺, and **Neumagen**, Germany's oldest wine
town. End the trip with a day and night in the city of 🚋 **Trier** ㊻–㊾,
making time in your schedule to see **Porta Nigra** (the Black Gate), one
of the grandest Roman buildings in northern Europe, and the **Kaiserthermen** (Imperial Baths), where slaves once labored in miles of underground
passageways to heat the water. Also visit the early Gothic **Liebfrauenkirche**
(Church of Our Lady), standing next to the **Dom** (Cathedral), which
bears traces of 1,000 years of history.

IF YOU HAVE 12 DAYS

Start your first day at 🚋 **Wiesbaden** ①, home to many of Germany's
turn-of-the-century millionaires, who left behind the magnificent buildings on the Wilhelmstrasse. Explore the Middle Rhine vineyards from
Eltville to **Bingen** ②–⑦ and from **Lorch** to **Oberwesel** ⑫–⑭. Also plan
to stop at some of the fabulous castles from **Burg Rheinstein** to **Burg**

Sooneck ⑧–⑪ and from **Burg Katz** to magnificent **Marksburg.** Spend two nights each at 🏨 **Bacharach** ⑬ and 🏨 **Boppard** ⑰. After stopping to see the sights of busy **Koblenz** ⑱–㉘, continue on to explore the Mosel Valley from **Winningen** ⑩ to **Trier** ㊻–㊾, staying two nights in 🏨 **Cochem** ㊷ and two in 🏨 **Trier.** On the tenth day, proceed to 🏨 **Köln** (Cologne) ⑳–⑳, the largest city on the Rhine. Towering over its Old Town is Germany's finest Gothic cathedral, the **Kölner Dom**; also noteworthy are the **Wallraf-Richartz-Museum, Museum Ludwig,** the **Römisch-Germanisches Museum,** with its enormous mosaic of Dionysius, and the Romanesque church, **St. Gereon's.** End the trip with a day and night in the elegant spa town of 🏨 **Aachen,** an important destination for anyone visiting the region. The stunning **Dom** (cathedral) remains the single greatest storehouse of Carolingian architecture in Europe, and the **Domschatzkammer** (cathedral treasury) is perhaps the richest in northern Europe.

When to Tour the Rhineland

You'll find the vineyards at their most luxurious in late spring and early summer, when the vines are in full flower, exuding their perfume. In summer, hotel prices are high because this is one of Germany's major tourist areas, drawing many visitors from around the world. Make reservations early. The majority of wine festivals are in late summer and early fall. In the winter some hotels and smaller museums are closed, and there are no more river cruises. But there are no crowds, either, and the snow can be as beautiful as the summer greenery.

THE MITTEL RHEIN

Most visitors to Germany envision the Rhineland resembling the Mittel Rhine (Middle Rhine). This area consists of steep and thickly wooded hills, terraced vineyards rising step by step above the riverbanks, massive hilltop castles, and tiny wine villages hugging river shores. Bonn, until recently the capital of Germany, is close to the legendary Siebengebirge (Seven Hills).

Numbers in the margin correspond to points of interest on the Rhineland map.

Wiesbaden

❶ *40 km (25 mi) west of Frankfurt. For the most scenic route, take B–42.*

Wiesbaden is on the east bank of the Rhine, almost opposite the town of Mainz (☞ Chapter 11), and marks the start of the most famous stretch of the Rhine, the **Rheingau,** home of Germany's finest wines and some of its most enchanting (and crowded) wine villages. Technically, the Rheingau begins just east of Wiesbaden, at Hochheim (the town that gave its name to Hock wine), but it's the sunny, southern stretch that people generally think of when they hear the name Rheingau.

Wiesbaden is one of the oldest cities in Germany, founded 2,000 years ago by Roman legions attracted by its hot springs. Its elegant 19th-century face, however, is what captures one's attention today. The compact city gained prominence in the mid-19th century when Europe's leisure classes rediscovered the hot springs. By 1900 Wiesbaden was home to the largest number of millionaires of any German city, Berlin included. The church of **St. Augustine of Canterbury,** built between 1863 and 1865 for English visitors, is an indication of how popular a destination Wiesbaden was.

Wander along **Wilhelmstrasse** to get a taste of its 19th-century opulence; this thoroughfare's mint-condition fin de siècle buildings and expensive stores provide eloquent proof of the city's continuing affluence. It hasn't always prospered in this century, however. The outbreak of World War I in 1914 halted the social whirl, and in the war's aftermath the city was occupied by French and British troops. The 19th-century residence of the dukes of Nassau, one-time rulers of Wiesbaden, is perhaps symbolic of Wiesbaden's fall from the social heights. Today behind the classical facade of the former palace are the mundane offices of the provincial government of Hessen.

NEED A BREAK? Sample Wiesbaden's 19th-century charm in the wood-paneled warmth of the centrally located **Café Maldaner** (⊠ Marktstr. 34). Don't be surprised if you think you're in Vienna—the café was opened in 1859 as a Viennese coffeehouse catering to the city's Austrian visitors.

At the end of June, when the **Wilhelmstrassenfest** is held, it's party time along Wilhelmstrasse—Rheingau wine and *Sekt* (sparkling wine) flow in abundance. Every August Wiesbaden hosts the **Rheingau Wine Festival,** the largest such event in Germany. The festival takes its name from the vine-covered slopes along the river between Wiesbaden and Bingen, 25 kilometers (15 miles) to the west, where the Rhine abruptly turns north.

Dining and Lodging

$$$$ ✕ **Die Ente vom Lehel.** The formal and elegant restaurant of the Nassauer Hof (☞ *below*) provides one of the most memorable dining experiences in Germany. Nouvelle cuisine is king here. ⊠ *Kaiser-Friedrich-Pl. 3,* ☎ *0611/133–666. Reservations essential. Jacket and tie. AE, DC, MC, V. Closed Sun., Mon., holidays, and 4 wks in July–Aug.*

$$ ✕ **Weihenstephan.** Bavarian specialties are offered in this Alpine-style restaurant 5 kilometers (3 miles) south of the city center in suburban Biebrich. Even Bavarian beer is available, despite this being the most famous wine-producing area of the country. The mood is as hearty as the cooking. ⊠ *Armenruhstr. 6,* ☎ *0611/61134. AE. Closed Sat.*

$$$$ ✕🛏 **Nassauer Hof.** Opposite the Kurpark, the Nassauer Hof epitomizes elegance and style. Set in a turn-of-the-century building, it combines the best of Old World graciousness with German efficiency and comfort. Rooms are large and classy; the bar is a chic place for a rendezvous. ⊠ *Kaiser-Friedrich-Pl. 3–4, D–65183,* ☎ *0611/1330,* FAX *0611/133–632. 202 rooms and 9 suites with bath. Restaurant, bar, indoor pool, massage, sauna. AE, DC, MC, V.*

$$$$ 🛏 **Radisson Schwarzer Bock.** For period charm few hotels beat the stylish Schwarzer Bock. The building dates from 1486, though most of what you see today is from the 19th century. The lavish public rooms are filled with antiques, flowers, and paintings; the opulent bedrooms are individually decorated in styles ranging from Baroque to modern. The thermal swimming pool will soothe away the pain of paying the bill. The recent purchase and renovation of the hotel by the Radisson group has improved the facilities, with new carpeting and bathrooms, without changing the atmosphere. ⊠ *Kranzpl. 12, D–65183,* ☎ *0611/1550,* FAX *0611/155–111. 127 rooms and 22 suites with bath. Restaurant, bar, indoor pool, massage, sauna. AE, DC, MC, V.*

Nightlife and the Arts

Wiesbaden's nightlife centers on the historic **Kurhaus** complex, which houses a magnificent concert hall, an elegant **casino,** and two gourmet restaurants. During the summer spa guests, locals, and tourists mingle in the *Bier Garten* and on the Kurhaus terrace. You'll find a mix of casino winners and losers celebrating or drowning their sorrows in the Kurhaus's **Pavillon Bar.**

MUSIC
Wiesbaden's symphony orchestra gives concerts in the **Staatstheater's Grosses Haus** and in the **Kurhaus.** Organ recitals are given every Saturday at 11:30 in the Gothic **Marktkirche** (⊠ Marktpl.).

THEATER
The **Hessisches Staatstheater** is based in a fine late-19th-century theater on Christian-Zais-Strasse (opposite the Kurhaus and casino). The **Staatstheater's Grosses Haus** (☎ 06121/132–325) presents classical drama, opera, ballet, and musicals are presented; less ambitious productions are given in the **Kleines Haus** (☎ 06121/132–327). The Grosses Haus is also the scene in early summer of Wiesbaden's annual **International May Arts Festival.**

Shopping

Broad, tree-lined **Wilhelmstrasse,** with designer boutiques housed in its fin de siècle buildings, is one of Germany's most elegant shopping streets.

Lovers of antiques will also do well in Wiesbaden, known as one of the best places in the country to find them; **Taunusstrasse** has some excellent antique shops.

Tennis

Wiesbaden's **Henkell ice stadium** (⊠ Höllerbornstr.) becomes a tennis court during the summer.

Eltville

❷ *14 km (9 mi) west of Wiesbaden, 16 km (10 mi) north of Mainz.*

Eltville is the geographic heart of the Rheingau. Its half-timbered buildings crowd narrow streets that date from Roman times. Although the Romans planted the first wine grapes in Germany, they never did it here. It was Charlemagne, so the story goes, who during the 9th century first realized the sunny slopes of the Rheingau could be used to produce wines. Eltville's vineyards may not go that far back, but some, including **Hanach** and **Rheinberg,** have been in continuous use since the 12th century. Today the town is best known for the production of *Sekt,* sparkling German wine (champagne by any other name, though the French ensured it could not legally be called that by including a stipulation in the Treaty of Versailles in 1919). Sekt cellars rest coolly beneath the town's winding streets. Those of the **Matheus Muller Company** are several miles long and hold up to 15 million bottles. Although the cellars are not open to the public, you can amble through the courtyards of some formidable old vineyard buildings, including the white-walled, slate-roof **Eltzerhof,** one of the more beautiful.

Eltville has its own **castle,** commissioned by the archbishop of Trier in 1330. The prince-archbishop of Mainz admitted Johannes Gutenberg, father of the modern printing press, to the court in Eltville, thereby saving the inventor from financial ruin.

The Gothic parish church of **Sts. Peter and Paul** has some fine 14th-century stained glass and ceiling frescoes; its walls are lined with the tombstones and monuments of noble families who rose to prominence on the prestige of the local wine.

❸ A mile or so from Eltville lies the village of **Kiedrich,** where you can see one of Germany's oldest church organs, dating from around 1500,

The west entrance to the church, where the organ is ensconced, is richly carved.

❹ The drive from Kiedrich back to the Rhine at **Oestrich-Winkel** takes you past the largest vineyard in the Rheingau. Oestrich-Winkel is the site of the oldest stone dwelling in the country, the **Graues Haus** (Gray House). It dates from the 9th century and is now a very good restaurant.

Dining and Lodging

$$$ ✕🏨 **Romantik Hotel Schwan.** The Romantik chain lives up to its name
★ with this half-timbered Renaissance building right on the Rhine—with green shutters, tubs of flowers, high gables, and sloping roofs. The restaurant offers fine local specialties and an extensive wine list; wine-tasting sessions are held among the oak casks in the ancient cellars. ⊠ *Rheinallee 5–7, D–65375 Oestrich,* ☎ *06723/8090,* 🝱 *06723/7820. 45 rooms with bath. Restaurant. AE, DC, MC, V. Restaurant closed Nov.–mid-Feb.*

Geisenheim

❺ *17 km (11 mi) west of Wiesbaden.*

The name *Geisenheim* is inextricably linked with Rheingau wines at their finest. "Rhineland is wineland" is a saying in this part of the world, and, indeed, you'll see a checkerboard of terraced vineyards stretching from the Rhine's riverside villages all the way back to a protective line of forests at the base of the Taunus Mountains. Geisenheim has some of the most renowned vineyards in the area, with grapes that create wines on a par with those from the Loire Valley and Burgundy.

From the vintner's point of view, this part of Germany has the ideal conditions for the cultivation of the noble Riesling grapes: a perfect southern exposure; shelter from cold north winds; slopes with the proper pitch for drainage; soil containing slate and quartz to reflect the sun and to hold heat through the night and moisture in the morning; and long sunny days from early spring until late fall. (Although the Rheingau is at approximately the same latitude as Newfoundland, you'd never know it from the weather.)

In Geisenheim visit the 18th-century **Schloss Johannisberg,** built on the site of a 12th-century abbey and still owned by the von Metternich family. Schloss Johannisberg produces what is generally regarded as one of the very best Rheingau wines, along with a renowned Sekt. On the castle terrace you can order the elegant estate-bottled golden wine by the glass. As you savor the cool, rich, clear-as-crystal drink, you can contemplate all that makes this corner of Europe so special. Views across the vineyards take in the river at its calmest. If you're lucky, the Rhine will be enveloped in a pastel mood worthy of a Turner painting. As you leave the castle, you can buy a bottle or two of the excellent wine at a shop just outside the walls.

Rüdesheim

❻ *25 km (16 mi) west of Wiesbaden.*

Rüdesheim is the Rhine Valley's most popular wine town and a place for day-trippers—it is to Frankfurt what Coney Island is to New York. Set along the river's edge, it is a truly picturesque place of half-timbered and gabled medieval houses, where everything is somehow related to wine or tourists or both. You can visit wine cellars to inspect great casks with elaborate and lovingly carved heads.

Angling up from the river toward the romantic Old Town is the region's most famous **Weingasse** (wine alley), the extraordinary **Drosselgasse** (Thrush Lane). This narrow, 200-yard-long cobbled lane is lined with cozy wine taverns and rustic restaurants. At night, voices raised in song and brass bands create a cacophony, shattering whatever peace the town may have known by day.

Rüdesheim can be a very plus-and-minus affair. You can love it in the morning, before the day's quota of tour buses start disgorging their passengers, and hate it at night, when it gets far too crowded for comfort. Still, all in all, it is definitely worth a visit.

Schloss Brömserburg will appeal to wine buffs and those who enjoy wandering through old castles. This is one of the oldest castles on the Rhine, built more than 1,000 years ago by the Knights of Rüdesheim on the site of a Roman fortress. Inside its stout walls are wine presses, drinking vessels, and collections related to viticulture from prehistoric times to the present. ⊠ *Weinmuseum in der Brömserburg, Rheinstr. 2,* ☎ *06722/2348.* ☜ *DM 3.* ☉ *Mid-Mar.–Oct., daily 9–6.*

The **Niederwald-Denkmal** stands above Rüdesheim at an elevation of 1,000 feet. This colossal stone statue represents Germania, the heroically proportioned woman who symbolizes the unification of the German Empire in 1871. Built between 1876 and 1883 on the orders of Bismarck, this giant figure came within an inch of being blown to smithereens during the dedication ceremonies. At the unveiling, held in the presence of the kaiser and Bismarck, an anarchist attempted to blow up the statue—and the assembled dignitaries. However, in true comic-opera style, a rain shower put out the fuse on the bomb, and all was well.

Niederwald can be reached by car or chairlift, or you can climb to the statue's steep perch. Whichever way you choose, the ascent offers splendid views, including one of the little island in the middle of the Rhine where the Mäuseturm (Mouse Tower) is situated (☞ *below*). The chairlift station to the monument is a short walk from the Drosselgasse. It operates continually every day from late March to early November; the round-trip fare is DM 8.

Dining and Lodging

$$–$$$ ✕ **Krone.** The extensive restoration work carried out on the 450-year-old Krone Hotel included a complete renovation of its restaurant, which now ranks among the most outstanding in the region. Chef Herbert Pucher's terrines and pâtés draw regular customers from as far away as Frankfurt. His fish dishes are supreme, and the Rhine wines are the best. ⊠ *Rheinuferstr. 10, Assmannshausen,* ☎ *06722/4030. AE, DC, MC, V.*

$$$–$$$$ ✕🗙 **Hotel Jagdschloss Niederwald.** This is not so much a place to stay overnight as a luxury resort hotel where you might want to spend your entire vacation. It's set in the hills 5 kilometers (3 miles) outside Rüdesheim, with predictably good views over the Rhine and the Rheingau. The former hunting lodge of the dukes of Hesse, it has a lavish, baronial atmosphere. The restaurant, with panoramic views, can be magnificent. The chef, who was trained in France, transforms traditional German recipes into something more exciting. Families will appreciate the wide range of activities offered, and night owls will appreciate the late hours of the bar. ⊠ *Auf dem Niederwald 1, D–65383,* ☎ *06722/1004,* ℻ *06722/47970. 52 rooms with bath. Restaurant, bar, indoor pool, sauna, tennis courts, health club, horseback riding. AE, DC, MC, V. Closed Jan.–Feb. 14.*

$$ ✕🔢 **Hotel und Weinhaus Felsenkeller.** Just around the corner from Drosselgasse, Hotel und Weinhaus Felsenkeller is a traditional 18th-century establishment providing modern comforts. The restaurant has a patio and seats 150. ✉ *Oberstr. 39–41, D–65385,* ☎ *06722/2094,* FAX *06722/47202. 60 rooms with shower. Restaurant. AE, MC, V.*

$$ ✕🔢 **Rüdesheimer Hof.** For a taste of Rheingau hospitality, try this typical inn. There's a terrace for summer dining, where you can enjoy excellent local specialties along with any of the many wines offered. ✉ *Geisenheimerstr. 1, D–65385,* ☎ *06722/2011,* FAX *06722/48194. 42 rooms with bath. Restaurant. AE, DC, MC, V. Closed mid-Nov.–mid-Feb.*

$$ ✕🔢 **Rüdesheimer Schloss.** The modern comforts border on the luxurious in this historic wine tavern that goes back 265 years. Most of the rooms have a view of the hillside vineyards. The three suites have avant-garde decor. Room 20 is popular for its large terrace. ✉ *Steingasse 10, D–65385,* ☎ *06722/90500,* FAX *06722/47960. 21 rooms with bath. Restaurant. AE, DC, MC, V. Closed during Christmas and Dec. 31.*

Bingen

❼ *25 km (16 mi) west of Wiesbaden, on the opposite side of the riverbank from Rüdesheim.*

The town of Bingen celebrates the festival of St. Rochus every year in mid-August. In **St. Rochus chapel,** built in 1666 in memory of Bingen's plague victims, is a portrait of Goethe, the great German writer, posing improbably as the saint. Another Bingen luminary was the 12th-century Benedictine abbess Hildegard, one of the first great women artist/scholars, who wrote on everything from the natural sciences to her religious visions; recordings of her music are also available. To get to Bingen, take the short ferry ride from the Adlerturm jetty in Rüdesheim. The fare is DM 1.40, DM 2.50 round-trip.

❽ The boat ride to the romantic castle of **Burg Rheinstein** is the number one excursion from Bingen. It was Prince Friedrich von Preussen, a cousin of Emperor Wilhelm I, who acquired the original medieval castle in 1825 and transformed it into the picture-book castle you see high above the Rhine today. The prince is buried in the castle's fanciful Gothic chapel. ☎ *06721/6377.*

❾ The ride to Burg Rheinstein takes you past one of the most famous sights on the Rhine, the **Mäuseturm** (Mouse Tower), a 13th-century edifice clinging to a rock on a tiny island in the river. According to legend, it was constructed by an avaricious bishop as a customs post to exact taxes from passing river traffic. The story suggests the greedy bishop grew so unpopular that he was forced to hole up in the tower, where he was eventually devoured by mice.

❿ Beyond the Mäuseturm there are two other medieval castles you can visit. **Burg Reichenstein** towers high above the enchanting wine town of **Trechtingshausen.** Reichenstein Castle is now a luxurious hotel where you can enjoy lunch in an excellent restaurant with a sensational view.

⓫ **Burg Sooneck** was the most feared stronghold in the Rhineland during the 12th century. It rises above the Rhine on a rocky outcrop and was destroyed several times during its colorful history and rebuilt in its present form in 1840 by the Prussian king Friedrich Wilhelm IV. From the castle you can follow a path through vineyards to one of the most spectacular vantage points of the entire Rhineland: the **Siebenburgenblick** (Seven-Castle View). ☎ *06743/6064.* ☾ *Tues.–Sun.*

Lodging

$$ 🔲 **Rheinhotel Starkenburger Hof.** In business since the middle of the 19th century, the Starkenburger Hof, decorated throughout in warm shades of brown and gold, is the number one choice in Bingen. It overlooks the Rhine, so don't settle for a room without a view. There's no restaurant, but a large buffet breakfast is included in the room rate. ⊠ *Am Rheinkai 1, D–55411 Bingen,* ☎ *06721/14341,* FAX *06721/13350. 30 rooms with bath or shower. Breakfast room. AE, DC. Closed Jan.–Feb.*

Lorch

12 *18 km (11 mi) northwest of Rüdesheim, 3 km (2 mi) north of Burg Sooneck, a ferry ride back across the Rhine at the village of Niederheimbach.*

The historic little wine town of Lorch has ancient walls that mark the northernmost limit of the Rheingau. Its parish church of **St. Martin** has a Gothic high altar and 13th-century carved choir stalls.

North of Lorch there are so many attractions on both banks of the river that the only way to see them all would be to zigzag back and forth across the river by ferry. Fortunately, there are small ferries all along the Rhine between here and Koblenz.

Bacharach

13 *4 km (2 mi) north of Lorch.*

Bacharach has a long association with wine, indicated by its name, which comes from the Latin *Bacchi ara,* meaning "altar of Bacchus," the Roman god of wine. The town was a thriving center of Rhine wine trade in the Middle Ages. Something of its medieval atmosphere can still be found in the narrow streets within its 14th-century defensive walls and towers.

NEED A BREAK? Stop by the old marketplace and look for the gold-painted sign of the **Weinhaus Altes Haus** (⊠ Marktpl.). Wine has been served in this half-timbered tavern for four centuries. Ask for any Bacharach Riesling and you won't be disappointed.

Dining and Lodging

$ ✕ **Hotel-Restaurant Steeger Weinstube.** Less than DM 20 buys you three hearty courses at this friendly, family-run tavern-restaurant just off the Rhine tourist route. The menu changes daily, but Rhineland-style sauerbraten, homemade potato dumplings, and venison (in season) are often featured. ⊠ *Blucherstr. 149, Bacharach-Steeg,* ☎ *06743/1240. AE, MC. Closed Wed.*

$$ ✕🔲 **Altkölnischer Hof.** Tucked in a quiet square in medieval Bacharach, the Altkölnischer is a small, half-timbered hotel built at the turn of the century. Colorful geraniums line the small windows; rooms are simply but attractively furnished in country style; and the rustic restaurant offers typical local dishes and some excellent wines. ⊠ *Blücherstr. 2, D–55422,* ☎ *06743/1339,* FAX *06743/2793. 20 rooms with bath. Restaurant. AE, V. Closed Nov.–Mar.*

Shopping

The **Weingut Wilhelm Wasum** cellar (⊠ Mainzerstr. 20–23, Bacharach, ☎ 06743/1234) is one of the best places to stop for wine on the Rhine, offering tours with English-speaking guides. The **Weingut Wolfgang**

Eberhard cellar (✉ Borbacherstr. 6–7, ☎ 06743/1591) has been in the same family for more than 250 years and has wine for sale.

The **Phil Jost** shop (✉ Rosenstr. 16, ☎ 06743/1224) has wineglasses and Westerwald ceramics. This store is known for offering factory, rather than retail, prices on high-quality goods; it also specializes in beer mugs.

Oberwesel

⓮ *8 km (5 mi) north of Bacharach, 20 km (12 mi) from Bingen.*

Oberwesel retains its medieval look. Sixteen of the original 21 towers that studded the town walls still stand; one does double duty as the bell tower of the 14th-century church of **St. Martin.** Towering above the town are the remains of the 1,000-year-old **Burg Schönburg,** whose massive walls, nearly 20 feet thick in places, were not strong enough to prevent its destruction by rampaging French troops in 1689. Part of the castle has been restored and today houses a comfortable hotel.

St. Goar

⓯ *7 km (4 mi) north of Oberwesel.*

The town of St. Goar was named after an early missionary who became the patron saint of Rhine boatmen and tavern keepers. At the outskirts of St. Goar stands what is left of the medieval castle, **Burg Rheinfels.** The Rhine near St. Goar narrows dramatically, funneling its waters into a treacherous maelstrom of fast-flowing currents and eddies.

⓰ Just outside **St. Goarshausen,** the town on the opposite side of the river, is the Lorelei, a grim, 400-foot-high rock that protrudes from the river. So many boats were wrecked on it because of the rushing torrents in the area that people began to credit a bewitching water nymph with golden tresses who inhabited the rock and lured sailors to watery graves using her beauty and strange songs.

These days, in season, the Lorelei's siren song can serve as a trap for tourists rather than sailors. Excursion boats leave regularly from Koblenz and Bingen on Lorelei cruises, and as these overcrowded vessels pass within sight of the famed cliffs, each and every one plays a loud taped version of the Lorelei song (a Heinrich Heine poem set to music) above the roar of the river.

You can see a statue of the Lorelei in St. Goarshausen. To get there, take the ferry from St. Goar.

If you visit this area in September, stay for the **Rhein in Flammen** (Rhine in Flames) **Festival,** a pyrotechnic orgy of rockets and flares that lights up St. Goar and St. Goarshausen and their surrounding vineyards.

Dining and Lodging

$$ ✗ **Roter Kopf.** This is a historic wine restaurant brimming with rustic Rhineland atmosphere. ✉ *Burgstr. 5, St. Goarshausen,* ☎ *06771/2698. No credit cards.*

$$$ ✗⬚ **Schlosshotel auf Burg Rheinfels.** Directly opposite Burg Maus, this castle-hotel breathes a regal air. Its ponderously grand interior is furnished with intricate French and Spanish antiques. Ask for a room with a view. The restaurant offers hearty regional specialties. ✉ *Schlossberg 47, D–56329 St. Goar,* ☎ *06741/8020,* ⛶ *06741/7652. 58 rooms with bath. Restaurant, bar, indoor and outdoor pools, miniature golf, fishing. AE, DC, MC, V.*

$ ✕🏨 **Herrmannsmühle.** This Alpine chalet-style hotel has heavy pine furnishings decorated with floral patterns. It stands just outside town by its own vineyards and offers good value at low prices, with an especially warm welcome extended by its host, Herr Herrmann. ✉ *Forstbachstr. 46, D–56346 St. Goarshausen,* ☎ *06771/7317. 10 rooms with bath. Restaurant. MC, V. Closed mid-Nov.–Feb.*

En Route North and south of St. Goarshausen are two castles whose 14th-century owners feuded so unrelentingly that the fortresses came to be known as Katz (cat) and Maus (mouse). **Burg Katz,** just north of St. Goarshausen, was built in 1371 by Count Wilhelm II von Katzenellbogen (literally, "cat's elbow"). **Burg Maus,** the rival castle south of St. Goarshausen, was named by Von Katzenellbogen. The rivalry, however, was a serious matter. There was constant competition between many of the castle-bound nobles of the Rhine to decide who would extract tolls from passing river traffic, a lucrative and vicious business. Napoléon, not one to respect medieval traditions, put an end to the fighting in 1806 when he destroyed Burg Katz. It was later reconstructed using the original medieval plans. Neither of the castles is open to the public.

Rivalry between neighboring castles was common even when they belonged to members of the same family. At **Kamp-Bornhofen,** 12 kilometers (8 miles) north of St. Goar, are **Burg Sterrenberg** and **Burg Liebenstein,** once owned by two brothers. When their relations deteriorated over a river-toll feud, they built a wall between them. Today competing wine taverns in the castles keep the rivalry going.

Boppard

⑰ *17 km (11 mi) northwest of St. Goar.*

Across from Kamp-Bornhofen is elegant Boppard, with its mile-long promenade usually lined with excursion and pleasure boats. Luxurious hotels, restaurants, and spa facilities are Boppard's hallmarks. There are also wine taverns of every caliber and substantial ruins from a 4th-century Roman fort here. The old quarter is part of a walking tour marked by signs starting from the 14th-century **Carmelite Church** on Karlmeliterstrasse. (Inside the church, grotesque carved figures peer from the choir stalls.) Take the chairlift up **Gedeonseck** to view this stretch of the Rhine from on high.

Dining and Lodging

$$$$ ✕🏨 **Hotel Klostergut Jakobsberg.** Stay here for the amazing location
★ on the north bank of the Rhine (the hotel's about 12 kilometers, or 8 miles, north of Boppard), the array of sports facilities, the excellent food, and the sumptuous furnishings. The hotel is in a castle (make sure you see its chapel) and has a sophisticated baronial atmosphere, due in part to an extensive collection of hunting trophies and rifles, a considerable assembly of paintings and prints, and imposing tapestries—real *Prisoner of Zenda* stuff. The hotel raises its own cattle and cultivates Japanese shiitake mushrooms, and puts both to good use in its restaurant. The veal medallions in goose-liver sauce are superb. ✉ *D–56154 Boppard-Rhein,* ☎ *06742/8080,* 𝔽𝔸𝕏 *06742/3069. 104 rooms and 7 suites with bath. Restaurant, indoor pool, sauna, golf course, tennis courts, bowling, horseback riding, squash, helipad. AE, DC, MC, V.*

En Route At Boppard the river swings east and then north to **Rhens,** a town that traces its origins back some 1,300 years. A vital center of the Holy Roman Empire, Rhens was where German kings and emperors were elected and then presented to the people. The **Königstuhl** (King's Chair), the monumental site where the ceremonies took place, is on a hilltop just outside Rhens, on the road to Waldesch. It was here in 1388 that the rift between the Holy Roman Empire and the papacy (to which the emperor was nominally subject) proved final. The six German prince-electors who nominated the emperor declared that henceforward their decisions were final and need no longer be given papal sanction.

★ **Marksburg,** the final castle on this fortress-studded stretch of the Rhine, is on the opposite bank of the river, 500 feet above the town of Braubach. Marksburg was built during the 12th century to protect silver and lead mines in the area; so successful were its medieval builders that the castle proved impregnable—it is the only one in the entire Middle Rhine Valley to have survived the centuries intact. Within its massive walls are a collection of weapons and manuscripts, a medieval botanical garden, and a restaurant. ☎ 02627/206. ⌨ DM 7. ⊙ *Easter–Oct., daily 10–5; Nov.–day before Easter, daily 11–4.*

Koblenz

🔞 *88 km (55 mi) northwest of Mainz, 55 km (34 mi) south of Bonn.*

The ancient city of Koblenz is at a geographic nexus known as the **Deutsches Eck** (corner of Germany) in the heart of the Middle Rhine region. Rivers and mountains converge here: The Mosel flows into the Rhine on one side; the Lahn flows in on the other; and three mountain ridges also intersect.

Koblenz serves as the cultural, administrative, and business center of the Middle Rhine. Its position at the confluence of two rivers bustling with steamers, barges, tugs, and every other kind of river boat makes it one of the most important traffic points on the Rhine.

Founded by the Romans in AD 9, historic Koblenz is close to the point where the Rhine and Mosel meet. Its Roman name, Castrum ad Confluentes (the Camp at the Confluence), was later corrupted to Koblenz. It became a powerful city in the Middle Ages, when it controlled trade on both rivers. Air raids during World War II destroyed 85% of the city, but extensive restoration has done much to re-create the atmosphere of old Koblenz. English-speaking walking tours of the Old Town can be arranged by the tourist office on request.

Numbers in the margin correspond to points of interest on the Koblenz map.

🔟 Koblenz is centered on the west bank of the Rhine. On the east bank of the Rhine, Europe's largest fortress, **Festung Ehrenbreitstein,** offers a commanding view from 400 feet above the river (the view alone justifies a visit). Take the cable car (Sesselbahn) if the walk is too daunting; the round-trip fare is DM 8. The earliest buildings date from about 1100, but the bulk of the fortress was constructed during the 16th century. In 1801 Napoléon's forces partially destroyed Festung Ehrenbreitstein; the French then occupied Koblenz for 18 years, which some claim accounts for the city's Gallic joie de vivre. More concrete evidence of French occupation can be found in the shape of the fortress's 16th-century **Vogel Greif cannon.** The French absconded with it in 1794; the Germans took it back in 1940; and the French commandeered it again in 1945. The 15-ton cannon was peaceably returned in 1984 by French president François Mitterrand. It is part of the exhibit of the history of local technologies, from wine-growing to industry, in the **County Museum** (Landesmuseum) in the fortress. ☎ 0261/71012. ⌨ *Fortress and museum free.* ⊙ *Museum mid-Mar.–mid-Nov., daily 9–12:30 and 1–5; fortress year-round; cable car Good Fri.–May, daily 10–5, and June–Nov. 1, daily 9:30–6. Fortress may be reached by ferry*

(DM 1.30) from Pegelhaus (Rhine Gardens) on the Koblenz side of the Rhine.

20 The bridge **Pfaffendorfer Brücke** marks the beginning of the Old Town. At its west end, between the modern blocks of the Rhein-Mosel Halle

21 and the Scandic Crown Hotel, is the **Weindorf,** a wine "village" constructed for a mammoth exhibition of German wine in 1925. It continues to attract tourists today and is especially lively around carnival time. If the weather's good, sample a glass of wine in the Weindorf's leafy gardens; in summer live music spices up the scene after 7 PM and at jazz brunches on Sundays and holidays.

22 The **Rheinanlagen,** a 10-kilometer (6-mile) promenade, one of the longest in the Rhineland, runs along the riverbank past the Weindorf.

23 Strolling the promenade toward town, you'll pass the gracious **Residenzschloss,** the prince-elector's palace. It was built in 1786 by Prince-Elector Clemens Wenceslaus as an elegant replacement for the grim Ehrenbreitstein fortress. He lived here for only three years, however; in 1791 he was forced to flee to Augsburg when the French stormed the city. Today the palace is used for city offices and is closed to visitors.

24 The squat form of the **Rheinkran,** a crane built in 1611, is one of the landmarks of Koblenz. Marks on the side of the building indicate the heights reached by floodwaters of bygone years. In the mid-19th century, a pontoon bridge consisting of a row of barges spanned the Rhine here; when ships approached, two or three barges were simply moved out of the way to let them through.

25 The **Deutsches Eck** is at the sharp intersection of the Rhine and Mosel, a pointed piece of land jutting into the river like the prow of some early ironclad warship. One of the more effusive manifestations of German nationalism—an 1897 statue of Kaiser Wilhelm I, first emperor of the newly united Germany—was erected here. It was destroyed at the end of World War II and replaced in 1953 with a ponderous, altarlike monument to German unity. After German reunification a new statue of Wilhelm was placed atop this monument in 1993, despite protest from those who felt it could be sending out some less-than-positive signals about the "new Germany." Pieces of the Berlin Wall stand behind it—a memorial to those who died as a result of the partitioning of the country.

26 **Museum Ludwig** stands just behind the Deutsches Eck, housed in the spic-and-span Deutschherrenhaus, a restored 13th-century building. Industrialist Peter Ludwig, one of Germany's leading contemporary art collectors, has founded museums in many Rhineland cities (☞ Cologne and Aachen, *below*); he's filled this museum, too, with part of his huge collection of modern art. ✉ *Danziger Freiheit 1,* ☎ *0261/304–040.* 💰 *DM 5.* ☉ *Tues.–Wed. and Fri.–Sat. 11–5, Thurs. 11–8, Sun. 11–6.*

27 **St. Kastor Kirche** is a sturdy Romanesque basilica consecrated in 836. It was here in 843 that the Treaty of Verdun was signed, formalizing the division of Charlemagne's great empire and leading to the creation of Germany and France as separate states. Inside, compare the squat Romanesque columns in the nave with the intricate fan vaulting of the Gothic sections. The **St. Kastor fountain** outside the church is an intriguing piece of historical one-upmanship. It was built by the occupying French to mark the beginning of Napoléon's ultimately disastrous Russian campaign of 1812. When the Russians, having inflicted a crushing defeat on Napoléon, reached Koblenz, they added an ironic SEEN AND APPROVED to the inscription on the fountain. ✉ *Kastorhof.*

The **Altstadt** (Old Town) may be reached from the Deutsches Eck via the **Moselanlagen** (Mosel Promenade). This walkway leads to Koblenz's

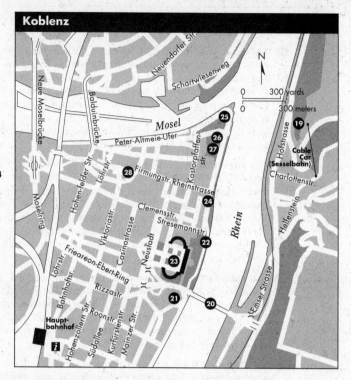

oldest restaurant, **Deutscher Kaiser,** which marks the start of the Old Town. The damage of war is evidenced in the blend of old buildings and modern store blocks on and around the central square of **Am Plan.** Near Am Plan, the **Middle Rhine Museum** houses the city's art collection in a lovely 16th-century building. ✉ *Florinsmarkt 15,* ☎ *0261/129–2501.* 🔒 *DM 5.* ☉ *Tues. and Thurs–Sat. 10–5, Wed. 11–8, Sun. 10–6.*

㉘ On one side of the Am Plan on An der Liebfrauenkirche is the **Liebfrauenkirche** (Church of Our Lady), which stands on Roman foundations at the Old Town's highest point. The bulk of the church is of Romanesque design, but its choir is one of the Rhineland's finest examples of 15th-century Gothic architecture, and the west front is graced with two 17th-century Baroque towers. Behind the church is the 17th-century Town Hall, formerly a Jesuit college, and the little statue called the **Schängelbrunnen** (literally "scalawag fountain"), a boy who spouts water every three minutes at unwary passersby. Another highlight of the Old Town is the **Four Towers,** restored 17th-century half-timbered houses.

Dining and Lodging

$$–$$$ ✕ **Fährhaus am Stausee.** The garden terrace where you can dine on warm, sunny days extends to the banks of the Mosel. The name comes from the ancient river-ferry crossing point that existed here until a bridge was built. A range of dishes, predominantly fish, fills the menu of this old, established restaurant. Rooms are available. ✉ *An der Fähre 3, Metternich,* ☎ *0261/2093. AE, DC, MC, V.*

$$ ✕ **Wacht am Rhein.** Watch on the Rhine, as the name translates, sums it up. In summer take a table on the outside terrace and watch the river traffic roll by; in winter choose a window table and dine with the Rhine outside and the atmospheric warmth of the fin de siècle fittings and

furnishings inside. Fish is the basis of the extensive menu. ☒ *Adenauer-Ufer 6,* ☎ *0261/15313. AE.*

$–$$ ✕ **Cafe Faustus.** Try to arrive early. The nondescript building packs a hothouse of trendy types within its wood-paneled walls. The unfinished floor provides them with a stage. The decidedly non-German food is good, more under the influence of the Mediterranean than the Rhine. ☒ *Florinsmarkt. No credit cards.*

$–$$ ✕ **Salat–Garten.** Here's the place for a vitamin fix, from A to zinc. Your cafeteria tray slides along rails past course after course of savory vegetarian food and pyramids of crisp salads; at the end you can buy Rhine wines by the glass or bottled beer. The atmosphere is almost as sterile as McDonald's and just as clean. ☒ *Gymnasialstr./Zentralpl.,* ☎ *0261/36455. No credit cards. Closed Sun. No dinner Sat. (except 1st Sat. of month).*

$–$$ ✕ **Weinhaus Hubertus.** This atmospheric old wine tavern is a great place to sample the flavors of old Koblenz. The flower-laden, half-timbered 17th-century exterior is in keeping with the rustic ambience inside. The food is ample and cooked with gusto, and the dishes are what you'd expect from a place named after the patron saint of hunting. ☒ *Florinsmarkt 6,* ☎ *0261/31177. No credit cards. Closed Tues. No lunch.*

$ ✕ **Stresemann.** Very popular among locals, this cheerful restaurant serves German specialties like sauerbraten in no-nonsense portions as well as enormous salads. Most of the guests drink beer, but there are a few good wines by the glass. The Rhine is just a couple of steps away. ☒ *Rheinzollstr. 8,* ☎ *0261/15464. Reservations essential. No credit cards.*

$$$$ ✕🏨 **Scandic Crown.** While this may be Koblenz's best hotel in terms of modernity, it lacks charm. Except for the views of the Rhine, the uniformity of the largish rooms suggests you're staying at a chain hotel. Bathrooms have spacious showers, but no tubs. The reception staff provides polished service, and the dining room serves French-influenced cooking. The hotel is a 10-minute walk from the Old Town and two minutes from the Weindorf (Wine Village). ☒ *Julius-Wegeler-Str. 6, D–56068,* ☎ *0261/1360,* 🖷 *0261/136–1199. 159 rooms with bath. 2 restaurants, bar, sauna. AE, DC, MC, V.*

$$$ 🏨 **Kleiner Riesen.** This is a well-run, straightforward hotel that gives value for your money. Another plus is the quiet riverside location that's still within walking distance of the train station and the Old Town. There's a good breakfast buffet but no restaurant. ☒ *Kaiserin-Augusta-Anlagen 18, D–56068 Koblenz,* ☎ *0261/32077,* 🖷 *0261/160–725. 27 rooms with bath. AE, DC, MC, V.*

Nightlife and the Arts

Singles go to the **Tanzcafé Besselink** (opposite the main train station)—it's open until 3 AM. Disco fans favor **Studio 54** (☒ Schulgasse 9) and the **Metro Club** in Koblenz-Hochheim (☒ Alte Heerstr. 130). The nightclub scene in Koblenz is dominated by the **Klapsmühle** (☒ Poststr. 2a). The **Petit Fleur** (☒ Rheinstr. 30) is also popular.

Koblenz has a theatrical tradition dating back to the 18th-century rule of the Prince-Elector Clemens Wenzeslaus. The gracious neoclassical theater he built in 1787 is still in regular use (☎ 0261/34629 for program details and tickets).

The Rheinische Philharmonie Orchestra plays regularly in the **Rhein-Mosel-Halle** (☒ Julius-Wegeler-Str., ☎ 0261/129–1651). Organ recitals are frequently given in two fine churches: the **Christuskirche** and the **Florinskirche.**

Shopping

Koblenz's most pleasant shopping is in the old city streets around the market square of **Am Plan. Löhr Center,** a modern, American-style, windowless mall, has some 130 shops and restaurants and will give you an authentic taste of the postwar German shopping experience.

Tennis

The **Freizeit Park** (☎ 02603/81095) in Koblenz's Industriekreisel has eight indoor tennis courts, plus a swimming pool and a sauna for postmatch relaxation.

En Route   At the **Garden of Living Butterflies,** you can rub elbows with gargantuan tropical butterflies. In a glass pavilion zoo, butterflies from South America, Asia, and Africa flit back and forth over the visitors' heads between the branches of banana trees and palms. It is far more inspiring than seeing them pinned to the bottom of a dusty museum case. You'll find it 15 kilometers north of Koblenz (Bendorf exit off the B–42). ✉ *Im Schlosspark, Bendorf–Sayn,* ☎ *02622/15478.* 💰 *DM 7.* 🕐 *Mid-Mar.–mid-Nov. daily, 9–6; Dec.–mid-Mar., daily 9–5.*

Numbers in the margin correspond to points of interest on the Rhineland map.

Bonn

29   *28 km (17 mi) south of Köln, 175 km (109 mi) north of Frankfurt.*

Bonn, the quiet university town on the Rhine, is now the interim seat of reunited Germany's federal government and parliament, but in a parliamentary vote on June 20, 1991, it lost out to Berlin as the permanent capital of the country. In reality Bonn will continue to share the responsibility of governing Germany with Berlin. The upper house of parliament—the **Bundesrat**—will remain in Bonn, as will nearly half the ministries and two-thirds of the civil servants. Moving the rest of the government to Berlin is expected to take 12 years and will be costly—as much as $30 billion.

The choice of Bonn as capital of the newly created Federal Republic of Germany in 1949 was never meant to be permanent. At the time few Germans thought the division of their country would prove anything other than temporary, and they were certain that Berlin would again become the capital before long. Popular legend now has it that Bonn, aptly described in the title of John Le Carré's spy novel *A Small Town in Germany,* was chosen as a stopgap measure to prevent such weightier contenders as Frankfurt from becoming the capital, a move that would have lessened Berlin's chances of regaining its former status.

In the city's streets, old markets, stores, pedestrian malls, parks, and the handsome Südstadt residential area, life is unhurried and unsophisticated by the standard of larger cities. The town center is a car-free zone. An inner-ring road circles it with parking garages on the perimeter. A convenient parking lot is just across from the railway station and within 50 yards of the tourist office.

Numbers in the margin correspond to points of interest on the Bonn map.

Bonn's status may be new, but its roots are ancient. The Romans settled this part of the Rhineland 2,000 years ago, calling it Castra Bonnensia. Bonn's cathedral, the **Münster,** stands where two Roman soldiers **30** were executed in AD 253 for holding Christian beliefs. **Münsterplatz,** site of the cathedral and a short walk from the tourist office at Münsterstrasse 20, is the logical place to begin your tour. The 900-year-old cathedral is vintage late-Romanesque, with a massive octagonal main tower and a soaring spire. It was chosen by two Holy Roman emperors for their coronations (in 1314 and 1346) and was one of the Rhineland's most important ecclesiastical centers in the Middle Ages. The bronze 17th-century figure of St. Helen and the ornate rococo pulpit are highlights of the interior. ⊠ *Münsterpl.*, ☎ *0228/633–344.* ☉ *Daily 7–7.*

㉛ The grand **Kurfürstliches Schloss** faces Bonn's Münster. Built during the 18th century by the prince-electors of Köln; it now houses a university. If it's a fine day, stroll through the Hofgarten (Palace Gardens).

㉜ **Poppelsdorfer Schloss** may be reached from Kurfürstliches Schloss by following the chestnut-tree avenue called Poppelsdorfer Allee southward. This former electors' palace was built in Baroque style between 1715 and 1753. The building houses the university's botanical garden, with an impressive display of tropical plants. ⊠ *Meckenheimer Allee 171*, ☎ *0228/732–259.* ☒ *Free.* ☉ *Apr.–Sept., weekdays 9–6, weekends and holidays 9–1; Oct.–Mar., weekdays 9–4.*

㉝ The **Rheinisches Landesmuseum** may be reached by taking Meckenheimer Allee and then Colmantstrasse (the walk is about ¼-mile long) on the way back to the Old Town. This large museum charts the history and culture of the Rhine Valley from Roman times to the present. The main draw is the skull of a Neanderthal man, put together from fragments found in the Neander Valley near Düsseldorf in 1856 and regarded as a vital link in the evolutionary chain. ⊠ *Colmantstr. 14–16*, ☎ *0228/72941.* ☒ *DM 4.* ☉ *Tues. and Thurs. 9–5, Wed. 9–8, Fri. 9–5, weekends 10–5.*

㉞ The **Alter Friedhof** (Old Cemetery), an ornate graveyard, is the resting place of many of the country's most celebrated sons and daughters. Look for the tomb of composer Robert Schumann and his wife, Clara. To get to the cemetery, go to the end of Colmantstrasse, take the underpass below the railroad line, and follow Thomastrasse 300 yards to the site. ⊠ *Am Alten Friedhof.* ☉ *Mar.–Aug., daily 7:15 AM–8 PM; Sept. and Feb., daily 8–8; Oct., daily 8–7; Nov.–Jan., daily 8–5.*

㉟ The Markt (market) is situated in the Old Town Center. Here you'll find an 18th-century **Rathaus** (Town Hall) that looks like a pink doll's house. ⊠ *Am Markt.*

★ **㊱** The **Beethovenhaus** (Beethoven House) is just north of the Town Hall on Bonngasse. The residence has been converted into a museum celebrating the life of the great composer. Here you'll find scores, paintings, a grand piano (his last, in fact), and an ear trumpet or two. Perhaps the most impressive exhibit is the room in which Beethoven was born—empty save for a bust of the composer. ⊠ *Bonngasse 20*, ☎ *0228/635–188.* ☒ *DM 8.* ☉ *Apr.–Sept., Mon.–Sat. 10–5, Sun. 11–4; Oct.–Mar., Mon.–Sat. 10–4, Sun. 10–1.*

㊲ A tour of Bonn would not be complete without mention of the **government buildings,** in a complex about a mile south of downtown. Strung along the Rhine amid spacious, leafy grounds are the offices of the federal president, the high-tech Chancellery, and the federal parliament; the '60s high-rise you see contains the offices of members of parliament.

㊳ A trio of museums near the government buildings has brought Bonn more into the swing of things cultural. The **Bundeskunsthalle** (Art Hall of the German Federal Republic) is a space for major traveling exhibitions. ⊠ *Friedrich-Ebert-Allee 2*, ☎ *0228/776–260.* ☒ *Free.* ☉ *Tues.–Sun. 10–7.*

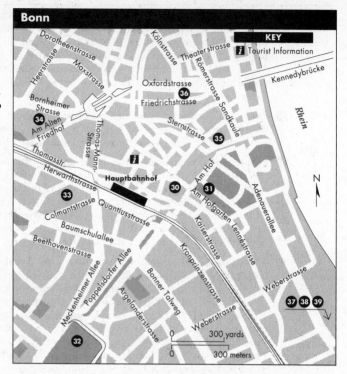

The **Kunstmuseum,** which is next door to the Bundeskunsthalle, is a large museum of contemporary art. ✉ *Friedrich-Ebert-Allee 4,* ☎ *0228/9171–2000.* 🎟 *Free.* 🕐 *Tues.–Sun. 10–7.*

39 The **Haus der Geschichte** is a controversial museum devoted to post–World War II German history. It displays an overwhelming amount of documentary material but avoids delving too deeply into some of the heavier issues of the period. ✉ *Adenauerstr. 250,* ☎ *0228/91650.* 🎟 *Free.* 🕐 *Tues.–Sun. 9–7.*

Dining and Lodging

$$ ✕ **Haus Daufenbach.** The stark white exterior of the Daufenbach, by the church of St. Remigius, disguises one of the most distinctive restaurants in Bonn. The mood is rustic, with simple wood furniture and antlers on the walls. Specialties include *Spanferkel* (suckling pig) and a range of imaginative salads. Wash them down with wines from the restaurant's own vineyards. ✉ *Brüdergasse 6,* ☎ *0228/637–944. No credit cards. Closed Mon. No dinner Sun. in summer.*

$ ✕ **Em Höttche.** Travelers have been given sustenance at this tavern since the late 14th century, and today it offers one of the best-value lunches in town. The interior is rustic; the food, stout and hearty. ✉ *Markt 4,* ☎ *0228/690–009. Reservations not accepted. No credit cards. Closed last 2 wks in Dec.*

$$$$ ✕🖭 **Bristol.** The Bristol could be in Dallas for all the German atmosphere it has, but for modern comfort and a terrific central location, it's an established favorite. ✉ *Prinz-Albert-Str. 2, D–53115,* ☎ *0228/26980,* 🖷 *0228/269–8222. 120 rooms with bath. Restaurant, indoor pool, sauna, bowling. AE, DC, MC, V.*

$$$$ ✕🖭 **Domicil.** A group of buildings around a quiet, central courtyard has been converted into a hotel of great charm and comfort. The rooms are individually furnished and decorated—in styles ranging from fin de siècle romantic to Italian modern. Lots of glass gives the public rooms a friendly airiness. ⊠ *Thomas-Mann-Str. 24–26, D–53111,* ☎ *0228/729–090,* FAX *0228/691—207. 42 rooms with bath. Restaurant, coffee shop, beauty salon, sauna. AE, DC, MC, V. Closed Dec. 25–Jan. 1.*

$$–$$$ 🏨 **Sternhotel.** For good value, solid comfort, and a central location in the Old Town, the family-run Stern is tops. Rooms can be small, but all are pleasantly furnished. There's no restaurant, but the bar has snacks. ⊠ *Markt 8, D–53111 Bonn,* ☎ *0228/72670,* FAX *0228/726–7125. 81 rooms with bath. Weekend rates. AE, DC, MC, V.*

$$ 🏨 **Rheinland.** This modest lodging has the advantage of being a short walk from the center of the Old Town. Rooms are comfortable, and although there is no restaurant, a good buffet breakfast greets the day. ⊠ *Berliner Freiheit 11, D–53111 Bonn,* ☎ *0228/658–096,* FAX *0228/472–844. 31 rooms with bath. AE, MC.*

Nightlife and the Arts

Nightlife in Bonn? There's the story of the visitor who asked where he could find. "She's taken the night off to visit her aunt in Köln," was the reply. Things have changed since then, however—there are now any number of bars and taverns in the Altstadt.

Try a Budweiser or Pilsener Urquell in the **Lampe** (⊠ Breitestr. 35). After midnight move on to the **Locke** (⊠ Prinz-Albertstr. 20). **Die Falle** (⊠ Belderberg 15) is a bar that attracts singles. The **Cave Club '77** (⊠ Bertha von Süttnerpl. 25) and the **CD Nightclub** (⊠ Rheingasse 14) have music and some adult spice. The **Jazz Galerie** (⊠ Oxfordstr. 24) has live jazz and rock many nights, starting at 9 PM. The **Pinte** (⊠ Breitestr. 46) is small, smoky, and fun. Disco goers head for **Sky** (⊠ Bonnerstr. 48) in Bad-Godesburg, where the suburb's resident diplomats let their hair down. **La Grange** (⊠ Wesselst. 5) is a popular dance club in downtown Bonn. Bonn's gamblers head to nearby Bad Neuenahr, where the casino is open daily 2 PM–3 AM.

On the first Saturday of May each year, the Rhine in Bonn goes up in flames—well, almost. It is one of the greatest fireworks display in the Rhine area.

MUSIC

Bonn means Beethoven, and every three years the city hosts a **Beethoven Festival**; the next one is in 1997. Contact the Bonn tourist office (☎ 0228/773–466) for program and ticket information.

The Bonn **Symphony Orchestra** opens its season in grand style every September with a concert on the market square, in front of City Hall. Otherwise, concerts are held in the **Beethovenhalle** (⊠ Wachsbleiche 26, ☎ 0228/631–321); they're free on Sunday morning. Chamber-music concerts are given regularly at the **Schumannhaus** (☎ 0228/773–6666). In May and June free concerts are held on Sunday evening in the **Bad Godesberg Redoute** (⊠ Auf dem Godesberg, ☎ 0228/316–071). The **Pantheon** theater (⊠ Bundeskanzlerpl., ☎ 0228/212521) has become a leading venue for all manner of pop concerts and cabaret.

Opera productions are staged regularly at the **Oper der Stadt Bonn** (⊠ Am Böselagerhof 1, ☎ 0228/773–666), popularly known as "La Scala of the Rhineland" and led by the colorful stage director Giancarlo del Monaco.

THEATER AND DANCE

Musicals and ballet are performed at the **Oper der Stadt Bonn** (☞ *above*). Bonn hosts a famous dance festival, the **International Dance Workshop,** in July and August. Call for program details and tickets (☎ 0228/11517). From May through October the **Bonner Sommer** festival offers folklore, music, and street theater, much of it outdoors and most of it free.

Shopping

The international comings and goings in Bonn keep antiques shops busy in this little town. **Paul Schweitzer** (✉ Muffendorfer Hauptstr. 37, ☎ 0228/362–659 is a respected dealer; closed Monday. The family-run **Ehlers Antiquitäten** (✉ Berliner Freiheit 28, ☎ 0228/676–853) is a reliable antiques outlet.

Despite its name, Bonn's **Wochenmarkt** (Weekly Market) is open daily, filling Marktplatz with vendors of produce and various edibles. Bargain-hunters flock to the city's renowned, and huge, **flea market** (*Flohmarkt*) held on the third Saturday of each month between April and October at **Rheinaue** (Ludwig-Erhard-Str.), where you can find secondhand goods and knickknacks of all descriptions. **Pützchens Markt,** a huge country fair, is held in the Bonn area the second weekend of September.

Königswinter

12 km (7 mi) northeast of Bonn.

The town of Königswinter has one of the most visited castles on the Rhine, the **Drachenfels.** Its ruins crown one of the highest hills in the **Sibengebirge** (Seven Hills), Germany's oldest nature reserve, with a spectacular view of the Rhine. The reserve has more than 100 kilometers (62 miles) of hiking trails. The castle was built during the 12th century by the archbishop of Köln. Its name commemorates a dragon said to have lived in a nearby cave. As legend has it, the dragon was slain by Siegfried, hero of the epic poem *The Nibelungenlied.*

Dining

$$ ✕ Gasthaus Sutorius. Across from the church of St. Margaretha, this wine tavern serves refined variations on German culinary themes with an intelligent selection of local wines. In summer food is served outdoors beneath the lime trees. ✉ *Oelinghovener Str. 7,* ☎ *02244/4749. No credit cards. Closed 2 wks in Jan., 4 wks in Sept. No lunch Mon.–Sat.*

Brühl

20 km (12 mi) southwest of Bonn.

In the heart of Brühl you'll discover Rhineland's most important Baroque palace, along with another important late-Baroque castle. ★ **Schloss Augustusburg** was constructed in the time of Prince Clemens-August between 1725 and 1768, along with the magnificent pleasure park that surrounds it. Augustusburg contains one of the most famous achievements of rococo architecture, a staircase by Balthasar Neumann. In summer the Brühl castle concerts are held here. ✉ *Schloss Str. 6,* ☎ *02232/42471.* 🎫 *DM 4.* ☉ *Feb.–Nov., Tues.–Sun. 9–noon and 1:30–4.*

Jagdschloss Falkenlust (Falcon Hunting Castle) is reached by a straight avenue leading to this courtly hunting palace at the other end of the park surrounding Schloss Augustusburg. It was built here because of its favorable location for falconry, a sport for which the electoral prince had a great passion. ⊠ *Schloss Str. 6,* ☎ *02232/42471.* 🖅 *DM 2.50.* 🕐 *Feb.–Nov., Tues.–Sun. 9–noon and 1:30–4.*

THE MOSEL VALLEY

The Mosel is one of the most hauntingly beautiful river valleys on earth: turreted castles look down from its leafy perches; its hilltops are crowned with bell towers; and throughout its expanse, skinny church spires stand against the sky. For more than 160 kilometers (100 miles), the silvery Mosel River meanders past a string of storybook medieval wine villages, each more attractive than the last.

The city of Trier, at the western end of the Mosel, could easily qualify as Germany's best-kept secret. The road from Koblenz, which follows the banks of the Mosel with all its loops and turns, takes three hours of driving. On the autobahn the distance of 125 kilometers (84 miles) between Koblenz and Trier can be covered in less than an hour.

Numbers in the margin correspond to points of interest on the Rhineland map.

Winningen

⓵ *15 km (10 mi) from Koblenz.*

Winningen is the center of the valley's largest vineyards. Another reason to stop here is to admire Germany's oldest half-timbered house in **Kirchenstrasse** (No. 1); it was built in 1320. On the slopes above Winningen's narrow medieval streets is a mile-long path, reached by driving up Fährstrasse to Am Rosenhang. Once there, high above the Mosel, you'll get a bird's-eye view of the **Uhlen, Röttgen, Bruckstück, Hamm,** and **Domgarten** vineyards.

OFF THE BEATEN PATH
KOBERN-GONDORF – For an even finer view of the river and its rich valley, follow the road 8 kilometers (5 miles) to this town on the north bank of the river, and turn off into the idyllic little Mühlental Valley. You can climb through the steep vineyards above Mühlental Valley to the remains of **Oberburg Castle,** built during the 12th century by the powerful Knights of Leyen. On the way you'll pass **St. Matthew's,** a 13th-century Romanesque chapel.

Dining and Lodging

$$$ ✕🖾 **Weinhaus Gries.** Come here to eat, drink, and daydream, on the shore of the gently flowing Mosel. You can also spend the night, if the road ahead seems too long. Across the river the imposing castle of Thurant rises. But the place offers more than a pretty view. Chef Peter Manca makes the most of in-season game from the local woods and performs fine variations on German standards like *Tafelspitz.* (marinated boiled beef). ⊠ *Moselufer 14, D–56332 Kattenes,* ☎ *02605/646,* 🖹 *02605/1643. 11 rooms with bath. Restaurant.*

Moselkern

15 km (10 mi) from Kobern-Gondorf.

★ ⓶ The Mosel has almost as many castles as the Rhine. Above the village of Moselkern is **Burg Eltz,** a castle that many deem the most impressive in the country. One way to reach this local landmark from Moselkern is on foot from the Wanderparkplatz (hiker's parking lot), a one-hour walk covering 3 kilometers (2 miles) on a footpath through the wild valley. If you drive, take B–416 from Koblenz along the Mosel until the road to Hatzenport; from there, follow the signs to "Münstermaifeld" and then to "Burg Eltz PP Antoniuskapelle." You will still have to walk (about 15 minutes) from the parking lot up the road from the castle; you can also take the small shuttle bus (fare: DM 1.50) from the parking lot. Either way it's worth the trek to see what may well be the most perfectly proportioned medieval castle in Germany. Perched on the spine of an isolated rocky outcrop, bristling with towers and pinnacles, it looks like a dream at first sight, the apotheosis of all one expects of a medieval castle, easily as impressive as "Mad" King Ludwig's fantasy creation, Neuschwanstein. But Burg Eltz is the real thing: an 800-year-old castle, with modifications from the 16th century. The magic continues in the interior, which is decorated with heavy Gothic furnishings. There is also an interesting collection of old weapons. The castle is depicted on the DM 500 banknote. ☎ 02672/1300. ✆ DM 8, includes guided tour. ☉ Apr.–Oct., daily 9:30–5:30.

Cochem

42 *15 km (10 mi) from Moselkern and Burg Eltz, 50 km (31 mi) southwest of Koblenz.*

Cochem is one of the most attractive towns of the Mosel Valley, with a riverside promenade to rival any along the Rhine. If you're traveling by train, just south of Cochem you'll be plunged into Germany's longest railway tunnel, the Kaiser-Wilhelm, an astonishing 4-kilometer-long (2½-mile-long) example of 19th-century engineering that saves travelers a 21-kilometer (13-mile) detour along one of the Mosel's great loops.

The **Reichsburg** (Imperial Fortress), Cochem's famous 900-year-old castle, was destroyed when Louis XIV stormed it in 1689. It was rebuilt during the 19th century in a romantic baronial style. Today it stands majestically over the town. The fortress has a good view overlooking the Mosel. ☎ 02671/1787. ✆ DM 5. ☉ Mid-Mar.–Nov., daily 9–6; Nov.–Dec. hourly tours 11–3.

Dining and Lodging

$$$ ✕🏨 **Alte Thorschenke.** There are few more authentic or atmospheric
★ old inns in the Rhineland than this picturesque spot in the heart of Cochem, dating from the 14th century. Creaking staircases, four-poster beds, river views, and exposed beams combine to produce an effect that is almost too good to be true. Avoid the modern annex if you want to experience the full charm of this romantic haunt. The restaurant's selection of local wines is extensive. ✉ Brückenstr. 3, D–56812, ☎ 02671/7059, 🖷 02671/4202. 51 rooms with bath. Restaurant. AE, DC, MC, V. Closed Jan.–mid-Mar.

$$ ✕🏨 **Brixiade.** Despite its modern-looking facade, the Brixiade has been welcoming guests—Kaiser Wilhelm II among them—for more than 100 years. Ask for a room with a view over the town and the river. A few of the rooms also have a balcony. The restaurant offers a fixed-price menu and magnificent local wines. Dine on the terrace in summer. ✉ Uferstr. 13, D–56182, ☎ 02671/9810, 🖷 02671/981–100. 35 rooms with bath. Restaurant, wine bar. AE, DC, MC, V.

$–$$ ✕🏨 **Weissmühle.** You'll want to stay—or eat—here as much to see the
★ picture-book village of Endertal, just outside of Cochem, as to lay your head on the hotel's ample pillows. The place is decorated in that inimitable German gingerbread style, with carved beams and lace curtains galore. Try the trout or the spit-roasted kebabs. ✉ D–56812 Cochem-Endertal, ☎ 02671/8955, 🖷 02671/8207. 36 rooms with shower. Restaurant, parking. DC, MC, V.

Shopping

Cochem's Herrenstrasse is lined with shops. You'll find local souvenirs at **Die Geschenkidee Heimes** (✉ Herrenstr. 13, ☎ 02671/91122).

En Route The little town of **Beilstein,** 8 kilometers (5 miles) past Cochem, has a mixture of all the picture-pretty features of a German river and wine town in this romantic area of the country. Take a look at the marketplace carved into the rocky slope.

NEED A
BREAK?

At the village of Ediger-Eller, 10 kilometers (6 miles) from Beilstein, stop at **Freiherr von Landenberg** (✉ Moselweinstr. 60, ☎ 02675/277), a roadside vineyard. Sample a glass of wine from the baron's vines and visit his private viticulture museum.

Zell

43 *12 km (8 mi) upriver from Cochem.*

Zell is a typical Mosel River town on a great loop in the river, much like Cochem. About midway between Koblenz and Trier, this small historic town is made up of picturesque red-roof homes and age-old fortifications falling into ruin. A scenic backdrop is provided by the vineyards that produce the famous Schwarze Katz (Black Cat) wine, rated one of Germany's very best whites. Stroll the town's medieval arc along the river. On your way you'll notice a small, twin-towered castle, Schloss Zell, dating from the 14th century. A restaurant here serves regional cuisine and wine from the owner's own Black Cat vineyards.

44 **Traben-Trarbach** straddles the Mosel 18 kilometers (11 miles) farther south. This two-town combination serves as headquarters for the regional wine trade and offers a popular wine festival in summer. Visit the ruins of **Mont Royal** high above Traben, on the east bank. This enormous fortress was built around 1687 by Louis XIV of France, only to be dismantled 10 years later under the terms of the Treaty of Rijswijk. Partially restored by the Nazis, the fortress retains some of its original forbidding mass.

Bernkastel-Kues

45 *22 km (14 mi) by road from Traben-Trarbach; 2 hrs by foot.*

Bernkastel-Kues can be reached by foot from Traben-Trarbach by taking the path that cuts across the tongue of land formed by the exaggerated loop of the river. The road, following the river, practically doubles back on itself as it winds leisurely along. Bernkastel, on the north bank of the river, and Kues, on the south were officially linked early in this century. The heart of **Bernkastel, Marktplatz,** meets all the requirements for the ideal small-town German market square. Most of the buildings are late-Gothic/early Renaissance, with facades covered with intricate carvings and sharp gables stabbing the sky. In the center of the square is **Michaelsbrunnen** (Michael's fountain), a graceful 17th-century work. Wine used to flow from it on special occasions in bygone years. Today, although wine flows freely in the town—especially during the local wine festival in the first week of September—only water ever comes from the fountain.

Burg Landshut, a 13th-century castle glowers above the town. Visit it for some amazing views of the river, either from its ramparts or from the terrace of the restaurant within its old walls, and to wander around its flower-strewn remains. In summer a bus makes the trip up to the castle every hour from the parking lot by the river.

Bernkasteler Doktor is the town's most famous wine. According to local lore, the wine got its unusual name after it saved the life of the prince-bishop of Trier, who lay dying in the castle. After all medicinal treatments had failed to cure him, he was offered a glass of the local wine—which miraculously put him back on his feet. Try a glass of it yourself at the castle (or buy a bottle from the vineyard bordering the street called Hinterm Graben).

The town of **Kues** owes its existence to Cardinal Nikolaus Cusanus (Kues), a 15th-century philosopher and pioneer of German humanist thought. He founded a religious and charitable institution, complete with a vineyard, on the riverbank in Kues. The vineyard is still going strong; ask about the regular tastings in the **St. Niklaus-Hospital.** The buildings here comprise the largest Gothic ensemble on the Mosel. Among them is the Mosel-Weinmuseum. ⊠ *Cusanusstr. 2,* ☎ *06531/4023.* ⚏ *DM 2.* ☉ *May–Oct., daily 10–5; Nov.–Apr., daily 2–5.*

Dining and Lodging

$$–$$$ ✕☗ **Zur Post.** Picture-book Germany is alive and well at the appealing, early-19th-century Zur Post. Behind its colorful, flower-laden facade lurk the obligatory exposed wood beams and a dark-paneled restaurant (with more than 100 wines). Bedrooms are tastefully decorated. ⊠ *Gestade 17, D–54470 Bernkastel-Kues,* ☎ *06531/2022,* ⅨⅩ *06531/2927. 42 rooms with bath. Restaurant, parking. AE, DC, MC, V. Closed Jan.*

$$ ✕☗ **Hotel Römischer Kaiser.** What better way to appreciate the views of the waterway and the surrounding vineyards than from a balcony at this riverside location on the promenade. Fortunately, all rooms here have one. The hotel's restaurant is noted for its good, reasonably priced regional wines. ⊠ *Markt. 29, D–54470 Bernkastel-Kues,* ☎ *06531/3038,* ⅨⅩ *06531/7672. 35 rooms with bath. Restaurant. AE, DC, MC, V. Closed Jan.–Feb.*

En Route From Bernkastel-Kues to Trier is farther south, a 66-kilometer (41- mile) drive of twisting river road. You can also board a cruise boat (☎ 02673/1515) from May through October that takes 4½ hours to reach Trier, with six stops along the way. The fare is DM 34 one-way, DM 44 round-trip. Boats depart from Bernkastel-Kues at 3:15, from Trier for Bernkastel-Kues at 9:15 AM; an additional boat runs Tuesday at 10 AM.

Endless vineyards and little river towns punctuate the snaking path of the Mosel. **Neumagen** was settled by the Romans during the 4th century. In its main square there's a modern copy of the famous carved relief of a Roman wine ship plying a choppy-looking Mosel. The original is in the Landesmuseum in Trier.

Numbers in the margin correspond to points of interest on the Rhineland map.

Trier

㊻ *66 km (41 mi) southeast of Bernkastel-Kues; 4½ hrs by cruise boat.*

Trier (known as Treves in English) claims to be the oldest town in Germany. It dates from 2000 BC, when Prince Trebeta, son of an Assyrian queen, arrived here and set up residence on the banks of the Mosel; he named the place Treberis, after himself. An inscription on a historic old house on Trier's marketplace claims: *"Ante Romam Treveris stetit annis mille trecentis"* ("1,300 years before Rome stood Trier").

Eventually the legions of Julius Caesar set up camp at this strategic point of the river, and Augusta Treverorum (the town of Emperor Augustus in the land of the Treveri) was founded in 16 BC. It was described as *"urbs opulentissima"*—a most opulent city, as beautiful as any outside Rome.

Around AD 275 an Alemannic tribe stormed Augusta Treverorum and reduced it to rubble. But it was rebuilt in even grander style and renamed Treveris. Eventually it evolved into one of the leading cities of the empire and was promoted to *Roma Secunda,* "a second Rome" north of the Alps. As a powerful administrative capital it was adorned with all the noble civic buildings of a major Roman settlement, as well as public baths, palaces, barracks, an amphitheater, and temples. The Roman emperors Diocletian (who made it one of the four joint capitals of the empire) and Constantine lived in Trier for years at a time.

Trier survived the collapse of Rome and became an important center of Christianity; it later became one of the most powerful archbishoprics in the Holy Roman Empire. The city thrived throughout the Renaissance and Baroque periods, taking full advantage of its location at the meeting point of major east–west and north–south trade routes and growing fat on the commerce that passed through. It also became one of Germany's most important wine-exporting centers. A later claim to fame is the city's status as the birthplace of Karl Marx. To do justice to Trier, consider staying for at least two full days. A ticket good for all the Roman sights in Trier costs DM 9. Between May and October there are walking tours of the city conducted in English by the local tourist board (☞ Contacts and Resources *in* The Rhineland A to Z, *below*).

Numbers in the margin correspond to points of interest on the Trier map.

★ **47** **Porta Nigra** (the Black Gate) is by far the best-preserved Roman structure in Trier and one of the grandest Roman buildings in northern Europe. It's a city gate, built during the 2nd century. Its name is misleading, however; the sandstone gate is not black but dark gray. Those with an interest in Roman construction techniques should look for the holes left by the original iron clamps that held the entire structure together. This city gate also served as part of Trier's defenses and was proof of the sophistication of Roman military might and ruthlessness. Attackers were often lured into the two innocent-looking arches of the Porta Nigra, only to find themselves enclosed in a courtyard—and at the mercy of the defending forces. ✍ *DM 4.* ☉ *Apr.–Oct., daily 9–6; Nov. and Jan.–Mar., daily 9–5; Dec., daily 10–4.*

48 The **Städtisches Museum Simeonstift,** near Porta Negra, contains the remains of the Romanesque Simeonskirche, a church built during the 11th century by Archbishop Poppo in honor of the early medieval hermit Simeon, who for seven years shut himself up in the east tower of the Porta Nigra. Collections of art and artifacts produced in Trier from the Middle Ages to the present now commemorate Simeon's feat. ⊠ *Porta Nigra,* ☎ *0651/718–2449.* ✍ *DM 3.* ☉ *Apr.–Oct., Tues.–Fri. 9–5, weekends 9–3; Nov.–Mar., Tues.–Fri. 9–5, weekends 9–1.*

49 The **Hauptmarkt,** the main square of old Trier, is easily reached via Simeonstrasse. A 1,000-year-old market cross and a richly ornate 16th-century fountain stand in the square.

50 The 13th-century **Liebfrauenkirche** (Church of Our Lady), which adjoins Trier's Dom, is one of the oldest purely Gothic churches in the

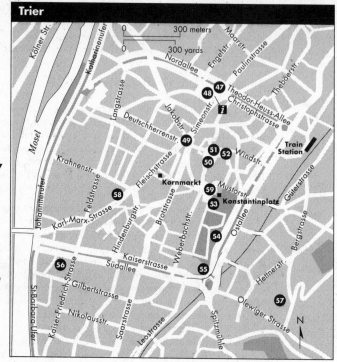

country. The interior is elegantly attenuated. ✉ Liebfrauenstr., ☎
0651/75801.

★ ❺❶ The **Dom** (cathedral) is a history of Trier in stone. There is almost no
period of the city's past that is not represented. It stands on the site of
the Palace of Helen, named for the mother of the emperor Constantine, who knocked the palace down in AD 330 and put up a large church
in its place. The church burned down in 336 and a second, even larger
one was built. Parts of the foundations of this third building can be
seen in the east end of the current structure (begun in about 1035).
The cathedral you see today is a weighty and sturdy edifice with small,
round-head windows, rough stonework, and asymmetrical towers, as
much a fortress as a church. Inside, Gothic styles predominate—the
result of remodeling in the 13th century—although there are also
many Baroque tombs, altars, and confessionals. This architectural
jumble of Romanesque, Gothic, and Baroque styles gives the place the
air of a vast antiques shop. The Gothic **Domschatzmuseum** (Treasury
Museum) in Trier's cathedral is the site of two extraordinary objects.
One is the 10th-century **Andreas Tragalter** (St. Andrew's Portable
Altar), constructed of gold by local craftsmen. It is smaller than the
Dom's main altar, but it is no lightweight. The other treasure is the
Holy Robe, the garment Christ is said to have worn at the time of his
trial before Pontius Pilate, which was then gambled for by Roman soldiers. As the story goes, it was brought to Trier by Constantine's
mother, Helen, a tireless collector of holy relics. It is so delicate and
old that it is seldom displayed. For lucky visitors 1996 was such a year,
when it was taken out from its regular abode—under a faded piece of
9th-century Byzantine silk. ✉ Domfriehof, ☎ 0651/75801. 🎫 Domschatzmuseum DM 2. ⏲ Apr.–Oct., Mon.–Sat. 10–noon and 2–5, Sun.
2–5; until 4 PM Nov.–Mar.

52 The **Bischöfliches Museum** (Episcopal Museum), just behind the cathedral, houses most of a series of antiquities unearthed by excavations around the cathedral of Trier. The exhibits include a 4th-century ceiling painting believed to have adorned the emperor Constantine's palace. ✉ *Windstr. 6–8,* ☎ *0651/710-5255.* 🎫 *DM 2.* 🕐 *Mon.–Sat. 9–1 and 2–5, Sun. 1–5.*

NEED A
BREAK?

There's a time-honored welcome at the **Steine Ratskeller** (✉ Hauptmarkt 14, ☎ 0651/75052) in the cellars beneath the Rathaus (Town Hall), where you can plunge into the hearty local fare or just order a coffee, beer, or glass of Mosel wine.

★ **53** The **Römische Palastaula** (Roman Basilica), south of the cathedral, is an impressive reminder of Trier's Roman past. Today this is the major Protestant church of Trier. When first built by the emperor Constantine around AD 310, it was the Imperial Throne Room of the palace. At 239 feet long, 93 feet wide, and 108 feet high, it demonstrates the astounding ambition of its Roman builders and the sophistication of their building techniques. It is one of the two largest Roman interiors in existence (the other is the Pantheon in Rome). Look up at the deeply coffered ceiling; more than any other part of the building, it conveys the opulence of the original structure. ✉ *Konstantinpl.,* ☎ *0651/978–080.* 🕐 *Apr.–Oct., weekdays 9–6, Sun. and holidays 11–6; Nov.–Mar., limited opening hrs.*

54 The **Rheinisches Landesmuseum** (Rhineland Archaeological Museum) lies south of the Palastaula, facing the grounds of the prince-elector's palace. The museum houses the largest collection of Roman antiquities in Germany. Pride of place goes to the 3rd-century stone relief of a Roman ship transporting immense barrels of wine up the river. If you stopped off in Neumagen on the way to Trier, you probably saw the copy in the town square. ✉ *Weimarerallee 44.* 🎫 *DM 2.* 🕐 *Tues.–Fri. 9:30–5, weekends 10:30–5.*

55 The ruins of the **Kaiserthermen** (Imperial Baths) are just 200 yards from the Rhineland Architectural Museum. Begun by Constantine during the 4th century, these were once the third-largest public baths in the Roman Empire, exceeded only by Diocletian's baths in Croatia and the baths of Caracalla in Rome. The Imperial Baths covered an area 270 yards long and 164 yards wide. Today only the weed-strewn fragments of the **Calderium** (hot baths) are left, but they are enough to give a fair idea of the original splendor and size of the complex. When the Romans pulled out, the baths were turned into a fortress (one window of the huge complex served as a city gate for much of the Middle Ages), then a church, and then a fortress again. 🎫 *DM 4.* 🕐 *Apr.–Oct., daily 9–6; Jan.–Mar. and Nov., daily 9–5; Dec., daily 10–4.*

56 The **Barbarathermen,** which have been excavated in Südallee, are much smaller baths than the Kaiserthermen, but still worth a look. ✉ *Südallee.* 🎫 *DM 4.* 🕐 *Apr.–Sept., daily 9–6; Oct.–Mar., daily 9–1 and 2–5.*

57 The remains of the **Amphitheater** lie just east of the Kaiserthermen. The Amphitheater was built around AD 100, the oldest Roman building in Trier. In its heyday it seated 20,000 people. You can climb down to the cellars beneath the arena to see what's left of the machines that were used to change the scenery; in the walls are the cells where lions and other wild animals were kept before being unleashed to devour maidens and do battle with gladiators. ✉ *Olewigerstr.* 🎫 *DM 4.* 🕐 *Apr.–Oct., daily 9–6; Nov. and Jan.–Mar., daily 9–5; Dec., daily 10–4.*

58 The **Karl-Marx-Haus,** south of Kornmarkt in the Old Town, offers a glimpse of a completely different time than that of the Romans. It was here that Marx was born in 1818. Serious social historians will feel at home in the little house, which has been converted into a museum charting Marx's life and the development of socialism around the world. A signed first edition of *Das Kapital,* the tome in which Marx sought to prove the inevitable decline of capitalism, may prove a highlight for some. ✉ *Brockenstr.,* ☎ *0651/43011.* 🎫 *DM 3.* ☉ *Apr.–Oct., Mon. 1–6, Tues.–Sun. 10–6; Nov.–Mar., Mon. 3–6, Tues.–Sun. 10–1 and 3–6.*

Trier is, of course, also a city of wine, and beneath its streets are cellars capable of storing nearly 8 million gallons. Drop in for a tasting

59 at the **Weininformation Mosel-Saar-Ruwer** (✉ *Konstantinpl. 11,* ☎ *0651/73690)* to get to know the wines of the region. The city also has a wine trail, a picturesque 1½-mile walk studded with information plaques that lead to the wine-growing suburb of **Olewig.** A free map of the trail along with information on Trier's wine making is available from the tourist office.

Dining and Lodging

$$$ ✕ **Pfeffermühle.** The stately Pfeffermühle stands alongside the Mosel,
★ by the cable-car station. This former fisherman's home is now considered to be the best restaurant in town, and it has recently added an outdoor terrace for summer dining. The food is nouvelle French. Rabbit in sherry sauce is outstanding, as is the lobster in champagne gelée with asparagus tips. The extensive wine list features vintage Mosels. ✉ *Zurlaubener Ufer 76,* ☎ *0651/26133. Reservations essential. MC, V. Closed Sun. and Feb. 19–Mar. 2. No lunch Mon.*

$$ ✕ **Ratskeller zur Steipe.** Buried in the vaults beneath the Town Hall, the Ratskeller's Teutonic mood and fare has a Russian flavor thanks to two Russian chefs. In summer you can move upstairs and eat on the terrace. ✉ *Hauptmarkt 14,* ☎ *0651/75052. AE, DC, V. Closed Tues. and mid-Jan.–mid-Feb.*

$$ ✕ **Zum Domstein.** This centrally located, bustling weinstube is built
★ above a Roman cellar, and it takes its history seriously—keeping its wines stored within its ancient walls, as the Romans did, and serving authentic Roman dishes as well as German fare in the restaurant above. Many of them are the staples of today's Italian cuisine, with sauces so rich they could have contributed to the downfall of the Roman Empire. ✉ *Am Hauptmarkt 5,* ☎ *0651/74490. Reservations not accepted. DC, MC, V. Closed Dec. 25.*

$$ ✕🏠 **Petrisberg.** This will be the choice of anyone who values classic
★ modern design and a location away from the downtown area. The building is unimposing externally, but inside features striking antiques and rooms with superb views overlooking vineyards, forests, and parklands. The rooms are large for the price and smartly furnished in a mixture of contemporary styles. For all that, it's no more than a 10-minute walk from the Old Town. Old farm implements and an eclectic assortment of artifacts lend a homey ambience to the tiny weinstube and dining room. The owner, Herr Pantenburg, provides a warm welcome. ✉ *Sickingerstr. 11–13, D-54296,* ☎ *0651/4640,* 📠 *0651/46450. 30 rooms and 3 suites with shower. Dining room, weinstube. No credit cards.*

$$ 🏠 **Hotel-Cafe Astoria.** This beautifully renovated 19th-century city villa is ideally located between the Mosel River and the Old Town. Ask for a room on the first floor, as they are larger. All rooms are cozy and comfortably furnished. ⊠ *Bruchhausenstr. 4, D–54290,* ☎ *0651/978-350,* FAX *0651/41121. 14 rooms with shower. Bar, café. AE, MC, V.*

Nightlife and the Arts

Trier's cathedral is the magnificent setting for much of the sacred music to be heard in the city; there are organ recital festivals in May, June, August, and September.

Shopping

For local crafts, explore **Kunsthandwerkerhof,** or Artisans' Court (⊠ Simeonstiftpl. 2, ☎ 0651/42991) with four artisans' workshops. Here you can watch glassblowers and engravers, stained-glass painters, and batik artists at work.

Tennis and Squash

The **Ferienpark Hochwald** (☎ 06589/1011) at Kell, near Trier, is one of the leading tennis complexes in Germany.

THE COLOGNE LOWLANDS

The lowlands are a region of gently rolling hills. The drama of the Rhine Gorge is lacking farther downstream. Instead you have the ancient cathedral city of Köln (Cologne) and Düsseldorf, an elegant city of art and fashion. Although not geographically in the Rhineland proper, Aachen is an important destination for anyone visiting the region. Its stunning cathedral and treasury are the single greatest storehouse of Carolingian art and architecture in Europe.

Numbers in the margin correspond to points of interest on the Rhineland map.

Köln

60 *28 km (17 mi) north of Bonn, 47 km (29 mi) south of Düsseldorf, 70 km (43 mi) southeast of Aachen.*

Köln (Cologne) is the largest city on the Rhine (the fourth-largest in Germany) and one of the most interesting. Although not as old as Trier, it has been a dominant power in the Rhineland since Roman times. Known throughout the world for its scented toilet water, eau de cologne (first produced here in 1705, from an Italian formula), the city is today a major commercial, intellectual, and ecclesiastical center. The numerous trade fairs, held in the two massive convention centers on the Deutzer side of the Rhine, are a draw for many.

Köln is a vibrant, bustling city, with something of the same sparkle that makes Munich so memorable. It claims to have more bars than any other German city, and it has a host of excellent eating establishments. It also puts on a wild carnival every February, with three days of orgiastic revelry, bands, parades, and parties that last all night.

Köln was first settled by the Romans in 38 BC. For nearly a century it grew slowly, in the shadow of imperial Trier, until a locally born noblewoman, Julia Agrippina, daughter of the Roman general Germanicus, married the Roman emperor Claudius. Her hometown was elevated to the rank of a Roman city and given the name Colonia Claudia Ara Agrippinensium. For the next 300 years Colonia (hence Cologne, or Köln) flourished. Today there's evidence of the Roman city's richness in the Römisch-Germanisches Museum, or Roman-German Museum (☞ *below*). When the Romans left, Köln was ruled first by the Franks, then by the Merovingians. During the 9th century, Charlemagne, the towering figure who united the sprawling German lands (and ruled much of present-day France) and was the first Holy Roman

Emperor, restored Köln's fortunes and elevated it to its preeminent role in the Rhineland. Charlemagne also appointed the first archbishop of Köln. The ecclesiastical heritage of Köln forms one of the most striking characteristics of the city, which has no fewer than 12 Romanesque churches. Its Gothic cathedral is the largest and the finest in Germany.

Köln eventually became the largest city north of the Alps and in time evolved into a place of pilgrimage second only to Rome. In the Middle Ages it was a member of the powerful Hanseatic League, occupying a position of greater importance in European commerce than either London or Paris.

Köln entered modern times as the number one city of the Rhineland. Then, in World War II, bombings destroyed 90% of it. Only the cathedral remained relatively unscathed. Almost everything else had to be rebuilt, more or less from the ground up, including all of the glorious Romanesque churches.

Early reconstruction was accomplished in a big rush—and it shows. Like many German cities that sprang up, mushroomlike, in the "Economic Miracle" of the 1950s, Köln is a mishmash of old and new, sometimes awkwardly juxtaposed. A good part of the former Old Town along the Hohe Strasse (old Roman High Road) was turned into one of Germany's first yet remarkably charmless pedestrian shopping malls, since emulated in so many other cities. Contrasting with its square, blocky forms are the totally re-created facades of the Old Town dwellings facing the river, which bring to mind Disneyland rather than recapturing their former dignified, venerable air. The ensemble is framed by six-lane expressways winding along the rim of the city center—barely yards from the cathedral—perfectly illustrating the problems, as well as the blessings, of postwar reconstruction.

Among the blessings is the fact that much of the Altstadt (Old Town), ringed by streets that follow the line of the medieval city walls, is closed to traffic; most major sights are within this area and are easily reached on foot. Here, too, you'll find the best shops.

The **tourist office** (☎ 0221/221–3345), across from the cathedral, can make hotel bookings for you at a cost of DM 6. From the tourist office or your hotel you can purchase a Köln-Bonbon card for DM 26; it provides admission to museums and a bus tour of the city (cost without the tour is DM 15). For information about guided tours of Köln, *see* Contacts and Resources *in* The Rhineland A to Z, *below.*

Numbers in the margin correspond to points of interest on the Köln map.

★ ⓺¹ The extraordinary Gothic cathedral, the **Kölner Dom,** dedicated to Sts. Peter and Mary, towers over the Old Town. It's comparable to the best French cathedrals; a visit here may prove a highlight of your trip to Germany. What you'll see is one of the purest expressions of the Gothic spirit in Europe. Here the desire to pay homage to God took the form of building as large and as lavish a church as possible, a tangible expression of God's kingdom on earth. Its spires soar heavenward, and its immense interior is illuminated by light filtering through acres of stained glass. Spend some time admiring the outside of the building (you can walk almost all the way around it). Notice how there are practically no major horizontal lines—all the accents of the building are vertical. It may come as a disappointment to learn that the cathedral, begun in 1248, was not completed until 1880. Console yourself with the knowledge that it was still built to original plans. At 515 feet high, the two west towers of the cathedral were by far the tallest structures in the world when they were finished.

The cathedral was built to house what were believed to be the relics of the Magi, the three kings who paid homage to the infant Jesus (the trade in holy mementos was big business in the Middle Ages—and not always scrupulous). Since Köln was by then a major commercial and political center, it was felt that a special place had to be constructed to house the relics. Anxious to surpass the great cathedrals then being built in France, the masons set to work. The size of the building was not simply an example of self-aggrandizement on the part of the people of Köln, however; it was a response to the vast numbers of pilgrims who arrived to see the relics. The ambulatory, the passage that curves around the back of the altar, is unusually large, allowing cathedral authorities to funnel large numbers of visitors up to the crossing (where the nave and transepts meet, and where the relics were originally displayed), around the back of the altar, and out again. Today the relics are kept just behind the altar, in the original enormous gold-and-silver **reliquary.** The other great treasure of the cathedral is the **Gero Cross,** a monumental oak crucifix dating from 971, in the last chapel on the left as you face the altar. Other highlights are the stained-glass windows, some dating from the 13th century; the 15th-century altarpiece; and the early 14th-century high altar with its glistening white figures and intricate choir screens.

There are more treasures in the **Dom Schatzkammer,** the cathedral treasury, including the silver shrine of Archbishop Engelbert, who was stabbed to death in 1225. *Dompl.,* ☎ *0221/135–130.* ▨ *Treasury DM 3.* ☉ *Mon.–Sat. 9–5, Sun. 1–5.*

★ ⑫ Grouped around Köln's cathedral is a collection of superb museums. The **Wallraf-Richartz-Museum** and **Museum Ludwig** complex (which includes the Philharmonic concert hall) together form the largest art collection in the Rhineland. The Wallraf-Richartz-Museum contains pictures spanning the years 1300 to 1900, with Dutch and Flemish schools particularly well represented. Rubens, who spent his youth in Köln, has a place of honor, but there are also outstanding works by Rembrandt, Van Dyck, and Frans Hals. Other Old Masters include Tiepolo, Canaletto, and Boucher. Some of the great Impressionists bring the collection into the 20th century, but it's here that the Museum Ludwig takes over. Devoted exclusively to 20th-century art, with a collection that is said to be second only to that of New York's Guggenheim, this is the flagship of the Rhineland museums donated by chocolate tycoon and megacollector Peter Ludwig (☞ Koblenz and Aachen). The Picassos are so meritorious that a new, all-Picasso museum will be constructed for them in the next few years. ⊠ *Bischofsgartenstr. 1,* ☎ *0221/221–2372 or 0221/221–3491.* ▨ *Both museums DM 10.* ☉ *Tues.–Fri. 10–6, weekends 11–6.*

⑬ The **Römisch-Germanisches Museum,** opposite the cathedral, was built from 1970 to 1974 around the famous Dionysus mosaic that was uncovered there during the construction of an air-raid shelter in 1941. The huge mosaic, more than 100 yards square, once covered the dining-room floor of a wealthy Roman trader's villa. Its millions of tiny earthenware and glass tiles depict some of the adventures of Dionysius, the Greek god of wine and, to the Romans, the object of a widespread and sinister religious cult. The pillared 1st-century tomb of Lucius Publicius, a prominent Roman officer, some stone Roman coffins, and a series of memorial tablets are among the museum's other exhibits. Bordering the museum on the south is a restored 90-yard stretch of the old Roman harbor road. ⊠ *Roncallipl. 4,* ☎

Köln (Cologne)

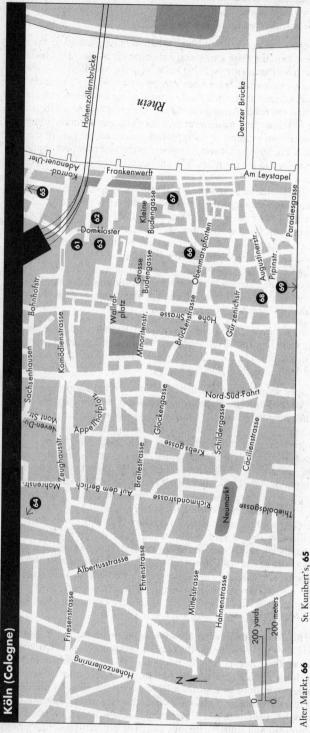

Alter Markt, **66**
Gross St. Martin, **67**
Gürzenich, **68**
Kölner Dom, **61**
Römisch-
Germanisches
Museum, **63**
St. Gereon's, **64**

St. Kunibert's, **65**
St. Maria im
Kapitol, **69**
Wallraf-Richartz-
Museum and
Museum Ludwig, **62**

yard stretch of the old Roman harbor road. ⊠ *Roncallipl. 4,* ☎ *0221/221–4438.* ▦ *DM 5.* ◷ *Tues.–Fri. 10–4, weekends 11–4.*

64 **St. Gereon's,** one of the most exquisite of the city's many Romanesque churches, stands on the site of an old Roman burial ground six blocks west of the train station. Experts regard St. Gereon's as one of the most noteworthy medieval structures still in existence, although the postwar restorations have been carried out with more care than taste. An enormous dome rests on walls that were once clad in gold mosaics. Roman masonry still forms part of the structure, which is believed to have been built over the grave of its namesake, the 4th-century martyr and patron saint of Köln. ⊠ *Gereonshof 4.*

65 **St. Kunibert's,** the most lavish of the churches from the late Romanesque period, is on the west side of the city, by the Rhine, just three blocks north of the train station. Consecrated in 1247, the church contains an unusual room, concealed under the altar, which gives access to a pre-Christian well once believed to promote fertility in women. ⊠ *Kunibertkloster 6.*

66 **Alter Markt** and its **Altes Rathaus,** are just south of St. Kunibert's. The Altes Rathaus is the oldest Town Hall in Germany (if you don't count that the building was entirely rebuilt after the war). The square has a handsome assembly of buildings—the oldest dating from 1135—in a range of styles. There was a seat of local government here in Roman times, and directly below the current Rathaus are the remains of the Roman city governor's headquarters, the Praetorium. The 14th-century **Hansa Saal** has tall Gothic windows and a barrel-vaulted wood ceiling, both potent expressions of medieval civic pride. The figures of the prophets, standing on pedestals at one end, are all from the early 15th century. Ranging along the south wall are nine additional statues, the so-called *Nine Good Heroes,* carved in 1360. Charlemagne and King Arthur are among them. ▱ *Free guided tour Mon., Wed., Sat. at 3.*

67 **Gross St. Martin** is one of the most outstanding of Köln's 12 Romanesque churches. Rebuilt after being flattened in World War II, its massive 13th-century tower, with distinctive corner turrets and an imposing central spire, is another landmark of Köln. The church was built on the site of a Roman granary.

Gross St. Martin is the parish church of the **Martinsviertel,** Köln's colorful old city, which is an attractive combination of reconstructed, high-gabled medieval buildings, winding alleys, and tastefully designed modern apartments and business quarters. Head here at night—the place comes alive at sunset.

68 **Gürzenich** is an attractive cultural center at the south end of Martinsviertel. This Gothic structure, all but demolished in the war but carefully reconstructed, takes its name from a medieval knight (von Gürzenich), from whom the city acquired a quantity of valuable real estate in 1437. The official reception and festival hall built on the site has played a central role in the city's civic life through the centuries. At one end of the complex are the remains of the 10th-century Gothic church of **St. Alban,** which were left ruined after the war as a memorial. On what's left of the church floor, you can see a sculpture of a couple kneeling in prayer, *Mourning Parent* by Käthe Kollwitz, a fitting memorial to the ravages of war. ⊠ *Gürzenichstr.*

69 The Romanesque church of **St. Maria im Kapitol** lies directly south of the Gürzenich, across Pipinstrasse. Built during the 11th and 12th centuries on the site of a Roman temple, St. Maria's is best known for its two beautifully carved 16-foot-high doors and its enormous crypt, the second-largest in Germany (after the one in Speyer Cathedral). ⊠ *Kasinostr. 6.*

🖐 Köln's **zoo**, founded in 1860, is West Germany's third oldest and one of the most interesting. Local children love it, perhaps because of its large monkey population and jungle house. ⊠ *Riehlerstr. 73.* 🖅 *DM 10.* ⊙ *Mar.–Sept., daily 9–6; Oct.–Mar., daily 9–5.*

Dining and Lodging

$$$$ ✗ **Bado-La Poêle d'Or.** At first glance the heavy furnishings and hushed
★ atmosphere of the Poêle d'Or make it seem like the last place you'd find light classical cuisine in Germany. But for some years those in the know have been claiming this as one of the finest dining establishments in Europe. Even such apparently simple dishes as onion soup win plaudits. Order salmon with lemon-ginger sauce or goose with truffle sauce, if you want to sample the full capabilities of the place. ⊠ *Komödienstr. 50–52,* ☎ *0221/134–100. Reservations essential. AE, DC, MC, V. Closed Sun. No lunch Mon.*

$$$ ✗ **Weinhaus im Walfisch.** The black-and-white gabled facade of this 400-year-old restaurant lets you know what to expect inside—though the local offerings are spruced up for an upmarket clientele. The menu presents fine quasi-traditional dishes with a French accent, at corresponding prices, and a wide range of wines. Drink a Riesling or a light-bodied red wine from the Ahr Valley. The restaurant is tucked away between the *Heumarkt* (haymarket) and the river. ⊠ *Salzgasse 13,* ☎ *0221/258–0397. AE, DC, MC, V. Closed weekends and holidays.*

$$ ✗ **Die Tomate.** If you don't like tomatoes, stay away from this popular little restaurant. The red fruit may be seen growing at the door, and the menu may feature tomato carpaccio with tomato paste and escallop of pork, as well as dishes without tomatoes, such as steak in a red-wine sauce. For dessert try the delicious pancakes filled with apples. ⊠ *Aachenerstr. 11,* ☎ *0221/257–4307. AE. No lunch Sun.*

$$ ✗ **Früh am Dom.** For real down-home German food, there are few places that compare with this time-honored former brewery. Bold frescoes on the vaulted ceilings establish the mood; the authentically Teutonic experience is complete with such dishes as *Hämmchen* (pork knuckle). The beer garden is delightful for summer dining. ⊠ *Am Hof 12–14,* ☎ *0221/258–0389. No credit cards.*

$$ ✗ **Ratskeller.** Here you can eat *Rheinische* sauerbraten and variations on the potato a la Cologne in the basement of the Altes Rathaus or in the courtyard, weather permitting. There is a "shopping buffet" on Thursday nights, when Germany's shops are open in the evening. ⊠ *Rathauspl. 1,* ☎ *0221/257–6929. AE, DC, MC, V.*

$ ✗ **Haus Töller.** There is no better place in Köln to imbibe Kölsch, the city's home brew. You won't sit long before an empty glass in the venerable *Bierstübe* before another is placed before you. The Teutonic specialties include bean soup, schnitzel, *Hämmchen* (pork knuckle), and potato pancakes. ⊠ *Weyerstr. 96,* ☎ *0221/214–086. No credit cards. Closed Wed. and Sun.*

$$$$ ✗▥ **Dom-Hotel.** Old-fashioned, formal, and gracious, with a stun-
★ ning location right by the cathedral, the Dom offers the sort of Old World elegance and discreetly efficient service few hotels aspire to these days. The antiques-filled bedrooms, generally in Louis XV or Louis XVI style, are subdued in color, high-ceilinged, and spacious. Each room is individually furnished. Service is, for the most part, exemplary, unhurried, and personal. The view of the cathedral is something to treasure. Enjoy it from the glass-enclosed Atelier am Dom, where you can dine informally on such specialties as marinated lamb carpaccio with

grated Parmesan, for a light meal, or sautéed mullet on a bed of spicy tomato ragout and basil noodles. The weekend package of DM 230 per night for a double room is a bargain, including champagne on arrival and reduced museum entrance fees. ⊠ *Domkloster 2A, D–50667,* ☎ *0221/20240,* FAX *0221/202–4444. 126 rooms with bath. 2 restaurants, bar, café. AE, DC, MC, V.*

$$$$ ✕⌘ **Excelsior Hotel Ernst.** The Empire-style lobby in sumptuous royal
★ blue, bright yellow, and gold is striking, and a similarly bold grandeur extends to the other public rooms in this 1863 hotel. Old Master paintings (including a Van Dyck) are everywhere; you'll be served breakfast in a room named after the Gobelin tapestries that hang there. Ultimately, it's the genuine warmth and helpfulness of the staff that make dining here a memorable experience. The restaurant Hansestube, which attracts a local business crowd with gourmet lunch specials, has a more hushed ambience in the evening, when it serves French haute cuisine with an occasional nod to the health conscious. Mushroom lovers will want to try the veal medallions in a rich cream sauce with a huge mound of morels. The wine cellar is famous for its French Burgundies and Bordeaux. ⊠ *Trankgasse 1, D–50667,* ☎ *0221/2701,* FAX *0221/135–150. 160 rooms with bath, 20 suites. Restaurant, bar, beauty salon, massage, exercise room. AE, DC, MC, V.*

$$ ✕⌘ **Stapelhäuschen.** One of the few houses along the riverbank to have survived World War II bombings, this is one of the oldest buildings in Köln. You can't beat the location, overlooking the river and right by Gross St. Martin; yet the rooms are reasonably priced, making up in age and quaintness for what they lack in luxury. The restaurant is in a slightly higher price bracket and does a respectable enough job with spruced-up versions of German specialties. ⊠ *Fischmarkt 1-3, D–50667,* ☎ *0221/257–7862,* FAX *0221/257–4232. Restaurant. AE, DC, MC, V.*

$$$$ ⌘ **Hotel im Wasserturm.** What used to be Europe's tallest water tower is now an 11-story luxury hotel-in-the-round, opened at the end of 1989 after a four-year, $70 million conversion. The neoclassic look of the brick exterior was retained by order of Cologne conservationists. The ultramodern interior was the work of the French designer Andrée Putman, renowned in the United States for her work on Morgan's, in New York. The 11th-floor restaurant has a view of the city. ⊠ *Kaygasse 2, D–50676,* ☎ *0221/20080,* FAX *0221/200–8888. 47 rooms and 40 suites and maisonettes with bath. Restaurant, café, room service, sauna. AE, DC, MC, V.*

$$ ⌘ **Altstadt.** Near the river in the Old Town, this is the place for charm
★ and low rates. All the rooms are individually decorated, and the service is impeccable—both welcoming and efficient. There's no restaurant. ⊠ *Salzgasse 7, D–50667,* ☎ *0221/257–7851,* FAX *0221/257–7853. 28 rooms with bath. Sauna. AE, DC, MC, V. Closed Dec. 25–Jan. 1.*

Nightlife and the Arts

BARS AND CLUBS

Köln's nightlife is found in three distinct areas: between the Alter Markt and Neumarkt in the old city; in **Zulpicherstrasse**; and around the **Friesenplatz** S-bahn station.

In summer head straight for the **Stadtgarten** (⊠ Venloerstr. 40, ☎ 0221/516–037) and sit in the Bier Garten for some good outdoor *Gemütlichkeit.* Any other time of year it is still worth a visit for its excellent jazz club that regularly brings class acts to the city. **Papa Joe's Biersalon** (⊠ Alter Markt 50–52, ☎ 258–2132) is kind of kitschy but often has classic jazz and draws locals as well as tourists. **Subway** (⊠ Aachnerstr. 82, ☎ 517–969) has disco and jazz, almost within earshot of the train station.

Many streets off the Hohenzollernring and Hohenstaufenring, particularly Roonstrasse, also provide a broad range of nightlife. **Das Ding** (⊠ Hohenstaufenring 30-32, ☎ 246–348), or "The Thing," is a student club that is never empty, even on weeknights. **Disco 42** (⊠ Hohenstaufenring 25, ☎ 247–971) is devoted to house and techno. For the last word in disco experience, make for the **Alter Wartesaal** (⊠ Am Hauptbahnhof, Johannisstr. 11, ☎ 912–8850) in the Hauptbahnhof on Friday or Saturday night. The old waiting room has been turned into a concert hall and disco, enabling Köln's boppers to get down on ancient polished parquet and check their style in original mahogany-framed mirrors.

THEATER, DANCE, AND OPERA

Köln's opera company, the **Oper der Stadt Köln,** is known for exciting classical and contemporary productions. The city's small ballet company, the **Kölner Tanzforum,** hosts an international festival, the Internationale Sommerakademie des Tanzes, every July. Köln's principal theater is the **Schauspielhaus** (⊠ Offenbachpl. 1). The Schauspielhaus is also home to the 20 or so private theaters in the city. Call (☎ 0221/221–8400) for program details and tickets. **Der Keller** (⊠ Kleingedankstr. 6, ☎ 0221/318–059) is the best-known venue for contemporary drama.

For children, Köln has a **puppet theater** (⊠ Rösratherstr. 133, ☎ 02208/2408).

MUSIC

Köln's **Westdeutsche Rundfunk Orchestra** performs regularly in the city's excellent concert hall, the **Philharmonie** (⊠ Bischofsgarten 1, ☎ 0221/2801). The **Gürzenich Orchestra** also gives regular concerts in the Philharmonie, but the natural setting for its music is the restored **Gürzenich,** medieval Köln's official reception mansion. Year-round **organ recitals** in Köln's cathedral are supplemented from June to August with a summer season of organ music. Organ recitals and chamber concerts are also presented in the churches of **St. Maria Himmelfahrt** (⊠ Marzellenstr. 26), **St. Aposteln** (⊠ Neumarkt 30), and **Trinitätskirche** (⊠ Filzengraben 4). Call for details on all church concerts (☎ 0221/534–856).

Shopping

Köln's shopping district begins at nearby **Wallrafplatz,** and a recommended shopping tour will take you down Hohe Strasse, Schildergasse, Neumarkt, Mittelstrasse, Hohenzollernring, Ehrenstrasse, Breite Strasse, Tunisstrasse, Minoritenstrasse, and then back to Wallrafplatz.

Hohe Strasse, south of the cathedral, is the main artery of Köln's huge pedestrian shopping zone. The area's stores, including many of the main German department-store chains—Kaufhof, Hertie, and Karstadt—are rich in quantity if not always in quality, and certainly a center of city life. **Mittelstrasse** and **Hohestrasse** are best for German fashions and luxury goods. **Offermann's** (⊠ Breite Str. 48-50, ☎ 0221/252–018) has a large selection of fine leather items and beautifully finished travel accessories.

Köln's most celebrated product is, of course, **eau de cologne.** In Glockengasse (⊠ No. 4711, of course, ☎ 0221/925–0450) you can visit the house where the 18th-century Italian chemist Giovanni-Maria Farina first concocted it. The shop has extended its selection to include other scents in addition to 4711, but the original product remains the centerpiece, available in all sizes from a purse-sized bottle to a container that holds a quart or so.

Chocolate is a quintessential Köln product; try **Ludwig chocolate,** if only in honor of all the Ludwig museums you'll encounter along your trip. You'll have no difficulty finding it in any of the delicatessens in the city center.

The **Alter Markt** in the Old Town holds a flea market every third Saturday. **Nippes** (⊠ Wilhelmpl.) has a flea market every fourth Sunday.

A visit to the **Gebrüder Grimm** (Brothers Grimm) book and toy shop (⊠ Mauritiussteinweg 110) is one of the most popular children's outings in Köln.

Tennis and Squash

Try **City Sport** (⊠ Rhöndroferstr. 10, ☎ 0221/411–092) for tennis. For squash, **Squashpark** is the best address (⊠ Neusserstr. 718a, ☎ 0221/740–8866).

Aachen

70 km (45 mi) west of Köln.

At the center of Aachen the characteristic *drei-Fenster* facades of residences, three windows wide, give way to buildings dating from the days when Charlemagne made Aix-la-Chapelle (as it was then called) one of the great centers of the Holy Roman Empire. Roman legions had pitched camp here because of the healing properties of the sulfur springs emanating from the nearby Eifel Mountains. Charlemagne's father, Pepin the Short, also settled here to enjoy the waters that gave Bad Aachen—as the town is also known—its name and continue to attract visitors today. But it was certainly Charlemagne who was responsible for the town's architectural wealth. After his coronation in Rome in 800, he spent more and more time in Aachen, building his spectacular palace and ruling his vast empire from within its walls. One-hour walking tours depart from the tourist information office weekdays at 2, weekends at 11, April–October. English tours can be set up by prior arrangement (☎ 0241/180–2960).

★ The stunning **Dom** (cathedral) in Aachen, the "Chapelle" of the town's previous name, remains the single greatest storehouse of Carolingian architecture in Europe. Though it was built over the course of 1,000 years and reflects architectural styles from the Middle Ages to the 19th-century, the commanding image is the magnificent octagonal royal chapel, rising up two arched stories to end in the cap of the dome. It was this section, the heart of the church, that Charlemagne saw completed in AD 800. His bones now lie in the Gothic choir interred in a golden shrine surrounded by wonderful carvings of saints. Another treasure is Charlemagne's marble throne. Charlemagne had to journey all the way to Rome for his coronation, but the next 32 Holy Roman emperors were crowned here in Aachen, and each marked the occasion by presenting a lavish gift to the cathedral. In the 12th century, Barbarossa donated the great chandelier now hanging in the center of the imperial chapel; his grandson, Friedrich II, donated Charlemagne's shrine. Emperor Karl IV journeyed from Prague in the late 14th century for the sole purpose of commissioning a bust of Charlemagne for the cathedral; now on view in the treasury, this bust contains a piece of Charlemagne's skull. ⊠ *Muensterpl.,* ☎ *0241/4770–9127.* ☉ *Daily 7–7.*

The **Domschatzkammer** (cathedral treasury) houses sacred art from late antiquity and the Carolingian, Ottonian, and Staufian eras; highlights include the famous Cross of Lothair, the Bust of Charlemagne, and the

Persephone sarcophagus. 🖼 *DM 5.* 🕑 *Mon. 10–1, Tues.–Wed. and Fri.–Sun. 10–6:30, Thurs. 10–9.*

The back of the **Rathaus** (Town Hall) is opposite the cathedral, across Katschhof Square. It was built beginning in the early 14th century on the site of the *Aula,* or "great hall," of Charlemagne's palace. Its first major official function was the coronation banquet of Emperor Karl IV in 1349, held in the great Gothic hall you can still see today (though this was largely rebuilt after the war). On the north wall of the building are statues of 50 emperors of the Holy Roman Empire. The greatest of them all, Charlemagne, stands in bronze atop the fountain Kaiserbrunnen in the center of the square. ⊠ *Marktpl.,* 🕿 *0241/432–7310.* 🖼 *DM 3.* 🕑 *Daily 10–1 and 2–5.*

<table>
<tr><td>NEED A
BREAK?</td><td>To locals, Aachen is no more famous for its architecture than for its *Printen,* a kind of gingerbread. One of the best places to try this sweet is the enchanting coffee shop called **Alte Aachener Kaffeestuben** (⊠ Buchel 18, 🕿 0241/35724). The house was built in 1655 and has retained its original character—wood paneling, tile ovens, low ceilings, and all. In addition to Printen and spice cookies called *Spekulatius,* formed in fancifully carved old wooden molds, the café serves meals.</td></tr>
</table>

An old Aachen tradition that continues today is "taking the waters." The arcaded, neoclassical **Elisenbrunnen** (Elisa Fountain), built in 1822, is situated south of the cathedral. It contains two fountains with thermal drinking water. Experts agree that the spa waters here—the hottest north of the Alps—are effective in helping to cure a wide range of ailments. Drinking the sulfurous water in the approved manner can be unpleasant; but as you hold your nose and gulp away, you can console yourself with the thought that you're emulating the likes of Dürer, Frederick the Great, and Charlemagne. In Dürer's time, the baths were enjoyed for more than their health-giving properties, and there were regular crackdowns on the orgylike goings-on—a far cry from today's rather clinical atmosphere. You can try sitting in the spa waters at the **Kurbad** (⊠ Monheimsallee 52, 🕿 0241/180–2922); admission is DM 16. The **Römerbad** (⊠ Buchkremerstr. 1, 🕿 0241/180–2923) is open longer hours than the Kurbad; admission is DM 11.

Like many famous German spa towns, Aachen has its **Spielbank** (casino). It's housed in the porticoed former Kurhaus, on the parklike grounds fronting Monheimsallee and facing the Kurbad Quellenhof. ⊠ *Monheimsallee 44,* 🕿 *0241/18080.* 🖼 *DM 5.* 🕑 *Weekdays 3 PM–2 AM, weekends until 3 AM. Jacket and tie. Bring passport for identification.*

Aachen has its modern side as well—one of the world's most important art collectors, Peter Ludwig, comes from Aachen and has endowed two museums in his hometown. The **Ludwig Forum für Internationale Kunst,** opened in 1993, is a space for a portion of Ludwig's truly enormous collection of contemporary art, as well as a venue for traveling exhibitions ⊠ *Jülicher Str. 97–109,* 🕿 *0241/18070.* 🖼 *DM 6.* 🕑 *Tues., Wed., Fri.–Sun. 11–7; Thurs. 11–10.*

The **Suermont-Ludwig Museum** was inaugurated in 1994. It's devoted to classical painting up to the beginning of this century. ⊠ *Wilhelmstr. 18,* 🕿 *0241/47980.* 🖼 *DM 6.* 🕑 *Tues., Thurs., Fri.–Sun. 11–7; Wed. 11–9.*

Dining and Lodging

$$$$ ✕ **Gala.** For the most elegant dining in Aachen, reserve a table at the
★   Gala restaurant, adjoining the casino. Dark-paneled walls and origi-

nal oil paintings make the mood discreetly classy; Chef Gerhard Gartner's cooking is regional, with nouvelle and other creative touches. ⊠ *Monheimsallee 44,* ☎ *0241/153–013. Reservations essential. Jacket and tie. AE, DC, MC, V. Closed Sun.–Mon. No lunch.*

$$$ ✕ **La Becasse.** Sophisticated French nouvelle cuisine is offered in this upscale modern restaurant, just outside the Old Town by the Westpark. Try the distinctively light calves' liver. ⊠ *Hanbrucherstr. 1,* ☎ *0241/74444. Reservations essential. Jacket and tie. AE, DC, MC, V. Closed Sun. and 3 wks in July–Aug. No lunch Sat. and Mon.*

$$ ✕ **Der Postwagen.** This annex of the more upscale Ratskeller is worth a stop for the building alone: an original half-timbered medieval edifice at one corner of the old Rathaus. Sitting at one of the low wooden tables, surveying the marketplace through the wavy old glass, you can dine very respectably on solid German fare. If you want to go really local, try *Unser Puttes,* a kind of blood sausage. ⊠ *Am Markt,* ☎ *0241/35001. No credit cards.*

$ ✕ **Am Knipp.** At this historic old Aachen Bierstübe, guests sit at low wooden tables next to the tiled stove. Pewter pots and beer mugs hang from the rafters. ⊠ *Bergdriesch 3,* ☎ *0241/33168. No credit cards.*

$$$$ ✕⊡ **Hotel Quellenhof.** The pampered luxury at the Quellenhof is
★ especially appealing to older guests. Built during World War I as a country home for the kaiser, it's one of Europe's grande dames: spacious, elegant, and formal. The rooms have high ceilings, a mix of conservative-style furniture, a walk-in baggage room, and huge, dated bathrooms that were converted from single bedrooms. The flower-filled Parkrestaurant, one of the best restaurants in northern Germany, serves haute cuisine in the grand manner. The hotel is near the Kurpark and the casino, and guests have direct access by lift to the thermal baths. ⊠ *Monheimsallee 52, D–52062,* ☎ *0241/152–081; for reservations in the U.S., 800/223–5652;* FAX *0241/154–504. 160 rooms with bath. Restaurant, pool. AE, DC, MC, V.*

$$ ✕⊡ **Hotel Brülls am Dom.** In the historic heart of the city, this family-run hotel offers not only tradition and convenience but also considerable comfort. It's a short walk to nearly all the major attractions. ⊠ *Hühnermarkt, D–52062,* ☎ *0241/31704,* FAX *0241/404–326. 10 rooms with bath. Café-bar. AE, DC, MC, V.*

$$–$$$ ⊡ **Benelux.** The centrally located Benelux is one of the best deals in Aachen. Small and family-run, it has comfortable modern rooms and a smattering of antiques in the public areas. ⊠ *Franzstr. 21, D–52064,* ☎ *0241/22343,* FAX *0241/22345. 33 rooms with bath. AE, DC, MC, V.*

Nightlife and the Arts

Aachen has a municipal orchestra that gives regular concerts in the **Kongresszentrum Eurogress** (⊠ Monheimsallee 52, ☎ 0241/151–011). The Irish pub, **Wild Rover** (⊠ Hirschgraben 13, ☎ 0241/35453), serves Guinness on tap to live music every night, starting at 9:30. **Intensivstation** (⊠ Hirschgraben 13, ☎ 0241/39936) has a late-night dance scene with indie, hip-hop, jazz, and soul.

Shopping

Don't leave Aachen without stocking up on the traditional local gingerbread, *Aachener Printen.* Most bakeries in town offer assortments. Some of the best is at the Alte Aachener Kaffeestuben, also known as the **Konditorei van den Daele** (⊠ Büchel 18, ☎ 0241/35724). The store-café is worth a visit for its atmosphere and tempting aromas, whether or not you intend to buy anything. It also ships goods.

Düsseldorf

47 km (29 mi) north of Köln.

At first glance, Düsseldorf may suffer in comparison to Köln, with its cathedral and remarkable skyline, but the elegant city has more than enough charm and beauty to justify including it on a Rhineland itinerary.

Düsseldorf has gained the reputation for being the richest city in Germany, with an extravagant lifestyle that long epitomized the success of the postwar "economic miracle." It is a glittering showcase for all the good things the deutsche mark can buy. A center for the advertising industry, the city is also known as Germany's fashion capital.

Although 80% of prewar Düsseldorf was destroyed in World War II, the city has since been more or less rebuilt from the ground up—in part re-creating landmarks of long ago and restoring a medieval riverside quarter, but in the main initiating what may well be the most successful updating of a major German city.

Hard as it may be to believe, this dynamic city at the confluence of the rivers Rhine and Düssel started as a small fishing town. The name means "village (*Dorf*) on the Düssel," but obviously this Dorf is a village no more. Raised expressways speed traffic past towering glass-and-steel structures; within them, glass-enclosed shopping malls showcase the fanciest outfits, furs, jewelry, and leather goods that famous designers can create and those with plenty of money can buy.

★ **Königsallee,** the main shopping avenue, is the epitome of Düsseldorf affluence; it's lined with the crème de la crème of designer boutiques and stores. Known as the Kö, this wide, double boulevard is divided by an ornamental waterway that is actually a part of the river Düssel. In the city about 80% of the Düssel runs underground; this is one of the few places where you can see it. Rows of chestnut trees line the Kö, affording shade for a string of sidewalk cafés. Beyond the Triton Fountain, at the street's north end, begins a series of parks and gardens. In these patches of green one senses a joie de vivre hardly expected in a city devoted to big business and overachieving.

The lovely **Hofgarten Park,** once the garden of the Elector's Palace, is reached by heading north to Corneliusplatz. Laid out in 1770 and completed 30 years later, the Hofgarten today serves as an oasis of greenery at the heart of downtown and as a focal point for Düsseldorf culture.

The Baroque **Schloss Jägerhof** in the Hofgarten is more a combination town house and country lodge than a castle. It houses the Goethe Museum, featuring original manuscripts, first editions, personal correspondence, and other memorabilia of one of Germany's greatest writers. ⊠ *Jacobistr. 2,* ☎ *0211/899–6262.* 🎫 *DM 4.* ☉ *Tues.–Fri. and Sun. 11–5, Sat. 1–5.*

The city's opera house is at the other end of the park from Schloss Jägerhof, on Heinrich-Heine-Allee. The **North Rhineland-Westphalia Art Collection,** removed some time ago from the Schloss Jägerhof, is now on display in a spacious new building across the street from the city opera house. Here you will encounter a dazzling array of 20th-century paintings of the classical modern, including works by Bonnard, Braque, Matisse, Léger, Johns, and Pollock; there are so many by Paul Klee because the Swiss painter lived in Düsseldorf for a time and taught at the National Academy of Art. ⊠ *Grabbepl. 5,* ☎ *0211/83810.* 🎫 *DM 5.* ☉ *Tues.–Sun. 10–6.*

The **Kunstmuseum** (Museum of Fine Arts) lies at the northern extremity of the Hofgarten, close to the Rhine. It features a collection of paintings by Old Masters and German Expressionists, running the gamut from Rubens, Goya, Tintoretto, and Cranach the Elder to the romantic Düsseldorf School and such modern German painters as Beckmann, Kirchner, Nolde, Macke, and Kandinsky. ⊠ *Ehrenhof 5,* ☎ *0211/899–2460.* ☑ *DM 10.* ☉ *Tues. and Thurs.–Sun. 10–5, Wed. 10–8.*

The restored **Altstadt** (Old Town) faces the Rhine. Narrow alleys thread their way to some 200 restaurants and taverns offering a wide range of foreign and local cuisines, all crowded into the 1-square-kilometer area between the Rhine and Heine Allee. Occasionally you can still see the *Radschläger,* young boys who demonstrate their cartwheeling ability, a Düsseldorf tradition, for the admiration (and tips) of visitors.

A plaque at Bolkerstrasse 53 indicates where Heinrich Heine was born in 1797. The **Heinrich Heine Institute** has a museum and an archive of significant manuscripts of this early 19th-century poet. Part of this complex is a former residence of the composer Robert Schumann. ⊠ *Bilkerstr. 12–14,* ☎ *0211/899–5571.* ☑ *DM 3.* ☉ *Tues.–Sun. 2–6.*

<table>
<tr><td>NEED A
BREAK?</td><td>Among beer buffs, Düsseldorf is famous for its *Altbier,* so called because of the old-fashioned brewing method still used. The mellow and malty copper-color brew is produced by eight breweries in town. The most atmospheric place to drink it is **Zum Verige** (⊠ Bergerstr. 1, ☎ 0211/84455). Here the beer is poured straight out of polished oak barrels and dished out by bustling waiters in long blue aprons.</td></tr>
</table>

The cobbled, traffic-free streets of the Old Town lead to Burgplatz. The 13th-century **Schlossturm** (Castle Tower) on Burgplatz is all that remains of the castle built by the de Berg family, who founded Düsseldorf. The tower also houses the **Schiffahrt Museum**, which charts 2,000 years of Rhine boatbuilding and river history. ⊠ *Burgpl. 30,* ☎ *0211/899–4195.* ☑ *DM 3.* ☉ *Tues.–Sat. 2–6, Sun. 11–6.*

The Gothic **St. Lambertus Church** is near Burgplatz, on Stiftsplatz. Its spire became distorted because unseasoned wood was used in its construction. The Vatican elevated the 14th-century brick church to a Basilica Minor (small cathedral) in 1974 in recognition of its role in church history. Built during the 13th century, with additions from 1394, St. Lambertus contains the tomb of William the Rich and a graceful late-Gothic tabernacle.

☾ **Aqua-Zoo** in the Nordpark offers a unique exhibition of aquatic creatures in their natural habitats. Among the highlights are the tropical park with crocodiles and the penguin habitat. All tanks can be viewed from above and through glass walls. ⊠ *Kaiserwertherstr. 380,* ☎ *0211/899–6150.* ☑ *DM 9.*

Dining and Lodging

$$$$ ✗ **Im Schiffchen.** Although it's a bit out of the way, dining in one of Germany's best restaurants makes it worth a trip. This is grande luxe, with cooking that's a fine art. The restaurant Aalschokker, on the ground floor, features local specialties created by the same chef but at lower prices. ⊠ *Kaiserwerther Markt 9,* ☎ *0211/401–050 or 0211/401–948. Reservations essential. AE, DC, MC, V. Closed Sun.–Mon. No lunch.*

$$$$ ✗ **Rôtisserie.** The decor is subdued and the atmosphere hushed, but
★ the food sparkles at this gourmet restaurant in the Steigenberger Parkhotel. Chef Alfred Schreiber serves classic French cuisine prepared with imagination and a light touch. Starters might include

whipped sorrel-chervil soup and a gossamer parfait of quail with raisins and green pepper, followed by such entrées as shellfish lasagna layered with asparagus, wild mushrooms, and lobster sauce. Some German classics are always on the menu; the restaurant's rendition of *Rote Grütze* (a red fruit compote) with vanilla sauce is especially admirable. ⊠ *Corneliuspl. 1,* ☎ *0211/13810,* ⨎⨋ *0211/131–679. Jacket and tie. AE, DC, MC, V.*

$$$$ ╳ **Weinhaus Tante Anna.** This charming restaurant is furnished with antiques; the cuisine presents another facet of German tradition and shows there's a lot more to this country's cooking than the standard platters of hearty wurst- and sauerkraut-based fare. The wine selection is particularly fine. ⊠ *Andreasstr. 2,* ☎ *0211/131–163,* ⨎⨋ *0211/132–974. AE, DC, MC, V. No lunch.*

$$ ╳ **Zum Schiffchen.** Not to be confused with the luxurious Im Schiffchen (☞ *above*), this is a colorful old riverside brewery tavern in the Altstadt, in business since 1628. Napoléon ate here in 1811. Today, as then, one sits at long, scrubbed wooden tables and dines family style on down-to-earth fare. Beer comes straight from the barrel, including the local *Altbier.* The day's specials invariably include grilled pork chops that come to the table sizzling; eels are another good bet. ⊠ *Hafenstr. 5,* ☎ *0211/132–422. Reservations essential. AE, DC, MC, V. Closed Sun. and holidays.*

$ ╳ **Füchschen.** At one of a handful of traditional beer taverns in the Altstadt that have held their own against time, guests rub elbows on the long wooden tables and quaff the *Altbier* fresh from the tap. The place has its own butcher and feeds its carnivorous clientele very well. One advantage over other places is that you can order food in small portions. ⊠ *Ratinger Str. 28/30,* ☎ *0211/84062. No credit cards.*

$$$$ ╳▥ **Hotel Breidenbacher Hof.** Rated among the two or three top ★ choices in Germany, this superluxurious hotel offers understated elegance with superb, white-glove service. The location is as central as you can get. The palatial lobby is studded with 17th- and 18th-century antiques, with the theme continuing in the beautifully appointed rooms. ⊠ *Heinrich Heine Allee 36, D–40213,* ☎ *0211/13030,* ⨎⨋ *0211/130–3830. 132 rooms with bath. 2 restaurants, bar. AE, DC, MC, V.*

$$$ ╳▥ **Hotel Esplanade.** This small modern hotel has an exceptionally quiet, leafy location still close the action. From the inviting lobby to attractive decor in the rooms, the sense here is one of intimacy. ⊠ *Fürstenpl. 17, D–40215 ,* ☎ *0211/375–010,* ⨎⨋ *0211/374–032. 80 rooms with bath. 2 restaurants, bar, pool, exercise room. AE, DC, MC, V.*

$$$$ ▥ **Steigenberger Parkhotel.** Miraculously quiet despite its central location on the edge of the Hofgarten and at the beginning of the ★ Königsallee, this old hotel is anything but stodgy. The soaring ceilings add to the spaciousness of the guest rooms, each individually decorated in a restrained, elegant style. The pampering continues at the breakfast buffet, served in the Rôtisserie (☞ *Dining, above*), where champagne and smoked salmon are appropriate starters for a shopping expedition on the Kö. ⊠ *Corneliuspl. 1, D–40213,* ☎ *0211/13810,* ⨎⨋ *0211/138–1570. 160 rooms with bath. Restaurant, 2 bars, café. AE, DC, MC, V.*

$$ ▥ **Hotel Cristallo.** Clearly someone took great pains with the slightly tacky but nonetheless striking decor of this well-located, midprice hotel. If you like gilt angels in the breakfast room, this is the place for you. Less subjectively judged attributes include a central location near the Kö and pleasant, eclectically furnished rooms, with comfortable sofas and color TVs even in singles. ⊠ *Schadowpl. 7,* ☎ *0211/84525,* FAX *0211/322–632. 35 rooms. AE, DC, MC, V.*

Nightlife and the Arts

Düsseldorf nightlife is mostly concentrated in the **Altstadt,** a landscape of pubs, discotheques, ancient restored brewery houses, and jazz clubs in the vicinity of the Marktplatz and along cobbled streets named Bolker, Kurze, Flinger, and Mühlen. These places may be crowded, but some are very atmospheric. A more sophisticated mood is set in the modern part of the city. **Bei Tony** (⊠ Lorettostr. 12) is a fashionable upscale bar. **Front Page** (Mannesman Ufer) is a slick water hole. **Sam's West** on the Kö is a number one disco.

MUSIC

Düsseldorf, once home to Mendelssohn, Schumann, and Brahms, has the finest concert hall in Germany after Berlin's Philharmonie: the **Tonhalle** (⊠ Ehrenhof 1, ☎ 0211/899–5540), a former planetarium on the edge of the Hofgarten. It's the home of the **Düsseldorfer Symphoniker,** which plays from September to mid-June. **Deutsche Oper am Rhein** (⊠ Heinrich Heine Allee 16a, ☎ 0211/133–949) showcases the city's highly regarded opera company and ballet troupe.

The **Düsseldorfer Marionettentheater** (⊠ Bolkerstr. 7, ☎ 0211/328–432) has puppet shows.

Shopping

The east side of the **Königsallee** is lined with some of Germany's trendiest boutiques, grandest jewelers, and most extravagant furriers. **Kö Center** (⊠ Königsallee 30), an upscale shopping arcade, features the most famous names in fashion, from Chanel to Louis Vuitton. **Kö Galerie** (⊠ Königsallee 60) has trendy fashion boutiques, where you can find the creations of such local designers as Ute Raasch. Kö Galerie also includes the Mövenpick restaurant on its luxurious two-story premises. **Schadow Arcade** (off Schadowplatz, at the end of the Kö Galerie) caters to normal pocketbooks, with such stores as Hennes and Mauritz and Habitat. Antiques in Düsseldorf can be found in the area around Hohe Strasse. Try the shop **Arts Decoratifs** (⊠ Hohe Str. 28, ☎ 0211/324–553) for art deco furniture, tableware, and knickknacks.

Tennis and Squash

Rhinestadium (⊠ Europapl. 5, ☎ 0211/899–5204) has 18 public courts.

THE RHINELAND A TO Z

Arriving and Departing

By Plane

The Rhineland is served by three international airports: Frankfurt, Düsseldorf, and Köln-Bonn. There are direct flights from the United States and Canada to all three, and all are also part of a comprehensive network of air services throughout Europe. Bus and rail lines connect each airport with its respective downtown area and provide rapid access to the rest of the region.

Getting Around

By Bicycle

The Mosel Valley, with its small hamlets lining the riverbanks, is an excellent area for biking. The Trier tourist office (☎ 0651/978–080) offers a free trail map. Most local train stations have bikes to rent from

April 1 to October 31 for DM 11–DM 13 per day, DM 7–DM 9 if
you have a valid rail ticket. Listings of additional outlets for rental bikes
are available from train stations.

By Boat

No visit to the Rhineland is complete without at least one river trip.
Fortunately, there are many cruise options from which to choose (☞
Guided Tours *in* Contacts and Resources, *below*).

Rowboats and canoes can be rented at most Rhine and Mosel river resorts. A list of rental outlets is included in the brochure "News," issued by the Rheinland-Pfalz tourist office (☞ Contacts and Resources,
below).

By Bus

There are two Europabus routes running across the Rhineland: One
originates in Britain and terminates in Munich, crossing the Rhineland
between Köln and Frankfurt; the other runs between Frankfurt and
Trier, stopping at the Frankfurt Airport, Wiesbaden, Mainz, Bingen,
and several towns along the Mosel River. All Europabuses are comfortable and fast. For details on services and reservations, contact
Deutsche Touring (✉ Am Römerhof 17, D–60486 Frankfurt/Main, ☎
069/790–3268). Local bus services connect most smaller towns and
villages throughout the Rhineland.

By Car

The autobahns and other highways of the Rhineland are busy, so
allow plenty of time for driving. Frankfurt is 126 kilometers (79 miles)
from Koblenz, 175 kilometers (110 miles) from Bonn, 190 kilometers
(119 miles) from Köln, and 230 kilometers (143 miles) from Düsseldorf. The most spectacular stretch of the Rhineland is along the Middle Rhine, between Mainz and Koblenz. Highways (though not
autobahns) hug the river on each bank, and car ferries crisscross the
Rhine at many points. Road conditions throughout the region are
excellent.

By Train

InterCity and EuroCity expresses connect all the cities and towns of
the area. Hourly InterCity routes run between Düsseldorf, Köln, Bonn,
and Mainz, with most services extending as far south as Munich and
as far north as Hamburg. The Mainz–Bonn route runs beside the
Rhine, between the river and the vine-covered heights, offering spectacular views all the way. The city transportation networks of Bonn,
Köln, and Düsseldorf are linked by S-bahn (for information contact
the Verkehrsverband in Köln, ☎ 0221/547–3333).

Contacts and Resources

Car Rentals

Avis: ✉ Adenauerallee 4–6, ☎ 0228/223–047, **Bonn**; ✉ Berliner
Allee 32, ☎ 0211/329–050, **Düsseldorf**; ✉ Schmidtstr. 39, ☎ 069/730–
111, **Frankfurt**; ✉ Andernacher Str. 203, ☎ 0261/800–366, **Koblenz**;
✉ Clemensstr. 29, ☎ 0221/234–333, **Köln**; ✉ Herzogenbuscher Str.
31, ☎ 0651/12722, **Trier.**

Europcar: ✉ Potsdamer Pl. 7, ☎ 0228/652–961, **Bonn**; ✉ Burgunderstr.
40, ☎ 0211/504–7041, **Düsseldorf**; ✉ Schlossstr. 32, ☎ 069/775–033,
Frankfurt; Köln-Bonn Airport, ☎ 02203/53088, **Köln.**

Hertz: ✉ Juelicherstr. 250, ☎ 0241/162–686, **Aachen**; ✉ Adenauerallee 216, ☎ 0228/217–041, **Bonn**; ✉ Immermannstr. 65, ☎ 0211/357–
025, **Düsseldorf**; ✉ Bismarckstr. 19-21, ☎ 0221/515–0847, **Köln**; ✉
Gutleutstr. 87, ☎ 069/2425–2627, **Frankfurt.**

Sixt-Budget: ✉ Tilde-Klose-Weg 6, ☎ 0211/471–310, **Düsseldorf**; ✉ Im Niedergarten 24, ☎ 06131/46173, **Mainz-Gonzenheim**; ✉ Eurenerstr. 5, ☎ 0651/820–821, **Trier.**

Embassies

United States, ✉ Deichmanns Aue 29, D–53113 Bonn, ☎ 0228/3391.

Great Britain, ✉ Friedrich-Ebert-Allee 77, D–53113 Bonn, ☎ 0228/234–061.

Canada, ✉ Friedrich-Wilhelmstr. 18, D–53113 Bonn, ☎ 0228/231–061.

Guided Tours

BOAT TRIPS

Trips along the Rhine and Mosel range from a few hours to days or even a week or more in length. One of the major lines is **Köln-Düsseldorfer Rheinschiffahrt** (✉ Frankenwerft 15, D–50667 Köln, ☎ 0221/208–8288); in the United States, **JFO CruiseService Corp.** (✉ 2500 Westchester Ave., Purchase, NY 10577, ☎ 914/696–3600 or 800/346–6525) and **KD River Cruises of Europe** (✉ 323 Geary St., Suite 603, San Francisco, CA 94102, ☎ 415/392–8817 or 800/858–8587). Its ships travel daily between Köln and Frankfurt, from Easter to late October, as well as cruises along the entire length of the Rhine and up the Mosel as far as Trier. Passengers have a choice of buying an excursion ticket or a ticket to a single destination or combined river-rail tickets, which allow you to break your river trip at any place the boats stop and continue by train. The K-D line has a weeklong "floating wine seminar" aboard the pride of its fleet, the motor ship *Helvetia,* which makes stops at vineyards on both the Mosel and Rhine rivers on a wine-tasting route that ends in Basel, Switzerland. The K-D Rhine line also organizes three- and four-day cruises along the Mosel that stop at most of the wine villages between Koblenz and Trier.

From March through November the **Hebel-Line** (☎ 06742/2420) in Boppard cruises the Lorelei Valley; night cruises have music and dancing. Trips along the Mosel are also available through **Mosel-Personenschiffahrt Bernkastel-Kues** (✉ Goldbachstr. 52, Bernkastel-Kues, ☎ 06531/8222).

Several shipping companies in Koblenz organize short "castle cruises" from Easter through September. Two boats, the *Undine* and the *Marksburg,* ply the Rhine between Koblenz and Boppard, passing 10 castles during the 75-minute, one-way voyage. Details and reservations are available from **Personenschiffahrt Merkelbach** (✉ Emserstr. 87, Koblenz-Pfaffendorf, ☎ 0261/76810). **Personenschiffahrt Josef Vomfell** (✉ Koblenzer Str. 64, Spay/Rhein, ☎ 02628/2431) organizes cruises on the Middle Rhine. The Koblenz operator, **Rhein und Moselschiffahrt Gerhard Collee-Holzenbein** (✉ Rheinzollstr. 4, ☎ 0261/37744), runs day cruises as far as Rüdesheim on the Rhine and Cochem on the Mosel.

From Köln, three shipping companies operate boat tours on the Rhine (all tours leave from the landing stages near the Hohenzollern Brücke, a short walk from the cathedral). The **Köln-Düsseldorfer** line (☞ *above*) has hourly trips starting at 9:30, daily April through September. The **Rhein-Mosel Schiffahrt** (✉ Konrad Adenauer-Ufer, ☎ 0221/121–714) has daily departures every 45 minutes starting at 10, April through September. The **Dampfschiffahrt Colonia** (✉ Lintgasse 18, ☎ 0221/211–325) has daily departures every 45 minutes beginning at 10, April through October. .

Limousine Travel Service (⊠ Wiesenhüttenpl. 39, Frankfurt, ☎ 069/230–
492) has a daily bus trip from Frankfurt along the "Riesling Route"
that encompasses the vineyards of the Rhineland between Frankfurt
and Rüdesheim. The tour includes a wine-tasting and a trip along the
Rhine to the wine village of St. Goar.

Bus trips into the countryside around Köln (to the Eifel Hills, the Ahr
Valley, and the Westerwald) are organized by several city travel agencies. Three leading tour operators are: **Globus Reisen** (⊠ Hohenzollernring 86, ☎ 0221/912–8270); **Univers-Reisen** (⊠ Am Rinkenpfuhl
57, ☎ 0221/209–020); and **Küppers-Reisebüro-Etrav** (⊠ Longericher-
Str. 183, ☎ 0221/210–966).

City tours of **Bonn** start from the tourist office (⊠ Münsterstr. 20, ☎
0228/773–466). Two-hour tours are conducted April–October, Monday–Saturday at 2; May–September, also weekends at 10:30; November–March, only Saturday at 10:30. The tour costs DM 18.

Between May and October walking tours of Trier are conducted by
the local tourist board (⊠ An der Porta Nigra, Postfach 3830, DM–3830,
☎ 0651/978–080). Tours leave from the Porta Nigra at 2. The cost
is DM 9.

Bus tours of **Köln** leave from outside the tourist office (opposite the
main entrance to the cathedral) hourly 10–3, April through October,
and at 11 and 2 November through April. The tour lasts two hours
and costs DM 23 for adults and DM 8 for children; it is conducted in
English and German. **"Köln by Night"** bus tours are offered Friday and
Saturday during July and August. These trips leave the tourist office
at 7 PM and include a tour of the city, a boat ride on the Rhine, a cold
supper, and a visit to a wine tavern; the cost is DM 49. A two-hour
walking tour of Köln is available with prior arrangement with the tourist
office. Most central hotels offer a special tourist package, the **"Kölner
Knüller,"** which includes a sightseeing tour voucher, a pass for all the
city's museums, and other reductions. The package costs DM 20.

City tours of **Düsseldorf** leave from Bus Quay 10, Friedrich-Ebert-Strasse
(across from the Hauptbahnhof) daily at 11:15 and 2:45. The 2½-hour
tour includes a visit to the top of the 700-foot Rhine television tower.
The cost is DM 23. After May the cost for the afternoon tour is DM
25, because the tour expands to include a boat trip on the Rhine.

Travel Agencies
American Express: ⊠ Burgmauer 14, D–50667 Köln, ☎ 0221/
925–9010.

⊠ Kaiserstr. 8, Postfach 100146, D–60311 Frankfurt, ☎ 069/21051.

⊠ Webergasse 8, D–65183 Wiesbaden, ☎ 0611/39144.

⊠ Heinrich-Heine-Allee 14, D–40213 Düsseldorf, ☎ 0211/82200.

Visitor Information
The Rhineland regional tourist office, **Fremdenverkehrsverband Rheinland Pfalz** (⊠ Postfach 1420, D–56014 Koblenz, ☎ 0261/915–200),
provides general information on the entire region. There are also local
tourist information offices in the following towns and cities:

Aachen: Verkehrsverein Bad Aachen, ⊠ Friedrich-Wilhelm-Pl., Postfach 2007, D–52022, ☎ 0241/180–2960.

Bernkastel-Kues: Stadt Verkehrsbüro, ⊠ Am Gestade 5, D–54464, ☎
06531/4023.

Bonn: Tourist Information Cassius-Bastei, ✉ Münsterstr. 20, D–53111, ☎ 0228/773–466.

Cochem: Verkehrsamt, ✉ Endertpl., D–56812, ☎ 02671/3971.

Düsseldorf: Verkehrsverein, ✉ Konrad Adenauer Pl. 12, D–40210, ☎ 0211/172–020.

Koblenz: Fremdenverkehrsamt der Stadt Koblenz, Verkehrspavillon am Hauptbahnhof, ✉ Postfach 2080, D–56020, ☎ 0261/915–200.

Köln: Verkehrsamt der Stadt Köln, ✉ Unter Fettenhenen 19, D–50667, ☎ 0221/221–3340.

Rüdesheim: Städtisches Verkehrsamt, ✉ Rheinstr. 16, D–65385, ☎ 06722/2962.

St. Goarshausen: Verkehrsamt, ✉ Bahnhofstr. 8, D–56346, ☎ 06771/427.

Trier: Tourist Information, ✉ an der Porta Nigra, Postfach 3830, D–54290, ☎ 0651/978–080.

Wiesbaden: Verkehrsbüro, ✉ Rheinstr. 15, corner of Wilhelmstr., D–65185, ☎ 0611/172–9780.

13 The Fairy-Tale Road

If you're in search of Cinderella, Hansel and Gretel, the Pied Piper, and Rumpelstiltskin, the Fairy-Tale Road is the place to look. One of Germany's special tourist routes, it leads through parts of Germany where the brothers Grimm lived and worked. From its start in Hanau, just east of Frankfurt, to its end in Bremen, 600 kilometers (370 miles) north, it passes dozens of picturesque towns full of half-timbered houses and guarded by castles. Hannover is the site of a magnificent Baroque park.

THE MAJORITY OF TRAVELERS who begin their Germany vacations at Frankfurt Airport head west to the Rhineland or south into the Black Forest or Bavaria. Some may find their way into the Taunus Mountains on Frankfurt's doorstep. Relatively few, however, venture north to follow a fascinating trail that leads deep into the heart of the country, not only into the land but into the German character as well.

This is the Fairy-Tale Road, or Märchenstrasse. It starts just a 20-minute rail or car journey east of Frankfurt in the town of Hanau and from there wends its way north some 600 kilometers (about 370 miles) through parts of Germany that shaped the lives and imagination of the two most famous chroniclers of German folk history and tradition, the brothers Grimm. Although the route is best explored by car, many of the attractions along its meandering path can also be reached by train.

The Fairy-Tale Road is among the most recent of Germany's special tourist routes. It doesn't have the glamour of the Romantic Road, but in its own way it is, perhaps, a route more in tune with romantics. It certainly doesn't suffer from the commercialism of the Wine Road.

The zigzag course detailed in this chapter follows the spine of the Fairy-Tale Road and includes a number of side trips and detours to nearby destinations worthy of a visitor's attention. Fairy tales come to life in forgotten villages where black cats snooze in the windows of half-timbered houses; in ancient forests where wild boar snort at timid deer; in misty valleys where the silence of centuries is broken only by the splash of a ferryman's oar. In a way, this could be considered a dual trip: going forward geographically and at the same time backward historically, into the reaches of childhood, imagination, and German folk consciousness, to visit Old World settings steeped in legend and fantasy.

From early childhood the Grimms were enthralled by tales of enchantment, of kings and queens, of golden-haired princesses saved from disaster by stalwart princes—folk tales, myths, epics, and legends that dealt with magic and wicked witches, predatory stepmothers, along with a supporting cast of goblins and wizards.

The Grimms did not invent these tales; they were in the public domain long before the brothers began collecting them. The Grimms' devotion to fairy tales could be considered merely a sideline to their main careers. Jacob was a grammarian who formulated Grimm's Law, a theory of linguistics relating Greek and Latin to German. Wilhelm was a literary scholar and critic. Together they spent most of their energies compiling a massive dictionary of the German language. But it is as the authors of *Kinder und Hausmärchen (Children's and Household Tales),* a work that has been called the best-known book after the Bible, that they are remembered. In 1812 the Grimms introduced the world to some 200 of their favorite stories, with a cast of characters that included Cinderella, Hansel and Gretel, Little Red Riding Hood, Rapunzel, Rumpelstiltskin, Sleeping Beauty, Snow White, and other unforgettable stars of the world of make-believe.

The Fairy-Tale Road leads through parts of Germany in which the brothers lived and gathered and situated their tales. It travels through the states of Hesse and Lower Saxony, to follow along the Fulda and Weser rivers via a string of highways and byways through a countryside as beguiling as any in Europe.

Pleasures and Pastimes

Dining

If you are in the western area of the region, try Westphalian ham, famous for more than 2,000 years. The hams can weigh as much as 33 pounds and are considered particularly good for breakfast, when a huge slice is served on a wood board with rich, dark pumpernickel bread baked for about 20 hours. If you're keen to do as the locals do, you'll wash it down with a glass of strong, clear Steinhäger schnapps. A favorite main course is *Pfefferpothast,* a sort of heavily browned goulash with lots of pepper. The "hast" at the end of the name is from the old German word *Harst,* meaning "roasting pan." Rivers and streams filled with trout and eels are common around Hameln. Göttinger *Speckkuchen* is a heavy and filling onion tart. In Bremen, *Aalsuppe grün,* eel soup seasoned with dozens of herbs, is a must in summer.

CATEGORY	COST*
$$$$	over DM 90
$$$	DM 55–DM 90
$$	DM 35–DM 55
$	under DM 35

*per person for a three-course meal, including tax and excluding drinks and service charge

Golf

There are golf courses at Bad Orb, Bad Pyrmont, Bremen, Fulda, Göttingen, Hanau, Kassel, and Polle-Holzminden; guests are welcome at all locations. The courses at Hanau (on the former hunting grounds at Wilhelmsbad) and Kassel (high above the city on the edge of Wilhelmshöhe Park) are particularly attractive. At Schloss Schwöbber, near Hameln, golfers tee off on the extensive castle grounds.

Hiking

The hills and forests between Hanau and Hameln are a hiker's paradise. The valleys of the Fulda, Werra, and Weser rivers make enchanting walking country, with ancient waterside inns positioned along the way. Local tourist information offices of the area have established a hiking route from Münden in the south to Porta-Westfalica, where the Weser River breaks through the last range of north German hills and into the lower Saxony Plain.

Horseback Riding

This part of Germany is horse country, and most resorts have riding stables. There are large and well-equipped equestrian centers at Löwensen, near Bad Pyrmont, and Hameln.

Lodging

Make reservations well in advance if you plan to visit during the summer. Though it's one of the less-traveled tourist routes in Germany, the main points of the Fairy-Tale Road are popular. Hannover is particularly busy during trade-fair times. Accommodations cover the spectrum from modern high-rises to ancient and crooked half-timbered buildings.

CATEGORY	COST*
$$$$	over DM 250
$$$	DM 175–DM 250
$$	DM 125–DM 175
$	under DM 125

*All prices are for two people in a double room, excluding service charges.

Water Sports
Great canoeing and motorboating can be enjoyed on the Fulda, Weser, and Werra rivers.

EXPLORING THE FAIRY-TALE ROAD

This isn't a route for travelers in a hurry. The road extends about half the length of Germany, from the banks of the Main River, which marks the border between northern and southern Germany, to the North Sea ports of Bremen and Bremerhaven. And it should be remembered that it's an artificial route, put together by German tourism experts who found a theme to hold the diverse regions together, namely their connection with the Grimm brothers and their stories. Some towns on the journey—Bremerhaven and Hanau, for example—have little of the fairy-tale atmosphere, while others, such as Steinau an der Strasse, Münden, and Hameln, might have stepped right out of a Grimm story.

Numbers in the text correspond to numbers in the margin and on the Fairy-Tale Road map.

IF YOU HAVE 3 DAYS
You won't get much farther than the first stretch of the route, from Hanau to Fulda, but that's enough for an introduction to the influence of the region on the Grimm brothers. Start your first day at **Hanau** ①, the southern end of the Fairy-Tale Road, which won't detain you for long. Although it's an unlovely town, reconstructed too hurriedly after the war, you should take a look at the 100-year-old statue of the Grimm brothers (in the Neustädter Marktplatz square), a charming representation of their relationship. Plan a short detour to **Schloss Philippsruhe,** the oldest French-style Baroque palace east of the Rhine, and to the spa town of **Wilhelmsbad** ②, where European royalty and nobility once took the waters. Make ⌘ **Gelnhausen** ③ your next stop, for a visit to the remains of Barbarossa's greatest castle. Plan an overnight stay at the **Romantisches Hotel Burg Mühle,** or at least dinner in its restaurant, where the mill's waterwheel turns as you eat. Devote your second day to exploring **Steinau an der Strasse** ④, where the Grimm brothers spent much of their childhood, and then continue on to ⌘ **Fulda** ⑤, where the impressive bishop's palace and the cathedral will take up much of what's left of your three days.

IF YOU HAVE 5 DAYS
Begin your tour by following the itinerary described above. On your third day proceed north of Fulda, calling at the medieval towns of **Lauterbach** and **Alsfeld,** both of which are perfect settings for Grimm tales. Spend the night in ⌘ **Kassel** ⑥ and try to catch the sunset from the heights of the Wilhelmshöhe. On the fourth day, traverse the valley of the Fulda River to where it meets the Weser, at **Münden** ⑦, which claimed a place on geographer Alexander von Humboldt's list of the world's most beautiful towns. Follow the lazily winding Weser northward now, making a short detour to **Göttingen** ⑧ for lunch in one of the student taverns in this busy university city. Try to fit in an overnight stay at one of Germany's most romantic hotels, Sleeping Beauty's castle, the ⌘ **Sababurg** ⑨, half-hidden in the depths of the densely wooded Reinhardswald. On the fifth day return to the Weser River valley road and find time for stops at **Bad Karlshafen** ⑩, **Höxter** ⑪, and **Bodenwerder** ⑫, to explore their streets of half-timbered houses, examples of the Weser Renaissance building style. End your trip at ⌘ **Hameln** ⑬, the Pied Piper's town.

The Fairy-Tale Road

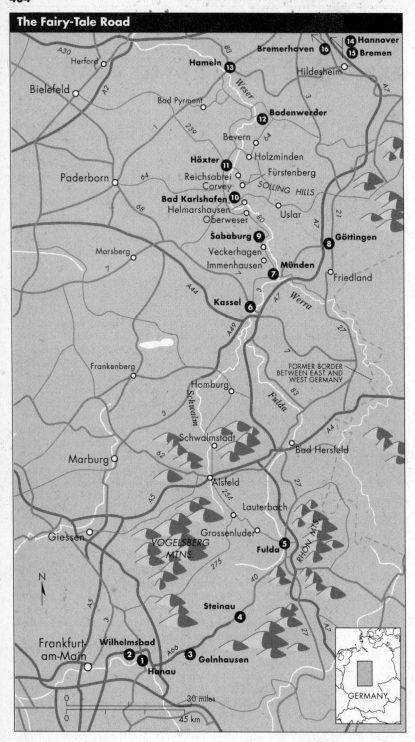

Bremerhaven
14 Hannover
15 Bremen
Hildesheim

A30
Herford
A2
Bielefeld

Hameln 13
Weser

Bad Pyrmont
Bodenwerder 12

Bevern
Paderborn
64
Höxter 11
Holzminden
Reichsabtei
Fürstenberg
Corvey
SOLLING HILLS
68
Bad Karlshafen 10
Helmarshausen
Uslar
Oberweser
21
A7
Marsberg
Sababurg 9
1
Veckerhagen
Göttingen 8
Immenhausen
Münden 7
Friedland
A44
3
Kassel 6
A7
Werra
27
A49
7
Frankenberg
FORMER BORDER
BETWEEN EAST AND
WEST GERMANY
83
Homburg
Fulda
A4
Schwalm
Marburg
Schwalmstadt
Bad Hersfeld
62
Alsfeld
A5
254
Lauterbach
27
Giessen
Grossenluder
VOGELSBERG
Fulda 5
RHÖN MTS.
MTNS.
3
275
40
A7
27
N
Steinau 4
A5
3
Frankfurt-
Wilhelmsbad
am-Main
2
1
A66
3 Gelnhausen
Hanau

0   30 miles
0   45 km

GERMANY

Follow the five-day itinerary described above. Leave the Fairy-Tale Road at Hameln for a detour to ⊞ **Hannover** ⑭, devoting at least half a day to the city's magnificent royal park of Herrenhausen. An overnight stay in Hannover will give you the opportunity to enjoy some nightlife after the tranquillity of much of the Weser Valley route. Or you can postpone that amusement until your arrival in ⊞ **Bremen** ⑮, 110 kilometers (66 miles) northwest. Bremen is the northernmost frontier of the Grimm brothers' influence, represented by several statues of the figures in the Bremen town musicians fable. It would be a shame to travel all this way without venturing the final 48 kilometers (30 miles) to the seaport of **Bremerhaven** ⑯, where a visit to Germany's largest maritime museum, the Deutsches Schiffahrtsmuseum, brings your tour to a memorable close.

When to Tour the Fairy-Tale Road

Summer is the ideal time to travel through this varied landscape, although in spring you'll find the river valleys carpeted in the season's first flowers while in fall the sleepy current of the Weser is often blanketed in mist; both sights linger in the mind. Travel the Weser Valley road early in the morning or late in the afternoon, when the light has a softening touch on the river.

Hanau

❶ *16 km (10 mi) east of Frankfurt.*

The Fairy-Tale Road begins in "once upon a time" fashion at Hanau, the town where the brothers were born: Jacob in 1785, Wilhelm a year later. Although travelers devoted to the Grimms will want to start their pilgrimage here, they should be forewarned that Hanau has become a traffic-congested suburb of Frankfurt, with post–World War II buildings that are not particularly attractive. Hanau was almost completely obliterated by wartime bombing raids, and there's little of the Altstadt (Old Town) that the Grimm brothers would recognize now.

Hanau's main attraction can reach be reached only on foot—the **Brothers Grimm Memorial** in the Neustädter Marktplatz. The bronze memorial, erected in 1898, is a larger-than-life-size statue of the brothers: one seated, the other leaning on his chair, the two of them deep in conversation—a fitting pose for these scholars who unearthed so many medieval myths and legends, earning their reputation as the fathers of the fairy tale.

The degree to which the brothers have influenced the world's concept of fairy tales—those of *The Arabian Nights* excepted—is remarkable. But it would be a mistake to imagine them as kindly, bewhiskered old gents telling stories in their rose-clad cottage for the pleasure of village children. As already mentioned, they were serious and successful academics, with interests ranging far beyond what we may think of as children's light amusements. Their stories probe deep into the German psyche and deal with far more complex emotions than is suggested by the occasional happily-ever-after endings; witness the Stephen Sondheim–James Lapine musical *Into the Woods,* based largely on the Grimms' works.

The solid bulk of Hanau's 18th-century **Rathaus** (Town Hall) stands behind the Grimm brothers statue. Every day at noon its bells play tribute to another of the city's famous sons, the composer Paul Hindemith (1895–1963), by chiming out one of his canons. At 10 AM the carillon plays a choral composition; at 2 PM, a minuet; and at 4 PM, a piece entitled *Guten Abend* (Good Evening) rings out for the crowds hurrying across the Marktplatz to complete their shopping before returning home. ☒ *Neustädter Marktpl.*

The **Altes Rathaus** (Old Town Hall), behind the Rathaus, dominates a corner that has been faithfully reconstructed. This handsome 16th-century Renaissance building has two half-timbered upper stories weighted down by a steep slate roof. Today it's the home of the German goldsmiths' craft. Known as the **Deutsches Goldschmiedehaus** (German Goldsmiths' House), it contains a permanent exhibit and regular national and international displays of goldsmiths' and silversmiths' crafts. ☒ *Altstädter Markt 6.* ☎ *Free.* ☉ *Tues.–Sun. 10–noon and 2–5.*

OFF THE
BEATEN PATH
SCHLOSS PHILIPPSRUHE – This palace on the banks of the Main River in the suburb of Kesselstadt (Bus 1 or 10 will take you there in 10 minutes) has much more than Grimm exhibits to offer: It's the oldest French-style Baroque palace east of the Rhine. Philippsruhe may remind you of Versailles, although its French-trained architect, Julius Ludwig Rothweil, planned it along the lines of another palace in the Paris area, the much smaller Clagny Palace. Philippsruhe—as its name, "Philipp's Rest," suggests—was built for Count Philipp Reinhard von Hanau. He didn't enjoy its riverside peace for long, however; he died less than three months after moving in. After the French builder Jacques Girard completed work on the palace, creating its very French appearance, the invading French confiscated it in 1803. Later Napoléon gave it as a present to his sister Pauline Borghese, who then put it up for sale. American forces took over Philippsruhe as a military quarters for a time in 1945, and until the postwar reconstruction of Hanau was complete, it served as the Town Hall. Every year on the first weekend of September, the palace grounds are invaded again—this time by the people of Hanau, for a magnificent party to commemorate the rebuilding of their war-ravaged town.

During the early 19th century, following the withdrawal of the French from Hanau, the original formal gardens were replanned as an informal, English-style park. You'll find the contrast between formal palace and informal wooded grounds striking. As you leave or enter, pause to study the entrance gate; the 19th-century gilding, made by Parisian masters, is real gold. ☒ *Schloss Philippsruhe, Kesselstadt.* ☎ *DM 3.* ☉ *Tues.–Sun. 11–6.*

NEED A
BREAK?
If the weather's good, seek out a place beneath the white-canvas sunshades on the palace terrace, now a café with a view overlooking the Main River that was once enjoyed by Count Philipp Reinhard. In inclement weather head for the palace's bistro, with its open fire and hot, strong coffee.

Dining and Lodging

$$$$ ✕🏠 **Brüder Grimm Hotel.** A few minutes' walk from the Brüder Grimm Memorial in Hanau's central market square, the hotel that carries their name has a fairy-tale restaurant on the top floor. Accommodations are modern and comfortable. Try for the "Eckzimmer"; it's the largest and best-decorated room. Several rooms have tiled floors instead of wall-to-wall carpet for the comfort of guests with allergies. The La Fontana restaurant has an excellent menu distinguished by Italian flair. ☒ *Kurt-Blaum-Pl. 6,* ☎ *06181/3060,* 𝖥𝖠𝖷 *06181/306–512. 80 rooms and 15 apartments with bath or shower. Restaurant, hot tub, sauna, exercise room. AE, DC, MC, V.*

Wilhelmsbad

❷ *3 km (2 mi) west of Hanau.*

Just north of Schloss Philippsruhe and a short bus ride from the center of Hanau is the city spa of Wilhelmsbad. It was built at the end of the 18th century by Crown Prince Wilhelm von Hessen-Kassel at the site where two peasant women, out gathering herbs, discovered mineral springs. For a few decades Wilhelmsbad rivaled Baden-Baden as Germany's premier spa and fashionable playground. Then, about 100 years ago, the springs dried up, the casino closed, and Europe's wealthy and titled looked for other amusements. But this is still Grimm fairy-tale land, and Wilhelmsbad, the sleeping-beauty spa, awoke from its slumber in the '60s to become a rejuvenated resort. The fine Baroque buildings and bathhouses were restored, parkland cleared and redesigned in informal English style, riding stables opened, and one of Germany's loveliest golf courses laid out where the leisure classes once hunted pheasants.

Gelnhausen

❸ *20 km (12 mi) northeast of Hanau.*

At Gelnhausen you'll find an island in the sleepy little Kinzig River with the remains of a castle that may well have stimulated the imagination of the Grimm brothers. Emperor Friedrich I—known as Barbarossa, or Red Beard—built the castle in this idyllic spot during the 12th century; in 1180 it was the scene of the first all-German Imperial Diet. Although on an island, the castle was hardly designed as a defensive bastion and was accordingly sacked in the Thirty Years' War. Today only parts of the russet walls and colonnaded entrance remain. Still, stroll beneath the castle's ruined ramparts on its watery site, and you'll get a tangible impression of the medieval importance of the court of Barbarossa. ⊠ *Follow signs to Burg Barbarossa,* ☎ *06051/820–054.* 🎫 *DM 2.* ☉ *Castle Mar.–Oct., Tues.–Sun. 10–1 and 2–5:30; Nov.–Feb., Tues.–Sun. 10–1 and 2–4:30.*

The **Hexenturm** (Witches Tower), a grim prison, remains from the time when Gelnhausen was the center of a paranoiac witch-hunt in the late 16th century; dozens of local women were burned at the stake or thrown—bound hand and foot—into the Kinzig River. Suspects were held in the Hexenturm of the town battlements. Today it houses a blood-curdling collection of medieval torture instruments. ⊠ *Barbarossastr.* 🎫 *DM 3.* ☉ *Tower can be visited only during regular guided tours, May–Sept., Sun. 2:30 (starting point: Rathaus).*

Dining and Lodging

$$–$$$ ✕🏨 **Romantisches Hotel Burg Mühle.** *Mühle* means "mill," and this hotel was once the tithe mill of the neighboring castle, delivering flour to the community until 1948. In the restaurant the mill wheel churns away as you eat. Special weekend deals include two nights' accommodation and two three-course dinners for DM 195 per person. The restaurant is closed for Sunday dinner. ⊠ *Burgstr. 2,* ☎ *06051/82050,* 📠 *06051/820–554. 34 rooms with bath. Restaurant, sauna, exercise room. DC, MC, V.*

Steinau an der Strasse

❹ *18 km (12 mi) northeast of Gelnhausen.*

For clear evidence of its formative influence on the brothers Grimm, you need only travel to the little town of Steinau—full name Steinau an der Strasse (Steinau "on the road," referring to an old trade route between Frankfurt and Leipzig). Here Father Grimm served as local magistrate and the Grimm brothers spent much of their childhood.

Steinau dates from the 13th century and is typical of villages in the region. Marvelously preserved half-timbered houses are set along cobblestone streets; imposing castles bristle with towers and turrets. In its woodsy surroundings one can well imagine encountering Little Red Riding Hood, Snow White, or Hansel and Gretel. The main street is named after the brothers; the building where paterfamilias was employed is now known as the "fairy-tale house."

★ A **castle** straight out of a Grimm fairy tale stands at the top of the town. Originally an early medieval fortress, it was rebuilt in Renaissance style between 1525 and 1558 and used by the counts of Hanau as their summer residence and later to guard the increasingly important trade route between Frankfurt and Leipzig. It's not difficult to imagine the young Grimm boys playing in the shadow of its great gray walls, perhaps venturing into the encircling dry moat.

The castle houses a **Grimm Museum,** one of two in Steinau. Climb the tower for a breathtaking view of Steinau and the countryside where the Grimm brothers once roamed. *Museum* ☎ *0663/6843.* ☜ *DM 2, guided tour of castle and museum DM 4, tower DM 1.* ☼ *Mar.–Oct., Tues.–Sun. 10–5; Nov.–Dec. and Feb., Tues.–Sun. 10–4.*

★ The **Amtshaus,** a few hundred yards from the castle, is a fine half-timbered, turreted house where the Grimm family resided from 1791 to 1796. It now contains the tourist office and a local history museum with a special section devoted to the Brothers Grimm. ☜ *DM 2.50.* ☼ *Apr.–Oct., weekdays 2–5.*

The Gothic church of **St. Catherine,** where the Grimm brothers' grandfather, Friedrich, was parson, stands in front of the castle in Steinau's ancient market square. ⊠ *Am Kumpen.*

The **Steinauer Marionettentheater,** a small puppet theater, is housed in the former stables of the town castle; here presentations of Grimm fairy tales are staged. ☎ *06663/245 for program details.*

A **Grimm memorial fountain** lies in the center of the Am Kumpen market square. It was built only in 1985, but its timeless design blends well with the rest of the town.

The 16th-century **Rathaus** (Town Hall) has six bronze figures on its white stucco facade; they represent a cross section of 16th-century Steinau's population—from the builder who helped construct the town to the mother and child who continue its traditions.

☾ **Erlebnispark Steinau an der Strasse,** one of the region's largest leisure parks, is 3 kilometers (2 miles) south of Steinau. It has a small zoo, various fairground rides, and a toboggan run that could be described as dry if it weren't for the water traps it runs through. There's a restaurant, too. One big advantage for families visiting this park: The very reasonably priced ticket covers all the attractions and as many toboggan rides as the kids can pack into the day. ⊠ *On the Marjoss road,* ☎ *0663/6889,* ☜ *DM 10.* ☼ *Apr.–Oct., daily 9–6.*

A 3-kilometer (2-mile) detour north of Steinau brings you to the chillingly named **Teufelshöhle** (Devil's Caves), a series of caves that would have given further inspiration to the Grimm brothers if only they had known of their existence. Although first explored by a local daredevil on the end of a rope in 1830, they weren't opened to the public until a century later. The caves are 2.5 million years old and have two im-

mense chambers, the *Dom* (cathedral) and *Kapelle* (chapel). Weird sta-
lactite formations have accumulated over the millenia, including one
in the shape of a giant beehive. The caves are an easy walk from
Steinau. ⊠ *On the Freiensteinau road (L3179).* ☎ *DM 3.* ☉ *Apr.–Oct.,
Sat. 1–6, Sun. and holidays 9–6.*

Dining and Lodging

$ ✕⊞ **Burgmannenhaus.** This sturdy, steep-eaved Steinau house calls it-
self a "romantic hotel-restaurant," and not without cause. Its rooms
are small, cozy, and traditionally furnished, and those under the eaves
have exposed beams and woodwork. The restaurant has a very good
menu with a French touch. The Fairy-Tale Road Bicycling Association
meets regularly here, so you might pick up some good tips. ⊠ *Brüder-
Grimmstr. 49, D–36396,* ☎ *0663/5084,* FAX *0663/50987. 5 rooms
with bath or shower. Restaurant. No credit cards.*

$ ✕⊞ **Weisses Ross.** If the nearby Burgmannenhaus is full, this is a good
second choice. It may be a simple inn, but you can sleep within its gnarled
walls in the knowledge that the Grimm brothers overnighted here almost 200 years ago. Rooms facing the street have views of ancient buildings but suffer a little from traffic noise. ⊠ *Brüder-Grimmstr. 48,
D–36396,* ☎ *06663/5804. 8 rooms, most with bath. Restaurant. No
credit cards.*

Shopping

Steinau an der Strasse was for centuries a renowned pottery center,
and in the mid-1880s, 40 potters were at work in the small town. Today
there's only one: **Hans Krüger.** But he's turning out the kind of work
that made Steinau so famous (Hans Krüger Kunsttöpferei, ⊠ Ringstr.
52, ☎ 06663/6413). The pottery tradition was mentioned first in official records in 1391 in the neighboring village of Marjoss, 3 kilometers (2 miles) south of Steinau, and two pottery firms are still
functioning there: the **Georg Ruppert family** (⊠ Brückenauer Str. 21,
☎ 06660/304) and Bernhard Breitenberger's **Bauerntöpferei** (⊠ Dis-
telbachstr. 24, ☎ 06660/1224).

En Route   Gelnhausen and Steinau an der Strasse both lie on another tourist trail,
the "German Half-timbered Road". It's not the road itself that is half-
timbered but the historic buildings in towns along its route. The route
stretches from near Frankfurt to north of Bremen and meets the Fairy-
Tale Road at several points along the way. A map and information
brochure can be obtained from the organization that plotted the
route, the Deutsche Geschäftstelle im Deutschen Zentrum für Hand-
werk und Denkmalpflege (⊠ Propstei Johannesberg, D–36041 Fulda,
☎ 0661/4953133).

The Fairy-Tale Road parts company with the half-timbered-towns route
at Steinau an der Strasse and heads directly north through the rural uplands of the Vogelsberg. At the region's highest point, near the village
of Obermoos, turn right and take the country road to Fulda. Alternatively, take another holiday route from Steinau an der Strasse, the Rhön
und Spessartfahrt, through the forested northern edge of the Rhön region and branch off for Fulda at the little spa of Bad Bruckenau.

Fulda

⑤ *32 km (19 mi) northeast of Steinau an der Strasse.*

The ancient episcopal city of Fulda is a treasure trove of Baroque architecture. Its grandest example is the immense **bishops' palace** on
Schlossstrasse, crowning the heights of the city. This great collection
of buildings began as a Renaissance palace in the early 17th century
and was transformed into its present Baroque splendor a century later

by Johann Dientzenhofer. Much of the palace is now used as municipal offices, but you can visit several of the former public rooms. The Fürstensaal (Princes' Hall) on the second floor provides a breathtaking display of Baroque decorative artistry, with ceiling paintings by the 18th-century Bavarian artist Melchior Steidl. Concerts are regularly held within its fabric-clad walls (contact the city tourist office in the palace for program details, ☎ 0661/102–345). The palace also has permanent displays of the faience ceramics for which Fulda was once famous, as well as some fine local glassware.

Pause at the windows of the great Fürstensaal to take in the view across the palace park to the **Orangerie,** a large garden with summer flowering shrubs and plants. If you have time after your palace tour, stroll over for a visit. There's a pleasant café on the first floor. ⊠ *Schlossstr. DM 4, guided tours 50 pf. ☉ Sat.–Thurs. 10–6, Fri. 2–6. Guided tours Apr.–Oct., Sat.–Thurs. 10:30 and 2:30, Fri. at 2:30; Nov.–Mar., weekdays 2:30, weekends 10:30 and 2:30.*

The **Dom,** Fulda's 18th-century cathedral with tall twin spires, stands across the broad boulevard that borders the palace park. The cathedral was built by Dientzenhofer on the site of an 8th-century basilica, which at the time was the largest church north of the Alps. The basilica had to be big enough to accommodate the ever-growing number of pilgrims from all parts of Europe, who converged on Fulda to pray at the grave of the martyred St. Boniface, the "Apostle of the Germans." A black alabaster bas-relief depicting his death marks the martyr's grave in the crypt. The cathedral museum contains a document bearing his writing, along with several other treasures, including a fine 16th-century painting by Lucas Cranach of the Elder of Christ and the adulteress (who looks very comely in her velvet Renaissance costume). *Dom Museum, ⊠ Dompl. DM 4. ☉ Apr.–Oct., Tues.–Sat. 10–5:30, Sun. and holidays 12:30–5:30; Nov.–Dec. and Feb.–Mar., Tues.–Sat. 10–12:30, Sun. and holidays 12:30–4.*

The **Vonderau Museum,** housed in the former Jesuit seminary, displays many outstanding historical works of religious art and sculpture. A popular section of the museum is its **planetarium.** It has only 35 seats, so you get a unique impression of wandering alone through the stars. ☎ *0661/928–3512. Museum DM 4, planetarium DM 5. ☉ Tues.–Sun. 10–6. Guided tours Fri.–Sun. 3:30. Planetarium performance times vary (call ☎ 0661/9283512 for program details).*

The **Michaelskirche** (Church of St. Michael) is one of Germany's oldest churches, built during the 9th century along the lines of the Church of the Holy Sepulchre in Jerusalem. It has a harmony and dignity that match the majesty of the Baroque facade of the neighboring Dom.

The central **Rathaus** is quite possibly the finest Renaissance half-timbered town hall in this part of the country. The half-timbering, separating the arcaded first floor from the steep roof and its incongruous but charming battery of small steeples, is particularly delicate.

Dining and Lodging

$–$$ ✕ **Zum Stiftskämmerer.** This former episcopal treasurer's home is now a charming tavern-restaurant, its menu packed with local fare prepared with imagination and flair. A four-course menu priced around DM 60 is an excellent value, although à la carte dishes can be ordered for as little as DM 12. Try the *Schlemmertöpfchen,* a delicious (and very filling) combination of pork, chicken breast, and venison steak. ⊠ *Kämmerzeller Str. 10,* ☎ *0661/52369. AE, MC, V.*

$$$$ ✕⌂ **Maritim Hotel am Schlossgarten.** This is the luxurious showpiece of the Maritim chain, housed in an 18th-century Baroque building overlooking Fulda Palace Park. Chandeliers, oil paintings, and antiques maintain the historic style, which contrasts with the hotel's modern atrium. The historic atmosphere of the grand old building, however, extends to the basement foundations, where you can dine beneath centuries-old vaulted arches in the Dianakeller restaurant. Many rooms have fine views overlooking the Fulda Palace Park; to be sure, order one of the two suites, which have spacious terraces. ✉ *Pauluspromenade 2, D–36037,* ☎ *0661/2820,* FAX *0661/282499. 111 rooms and 2 suites with bath. 2 restaurants, bar, café, indoor pool, sauna, bowling, bicycles. AE, DC, MC, V.*

$$$$ ✕⌂ **Romantik Hotel Goldener Karpfen.** Fulda is famous for its Baroque
★ buildings, and this hotel is a short walk from the finest of them. The hotel, too, dates from the Baroque era but has a later facade. Inside it has been renovated to a high standard of comfort. Afternoon coffee in the comfortable, tapestry-upholstered chairs of the hotel's lounge is one of Fulda's delights, while dining in the elegant restaurant, with its crisp white linen, Persian rugs, and subdued lighting, is another. ✉ *Simpliciusbrunnen. 1, D–36037,* ☎ *0661/70044,* FAX *0661/73042. 55 rooms with bath or shower. Restaurant, weinstube, sauna, exercise room. AE, DC, MC, V.*

$$ ⌂ **Zum Kurfürsten.** In the heart of the Old Town, this lodging is itself part of Fulda's Baroque face. But behind the venerable facade guests are assured of modern facilities. ✉ *Schlossstr. 2, D–36037,* ☎ *0661/70001,* FAX *0661/77919. 50 rooms with bath. Restaurant, sauna. AE, DC, MC, V.*

Nightlife and the Arts

Chamber-music concerts are held regularly from September through May in the chandelier-hung splendor of the **bishops' palace.** One wing of the palace is now the city's main theater Organ recitals are given regularly in Fulda's **Dom.** Call (☎ 0661/102–326) for program details of all Fulda cultural events.

En Route   Kassel is the next major stop on the road north. If you're in a hurry, you can reach Kassel from Fulda in less than an hour via Autobahn 7. But the Fairy-Tale Road gives Autobahns a wide berth, so if you have time, take B–254 into the Vogelsberg Mountains via Grossenluder to Lauterbach, some 25 kilometers (15 miles) northeast of Fulda.

Lauterbach, a resort town of many medieval half-timbered houses, has not just one castle but two—the **Riedesel** and the **Eisenbach.** The town is the setting of one of the Grimm's fairy tales, the one in which the Little Scalawag loses his sock. Lauterbach's other claim to fame is its **garden gnomes,** turned out here by the thousands and exported all over the world. These ornaments are made in all shapes and sizes, from 3 inches to 3 feet tall, by the firm of Heissner Keramik. Several shops in Lauterbach sell the gnomes, if you'd like to take one home with you. A good selection featuring Grimm fairy-tale characters is available at the **Heissner Shops** (✉ Schlitzerstr. 24 and Schubertstr. 14, ☎ 06641/860 for both).

The Fairy-Tale Road continues north to **Alsfeld,** (34 kilometers/21 miles northwest of Fulda), notable for its medieval town center of beautifully preserved half-timbered houses, some that lean out, almost touching one another across narrow, winding cobbled streets. Seek out **Kirchplatz,** a small square behind the late-Gothic Walpurgiskirche off the main square, and **No. 12,** whose rightward lurch seems to defy gravity. So, too, does the jewel of Alsfeld—and one of Germany's showpieces—the **Altes Rathaus** (Old Town Hall), built in 1512. Its facade—combining a stone-colonnade ground floor, half-timbered upper reaches, and a dizzily steep, top-heavy slate roof punctured by two pointed towers shaped like witches' hats—would look right at home in Walt Disney World. If you want to get an unobstructed view of this remarkable building (which is not open to the public) for your photo album, avoid the Marktplatz on Tuesday and Friday, when market stalls clutter the square.

From there the routing follows the little Schwalm River through a picturesque region so inextricably linked with the Grimm fairy tales that it's known as Rotkäppchenland (Little Red Riding Hood country). On a side road, **Neustadt** is the home of the 13th-century circular tower from which Rapunzel supposedly let down her golden tresses. About 10 kilometers (6 miles) north is **Schwalmstadt,** the capital of the area. If you happen to be here on one of the town's many festival days, you'll see local people decked out in the traditional folk costumes that are still treasured in these parts. If you're interested in buying regional costumes, such as Hessen *Trachten* dresses, try **Berdux** (⊠ Hirschberg 1, ☎ 06691/23029).

Of passing interest is **Marburg,** some 40 kilometers (25 miles) southwest on the Route 3 Kassel Highway, where the Grimm brothers attended the university and began their folktale research.

NEED A BREAK? : At Homberg, 19 kilometers (12 miles) north of Schwalmstadt, stop at the 15th-century **Krone Inn** (☎ 05681/2407), on the market square; it's the oldest guest house in Germany. Within its half-timbered walls you can eat and drink and dream of centuries past.

Kassel

6 *40 km (24 mi) north of Homburg, 100 km (60 mi) north of Fulda.*

The Brothers Grimm worked for a time in Kassel as librarians at the court of the king of Westphalia, Jerome Bonaparte, Napoléon's youngest brother. The Grimms continued to collect stories and legends. Many French tales were recounted to them by Dorothea Viehmann, "the Fairy-tale Lady," who lived in the neighboring village of Baunatal.

The **Brüder Grimm Museum,** in the center of Kassel, occupies five rooms of the Palais Bellevue, where the brothers once lived and worked. Exhibits include furniture, memorabilia, letters, manuscripts, and editions of their books, as well as paintings, aquarelles, etchings, and drawings by Ludwig Emil Grimm, a third brother and a graphic artist of note. ⊠ *Palais Bellevue, Schöne Aussicht 2,* ☎ *0561/787–2033.* ▣ *DM 3.* ☉ *Daily 10–5.*

★ The **Staatliche Kunstsammlungen** (State Art Collection), Kassel's leading art gallery, is one of Germany's best museums, situated in Wilhelmshöhe Palace. It houses 17 Rembrandts, along with outstanding works by Rubens, Hals, Jordaens, Van Dyck, Dürer, Altdorfer, Cranach, and Baldung Grien. ⊠ *Schloss Wilhelmshöhe,* ☎ *0561/93777.* ▣ *DM 3.* ☉ *Tues.–Sun. 10–5.*

The 18th-century **Wilhelmshöhe** Palace served as a royal residence from 1807 to 1813, when Jerome was king of Westphalia. Later it became the summer residence of the German emperor Wilhelm II. The great palace stands at the end of the 5-kilometer-long (3-mile-long) Wilhelmshöher Allee, an avenue that runs straight as an arrow from one side of the city to the other. Beyond the palace the Wilhelmshöhe heights are crowned by an astonishing monument, a red-stone octagon bearing a giant statue of **Hercules,** built at the beginning of the 18th century. The statue is now closed to the public after being designated a security risk, so it's no longer possible to climb inside for the best view of Kassel. Nevertheless, from the base of the statue you get a very fine look over the entire city, spread out over the plain below and bisected by the straight line of the Wilhelmshöher Allee. But that's only for starters: At 2 PM on Sunday and Wednesday from mid-May through September, water gushes from a fountain beneath the Hercules statue, rushes down a series of cascades to the foot of the hill, and ends its precipitous journey on a 175-foot-high jet of water. It's a natural phenomenon, with no pumps. It takes so long to accumulate enough water that the sight can be experienced only on those two days, on holidays, and during the summer on the first Saturday of each month, when the cascades are also floodlit. Bus 1 runs from the city to the Wilhelmshöhe. Bus 23 climbs the heights to the octagon and the Hercules statue. A café lies a short walk from the statue, and there are several restaurants in the area.

The Wilhelmshöhe was laid out as a Baroque park—Europe's largest palace grounds—its elegant lawns separating the city from the thick woods of the Habichtswald (Hawk Forest). It comes as something of a surprise to see the turrets of a romantic medieval castle, the **Löwenburg** (Lion Fortress), breaking the harmony. There are more surprises, for this is no true medieval castle but a fanciful, stylized copy of a Scottish castle, built 70 years after the Hercules statue that towers above it. The architect was a Kassel ruler who displayed an early touch of the mania later seen in the castle-building excesses of Bavaria's eccentric Ludwig II. The Löwenburg contains a collection of medieval armor and weapons, tapestries, and furniture. ✉ *DM 4, includes guided tour.* ☉ *Mar.–Oct., Tues.–Sun. 10–5; Nov.–Apr., Tues.–Sun. 10–4.*

The **Deutsches Tapeten Museum,** the world's most comprehensive museum of tapestry, has more than 600 exhibits tracing the history of the art through the centuries. ✉ *Brüder-Grimm-Pl. 5,* ☎ *0561/775712.* ✉ *DM 4.* ☉ *Tues.–Sun. 10–5.*

Dining and Lodging

$$ ✕ **Die Pfeffermühle.** The "Peppermill" is in Kassel's Gude Hotel, but it's no conventional hotel restaurant. The menu is truly international: Indian and Russian dishes share space with traditional German fare. ✉ *Frankfurterstr. 299,* ☎ *0561/48050. AE, DC, MC, V. Closed Sun. evening.*

$ ✕ **Ratskeller.** Here you'll eat within the embracing surroundings of cellar vaults. Owner-chef Tomislav Mravicici is Croatian, and his Balkan specialties find their way onto the predominantly German menu, which changes daily. ✉ *Obere Konigstr. 8,* ☎ *0561/15928. AE, DC, MC, V.*

$$$$ ✕▥ **Schlosshotel Wilhelmshöhe.** Set in the beautiful Baroque Wilhelmshöhe Park, 5 kilometers (3 miles) from town, this is no ancient palace but a modern hotel with its own sports center to aid in attracting business seminars. ✉ *Schlosspark 8, D–34131,* ☎ *0561/30880,* 🅵🅰🆇 *0561/308–8428. 99 rooms, 7 suites with bath. Restaurant, bar, café, indoor pool, hot tub, sauna, golf, tennis, exercise room, horseback riding. AE, DC, MC, V.*

$$$ ✕▥ **City-Hotel.** This new hotel in the city center, just a few minutes from the Rathaus, is sympathetically designed to blend in with its ancient surroundings. Inside, rooms are stylishly decorated and furnished. ✉ *Wilhelmshöher Allee 38–42, D–34131,* ☎ *0561/72810,* 🅵🅰🆇 *0561/728–1199. 65 rooms with bath. Restaurant, bar, café, indoor pool, beauty salon, sauna, therapeutic baths. AE, DC, MC, V. Closed mid-Dec.–mid-Jan.*

Nightlife and the Arts

Kassel has a **casino** (⊠ Schlosspark 2, ☎ 0561/930850) in the suitably opulent setting of the Wilhelmshöhe Park. It's open daily 3 PM–3 AM.

Kassel is disco city. **Club 21** (⊠ Friedrich-Ebert-Str. 61a) and **Club 2000** (⊠ Weserstr. 15a) are two favorites.

Outdoor concerts are held in **Wilhelmshöhe Park** on Wednesday, Saturday, and Sunday afternoons from May through September. Classical-music concerts are also given by the city's municipal orchestra in the **Stadttheater.** Kassel holds a Gustav Mahler Festival every two years, one is being held in 1997; call (☎ 0561/10940) for program details of all concerts and tickets.

Kassel has no fewer than 35 theater companies. The principal venues are the **Schauspielhaus,** the **Tif-Theater,** the **Stadthalle,** and the **Komödie.** Call (☎ 0561/109–4222) for program details and tickets for all.

Kassel's famous international **Dokumenta X** art festival, held every two years, runs from June 21 to September 28, 1997.

Shopping

In the village of Immenhausen, just north of Kassel, you can visit a local glass foundry, the **Glashütte Süssmuth** (⊠ Am Bahnhof 3, ☎ 05673/2060), and watch glassblowers create fine works that are also for sale. The foundry is open weekdays 9–5 and Saturday 9–1. The very finest, however, find their way into a neighboring museum, where you'll get fascinating insight into the glassblower's craft. Museum hours are weekdays 9–5, Saturday 9–1, and Sunday 10–5.

Münden

★ ❼ *24 km (15 mi) north of Kassel.*

This town, whose official name is Hannoversch-Münden, shouldn't be missed if you're visiting the region. In the 18th century the German scientist and explorer Alexander von Humboldt included Münden in his short list of the world's most beautiful towns (Passau, in eastern Bavaria, was another choice). You just may agree with him when you get here.

A 650-year-old bridge crosses the Weser River to lead into this old walled settlement that appears untouched by recent history—frozen in the dim and distant past, you might think. You'll have to travel a long way through Germany to find a grouping of half-timbered houses as harmonious as those in this beautiful old town, surrounded by forests and the Fulda and Werra rivers, which join and flow as the Weser River to Bremen and the North Sea.

Take your camera with you on a stroll down Langenstrasse; No. 34 is where the famous Dr. Eisenbarth died in November 1727. The extraordinary doctor won a place in German folk history as a successful physician and a marketplace orator: a quack who delivered what he promised! A dramatization of his life is presented in the summer in front of the medieval Rathaus. (Contact the Verkehrsbüro Naturpark Münden, ☎ 05541/75313, for details.)

Göttingen

❽ *30 km (18 mi) northeast of Münden, 54 km (33 mi) northeast of Kassel.*

Although Göttingen is not strictly on the Fairy-Tale Road, it is closely associated with the Brothers Grimm, for they served as professors and librarians at the city's ancient university from 1830 to 1837.

The university appears to dominate every aspect of life in Göttingen, and there's scarcely a house more than a century old that doesn't bear a plaque linking it with a famous person who once studied or taught here. In one of the towers of the city's old defense wall, Otto von Bismarck, the Iron Chancellor and founder of the 19th-century German Empire, pored over his books as a 17-year-old law student. It looks like a romantic student's den now (the tower is open to visitors), but Bismarck was a reluctant tenant—he was banned from living within the city center because of "riotous behavior" and his fondness for wine. The taverns where Bismarck and his cronies drank are still there, all of them associated with Göttingen luminaries. Even the defiantly 20th-century Irish Pub has established itself within the half-timbered walls of a historic old house that once belonged to an 18th-century professor.

The statue of **Gänseliesel,** the little Goose Girl of German folklore, stands in the central market square, symbolizing the strong link between the students and their university city. The statue shows her carrying her geese and smiling shyly into the waters of a fountain. Above her pretty head is a charming wrought-iron *Jugendstil* (art nouveau) bower of entwined vines. The students of Göttingen contributed money toward the erection of the bronze statue and fountain in 1901, and they have given it a central role in a custom that has grown up around the university: Graduates who earn a doctorate traditionally give Gänseliesel a kiss of thanks. Göttingen's citizens say she's the most-kissed girl in the world. There was a time, however, when the city fathers were none too pleased with this licentious boast, and in 1926 they banned the tradition. A student challenged the ban before a Berlin court but lost the case. Officially the ban still stands, although neither the city council nor the university takes any notice of it.

The **Rathaus** (Town Hall) lies directly behind the Gänseliesel statue. It was begun during the 13th century but never completely finished. The result is the part-medieval, part-Renaissance building you see today. The bronze lion's-head knocker on the main door dates from early in the 13th century and is the oldest of its type in Germany. Step through the door, and in the lobby striking murals tell the city's story. The medieval council chamber served for centuries as the center of civic life. Within its painted walls and beneath its heavily beamed ceiling, the council met, courts sat in judgment, visiting dignitaries were officially received, receptions and festivities were held, and traveling theater groups performed.

In the streets around the Town Hall you'll find magnificent examples of Renaissance architecture. Many of these half-timbered, low-gabled buildings house businesses that have been there for centuries. The **Ratsapotheke** (pharmacy) across from the Town Hall is one of the town's oldest buildings; medicines have been doled out there since 1322.

The 16th-century Schrödersches Haus, a short stroll from the Town Hall up Weenderstrasse, is the most appealing shop front you're likely to find in all Germany. On the way to the Schrödershes Haus, you'll pass the ancient student tavern Zum Szültenbürger. Another tavern, Zum Altdeutschen, is around the corner on Prinzenstrasse (the street is named after three English princes, sons of King George III, who lived in a house here during their studies in Göttingen from 1786 to 1791). Don't be shy about stepping into either of these taverns or any of the others that catch your eye; the food and drink are inexpensive, and the welcome is invariably warm and friendly.

The **Sparkasse bank building** was once the Hotel zur Krone, where King George V of Hannover had his headquarters in June 1866 before setting off for the fateful battle of Langensalza, where he lost his kingdom to Bismarck's warrior-state of Prussia, soon to preside aggressively over the newly united Germany. ⊠ *Weenderstr. 13.*

The **Städtisches Museum** (City Museum) is in Göttingen's only noble home, a 16th-century palace. It has an instructive exhibition charting the architectural styles you'll come across in this part of Germany, as well as a valuable collection of antique toys and a reconstructed apothecary's shop. ⊠ *Ritterplan 7–8.* ⊠ *DM 3.* ☉ *Tues.–Fri. 10–5, weekends 10–1.*

Dining and Lodging

$$ ✕ **Historischer Rathskeller.** Here you'll dine in the vaulted underground chambers of Göttingen's 15th-century City Hall, choosing from a traditional menu, with the friendly assistance of chef Jens Bredenbeck. ⊠ *Am Markt 9,* ☎ *0551/56433. AE, DC, MC, V.*

$ ✕ **Zum Schwarzen Bären.** The "Black Bear" is one of Göttingen's old-
★ est tavern-restaurants, a 16th-century half-timbered house that breathes history and hospitality. The specialty of the house is *Bärenpfanne,* a generous portion of local meats. ⊠ *Kurzestr. 12,* ☎ *0551/58284. AE, DC, MC, V. Closed Mon. No dinner Sun.*

$$$$ ⊞ **Gebhards Hotel.** Though just across a busy road from the train station, this hotel stands aloof and unflurried on its own grounds, a sensitively modernized 18th-century building that's something of a local landmark. Guests are mostly visitors to the university, and consequently the majority of the hotel rooms are singles. ⊠ *Goethe-Allee 22-33, D–37073,* ☎ *0551/49680,* FAX *0551/496–8110. 62 rooms with bath or shower. Restaurant, indoor pool, sauna, exercise room. AE, DC, MC, V.*

$–$$ ⊞ **Hotel Beckman.** The Beckman family runs this pleasant and homey hotel with friendly efficiency. Rooms are furnished in modern style, with light woods and pastel shades. The family takes particular pride in the hotel garden, a quiet and lush retreat in all seasons. The hotel is 5 kilometers (3 miles) out of town, with good bus links to downtown. ⊠ *Ulrideshuser-Str. 44, Göttingen-Nikolausberg, D–37077,* ☎ *0551/209080,* FAX *0551/2090888. 27 rooms, 21 with bath or shower. Restaurant, café, sauna. AE, DC, MC, V.*

Nightlife and the Arts

The ancient student taverns that crowd the downtown area are the focus of local nightlife, but for something more sophisticated try the **Blue Note** jazz club and disco (⊠ Wilhelmspl. 3) or the Latin-style **Caribe** (⊠ Johannisstr. 33).

Göttingen's symphony orchestra presents about 20 concerts a year. In addition, the city has a nationally known boys choir and an annual Handel music festival in June. Call (☎ 0551/56700) for program details and tickets for all three.

Göttingen's two theater companies—the 100-year-old **Deutsches Theater** and the **Junge Theater**—are known throughout Germany; call (☎ 0551/496–911) for program details and tickets.

Not far from the city, near Gleichen, outdoor performances of Grimm fairy tales are presented on a woodland stage at Bremke on certain summer weekends. Check with the local tourist office for dates.

En Route To pick up the Fairy-Tale Road where it joins the scenic Weser Valley Road, return to Münden and head north on B–64. This is a beautiful drive. However, you do need your own car because there are no buses that connect Münden with Hameln, and the train takes another route from the one described below.

Sababurg

★ **9** *10 km (6 mi) north of Göttingen.*

In the village of Veckerhagen, take a left turn to the signposted Sababurg. You're now on the road to Dornröschen's, or Sleeping Beauty's Castle. It stands just as the Grimm fairy tale tells us it did, in the depths of the densely wooded Reinhardswald, still inhabited by deer and wild boar. Sababurg was built as a 14th-century fortress, by the archbishop of Mainz, to protect a nearby pilgrimage chapel. Later it was destroyed and then rebuilt as a turreted hunting lodge for the counts of Hessen. Today it is a fairly fancy hotel. Even if you don't stay the night, a drive to the castle will be a highlight of any stay in this region.

Dining and Lodging

$$$$ ✕▥ **Dornröschenschloss Sababurg.** The medieval fortress thought to
★   have been the inspiration for the Grimm brothers' tale of *The Sleeping Beauty* is now a small luxury hotel snugly set in the castle walls and surrounded by the oaks of the Reinhardswald. Concerts and plays are held on the grounds in summer. The castle was built in 1334, but many of the palatial improvements came during the 17th and 18th centuries. However, it was not until 1960 that it became a hotel. Since that time the Koseck family has been enthusiastically welcoming visitors and showing them the magic of the area. The restaurant serves a fine haunch of venison in the autumn, but the fresh trout with a Riesling-based sauce in the spring is equally satisfying. ✉ *Hofgeismar, D–34369,* ☎ *05671/8080,* ☏ *05671/808–200. 18 rooms with bath. Restaurant. AE, DC, MC, V. Closed mid-Jan.–mid-Feb.*

En Route From the castle, follow another road back to the Weser Valley riverside village of Oberweser. Turn left and take B–80 north. This is one of Germany's most haunting river roads, where the fast-flowing Weser snakes between green banks that hardly show where land ends and water begins. Standing sentinel along the banks are superb little towns, whose half-timbered architecture has given rise to the expression "Weser Renaissance." You'll see examples of that style wherever you travel in this area, from Münden to Hameln (where it reaches a spectacular climax).

Bad Karlshafen

10 *42 km (25 mi) north of Münden, 55 km (33 mi) northwest of Göttingen.*

From the inland harbor of the pretty little spa of Bad Karlshafen German troops of the state of Waldeck embarked to join the English Hannoverian forces in the American War of Independence. George III, the English king who presided over the loss of the American colonies, was a Hannoverian—his grandfather, George I, spoke only German when he became king of England in 1715—and although George III sent no Hannoverian forces to America, several neighboring German states did. Flat barges took the troops down the Weser to Bremen, where they were shipped across the North Sea for the long voyage west. Many American families can trace their heritage to this small spa and the surrounding countryside.

Viewed from one of the benches overlooking the harbor, there's scarcely a building that's not in the imposing Baroque style. The grand Rathaus behind you is the best example. Bad Karlshafen stands out in solitary splendor amid the homely Weser Renaissance style of other riverside towns.

Dining and Lodging

$ ✕ **Gaststätte-Hotel Weserdampfschiff.** You can step right from the deck of a Weser pleasure boat into the welcoming garden of this popular hotel-tavern. Fish from the river land straight in the tavern's frying pan. There are 13 cozy rooms, most of which have river views. ⊠ *Weserstr. 25,* ☎ *05672/2425. No credit cards. Closed Mon.*

$$–$$$$ ✕🏨 **Romantik Hotel Menzhausen.** The half-timbered exterior of this 16th-century establishment in the small town of Uslar, 12 kilometers (7 miles) east of the Weser River, is matched by the cozy interior of its comfortable, well-appointed restaurant. The 400-year-old wine cellar harbors outstanding vintages, served with reverence at excellent prices. The hotel itself has 41 pleasant rooms, many with antiques. Ask for one in the historic Mauerschlösschen if you're looking for the romance in Romantik. ⊠ *Langestr. 12, D–37170,* ☎ *05571/2051,* FAX *05571/5820. 41 rooms. Restaurant, indoor pool, sauna. AE, DC, MC, V.*

$ ✕🏨 **Hessicher Hof.** In the heart of town, the inn started as a tavern for the locals. There's still a bar, but the building has been extended and renovated, with the addition of several comfortably furnished bedrooms, all of them with showers. A few also have a small balcony. The restaurant serves good, hearty fare. Breakfast is included in the room price, or you may request half-pension. ⊠ *Carlstr. 13–15, D–34385,* ☎ *05672/1059,* FAX *05672/2515. 18 rooms with bath or shower. Restaurant, bar. AE, MC, V.*

Shopping

There are some excellent small, privately run **potteries** and **glassworks** in the area. In Bad Karlshafen you can watch the craftspeople at work in a studio in the Baroque Rathaus and buy goods directly from them.

Höxter

⓫ *24 km (14 mi) north of Bad Karlshafen.*

Stop at Höxter to admire its Rathaus (Town Hall), a perfect example of the Weser Renaissance style, combining three half-timbered stories with a romantically crooked tower.

OFF THE BEATEN PATH   **REICHSABTAEI CORVEY (THE IMPERIAL ABBEY OF CORVEY) –** Across the river and 3 kilometers (2 miles) east of Höxter lies this abbey, optimistically described by some as the "Rome of the North" and idyllically set between the wooded heights of the Solling region and the Weser. The 1,100-year history of the abbey is tightly bound up with the early development of German nationhood. It was chosen as the site of several sessions of the German Imperial Council during the 12th century, and in the 9th-century abbey church you can step into the lodge used by several Holy Roman emperors. The composer of the German national anthem, Hoffmann von Fallersleben, worked for 14 years in the abbey's vast library, where, in the 16th century, the first six volumes of the annals of the Roman historian Tacitus were discovered. 🎟 *DM 4.* ☉ *Apr.–Oct., daily 9–6.*

Dining

$$$ ✕ **Schloss Bevern.** You'll dine like a baron here, within the honey-color
★   old walls of a Renaissance castle in the little town of Bevern, just north of Höxter and Corvey. In the enchanting inner courtyard, a soli-

tary dome-top, half-timbered tower stands sentinel over a 17th-century fountain. This romantic mood carries into the stylish restaurant, where you'll dine on such traditional country dishes as roast pheasant or partridge at tables with glistening silverware and finely cut glassware. ✉ *Am Schoss,* ☎ *05531/8783. Reservations essential. AE, DC, MC, V. Closed Mon. No lunch Tues.*

$$ ✗ **Enzianhütte.** The Weser River winds lazily below this terraced restaurant. If it's too chilly to sit outside, there's a cozy room with an open fireplace. Some traditional dishes are cooked on the grill over the fire. ✉ *Am Ochsenbrink 2,* ☎ *05535/8710. AE, DC, MC. Closed Wed.*

$$ ✗ **Schlossrestaurant Corvey.** The attractions of Corvey Abbey include
★ an excellent restaurant. You can dine outside under centuries-old trees in summer and inside before a blazing hearth in winter (although the restaurant is open only on Sundays from November until Easter). The lunchtime menu is a particularly good value. ✉ *Reichsabtei Corvey,* ☎ *05271/8323. AE, MC.*

Shopping

Germany's oldest **porcelain** factory is at Fürstenberg, 8 kilometers (5 miles) south of Höxter, in a Baroque castle high above the Weser River. The crowned gothic letter *F*, which serves as its trademark is world famous. You'll find Fürstenberg porcelain in shops throughout the area and in such towns as Bad Karlshafen and Höxter. By far the most satisfying way of starting a Fürstenberg collection, or adding to it, is to make the journey up to the 18th-century castle, where production first began in 1747, and buy directly from the manufacturer. Fürstenberg and most dealers will take care of shipping arrangements and any tax refunds. ☉ *Factory and showrooms Tues.–Sat. 9–5, Sun. 10–5.*

Bodenwerder

🄬 *34 km (21 mi) north of Höxter.*

The charming Weser town of Bodenwerder plays a central role in German popular literature. It is the birthplace of the Lügenbaron (Lying Baron) von Münchhausen, who used to entertain friends with a pipe of rich Bremen tobacco, a glass of good wine, and stories of his exploits as a captain in wars against the Turks and the Russians. They were preposterous, unbelievable stories that one of his friends, on the run from the German authorities, had published in England. From England they found their way back to Germany, and the baron became a laughingstock—as well as a famous figure in German literary history. The imposing family home in which he grew up is now the Rathaus; one room has been turned into the **Münchhausen Museum,** crammed with mementos of the baron's adventurous life. Included is a cannonball on which the baron claimed to have ridden into orbit during the Russo-Turkish War of 1736, flying around Earth to reach the moon, or so he insisted. In front of the house you'll see a statue of Münchhausen in a scene from one of his most outlandish stories. He's riding half a horse; the other half, said Münchhausen, was chopped off by a castle portcullis, but he rode on without noticing the accident.

Dining and Lodging

$$ ✗ **Enzianhütte.** The Weser River winds lazily below this terraced restaurant. If it's too chilly to sit outside, there's a cozy room with an open fireplace. Some traditional dishes are cooked on the grill over the fire. ✉ *Am Ochsenbrink 2,* ☎ *05535/8710. AE, DC, MC. Closed Wed.*

$$ ✗🖫 **Hotel Deutsches Haus.** The fine half-timbered facade of this solidly comfortable country hotel vies for attention with the nearby

former home of Baron Münchhausen, now Bodenwerder's Town Hall.
There's a lot of wood inside, too, with original beams and oak paneling adding to the rural feel. The town park is outside the front door,
and the Weser River is a short walk away. ⊠ *Münchhausenpl. 4,
D–37619*, ☎ *05533/3925*, 🖷 *05533/4113. 42 rooms with bath or
shower. Restaurant, bowling, recreation room. AE, MC, V. Closed Jan.*

Hameln

★ ⑬   *24 km (15 mi) north of Bodenwerder, 47 km (28 mi) southwest of Hannover.*

Hameln (or Hamelin, in English) needs no introduction because children the world over are familiar with the story of the Pied Piper who
spirited away all the young people of the town. The story of the Pied
Piper of Hameln had its origins in an actual event. During the 13th century an inordinate number of young men in Hameln were being con-
scripted to fight in an unpopular war in Bohemia and Moravia. Citizens
became convinced they were being spirited away by the Devil playing
his flute. In later stories the Devil was changed to a gaudily attired rat
catcher who rid the town of rodents by playing seductive melodies on
his flute so that the rodents followed him willingly, waltzing their way
right into the Weser. However, when the town defaulted on its contract
and refused to pay the piper, he settled the score by playing his merry
tune to lead Hameln's children on the same route. As the children
reached the river, the Grimms wrote, "They disappeared forever."

This tale is included in the Grimms' other book, *German Legends*. A
variation of the Pied Piper tale appears on the plaque of a 17th-century
house at 28 Osterstrasse, fixing the date of the event as June 26, 1284.
In more recent times, the Pied Piper tale has been immortalized via an
ultramodern sculpture group set above a reflecting pool in a pedestrian
area of town. Today you'll find Hameln tied to its Pied Piper myth every
bit as much as the little Bavarian village of Oberammergau is dominated
by its Passion Play. There are even rat-shape pastries in the windows of
Hameln's bakeries. The house that bears the Pied Piper plaque—a brilliant example of Weser Renaissance—is known as the Rattenfängerhaus
(rat catcher's house), despite being built some time after the sorry story
is said to have occurred. To this day no music is played and no revelry
of any kind takes place on the street that runs beside the house, where
the children of Hameln are said to have followed the Piper.

The **Rattenfängerhaus** (now a restaurant) is one of several beautiful
half-timbered houses on the central Osterstrasse. At one end of the street
is the **Hochzeitshaus** (Wedding House), occupied by city government
offices. Every Sunday from mid-May to mid-September the story of
the Pied Piper is played out at noon by local actors and children on
the terrace in front of the building. The half-hour performance is free;
get there early to ensure a good place. The carillon of the Hochzeitshaus plays a "Pied Piper song" every day at 8:35 and 11:05, and mechanical figures enacting the story appear on the west gable of the
building at 1:05, 3:35, and 5:35.

NEED A
BREAK?   Just up the street is the historic old hostelry **Zur Krone** (⊠ Osterstr. 30,
☎ 05151/9070). If it's a sunny day, take a seat on the terrace in front
of the hotel's half-timbered facade. If it's cool, there's a warm welcome
inside. In the evening, in the middle of Old Town, the popular wood-
beamed watering hole is **Die Alte Post** (⊠ Hummlstr. 23, ☎ 05151/
43444), where beer flows freely and baguette sandwiches are served.

Dining and Lodging

$-$$ ✕ **Rattenfängerhaus.** This is Hameln's most famous building, reput-
★ edly the place where the Pied Piper stayed during his rat-removing as-
signment. Rats are all over the menu, from "rat-remover cocktail" to
a "rat-tail dessert." But don't be put off: The traditional dishes are excellent, and the restaurant is guaranteed rodent free. ⊠ *Osterstr. 28,*
☎ *05151/3888. AE, DC, MC, V.*

$$$-$$$$ 🏠 **Hotel zur Kröne.** If you fancy a splurge, ask for the split-level suite.
★ With prices starting at DM 380 a night, it's an expensive but delight-
ful luxury. The building dates from 1645 and is a half-timbered mar-
vel. Avoid the modern annex, however; it lacks all charm. ⊠ *Osterstr.*
30, D–31785, ☎ *05151/9070,* 🖷 *05151/907–217. 29 rooms, 5 apart-*
ments, all with bath or shower. Restaurant. AE, DC, MC, V.

$$ 🏠 **Hotel zur Börse.** A long-established, family-run property in the Old
Town, this hotel offers comfortable accommodations and friendly ser-
vice. Bathrooms were all lavishly renovated in 1996. The hotel's attractive winter garden is a pleasant retreat. ⊠ *Osterstr. 41 (entrance*
on Kopmanshof), D–31785, ☎ *05151/7080,* 🖷 *05151/25485. 34*
rooms with bath or shower. Restaurant, pub. AE, DC, MC, V. Closed
Dec. 25, Jan. 1.

Nightlife and the Arts

Hameln's main theater, the **Weserbergland Festhalle** (⊠ Rathauspl.,
☎ 0515/3747), has a regular program of drama, concerts, opera, and
ballet from September through June.

Hannover

⓮ *48 km (27 mi) northeast of Hameln.*

Hannover, a city of commerce and culture, is way off the Fairy-Tale
Road but exerts a magnetic pull on visitors to this region of Germany.
Hannover is a successful example of how commercial and cultural in-
terests merge to the benefit of both. It is Germany's major trade-fair
center and at the same time an exemplary patron of the arts, with leading museums, an opera house of international repute, and the finest
Baroque park in the country. From 1714 until 1837 rulers of the
House of Hannover also sat on the British throne, as kings George I–V.
King George III presided over the loss of the American Revolutionary
War, and reminders of that period are to be found in several Hannover
museums. Today there are many more cities and towns named Hanover
in the United States than in Germany—63 of them, all spelled English
style (one *n*), but nonetheless mostly tracing their roots to the German
mother city. It's said that purist German is spoken in Hannover, although
no objective reason for this can be found.

Bomb damage to Hannover in World War II was so devastating that a
proposal to level the ruins and build a new city was seriously considered. The plan was mercifully never adopted, and Hannover arose to become once again a city of beauty and grace. Successive city administrations
encouraged a mix of old and modern, so you'll find startling sculptural
works vying for attention with stately rows of half-timbered houses.
Burgstrasse, with its steel, wind-driven kinetic sculpture, is an example.

In 1994 the city organized an unusual international competition for
bus-stop design, and the nine best entrants have remained as an integral part of the Hannover street scene. It's fun to pick out the winning
bus stops; one of them, at Braunschweiger Platz, is the work of the American architect Frank O. Gehry, designer of the world's largest concert

hall, in Los Angeles. Hannoverians have dubbed his bus stop "Frank's Dino" because of its humpbacked appearance. The British designer Jasper Morrison is also represented, with a bus stop at Aegidientorplatz that was highly praised for its "British understatement and lack of fussy decoration."

Schottisches Kreuz (Scottish Cross) by sculptor British Henry Moore, opposite the City Hall steps, is one of several outstanding and monumental sculptures by international masters that decorate the urban landscape.

The central point of Hannover's cultural life is its **Opernhaus** (⊠ Opernpl. 1, ☎ 0511/168–6161), which ranks as one of Germany's most beautiful 19th-century classical theaters; it was built in 1845–52 as a royal opera house and is still the setting of some truly regal productions.

The Gothic **Marktkirche St. Georg und St. Jacobus** (Market Church of Sts. George and James) dominates Hannover's central market square. It has a splendid Gothic carved altar and fine stained glass. Next to the Market Church is Hannover's first City Hall, the **Altes Rathaus,** dating from the 14th century and a notable example of Hannoverian brick architecture.

The former Hannoverian royal palace, the **Leineschloss,** stands above the River Leine and is now the seat of the Lower Saxony State Parliament. Call the tourist office (☎ 0511/301–410) if you'd like to visit. On the other side of the road from Leineschloss, facing Leinstrasse, is a smaller palace where King George V lived from 1851 to 1862. Next door is the vast bulk of the new **Rathaus** (City Hall), built at the start of the century in Wilhelmine style at a time when pomp and circumstance were important ingredients of heavy German bureaucracy.

Hannover has two of Germany's leading art museums. The **Niedersächsisches Landesmuseum** has some priceless early art, including work by Tilman Riemenschneider, Veit Stoss, Hans Holbein the Younger, and Lucas Cranach. ⊠ *Am Maschpark 5,* ☎ *0511/98075.* ☞ *Free (with tourist office's Hannover Card).* ☉ *Tues.–Sun. 10–5, Thurs. 10–7.*

The **Sprengel Museum** has one of Germany's leading collections of modern art, with important works by Max Beckmann, Max Ernst, Paul Klee, Emil Nolde, and Pablo Picasso. ⊠ *Kurt-Schwitters-Pl.,* ☎ *0511/168–3875.* ☞ *Free (with tourist office's Hannover Card).* ☉ *Tues. 10–10, Wed.–Sun. 10–6.*

Like Hamburg, Hannover has an inland lake that is a favorite local recreation area. In summer you can swim in its warm waters or hire a sailboat.

NEED A
BREAK?
> The **Strandbad café** (⊠ Karl-Thiele-Weg 28) on the edge of Hannover's lake is just the place for a reviving cup of coffee or something more substantial. For more impressive surroundings, try the restaurant in the casino on the north shore. It can be counted on for lunch, afternoon coffee, or dinner.

★ Hannover's showpiece—the gardens of the former royal summer residence at **Herrenhausen**—is outside the city center, a short ride on Tramline 5 or 16. The magnificent palace built there in the late 17th century by the Hannoverian ruler Herzog Johann Friedrich was ruined in wartime bombing and never rebuilt. But the Baroque park—unmatchable in Germany—was restored in all its formal precision, with the geometric pattern of walks, gardens, and copses framed by a placid moat. From Easter until October fountains play for a few hours daily and add their own element of Baroque grace (weekdays 11–noon and

3–4, weekends 10–noon and 3–5). An 18th-century residence at the edge of the park is now a museum, the **Fürstenhaus Herrenhausen-Museum,** affording fascinating insight into the Hannoverian court life and its links with England. ✉ *Herrenhausen Park:* 🎫 *Free;* ⊙ *Daily 8– 4:30. Fürstenhaus Herrenhausen-Museum:* ✉ *Alte Herrenhäuser Str. 14,* ☎ *0511/750–947;* 🎫 *DM 3.50;* ⊙ *Tues.–Sun. 10–5.*

Dining and Lodging

$–$$ ✕ **Grapenkieker.** An ancient pot steams in the aromatic farmhouse-style kitchen of the half-timbered Grapenkieker, and the hearty hot pots it produces form the basis of the menu. Proprietors Gabriele and Karl-Heinz Wolf are locally famous for their flair in the kitchen and the warm welcome they give their guests. The restaurant is 5 kilometers (3 miles) from the city center, in the Isernhagen District, but it's well worth seeking out. ✉ *Hauptstr. 56, Isernhagen,* ☎ *05139/88068. AE, DC, MC.* ⊙ *Tues.–Sat. evenings only.*

$$$–$$$$ ✕⊞ **Hotel Benther Berg.** This large country house hotel-cum-modern extension sits amid parkland and woods on the southern edge of Hannover, in the Ronneberg-Benthe District. Rooms are large and furnished mostly in modern dark woods and pastel shades. The restaurant attracts Hannover regulars who value its international cuisine. ✉ *Vogelsangstr. 18, Ronneberg-Benthe, D-30457,* ☎ *05108/64060,* 🄵🄰🄷 *05108/640–650. 65 rooms, 2 suites with bath. Restaurant, café, indoor pool, sauna. AE, DC, MC, V.*

$$–$$$ ✕⊞ **Hotel Körner.** The modern Körner has a traditional, almost old-fashioned feel about it, probably created by the friendly and personal service. Rooms are comfortably furnished in light veneers and pastel shades. The small courtyard and terrace, with their cooling fountain, are ideal for an alfresco summer breakfast. The Lüzower Jäger restaurant is decorated with memorabilia from the Hannoverian wars of liberation, and the menu is a harmonious blend of French cuisine and Lower Saxony specialties. ✉ *Körnerstr. 24–25, D-30159,* ☎ *0511/16360,* 🄵🄰🄷 *0511/18048. 75 rooms with bath. Restaurant, indoor pool, exercise room. AE, DC, MC, V.*

Nightlife and the Arts

Hannover has a very elegant **casino** (✉ Am Maschsee). It's open from 3 PM.

Hannover's **opera company** is internationally known, with productions staged in one of Germany's finest 19th-century classical opera houses. Call (☎ 0511/368–1711) for program details and tickets.

Shopping

Hannover has what it claims is Germany's oldest **flea market**—certainly one of the largest and most interesting. It's held every Saturday on the banks of the River Leine (Am Hohen Ufer) from 7 to 4. The colorful sculptures by Niki de St. Phalle you'll see on the opposite bank (Am Leibnitzufer) are not for sale—they were commissioned by the city, which then had to prevent them from being added to the flea-market junk. Artistic standards prevailed, and the Niki de St. Phalle sculptures (huge maternal "nanas") are now an indispensable part of the city landscape.

En Route The influences that shaped the lives and work of the Grimm brothers weaken north of Hameln and Hannover, but the Fairy-Tale Road continues as far as Bremen. You can get there in less than an hour on the A–27 autobahn or return to Hameln and follow the Weser as it breaks free of the Wesergebirge uplands at Porta Westfalica and flows in an idle, meandering course through the north German plains to the sea.

Bremen

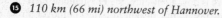

⑮   *110 km (66 mi) northwest of Hannover.*

Bremen is Germany's oldest and second-largest port—only Hamburg is bigger—and it has close historical seafaring ties with North America. Together with Lübeck and Hamburg, Bremen was an early member of the Hanseatic League, and its rivalry with the larger port on the Elbe is still tangible. Though Hamburg may still claim its historical title as Germany's "door to the world," Bremen likes to boast: "But we have the key."

Bremen is also central to the delightful fable of the Bremer Stadtmusikanten, or Bremen Town Musicians, a rooster, cat, dog, and donkey quartet that came to Bremen to seek its fortune. You'll find statues of this group in various parts of the city, the most famous being a handsome bronze of the four, each perched on the back of another to form a pyramid of sorts. This statue stands alongside the northwest corner of the Rathaus on one of Europe's most impressive market squares, bordered by the Rathaus, the imposing 900-year-old Gothic cathedral (St. Petri Dom), a 16th-century guild hall, and a modern glass-and-steel state parliament building, with a high wall of gabled town houses as backdrop. On the square stands the famous stone statue of the knight Roland, erected in 1400. Three times larger than life, the statue serves as Bremen's shrine, good-luck piece, and symbol of freedom and independence.

Charlemagne established a diocese here during the 9th century, and a 15th-century statue of him, together with seven princes, adorns the ancient **Rathaus** (City Hall), a Gothic building that acquired a Renaissance facade during the early 17th century. The two styles combine harmoniously in the magnificent beamed banquet hall. Hanging on the wall are painted scenes from Bremen's 1,200-year history, along with model galleons and sailing ships, vivid reminders of the importance of such vessels in the story of the seafaring city. In its massive vaulted cellars is further evidence of the riches accumulated by Bremen in its busiest years: barrels of fine 17th-century Rhine wine.

The **Übersee Museum** has a unique collection of items tracing the histories and cultures of the many peoples with whom the Bremen traders came into contact. One section is devoted to North America. ⊠ *Bahnhofspl. 13,* ☎ *0421/361–9203.* ▣ *DM 4.* ☉ *Tues.–Sun. 10–6.*

Don't leave Bremen without strolling down **Böttcherstrasse,** at one time inhabited by coopers, or barrel makers. Between 1924 and 1931 their houses were torn down and reconstructed in a style once historically sensitive and modern, by Bremen coffee millionaire Ludwig Roselius. (He was the inventor of decaffeinated coffee and held the patent for many years; Sanka was its brand name in the United States.) Many of the restored houses are used as galleries for local artists. At one end of Böttcherstrasse is the **Roselius-Haus,** a 14th-century building that is now a museum showcasing German and Dutch paintings, as well as wood carvings, furniture, textiles, and numerous examples of decorative arts from the 12th through the 18th centuries. Notice also the arch of Meissen bells at the rooftop. These chime daily at noon, 3, and 6. ⊠ *Böttcherstr. 8–10,* ☎ *0421/336–5077.* ▣ *DM 8.* ☉ *Tues.–Sun. 11–5.*

Walk, too, through the idyllic **Schnoorviertel,** a jumble of houses, taverns, and shops once occupied or frequented by fishermen and tradespeople. This is Bremen's oldest district, dating back to the 15th and 16th centuries. Over the last decade the area has become quite fashionable among artists and craftspeople, who have restored the tiny one-up-one-down cottages to serve as galleries and workshops. Other buildings have been converted into small cafés and pubs that attract locals and visitors alike.

16 Forty-eight kilometers (30 miles) upriver, at **Bremerhaven**, is the country's largest and most fascinating maritime museum, the **Deutsches Schiffahrtsmuseum**, with a harbor containing seven old trading ships. ✉ *Von-Renzelen-Str.,* ☎ *0471/482–070.* 🎟 *DM 5.* 🕐 *Tues.–Sun. 10–6.*

Dining and Lodging

$$$$ ✕ **Park Restaurant.** Chef Bernhard Stumpf, formerly of the renowned
★ Restaurant Français in Frankfurt, has transformed the Park into one of the finest dining establishments in Germany. In the Park Hotel Bremen (☞ *below*), it is somewhat small for a hotel restaurant, but the floor-to-ceiling windows and lacquered ceiling open up the room. Stunning in yellow, black, and cream, the dining room is decorated with shimmering crystal chandeliers, classical molding, marble urns, and Louis XVI chairs, all of which add to the sense of occasion. Chef Stumpf adds a dash of fantasy to his classic French dishes, which may include broccoli flan with autumn vegetables atop a pine-nut and celery sauce, sautéed fillet of beef with ox-marrow ragout, and cottage-cheese soufflé in fig-honey sauce. ✉ *Im Bürgerpark,* ☎ *0421/34080. Reservations essential. Jacket and tie. AE, DC, MC, V.*

$$ ✕ **Comturai.** The vaults of Bremen's ancient Church of the Holy Spirit (Heiliggeistkirche) were secularized some time ago, becoming a beer cellar and restaurant, where the cuisine is devilishly good if not exactly heavenly. Special medieval banquet menus are served to groups of more than 10, but there's often a place for a lone diner—and it's a great way to meet the locals. ✉ *Ostertorstr. 30-32,* ☎ *0421/325050. AE, MC, V.*

$$ ✕ **Grashoff's Bistro.** Locals say this is Bremen's number one lunchtime
★ bistro. You dine French style, at closely packed tables in a room whose walls are smothered with interesting old prints and photographs. The menu also has a French touch, with an accent on fish fresh from Bremen's market. ✉ *Contrescarpe 80,* ☎ *0421/14740. DC, V. Closed Sun. and weekday evenings.*

$$ ✕ **Ratskeller.** Said to be Germany's oldest and most renowned
★ Ratskeller restaurant, this one specializes in solid, typical northern German fare, including the finest poultry and the freshest seafood, prepared in ingenious ways. However, it's no place for beer drinkers. Shortly after the restaurant opened in 1408, the city fathers decreed that only wine could be served there, and the ban on beer still exists. You'll dine in a cellar lined with wine casks, including an 18th-century barrel that could house a family of wine drinkers. Connoisseurs have 600 labels from which to choose. ✉ *Am Markt,* ☎ *0421/321–676. AE, DC, MC, V.*

$$$$ ✕🏨 **Park Hotel Bremen.** The service doesn't get any more gracious than
★ at this grand hotel by a lake in the 800-acre Bürgerpark, near the main train station. Aside from the impressive central dome, the architecture—'50s international style—is banal. What does shine is the ever-accommodating staff, who'll be glad to provide you with suitable jogging clothes for the 15-minute run to the historic center or arrange a complimentary limousine into town, if you'd rather have a ride. No one would blame you, however, if you wanted to stay put in such luxurious digs. The guest rooms differ radically in decor—Moorish, Japanese, and Italian Modern are just some of the themes (a Roman-style Pompeian suite has just been added)—and the bathrooms are lined with 12 different kinds of marble. The rooms in the wing, added in the '70s, are not as large as those in the main building. ✉ *Im Bürgerpark, D–28195,* ☎ *0421/34080; for reservations in the U.S., 800/223–6800;* FAX *0421/3408–*

602. 138 rooms with bath, 13 suites. 2 restaurants, bar, café, beauty salon, massage, bicycles. AE, DC, MC, V.

$$$–$$$$ ✕⊡ **Mercure Columbus.** Elegantly renovated and now under the French management of the Accor group, this hotel is conveniently adjacent to the train station and only a short stroll from the Old Town attractions. An elegant restaurant was recently opened. The decor is modern, and many of the rooms are spacious. ⊠ *Bahnhofpl. 5–7, D–28195,* ☎ *0421/30120,* FAX *0421/15369. 143 rooms and 5 suites. Restaurant, bar, sauna. AE, DC, MC, V.*

$$–$$$ ✕⊡ **Hotel Landhaus Louisenthal.** American visitors particularly like this
★ family-run, half-timbered country-house hotel on the outskirts of Bremen—30% of its guests are from the United States. The 150-year-old building has old-world charm and a caring management. Bathrooms were recently renovated and are an additional touch of luxury. ⊠ *Leher Heerstr. 105, D–28195,* ☎ *0421/232–076,* FAX *0421/236–716. 58 rooms and 2 apartments, all with bath or shower. Restaurant, sauna. AE, DC, MC, V.*

Nightlife and the Arts

Bremen may be Germany's oldest seaport, but it can't match Hamburg for racy nightlife. Nevertheless, the streets around the central Marktplatz and in the historic Schnoor District are filled with atmospheric taverns and bars of various kinds.

Bremerhaven has a casino (⊠ Theodor–Heuss–Pl. 3, ☎ 0471/413–641) that attract gamblers from even Bremen and Hamburg. It's open daily from midday.

Bremen has a Philharmonic orchestra of national stature, which plays regularly throughout the year at the city's concert hall; call for program details and tickets (☎ 0421/361–2615).

The city also has three theaters, which regularly stage classical and modern dramas, comedies, and musical comedies: the **Schauspielhaus** (⊠ Goethepl. 1, ☎ 0421/36530), the **Concordia,** and the **Musiktheater.** Call (☎ 0421/365–3333) for program details and tickets.

Shopping

In Bremen bargain hunters should head to the idyllic Schnoorvier. Bremerhaven has one of Germany's oldest established shoemakers, **Leder-Koopmann** (⊠ Georgstr. 56, ☎ 0471/302–829), where you can buy first-class footwear and all kinds of leather goods, made with the kind of care that has kept the firm in business since 1898.

THE FAIRY-TALE ROAD A TO Z

Arriving and Departing

By Bus

Europabus, with services from Scandinavia through Germany to the Balkans, calls at Bremen, Kassel, and Göttigen. For information, timetables, and reservations, contact **Deutsche Touring GmbH.** (⊠ Am Römerhof 17, D–60486 Frankfurt/Main 90, ☎ 069/79030).

By Car

Important north–south and east–west autobahns crisscross the region, affording easy and speedy access from Hamburg (via the A–7), Frankfurt (the A–66) and Berlin (the A–2).

By Plane
Frankfurt, Hannover, and Hamburg are the closest international airports to the area. Frankfurt is less than half an hour from Hanau, the start of the route. Hamburg is less than an hour from Bremen, the route's end.

By Train
Hannover is an important railroad junction, served by InterCity and InterCity Express (ICE) trains and on the Hamburg–Munich and Frankfurt–Berlin rail routes.

Getting Around

By Boat
From May through September two companies—**Oberweser-Dampf-schiffahrt** and **Weisse Flotte Warnecke,** each with a fleet of six ships, operate daily on the Weser River between Hameln, Bodenwerder, and Bad Karlshafen. On Monday, Wednesday, Friday, and Saturday, the Oberweser-Dampfschiffahrt boats sail as far as Münden, and on Tuesday, Thursday, Saturday, and Sunday, from Münden to Hameln. On the days when there is no service between Bad Karlshafen and Münden, a bus service ferries boat passengers between the two towns. For further information and bookings, contact **Oberweser-Dampfschiffahrt** (✉ Inselstr. 3, D–31787 Hameln, ☎ 05151/22016) or **Weisse Flotte Warnecke** (✉ Hauptstr. 39, D–31785 Hameln, ☎ 05151/3975; ✉ Weserstr., D–37619 Bodenwerder, ☎ 05533/4864).

By Bus
Frankfurt, Kassel, Göttingen, and Bremen all have city bus services that extend into the countryside along the Fairy-Tale Road.

By Car
Germany's autobahn network penetrates deep into the area. Hanau, Fulda, Kassel, Göttingen, and Bremen are all served directly by autobahns. The Fairy-Tale Road itself incorporates one of Germany's loveliest scenic drives, the Wesertalstrasse, or Weser Valley Road, from Münden in the south to Hameln in the north.

By Train
Fulda, Kassel, and Göttingen are served by Germany's ultramodern InterCity Express line, which reduces traveling time between Frankfurt and Hamburg to three hours and 45 minutes. All other centers and most of the smaller towns are connected by rail, supplemented by railroad buses.

Contacts and Resources

Car Rentals
Avis: ✉ Kirchbachstr. 200, ☎ 0421/211–077, **Bremen;** ✉ Schmidtstr. 39, ☎ 069/730–111, **Frankfurt;** ✉ Drehbahn 15–25, ☎ 040/341–651, **Hamburg;** ✉ Am Klagesmarkt 22, ☎ 0511/14441, **Hannover.**

Hertz: ✉ Neuenland Airport, ☎ 0421/555–350, **Bremen;** ✉ Gutleutstr. 87, ☎ 069/2425–2627, **Frankfurt;** ✉ Kirchenallee 34–36, ☎ 040/280–1201, **Hamburg;** ✉ Schulenburger Landstr. 146, ☎ 0511/635–092, **Hannover.**

Sixt-Budget: ✉ Duckwitzstr. 55, ☎ 0421/510–055, **Bremen;** ✉ Am Römerhof, ☎ 069/705–018, and Frankfurt Airport, ☎ 069/697–0070, **Frankfurt;** ✉ Schulenburger Landstr. 66, ☎ 0511/352–1213, **Hannover;** ✉ Leipzigerstr. 56, ☎ 0561/54093, **Kassel.**

Emergencies
Police: ☎ 110. **Fire and emergency medical aid:** ☎ 112.

Guided Tours

Several towns on the Fairy-Tale Road offer guided tours. Fulda has a 2 PM daily tour of the Old Town, starting at the Stadtschloss. Göttingen shows visitors around April–October weekdays at 11 and on weekends at 2 (starting from the Old Town Hall). Hameln has daily tours May–September Monday–Saturday at 3 and Sunday at 10, beginning from the tourist office (⊠ Diesterallee 3). The major sights of Hannover are strung together on a tourist trail marked by red signs. The "Red Thread" is also clearly marked on a map of the city obtainable from the Tourist Information Office (⊠ Ernst August-Pl. 2, ☎ 0511/301420). Guided bus tours of Hannover start from outside the Tourist Information Office May through September, Monday–Saturday at 1:30 PM; October through April, Saturday only, at 1:30 PM. Guided bus tours of Kassel set off from Königsplatz every Saturday, May–mid-November, at 2 PM, while walking tours start from the Königsplatz steps every Wednesday, May–mid-October, at 11 AM.

The **Oberweser-Dampfschiffahrt Company** and Warnecke's **Weisse Flotte** (White Fleet) operate summer services on the Weser River between Hameln and Münden. Both companies will give you advice on how to combine a boat trip with a tour by bike, bus, or train. The Oberweser-Dampfschiffahrt Company also has a daily excursion from Hameln to the nearby Ohrberg Park and pleasure gardens; on Sunday afternoons it offers a 2½-hour *Kaffeereise* (coffee trip) on the river. From April through October an excursion boat makes a four-hour trip daily up the Fulda River from Kassel. It leaves the Altmarkt Pier at 2 and returns at 6. The trip costs DM 18. In summer the Oberweser-Dampfschiffahrt Company offers Sunday excursions that include a guided tour of Hameln, lunch in an old tavern, a cycle trip down the Weser riverbank to Bodenwerder and a boat ride back—all for DM 55 (including bike rental). Call for details and reservations (☎ 05151/22016).

A variety of enjoyable boat excursions leave from Bremerhaven, ranging from one-hour trips around the harbor to more ambitious cruises along the lower Saxony coast, and costing from DM 12 to DM 34. Call ☎ 0471/415–850 or 0471/477–1500 for information. There's also a daily round-trip flight from the Bremerhaven airport to the fortresslike North Sea island of Helgoland (☎ 0471/77188 for flight details).

Year-round tours of the region are offered by a Hameln company, **Rattenfänger-Reisen** (⊠ Bahnhofstr. 18/20, ☎ 05151/108–484) and by Sonnental–Reise (⊠ Hesslingen 89, Hessische Oldendorf, ☎ 05152/2172). Some local authorities—those in Bad Karlshafen, for example—also organize bus tours. Contact individual tourist offices for details.

Outdoor Activities and Sports

At Schloss Schwöbber, near Hameln, golfers tee off on the castle grounds (☎ 05154/9870).

Contact **Fremdenverkehrsverband Weserbergland-Mittelweser** (D–31785 Hameln, ☎ 05151/202–517) for information.

Contact equestrian centers at Löwensen, near Bad Pyrmont (☎ 05281/10606), and Hameln (☎ 05151/3513). Katrin Graf's Circle K ranch at Steinau-Marborn (☎ 06663/5321) rents horses trained to be ridden western style.

WATER SPORTS

For information on Fulda River trips and canoe rental, call ☎ 0561/22433. **Busch Bootstouristik** (✉ D–34399 Oberweser, ☎ 05574/818) rents canoes from April through October on the Fulda, Weser, and Werra and organizes trips of up to a week on all three rivers. Motorboats can be rented from **Weisse Flotte Warnecke** (☎ 05533/4864) in Bodenwerder.

Visitor Information

Information on the Fairy-Tale Road can be obtained from the **Deutsche Märchenstrasse** (✉ Postfach 102660, D–34117 Kassel, ☎ 0561/707–7140). There are local tourist information offices in the following towns:

Alsfeld: Verkehrsbüro, ✉ Rittergasse 5, D–36304, ☎ 06631/182–165.

Bad Pyrmont: Kur-und-Verkehrsverein, ✉ Arkaden 14, D–31812 ☎ 05281/4627.

Bodenwerder: Städtische Verkehrsamt, ✉ Bruckenstr. 7, D–37619, ☎ 05533/40541.

Bremen: Verkehrsverein, ✉ Hillmannpl. 6, D–28195, ☎ 0421/308–000.

Bremerhaven: Verkehrsamt der Seestadt Bremerhaven, ✉ Van-Ronzelen-Str. 2, D–27568, ☎ 0471/946–4610.

Fulda: Städtische Verkehrsbüro, ✉ Schlossstr. 1, D–36037, ☎ 0661/102–345.

Göttingen: Fremdenverkehrsverein, ✉ Altes Rathaus, D–37073, ☎ 0551/54000.

Hameln: Verkehrsverein, ✉ Deisterallee (am Bürgergarten), D–31785, ☎ 05151/202–617.

Hanau: Verkehrsbüro, ✉ Altstädter Markt 1, D–63450, ☎ 06181/2950.

Hannover: Hannover Information, ✉ Ernst-August-Pl. 2, D–30159, ☎ 0511/301–421.

Kassel: Tourist Information, ✉ Königspl. 53, D–34117, ☎ 0561/34054.

Münden: Verkehrsbüro, ✉ Rathaus am Markt, D–34346, ☎ 05541/75313.

Steinau an der Strasse: ✉ Verkehrsamt Am Kumpen 1–3, D–36396, ☎ 06663/5655.

14 Hamburg

The Free and Hanseatic City of Hamburg, the city's official title, is an apt description. Water—in the form of the Alster lakes and the River Elbe—is its defining feature and the secret of its success. Even before the formation of the Hanseatic League, Hamburg shipped to and from all parts of the world. This is evident in many of the city's attractions, including the Fischmarkt, its diverse restaurants, and the red-light district (the Reeperbahn).

UNTIL RECENTLY Hamburg could have been considered Germany's best-kept secret, virtually ignored by streams of foreign visitors whose itineraries invariably included the Rhine, the Romantic Road, and Munich, but not Hamburg. Now it's neck and neck with Munich as Germany's second-favorite city among foreign visitors (Berlin is first). And yet, for many tourists, it still has something of an image problem. Mention of the city invariably triggers thoughts of the gaudy night world of the Reeperbahn, that sleazy strip of clip joints, sex shows, and wholesale prostitution that has helped make Hamburg Europe's "sin city" supreme. Today the once infamous red-light district has become a hip meeting place for young Hamburgers and tourist crowds, who enjoy the bright lights and chic haunts of the not-so-sinful Reeperbahn, especially on warm summer nights.

Hamburg, or "Hammaburg," was founded in 810 by Charlemagne. For centuries it was a walled city, its gigantic outer fortifications providing a tight little world relatively impervious to outside influences. Situated at the mouth of the Elbe, one of Europe's great rivers and the 97-kilometer (60-mile) umbilical cord that ties the harbor to the North Sea, Hamburg's role as a port gained it world renown It was one of the kingpins of the Hanseatic League, that medieval union of north German merchant cities that dominated shipping in the Baltic and North seas, with trading satellites in Bergen, Visby, Danzig, Riga, Novgorod, and other points of the compass. The city-state's official title (yes, just like Berlin and Bremen, Hamburg is both)—the Free and Hanseatic City of Hamburg—still reflects the importance of that period. The Thirty Years' War left Hamburg unscathed. Napoléon's domination of much of the continent during the early 19th century hardly touched the city either. Indeed, it was in the 19th century that Hamburg reached the crest of its power, when the largest shipping fleets on the seas, with some of the fastest ships afloat, were based here; tentacles of its shipping lanes reached to the far corners of the earth. Ties to New York, Buenos Aires, and Rio de Janeiro were stronger than those to Berlin or Frankfurt. During the four decades leading up to World War I, Hamburg became one of the world's richest cities. Its aura of wealth and power was continued right up to the outbreak of World War II, and even today it shows. Each year about 15,000 ships sail up the lower Elbe carrying more than 50 million tons of cargo—from petroleum and locomotives to grain and bananas.

What you see today is the "new" Hamburg. The Great Fire of 1842 all but obliterated the original city; a century later World War II bombing raids destroyed port facilities and leveled more than half of the city proper. The miracle is that in spite of the 1940–44 raids, Hamburg now stands as a remarkably faithful replica of that glittering prewar city—a place of enormous style, verve, and elegance, with considerable architectural diversity. Of particular interest are the 14th-century houses of Deichstrasse—the oldest residential area in Hamburg—and the Kontorhausviertel (Business House Quarter). The latter contains some unique clinker-brick buildings from the '20s. A variety of turn-of-the-century *Jugendstil* (art nouveau) buildings can also be found in various parts of the city.

The comparison that Germans like to draw between Hamburg and Venice is—like all such comparisons with the *Serenissima*—somewhat exaggerated. But the city *is* threaded with countless canals and waterways spanned by about 1,000 bridges, even more than you'll find in Venice. Swans glide on the canals. Arcaded passageways run along the waterways. In front of the Renaissance-style Rathaus (City Hall) is a square that resembles the Piazza San Marco.

The distinguishing feature of downtown Hamburg is the Alster. Once an insignificant waterway, it was dammed during the 18th century to form an artificial lake. Divided at its south end, it is known as the Binnenalster (Inner Alster) and the Aussenalster (Outer Alster)—the two separated by a pair of graceful bridges, the Lombard Brücke and the John F. Kennedy Brücke. The Inner Alster is lined with stately hotels, department stores, fine shops, and cafés; the Outer Alster is framed by the spacious greenery of parks and gardens against a backdrop of private mansions. From late spring into fall, sailboats and surfboards skim across the surface of the Outer Alster. White passenger steamers zip back and forth. The view from these vessels (or from the shore of the Outer Alster) is of the stunning skyline of six spiny spires (five churches and the Rathaus) that is Hamburg's identifying feature. It all creates one of the most distinctive and appealing downtown areas of any European city.

Those accustomed to the warm *Gemütlichkeit* (conviviality) and jolly camaraderie of Munich should be advised that, as do most north German cities, Hamburg initially presents a more somber face. People here are reputed to be notoriously frugal and cool on the one hand, generous hosts on the other, with a penchant for indulging their tastes for the most refined delicacies. The city's proud past is still evident today, as *Hanseaten*—members of the distinguished city business and political elite—act with an understatement, modesty, and sincerity that has gained them a formidable reputation throughout Germany. Easily recognizable by their conservative dress code of navy blue and gray, Hanseaten are sometimes glimpsed in the downtown area or at fashionable restaurants. But in a vibrant and energetic city, these people work just as hard as they play and turn out to be friendlier than they first appear.

Pleasures and Pastimes

Dining
Hamburg is undoubtedly one of the best places in the country to enjoy fresh seafood, cooked and served in the traditional German way. The flotilla of fishing boats brings a wide variety of fish to the city—to sophisticated upscale restaurants as well as simple harborside taverns. One of the most celebrated dishes among the robust local specialties is *Aalsuppe* (eel soup), a tangy concoction not entirely unlike Marseilles's famous bouillabaisse. A must in summer is *Aalsuppe grün,* seasoned with dozens of herbs. Smoked eel, *Räucheraal,* is equally good. In the fall try *Bunte oder Gepflückte Finten,* a dish of green and white beans, carrots, and apples. Available anytime of year is *Küken* ragout, a concoction of sweetbreads, spring chicken, tiny veal meatballs, asparagus, clams, and fresh peas cooked in a white sauce. Other northern German specialties include *Stubenküken* (chicken), *Vierländer Mastente* (duck), *Birnen, Bohnen und Speck* (pears, beans, and bacon), and the sailors' favorite, *Labskaus*—a stew made from pickled meat, potatoes, and (sometimes) herring, garnished with a fried egg, sour pickles, and lots of beets.

The Harbor
Because the city's harbor is Germany's gateway to the world, a harbor cruise is a must for visitors. Traditionally Hamburg has derived its pride as a free city from its free port. The city gets much of its energy from the continuous ebb and flow of huge cargo vessels and container ships, and the harbor's prosperity and international flavor best symbolizes the spirit of this city. The narrow cobblestone streets and

late medieval storage houses in the older parts of town testify to Hamburg's past as a bustling and powerful Hanseatic city. Today bars and nightclubs have transformed some of the harbor area into a hot spot for both tourists and locals on the lookout for kinky entertainment.

Shopping

Shopping in Hamburg can be enjoyable but expensive. Although not as rich or sumptuous on first sight as Düsseldorf or Munich, Hamburg nevertheless ranks first among Germany's shopping experiences. As sophisticated as the city's style, the fancy boutiques primarily sell distinguished and somewhat conservative fashion; understatement is the idea here. Some of the country's premier designers, such as Karl Lagerfeld, Jil Sander, and Wolfgang Joop, are either native Hamburgers or have worked here for quite some time. In the last few years Hamburg has become the city with the most shopping malls in the country, mostly small but stylish shopping arcades in the downtown area offering entertainment, fashion, and fine food.

EXPLORING HAMBURG

Hamburg's most important sightseeing attractions are found in the downtown area, which stretches between the Alster Lakes to the north and the harbor and the river Elbe to the south. This area consists of three different quarters, each unique in character and each of interest to the tourist. The first is the business district around the Hauptbahnhof (Central Train Station) and the Rathaus (Town Hall); the second, the historic neighborhood clustered near the harbor; and the third, the shabby but thrilling district of St. Pauli, including the Reeperbahn, the strip of sex clubs and bars.

Great Itineraries

Though Hamburg, with more than 1.7 million citizens, is Germany's second-largest city, it is nevertheless easy to explore. Easily traversed on foot, the business district retains its relatively small medieval scale, yet it is dominated by broad shopping boulevards and modern buildings. You can reach the two other city sections of interest—the historic quarters with the harbor, and St. Pauli—by subway within minutes and then explore them on foot. In a minimum stay of two days you can see all the major sights in town. During a visit of four days you'll be able to make some side trips off the beaten path. Add one more day, and you can see sights beyond the classical landmarks, as well as add boat trips to your itinerary.

IF YOU HAVE 2 DAYS

Start your tour at the **Alster** lakes and head toward the city's main shopping boulevards of **Jungfernstieg** and **Mönckebergstrasse.** A short walk south of Mönckebergstrasse takes you to the **Rathaus** (Town Hall) with its majestic architecture, while a brief walk north of the same street leads you to the equally impressive **Hauptbahnhof** (Central Train Station), the largest steel-and-glass construction of its kind in Europe. The Kontorhausviertel with its **Chilehaus** is one of the nicest parts of town, a collection of old brick warehouses dating back to the 1920s.

The next day start with a visit to the harbor area, where you can make a quick tour of the **Freihafen Hamburg,** Hamburg's Free Port, one of the largest in the world. Compare the port's modern warehouses with their antique counterparts on the photogenic **Deichstrasse** in the oldest part of town. You may want to inspect at least one of the city's great churches; a good choice is the city's premier landmark, **St. Michaeliskirche** (St. Michael's Church), with its outstanding Baroque architecture. Finally, head over to **Landungsbrücken** (Landing Bridges), the starting

Hamburg

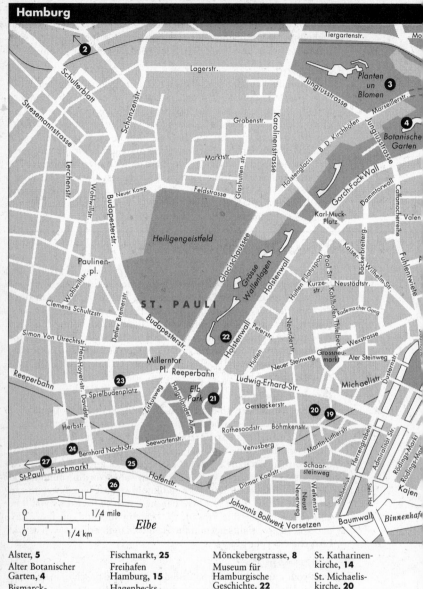

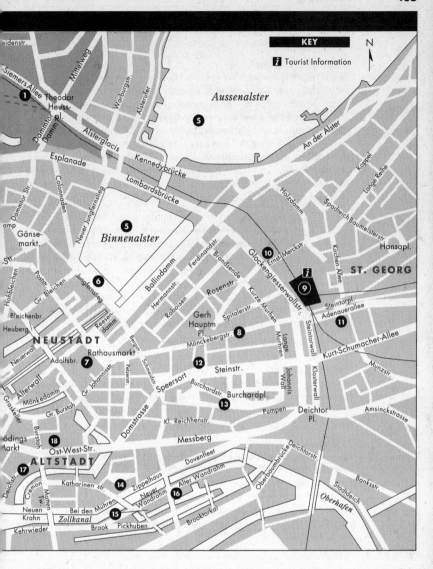

N

Aussenalster

Binnenalster

ST. GEORG

NEUSTADT

ALTSTADT

Zollkanal

Oberhafen

point of round-trip boat rides to the harbor and the river Elbe. And
don't leave Hamburg without taking a stroll down the **Reeperbahn,**
the red-light district.

IF YOU HAVE 3 DAYS

Begin your trip through downtown Hamburg at **Hagenbecks Tierpark**
(zoo) and enjoy watching wild animals roaming freely in their living
areas. Equally green are the two parks, **Planten un Blomen** (Plants and
Flowers) and the **Alter Botanischer Garten** (Old Botanical Gardens),
both beautifully laid-out landscapes amid the downtown business district. After exploring this business area's other main attractions, from
the **Alster** to the **Hauptbahnhof,** detour to Hamburg's two halls of art,
the **Kunsthalle** (Art Gallery) and the **Museum für Kunst und Gewerbe**
(Museum of Arts and Crafts), both showcasing some of the best paintings and artwork in Germany.

Devote your second day to historic Hamburg and the harbor. Commence your tour at the **Freihafen Hamburg** (Free Port of Hamburg)
and don't miss the **Speicherstadt** (Warehouse District), where 19th-cen-
tury warehouses hark back to its prosperous past. After a walk among
the charming houses on **Deichstrasse,** continue on to the **Krameramtswohnungen,** the late medieval shopkeepers guild's homes, which
have been meticulously restored. Next, visit the **Museum für Hamburgische Geschichte** (Museum of Hamburg History), which provides
an excellent overview of the city's dramatic past.

Spend the third day at the **Reeperbahn,** the red-light district. If you enjoy
the kinky sides of life, stop by the **Erotic Art Museum,** one of Europe's
largest and most explicit (yet tasteful) displays of erotic artwork. Before enjoying nightlife here, board one of the boats at **Landungsbrücken** (Landing Bridges) for a sightseeing tour through the harbor.
The next morning mingle with locals at the **Fischmarkt** (Fish Market),
one of Germany's most thrilling markets.

IF YOU HAVE 4 DAYS

To get a glimpse of Hamburg's playful turn-of-the-century art nouveau
architecture, start the first day at the **Dammtor Train Station** and make
quick trips to **Hagenbecks Tierpark** and the parks of **Planten un Blomen**
and **Alter Botanischer Garten.** The inner city district has many sightseeing highlights and museums, from the **Alster** to **Chilehaus,** including **St. Jacobikirche** (St. James's Church), a medieval house of worship
with Gothic altars.

On the second day explore Hamburg's past at the harbor and in other
old parts of town. Begin with the **St. Katharinenkirche** (St. Catherine's
Church), the city's perfectly restored Baroque church. Then spend the
afternoon at Hamburg's harbor and its historic attractions, from the
Freihafen Hamburg (Free Port) to **Krameramtswohnungen** (Shopkeepers-Guild Houses), including **St. Nikolaikirche** (St. Nicholas's
Church), a ruin now serving as a memorial. End the day by stopping
at the giant **Bismarck-Denkmal** (Bismarck Monument), rising high
above the city, for the panoramic view from its top. A third day might
well be spent in **St. Pauli,** exploring its various sights.

On the fourth day return to **Landungsbrücken** and embark on a boat
ride to the idyllic waterside village of **Blankenese** on the river Elbe.
This is old Hamburg at its best.

Downtown Hamburg

The city's heart is centered around two extensive shopping boulevards, the Jungfernstieg and the Mönckebergstrasse. The area was

heavily bombarded during the war, so most of the buildings here were constructed after World War II; they now house banks, insurance companies, and other big businesses. Downtown may not the most beautiful part of town, but its most bustling atmosphere can be invigorating.

A Good Walk
Numbers in the text correspond to numbers in the margin and on the Hamburg map.

Begin at **Dammtor Train Station** ①, a fine example of Hamburg's *Jugendstil* (art nouveau) architecture. Departing from the south exit, you can easily take a detour to Hamburg's zoo, **Hagenbecks Tierpark** ②, one of Germany's oldest and most popular urban animal habitats. It has its own subway stop on the U–2 line. After visiting the zoo, return to the south exit of Dammtor Station; on your right you'll see the **SAS Plaza Hotel** and the **Congress Centrum Hamburg (CCH),** a vast, modern conference-and-entertainment complex at the northeast corner of **Planten un Blomen** (Plants and Flowers) ③ park, which adjoins the **Alter Botanischer Garten** (Old Botanical Gardens) ④. Both the park and the gardens are situated in the larger Wallringpark, which encompasses four parks in all.

You'll need to cover a lot of ground on foot to see everything these two parks have to offer, but a trip on the light railway (which crosses all four of the parks in Wallringpark) will give you a taste of their many aspects. If you take the railway, aim to finish your journey at Stephansplatz.

Walkers may continue past the Congress Centrum and bear left in a sweeping arc through the ornamental **Planten un Blomen** park, with its main entrance off Stephansplatz. When you leave the park, make your way to the northeast entrance to the **Alter Botanischer Garten** at Stephansplatz and head south to cross over the Esplanade. Walk down the attractive Colonnaden to reach the **Alster** ⑤ lakes and **Jungfernstieg** ⑥, the most elegant boulevard in downtown Hamburg.

Turn off the Jungfernstieg onto Reesendamm street and make your way to the **Rathaus** (Town Hall) ⑦ and the square of the same name. Leave by its east side, perhaps pausing to join other visitors who are relaxing on the steps of the memorial to the poet Heinrich Heine, a real Hamburg fan.

Beyond the memorial lies **Mönckebergstrasse** ⑧, Hamburg's not so elegant but always bustling shopping boulevard. When you reach its end, you'll meet the busy main road of Steintorwall, which was the easternmost link of the defense wall encircling the Old Town during the 17th century. Rather than battling to cross against the fast-moving traffic, take the pedestrian underpass to the **Hauptbahnhof** ⑨, Hamburg's central train station, which is Europe's largest steel-and-glass construction of its kind. Leave the Hauptbahnhof the way you entered and turn right on Steintorwall, which continues as Glockengiesserwall, until you come to one of Germany's major art museums, the **Kunsthalle** (Art Gallery) ⑩, on the corner of Ernst-Merck-Strasse.

A quite different but equally fascinating perspective on art is offered by the nearby **Museum für Kunst und Gewerbe** (Museum of Arts and Crafts) ⑪. To reach it, head in the direction from which you came and turn left on Steintordamm, crossing over the railroad tracks. The large, yellow museum building is across the street, its entrance on Brockestrasse.

Return to the city center for a visit to the **St. Jacobikirche** (St. James's Church) ⑫, just off the Mönckebergstrasse. Turn right when leaving the museum, then right again onto Kurt-Schumacher-Allee. Cross over

Steintorwall near the subway and continue west along Steinstrasse to the Jacobikirche on your right—you'll recognize it by its needle spire. Upon leaving the Jacobikirche, cross over Steinstrasse and head down Mohlenhofstrasse, which will bring you to Burchardplatz. This area, south of the Jakobikirche between Steinstrasse and Messberg, is known as the Kontorhausviertel (Office Building Quarter), a nicely restored city quarter with redbrick commercial buildings dating back to the 1920s. Of particular interest here, at the south end of Burchardplatz, is the **Chilehaus** ⑬, the most famous building in the area, which resembles a huge ship.

TIMING

You could easily spend days in downtown Hamburg and always find something new to consider. You need half a day for just walking the proposed tour, depending on how much time you devote to the parks, the zoo (both are crowded but most enjoyable on summer weekends), and to shopping (which isn't advisable on Saturday mornings because of the crowds). If you add two hours for visits to the museums and the Town Hall and two more hours for the delightful boat tour on the Alster Lakes, you'll end up spending more than a full day on this itinerary.

Numbers in the margin correspond to points of interest on the Hamburg map.

Sights to See

❺ **Alster** (Alster Lakes). These twin lakes grant downtown Hamburg one of its most memorable vistas. In summer the boat landing at the Jungfernstieg, below the Alsterpavillion, is the starting point for the *Alsterdampfer,* the flat-bottom passenger boats that teem on the lakes. Small sailboats and rowboats, hired from yards on the shores of the Alster, are very much a part of the summer scene.

Every Hamburger dreams of living within sight of the Alster, but only the wealthiest can afford it. Hamburg has its fair share of millionaires, some of whom are lucky enough to own one of the magnificent garden properties around the Alster's perimeter, called "Millionaire's Coast" by the locals. But you don't have to own one of these estates to be able to enjoy the waterfront—the Alster shoreline offers 6 kilometers (4½ miles) of tree-lined public pathways. Popular among joggers, these trails are a lovely place for a stroll. ⊠ *Alster Lakes and canal tours, Jungfernstieg,* ☎ *040/3574–2419.* ⊡ *DM 14. A 3-hr combination lake and canal tour leaves at 9:45, 12:15, 2:45, and 5:15 and costs DM 19.* ☉ *50-min lake tours leave daily every ½ hr 10–6 Apr.–Oct., less often rest of yr.*

❹ **Alter Botanischer Garten** (Old Botanical Gardens). This green and open park in Wallringpark specializes in rare and exotic plants. Tropical and subtropical species are grown under glass in hothouses, with specialty gardens—including herbal and medicinal—clustered around the old moat. ⊠ *Stephanspl.,* ☎ *040/232–327.* ⊡ *Free.* ☉ *Daily 8–6.*

⑬ **Chilehaus.** This building is the most representative example of the northern German clinker-brick architecture of the '20s. The fantastical 10-story structure, which at first looks like a vast landlocked ship, was commissioned by businessman Henry Sloman, who traded in saltpeter from Chile. The building is the most famous in the surrounding **Kontorhausviertel,** a series of imaginative clinker-brick buildings designed in the New Objectivity style of 1920s civic architect Fritz Schumacher. *U-bahn: Messburg.*

❶ **Dammtorbahnhof** (Dammtor Train Station). Built in 1903, this elevated steel-and-glass Jugendstil structure is one of Hamburg's finest train stations. Recently renovated, it is one of many art nouveau buildings you'll see during your stay in Hamburg. You can buy a city map at the newsstand in the station to find your way through the city. ✉ *Ernst-Siemers-Allee.*

② Hagenbecks Tierpark (zoo). One of the country's oldest and most popular zoos, the park has been family-owned for five generations. Founded in 1848, it was the world's first city zoo to let wild animals roam freely in vast, open-air corrals. The Dolphinarium is particularly popular with kids. ✉ *Hagenbeckallee at Hamburg–Stellingen,* ☎ *040/5400–014748.* ☞ *DM 19, Dolphinarium DM 6.* ☉ *Daily 9–sunset. U-bahn: Hagenbecks Tierpark.*

⑨ Hauptbahnhof (Central Train Station). This train station's impressive architecture of steel and glass is a breathtaking example of imperial German pride. It was opened in 1906 and completely renovated in 1991. Today it caters to a heavy volume of international, national, and suburban rail traffic. Despite being badly damaged during the Second World War and being modernized many times, its architectural impact remains intact. The enormous 394-foot-long cast-iron-and-glass building is accentuated by a 460-foot-wide glazed roof that is supported only by pillars at each end. The largest structure of its kind in Europe, it is remarkably spacious and light inside. ✉ *Steintorpl.*

⑥ Jungfernstieg. This wide promenade looking out over the Alster lakes is the city's premier shopping boulevard. Its attractive promenade, laid out in 1665, used to be part of the muddy millrace that channeled water into the Elbe River. The two lakes meet at the 17th-century defense wall at Lombard Brücke, the first bridge visible across the water. Hidden from view behind the sedate facade of Jungfernstieg is a network of nine covered arcades that together account for almost a mile of shops offering everything from cheap souvenirs to expensive haute couture. Many of these air-conditioned passages have sprung up in the past two decades (☞ Shopping, *below*), but some existed during the 19th century; the first glass-covered arcade, called Sillem's Bazaar, was built in 1845.

NEED A BREAK? | Hamburg's best-known and oldest café, the newly refurbished **Alsterpavillon** (✉ Jungfernstieg 54, ☎ 040/3550–920) is an ideal vantage point from which to observe the constant activity on the Binnenalster (Inner Alster).

⑩ Kunsthalle (Art Gallery). One of the most important art collections in Germany, the Kunsthalle's 3,000 paintings, 400 sculptures, and coin and medal collection present a remarkably diverse picture of European artistic life from the 14th century to the present. One room of paintings shows works by local artists since the 16th century. There is also an outstanding collection of German Romantic paintings, including works by Runge, Friedrich, and Spitzweg. An exhibition of European art by such painters as Holbein, Rembrandt, Van Dyck, Tiepolo, and Canaletto is on display, as are examples of the late-19th-century Impressionist movement by artists ranging from Leibl and Lieberman to Manet, Monet, and Renoir. The Kunsthalle comprises two linked buildings: the Kunsthaus, exhibiting mainly contemporary works, and the Renaissance-style Kunsthalle. ✉ *Glockengiesserwall 1,* ☎ *040/2486–2612.* ☞ *DM 6.* ☉ *Tues.–Wed. and Fri.–Sun. 10–6, Thurs. 10–9. U-bahn: Hauptbahnhof.*

⑧ Mönckebergstrasse. This broad, bustling street of shops—Hamburg's major thoroughfare—cuts through both the historic and new downtown areas. It's a relatively new street, laid out in 1908, when this part of the Old Town was redeveloped. Although the shops here are not quite as exclusive as those of Jungfernstieg, the department stores and shopping precincts on both sides of the street provide a wide selection of goods at more easily affordable prices.

⓫ Museum für Kunst und Gewerbe (Museum of Arts and Crafts). The museum houses a wide range of exhibits from a collection of 15th- to 18th-century scientific instruments to an art nouveau room setting, complete with ornaments and furniture, all either original or faithfully reproduced. It was built in 1876 as a museum and school combined. Its founder, Justus Brinckmann, intended it to be a stronghold of the applied arts to counter what he saw as a decline in taste due to industrial mass production. A keen collector, Brinckmann amassed a wealth of unusual objects, including a fine collection of ceramics from all over the world. ⊠ *Steintorpl. 1,* ☎ *040/2486–2630.* ⌨ *DM 3.* ☼ *Tues.–Wed. and Fri.–Sun. 10–6, Thurs. 10–9. U-bahn: Hauptbahnhof.*

❸ Planten un Blomen (Plants and Flowers park). Opened in 1935, this park is famous all over Germany for its well-kept plant, flower, and water gardens and has many places to rest and admire the flora. The Japanese Garden here is the largest of its kind in Europe and provides the ideal setting for traditional tea ceremonies in the summer. The park lies within the remains of the 17th-century fortified wall that defended the city during the Thirty Years' War, the cataclysmic religious struggle that raged in middle Europe between 1618 and 1648. The remains of the old fortifications and moats have since been cleverly integrated into a huge, tranquil park on the edge of the city center. If you visit on a summer evening, you'll see the Wasserballet, an illuminated fountain "ballet" in the lake set to organ music. Make sure you get to the lake in good time for the show—it begins at 10 PM each evening during the summer (at 9 PM in September).

The Plants and Flowers park is part of the larger **Wallringpark,** which also includes the ☞ Alter Botanischer Garten, plus the Kleine and Grosse Wallanlagen parks to the south, whose special appeal is their well-equipped leisure facilities, including a children's playground and theater, a model-boat pond, roller- and ice-skating rinks, and outdoor chess. Planten un Blomen: ⊠ *Stephanspl.* ⌨ *Free.* ☼ *Mar.–Oct. daily, 9–4:45; Nov.–Feb. daily, 9–3:45.*

★ ❼ Rathaus (Town Hall). To most Hamburgers this large building is the symbolic heart of the city. As a city-state—an independent city and simultaneously one of the 16 federal states of reunited Germany—Hamburg has a city council and a state government, both of which have their administrative headquarters in the Rathaus. The Town Hall, a pompous neo-Gothic affair, dictates political manners in the city. To this day the mayor of Hamburg never welcomes VIPs at the foot of the stairway, but always awaits them at the very top —whether it's a president or the queen of England.

Both the Rathaus and the **Rathausmarkt** (Town Hall Market) lie on marshy land, which everyone was reminded of in 1962 when the entire area was severely flood. The large square, with its surrounding arcades, was laid out after Hamburg's Great Fire of 1842. The architects set out to create an Italian-style square, drawing on St. Mark's in Venice for inspiration. The rounded glass arcade bordered by trees was added in 1982. Building on the Nordic Renaissance–style Rathaus began in 1866 when 4,000 wooden piles were sunk into the moist soil to stabilize its mighty bulk. It was completed in 1892, the year a cholera epidemic claimed the lives of 8,605 people in 71 days. A fountain and monument to that unhappy chapter in Hamburg's history can be found in a rear courtyard of the Rathaus.

This immense building, with its 647 rooms (six more than Buckingham Palace!) and towering central clock tower, is not the most graceful structure in the city, but the sheer opulence of its interior is hard to beat. Although you get to see only the state rooms, the tapestries, huge staircases, glittering chandeliers, coffered ceilings, and grand portraits convey forcefully the wealth of the city during the last century and give insight into the bombastic municipal taste.

The starting point for tours of the Rathaus interior is the ground-floor Rathausdiele, a vast pillared hall. ⊠ *Rathausmarkt,* ☎ *040/3681–2470. English-language tours (✑ DM 2) given hourly Mon.–Thurs. 10:15–3:15, Fri.–Sun. 10:15–1:15. U-bahn: Mönckebergstr.*

⑫ **St. Jacobikirche** (St. James's Church). This 13th-century church was almost completely destroyed during the Second World War. Only the furnishings, put into storage until restoration of the building was completed in 1962, survived. The interior is not to be missed—it houses such treasures as the vast Baroque organ on which Bach played in 1720 and three Gothic altars from the 15th and 16th centuries. ⊠ *Steinstr.* ☺ *Mon.–Sat. 10–5, Sun. 10–noon. U-bahn: Mönckebergstr.*

The Harbor and Historic Hamburg

Hamburg's historic sections are a fascinating mixture of very old and very new features; the modern harbor stands in stark contrast to its late-medieval and 19th-century predecessors—the warehouses. Narrow cobblestone streets with richly decorated historic manors lead to the various churches, which give this part of town a distinctively venerable atmosphere.

A Good Walk

Numbers in the text correspond to numbers in the margin and on the Hamburg map.

This tour takes you southward to the historic and picturesque city quarters around the harbor area. Start with a visit to the restored **St. Katherinenkirche** (St. Catherine's Church) ⑭ en route: From the Messberg end of Pumpen Street, cross the busy Ost-West-Strasse by Messberg station and continue down Dovenfleet, which runs alongside the Zoll Kanal (Customs Canal). Continue until Dovenfleet turns into Bei den Mühren and you'll see the distinctive green-copper spire of the St. Katherinenkirche.

Head back a short ways to the bridge you previously passed, the Kornhausbrücke. Notice the sign on the bridge announcing your entrance to the **Freihafen Hamburg** (Free Port) ⑮ and the **Speicherstadt** (Warehouse District) ⑯, 19th-century warehouses lining the waterfront. As you leave the Free Port over the Brooksbrücke (two bridges down from the Kornhausbrücke), you'll pass through a customs control point, at which you may be required to make a customs declaration. Turn left after the bridge, where Bei den Mühren becomes Neuen Krahn. Take your second right—onto **Deichstrasse** ⑰, the city's 18th-century business district, which runs alongside Nikolaifleet, a former course of the Alster and one of Hamburg's oldest canals. After exploring this lovely area, take the Cremon Bridge at the north end of Deichstrasse. This angled pedestrian bridge spans Ost-West-Strasse. You may wish to make a small detour down one of the narrow alleys between the houses (Fleetgänge) to see the fronts of the houses facing the Nikolaifleet.

The Cremon Bridge will take you to Hopfenmarkt Square, just a stone's throw from the ruins of the **St. Nikolaikirche** (St. Nicholas's Church) ⑱. From here head west on Ost-West-Strasse and cross to the other side at the Rödingsmarkt U-bahn station. Continue along Ost-

West-Strasse, which turns into Ludwig-Erhard-Strasse, until you reach Krayenkamp, a side street to your left that will take you to the historic **Krameramtswohnungen** ⑲ (Shopkeepers-Guild Houses). The distance from the Nikolaikirche to Krayenkamp is about 1 kilometer (½ mile). Hamburg's best-loved and most famous landmark, **St. Michaeliskirche** (St. Michael's Church) ⑳, is on the other side of Krayenkamp Road.

From St. Michaeliskirche, walk west until you reach a park and the enormous **Bismarck-Denkmal** (Bismarck Monument) ㉑, rising high above the greenery. From the monument's northeast exit cross Ludwig-Erhard-Strasse and continue on Holstenwall to the **Museum für Hamburgische Geschichte** (Museum of Hamburg History) ㉒, with exhibits about the city's fascinating past.

TIMING

This can be a rather short walk, manageable in half a day if you only stroll through the historic harbor quarters. You may wish to spend another 1½ hours at the Museum of Hamburg History and still another hour taking a closer look at ecclesiastical art in the various churches.

Sights to See

Numbers in the margin correspond to points of interest on the Hamburg map.

㉑ **Bismarck-Denkmal** (Bismarck Memorial). The colossal 111-foot granite monument, erected between 1903 and 1906, is a mounted statue of Chancellor Bismarck, the Prussian "Iron Chancellor," who was the force behind the unification of Germany. The plinth features bas-reliefs of various German tribes. Created by sculptor Hugo Lederer, the statue calls to mind Roland, the famous warrior from the Middle Ages, and symbolizes the German Reich's protection of Hamburg's international trade. As you climb the pathway leading to it, you'll realize the sandy hill supporting it is responsible for part of its height. U-bahn: St. Pauli.

⑰ **Deichstrasse.** The oldest residential area in the Old Town of Hamburg, which dates from the 14th century, showcases houses lavishly restored, mostly from the 17th to the 19th century. Many of the original houses on Deichstrasse were destroyed in the Great Fire of 1842, which broke out in No. 42 and left approximately 20,000 people homeless; only a few of the early dwellings escaped its ravages.

Today Deichstrasse is a protected area of great historical interest. At No. 39 Deichstrasse, for example, is the Baroque facade of a house built in 1700. Farther along, No. 27, built in 1780 as a warehouse, is the oldest of its kind in Hamburg. All the buildings in the area have been painstakingly restored, thanks largely to the efforts of public-spirited individuals.

NEED A
BREAK?

There are three good basement restaurants in this area, all recommended if you are ready for a break. The **Alt Hamburger Aalspeicher** (✉ Deichstr. 43, ☎ 040/362–990) serves fresh-fish dishes; the **Alt Hamburger Bürgerhaus** (✉ Deichstr. 37, ☎ 040/373–633) specializes in traditional Hamburg fare; and the **Nikolaikeller** (✉ Cremon 36, ☎ 040/366–113), an upscale old Hamburg tavern, offers the biggest herring menu in Germany. All three are on Deichstrasse and Cremon.

⑮ **Freihafen Hamburg** (Free Port). The city's major attraction, Hamburg's Free Port has existed since the 12th century, when Emperor Barbarossa—the Holy Roman Emperor Frederick I—granted the city special privileges, which included freedom from customs dues on the Elbe River. The original Free Port was situated where the Alster meets the Elbe, near Deichstrasse, but it was moved farther south as Hamburg's trade increased during the following centuries. With Hamburg's membership in the German Empire's Customs Union in the late 1800s, major restructuring of the Free Port became necessary to make way for additional storage facilities. An entire residential area was torn down (including many Renaissance and Baroque buildings), and the Speicherstadt warehouses, the world's largest continuous storage space, came into being between 1885 and 1927.

⑲ Krameramtswohnungen (Shopkeepers-Guild Houses). This tightly packed group of courtyard houses was built between 1620 and 1626 for widows of shopkeepers-guild members. They became homes for the elderly after 1866, when the freedom to practice trades was granted. The half-timbered, two-story dwellings, with their unusual twisted chimneys and decorative brick facades, were restored in the 1970s and are now protected buildings. The house marked "C" is open to the public. A visit inside the furnished setting gives you a sense of what life was like in those 17th-century dwellings. Some of the houses have been converted to suit modern-day commercial purposes so you'll find a few shops and a bar-cum-restaurant in the style of Old Hamburg. ⊠ *Historic House "C," Krayenkamp 10,* ☎ *040/3110–2624.* ⊒ *DM 1.* ☉ *Tues.–Sun. 10–5. U-bahn: Rödingsmarkt.*

NEED A
BREAK?

Krameramtsstuben (⊠ Krayenkamp 10, ☎ 040/365–800) in the Krameramtswohnungen Quarter is a rustic dining spot where you can sample hearty traditional local dishes, mostly made with fish. The restaurant is open daily from 10 AM to midnight.

☚ ㉒ Museum für Hamburgische Geschichte (Museum of Hamburg History). A visit to this museum gives you an excellent overview of Hamburg's development through the centuries. The museum's vast and comprehensive collection of artifacts charts the history of Hamburg from its origins in the 9th century to the present. Among the museum's many attractions are an exhibit that describes, through pictures and models, the development of the port and shipping between 1650 and 1860, and a 16th-century architectural model of Solomon's Temple, measuring 11 square feet and made of five different types of wood.

Railway buffs will delight in the railway section and escape into past eras of train travel. Its centerpiece is a model layout of the Hamburg-to-Harburg rail link, complete with a puffing miniature steam locomotive. (Ask at the front desk for the schedule of model railway demonstrations.) ⊠ *Holstenwall 24,* ☎ *040/3504–2360.* ⊒ *DM 6.* ☉ *Tues.–Sat. 10–5, Sun. 10–6. U-bahn: St. Pauli.*

⑭ St. Katharinenkirche (St. Catherine's Church). Completed in 1660, this house of worship is dedicated to St. Catherine, a princess of Alexandria martyred at the beginning of the 4th century. Both the exterior and the interior were severely damaged during World War II, but it has since been carefully reconstructed in a Baroque design. Almost none of the original interior furnishings escaped destruction. Only two 17th-century epitaphs (to Moller and von der Feehte) remain. ⊠ *Bei den Mühren.* ☉ *Summer, daily 9–6; winter, daily 9–4. U-bahn: Messberg.*

★ ⑳ St. Michaeliskirche (St. Michael's Church). "Michel" as it is called locally, is Hamburg's principal church and northern Germany's finest Baroque ecclesiastical building. Constructed on this site from 1649 to 1661 (the tower followed in 1669), it was razed after lightning struck almost a century later. It was rebuilt between 1750 and 1786 in the decorative Nordic Baroque style but fell victim in 1906 to a terrible fire that destroyed all but the outside walls of the church. A replica

was completed in 1912, but it suffered during the Second World War.
By 1952 it was once again restored.

The Michel has a distinctive 433-foot brick-and-iron tower bearing the
largest tower clock in Germany, 26 feet in diameter. Just above the clock
is the viewing platform (accessible by elevator or stairs), which affords
a magnificent panorama of the city, the Elbe River, and the Alster
Lakes. Twice a day, at 10 AM and 9 PM (on Sundays at noon only), a
watchman plays a trumpet solo from the tower platform, and during
festivals an entire wind ensemble crowds onto the platform to perform.
St. Michaeliskirche: ⊙ *Apr.–Sept., daily 9–6 (Thurs. until 10); Oct.–Mar.,
daily 10–5 (Thurs. until 10). St. Michael's Tower:* ▨ *Elevator or staircase (449 steps) DM 4;* ⊙ *Apr.–Sept., Mon.–Sat. 9–6, Sun. 11:30–6;
Oct.–Mar., daily 10–5. U-bahn: Landungsbrücken or Rödingsmarkt.*

NEED A
BREAK?

Just opposite the Michel is one of Hamburg's most traditional restaurants, the **Old Commercial Room** (⊠ Englische Planke 10, ☎ 040/366–
319). Try one of the local specialties, such as *Labskaus* (a traditional
sailors' dish) or *Aalsuppe* (eel soup).

⑱ St. Nikolaikirche (St. Nicholas's Church). The tower and outside walls
of this 19th-century neo-Gothic church, which survived World War II,
today serves as a monument to those killed and persecuted during the
war. Adjacent to the tower is a center documenting the church. It is
run by a citizens organization that is also spearheading private efforts
to partially rebuild the church and redesign the surrounding area. Beneath the former church a wine cellar is open for browsing and wine
tasting, as well as for the purchase of wine. ⊠ *Ost-West-St. by Hopfenmarkt.* ⊙ *Information center Mon., Wed., and Fri. 10–6, Tues. and
Thurs. 10–2; wine cellar weekdays 11–6, Sat. 10–1. U-bahn: Rathaus
or Rödingsmarkt.*

⑯ Speicherstadt (Warehouse District). These imposing warehouses in the
☞ Freihafen Hamburg (Free Port) reveal yet another aspect of Hamburg's extraordinary architectural diversity. A Gothic influence is ap-
parent here, with a rich overlay of gables, turrets, and decorative
outlines. These massive rust-brown buildings are still used to store and
process every conceivable commodity, from coffee and spices to raw
silks and handwoven Oriental carpets. Although you won't be able to
enter the buildings, the nonstop comings and goings you'll see as you
stroll around this area will give you a good sense of a port at work.

St. Pauli and the Reeperbahn

The city district of St. Pauli is sometimes described as a "babel of sin,"
but that's not entirely fair. The Reeperbahn, its major thoroughfare,
offers a broad menu of entertainment in addition to the striptease and
sex shows. Beyond this strip of pleasure St. Pauli is dominated by its
waterfront at the river Elbe, giving this part of Hamburg a maritime,
though run-down, appeal.

A Good Walk

*Numbers in the text correspond to numbers in the margin and on the
Hamburg map.*

Starting from the St. Pauli U-bahn station, you are at the very beginning of a long, neon-lit street stretching nearly 1 kilometer (½ mile) as
far as the eye can see. This is the red-light **Reeperbahn** ㉓, Hamburg's
lively strip of nightlife entertainment and sex clubs. A not-to-be missed
peculiar gallery is the **Erotic Art Museum** ㉔, exhibiting all the hidden
sides of human sexuality. But as the bright lights begin to fade some-

time around daybreak, those who are made of stern stuff continue their entertainment at the **Fischmarkt** (Fish Market) ㉕, a shopper's paradise stocked with fresh fish, meat, vegetables, and plants.

From the market you can head back to the nearby landings at **Landungsbrücken** (Landing Bridges) ㉖, where ferries depart for short round-trips in the area. To find the booking hall and departure point from the Fischmarkt, retrace your original steps but instead of turning left up the hill to the U-bahn station, bear right toward the long limestone building instantly recognizable by its two towers.

One trip you should try to make is to the waterside village of **Blankenese** ㉗, 14½ kilometers (9 miles) west of Hamburg. To get there, take a 14-kilometer ferry ride from Landungsbrücken. From there you have a choice of transportation back to the city—by ferry, by S-bahn, or on foot. The celebrated Elbe River walk is long—about 13 kilometers (8 miles) from Blankenese to Landungsbrücken—but it's one of Hamburg's prettiest.

TIMING

This tour can last a full day and a long night, including a very enjoyable boat trip through the harbor, a few hours in the theaters and bars along the Reeperbahn, and finally a visit to the Fish Market when it opens in the wee hours. However, you might just want to stroll down the red-light strip and check out the Erotic Art Museum and the Landungsbrücken, all in less than three hours.

Sights To See

Numbers in the margin correspond to points of interest on the Hamburg map.

㉗ **Blankenese.** Blankenese is another of Hamburg's surprises—a suburb west of the city with the character of a quaint fishing village. Some Germans like to compare it to the French and Italian rivieras; many consider it the most beautiful part of Hamburg. During the 14th century Blankenese was an important ferry point, but it wasn't until the late 18th and 19th centuries that it became a popular residential area. The town has a lively fruit and vegetable market, open Tuesday 8–2, Friday 8–6, and Saturday 8–1. *Mid-Apr.–Aug., HADAG ferries depart from Pier 3 for Blankenese weekdays at 10:30 and 2:30, weekends at 11:30 and 3:30; they leave Blankenese weekdays at 1 and 6:30, weekends at 2 and 5:30. Ferries continue running on weekends only (at above times) through Sept.*

NEED A BREAK?	A fine view and good food await you at **Sägebiel's Fährhaus** (⌧ Blankeneser Hauptstr. 107, ☎ 040/861–514), a former farmhouse where Kaiser Wilhelm once celebrated his birthday. The fish dishes are recommended.

㉔ **Erotic Art Museum.** Sexually provocative art from 1520 to the present, 500 original works in all, are showcased here. The collection is presented with such great taste and decorum in an attractively renovated four-story building that it has won the respect of many who would not normally wish to view such an exhibit. ⌧ *Bernhard-Nocht-Str. 69,* ☎ *040/3174757. Minimum age is 18.* ⌹ *DM 15.* ☉ *Daily 10 AM–midnight. U-bahn: St. Pauli.*

㉕ **Fischmarkt** (Fish Market). The Altona Fischmarkt is by far the most celebrated of Hamburg's many markets, and it is worth getting out of bed early for. It swings into action every Sunday morning in summer at 5 and two hours later in winter. There is probably no other market in Germany where both vendors and customers are as fervently making deals. Offering real bargains, the market's barkers are famous for their sometimes rude though successful approaches to shoppers.

Sunday fish markets became a tradition in the 18th century, when fishermen sold their catch before church services. Today freshly caught fish are only part of a compendium of wares on sale at the popular Fischmarkt in Altona. In fact, you can find almost anything—from live parrots and palm trees to armloads of flowers and bananas, valuable antiques to second-, third-, and fourth-hand junk. ⊠ *Between Grosse Elbestr. and St. Pauli Landungsbrücken.* ⊙ *Sun. 5–10 AM in summer and 7–10 AM in winter. U-bahn: Landungsbrücken.*

🖐 **26** **Landungsbrücken** (Landing Bridges). The main passenger terminal for a whole range of ferry and barge rides, both one-way and round-trip, along the waterways in, around, and outside Hamburg is also the starting point for sightseeing tours of the harbor. For children, harbor tours are an obvious choice. A visit to the port is not complete without a tour of one of the most modern and efficient harbors in the world. Hamburg is Germany's largest seaport, with 33 individual docks and 500 berths lying within its 78 square kilometers (30 square miles).

There's usually a fresh breeze, so do dress warmly enough for your trip. Don't expect rolling surf and salty air, however, as Hamburg's port is 56 nautical miles from the North Sea. The HADAG line and other companies organize round-trips in the port, lasting about one hour and taking in several docks. ☎ *040/564–523.* 🎫 *1-hr trip DM 15.* ⊙ *Harbor tours run from Piers 1–7 at Landungsbrücken. In summer they depart every ½ hr; in winter, whenever a boat is full. An English-language tour leaves from Pier 1 daily at 11:15 Mar.–Nov.*

You can combine an evening trip around the harbor with a cold buffet dinner, including as much beer as you can drink. Other watery options include rowboat rentals on the Stadtpark Lake and surrounding canals and dancing on a "party ship." In the first-floor booking hall is the main ticket office and information desk. Book at the HADAG pavilion on Landungsbrücken (☎ *040/313–687).* 🎫 *DM 69.* ⊙ *Departures late Apr.–early Dec., Sat. at 8 PM. Inquire at information office about other special cruises.*

23 **Reeperbahn.** The hottest spots in town are concentrated in the St. Pauli Harbor area, on the Reeperbahn and on a little side street known as the Grosse Freiheit (Great Freedom, and that's putting it mildly!). The shows are expensive and explicit, but to walk through this area is an experience in itself, and you can soak up the atmosphere without spending anything. Indeed, compared with former times, it is quite tame. It's *not* advisable, however, to travel through this part of the city alone in the wee hours of the morning. Saturday night finds St. Pauli pulsating with people determined to have as much fun as possible.

It's no understatement to say that while some of the sex clubs may be relatively tame, a good many others are pornographic in the extreme. None of them get going until about 10 PM; all will accommodate you till the early hours. Order your own drinks rather than letting the hostess do it and then pay for them as soon as they arrive, double-checking the price list again before handing over the money.

Among the attractions in the St. Pauli area are theaters, clubs, music pubs, discos, and a bowling alley. The Schmidt Theater on Reeperbahn has a repertoire of live music, vaudeville, chansons, and cabaret, while the St. Pauli theater on Speilbudenplatz presents popular lowbrow productions in Hamburger dialect. *U-bahn: St. Pauli.*

DINING

CATEGORY	COST*
$$$$	over DM 95
$$$	DM 65–DM 95
$$	DM 45–DM 65
$	DM 25–DM 45

*per person for a three-course meal, excluding drinks

$$$$ ✕ **Landhaus Dill.** A fine fin de siècle building with views of the Elbe is home for this restaurant. It has an air of cool elegance, with crisp linen and glistening tile floors, and a high standard of cuisine. The lobster salad is still prepared at your table, and the rack of lamb comes hot from the kitchen with an aromatic thyme sauce. For dessert, try the rhubarb compote with vanilla cream. ✉ Elbchaussee 94, ☎ 040/390–5077. Jacket and tie. AE, DC, MC, V. Closed Mon.

$$$$ ✕ **Landhaus Scherrer.** Though this establishment is only minutes from ★ the downtown area, in Altona, its parklike setting seems worlds away from the high-rise bustle of the city. The mood is elegantly low-key—the building was originally a brewery—with wood-paneled walls and soft lighting. The food fuses sophisticated nouvelle specialties with more down-to-earth local dishes. The wine list is exceptional. ✉ Elbchaussee 130, ☎ 040/880–1325. Jacket and tie. AE, DC, MC, V. Closed Sun.

$$$$ ✕ **Le Canard.** One of Hamburg's top restaurants, Le Canard possesses ★ a much-coveted location overlooking the Elbe River, with enviably elegant decor and top-notch nouvelle cuisine to match. Chef Viehhauser's skills and creativity have kept the restaurant's standards high. Fish dishes predominate, but the roast lamb in thyme sauce is worth sampling. ✉ Elbchaussee 139, ☎ 040/880–5057. Reservations essential. Jacket and tie. AE, DC, MC, V. Closed Sun.

$$$ ✕ **Fischereihafen-Restaurant Hamburg.** For the best fish in Hamburg, ★ dine at this big, upscale restaurant in Altona, just west of the downtown area right on the Elbe. The menu changes daily according to what's available in the fish market that morning. It's a favorite with the city's beau monde. ✉ Grosse Elbestr. 143, ☎ 040/381–816. Reservations essential. AE, DC, MC, V.

$$$ ✕ **La Mer.** The elegant dining room of the Hotel Prem, this is just about the best hotel restaurant in the city, memorably located on the Aussenalster, a 10-minute ride from downtown. A host of subtle specialties, ever changing, is featured in this stylish restaurant, including marinated inoki mushrooms with imperial oysters and salmon roe, and spring venison with elderberry sauce. ✉ An der Alster 9, ☎ 040/245–454. Jacket and tie. AE, DC, MC, V. Closed Sun. No lunch Sat.

$$$ ✕ **Noblesse.** The elegant restaurant of Hamburg's Ramada Renaissance Hotel, in the Hanse arcades, has won awards for its cuisine and service, and it's rapidly becoming a choice eating haunt in the city center. The extensive menu combines German traditional fare and nouvelle cuisine, while the wine list includes fine selections from France, Germany, and Italy. The lunchtime menus and buffet are an especially good value. ✉ Grosse Bleichen, ☎ 040/349–180. Jacket and tie. AE, DC, MC, V.

$$$ ✕ **Peter Lembcke.** There's no better place to eat eel soup or Labskaus ★ (stew made with pickled meat and potatoes). The best of traditional northern German cuisine is served in this small, simply decorated, and long-established restaurant, just north of the train station. The restaurant is nearly always crowded; the service, though warm, can be uncertain. ✉ Holzdamm 49, ☎ 040/243–290. Jacket and tie. AE, DC, MC, V. Closed Sun. No lunch Sat.

$$ ✕ **Ahrberg.** This restaurant on the river in Blankenese has a pleasant terrace for summer dining and a cozy, wood-paneled dining room for

Hamburg Dining

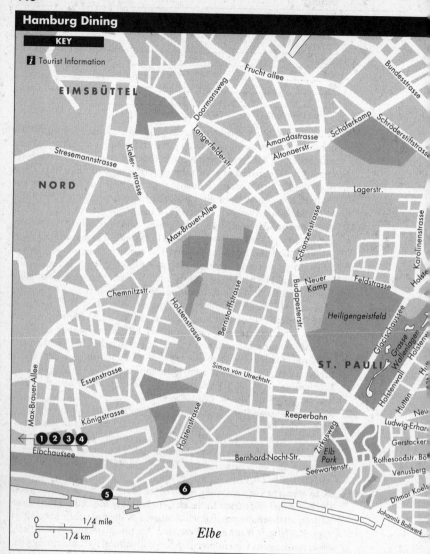

KEY

ℹ️ Tourist Information

Ahrberg, 3
At Nali, 7
Avocado, 14
Le Canard, 4
Fischereihafen-Restaurant Hamburg, 5
Fischerhaus, 6
Il Giardino, 10

Landhaus Dill, 1
Landhaus Scherrer, 2
La Mer, 13
Noblesse, 8
Peter Lembcke, 12
Ratsweinkeller, 11
Restaurant Royal Kopenhagen, 9

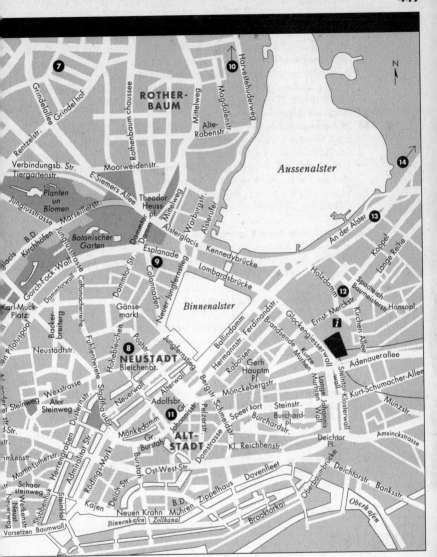

ROTHER-
BAUM

Aussenalster

Planten
un
Blomen

Botanischer
Garten

Binnenalster

Gänse-
markt

NEUSTADT

ALT-
STADT

Binnenhafen Zollkanal

Oberhafen

colder days. The menu features a range of traditional German dishes and seafood specialties. Try the shrimp-and-potato soup or, in season, the fresh carp. ⊠ *Strandweg 33,* ☎ *040/860–438. AE, MC. Closed Sun.*

$$ ✕ **Il Giardino.** The attractive courtyard garden here makes a delightful setting for low-key summer dining. The menu reflects a French influence, although the ambience is lively Italian. The wine list is extensive. ⊠ *Ulmenstr. 17–19,* ☎ *040/470–147. AE, DC, MC, V. Closed Sun. No lunch Mon.*

$$ ✕ **Ratsweinkeller.** For atmosphere and robust local specialties, there are few more compelling restaurants in Germany than this cavernous, late-19th-century haunt under the Town Hall. High stone-and-brick arches with ship models suspended from them and simple wood tables set the mood. You can order surprisingly fancy or no-nonsense meals. Fish specialties predominate, but there's a wide choice of other dishes, too. ⊠ *Grosse-Johannisstr. 2,* ☎ *040/364–153. AE, DC, MC, V. Closed Sun. and holidays.*

$$ ✕ **Restaurant Royal Kopenhagen.** Although most of the menu and all of the decor are maritime, red-meat eaters will find enough to make do here. A late-night menu is offered primarily for patrons of the nearby theater and opera house. If no table is available, try Stephans Keller downstairs (same management) for similar dishes at slightly lower prices. ⊠ *Esplanade 31, at Stephanpl.,* ☎ *040/343–672. AE, DC, MC, V. Closed Sun.*

$ ✕ **At Nali.** This is one of Hamburg's oldest and most popular Turkish restaurants, and it has the added advantage of staying open till 1 AM, handy for those after a late-night kebab. Prices are low, service is reliable and friendly, and the menu is extensive. ⊠ *Rutschbahn 11,* ☎ *040/410–3810. Reservations essential on weekends. AE, DC, MC, V.*

$ ✕ **Avocado.** The imaginative vegetarian menu at this popular, modern restaurant is an excellent value. In the pleasant Uhlenhorst District, close to the Aussenalster, it is Hamburg's only no-smoking restaurant. Try the salmon in Chablis. ⊠ *Kanalstr. 9,* ☎ *040/220–4599. Reservations essential. No credit cards. Closed Mon.*

$ ✕ **Fischerhaus.** Always busy (expect to share a table), this plainly dec-
★ orated waterfront establishment offers time-honored Hamburg fish specialties. It's hardly haute cuisine, but the standards, like the service, are ultrareliable. This is a great place to try eel soup. ⊠ *Fischmarkt 14,* ☎ *040/314–053. No credit cards.*

LODGING

Hamburg has a full range of hotels, from five-star, grande-dame luxury enterprises to simple pensions. The nearly year-round conference and convention business keeps most rooms booked well in advance, and the tariffs are high. But many of the more expensive hotels lower their weekend rates because all those businesspeople have gone home. The tourist office can help with reservations if you arrive with nowhere to stay (☞ Contacts and Resources *in* Hamburg A to Z, *below*); be sure to ask about the many Happy Hamburg special-accommodation packages.

CATEGORY	COST*
$$$$	over DM 325
$$$	DM 225–DM 325
$$	DM 150–DM 225
$	under DM 150

*All prices are for two people in a double room, including tax and service charge.

$$$$ ⊞ **Hotel Abtei.** On a quiet, tree-lined street a mile north of the downtown area, in Harvestehude, this elegant period hotel offers understated luxury and very friendly, personal service. You can have your breakfast in the beautiful garden and afternoon tea in the antiques-filled sitting room. In the evenings the intimate restaurant serves carefully prepared traditional German dishes. ⊠ *Abteistr. 14, D–20099,* ☎ *040/442–905,* ꜰꜱ *040/449–820. 11 rooms, all with bath. Restaurant. AE, DC, MC, V.*

$$$$ ⊞ **Kempinski Atlantic Hotel Hamburg.** There are few hotels in Germany
★ more sumptuous than this gracious Edwardian palace facing the Aussenalster. The mood is created with thick-carpeted, marble-inlaid panache, along with modern touches, especially in the lighting. The lobby is positively baronial: imposing marble pillars, leather armchairs, and a snack bar serving champagne and caviar. Whether the rooms are traditionally furnished or more modern, they all are typical of Hamburg in their understated luxury. All have spacious sitting areas with a writing desk and easy chairs, as well as large bathrooms, most with two washbasins, a bathtub, and a separate shower stall. The suites are little short of palatial; Madonna, Prince, and Michael Jackson have all found quarters in the Presidential Suite. Service at the Atlantic is hushed and swift, and the large and friendly staff will ensure that your every wish is fulfilled. In fine weather guests can lounge in the formal outdoor courtyard, where only the gurgling fountain disturbs the peace. The Atlantic Restaurant is a stunning example of post-modernism, with rich bird's-eye maple details, black columns, and inlaid marble. ⊠ *An der Alster 72–79, D–20149,* ☎ *040/28880,* ꜰꜱ *040/2163–297. 243 rooms and 13 suites, all with bath. 2 restaurants, 2 bars, room service, indoor pool, beauty salon, massage, sauna, parking. AE, DC, MC, V.*

$$$$ ⊞ **Marriott.** This is the first Marriott in Germany, and it remains the showpiece—from the extraordinary barrel-roof ceiling of the reception area to the expansive comfort of its guest rooms. Unlike other Marriott hotels in Germany (Munich's, for instance), this one has a central city location—an unbeatable spot on Hamburg's Gänsemarkt, in the center of the best shopping areas. The hotel's aptly named American Place restaurant is one of the best the city center has to offer. ⊠ *ABC-Str. 52, D–20354,* ☎ *040/35050,* ꜰꜱ *040/2165–871. 277 rooms, 10 suites, all with bath. Restaurant, bar, no-smoking rooms, room service, indoor pool, beauty salon, massage, sauna, fitness center, boutiques, parking. AE, DC, MC, V.*

$$$$ ⊞ **Vier Jahreszeiten.** Some claim this handsome 19th-century town
★ house on the edge of the Binnenalster is the best hotel in Germany. Friedrich Haerlin founded the hotel in 1897, and although it was acquired by a Japanese company in 1989, it is still run as perfectly as it was under Haerlin family ownership. Antiques—the hotel has a set of near-priceless Gobelin tapestries—line the public rooms and stud the stylish bedrooms; forests of flowers stand in massive vases; rare oil paintings hang on the walls; and, of course, all the rooms are individually decorated with superb taste. Of the four restaurants, the Haerlin is the most formal and features superb nouvelle and classic specialties. If you want a room with a view of the lake, especially one with a balcony, make reservations well in advance. ⊠ *Neuer Jungfernstieg 9–14, D–20354,* ☎ *040/34940,* ꜰꜱ *040/349–4602. 158 rooms, 23 apartments, all with bath. 4 restaurants, bar, room service, beauty salon, parking. AE, DC, MC, V.*

$$$ ⊞ **Aussen Alster.** Crisp and contemporary in design, this boutique hotel prides itself on giving personal attention to its guests. Rooms are compact; most have a full bathroom, but a few have a shower only. Stark white walls, white bedspreads, and light-color carpets create a bright, fresh ambience. A small bar is open in the evenings, and a tiny garden is available for summer cocktails. The restaurant serves Mediter-

Hamburg Lodging

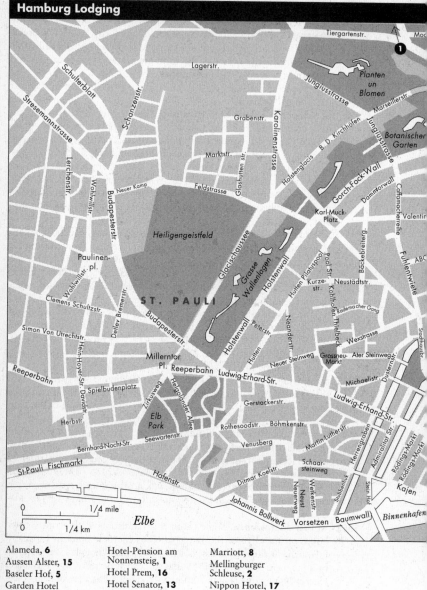

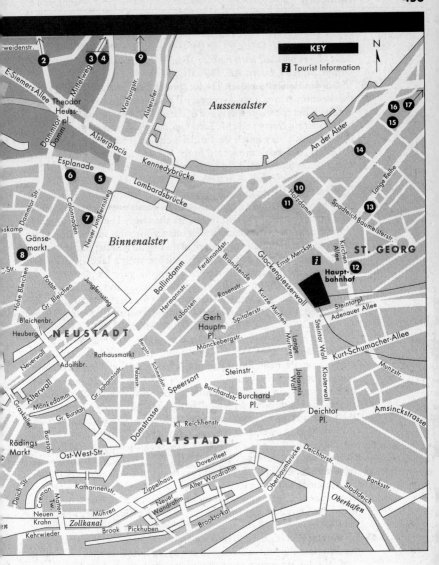

weidenstr.

2 ❷   **3** ❸ **4** ❹   **9** ❾

E-Siemers Allee

Theodor Heuss-pl.

Dammtor Damm

Mittelweg

Warburgstr.

Alsterufer

Aussenalster

KEY

i Tourist Information

N

16 ⓰ **17** ⓱

15 ⓯

Alsterglacis

Kennedybrücke

An der Alster

14 ⓮

Esplanade

6 ❻   **5** ❺

Lombardsbrücke

Dammtor Str.

Colonnaden

Neuer Jungfernstieg

Binnenalster

10 ❿

11 ⓫

Holzdamm

Lange Reihe

Spaadteich

Baumeisterstr.

13 ⓭

7 ❼

skamp

Gänse-markt.

8 ❽

Hohe Bleichen

Poststr.

Gr. Bleichen

Jungfernstieg

Ernst Merckstr.

Kirchen-Allee

ST. GEORG

i

12 ⓬

Haupt-bahnhof

Bleichenbr.

Heuberg

NEUSTADT

Neuerwall

Alterwall

Grakeller

Mönkedamm

Gr. Burstah

Adolfsbr.

Bergstr.

Gr. Johannisstr.

Pelzerstr.

Schmiedstr.

Rathausmarkt

Ballindamm

Hermannstr.

Ferdinandstr.

Brandende

Raboisen

Rosenstr.

Gerh Hauptm Pl.

Spitalerstr.

Mönckebergstr.

Kurze Mühren

Glockengiesserwall

Steintorpl. Adenauer Allee

Steintor Wall

Lange Mühren

Johannis Wall

Klosterwall

Kurt-Schumacher-Allee

Munzstr.

Steinstr.

Speersort

Burchardstr.

Burchard Pl.

Deichtor Pl.

Amsinckstrasse

Rödings Markt

Ost-West-Str.

Domstrasse

Kl. Reichenstr.

ALTSTADT

Deich Str.

Cremon

Matten Twi

Neuen Krahn

Katharinenstr.

Mühren

Zollkanal

Brook

Pickhuben

Zippelhaus

Neuer Wandrahm

Dovenfleet

Alter Wandrahm

Brooktorkai

Oberbaumbrücke

Deichtorstr.

Banksstr.

Stadtdeich

Oberhafen

Kehrwieder

ranean fare for lunch and dinner. At the bottom of the street is the Aussen Alster Lake, where the hotel has its own sailboat for guests' use. ✉ *Schmilinskystr. 11, D–20099,* ☎ *040/241–557, D–20099,* FAX *040/280–3231. 27 rooms, all with bath or shower. Restaurant, bar, sauna, solarium, bicycles, boats. AE, DC, MC, V.*

$$$ 🏨 **Garden Hotels Pöseldorf.** The location in chic Pöseldorf, a mile from
★ the downtown area, may discourage those who want to be in the thick of things, but otherwise this is one of the most appealing hotels in Hamburg, offering classy and chic accommodations in three attractive city mansions. It's very much the insider's choice. There's no restaurant, but light, cold meals are served in the bar and airy winter garden. ✉ *Magdalenenstr. 60, D–20148,* ☎ *040/414–040,* FAX *040/414–0420. 57 rooms, 3 suites, all with bath. Bar, parking. AE, DC, MC, V.*

$$$ 🏨 **Hotel Prem.** Facing the Aussen Alster, this extremely personable, quiet,
★ small hotel is Hamburg's gem. Most of its guests are repeats who have their favorite rooms; no two rooms are the same. The Adenauer Suite (named after West Germany's then-chancellor who stayed here), for example, is traditionally furnished, including an antique chaise longue and a period writing desk in a small alcove with a lake view. Room 102 across the hall has contemporary furnishings and a platform bed. Suite 2 has two rooms with modern furnishings and a terrace overlooking the lake. The intimate bar is perfect for an evening drink, and the dining at La Mer is superb (☞ *Dining, above*). ✉ *An der Alster 8–10, D–20099,* ☎ *040/2417–2628,* FAX *040/2803–851. 44 rooms, 11 suites, all with bath. Restaurant, bar, sauna. AE, DC, MC, V.*

$$$ 🏨 **Hotel Senator.** At this modern hotel, conveniently located two blocks from the main railway station, every room has a fresh look and modern conveniences, from hair dryers to cable TV. The largest and quietest rooms are on the fifth floor at the back of the building. Most rooms have bathrooms with a full bath; a few have only a shower. On the first floor the reception area has a pleasant glass-enclosed terrace for breakfast, as well as a bar and a lounge. ✉ *Lange Reihe 18–20, D–20099,* ☎ *040/241–203,* FAX *040/280–3717. 56 rooms, all with bath. Restaurant, bar, parking. AE, DC, MC, V.*

$$ 🏨 **Alameda.** Occupying the first two floors of a downtown building, the Alameda offers guests good, basic accommodations. The upstairs rooms are nicer and somewhat more spacious, but all rooms have TV, radio, and minibar. ✉ *Colonnaden 45, D–20354,* ☎ *040/344–000,* FAX *040/343–439. 18 rooms, all with shower. AE, DC, MC, V.*

$$ 🏨 **Baseler Hof.** It's hard to find fault with this hotel, which is centrally located near the Binnenalster and the opera house. Service is friendly and efficient, rooms are neatly if functionally furnished, and prices are quite reasonable for this expensive city. The hotel caters to individuals and convention groups, so at times the lounge area, with rather formal clusters of tables and chairs, can become crowded. ✉ *Esplanade 11, D–20354,* ☎ *040/359–060,* FAX *040/3590–6918. 149 rooms, all with bath. 2 restaurants, bar, room service. AE, DC, MC, V.*

$$ 🏨 **Hotel-Garni Mittelweg.** With chintz curtains, flowered wallpaper, old-fashioned dressing tables, and a country-house-style dining room that, unfortunately, serves only breakfast, this hotel possesses a small-town charm that seems almost out of place in bustling, big-business Hamburg. A converted turn-of-the-century mansion in upmarket Pöseldorf, it's well located on the fashionable Mittelweg, a short walk from the Aussenalster and a quick bus ride to the city center. ✉ *Mittelweg 59, D–20149,* ☎ *040/414–1010,* FAX *040/4141–0120. 35 rooms, 2 apartments, all with bath or shower. No credit cards.*

$$ 🏨 **Hotel-Pension am Nonnenstieg.** The owner, Frau Hodermann, is friendly and helpful and makes this unassuming little hotel homey. Extra beds for younger children can be put in rooms at no extra charge. Ask for a room with a kitchen alcove if you want to cook for yourself. There is no restaurant; only breakfast is offered. ☒ *Nonnenstieg 11, D–20149,* ☎ *040/480–6490,* ⓕⓐⓧ *040/4806–4949. 30 rooms, all with bath. No credit cards.*

$$ 🏨 **Ibis Hamburg Alster.** This French chain hotel may have few frills, but in this costly city it offers smart, uniformly decorated rooms at reasonable rates. Each room has a bathroom with a shower and just enough space to hang your clothes. On the ground floor the helpful, English-speaking staff is welcoming, and the lobby bar creates camaraderie among the guests. The location, across the street from the Atlantic Kempinski, is just a five-minute walk from the train station and two minutes from the Alster Lakes. ☒ *Holtzdamm 4–12, D–20099,* ☎ *040/248–290,* ⓕⓐⓧ *040/2482–9999. 165 rooms. Restaurant, bar, parking. AE, DC, MC, V.*

$$ 🏨 **Kronprinz.** For its down-market position (on a busy street opposite the railway station) and its moderate price, the Kronprinz is a surprisingly attractive hotel, with a whiff of five-star flair. Rooms are individually styled, modern but homey; ask for Number 45, which has mahogany and red-plush decor. ☒ *Kirchenallee 46,* ☎ *040/243–258, D–20099,* ⓕⓐⓧ *040/280–1097. 69 rooms, all with bath or shower. Restaurant, terrace. AE, DC, MC, V.*

$$ 🏨 **Mellingburger Schleuse.** If you want off-the-beaten-track lodgings while visiting Hamburg, this member of the Ringhotels association is the place for you. Only a 20-minute drive from the downtown area, it is idyllically located in a forest—the Alsterwanderweg hiking trail passes right by the doorstep. The hotel itself is more than 200 years old, with a thatch roof, peasant-style furnishings, and a restaurant that serves traditional northern German dishes. ☒ *Mellingburgredder 1, D–22395,* ☎ *040/602–400103,* ⓕⓐⓧ *040/602–7912. 40 rooms, all with bath. 2 restaurants, bar, indoor pool, fitness room, parking. AE, DC, MC.*

$$ 🏨 **Nippon Hotel.** You'll be asked to remove your shoes before entering your room at the Nippon, western Germany's second exclusively Japanese hotel (the first is in Düsseldorf). There are tatami on the floor, futon mattresses on the beds, and an attentive Japanese staff. The authenticity might make things a bit *too* spartan and efficient for some, but by cutting some Western-style comforts the hotel offers a good value in the attractive Uhlenhorst District. The hotel has a Japanese restaurant and sushi bar. ☒ *Hofweg 75, D–22085,* ☎ *040/227–1140,* ⓕⓐⓧ *040/2271–1490. 41 rooms, 1 suite, all with bath or shower. Restaurant. AE, DC, MC, V.*

$$ 🏨 **Wedina.** Rooms at this small hotel are neat and compact, with contemporary furnishings and bathrooms that have either a shower or a tub. A small bar and a restaurant area, used for breakfast only, are on the ground floor and face the veranda and small pool. The Swiss owners also have a small pension, Gästehaus Gurlitt, across the street, with 15 simpler and slightly smaller rooms, all with shower. Both lodgings are a half block from the Aussenalster and a brisk 10-minute walk from the station. ☒ *Gurlittstr. 23,* ☎ *040/243–011, D–20099,* ⓕⓐⓧ *040/280–3894. 27 rooms with bath or shower. Bar, pool. AE, DC, MC, V.*

NIGHTLIFE AND THE ARTS

Nightlife

The Reeperbahn

Whether you think it sordid or sexy, the Reeperbahn in the St. Pauli District is as central to the Hamburg scene as are the classy shops along Jungfernstieg. A walk down Herbertstrasse (men only, no women or children permitted), just two blocks south of the Reeperbahn, can be quite an eye-opener. Here prostitutes sit displayed in windows as they await customers. On nearby **Grosse Freiheit** (an appropriate name: it means Great Freedom) are a number of the better-known sex-show clubs: **Colibri** at No. 30, **Safari** at No. 24, and **Salambo** at No. 11. They cater to the package-tour trade as much as to those on the prowl by themselves. Prices are high. If you order a drink, ask for the price list, which legally must be on display, and pay as soon as you're served. Don't expect much to happen here before 10 PM.

Schmidt Theater and **Schmidts Tivoli** (Schmidt Theater, ⊠ Spielbudenpl. 24; Schmidts Tivoli, ⊠ Spielbudenpl. 27-28, both ☎ 040/311–231). These more recent arrivals on the scene along the Reeperbahn have become Germany's leading variety theaters. Their shows are nationally televised. The classy repertoire of live music, vaudeville, chansons, and cabaret in both houses is quite hilarious and worth the entrance fee. If you don't get a ticket (which is likely to happen), relax in one of their cafés.

St. Pauli-Theater (⊠ Spielbudenpl. 29, ☎ 040/314–344). A veteran of the age of velvet and plush, the St. Pauli-Theater serves up a popular brand of lowbrow theater in Hamburger dialect, which is even incomprehensible to other northern Germans.

Jazz Clubs

Birdland (⊠ Gärtnerstr. 122, ☎ 040/405–277). This is one of the leading clubs among Hamburg's more than 100 venues. The jazz scene in Hamburg is thriving as never before, and at the Birdland everything—from traditional New Orleans sounds to avant-garde electronic noises—is featured.

Cotton Club (⊠ Alter Steinweg 10, ☎ 040/343–878). Hamburg's oldest jazz club offers classical New Orleans jazz on most nights.

Fabrik (⊠ Barnerstr. 36, ☎ 040/391–079). The special feature here are Sunday-morning *Früschoppen* (brunch) concerts at 11. They're always packed, so get here early.

Discos

Die Insel (⊠ Alsterufer 35, ☎ 040/410–6955). This club, a disco and restaurant in one, is one of the biggest and most elegant nightspots in Hamburg. Prices can be high, but it's always chic.

Grosse Freiheit 36 (⊠ Grosse Freiheit 36, ☎ 040/420–3282). This disco has several dance floors and different clubs, spread over three stories.

Mojo Club (⊠ Reeperbahn 1, ☎ 040/319–1999). This funky club-disco plays primarily acid jazz and soul, proving that the Reeperbahn is more than just sex clubs.

Skyy (⊠ Spielbudenpl. 16b, ☎ 040/319–1711). Tiny as this club may seem, it's an always crowded and bustling hot spot. The DJs are mostly into African and R&B music.

Top of the Town (⊠ Marseiller Str. 2, ☎ 040/3502–3210). Both elegant and expensive, as most Hamburg discos are, this nightspot on the 26th floor of the SAS Plaza Hotel is a favorite of more mature businessmen.

The Arts

The arts flourish in this elegant metropolis. The city's ballet company is one of the finest in Europe, and the Ballet Festival in July is a cultural high point. Full information on upcoming events is available in the magazine *Hamburger Vorschau*—pick it up in tourist offices and most hotels for DM 2.30—and the magazine *Szene Hamburg*, sold at newsstands throughout the city for DM 5.

A number of travel agencies sell tickets for plays, concerts, and the ballet. There's also a ticket office in the main tourist office in the **Bieber-**

haus (✉ Hachmannpl., ☎ 040/280–2848). Or try these ticket agencies in the downtown area: **Theaterkasse im Alsterhaus** (✉ Jungfernstieg 16, ☎ 040/352–664) and **Theaterkasse Central** (✉ Gerhart-Hauptmann-Pl., ☎ 040/337–124).

Concerts

Musikhalle (✉ Karl-Muck-Pl., ☎ 040/346–920). At Hamburg's most important concert hall, both the Hamburg Philharmonic and the Hamburg Symphony Orchestra appear regularly. Visiting orchestras from overseas are also showcased here.

Norddeutscher Rundfunk Studio 10 (✉ Oberstr., ☎ 040/413–2504). The public radio station's symphony hall stages regular concerts by the symphony orchestra and guest appearances by visiting musicians.

Film

The British Council Film Club (✉ Rothenbaumchaussee 34, ☎ 040/446–057) shows films in English.

Opera and Ballet

Operettenhaus (✉ Spielbudenpl. 1, ☎ 040/270–75270). This stage that puts on light opera and musicals, at press time, was offering Andrew Lloyd Weber's *Cats*.

Staatsoper Hamburg (✉ Grosse Theaterstr. 35, ☎ 040/351–721). One of the most beautiful theaters in the country, this is the leading northern German venue for top-class opera and ballet.

Theater

Deutsches Schauspielhaus (✉ Kirchenallee 39, ☎ 040/248–713). Hamburg's leading drama stage is probably the most beautiful theater in the city, lavishly restored to its full 19th-century opulence in the early 1980s and now the most important venue in Hamburg for classical and modern theater.

English Theater (✉ Lerchenfeld 14, ☎ 040/227–7089). As the city's only stage to present English-language drama, it may be a solution for non-German-speaking tourists interested in a German theater encounter.

Hansa Theater (✉ Steindamm 17, ☎ 040/241–414). This variety-show dinner theater is a real German rarity, both for its nostalgia and the excellent artists and singers presenting premier evening entertainment.

Kampnagel (✉ Jarrestr. 20-24, ☎ 040/2709–4949). For alternative theater and dance productions, including groups of national and international renown, try Kampnagel, the best place of its type in northern Germany.

Neue Flora Theater (✉ Corner of Alsenstr. and Stresemannstr. 159a, ☎ 040/2707–5270). Hamburg is by far Germany's capital for musicals. The newly reopened Neue Flora, where at press time *The Phantom of the Opera* continued its long run, is the best deal for musicals in town.

Thalia-Theater (✉ Alstertor, ☎ 040/322–666). This is still one of the country's most controversial theater houses, where classical drama is staged in much disputed modern settings.

OUTDOOR ACTIVITIES AND SPORTS

Bicycling

There are bike paths throughout downtown and many outlying areas. You can rent bikes from the tourist office (☞ Contacts and Resources *in* Hamburg A to Z, *below*) for DM 2 per hour, April through September. A day's rental costs DM 10 (DM 20 for the weekend).

Golf

There are two leading clubs: **Hamburger Golf-Club Falkenstein** (✉ In de Bargen 59, ☎ 040/812–177); and **Golf-Club auf der Wendlohe** (✉

Oldesloerstr. 251, ☎ 040/550–5014). Visiting members of foreign clubs are welcome.

Jogging

The best places for jogging are around the Planten un Blomen and Alt Botanischer Garten parks and along the leafy promenade around the Alster. The latter is about 2½ kilometers (4 miles) long.

Sailing

You can rent rowboats and sailboats on the Alster in the summer between 10 AM and 9 PM for around DM 12 an hour, plus DM 3 per additional person. For more advanced sailing, contact the **Yacht-Schule Bambauer** (⊠ Schöne Aussicht 20a, ☎ 040/273–224).

Swimming

Don't even think about swimming in the Elbe or the Alster—they're health hazards. There are, however, pools—indoor and outdoor—throughout the city. A full listing is available from the tourist office. Two to try are **Alster Schwimmhalle** (⊠ Ifflandstr. 21., ☎ 040/223–012) and **Blankenese** (⊠ Simrockstr. 45, ☎ 040/862–392).

Tennis and Squash

The Hamburger Tennis Verband (⊠ Bei den Tennisplätzen 77, ☎ 040/651–2973) has a full listing of the many indoor and outdoor courts in the city. Listings are also available from the tourist office. For squash, try the **Squash Center Marquardt** (⊠ Hagenbeckstr. 124a, ☎ 040/546–074). It has 17 courts, a swimming pool, a sauna, and a solarium.

SHOPPING

Shopping Districts

Grosse Bleichen. The streets Grosse Bleichen and Neuer Wall, which lead off Jungfernsteig, is a high-price-tag zone. Hamburg's main shopping districts are among the most elegant on the Continent, and the city has Europe's largest area of covered shopping arcades, most of them packed with small, exclusive boutiques. The Grosse Bleichen also leads to three of the city's most important covered (or indoor) shopping malls: The marble-clad **Galleria** is modeled after London's Burlington Arcade. Daylight streams through the immense glass ceilings of the **Hanse-Viertel,** an otherwise ordinary reddish-brown brick building. The **Kaufmannshaus,** also known as the Commercie, is one of the oldest indoor malls. The malls all connect, and energetic shoppers may want to spend several hours exploring them. The mood is busily elegant, and you'll understand why Hamburgers call it their *Quartier Satin.*

Jungfernstieg. Hamburg's leading shopping street is just about the most upscale and expensive in the country. It's lined with classy jewelers—**Wempe, Brahmfeld & Guttruf,** and **Hintze** are the top names—and chic clothing boutiques such as **Linette, Ursula Aust, Selbach, Windmöller,** and **Jäger & Koch.** Prices are high, but the quality is tops.

Pöseldorf. Away from the downtown area in this fashionable district, take a look at Milchstrasse and Mittelweg. Both are bright and classy, with small boutiques, restaurants, and cafés. The leading name is **Jil Sander** (⊠ Milchstr. 8, ☎ 040/5530–2173), the city's best-known designer of women's clothing and accessories.

Spitalerstrasse. This boulevard, running from the main train station to Gerhard-Hauptmann-Platz, is a pedestrians-only shopping street that's lined with stores. Prices here are noticeably lower than those in Jungfernstieg.

Antiques

Antik-Center (⊠ Klosterwall 9–21, ☎ 040/326–285). This assortment of shops in the old market hall, close to the main train station, features a wide variety of pieces—large and small, valuable and not so valuable—from all periods.

St. Georg. Take a look at the shops in this city district, especially those between Lange Reihe and Koppel. You'll find a mixture of genuine antiques (*Antiquitäten*) and junk (*Trödel*). You won't find many bargains, however. ABC-Strasse is another happy hunting ground for antiques lovers.

Department Stores

Alsterhaus (⊠ Jungfernstieg 16–20, ☎ 040/359–010). Hamburg's most famous department store is both large and elegant; it's a favorite with locals and a must for visitors. Even Prince Charles and Princess Diana stopped here during a visit to Hamburg. Don't miss its amazing food department. Reward yourself for having braved the crowds by ordering a glass of champagne; it's a surprisingly good value.

Karstadt (⊠ Mönckebergstr. 16, ☎ 040/30940). This branch of one of Germany's leading department-store chains offers the same goods as the Alsterhaus at similar prices. Hamburg's downtown Karstadt is the city's best place to shop for sports clothing.

Kaufhof (⊠ Mönckebergstr. 3, ☎ 040/333–070). Equally large but not as classy, Kaufhof offers far more bargains than most other department stores here, in a setting that is nevertheless enjoyable.

Food and Flea Markets

Blankenese (Bahnhofstr., S-bahn: Blankenese). A lively fruit and vegetable market in the heart of this suburb manages to preserve the charm of a small village. It's open Tuesday 8–2, Friday 8–6, and Saturday 8–1.

Fischmarkt (Fish Market). Fish of all shapes and sizes can be purchased at this market, as can a wide range of other goods, including flowers, fruit and vegetables, antiques, and secondhand junk. For many it's also a traditional setting for a last beer after a night on the town. In summer it's open Sunday 5–10 AM. (S- or U-bahn: Landungsbrücken.)

Gift Ideas

Binikowski (⊠ Lokstedter Weg 68, ☎ 040/462–852). This nice little shop offers the most famous must-buy—*Buddelschiffe,* a ship in a bottle. There are few better places to shop for one, or for a blue-and-white striped sailor's shirt, a sea captain's hat, ship models, even ship's charts.

Brücke 4 (⊠ St. Pauli Landungsbrücken, ☎ 040/316–373). This Hamburg institution is an experience not to be missed, the best place for all of the city's specialty maritime goods

Gäth & Peine (⊠ Luisenweg 109, ☎ 040/213–599). This is the premier location for flags from around the world.

Seifarth and Company (⊠ Robert-Koch-Str. 17, ☎ 040/524–0027). You may find it bizarre, but Hamburg is one of the best cities in Europe for buying tea. Smoked salmon and caviar are also terrific buys. Seifarth and Company, the largest caviar mail-order business in Europe, also offers lobsters, salmon, and exotic teas.

SIDE TRIPS

Ahrensburg

One of Schleswig-Holstein's major attractions is the romantic 16th-century Schloss Ahrensburg (Ahrensburg Castle), in the town of Ahrensburg, about 25 kilometers (16 miles) northeast of Hamburg. Ahrensburg itself is mainly a commuter town, home to about 27,000 people. The magnificent castle and nearby Bredenbecker Teich Lake make it worth a visit—it's an ideal day excursion.

Schloss Ahrensburg (Ahrensburg Castle). Surrounded by lush parkland on the banks of the Hunnau, the whitewashed-brick, moated Renaissance castle stands much as it did when constructed at the end of the 16th century. Originally built by Count Peter Rantzau, it changed hands in 1759 and was remodeled inside by its new owner, the financier Carl Schimmelmann. The interior was again altered in the mid-19th century and recently underwent yet another renovation.

Inside are period furniture and paintings, fine porcelain, and exquisite crystal. On the grounds stands a simple 16th-century church erected at the same time as the castle, although the west tower was completed later and Baroque alterations were made in the 18th century. The church is nestled between two rows of 12 almshouses, or *Gottesbuden* (God's cottages). ☎ *04102/42510.* ✆ *DM 3.* ☺ *Apr.–Sept., Tues.–Sun. 10–12:30 and 1:30–5; Oct. and Feb.–Mar., Tues.–Sun. 10–12:30 and 1:30–4; Nov.–Jan., Tues.–Sun. 10–12:30 and 1:30–3.*

Ahrensburg A to Z

ARRIVING AND DEPARTING

By Car. Take the A–1 Autobahn for 25 kilometers (15 miles) and get off at the Ahrensburg exit. An alternative is Bundestrasse B–75.

By Train. Take the S-bahn line S-4 to Ahrensburg or the U-bahn line U-1 to Ahrensburg-Ost.

Altes Land

The marshy Altes Land extends 30 kilometers (19 miles) west from Hamburg along the south bank of the Elbe River to the town of Stade. This traditional fruit-growing region is dotted with huge half-timbered farmhouses and crisscrossed by canals. The fertile land is a popular hiking spot, especially in spring, when the apple and cherry trees are in blossom. Some of the prettiest walks take you along the dikes running next to the Rivers Este and Lühe. Much of the territory is best covered on foot, so wear your walking shoes. You may want to bring a picnic lunch as well and spend a long (summer) day here.

From the dock at Cranz, walk south into the suburb of **Neunfelde.** Here you can visit **St. Pancras Kirche** (St. Pancras Church), a Baroque church with an unusual painted barrel roof, worth a visit for its altar inside. It was built in 1688, and the organ, dating from the same period, was designed by Arp Schnitger, an organ builder and local farmer. ✉ *Am Organistenweg,* ☎ *040/745–9296.* ☺ *Daily 9–4.*

The village of **Jork** in Lower Saxony lies some 9 kilometers (5 miles) on foot to the west of Neunfelde, just beyond the confluence of the Este and Elbe rivers. Stroll through Jork and take in the early 18th-century church and decorative farmhouses. The old windmill in nearby **Borstel** is worth a short detour.

The town of **Stade** is about a 13-kilometer (8-mile) walk from the ferry docking point of Lühe. Stade is notable for the ruins of a rampart wall around the Altstadt (Old Town); it also contains the obligatory half-timbered houses. Four times the size of Jork, with a population of 45,000, it lies on the west edge of the Altes Land, on the River Schwinge, and was once a member of the Hanseatic League of trading towns.

Altes Land A to Z
ARRIVING AND DEPARTING

By Car. Take B–73 west from Harburg.

By Ferry. Ferries depart from the Landungsbrücken boat landing in the St. Pauli District twice daily during the week and four times daily on the weekends from mid-April through August and only on the weekends in September. Take the ferry to Lühe. To reach Cranz, take the ferry from Blankenese.

HAMBURG A TO Z

Arriving and Departing

By Bus
The **ZOB,** or **Zentral-Omnibus-Bahnhof,** Hamburg's bus station, is right behind the Hauptbahnhof (✉ Adenauerallee 78). For information ☎ 040/247–575, or contact the Deutsche Touring-Gesellschaft (✉ Am Römerhof 17, D–60486 Frankfurt/Main, ☎ 069/79030).

By Car
Hamburg can be reached by car from all other major German cities in fewer than seven hours. Incoming autobahns connect with Hamburg's three beltways, which then easily take you to the downtown area. Follow the signs for Stadtzentrum.

By Ferry
The **Ms. Hamburg** (☎ 040/383–930) carries passengers and cars three times a week for the 24-hour run between Hamburg and Harwich, England.

By Plane
Hamburg's international airport, **Fuhlsbüttel** (☎ 040/50750), is 11 kilometers (7 miles) northwest of the city. Many major U.S. airlines fly to Hamburg; there are also regular flights from Britain. There are frequent flights from all major German cities and European capitals.

BETWEEN THE AIRPORT AND DOWNTOWN

An **Airport-City-Bus** runs between the airport and Hamburg's Hauptbahnhof (main train station) daily at 20-minute intervals. Along the way buses stop at the hotels Reichshof, Atlantic, and Hamburg-Plaza, the central bus station at Adenauerallee 78, and at the fairgrounds. Buses run from 5:40 AM to 10:30 PM. Tickets are DM 8. The **Airport-Express** (Bus 110) runs every 10 minutes between the airport and the Ohlsdorf U- and S-bahn stations, a 17-minute ride from the main train station. The fare is DM 4. A taxi from the airport to the downtown area will cost about DM 30. If you're picking up a rental car at the airport, follow the signs to Stadtzentrum (downtown).

By Train
EuroCity and InterCity trains connect Hamburg with all German cities and many major European cities. Two InterCity Express "super train" lines link Hamburg with Frankfurt and Munich, and Würzburg and Munich, respectively. There are two principal stations: the centrally located **Hauptbahnhof** and **Hamburg-Altona,** west of the downtown area. For information, call 040/19419.

Getting Around

By Bicycle
Most major streets in Hamburg have paths reserved for bicyclists. From May through September rent bikes at the tourist information of-

fice at the main train station. Prices range from DM 2 per hour to DM 20 for the entire weekend. For information, call 040/3005–1244.

By Car

Hamburg is easier to handle by car than many other German cities, and is relatively uncongested by traffic. During business hours traffic, however, is as gridlocked as in any big German city, so avoid early morning and late afternoon hours.

By Public Transportation

The HVV, Hamburg's public transportation system, includes the U-bahn (subway), the S-bahn (suburban train), and buses. A one-way fare starts at DM 2.50, which covers approximately four stops; DM 4 covers about eight stops. Tickets are available on all buses and at the automatic machines in all stations and at most bus stops. A **Tageskarte** (an all-day ticket), valid from 9 AM to 1 AM, costs DM 7.70 for unlimited rides on the HVV system. If you're traveling with family or friends, a **Gruppen-od. Familienkarte** (group or family ticket) is a good value—a group of up to four adults and three children can travel for the entire day for only DM 13.20. Available from all of the Hamburg tourist offices, the **Hamburg CARD** allows unlimited travel on all public transportation within the city, admission to state museums, and approximately 30% discounts on most bus, train, and boat tours. The Hamburg CARD, which is valid for 24 hours (beginning at 6 PM through 6 PM the following day), costs DM 11.80 for one adult and up to three children under the age of 12; the family card costs DM 24 for four adults and up to three children under the age of 12. The Hamburg CARD for three days (valid starting at noon the first day) costs DM 23.80 and DM 38, respectively.

Tickets are not collected as you enter or leave the platform, but if you are found without a ticket, the fine is DM 80.

In the north of Hamburg the HVV system connects with the **A-bahn** (Alsternordbahn), a suburban train system that extends into Schleswig-Holstein.

Night buses (Nos. 600–640) serve the downtown area all night, leaving the Rathausmarkt and Hauptbahnhof every hour.

Information on the **HVV system** can be obtained directly from the **Hamburg Passenger Transport Board** by calling 040/322–911 (open daily 7 AM–8 PM).

By Taxi

Taxi meters start at DM 3.60, and the fare is DM 2.20 per kilometer, plus 50 pfennigs for each piece of luggage. To order a taxi, call 040/441–011, 040/686–868, or 040/611–061.

Contacts and Resources

Car Rentals

Avis, Airport, ☎ 040/5075–2314; ⊠ Drehbahn 15–25, ☎ 040/341–651. **Hertz,** Airport, ☎ 040/5075–2302; ⊠ Amsinckstr. 45, ☎ 040/230–045. **Sixt-Budget,** Airport, ☎ 040/5075–2305; ⊠ Friedrich-Ebert-Damm 160a, ☎ 040/693–9393.

Consulates

U.S. Consulate General, ⊠ Alsterufer 28, ☎ 040/411–710. **British Consulate General,** ⊠ Harvestehuder Weg 8a, ☎ 040/448–0320.

Emergencies

Police: ☎ 110. **Ambulance and Fire Department:** ☎ 112. **Medical Emergencies:** ☎ 040/228–022. **Dentist:** ☎ 040/468–3260 or 040/11500.

English Bookstore

Frensche (✉ Spitalerstr. 26e, ☎ 040/327–585) stocks books and news-papers.

Guided Tours

BOAT TOURS

Water dominates Hamburg, and there are few better ways to get to know the city than by taking a trip around the massive harbor. During the summer excursion boats and barges leave the Landungsbrücken (piers) every half hour for one-hour tours of the harbor. During the winter departures are not as frequent, with operators usually waiting for a full boat before setting off. The boats leave from Piers 1, 2, 3, and 7, and the trip costs DM 15. The Störtebeker line offers a six-course Baroque-style banquet with music during a four-hour tour of the harbor for DM 111. You must book in advance for this one (☎ 040/2274–2375). For additional information on harbor tours, call 040/311–7070, 040/313–130, 040/313–959, or 040/314–611.

Boat trips around the Alster Lakes and through the canals leave from the Jungfernstieg in the center of the city. From April through November they leave every half hour, less regularly in winter. The cost of the 50-minute tour is DM 14 for adults and DM 7 for children under 14; the complete two-hour tour costs DM 23.

From May through September there's a romantic, nighttime tour of the Alster Lakes leaving the Jungfernstieg every evening at 8 (the fare is DM 20). For information on these and other Alster tours, call 040/357–4240.

HAMBURG BY NIGHT

Stadtrundfahrt City Sightseeing (☎ 040/227–7595) offers adults-only tours of Hamburg hot spots nightly Tuesday–Saturday, from late March to early November and on Friday and Saturday nights the rest of the year. The tours leave Kirchenallee (in front of the Hauptbahn-hof) at 8 and take in a cross section of the city's night spots, including St. Pauli sex bars. The DM 99 fare includes drinks along the way. If you want a taste of Hamburg's no-holds-barred nightlife but don't want to head out on your own, this is a reasonable introduction.

ORIENTATION TOURS

Sightseeing bus tours of the city, all with English-speaking guides (☎ 040/227–1060) leave from Kirchenallee by the main train station. A bus tour lasting 1¾ hours sets off at 9, 11, noon, 1, 3, and 4 daily in summer, less frequently the rest of the year, and costs DM 26. A longer tour, lasting 2½ hours, starts at 10 and 2, costing DM 32. For an additional DM 12, both tours can be combined with a one-hour boat trip. Tours are conducted at irregular times, according to season. City tours aboard the nostalgic *Hummelbahn* (converted railroad wagons pulled by a tractor) are offered daily April–October, starting from the Kirchenallee stop hourly from 10 to 5; and at 10, noon, 2, and 4, November–March. The fare is DM 20 for 1½ hours. On Friday and Saturday at 8 PM May–August, the *Hummerbahn* (☎ 040/792–8979) also offers a three-hour evening tour of the city at a cost of DM 48 (including a drink). Some tours also leave from the Landungsbrücken; inquire at a tourist information office.

WALKING TOURS

Tours of the downtown area are organized by the **Museum für Arbeit.** They are held on weekends only May–September and are conducted in German only. Call 040/2984–2364 for information.

Late-Night Pharmacies

All pharmacies in Hamburg offer late-night service on a rotating basis. Every pharmacy displays a notice indicating the location of the nearest shop that is on duty. For **emergency pharmaceutical assistance** inquire at the police station nearest you.

Travel Agencies

American Express (✉ Rathausmarkt 5, ☎ 040/331–141). **Hapag-Lloyd** (✉ Verkehrspavillon Jungfernstieg, ☎ 040/3258–560).

Visitor Information

The main branch of the tourist office is in the **Bieberhaus** Hachmannplatz (next to the main railway station, ☎ 040/3005–1244). It's open weekdays 7:30 AM–6 PM, Saturday 8 AM–3 PM. In addition to its comprehensive hotel guide, the tourist office also publishes a monthly program of events in the city, *Hamburg Vorschau,* available for DM 2.30, which details upcoming shows, plays, movies, and exhibits. The illustrated magazine *Hamburg Tips* is issued quarterly and details major seasonal events; it's free of charge.

There's also a tourist office in the **Hauptbahnhof** (the main train station; ☎ 040/300–51200); it's open daily 7 AM–11 PM. The **airport tourist office** (☎ 040/300–51240) is open daily 8 AM–11 PM. At the harbor there's an office at the **St. Pauli Landungsbrücken** (boat landings; ☎ 040/300–51200); it's open daily 9:30–5:30. There's also an office in the **Hanse-Viertel** shopping mall (☎ 040/3005–1220), open weekdays 10–6:30 (Thurs. 10–8:30), Saturday 10–3 (10–6 on 1st Sat. of month).

All offices can help with accommodations, and there's a central booking office for telephone callers (☎ 040/3005–1300). A DM 5 fee is charged for every room reserved; the cost is then deducted from your bill at the hotel.

15 Berlin

Reunited Berlin is a metropolis born again, ready to assume its role as the capital of Germany and one of Europe's great cities. After almost 30 years of artificial division, it still remains at odds with its newly found unity. Today, due to burgeoning building development, the city has become the continent's largest construction site, with a skyline dominated by a forest of cranes. Yet Berlin maintains its youthful, dramatic, and mercurial atmosphere. Life here is literally on the razor's edge. As Central Europe's most important connection to the East, the city embraces a multitude of mingling cultures.

BERLIN'S ROLE AS THE FOCAL POINT and touchstone of a reuniting Germany began on November 9, 1989, when the infamous Berlin Wall fell, culminating two years later in the historic parliamentary vote to make the city once again the seat of the federal government and the parliament. Thus the end of the cold war was signaled in the city that was both the beginning cause and the permanent victim of one of the greatest geographic and political anomalies of all time. For nearly 30 years Berlin was split in two by a concrete wall more than 12 feet high—its larger western half an island of capitalist democracy surrounded by an East Germany run by hard-line Communists. Built in 1961 at the height of the cold war, the Berlin Wall symbolized the separation of two sharply different political and economic systems. Ironically, though, it also became a major tourist attraction, where viewing platforms along the western side enabled visitors to see the battlefront-like no-man's-land on the other side, guarded by soldiers and peppered with booby traps. The wall's demolition cast it once more as a symbol—this time of the change sweeping over former Iron Curtain countries. With the wall gone, and mostly recycled into street gravel, only four large chunks of the wall have been left standing as reminders of the grim past.

Compared to other German cities, Berlin is quite young and, ironically, began as two cities more than 750 years ago. Museum Island, on the Spree River, was once called Cölln, while the mainland city was always known as Berlin. As early as the 1300s, Berlin prospered from its location at the crossroads of important trade routes, and it filled with merchants and artisans of every description. After the ravages of the Thirty Years' War (1618–48), Berlin rose to power as the seat of the Hohenzollern dynasty, as the Great Elector (Friedrich Wilhelm), in his almost 50 years of reign, set off a renaissance in the city, especially in the construction of such academic institutions as the Academy of Arts and the Academy of Sciences. Later, Frederick the Great made Berlin and Potsdam his glorious centers of the enlightened yet autocratic Prussian monarchy.

The German Empire, dominated by Prussia with Berlin as its capital and ruled by the "Iron Chancellor," Count Otto von Bismarck in the late 19th century, proved to be the dominant force in unifying the many independent German principalities. Berlin maintained its status as the imperial German capital throughout the German Empire (1871–1918), the post–World War I Weimar Republic (1919–33), and Hitler's so-called Third Reich (1933–45). But the city's golden years were the Roaring '20s, when Berlin, the energetic, modern, and sinful counterpart to Paris, became a center for the cultural avant-garde. World-famous writers, painters, and artists met here while the impoverished bulk of its 4 million inhabitants lived in heavily overpopulated quarters. This "dance on the volcano," as those years of political and economic upheaval have been called, came to a grisly and bloody end after January 1933, when Adolf Hitler assumed power. The Nazis made Berlin their capital but ultimately failed to remodel the city into a silent monument to their iniquitous power based on fear and terror. During World War II Berlin was bombed to smithereens. At the end of the war, there was more rubble in Berlin than in all other German cities combined.

With the division of Germany after World War II, Berlin was also partitioned—with American, British, and French troops in the districts to the west, and the Soviet Union's forces to the east. With the advent of the cold war in 1947, Berlin became one of the world's hot spots. The three western occupied zones gradually merged, becoming West Berlin, while the Soviet-controlled eastern zone defiantly remained separate. A year later, in an attempt to force the Western Allies to relinquish their stake in the city, the U.S.S.R. set up a blockade cutting off all overland supply routes from the West. The Western Allies countered by mounting the Berlin Airlift. Some 750,000 flights delivered 2 million tons of goods, including an entire coal power plant, and kept West Berlin alive for most of a fateful year, until the Soviets finally lifted the blockade. Peace conferences repeatedly failed to resolve the question of Germany's division, and in 1949 the Soviet Union established East Berlin as the capital of its new puppet state, the German Democratic Republic. West Berlin was not legally part of the Federal Republic of Germany, although it was clearly tied to the western Federal Republic's political and economic system. The division of the city was cruelly finalized in concrete in August 1961, when the East German government constructed the infamous Berlin Wall, which broke up families and friendships.

With the wall now relegated to the junk pile of history, visitors can appreciate the qualities that mark the city as a whole. Its particular charm has always lain in its spaciousness, its trees and greenery, and its racy atmosphere. When the Greater City of Berlin, as the city-state is known today, was laid out in 1920, entire towns and villages far beyond the downtown area were incorporated. Most of the really stunning parts of the prewar capital are in the historic eastern part of town, which has grand avenues and monumental buildings, while the western downtown districts possess fancy shopping boulevards.

What really makes Berlin special, however, are the intangibles—the spirit and bounce of the city and its citizens. Berliners come off as brash, witty, no-nonsense types, who speak German with their own piquant dialect and are considered by their fellow countrymen as a most rude species. The bracing air, the renowned *Berliner Luft*, gets part of the credit for their high-voltage energy. It's attributable to the fact that many residents have faced adversity all their lives, and have managed to do so with a mordant wit and cynical acceptance of life. To many, crisis has been a way of life here for as long as they can remember. It is this particularly tense atmosphere that has attracted an international crowd from all walks of life.

Pleasures and Pastimes

Construction Sites

It may seem odd, but the latest addition to Berlin's sightseeing highlights is noisy and dirty construction sites. The city's historic downtown area is literally being rebuilt from scratch. Close to US$35 billion will have been spent here by the year 2000. Among the great development projects are the new government district in Tiergarten, between the Reichstag and the Brandenburger Tor, as well as the all-new company headquarters of Sony Europe, Mercedes Benz, and Asea Brown Boveri at Potsdamer Platz, which are still under construction. The first fancy shops on old Friedrichstrasse have already opened, but new arrivals make this traditional shopping boulevard in the heart of the city still worthy of investigating to see buildings in progress.

Fine Dining

As in few other German cities, dining in Berlin can either mean sophisticated nouvelle specialties in upscale restaurants with linen tablecloths and hand-painted porcelain plates or hearty local specialties in atmospheric and inexpensive inns; the range is as vast as the city itself. Specialties include *Eisbein mit Sauerkraut* (knuckle of pork with pickled cabbage), *Rouladen* (rolled stuffed beef), *Spanferkel* (suckling pig), *Berliner Schüsselsülze* (potted meat in aspic), *Schlachterplatte* (mixed grill), *Hackepeter* (ground beef), and *Kartoffelpuffer* (fried potato cakes). Spicy *Currywurst* is a chubby frankfurter that's served in a variety of ways at *Bockwurst* stands all over the city. Turkish specialties are an integral part of the Berlin food scene. On almost every street you'll find snack stands selling *Döner Kepab* (grilled lamb with salad in a flat-bread pocket).

Lodging

Berlin lost all its grand old luxury hotels in the bombing during World War II. A few were rebuilt, but today many of the best hotels are modern; although they lack little in service and comfort, you may find some short on atmosphere. For first-class or luxury accommodations, eastern Berlin is easily as good as the western parts of town. If you're seeking something more moderately priced, however, the better choice may be districts like Charlottenburg, Schöneberg, or Wilmersdorf, where there are large numbers of good-value pensions and small hotels; many of them date from the turn of the century, preserving some traditional character.

Museums

Berlin is home to some of the world's most unique museums, art galleries, and exhibition halls. Its more than 100 state and private museums showcase the arts, from ancient times through the medieval and Renaissance periods up to modern avant-garde; historic items of all ages; technology from all over the world; architecture and design of all styles; and nature's treasures. Among the jewels of Berlin's museum culture are original, life-size monuments of Greek, Byzantine, and Roman architecture, on the renowned Museum Island, and the collections of the two Egyptian museums, which include the famous bust of Egyptian queen Nefertiti.

Nightlife

Berlin is the only European city without official closing hours, so Berliners and tourists alike enjoy their drinks until the wee hours of the morning without fear of a last call. A peculiar leftover from the bygone days of Allied occupation, liberal handling of drinking hours has transformed Berlin into a nightlife El Dorado. More than 6,000 pubs, music and dancing clubs, cabarets, and theaters guarantee a thrilling variety of fun and entertainment. The city presents Germany's leading dramatic and musical productions, as well as lively variety shows in some of Europe's largest theaters, including the Friedrichstadtpalast. For dance buffs, the city will be just as pleasurable, as Berlin has turned into a mecca for acid jazz, house, and techno music.

EXPLORING BERLIN

Exploring Berlin is different from sightseeing in most other German big cities because, as a young and partly planned capital, its streets and boulevards are organized in a unusually clear manner. There are 23 boroughs in Berlin; for tourists, the three most important are Charlottenburg and Tiergarten in the downtown western area and Mitte in the historic eastern part of town. In addition, visitors should consider a few outlying districts south of the city.

Great Itineraries

Berlin is laid out on an epic scale—western Berlin alone is four times the size of the city of Paris. Although public transportation makes some sightseeing attractions convenient and inexpensive, the sheer magnitude of the city and its wealth of tourist attractions make it hard for strangers to reach many of the most important sights.

It takes only two days to explore both the western downtown and the eastern historic districts. Three days allow you a more leisurely pace that will give you time to gain a deeper insight into Berlin's dramatic history and exciting present, beyond the traditional tourist highlights. A trip of fewer than five days, however, is not enough time to experience the real, electrifying atmosphere of this city or to visit sights off the beaten track. If you stay here any longer, you may want to remain forever and become a Berliner.

IF YOU HAVE 2 DAYS

Start at famous **Kurfürstendamm** and stroll down the boulevard to **Kaiser-Wilhelm Gedächtniskirche** (Emperor Wilhelm Memorial Church) before doing some shopping or relaxing at the **Kaufhaus des Westens** (Department Store of the West), Europe's largest department store. Right in front of this building, Bus 100 will take you past the **Reichstag** (Parliament Building) to the **Brandenburger Tor** (Brandenburg Gate), where you should descend the bus and explore **Unter den Linden** and its various sights. First, make a detour to the **Gendarmenmarkt**, Berlin's finest square; then head over to the **St. Hedwigs-Kathedrale,** Berlin's only Catholic cathedral. Other nearby buildings in the historic center of old Berlin include the **Staatsoper Unter den Linden** (State Opera); the **Kronprinzenpalais** (Prince's Palace), the old palace residence for the royal family's heirs to the throne; and the **Deutsches Historisches Museum** (German History Museum), which showcases German history. Don't miss **Museumsinel** (Museum Isle) where—among other world-class monuments—the antique Pergamonaltar is on display. Equally impressive is the turn-of-the-century cathedral **Berliner Dom** (Berlin Cathedral), a reminder of Germany's imperial past. Finally, inspect Gothic **St. Marienkirche** (St. Mary's Church) at the beginning of the vast **Alexanderplatz,** the square that used to be former East Berlin's busiest spot.

The next day take a cab to the **Schloss Charlottenburg** with its art galleries and the **Ägyptisches Museum** (Egyptian Museum), with the portrait bust of Queen Nefertiti. In the afternoon head south to the greenery and lakes of the **Grunewald** and enjoy a leisurely afternoon at the favorite weekend spot of Berliners.

IF YOU HAVE 3 DAYS

Begin your tour of Berlin at one of the more western portions of the **Kurfürstendamm,** such as Olivaer Platz, and stroll down the thoroughfare to the east, doing some shopping in the elegant designer boutiques along your way. At Breitscheidplatz with its **Kaiser-Wilhelm-Gedächtniskirche,** you might want to stay a little bit longer to mingle with locals and street artists. Next, head over to the **Europa Center** and the **Zoologischer Garten** (Zoological Garden), and then spend some time at the **Kaufhaus des Westens** department store.

Start the next day at the greenery of **Tiergarten** (Animal Garden), the former hunting grounds for Prussian monarchs and now the city's largest landscaped park, with its **Siegessäule** (Victory Column) commemorating German military victories in the late 19th century. Take a quick look at **Schloss Bellevue,** the federal president's governmental seat, and look for German history at the **Reichstag** and the **Brandenburger Tor** before heading to the sights along **Unter den Linden.**

Spend your third day at the **Alexanderplatz** and continue on to the **Rotes Rathaus** (Red Town Hall), the late-medieval church **St. Nikolaikirche** (St. Nicholas's Church), and then to the capital's backyard around the **Neue Synagoge** (New Synagogue). At day's end make a quick tour of **Schloss Charlottenburg** and its surrounding attractions, including Ne-

Berlin

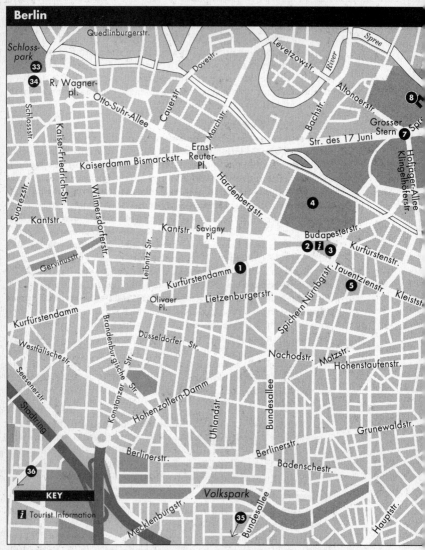

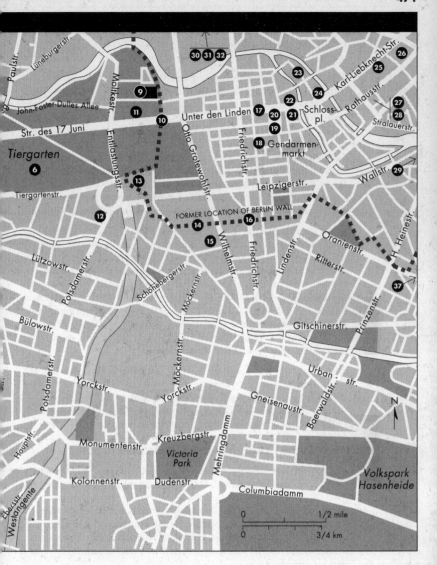

fertiti's portrait bust at the **Ägyptisches Museum** (Egyptian Museum). Before leaving town, make sure to stop by the **Dahlem Museums** and relax at the **Grunewald** forest.

IF YOU HAVE 5 DAYS

Start at the **Kurfürstendamm** and reserve a full day for its attractions. A thorough look at the **Tiergarten** with its greenery and sightseeing highlights makes for a pleasant second day. The next morning you might begin your walk on **Unter den Linden** at the **Brandenburger Tor,** moving along the grand boulevard towards the eastern part of the city, exploring all of its museums and historic buildings, including the **Sowjetisches Ehrenmal** (Soviet Honor Memorial), dedicated to the Red Army soldiers who died during the final battle of Berlin in World War II; the **Bertolt Brecht Museum and House,** the living quarters of playwright Bertolt Brecht; the **Märkisches Museum,** devoted to the city's history; and, finally, the **Jewish Cemetery,** the largest of its kind in Europe.

Begin your fourth day at the **Potsdamer Platz** (Potsdam Square) and continue through the district of Kreuzberg, with its various sights. A unique cluster of world-class museums, a music hall, and a state library awaits you at the **Kultuforum** (Cultural Forum). Next, investigate the **Preussischer Landtag** (Prussian State Legislature) and the **Prinz-Albrecht-Gelände** (Prince Albrecht Grounds), where former Nazi prison cellars were excavated. Proceed to one of Berlin's most historic spots— **Checkpoint Charlie,** the former border station at the Berlin Wall that was reserved for Allied personal and foreign visitors. End your day at the exhibitions of the **Schloss Charlottenburg.**

Spend your last day south of Berlin at the **Dahlem Museums** and the **Grunewald** forest. If you have time left, you may want to visit the **East Side Gallery,** a preserved section of the infamous Berlin Wall, now transformed into an open-air gallery; or the **Sachsenhausen Memorial** north of the city, with remnants of a Nazi concentration camp.

The Kurfürstendamm and Western Downtown Berlin

The Ku'damm, as Berliners (and most visitors as well) affectionately refer to the Kurfürstendamm, Berlin's busiest shopping street stretches for 3.2 kilometers (2 miles) through the heart of the city's western downtown section. The popular thoroughfare is lined with shops, department stores, art galleries, theaters, movie houses, and hotels, as well as some 100 restaurants, bars, clubs, and sidewalk cafés. Berlin's best-known boulevard bustles with shoppers and strollers most of the day and far into the night.

A Good Walk

Numbers in the text correspond to numbers in the margin and on the Berlin map.

Start your tour of the western downtown section of Berlin on the far western end of the **Kurfürstendamm** ①, either at Olivaer Platz or at Adenauerplatz farther west. As you make your way down the tree-lined boulevard in an easterly direction, stopping at elegant boutiques and one of the numerous cafés and restaurants along the way, you will eventually reach the **Kaiser-Wilhelm-Gedächtniskirche** (Emperor Wilhelm Memorial Church) ②, the very heart of western Berlin. The ruin serves as a memorial to the horrors of war and has become an urban meeting point for Berliners, outcasts and tourists alike, who contribute to the vibrant atmosphere on the square around the church.

Just steps away from the ruin is the **Europa Center** ③, one of the few Berlin shopping malls that still attracts masses of visitors and shoppers. The Berlin tourist information office is at the back of Europa Center on Budapester Strasse. Across from the entrance to the tourist office, you'll find the **Elefantentor** (Elephant Gate), the main entrance to the **Zoologischer Garten** ④, western Berlin's zoo and aquarium. Before visiting the zoo, take a stroll along Tauentzienstrasse, the boulevard that runs southeast away from the corner of Europa Center. Tauentzienstrasse, or the Tauentzien as Berliners prefer to call this not-very-fashionable shopping strip, leads you straight to Europe's largest department store, the **Kaufhaus des Westens** ⑤, nicknamed KaDeWe.

You could easily spend the whole day at this consumer's paradise. Instead, head back to the Zoologischer Garten. Catch the U-bahn subway near KaDeWe at Wittenbergplatz. This subway station, Berlin's first, was completed in 1913 and has been painstakingly restored. To reach the tour's final stop, **Zoologischer Garten,** take the subway one stop (to the station named after the zoo). You'll get out at the zoo's main entrance, on Hardenbergplatz, or you can backtrack and enter at the Elefantentor.

TIMING

To enjoy a leisurely walk from the western end of the Kurfürstendamm down to its beginning at Breitscheidplatz takes at least four hours, including a quick breakfast or lunch. If you wish to get a taste of urban life, you can easily spend at least three hours visiting the area around the Kaiser-Wilhelm-Gedächtniskirche, the Europa Center, and the shops along the Tauentzien and the KaDeWe. A trip to the zoo and the aquarium will take at least two hours. If you're in a hurry, you might consider spending less time shopping and more time watching the animals. Be mindful of the strict German store-closing hours and expect the Ku'damm to be extremely crowded on Saturday mornings; everybody is in a rush because all shops close at 2 PM.

Sights to See

Numbers in the margin correspond to points of interest on the Berlin map.

❸ **Europa Center.** This vast shopping and business complex was erected at the site of the renowned Romanisches Café, the hot spot for writers and actors during the Roaring '20s. Today, the plaza in front of the Europa Center is a "city within a city," where, in summer, Berliners, hippies, homeless people, and tourists mingle. This 1960s 22-story tower—dubbed "Pepper's Manhattan" after its owner, K. H. Pepper—houses more than 100 shops, restaurants and cafés, two cinemas, a theater, a casino, and the Verkehrsamt (tourist information center), with Berlin's largest thermal baths at the very top. You can even find two pieces of the Berlin Wall by the Tauentzienstrasse entrance. For a spectacular view of the city, take the lift to the i-Punkt restaurant and observation platform on the top floor. ⊠ *Breitscheidpl.*

★ ❷ **Kaiser-Wilhelm-Gedächtniskirche** (Emperor Wilhelm Memorial Church). This ruin stands as a dramatic reminder of the war's destruction. The bell tower, which Berliners call "hollow tooth," is all that remains of the once-imposing church, which was built between 1891 and 1895 and originally dedicated to the emperor, Kaiser Wilhelm I. On the hour you'll hear the chimes in the tower play a melody composed by the last emperor's great-grandson, the late Prinz Louis Ferdinand von Hohenzollern.

In stark contrast to the old bell tower are the adjoining Memorial Church and Tower built by famous German architect Professor Egon Eiermann in 1959–61. These ultramodern octagonal structures, with their myriad honeycomb windows, are perhaps best described by their nicknames:

the lipstick and the powder box. The interior is dominated by the brilliant blue of its stained-glass windows, imported from Chartres, France. Church music and organ concerts are presented in the church regularly.

An historic exhibition on the devastation of World War II inside the old tower features a religious cross constructed of nails that was recovered from the ashes of the burned-out Coventry Cathedral in England, destroyed in a German bombing raid in November 1940. ⊠ *Breitscheidpl.,* ☎ *030/218–5023.* ⊠ *Free.* ☉ *Tues.–Sat. 10–5; closed holidays.*

❺ Kaufhaus des Westens (Department Store of the West). The KaDeWe isn't just Berlin's classiest department store; it's also Europe's biggest department store, a grand-scale emporium in modern guise. An enormous selection of goods can be found on its seven floors, but it is best known for its food and delicatessen counters, restaurants, champagne bars, and beer bars covering the two upper floors, crowned by its rooftop winter garden. ⊠ *Tauentzienstr. 21,* ☎ *030/21–210.*

❶ Kurfürstendamm. This grand boulevard, known locally as Ku'damm, is certainly the liveliest and most exciting stretch of roadway in Berlin. The busy thoroughfare was first laid out during the 16th century as the path by which Elector Joachim II of Brandenburg traveled from his palace on the Spree River to his hunting lodge in the Grunewald. The Kurfürstendamm (Elector's Causeway) was developed into a major route in the late 19th century, thanks to the initiative of Bismarck, the "Iron Chancellor."

Don't look for house Number 1—when the Ku'damm was relocated in the early '20s, the first 10 address numbers were just dropped. Back then, the Ku'damm was a relatively new boulevard and by no means the city's most elegant one; it was fairly far removed from the old heart of the city, which was Unter den Linden in the eastern section of Berlin. The Ku'damm's prewar fame was due mainly to the rowdy bars and dance halls that studded much of its length and its side streets. Some of these were low-down dives, scenes of erotic circuses where kinky sex was the norm.

Along with the rest of Berlin, the Ku'damm suffered severe wartime bombing. Almost half of its 245 late-19th-century buildings were destroyed in the 1940s, and the remaining buildings were damaged in varying degrees. What you see today (as in most of western Berlin) is either restored or was constructed during the past decades. Although the street is frequently described as "glittering" and/or "sophisticated," there are those who are convinced it has lost whatever real charm and flair it may once have possessed.

★ ☻ ❹ Zoologischer Garten (Zoological Gardens). Germany's oldest zoo opened in 1844 and today has become Europe's largest. You'll find it in the southwestern corner of the 630-acre park called the Tiergarten (Wild Game Garden). After being destroyed during World War II, the zoo was carefully redesigned to create surroundings as close to the animals' natural environment as possible. The zoo houses more than 14,000 animals belonging to 1,700 different species and has been successful in breeding rare species. Among the zoo's claims to fame are Europe's largest and most modern birdhouse, a terrarium renowned for its crocodiles, and an aquarium with more than 10,000 fish, reptiles, and amphibians. The picturesque, Asian-style **Elefantentor** (Elephant Gate), which is the main entrance to the zoo, adjoins the aquarium. ⊠ *Budapester Str. 34,* ☎ *030/254–010.* ⊠ *Zoo DM 11, aquarium DM 10, combined ticket to zoo and aquarium DM 17.* ☉ *Zoo daily 9–6:30, 9–5 in winter; aquarium daily 9–6.*

Set some time aside for a coffee at **Einstein Cafe** (⊠ Kurfürstenstr. 58,
☎ 030/261–5096), where you can select from a variety of exotic cof-
fees. The Viennese-style coffeehouse is in the beautiful 19th-century mansion of German silent-movie star Henny Porten. Try its famous
Apfelstrudel; it's expensive but worth every pfennig.

The Tiergarten and the Brandenburger Tor

The Tiergarten, a beautifully laid-out park with lakes and paths is the
"green lung" of Berlin. In summer it is swamped by sunbathers and
families with their barbecues. Its eastern end between the grandiose
landmarks of the Reichstag (Parliament) and the Brandenburger Tor
(Brandenburg Gate) is currently being developed into the new seat of
the federal government.

A Good Walk
*Numbers in the text correspond to numbers in the margin and on the
Berlin map.*

From the Zoologischer Garten (☞ *above*), you can set off diagonally
through the greenery of idyllic **Tiergarten** (Animal Garden) ⑥, which
served as the hunting grounds of the Great Elector during the 17th century. At the center of the park you'll approach the traffic intersection
known as the **Grosser Stern** (Big Star), so called because five roads meet
here. This is the park's highest point and the site of the **Siegessäule** (Victory Column) ⑦. Follow the Spreeweg Road from the Grosser Stern to
Schloss Bellevue (Bellevue Palace) ⑧, the seat of the German federal president. Leave the Schloss Bellevue and head east along the John-Foster-
Dulles Allee, keeping the Spree River in sight on your left. You'll soon
pass the former **Kongresshalle** (Congress Hall), which houses exhibitions on modern art and cultures of Third World countries.

Continuing east, you'll reach the monumental **Reichstag** ⑨, the German Empire's old parliament building. By the year 2000, the historic
building will house the Bundestag, Germany's federal parliament. Due
to massive reconstruction, the Reichstag is closed, but you might be
lucky and get a glimpse of its facade or the new glass dome. Just south
of the Reichstag, where Strasse des 17. Juni meets Unter den Linden,
is another monumental symbol of German unity and of the long division of Berlin—the mighty **Brandenburger Tor** ⑩, probably the most
significant landmark of both German triumphs and defeats.

A short distance west, along Strasse des 17. Juni—a name that commemorates the 1953 uprising of former East Berlin workers that was
quashed by Soviet tanks—you will see the **Sowjetisches Ehrenmal** (Soviet Honor Memorial) ⑪. Turn south from the memorial onto the Ent-
lastungsstrasse and cross the tip of the Tiergarten to nearby Kemperplatz
with its **Kulturforum** (Cultural Forum) ⑫, a large square where you'll
find a series of fascinating museums and galleries, such as the **New National Gallery,** and the **Philharmonie** music hall. At its eastern side behind the **Staatsbibliothek** (National Library) lies the **Potsdamer Platz** ⑬,
Europe's biggest construction site, where several companies are erect-
ing their headquarters. To get a good look at the continuing build-up
of concrete and steel, head southeast along Stresemannstrasse. Then
follow Niederkirchnerstrasse, tracing the Berlin Wall's former location
in this area.

This is yet another strip of German history, with the old **Preussischer
Landtag** (Prussian State Legislature) ⑭, the seat of Berlin's parliament,
and the **Prinz-Albrecht-Gelände** (Prince Albrecht Grounds) ⑮, with
the cellar ruins of Nazi SS headquarters. The history of the hideous

Berlin Wall can be followed in the museum that arose at the former **Checkpoint Charlie** ⑯ crossing point at Friedrichstrasse, the second cross street heading east on Niederkirchnerstrasse. Almost nothing here remains of the days of the cold war, but the museum tells the fascinating stories of the wall, refugees, and spies.

TIMING

You can do the whole tour in a day, providing you take Berlin's least expensive public-transportation vehicle, Bus 100. It starts at the U-bahn station Zoologischer Garten and has several stops along the Kurfürstendamm and all major streets in the Tiergarten. You can leave and reboard the bus whenever you like. All buildings in the Tiergarten, with the exception of the Kongresshalle, are closed to the public, so you can explore Tiergarten in less than two hours, even if you walk. The Brandenburger Tor and the Kulturforum won't take long to see either. If you want to spend some time in the museums around Kemperplatz, reserve at least three hours before heading to the Preussischer Landtag and the Prinz-Albrecht-Gelände. Depending on the exhibitions shown, you might stay at those two places for another two hours minimum before exploring the area around Checkpoint Charlie. Walking distances between all major areas is less than 30 minutes.

Sights to See

Numbers in the margin correspond to points of interest on the Berlin map.

★ ⑩ **Brandenburger Tor** (Brandenburg Gate). This massive gate, once the pride of imperial Berlin, was left an eerie no-man's-land when the wall was built. After its demise the gate was the focal point of much celebrating, for this evocative symbol of Berlin was finally returned to all the people of the newly united city. The Brandenburger Tor, the only remaining gate of an original group of 14 built by Carl Langhans in 1788–91, was designed as a triumphal arch for King Frederick Wilhelm II in virile classical style paying tribute to Athens's Acropolis. The quadriga, a chariot drawn by four horses and driven by the Goddess of Peace, was added in 1794. Troops paraded through the gate after successful campaigns—the last time in 1945, when victorious Red Army troops took Berlin. The upper part of the gate, together with its chariot and Goddess of Peace, was destroyed in the war. In 1957 the original molds were discovered in West Berlin, and a new quadriga was cast in copper and presented as a gift to the people of East Berlin—a remarkable and rare instance of cold-war-era East–West cooperation, even though the Prussian Iron Cross on top of it, a symbol of western militarism to East Germans, was only added in 1991.

⑯ **Checkpoint Charlie.** This was the most famous crossing point between the two Berlins during the cold war; it was here that American and Soviet tanks faced each other during the tense months of the Berlin blockade in 1948–49. The crossing point disappeared along with the wall,
★   but the **Haus am Checkpoint Charlie** (House at Checkpoint Charlie— The Wall Museum) is still there. The museum reviews the history of the events leading up to the construction of the wall and displays actual tools and equipment, records, and photographs documenting methods used by East Germans to cross over to the West (one of the most ingenious instruments of escape was a miniature submarine). You can also see paintings, drawings, and exhibits of Berlin history since the erection of the wall and watch documentary films related to the exhibitions. ⊠ *Friedrichstr. 44,* ☎ *030/251–1031.* ☒ *DM 7.50.* ☉ *Daily 9 AM–10 PM.*

NEED A
BREAK?

While trying to imagine the former Checkpoint Charlie crossing and the wall, get a window seat at **Cafe Adler** (✉ Friedrichstr. 206, ☎ 030/ 251-8965), which once bumped right up against the wall. The soups and salads are all tasty—and cheap.

⓬ **Kulturforum** (Cultural Forum). With its unique ensemble of museums, galleries, libraries, and the philharmonic hall, the complex is considered one of Germany's cultural jewels. The exhibitions at the **Kupferstichkabinett** include European woodcuts, engravings, and illustrated books from the 15th century to the present. Also on display are several pen-and-ink drawings by Dürer, 150 drawings by Rembrandt, and a photographic archive. The Kunstbibliothek contains art posters, a costume library, ornamental engravings, and a commercial art collection. A new building opened in 1994, housing the Kupferstichkabinett (Drawings and Prints Collection) and the **Kunstbibliothek** (Art Library). Another building displays paintings dating from the late Middle Ages to 1800. ✉ *Matthäikirchpl. Kupferstichkabinett,* ☎ *030/ 266–2002; Kunstbibliothek,* ☎ *030/266–2030.* ⌖ *Free.* ⊙ *Tues.–Fri. 9–4, weekends 10–5. A Tageskarte (day card), covers 1-day admission to all museums at Kulturforum. Card (DM 8) is available at each museum.*

The roof that resembles a great tent belongs to the **Philharmonie** (Philharmonic Hall), the home to the renowned Berlin Philharmonic Orchestra since 1963 (☞ Nightlife and the Arts, *below*). The smaller Chamber Music Hall adjoining it was built in 1987. Both these buildings and the **Staatsbibliothek** (National Library), one of the largest libraries in Europe, were designed by Hans Scharoun.

The Philharmonie added the **Musikinstrumenten-Museum** (Musical Instruments Museum) in 1984. It is well worth a visit for its fascinating collection of keyboard, string, wind, and percussion instruments. ✉ *Tiergartenstr. 1,* ☎ *030/254–810.* ⌖ *DM 4; free Sun. and holidays.* ⊙ *Tues.–Fri. 9–5, weekends 10–5. Guided tours Sat. at 11; presentation of the Wurlitzer organ 1st Sat. of month at noon. Tour DM 3.*

Inside the **Kunstgewerbemuseum** (Museum of Decorative Arts), which is opposite the Philharmonie, you'll find a display of arts and crafts in Europe from the Middle Ages to the present. Among its notable exhibits are the Welfenschatz (Welfen Treasure), a collection of 16th-century gold and silver plates from Nürnberg, as well as ceramics and porcelains. ✉ *Matthäikirchpl.,* ☎ *030/266–2911.* ⌖ *DM 4; free Sun. and holidays.* ⊙ *Tues.–Fri. 9–5, weekends 10–5.*

The **Neue Nationalgalerie** (New National Gallery) collection comprises paintings, sculptures, and drawings from the 19th and 20th centuries, with an accent on works by such Impressionists as Manet, Monet, Renoir, and Pissarro. Other schools represented are German Romantics, Realists, Expressionists, and Surrealists. In a modern glass-and-steel building designed by Mies van der Rohe and built in the mid-1960s, the gallery frequently showcases outstanding international art exhibitions. ✉ *Potsdamer Str. 50,* ☎ *030/266–2662.* ⌖ *DM 4; free Sun. and holidays.* ⊙ *Tues.–Fri. 9–5, weekends 10–5.*

⓭ **Potsdamer Platz** (Potsdam Square). The once-divided capital is being rebuilt on this square, Berlin's former inner-city center, which was Europe's busiest plaza before World War II. Looking at today's constructions of steel, glass, and concrete, it is hard to imagine the square as the no-man's-land it was when the wall cut across it. Where the British, American, and Russian sectors once met, Sony, Mercedes Benz, Asea Brown Boveri, and Hertie are building their new company headquarters; the area will also contain a huge artificial city with apartments, theaters, cafés, a hotel, a movie complex, and a casino. The best overview of the site can be found at a futuristic, bright-red Information Center, which resembles an oversize container, at the eastern end of the Potsdamer Platz. You can also take a ride on U-bahn 2 between the stations Bülowstrasse and Mohrenstrasse or take a break at the National Library's cafeteria at the ☞ **Kulturforum** to get a spectacular look at the construction. ⊠ *Infobox, Leipziger Pl. 21,* ☎ *030/2266–2424.* 🎫 *Free.* 🕓 *Mon.–Wed. and Fri. 9–7, Thurs. 9–9, weekends 9–7.*

★ ⑭ **Preussischer Landtag** (Prussian State Legislature). The monumental parliamentary building on the northern side of Niederkirchnerstrasse now houses Berlin's House of Deputies and is one of Germany's most impressive administration buildings. Even if the House isn't in session, you should take a look inside and admire the huge entrance hall. Opposite is the **Martin-Gropius-Bau,** a renowned exhibition hall and home to a city museum, a gallery of local art, and a museum on Jewish culture in Berlin. Along Niederkirchnerstrasse is one of only four still-standing sections of the infamous Berlin Wall; the other three sections may be found along the Schiffahrtskanal by the Invaliden Cemetery in the Mitte District; along the southern end of Bernauer Strasse, also in Mitte (a museum is planned here); and along the Spree in the Friedrichshain District. ⊠ *Niederkirchnerstr. 5,* ☎ *030/2325–2325.* 🕓 *Weekdays 8–6.*

⑮ **Prinz-Albrecht-Gelände** (Prince Albrecht Grounds). Buildings here housed the headquarters of the SS, the Main Reich Security Office, and other Nazi security organizations from 1933 until 1945. After the war the grounds were leveled. They remained untouched until 1987, when the basements of the buildings, which were used as so-called "house prisons" by the SS, were excavated, and an exhibit documenting their history and Nazi atrocities was opened. ⊠ *Topography of Terror, Stresemannstr. 110,* ☎ *030/2548–6703.* 🎫 *Free.* 🕓 *Daily 10–6. Tours by appointment only.*

★ ⑨ **Reichstag** (Parliament Building). This gray and monolithic-looking building became world famous when, in the summer of 1995, American artists Christo and Jeanne-Claude wrapped the traditional seat of German parliament. The Reichstag was erected between 1884 and 1894 to house the German parliament during the time of the German Empire and later served a similar function during the ill-fated Weimar Republic. On the night of February 28, 1933, the Reichstag and its pompous glass dome were burned to a shell under mysterious circumstances, an event that provided the Nazis with a convenient pretext for outlawing all opposition parties. The Reichstag was rebuilt, but it was again badly damaged in 1945 in the Battle of Berlin, the final struggle between the Red Army and the German Wehrmacht. After extensive remodeling by British architect Sir Norman Foster, who is adding a new, futuristic glass cupola, the Reichstag is once again scheduled to host the Bundestag, starting in the year 2000. Until then it will be closed to the public.

⑧ **Schloss Bellevue** (Bellevue Palace). This small palace has served as the West German federal president's official residence in West Berlin since 1959. It was built on the Spree River in 1785 for Frederick the Great's youngest brother, Prince August Ferdinand. In 1994 then-president Richard von Weizsäcker made it his main residence. Since then it has been closed to the public. ⊠ *Schloss Bellevue Park.*

⑦ **Siegessäule** (Victory Column). The 227-foot-high granite, sandstone, and bronze column has a splendid view across much of Berlin. It was originally erected in 1873 to commemorate the successful Prussian military campaigns and was set up in front of the Reichstag. In 1938, when Hitler was having Berlin redesigned according to his megalomaniacal plans, the column was moved to its present site. A climb of 285 steps up through the column to the observation platform can be tiring, but the view makes it worth the effort. ⊠ *Am Grossen Stern.,* ☎ *030/391–2961.* 🖾 *DM 1.50.* 🕙 *Mon. 1–6, Tues.–Sun. and holidays 9–6.*

⓫ **Sowjetisches Ehrenmal** (Soviet Honor Monument). Built directly after World War II, this semicircular monument stands as a reminder of the bloody victory of Soviet troops over the shattered German army in Berlin in May 1945. The structure, which shows a bronze statue of a soldier, rests on a marble plinth taken from Hitler's former Berlin monumental Reichkanzlei. The memorial is flanked by what are said to be the first two T-34 tanks to have fought their way into the city during the last days of the war. ⊠ *Str. des 17. Juni.*

❻ **Tiergarten** (Animal Garden). For Berliners, the quiet greenery of Tiergarten is the equivalent of what Central Park is to New Yorkers—a green oasis in the heart of urban turmoil. The park with its 6½ acres of lakes and ponds was landscaped by famous garden architect Joseph Peter Lenné. In summer this park, with some 23 kilometers (14 miles) of footpaths along white marble sculptures, becomes the epitome of peaceful and multicultural Berlin: Turkish families frolic in the green meadows and have spicy barbecues, while children play soccer and gay couples sunbathe. The park suffered severe damage from World War II bombing raids. Then, during the freezing winter of 1945–46, Berliners desperate for fuel cut down many of the remaining trees. Replanting finally began in 1949. In the center of the Tiergarten you'll find the **Kongresshalle,** which was an engineering feat in 1957 when Americans built it; it collapsed in 1981, killing an American journalist. Nicknamed the "pregnant oyster," the rebuilt hall is now home to the World Culture House.

Unter den Linden and Historic Berlin

Behind the Brandenburger Tor (Brandenburg Gate; ☞ Tiergarten *and* Brandenburger Tor, *above*), Unter den Linden, the main street of the eastern part of Berlin, welcomes visitors with restored historic landmarks, museums, and hastily erected new office buildings. At the very end of this distinguished boulevard, around Alexanderplatz, Berlin's handful of skyscrapers bear witness to a bustling urban atmosphere.

A Good Walk

Numbers in the text correspond to numbers in the margin and on the Berlin map.

Begin your walk at the **Pariser Platz,** right behind the Brandenburger Tor, and take a long walk down **Unter den Linden** ⑰ to the east. This eastern and older counterpart to western Berlin's Kurfÿrstendamm is both more historic and more elegant, and often deserted. Continue down to the intersection of Unter den Linden and Friedrichstrasse, which from the turn of the century until the beginning of World War II was the busiest intersection in all Berlin. Turn right into Friedrichstrasse, passing the new and fancy shops, until you reach **Gendarmenmarkt** ⑱, one of Europe's finest plazas.

Head down Französische Strasse to **St. Hedwig's Kathedrale** ⑲, Berlin's leading Catholic church, and the **Staatsoper Unter den Linden** ⑳, the city's premier opera house. These buildings, along with the **Kronprinzenpalais** (Prince's Palace) ㉑—which adjoins the opera house— and **Humboldt-Universität** (Humboldt University), form the so-called

Forum Fridericianum, the epitome of Prussian glory, designed by Frederick the Great himself. Opposite the Kronprinzenpalais and next to Humboldt-Universität is the **Deutsches Historisches Museum** ㉒, the old Prussian armory that now houses Germany's National History Museum. Turn left and follow the Spree Canal, and you'll come to **Museumsinsel** (Museum Island) ㉓, on the site of Berlin's two original medieval settlements. Among the cultural treasures on this little isle is the Pergamon Altar, a monumental Greek temple that was shipped to Berlin in the late 19th century. From the museum complex follow the Spree Canal back to Unter den Linden and the enormous cathedral **Berliner Dom** ㉔ with its adjacent modern buildings left over from Communist rule.

Next, follow Karl-Liebknecht-Strasse to take a look at the 13th century **St. Marienkirche** (St. Mary's Church) ㉕ and the bordering **Alexanderplatz** ㉖, the wide-open square that formed the hub of eastern Berlin's city life. Walk across the lower end of the square past the **Rotes Rathaus** (Red Town Hall) ㉗, the city's Town Hall, and medieval **St. Nikolaikirche** (St. Nicholas Church) ㉘. Wander back down Rathausstrasse and cross Fischerinsel and Gertraudenstrasse before heading up the south bank of the canal to the redbrick **Märkisches Museum** ㉙, which displays the history of Berlin.

From here take the U-2 subway three stops to the Stadtmitte station, then change to the U-6, traveling three more stops to Oranienburger Tor. Walk north on Friedrichstrasse beyond the bend where the street turns into the Chausseestrasse to find the **Bertolt Brecht House and Museum** ㉚ and the bordering graveyard, where many historic figures are buried. Head back toward the Unter den Linden historic district and turn left down Oranienburger Strasse to the massive **Neue Synagoge** (New Synagogue) ㉛, which was recently restored. This synagogue, the largest in the city, lies at the southwestern end of Berlin's old Jewish Quarter and seems a bit out of place because a lot of other buildings in the area haven't been restored since the end of World War II. Just north of here, in the district of Weissensee, Europe's largest **Jewish Cemetery** ㉜ can be found.

TIMING

Exploring the historic heart of Berlin might seem just as exhausting as the city's past has been dramatic. The walk down Unter den Linden past Alexanderplatz to the St. Nikolaikirche and the Jewish Quarter takes about two hours if you don't take a closer look at any museums or other highlights. You should, however, allow at least the same amount of time for the Museumsinsel. You won't regret one minute of your visit. Most of the other sights, including the museums and cemeteries, can be seen in less than one hour each. If you're short on time, make sure to set clear priorities. Bear in mind that on weekends, Museumsinsel is crowded with tourists, so try to visit there early or during the week.

Sights to See

Numbers in the margin correspond to points of interest on the Berlin map.

★ ㉖ **Alexanderplatz.** This square once formed the hub of East Berlin city life. German writer Alfred Döblin dubbed it the "heart of a world metropolis." It's a bleak sort of place today, open and windswept and surrounded by grimly ugly modern buildings, with no hint of its prewar bustling activity—a reminder not just of the Allied bombing of Berlin but of the ruthlessness practiced by the East Germans when they demolished the remains of the old buildings. The square, named for Czar

Alexander I, and the surrounding area will hardly be recognizable after the completion of a planned radical transformation. After construction, due to run late into the first decade of the 21st century, Berliners may have a mini-Manhattan downtown with a dozen 40-story skyscrapers.

Finding Alexanderplatz from any other part of the city is no problem; just head toward the **Fernsehturm**, the soaring TV tower, completed in 1969 and 1,198 feet high (not accidentally 710 feet higher than western Berlin's broadcasting tower and 98 feet higher than the Eiffel Tower in Paris). The tower's observation platform offers the best view of Berlin; on a clear day you can see for 40 kilometers (24 miles). You can also enjoy a coffee break up there in the city's highest café, which rotates for your panoramic enjoyment. ⊠ *Panoramastr. 1a,* ☎ *030/242– 3333.* ⊡ *DM 6.* ☉ *Daily 9* AM*–midnight.*

㉔ Berliner Dom (Berlin Cathedral). The impressive 19th-century cathedral with its enormous green copper dome is one of the great ecclesiastical buildings in Germany. Its main nave was reopened in June 1993 after a 20-year renovation. There's an observation balcony that allows a view of the cathedral's ceiling and interior. More than 80 sarcophagi of Prussian royals are on display in the cathedral's catacombs. ⊠ *Am Lustgarten.* ⊡ *Balcony DM 3, museum free.* ☉ *Church Mon.–Sat. 9– 6:30, Sun. and holidays 11:30–6:30; balcony Mon.–Sat. 10–6, Sun. 11:30–6; museum Wed.–Sun. 10–6.*

Opposite the cathedral on Schlossplatz is a colossal modern building in bronze mirrored glass—the **Palast der Republik** (Palace of the Republic), a postwar monument to socialist progress that housed East Germany's so-called People's Chamber (parliament). Since 1991 the Palast has been closed and is still undergoing renovation while politicians try to find a meaningful use for the asbestos-poisoned building. Nothing about the structure and the vast square in front of it suggests that this was the very spot where the Hohenzollern city palace once stood. It was heavily damaged by bombings during the war and was then dynamited by the Communist regime. In 1993, to win support for reconstruction of the palace—an endeavor that would cost several billion dollars—a group of businessmen had a steel-and-plastic replica erected. But in spite of this massive and gallant effort, the city fathers are unwilling and unable to provide the necessary funds to make come true a dream for which a lot of their citizens still hope. The building at the southern end of Schlossplatz used to house East Germany's **Staatsrat** (Federal Senate).

㉚ Bertolt Brecht House and Museum. You can visit the former working and living quarters of playwright Bertolt Brecht and his wife, Helene Weigel, and there's a library for Brecht scholars. The downstairs restaurant serves Viennese cuisine using Weigel's recipes. Brecht is buried next door, along with his wife and more than 100 other celebrated Germans, in the **Dorotheenstädtischer Friedhof** (Doretheer Cemetery). ⊠ *Chausseestr. 125,* ☎ *030/282–9916. Apartment:* ⊡ *DM 4;* ☉ *Tues.–Fri. 10–noon, Thurs. 10–noon and 5–7, Sat. 9:30–noon and 12:30–2; tours every ½ hr. Library:* ⊡ *Free;* ☉ *Tues.–Fri. 9–3. Cemetery:* ☎ *030/ 461–7279;* ☉ *Daily 8–4.*

㉒ Deutsches Historisches Museum (German History Museum). The onetime Prussian arsenal (Zeughaus), a magnificent Baroque building constructed 1695–1730, houses Germany's National History Museum. The oldest building on Unter den Linden, it was used as a hall of fame glorifying Prusso-German militarism. The museum's permanent exhibit provides a compendium of German history from the Middle Ages to the present. ✉ *Unter den Linden 2,* ☎ *030/215–020.* 🎫 *Free.* ☉ *Thurs.–Tues. 10–6. Tours by appointment only. English-speaking guides available for DM 50.*

⑱ Gendarmenmarkt. One of Europe's finest piazzas, this large square is the site of the beautifully reconstructed 1818 **Schauspielhaus,** one of Berlin's main concert halls, and the **Deutscher and Französischer Dom** (German and French Cathedrals). At press time, the German cathedral on the south side was still undergoing restoration. The French cathedral contains the Hugenottenmuseum, with exhibits charting the history and the art of the Protestant refugees from France—the Huguenots—expelled at the end of the 17th century by King Louis XIV. Their energy and commercial expertise did much to help boost Berlin during the 18th century. ✉ *Gendarmenmarkt,* ☎ *030/229–1760.* 🎫 *DM 2.* ☉ *Wed.–Sat. noon–5, Sun. 1–5.*

㉜ Jewish Cemetery. More than 150,000 graves make this peaceful retreat Europe's largest Jewish cemetery. It can be found in Berlin's Weissensee District. The cemetery and tombstones are in excellent condition—a seeming impossibility, given its location in the heart of the so-called Third Reich. The cemetery lies just north of the old Jewish Cemetery on Grosse Hamburger Strasse. Destroyed by the Nazis, only a plaque and a few broken tombstones remain today. To reach the Weissensee cemetery, take Tram 2, 3, 4, 13, or 23 from Hackescher Markt to Berliner Allee and head south on Herbert-Baum-Strasse. ☉ *Sun.–Thurs. 8–4, Fri. 8–3; closed Jewish holidays.*

㉑ Kronprinzenpalais (Prince's Palace). Now used as a government guest house, this magnificent building designed in the Baroque style was originally constructed in 1732 by Philippe Gerlach for Crown Prince Friedrich (who later became Frederick the Great) and was chosen as the new federal president's seat in the German capital. But after a long legal dispute with the owner of the adjacent Opernpalais, the government gave up its plans and made Schloss Bellevue its first choice. During 1856–57, the palace was remodeled by Johann Heinrich Strack, when it received its current roof, the portico columns, and two side wings. ✉ *Unter den Linden 3.*

㉙ Märkisches Museum. At this showcase for Berlin's history, you can see exhibits on the city's theatrical past and a fascinating collection of mechanical musical instruments. They are demonstrated on Sunday at 11 and Wednesday at 3. ✉ *Am Köllnischen Park 5,* ☎ *030/308–660.* 🎫 *DM 3, instrument demonstration DM 2.* ☉ *Tues.–Sun. 10–6.*

★ ㉓ Museumsinsel (Museum Island). On the site of one of Berlin's two original settlements, Cölln, this unique complex of four world-class museums is an absolute must—and not just for museum buffs. The **Altes Museum** (Old Museum) is an austere neoclassical building just north of old Lustgarten that features postwar East German art; its large etching and drawing collection, from the Old Masters to the present, is a treasure trove. The **Alte Nationalgalerie** (Old National Gallery, entrance on Bodestrasse) houses an outstanding collection of 18th-, 19th, and early 20th-century paintings and sculptures and often hosts special temporary exhibits. Works by Cézanne, Rodin, Degas, and one of Germany's most famous portrait artists, Max Liebermann, are part of the permanent exhibition.

★ Even if you aren't generally interested in exhibits about the ancient world, make an exception for the **Pergamonmuseum** (entrance on Am Kupfergraben). It is not only the standout in this complex, but one of the world's greatest museums. The museum's name is derived from its principal and best-loved display, the Pergamon Altar, a monumental Greek temple discovered in what is now Turkey and dating from 180 BC. Equally impressive is the Babylonian Processional Way in the Asia Minor department.

Last in the complex, with an entrance on Monbijoubrücke, is the **Bodemuseum,** with its superb Egyptian, Byzantine, and early Christian relics, sculpture collections, and coin gallery. The Sphinx of Hatshepsut, from around 1500 BC, is stunning, as are the Burial Cult Room and the world's largest papyrus collection.

For all Museumsinsel: ☎ *030/203–550.* ✉ *Each museum on Museum Island DM 4, free Sun. and holidays. A Tageskarte (day card), available at each museum, covers 1-day admission to all museums for DM 8.* ☺ *All museums Tues.–Sun. 10–6.*

③① Neue Synagoge (New Synagogue). This meticulously restored landmark, built between 1859 and 1866, is an exotic amalgam of styles, the whole faintly Middle Eastern. When its doors opened it was the largest synagogue in Europe, with 3,200 seats. The synagogue was largely ruined on the night of November 9, 1938, the infamous Kristallnacht (Night of the Broken Glass), when Nazi looters rampaged across Germany, burning synagogues and smashing the few Jewish shops and homes left in the country. Further destroyed by Allied bombing in 1943, it remained untouched until restoration began under the East German regime in the mid-'80s. Its interior was partially restored and reopened in 1995, while its facade was restored between 1983–1990. The building is connected to the modern Centrum Judaicum, a center for Jewish culture and learning. ✉ *Oranienburger Str. 28/30,* ☎ *030/280–1250.* ☺ *Sun.–Thurs. 10–6, Fri. 10–2.*

The area to the northeast of the synagogue is known as the **Scheunenviertel** (Stable Quarters) or Jüdisches Viertel (Jewish Quarter). During the second half of the 17th century, the Great Elector brought artisans, small-business men, and Jews into the country to improve his finance situation. They moved here just outside one of the city's walls, along with many of the city's poor and a substantial number of military personnel (hence the stables). Early in the 18th century the city wall and the stables were moved in order to accommodate the city's growth. As industrialization intensified, the quarter became poorer, and in the 1880s many East European Jews escaping pogroms settled here. By the 20th century the quarter had a number of bars, stores, and small businesses frequented by gamblers, prostitutes (they're still here, along Oranienburger Strasse), and poor customers from the area. Jewish religious and business life flourished here until 1933, when the Nazis conducted their first raid and made arrests.

NEED A BREAK?   For coffee, cake, or an Israeli snack of eggplant and pita bread, stop at the **Beth Cafe** (✉ Tucholskystr. 40, ☎ 030/281–3135), one of the first Jewish businesses to open in the city's former Jewish district. The place is small and always full, so be prepared to share a table. Just around the corner from the synagogue, the café is run by the Adass Jisroel Jewish community.

②⑦ Rotes Rathaus (Red Town Hall). The renamed Berliner Rathaus is known for its redbrick design and friezes depicting the city's history. After the city's reunification, this pompous symbol of Berlin's 19th-century urban pride again became the seat of the city government. ✉ *Jüdenstr./Rathausstr.,* ☎ *030/24010.* ✉ *Free.* ☺ *Weekdays 9–6.*

①⑨ St. Hedwig's Kathedrale (St. Hedwig's Cathedral). Similar to the Pantheon in Rome, this substantial, circular building is Berlin's premier

Catholic church. When the cathedral was erected in 1747, it was the first Catholic church built in resolutely Protestant Berlin since the Reformation during the 16th century. Frederick the Great thus tried to silence Prussia's Catholic population after his invasion of Catholic Silesia. ⊠ *Hinter der Katholischen Kirche 3,* ☎ *030/203–4870.* ⊙ *Weekdays 10–5, Sun. 1–5.*

㉕ **St. Marienkirche** (St. Mary's Church). This medieval church, one of the finest in Berlin, is worth a visit for its late-Gothic fresco *Der Totentanz* (*Dance of Death*). Obscured for many years, it was restored in 1950, revealing the original in all its macabre allure. The cross on top of the church tower was an everlasting annoyance to Communist rulers, as its golden metal was always mirrored in the windows of the Fernsehturm TV tower, the pride of socialist construction genius. ⊠ *Karl-Liebknecht-Str. 8.,* ☎ *030/242–4467.* ⊙ *Mon.–Thurs. 10–noon and 1–4, weekends noon–4. Free tours Mon.–Thurs. at 1, Sun. at 11:45.*

㉘ **St. Nikolaikirche** (St. Nicholas Church). The complex of buildings centering around this medieval twin-spire church gives you an idea of what the old Berlin looked like. The quarter with its tiny cobblestone streets that has grown around Berlin's oldest parish church, dating from 1230, is filled with stores, cafés, and restaurants. The adjacent **Fischerinsel** (Fisherman's Island) area was the heart of Berlin 750 years ago, and today retains some of its medieval character. At Breite Strasse you'll find two of Berlin's oldest buildings: No. 35 is the Ribbeckhaus, the city's only surviving Renaissance structure, dating from 1624, and No. 36 is the early Baroque Marstall, built by Michael Matthais from 1666 to 1669. ⊠ *Nikolaikirchpl.,* ☎ *030/2380–900.* 🎫 *DM 3.* ⊙ *Tues.–Sun. 10–6.*

⑳ **Staatsoper Unter den Linden** (State Opera). The lavishly restored opera house, Berlin's prime opera stage, lies at the heart of the Forum Fridericianum. This ensemble of surrounding buildings was designed by Frederick the Great himself to showcase the splendor of his enlightened rule. A performance at the opera house with its maestro, Daniel Barenboim, is often memorable. ⊠ *Unter den Linden 7,* ☎ *030/2035–4555.* ⊙ *Box office weekdays noon–5:45.*

NEED A BREAK?	·The **Opernpalais** (⊠ Unter den Linden 5, ☎ 030/204–2269) right next to the opera house is home to four different restaurants and cafés, all famous for their rich German cakes, pastries, and brunches.

⑰ **Unter den Linden.** Thanks to several new buildings, the central thoroughfare of old Berlin has slowly transformed back into the elegant avenue it was during prewar times. Its name means "under the linden trees"—no wonder Marlene Dietrich once sang: "As long as the old linden trees still bloom, Berlin is still Berlin." Among the sightseeing attractions worth visiting on Unter den Linden are the ☞ **Kronprinzpalais,** the ☞ **Deutsches Historiches Museum,** and **Humboldt-Universität** (Humboldt University), originally built in 1766 as a palace for the brother of Friedrich II of Prussia. It became a university in 1810, and Karl Marx and Friedrich Engels were once among its students. The main hall of the university (⊠ Unter den Linden 6, ☎ 030/20930) is open Monday–Saturday 6 AM–10 PM.

Adjacent to the University is the **Neue Wache** (New Guardhouse). Constructed in 1818, it served as the Royal Prussian War Memorial until the declaration of the Weimar Republic in 1918. Badly damaged in World War II, it was restored by the East German state and rededicated in 1960. After unification it was restored to its Weimar Republic appearance and, in November 1993, inaugurated as Germany's central war memorial.

Of particular historic interest is the crossing of Unter den Linden and **Friedrichstrasse,** once lined with clubs, along with cabarets and avant-garde theaters. Even though Friedrichstrasse has been significantly transformed from its dreary pre-unification days and now offers a growing number of shops, restaurants, and bars, it still can't compete with the glitz and glamour of Ku'damm and the sheer number of establishments there.

Palaces and Parks in Outer Berlin

Berlin might appear to be a highly energetic city, but beyond its inner district, it is surprisingly green and idyllic. In addition to the Tiergarten, there are several palaces, parks, and museums in the southwestern parts of town that are well worth a visit.

A Good Tour

Numbers in the text correspond to numbers in the margin and on the Berlin map.

Besides Berlin's main attractions in the western downtown and eastern historic district, the city has sightseeing spots in outlying areas to the south, the east, and the north that should not to be missed. In the far west of the Charlottenburg District lies the Baroque palace that gave this part of town its name: **Schloss Charlottenburg** ㉝, with its museums and the adjacent **Ägyptisches Museum** ㉞. To get to Schloss Charlottenburg from western downtown Berlin, take the U-bahn 2 from Wittenbergplatz or Zoologisher Gerten station in the direction of Ruhleben. Get off at the Bismarckstrasse stop and then take the U-bahn 7 in the direction of Rathaus Spandau to Richard-Wagner-Platz station. From here, walk northwest on Otto-Suher-Allee toward the dome of the palace. The total U-bahn ride takes about 15 minutes.

South of Berlin is a cluster of fine museums, known as the **Dahlem Museums** ㉟, which includes the Gamädegalerie, with its superb collection of European paintings. The best way to get there from downtown Berlin is by the U-bahn 1 to Dahlem Dorf station. To reach the Dahlem Museums from Schloss Charlottenburg, walk to Richard-Wagner Platz station and ride the U-bahn 7 in the direction of Rudow until you reach the stop Feherbelliner Platz. Change trains here and take U-bahn 1 in the direction of Krumme Lanke, getting off at Dahlem Dorf. The trip from the palace to the museums takes about a half hour.

From the Dahlem Museums, it is a short ride via the U-bahn 1 line to the Krumme Lanke station. Change trains at the suburban railway station at nearby Mexikoplatz and take a ride on the S-bahn 3 (in the direction of Potsdam Stadt) or 7 (in the direction of Wannsee) to the Nikolassee, Wannsee, or Grunewald stations. Each serves as a starting point for hour-long hikes through the greenbelt of the **Grunewald** ㊱ and the Wannsee lakes.

It's quite a ride on the S-bahn line toward the east and the **East Side Gallery** ㊲, with a remaining section of the Berlin Wall; there are more than a hundred paintings on the once infamous concrete. From Wannsee, take S-bahn 3 (in the direction of Erkner) or 7 (in the direction of Ahrensfelde). Leave the train at Hauptbahnhof and walk toward the Spree, to the southern end of Strasse der Pariser Commune, to reach the East Side Gallery. The trip from Wannsee to the gallery will take between 45 minutes and an hour.

Finally, you can also make a trip to Sachsenhausen, 35 kilometers (22 miles) north of Berlin, where you'll find the **Sachsenhausen Memorial** ㊳, the only Nazi concentration camp near Berlin. To reach Sachsenhausen, take the suburban S-bahn 1 from Friedrichstrasse to Oranienburg, the last stop. The ride will take 45 to 50 minutes. From the station it's a 25-minute walk, or you can take a taxi. To reach Sachsenhausen from the East Side Gallery, take any S-bahn (3, 5, 7, or 9) from Hauptbahnhof to Friedrichstrasse, and then change trains to Line 1, getting off at Oranienburg. The total trip from Hauptbahnhof to Oranienburg lasts about an hour.

TIMING

To take in all the attractions above, you will need at least two full days, with one of them devoted to Schloss Charlottenburg, the Dahlem Museums, and the Grunewald area alone. A second day may be spent seeing the sights in the east and north of Berlin. If you skip the two museums at Schloss Charlottenburg and Dahlem, you will still need a full day to visit the other places.

Sights to See

Numbers in the margin correspond to points of interest on the Berlin map.

㉞ Ägyptisches Museum (Egyptian Museum). The former east guardhouse and residence of the king's bodyguard is now home to the famous portrait bust of the exquisite **Queen Nefertiti.** The 3,300-year-old sculpture of the Egyptian queen is the centerpiece of a collection of works that spans Egypt's history since 4000 BC and includes some of the best-preserved mummies outside Cairo. The museum is across from ☞ **Schloss Charlottenburg.** ✉ *Schlossstr. 70,* ☎ *030/320–911.* ▣ *DM 4.50.* ☉ *Mon.–Thurs. 9–5, weekends 10–5.*

㉟ Dahlem Museums. This unique complex of seven museums includes the **Gemäldegalerie** (Painting Gallery), the **Museum fur Völkerkunde** (Ethnographic Museum), and the **Skulpturensammlung** (Sculpture Collection). The **Gemäldegalerie,** considered to be one of Germany's finest art galleries, houses an extensive selection of European paintings from the 13th to the 18th century. Several rooms on the first floor are reserved for paintings by German masters, among them Dürer, Cranach the Elder, and Holbein. An adjoining gallery houses the works of the Italian masters—Botticelli, Titian, Giotto, Lippi, and Raphael—and another gallery on the first floor is devoted to paintings by Dutch and Flemish masters of the 15th and 16th centuries: van Eyck, Bosch, Brueghel the Elder, and van der Weyden. Flemish and Dutch paintings from the 17th century are displayed on the floor above; it contains the world's second-largest Rembrandt collection.

The **Museum für Völkerkunde** is internationally famous for its arts and artifacts from Africa, Asia, the South Seas, and the Americas. The large collection of Mayan, Aztec, and Incan ceramics and stone sculptures should not be missed. The **Skulpturensammlung** houses Byzantine and European sculpture from the 3rd to the 18th century. Included in its collection is Donatello's *Madonna and Child,* sculpted in 1422. *Dahlem Museums:* ☎ *030/83011.* ▣ *Individual admission to Gemäldegalerie (entrance at Arnimallee 23–27), Museum für Völkerkunde, (entrance at Lansstr. 8), and Skulpturensammlung (entrance at Arnimallee 23–27) is DM 4; free Sun. and holidays.* ☉ *Tues.–Fri. 9–5, weekends 10–5.*

㊲ East Side Gallery. This section of concrete amounts to nothing less than the largest open-air gallery in the world. Between February and June of 1990, 118 artists from around the globe created unique works of art on the longest—1.3 kilometers (2 miles)—remaining section of the Berlin Wall; it has been declared an historic monument. One of the most well-known works, by Russian artist Dmitri Vrubel, depicts Brezhnev and Honnecker (the former East German leader) kissing, with the caption "My God. Help me survive this deadly love." ✉ *Mühlenstr./Oberbaumbrücke.* ⊘ *Summer, daily 10–5; rest of yr, weekends 10–5.*

36 **Grunewald** (Green Forest). Together with its Wannsee lakes, this splendid forest is the most popular green retreat for Berliners. On weekends in spring and fall and daily in summer, Berliners come out in force, swimming, sailing their boats, tramping through the woods, and riding horseback. In winter a downhill ski run and even a ski jump operate on the modest slopes of Teufelsberg Hill. In no other European city has such an expanse of uninterrupted natural surroundings been preserved. In addition, some 60 lakes, connected by rivers, streams, and canals in a verdant setting of meadows, woods, and forests are situated along the city's fringe. Excursion steamers ply the water wonderland of the Wannsee, the Havel River, and the Müggelsee. (☞ Guided Tours *in* Berlin A to Z, *below.*)

38 **Sachsenhausen Gedenkstätte** (Sachsenhausen Memorial). The only Nazi concentration camp near the so-called Third Reich capital was established in 1936, later becoming a Soviet internment and prison camp for German soldiers. In 1961 the camp was made into a memorial to its more than 100,000 victims. The area has a few preserved facilities and barracks, as well as a memorial and museum. ✉ *Oranienburger Str. der Nationen 22,* ☎ *03301/803–719.* ▣ *Free.* ⊘ *Tues.–Sun. 8.30–4:30.*

33 **Schloss Charlottenburg** (Charlottenburg Palace). This showplace of western Berlin, the most monumental reminder of imperial days, served as a city residence for the Prussian rulers. You can easily spend a full day at Charlottenburg. In addition to the apartments of the Prussian nobility, you may explore the landscaped gardens and several excellent museums set within and just outside the grounds.

The gorgeous palace started as a modest royal summer residence in 1695, built on the orders of King Friedrich I for his wife, Queen Sophie-Charlotte. During the 18th century, Frederick the Great made a number of additions, such as the dome and several wings designed in the rococo style. By 1790 the complex had evolved into the massive royal domain you see today. The palace was severely damaged during World War II but has been painstakingly restored. Many of the original furnishings and works of art survived the war and are now on display. Behind heavy iron gates the Court of Honor—the courtyard in front of the palace—is dominated by a fine Baroque statue, the Reiterstandbild des Grossen Kurfürsten (the equestrian statue of the Great Elector).

Inside the main building the suites of Friedrich I and his wife are furnished in the prevailing style of the era. Paintings include royal portraits by Antoine Pesne, a noted court painter of the 18th century. On the first floor you can visit the Oak Gallery, the early 18th-century palace chapel, and the suites of Friedrich Wilhelm II and Friedrich Wilhelm III, furnished in the Biedermeier style.

A gracious staircase leads up to the sumptuous state dining room and the 138-foot-long **Golden Gallery.** West of the staircase are the rooms of Frederick the Great, in which the king's extravagant collection of works by Watteau, Chardin, and Pesne are displayed. Also in the so-called New Wing is the **Galerie der Romantik,** the National Gallery's collection of masterpieces from such 19th-century German painters as Karl Friedrich Schinkel and Caspar David Friedrich, the leading member of the German Romantic school. Visits to the royal apartments are by guided tour only; tours leave every hour on the hour from 9 to 4. Parks and gardens can be visited for free and offer a pleasant respite from sightseeing. ✉ *Luisenpl.,* ☎ *030/320–911.* ▣ *Galerie der Romantik DM 4, guided tour DM 4.* ⊘ *Tues.–Fri. 9–5, weekends 10–5.*

The **Antikensammlung** (antique collection) in the former west guard-house is home to a collection of ceramics and bronzes as well as everyday utensils from ancient Greece and Rome and a number of Greek vases from the 6th to the 4th century BC.

The **Museum für Vor- und Frügeschichte** (Museum of Pre- and Early History) depicts the stages of the evolution of humanity from 1 million BC to the Bronze Age. It is in the western extension of the palace opposite Klausener Platz. ☎ *030/320–911 for all 3 museums.* ✉ *Individual admission to Ägyptisches Museum, Antikensammlung, and Museum für Vor- and Frügeschichte: DM 4; free Sun. and holidays. A Tageskarte (day card), available at each museum, covers 1-day admission to all 3 museums. The card is DM 8 and includes a guided tour of Schloss Charlottenburg.* ☉ *Mon.–Thurs. 9–5, weekends 10–5.*

The park behind the palace was laid out beginning in 1697 as a baroque French (its only remains are near the palace) and was transformed into an English garden in the early 19th century. There are several buildings in the park that deserve particular attention, including the Belvedere, a teahouse (overlooking the lake and Spree River) that now houses a collection of Berlin porcelain, and the Schinkel Pavilion behind the palace near the river.

DINING

CATEGORY	COST*
$$$$	over DM 100
$$$	DM 75–DM 100
$$	DM 50–DM 75
$	under DM 50

per person for a three-course meal, excluding drinks

$$$$ ★ ✗ **Bamberger Reiter.** One of the city's leading restaurants, Bamberger is presided over by Tyrolean chef Franz Raneburger. He relies on fresh market produce for his *Neue Deutsche Küche* (new German cuisine), so the menu changes daily. Fresh flowers set off this attractive, oak-beamed restaurant. ✉ *Regensburgerstr. 7,* ☎ *030/218–4282. Reservations essential. AE, DC, V. Closed Sun., Mon., and Jan. 1–15. No lunch.*

$$$$ ✗ **Ermeler-Haus.** The rococo grandeur of this wine restaurant reflects the elegance of the restored patrician home whose upstairs rooms it occupies. The house dates from the mid-16th century and was moved to its present location in 1969. The restaurant's atmosphere is subdued and formal, the wines are imported, and the service and German cuisine are excellent. There's dancing every Saturday evening. ✉ *Märkisches Ufer 10,* ☎ *030/279–4028. AE, DC, MC, V. Closed Mon.*

$$$$ ✗ **Frühsammer's Restaurant an der Rehwiese.** Here you can watch chef Peter Frühsammer at work in his open kitchen. He's ready with advice on the daily menu; salmon is always a treat. The restaurant is in the annex of a turn-of-the-century villa in the Zehlendorf District (U-bahn to Krumme Lanke and then Bus 53 to Rehwiese). ✉ *Matterhornstr. 101,* ☎ *030/803–8023. Reservations essential. AE, MC. No lunch.*

$$$$ ★ ✗ **Rockendorf's.** The city's premier restaurant only has fixed-price menus, some with up to nine courses. Exquisitely presented on fine porcelain, the mainly nouvelle specialties are sometimes fused with classic German cuisine. The wine list—with 800 choices, one of the world's best—has the appropriate accompaniment to any menu. ✉ *Düsterhauptstr. 1,* ☎ *030/402–3099. Reservations essential. AE, DC, MC, V. Closed Sun., Mon., 3 wks in summer, Dec. 25, and Jan. 1.*

$$$ ✗ **Alt-Luxemburg.** In the Charlottenburg District, this popular restaurant is tastefully furnished, and attentive service enhances the intimate

setting. Chef Karl Wannemacher uses only the freshest ingredients for his French-German dishes, including his divine lobster lasagna. ⊠ *Windscheidstr. 31,* ☎ *030/323–8730. AE, DC, V. Closed Sun.*

$$$ ✕ **Borchardt.** This is one of the most fashionable of the meeting places
★ that have sprung up in historic Berlin. The high ceiling, columns, red plush benches, and Art Nouveau mosaic (discovered during renovations) help create the impression of a 1920s café where today's celebrities like Karl Lagerfeld or Claudia Schiffer meet. The restaurant serves entrées with a French accent and is well known for its luscious seafood platter (DM 58). Desserts include whiskey parfait with honey sauce and strawberry parfait with rhubarb foam. Sunday brunches are particularly popular, so plan ahead. ⊠ *Französische Str. 47,* ☎ *030/229–3144. AE, V.*

$$$ ✕ **Paris Bar.** Just off the Ku'damm, this trendy restaurant attracts a polyglot clientele of film stars, artists, entrepreneurs, and executives who care more for glamour than gourmet food. The cuisine, including such delights as Jacques oysters and lamb chops with Provençal herbs, is high-powered, medium-quality French. ⊠ *Kantstr. 152,* ☎ *030/313–8052. AE.*

$$$ ✕ **Tucci.** This Italian restaurant, where light dishes are served along with
★ fine wines, is still a well-kept secret. As in few upscale Charlottenburg eateries, service is friendly and quick; in summer you can sit down at one of their outside tables and enjoy people-watching. Ask for their specials of the day. ⊠ *Grolmanstr. 52,* ☎ *030/313–9335. No credit cards.*

$$ ✕ **Französischer Hof.** The ceilings in this classy restaurant are high, and the wine list is long. International fare, with an emphasis on French dishes, is served with impeccable service. The maître d' claims guests can find "an oasis of calm and relaxation" here, and he's right. The summer terrace offers a seat practically on the Gendarmenmarkt. ⊠ *Jägerstr. 56,* ☎ *030/229–3969. AE, DC, MC, V.*

$$ ✕ **März am Ufer.** Come here for nouvelle German and Continental cuisine at its best. The creative concoctions include fresh homemade pasta with organic spinach leaves. It's near the New National Gallery, overlooking the Schöneberger Ufer. Because this is a relatively small place, ask for a table in the room away from the hustle of the bar. The marble walls and striking lighting effects may remind you of a sleek New York restaurant. ⊠ *Schöneberger Ufer 65,* ☎ *030/261–3882. No credit cards. Closed Mon. and Dec. 25–Jan. 1. No lunch.*

$$ ✕ **Reinhard's.** In the Nikolai Quarter, you'll discover one of eastern Berlin's popular eating establishments. Friends meet here to enjoy the carefully prepared entrées and to sample spirits from the amply stocked bar, all served by friendly, colorful tie–wearing waiters. The honey-glazed breast of duck, *Adlon,* is one of the house specialties. If you just want to hug the bar but find no room here, don't despair; head two doors down to Italian Otello (under the same management). ⊠ *Poststr. 28,* ☎ *030/242–5295. AE, DC, MC, V.*

$$ ✕ **Turmstuben.** Not for the infirm or those who are afraid of heights, this restaurant, tucked away below the cupola of the French Cathedral at the north side of the Gendarmenmarkt, is reached by a long, winding staircase. Your reward at the top of the stairs is a table at one of Berlin's most original and attractive restaurants. The menu is short, but there's an impressive wine list. ⊠ *Gendarmenmarkt 5,* ☎ *030/229–9313. Reservations essential on weekends. AE, MC, V.*

$$ ✕ **Zitadellen-Schänke.** Here you'll dine like a medieval noble, served a multicourse menu by Prussian wenches and serenaded by a minstrel group. In winter a roaring fire helps to light and warm the vaulted restaurant, which is part of Spandau's historic Zitadelle. These medieval banquets are popular, so be sure to reserve your spot at one of the heavy,

Berlin Dining

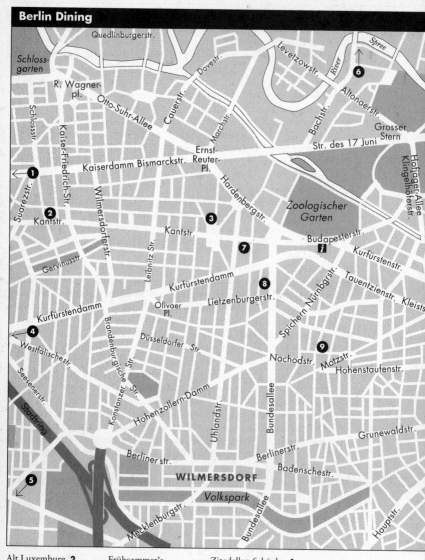

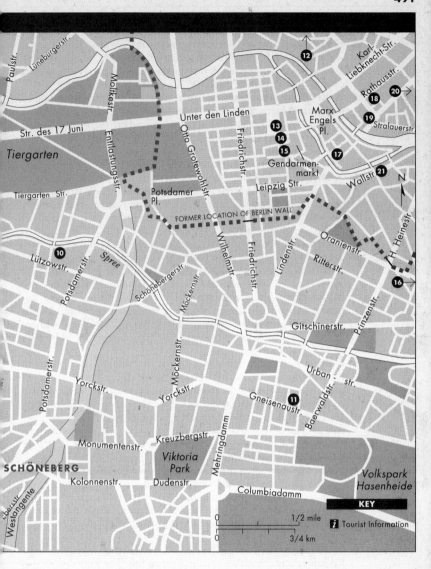

Paulstr.

Lüneburgerstr.

Moltkestr.

Str. des 17 Juni

Tiergarten

Tiergarten Str.

Entlastungsstr.

Otto Grotewohlstr.

Unter den Linden

Friedrichstr.

Karl-
Liebknecht-Str.

Rathausstr.

Stralauerstr.

Marx
Engels
Pl.

Gendarmen-
markt

Leipzig Str.

Potsdamer
Pl.

Wallstr.

N

FORMER LOCATION OF BERLIN WALL

Wilhelmstr.

Friedrichstr.

Lindenstr.

Oranienstr.

Ritterstr.

H. Heinestr.

Lützowstr.

Spree

Potsdamerstr.

Schönebergerstr.

Möckernstr.

Gitschinerstr.

Prinzenstr.

Urban str.

Potsdamerstr.

Yorckstr.

Yorckstr.

Möckernstr.

Gneisenaustr.

Baerwaldstr.

Monumentenstr.

Kreuzbergstr.

Mehringdamm

*Viktoria
Park*

SCHÖNEBERG

Kolonnenstr.

Dudenstr.

Columbiadamm

*Volkspark
Hasenheide*

Oberstr.

Westtangente

10

11

12

13

14

15

16

17

18

19

20

21

KEY

i Tourist Information

0   1/2 mile

0   3/4 km

antique oak tables. ✉ *Am Juliusturm, Spandau,* ☎ *030/334–2106. AE, DC, MC, V. Closed Mon.*

$$ ✕ **Zur Rippe.** This popular eating place in the Nikolai Quarter serves wholesome food in an intimate setting characterized by oak paneling and ceramic tiles. Specialties include the cheese platter and a herring casserole. ✉ *Poststr. 17,* ☎ *030/242–4248. AE, DC, MC, V.*

$ ✕ **Alt-Cöllner Schankstuben.** A tiny restaurant and pub are contained within this charming, historic Berlin house. The section to the side of the canal on the Kleine Gertraudenstrasse, where there are tables set outside, serves as a café. The menu is relatively limited, but the quality—like the service—is good. ✉ *Friederichsgracht 50,* ☎ *030/242–5972. Reservations not accepted. AE, DC, MC, V.*

$ ✕ **Blockhaus Nikolskoe.** Prussian king Frederick Wilhelm III built this Russian-style wooden lodge for his daughter Charlotte, wife of Russian czar Nicholas I. South of the city, in Glienecker Park, it offers open-air, riverside dining in summer. Game dishes are prominently featured. ✉ *Nikolskoer Weg 15,* ☎ *030/805–2914. AE, DC, MC, V. Closed Thurs.*

$ ✕ **Café Oren.** This popular vegetarian eatery is next to the Neue Syn-
★ agoge on Oranienburger Strasse, not far from Friedrichstrasse. The restaurant buzzes with loud chatter all evening, and the atmosphere and service are welcoming and friendly. The intimate back courtyard is a wonderful place to enjoy a cool summer evening or a warm autumn afternoon. The extensive menu offers mostly Israeli and Middle Eastern fare—including delicious, filled "Moroccan Cigars"—in addition to numerous dessert offerings. ✉ *Oranienburger Str. 28,* ☎ *030/282–8228. No credit cards.*

$ ✕ **Diyar.** In a city with nearly a quarter of a million Turks, many of them residents since the mid-1960s, Turkish food is typical, not exotic. Ergo, what better place to try something more than a Döer Kepab street-side than this large, spacious Turkish restaurant in Kreuzberg. It serves a wide selection of traditional meat dishes and also has a decent amount of vegetarian fare. In the traditional Turkish no-chair corner you can immerse yourself even further. ✉ *Dresdner Str. 9,* ☎ *030/615–2708. No credit cards.*

$ ✕ **Hardtke.** Just about the most authentic old Berlin restaurant in the
★ city, this simply decorated dining spot, with paneled walls and a wood floor, is very popular with tourists. The food is traditional and hearty. It's a great place to try *Eisbein* (knuckle of pork). Wash it down with a large stein of beer. ✉ *Meinekestr. 27,* ☎ *030/881–9827. No credit cards.*

$ ✕ **Thürnagel.** The great food served in this vegetarian restaurant in the Kreuzberg District makes healthful eating fun. The *Seitan* (vegetable protein) in sherry sauce and the tempeh curry are good enough to convert a seasoned carnivore. ✉ *Gneisenaustr. 57,* ☎ *030/691–4800. No credit cards. No lunch.*

$ ✕ **Zur Letzten Instanz.** Established in 1621, Berlin's oldest restaurant
★ combines the charming atmosphere of old Berlin with a limited (but very tasty) choice of dishes. Napoléon is said to have sat alongside the tile stove in the front room, and Mikhail Gorbachev enjoyed a beer during a visit in 1989. The emphasis here is on beer, both in the recipes and in the mugs. Service can be erratic, though always engagingly friendly. ✉ *Waisenstr. 14–16,* ☎ *030/242–5528. AE, DC, MC, V.*

LODGING

Year-round business conventions and the influx of summer tourists mean you should make reservations well in advance. If you arrive without reservations, consult hotel boards at airports and train stations, which show hotels with vacancies, or go to the tourist office at Tegel Airport or at the Hauptbahnhof or Zoologischer Garten train stations. The main tourist office in the Europa Center can also help with reservations (☞ Contacts and Resources *in* Berlin A to Z, *below*).

CATEGORY	COST*
$$$$	over DM 350
$$$	DM 270–DM 350
$$	DM 180–DM 270
$	under DM 180

All prices are for two people in a double room, including tax and service.

$$$$ 🏨 **Berlin Hilton.** The Hilton overlooks the historic Gendarmenmarkt and the German and French cathedrals, as well as the classic Schaupielhaus (concert hall). All the right touches are here, from heated bathtubs to special rooms for businesswomen and travelers with disabilities. ⊠ *Mohrenstr. 30,* ☎ *030/20230,* 🖷 *030/2023–4269, D–10117, 355 rooms with bath, 24 suites. 3 restaurants, 2 bars, cafeteria, pub, no-smoking rooms, room service, indoor pool, massage, sauna, bowling, exercise room, squash, dance club. AE, DC, MC, V.*

$$$$ 🏨 **Bristol Hotel Kempinski.** Destroyed in the war, rebuilt in 1952, and
★ renovated in 1980, the "Kempi" is a renowned Berlin classic. On the Ku'damm in the heart of the city, it has the best shopping at its doorstep and some fine boutiques of its own within. All rooms and suites are luxuriously decorated and equipped with marble bathrooms, air-conditioning, and cable TV. Children under 12 stay for free if they share their parents' room. ⊠ *Kurfürstendamm 27, D–10719,* ☎ *030/884–340,* 🖷 *030/883–6075. 315 rooms with bath, 52 suites. 2 restaurants, bar, room service, indoor pool, beauty salon, massage, sauna, exercise room. AE, DC, MC, V.*

$$$$ 🏨 **Grand Hotel Esplanade.** Opened in 1988, the Grand Hotel Esplanade exudes luxury. Uncompromisingly modern architecture, chicly stylish rooms, and works of art by some of Berlin's most acclaimed artists are its outstanding visual aspects. Then there are the superb facilities and impeccable service. The enormous grand suite comes complete with sauna, whirlpool, and a grand piano—for DM 2,500 per night. ⊠ *Lützowufer 15, D–10785,* ☎ *030/254–780,* 🖷 *030/265–1171. 369 rooms with bath, 33 suites. 2 restaurants, 2 bars, room service, pool, hot tub, sauna, steam room, exercise room. AE, DC, MC, V.*

$$$$ 🏨 **Inter-Continental Berlin.** In conjunction with the recent addition of a major conference center, the entire hotel was substantially improved. The rooms and suites are all of the highest standard, and their decor shows exquisite taste, with such refinements as luxurious carpets and elegant bathrooms. ⊠ *Budapester Str. 2, D–10787,* ☎ *030/26020,* 🖷 *030/2602–80760. 511 rooms with bath, 70 suites. 3 restaurants, 2 bars, no-smoking floors, room service, indoor pool, hot tub, sauna. AE, DC, MC, V.*

$$$$ 🏨 **Maritim ProArte Hotel Berlin.** French designer Philippe Starck (responsible for Manhattan's Paramount and Royalton hotels) took the old Metropol Hotel and transformed it into this modern, futuristic accommodation. Some space is devoted to original works by modern artists of national and international reputation. It's still a choice facility for business travelers, with a large desk, two telephones, and fax and PC connections in every room. Other luxuries—minibars, on-line movies, and bathrooms furnished with marble and black amethyst granite— will be appreciated by all. ⊠ *Friedrichstr. 150–153, D–10117,* ☎ *030/ 20335,* 🖷 *030/2033–4209. 403 rooms with bath, 29 suites. 3 restaurants, bar, in-room safes, minibars, no-smoking floors, indoor pool, massage, sauna, solarium, exercise room. AE, DC, MC, V.*

$$$$ 🏨 **Schlosshotel Vier Jahreszeiten.** This latest newcomer to the top
★ luxury hotels in Berlin is in the beautiful, verdant setting of Grunewald forest. The palace-like building is full of high style, and the renowned

Berlin Lodging

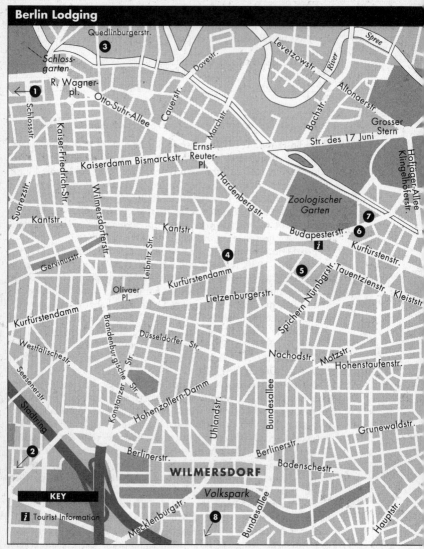

Berlin Hilton, **15**	Hotel Casino, **1**	Schlosshotel Vier
Bristol Hotel	Hotel Müggelsee, **11**	Jahreszeiten, **8**
Kempinski, **4**	Inter–Continental	Schweizerhof
Charlottenhof, **13**	Berlin, **7**	Intercontinental
Econtel, **3**	Landhaus	Berlin, **6**
Forum Hotel, **16**	Schlachtensee, **2**	Steigenberger
Gendarm Garni	Maritim ProArte	Berlin, **5**
Hotel, **14**	Hotel Berlin, **12**	
Grand Hotel	Riehmers	
Esplanade, **9**	Hofgarten, **10**	

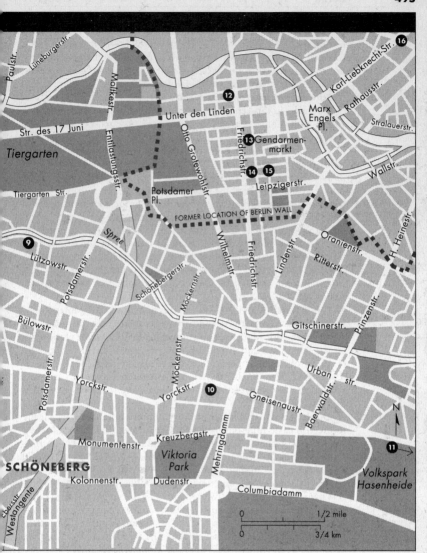

Paulstr.

Lüneburgerstr.

Moltkestr.

Str. des 17 Juni

Tiergarten

Entlastungsstr.

Unter den Linden

Otto Grotewohlstr.

12

Marx Engels Pl.

Karl-Liebknecht-Str.

Rathausstr.

16

Stralauerstr.

Friedrichstr.

13 Gendarmen-markt

Wallstr.

Tiergarten Str.

Potsdamer Pl.

14 **15**

Leipzigerstr.

FORMER LOCATION OF BERLIN WALL

H. Heinestr.

9

Lützowstr.

Spree

Potsdamerstr.

Schönebergerstr.

Mäckernstr.

Wilhelmstr.

Friedrichstr.

Lindenstr.

Oranienstr.

Ritterstr.

Prinzenstr.

Bülowstr.

Gitschinerstr.

Mäckernstr.

Urban - str.

Yorckstr.

Yorckstr.

10

Gneisenaustr.

Baerwaldstr.

N

Monumentenstr.

Kreuzbergstr.

Mehringdamm

11

SCHÖNEBERG

Viktoria Park

Volkspark Hasenheide

Kolonnenstr.

Dudenstr.

Potsdamerstr.

Ebersstr.

Westtangente

Columbiadamm

0   1/2 mile

0   3/4 km

Karl Lagerfeld designed the interior and all the rooms, which are extravagantly decorated and grand in size. Service is more than smooth. ✉ *Brahmsstr. 10,* ☎ *030/895–840,* FAX *030/8958–4800, D–14193, 52 rooms with bath, 12 suites. 2 restaurants, bar, in-room safes, minibars, no-smoking rooms, room service, indoor pool, beauty salon, massage, sauna, solarium, exercise room. AE, DC, MC, V.*

$$$$ ☷ **Schweizerhof Intercontinental.** There's a rustic, alpine look about most of the rooms in this centrally located hotel; the extras, such as on-line videos and minibars, are up-to-the-minute. Ask to stay in the west wing, where rooms are larger, but standards are high throughout. The indoor pool is the largest of any Berlin hotel. ✉ *Budapester Str. 21– 31, D–10787,* ☎ *030/26960,* FAX *030/269–6900. 430 rooms with bath, 26 suites. 2 restaurants, bar, no-smoking floor, room service, indoor pool, sauna, steam room, exercise room. AE, DC, MC, V.*

$$$$ ☷ **Steigenberger Berlin.** The Steigenberger group's exemplary Berlin hotel is centrally situated, only a few steps from the Ku'damm, but remarkably quiet. Small touches that lift the hotel above the usual run of chain establishments include a safe in every room and complimentary shoe-shine service. ✉ *Los-Angeles-Pl. 1,* ☎ *030/21270, D–10789,* FAX *030/212–7799. 397 rooms with bath, 11 suites. 2 restaurants, bar, café, piano bar, no-smoking floor, room service, indoor pool, massage, sauna. AE, DC, MC, V.*

$$$ ☷ **Forum Hotel.** With its 40 stories, this hotel (owned by Inter-Continental) at the top end of Alexanderplatz competes with the nearby TV tower for the title of premier downtown landmark. As one of the city's largest hotels, it is understandably less personal. Its casino is the highest in Europe and is open until 3 AM. ✉ *Alexanderpl., D–10178,* ☎ *030/23890,* FAX *030/2389–4305. 943 rooms with bath, 13 suites. 2 restaurants, bar, no-smoking floors, sauna, exercise room, casino. AE, DC, MC, V.*

$$ ☷ **Charlottenhof.** This small but very popular hotel-pension, ideally located on eastern Berlin's beautiful Gendarmenmarkt, has a homey, friendly atmosphere. Ask for the weekend bargain rates. ✉ *Charlottenstrasse 52, D–10117,* ☎ *030/238–060,* FAX *030/2380–6100. 86 rooms with bath. Restaurant, bar. AE, DC, MC, V.*

$$ ☷ **Hotel Casino.** What were once the main quarters of imperial officers have been skillfully converted into an appealing hotel with large, comfortable rooms, all tastefully furnished and well equipped—the Prussian soldiers never had it so good! The Casino is in the Charlottenburg District. ✉ *Königen-Elisabeth-Str. 47a, D–14059,* ☎ *030/303–090,* FAX *030/303–0945. 23 rooms with bath. Bar. AE, DC, MC, V.*

$$ ☷ **Hotel Müggelsee.** Berlin's largest and some say most beautiful lake in the southeastern outskirts of Berlin is just beyond your balcony at this reliable hotel, which was once a favorite among East Germany's communist leaders. The rooms are not luxurious, but they are comfortable and fairly spacious. The hotel can arrange for forest picnics and even has its own yacht for guests' use. ✉ *Am Grossen Müggelsee, D–12559,* ☎ *030/658–820,* FAX *030/6588–2263. 174 rooms with bath. 4 restaurants, bar, massage, sauna, tennis court, boating, bike rental. AE, DC, MC, V.*

$$
★ ☷ **Landhaus Schlachtensee.** Opened in 1987, this former villa (built in 1905) is now a cozy bed-and-breakfast hotel. The Landhaus Schlachtensee offers personal and efficient service, well-equipped rooms, and a quiet location in the Zehlendorf District. The nearby Schlachtensee and Krumme Lanke lakes beckon you to swim, boat, or walk along their shores. ✉ *Bogotastr. 9, D–14163,* ☎ *030/816–0060,* FAX *030/8160– 0664. 18 rooms with bath. Breakfast room. AE, DC, MC, V.*

$$　**☆**　🏨 **Riehmers Hofgarten.** A few minutes' walk from Kreuzberg Hill and the colorful district's restaurants and bars, and also near Tempelhof Airport, this small hotel has fast connections to the center of town. The beautifully restored late-19th-century building has high-ceiling rooms that are comfortable, with crisp linens and firm beds. ✉ *Yorckstr. 83, D–10965,* ☎ *030/781–011,* FAX *030/786–6059. 21 rooms with bath. Restaurant, bar. AE, DC, MC, V.*

$　🏨 **Econtel.** This family-oriented hotel is within walking distance of Charlottenburg Palace. The spotless rooms have a homey feel and provide closet safes and cable TV. A crib, bottle warmer, and kiddie toilet are available on request free of charge. The breakfast buffet provides a dazzling array of choices to fill you up for a day of sightseeing. ✉ *Sömmeringstr. 24,* ☎ *030/346–810, D–10589,* FAX *030/344–7034. 205 rooms with bath. Bar, in-room safes. AE, MC, V.*

$　**☆**　🏨 **Gendarm Garni Hotel.** This well-run hotel is situated by the Gendarmenmarkt, in the heart of old Berlin. All the rooms are neat and pleasantly furnished. Ask for the corner suite facing the square; the view and the large living room (for DM 225) make for one of the better deals in town. ✉ *Charlottenstr. 60, D–10117,* ☎ *030/204–4180,* FAX *030/208-2482. 25 rooms with bath, 4 suites. Bar. AE, MC, V.*

NIGHTLIFE AND THE ARTS

Nightlife

Bars

Bar am Lützowplatz (✉ Am Lützowpl. 7, ☎ 030/2626–807). A Berlin classic, this fancy bar with the longest counter in town is a must for nighthawks. The bar attracts some of the town's most beautiful women, who enjoy American cocktails while flirting with the handsome bartenders.

Champussy (✉ Uhlandstr. 171, ☎ 030/8812—220). At this elegant spot, bartenders devote all their knowledge to serving the best champagne cocktails in town. The interior is definitely first class, with the bar hidden behind massive white columns.

Harry's New York Bar (✉ Am Lützowufer 15, ☎ 030/2547–8821). This is probably the best hotel bar in town, situated in the lobby of Berlin's Grand Hotel Esplanade. It's also one of the few in the city that features live piano music. Businessmen try to relax under the portraits of American presidents and modern paintings hanging on the wall.

Kumpelnest 3000 (✉ Lützowstr. 23, ☎ 030/2616–918). After you've been here, you might argue about whether this place is really a bar. It's a hot spot for kinky nightclubbers only, where a crowd of both gays and heteros mingle. Nobody really cares about the quality of the drinks, although the beer is good.

Kneipen

The city's roughly 6,000 bars and pubs all come under the heading of *Kneipen*—the place around the corner where you stop in for a beer, a snack, and conversation—and sometimes to dance. Other than along Ku'damm and its side streets, the happening places in western Berlin are around **Savignyplatz** in Charlottenburg, **Nollendorfplatz, Winterfeldplatz** in Schöneberg, **Ludwigkirchplatz** in Wilmersdorf, and along **Oranienstrasse** and **Wienerstrasse** in Kreuzberg. In eastern Berlin most of the action is along **Oranienburger Strasse,** north in Mitte, and around **Kollwitzplatz** in Prenzlauer Berg.

Bierhimmel (✉ Oranienstr. 183, ☎ 030/6217–434). The name translates as "beer heaven," and this joint is a funky mix of kitsch and class for a typical Kreuzberg crowd—it's neither stylish nor extremely friendly. But the "secret" back room is worth a visit; it's a red-leather-padded '50s cocktail bar that's fit for Elvis.

Café Westphall (✉ Käthe-Kollwitz-Str. 64, ☎ 030/4483–289). This Kneipe was one of only a few alternative places during the Communist era. Right on Kollwitzplatz, it still has an alternative feel, with great atmosphere and food.

Dralle's (✉ Schlüterstr. 69, ☎ 030/3135–038). At this Charlottenburg classic the city's media crowd gets together for a drink. The all-red pub and bar stay open until the early morning hours.

Leydicke (✉ Mansteinstr. 4, ☎ 030/2162–973). This historic spot is a must for out-of-towners. The proprietors operate their own distillery and have a superb selection of wines and liqueurs.

Silberstein (✉ Oranienburger Str. 34, ☎ 2812–095). You might pass this place up at first, mistaking it for an art gallery, and you wouldn't be entirely wrong—it's that *and* also one of the city's trendiest meeting places.

Tacheles (✉ Oranienburger Str. 53–56, ☎ 030/2826–185). This huge ruin dates back from the days of war. Inside, a variety of clubs, pubs, bars, and off-stages showcases the finest of Berlin's alternative scene. In summer the backyard becomes a crowded beer garden.

Discos

Far Out (✉ Kurfürstendamm 156, ☎ 030/320–007). This formerly Bhagwan-operated disco has the cleanest air in the city and one of the biggest dance floors, where the mostly young crowd—in their early twenties—enjoys mostly old hits. Tuesday is no-smoking night; closed Monday.

Metropol (✉ Nollendorfpl. 5, ☎ 030/2162–787). Berlin's largest disco, which also stages concerts, is a hot spot for younger tourists. The black dance floor upstairs is the scene of a magnificent laser light show. Its occasional gay dances are hugely popular. The DM 10 cover includes your first drink. The disco is open Friday and Saturday only.

90 Grad (✉ Dennewitzstr. 37, ☎ 030/2628–984). This jam-packed disco plays hip-hop, soul, and some techno and really gets going around 2 AM. Women come fashionably dressed and go right in, but men usually have to wait outside until they get picked by the doorman.

Pleasure Dome (✉ Hasenheide 13, ☎ 030/6934–061). Here you'll find one of Berlin's biggest dancing areas, with multiple levels and full high-tech equipment. There's a '70s atmosphere populated by '90s kids under 20.

Sophienklub (✉ Sophienstr. 6, ☎ 030/2824–552). A gathering spot for mostly local former East Berliners, this cramped disco always serves up a formidable music mix. It's heavy on acid jazz.

Jazz Clubs

Berlin's lively music scene is dominated by jazz and rock. For jazz enthusiasts *the* events of the year are the summer's **Jazz in the Garden** festival and the autumn international **Jazz Fest Berlin.** For information, call the tourist information center (☎ 030/262–6031).

A-Trane Jazzclub (✉ Pestalozzistr. 105, ☎ 030/3132–550). A stylish newcomer, the A-Trane has found its fans among Berlin's jazz community. The club has studio-like equipment and is often used for radio recordings.

Eierschale (I) (✉ Podbielskiallee 50, ☎ 030/832–7097). A variety of jazz groups appears here at the "Egg Shell," one of Berlin's oldest jazz clubs, open daily from 8:30 PM. Admission is free.

Flöz (✉ Nassauische Str. 37, ☎ 030/861–1000). The sizzling jazz at this club sometimes accompanies theater presentations.

Franz-Club (✉ Schönhauser Allee 36–39, ☎ 030/442–8203). This eastern Berlin club brings in big jazz names and follows up the acts with hours of dancing. Admission is DM 5 after the show.

Quasimodo (✉ Kantstr. 12a, ☎ 030/312–8086). The most established and popular jazz venue in the city has a great basement atmosphere and a good seating arrangement.

Casinos

Spielbank Berlin (✉ Europa Center, ☎ 030/2500–890). Berlin's leading casino with 10 roulette tables and three blackjack tables stays open 3 PM–3 AM.

Gay Nightlife

Berlin is unmistakably Germany's gay capital, and many visitors from other European countries also come to partake of the city's gay scene. Concentrated in Schöneberg (around Nollendorfplatz) and Kreuzberg, and growing in Mitte and Prenzlauer Berg in eastern Berlin, the scene offers great diversity.

The following places are a good starting point for information. Also check out the magazine *Siegessäule* (free and available at the places listed below as well as many others around town).

Mann-O-Meter (✉ Motzstr. 5, ☎ 030/216–8008). You can get extensive information about gay life, groups, and events. Talks are held in the café, which has a variety of books and magazines. Open Monday–Saturday 3–11, Saturday 3–9.

Schwuz (✉ Hasenheide 54, ☎ 030/694–1077). This gay gathering spot sponsors different events. Every Saturday starting at 11 PM there is an "open evening" for talk and dance.

KNEIPEN

Anderes Ufer (✉ Hauptstr. 157, ☎ 030/7841–578). A young gay and lesbian crowd frequents this hip Kneipe. It has a mellow atmosphere and '50s and '60s music.

Hafenbar (✉ Motzstr. 19, ☎ 030/2114–118). The interior and the energetic crowd make this gay bar endlessly popular and a favorite singles place. At 4 AM people move next door to Tom's Bar, open until 6 AM.

DISCOS

Connection (✉ Welserstr. 24, ☎ 030/2181–432). Close to Wittenbergplatz, this disco offers heavy house music and lots of dark corners. It's open Friday and Saturday, midnight until 6.

Metropol (☞ *Discos, above*).

Schwuz (☞ *above*).

The Arts

Today's Berlin has a tough task living up to the reputation it gained from the film *Cabaret,* but if nightlife has been a little toned down since the '20s and '30s, the arts still flourish. In addition to the many hotels that book seats, there are several ticket agencies, including **Ticket Counter** (✉ Europa Center, ☎ 030/264–1138), **Theaterkasse Centrum** (✉ Meinekestr. 25, ☎ 030/882–7611), and the **Hekticket** office at Alexanderplatz (✉ Rathausstr. 1, ☎ 030/883–6010), that offer discounted and last-minute tickets. Most of the big stores (Hertie, Wertheim, and Karstadt, for example) also have ticket agencies. Detailed information about what's going on in Berlin can be found in *Metropolis,* an English-language monthly cultural magazine; *Berlin Programm,* a monthly tourist guide to Berlin arts, museums and theaters; and the magazines *Prinz, tip,* and *Zitty,* which appear every two weeks and provide full arts listings.

Concerts

Berlin is the home of one of the world's leading orchestras, the **Berliner Philharmonisches Orchester** (☞ Philharmonie, *below*), in addition to a number of other major symphony orchestras and orchestral ensembles. The **Berlin Festival Weeks,** held annually from August through September, combine a wide range of concerts, operas, ballet, theater, and art exhibitions. For information and reservations, write **Festspiele GmbH** (Kartenbüro, ⊠ Budapester Str. 50, 10787 Berlin).

CONCERT HALLS

Deutschlandhalle (⊠ Messedamm 26, 030/303–81). Big rock acts and extravagant opera and musicals productions can be seen in this immense hall.

Grosser Sendesaal des SFB (⊠ Haus des Rundfunks, Masurenallee 8–14, ☎ 030/303–10). Part of the Sender Freies Berlin, one of Berlin's broadcasting stations, the Grosser Sendesaal is the home of the Radio Symphonic Orchestra.

Konzerthaus Berlin (⊠ In the Schauspielhaus; Gendarmenmarkt, ☎ 030/2030–92100). This beautifully restored hall is a prime venue for concerts in historic Berlin.

Konzertsaal der Hochschule der Künste (⊠ Hardenbergstr 33, ☎ 030/3185–2374). The concert hall of the Academy of Fine Arts is Berlin's second largest.

Philharmonie (⊠ Matthäikircherstr. 1, 030/261–4383). The Berlin Philharmonic is based here. The hall also houses the new Kammermusiksaal, dedicated to chamber music.

Waldbühne (⊠ Am Glockenturm, close to the Olympic Stadium, ☎ 030/305–5079). Modeled after an ancient Roman theater, this open-air site accommodates nearly 20,000 people.

Film

Berlin has about 110 movie theaters, showing about 100 films a day. International and German movies are shown in the big theaters around the Ku'damm; the off-Ku'damm theaters show less-commercial movies. For (undubbed) movies in English, go to the **Babylon** (⊠ Dresdnerstr. 126, ☎ 030/614–6316), the **Kurbel** (⊠ Giesebrechtstr. 4, ☎ 030/883–5325), or the **Odeon** (⊠ Hauptstr. 116, ☎ 030/781–5667).

In February, Berlin hosts the **Internationale Filmfestspiele,** an internationally famous film festival, conferring the Golden Bear award on the best films, directors, and actors. Call 030/254–890 for information.

Opera, Musicals, and Dance

After unification Berlin decided to keep its three opera houses, all of which have their own ballet companies: the **Deutsche Oper Berlin** (⊠ Bismarckstr. 34–37, ☎ 030/343–81), one of Germany's leading opera houses; the **Staatsoper Unter den Linden** (⊠ Unter den Linden 7, ☎ 030/2035–4555); and the **Komische Oper** (⊠ Behrenstr. 55–57, ☎ 030/2026–0360). At the **Neuköllner Oper** (⊠ Karl-Marx-Str. 131–133, ☎ 030/6889–0777), you'll find showy, fun performances of long-forgotten operas as well as humorous musical productions. At the **Theater des Westens** (⊠ Kantstr. 12, ☎ 030/882–2888), the **Metropol Theater** (⊠ Friedrichstr. 101, ☎ 030/2024–6117), and the **Musical Theater Berlin** (⊠ Schaperstr. 24, ☎ 030/8842–0884), comic operas and musicals, such as *West Side Story, A Chorus Line,* and *Cabaret,* are presented.

Experimental and modern-dance performances are presented at **Podewil** (⊠ Klosterstr. 68–70, ☎ 030/247–49777), **Tanzfabrik** (⊠ Möckernstr. 68, ☎ 030/786–5861), **Tacheles** (☞ *below*), and **Theater am Halleschen Ufer** (☞ *below*).

Outdoor Activities and Sports **501**

Theater

Theater in Berlin is outstanding, but performances are usually in German. The exceptions are operettas and the (nonliterary) cabarets. Of the city's impressive number of theaters, the most renowned for both their modern and classical productions are the **Schaubühne am Lehniner Platz** (⌧ Kurfürstendamm 153, ☎ 030/890–023) and the **Deutsches Theater** (⌧ Schumannstr. 13, ☎ 030/284–41225), which has an excellent studio theater next door, the **Kammerspiele** (☎ 030/284–41226).

Other notable theaters include the **Berliner Ensemble** (⌧ Bertolt Brecht-Pl. 1, ☎ 030/282–3160), dedicated to Brecht and works of other international playwrights; the **Hebbel Theater** (⌧ Stresemannstr. 29, ☎ 030/251–0144), showcasing international theater and dance troupes; the **Maxim Gorki Theater** (⌧ Am Festungsgraben 2, ☎ 030/2022–1115), which also has a superb studio theater; the **Renaissance-Theater** (⌧ Hardenbergstr. 6, ☎ 030/312–4202); and **Volksbühne** (⌧ Rosa-Luxemburg-Pl., ☎ 030/3087–4630), known for its radical interpretations of dramas. For *Boulevard* plays (fashionable social comedies), try the **Hansa Theater** (⌧ Alt-Moabit 48, ☎ 030/391–4460), the **Komödie** (⌧ Kurfürstendamm 206, ☎ 030/883–001), and, at the same address, the **Theater am Kurfürstendamm** (☎ 030/883–1001).

For smaller, more alternative theaters, which generally showcase different guest productions, try **Tacheles** (⌧ Oranienburger Str. 53–56, ☎ 030/282–6185), **Theater am Halleschen Ufer** (⌧ Hallesches Ufer 32, ☎ 030/251–0941), or **Theater Zerbrochene Fenster** (⌧ Fidicinstr. 3, ☎ 030/694–2400).

Social and political satire has a long tradition in cabaret theaters here. The **Stachelschweine** (⌧ Europa Center, ☎ 030/261–4795) and **Die Wühlmäuse** (⌧ Nümbergerstr. 33, ☎ 030/213–7047) carry on that tradition with biting wit and style. Eastern Berlin's equivalent is **Distel** (⌧ Friedrichstr. 101, ☎ 030/200–4704). For children's theater, head for the world-famous **Grips Theater** (⌧ Althonaerstr. 22, ☎ 030/391–4004) or **Hans Wurst Nachfahren** (⌧ Gleditschstr. 5, ☎ 030/216–7925). Both are nominally for children but can be good entertainment for adults as well.

Variety Shows

During the past few years Berlin has become Germany's prime hot spot for variety shows, presenting magic, artistic, and circus performances, sometimes combined with music and classic cabaret. The world's largest variety show is presented at the **Friedrichstadtpalast** (⌧ Friedrichstr. 107, ☎ 030/2326–2474), a glossy showcase for revues, famous for its female dancers. Much smaller but classier in style is the **Wintergarten** (⌧ Potsdamer Str. 96, ☎ 030/2627–070), a romantic homage to the old days of Berlin's original variety theater in the '20s. Equally intimate and intellectually entertaining is the **Bar jeder Vernunft** (⌧ Spiegelzelt, Schaperstr. 24, ☎ 030/8831–582), whose name is a pun, literally meaning "devoid of any reason." A larger stage, which has risen to near stardom in the city's off-scene thanks to its extremely funny shows, is the **Chamäleon Varieté** (⌧ Rosenthaler Str. 40/41, ☎ 030/2827–118).

OUTDOOR ACTIVITIES AND SPORTS

Bicycling

There are bike paths throughout the downtown area and the rest of the city. *See* Getting Around *in* Berlin A to Z, *below,* for details on renting bikes.

Golf

Berlin's leading club is the **Golf- und Land Club Berlin-Wannsee** (⌂ Am Stölpchenweg, Wannsee, ☎ 030/805–5075).

Jogging

The **Tiergarten** is the best place for jogging in the downtown area. Run its length and back and you'll have covered 8 kilometers (5 miles). Joggers can also take advantage of the grounds of **Charlottenburg Palace**, 3 kilometers (2 miles) around. For longer runs, anything up to 20 miles, make for the **Grunewald.**

Riding

Horses can be rented at the **Reitsportschule Onkel Toms Hütte** (⌂ Onkel-Tom-Str. 172, ☎ 030/813–2082), **Reitsportschule Pichelsberg** (⌂ Schirwindter Allee 45, ☎ 030/304–0608), and **Reitsportshcule Haflinger Hof** (⌂ Feldweg 21, in Fredersdorf, close to Berlin, ☎ 033439/6371).

Sailing and Windsurfing

Boats and boards of all kinds are rented by **Albrecht Wassersport** (⌂ Kaiserdamm 95, ☎ 030/301–9555). **Windschief** (⌂ Havelchaussee am Wasser, ☎ 030/803–663) rents Windsurfers mid-April through mid-October.

Swimming

The **Wannsee,** the **Halensee** and the **Plötzensee** all have beaches; they get crowded during summer weekends, however. There are public pools throughout the city, so there's bound to be at least one near where you're staying. For full listings ask at the tourist office. Berlin's most impressive pool is the **Olympia-Schwimmstadion** at Olympischer Platz (U-bahn: Olympiastadion). The **Blub Badeparadies** lido (⌂ Buschkrugallee 64, ☎ 030/606–6060) has indoor and outdoor pools, a sauna garden, hot whirlpools, and a solarium (U-bahn: Grenzallee).

Tennis and Squash

There are tennis courts and squash centers throughout the city; ask your hotel to direct you to the nearest of these. **Tennis & Squash City** (⌂ Brandenburgische Str. 53, Wilmersdorf, ☎ 030/879–097) has six tennis courts and 11 squash courts. At **Tennisplätze am Ku'damm** (⌂ Cicerostr. 55A, ☎ 030/891–6630), you can step right off the Ku'damm and onto a tennis court.

SHOPPING

Shopping Districts

Bleibtreustrasse. For trendier clothes, try the boutiques along this side street of the Ku'damm. One of the more avant-garde fashion boutiques is **Durchbruch** (⌂ Schlüterstr. 54, ☎ 030/881–5568), just off Bleibtreustrasse. The name means "breakthrough," and the store lives up to its name by selling different designers' outrageous styles (women's clothing only). Less trendy and much less expensive is the outdoor shopping mall along **Wilmersdorfer Strasse** (U-7 station of same name), where price-conscious Berliners do their shopping. It's packed on weekends. **Friedrichstrasse.** This rebuilt boulevard offers the most elegant shops in historic Berlin, including a brand new **Galeries Lafayette** department store. Nearby Unter den Linden has a mix of expensive boutiques, including a Meissen ceramic showroom, and tourist souvenir shops. Around **Alexanderplatz,** more affordable stores offer everything from clothes to electronic goods to designer perfumes. A large number of clothing and specialty stores have sprung up in and around the **Nikolai Quarter.**

Kurfürstendamm. The city's liveliest and most famous shopping area is still found around Kurfürstendamm and its side streets, especially between **Breitscheidplatz** and **Olivaer Platz.** The **Europa Center** (☎ 030/ 348–0088) at Breitscheidplatz encompasses more than 100 stores, cafés, and restaurants—although this is not the place to hunt for bargains. Running east from Breitscheidplatz is **Tauentzienstrasse,** another shopping street. At the end of it is Berlin's most celebrated department store, the **Kaufhaus des Westens** or KaDeWe. The elegant **Uhland-Passage** (✉ 170 Uhlandstr.) has leading name stores as well as cafés and restaurants. The new **Kempinski Plaza** (✉ Uhlandstr. 181–183) features exclusive boutiques and a pleasant atrium café.

Antiques
Not far from Wittenbergplatz lies Keithstrasse, a street full of antiques stores. Eisenacher Strasse, Fuggerstrasse, Kalckreuthstrasse, Motzstrasse, and Nollendorfstrasse—all close to Nollendorfplatz—have many antiques stores of varying quality. Another good street for antiques is Suarezstrasse, between Kantstrasse and Bismarckstrasse.

Berliner Antik- und Flohmarkt. This is one of the largest, more established, and expensive places dealing in antique art. It offers everything from costly antique lamps to bargain books. Many antiques stores are found under the tracks at the Friedrichstrasse station (☎ 030/208– 2645), open Monday and Wednesday to Sunday 11–6).

Berliner Kunstmarkt (Berlin Art Market). On Saturdays and Sundays from 10 to 5, the colorful and lively antiques and handicrafts fair on **Strasse des 17. Juni** swings into action. Don't expect to pick up many bargains—or to have the place to yourself.

Christie's (✉ Fasanenstr. 72, ☎ 030/881–4164). The venerable auction house has an outpost just off the Ku'damm.

Sotheby's (✉ Palais am Festungsgraben on Unter den Linden, ☎ 030/ 204–4119). The international auction house has set up shop in one of historic Berlin's more beautiful buildings, staging auctions on a regular basis.

Department Stores
Kaufhaus des Westens (KaDeWe) (✉ Tauentzienstr. 21, ☎ 030/21210). The largest department store in continental Europe, the undeniably classy KaDeWe carries a grand selection of goods on seven floors, as well as food and deli counters, champagne bars, restaurants, and beer bars on its two upper floors.

Kaufhof (✉ Alexanderpl., ☎ 030/24640). Situated at the north end of Alexanderplatz, the former Centrum department store has been taken over by the west German department-store chain.

Wertheim (✉ Kurfürstendamm 181, ☎ 030/8800–3206). The other main department store downtown is neither as big nor as attractive as the KaDeWe, but Wertheim nonetheless offers a large selection of fine wares.

Gift Ideas
Berlin is a city of alluring stores and boutiques. Despite its cosmopolitan gloss, shop prices are generally lower than in cities like Munich and Hamburg. Most stores offer tax-free shopping for non–European Union citizens, so be sure to ask about it before making your purchase.

Gipsformerei der Staatlichen Museen Preussischer Kulturbesitz (✉ Sophie-Charlotte-Str. 17, ☎ 030/321–7011). If you long to have the Egyptian Museum's Queen Nefertiti bust on your mantelpiece at home, check out the state museum's shop, open weekdays 9 to 4, which sells plaster casts of treasures from the city's museums.

Königliche Porzellan Manufaktur. Fine porcelain is still produced by this former Royal Prussian Porcelain Factory, also called KPM. You can buy this delicate handmade, hand-painted china at KPM's store (✉ Kurfürstendamm 26A, ☎ 030/881–1802), but it may be more fun to visit the factory salesroom (✉ Wegelystrasse 1, ☎ 030/310–802), which also sells seconds at reduced prices.

Specialty Stores

JEWELRY
Galerie "re" (✉ Friedrichstr. 58, ☎ 030/208–6870) in Central Berlin has good jewelry values.
Wurzbacher (✉ Kurfürstendamm 36, ☎ 030/883–3892) carries fine handcrafted jewelry.

MEN'S CLOTHING
Budapester Schuhe (✉ Kurfürstendamm 199, ☎ 030/881–1707). A Berlin classic, this old-style shop for men's shoes offers the largest selection of business shoes in all designs and colors.
Mientus (✉ Wilmersdorfer Str. 73 and Kurfürstendamm 52, ☎ 030/323–9077 for both). This large, exclusive men's store caters to expensive tastes. It offers both conventional and business wear, as well as sporty and modern looks, and carries many top designer labels.
Selbach (✉ Kurfürstendamm 195/196, ☎ 030/262–7038). Come here for elegant evening clothes and fashionable designer labels for the young crowd—at a high price.

WOMEN'S CLOTHING
Bogner-Shop Zenker (✉ Kurfürstendamm 45, ☎ 030/881–1000). For German designer wear, try this boutique. It's not cheap, but the styling is classic.
Granny's Step (✉ Kurfürstendamm 56, ☎ 030/323–7660). Next to Kramberg you'll find evening wear styled along the lines of bygone times.
Kramberg (✉ Kurfürstendamm 56, ☎ 030/327–9010). If you're looking for international labels, including Gucci, Armani, and Chanel, drop by here and enjoy the first-class atmosphere in this top-of-the-world store.
Nouvelle (✉ Bleibtreustr. 24, ☎ 030/881–4737). Browse through this extraordinary lingerie store if you're feeling daring. Elegant '20s intimate wear made of fine, old-fashioned materials is its specialty.

SIDE TRIPS

A trip to Berlin wouldn't be complete without paying a visit to Brandenburg, the poor rural state which surrounds the city. Even if you have only a few days left, you should spare a day or two for visiting it. In contrast to Berlin's vibrant urbanity, Brandenburg's lovely countryside is a pleasant surprise, with green meadows to the north and pine barrens to the east and south. Sightseeing highlights include the palace of Sanssouci, near Potsdam, the old capital of Brandenburg, and Frankfurt an der Oder, a frontierlike small town at the German-Polish border. While Sanssouci is definitely a not-to-be-missed side trip, you might want to skip Frankfurt an der Oder unless you are interested in observing firsthand the new European order at work. In 1995, in a historic popular vote, the peoples of both states, Berlin and Brandenburg, decided to become one state by the turn of the century.

Potsdam

Prussia's most famous king, Friedrich II—Frederick the Great—spent more time at his summer residence, **Sanssouci** in Potsdam, than at the official court in Berlin, and it's no wonder. Frederick was an aesthetic ruler, and he clearly fell for the sheer beauty of the sleepy township lost among the hills, meadows, and lakes of this rural corner of mighty Prussia. The residence, one of Europe's most important at the time, is contained in a beautifully landscaped park, yet what you see is largely the result of a magnificent restoration job by the East Germans. The vine-covered terraces on which Sanssouci stands rise in majestic steps from a side stream of the Havel, a few minutes' walk from the center of Potsdam.

Its name means "without a care" in French, the language Frederick tried to cultivate in his own private circle and within the court. Some experts believe Frederick actually named the palace "Sans, Souci," which they translate as "with and without a care," a more apt name; its construction caused him a lot of trouble and expense and sparked furious rows with his master builder, Georg Wenzeslaus von Knobelsdorff. His creation nevertheless became one of Germany's greatest tourist attraction—5 million visitors a year file through the palace and grounds.

Frederick wanted to be buried, with no pomp and circumstance, beside his hunting dogs on the terrace of his beloved Sanssouci; a "philosopher's funeral" was what he decreed. His shocked nephew and successor, Friedrich Wilhelm II, ordered the body to be laid out in state and then consigned Frederick's remains to the garrison church of Potsdam. The coffin was removed to safety during World War II, after which it went on a macabre peregrination that ended in the chapel of the Hohenzollern Castle in southern Germany. The unification of Germany in 1991 made it possible to grant Frederick his last wish.

Executed according to Frederick's impeccable French-influenced taste, the palace, built from 1745 to 1747, is extravagantly rococo, with scarcely a patch of wall left unadorned. Strangely, Frederick occupied only five rooms; his bedroom, study, and circular library (beautifully paneled with cedar wood) can be visited. Another five rooms were kept for guests, one exclusively reserved for the French writer and philosopher Voltaire. To the west of the palace is the **New Chambers** (1747), which housed guests of the king's family; originally it functioned as a greenhouse until it was remodeled in 1771–74. Just east of Sanssouci Palace is the Picture Gallery (1755–63), which still displays Frederick's collection of 17th-century Italian and Dutch paintings. It is under reconstruction and will not reopen until early 1997. *Information Center, Sanssouci:* ☎ *0331/9694-202.* ✉ *Schloss Sanssouci (guided tours only) DM 8.* ◷ *Apr.–Oct., daily 9–5, except 1st and 3rd Mon. of month; Feb. and Mar., daily 9–4, except 1st and 3rd Mon.; Nov.–Jan., daily 9–3, except 1st and 3rd Mon. New Chambers:* ✉ *DM 5.* ◷ *Apr.–Oct., daily 9–5; Feb. and Mar. 9–4; Nov.–Jan., Sat.–Thurs. 9–3.*

Neues Palais (New Palace), a much larger and grander palace than Sanssouci, stands at the end of the long straight avenue that runs through Sanssouci Park. It was built after the Seven Years' War (1756–63), when Frederick loosened the purse strings. It's said he wanted to demonstrate to his subjects that the state coffers hadn't been depleted too severely by the long conflict. Frederick rarely stayed here, however, preferring the relative coziness of Sanssouci. Still, the Neues Palais has much of interest, including an indoor grotto hall, an extravaganza out of a Jules Verne novel, with walls and columns set with shells, coral, and other aquatic decoration. The upper gallery contains paintings by 17th-century Italian masters and a bijou court theater in which performances are still given. ✉ *DM 8, including guided tour.* ◷ *Apr.–Oct., daily 9–5, except 2nd and 4th Mon. of month; Feb.–Mar. 9–4, except 2nd and 4th Mon.; Nov.–Jan. 9–3, except 2nd and 4th Mon.*

Schloss Charlottenhof stands on its own grounds in the southern part of Sanssouci Park. After Frederick died in 1786, the ambitious Sanssouci building program ground to a halt, and the park fell into neglect. It

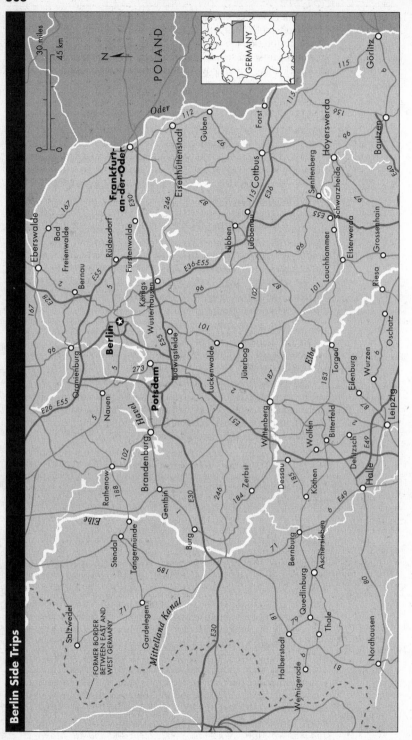

was 50 years before another Prussian king, Frederick William III, restored Sanssouci's earlier glory. He engaged the great Berlin architect Karl Friedrich Schinkel to build a small palace for the crown prince, Schloss Charlottenhof. Schinkel gave it a classical, almost Roman appearance, and he let his imagination loose in the interior, too—decorating one of the rooms as a Roman tent, with its walls and ceiling draped in striped canvas. ▣ *DM 6 (guided tour only).* ⊘ *Mid-May–mid-Oct., daily 9–5, except 4th Mon. of month.*

Römische Bäder (Roman Baths), **Orangerie,** and **Chinesisches Teehaus** (Chinese Teahouse), just north of the Schloss Charlottenhof on the path back to Sanssouci, were later additions to the park. Friedrich Wilhelm II built the Roman Baths (1836), while the teahouse was constructed in 1757 in the Chinese style, which was the rage then. The Orangerie (completed in 1860), with two massive towers linked by a colonnade, evokes an Italian Renaissance palace. Today it houses 47 copies of paintings by Raphael. Elsewhere in the park the Mosque, resembling a delicious layer cake, disguises pump works that operated the fountains in Sanssouci Park; the minaret concealed the chimney. The Italianate Peace Church (1845–48) houses a 12th-century Byzantine mosaic taken from an island near Venice. *Roman Baths:* ▣ *DM 3 (additional charge for special exhibitions);* ⊘ *Mid-May–Oct., daily 9–5, except 3rd Mon. of month. Chinese Teahouse:* ▣ *DM 4;* ⊘ *Mid-May–mid-Oct., daily 9–5, except every 2nd Mon. Orangerie:* ▣ *DM 4 (without guided tour; additional charge for special exhibitions);* ⊘ *May–Oct., daily 9–5. Mosque:* ▣ *DM 2;* ⊘ *Mid-May–mid-Oct., Wed.–Sun. 9–5; mid-Oct.–mid-May, weekends 9–4.*

NEED A BREAK? Halfway up the park's Drachenberg Hill, above the Orangerie, stands the curious **Drachenhaus** (Dragon House), modeled in 1770 after the Pagoda at London's Kew Gardens and named for the gargoyles ornamenting the roof corners. It now houses a popular café.

Schloss Cecilienhof, the final addition to Sanssouci Park, is equally exotic. Resembling a rambling, half-timbered country manor house, the Schloss Cecilienhof was built for Crown Prince Wilhelm in 1913 in a newly laid out stretch of the park bordering the Heiliger See, called the New Garden. It was here that the Allied leaders Truman, Attlee, and Stalin hammered out the fate of postwar Germany, at the 1945 Potsdam Conference. ⊠ *Schloss Cecilienhof.* ▣ *DM 5 (with guided tour).* ⊘ *Daily 9–5, except 2nd and 4th Mon. of month.*

Potsdam City itself still retains the imperial character lent it by the many years during which it served as royal residence and garrison quarters. It shouldn't be overlooked. The central market square, the **Alter Markt,** sums it all up: the stately, domed **Nikolaikirche** (built in 1724), a square Baroque church with classical columns; an **Egyptian obelisk** erected by Sanssouci architect von Knobelsdorff; and the officious facade of the old **City Hall** (built in 1755) with a gilded figure of Atlas atop the tower. Wander around some of the adjacent streets, particularly Wilhelm-Külz-Strasse, to admire the handsome restored burghers' houses.

Holländisches Viertel (Dutch Quarter) lies three blocks north of the Alter Markt. This settlement was built by Friedrich Wilhelm I in 1732 to induce Dutch artisans to settle in a city that needed migrant labor to support its rapid growth. (Few Dutch came, and the gabled, hip-roofed brick houses were largely used to house staff.) The Dutch government has promised to finance some of the cost of repairing the damage done by more than four decades of communist neglect.

Dining and Lodging

$ ✕ **Am Stadttor.** A five-minute walk from Sanssouci Palace and on Potsdam's main shopping street, the Stadttor is the ideal spot for lunch. The menu isn't exactly imperial Prussian, but the dishes are filling and inexpensive. The soups are particularly wholesome, and the liver Berlin style is as good as any you'll find in the city. ⊠ *Brandenburger Str. 1–3,* ☎ *0331/291–729. No credit cards.*

$$ ⊡ **Schlosshotel Cecilienhof.** This English country–style mansion is where Truman, Atlee, and Stalin drew up the 1945 Potsdam Agreement, and where Truman received news of the first successful atom bomb test, which occurred July 16, 1945. The hotel rooms are somewhat mundane, although comfortable and adequately equipped. The Schloss is set in its own parkland bordering a lake and is a pleasant 15-minute stroll from Sanssouci and the city center. ⊠ *Neuer Garten,* ☎ *0331/ 37050,* FAX *0331/292–498. 42 rooms with bath. Restaurant, room service, sauna. AE, D, MC, V.*

Potsdam A to Z

ARRIVING AND DEPARTING

Potsdam is virtually a suburb of Berlin, some 20 kilometers (12 miles) southwest of the city center and a half-hour journey by car or bus, or 45 minutes by S-bahn. City traffic is heavy, however, and a train journey is recommended. Perhaps the most effortless way to visit Potsdam and its attractions is to book a tour with one of the big Berlin operators (☞ Guided Tours *in* Berlin A to Z, *below*).

By Boat. Boats leave Wannsee, landing hourly, between 10 AM and 6 PM; until 8 PM in summer.

By Bus. There is regular bus service from the bus station at the Funkturm, Messedamm 8 (U-1 U-bahn station Kaiserdamm).

By Car. From Berlin center (Str. des 17. Juni), take the Postdamer Strasse south until it becomes Route 1 and then follow the signs to Postdam. A faster way is taking the highway from Funkturm through Zehlendorf to Potsdam.

By Train. Take the S-bahn, either the S-3 or the S-7 line, to Potsdam Stadt (for the city and Schloss Sanssouci). Change there for the short rail trip to the Potsdam–Charlottenhof (for Schloss Charlottenhof) and Wildpark (for Neues Palais) stations. You can also take Bus 116 from Wannsee to the Glienecker Brücke, and then take a ride on the streetcar to Potsdam's Bassanplatz station. From there you can walk down Brandenburger Strasse to Platz der Nationen and on to the Green Gate, the main entrance to Sanssouci Park.

GUIDED TOURS

All major sightseeing companies (☞ Guided Tours *in* Berlin A to Z, *below*) offer three- to four-hour-long tours of Potsdam and Sanssouci for DM 54. The **Potsdam Tourist Office** also runs two tours April through October. Its three-hour tour, including Sanssouci, costs DM 35; the 1½-hour tour of the city alone is DM 27 (☞ Visitor Information, *below*).

VISITOR INFORMATION

The **Potsdam Tourist Office** has information on tours, attractions, and events, and also reserves hotel rooms for tourists. ⊠ *Friedrich-Ebert-Str. 5, Postfach 601220, D–14467 Potsdam,* ☎ *0331/291–100.* ☉ *Apr.–Oct., weekdays 9–8, weekends 9–6; Nov.–Mar., weekdays 10– 6, weekends 10–2.*

Frankfurt an der Oder

Frankfurt an der Oder sits in its faded Prussian glory on the banks of the Oder River. Ninety percent of the historic center of town was destroyed in May 1945, not by Allied bombing but in a devastating fire that broke out after Germany's capitulation. The fire was sparked by a confrontation between remaining units of the Nazi "Werwolf" resistance and Polish forces from across the Oder. The flames spread rapidly because the conquered city had no fire brigade. Until then 80% of the city had survived the war undamaged. Today the strong undercurrent of anti-Polish feeling in Frankfurt an der Oder is palpable, and local police are kept busy smoothing over quarrels between the locals and Poles from across the river.

The **Rathaus** (City Hall), 100 yards west of the Oder, is the oldest building in town and also the most imposing. First mentioned in official records in 1348, the building has a 17th-century Baroque facade that now looks out over the hustle and bustle of central Frankfurt. ⊠ *Marktpl.*

Kleist Gedenk- und Forschungsstätte (Kleist Memorial and Research Center) is an elegant and finely restored Baroque structure situated on the Oder Riverbank behind City Hall. It's the world's only museum devoted to the great German writer Heinrich von Kleist (1777–1811). Kleist's birthplace in Frankfurt an der Oder was among the buildings consumed by fire in 1945, but the house containing this Kleist memorial site dates from the year of the dramatist's birth. Kleist lived only 34 years—he shot himself in a suicide pact with his lover in Berlin—but his contribution to German literature was monumental. His works, notably the famous history play *Das Kätchen von Heilbronn* (source of one of Carl Orff's greatest compositions) and the comedy *Der Zerbrochene Krug* (premiered by Goethe in Weimar in 1808), avoid all attempts at categorization. The original manuscripts of both plays are in the museum, which traces Kleist's life and work with exemplary clarity and care. It's behind City Hall, on the banks of the Oder. ⊠ *Faberstr. 7,* ☎ *0335/23185.* ⊡ *DM 3.50.* ⊙ *Tues.–Fri. 10–noon and 2–4, weekends 2–5.*

Dining and Lodging

$$ ✕⊡ **Graham's.** This pension-hotel, run by a friendly staff, has a direct streetcar connection to much of the city. All the rooms have been modernized. The restaurant gives guests a choice of a rustic inn feel or a colorful café atmosphere. Both areas have the same menu, a variety of traditional German dishes and six different kinds of beer on tap. ⊠ *August-Bebel-Str. 11, D–15234 Frankfurt/Oder,* ☎ *0335/433–5429,* ℻ *0335/433–3991. 30 rooms, all with showers. Restaurant. AE, MC, V.*

Frankfurt an der Oder A to Z

ARRIVING AND DEPARTING

By Car. Frankfurt an der Oder is 90 kilometers (55 miles) east of Berlin, about an hour's drive. Head east on eastern Berlin's Landsberger Allee, joining the E–55 Ring-Autobahn and heading south until the Frankfurt/Oder turnoff. Exit at Frankfurt-Stadtmitte.

By Train. Trains depart every two hours from Berlin's Hauptbahnhof.

VISITOR INFORMATION

Frankfurt Tourist Information, ⊠ Karl-Marx-Str. 8a, D–15230 Frankfurt/Oder, ☎ 0335/325–216, ℻ 0335/22565.

BERLIN A TO Z

More than five years after the official unification of the two Germanys,
the nuts-and-bolts work of joining up the halves is not complete, and
uncertainties abound. We have given addresses, telephone numbers, and
other logistical details based on the best available information, but
please understand that everything from telephone numbers to street names
are still changing at a furious pace. Inquire at one of Berlin's tourist information offices for the most up-to-date information.

Arriving and Departing

By Bus

Buses are slightly cheaper than trains. Berlin is linked by bus to 170
European cities. The main station is at the corner of Masurenallee 4–
6 and Messedamm. Reserve through DER (state agency), commercial
travel agencies, or the station itself. For information, call 030/301–
8028 between 9 and 5:30.

By Car

The "transit corridor" roads linking former West Germany with western Berlin are still there, but the strict restrictions that once confined
foreign motorists driving through East Germany have vanished, and
today you can travel through the country at will. Expressways link Berlin
with the eastern German cities of Magdeburg, Leipzig, Rostock, Dresden, and Frankfurt an der Oder. At press time speed restrictions of 130
kilometers per hour (80 miles per hour) still applied, and you must carry
your driver's license, car registration, and insurance documents with
you. Seat belts must be worn at all times, even in the backseat.

By Plane

Most international airlines fly to western Berlin's **Tegel Airport** (☎ 030/
410–2306) from all major U.S. and European cities. Because of increased
air traffic following unification, the former military airfield at **Tempelhof** (☎ 030/691–510) is also used. Eastern Berlin's **Schönefeld Airport**
(☎ 030/60910) is about 24 kilometers (15 miles) outside the downtown
area. It is used principally by Russian and Eastern European airlines,
although it's been taking more and more charter traffic.

BETWEEN THE AIRPORT AND DOWNTOWN

Tegel Airport is only 6 kilometers (4 miles) from the downtown area.
The No. 109 and X09 airport buses run at 10-minute intervals between
Tegel and downtown via Kurfürstendamm (downtown western Berlin),
Bahnhof Zoologischer Garten, and Budapester Strasse. The trip takes
30 minutes; the fare is DM 3.70. Expect to pay about DM 25 for the
same trip by taxi. If you rent a car at the airport, take the Stadtauto-
bahn (there are signs) into Berlin. The Halensee exit leads to Kurfürstendamm. Tempelhof is linked directly to the city center by the U-6 subway
line. From Schönefeld, a shuttle bus leaves every 10–15 minutes for the
nearby S-bahn station; S-bahn trains leave every 20 minutes for the
Friedrichstrasse station in downtown eastern Berlin and for the Zoologischer Garten station in downtown western Berlin. Bus 171 also
leaves every 10 or 15 minutes for the western Berlin Rudow subway
station. A taxi ride from the airport takes about 40 minutes and will
cost around DM 55. By car, follow the signs for Stadtzentrum Berlin.

By Train

There are six major rail routes to Berlin from the western part of the
country (from Hamburg, Hannover, Köln, Frankfurt, Munich, and Nürnberg), and the rail network in the east has expanded considerably, making all of eastern German more accessible. Service between Berlin and

eastern Europe has also improved significantly, resulting in shorter traveling times. Ask about reduced fares within Germany; three people or more can often travel at discounted rates. Some trains now stop at and depart from more than one of Berlin's four main train stations, but generally west- and north-originating trains arrive at Friedrichstrasse and Zoologischer Garten, and east- and south-originating trains at Hauptbahnhof and Lichtenberg. For details on rates and information, call **Deutsche Bahn Information** (☎ 030/19419).

Getting Around

By Bicycle

Bicycling is popular in Berlin. While it's not recommended in the downtown area, it's ideal in outlying areas. Bike paths are generally marked by red bricks on the walkways; many stores that rent or sell bikes carry the Berlin biker's atlas to help you find the paths. Call **Fahrrad Mietzner** (✉ Hagelbergerstr. 53, ☎ 030/785–9488) for information and rental locations, or rent your bikes at most of the major hotels for approximately DM 30 for 24 hours.

By Car

Berliners are famous for their reckless driving, so exploring the city by car can be extremely frustrating for out-of-towners. Due to the many construction sites, traffic on many streets is often detoured, and business traffic in the morning and late afternoon hours is stop-and-go for every driver. It's best to leave your car at the hotel and take the public transit system.

By Subway

Berlin is too large to be explored on foot. To compensate, the city has one of the most efficient public-transportation systems in Europe, a smoothly integrated network of subway (U-bahn) and suburban (S-bahn) train lines, buses, trams (in eastern Berlin only), and even a ferry across the Wannsee Lake, making every part of the city easily accessible. Extensive all-night bus and tram service operates seven nights a weeks (indicated by the letter N next to route numbers), and the subway lines U-9 and U-12 run all night on weekends. In summer excursion buses link downtown with popular recreational areas.

Sometime in 1997 most of the fares listed below will be slightly higher. At press time a DM 3.90 ticket covers the entire system for two hours and allows you to make an unlimited number of changes between trains, buses, and trams. Four such fares, discounted when sold together, are a good value (DM 13). If you are just making a short trip, buy a **Kurzstreckentarif.** It allows you to ride six bus stops or three U-bahn or S-bahn stops for DM 2.50. Packs of four cost DM 8.50. The best deal for visitors who plan to travel around the city extensively is the **day card** for DM 15, valid for 24 hours and good for all trains and buses. The **group day card,** DM 24, offers the same benefits for two adults and up to three children. A seven-day **tourist pass** costs DM 40 and allows unlimited travel on all city buses and trains. Another option is the **Berlin WelcomeCard,** which costs DM 16 and entitles one adult and up to three children to 24 hours or two days (DM 29) of unlimited travel as well as free admission or reductions of up to 50% for sightseeing trips, museums, theaters, and other events and attractions. If you're caught without a ticket, the fine is DM 60.

All tickets are available from vending machines at U-bahn and S-bahn stations. Punch your ticket into the red machine on the platform. For information about public transportation, call the **BVG** or go to the in-

Berlin Public Transit System

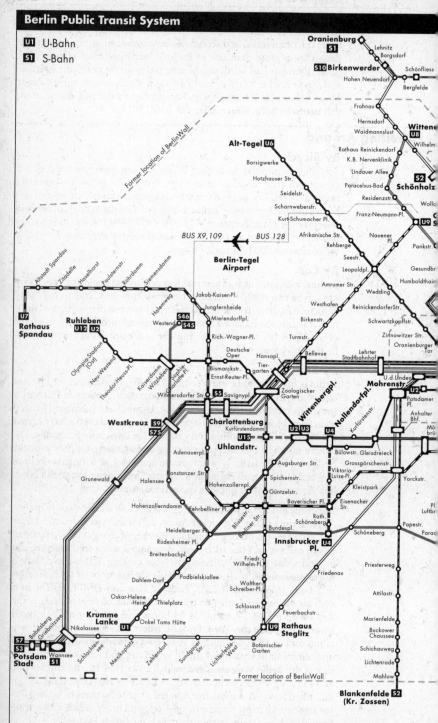

U1 U-Bahn
S1 S-Bahn

Oranienburg S1
Lehnitz
Borgsdorf
S10 Birkenwerder
Schönfliess
Hohen Neuendorf
Bergfelde
Frohnau
Hermsdorf
Wittene
Waidmannslust
U8
Alt-Tegel U6
Wilhelm
Borsigwerke
Rathaus Reinickendorf
Hotzhauser Str.
K.B. Nervenklinik
Lindauer Allee
Seidelstr.
Paracelsus-Bad
S2
Scharnweberstr.
Residenzstr.
Schönholz
Kurt-Schumacher-Pl.
Franz-Neumann-Pl.
Wolla
U9
BUS X9,109   BUS 128
Afrikanische Str.
Nauener
Pl.
Berlin-Tegel
Rehberge
Pankstr.
Airport
Seestr.
Gesundbr
Leopoldpl.
Humboldthain
Amrumer Str.
Wedding
Jakob-Kaiser-Pl.
Westhafen
ReinickendorferStr.
Jungfernheide
U7
Ruhleben
Halemweg
S46
Mierendorffpl.
Birkenstr.
Schwartzkopffstr.
Rathaus   U12 U2
Westend
S45
Rich.-Wagner-Pl.
Turmstr.
Zinnowitzer Str.
Spandau
Olympia-Stadion
Deutsche
Oranienburger
(Ost)
Oper
Hansapl.
Bellevue
Lehrter
Tor
Neu-Westend
Bismarckstr.
Tier-
Stadtbahnhof
U.d.Linden
Theodor-Heuss-Pl.
Ernst-Reuter-Pl.
garten
Mohrenstr.
U2
Kaiserdamm
Sophie-
Zoologischer
Potsdamer
Witzleben
Charlotte-Pl.
Garten
Pl.
Wittersdorfer Str.
S5 Savignypl.
Anhalter
Mö
Westkreuz S9
Charlottenburg
Bhf.
brü
S75
Kurfürstendamm
Wittenbergpl.
Nollendorfpl.
Adenauerpl.
Uhlandstr.
U1 U3
U4
Kurfürstenstr.
Konstanzer Str.
U15
Bülowstr. Gleisdreieck
Pl
Grunewald
Halensee
Augsburger Str.
Grossgörschenstr.
Luftbr
Hohenzollernpl.
Spichernstr.
Viktoria-
Yorckstr.
Luise-Pl.
Hohenzollerndamm
Güntzelstr.
Kleistpark
Fehrbelliner Pl.
Bayerischer Pl.
Eisenacher
Papestr.
Heidelberger Pl.
Rath.
Str.
Parad
Schöneberg
Rüdesheimer Pl.
Bundespl.
Schöneberg
Breitenbachpl.
Innsbrucker U4
Priesterweg
Friedr.
Pl.
Dahlem-Dorf
Podbielskiallee
Wilhelm-Pl.
Friedenau
Attilastr.
Oskar-Helene
Walther-
-Heim
Thielplatz
Schreiber-Pl.
Krumme
Schlossstr.
Marienfelde
Lanke
U1
Feuerbachstr.
Buckower
Onkel Toms Hütte
U9 Rathaus
Chaussee
Nikolassee
Steglitz
Schichauweg
S7
Botanischer
S3
Garten
Lichtenrade
Babelsberg
Griebnitzsee
Potsdam
Schlachten-
Mahlow
Stadt S1
Wannsee
see
Mexikoplatz
Zehlendorf
Sundgauer
Lichterfelde-
Str.
West
Former location of BerlinWall
Blankenfelde S2
(Kr. Zossen)

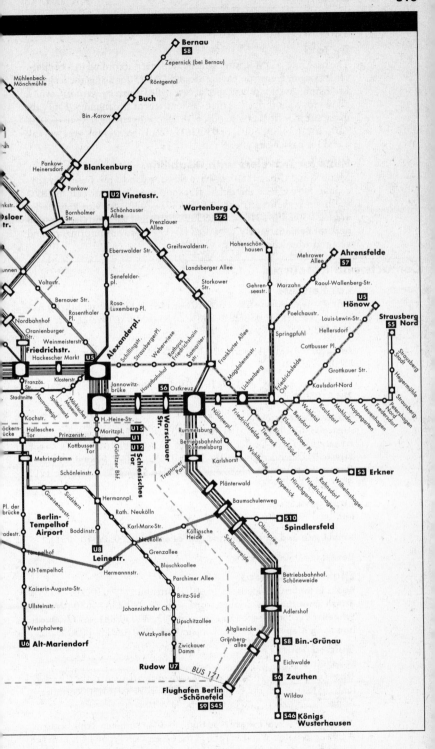

formation office on Hardenbergplatz, directly in front of the **Bahnhof Zoo** train station or call **Berliner Verkehrsbetriebe,** ☎ 030/752–7020.

By Taxi
The base rate is DM 4, after which prices vary according to a complex tariff system. Figure on paying around DM 15 for a ride the length of Ku'damm. Ask for a new special fare called *Kurzstreckentarif,* which allows for a short ride less than 2 kilometers or five minutes. Hail cabs in the street or from taxi stands, or order one by calling 030/9644, 030/210–202, 030/691–001, or 030/261–026. U-bahn employees will call a taxi for passengers after 8 PM.

Hints for Travelers with Disabilities
Many S- and U-bahn stations have elevators, and a few buses have hydraulic lifts. Check the public transportation maps or call the **BVG** (Berliner Verkehrsbetriebe, ☎ 030/752–7020). **Service-Ring-Berlin e.V.** (☎ 030/859–4010 or 030/9389–2410) and **Verband Geburts- und anderer Behinderter e.V.** (☎ 030/341–1797) provide information and van and wheelchair rentals.

Contacts and Resources
Car Rentals
Avis (✉ Tegel Airport, ☎ 030/4101–3148; ✉ Budapester Str. 43, Am Europa Center, ☎ 030/261–1881; ✉ Karl-Marx-Allee 264, ☎ 030/685–2093).

Europcar (✉ Tegel Airport, ☎ 030/4101–3354; ✉ Kurfürstenstr. 101, ☎ 030/213–1031).

Hertz (Tegel Airport, ☎ 030/4101–3315; ✉ Budapester Str. 39, ☎ 030/261–1053).

Consulates
Australia (✉ Uhlandstr. 181–183, ☎ 030/880–0880). **Canada** (✉ International Trade Center, Friedrichstr. 95, ☎ 030/261–1161). **Great Britain** (✉ Unter den Linden 32–34, ☎ 030/201–840). **Ireland** (✉ Ernst-Reuter-Pl. 10, ☎ 030/3480–0822). **United States** (✉ Clayallee 170, ☎ 030/832–9233).

Emergencies
Police (☎ 030/110).

Ambulance and emergency medical attention (☎ 030/310–031).

Dentist (☎ 030/01141).

English Bookstores
Books in Berlin (✉ Goethestr. 69, Charlottenburg, ☎ 030/313–1233). **British Bookshop** (✉ Mauerstr. 82–84, ☎ 030/238–4680). **Marga Schoeller Bücherstube** (✉ Knesebeckstr. 33, ☎ 030/881–1112). **Buchhandlung Kiepert** (✉ Hardenbergstr. 4–5, ☎ 030/311–0090).

Guided Tours
BOAT TRIPS
Tours of downtown Berlin's **canals** take in sights such as the Charlottenburg Palace and the Congress Hall. Tours depart from Kottbusser Bridge in Kreuzberg and cost around DM 10.

A tour of the **Havel Lakes** is the thing to do in summer. Trips begin at Wannsee (S-bahn: Wannsee) and at the Greenwich Promenade in Tegel (U-bahn: Tegel). You'll sail on either the whale-shaped vessel *Moby Dick* or the *Havel Queen,* a Mississippi-style boat, and cruise 27½ kilometers (17 miles) through the lakes and past forests. Tours last 4½ hours and cost between DM 15 and DM 20. There are 20 operators. The following are the leading ones:

Reederei Bruno Winkler (⊠ Levetzowstr. 12a, ☎ 030/391−7010).

Reederei Heinz Riedel (⊠ Planufer 78, ☎ 030/693−4646).

Stern- und Kreisschiffahrt (⊠ Puschkinallee 16-17, ☎ 030/617−3900).

BUS TOURS

Four companies offer more or less identical tours (in English) covering all major sights in Berlin, as well as all-day tours to Potsdam, Dresden, and Meissen. The Berlin tours cost DM 25−DM 45; those to Potsdam, DM 50−DM 70; and to Dresden and Meissen, approximately DM 100.

Berliner Bären Stadtrundfahrten (BBS, ⊠ Rankestr. 35, ☎ 030/214−8790). Groups depart from the corner of Rankestrasse and Kurfürstendamm and in eastern Berlin, from Alexanderplatz, in front of the Forum Hotel.

Berolina Stadtrundfahrten (⊠ Kurfürstendamm 22, corner Meinekestr., ☎ 030/882−2091). Groups depart from the corner of Kurfürstendamm and Meinekestrasse and in eastern Berlin, from Karl-Liebknecht-Strasse, in front of the Radisson Plaza Hotel.

Bus Verkehr Berlin (BVB, ⊠ Kurfürstendamm 225, ☎ 030/885−9880). Tours leave from Kurfürstendamm 225.

Severin & Kühn (⊠ Kurfürstendamm 216, ☎ 030/883−1015). Groups leave from clearly marked stops along the Kurfürstendamm and in eastern Berlin, at the corner of Unter den Linden and Universitätstrasse.

SPECIAL-INTEREST TOURS

Sightseeing tours with a cultural/historical bias are offered weekends at a cost of approximately DM 15 by **StattReisen** (⊠ Malplaquetstr. 5, ☎ 030/455−3028). Tours include "Jewish History" and "Prenzlauer Berg Neighborhoods" and are in German; in summer English tours are offered as well. All **Berlin Walks** (⊠ Eislebener Str. 1, ☎ 030/211−6663) tours are in English. The introductory "Discover Berlin" tour takes in the major downtown sites in 2½ to 3 hours. Other theme tours (so-called Third Reich sites, Jewish life, cabaret tour) are shorter and run April−October. Tours depart from outside the McDonald's opposite the main entrance to the Zoologischer Garten train station and cost DM 14, plus S-bahn transportation.

Late-Night Pharmacies

Pharmacies in Berlin offer late-night service on a rotating basis. Every pharmacy displays a notice indicating the location of the nearest shop with evening hours. For **emergency pharmaceutical assistance,** call 030/01141.

Travel Agencies

American Express Reisebüro (⊠ Bayreuther Str. 23, ☎ 030/2149−8363; ⊠ Uhlandstr. 173, ☎ 030/882−7575; ⊠ Friedrichstr. 172, ☎ 030/238−4102).

American Lloyd (⊠ Kurfürstendamm 209, ☎ 030/20740).

Visitor Information

The **Verkehrsamt Berlin** (main tourist office) is in the heart of the city in the Europa Center (☎ 030/262−6031). If you want materials on the city before your trip, write **Verkehrsamt Berlin Europa Center** (⊠ Martin-Luther-Str. 105, 10825 Berlin). For information on the spot, the office is open Monday−Saturday 8 AM−10:30 PM, Sunday 9−9. There are also offices at the Brandenburger Tor (☎ 030/229−1258), open daily 10 AM–6 PM); at the **Tegel Airport** (☎ 030/4101–3145), open daily 8 AM–11 PM; and at the train stations **Zoologischer Garten** (☎ 030/313–9063), open Monday–Saturday 8 AM–10.30 PM, and **Hauptbahnhof** (☎ 030/279–5209), open daily 8–8. Berlin has an information center geared toward women that helps with accommodations and gives information on upcoming events. Contact **Fraueninfothek Berlin** (✉ Dircksenstr. 47, ☎ 030/282–3980), open Tuesday–Saturday 9–9, Sunday and holidays 9–3.

For information in English on all aspects of the city, pick up a copy of *Berlin Turns On*, free from any tourist office.

16 Thuringia and Saxony

Traditional tourist sites and the opportunity to see an area in transition—for 45 years it was bound more closely with the Soviet Union than with West Germany—make this region worth visiting. Dresden's Zwinger Palace complex is a cultural wonder; Leipzig, the largest eastern German city after Berlin, is an important commercial center (avoid the trade-fair dates); and Weimar's days as a 19th-century cultural center are still appreciable.

MENTION OF THE FORMER German Democratic Republic generally conjures up images of dour landscapes and grim industrial cities, even since the collapse of the Communist government. It will take years before the polluted, dying forests in the south can be rejuvenated and the ancient soot-stained factories replaced. The deteriorating public housing projects of the '50s and '60s cannot be razed overnight, any more than the acrid smell of brown coal smoke can be eliminated that quickly. But the small towns of eastern Germany—in the federal states of Thuringia and Saxony—will tell much more about an older Germany than the frenetic lifestyles of Frankfurt, Hamburg, Stuttgart, or Köln. The Communist influence here—hard-line as it was—never penetrated as deeply as did the American impact on West Germany. East Germany clung to its German heritage, proudly preserving connections with such national heroes as Luther, Goethe, Schiller, Bach, Händel, Wagner, and Hungarian-born Liszt. And although bombing raids in World War II devastated most of its cities, the East Germans extensively rebuilt and restored their historic neighborhoods. Meissen porcelain, Frederick the Great's palace at Potsdam, the astounding collections of the Pergamon and Bode museums in Berlin, and those in the Zwinger in Dresden are now part of the total national heritage.

Traditional tourist sights aside, eastern Germany is also worth visiting precisely because it *is* in transition. In the wake of ebullient newspaper headlines and photographs of wild parties amid the rubble of the Berlin Wall, it's all too easy to simplify what's going on in the former GDR as a quest for Western-style democracy. The initiative for unification came as much from the West as it did from the East, and the former East Germans have not been altogether happy with the consequences. Though they had the highest standard of living of any Eastern Bloc country, many erstwhile East Germans still see their western compatriots as the "haves" and themselves as the "have-nots."

These people, bound politically and economically to the Soviet Union for 45 years, are still not entirely comfortable with their newly acquired freedoms and responsibilities. For most of those years, despite being Communism's "Western Front," the GDR was largely isolated from Western ideas, and many now resent having the less savory elements of Western society imposed on what was an orderly, if unexciting, way of life. Time has not stood still east of the former border, but it has taken much less of a toll than in the west.

The main differences for travelers are the absence of a border, not having to change currencies, and—regrettably—higher prices. But most important is the complete freedom that visitors now have to go wherever they want, choose their hotels, and wander off the former "transit corridors" and explore eastern Germany at will.

Pleasures and Pastimes

Dining
Although enterprising and mostly young managers and chefs are beginning to establish themselves in the east, many of the best restaurants are still in the larger hotels. Regional specialties include *Thüringer Sauerbraten mit Klössen* (roast corned beef with dumplings), spicy *Thüringer Wurst* (sausage), *Bärenschinken* (cured ham), and *Harzer Köhlerteller mit Röstkartoffeln* (charcoal-grilled meat with roast potatoes). Seafood is plentiful in the lake areas.

CATEGORY	COST*
$$$$	over DM 60
$$$	DM 40–DM 60
$$	DM 25–DM 40
$	under DM 25

per person for a three-course meal and a beer or glass of wine, including tax and tip

Lodging

A crash building program is filling the accommodation gaps in Thuringia and Saxony, although there's still a shortage of reasonably priced rooms, particularly in Leipzig and Dresden. Tourist offices are invariably sympathetic and helpful, and most have lists of private households offering bed and breakfast for as little as DM 50. If you're planning to travel during peak season, try to book in advance.

Note that during the Leipzig Fair—early March and early September—most Leipzig hotels increase their prices.

CATEGORY	COST*
$$$$	over DM 250
$$$	DM 200–DM 250
$$	DM 160–DM 200
$	under DM 160

All prices are for two people in a double room, including tax and service charge.

Old Railway Engines and Boats

Eastern Germany turns out to be a treasure house of old steam-driven tractors, factory engines, train engines, and riverboats, many lovingly restored by enthusiasts. German Railways (Deutsche Bahn) regularly runs trains from the years 1899–1930 on a small-gauge line that penetrates deep into the Saxony countryside and the Fichtelberg Mountains. Since the early 1990s the world's largest and oldest fleet of paddle steamers has been assembled on the Elbe. Eight wonderful old steamers (all of them under official technical-preservation orders) and two reconstructed ships ply up and down the Elbe, following the Saxony wine route, as far as the neighboring Czech Republic.

Outdoor Activities and Sports

WATER SPORTS

The Elbe, Gera, and Saale rivers all offer good canoeing, often on waters where you'll scarcely see another paddle. Contact the tourist offices in Dresden, Gera, or Halle for rental information.

WINTER SPORTS

The upland, heavily forested Thüringer Wald is eastern Germany's second-favorite holiday destination in summer and in winter. Its center is Suhl, administrative heart of an area where every 10th town and village is a spa or mountain resort. The region south of Erfurt, centering around Oberhof, is also popular, with comfortable hotels and full sports facilities.

Exploring Thuringia and Saxony

The federal states of Thuringia and Saxony cover the southeastern part of the former East Germany, and the region's still-run-down industrial towns and unattractive farm estates remind you of its proximity to other formerly Communist-run countries—Poland and what was Czechoslovakia. But some of Germany's most historically important cities are here, and energetic reconstruction programs are slowly restoring them. Dresden, for instance, is within a year or two of recapturing its reputation as the "Florence of the Elbe," and, just upstream, Meissen is being given an impressive face-lift. Even industrial Leipzig has washed off a lot of grime and has an old city center that rivals many in the richer west.

Great Itineraries

Rail communications in the east have improved rapidly and most of the old problems—unreliable and slow services, ancient rolling stock and lines—have disappeared, so the region can be comfortably toured by train. East–west and north–south autobahns crisscross the two states, and most of the old horrors of driving in the east have been removed by crash road-building.

Numbers in the text refer to numbers in the margin and on the Eastern Germany map.

IF YOU HAVE 3 DAYS

Spend a day in ⊞ **Dresden** ㉗, with its amazing Zwinger complex and richly stocked museums, and then make for the city of Bach, ⊞ **Leipzig** ⑦, stopping in **Meissen** ㉖ to see how the famous porcelain is produced. If there's still time, visit **Weimar** ③, the city of Goethe and Schiller.

IF YOU HAVE 5 DAYS

Plan your itinerary in an eastward direction, starting at **Eisenach** ① and prowling through one of Germany's most famous castles, the Wartburg. The next stop is **Erfurt** ②, a city of towers that mostly managed to escape wartime bombing. Plan a whole day for ⊞ **Weimar** ③, and consider overnighting in its most famous hotel, the charming, luxurious Elephant, where you'll be following a distinguished line of guests. **Gera** ④, farther east on the E–40 Autobahn, is worth visiting for the permanent exhibition of works by the painter Otto Dix in the house where he was born. From there it's a short journey north to ⊞ **Leipzig** ⑦ for another overnight stay and an evening out in the old city. The Elbe River is an hour's drive or train journey east. Pick up the course of the great river at **Meissen** ㉖, stopping long enough for a visit to the porcelain factory before heading upstream to ⊞ **Dresden** ㉗ for a day or two of exploring its riches.

IF YOU HAVE 7 DAYS

Linger longer in **Eisenach** ①, **Erfurt** ②, and ⊞ **Weimar** ③, and then head north to **Halle** ⑤, the birthplace of Händel and home of a fascinating museum devoted to the composer. If time allows, continue farther north to **Dessau** ⑥, where the original Bauhaus building that gave its name to a whole artistic movement still stands. Stop at the beautiful Baroque palace of Mosigkau, 9 kilometers (6 miles) southwest of Dessau. Return south on the E–51 Autobahn to ⊞ **Leipzig** ⑦, making a brief detour to Bitterfeld to get an idea of the industrial decline suffered by East Germany under Communist rule. Leave enough time in Leipzig for visits to its outstanding museums, including the Grassimuseum complex and Museum der Bildende Künste. From Leipzig head south to a city that acquired symbolic importance in the GDR years, **Chemnitz** ㉔. Although it changed its name from Karl-Marx-Stadt, a monumental bust of the city patron still sits defiantly in front of the district council building. From Chemnitz it's east to **Freiberg** ㉕; find time to visit the ancient silver workings that once made the town prosperous. Follow the picturesque Freital road to ⊞ **Dresden** ㉗, where you'll need at least two days to get to know the city and its cultural attractions—although you should save half a day for an excursion to **Meissen** ㉖.

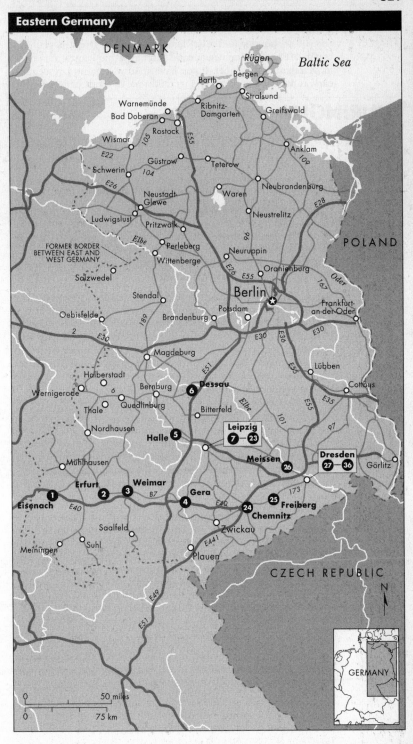

Eastern Germany

DENMARK

Baltic Sea

Rügen

Barth
Bergen

Warnemünde
Bad Doberan
Rostock
Ribnitz-
Damgarten
Stralsund
Greifswald

Wismar
E22
105
Güstrow
104
Teterow
Anklam
109

Schwerin
E26
Neustadt-
Glewe
Waren
Neubrandenburg

Ludwigslust
Pritzwalk
Neustrelitz
E28

Elbe
Perleberg
96

Salzwedel
Wittenberge
Neuruppin
E26
E55
Oranienburg
Oder
167

Stendal
189
Brandenburg
Berlin
Potsdam
Frankfurt-
an-der-Oder

Oebisfelde
2
E30
E30
E36
E30

POLAND

Magdeburg
E51
E55
Lübben

Halberstadt
6
Bernburg
Dessau **6**
E35
Cottbus

Wernigerode
Quedlinburg
Bitterfeld
Elbe
101
E55

Thale
Nordhausen
Halle **5**
Leipzig
7 **23**
97

Mühlhausen
Meissen **26**
Dresden
27—**36**
Görlitz

Erfurt
2 **3** Weimar
B7
Gera
4
E40
173

Eisenach **1**
E40
Chemnitz **24** **25** Freiberg

Saalfeld
Zwickau

Meiningen
Suhl
E441
Plauen

E49

CZECH REPUBLIC

N

E51

FORMER BORDER
BETWEEN EAST AND
WEST GERMANY

0   50 miles
0   75 km

GERMANY

When to Tour Thuringia and Saxony

Winters in this part of Germany can be cold, wet, and dismal, so unless you are heading for the city lights of Leipzig or Dresden, plan your trip in late spring, summer, or early autumn. Avoid Leipzig at fair time in March and September. If you have good weather in Dresden, rise early to see the sun burst onto its sandstone riverside panorama.

THURINGIA

Eisenach, Erfurt, Weimar, Gera, Halle, Dessau

Eisenach

❶ *95 km (48 mi) northwest of Fulda (nearest ICE rail station).*

Standing in Eisenach's ancient market square, ringed by half-timbered houses, it's difficult to imagine this town as an important center of the eastern German automobile industry, home of the now-shunned Wartburg. This solid, noisy staple of the East German auto trade was named after the famous castle that broods over Eisenach, high atop one of the foothills of the Thuringian Forest.

★ Begun in 1067 (and added to throughout the centuries), **Wartburg Castle** hosted the German minstrels Walter von der Vogelweide and Wolfram von Eschenbach, Martin Luther, Richard Wagner, and Goethe. Johann Sebastian Bach was born in Eisenach in 1685 and must have climbed the hill to the castle often. Legend has it that von der Vogelweide, Germany's most famous minstrel, won the celebrated "contest of the *Minnesingers*" here, later immortalized by the Romantic writer Novalis and in Wagner's *Tannhäuser.* Luther sought shelter within its stout walls from papal proscription from May 1521 until March 1522 while he translated the New Testament from Greek into German, an act that paved the way for the Protestant Reformation. The study in which Luther worked can be visited; it's basically the same room he used, although the walls have been scarred by souvenir hunters who, over the centuries, scratched away the plaster and much of the wood paneling. Luther's original desk was vandalized; the massive table you'll see is a later addition, although it belonged to Luther's family.

There's much more of interest in this fascinating castle, including a portrait of Luther and his wife, by Cranach the Elder, and a very moving sculpture, the *Kneeling Angel,* by the great 15th-century artist Tilman Riemenschneider. The 13th-century great hall is breathtaking; it's here that the minstrels are said to have sung for courtly favors. Don't leave without climbing the belvedere for a panoramic view of the distant Harz Mountains and the Thuringian Forest, and soak in the medieval atmosphere of the half-timbered, cottage-style interior courtyards of the castle. ☎ *03643/2500.* ▨ *DM 10 (including guided tour).* ☉ *Nov.–Mar., daily 9–3:30; Apr.–Oct., daily 8:30–4:30.*

The **Lutherhaus** has many fascinating exhibits illustrating the life of Luther. ✉ *Lutherpl. 8,* ☎ *03691/29830.* ▨ *DM 3.* ☉ *May–Sept., daily 9–5; Oct.–Apr., Mon.–Sat. 9–5, Sun. 2–5.*

The **Bachhaus** has exhibits devoted to the entire Bach family and includes a collection of historical musical instruments. ✉ *Frauenplan 21,* ☎ *03691/203–714.* ▨ *DM 5.* ☉ *Apr.–Sept., Mon. noon–5:45, Tues.–Sun. 9–5:45; Oct.–Mar., Mon. 1–4:45, Tues.–Sun. 9–4:45.*

The composer Richard Wagner gets his due at the **Reuter-Wagner Museum,** which has the most comprehensive exhibition on Wagner's life and work outside Bayreuth. ✉ *Reuterweg 2,* ☎ *03691/203–971.* ▣ *DM 4.* ◷ *Tues.–Sun. 10–5.*

At Johannesplatz 9 look for what is said to be the **narrowest house** in eastern Germany, built in 1890; its width is just over 6 feet, 8 inches; its height, 24½ feet; and its depth, 34 feet.

Dining and Lodging

$$–$$$ ✕▣ **Fürstenhof.** Every room in this beautifully restored *Jugendstil* mansion has a fine view of the Wartburg. The corner oriel rooms are particularly attractive, with traditional furnishings such as long velvet drapes and floral fabrics. The hotel restaurant has rapidly established itself as a premier address in eastern Germany; you dine in princely style in a room with many 100-year-old features, including a gleaming parquet floor and floor-to-ceiling windows looking out over Eisenach. The international menu embraces the best traditional German dishes (the marinated fillet of veal melts on the tongue). ✉ *Luisenstr. 11–13, D–99817,* ☎ *03691/7780,* FAX *03691/203–682. 51 rooms with bath. Restaurant. AE, DC, MC, V.*

$$ ✕▣ **Auf der Wartburg.** In this castle hotel, where Martin Luther, Johann Sebastian Bach, and Richard Wagner were also guests, you'll get a splendid view over the town and the surrounding countryside. The standard of comfort is above average, and antiques and Oriental rugs mix with modern, moderately stylish furnishings. The hotel runs a shuttle bus to the rail station. ✉ *Wartburg, D–99817,* ☎ *03691/5111,* FAX *03691/5111, 26 rooms with bath, 4 suites. Restaurant, exercise room. AE, DC, MC, V.*

$–$$ ✕▣ **Hotel Glockenhof.** At the base of Wartburg Castle, this former church-run hostel has blossomed into a handsome, luxurious hotel, cleverly incorporating the original half-timbered city mansion into a modern extension. The excellent restaurant has been joined by a brasserie. ✉ *Grimmelgasse 4, D–99817,* ☎ *03691/2340,* FAX *03691/234–141. 37 rooms, 3 suites, all with bath. Restaurant, brasserie. AE, MC, V.*

Erfurt

❷ *55 km (36 mi) east of Eisenach.*

The "flowers and towers" city of Erfurt emerged from World War II relatively unscathed, with most of its innumerable towers intact (to be restored during the early 1970s). Flowers? Erfurt is the center of the eastern German horticultural trade and Europe's largest flower- and vegetable-seed producer, a tradition begun by local botanist Christian Reichart, who pioneered seed research. The outskirts of the city are smothered in greenhouses and plantations, and one of Germany's biggest horticultural shows, the Internationale Gartenbauausstellung, takes place here every year from the end of March through September.

With its highly decorative and colorful facades, this is a fascinating city to discover on foot (though you might be tempted to climb aboard one of the old-fashioned horse-drawn open carriages that tour the Old Town center every Saturday and Sunday, leaving from outside the cathedral at 10 and 4). Erfurt is a photographer's delight: a city of narrow, busy ancient streets dominated by the magnificent 14th-century Gothic cathedral, the **Erfurter Dom.** The **cathedral square** is bordered by attractive old houses dating from the 16th century and by the **Rathaus.** The pedestrian-zone **Anger** is also lined with restored Renaissance houses. The **Bartholomäusturm,** base of a 12th-century tower, holds a 60-bell carillon.

The **Erfurter Dom** is reached by a broad staircase from the expansive cathedral square. Its Romanesque origins (Romanesque foundations can still be seen in the crypt) are best preserved in the choir, where you'll find glorious stained-glass windows and beautifully carved choir stalls. They have a worldly theme, tracing the vintner's trade back through the centuries. Nearby, look for a remarkable group of freestanding figures: a man flanked by two women. The man is the 13th-century Count von Gleichen. But the two women? There are two stories: The more respectable version says they are the count's wives, one of whom he married after the death of the other; the other, possibly older, story claims one woman is his wife, the other his mistress, a Saracen beauty who saved his life under mysterious circumstances during a crusade. The cathedral's biggest bell, the Gloriosa, is the largest free-swinging bell in the world. Cast in 1497, it took three years to install in the tallest of the three sharply pointed towers, painstakingly lifted inch by inch with wooden wedges. No chances are taken with this two-ton treasure; it rings only on special occasions, such as at Christmas and to ring in the New Year, its deep boom sounding across the entire city. 📧 *Tour DM 2.* ☉ *May–Oct., weekdays 9–11:30 and 12:30–5, Sat. 9–11:30 and 12:30–4:30, Sun. and public holidays 2–4; Nov.–Apr., Mon.–Sat. 10–11:30 and 12:30–4, Sun. and public holidays 2–4.*

The Gothic church of **St. Severus** has an extraordinary font, a masterpiece of intricately carved sandstone that reaches practically to the roof of the church. It is linked to the cathedral by a 70-step open staircase.

Behind the predominantly neo-Gothic City Hall, the **Rathaus,** on the central square, you'll find Erfurt's most outstanding attraction spanning the Gera River, the **Krämerbrücke** (Shopkeepers' Bridge). You'd have to travel to Florence to see anything else like this, a Renaissance bridge incorporating shops and homes. Built in 1325 and restored in 1967–73, the bridge served for centuries as an important trading center, where goldsmiths, artisans, and merchants plied their trades. Today antiques shops fill the majority of the timber-frame houses that are incorporated into the bridge, some dating from the 16th century. The area around the bridge, crisscrossed with ancient streets lined with picturesque and often crumbling homes, is known as **Klein Venedig** (Little Venice)—not because of any real resemblance to the lagoon city but for the recurrent flooding caused by the river.

The young Martin Luther spent his formative years in the **St. Augustine cloisters.** Today it's a seminary. ✉ *Gotthardstr.*

Erfurt's interesting local-history museum is housed in a late-Renaissance house, **Zum Stockfisch.** ✉ *Johannesstr. 169,* ☎ *0361/562–4888.* 📧 *Free.* ☉ *Tues. and Thurs.–Sun. 10–5, Wed. 10–8.*

Dining and Lodging

$ ✕ **Dasdie.** Wolfgang Staub's Dasdie combines restaurant, bistro, bar, cabaret stage, and dance floor under one roof, so you can lunch here (for less than DM 8), return for an early supper, enjoy a show, and end the day with a dance. The food is hit-or-miss, but the place is always lively and prices are low. ✉ *Marstallstr. 12,* ☎ *0361/646–1385. AE, DC, MC, V.*

$ ✕ **Restaurant zur Penne.** This is Erfurt's oldest beer cellar, with a virtually unbroken history reaching back to 1515. It has eight different beers on tap and a menu bursting with hearty Thuringian fare (wild boar is a must if it's offered). In summer a shady beer garden beckons diners to leave the shadowy but atmospheric cellar-restaurant. ✉ *Grosse Arche 3–5,* ☎ *0361/643–7469. AE, DC, MC, V.*

ownership. Frantic efforts were launched to solve the problem, and there were hopes that the famous old "White Swan" would open again before the end of the year. If it *is* open in 1997 (and it will be a tragedy if it isn't), this is the place to wine and dine in Weimar. History breathes from the ancient, exposed timbers and centuries-old wall paintings. ⊠ *Frauenstorstr. 23,* ☎ *03643/61715. Reservations essential. Jacket and tie. AE, DC, MC, V. Closed Mon.*

$$ ✕ **Hotel Thüringen.** The plush elegance of the Thüringen's restaurant, complete with velvet drapes and chandeliers, makes it seem expensive, but there's a pleasant surprise in store: The international and regional dishes served are remarkably moderate in price. An excellent Thüringer roast beef, for instance, costs less than DM 20. ⊠ *Brennerstr. 42,* ☎ *03643/3675. AE, DC, MC, V.*

$ ✕ **Ratskeller.** This is one of the region's most authentic city hall–cellar restaurants, its whitewashed, barrel-vaulted ceiling attesting to centuries of tradition. Tucked away at the side is a cozy bar where you can enjoy a preprandial drink beneath a spectacular art-nouveau colored skylight. The delicious Madagascar green-pepper soup is the only exotic touch to the otherwise traditional Thuringian menu. If venison is in season, try it—likewise the wild duck or wild boar in red-wine sauce. ⊠ *Markt 10,* ☎ *03643/64142. AE, MC, V.*

$ ✕ **Sharfe Ecke.** Thuringia's traditional *Knödel* are at their best here—but be patient, they're made to order and take 20 minutes. The Knödel come with just about every dish, from roast pork to venison stew, and the wait is well worth it. The ideal accompaniment for virtually anything on the menu is the locally brewed beer. ⊠ *Eisfeld 2,* ☎ *03643/202–430. No credit cards. Closed Mon.*

$$$$ ✕⊞ **Weimar Hilton.** Weimar's most modern hotel combines luxury with sleek and smooth-running service. The riverside Belvedere Park that Goethe helped to plan is just across the road, and the rococo Belvedere Palace, with its museum of ancient vehicles, is a short walk away. Weimar's center is quite a hike in the other direction, but buses are frequent. ⊠ *Belvederer Allee 25, D–99425,* ☎ *03643/7220,* FAX *03643/722–741. 294 rooms, 6 suites with bath. 2 restaurants, 4 bars, café, indoor pool, sauna, spa, bowling, exercise room. AE, DC, MC, V.*

$$$–$$$$ ✕⊞ **Flamberg Hotel Elephant.** The historic Elephant, dating from ★ 1696, is now in the hands of the Flamberg group, which has thankfully kept the individual charm that made it one of Germany's most famous hostelries, even in Communist times. Book here (well ahead) and you'll follow the choice of Goethe, Schiller, Herder, Liszt (after whom the hotel bar is named)—and Hitler—all of whom have been guests. Behind the sparkling white facade are comfortable modern rooms, thanks to renovations, but a feeling for the past is ever present. ⊠ *Am Markt 19, D–99423,* ☎ *03643/8020,* FAX *03643/65310. 97 rooms with bath, 5 suites. 2 restaurants, bar, sauna, nightclub. AE, DC, MC, V.*

$$ ✕⊞ **Christliches Hotel Amalienhof.** Book far ahead to secure a room at the hotel that is rapidly becoming everyone's "inside tip." The now historic and officially protected building began life in 1826 as a church hostel, but subsequent remodelings turned it into a comfortable, cozy, and friendly little hotel, central to Weimar's chief attractions. Double rooms are furnished with high-class antique reproductions, while public rooms have the real thing. ⊠ *Amalienstr. 2, D–99423,* ☎ *03643/5490,* FAX *03643/549–110. 22 rooms with shower. Restaurant, bar. MC, V.*

Nightlife and the Arts

For a cultural city Weimar has a surprisingly lively after-dark scene, concentrating on piano vars and nightclubs at the Hilton and Elephant hotels.

Shopping

Goethe planted Germany's first ginkgo in Weimar, and the tree's distinctive leaf is a favorite motif for goldsmiths and jewelry makers. You can admire the fanciful pieces at **Uwe Matthiessen's workshop** at Kupfergasse 3.

OFF THE
BEATEN PATH

BUCHENWALD – In the Ettersberg Hills just north of Weimar is a blighted patch of land that contrasts cruelly with the verdant countryside that so inspired Goethe: Buchenwald, one of the most infamous Nazi concentration camps. Sixty-five thousand men, women, and children from 35 countries met their deaths here through forced labor, starvation, disease, and gruesome medical experiments. Each is commemorated by a small stone placed on the outlines of the barracks, which have long since disappeared from the site, and by a massive memorial tower built in a style that some critics find reminiscent of the Nazi megalomania it seeks to condemn. The tower stands on the highest point of Buchenwald, approached by a broad, long flight of steps and sheltering at its base a sculpted group representing the camp's victims. ⊡ Free. ⊙ May–Sept., Tues.–Sun. 9:45–5:15; Oct.–Apr., Tues.–Sun. 8:45–4:15. Bus tours to the site are organized by Weimar's tourist office, Weimar-Information, ⊠ Markt 10, ☎ 03643/24000. City buses to Buchenwald leave bus station, calling at the railway station, every 2 hrs, between 7:10 AM and 3:30 PM.

Gera

❹   65 km (39 mi) east of Weimar.

Once a princely residence and center of a thriving textile industry, the city has largely been rebuilt after the heavy damage sustained in World War II. Gera has often been compared with old Vienna, although today you have to search long and hard—and even then exercise some imagination—to discover any striking similarities between the German provincial town and the Hapsburg capital. After the combined destruction of a world war and more than four decades of Communist mismanagement, some ornate, albeit crumbling, house facades, however, do betray Gera's rich past.

Although the palace in which prince-electors once held court was destroyed in the final weeks of World War II and never rebuilt, the palace's 16th-century **Orangerie** does still stand, in the former Küchengarten in the suburb of Untermhaus. It's an imposing semicircular Baroque pavilion, irreverently dubbed the "roast sausage" by the people of Gera, which now houses an art gallery. ⊠ Küchengartenallee 4. ⊡ DM 3. ⊙ Tues. 1–8, Wed.–Fri. 10–5, weekends 10–6.

Gera's real claim to fame is artist **Otto Dix** (1891–1969). The house where the satirical Expressionist painter was born is now a **museum,** with a gallery of his work and a permanent exhibition on his life. Otto–Dix–Haus, ⊠ Mohrenpl. 4, ☎ 03643/832–4927. ⊡ DM 5 (includes admission to Orangerie). ⊙ Tues.–Fri. 10–5, weekends 10–6.

Don't leave Gera without checking out the central town square, the **Marktplatz,** its Renaissance buildings restored with rare (for eastern Germany) care. The 16th-century City Hall, the **Rathaus,** has a vividly decorated entrance. Note the weird angles of the lower-floor windows; they follow the incline of the staircase winding up the interior of the building's picturesque 185-foot-high tower.

NEED A BREAK?	At the City Hall's vaulted cellar restaurant, the **Ratskeller,** Gera's me-dieval past crowds in on you from all sides, with painted scenes on glass partitions and on the gnarled walls themselves. The restaurant is open daily from mid-morning until midnight, so it's an ideal place for coffee, lunch, or dinner.

Lodging

$$ 🏨 **Galerie-Hotel.** This small, friendly hotel near the center of town takes pride in its artistic ambience, evidence of which can be found in the modern, brightly colored furnishings and the regular exhibitions of work by Thuringian artists. Some of their work even finds its way onto the walls of the rooms, which are comfortable and well-appointed, all with satellite TV and fax outlets. The very reasonable rate includes an ex-tensive breakfast buffet. ⊠ *Leibnitzstr. 21, D–07548,* ☎ *0365/20150,* FAX *03651/201–522. 17 rooms with bath. AE, DC, V.*

OFF THE BEATEN PATH	**BELVEDERE PALACE –** Just south of Gera, the lovely 18th-century yellow-stucco Belvedere Palace once served as a hunting and pleasure castle; today you'll find a Baroque museum and an interesting collection of coaches and other historic vehicles inside. The formal gardens were in part laid out according to Goethe's concepts. ☎ *03643/64039.* ☞ *DM 4.* ☉ *Apr.–Oct., Tues.–Sun. 10–6.*

Halle

❺ *52 km (31 mi) south of Dessau, 32 km (19 mi) northwest of Leipzig.*

Like many eastern German cities, Halle has acquired a reputation that, on closer inspection, it doesn't really deserve, particularly in these times of reconstruction. The 1,000-year-old city, built on the salt trade, is one of eastern Germany's worst examples of Communist urban planning, with a hastily built residential area, whose name, Halle-Neustadt, has been shortened cynically by the locals to "Hanoi." Yet precisely the part of Halle that suffered most from decades of ne-glect—its old city—has an unusual beauty, particularly its spacious cen-tral marketplace, the **Markt,** its northern side bristling with five distinctive sharp-steepled towers. Four of them are claimed by a church, St. Mary's (the **Marienkirche**), but the fifth is Halle's celebrated **Roter Turm** (Red Tower), built between 1418 and 1506 as an expression of the city's power and wealth; it houses a bell carillon and the local tourist office. The tower looks a bit incongruous against the backdrop of mod-ern Halle, like an elaborate sand castle stranded by the tide.

The four towers of the late-Gothic **Marienkirche** (two connected by a vertiginous catwalk bridge) dominate the skyline of Halle's Markt. Mar-tin Luther preached in it; George Friedrich Händel, born in Halle in 1685, was baptized in its font and went on to learn to play the organ beneath its high, vaulted ceiling.

The **Händelhaus,** where Händel was born, is now a museum devoted to the composer; in the entrance hall is a display of glass harmoniums, curious musical instruments perfected by Benjamin Franklin when he was ambassador to England in the 1760s. ⊠ *Grosse Nikolaistr. 5–6,* ☎ *0345/500–900.* ☞ *DM 2.* ☉ *Tues., Wed., and Fri.–Sun. 9:30–5:30, Thurs. 9:30–7.*

The **Marktschlösschen,** a late-Renaissance structure just off the mar-ket square, contains an interesting collection of historical musical in-struments, some of which could have been played by Händel and his contemporaries. *Musikinstrumentensammlung des Händel-Hauses,* ⊠

Marktschlösschen, Markt 13, ☎ *0345/202–5977.* 🎟 *DM 1.* ☉
Wed.–Sun. 1:30–5:30.

The **Moritzburg,** a castle built in the late 15th century by the archbishop
of Magdeburg after he had claimed the city for his archdiocese, is testament to Halle's early might, which vanished with the Thirty Years'
War. The castle is a typical late-Gothic fortress, with a dry moat and
a sturdy round tower at each of its four corners. There's a cloisterlike
peace in the central courtyard today, quite a contrast to the years
when one army of occupation followed another with bloody regular-
ity. In prewar years the castle contained a leading gallery of **German
Expressionist paintings,** which were ripped from the walls by the Nazis
and condemned as "degenerate." Some of the works so disdained by
the Nazis are back in place, together with some outstanding late-19th-
and early 20th-century art. You'll find Rodin's famous sculpture the
Kiss here. *Staatliche Galerie Moritzburg,* ✉ *Friedemann-Bach-Pl. 5,*
☎ *0345/37031.* 🎟 *DM 3.* ☉ *Tues. 11–8:30, Wed.–Fri. 10–5:30,
weekends 10–6.*

Halle's cathedral, the **Dom,** is the city's only early-Gothic church. Its
nave and side aisles are of equal height, a characteristic of much Gothic
church design in this part of Germany. ✉ *About 200 yards southeast
of the Moritzburg.*

The former Episcopal residence, the 16th-century **Neue Residenz,** now
houses a world-famous collection of **fossils** dug from brown coal deposits in the Geiseltal Valley near Halle. *Geiseltalmuseum,* ✉ *Dompl.
5,* ☎ *0345/37781.* ☉ *Weekdays 9–noon and 1–5.*

The salt trade on which Halle built its prosperity is documented in the
Halloren- und Salinemuseum. The full-scale replica of a salt mine gives
a depressing picture of how the miners toiled underground. The museum is on the south side of the Saale River (cross the Schiefer Bridge
to get there). ✉ *Mansfelderstr. 52,* ☎ *0345/202–5034.* 🎟 *DM 1.50.*
☉ *Tues.–Sun. 10–5.*

Dining and Lodging

$ ✗ **Gildenhaus St. Nikolaus.** This massive, early 19th-century colossus
of a building, on the same street as the Händelhaus, served as a guild-
hall and a clothing-factory canteen before it opened as a restaurant.
The food betrays its canteen past—big portions, inconsistent quality,
and low prices. If you're in luck, the venison stew might be at its peak.
Berlin-style liver and onions can also be recommended. But the surroundings invite lingering, and it takes time to absorb all its medieval-
style decoration—from the stained-glass windows to the rural
paraphernalia hanging on the paneled walls. In the middle of all the
jumble is a mock English-style telephone booth, with a phone that's
about as reliable as the cuisine. ✉ *Grosse Nikolaistr. 9–11,* ☎
0345/502–067. AE, DC, MC, V.

$$$ ✗🏠 **Hotel-restaurant zum Kleinen Sandberg.** On a quiet side street off
the main pedestrian mall, where the city prison once cast its grim
shadow, stands one of Halle's prettiest medieval houses, now a small,
exclusive restaurant and hotel. Behind its bright brown-and-white
half-timbered facade is a variety of individually furnished rooms, some
with their own whirlpool baths. The restaurant is small, divided by cross
beams and an intimate bar, and serves predominantly Baden special-
ties—marinated meats with such regional trimmings as spaetzle (home-
made egg noodles)—with a wine list of Baden vintages. ✉ *Kleiner
Sandberg 5, D–06108,* ☎ 🆊 *0345/770–0269. 9 rooms with bath.
Restaurant. AE, V.*

Nightlife and the Arts

The city of Händel is naturally an important music center, and Halle is famous for its opera productions, orchestral concerts, and particularly for its choirs. For **opera** schedules call 345/5110–0355 and **Philharmonic Orchestra** information 0345/202–3278. The annual Händel Festival takes place in the first half of June, and two youth-choir festivals occur in May and October.

En Route If you're driving to Dessau, take the country road to Zorbig, branch off on the B–183 to Köthen and then the B–185 in the direction of Dessau. After 11 kilometers (7 miles) you'll come to Mosigkau and its 18th-century late-Baroque **Schloss Mosigkau.** Try to visit this exquisite mid-18th-century country palace in late afternoon or early evening, when the setting sun lends a warm glow to the biscuit-color facades of the three wings. Prince Leopold of Anhalt-Dessau commissioned the palace for his favorite daughter, Anna Wilhelmine. Never married, she lived there alone, and when she died, she left the property to an order of nuns. They immediately tore up the formal grounds to make an English-style park, and after a post–World War II attempt to restore the original Baroque appearance, money and enthusiasm ran out. The palace itself, however, was always well maintained, and the present custodians are so concerned about its preservation that you'll be asked to put on felt slippers for your tour of its rooms. Only a quarter of the rooms can be visited, but they include one of Germany's very few Baroque picture galleries. Its stucco ceiling is a marvel of rococo decoration, a swirling composition of pastel-color motifs. ☎ *0340/831–139.* *Palace DM 5, palace gardens DM 1 (admission in both cases includes guided tour).* ☉ *May–Sept., Tues.–Sun. 10–6; Nov.–Mar., Tues.–Fri. 10–4, weekends 11–4; Apr. and Oct., Tues.–Sun. 10–5.*

Dessau

❻ *55 km (38 mi) northeast of Halle.*

The name Dessau is known to every student of modern architecture. Here in 1925–26 the architect Walter Gropius set up his Bauhaus school of design, which has probably had the greatest influence of any art movement on 20th century architecture and design. Gropius's concept was to simplify design to allow mechanized construction; 316 villas in the Törten section of the city were built in the '20s using his ideas and methods. Stop to view the refurbished Bauhaus building—this was the fountainhead of ideas that have determined the appearance of such cities as New York, Chicago, and San Francisco. Still used as an architecture school, the building can be visited weekdays 10–5, and exhibits are also open weekends 10–12:30 and 2–5.

For a contrast to the no-nonsense Bauhaus architecture, look at Dessau's older buildings, including St. George's Church, built in 1712 in Dutch Baroque style.

SAXONY

Crossing the border from Thuringia into Saxony you will be forgiven for noticing no marked difference. Only as you travel east do the villages and landscape show signs of having languished for decades in this almost forgotten corner of Germany, close to the Czech and Polish borders. Two cities, however, are recovering magnificently: Dresden and Leipzig. As you make your way toward Dresden from Freiberg, you have the choice of following the Freital road to Dresden or cutting north to the Elbe River and the enchanting little city of Meissen. Either way, Dresden should be the climax of any tour of this part of Germany.

Leipzig

7 *32 km (19 mi) southeast of Halle, 65 km (39 mi) south of Dessau.*

With a population of about 560,000, Leipzig is the second-largest city in eastern Germany (after Berlin) and has long been a center of printing and bookselling. Astride major trade routes, it was an important market town in the Middle Ages, and it continues to be a trading center, thanks to fairs that twice a year (March and September) bring together buyers from east and west.

Those familiar with music and German literature will associate Leipzig with the great composer Johann Sebastian Bach (1685–1750), who was organist and choir director at the Thomaskirche (St. Thomas's Church); with the 19th-century composer Richard Wagner, who was born here in 1813; and with German Romantic poets Goethe and Schiller, both of whom lived and worked in the area.

In 1813, on the city's outskirts, the Battle of the Nations was fought, in which Prussian, Austrian, Russian, and Swedish forces stood ground against Napoléon's troops. This battle (*Völkerschlacht*) was instrumental in leading to the French general's defeat two years later at Waterloo and thus helped to decide European national boundaries for the remainder of the century.

Following the devastation of World War II, little is left of old Leipzig. Considerable restoration has been undertaken in the old city, however, and the result certainly conveys touches of Renaissance character and Jugendstil flair, although some of the newer buildings (notably the university's skyscraper tower) distort the perspective and proportions of the old city.

Numbers in the margin correspond to points of interest on the Leipzig map.

8 Leipzig's main train station, the **Hauptbahnhof,** is alone a major city attraction (there's a tourist information office opposite Platform 3, open weekdays 9–5). In 1991 it was expanded to accommodate the anticipated post-reunification increase in traffic, and with its 26 platforms the station is the largest in Europe. But its fin de siècle grandness remains, particularly in the staircases that lead majestically up to the platforms. As you climb them, take a look at the great arched ceilings high above you; they're unique among German railway stations.

9 Leipzig's showpiece is its old market square, the **Markt,** only slightly smaller than St. Mark's Square in Venice. One side is occupied completely by the recently restored Renaissance City Hall, the **Altes Rathaus,** which now houses the **Stadtgeschichtliches Museum,** where Leipzig's past is well documented. ✉ *Markt 1,* ☎ *0341/965310.* ⌦ *DM 3.* ☉ *Tues.–Fri. 10–6, weekends 10–4.*

Starting from all sides of the Markt, small streets attest to Leipzig's rich trading past. Tucked in among them are glass-roof arcades of surprising beauty and elegance. Invent a headache and step into the *Apotheke* at Hainstrasse 9. You'll find yourself in surroundings that haven't changed for 100 years or more, redolent of powders and perfumes, home cures, and foreign spices. It's spectacularly Jugendstil, with finely etched and stained glass and rich mahogany. Or head to the antiquarian bookshops of the nearby Neumarkt Passage.

10 The **Mädlerpassage,** accessible from Grimmaischesstrasse, is Leipzig's finest arcade, where the ghost of Goethe's Faust lurks in every marble corner. Here you'll find the famous Auerbachs Keller restaurant, at No.

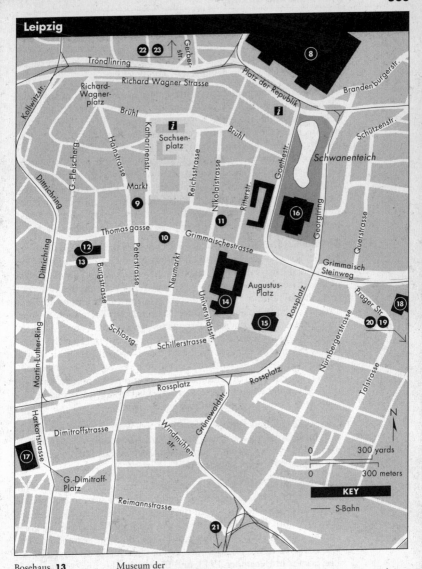

Leipzig

Bosehaus, **13**

Exhibition
Pavilion, **20**

Gohliser
Schlösschen, **22**

Grassimuseum, **18**

Hauptbahnhof, **8**

Leipzig University
tower, **14**

Mädlerpassage, **10**

Markt, **9**

Museum der
Bildenden Künste, **17**

Neues
Gewandhaus, **15**

Nikolaikirche, **11**

Opera House, **16**

Schiller's House, **23**

Thomaskirche, **12**

Torhaus Dölitz, **21**

Völkerschlacht-
denkmal, **19**

2, where Goethe set a scene in *Faust* (☞ Dining and Lodging, *below*). A bronze group of characters from the play, sculpted in 1913, beckons you down the stone staircase to the cellar restaurant. A few yards away down the arcade is a delightful Jugendstil coffee shop called Mephisto, decorated in devilish reds and blacks.

★ ⓫   The **Nikolaikirche** has taken a central place in Leipzig's contemporary life as well as the city's history—demonstrations here are credited with helping to bring down the Communist regime. Every Monday for months before the government collapsed, thousands of citizens gathered in front of the church chanting, "*Wir sind das Volk*" ("We are the people"). Inside the church, which is much more impressive than the undistinguished facade would have you believe, is a soaring Gothic choir and nave. Notice the unusual patterned ceiling supported by classical pillars that end in palm-tree-like flourishes, a curious combination of styles that meld successfully. Luther is said to have preached from the ornate 16th-century pulpit. ⊠ *Just off Grimmaischesstr.*

★ ⓬   The **Thomaskirche** is the Gothic church where Bach was choirmaster for 27 years and where Martin Luther preached on Whit Sunday 1539, signaling the arrival of Protestantism in Leipzig. Originally the center of a 13th-century monastery, which was rebuilt during the 15th century, the tall church now stands by itself, but the names of adjacent streets recall the cloisters that once surrounded it. Bach wrote most of his cantatas for the church's famous boys choir, the Thomasknabenchor, which was founded during the 13th century; the church continues as the choir's home as well as a center of Bach tradition. In the Middle Ages the choir was assembled to sing at every public function—from the installation of bishops to the execution of criminals. Its ranks thinned rapidly when the boys were engaged to sing while plague victims were carted to graves outside the city walls.

Bach's 12 children and the infant Richard Wagner were baptized in the church's early 17th-century font; Karl Marx and Friedrich Engels also stood before this same font, godfathers to Karl Liebknecht, who grew up to be a revolutionary, too!

The great music Bach wrote during his Leipzig years commanded little attention in his lifetime, and when he died, he was given a simple grave, without a headstone, in the city's Johannisfriedhof Cemetery. It wasn't until 1894 that an effort was made to find where the great composer lay buried, and after a thorough, macabre search his coffin was removed to the Johanniskirche. The church was destroyed by Allied bombs in December 1943, and Bach found his final resting place in the church he would have selected: the Thomaskirche. It's now a place of pilgrimage for music lovers the world over, and his gravestone below the high altar is never without a floral tribute. Fresh flowers also constantly decorate the statue of Bach that stands before the church, erected on the initiative of the composer Mendelssohn, who performed his own music in the church and revered its great master. ⊠ *Thomaskirchhof, just off Grimmaischesstr.* 🎫 *Free.* ☉ *Daily 9–6.*

⓭   The Bach family home, the **Bosehaus,** still stands opposite the Thomaskirche and is now a museum devoted to the composer's life and work. (The exhibits are in German only; an English-language guide can be purchased in the shop.) Of particular interest is the display of musical instruments dating from Bach's time. ⊠ *Thomaskirchhof 16,* ☎ *0341/964–4135.* 🎫 *DM 2.* ☉ *Mon.–Sun. 10–5.*

NEED A   If the weather's good, take an outdoor table at the **Cafe Concerto** (⊠
BREAK?   Thomaskirchhof 13), open daily 9–8, and absorb the peace and quiet

of the little square, dominated by a statue of Bach. Street musicians regularly play the man's works, literally at his feet. The Jugendstil interior of the café beckons in all weather, with a menu of light meals, local beers and wines, and coffee.

⑭ Towering over Leipzig's city center is the 470-foot-high **Leipzig University tower,** which houses administrative offices and lecture rooms. Some of the young wags who study there have dubbed it the "Jagged Tooth"; they were also largely responsible for changing the official name of the university, replacing the postwar title of Karl Marx University with its original one.

Augustus Platz spreads out below the university tower like a space-age campus. In the shadow of the skyscraper is the glass-and-concrete **⑮ Neues Gewandhaus,** the modernistic home of the eponymous orchestra, one of Germany's greatest. (Its popular director, Kurt Masur, recently added to his duties the directorship of the New York Philharmonic Orchestra.) In the foyer you can see one of Europe's largest ceiling paintings, a staggering 716-square-meter allegorical work by Sighard Gilles devoted to the muse of music. The statue of Beethoven that stands in the foyer, by sculptor Max Klinger, won first prize at the 1912 World Art Exhibition in Vienna. The world-renowned acoustics of the Gewandhaus enhance the resonance of every tone by a full two seconds.

⑯ Leipzig's **Opera House** was the first postwar theater to be built in Communist East Germany. Its solid, boxy style is an enduring subject of local controversy. ⊠ *Directly opposite Gewandhaus, on north side of Augustus-Pl.*

⑰ The **Museum der Bildenden Künste,** near the 19th-century neo-Gothic monstrosity that serves as Leipzig's City Hall, is the city's leading art gallery. The art collection occupies the ground floor of the former Reichsgericht, the court where the Nazis held a show trial against the Bulgarian Communist Georgi Dimitroff on a trumped-up charge of masterminding a plot to burn down the Reichstag in 1933. ⊠ *Georgi-Dimitroff-Pl. 1, ☎ 0341/216–9914. ⊠ DM 5, free 2nd Sun. of month. ⊙ Tues. and Thurs.–Sun. 9–5, Wed. 1–9:30.*

⑱ The **Grassimuseum** complex (⊠ Johannespl. 5–11, ☎ 0341/21420) is not only a major cultural venue in its own right but a fine example of German art deco, as well. It was built in 1925–29 to house three important museums: the newly renovated **Museum of Arts and Crafts,** the **Ethnological Museum,** and the **Musical Instruments Museum** (enter from Täubchenweg 2). ⊠ *Museum of Arts and Crafts: ⊠ DM 4; ⊙ Tues.–Fri. 10–6, Wed. 10–8, weekends 10–5. Ethnological Museum: ⊠ DM 5; ⊙ Tues.–Fri. 10–5:30, weekends 10–4:30. Musical Instruments Museum: ⊠ DM 5; ⊙ Tues.–Fri. 9–5, Sat. 10–5, Sun. 10–1.*

OFF THE
BEATEN PATH
BOTANISCHER GARTEN (BOTANICAL GARDEN) – This set of splendid open-air gardens and greenhouses incorporates Germany's oldest university botanical garden, which dates from 1542. The journey to the Botanischer Garten stop takes about 15 minutes on Tram 1. ⊠ *Linnestr. 1. ☎ 0341/9736850. ⊠ Free. ⊙ Gardens Apr.–Sept., daily 9–6; Oct.–Mar., daily 9–4. Greenhouses Apr.–Sept., Wed. 1–6, Sun. 9–6; Oct.–Mar., Wed. 1–6, Sun. 9–4.*

⑲ The battle that put Leipzig on the military map of Europe, the 1813 Battle of the Nations (*Völkerschlacht*), is commemorated by the **Völkerschlachtdenkmal,** an enormous memorial on the outskirts of the city (via Streetcars 15, 20, 21 or 25). Rising out of suburban Leipzig like some great Egyptian tomb, the somber, gray pile of granite and concrete is more than 300 feet high. Despite its ugliness, the site is well worth a visit, if only to wonder at the lengths—and heights—to which the Prussians went to celebrate their military victories, and to take in the view from a windy platform near the top (provided you can climb the 500 steps to get there). The Prussians did make one concession to Napoléon in designing the monument: A stone marks the spot where he stood during the three-day battle. ☎ *0341/878–0471.* ⚏ *DM 3.50.* ☉ *May–Oct., daily 10–5; Nov.–Apr., daily 9–4. Guided tours daily at 10:30, 11:30, 1:30, and 2:30.*

㉔ The **Exhibition Pavilion,** also reached via Streetcars 15, 20, 21, or 25, has a vast diorama portraying the Battle of the Nations and a display of weapons and uniforms of those times. ✉ *Prager Str. 210, in Wilhelm-Külz Park,* ☎ *0341/878–1392.* ⚏ *DM 2.* ☉ *May–Sept., Wed.–Sun. 10–6; Oct.–Apr., Wed.–Sun. 9–4.*

㉑ The **Torhaus Dölitz,** the gatehouse of the Dölitz Palace (Streetcar 22 or 24 and then a walk up Helenenstrasse), has exhibition of toy soldiers re-creating the Battle of the Nations. ✉ *Helenenstr. 24,* ☎ *0341/323–307.* ⚏ *DM 2.* ☉ *Wed.–Sun. 10–5.*

㉒ Outside of the center of Leipzig but reachable by public transportation (Streetcars 20 and 24, then walk left up Poetenweg, or Streetcar 6 to Menckestr.) is the delightfully rococo **Gohliser Schlösschen** (Gohliser House), the site of frequent concerts. ✉ *Menckestr. 23,* ☎ *0341/52979.* ☉ *Mon. and Fri. 1–5; Tues., Thurs., and Sat. 9–1; Wed. 1–8.*

㉓ **Schiller's House** was for a time the home of the German poet and dramatist Friedrich Schiller. *Schillerhaus,* ✉ *Menckestr. 42, up the street from Gohliser Schlösschen,* ☎ *0341/566–2170.* ⚏ *DM 2.* ☉ *Tues., Wed., and Fri., 10–5; Thurs. 10–6; Sat. 11–5.*

Dining and Lodging

$$ ✕ **Apels Garten.** The garden associations of this elegant little restaurant in the city center are to be found in the landscape paintings on the wall, the floral arrangements on the tables, and the fresh produce on the imaginative menu. The wild-duck soup with homemade noodles is an obligatory starter—you won't find another soup like it in Leipzig. ✉ *Kolonnadenstr. 2,* ☎ *0341/285–093. AE, DC, MC, V. No dinner Sun.*

$$ ✕ **Auerbachs Keller.** Amazingly, this most famous of Leipzig's restau-
★ rants went bankrupt in 1995, indicative of the turmoil still existing in eastern Germany. But it was such an established part of the eastern German scene that vigorous efforts were being made to rescue it, and regulars strongly believe it will soon be back in business. It's been around since 1530, after all, and Goethe immortalized it in his *Faust.* The menu features regional dishes from Saxony, often with Faustian names. There is also a good wine list. ✉ *Mädler-Passage 2–4,* ☎ *0341/216–1040. Reservations essential. Jacket and tie. AE, DC, MC, V.*

$$ ✕ **Deutscher Hof.** The Hotel Deutscher Hof's beamed and paneled restaurant is a fine example of Leipzig Jugendstil, with elegant woodwork and glass. The menu is heartily Thuringian with an international touch. If you have problems getting a table, try instead the cellar restaurant, Zur Laderne, where you'll eat beneath the original vaulted ceiling and between warm brick walls. ✉ *Waldstr. 31–33,* ☎ *0341/71100. MC, V.*

$$ ✕ **Paulaner Palais.** Munich's Paulaner Brewery has transformed a historic corner of Leipzig into a vast complex combining restaurants, a banquet hall, a café, and a beer garden. There's something here for everybody, from intimate dining to noisy, Bavarian-style tavern-table jollity.

The food is a hearty mix of Bavarian and Thuringian, and the Paulaner beer is a perfect accompaniment. ⊠ *Klostergasse 3–5,* ☎ *0341/211–3115. AE, MC, V.*

$$ ✕ **Zill's Tunnel.** The "tunnel" refers to the barrel-ceiling, ground-floor restaurant, where foaming glasses of excellent local beer are served with a smile. The friendly staff will also help you decipher the Old Saxon descriptions of the menu's traditional dishes. Upstairs there's a larger wine restaurant with a welcoming open fireplace. Despite the distinction between the two, you can drink whatever you choose on either floor; wine buffs will single out the rare Saxon wine from a Saale Valley vineyard. Goose prepared in a variety of ways is a staple here, and among the soups is one made with vegetables, beer, and gin—a potent mixture. ⊠ *Barfussgässchen 9,* ☎ *0341/200–446. No credit cards.*

$$$$ ✕▥ **InterContinental.** The city's newest and by far most luxurious hotel is imposing, with its high-rise profile as well as its Japanese restaurant and garden. Rooms in this Japanese-built hotel offer every luxury, including bathrooms with marble floors and walls and full air-conditioning—and you'll be close to the main train station. ⊠ *Gerberstr. 15, D–04105,* ☎ *0341/9880,* ℻ *0341/988–1229. 429 rooms with bath, 18 suites. 4 restaurants, 2 bars, coffee shop, indoor pool, massage, sauna, spa, bowling, exercise room, shops, billiards, casino, nightclub. AE, DC, MC, V.*

$$$$ ✕▥ **Maritim Hotel Astoria.** Many prefer this older hotel for its grandness and solid comfort, as well as for its proximity to the main train station. There's considerable traffic in the area, so you'll do best with a room on the side rather than the front. If you eat lunch or dinner in the Galerie restaurant, you'll literally be dining in an art museum. ⊠ *Pl. der Republik 2, D–04109,* ☎ *0341/72220,* ℻ *0341/722–4747. 309 rooms with bath. 2 restaurants, bar, café, sauna, nightclub. AE, DC, MC, V.*

$$$ ✕▥ **Holiday Inn Garden Court.** The former, slightly seedy Hotel Zum
★ Löwen has undergone two consecutive transformations in as many years and has metamorphosed into a smart and very comfortable hotel. The change is dazzling, and unchanged, of course, is the excellent location, just across the street from Leipzig's main railway station. Rooms are still on the small side, but they lack nothing in terms of comfort and facilities and are decorated and furnished in a warm combination of American cherry wood and rich blues and golds. The open-plan bar and lounge are a lively evening meeting spot. The Partout restaurant confidently proclaims that its chef "will not tolerate monotony," and the Partout bistro serves light snacks until the early hours. ⊠ *Rudolf-Breitscheid-Str. 3, D–04103,* ☎ *0341/125–100,* ℻ *0341/125–1100. 121 rooms, 9 suites with bath or shower. Restaurant, bar, sauna, exercise room. AE, DC, MC, V.*

$$ ✕▥ **Balance Hotel Leipzig.** The small Balance group keeps prices in its hotels down by trimming extras. Basic comforts, however, are guaranteed, and rooms are well furnished and surprisingly large, with some family suites designed as two-story maisonettes. Tea- and coffee-making facilities in the rooms are a substitute for the lack of all-night room service. The group's Leipzig hotel is its newest, a sleek and stylish addition to Leipzig's southeastern skyline. ⊠ *Wasserturmstr. 33, D–04299,* ☎ *0341/86790,* ℻ *0341/867–944. 134 rooms and suites with bath. Restaurant. AE, DC, MC, V.*

$$$ ▥ **Hotel Silencium.** This new hotel is part of the Silencium group, which guarantees its guests a peaceful night. So although it's on a busy thoroughfare, hush permeates the entire house, a beautifully converted city mansion filled with modern, comfortable rooms outfitted with attractive cane furniture and equipped with satellite TV and fax outlets. Though the hotel is about 3 kilometers (2 miles) from the city center, tram stops are nearby. It does not have a restaurant, but there is a fairly wide choice of places to eat in the immediate area. ⊠ *Georg-Schumann-Str. 268, Leipzig-Möckern, D–04159,* ☎ *0341/901–2990,* FAX *0341/901–2991. 34 rooms with bath. AE, DC, MC, V.*

Nightlife and the Arts

The Neues Gewandhaus, a controversial piece of architecture, is home to an undeniably splendid **orchestra.** Tickets to concerts are very difficult to obtain unless you reserve well in advance and in writing only (Gewandhaus zu Leipzig, ⊠ Augustuspl. 8, D–04109). Sometimes spare tickets are available at the box office a half hour before the evening performance. Leipzig holds an annual music festival, **"Music Days,"** in June. One of Germany's most famous **cabarets,** the Pfeffermühle (Peppermill), has a lively bar off a courtyard opposite the Thomaskirche (⊠ Thomaskirchhof 16). On pleasant evenings the courtyard fills with benches and tables, and the scene rivals the indoor performance for entertainment. Top **discos** include the revamped **Schorsch'l** (⊠ Dufourstr. 8, ☎ 0341/213–0556), which assures over-thirties they'll also feel at home; the ever-popular **Esplanade** (⊠ Richard-Wagner-Str. 10, ☎ 0341/282–330); and the **Tanzpalast,** in the august setting of the city theater, the Schauspielhaus (⊠ Bosestr. 1, ☎ 0341/281–023). Another magnet for young people is the **Moritzbastei** (⊠ Universitätstr. 9, ☎ 0341/960–5191), reputedly Europe's largest student club, with bars, a disco, a café, a theater, and a cinema. It attracts 350,000 young people a year, and foreign visitors are welcome. The lively **after-dark scene** also includes an exotic café-bar, **VIS–A–VIS** (⊠ Rudolf-Breitscheid-Str. 33, ☎ 0341/292–718), which has a particular welcome for "gay people, artists, birds of paradise and other aesthetes."

Shopping

One of Leipzig's greatest pleasures is exploring the beautifully restored Jugendstil **arcades** that thread through the city center. In such restored precincts as the Mädlerpassage you can now find boutiques as chic as any in Hamburg or Munich.

En Route   Most roads now lead to Dresden, but leave the autobahn (or change trains) at Grimma, 25 kilometers (17 miles) east of Leipzig, and head for **Colditz,** following a pretty river valley that leads directly to the town whose name still sends a chill through soldiers who fought the Germans in World War II. During the war the Germans converted the massive, somber castle looming over the little town to what they believed would be an escape-proof abode for allied prisoners regarded as security risks. But many managed to flee, employing a catalog of ruses that have since been the stuff of several films and books. The castle is now a home for senior citizens, but the courtyards and some of the installations used during the war can be visited.

Chemnitz

㉔ *80 km (50 mi) southeast of Leipzig.*

On older maps Chemnitz may appear as Karl-Marx-Stadt, an appellation thrust on the city in 1953 to honor the East German working community with a dedication to the man who really started it all. In 1990 the inhabitants, free to express a choice, overwhelmingly voted to restore the original name. Still, in front of the district council building in the new city center is one of few remaining **Karl Marx memorials** in eastern Germany (thanks to the hard-fighting pro-Marx lobby), a massive stylized head sculpted by the Soviet artist Lew Kerbel. Behind it is the motto "Working Men of All Countries, Unite!"—in German, Russian, French, and English. Badly damaged during World War II, Chemnitz has revived as a center of heavy industry, but it never had the architectural attractions of other cities in the area.

Chemnitz's main visual attraction is its 12th-century **Red Tower** in the center of the city. The **Altes Rathaus** (Old City Hall), dating from 1496 to 1498, incorporates a variety of styles, after many reconstructions. Outside the city museum (which is not particularly exciting) is a group of 250-million-year-old **petrified tree trunks,** unique in Europe and looking for all the world like a modern work of sculpture.

Dining and Lodging

$$$$ ✕🏨 **Günnewig Hotel Chemnitzer Hof.** You might enjoy the sense of living in another era at this city-center hotel with origins in the early Bauhaus style, in which ornamentation was discarded in favor of abstract design (it was built in 1930 and is now on the national historic register). The spacious rooms are furnished with fine veneers and attractive shades of blue. ⊠ *Theaterpl. 4, D–09111,* ☎ *0371/6840,* 𝖥𝖠𝖷 *0371/62587. 104 rooms with bath. 2 restaurants, bar, Bierstube, sauna, nightclub. AE, DC, MC, V.*

$$$ ✕🏨 **Adelsberger Parkhotel Hoyer.** The first hotel built in Chemnitz since reunification proudly claims its position in the modern, graceful styling of the exterior and in the elegant comfort of the guest rooms. The apartments under the steeply sloping eaves are particularly attractive, with cozy nooks lit by large dormer windows. The royal-blue-and-white furnishings of the restaurant, flooded with light from floor-to-ceiling bay windows, are a perfect accompaniment to an imaginative menu in which an international cuisine embraces some hearty Thuringian specialties. ⊠ *Wilhelm-Busch-Str. 61, D–09127,* ☎ *0371/773–303,* 𝖥𝖠𝖷 *0371/773–377. 22 rooms with bath, 5 apartments. Restaurant, sauna, exercise room. AE, MC, V.*

$$$ ✕🏨 **Hotel Mercure Kongress.** This Communist-era, 26-story skyscraper hotel was once uninspiring in its uniform decor, but now you'll notice a sleek Western style. Even the address is new—the hotel stands on a renamed version of Karl-Marx-Strasse. For a fantastic view of the city try for a room on one of the upper floors or book a table in the newly opened Panorama restaurant, on the 26th floor. But book early—this is a favorite on the convention and meeting circuit. ⊠ *Brückenstr. 19, D–09111,* ☎ *0371/6830,* 𝖥𝖠𝖷 *0371/683–505. 386 rooms with bath. 2 restaurants, bar, beauty salon, sauna. AE, DC, MC, V.*

En Route From Chemnitz take the winding Freital Valley road east to Freiberg. You'll pass through a village called Frankenstein on the way, and although there are some ancient castle ruins in the vicinity, nobody claims this is where the scientist-baron conducted his experiments.

Freiburg

㉕ *35 km (22 mi) east of Chemnitz.*

Once a prosperous silver-mining community, Freiberg is highlighted by two picturesque Gothic town squares, the Upper and Lower markets. The late-Gothic cathedral, with its Golden Gate, constructed in 1230, has a richly decorated interior and a Silbermann organ dating from 1711.

The 800-year-old **mine** that yielded riches great enough to merit the name Reiche Zeche (Wealthy Mine) can still be visited. ⊠ *Fuchsmuhlenweg 9,* ☎ *03731/22044.* 🎫 *DM 15, includes guided tour, conducted Apr.–Sept., weekdays at 9:30, Sat. 8, 11, and 2; Oct.–Mar., 1st Sat. of month.*

The **city museum,** on central Domplatz, vividly describes the history of silver mining in and around Freiberg. ⊠ *Stadt- und Bergbaumuseum, Am Dom 1,* ☎ *03731/23197.* 🖅 *DM 3.* ⏱ *Tues.–Sun. 9–5.*

Meissen

 40 km (24 mi) north of Freiberg, 25 km (15 mi) northwest of Dresden.

This romantic city on the Elbe River is known the world over for its porcelain, bearing the trademark crossed blue swords. The first European porcelain was made in this area in 1708, and in 1710 the royal porcelain manufacturer was established in Meissen, close to the local raw materials.

The story of how porcelain came to be produced in Meissen reads like a German fairy tale: Saxony ruler August the Strong (who ruled 1697–1704 and 1710–33) urged alchemists at his court to search for the secret of making gold, something he badly needed to refill a Saxon state treasury depleted by his expensive building projects and extravagant lifestyle. The alchemists failed to produce gold, but one of them, Johann Friedrich Böttger, discovered a method for making something almost as precious: fine hard-paste porcelain. Prince August consigned Böttger and a team of craftsmen to a hilltop castle—Albrechtsburg, in Meissen—and set them to work. August hoped to keep their recipe a state secret, but within a few years fine porcelain was being produced by Böttger's method in many parts of Europe. Meissen porcelain is to be found in one form or another all over town. A set of porcelain bells at the late-Gothic **Frauenkirche,** on the central market square, the Marktplatz, was the first of its kind anywhere when installed in 1929. The largest set of porcelain figures ever crafted can be found in the **Nikolaikirche,** which also houses remains of early Gothic frescoes. Also of interest in the town center are the 1569 **Old Brewery,** graced by a Renaissance gable; **St. Francis,** now housing a city museum; and **St. Martin's,** with a late-Gothic altar.

The **Albrechtsburg castle,** where the story of Meissen porcelain really began, sits high above old Meissen, towering over the river far below. It's a bit of a climb up Burgstrasse and Amtsstrasse to the castle, although a bus runs regularly up the hill from the central market square. The 15th-century Albrechtsburg is Germany's first truly residential castle, a complete break with the earlier style of fortified bastion. It fell into disuse and neglect as nearby Dresden rose to local prominence, but it's still an imposing collection of late-Gothic and Renaissance buildings. In the central courtyard, a typical Gothic *Schutzhof* protected on three sides by high rough-stone walls, is an exterior spiral staircase, the **Wendelstein,** a masterpiece of early masonry, which was hewn in 1525 from one massive stone block. The ceilings of the castle halls are richly decorated, although many date only from a restoration in 1870. Adjacent to the castle is a towered early Gothic cathedral. ☎ *03521/47070.* 🖅 *DM 6 (guided tours an extra DM 2).* ⏱ *Mar.–Nov., daily 10–6; Dec. and Feb. 10–5.*

The **porcelain works** outgrew their castle workshop during the mid-19th century, and today you'll find them on the outskirts of town. There you can see porcelain production demonstrations. In the same building a museum displays Meissen porcelain, a collection that rivals that of the Porcelain Museum in Dresden. ⊠ *Talstr. 9,* ☎ *0351/468–700 or 0351/468–208.* 🖅 *Museum DM 5, workshops DM 5 (including guided tour).* ⏱ *Daily 9–5.*

Dining and Lodging

$–$$ ✕ **Burgkeller.** This ancient and popular hostelry, part of the centuries-old complex of buildings ringing the castle, was closed in 1996 because of ownership problems, but the people of Meissen fervently hoped it would reopen by 1997. If their hopes are fulfilled, this will be *the* place to wine and dine in Meissen, if only because of the sensational view of the Elbe River valley from its large dining room and tree-shaded terrace. ⊠ *Dompl. 9 (no ☎ at press time).*

$$$–$$$$ ✕🖬 **Pannonia Parkhotel.** This Jugendstil villa on the banks of the Elbe, across the river from the hilltop castle, is now in the hands of an energetic and imaginative young American hotel director who envisions a culinary and cultural center. The first part of the plan has been realized, with cuisine of international flair and a dining room that makes use of such features of the old house as its original stained glass and its elegantly framed doors. By 1997 it should also be the scene of regular chamber-music evenings. Although most of the luxuriously furnished and appointed rooms are in the newly built annexes, try for one in the villa—and for an unforgettable experience book the top suite (in every sense) under the eaves (around DM 400 a night). The view of the river and the castle from its two rooms and from the badminton-court-size private terrace is sensational. On weekends room rates drop by as much as half. ⊠ *Hafenstr. 27–31, D–01662,* ☎ *03521/72250,* 䤸 *03521/722–904. 76 rooms with bath, 17 apartments, 4 suites. Restaurant, bars, sauna, exercise room. AE, DC, MC, V.*

Nightlife and the Arts

Meissen's cathedral, the **Dom,** has a year-long music program, with organ and choral concerts every Saturday during the summer. Call ☎ 03521/452–490 for details. Regular **concerts** are held at the Albrechtsburg, and in summer open-air evening performances are staged in the castle's romantic courtyard, the Burghof (☎ 03521/47070 for details).

Shopping

Meissen **porcelain** can be bought directly from the manufacturer in Talstrasse and in every china and gift shop in town. To **wine** connoisseurs, the name Meissen is associated with something almost as precious as porcelain: Vineyards around Meissen produce a top-quality wine that is much in demand throughout Germany—if you enjoy a good vintage, don't leave without a bottle.

En Route   Follow the road north of the Elbe to Dresden. The small town of **Radebeul,** halfway between Meissen and Dresden, is a mecca for fans of Westerns from all over the world. Radebeul is the birthplace of Germany's well-loved novelist Karl May, who wrote highly popular, convincing Westerns without once visiting America. A museum explains just how he did it. ⊠ *Karl-May-Str. 5.* ⊙ *Mar.–Oct., Tues.–Sun. 9–6, Nov.–Feb., Tues.–Sun. 10–4.*

Hellerau, on the outskirts of Dresden (adjacent to the airport), is the site of one of Europe's first experiments in "garden town" planning. It was founded in 1910 by a Dresden furniture maker who wanted to prove that artifacts of lasting beauty could be produced by workers housed in pleasant surroundings. He was helped by an enthusiastic arts lover, Wolf Dohrn, who established at Hellerau a revolutionary new school of dance theory, building Germany's first modern-style theater for the new company. The experiment foundered with Dohrn's death in a skiing accident in 1914 and with the outbreak of World War I. There was a brief renaissance after the war, but the Nazis and then World War II finally obliterated Hellerau as a cultural center. The Red Army took the theater and surrounding buildings over as a military hospital and barracks after the war but in 1992 gave them back to the people of Hellerau, who now plan to revive them as a pan-European cultural center, with the possible assistance of an American institute.

Dresden

㉗ *25 km (15 mi) southeast of Meissen, 205 km (123 mi) south of Berlin).*

Saxony's capital city sits in rococo splendor on a wide sweep of the Elbe River, and its proponents are working with German thoroughness to recapture the city's old reputation as the "Florence of the North," after war and official neglect exacted their heavy toll. In its rococo yellows and greens, it is enormously appealing, and the effect is even more overwhelming when you compare what you see today—or what Canaletto paintings reflect of a Dresden centuries earlier—with the photographs of Dresden in 1945, after a British bombing raid almost destroyed it overnight. It was one of the architectural and cultural treasures of the Western world, and despite lack of funds and an often uncooperative Communist bureaucracy, the people of Dresden succeeded in rebuilding it—an enormous tribute to their skills and dedication.

Their efforts restored at least the riverside panorama to the appearance Canaletto would have recognized, but some of the other parts of the city center look halfway between construction and demolition. In the coming years the city will look more like a building site as 20 new hotels are added to provide the accommodations it so desperately needs. Don't think of visiting Dresden without reserving a place to stay well in advance.

Dresden was the capital of Saxony as early as the 15th century, although most of its architectural masterpieces date from the 18th century, when the enlightened Saxon ruler August the Strong and his son, Frederick Augustus II, brought leading Italian and Bavarian architects and designers up from the south. The predominantly Italianate influence is evident today in gloriously overblown rococo architecture.

The best introduction to Dresden is to arrive by boat (☞ Getting Around *in* Thuringia and Saxony A to Z, *below*), but for motorists or train passengers, the starting point of a Dresden tour will be the main railway station (which has adequate parking). To reach the old part of the city and its treasures, you'll first have to cross a featureless expanse surrounded by postwar high-rises, leading into the pedestrians-only Pragerstrasse (the tourist information office is at No. 8).

Numbers in the margin correspond to points of interest on the Dresden map.

㉘ The true center of Dresden is its broad **Altmarkt,** whose colonnaded beauty survived the disfiguring efforts of city planners to turn it into a huge outdoor parking lot. The Altmarkt's church, the **Kreuzkirche,** is an interesting combination of Baroque and Jugendstil architecture and decoration. A church stood here during the 13th century, but the present structure dates from the late 1700s. Other interesting buildings bordering the Altmarkt include the rebuilt **Rathaus,** and the yellow-stucco, 18th-century Landhaus, which contains the **Museum für Geschichte der Stadt Dresden** (City Historical Museum). ▣ *DM 3.* ⊙ *Mon.–Thurs. and weekends 10–6 (until 8 on Wed. May–Sept.).*

Despite its name, the **Neumarkt** (New Market), adjacent to the Altmarkt, is Dresden's historic heart. The ruins that scar the square are all that remain of Germany's greatest Protestant church after the February 1945 bombing raid. These jagged, precariously tilting walls were
㉙ once the mighty Baroque **Frauenkirche,** so sturdily built that it with-

Dresden

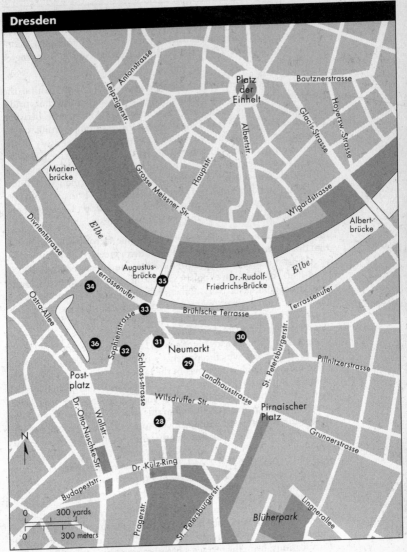

Albertinum, **30**
Altmarkt, **28**
Augustusbrücke, **35**
Frauenkirche, **29**
Johanneum, **31**
Katholische
Hofkirche, **33**

Residenzschloss, **32**
Semperoper, **34**
Zwinger, **36**

stood a three-day bombardment during the Seven Years' War, only to fall victim to the flames that followed the World War II raid. The church is painstakingly being reconstructed with the aim of holding a reconsecration in the year 2006, the 800th anniversary of the founding of Dresden.

㉚ The massive, imperial-style **Albertinum,** which looms behind the Frauenkirche, is Dresden's leading art museum and one of the world's great galleries. It is named after Saxony's King Albert, who between 1884 and 1887 converted a royal arsenal into a suitable setting for the treasures he and his forebears had collected. The upper story of the Albertinum, accessible from the Brühlsche Terrasse, houses the **Gemäldegalerie Neue Meister** (Gallery of Modern Masters), with displays of 19th- and 20th-century paintings and sculpture. Permanent exhibits include outstanding work by German masters of the 19th and 20th centuries (Caspar David Friedrich's haunting *Das Kreuz im Gebirge* is here) and French Impressionists and post-Impressionists.

Impressive as the art gallery is, it's the **Grüne Gewölbe** (Green Vault) that draws the most attention. Named after a green room in the palace of August the Strong, this part of the Albertinum (entered from Georg-Treu-Platz) contains an exquisite collection of unique objets d'art fashioned from gold, silver, ivory, amber, and other precious and semiprecious materials. Among the crown jewels are the world's largest "green" diamond, 41 carats in weight, and a dazzling group of tiny gem-studded figures entitled *Hofstaat zu Delhi am Geburtstag des Grossmoguls Aureng-Zeb.* The unwieldy name gives a false idea of the size of the work, dating from 1708, which represents a birthday gathering at the court of an Indian mogul; some parts of the tableau are so small they can be admired only through a magnifying glass. Somewhat larger and less delicate is the drinking bowl of Ivan the Terrible, perhaps the most sensational of the treasures to be found in this extraordinary museum. Next door is the **Skulpturensammlung** (Sculpture Collection), which includes ancient Egyptian and classical works and examples by Giovanni da Bologna and Adriaen de Vries. *Albertinum,* ⊠ *Am Neumarkt,* ☎ *0351/495–3056.* 🖾 *DM 7, includes admission to Gemäldegalerie Neue Meister, Grünes Gewölbe, Münzkabinett (coin collection), and Skulpturensammlung.* ☉ *Mon.–Wed. and Fri.–Sun. 10–6.*

If you leave the Albertinum by the **Brühlsche Terrasse** exit you'll find yourself on what was once known as the "Balcony of Europe," a terrace high above the Elbe, carved from a 16th-century stretch of the city fortifications; from the terrace a breathtaking vista of the Elbe and the Dresden skyline opens up.

NEED A
BREAK?

You can enjoy the view and also take a break after so much gallery viewing by stepping into the nearby **Cafe Vis-a-Vis,** which sits handsomely in a Baroque mansion on the Brühlsche Terrasse.

㉛ Like the Albertinum, the **Johanneum,** accessible by steps leading down from the Brühlsche Terrasse, is a former royal building that now serves as a museum. The 16th-century Johanneum was once the regal stables. Instead of horses, it now houses the **Verkehrsmuseum,** a collection of historical vehicles, including vintage automobiles and engines. ⊠ *Am Neumarkt,* ☎ *0351/495–3002.* 🖾 *DM 4; Fri. DM 2.* ☉ *Tues.–Sun. 10–5.*

The former **stable exercise yard,** behind the Johanneum and enclosed by elegant Renaissance arcades, was used during the 16th century as an open-air festival ground. To spare the royalty on horseback the trouble of dismounting before ascending to the upper story to watch the jousting and jollities in the yard below, a ramp was built to accommodate both two- and four-legged guests. You'll find the scene today much as it was centuries ago, complete with jousting markings in the ground. More popular even than jousting in those days was *Ringelstechen,* a risky pursuit in which riders at full gallop had to catch small rings on their lances. Horses and riders often came to grief in the narrow confines of the stable yard.

On the outside wall of the Johanneum is a remarkable example of **Meissen porcelain art:** a painting on Meissen tiles of a royal procession, 336 feet long. More than 100 members of the royal Saxon house of Wettin, half of them on horseback, are represented on the giant jigsaw made up of 25,000 porcelain tiles, painted in 1904–1907 and based on a design by Wilhelm Walther.

㉜ The former royal palace, the **Residenzschloss,** where restoration work is under way behind the fine Renaissance facade, is at the end of the street bearing the porcelain-tile procession. Although work is not complete, some of the finished rooms are hosting historical exhibitions. The main gate of the palace, the **Georgentor,** has been restored to its original appearance, complete with an enormous statue of the fully armed Saxon count George guarding the portal that carries his name. The palace housed August the Strong's Grünes Gewölbe before it was moved in its entirety to the Albertinum. ✉ *Sophienstr.,* ☎ *0351/495–3110.* 🖅 *DM 3.* ◷ *Mon.–Wed. and Fri.–Sun. 10–6.*

㉝ The **Katholische Hofkirche,** next to the Herzogschloss, is the largest church in Saxony and is also known as the Cathedral of St. Trinitas. The son of August the Strong, Frederick Augustus II (who ruled 1733–63), brought architects and builders from Italy to construct a Catholic church in a city that had been the first large center of Lutheran Protestantism. They worked away in secret, so the story goes, and Dresden's Protestant burghers were presented with a fait accompli when the church was finally consecrated in 1754. Seventy-eight historical and biblical figures decorate the Italian High Baroque facade; inside, the treasures include a beautiful stone pulpit by the royal sculptor Balthasar Permoser and a 250-year-old church organ, said to be one of the finest ever to come from the mountain workshops of the famous Silbermann family. In the cathedral's crypt are the tombs of 49 Saxon rulers and a precious vessel containing the heart of August the Strong.

㉞ The **Semperoper** (Semper Opera House), opposite the cathedral, on the Theaterplatz, is justifiably one of Germany's best-known and most popular theaters. Richard Wagner's *Rienzi, Der fliegende Holländer,* and *Tannhäuser,* and Richard Strauss's *Salome, Elektra,* and *Der Rosenkavalier* all premiered here. The masterful Dresden architect Gottfried Semper built the opera house in 1838–41, in Italian Renaissance style, and then saw his work razed in a fire caused by a careless candlelighter. Semper had to flee Dresden because of his participation in a democratic uprising, so his son Manfred rebuilt the theater in the neo-Renaissance style you see today. Even Manfred Semper's version had to be rebuilt after the devastating bombing raid of February 1945. On the 40th anniversary of that raid—February 13, 1985—the Semperoper reopened with a performance of *Der Freischutz* by Carl Maria von Weber, another composer who did much to make Dresden a leading center of German music and culture. The demand to experience the Semper Opera is enormous, and tickets are difficult to obtain, even in advance. If you're lucky enough to get in, however, an overwhelming experience awaits you. Even if you're no opera buff, the Semper's lavish interior—predominantly crimson, white, and gold—can't fail to impress. Marble, velvet, and brocade create an atmosphere of intimate luxury (it seats 1,323), and the uninterrupted views and flawless acoustics are renowned. Tours of the Opera House are given Monday–Saturday 2–4 and cost DM 8.

On Theaterplatz, across from the opera and next to the Schloss, is a busy little café-bistro where you can pause for a coffee or a snack, surrounded by Dresden businesspeople taking a break from nearby offices. ✉ *Am Schloss. Schlossstr. 1.*

35 The **Augustusbrücke,** which spans the river in front of the cathedral, is a rebuilt version of a historic 17th-century bridge blown up by the SS shortly before the end of World War II. The bridge was restored and renamed for Georgi Dimitroff, the Bulgarian Communist accused by the Nazis of instigating the Reichstag fire; after the fall of Communism the original name, honoring August the Strong, was reinstated.

36 The **Zwinger,** which borders Theaterplatz, is Dresden's magnificent Baroque showpiece and perhaps one of the greatest examples of Baroque architecture in Europe. There are two entrances; the Kronentor (Crown Gate), off Ostra-Allee, is the one through which August the Strong and his royal retinue once paraded. August hired a small army of artists and artisans to create a "pleasure ground" worthy of the Saxon court, building it on a section of the original city fortifications (the Zwinger). They were placed under the general direction of the architect Matthaus Daniel Pöppelmann, who was called reluctantly out of retirement to design what came to be his greatest work, begun in 1707 and completed in 1728. Completely enclosing a central courtyard filled with lawns and pools, the complex is composed of six linked pavilions, one of which boasts a carillon of Meissen bells, hence its name: Glockenspielpavillon.

The Zwinger is an extraordinary scene—a riot of garlands, nymphs, and other Baroque ornamentation and sculpture on the edge of an urban landscape etched in somber gray. The contrast would have been much greater had Semper not closed in one side of the Zwinger, which was originally open to the riverbank. Stand in the center of this quiet oasis, where the city's roar is kept at bay by the palatial wings that form the outer framework of the Zwinger, and imagine the summer evenings when August the Strong invited his favored guests to celebrate with him—the wedding, for instance, of his son, Prince Friedrich August, to Maria Joseph, archduchess of Austria. The ornate carriage-style lamps shone; the fountains splashed in the shallow pools; and wide staircases beckoned to galleried walks and to the romantic Nymphenbad, a coyly hidden courtyard where statues of nude women perch in alcoves to protect them from a fountain that spits unexpectedly at unwary visitors.

The **Sempergalerie,** in the northwestern corner of the Zwinger complex, was built by the great architect to house parts of the art collections of the Saxon royal house. It contains the world-renowned Gemäldegalerie Alte Meister (Gallery of Old Masters). The Zwinger Palace complex also contains a porcelain collection, a zoological museum, and the Mathematisch-Physikalischer Salon, which displays old scientific instruments.

Among the priceless paintings in the Sempergalerie collection are works by Dürer, Holbein, Jan van Eyck, Rembrandt, Rubens, van Dyck, Hals, Vermeer, Raphael (*The Sistine Madonna*), Titian, Giorgione, Veronese, Velázquez, Murillo, Canaletto, and Watteau. On the wall of the entrance archway you'll see an inscription in Russian, one of the few amusing reminders of World War II in Dresden. It reads, in rhyme: "Museum checked. No mines. Chanutin did the checking." Chanutin, presumably, was the Russian soldier responsible for checking one of Germany's greatest art galleries for anything more explosive than a Rubens nude. ☎ *0351/491–4619.* ✆ *DM 7.* ⏰ *Tues.–Sun. 10–6.*

The Zwinger's **Porcelain Museum**, stretching from the curved gallery that adjoins the Glockenspielpavillon to the long gallery on the east side, is considered one of the best of its kind in the world. The focus, naturally, is on Dresden and Meissen china, but there are also outstanding examples of Japanese, Chinese, and Korean porcelain. The **Zoological Museum** has a small but very interesting collection of natural history exhibits, including skeletons of wild animals that once roamed the Elbe Valley. The **Mathematics and Physics Salon** is packed with rare and historic scientific instruments. *Porcelain Museum:* ☎ *0351/491–4619;* ✆ *DM 3;* ⏰ *Fri.–Wed. 10–6. Zoological Museum:* ☎ *0351/495–2503;* ✆ *DM 2;* ⏰ *Tues.–Sun. 9–4. Mathematisch-Physikalischer Salon:* ☎ *0351/495–1364;* ✆ *DM 3;* ⏰ *Fri.–Wed. 9:30–5.*

Theaterplatz has as its centerpiece a proud equestrian **statue of King Johann,** who ruled Saxony when Gottfried Semper was at work. Don't be misled by Johann's confident pose in the saddle—he was terrified of horses and never learned to ride.

OFF THE BEATEN PATH

ARMEE-MUSEUM (MILITARY MUSEUM) – This museum covers military history predating the German Democratic Republic (✉ Olbrichtpl. 3). It's open Tuesday to Sunday 9–5; admission is DM 1.50. The **Buch Museum** (Book Museum) traces the history of books from the Middle Ages to the present (✉ Marienallee 12). It's open weekdays 9–4 and a guided tour is conducted Saturday at 2; admission is free. The **Deutsches Hygiene Museum** (German Museum of Health) has historical displays of medical equipment and a unique glass anatomical figure (✉ Lingnerpl. 1). It's open Tuesday to Saturday 9–5; admission is DM 5.

Dining and Lodging

$–$$ ✕ **Haus Altmarkt.** The choice of cuisine in this busy corner of the colonnaded Altmarkt is enormous—from the McDonald's that has surreptitiously wormed its way into the city landscape to the upscale Amadeus restaurant on the first floor. Between these extremes are a jolly, bistrolike café and, downstairs, a vaulted restaurant with a secluded bar. The Zum Humpen restaurant is the best value, with midday menu offerings of less than DM 20. In warm weather you can eat outside on a terrace and watch the marketplace bustle. ✉ *Am Altmarkt 1,* ☎ *0351/495–1212. AE, MC, V.*

$–$$ ✕ **Italienisches Dörfchen.** The name, which means "Italian village," is a reference to the fact that this historic building on the banks of the Elbe once housed Italian craftsmen. They had been brought to Dresden to work on the Hofkirche. Today the rooms offer a warm welcome to all visitors. There's a beer tavern, a café, and a shady garden for alfresco eating. ✉ *Theaterpl. 3,* ☎ *0351/498–160. AE, DC, MC, V.*

$$$$ ✕🏨 **Hotel am Terrassenufer.** Canaletto painted the same vistas that latter-day guests can enjoy from within this sleek, new, 12-story hotel on the Elbe River terrace; all rooms have panoramic views of the river and the Old Town, and on clear days even to the hills of the Sächsische Schweiz. The rooms are decorated in fresh pastel shades, the furniture in bright cherry-wood veneers. The old city center and all major sights are a few minutes' walk away. ✉ *Am Terrassenufer 12,* ☎ *0351/440–9500, D–01067,* 📠 *0351/440–9600. 190 rooms with bath, 6 suites. Restaurant, bar. AE, DC, MC, V.*

$$$$ ✕🏨 **Kempinski Hotel Taschenbergpalais.** Destroyed in wartime bombing but now rebuilt, the historic Taschenberg Palace—the work of the

Zwinger architect Matthäus Daniel Pöppelmann—reopened as a magnificent hotel in early 1995. It's Dresden's premier address, a new showpiece of the Kempinski group and the last word in luxury, as befits the former residence of the Saxon crown princes. Rooms are as big as city apartments, while suites earn the adjective palatial. Business travelers are particularly well catered to, with fax/modem outlets in all rooms and a special business center, equipped with every high-tech device, including laptops. But the hotel is recommended for anyone looking for expensive pampering in the romantic heart of old Dresden. ⊠ *Am Taschenberg, D–01067,* ☎ *0351/49120,* ℻ *0351/491–2812. 188 rooms, 25 suites. 2 restaurants, bars, indoor pool, sauna, steam room. AE, DC, MC, V.*

$$$$ ✕▥ **Maritim Hotel Bellevue.** Across the river from the Zwinger Palace, opera, and main museums, this modern hotel cleverly incorporates an old restored mansion. Rooms are luxurious and service is good, lagging only when the tour groups arrive and depart. ⊠ *Grosse Meissner Str. 15, D–01097 Dresden,* ☎ *0351/56620,* ℻ *0351/55997. 326 rooms with bath, 16 suites and apartments. 4 restaurants, bar, café, indoor pool, sauna, bowling, exercise room, jogging. AE, DC, MC, V.*

$$ ✕▥ **Hotelschiff Florentina.** Dresden's celebrated river panorama is right outside your cabin window on this cruise-liner hotel, moored just below the historic Augusta Bridge and a catwalk stroll from all the major sights. The boat has spacious public lounges and a restaurant with the finest view in town. In summer you can eat on deck; if the weather cools you can move inside to a plant-hung winter garden. Cabins—furnished "maritime-style"—all have showers and toilets and come equipped with TV, radio, and telephone. ⊠ *Terrassenufer, D–01069 Dresden,* ☎ *0351/459–0169,* ℻ *0351/459–5036. 63 cabins with shower. Restaurant, bar, indoor pool, sauna. AE, DC, MC, V.*

$$ ✕▥ **Ibis Hotels Bastei, Königstein, Lilienstein.** This is three hotels in one, all part of a massive, modern complex on the Prager Strasse central shopping mall, between the main railway station and the old city center. The three Communist-era hotels were taken over by the Ibis group, which lost no time in giving the drab quarters, once occupied by Communist Party guests, the veneered, pastel-shade, polished Ibis touch, including satellite TV. ⊠ *Prager Str., D–01069,* ☎ *0351/485–6666,* ℻ *0351/485–6667. 297 rooms with bath, 9 apartments. 4 restaurants, bars. AE, DC, MC, V.*

$ ✕▥ **Schloss Röhrsdorf.** This beautifully restored Saxon country palace, surrounded by rolling parkland, is just a short drive from Dresden. Rooms have been renovated to a high standard of comfort, with mostly modern furnishings, but keeping some of the original antique touches. The vaulted restaurant is of equally high standard. The hotel has its own stables, and the terrain is ideal for riding. ⊠ *Hauptstr. 3, D–01809 Röhrsdorf,* ☎ *0351/285–770,* ℻ *0361/2857–7263. 22 rooms with bath. Restaurant, bar, stables. AE, DC, MC, V.*

Nightlife and the Arts

The **opera** in Dresden has regained its international reputation since the Semper Opera House (Sächsische Statsoper Dresden, ⊠ Theaterpl., D–01067 Dresden) reopened in 1985 following an eight-year reconstruction. Just seeing the magnificent house is worth the trip; a performance is that much better. Tickets are reasonably priced but also hard to get; they're often included in package tours. Try your luck at the evening box office (the Abendkasse, left of the main entrance, ☎ 0351/49110, 0351/491–1716, or 0351/491–1731) about a half hour before the performance; there are usually a few dozen tickets available. If you're unlucky, take one of the opera house tours (☞ *above*).

Sixt-Budget: ☒ Mohrenstr. 30 (in the Hilton Hotel), ☎ 030/242–4800, and Schönefeld Airport, ☎ 030/609–15690, **Berlin**; ☒ An der Frauenkirche 5 (Hilton Hotel), ☎ 0351/484–1696, ☒ St. Petersburger Str. 34 (in Hotel Mercure Newa), ☎ 0351/495–6012, and Dresden Airport, ☎ 0351/589–4570, **Dresden**; ☒ Gerberstr. 15 (Hotel Inter-Continental), ☎ 0341/988–1149, and Leipzig Airport, ☎ 0341/224–1868, **Leipzig**.

Emergencies

Police: ☎ 110. **Fire:** ☎ 110. For **ambulance** or **medical emergency:** ☎ 112.

Guided Tours

Information on travel and tours to and around eastern Germany is available from most travel agents. Most Berlin tourist offices carry brochures about travel in eastern Germany. For information about guided tours around the region, contact **Berolina Berlin-Service** (☒ Meinekestr. 3, D–10719 Berlin, ☎ 030/882–2091) or **DER** Deutsches Reisebüro GmbH. (☒ Augsburger Str. 27, D–12309 Berlin, ☎ 030/2199–8100). German Railways' small-gauge line penetrates deep into the Saxony countryside and the Fichtelberg Mountains. Call the Deutsche Bahn office in Dresden, 0351/461–3558, for schedule and fare information. For information on paddle-steam tours of the Elbe, contact the Sächsische Dampfschiffahrts GmbH., ☎ 0351/496–9203.

Guided bus tours of **Leipzig** (in English) run daily at 1:30 (May–Sept., also on weekends at 10:30); tours leave from outside the Opera House in Goethestrasse. A walking tour of Leipzig (also in English) sets off from the **tourist information office** (☒ Sachsenpl. 1, ☎ 0341/710–4280) May–September, Monday–Saturday at 4; October–April, Tuesday–Thursday at 4. Tickets can be booked at the tourist information office.

Dresden streetcar tours leave from Postpl. (Tues.–Sun. at 9, 11, and 1:30); bus tours, leaving from Dr.-Külz-Ring, run Tuesday–Thursday at 11 (☎ 0351/495–5025 for details).

Travel Agencies

American Express: ☒ Hotel Bellevue, Köpckestr., Dresden, 15, ☎ 0351/56620; ☒ Europaisches Reisebüro, Katherinenstr., Leipzig, ☎ 0341/79210.

Visitor information

Chemnitz: ☒ Str. der Nationen 3, D–09008, ☎ 0371/62051.

Dessau: ☒ Rathaus, Zerbster Str., D–06813, ☎ 0340/214–804.

Dresden: ☒ Box 201, Pragerstr. 10/11, D–01069, ☎ 0351/495–5025.

Eisenach: ☒ Bahnhofstr. 3–5, D–99817, ☎ 03691/69040.

Erfurt: ☒ Bahnhofstr. 37, D–99084, ☎ 0361/562–3436.

Freiburg: ☒ Burgstr. 1, D–09595, ☎ 03731/23602.

Gera: ☒ Breitscheidstr. 1, D–07545, ☎ 0365/26432

Halle: ☒ Steinweg 7, D–06110, ☎ 0345/202–4700.

Leipzig: ☒ Sachsenpl. 1, D–04109, ☎ 0341/71040.

Meissen: An der Frauenkirche 3, D–01662, ☎ 03521/454–470.

Suhl: ☒ Steinweg 1, ☎ 03681/20052.

Weimar: ☒ Markt 10, D–99423, ☎ 03643/24000.

17 The Baltic Coast

If you're looking for a quiet vacation, you can head for the endless miles of sandy beaches interspersed with stretches of chalk cliffs and charming little coves that make up the Baltic Coast, along eastern Germany's shoreline. This flat countryside with its lush green marshes, deep-blue sea and lakes under a wide sky, is only slowly emerging as Germany's new premier vacation hot spot. Its remote villages and towns still seem trapped in the '30s, providing a wealth of architectural delights—from well-preserved medieval town squares to simple, whitewashed seaside cottages with thatched roofs.

WHEN THE LORD MADE THE EARTH, He started with Mecklenburg," is a well-known quip by the German writer Fritz Reuter, whose praise for his home state is more than justified. Mecklenburg-Vorpommern contains the Baltic Coast, Germany's half-forgotten eastern shoreline, as unfamiliar to most former West Germans as it is to foreigners. It's a region of white, sandy beaches, coves, chalk cliffs, ancient ports, and fishing villages where time and custom seem to have stood still. Some of the beach resorts have been popular holiday destinations since the mid-19th century, when sunbathing and sea swimming first became fashionable. But the entire 1,130-kilometer (706-mile) weaving coastline— from the Trave River estuary, above Lübeck, to Swinemünde, at the Polish border—was plunged into isolation when the Iron Curtain came down just east of Lübeck. Although the Baltic Coast was considered the Riviera of the Eastern Bloc, and was correspondingly full each summer, the communist regime did not invest in the restoration or development of the area's resort centers. On the islands of Hiddensee and Rügen, for example, the clock appears to have stopped in the 1920s and '30s; the architecture, the pace of life, even the old-fashioned trains are caught in a time warp.

Until 1989 Lübeck was the eastern outpost of the West. Three kilometers (2 miles) away were the watchtowers of Communist East Germany. Today the sense of crossing a border still prevails. Lübeck has spent the last 40 years reconstructing and restoring its Hanseatic heritage, and it is a charming town in the state of Schleswig-Holstein.

The neighboring state of Mecklenburg-Vorpommern in the former East Germany, in contrast, is a depressing mixture of cheaply constructed apartment houses and neglected buildings of the past. Forty years of communism worked to create a workers' paradise, not a mecca for tourists.

This chapter follows a route through five leading Hanseatic League ports, whose medieval merchants became rich by monopolizing trade across the Baltic Sea between the 12th and 16th centuries. Much of their wealth was invested in buildings; some of the finest examples of north German Gothic and Renaissance redbrick architecture, with its tall, stepped gables, are found here. Except for the cities of Schwerin and Rostock, the Baltic Coast is a rural region in which the sea has long played a pivotal role. Since its development more than 800 years ago, this area has been populated largely with seafaring folk, traders, and fisherman. Despite meager attempts by the East German government to industrialize the region's larger cities in the 1960s and '70s, they remain economically depressed and uncompetitive with the West. In 1995–96 both Rostock and Stralsund suffered another major blow to their economies, when the shipbuilding industry went bankrupt and thousands of workers were laid off. The state's unemployment rates are among the highest in Germany.

Thus this region has desperately embarked on both intensive restoration of historic buildings and development of the tourist industry to revitalize not only the economy but also pride in the Hanseatic heritage.

This chapter's tours take you east from Lübeck to Usedom Island, parallel to the coast but slightly inland. If you see an interesting road that wanders off to the north, it's likely to lead to the coast and could be worth a detour.

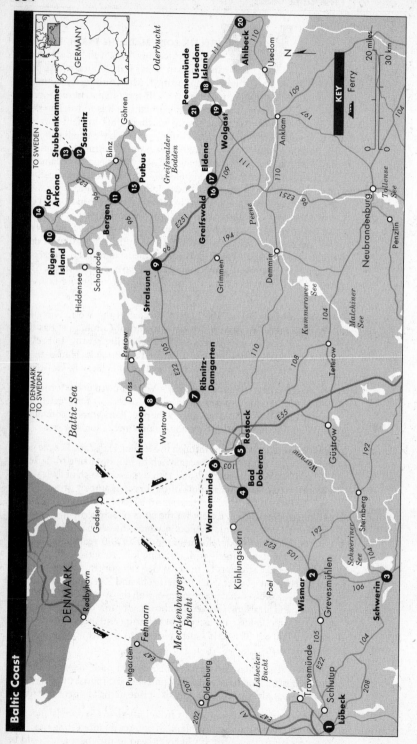

Baltic Coast

GERMANY

Oderbucht

N

KEY

▬▬ Ferry

0   20 miles
0   30 km

TO SWEDEN

Usedom

Ahlbeck **20**
Usedom Island
Peenemünde **18**
21
19 Wolgast

Anklam

Neubrandenburg

Tollense See

Penzlin

Stubbenkammer
Sassnitz **12** **13**
Göhren
Binz
Kap Arkona **14**
Putbus **15**
11 Bergen
Rügen Island **10**
Schaprode
Hiddensee

Greifswalder Bodden

Eldena **17**
Greifswald **16**
Stralsund **9**

Grimmen

Demmin

Kummerower See

Malchiner See

Teterow

Prerow

Darss

Ribnitz-Damgarten **7**
Ahrenshoop **8**
Wustrow

Baltic Sea

TO DENMARK
TO SWEDEN

Gedser

Rostock
Bad Doberan **5**
6 **4**
Warnemünde

Güstrow

Sternberg

Warnow

DENMARK

Rødbyhavn

Fehmarn

Puttgarden

Oldenburg

Kühlungsborn

Poel

Mecklenburger Bucht

Wismar **2**
Grevesmühlen

Schweriner See

Schwerin **3**

Lübecker Bucht

Travemünde
Schlutup
Lübeck **1**

Pleasures and Pastimes

Beaches

Good beaches exist all along the Baltic Coast. Virtually all the sandy beaches are clean and safe, sloping gently into the water. At the height of the season (July–August), the seaside resort beaches with food services and toilets are packed. Water temperature in August rarely exceeds 20°C (65°F). The busiest beaches are at **Bansin** (Usedom Island), **Binz** (Rügen Island), **Ostseebad Kühlungsborn**, and **Warnemünde**. More remote and quieter beaches can be found at **Timmendorf** on Poel Island, where the water quality is particularly good (you can drive there from Wismar or take a White Fleet boat); **Kap Arkona** (reachable only on foot); and **Hiddensee Island**, off Rügen. The prettiest coves and beaches are located at **Ahrenshoop Weststrand**, on the Darss Peninsula; **Nienhagen**, (near Warnemünde); and the **Grosser Jasmunder Bodden**, on Rügen Island to the west of Lietzow.

Some beaches allow nude bathing; in German it's known as *Freikörperkultur* (literally, "free body culture"), FKK for short. The most popular of these bare-all beaches are at **Nienhagen** and **Prerow** (on Darss).

Churches

Throughout the region medieval churches make for a special German style of Gothic architecture called red tile or redbrick Gothic. Its blend of red and white facades is a familiar sight in all of northern Germany, but there is no other place on earth with as many fine examples of this style than in Mecklenburg-Vorpommern. Here even the smallest village proudly boasts a redbrick church, and the cathedrals in cities like Wismar or Stralsund testify to the region's prosperous past as Hanse seaports. Today many of these churches are being restored, causing their partial or total closure to the public. Check with the nearest tourist information beforehand for accessibility or current opening hours.

Dining

Among the local specialties to look for are *Mecklenburger Griebenroller,* a custardy casserole of grated potatoes, eggs, herbs, and chopped bacon; *Mecklenburger Fischsuppe,* a hearty fish soup with vegetables, tomatoes, and sour cream; *Gefüllte Ente* or *Gefüllte Schweinebraten Mecklenburger Art,* baked duck or pork stuffed with bread crumbs, apples, prunes, and raisins; and *Pannfisch,* the region's own fish patty. A delicacy that originated during the time of Sweden's influence is *Grützwurst,* an oatmeal-based liver sausage sweetened with raisins. A favorite local nightcap since the 17th century is *Eierbier* (egg beer), a concoction of egg whites, beer, ginger, cinnamon, sugar, and water, stirred vigorously and served warm. It's said to soothe the stomach, and it's guaranteed to give you a sound night's sleep. In general, you will find the menus offer fare similar to dishes served in western Germany, although you will usually find the food more simply prepared.

CATEGORY	COST*
$$$$	over DM 50
$$$	DM 40–DM 50
$$	DM 25–DM 40
$	under DM 25

*per person for a three-course meal, excluding drinks

Lodging

Expect to pay inflated prices at recently constructed, fully equipped large hotels and at the renovated high-rises dating from the former regime. Because much of the new entrepreneurial spirit of the east has been directed toward the tourism industry, potentially a major player in reviving this region's sagging economy, many local, privately owned small hotels and pensions have opened up. As a rule, the staffs of these new establishments provide personalized and enthusiastic service. In high season all accommodations, especially along the coast, are in great demand. If you can't book well in advance, throw yourself at the mercy of the local tourist office; it will probably be able to find you simple, inexpensive bed-and-breakfast accommodations in a private home.

CATEGORY	COST*
$$$$	over DM 250
$$$	DM 175–DM 250
$$	DM 125–DM 175
$	under DM 125

All prices are for a standard double room, including tax and service charge.

Exploring Mecklenburg-Vorpommern

The state's coastal region offers two major areas of interest, Mecklenburg in the west and Vorpommern, adjoining the Polish border in the east. While western Mecklenburg, which includes the state capital, Schwerin, enjoys a beautiful countryside of lakes, lush green meadows, fertile fields, and tree-lined avenues, the state's eastern part, called Vorpommern, has a secluded tundralike landscape with sandy grounds and vast areas of heath and dunes.

Great Itineraries

You could easily drive through the whole state from west to east in well under a day. But that would be the surest way to miss all the hidden treasures of churches and little sightseeing gems in the quaint villages and medieval cities along the way. Instead, try to do it like the natives—at a slow pace. Three days make for a pleasant and unforgettable visit, touring most of the major sightseeing spots. Add two more days to your schedule, and you'll enjoy a full day of relaxation on the beach. A whole week will offer deeper insight into this region and its laid-back people. Should you indulge in such a long sojourn, especially spending time in the fishing villages, you will certainly perceive the rest of the world as they do—just a faint memory far, far away.

Numbers in the text correspond to numbers in the margin and on the Baltic Coast map.

IF YOU HAVE 3 DAYS

Start your trip in **Lübeck** ①, western Germany's only authentic Hanseatic town, which retains its medieval atmosphere. Continue from Lübeck toward 🏛 **Wismar** ②. After a visit to this city with its market square and equally delightful churches, begin the second day with a side trip to **Schwerin** ③, its lakes, and the magnificent castle, Schweriner Schloss. Then return to Wismar and proceed to the cloister church at **Bad Doberan** ④ and to 🏛 **Rostock** ⑤, the center of eastern Germany's shipbuilding industry. Stay the night in this old Hanseatic port before enjoying a last day in **Stralsund** ⑨, a much smaller but more charming medieval town. Use it as a gateway to the most remote and solitary part of the Baltic Coast: the island of **Rügen** ⑩, which contains the **Stubbenkammer** ⑬ and the **Königstuhl,** the most outstanding chalk cliffs of the island's coastline.

IF YOU HAVE 5 DAYS

Devote a full day to **Lübeck** ① and **Wismar** ② before heading south to 🏛 **Schwerin** ③ to spend the night there. The next day, after a tour of the Schweriner lakes and the Schweriner Schloss, continue your trip to the east via **Bad Doberan** ④ and **Kühlungsborn,** a premier beach resort. The little Molli train driven by a steam locomotive connects the resort and Bad Doberan. Spend the night in ⊞ **Rostock** ⑤. The third day may be devoted to this seaport and a side trip to the seaside resort of **Warnemünde** ⑥. Return to Rostock and continue on to the medieval port of **Stralsund** ⑨. You may well want to spend the last two days here and on the island of **Rügen** ⑩. Not to be missed on the island are the city of **Bergen** ⑪; the small seaport of ⊞ **Sassnitz** ⑫, where ferries depart to Sweden; the **Stubbenkammer** ⑬; and the endless dunes at **Kap Arkona** ⑭. A visit to Vorpommern wouldn't be complete without a trip to ⊞ **Greifswald** ⑯, the last of the medieval Hanseatic towns on eastern Germany's coastline. Continue east toward **Wolgast** ⑲ and take the causeway to another deserted island, Usedom. Its beaches seem to stretch on forever; the coast near the village of **Ahlbeck** ⑳ offers the finest sand and the best water.

IF YOU HAVE 7 DAYS

You can take in the scenery between **Lübeck** and ⊞ **Rostock** ①–⑤ in a leisurely three days, depending on your interests and whether you take a side trip to **Grevesmühlen,** where you find the Gothic St. Nikolai Parish Church. From Rostock head eastward until you reach **Ribnitz-Damgarten** ⑦, the center of Germany's amber industry. If you don't find an appealing souvenir or present here, you might be luckier in **Ahrenshoop** ⑧, a small coastal village that used to be an artists' colony. On the fourth and fifth day, visit the sights between ⊞ **Stralsund** and **Kap Arkona** ⑨–⑭, on the island of Rügen. A nice little excursion is a train ride to the island's southeastern corner between **Putbus** ⑮ and Göhren. The next destination is **Greifswald** ⑯, where the suburb of **Eldena** ⑰ reveals the ruins of a 12th-century Cistercian monastery. Your two final days can be spent in a most relaxing fashion, with a leisurely drive to **Wolgast** ⑲ and ⊞ **Ahlbeck** ⑳ on the island of Usedom, which is also known for its beaches. You might stop at **Peenemünde** ㉑, the former launch sites for Nazi Germany's dreaded V1 and V2 rockets.

When to Tour the Baltic Coast

Unfortunately, the region's climate is at its best when Mecklenburg-Vorpommern is also most crowded—in summer, the high season for vacationers from Hamburg or Berlin. Winter is extremely harsh in this area, and even spring and fall are rather windy, chilly, and rainy. The best times to visit are July and August. If you want to avoid the tourist crowds, schedule your trip for June or September. But don't expect reasonable water temperatures or hot summer days on the beach.

WESTERN MECKLENBURG

This long-forgotten coastal region of eastern Germany, pinned between two sprawling urban areas—the state capital of Schwerin in the west and Rostock in the east—is thriving again. Despite its perennial economic woes, this part of Germany, and Schwerin in particular, has attracted many new businesses, which suggests a light at the end of the tunnel. Though the region is close to the sea, it is made up largely of endless fields of wheat and yellow rape and a dozen or so wonderful lakes.

Numbers in the margin correspond to points of interest on the Baltic Coast map.

Lübeck

★ ❶ *56 km (35 mi) northeast of Hamburg.*

The ancient core of Lübeck, one of Europe's largest Old Towns dating from the 12th century, was a chief stronghold of the Hanseatic merchant princes who controlled trade on the Baltic. But it was the roving King Henry the Lion (Heinrich der Löwe) who established the town and, in 1173, laid the foundation stone of the redbrick Gothic cathedral.

Until two years ago, Lübeck was near to every German's heart, but even closer to every hip pocket: The town's famous landmark, the Holstentor Gate, appeared on the DM 50 note. This ancient gate on Holstentor Platz, built between 1464 and 1478, is flanked by two round, squat towers—solid symbols of Lübeck's prosperity as a trading center.

In the **Old Quarter,** proof of Lübeck's former position as the golden queen of the Hanseatic League is found at every step. More 13th- to 15th-century buildings stand in Lübeck than in all other large northern German cities combined, which, in 1987, prompted UNESCO to list Lübeck's Old Quarter in its register of the world's greatest cultural and natural treasures. The **Rathaus** (Town Hall), dating from 1240, is among the buildings lining the arcaded Marktplatz, one of Europe's most striking medieval market squares. The Town Hall is particularly noteworthy; it has been subjected to several architectural face-lifts that have added Romanesque arches, Gothic windows, and a Renaissance roof. ⊠ *Breitestr. 63,* ☎ *0451/122–1005.* ▨ *Guided tours (in German) DM 4.* ☉ *Tours weekdays 11, noon, and 3.*

The impressive redbrick Gothic **Marienkirche** (St. Mary's Church), which has the highest brick nave in the world, looms behind the Rathaus. ⊠ *Marienkirchhof,* ☎ *0451/74901.* ☉ *Daily 10–6.*

NEED A
BREAK?

At the traditional **Café Niederegger** (⊠ Breitestr. 89, ☎ 0451/530–1126), across from the Rathaus, don't miss the opportunity to sample the world-renowned Niederegger marzipan fresh from its source. The firm has been producing marzipan in Lübeck since 1825; the café, a virtual museum of marzipan, showcases more than 300 specialties.

The **Buddenbrookhaus,** a respectful and Puritan-looking mansion, was made famous by German novelist Thomas Mann's saga *Buddenbrooks.* Mann's family once lived in the house, which has recently opened as the **Heinrich and Thomas Mann Zentrum.** This museum documents the life and works of these brothers, both among the most important Geržman writers of this century. A tour and video in English are offered. ⊠ *Mengstr. 4,* ☎ *0451/122–4192.* ▨ *DM 4.* ☉ *Daily 10–5.*

The Gothic **Heiligen-Geist-Hospital** (Hospital of the Holy Ghost), built during the 14th century by the town's rich merchants, is still caring for the infirm. ⊠ *Am Koberg,* ☎ *0451/122–2040.* ☉ *Tues.–Sun. 10–5; winter Tues.–Sun. 10–4.*

The **Lübecker Dom,** or cathedral, the oldest building in Lübeck, had its foundation stone laid in 1173 by that gadabout royal Henry the Lion. The Gothic Dom, incorporating late-Romanesque and Renaissance features, was severely damaged in World War II but rebuilt from 1958 to 1977. The Dom and Marienkirche (☞ *above*) regularly present organ concerts, a real treat in these magnificent redbrick Gothic churches. ⊠ *Domkirchhof,* ☎ *0451/74704.* ☉ *Daily 10–6.*

Dining and Lodging

$$$–$$$$ ✕ **Wullenwever.** Culinary experts say this restaurant has set a new
   ★   standard of dining sophistication for Lübeck. It is certainly one of the most attractive establishments in town, with dark furniture, chandeliers, and oil paintings on pale pastel walls. In summer tables are set in a quiet flower-strewn courtyard. Try the homemade pasta in truf-

fle cream or baked pigeon with chanterelle mushrooms. ✉ *Becker-grube 71,* ☎ *0451/704–333. Reservations essential. Jacket and tie. AE, DC, V. Closed Sun. and Mon.*

$$–$$$
★ ✕ **Schiffergesellschaft.** Not even the scent of a woman was allowed in Schiffergesellschaft from its opening in 1535 until 1870. Today men and women alike sit in church-style pews at long, 400-year-old oak tables. You'll note that at each end of the pew is a sculpted coat of arms of a particular city. Ship owners had their set routes (between Lübeck and Bremen, for example), and they each had their own pew and table. A good way to begin your meal is with the *Krebssuppe* (crab soup), made from things best not known but that will cure all ills; follow this with the *Kapitänschüssel,* a kind of goulash consisting of three different meats. For dessert you might try the regional specialty *Rote Grütze,* made from red berries and topped with a vanilla sauce. Dinner may be washed down with *Rotspon,* Lübeck's locally bottled French red wine. Make reservations for the Historische Halle rather than for the other rooms. ✉ *Breite Str. 2,* ☎ *0451/76776. No credit cards.*

$$$$
✕▦ **Mövenpick Hotel Lysia.** The location of this ultramodern member of the Swiss-owned chain is perfect—a two-minute walk from the famous Holsten Gate and the Old Town and five minutes from the main train station. If you fancy an Old World atmosphere, however, the Mövenpick is not for you. Rattan furniture, lots of brass details, and vividly colored contemporary paintings create a bright, breezy look throughout, although the built-in furniture in the guest rooms smacks of motel decor. The menu in the sprawling, overlit restaurant is daunting in its variety—from such Swiss specialties as *Rösti* to venison with lingonberries and other local seasonal fare—and the chef succeeds beyond all expectations. Save room for the dizzying array of gooey ice-cream concoctions. ✉ *Willy-Brandt-Allee 3-5, beim Holstentor, D–23554,* ☎ *0451/15040,* ℻ *0451/150–4111. 197 rooms, all with bath. Restaurant, bar, no-smoking rooms, room service, car rental. AE, DC, MC, V.*

$$$
★ ✕▦ **Jensen.** Only a stone's throw from the Holstentor and within the inner city, this long-established hotel is ideally situated for viewing all the main attractions and faces the moat that surrounds the Old Town. It's family-run and very comfortable, with modern, renovated rooms. Though not large, the rooms are big enough for adjacent twin beds and a coffee table and come with either a shower or a bath. The popular Yachtzimmer restaurant, with exposed stone walls and an open kitchen, offers a mix of regional and international dishes. ✉ *An der Obertrave 4, D–23552,* ☎ *0451/71646,* ℻ *0451/73386. 42 rooms, 1 suite, all with bath. Restaurant. AE, DC, MC, V.*

$$$
▦ **Kaiserhof.** The most comfortable hotel in Lübeck consists of two early 19th-century merchant's houses linked together, tastefully renovated and retaining many of the original architectural features. It's just outside the moated Old Town center—a five-minute walk from the cathedral. Although the hotel lacks a full restaurant, a marvelous breakfast (included in the room cost) is served, and there's also a cozy bar. Bedrooms vary, but all have a restful, homey ambience, and the quietest of them overlook the garden at the back. ✉ *Kronsforder Allee 11–13, D–23560,* ☎ *0451/703–301,* ℻ *0451/795–083. 65 rooms, 6 suites, all with bath. Bar, indoor pool, sauna, exercise room. AE, DC, MC, V.*

$
▦ **Altstadt.** Behind the landmark old facade stands a hotel that opened in 1984. The Altstadt offers modern but not luxurious comforts. The studios, fitted with small kitchens, are a particularly good value if you plan to stay a few days. There is no restaurant, but breakfast (included in the price) is served in the hotel. ✉ *Fischergrube 52,*

D–23552, ☎ 0451/72083, ℻ 0451/73778. *20 rooms and 9 studios, some with bath. No credit cards.*

Nightlife and the Arts

Contact the **Musik und Kongresshallen Lübeck** (✉ Willy-Brandt-Allee 10, D–23552 Lübeck, ☎ 0451/790–400) for schedules of the myriad concerts, operas, and theater in Lübeck.

In summer try to catch a few performances of the **Schleswig-Holstein Music Festival** (late June–late Aug.), which features orchestras composed of young musicians from more than 25 countries, performing in the Dom or Marienkirche. Some of the concerts in small towns and villages nearby are even staged in barns. The sight of the late Leonard Bernstein conducting a complete classic orchestra, where otherwise cows and chicken are fed, is still remembered. For exact dates and tickets, contact **Schleswig–Holstein Konzertorganisation** (✉ Kartenzentrale Kiel, Postfach 3840, D–24037 Kiel, ☎ 0431/567–080).

En Route Leave Lübeck on Route 105. Don't expect a fast highway. Route 105 is a narrow two-lane road all the way to Poland, heavily traveled by slow-moving trucks. Stop at **Grevesmühlen** to view a pretty Renaissance Town Hall and the Gothic **St. Nikolaikirche**, a parish church. ✉ *Kirchpl. 4,* ☎ *03881/2524.*

The **Iserberg,** one of the highest hills in the region, is several miles east of Grevesmühlen, where you can see the coastline and the island of Poel. This region has been buffeted by stiff storms and more: Over the centuries the armies of Sweden, Denmark, Prussia, and France fought here for control of the coast. In nearby **Tannenberg** a grim reminder of a more recent conflict can be found—the site of a memorial cemetery for some of the 8,000 Nazi concentration camp victims who drowned when four ships transporting them were mistakenly attacked by Allied planes and sunk in the Lübecker Bay only days before the war ended.

Wismar

★ ❷ *60 km (37 mi) east of Lübeck on Rte. 105.*

The old city of Wismar was one of the original three sea-trading towns, along with Lübeck and Rostock, that banded together in 1259 to combat Baltic pirates. From this mutual defense pact grew the great and powerful private trading block, the Hanseatic League, which dominated the Baltic for centuries. The Thirty Years' War was particularly devastating for this region—it halved the prewar population—and the power of the Hanseatics was broken. Wismar became the victim of regular military tussles and finally fell to Sweden. In 1803 the town was leased for 100 years to a German Mecklenburg duke, and only when the lease expired did Wismar legally rejoin Germany. Despite this checkered history, the wealth generated by the Hanseatic merchants can still be seen in Wismar's ornate architecture.

★ The **Marktplatz,** one of the largest and most colorful in Europe, is framed by patrician gabled houses, evidence of the city's prosperous past. The style of buildings on the square ranges from redbrick late-Gothic through Dutch Renaissance to 19th-century neoclassical. Of particular interest is the **Wasserkunst**, the ornate pumping station in Dutch Renaissance style, built 1580–1602 by the Dutch master Philipp Brandin. Not only was it a work of art, it supplied the town with water until the mid-19th century. In 1922 filmmaker Friedrich Wilhelm Murnau used the tortuous streets of Wismar's Old Town in his Expressionist horror movie classic, *Nosferatu.*

NEED A
BREAK?

The **Alter Schwede** (✉ Am Markt 19, ☎ 03841/283–552), a colorful seamen's tavern since 1878, has entertained guests ranging from sailors to the Swedish royal family. Dating from 1380, it's the oldest building on the Marktplatz and can be easily identified by its stepped gables and red-brick facade. The present owner has made this restaurant one of the best places for fish dishes in town. Try their *Neptun's Füllhorn*, a dish of various fish, including salmon and pike fillets, in a spicy sauce of dill and mustard.

The ruins of the **Marienkirche** (St. Mary's Church) with its 250-foot high tower, bombed in World War II, lie just behind the Marktplatz; the church is still undergoing repairs. At noon, 3 PM, and 5 PM, listen for one of 14 hymns played on its clarion bells. The **Fürstenhof,** home of the former dukes of Mecklenburg, stands next to Marienkirche. It is an early 16th-century Italian Renaissance structure with touches of late-Gothic. The facade is a series of fussy friezes depicting scenes from the Trojan War. The **Georgenkirche** (St. George's Church), an-other victim of the war, is adjacent to the Fürstenhof. Today it's the biggest Gothic religious ruin in Europe.

The late-Gothic **St. Nikolaikirche** (St. Nicholas's Church), with a 120-foot-high nave, was built from 1381 to 1487. A remnant of the town's long domination by Sweden is the additional altar built for Swedish sailors. Important architectural relics rescued from the bombed ruins of other Wismar churches are displayed here, notably the Gothic high altar from the Georgenkirche. ✉ *Hinter dem Chor,* ☎ *03841/213–615.* ☉ *Mon.–Sat. 10–noon and 1–5, Sun. and holidays 1–5.*

The **Dutch Renaissance Schabbellhaus** houses a fascinating museum of local history. It is just across the street from Nikolaikirche. ✉ *Schweins-brücke 8,* ☎ *03841/282–350.* ▣ *DM 2.* ☉ *Tues., Wed., and Fri.–Sun. 10–4:30, Thurs. 10–8.*

If you've got an hour to spare, wander among the jetties and quays of the port, a mix of the medieval and the modern. **To' n Zägenkrog,** a seaman's haven decorated with shark's teeth, stuffed seagulls, and maritime gear, is a picturesque pit stop along the harbor. ✉ *Ziegen-markt 10,* ☎ *03841/282–716.*

Dining and Lodging

$$ ✕ **Alter Schwede.** Regarded as one of the most attractive, authentic
★ taverns on the Baltic—and correspondingly busy—this eatery has a cook-ing staff intent on reviving Mecklenburg's traditional cuisine, which features both game and fish dishes. The restaurant is famous for its chicken liver with onions and apple rings, an equally hearty and tra-ditional Mecklenburg-dish. ✉ *Am Markt 19,* ☎ *03841/283–552. AE, MC, V.*

$ ✕ **Kartoffelhaus Nr. 1.** Potato lovers come here for the potato pizza, potato crepes, potato schnapps, and the dozens more dishes and del-icacies made from the humble tuber that is this restaurant's specialty and namesake (the name translates as "Potato House Number One"). You'd never guess from the menu's unique theme and the mix-and-match decor that this is one link in a Germany-wide chain; this *does* explain the very reasonable prices, however. In addition to serving all things potato, Kartoffelhaus Nr. 1 also offers a good selection of steaks. ✉ *Frische Grube 31,* ☎ *03841/200–030. AE, MC.*

$ ✕ **Seehase.** This small, no-frills fish restaurant is favored by locals as well as visitors. Ask for the rich fish-and-sour-cream soup, *Fischsol-janka,* a rather hearty eastern German version of minestrone. ✉ *Alt-böterstr. 6,* ☎ *03841/282–134. No credit cards.*

$$-$$$ X🏨 **Hotel Stadt Hamburg.** Why is this tasteful, first-class hotel, opened
★   in 1993, less expensive than its equally luxurious neighbors? Because
         use of several of the facilities (i.e., health club, parking) costs extra here,
         so you pay only for what you actually use. Behind the hotel's histori-
         cal facade is a modern, open, airy interior, with skylights and a posh
         lobby that would be perfectly at home in southern California. The rooms
         are elegantly decorated with cherry wood art deco–style furnishings.
         Downstairs, the hotel's Bierkeller, a cavernous 17th-century room with
         vaulted ceilings, is now a trendy nightspot adorned with avant-garde
         paintings, bar stools elaborately sculpted from wrought iron, and a very
         chic crowd. ⊠ *Am Markt 24, D–23966 Wismar,* ☎ *03841/2390,* ℻
         03841/239–239. 106 rooms, all with bath. Restaurant, beer cellar, café,
         minibars, no-smoking floor, massage, sauna, exercise room, fax ma-
         chines. AE, DC, MC, V.

Nightlife and the Arts

At the **Stadttheater** (⊠ Philipp-Müllerstr. 5, ☎ 03841/507–206), plays
in German and operas are performed regularly, and concerts are occasionally presented.

Schwerin

★ ❸   *32 km (20 mi) south of Wismar on Rte. 106.*

Schwerin, the second-largest town in the region after Rostock and capital of the state of Mecklenburg-Vorpommern, is worth a trip just to
visit the giant **Schweriner Schloss** (Schwerin Palace) of the Mecklenburg royal family, on an island on the edge of Lake Schwerin, close to
the Old Town. The earliest palace on this site dates back to 1018. When
Henry the Lion founded Schwerin in 1160, he ordered the enlargement
of the existing castle. The castle you see today is a unique pastiche of
historical styles, due to 800 years of fires, renovations, and additions.
Surmounted by 15 turrets large and small, the palace is reminiscent of
a French château, and, indeed, parts were modeled on Chambord in
the Loire Valley. Its present-day neo-Renaissance aspect and many
ducal staterooms date from between 1845 and 1857.

North of the main tower is the **Neue Lange Haus** (New Long House),
built from 1553 to 1555. The Communist government restored and
maintained the fantastic opulence of this rambling, 80-room reminder
of an absolutist monarchy for use in the 1960s and 1970s as a boarding school for the education of kindergarten teachers. Since the relo-
cation of the regional capital to Schwerin, however, a fifth of the
rooms are now used for regional government offices. Antique furniture, objets d'art, silk tapestries, and paintings are sprinkled throughout the salons (the Throne Room is particularly extravagant), but of
special interest are the ornately patterned and highly burnished inlaid
wooden floors and wall panels. The many tales of the good-spirited
castle ghost, Petermännchen (Little Man Peter), who aids the poor and
oppressed, will delight the entire family. The castle is surrounded by
parkland laid out in the 18th century that contains many beautiful and
rare species of trees. Sandstone replicas of the sculptures of Permoser
adorn the tree-lined avenues. ⊠ *Lennéstr.,* ☎ *0385/562–738.* 🖼 *DM*
6. ☉ *Palace and gardens open June–Oct., Tues.–Sun. 10–6; Nov.–May,*
Tues.–Sun. 10–5.

NEED A   **Schlosscafé** (⊠ Lennéstr., ☎ 0385/525-2963), today Schwerin's most
BREAK?   picturesque coffee shop, is in the King's Hall of the palace. It is
              renowned for its creative ice-cream desserts.

A visit to Schwerin wouldn't be complete without a boat tour on the city's surrounding lakes. (☞ Contacts and Resources *in* Mecklenburg-Vorpommern A to Z, *below.*)

The **Alte Garten,** the town's showpiece square, was the scene of military parades during the years of Communist rule. It is dominated by two buildings, the ornate neo-Renaissance state theater, constructed 1883–86, and the **Staatliches Museum,** which houses an interesting collection of paintings by such 19th-century German artists as Max Liebermann and Lovis Corinth, plus an exhibition of Meissen porcelain. ☎ 0385/592–400. ➳ Free. ۞ Wed.–Sun. 10–5, Tues. 10–2.

The **Dom,** a Gothic cathedral, is the oldest building (built 1222–48) in the city and another noteworthy sight in Schwerin's Old Town. The bronze baptismal font is from the 14th century; the altar was built in 1440. Religious scenes painted on the walls of the adjoining **Schweriner Dom** date from the Middle Ages. Sweeping views of the Old Town and lake await those with the energy to climb the 219 steps to the top of the 320-foot-high cathedral tower. The Alte Garten is opposite the entrance to the palace island. ✉ Am Marktpl., ☎ 0385/565–014. ۞ Tower Mon. 11–4, Tues.–Sat. 11–noon and 2:30–4:30, Sun. 2:30–4:30.

The **Freilichtmuseum Schwerin-Muess** (Open-air Museum) is a living-history museum representing traditional work and farm life in Germany. Children in particular and history buffs in general will enjoy wandering through the 17 preserved buildings, which include a blacksmith's shop dating from 1736, a village school from the 19th century, a traditional fire station, a carriage house, and a barn. All buildings are precisely decorated with antiques of their era. You can watch demonstrations of the tools and traditional methods used to bake bread and work metal. ✉ 6 km (4 mi) south of Schwerin, ☎ 0385/213–011. ➳ DM 3. ۞ May–Oct., Tues.–Sun. 10–6.

Dining and Lodging

$$$ ✗ **Weinhaus Uhle.** One of the most traditional and popular eating places
★ in Schwerin, this restaurant is named after the wine merchant who opened the restaurant back in 1740. You can dine on regional specialties and international mixed grills served in a colorful, unspoiled setting, accompanied by a small band that plays nightly. ✉ Schusterstr. 13–15, ☎ 0385/562–956. AE, MC.

$$–$$$ ✗ **Zum Goldenen Reiter.** The classic elegance of this restaurant pro-
★ vides a sharp contrast to the current crop of glossy restaurant chains and mossy, old taverns. The dark-wood, candlelit rooms generate a sophisticated yet comfortable atmosphere. Head Chef Ulrich Armster serves *Mecklenburger Entenbrust,* a tender breast of duck stuffed with apples and red cabbage, a recipe lifted from an 1896 cookbook of regional specialties. ✉ Puschkinstr. 44, ☎ 0385/565–036. AE, MC.

$$ ✗ **Ritterstübe.** Pleasant service and solid regional specialties characterize this remnant of the Communist era. House specialties include *gefüllter Nackenbraten,* green cabbage soup, and a local favorite, *Rumpsteak Mecklenburger Art,* prepared with raisins and horseradish. ✉ Ritterstr. 3, ☎ 0385/565–240. MC. Closed Mon.

$$$$ ✗⌂ **Hotel Plaza Schwerin.** The winner of the "Best Quality Award Eu-
★ rope," this Best Western hotel's interior was completely remodeled and exudes a first-class atmosphere of marble and selected woods. Designed for business types, the prices are exorbitant on weekdays, but the hotel cuts rates in half for most rooms on the weekends. ✉ Am Grünen Tal/Hamburger Allee, D–19063, ☎ 0385/34820, ℻ 0385/341–053.

78 rooms and 1 suite, all with bath. Restaurant, piano bar, no-smoking floor, room service, sauna. AE, DC, MC, V.

$$–$$$ ✕⚏ **Hotel Arte Schwerin.** This new hotel is small and distinguished. The redbrick building is a fully restored farmhouse whose exterior has a small-town appearance in contrast to its modern and luxurious interior. The hotel is found at the peaceful Ostorfer Lake, close to the Schweriner Schloss. ✉ *Dorfstr. 6, D–19063,* ☎ *0385/63450,* 𝔽𝔸𝕏 *0385/634–5100. 40 rooms with bath. Restaurant, bar, in-room safes, minibars, hot tub, sauna. AE, MC, V.*

$ ✕⚏ **Strand-Hotel.** Built in 1910, this perfect summer getaway spot is one of the few remaining luxury resorts from Communist times. It's a four-story yellow hotel with bright-blue awnings on the shore of Lake Schwerin. A walk along the beach and through the Baroque palace gardens leads directly to the castle and Old Town. Boxy minibathrooms, haphazardly added to many rooms during renovations, detract from the otherwise clean, refreshing atmosphere. But at these prices—and breakfast is included—it's a steal. Book at least a month in advance, and request a lakeside room with a balcony. ✉ *Am Strand 13, D–19063 Schwerin-Zippendorf,* ☎ *0385/213–053,* 𝔽𝔸𝕏 *0385/321–174. 26 rooms with bath. Restaurant, bar, café. AE, MC, V.*

Nightlife and the Arts

The **MEXX disco** (✉ Arsenalstr. 16), next door to the sleek coffeehouse Lesecafé am Pfaffenteich, attracts a stylish young crowd.

Mecklenburger Staatstheater (✉ Am Alten Garten, ☎ 0385/83993) stages German drama. In June, the **Sommerfest** on the Lankower See (Lankower Lake) offers classical music at its best.

Shopping

Antiques and bric-a-brac that have languished in cellars and attics since World War II are still surfacing throughout eastern Germany, and the occasional bargain can be found. The best places to look in Schwerin are on and around Schmiedestrasse, Schlossstrasse, and Mecklenburgstrasse.

Bad Doberan

❹ *60 km (37 mi) east of Wismar on Rte. 105. 90 km (56 mi) northeast of Schwerin.*

★ Bad Doberan has a meticulously restored redbrick **cloister church,** one of the finest of its kind in the region. It was built by Cistercian monks between 1294 and 1368 in the northern German Gothic style, with a central nave and transept. The main altar dates from the early 14th century and features a 45-foot-tall cross. Many of the monastic buildings have been preserved; the former corn granary is now a youth center. ✉ *Klosterstr. 2,* ☎ *038203/2716.* ▣ *DM 2.* ☉ *May–Sept., Mon.–Sat. 9–6, Sun. noon–6; Mar., Apr., and Oct., Mon.–Sat. 9–4, Sun. noon–4; Nov.–Feb., Tues.–Fri. 9–noon and 2–4, Sat. 9–4, Sun. noon–4. Guided tours at 1, 2, and 3.*

Horse-racing fans may be interested to know that the first race course in Europe outside Britain was established in Bad Doberan in 1822. Racing took place until the beginning of the 1950s. In 1993 the renovated track was reopened to initiate the annual international festival, **Rennwochenende** (Race Weekend), which features two days of racing during the last weekend of July.

No visit to this part of the world would be complete without a ride on ★ ☾ *Molli,* a quaint little steam train that has been chugging up and down a 10-mile-long narrow-gauge track between Bad Doberan and the nearby beach resorts of **Heiligendamm** and **Kühlungsborn** since 1886. The train was nicknamed after a little local dog that barked its approval every time the smoking iron horse passed by. At the start of the 40-minute journey the engine and its old wooden carriages make their way through the center of Bad Doberan's cobbled streets. *Molli* runs 13 times daily in both directions between Bad Doberan and Kühlungsborn. In the Salonwagen of the train you can have a cup of coffee while viewing the impressive Mecklenburg meadows and forests. ⊠ *Mecklenburgische Bäderbahn Molli, c/o Küstenbus GmbH,* ☎ *038203/2051,* ℻ *038203/2470.* ⌔ *DM 4–DM 9.90, depending on the number of stops.* ☼ *May–Sept., daily 5:30 AM–8:30 PM; Oct.–Apr., daily 5:10 AM–4:10 PM.*

Dining and Lodging

$$ ✗ **Weisser Pavillon.** A Chinese pagoda–type structure built during the
★ 19th century in an English-style park is an exotic setting for lunch or high tea (in summer the café closes at 10 PM). But it's regional specialties that are featured here. ⊠ *Auf dem Kamp,* ☎ *038203/2326. No credit cards.*

$$$–$$$$ ✗⊟ **Romantik-Kurhotel.** Built in 1793 for a Mecklenburg duke, this
★ historic whitewashed member of the Romantik Hotel group has been accommodating visitors for more than 200 years. Completely restored and renovated, each room exudes Old World elegance with modern comforts. The individual touches of manager Dr. Horst Metz and the friendly staff provide pleasant, personalized service in a regal setting. ⊠ *August-Bebel-Str. 2, D–18209 Bad Doberan,* ☎ *038203/3036,* ℻ *038203/2126. 59 rooms, all with shower. Restaurant, café, sauna. AE, DC, MC, V.*

$$–$$$ ✗⊟ **Röntgen.** This hotel, housed in a white mansion dating from
★ 1902, offers spacy one- to three bedroom apartments with kitchenettes, as well as a nice little restaurant specializing in fish dishes and a café. Situated in the heart of Kühlungsborn, it is run by the Röntgen family, which is not only proud of its tradition as bakers, but also of its highly personalized service. The hotel is especially well suited to accommodate families or groups. ⊠ *Strandstr. 30a, D–18225 Kühlungsborn,* ☎ *038293/7810,* ℻ *038293/78199. 17 apartments, all with kitchenette and bath. Restaurant, café.*

$$ ✗⊟ **Am Strand.** This small yellow hotel has been a private vacation home since its construction in the 1920s. Its guests get modest, modern comfort right on the beach promenade. ⊠ *Str. des Friedens 16, D–18225 Kühlungsborn,* ☎ *038293/6611,* ℻ *038293/80118. 39 rooms, all with bath or shower. Restaurant, sauna. DC, MC, V.*

Rostock

⑤ *14 km (9 mi) east of Bad Doberan on Rte. 105.*

Rostock, the biggest port and shipbuilding center of former East Germany, was founded around 1200. The once-thriving city suffered most from the dissolution of the Hanseatic Pact in 1669, as the area was fought over and trade declined. While Hamburg, Kiel to the west, and Stettin to the east (now part of Poland) became leading port cities, Rostock languished until the late 1950s, when the newly formed German Democratic Republic found it needed a sea outlet and reestablished Rostock as a major port. Since reunification, work at the port has been halved and, except for ferries coming from Gedser (Denmark) and Trelleborg (Sweden), there is little scheduled traffic. In 1995 mass layoffs of shipyard workers were a major blow to the city's weak economy.

Today the biggest local attraction is *Hanse Sail,* a week of yacht racing held in August. One of the best views of old Rostock is from the harbor. The city suffered severe damage in the World War II bombings of the Heinkel (the Luftwaffe's bombers) and armaments factories, but much of the Old Town's core has been rebuilt, including large segments of the medieval town wall.

The main street, the pedestrian-only **Kröpelinerstrasse,** begins at the old western gate, the Kröpeliner Tor. On this street you'll find the finest examples of the late-Gothic and Renaissance houses of the rich *Hanse* merchants. The triangular **Universitätsplatz,** commemorating the founding of northern Europe's first university here in 1419, is home to the Rostock University's Italian Renaissance–style main building, finished in 1867. It now stands on the site of the original construction.

At the **Neue Markt** (town square), you'll immediately notice the architectural potpourri that is the **Rathaus** (Town Hall). Basically 13th-century Gothic with a Baroque facade, the building spouts seven slender, decorative towers, looking like candles on a peculiar birthday cake. The square is surrounded by historic gabled houses.

Four-centuries-old **St. Marienkirche** (St. Mary's Church), the Gothic architectural prize of Rostock, boasts a bronze baptismal font from 1290 and some interesting Baroque features, notably the oak altar (1720) and organ (1770). The unique attraction, however, is the huge astronomical clock dating from 1472; it has a calendar extending to the year 2017. ⊠ *Am Ziegenmarkt,* ☎ *0381/492–3396.* ⓢ *Mon.–Sat. 10–5, Sun. 11–noon.*

The **Münze,** Rostock's former mint, stands at the rear of St. Marienkirche. The town started producing its own coins in 1361 and only relinquished this right in 1864. The Münze has a fine Renaissance arched entrance and a stone relief depicting coin makers going about their work. ⊠ *Am Ziegenmarkt 3.*

ⓒ The **Schiffahrtsmuseum** traces the history of shipping on the Baltic and displays models of ships, which are especially interesting for children. It is just beyond the city wall, at the Steintor. ⊠ *August-Bebel-Str. 1,* ☎ *0381/492–2697.* ⓢ *DM 4.* ⓢ *Tues.–Sun. 9–5.*

ⓒ The **Schiffbaumuseum,** Rostock's shipbuilding museum, is housed in the hold of the *Dresden,* a 10,000-ton old freighter. Built in 1952, the ship also contains a youth hostel. The *Dresden* is moored to the riverbank on the right-hand side of the road, along the Warnow River about 5 kilometers (3 miles) north of the center of Rostock. ⊠ *Traditionsanlegepl. Schmarl,* ☎ *0381/1219–726.* ⓢ *DM 4.* ⓢ *Tues.–Sun. 9–5.*

The **Port Centre** is a ship that was commandeered and moored alongside the riverbank to become a complex of stores, boutiques, bars, and restaurants. With the collapse of state communism, there were not enough buildings to house shops, so the ship offered additional space. ⊠ *Kapuzenhof.*

ⓒ The **Zoologischer Garten** (Zoological Garden) has one of the largest collections of exotic animals and birds in northern Germany. This zoo is particularly noted for its polar bears, some of which were bred in Rostock. If you're traveling with kids, a visit is a must. ⊠ *Rennbahnallee 21,* ☎ *0381/37111.* ⓢ *DM 7; DM 5 Oct.–Mar.* ⓢ *Oct.–Mar., daily 9–4; Nov.–Apr., daily 9–5.*

Dining and Lodging

$ ✕ **Zur Kogge.** Looking like the cabin of some ancient sailing vessel,
★   the oldest sailors' beer tavern in town serves mostly fish. Order the

Mecklenburger Fischsuppe if it's on the menu; *Räucherfisch* (smoked fish) is also a popular choice. Starting at 8 PM, Tuesday–Saturday, live music adds to the restaurant's authentic maritime atmosphere. ⊠ *Wokrenter Str. 27,* ☎ *0381/493–4493. Reservations essential. AE, DC, MC, V.*

$$$ ✕▥ **Ramada Hotel Rostocker Hof.** This newly opened hotel in an old
★ 19th-century mansion is a genuine part of Rostock's historic Old Town. It provides smooth service, and the modern rooms are tastefully decorated. Despite its downtown location, it is a quiet place to stay. ⊠ *Schwaansche/Kröpeliner Str., D–18055,* ☎ *0381/49700,* ⨳ *0381/4970–700. 150 rooms, all with bath. Restaurant, bar, sauna, exercise room. AE, DC, MC, V.*

Nightlife and the Arts
The bar/café **Käjahn** (⊠ Patriotischer Weg 126) is a stylish nightspot. **Speicher** (⊠ Am Strande 3, ☎ 0381/492–3031), a split-level disco, appeals to all ages.

The **Volkstheater** (⊠ Doberanerstr. 134/35, ☎ 0381/2440) presents plays (German only) and concerts.

The summer season brings with it a plethora of special concerts, the highlights are the **"Music in May"** concerts, primarily at Rostock and also at nearby Stralsund.

Shopping
Echter Rostocker Doppel-Kümmel und -Korn, a kind of schnapps made from various grains, is a traditional liquor of the region around Rostock. Fishermen have numbed themselves to the cold for centuries with this 40% alcoholic beverage; a 7-liter bottle costs DM 18.

Warnemünde

❻ *14 km (9 mi) north of Rostock on Rte. 103.*

Warnemünde is a quaint seaside resort with the best hotels and restaurants in the area, as well as 20 kilometers (12 miles) of beautiful white beach. This former fishing village was annexed to Rostock in 1323 to secure safe entrance to the Hanseatic city's harbor. For years it has been a popular summer holiday destination for families in eastern Germany—they're drawn by a 2-mile-long sandy beach and a giant, heated saltwater pool with artificial waves as high as 4 feet, among other attractions. ⊠ *Meeresschwimmhalle, on the promenade next to Hotel Neptun,* ☎ *0381/777–865.* ⊟ *DM 7.* ☉ *Mon. 1–8, Tues.–Fri. 10–8, Sat. 9–8, Sun. 8–8.*

Children will also enjoy climbing to the top of the town landmark, a 115-foot-high **Leuchtturm** (lighthouse), dating from 1898; on clear days it offers views of the coast and Rostock Harbor. Inland from the lighthouse is the area known as **Alter Strom,** once the entry into the port of Warnemünde and now a marina for yachts that has bars, cozy restaurants, and specialty shops.

Dining and Lodging
$$ ✕ **Fischerklause.** Sailors have stopped in at this restaurant's bar since the turn of the century, but it's not *that* kind of place. Locals come here, too, although they tend to go farther inside, to the dining room, where they dig into some of the wide variety of seafood dishes; the smoked fish sampler served on a lazy Susan is delicious, but the house specialty is the fish soup—best washed down with some Rostocker Kümmel schnapps. An accordionist entertains the crowd on Friday and Satur-

day evenings. ✉ *Am Strom 123,* ☎ *0381/52516. Reservations essential. AE, MC, V.*

$ ✕ **Café 28.** This candlelit bistro exudes a bohemian air, from the local artwork on its walls and the soft acoustic music in the background to its light, tasty, and very reasonably priced salads and pastas. It's also a fine place to stop for a cappuccino or a drink in the romantic, youthful, artsy atmosphere. ✉ *Mühlenstr. 28,* ☎ *0381/52467. No credit cards.*

$$$$ ✕▥ **Hotel Neptun.** The 19-story concrete-and-glass Neptun is an eyesore on the outside, but inside it has the redeeming qualities of a luxury hotel. Every one of the neat and lovingly decorated rooms has a sea view. To get first-class atmosphere for less money, ask for the hotel's special "happy weekend" and "vacation on the sea" rates. ✉ *Seestr. 19, D–18119,* ☎ *0381/7770,* FAX *0381/54023. 350 rooms, 4 suites with bath. 3 restaurants, 2 bars, café, outdoor and indoor pools, beauty salon, sauna, spa, dance club. AE, DC, MC, V.*

$–$$ ✕▥ **Landhotel Ostseeraum.** The family-owned hotel is an outstanding example of blending modern style with rural architecture. This old farmhouse with a thatched roof is fairly secluded, in an area outside Warnemünde, just 500 yards from the beach. ✉ *Stolteraaweg 34b, D–18119 Warnemünde-Diedrichshagen,* ☎ FAX *0381/51719. 18 rooms, half with private bath. Restaurant, bar. No credit cards.*
★

$$–$$$ ▥ **Hotel Germania.** Set at the harbor entrance and only one block from
★   the beach, the Alter Strom promenade, and some of the best restaurants in town, this small hotel's location alone makes it a good choice, and then there are the rooms; newly renovated, they are tastefully decorated in pleasing pale-blue tones and mahogany furnishings and equipped with TV and minibar. With so many good eateries nearby you probably won't miss having a hotel restaurant, but sybarites may object to the lack of an on-site spa, sauna, pool, or fitness room. ✉ *Am Strom 110–111, D–18119,* ☎ *0381/519–850,* FAX *0381/519–8510. 18 rooms, all with shower. Minibars. AE, D, MC, V.*

Nightlife and the Arts

In Warnemünde nearly all the seaside hotels and resorts, down to the smallest, have almost nightly dances during the summer months. Head to the large hotels to search for fun. The pubs in **Alter Strom** are gathering places for locals and visitors alike.

The **Skybar** is on the 19th floor of the Neptun Hotel (✉ Seestr. 19, ☎ 0381/7770). Open until 4 AM, this bar, whose roof opens, gives you the chance to sit under the stars and watch ship lights twinkle on the sea.

Outdoor Activities and Sports

FISHING

Fishing is a rapidly expanding leisure industry in the area. Every port along the coast now has small boats for hire, and some boatmen will lead you to the shoals. For information on equipment availability, contact the Rostock tourist office (☎ 0381/459–0860) for **Warnemünde Harbor.**

Ribnitz-Damgarten

❼   *30 km (19 mi) northeast of Warnemünde. 26 km (16 mi) east of Rostock on Rte. 105.*

Ribnitz-Damgarten is the center of the **amber** (in German, *Bernstein*) business, unique to the Baltic Coast. In the **Bernsteinmuseum,** which adjoins the main factory, you can see a fascinating exhibition of how this precious "Baltic gold" is collected from the sea and refined to make jewelry and objets d'art. The museum has examples of amber dating from 35 to 50 million years. The biggest lump of raw amber ever harvested from the sea weighed more than 23 pounds. If it were ever cut, it could make 30 necklaces, but instead it is on exhibit in the Museum für Naturkunde in Berlin. ⊠ *Im Kloster 1–2,* ☎ *03821/2931.* ⊠ *DM 4.* ⊙ *May–Sept., daily 9:30–5; Apr. and Oct., Tues.–Sat. 9:30–4:30, Sun. 1–4:30; Nov.–Mar., Wed.–Sat. 10–4, Sun. 1–4.*

Shopping

The precious Bernstein stones, formed from the sap of ancient conifers, are more than 35–50 million years old. You can buy amber jewelry, chess figures, and ornate jewelry boxes in the Bernsteinmuseum. The jewelry, often designed with gold and silver as well as amber, costs from DM 100 to DM 1,000. Fossils are often embedded in the stone—a precious find. (Hint: Only true amber floats in a glass of water stirred with 2 teaspoons of salt.) There is a less expensive way to acquire these gems: Head for a beach and join the locals in the perennial quest for amber stones washed up among the seaweed after a storm. Your children may also stumble upon a little pebble with a hole worn in the middle. Prevalent on this coast, they are called *Hühnergötter* (chicken gods) by the locals, who believe they bring good luck.

VORPOMMERN

The best description of this region is found in its name, which simply means "before Pommerania." This area, indeed, seems trapped between Mecklenburg and the authentic, old Pommerania further east, now part of Poland. Most people think this area is neither fish nor fowl. Although Vorpommern is not the dull, monotonous backwater it is made out to be, it is not a typical tourist attraction, either. Its very remoteness and poverty ensure an unforgettable view of unspoiled nature, primarily attracting families and a young crowd. At first glance, the countryside—with its tundralike appearance, pine barrens, sandy heaths, and dunes—seems harsh and deserted. But to the mindful traveler, its beauty will slowly unfold as one explores its quiet terrain.

Ahrenshoop

8 *75 km (46 mi) north of Ribnitz-Damgarten.*

The village of Ahrenshoop was the site of an art colony, begun in the late 19th century, which brought together painters from across Germany and beyond. Even today it is especially picturesque. After World War II Ahrenshoop became a mecca of sorts to artists, musicians, and writers of the GDR. Continue toward Prerow to get back to the mainland, but be sure to stop at the 17th-century seamen's church on the edge of town. The powerful simplicity of this rustic church and cemetery reflects the importance of religion in the local fishermen's lives.

Ahrenshoop is typical of the seaside villages on the half island of **Darss,** as Germans call it. This half-moon-shape finger of land was once three islands that became one from centuries of shifting sand. Since 1966 much of Darss has been a nature reserve, partly to protect the ancient forest of beech, holly, and juniper, but also because of its topographical uniqueness. The area contains many rare plants and provides shelter for a huge variety of seabirds. The peacefulness and seclusion of this preserve make its many paths ideal for biking and hiking. The island's best beach is **Weststrand** (West Beach), a broad stretch of fine, white sand that is free of auto traffic and most development. Wind-sculptured trees, veterans of a long-standing battle with nature, border the beach. Darss is also noted for its old fisherman's cottages, with

brightly painted doors and reed-thatched roofs. All new constructions
are *required* to have thatched roofs in keeping with the traditional style
of the island.

Stralsund

❾ *59 km (36 mi) east of Ahrenshoop, 42 km (26 mi) east of Ribnitz-
Damgarten on Rte. 105.*

Although it was rapidly industrialized, this jewel of the Baltic features
a historic, rebuilt, and restored city center. In 1815 the Congress of Vienna awarded the city, which had been under Swedish control, to the
Prussians. Following an attack by the Lübeck fleet in 1249, a defensive wall was built around Stralsund, parts of which you'll see on your
left as you come into the Old Town.

The old market square, the **Alter Markt,** has the best local architecture,
ranging from Gothic through Renaissance to Baroque. Most of the buildings were rich merchants' homes, notably the late-Gothic **Wulflamhaus,**
with 17 ornate, steeply stepped gables. Stralsund's architectural masterpiece, however, is the 13th-century **Rathaus** (Town Hall), considered by many to be the finest secular example of redbrick Gothic in
northern Germany. Note the coats of arms of the main towns that formed
the exclusive membership of the Hanseatic League.

The 13th-century Gothic **St. Nikolaikirche** (St. Nicholas's Church) faces
the market square. Its treasures include a 15-foot-high crucifix from the
14th century, an astronomical clock from 1394, and a Baroque altar.
⊠ *Badenstr.,* ☎ *03831/297–199.* ۝ *Tues.–Fri. 10–noon and 2–4,
Sat. 10–noon, Sun. 11:30–noon.*

Walk down the pedestrian street **Ossenreyerstrasse** for a glimpse of
the grandiose beginnings of modern consumer culture at the turn-of-
the-century department store at Ossenreyerstrasse 8–13, the site of the
first in the famous Wertheim chain. Alas, fame is fleeting, and the building—with its magnificent glassed-in courtyard—is now part of the Horten
chain of stores.

The **Katherinenkloster** is a former cloister on Mönchstrasse. Forty
rooms of the cloister now house two museums: the famed **Meeresmuseum**
with aquarium (☞ *below*) and the **Kulturhistorisches Museum,** exhibiting a diverse selection of artifacts from more than 10,000 years
of this coastal region's history. Highlights include the toy collection and
10th-century Viking gold jewelry found on Hiddensee. You'll reach the
museums by walking along Ossenreyerstrasse through the Apol-
lonienmarkt on Mönchstrasse. ⊠ *Kulturhistorisches Museum, Mönchstr. 25–27,* ☎ *03831/292–180.* 💲 *DM 4.* ۝ *Tues.–Sun. 10–5.*

The Stralsund aquarium of Baltic Sea life is part of the maritime mu-
seum **Meeresmuseum,** which also displays the skeleton of a giant
whale, a hammerhead shark, and a 25-foot-high chunk of coral. ⊠
Katharinenberg 14–20, entrance on Mönchstr., ☎ *03831/295–135.*
💲 *DM 7.* ۝ *May.–Oct., daily 10–5; Nov.–Apr., Tues.–Sun. 10–5;
July–Aug., Mon.–Thurs. 9–4.*

Monstrous **St. Marienkirche** (St. Mary's Church) is the largest of the
three redbrick Gothic churches of Stralsund. With 4,000 pipes and intricate decorative figures, the magnificent 17th-century Stellwagen-Organ
is a delight to see and hear (there are concerts regularly). The view from
the church tower of Stralsund's old city center, the surrounding coast,
and Rügen Island is well worth the 349 steps you must climb to reach
the top. ⊠ *Neuer Markt, entrance at Bleistr.,* ☎ *03831/293–529.* ۝

Mon.–Sat. 10–4, Sun. 11:30–4. 🖼 *Guided tours daily of church tower DM 2.*

Dining and Lodging

$$
★
✕ **Scheelehaus.** A high, beamed ceiling and half-timbered walls of red-brick give this centuries-old restaurant the air of a baronial hall. The 10-foot-high windows still have the original thick, bull's-eye panes. Specialties of this acclaimed restaurant include *Stralsunder Fischsuppe,* one of the best local versions of the regional dish, *Gefüllter Schweinebraten,* and *Kartoffelbällchen*—potato balls filled with an almond, apple, and cinnamon mixture. ⊠ *Fährstr. 23,* ☎ *03831/292–987. AE, MC, V. Closed Sun. and Mon. in Jan. and Feb.*

$$
★
✕ **Wulflamstuben.** The atmosphere of this restaurant perfectly suits its historic location on the ground floor of *Wulflamhaus,* a 14th-century gabled house on the old market square. Copperplate engravings and ornate woodwork on the walls provide a regal yet pleasant setting. Steaks and fish are the specialty of the house; if you plan to visit in late spring or early summer, get the light and tasty *Maischolle* (May fish), fresh from the North Sea. The roast duck stuffed with apples, black bread, and plums and served in sweet sauce melts in your mouth. ⊠ *Alter Markt 5,* ☎ *03831/291–533. Reservations essential. AE, DC, MC, V.*

$–$$
★
✕ **Zum Alten Fritz.** This place a few miles outside Stralsund is worth a visit for its rustic interior and copper brewing equipment alone. Good, old German beer and ale of all colors are the main attractions here. Besides serving beer from Zwickelfritz, the city's brewery, the pub also carries a wide variety of surf-and-turf regional specialties. In summer the atmosphere becomes rambunctious, as both locals and tourists enjoy their drinks in the outside beer garden. ⊠ *Greifswalder Chaussee 84-85, at route B–96a,* ☎ *03831/255–500,* 𝗙𝗔𝗫 *03831/255–513.*

$$
★
🏨 **Hotel zur Post.** This small hotel is a great deal for travelers who want to enjoy a homey and yet first-class atmosphere. It is on the market square near the heart of the Old Town of Stralsund. The hotel's interior is a thoughtful blend of traditional North German furnishing and state-of-the-art design. ⊠ *Am Neuen Markt, Tribseer Str. 22, D–18439,* ☎ *03831/200–500,* 𝗙𝗔𝗫 *03831/200–510. 104 rooms, 2 suites, 8 apartments, all with bath. AE, MC, V.*

$$
🏨 **Norddeutscher Hof.** It's in the old section of the city across from Marienkirche, but don't let the weathered facade fool you; the hotel was completely renovated a few years ago. Unfortunately, the lobby and restaurant were not as simply and tastefully redecorated as the guest rooms. Still, you get the basics at a fair price. ⊠ *Neuer Markt 22, D–18439,* ☎ 𝗙𝗔𝗫 *03831/293–161. 13 rooms with bath. AE, MC, V.*

Nightlife and the Arts

The disco **Kiss Nacht** (⊠ Bartherstr. 58, ☎ 03831/292–449) offers dancing for a youthful crowd. **Störtebeker Keller** (⊠ Ossenreyerstr. 49, ☎ 03831/292–758) has dancing and cabaret.

Shopping

The **spring markets** held during April and May include a multitude of flea-market stalls.

Buddelschiffe (ships in a bottle) are a symbol of the once-magnificent sailing history of this region. They look easy to build, but they are not, and they are quite delicate. Expect to pay more than DM 120 for a small, 1-liter bottle.

Look out for **Fischerteppiche** (Fisherman's carpets). One square meter of these traditional carpets takes 150 hours to create, which explains why they're only meant to be hung on the wall and why they cost from DM 500 to DM 2,000. They're decorated with traditional symbols of the region, such as the mythical griffin, along with pine trees, eels, sea roses, and thistles.

Rügen Island

⑩ *4 km (2½ mi) northeast of Stralsund on Rte. 96.*

What Rügen lacks in architectural allure it makes up for in natural beauty. Its diverse and breathtaking landscapes have inspired poets and painters for more than a century. The island first became popular as a holiday destination with the development of the railways in the mid-19th century, and many of the grand mansions and villas on the island date from this period. Despite its continuing popularity during the Communist years, little development has taken place since the mid-1930s, leaving the entire island in a kind of time warp. For example, dances—all the rage in the 1920s and '30s—continue on Rügen, with afternoon coffee dances at cafés and dinner dances at hotels. Near the city of Prora (between Binz and Sassnitz) stands another fascinating remnant of Germany's past: the ruins of an abandoned Nazi scheme to create the world's largest resort. Planned for 20,000 people, the not even half-finished construction was pushed aside for more pressing matters. The East German army practiced within the complex's grounds. The island's main route runs between the **Grosser Jasmunder Bodden,** a giant sea inlet, and a smaller expanse of water—the **Kleiner Jasmunder Bodden Lake**— to the port of Sassnitz. Travelers are best off at any of the island's four main vacation centers—Sassnitz, Binz, Sellin, and Göhren.

Bergen

⑪ *34 km (21 mi) northeast of Stralsund on Rte. 96.*

Bergen, the island's administrative capital, is worth a visit for the **Rugard,** a small hill 91 meters (298 feet) above sea level that offers a fantastic panorama view of the whole island. Bergen was founded as a Slavic settlement some 900 years ago. Today only some remnants of the old fortification wall are to be found on the Rugard.

Sassnitz

⑫ *25 km (16 mi) northeast of Bergen on Rte. 96.*

From Sassnitz, where ferries run to Sweden, walk into **Jasmund National Park** to stare in awe at the Königstuhl cliffs. For information about the national park, contact the Sassnitz tourist office (☞ Contacts and Resources in The Baltic Coast A to Z below). Off the northwest corner of Rügen is a smaller island, the Hiddensee. The undisturbed solitude of this sticklike island has attracted such vacationers as Albert Einstein, Thomas Mann, Rainer Maria Rilke, and Sigmund Freud. You will find no tennis courts, discos, ritzy tourist accommodations, or even cars here. As Hiddensee is an auto-free zone, you must leave your car in Schaprode and take a ferry to this virtually undisturbed oasis, whose inhabitants are fighting hard to retain its tranquility.

⑬ Ten kilometers (6 miles) north of Sassnitz are the twin chalk cliffs of Rügen's main attraction, **Stubbenkammer** headland, on the east coast of the island. From here the much photographed chalk cliff **Königstuhl,** rising 351 feet from the sea, can be seen best. A steep trail leads down to beach.

Kap Arona

⑭ *21 km (13 mi) northwest of Stubbenkammer.*

Kap Arkona has a lighthouse marking the northernmost point in eastern Germany, and you can see the Danish island of Moen from a restored watchtower next door. The blustery sand dunes of Kap Arkona in the north and the quiet waters and coves of the Grosser Jasmunder Bodden in the center of Rügen are a nature lover's paradise.

Putbus

⑮ *59 km (37 mi) southeast of Kap Arkona, 8 km (5 mi) south of Bergen.*

From **Putbus,** you can take a ride on the 90-year-old miniature steam train, the *Rasender Roland* (Racing Roland), which runs 24½ kilometers (15 miles) to Göhren, at the southeast corner of the Rügen. Trains leave hourly during the day; the ride takes 45 minutes one-way and costs DM 10. For a splendid view in all directions, climb the cast-iron spiral staircase of the lookout tower of **Jagdschloss Granitz,** a hunting lodge near Binz built in 1836 by Karl Friedrich Schinkel. It stands on the highest point of East Rügen and has an excellent hunting exhibit. ☎ 038393/2263. 🎫 *DM 4.50.* ⊗ *Apr.–Oct., daily 9–5:30; Nov.–Mar., weekends only 10–5.*

Dining and Lodging

$$–$$$$ ✕🏨 **Hotel Vineta.** This great white building is one of the most beau-
★ tiful on the Rügen Island. Its name derives from a local fairy tale that tells of the destruction of the prosperous but sinful city of Vineta in a winter storm. According to the legend you can still hear the golden bells of the sunken city's towers ringing through the fog. Apart from that, the Vineta is pleasant and quiet; it is at the promenade in Binz. ⊠ *Hauptstr. 20, D–18609 Binz–Rügen,* ☎ *038393/390,* 🖷 *038393/39–444. 25 rooms, 8 suites, 5 apartments with bath. 2 restaurants, bar, sauna. AE, DC, MC, V.*

$$$ ✕🏨 **Nordperd.** Built in 1990, with an addition in 1994, this four-story hotel is one of the better-equipped accommodations on the island—all rooms have a TV, phone, minibar, and safe. The decor is white and bright, with cheerful patterned upholstery and curtains, although space is at a premium. Some rooms have coastal views, thanks to the hotel's location: on a hill at the southeast tip of the island, at the seaside resort village of Göhren. At the restaurant, which serves regional dishes, look for *Rügenwild,* a pot roast made with game. ⊠ *Nordperdstr. 11, D–18586 Göhren-Rügen,* ☎ *038308/70,* 🖷 *038308/7160. 70 rooms, all with bath or shower. Restaurant, bar, beer garden, sauna. AE, DC, MC, V.*

$–$$ ✕🏨 **Rügen-Hotel Sassnitz.** Many rooms here provide views of the busy little port of Sassnitz, where ferries operate to Trelleborg, Sweden. Except for the coastal views, you'll find at best utilitarian comfort and an impersonal, efficient manner within these nine stories. ⊠ *Seestr. 1, D–18546 Sassnitz,* ☎ *038392/320–90,* 🖷 *038392/321–75. 115 rooms, 2 suites with bath. Restaurant, 2 bars, café, room service.*

$ ✕🏨 **Hotel Godewind.** Two hundred meters from the beaches of Hid-
★ densee that have so inspired writers, this small hotel offers solid food and lodging at very reasonable prices. The apartments are a good value if you intend to stay for more than a few days. Godewind's restaurant is known on the island for its traditional regional dishes. ⊠ *Süderende 53, D–18565 Vitte-Hiddensee,* ☎ *038300/235,* 🖷 *038300/50161. 25 rooms, most with bath. Restaurant, bar, bicycles. No credit cards.*

$$ 🏨 **Hotel Villa Granitz.** The little town of Baabe considers itself the most
★ beautiful beach on Rügen Island. This newly erected mansion, in the romantic art nouveau style popular at the turn of the century, is a small and quiet retreat for travelers who want to avoid the tourist masses in the island's other resorts. All rooms are fully equipped with cable TV, safe, and refrigerator. Many rooms and some of the apartments even have

their own decks or balconies. ✉ *Birkenallee 17, D–18586 Baabe,* ☎ *038303/1410,* ℻ *038303/141–44. 52 rooms with bath. No credit cards.*

Outdoor Activities and Sports
WATER SPORTS

As private enterprise revives, a wide range of water-based activities is becoming available: windsurfing, sailing, surfing (although, to be truthful, the waves here are modest), and pedal-boat riding. Equipment is available for hire at the beach resorts. If you have difficulty locating what you want, contact the local tourist offices. The best-protected area along the coast for sailing is **Grosser Jasmunder Bodden,** a huge bay on Rügen Island. Boats for the bay can be hired at Lietzow and Ralswiek. Warnemünde has an international sailing regatta in July.

Shopping

Replicas of the **Hiddensee Golden Jewelry** aren't as valuable as the originals but are nevertheless a great souvenir. At the end of the 19th-century 16 pieces of 10th-century Viking jewelry were discovered (presently housed in the Kulturhistorisches Museum in Stralsund). Gold and silver replicas of their distinctive patterns are found in shops on Rügen Island and on Hiddensee Island.

Greifswald

⑯ *64 km (40 mi) southeast of Putbus, 32 km (20 mi) southeast of Stralsund on Rte. 96.*

Griefswald is the last in the string of Hanseatic ports on the Baltic Coast. The town was a busy sea trading center in the Middle Ages but became a backwater during the 19th century, when larger ships couldn't negotiate the shallow Ryck River leading to the sea. Today's visitors have German army commander Colonel Rudolf Petershagen to thank for the opportunity to see many of the town's original buildings. In charge of Greifswald in early 1945, he surrendered the town to the approaching Soviet forces rather than see it destroyed. So it's ironic that lack of funds for restoration over the next 40 years have left some historic buildings in desperate need of repair.

The **Marktplatz** (market square), presided over by a medieval Rathaus, rebuilt in 1738–50 following a fire, was modified during the 19th century and again in 1936. The square is surrounded by splendid old houses in redbrick Gothic styles.

Three churches shape the silhouette of the city. The 13th-century **Dom St. Nikolai** (St. Nicholas's Cathedral), at the start of Martin-Luther-Strasse, is a Gothic church from whose 300-foot-high tower one can get an impressive view. ✉ *Domstr.,* ☎ *03834/2627.* ☉ *Daily 9–3:30.*

The 14th-century **Marienkirche** (St. Mary's Church), the oldest surviving church in Greifswald, has remarkable 60-foot-high arches and a striking four-corner tower. ✉ *Friedrich-Loeffler-Str. 68, at corner of Brüggstr.,* ☎ *03834/2263.* ☉ *Weekdays 10–noon and 2–4.*

St. Jacobikirche (St. Jacob's Church) dates from the 13th century and was later rebuilt to a three-nave design. ✉ *Karl-Marx-Pl. 4,* ☎ *03834/502–209.* ☉ *Weekdays 10–noon and 2–4, Sat. 10–noon, Sun. noon–1.*

⑰ Just outside Greifswald, in what is now the suburb of **Eldena,** stand the ruins of a 12th-century **Cistercian monastery** made famous in a painting by Caspar David Friedrich (now at the Gallery of Romantic Painting in Berlin), who was born in Greifswald in 1774. The monastery, which led to the founding of Greifswald, was plundered by rampaging Swedish soldiers early in the Thirty Years' War and abandoned. The Gothic structure was further cannibalized by townsfolk over the next two centuries until it was made a protected national monument, a result of the publicity it gained from the celebrated Friedrich painting.

Dining and Lodging

$–$$ ✕ **Alter Speicher.** Its broad selection of delectable grilled items and
★ its wine list have brought this comfortable steak house regional renown. To warm up your taste buds for the grilled treats, try the *Kleines Ragout Fin* baked with Parmesan. And to round out your meal, try one of the many tasty dessert selections. The restaurant is conveniently located on the edge of the old city center. ✉ *Rossmühlenstr. 25,* ☎ *03834/2974. Reservations essential. AE, MC.*

$$ ✕🏨 **Europa Hotel Greifswald.** The hotel's unique decoration—curtains, bedcovers, and lamp shades covered in bold stripes and flowers—stands out from the standard pastel Southwestern-style palette and patterns common in newly constructed hotels of this region. To make up for the garishly bright rooms, the hotel provides modern amenities, a convenient location, a helpful staff, and an excellent restaurant. ✉ *Hans-Beimler-Str. 1–3, D–17491,* ☎ *03834/8010,* 𝔉𝔄𝔛 *03834/801–100. 51 rooms, all with bath, 4 apartments with kitchenettes. Restaurant, bar, no-smoking rooms, sauna, exercise room. AE, DC, MC, V.*

$ ✕🏨 **Hotel Maria.** Though not exactly luxurious, the facilities at this
★ recently built hotel are clean and modern—and the friendly service is what you'd hope for from such a small, family-owned place. The hotel is right on the harbor, just a short walk from the Wiecker Drawbridge; its terrace is the perfect place to linger over a drink while watching the panorama of summer sailboats. ✉ *Dorfstr. 45, D–17493,* ☎ *03834/841–426,* 𝔉𝔄𝔛 *03834/840–136. 13 rooms, all with bath. Restaurant. MC.*

Nightlife and the Arts

Greifswald's **Bach Week** in June offers a variety of classical concerts featuring the maestro's compositions, including open-air concerts at the ruins of the Eldena Cloister.

Usedom Island

⓲ On its seaboard side 40-kilometer-long (25-mile-long) **Usedom Island** has almost 32 kilometers (20 miles) of sandy shoreline and a string of resorts. Much of the island, whose untouched landscape is rivaled only by Poland's pristine pine barrens further east, is a nature preserve that provides refuge for a number of rare birds, including the giant sea eagle, which has a wingspan of up to 8 feet. Even in the summer this island is more or less deserted, and visitors can explore it at their leisure on foot or by bicycle. Boating is also possible around the many inlets and on the small inland rivers.

Wolgast

⓳ *32 km (20 mi) northeast of Greifswald on Rte. 109, then Rte. 111.*

Wolgast is near the causeway crossing to Germany's other main Baltic island, **Usedom.** Wolgast's chief attraction is the Old Town square, **Rathausplatz,** where the pretty mid-17th-century half-timbered house known locally as the Kaffeemühle (Coffee House) and a Baroque Town Hall are situated. The Kaffeemühle, far from serving coffee, contains the local history museum, **Stadtgeschichtliches Museum,** which tells the life story of another locally born artist of the Romantic era—Philipp Otto Runge. The museum also has an exhibition detailing the development of Germany's V2 rocket during World War II, spearheaded by scientist Werner von Braun, who later developed the U.S. space program. ⊠ *Rathauspl. 6,* ☎ *03836/203–041.* 🎫 *DM 3.* ☉ *Tues.–Sun. 10–5.*

The massive redbrick Gothic **St. Petri Kirche** sits on the highest point of the Old Town. The church has 24 paintings of the *Hohlbeinschen Totentanz* (Dance of Death). ⊠ *Kirchpl. 7.* 🎫 *DM 3 to enter tower.* ☉ *Weekdays 10–11:30 and 1:30–5.*

Ahlbeck

⍝ *36 km (22 mi) northeast of Wolgast on Rte. 111.*

Ahlbeck, one of the best resorts on Usedom and the island's main town, features an unusual 19th-century wooden pier with four towers. Ahlbeck's promenade is lined with turn-of-the-century villas, some of which are now small but as yet unsophisticated hotels. If you stroll along the beach to the right of Ahlbeck's pier, you'll arrive at the Polish border—the easternmost corner of the island belongs to Poland. Just west of Ahlbeck is Heringsdorf, the oldest resort on the island and the place chosen by Russian playwright Maxim Gorky for a quiet sojourn in 1922. He stayed in the villa called Irmgard, now a protected monument.

Peenemünde

㉑ *46 km (29 mi) northwest of Ahlbeck.*

At the northern end of Usedom Island is **Peenemünde,** the launch site of the world's first jet rockets, the V1 and V2, developed by Germany toward the end of World War II and fired at London (☞ Wolgast, *above*). One can view these rockets as well as models of early airplanes and ships at the popular **Historisch-Technisches Informationszentrum.** A playground and a hands-on exhibit explaining alternative energy sources make this museum especially good for children. There is also an exhibit about the concentration camps. ⊠ *Bahnhofsstr. 28,* ☎ *038371/20573.* 🎫 *DM 6.* ☉ *Apr.–Oct., Tues.–Sun. 9–6; Nov.–Mar., Tues.–Sun. 9–4.*

Dining and Lodging

$$–$$$ ✕ **Seebrücke.** Perched on pilings over the Baltic, the "Sea Bridge" is
★ the historic center of Ahlbeck. The emphasis is on seafood, but the menu has other choices, from *Königsberger Klops* (spicy meatballs in a thick, creamy sauce) to a tender fillet of lamb. If you don't want a full meal, stop in to enjoy the building and the view, over coffee and a piece of one of the delectable cakes. ⊠ *Dünenstr.,* ☎ *03878/8320. AE, MC, V. Closed Oct.–Apr.*

$$ ✕ **Café Asgard.** A visit here is a step back into the 1920s, which is when
★ this restaurant with dancing first opened its doors. You'll dine amid silk wallpaper, potted plants, crisp white napery, and fresh flowers. The specialty is *Feuerfleisch,* a spicy beef dish. The Asgard is open all day, so if you stop by between meal times, settle for a homemade pastry. If you're in a foot-tapping mood, visit the Golden Twenties dance hall above the restaurant. ⊠ *Strandpromenade 15, Bansin,* ☎ *038378/294– 88. No credit cards.*

$$–$$$ ✕🏨 **Esplanade Hotel.** A hundred years ago this first-class hotel was
★ the island's prime venue for the upper class vacationing here. Two years ago the hotel was restored to its traditional glory. The rooms are spacious but discreetly furnished. The hotel's restaurant, however, serving light German nouvelle cuisine, is in splendid Victorian style. ⊠ *Seestr. 5, D–17424 Heringsdorf,* ☎ *038378/700,* 𝖥𝖠𝖷 *038378/70–400. 40 rooms, 1 suite, all with bath or shower. Restaurant, no-smoking floor.*

$$ ✕🏨 **Ostseehotel.** Generations of vacationing families have stayed at
★ this snug, if slightly dated, hotel in a 19th-century villa on Ahlbeck's promenade. Rooms are airy but spartan, and most have sea views. The

restaurant serves mainly hearty local pork-and-potato dishes, but the goulash soup is exceptional; also look for fresh pike-perch in season. Dances are held several times a week during the summer. ⊠ *Dünen-str. 41, D–17419 Ahlbeck,* ☎ *038378/600,* ⅀X *03378/60100. 42 rooms. Bar, bicycles. AE, MC, V. Closed Sept.–March.*

Outdoor Activities and Sports

BIKING

The coastal region and the islands in particular are ideal for cycling (read: flat), which numerous entrepreneurs have been quick to note. Most large hotels provide bicycles for guests, and many shops rent bikes at modest rates on a daily or weekly basis. More and more train stations in this region also rent bicycles. Escorted tours are organized by the tourist offices; contact the regional tourist office (☞ Contacts and Resources *in* Mecklenburg-Vorpommern A to Z, *below*) for more information.

CAMPING

There are 150 campsites scattered along the coast and on the islands. Contact the local tourist offices for a list of locations and facilities offered.

MECKLENBURG-VORPOMMERN A TO Z

Arriving and Departing

By Car
Lübeck is 56 kilometers (35 miles) from Hamburg via autobahn A–1 (E–22).

By Plane
The international airport closest to the beginning of the tour is in **Hamburg,** just 45 minutes southwest of Lübeck by train or car. **Berlin,** with two international airports (Tegel and Schönefeld), is 280 kilometers (175 miles) south.

By Train
Lübeck is linked to the InterCity train network, with hourly connections to Hamburg, just 45 minutes away. There is also train service from Berlin to Lübeck.

Getting Around

By Boat
The **Weisse Flotte** (White Fleet) line operates a number of ferries linking the Baltic ports, as well as short harbor and coastal cruises. Boats depart from Warnemünde, Wismar, Sassnitz, and Stralsund. For information and the latest schedule, call 0381/519–860 for boats departing Warnemünde, 0381/268–116 for all other ports; or call the city's tourist office (☞ *below*). Harbor and coastal cruises also operate from Lübeck; contact the Lübeck tourist office for details (☎ 0451/122–8109). In addition, ferries run between Rostock, Warnemünde, Stralsund, and Sassnitz and Sweden, Denmark, and Finland.

Due to severe reductions in the fishing industry, many of the former fishermen in these towns supplement their income by giving sunset tours of the harbors or shuttling visitors between neighboring towns. This is a unique opportunity to ride on an authentic fishing ship, boost the local economy, *and* get a very personalized tour. Ask the tourist offices for more information.

By Bus
Local buses link the main train stations with outlying towns and villages, especially the coastal resorts. Buses operate throughout Rügen and Usedom islands.

By Car
With the exception of high summer (July and August), roads along the coast are not overcrowded. Route 105 covers much of the journey. The main road over the causeway from Stralsund (Route 96) cuts straight across the Rügen Island southwest to northeast, a distance of 51 kilometers (32 miles). If you are returning to Berlin from Usedom Island, you can leave the island by a causeway at the southwest corner, reached from the town of Usedom and emerging on the mainland at Anklam. From Anklam you can take Route 109 all the way to Berlin, a distance of 162 kilometers (101 miles). Road surfaces in eastern Germany are generally not good, although major improvements are under way. There is a maximum speed limit of 130 kph (80 mph) on motorways in eastern Germany, and 80 kph (48 mph) on other main out-of-town roads.

By Train
A north–south train line links Berlin with Schwerin and Rostock. An east–west route connects Hamburg, Lübeck, and Rostock, and some trains continue through to Stralsund and Sassnitz on Rügen Island. Train service between the smaller cities of former East Germany is generally much slower than in the west, due to poor track conditions. Routes between major cities, such as Leipzig, Berlin, Lübeck, and Rostock, are served by the faster InterCity trains.

Contacts and Resources

Car Rentals
Avis: ✉ Willy-Brandt-Allee 7, ☎ 0451/72008, **Lübeck**; ✉ Am Warnowufer 6, ☎ 0381/459–0475, **Rostock.**

Hertz: ✉ Wahlhalb Insel 1–5, ☎ 0451/71747, **Lübeck**; ✉ Röverzhagener Chaussee, ☎ 0381/683–065, **Rostock.**

Emergencies
There is no state-wide emergency number, so call ☎ 110 for **police** and **ambulance.**

Guided Tours
Although tourist offices and museums have worked to improve the quality and amount of English-language literature about this area, the availability of English-speaking tours should not be taken for granted; they must be ordered ahead of time at the local tourist office, and because most are designed for groups, there is usually a flat fee of DM 40–DM 60. Towns currently offering tours are: Lübeck, Stralsund, and Rostock. For the latest schedules, contact the regional tourist office, **Landesfremdenverkehrverband Mecklenburg-Vorpommern** (✉ Pl. der Freundschaft 1, ☎ 0381/448–426).

Guided tours of **old Lübeck** depart daily from one of Lübeck's tourist offices, on the old Markt (☎ 0451/122–8106), between mid-April and mid-October and on weekends only from mid-October to mid-April.

In **Schwerin** Weisse Flotte has two-hour tours of the region's unspoiled seven lakes. A trip to the island of Kaninchenwerder, a small nature preserve serving as sanctuary for more than 100 species of water birds, offers an unforgettable nature experience. Boats depart at the Schweriner Lake, adjacent to the Schweriner Schloss. ✉ *Weisse Flotte Schwerin, Anlegestelle Schloss pier, Box 010224, D–19002 Schwerin,* ☎ *0385/581–1596,* FAX *0381/5811-595.* ☉ *Ships depart daily May–Sept., 10–6.*

Visitor Information

The principal regional tourist office for the Baltic Coast is **TOURBU-Zentrale, Landesfremdenverkehrsverband, Mecklenburg-Vorpommen e.V.** (⊠ Platz der Freundschaft 1, D–18059 Rostock, ☎ 0381/448–428, ℻ 0381/448–423).

There are local tourist information offices in the following towns and cities:

Bad Doberan: Informationszentrum, ⊠ Goethestr. 1, D–18209, ☎ ℻ 038203/2154.

Greifswald: Informationsbüro, ⊠ Schuhhagen 22, D–17489, ☎ 03834/3460.

Lübeck: Amt für Lübeck-Werbung und Tourismus, ⊠ Beckergrube 95, D–23539, ☎ 0451/122–8109.

Rostock: Touristbüro, ⊠ Schnickmannstr. 13–14, D–18055, ☎ 0381/497–990, ℻ 0381/497–9923.

Rügen Island: Rügen Island Touristik Service, ⊠ Bahnhofstr. 28b, D–18573 Altefähr, ☎ 038306/6160, ℻ 038306/61666.

Sassnitz: Fremdenverkehrsbüro Sassnitz, ⊠ Hauptstr. 1, D–18546, ☎ 038392/32037, ℻ 038392/36080.

Schwerin: Tourist-Information, ⊠ Am Markt 11, D–19055, ☎ 0385/560–931, ℻ 0385/555–094.

Stralsund: Stadtinformation, ⊠ Ossenreyerstr. 1–2, D–18439, ☎ 03831/252–251, ℻ 03831/252–2195.

Usedom Island: Fremdenverkehrsverband Insel Usedom, ⊠ Bäderstr. 4, D–17459, ☎ 038375/21693, ℻ 038375/23429.

Warnemünde: Kurbetrieb Seebad Warnemünde, ⊠ Weidenweg 2, Postfach 23, D–18119, ☎ 0381/52456, ℻ 0381/52457.

Wismar: Wismar Information, ⊠ Stadthaus, Am Markt 11, D–23966, ☎ ℻ 03841/282–958.

18 Portrait of Germany

Germany at a Glance: A Chronology

Books

GERMANY AT A GLANCE: A CHRONOLOGY

ca. 5000 BC   Tribes settle in the Rhine and Danube valleys

ca. 2000–   Distinctive German Bronze Age culture emerges, with
800 BC   settlements ranging from coastal farms to lakeside villages

ca. 450–   Salzkammergut people, whose prosperity is based on abundant salt
50 BC   deposits (in the area of upper Austria), trade with Greeks and
Etruscans; they spread as far as Belgium and have first contact with
the Romans

9 BC–AD 9   Roman attempts to conquer the "Germans"—the tribes of the Cibri,
the Franks, the Goths, and the Vandals—are only partly successful;
the Rhine becomes the northeastern border of the Roman Empire
(and remains so for 300 years)

212   Roman citizenship is granted to all free inhabitants of the Empire

ca. 400   Pressed forward by Huns from Asia, such German tribes as the
Franks, the Vandals, and the Lombards migrate to Gaul (France),
Spain, Italy, and North Africa, scattering the Empire's populace and
eventually leading to the disintegration of central Roman authority

486   The Frankish kingdom is founded by Clovis; his court is in Paris

497   The Franks convert to Christianity

776   Charlemagne becomes king of the Franks

800   Charlemagne is declared Holy Roman Emperor; he makes Aachen
capital of his realm, which stretches from the Bay of Biscay to the
Adriatic and from the Mediterranean to the Baltic. Under his
enlightened patronage, there is an upsurge in art and architecture—
the Carolingian renaissance

843   The Treaty of Verdun divides Charlemagne's empire among his three
sons: West Francia becomes France; Lotharingia becomes Lorraine
(territory to be disputed by France and Germany into the 20th
century); and East Francia takes on, roughly, the shape of modern
Germany

911   Five powerful German dukes (of Bavaria, Lorraine, Franconia,
Saxony, and Swabia) establish the first German monarchy by
electing King Conrad I

962   Otto I is crowned Holy Roman Emperor by the Pope; he establishes
Austria—the East Mark. The Ottonian renaissance is marked
especially by the development of Romanesque architecture

1024–1125   The Salian Dynasty is characterized by a struggle between emperors
and Church that leaves the empire weak and disorganized; the great
Romanesque cathedrals of Speyer, Trier, Mainz, and Worms are
built

1138–1254   Frederick Barbarossa leads the Hohenstaufen Dynasty; there is
temporary recentralization of power, underpinned by strong trade
and Church relations

1158   Munich, capital of Bavaria, is founded by Duke Henry the Lion;
Henry is deposed by Emperor Barbarossa, and Munich is presented
to the House of Wittelsbach, which rules it until 1918

1241   The Hanseatic League is founded to protect trade; Bremen,
Hamburg, Köln, and Lübeck are early members. Agencies soon

extend to London, Antwerp, Venice, and the Baltic and North seas; a complex banking and finance system results

mid-1200s The Gothic style, exemplified by the grand Köln Cathedral, flourishes

1456 Johannes Gutenberg (1397–1468) prints first book in Europe

1471 The painter Albrecht Dürer (dies 1528) is born during the Renaissance. The Dutch-born philosopher Erasmus (1466–1536), and the painters Hans Holbein the Younger (1497–1543), Lucas Cranach the Elder (1472–1553), and Albrecht Altdorfer (1480–1538) help disseminate the new view of the world. Increasing wealth among the merchant classes leads to strong patronage of the revived arts

1517 The Protestant Reformation begins in Germany when Martin Luther (1483–1546) nails his "Ninety-Five Theses" to a church door in Wittenberg, contending that the Roman Church has forfeited divine authority through the corrupt sale of indulgences. Though Luther is outlawed, his revolutionary doctrine splits the church; much of north Germany embraces Protestantism

1524–25 The (Catholic) Hapsburgs rise to power; their empire spreads throughout Europe (and as far as North Africa, the Americas, and the Philippines). In 1530, Charles V (a Hapsburg) is crowned Holy Roman Emperor; he brutally crushes the Peasants' War, one in a series of populist uprisings in Europe

1545 The Council of Trent marks the beginning of the Counter-Reformation. Through diplomacy and coercion, most Austrians, Bavarians, and Bohemians are won back to Catholicism, but the majority of Germany remains Lutheran; persecution of religious minorities grows

1618–48 Germany is the main theater for combat in the Thirty Years' War. The powerful Catholic Hapsburgs are defeated by Protestant forces, swelled by disgruntled Hapsburg subjects and the armies of King Gustav Adolphus of Sweden. The bloody conflict ends with the Peace of Westphalia (1648); Hapsburg and papal authority are severely diminished

1689 Louis XIV of France invades the Rhineland Palatinate and sacks Heidelberg. Elsewhere at the end of the 17th century, Germany consolidates its role as a center of scientific thought

1708 Johann Sebastian Bach (1685–1750) becomes court organist at Weimar and launches his career; he and Georg Friederic Händel (1685–1759) fortify the great tradition of German music. Baroque and, later, Rococo art and architecture flourish

1740–86 Reign of Frederick the Great of Prussia; his rule sees both the expansion of Prussia (it becomes the dominant military force in Germany) and the growth of Enlightenment thought

ca. 1790 The great age of European orchestral music is raised to new heights in the works of Joseph Haydn (1732–1809), Wolfgang Amadeus Mozart (1756–91), and Ludwig van Beethoven (1770–1827)

early 1800s Johann Wolfgang von Goethe (1749–1832) helps initiate Romanticism. Other German Romantics include the writers Friedrich Schiller (1759–1805) and Heinrich von Kleist (1777–1811); the composers Robert Schumann (1810–56), Hungarian-born Franz Liszt (1811–86), Richard Wagner (1813–83), and Johannes Brahms (1833–97); and the painter Casper David

Friedrich (1774–1840). In architecture, the severe lines of neoclassicism become popular

1806 Napoléon's armies invade Prussia; it briefly becomes part of the French Empire

1807 The Prussian prime minister Baron vom und zum Stein frees the serfs, creating a new spirit of patriotism; the Prussian army is rebuilt

1813 The Prussians defeat Napoléon at Leipzig

1815 Britain and Prussia defeat Napoléon at Waterloo. At the Congress of Vienna, the German Confederation is created as a loose union of 39 independent states, reduced from more than 300 principalities. The *Bundestag* (national assembly) is established at Frankfurt. Already powerful Prussia increases, gaining the Rhineland, Westphalia, and most of Saxony

1848 The "Year of the Revolutions" is marked by uprisings across the fragmented German Confederation; Prussia uses the opportunity for further expansion. A national parliament is elected, taking the power of the Bundestag to prepare a constitution for a united Germany

1862 Otto von Bismarck (1815–98) becomes prime minister of Prussia; he is determined to wrest German-populated provinces from Austro-Hungarian (Hapsburg) control

1866 Austria-Hungary is defeated by the Prussians at Sadowa; Bismarck sets up the Northern German Confederation in 1867. A key figure in Bismarck's plans is Ludwig II of Bavaria (the Dream King). Ludwig—a political simpleton—lacks successors, making it easy for Prussia to seize his lands

1867 Karl Marx (1818–83) publishes *Das Kapital*

1870–71 The Franco-Prussian War: Prussia lays siege to Paris. Victorious Prussia seizes Alsace-Lorraine but eventually withdraws from all other occupied French territories

1871 The four south German states agree to join the Northern Confederation; Wilhelm I is proclaimed first Kaiser of the united Empire

1882 Triple Alliance is forged between Germany, Austria-Hungary, and Italy. Germany's industrial revolution blossoms, enabling it to catch up with the other great powers of Europe. Germany establishes colonies in Africa and the Pacific

ca. 1885 Daimler and Benz pioneer the automobile

1890 Kaiser Wilhelm II (rules 1888–1918) dismisses Bismarck and begins a new, more aggressive course of foreign policy; he oversees the expansion of the Navy

1890s A new school of writers, including Rainer Maria Rilke (1875–1926), emerges. Rilke's *Sonnets to Orpheus* gives German poetry new lyricism

1905 Albert Einstein (1879–1955) announces his theory of relativity

1906 Painter Ernst Ludwig Kirchner (1880–1938) helps organize *Die Brücke,* a group of artists who along with *Der Blaue Reiter* forge the avant-garde art movement Expressionism

1907 Great Britain, Russia, and France form the Triple Entente, which, set against the Triple Alliance, divides Europe into two armed camps

1914–18 Austrian Archduke Franz-Ferdinand is assassinated in Serbia. The attempted German invasion of France sparks World War I; Italy and Russia join the Allies, and four years of pitched battle ensue. By 1918, the Central Powers are encircled and must capitulate

1918 Germany is compelled by the Versailles Treaty to give up its overseas colonies and much European territory (including Alsace-Lorraine to France) and to pay huge reparations to the Allies; the tough terms leave the new democracy (the Weimar Republic) shaky

1919 The Bauhaus school of art and design, the brainchild of Walter Gropius (1883–1969), is born. Thomas Mann (1875–1955) and Hermann Hesse (1877–1962) forge a new style of visionary intellectual writing—until quashed by Nazism

1923 Germany suffers runaway inflation. Adolf Hitler's "Beer Hall Putsch," a rightist revolt, fails; leftist revolts are frequent

1925 Hitler publishes *Mein Kampf* (*My Struggle*)

1932 The Nazi Party gains the majority in the Bundestag

1933 Hitler becomes chancellor; the Nazi "revolution" begins

1934 President Paul von Hindenburg dies; Hitler declares himself *Führer* (leader) of the Third Reich (empire). Nazification of all German social institutions begins, spreading a policy that is virulently racist and anti-Communist. Germany recovers industrial might and rearms

1936 Germany signs anti-Communist agreements with Italy and Japan, forming the Axis; Hitler reoccupies the Rhineland

1938 The *Anschluss* (annexation): Hitler occupies Austria; Germany occupies the Sudetenland in Czechoslovakia

1939–40 In August, Hitler signs a pact with the Soviet Union; in September he invades Poland; war is declared by the Allies. Over the next three years, there are Nazi invasions of Denmark, Norway, the Low Countries, France, Yugoslavia, and Greece. Alliances form between Germany and the Baltic states

1941–45 Hitler launches his anti-Communist crusade against the Soviet Union, reaching Leningrad in the north and Stalingrad and the Caucasus in the south. In 1944, the Allies land in France; their combined might brings the Axis to its knees. In addition to the millions killed in the fighting, more than 6 million Jews die in Hitler's concentration camps. Germany is again in ruins. Hitler kills himself. Berlin (and what becomes East Germany) is occupied by the Soviet Union

1945 At the Yalta Conference, France, the United States, Britain, and the Soviet Union divide Germany into four zones; each country occupies a sector of Berlin. The Potsdam Agreement expresses the determination to rebuild Germany as a democracy

1948 The Soviet Union tears up the Potsdam Agreement and attempts, by blockade, to exclude the three other Allies from their agreed zones in Berlin. Stalin is frustrated by a massive airlift of supplies to West Berlin

1949 The three Western zones are combined to form the Federal Republic of Germany; the new West German parliament elects Konrad Adenauer as chancellor (a post held until his retirement in 1963). Soviet-held East Germany becomes the Communist German Democratic Republic

1950s   West Germany, aided by the financial impetus provided by the Marshall Plan, rebuilds its devastated cities and economy—the *Wirtschaftswunder* (economic miracle) gathers pace

1957   The Treaty of Rome heralds the formation of the European Economic Community (EEC); Germany is a founding member

1961   Communists build the Berlin Wall to stem the outward tide of refugees. The writers Heinrich Böll and Günter Grass emerge

1969–1974   The vigorous chancellorship of Willy Brandt pursues Ostpolitik, improving relations with Eastern Europe, the Soviet Union, and recognizing East Germany's sovereignty

mid-1980s   The powerful German Green Party emerges as the leading environmentalist voice in Europe

1989   Discontent in East Germany leads to a flood of refugees westward and to mass demonstrations; Communist power collapses across Eastern Europe; the Berlin Wall falls

1990   Political instability ushers in the year. In March the first free elections in East Germany bring a center-right government to power. The Communists, faced with corruption scandals, suffer a big defeat, but are represented in the new, democratic parliament. The World War II victors hold talks with the two German governments and the Soviet Union gives its support for reunification. Economic union takes place on July 1, with full political unity on October 3. In December, in the first democratic national German elections for 58 years, Chancellor Helmut Kohl's three-party coalition is reelected. Support for the Green Party wanes, and the Communists—renamed the Democratic Socialists—win 17 seats in the new parliament

1991   Nine months of emotional debate about the future capital of the reunited country ends on June 20, when parliamentary representatives vote in favor of quitting Bonn—seat of the West German government since 1949—and moving to Berlin, which was the capital until the end of World War II

BOOKS

Germany is the setting for many good spy novels, including *The Odessa File,* by Frederick Forsyth; John Le Carré's *A Small Town in Germany;* Alistair MacLean's *Where Eagles Dare;* Walter Winward's *The Midas Touch;* and *The Leader and the Damned,* by Colin Forbes.

If you like to travel with a historical novel, look for Christine Bruckner's *Flight of Cranes;* Timothy Findley's *Famous Last Words;* and Fred Uhlman's *Reunion.* Also, Silvia Tennenbaum's *Yesterday's Streets* covers three generations of a wealthy German family.

Other suggested titles include Günter Grass's *The Tin Drum;* Christa Wolf's *No Place on Earth;* Thoman Mann's *Buddenbrooks,* Hermann Hesse's *Narcissus and Goldmund,* Heinrich Böll's *The Lost Honor of Katarina Blum* and Peter Handke's *A Sorrow Beyond Dreams.* For a contemporary study of the Germans, read *Germany and the Germans* by British author John Ardagh. Peter Schneider's *The German Comedy* deals with German life after the fall of the Berlin Wall.

For books about pre-war Berlin, pick up Vicki Baum's *Grand Hotel* or Christopher Isherwood's *Berlin Stories.* Leon Uris's *Armageddon: A Novel of Berlin* is set at the end of World War II. Contemporary novels with a Berlin setting include Len Deighton's *Berlin Game* and Peter Schneider's *The Wall Jumper.*

For a good introduction to German history, try Mary Fulbrook's *A Concise History of Germany.* For coverage of World War II and Nazism, consult William Shirer's *The Rise and Fall of the Third Reich.*

GERMAN VOCABULARY

English	German	Pronunciation
Basics		
Yes/no	Ja/nein	yah/nine
Please	Bitte	**bit**-uh
Thank you (very much)	Danke (vielen Dank)	**dahn**-kuh (**fee**-lun dahnk)
Excuse me	Entschuldigen Sie	ent-**shool**-de-gen zee
I'm sorry	Es tut mir leid.	es toot meer lite
Good day	Guten Tag	**goo**-ten tahk
Good bye	Auf Wiedersehen	auf **vee**-der-zane
Mr./Mrs.	Herr/Frau	hair/frau
Miss	Fräulein	**froy**-line
Pleased to meet you.	Sehr erfreut.	zair air-**froit**
How are you?	Wie geht es Ihnen?	vee **gate** es **ee**-nen?
Very well, thanks.	Sehr gut, danke.	zair goot **dahn**-kuh
And you?	Und Ihnen?	oont **ee**-nen
Numbers		
1	ein(s)	eint(s)
2	zwei	tsvai
3	drei	dry
4	vier	fear
5	fünf	fumph
6	sechs	zex
7	sieben	**zee**-ben
8	acht	ahkt
9	neun	noyn
10	zehn	tsane
Days of the Week		
Sunday	Sonntag	**zone**-tahk
Monday	Montag	**moan**-tahk
Tuesday	Dienstag	**deens**-tahk
Wednesday	Mittwoch	**mit**-voah
Thursday	Donnerstag	**doe**-ners-tahk
Friday	Freitag	**fry**-tahk
Saturday	Samstag/Sonnabend	**zahm**-stakh/**zonn**-a-bent
Useful Phrases		
Do you speak English?	Sprechen Sie Englisch?	**shprek**-hun zee **eng**-glish?
I don't speak German.	Ich spreche kein Deutsch.	ich **shprek**-uh kine doych
Please speak slowly.	Bitte sprechen Sie langsam.	**bit**-uh **shprek**-en zee **lahng**-zahm

I am American/ British	Ich bin Amerikaner(in)/ Engländer(in)	ich bin a-mer-i-**kahn**-er(in)/**eng**-glan-der(in)
My name is . . .	Ich heiße . . .	ich **hi**-suh
Yes please/No, thank you	Ja bitte/Nein danke	yah **bi**-tuh/**nine** dahng-kuh
Where are the restrooms?	Wo ist die Toilette?	vo ist dee twah-**let**-uh
Left/right	links/rechts	links/rechts
Open/closed	offen/geschlossen	O-fen/geh-**shloss**-en
Where is . . .	Wo ist . . .	**vo** ist
the train station?	der Bahnhof?	dare **bahn**-hof
the bus stop?	die Bushaltestelle?	dee **booss**-hahlt-uh-**shtel**-uh
the subway station?	die U-Bahn-Station?	dee oo-bahn-**staht**-sion
the airport?	der Flugplatz?	dare **floog**-plats
the post office?	die Post?	dee **post**
the bank?	die Bank?	dee **banhk**
the police station?	die Polizeistation?	dee po-lee-**tsai**-staht-sion
the American/ British consulate?	das amerikanische/ britische Konsulat?	dahs a-mare-i-**kahn**-ishuh/**brit**-ish-uh cone-tso-**laht**
the Hospital?	das Krankenhaus?	dahs **krahnk**-en-house
the telephone	das Telefon	dahs te-le-**fone**
I'd like to	Ich hätte gairnhave . . .	ich **het**-uh gerne . . .
a room	ein Zimmer	I-nuh **tsim**-er
the key	den Schlüssel	den **shluh**-sul
a map	eine Stadtplan	I-nuh **staht**-plahn
a ticket	eine Karte	I-nuh **cart**-uh
How much is it?	Wieviel kostet das?	**vee**-feel **cost**-et dahs?
I am ill/sick	Ich bin krank	ich bin **krahnk**
I need . . .	Ich brauche . . .	ich **brow**-khuh
a doctor	einen Arzt	I-nen **artst**
the police	die Polizei	dee po-li-**tsai**
help	Hilfe	**hilf**-uh
Stop!	Halt!	hahlt
Fire!	Feuer!	**foy**-er
Look out/Caution!	Achtung!/Vorsicht!	**ahk**-tung/**for**-zicht

Dining Out

A bottle of . . .	eine Flasche . . .	I-nuh **flash**-uh
A cup of . . .	eine Tasse . . .	I-nuh **tahs**-uh
A glass of . . .	ein Glas . . .	ein **glahss**
Ashtray	der Aschenbecher	dare **Ahsh**-en-bekh-er
Bill/check	die Rechnung	dee **rekh**-nung
Do you have . . . ?	Haben Sie . . . ?	**hah**-ben zee

Food	Essen	**es**-en
I am a diabetic.	Ich bin Diabetiker(in)	ich bin dee-ah-**bet**-ik-er
I am on a diet.	Ich halte Diät.	ich **hahl**-tuh dee-**et**
I am a vegetarian.	Ich bin Vegetarier(in)	ich bin ve-guh-**tah**-re-er
I cannot eat . . .	Ich kann . . .nicht essen	ich kan . . .nicht **es**-en
I'd like to order . . .	Ich möchte . . . bestellen	ich **mohr**-shtuh buh-shtel-en . . .
Menu	die Speisekarte	dee **shpie**-zeh-car-tuh
Napkin	die Serviette	dee zair-vee-**eh**-tuh
Separate/all	Getrennt/alles	ge-**trent/ah**-les
together	zusammen	tsu-**zah**-men

MENU GUIDE

English	German
Made to order	Auf Bestellung
Side dishes	Beilagen
Extra charge	Extraaufschlag
When available	Falls verfügbar
Entrées	Hauptspeisen
Home made	Hausgemacht
(not) included	. . .(nicht) inbegriffen
Depending on the season	je nach Saison
Local specialties	Lokalspezialitäten
Set menu	Menü
Lunch menu	Mittagskarte
Desserts	Nachspeisen
style	. . . nach .. . . Art
at your choice	. . . nach Wahl
at your request	. . . nach Wunsch
Prices are . . .	Preise sind . . .
Service included	*inklusive Bedienung*
Value added tax included	*inklusive Mehrwertsteuer (Mwst.)*
Specialty of the house	Spezialität des Hauses
Soup of the day	Tagessuppe
Appetizers	Vorspeisen
Is served from . . . to . . .	Wird von . . . bis . . . serviert

Breakfast

Bread	Brot
Roll(s)	Brötchen
Butter	Butter
Eggs	Eier
Hot	heiß
Cold	kalt
Decaffeinated	koffeinfrei
Jam	Konfitüre
Milk	Milch
Orange juice	Orangensaft
Scrambled eggs	Rühreier
Bacon	Speck
Fried eggs	Spiegeleier
White bread	Weißbrot
Lemon	Zitrone
Sugar	Zucker

Appetizers

Oysters	Austern
Frog legs	Froschschenkel
Goose liver paté	Gänseleberpastete
Lobster	Hummer
Shrimp	Garnelen
Crayfish	Krebs
Salmon	Lachs
Mussels	Muscheln

Prosciutto with melon	Parmaschinken mit Melone
Mushrooms	Pilze
Smoked …	Räucher …
Ham	Schinken
Snails	Schnecken
Asparagus	Spargel

Soups

Stew	Eintopf
Semolina dumpling soup	Grießnockerlsuppe
Goulash soup	Gulaschsuppe
Chicken soup	Hühnersuppe
Potato soup	Kartoffelsuppe
Liver dumpling soup	Leberknödelsuppe
Oxtail soup	Ochsenschwanzsuppe
Tomato soup	Tomatensuppe
Onion soup	Zwiebelsuppe

Methods of Preparation

Blue (boiled in salt and vinegar)	Blau
Baked	Gebacken
Fried	Gebraten
Steamed	Gedämpft
Grilled (broiled)	Gegrillt
Boiled	Gekocht
Sauteed	In Butter geschwenkt
Breaded	Paniert
Raw	Roh

When ordering steak, the English words "rare, medium, (well) done" are used and understood in German.

Fish and Seafood

Eel	Aal
Oysters	Austern
Trout	Forelle
Flounder	Flunder
Prawns	Garnelen
Halibut	Heilbutt
Herring	Hering
Lobster	Hummer
Scallops	Jakobsmuscheln
Cod	Kabeljau
Crab	Krabbe
Crayfish	Krebs
Salmon	Lachs
Spiny lobster	Languste
Mackerel	Makrele
Mussels	Muscheln
Red sea bass	Rotbarsch
Sole	Seezunge
Squid	Tintenfisch
Tuna	Thunfisch

Meats

Mutton	Hammel
Veal	Kalb(s)
Lamb	Lamm
Beef	Rind(er)
Pork	Schwein(e)

Cuts of Meat

Example: For "Lammkeule" see "Lamm" (above) + "...keule" (below)

breast	...brust
scallopini	...geschnetzeltes
knuckle	...haxe
leg	...keule
liver	...leber
tenderloin	...lende
kidney	...niere
rib	...rippe
Meat patty	Frikadelle
Meat loaf	Hackbraten
Cured pork ribs	Kasseler Rippchen
Liver meatloaf	Leberkäse
Ham	Schinken
Bacon and sausage with sauerkraut	Schlachtplatte
Brawn	Sülze
Cooked beef with horseradish and cream sauce	

Game and Poultry

Duck	Ente
Pheasant	Fasan
Goose	Gans
Chicken	Hähnchen (Huhn)
Hare	Hase
Deer	Hirsch
Rabbit	Kaninchen
Capon	Kapaun
Venison	Reh
Pigeon	Taube
Turkey	Truthahn
Quail	Wachtel

Vegetables

Eggplant	Aubergine
Red cabbage	Blaukraut
Cauliflower	Blumenkohl
Beans	Bohnen
green	*grüne*
white	*weiße*
Button mushrooms	Champignons
Peas	Erbsen
Cucumber	Gurke
Cabbage	Kohl

Lettuce	Kopfsalat
Leek	Lauch
Asparagus, peas and carrots	Leipziger Allerlei
Corn	Mais
Carrots	Mohrrüben
Peppers	Paprika
Chanterelle mushrooms	Pfifferlinge
Mushrooms	Pilze
Brussels sprouts	Rosenkohl
Red beets	Rote Beete
Celery	Sellerie
Asparagus (tips)	Spargel(spitzen)
Tomatoes	Tomaten
Cabbage	Weißkohl
Onions	Zwiebeln
Spring Onions	Frühlingszwiebeln

Side dishes

Potato(s)	Kartoffel(n)
fried	*Brat . . .*
boiled in their jackets	*Pell . . .*
with parsley	*Petersilien . . .*
fried	*Röst . . .*
boiled in saltwater	*Salz . . .*
mashed	*. . . brei*
dumplings	*. . . klöße (knödel)*
pancakes	*. . . puffer*
salad	*. . . salat*
Pasta	Nudeln
French fries	Pommes frites
Rice	Reis
buttered	*Butter . . .*
steamed	*gedämpfter . . .*

Condiments

Basil	Basilikum
Vinegar	Essig
Spice	Gewürz
Garlic	Knoblauch
Herbs	Kräuter
Caraway	Kümmel
Bay leaf	Lorbeer
Horseradish	Meerettich
Nutmeg	Muskatnuß
Oil	Öl
Parsley	Petersilie
Saffron	Safran
Sage	Salbei
Chives	Schnittlauch
Mustard	Senf
Artificial sweetener	Süßstoff
Cinnamon	Zimt
Sugar	Zucker
Salt	Salz

Cheese

Mild	Allgäuer Käse, Altenburger (goat cheese), Appenzeller, Greyerzer, Hüttenkäse (cottage cheese), Kümmelkäse (with caraway seeds), Quark, Räucherkäse (smoked cheese), Sahnekäse (creamy), Tilsiter, Ziegekäse (goat cheese).
Sharp	Handkäse, Harzer Käse, Limburger.
curd	frisch
hard	hart
mild	mild

Fruits

Apple	Apfel
Orange	Apfelsine
Apricot	Aprikose
Blueberry	Blaubeere
Blackberry	Brombeere
Strawberry	Erdbeere
Raspberry	Himbeere
Cherry	Kirsche
Grapefruit	Pampelmuse
Cranberry	Preiselbeere
Raisin	Rosine
Grape	Weintraube
Banana	Banane
Pear	Birne
Kiwi	Kiwi

Nuts

Peanuts	Erdnüsse
Hazelnuts	Haselnüsse
Coconut	Kokosnuß
Almonds	Mandeln
Chestnuts	Maronen

Desserts

. . . soufflé	. . . auflauf
ice cream	. . . eis
cake	. . . kuchen
Honey-almond cake	Bienenstich
Fruit cocktail	Obstsalat
Whipped cream	(Schlag)sahne
Black Forest cake	Schwarzwälder Kirschtorte

Drinks

chilled	eiskalt
with/without ice	mit/ohne Eis
with/without water	mit/ohne Wasser
straight	pur
room temperature	Zimmertemperatur
brandy	. . . geist

distilled liquor	. . . korn
liqueur	. . . likör
schnapps	. . . schnaps
Egg liquor	Eierlikör
Mulled claret	Glühwein
Caraway-flavored liquor	Kümmel
Fruit brandy	Obstler
Vermouth	Wermut

When ordering a Martini, you have to specify "gin (vodka) and vermouth," otherwise you will be given a vermouth (Martini & Rossi).

Beer and Wine

non-alcoholic	Alkoholfrei
A dark beer	Ein Dunkles
A light beer	Ein Helles
A mug (one quart)	Eine Maß
Draught	Vom Faß
Dark, bitter, high hops content	Altbier
Strong, high alcohol content	Bockbier (Doppelbock, Märzen)
Wheat beer with yeast	Hefeweizen
Light beer, strong hops aroma	Pils(ener)
Wheat beer	Weizen(bier)
Light beer and lemonade	Radlermaß
Wines	Wein
Rosé wine	Rosëwein
Red wine	Rotwein
White wine and mineral water	Schorle
Sparkling wine	Sekt
White wine	Weißwein
dry	herb
light	leicht
sweet	süß
dry	trocken
full-bodied	vollmundig

Non-alcoholic Drinks

Coffee	Kaffee
decaffeinated	*koffeinfrei*
with cream/sugar	*mit Milch/Zucker*
with artificial sweetener	*mit Sülßstoff*
black	*schwarz*
Lemonade	Limonade
orange	*Orangen . . .*
lemon	*Zitronen . . .*
Milk	Milch
Mineral water	Mineralwasser
carbonated/non-carbonated	*mit/ohne Kohlensäure*
juice	*. . . saft*
(hot) Chocolate	(heiße) Schokolade
Tea	Tee
iced tea	*Eistee*
herb tea	*Kräutertee*
with cream/lemon	*mit Milch/Zitrone*

INDEX

X = restaurant, ⊠ = hotel

Escape to ancient cities and

journey to  *exotic islands with*

CNN Travel Guide, a wealth of valuable advice. Host

Valerie Voss will take you to

all of your favorite destinations,

including those off the beaten

path. Tune-in to your passport to the world.

CNN TRAVEL GUIDE
SATURDAY 12:30 PMᴇᴛ   SUNDAY 4:30 PMᴇᴛ

CNN®

CNN ✈
Airport Network

Your
Window
To The
World
While You're
On The
Road

Keep in touch when you're traveling. Before you take off, tune in
to CNN Airport Network. Now available in major airports across
America, CNN Airport Network provides nonstop news, sports,
business, weather and lifestyle programming. Both domestic and
international. All piloted by the top-flight global resources of CNN.
All up-to-the minute reporting. And just for travelers, CNN Airport
Network features two daily Fodor's specials. "Travel Fact" provides
enlightening, useful travel trivia, while "What's Happening" covers
upcoming events in major cities worldwide. So why be bored
waiting to board? TIME FLIES WHEN YOU'RE WATCHING THE
WORLD THROUGH THE WINDOW OF CNN AIRPORT NETWORK!

WHEREVER YOU TRAVEL, $\mathcal{H}$ELP IS NEVER FAR AWAY.

From planning your trip to providing travel assistance along the way, American Express® Travel Service Offices are always there to help.

Germany

American Express Reisebüro
Haugerpfarrgasse 1
Bavaria Reisebüro, Würzburg
931/355-690

American Express Travel Service
Savignyplatz 6
Berlin
30/315-9300

American Express Travel Service
Bundeskanzlerplatz 2-10
Bonn
228/260-080

American Express Travel Service
Honinger Weg 100
Cologne
221/936-4060

American Express Travel Service
Wilsdruffer Strasse 2
Dresden
351/495-2152

American Express Travel Service
Hafenstrasse 1
Frankfurt
69/255-8035

American Express Travel Service
Hohe Brücke 1
Hamburg
40/372-677

American Express Travel Service
Zentralbereich
Airport, Munich
89/975-99-420

Travel

http://www.americanexpress.com/travel

American Express Travel Service Offices are found in central locations throughout Germany.

Listings are valid as of May 1996. Not all services available at all locations.
© 1996 American Express Travel Related Services Company, Inc.